TENTH EDITION

Programming iOS 13
*Dive Deep into Views, View Controllers,
and Frameworks*

Matt Neuburg

Beijing · Boston · Farnham · Sebastopol · Tokyo

Programming iOS 13, Tenth Edition

by Matt Neuburg

Copyright © 2020 Matt Neuburg. All rights reserved.

Printed in Canada.

Published by O'Reilly Media, Inc., 1005 Gravenstein Highway North, Sebastopol, CA 95472.

O'Reilly books may be purchased for educational, business, or sales promotional use. Online editions are also available for most titles (*http://oreilly.com*). For more information, contact our corporate/institutional sales department: 800-998-9938 or *corporate@oreilly.com*.

Editor: Rachel Roumeliotis

Production Editor: Kristen Brown

Illustrator: Matt Neuburg

Proofreader: O'Reilly Production Services

Indexer: Matt Neuburg

Cover Designer: Randy Comer

Interior Designer: David Futato

May 2011:	First Edition
March 2012:	Second Edition
March 2013:	Third Edition
December 2013:	Fourth Edition
December 2014:	Fifth Edition
November 2015:	Sixth Edition
November 2016:	Seventh Edition
December 2017:	Eighth Edition
October 2018:	Ninth Edition
October 2019:	Tenth Edition

Revision History for the Tenth Edition:

2019-12-05:   First release

See *http://oreilly.com/catalog/errata.csp?isbn=9781492074618* for release details.

978-1-492-07461-8

[MBP]

Table of Contents

Part II. Interface

Part III.   Some Frameworks

Part IV.   Final Topics

Preface

With the arrival of Swift 5 in early 2019, the stamp of maturity has been placed upon the Swift language. When Swift was introduced to the public in 2014, it was a sort of second-class citizen. The Cocoa frameworks that give an iOS app its functionality expect to be spoken to in Objective-C, and several megabytes of libraries had to be included in every Swift app, effectively containing the whole of the Swift language and translating everything into Objective-C. But Swift 5 introduces ABI stability, which means that, since iOS 12.2, the Swift language has become part of the system. Swift is now on a par with Objective-C, and Swift apps are smaller and faster.

Swift is the programming language used throughout this book. Still, some awareness of Objective-C (including C) can be useful. The Foundation and Cocoa APIs are still written in C and Objective-C. In order to interact with them, you might have to know what those languages would expect.

The Scope of This Book

Programming iOS 13 is the second of a pair with my other book, *iOS 13 Programming Fundamentals with Swift*; it picks up where the other book leaves off. If writing an iOS program is like building a house of bricks, *iOS 13 Programming Fundamentals with Swift* teaches you what a brick is and how to handle it, while *Programming iOS 13* hands you some actual bricks and tells you how to assemble them.

So this book, like Homer's *Iliad*, begins in the middle of the story. The reader is expected to jump with all four feet into views and view controllers. Topics such as the Swift programming language, the Xcode IDE, including the nature of nibs, outlets, and actions, and the mechanics of nib loading, and the fundamental conventions, classes, and architectures of the Cocoa Touch framework, including delegation, the responder chain, key–value coding, key–value observing, memory management, and so on, were all taught in *iOS 13 Programming Fundamentals with Swift*.

So if something appears to be missing from this book, that's why! If you start reading *Programming iOS 13* and wonder about such unexplained matters as Swift language basics, the `UIApplicationMain` function, the nib-loading mechanism, Cocoa patterns of delegation and notification, and retain cycles, wonder no longer! I don't explain them here because I have already explained them in *iOS 13 Programming Fundamentals with Swift*. If you're not sufficiently conversant with those topics, you might want to read that book first; you will then be completely ready for this one.

Here's a summary of the major sections of *Programming iOS 13*:

- Part I describes views, the fundamental units of an iOS app's interface. Views are what the user can see and touch in an iOS app. To make something appear before the user's eyes, you need a view. To let the user interact with your app, you need a view. This part of the book explains how views are created, arranged, drawn, layered, animated, and touched.

- Part II starts by discussing view controllers. Perhaps the most important aspect of Cocoa programming, view controllers enable views to come and go coherently within the interface, allowing a single-windowed app running on what may be a tiny screen to contain multiple screens of material. View controllers are used to manage interface and to respond to user actions; most of your app's code will be in a view controller. This part of the book talks about how view controllers work, and the major built-in types of view controller that Cocoa gives you. It also describes every kind of view provided by the UIKit framework — the primary building blocks with which you'll construct an app's interface.

- Part III surveys the most commonly used frameworks provided by iOS. These are clumps of code, sometimes with built-in interface, that are not part of your app by default, but are there for the asking if you need them, allowing you to work with such things as sound, video, user libraries, maps, and the device's sensors.

- Part IV wraps up the book with some miscellaneous but significant topics: files, networking, threading, and how to implement undo.

- Appendix A summarizes the basic lifetime event messages sent to your app.

- Appendix B catalogs some useful utility functions that I've written. My example code takes advantage of these functions, so you should keep an eye on this appendix, consulting it whenever a mysterious method name appears.

- Appendix C is an excursus discussing an often misunderstood aspect of iOS programming: asynchronous code.

Someone who has read this book and is conversant with the material in *iOS 13 Programming Fundamentals with Swift* should be capable of writing a real-life iOS app with a clear understanding of the underlying fundamentals and techniques and a good sense of where the app is going as it grows and develops. The book itself doesn't show how to write any particularly interesting iOS apps, but it is backed by dozens of example projects that you can download from my GitHub site, *http://github.com/ mattneub/Programming-iOS-Book-Examples*, and it uses my own real apps and real programming situations to illustrate and motivate its explanations.

What's Not in This Book

iOS programming is a vast subject. I can't possibly cover it all, so this book is intended to prepare you for your own further explorations. Certain chapters, especially in Parts III and IV, introduce a topic, providing an initial basic survey of its concepts, its capabilities, and its documentation, along with some code examples; but the topic itself may be far more extensive. My goal is to set your feet firmly on the path; after reading the discussion here, you'll be equipped to proceed on your own whenever the need or interest arises.

In addition, many entire areas of iOS have had to be excluded from this book entirely:

SpriteKit
SpriteKit provides a built-in framework for designing 2D animated games.

SceneKit
Ported from macOS, the SceneKit framework makes it much easier to create 3D games and interactive graphics.

GameplayKit
This framework provides the architectural underpinnings for writing a game app.

Metal
Metal performs intensive computation, especially for 3D graphics. It supersedes OpenGL and GLKit.

GameKit
The GameKit framework covers areas that can enhance your user's multiplayer game experience, such as peer-to-peer device communication (including voice communication) and Game Center.

Printing
See the "Printing" chapter of Apple's *Drawing and Printing Guide for iOS*.

Security
This book does not discuss security topics such as keychains, certificates, and encryption. See Apple's *Security Overview* and the Security framework.

Accessibility

VoiceOver assists visually impaired users by describing the interface aloud. To participate, views must be configured to describe themselves usefully. Built-in views already do this to a large extent, and you can extend this functionality. See Apple's *Accessibility Programming Guide for iOS*.

Telephone

The Core Telephony framework lets your app get information about a particular cellular carrier and call. CallKit allows VoIP apps to integrate with the built-in Phone app.

PassKit

The PassKit framework allows creation of downloadable passes to go into the user's Wallet app.

HealthKit

The HealthKit framework lets your app obtain, store, share, and present data and statistics related to body activity and exercise.

Externalities

The user can attach an external accessory to the device, either directly via USB or wirelessly via Bluetooth. Your app can communicate with such an accessory. See Apple's *External Accessory Programming Topics*. The HomeKit framework lets the user communicate with devices in the physical world, such as light switches and door locks. This book also doesn't discuss iBeacon or near field communication (the Core NFC framework).

Handoff

Handoff permits your app to communicate a record of what the user is doing, so that the user can switch to another copy of your app on another device and resume doing the same thing. See Apple's *Handoff Programming Guide*.

Spotlight

The user's Spotlight search results can include data supplied by your app. See Apple's *App Search Programming Guide*.

SiriKit

The SiriKit framework lets you configure your app so that the user can talk to the device to tell it what to do.

Augmented Reality

Certain devices can impose drawn objects into the world viewed live through the device's camera by means of the ARKit framework.

Machine Learning

> The Core ML framework embraces image analysis (the Vision framework) as well as decision trees (GameplayKit). Language analysis classes (such as Foundation NSLinguisticTagger) are now part of the Natural Language framework.

Low-Level Networking

> The Network framework lets you implement low-level networking protocols such as TLS, TCP, and UDP without resorting to BSD sockets.

PencilKit

> New in iOS 13, PencilKit provides tools for implementing drawing and graphical annotations.

SwiftUI

> SwiftUI, introduced to the public in mid-2019, is a domain-specific language wrapped around Swift plus a framework that uses its own hooks into the iOS interface and its own characteristic data-driven messaging. It promises to make it easier to program for multiple platforms (not only iOS but also tvOS, watchOS, and so on) and to escape the dictates of Cocoa's event-driven architecture. But it is *not* Cocoa and is not discussed in this book. This is a Cocoa book! However, even if you're using SwiftUI, you are likely to use other frameworks as well, so there are many topics in this book that might be of interest to you, especially starting in Part III.

From the Programming iOS 4 Preface

A programming framework has a kind of personality, an overall flavor that provides an insight into the goals and mindset of those who created it. When I first encountered Cocoa Touch, my assessment of its personality was: "Wow, the people who wrote this are really clever!" On the one hand, the number of built-in interface objects was severely and deliberately limited; on the other hand, the power and flexibility of some of those objects, especially such things as UITableView, was greatly enhanced over their OS X counterparts. Even more important, Apple created a particularly brilliant way (UIViewController) to help the programmer make entire blocks of interface come and go and supplant one another in a controlled, hierarchical manner, thus allowing that tiny iPhone display to unfold virtually into multiple interface worlds within a single app without the user becoming lost or confused.

The popularity of the iPhone, with its largely free or very inexpensive apps, and the subsequent popularity of the iPad, have brought and will continue to bring into the fold many new programmers who see programming for these devices as worthwhile and doable, even though they may not have felt the same way about OS X. Apple's own annual WWDC developer conventions have reflected this trend, with their emphasis shifted from OS X to iOS instruction.

The widespread eagerness to program iOS, however, though delightful on the one hand, has also fostered a certain tendency to try to run without first learning to walk. iOS gives the programmer mighty powers that can seem as limitless as imagination itself, but it also has fundamentals. I often see questions online from programmers who are evidently deep into the creation of some interesting app, but who are stymied in a way that reveals quite clearly that they are unfamiliar with the basics of the very world in which they are so happily cavorting.

It is this state of affairs that has motivated me to write this book, which is intended to ground the reader in the fundamentals of iOS. I love Cocoa and have long wished to write about it, but it is iOS and its popularity that has given me a proximate excuse to do so. Here I have attempted to marshal and expound, in what I hope is a pedagogically helpful and instructive yet ruthlessly Euclidean and logical order, the principles and elements on which sound iOS programming rests. My hope, as with my previous books, is that you will both read this book cover to cover (learning something new often enough to keep you turning the pages) and keep it by you as a handy reference.

This book is not intended to disparage Apple's own documentation and example projects. They are wonderful resources and have become more wonderful as time goes on. I have depended heavily on them in the preparation of this book. But I also find that they don't fulfill the same function as a reasoned, ordered presentation of the facts. The online documentation must make assumptions as to how much you already know; it can't guarantee that you'll approach it in a given order. And online documentation is more suitable to reference than to instruction. A fully written example, no matter how well commented, is difficult to follow; it demonstrates, but it does not teach.

A book, on the other hand, has numbered chapters and sequential pages; I can assume you know views before you know view controllers for the simple reason that Part I precedes Part II. And along with facts, I also bring to the table a degree of experience, which I try to communicate to you. Throughout this book you'll find me referring to "common beginner mistakes"; in most cases, these are mistakes that I have made myself, in addition to seeing others make them. I try to tell you what the pitfalls are because I assume that, in the course of things, you will otherwise fall into them just as naturally as I did as I was learning. You'll also see me construct many examples piece by piece or extract and explain just one tiny portion of a larger app. It is not a massive finished program that teaches programming, but an exposition of the thought process that developed that program. It is this thought process, more than anything else, that I hope you will gain from reading this book.

Versions

This book is geared to Swift 5.1, iOS 13, and Xcode 11.

In general, only very minimal attention is given to earlier versions of iOS and Xcode. Earlier versions can be very different from the current version, and it would be impossible to go into detail about all that has changed over the years. Besides, that information is readily and compendiously available in my earlier books. Recent innovations are called out clearly. The book does contain some advice about backward compatibility, especially with regard to scene support.

I generally give method names in Swift, in the style of a function reference — the name plus parentheses containing the parameter labels followed by colon. Now and then, if a method is already under discussion and there is no ambiguity, I'll use the bare name. In a few places, where the Objective-C language is explicitly under discussion, I use Objective-C method names.

I have tried to keep my code up-to-date right up to the moment when the manuscript left my hands; but if, at some future time, a new version of Xcode is released along with a new version of Swift or with revisions to the Cocoa APIs, some of the code in this book might be slightly incorrect. Please make allowances, and be prepared to compensate.

Screenshots of Xcode were taken using Xcode 11 under macOS 10.14 Mojave. The interface on 10.15 Catalina is slightly different from the screenshots (especially if you're using "dark mode"), but this difference will be minimal and shouldn't cause any confusion.

Acknowledgments

This book was written with the aid of some wonderful software:

- git (*http://git-scm.com*)
- Sourcetree (*http://www.sourcetreeapp.com*)
- TextMate (*http://macromates.com*)
- AsciiDoc (*http://www.methods.co.nz/asciidoc*)
- Asciidoctor (*http://asciidoctor.org*)
- BBEdit (*http://barebones.com/products/bbedit*)
- EasyFind (*https://www.devontechnologies.com/support/download*)
- Snapz Pro X (*http://www.ambrosiasw.com*)
- GraphicConverter (*http://www.lemkesoft.com*)
- OmniGraffle (*http://www.omnigroup.com*)

The book was typed and edited almost entirely on my faithful Unicomp Model M keyboard (*http://pckeyboard.com*).

At O'Reilly Media, many people have made writing this book fun and easy; particular thanks go to Kristen Brown, Rachel Roumeliotis, Dan Fauxsmith, Adam Witwer, Nick Adams, Heather Scherer, Melanie Yarbrough, Sarah Schneider, and Sanders Kleinfeld. My first editor was Brian Jepson; his influence is present throughout.

Finally, a special thanks to my beloved wife, Charlotte Wilson, for her sharp eye, her critical ear, and her unflagging encouragement. This book could not have been written without her.

Conventions Used in This Book

The following typographical conventions are used in this book:

Italic
: Indicates new terms, URLs, email addresses, filenames, and file extensions.

`Constant width`
: Used for program listings, as well as within paragraphs to refer to program elements such as variable or function names, databases, data types, environment variables, statements, and keywords.

`Constant width bold`
: Shows commands or other text that should be typed literally by the user.

`Constant width italic`
: Shows text that should be replaced with user-supplied values or by values determined by context.

 This element signifies a tip or suggestion.

 This element signifies a general note.

 This element indicates a warning or caution.

Using Code Examples

Supplemental material (code examples, exercises, etc.) is available for download at *https://github.com/mattneub/Programming-iOS-Book-Examples*.

If you have a technical question or a problem using the code examples, please send email to *bookquestions@oreilly.com*.

This book is here to help you get your job done. In general, if example code is offered with this book, you may use it in your programs and documentation. You do not need to contact us for permission unless you're reproducing a significant portion of the code. For example, writing a program that uses several chunks of code from this book does not require permission. Selling or distributing examples from O'Reilly books does require permission. Answering a question by citing this book and quoting example code does not require permission. Incorporating a significant amount of example code from this book into your product's documentation does require permission.

We appreciate, but do not require, attribution. An attribution usually includes the title, author, publisher, and ISBN. For example: "*Programming iOS 13* by Matt Neuburg (O'Reilly). Copyright 2020 Matt Neuburg, 978-1-492-07461-8."

If you feel your use of code examples falls outside fair use or the permission given above, feel free to contact us at *permissions@oreilly.com*.

O'Reilly Online Learning

 For more than 40 years, *O'Reilly Media* has provided technology and business training, knowledge, and insight to help companies succeed.

Our unique network of experts and innovators share their knowledge and expertise through books, articles, conferences, and our online learning platform. O'Reilly's online learning platform gives you on-demand access to live training courses, in-depth learning paths, interactive coding environments, and a vast collection of text and video from O'Reilly and 200+ other publishers. For more information, please visit *http://oreilly.com*.

How to Contact Us

Please address comments and questions concerning this book to the publisher:

O'Reilly Media, Inc.
1005 Gravenstein Highway North
Sebastopol, CA 95472
800-998-9938 (in the United States or Canada)
707-829-0515 (international or local)
707-829-0104 (fax)

We have a web page for this book, where we list errata, examples, and any additional information. You can access this page at *https://oreil.ly/programming_iOS13*.

Email *bookquestions@oreilly.com* to comment or ask technical questions about this book.

For more information about our books, courses, conferences, and news, see our website at *http://www.oreilly.com*.

Find us on Facebook: *http://facebook.com/oreilly*

Follow us on Twitter: *http://twitter.com/oreillymedia*

Watch us on YouTube: *http://www.youtube.com/oreillymedia*

PART I

Views

Views are what your user sees on the screen and interacts with by touching the screen. The book begins by explaining how they work:

- Chapter 1 discusses views in their most general aspect — their hierarchy, visibility, position, and layout.

- Chapter 2 is about drawing. A view knows how to draw itself; this chapter explains how to tell a view what you want it to draw.

- Chapter 3 explains about layers. The drawing power of a view comes ultimately from its layer.

- Chapter 4 talks about animation, which you'll use to enliven your app's interface.

- Chapter 5 explains how your app senses and responds to the user touching the screen.

CHAPTER 1

Views

A *view* (an object whose class is UIView or a subclass of UIView) knows how to draw itself into a rectangular area of the interface. Your app has a visible interface thanks to views; everything the user sees is ultimately because of a view. Creating and configuring a view can be extremely simple: "Set it and forget it." You can configure a UIButton in the nib editor; when the app runs, the button appears, and works properly. But you can also manipulate views in powerful ways, in real time. Your code can do some or all of the view's drawing of itself (Chapter 2); it can make the view appear and disappear, move, resize itself, and display many other physical changes, possibly with animation (Chapter 4).

A view is also a responder (UIView is a subclass of UIResponder). This means that a view is subject to user interactions, such as taps and swipes. Views are the basis not only of the interface that the user sees, but also of the interface that the user touches (Chapter 5). Organizing your views so that the correct view reacts to a given touch allows you to allocate your code neatly and efficiently.

The *view hierarchy* is the chief mode of view organization. A view can have subviews; a subview has exactly one immediate superview. We may say there is a *tree* of views. This hierarchy allows views to come and go together. If a view is removed from the interface, its subviews are removed; if a view is hidden (made invisible), its subviews are hidden; if a view is moved, its subviews move with it; and other changes in a view are likewise shared with its subviews. The view hierarchy is also the basis of, though it is not identical to, the responder chain.

A view may come from a nib, or you can create it in code. On balance, neither approach is to be preferred over the other; it depends on your needs and inclinations and on the overall architecture of your app.

Window and Root View

The top of the view hierarchy is a window. It is an instance of UIWindow (or your own subclass thereof), which is a UIView subclass. At launch time, a window is created and displayed; otherwise, the screen would be black. New in iOS 13, your app might support multiple windows on an iPad (Chapter 9); if it doesn't, or if we're running on an iPhone, your app will have exactly one window (the *main* window). A visible window forms the background to, and is the ultimate superview of, all your other visible views. Conversely, all visible views are visible by virtue of being subviews, at some depth, of a visible window.

In Cocoa programming, you do not manually or directly populate a window with subviews. Rather, the link between your window and the interface that it contains is the window's *root view controller*. A view controller is instantiated, and that instance is assigned to the window's `rootViewController` property. That view controller's *main view* — its `view` — henceforth occupies the entirety of the window. It is the window's sole subview; all other visible views are subviews (at some depth) of the root view controller's view. (The root view controller itself will be the top of the *view controller hierarchy,* of which I'll have much more to say in Chapter 6.)

How an App Launches

How does your app, at launch time, come to have its window in the first place, and how does that window come to be populated and displayed? If your app uses a main storyboard, it all happens automatically. But "automatically" does *not* mean "by magic!" The procedure at launch is straightforward and deterministic, and your code can take a hand in it. It is useful to know how an app launches, not least because, if you misconfigure something and app launch goes wrong, you'll be able to figure out why.

Your app consists, ultimately, of a single call to the `UIApplicationMain` function. (Unlike an Objective-C project, a typical Swift project doesn't make this call explicitly, in code; it is called for you, behind the scenes.) This call creates some of your app's most important initial instances; if your app uses a main storyboard, those instances include the window and its root view controller.

Exactly how `UIApplicationMain` proceeds depends on what it discovers as it gets going. New in iOS 13, your app can use scenes and scene-related classes and protocols (UISceneSession, UIScene, UIWindowScene, UIWindowSceneDelegate). The runtime knows whether your app does this because of the presence of the "Application Scene Manifest" dictionary in the *Info.plist.* By default, new app projects that you create from Xcode's built-in app templates have this dictionary and use scenes (even if they do not support multiple windows on iPad). But you might also have older projects, or you might want your app to be backward compatible to iOS 12 and before. So I'll show two different launch trajectories — what happens in iOS 12 and before, and what happens in iOS 13 in an app that supports window scenes.

iOS 12 and before

Here's how `UIApplicationMain` bootstraps your app as it launches on iOS 12 and before:

1. `UIApplicationMain` instantiates UIApplication and retains this instance, to serve as the shared application instance, which your code can later refer to as `UIApplication.shared`. It then instantiates the app delegate class; it knows which class that is because it is marked `@UIApplicationMain`. It retains the app delegate instance, ensuring that it will persist for the lifetime of the app, and assigns it as the application instance's `delegate`.

2. `UIApplicationMain` looks to see whether your app uses a main storyboard; it knows whether you are using a main storyboard, and what its name is, by looking at the *Info.plist* key "Main storyboard file base name" (`UIMainStoryboard-File`). If so, it instantiates that storyboard's initial view controller. (I'll talk more about that in Chapter 6.)

3. If your app uses a main storyboard, `UIApplicationMain` instantiates UIWindow and assigns the window instance to the app delegate's `window` property, which retains it, ensuring that the window will persist for the lifetime of the app.

4. If your app uses a main storyboard, `UIApplicationMain` assigns the initial view controller instance to the window's `rootViewController` property, which retains it. The view controller's view becomes the window's sole subview.

5. `UIApplicationMain` calls the app delegate's `application(_:didFinish-LaunchingWithOptions:)`.

6. Your app's interface is not visible until the window, which contains it, is made the app's key window. Therefore, if your app uses a main storyboard, `UIApplicationMain` calls the window's instance method `makeKeyAndVisible`.

iOS 13 with window scene support

Here's how `UIApplicationMain` bootstraps your app with window scene support as it launches on iOS 13:

1. `UIApplicationMain` instantiates UIApplication and retains this instance, to serve as the shared application instance, which your code can later refer to as `UIApplication.shared`. It then instantiates the app delegate class; it knows which class that is because it is marked `@UIApplicationMain`. It retains the app delegate instance, ensuring that it will persist for the lifetime of the app, and assigns it as the application instance's `delegate`.

2. `UIApplicationMain` calls the app delegate's `application(_:didFinish-LaunchingWithOptions:)`.

3. `UIApplicationMain` creates a UISceneSession, a UIWindowScene, and an instance that will serve as the window scene's delegate. The *Info.plist* specifies, as a string, what the class of the window scene delegate instance should be ("Delegate Class Name" inside the "Application Scene Manifest" dictionary's "Scene Configuration"). In the built-in app templates, it is the SceneDelegate class; this is written in the *Info.plist* as `$(PRODUCT_MODULE_NAME).SceneDelegate` to take account of Swift "name mangling."

   (In iOS 13, `UIApplicationMain` *always* creates a UISceneSession and a UIWindowScene even if your app does *not* declare support for window scenes — in fact, even if your app is linked against iOS 12 or earlier. They are present as part of the architecture even if your app never needs to refer to them.)

4. `UIApplicationMain` looks to see whether your initial scene uses a storyboard. The *Info.plist* specifies, as a string, the name of its storyboard ("Storyboard Name" inside the "Application Scene Manifest" dictionary's "Scene Configuration"). If so, it instantiates that storyboard's initial view controller.

5. If the scene uses a storyboard, `UIApplicationMain` instantiates UIWindow and assigns the window instance to the scene delegate's `window` property, which retains it.

6. If the scene uses a storyboard, `UIApplicationMain` assigns the initial view controller instance to the window instance's `rootViewController` property, which retains it. The view controller's view becomes the window's sole subview.

7. `UIApplicationMain` causes your app's interface to appear, by calling the UIWindow instance method `makeKeyAndVisible`.

8. The scene delegate's `scene(_:willConnectTo:options:)` is called.

The most important differences between this procedure and the iOS 12 procedure are:

- The call to `application(_:didFinishLaunchingWithOptions:)` is much earlier in the sequence. This won't matter if you confine your use of this method to initializations that affect the app as a whole. If you need to know that the launch process is over and your window is visible, implement `scene(_:willConnectTo:options:)`.

- The `window` property belongs to the scene delegate, not the app delegate.

App Without a Storyboard

It is possible to write an app that lacks a main storyboard:

- In iOS 12 and before, this means that the *Info.plist* contains no "Main storyboard file base name" entry.

- In iOS 13 with scene support, it means that there is no "Storyboard Name" entry under "Application Scene Configuration" in the "Application Scene Manifest" dictionary.

Such an app simply does in code everything that `UIApplicationMain` does automatically if the app has a main storyboard. In iOS 12 and before, you would do that in the app delegate's `application(_:didFinishLaunchingWithOptions:)`. In iOS 13, with a window scene, you do it in the scene delegate's `scene(_:willConnect-To:options:)`:

```
func scene(_ scene: UIScene,
    willConnectTo session: UISceneSession,
    options connectionOptions: UIScene.ConnectionOptions) {
        if let windowScene = scene as? UIWindowScene {
            self.window = UIWindow(windowScene: windowScene)  ❶
            let vc = // ...                                    ❷
            self.window!.rootViewController = vc               ❸
            self.window!.makeKeyAndVisible()                   ❹
        }
}
```

❶ Instantiate UIWindow and assign it as the scene delegate's `window` property. It is crucial to make the connection between the window scene and the window by calling `init(windowScene:)`.

❷ Instantiate a view controller and configure it as needed.

❸ Assign the view controller as the window's `rootViewController` property.

❹ Call `makeKeyAndVisible` on the window, to show it.

(That's how a SwiftUI app works. SwiftUI doesn't use storyboards; step 2 creates a UIHostingController that hosts the app's initial View, and after that the SwiftUI code takes over.)

A variant that is sometimes useful is an app that has a storyboard but doesn't let `UIApplicationMain` see it at launch. That way, we can dictate at launch time which view controller from within that storyboard should be the window's root view controller. A typical scenario is that our app has something like a login or registration screen that appears at launch if the user has not logged in, but doesn't appear on subsequent launches once the user *has* logged in:

```
func scene(_ scene: UIScene,
    willConnectTo session: UISceneSession,
    options connectionOptions: UIScene.ConnectionOptions) {
        if let windowScene = scene as? UIWindowScene {
```

```
            self.window = UIWindow(windowScene: windowScene)
            let userHasLoggedIn : Bool = // ...
            let vc = UIStoryboard(name: "Main", bundle: nil)
                .instantiateViewController(identifier: userHasLoggedIn ?
                    "UserHasLoggedIn" : "LoginScreen") // *
            self.window!.rootViewController = vc
            self.window!.makeKeyAndVisible()
        }
    }
```

Referring to the Window

Once the app is running, there are various ways for your code to refer to the window:

From a view

If a UIView is in the interface, it automatically has a reference to the window that contains it, through its own `window` property. Your code will probably be running in a view controller with a main view, so `self.view.window` is usually the best way to refer to the window.

You can also use a UIView's `window` property as a way of asking whether it is ultimately embedded in the window; if it isn't, its `window` property is `nil`. A UIView whose `window` property is `nil` cannot be visible to the user.

From the scene delegate

The scene delegate instance maintains a reference to the window through its `window` property.

From the application

The shared application maintains a reference to the window through its `windows` property:

```
let w = UIApplication.shared.windows.first!
```

 Do not expect that the window you know about is the app's only window. The runtime can create additional mysterious windows, such as the UITextEffectsWindow and the UIRemoteKeyboardWindow.

Experimenting with Views

In the course of this and subsequent chapters, you may want to experiment with views in a project of your own. If you start your project with the Single View App template, it gives you the simplest possible app — a main storyboard containing one scene consisting of one view controller instance along with its main view. As I described in the preceding section, when the app runs, that view controller will become the window's `rootViewController`, and its main view will become the window's root view. If you can get *your* views to become subviews of that view controller's main view, they will be present in the app's interface when it launches.

In the nib editor, you can drag a view from the Library into the main view as a subview, and it will be instantiated in the interface when the app runs. However, my initial examples will all create views and add them to the interface *in code*. So where should that code go? The simplest place is the view controller's viewDidLoad method, which is provided as a stub by the project template code; it runs once, before the view appears in the interface for the first time.

The viewDidLoad method can refer to the view controller's main view by saying self.view. In my code examples, whenever I say self.view, you can assume we're in a view controller and that self.view is this view controller's main view:

```
override func viewDidLoad() {
    super.viewDidLoad() // this is template code
    let v = UIView(frame:CGRect(x:100, y:100, width:50, height:50))
    v.backgroundColor = .red // small red square
    self.view.addSubview(v) // add it to main view
}
```

Try it! Make a new project from the Single View App template, and make the ViewController class's viewDidLoad look like that. Run the app. You will actually *see* the small red square in the running app's interface.

Subview and Superview

Once upon a time, and not so very long ago, a view owned precisely its own rectangular area. No part of any view that was not a subview of this view could appear inside it, because when this view redrew its rectangle, it would erase the overlapping portion of the other view. No part of any subview of this view could appear outside it, because the view took responsibility for its own rectangle and no more.

Those rules were gradually relaxed, and starting in OS X 10.5, Apple introduced an entirely new architecture for view drawing that lifted those restrictions completely. iOS view drawing is based on this revised architecture. In iOS, some or all of a subview can appear outside its superview, and a view can overlap another view and can be drawn partially or totally in front of it without being its subview.

Figure 1-1 shows three overlapping views. All three views have a background color, so each is completely represented by a colored rectangle. You have no way of knowing, from this visual representation, exactly how the views are related within the view hierarchy. In actual fact, View 1 is a sibling view of View 2 (they are both direct subviews of the root view), and View 3 is a subview of View 2.

When views are created in the nib, you can examine the view hierarchy in the nib editor's document outline to learn their actual relationship (Figure 1-2). When views

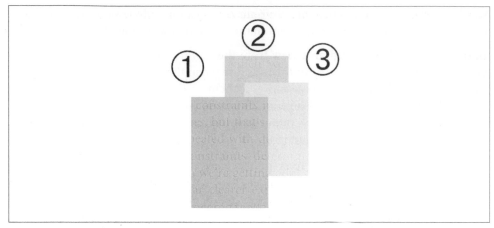

Figure 1-1. Overlapping views

Figure 1-2. A view hierarchy as displayed in the nib editor

are created in code, you know their hierarchical relationship because you created that hierarchy. But the visible interface doesn't tell you, because view overlapping is so flexible.

Nevertheless, a view's position within the view hierarchy is extremely significant. For one thing, the view hierarchy dictates the *order* in which views are drawn. Sibling subviews of the same superview have a definite order; an earlier sibling is drawn before a later sibling, so if they overlap, the earlier one will appear to be behind the later one. Similarly, a superview is drawn before its subviews, so if the subviews overlap their superview, the superview will appear to be behind them.

You can see this illustrated in Figure 1-1. View 3 is a subview of View 2 and is drawn on top of it. View 1 is a sibling of View 2, but it is a later sibling, so it is drawn on top of View 2 and on top of View 3. View 1 *cannot* appear behind View 3 but in front of View 2, because Views 2 and 3 are subview and superview and are drawn together — both are drawn either before or after View 1, depending on the ordering of the siblings.

This layering order can be governed in the nib editor by arranging the views in the document outline. (If you click in the canvas, you may be able to use the menu items of the Editor → Arrange menu instead — Send to Front, Send to Back, Send Forward,

Send Backward.) In code, there are methods for arranging the sibling order of views, which we'll come to in a moment.

Here are some other effects of the view hierarchy:

- If a view is removed from or moved within its superview, its subviews go with it.
- A view's degree of transparency is inherited by its subviews.
- A view can optionally limit the drawing of its subviews so that any parts of them outside the view are not shown. This is called *clipping* and is set with the view's clipsToBounds property.
- A superview *owns* its subviews, in the memory-management sense, much as an array owns its elements; it retains its subviews, and is responsible for releasing a subview when that subview is removed from the collection of this view's subviews, or when the superview itself goes out of existence.
- If a view's size is changed, its subviews can be resized automatically (and I'll have much more to say about that later in this chapter).

A UIView has a superview property (a UIView) and a subviews property (an array of UIView objects, in back-to-front order), allowing you to trace the view hierarchy in code. There is also a method isDescendant(of:) letting you check whether one view is a subview of another at any depth.

If you need a reference to a particular view, you will probably arrange it beforehand as a property, perhaps through an outlet. Alternatively, a view can have a numeric tag (its tag property), and can then be referred to by sending any view higher up the view hierarchy the viewWithTag(_:) message. Seeing that all tags of interest are unique within their region of the hierarchy is up to you.

Manipulating the view hierarchy in code is easy. This is part of what gives iOS apps their dynamic quality. It is perfectly reasonable for your code to rip an entire hierarchy of views out of the superview and substitute another, right before the user's very eyes! You can do this directly; you can combine it with animation (Chapter 4); you can govern it through view controllers (Chapter 6).

The method addSubview(_:) makes one view a subview of another; removeFrom-Superview takes a subview out of its superview's view hierarchy. In both cases, if the superview is part of the visible interface, the subview will appear or disappear respectively at that moment; and of course the subview may have subviews of its own that accompany it. Removing a subview from its superview releases it; if you intend to reuse that subview later on, you will need to retain it first by assigning it to a variable.

Events inform a view of these dynamic changes. To respond to these events requires subclassing. Then you'll be able to override any of these methods:

- willRemoveSubview(_:), didAddSubview(_:)

- `willMove(toSuperview:)`, `didMoveToSuperview`
- `willMove(toWindow:)`, `didMoveToWindow`

When `addSubview(_:)` is called, the view is placed last among its superview's sub-views, so it is drawn last, meaning that it appears frontmost. That might not be what you want. A view's subviews are indexed, starting at 0 which is rearmost, and there are methods for inserting a subview at a given index or below (behind) or above (in front of) a specific view; for swapping two sibling views by index; and for moving a subview all the way to the front or back among its siblings:

- `insertSubview(_:at:)`
- `insertSubview(_:belowSubview:)`, `insertSubview(_:aboveSubview:)`
- `exchangeSubview(at:withSubviewAt:)`
- `bringSubviewToFront(_:)`, `sendSubviewToBack(_:)`

Oddly, there is no command for removing all of a view's subviews at once. However, a view's `subviews` array is an immutable copy of the internal list of subviews, so it is legal to cycle through it and remove each subview one at a time:

```
myView.subviews.forEach {$0.removeFromSuperview()}
```

Color

A view can be assigned a background color through its `backgroundColor` property. A view distinguished by nothing but its background color is a colored rectangle, and is an excellent medium for experimentation, as in Figure 1-1.

A view whose background color is `nil` (the default) has a transparent background. If this view does no additional drawing of its own, it will be invisible! Such a view is perfectly reasonable; a view with a transparent background might act as a convenient superview to other views, making them behave together.

A color is a UIColor, which will typically be specified using `.red`, `.blue`, `.green`, and `.alpha` components, which are CGFloat values between 0 and 1:

```
v.backgroundColor = UIColor(red: 0, green: 0.1, blue: 0.1, alpha: 1)
```

There are also numerous named colors, vended as static properties of the UIColor class:

```
v.backgroundColor = .red
```

New in iOS 13, you may need to be rather more circumspect about the colors you assign to things. The problem is that the user can switch the device between light and dark modes. This can cause a cascade of color changes that can make hard-coded colors look bad. Suppose (in a new project created in Xcode 11) we give the view controller's main view a subview with a dark color:

```
override func viewDidLoad() {
    super.viewDidLoad()
    let v = UIView(frame:CGRect(x:100, y:100, width:50, height:50))
    v.backgroundColor = UIColor(red: 0, green: 0.1, blue: 0.1, alpha: 1)
    self.view.addSubview(v)
}
```

If we run the project in the simulator, we see a small very dark square against a white background. But now suppose we switch to dark mode. Now the background becomes black, and we don't see our dark square any longer. The reason is that the view controller's main view has a *dynamic* color, which is white in light mode but black in dark mode, and now our dark square is black on black.

One solution is to make our UIColor dynamic. We can do this with the initializer init(dynamicProvider:), giving it as parameter a function that takes a trait collection and returns a color. I'll explain more about what a trait collection is later in this chapter; right now, all you need to know is that its userInterfaceStyle may or may not be .dark:

```
v.backgroundColor = UIColor { tc in
    switch tc.userInterfaceStyle {
    case .dark:
        return UIColor(red: 0.3, green: 0.4, blue: 0.4, alpha: 1)
    default:
        return UIColor(red: 0, green: 0.1, blue: 0.1, alpha: 1)
    }
}
```

We have created our own custom dynamic color, which is different depending what mode we're in. In dark mode, our view's color is now a dark gray that is visible against a black background.

 To switch to dark mode in the simulator, click the Environment Overrides button in the debug bar. In the popover that appears, click the first switch, at the upper right.

A more compact way to get a dynamic color is to use one of the many dynamic colors vended as static properties by UIColor in iOS 13. Most of these have names that start with .system, such as .systemYellow; others have *semantic* names describing their role, such as .label. For details, see Apple's *Human Interface Guidelines*.

You can also design a custom named color in the asset catalog. When you do, you can choose from the Appearances pop-up menu in the Attributes inspector and switch to Any, Dark. Now there are two colors, one for dark mode and the other for everything else, just as in our earlier code. Let's say we've done that, and our color in the asset catalog is called myDarkColor. Then you could say:

```
v.backgroundColor = UIColor(named: "myDarkColor")
```

Custom named colors from the asset catalog also appear in the Library and in the color pop-up menus in the Attributes inspector when you select a view.

Visibility and Opacity

Three properties relate to the visibility and opacity of a view:

isHidden

A view can be made invisible by setting its isHidden property to true, and visible again by setting it to false. Hiding a view takes it (and its subviews, of course) out of the visible interface without actually removing it from the view hierarchy. A hidden view does not (normally) receive touch events, so to the user it really is as if the view weren't there. But it is there, so it can still be manipulated in code.

alpha

A view can be made partially or completely transparent through its alpha property: 1.0 means opaque, 0.0 means transparent, and a value may be anywhere between them, inclusive. This property affects both the apparent transparency of the view's background color and the apparent transparency of its contents. If a view displays an image and has a background color and its alpha is less than 1, the background color will seep through the image (and whatever is behind the view will seep through both). Moreover, it affects the apparent transparency of the view's subviews! If a superview has an alpha of 0.5, none of its subviews can have an *apparent* opacity of more than 0.5, because whatever alpha value they have will be drawn relative to 0.5. A view that is completely transparent (or very close to it) is like a view whose isHidden is true: it is invisible, along with its subviews, and cannot (normally) be touched.

(Just to make matters more complicated, colors have an alpha value as well. A view can have an alpha of 1.0 but still have a transparent background because its backgroundColor has an alpha less than 1.0.)

isOpaque

This property is a horse of a different color; changing it has no effect on the view's appearance. Rather, it is a hint to the drawing system. If a view is completely filled with opaque material and its alpha is 1.0, so that the view has no effective transparency, then it can be drawn more efficiently (with less drag on performance) if you inform the drawing system of this fact by setting its isOpaque to true. Otherwise, you should set its isOpaque to false. The isOpaque value is *not* changed for you when you set a view's backgroundColor or alpha! Setting it correctly is entirely up to you; the default, perhaps surprisingly, is true.

Frame

A view's `frame` property, a CGRect, is the position of its rectangle within its superview, *in the superview's coordinate system*. By default, the superview's coordinate system will have the origin at its top left, with the x-coordinate growing positively rightward and the y-coordinate growing positively downward.

Setting a view's frame to a different CGRect value repositions the view, or resizes it, or both. If the view is visible, this change will be visibly reflected in the interface. On the other hand, you can also set a view's frame when the view is not visible, such as when you create the view in code. In that case, the frame describes where the view *will* be positioned within its superview when it is given a superview.

UIView's designated initializer is `init(frame:)`, and you'll often assign a frame this way, especially because the default frame might otherwise be `CGRect.zero`, which is rarely what you want. A view with a zero-size frame is effectively invisible (though you might still see its subviews). Forgetting to assign a view a frame when creating it in code, and then wondering why it isn't appearing when added to a superview, is a common beginner mistake. If a view has a standard size that you want it to adopt, especially in relation to its contents (like a UIButton in relation to its title), an alternative is to call its `sizeToFit` method.

We are now in a position to generate programmatically the interface displayed in Figure 1-1; we determine the layering order of v1 and v3 (the middle and left views, which are siblings) by the order in which we insert them into the view hierarchy:

Figure 1-3. A subview inset from its superview

```
let v1 = UIView(frame:CGRect(113, 111, 132, 194))
v1.backgroundColor = UIColor(red: 1, green: 0.4, blue: 1, alpha: 1)
let v2 = UIView(frame:CGRect(41, 56, 132, 194))
v2.backgroundColor = UIColor(red: 0.5, green: 1, blue: 0, alpha: 1)
let v3 = UIView(frame:CGRect(43, 197, 160, 230))
v3.backgroundColor = UIColor(red: 1, green: 0, blue: 0, alpha: 1)
self.view.addSubview(v1)
v1.addSubview(v2)
self.view.addSubview(v3)
```

 That code, and all subsequent code in this book, uses a custom CGRect initializer with no argument labels. Please read the sidebar "Core Graphics Initializers" on page 14 right now!

When a UIView is instantiated from a nib, its `init(frame:)` is *not called* — `init(coder:)` is called instead. Implementing `init(frame:)` in a UIView subclass, and then wondering why your code isn't called when the view is instantiated from a nib, is a common beginner mistake.

Bounds and Center

Suppose we have a superview and a subview, and the subview is to appear inset by 10 points, as in Figure 1-3. So we want to set the subview's frame. But to what value? CGRect methods like `insetBy(dx:dy:)` make it easy to derive one rectangle as an inset from another. But *what* rectangle should we inset from? Not from the superview's frame; the frame represents a view's position within *its* superview, and in that superview's coordinates. What we're after is a CGRect describing our superview's rectangle in its *own* coordinates, because those are the coordinates in which the subview's frame is to be expressed. The CGRect that describes a view's rectangle in its own coordinates is the view's bounds property.

So, the code to generate Figure 1-3 looks like this:

Figure 1-4. A subview exactly covering its superview

```
let v1 = UIView(frame:CGRect(113, 111, 132, 194))
v1.backgroundColor = UIColor(red: 1, green: 0.4, blue: 1, alpha: 1)
let v2 = UIView(frame:v1.bounds.insetBy(dx: 10, dy: 10))
v2.backgroundColor = UIColor(red: 0.5, green: 1, blue: 0, alpha: 1)
self.view.addSubview(v1)
v1.addSubview(v2)
```

You'll very often use a view's bounds in this way. When you need coordinates for positioning content inside a view, whether drawing manually or placing a subview, you'll refer to the view's bounds.

If you change a view's bounds *size*, you change its *frame*. The change in the view's frame takes place around its *center*, which remains unchanged:

```
let v1 = UIView(frame:CGRect(113, 111, 132, 194))
v1.backgroundColor = UIColor(red: 1, green: 0.4, blue: 1, alpha: 1)
let v2 = UIView(frame:v1.bounds.insetBy(dx: 10, dy: 10))
v2.backgroundColor = UIColor(red: 0.5, green: 1, blue: 0, alpha: 1)
self.view.addSubview(v1)
v1.addSubview(v2)
v2.bounds.size.height += 20
v2.bounds.size.width += 20
```

What appears is a single rectangle; the subview completely and exactly covers its superview, its frame being the same as the superview's bounds. The call to `insetBy` started with the superview's bounds and shaved 10 points off the left, right, top, and bottom to set the subview's frame (Figure 1-3). But then we added 20 points to the subview's bounds height and width, which added 20 points to the subview's frame height and width as well (Figure 1-4). The subview's center didn't move, so we effectively put the 10 points back onto the left, right, top, and bottom of the subview's frame.

If you change a view's bounds *origin*, you move the *origin of its internal coordinate system*. When you create a UIView, its bounds coordinate system's zero point (0.0,0.0) is at its top left. Because a subview is positioned in its superview with respect to its superview's coordinate system, a change in the bounds origin of the

Figure 1-5. The superview's bounds origin has been shifted

superview will change the apparent position of a subview. To illustrate, we start once again with our subview inset evenly within its superview, and then change the bounds origin of the superview:

```
let v1 = UIView(frame:CGRect(113, 111, 132, 194))
v1.backgroundColor = UIColor(red: 1, green: 0.4, blue: 1, alpha: 1)
let v2 = UIView(frame:v1.bounds.insetBy(dx: 10, dy: 10))
v2.backgroundColor = UIColor(red: 0.5, green: 1, blue: 0, alpha: 1)
self.view.addSubview(v1)
v1.addSubview(v2)
v1.bounds.origin.x += 10
v1.bounds.origin.y += 10
```

Nothing happens to the superview's size or position. But the subview has moved up and to the left so that it is flush with its superview's top-left corner (Figure 1-5). Basically, what we've done is to say to the superview, "Instead of calling the point at your upper left (0.0,0.0), call that point (10.0,10.0)." Because the subview's frame origin is itself at (10.0,10.0), the subview now touches the superview's top-left corner. The effect of changing a view's bounds origin may seem directionally backward — we increased the superview's origin in the positive direction, but the subview moved in the negative direction — but think of it this way: a view's bounds origin point coincides with its frame's top left.

We have seen that changing a view's bounds size affects its frame size. The converse is also true: changing a view's frame size affects its bounds size. What is *not* affected by changing a view's bounds size is the view's center.

A view's center is a single point establishing the positional relationship between the view's bounds and its superview's bounds. It represents a subview's position within its superview, in the superview's coordinates; in particular, it is the position *within the superview* of the subview's own *bounds center*, the point derived from the bounds like this:

```
let c = CGPoint(theView.bounds.midX, theView.bounds.midY)
```

Changing a view's bounds does not change its center; changing a view's center does not change its bounds. A view's bounds and center are orthogonal (independent), and completely describe the view's size and its position within its superview. The view's frame is therefore superfluous! In fact, the frame property is merely a convenient expression of the center and bounds values. In most cases, this won't matter to you; you'll use the frame property anyway. When you first create a view from scratch, the designated initializer is init(frame:). You can change the frame, and the bounds size and center will change to match. You can change the bounds size or the center, and the frame will change to match. Nevertheless, the proper and most reliable way to position and size a view within its superview is to use its bounds and center, not its frame; there are some situations in which the frame is meaningless (or will at least behave very oddly), but the bounds and center will always work.

We have seen that every view has its own coordinate system, expressed by its bounds, and that a view's coordinate system has a clear relationship to its superview's coordinate system, expressed by its center. This is true of every view in a window, so it is possible to convert between the coordinates of any two views in the same window. Convenience methods are supplied to perform this conversion both for a CGPoint and for a CGRect:

- convert(_:to:)
- convert(_:from:)

The first parameter is either a CGPoint or a CGRect. The second parameter is a UIView; if the second parameter is nil, it is taken to be the window. The recipient is another UIView; the CGPoint or CGRect is being converted between its coordinates and the second view's coordinates. If v1 is the superview of v2, then to center v2 within v1 you could say:

```
v2.center = v1.convert(v1.center, from:v1.superview)
```

A more common approach is to place the subview's center at the superview's *bounds* center, like this:

```
v2.center = CGPoint(v1.bounds.midX, v1.bounds.midY)
```

That's such a common thing to do that I've written an extension that provides the center of a CGRect as its center property (see Appendix B), allowing me to talk like this:

```
v2.center = v1.bounds.center
```

Observe that the following is *not* the way to center a subview v2 in a superview v1:

```
v2.center = v1.center // that won't work!
```

Trying to center one view within another like that is a common beginner mistake. It can't succeed, and will have unpredictable results, because the two center values are in different coordinate systems.

When setting a view's position by setting its center, if the height or width of the view is not an integer (or, on a single-resolution screen, not an even integer), the view can end up *misaligned*: its point values in one or both dimensions are located between the screen pixels. This can cause the view to be displayed incorrectly; if the view contains text, the text may be blurry. You can detect this situation in the Simulator by checking Debug → Color Misaligned Images. A simple solution is to set the view's frame to its own integral.

Transform

A view's transform property alters how the view is drawn, changing the view's *apparent* size, location, or orientation, without affecting its *actual* bounds and center. A transformed view continues to behave correctly: a rotated button is still a button, and can be tapped in its apparent location and orientation. Transforms are useful particularly as temporary visual indicators. You might call attention to a view by applying a transform that scales it up slightly, and then reversing that transform to restore it to its original size, and animating those changes (Chapter 4).

A transform value is a CGAffineTransform, which is a struct representing six of the nine values of a 3×3 transformation matrix (the other three values are constants, so there's no need to represent them in the struct). You may have forgotten your high-school linear algebra, so you may not recall what a transformation matrix is. For the details, which are quite simple really, see the "Transforms" chapter of Apple's *Quartz 2D Programming Guide* in the documentation archive, especially the section called "The Math Behind the Matrices." But you don't really need to know those details, because initializers are provided for creating three of the basic types of transform: rotation, scale (size), and translation (location). A fourth basic transform type, skewing or shearing, has no initializer and is rarely used.

By default, a view's transformation matrix is CGAffineTransform.identity, the identity transform. It has no visible effect, so you're unaware of it. Any transform that you do apply takes place around the view's center, which is held constant.

Here's some code to illustrate use of a transform:

```
let v1 = UIView(frame:CGRect(113, 111, 132, 194))
v1.backgroundColor = UIColor(red: 1, green: 0.4, blue: 1, alpha: 1)
let v2 = UIView(frame:v1.bounds.insetBy(dx: 10, dy: 10))
v2.backgroundColor = UIColor(red: 0.5, green: 1, blue: 0, alpha: 1)
```

Figure 1-6. A rotation transform

```
self.view.addSubview(v1)
v1.addSubview(v2)
v1.transform = CGAffineTransform(rotationAngle: 45 * .pi/180)
print(v1.frame)
```

The `transform` property of the view `v1` is set to a rotation transform. The result (Figure 1-6) is that the view appears to be rocked 45 degrees clockwise. (I think in degrees, but Core Graphics thinks in radians, so my code has to convert.) Observe that the view's `center` property is unaffected, so that the rotation seems to have occurred around the view's center. Moreover, the view's `bounds` property is unaffected; the internal coordinate system is unchanged, so the subview is drawn in the same place relative to its superview.

The view's `frame` is now useless, as no mere rectangle can describe the region of the superview apparently occupied by the view; the frame's actual value, roughly (63.7,92.7,230.5,230.5), describes the minimal bounding rectangle surrounding the view's apparent position. The rule is that if a view's `transform` is not the identity transform, you should not set its `frame`; also, automatic resizing of a subview, discussed later in this chapter, requires that the superview's transform be the identity transform.

Suppose, instead of a rotation transform, we apply a scale transform, like this:

```
v1.transform = CGAffineTransform(scaleX:1.8, y:1)
```

The `bounds` property of the view `v1` is still unaffected, so the subview is still drawn in the same place relative to its superview; this means that the two views seem to have stretched horizontally together (Figure 1-7) No bounds or centers were harmed by the application of this transform!

Methods are provided for transforming an existing transform. This operation is not commutative; order matters. (That high school math is starting to come back to you now, isn't it?) If you start with a transform that translates a view to the right and then

Figure 1-7. A scale transform

Figure 1-8. Translation, then rotation

apply a rotation of 45 degrees, the rotated view appears to the right of its original position; on the other hand, if you start with a transform that rotates a view 45 degrees and then apply a translation to the right, the meaning of "right" has changed, so the rotated view appears 45 degrees down from its original position. To demonstrate the difference, I'll start with a subview that exactly overlaps its superview:

```
let v1 = UIView(frame:CGRect(20, 111, 132, 194))
v1.backgroundColor = UIColor(red: 1, green: 0.4, blue: 1, alpha: 1)
let v2 = UIView(frame:v1.bounds)
v2.backgroundColor = UIColor(red: 0.5, green: 1, blue: 0, alpha: 1)
self.view.addSubview(v1)
v1.addSubview(v2)
```

Then I'll apply two successive transforms to the subview, leaving the superview to show where the subview was originally. In this example, I translate and then rotate (Figure 1-8):

```
v2.transform =
    CGAffineTransform(translationX:100, y:0).rotated(by: 45 * .pi/180)
```

In this example, I rotate and then translate (Figure 1-9):

Figure 1-9. Rotation, then translation

```
v2.transform =
    CGAffineTransform(rotationAngle: 45 * .pi/180).translatedBy(x: 100, y: 0)
```

The `concatenating` method concatenates two transform matrices using matrix multiplication. Again, this operation is not commutative. The order is the *opposite* of the order when chaining transforms. This code gives the same result as the previous example (Figure 1-9):

```
let r = CGAffineTransform(rotationAngle: 45 * .pi/180)
let t = CGAffineTransform(translationX:100, y:0)
v2.transform = t.concatenating(r) // not r.concatenating(t)
```

To remove a transform from a combination of transforms, apply its inverse. The `inverted` method lets you obtain the inverse of a given affine transform. Again, order matters. In this example, I rotate the subview and shift it to its "right," and then remove the rotation, demonstrating how to translate a view at an angle (Figure 1-10):

```
let r = CGAffineTransform(rotationAngle: 45 * .pi/180)
let t = CGAffineTransform(translationX:100, y:0)
v2.transform = t.concatenating(r)
v2.transform = r.inverted().concatenating(v2.transform)
```

CGPoint, CGSize, and CGRect all have an `applying(_:)` method that permits you to apply an affine transform to them. With it, you can calculate what the result *would* be if you were to apply the transform to a view. However, the transform is centered at the origin, so if that isn't what you want, you have to translate the rotation point to the origin, apply the real transform, and then invert the translation transform. Earlier we rotated a view and printed its `frame`, like this:

```
let v1 = UIView(frame:CGRect(113, 111, 132, 194))
v1.transform = CGAffineTransform(rotationAngle: 45 * .pi/180)
print(v1.frame) // 63.7,92.7,230.5,230.5
```

We can get the same result without actually rotating any views:

Figure 1-10. Rotation, then translation, then inversion of the rotation

```
let rect = CGRect(113, 111, 132, 194)
let shift = CGAffineTransform(translationX: -rect.midX, y: -rect.midY)
let rotate = v1.transform
let transform = shift.concatenating(rotate).concatenating(shift.inverted())
let rect2 = rect.applying(transform)
print(rect2) // 63.7,92.7,230.5,230.5
```

Transform3D

New in iOS 13, a UIView has a `transform3D` property. This is actually the underlying layer's `transform` property (Chapter 3), but since it is now exposed through the view, I'll explain it here.

As the name implies, a `transform3D` takes place in three-dimensional space; its description includes a z-axis, perpendicular to both the x-axis and y-axis. (By default, the positive z-axis points out of the screen, toward the viewer's face.) The result of such a transformation does not necessarily *look* three-dimensional; but it *operates* in three dimensions, quite sufficiently to give a cartoonish but effective sense of reality, especially when performing an animation. We've all seen the screen image flip like turning over a piece of paper to reveal what's on the back; that's a rotation in three dimensions.

Like a view's `transform`, a `transform3D` takes place by default around the view's center, which is unaffected. (You can get finer control by dropping down to the level of the layer.) The transform itself is described mathematically by a struct called a CATransform3D. The Core Animation *Transforms* documentation lists the functions for working with these transforms. They are a lot like the CGAffineTransform functions, except they've got a third dimension. A 2D scale transform depends upon two values, the scale on the x-axis and the y-axis; for a 3D scale transform, there's also a z-axis so you have to supply a third parameter.

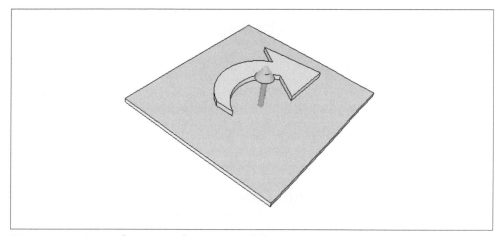

Figure 1-11. An anchor point plus a vector defines a rotation plane

The rotation 3D transform is a little more complicated. In addition to the angle, you also have to supply three coordinates describing the *vector* around which the rotation is to take place. Perhaps you've forgotten from your high-school math what a vector is, or perhaps trying to visualize three dimensions boggles your mind, so here's another way to think of it.

For purposes of discussion, imagine a coordinate system in which the center of the rotation (by default, the view's center) is at the origin (0.0,0.0,0.0). Now imagine an arrow emanating from that origin; its other end, the pointy end, is described by the three coordinates you provide in that coordinate system. Now imagine a plane that intersects the origin, perpendicular to the arrow. That is the plane in which the rotation will take place; a positive angle is a clockwise rotation, as seen from the side of the plane with the arrow (Figure 1-11). In effect, the three coordinates you supply describe (relative to the origin) where your eye would have to be to see this rotation as an old-fashioned two-dimensional rotation.

A vector specifies a direction, not a point. It makes no difference on what scale you give the coordinates: (1.0,1.0,1.0) means the same thing as (10.0,10.0,10.0), so you might as well say (1.0,1.0,1.0), sticking to the unit scale; when you do, the vector is said to be *normalized*.

If the three normalized values are (0.0,0.0,1.0), with all other things being equal, the case is collapsed to a simple CGAffineTransform, because the rotational plane is the screen. If the three normalized values are (0.0,0.0,-1.0), it's a backward CGAffineTransform, so that a positive angle looks counterclockwise (because we are looking at the "back side" of the rotational plane).

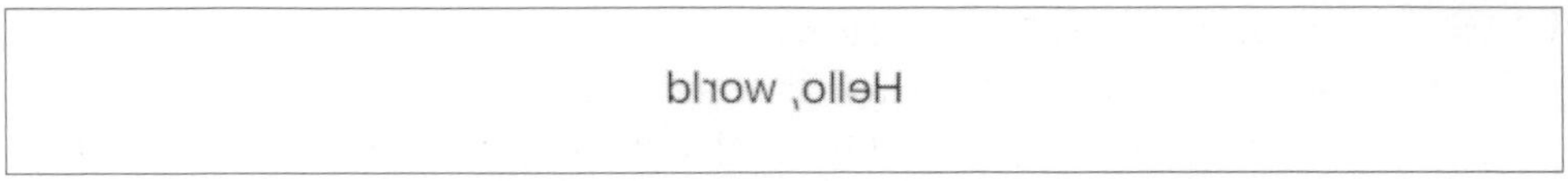

```
                          blɿow ,olləH
```

Figure 1-12. A backward label

In this example, I'll flip a UIView around its vertical axis. If this view is a UILabel whose text is "Hello, world", the result is that we see the words "Hello, world" written *backward* (Figure 1-12):

```
v.transform3D = CATransform3DMakeRotation(.pi, 0, 1, 0)
```

Window Coordinates and Screen Coordinates

The device screen has no frame, but it has bounds. The window has no superview, but its frame is set automatically to match the screen's bounds. The window starts out life filling the screen, and generally continues to fill the screen, and so, for the most part, *window coordinates are screen coordinates*. (I'll discuss the possible exceptions on an iPad in Chapter 9.)

In iOS 7 and before, the screen's coordinates were invariant. The transform property lay at the heart of an iOS app's ability to rotate its interface: the window's frame and bounds were locked to the screen, and an app's interface rotated to compensate for a change in device orientation by applying a rotation transform to the root view, so that its origin moved to what the user now saw as the top left of the view.

But iOS 8 introduced a major change: when the app rotates to compensate for the rotation of the device, the screen (and with it, the window) is what rotates. None of the views in the story — neither the window, nor the root view, nor any of its subviews — receives a rotation transform when the app's interface rotates. Instead, there is a transposition of the dimensions of the screen's bounds (and a corresponding transposition of the dimensions of the window's bounds and its root view's bounds): in portrait orientation, the size is taller than wide, but in landscape orientation, the size is wider than tall.

Therefore, there are actually *two* sets of screen coordinates. Each is reported through a UICoordinateSpace, a protocol (also adopted by UIView) that provides a bounds property:

UIScreen's coordinateSpace *property*
> This coordinate space *rotates*. Its bounds height and width are transposed when the app rotates to compensate for a change in the orientation of the device; its bounds origin is at the top left of the *app*.

UIScreen's `fixedCoordinateSpace` *property*

> This coordinate space is *invariant*. Its bounds origin stays at the top left of the *physical device*, remaining always in the same relationship to the device's hardware buttons regardless of how the device itself is held.

To help you convert between coordinate spaces, UICoordinateSpace provides methods parallel to the coordinate-conversion methods I listed earlier:

- `convert(_:from:)`

- `convert(_:to:)`

The first parameter is either a CGPoint or a CGRect. The second parameter is a UICoordinateSpace, which might be a UIView or the UIScreen; so is the recipient. Suppose we have a UIView v in our interface, and we wish to learn its position in fixed device coordinates. We could do it like this:

```
let screen = UIScreen.main.fixedCoordinateSpace
let r = v.superview!.convert(v.frame, to: screen)
```

Imagine that we have a subview of our main view, at the exact top left corner of the main view. When the device and the app are in portrait orientation, the subview's top left is at (0.0,0.0) both in window coordinates and in screen `fixedCoordinate-Space` coordinates. When the device is rotated left into landscape orientation, and if the app rotates to compensate, the window rotates, so the subview is *still* at the top left from the user's point of view, and is *still* at the top left in window coordinates. But in screen `fixedCoordinateSpace` coordinates, the subview's top left x-coordinate will have a large positive value, because the origin is now at the lower left and its x grows positively upward.

Occasions where you need such information will be rare. Indeed, my experience is that it is rare even to worry about window coordinates. All of your app's visible action takes place within your root view controller's main view, and the bounds of that view, which are adjusted for you automatically when the app rotates to compensate for a change in device orientation, are probably the highest coordinate system that will interest you.

 New in iOS 13, the window's UIWindowScene also vends a `coordinateSpace`. It isn't clear to me under what circumstances this would differ from the window's coordinate space.

Trait Collections

Because of the dynamic nature of the larger environment in which views live, it is useful to have an object describing that environment that propagates down through the hierarchy of view controllers and views, along with a way of alerting each element of that hierarchy that the environment has changed. This is managed through the *trait collection.*

The trait collection originates in the screen (UIScreen) and works its way down through the window and any view controllers whose view is part of the interface all the way down to every individual subview. All the relevant classes (UIScreen, UIViewController and UIPresentationController, and UIView) implement the UITraitEnvironment protocol, which supplies the `traitCollection` property and the `traitCollectionDidChange` method.

The `traitCollection` is a UITraitCollection, a value class. It is freighted with a considerable number of properties describing the environment. Its `displayScale` tells you the screen resolution; its `userInterfaceIdiom` states the general device type, iPhone or iPad; it reports such things as the device's force touch capability and display gamut; and so on.

Both at app launch time and if any property of the trait collection changes while the app is running, the `traitCollectionDidChange(_:)` message is propagated down the hierarchy of UITraitEnvironments; the old trait collection (if any) is provided as the parameter, and the new trait collection can be retrieved as `self.traitCollection`.

 If you implement `traitCollectionDidChange(_:)`, always call `super` in the first line. Forgetting to do this is a common beginner mistake.

It is also possible to construct a trait collection yourself. Oddly, though, you can't set any trait collection properties directly; instead, you form a trait collection through an initializer that determines just *one* property, and if you want to add further property settings, you have to combine trait collections by calling `init(traitsFrom:)` with an array of trait collections:

```
let tcdisp = UITraitCollection(displayScale: UIScreen.main.scale)
let tcphone = UITraitCollection(userInterfaceIdiom: .phone)
let tc1 = UITraitCollection(traitsFrom: [tcdisp, tcphone])
```

The `init(traitsFrom:)` array works like inheritance: an *ordered intersection* is performed. If two trait collections are combined, and they both set the same property, the winner is the trait collection that appears later in the array or further down the inheritance hierarchy. If one sets a property and the other doesn't, the one that sets the property wins. If you create a trait collection, the value for any unspecified property will be inherited if the trait collection finds itself in the inheritance hierarchy.

To compare trait collections, call `containsTraits(in:)`. This returns `true` if the value of every *specified* property of the parameter trait collection matches that of this trait collection.

The trait collection properties that are of chief concern with regard to UIViews in general are the interface style and the size classes, so I'll talk about those now.

Interface Style

The trait collection's `userInterfaceStyle` (a UIUserInterfaceStyle, new in iOS 13) reports whether the environment is in light mode (`.light`) or dark mode (`.dark`). For the significance of these for your app, see the discussion of colors earlier in this chapter. If your colors are dynamic colors, then for the most part everything will happen automatically; the user switches modes, and your colors change in response. However, there are circumstances under which you may be managing some colors manually, and you'll want to know when the interface style changes so that *you* can change a color in response.

Let's say we're applying a custom named dynamic color from the asset catalog to the border of a view. This is actually done at the level of the view's layer (Chapter 3), and requires that we take the color's `cgColor` property:

```
self.otherView.layer.borderWidth = 4
self.otherView.layer.borderColor =
    UIColor(named: "myDarkColor")?.cgColor
```

The problem is that neither a layer nor a color's `cgColor` knows anything about the trait collection. So it is up to us to listen for trait collection changes and apply our dynamic color *again*. We can save ourselves from doing unnecessary work, thanks to the trait collection `hasDifferentColorAppearance` method:

```
override func traitCollectionDidChange(_ prevtc: UITraitCollection?) {
    super.traitCollectionDidChange(prevtc)
    if prevtc?.hasDifferentColorAppearance(
        comparedTo: self.traitCollection) ?? true {
            self.otherView.layer.borderColor =
                UIColor(named: "myDarkColor")?.cgColor
    }
}
```

Observe that we don't have to know what the `userInterfaceStyle` actually is; we simply take our dynamic color's `cgColor` and apply it, exactly as we did before. How can this be? It's because the act of accessing the named color from the asset catalog — `UIColor(named: "myDarkColor")` — takes place in the presence of a global value, `UITraitCollection.current`. In `traitCollectionDidChange` and various other places, the runtime sets this value for us, and so our dynamic color arrives in the correct interface style variant and our derived `cgColor` is the correct color. In contexts where `UITraitCollection.current` is *not* set automatically, you are free to set it manually, ensuring that subsequent operations involving dynamic colors will take place in the correct environment.

The trait collection is also the key to understanding what color a named dynamic color really is. What color is `.systemYellow`? Well, it depends on the trait collection. So to find out, you have to *supply* a trait collection. That's easy, because you can *make* a trait collection. Now you can call `resolvedColor`:

```
let yellow = UIColor.systemYellow
let light = UITraitCollection(userInterfaceStyle: .light)
let dark = UITraitCollection(userInterfaceStyle: .dark)
let yellowLight = yellow.resolvedColor(with: light)
// 1 0.8 0 1
let yellowDark = yellow.resolvedColor(with: dark)
// 1 0.839216 0.0392157 1
```

In addition to the `userInterfaceStyle`, the trait collection also has a `userInterface-Level`, which is `.base` or `.elevated`. This affects dynamic background colors. Only confined regions in front of the main interface are normally affected. An alert (Chapter 13) has an `.elevated` interface level, even if the main interface behind the alert does not.

Size Classes

The salient fact about app rotation and the like is not the rotation *per se* but the change in the app's dimensional proportions. Consider a subview of the root view, located at the bottom right of the screen when the device is in portrait orientation. If the root view's bounds width and bounds height are effectively transposed, then that poor old subview will now be outside the bounds height, and therefore off the screen — unless your app responds in some way to this change to reposition it. (Such a response is called *layout*, a subject that will occupy most of the rest of this chapter.)

The dimensional characteristics of the environment are embodied in a pair of *size classes* which are vended as trait collection properties:

`horizontalSizeClass`
`verticalSizeClass`
    A UIUserInterfaceSizeClass value, either `.regular` or `.compact`.

In combination, the size classes have the following meanings when, as will usually be the case, your app's window occupies the entire screen:

Both the horizontal and vertical size classes are `.regular`
    We're running on an iPad.

The horizontal size class is `.compact` *and the vertical size class is* `.regular`
    We're running on an iPhone with the app in portrait orientation.

The horizontal size class is `.regular` *and the vertical size class is* `.compact`
    We're running on a "big" iPhone with the app in landscape orientation.

Both the horizontal and vertical size classes are `.compact`

> We're running on an iPhone (other than a "big" iPhone) with the app in landscape orientation.

 The "big" iPhones are the iPhone 6/7/8 Plus, iPhone XR, and iPhone XS Max. New at the time of this writing, the iPhone 11 and iPhone 11 Pro Max are also "big" iPhones.

Clearly, a change in the size classes detected through `traitCollectionDidChange` is *not* the way to learn simply that the interface has rotated. Size classes don't distinguish between an iPad in portrait orientation and an iPad in landscape orientation. They distinguish between the most important extreme situations: if the horizontal size class goes from `.regular` to `.compact`, the app is suddenly tall and narrow, and you might want to compensate by changing the interface in some way. In my experience, however, you won't typically implement `traitCollectionDidChange` in order to hear about a change in size classes; rather, the size classes are something you'll *consult* in response to some *other* event. (I'll talk more in Chapter 6 about how to detect actual rotation at the level of the view controller.)

Overriding Trait Collections

Under certain circumstances, it can be useful to isolate part of the UITraitEnvironment hierarchy and lie to it about what the trait collection is. You might like part of the hierarchy to believe that we are on an iPhone in landscape when in fact we are on an iPhone in portrait. (I'll give an example in Chapter 6.) Or there might be some area of your app that should not respond to a change between light and dark mode.

You cannot insert a trait collection directly into the inheritance hierarchy simply by setting a view's trait collection; `traitCollection` isn't a settable property. However, in a UIViewController you can inject your own trait collection by way of the `overrideTraitCollection` property (and UIPresentationController has a method that is similar).

For the user interface style, there is a simpler facility available both for a UIViewController and for a UIView: the `overrideUserInterfaceStyle` property (new in iOS 13). It isn't a trait collection; it's a UIUserInterfaceStyle. The default value is `.unspecified`, which means that the interface style of the trait collection should just pass on down the hierarchy. But if you set it to `.light` or `.dark`, you block inheritance of just the `userInterfaceStyle` property of the trait collection starting at that point in the hierarchy, substituting your own custom setting.

 To make your *entire* app unresponsive to the user's specified interface style, set the "User Interface Style" key (`UIUserInterfaceStyle`) in the *Info.plist* to `Light` or `Dark`.

Layout

We have seen that a subview moves when its superview's bounds *origin* is changed. But what happens to a subview when its superview's *size* is changed?

Of its own accord, *nothing* happens. The subview's bounds and center haven't changed, and the superview's bounds origin hasn't moved, so the subview stays in the same position relative to the top left of its superview. In real life, that usually won't be what you want. You'll want subviews to be resized and repositioned when their superview's size is changed. This is called *layout*.

Here are some ways in which a superview might be resized dynamically:

- Your app might compensate for the user rotating the device 90 degrees by rotating itself so that its top moves to the new top of the screen, matching its new orientation — and, as a consequence, transposing the width and height values of its bounds.

- An iPhone app might launch on screens with different aspect ratios: for instance, the screen of the iPhone SE is relatively shorter than the screen of later iPhone models, and the app's interface may need to adapt to this difference.

- A universal app might launch on an iPad or on an iPhone. The app's interface may need to adapt to the size of the screen on which it finds itself running.

- A view instantiated from a nib, such as a view controller's main view or a table view cell, might be resized to fit the interface into which it is placed.

- A view might respond to a change in its surrounding views. For instance, when a navigation bar is shown or hidden dynamically, the remaining interface might shrink or grow to compensate, filling the available space.

- The user might alter the width of your app's window on an iPad, as part of the iPad multitasking interface.

In any of those situations, and others, layout will probably be needed. Subviews of the view whose size has changed will need to shift, change size, redistribute themselves, or compensate in other ways so that the interface still looks good and remains usable.

Layout is performed in three primary ways:

Manual layout

The superview is sent the `layoutSubviews` message whenever it is resized; so, to lay out subviews manually, provide your own subclass and override `layout-Subviews`. Clearly this could turn out to be a lot of work, but it means you can do anything you like.

Autoresizing

    Autoresizing is the oldest way of performing layout automatically. When its superview is resized, a subview will respond in accordance with the rules prescribed by its own `autoresizingMask` property value, which describes the resizing relationship between the subview and its superview.

Autolayout

    Autolayout depends on the *constraints* of views. A constraint is a full-fledged object with numeric values describing some aspect of the size or position of a view, often in terms of some other view; it is much more sophisticated, descriptive, and powerful than the `autoresizingMask`. Multiple constraints can apply to an individual view, and they can describe a relationship between *any* two views (not just a subview and its superview). Autolayout is implemented behind the scenes in `layoutSubviews`; in effect, constraints allow you to write sophisticated `layoutSubviews` functionality without code.

Your layout strategy can involve any combination of those. The need for manual layout is rare, but you can implement it if you need it. Autoresizing is the default. Autolayout is an opt-in alternative to autoresizing. But in real life, it is quite likely that *all* your views will opt in to autolayout, because it's so powerful and best suited to help your interface adapt to a great range of screen sizes.

The default layout behavior for a view depends on how it was created:

In code

    A view that your code creates and adds to the interface, by default, uses autoresizing, not autolayout. If you want such a view to use autolayout, you must deliberately suppress its use of autoresizing.

In a nib file

    All new *.storyboard* and *.xib* files opt in to autolayout. Their views are ready for autolayout. But a view in the nib editor can still use autoresizing if you prefer.

Autoresizing

Autoresizing is a matter of conceptually assigning a subview "springs and struts." A spring can expand and contract; a strut can't. Springs and struts can be assigned internally or externally, horizontally or vertically. With two internal springs or struts, you specify whether and how the view can be resized; with four external springs or struts, you specify whether and how the view can be repositioned:

- Imagine a subview that is centered in its superview and is to stay centered, but is to resize itself as the superview is resized. It would have four struts externally and two springs internally.

- Imagine a subview that is centered in its superview and is to stay centered, and is *not* to resize itself as the superview is resized. It would have four springs externally and two struts internally.

- Imagine an OK button that is to stay in the lower right of its superview. It would have two struts internally, two struts externally from its right and bottom, and two springs externally from its top and left.

- Imagine a text field that is to stay at the top of its superview. It is to widen as the superview widens. It would have three struts externally and a spring from its bottom; internally it would have a vertical strut and a horizontal spring.

In code, a combination of springs and struts is set through a view's `autoresizing-Mask` property, which is a bitmask (UIView.AutoresizingMask) so that you can combine options. The options represent springs; whatever isn't specified is a strut. The default is the empty set, apparently meaning all struts — but of course it can't really be *all* struts, because if the superview is resized, *something* needs to change, so in reality an empty `autoresizingMask` is the same as `.flexibleRightMargin` together with `.flexibleBottomMargin` (and the view is pinned by struts to the top left).

In debugging, when you log a UIView to the console, its `autoresizingMask` is reported using the word `autoresize` and a list of the springs. The external springs are `LM`, `RM`, `TM`, and `BM`; the internal springs are `W` and `H`. `autoresize = LM+TM` means there are external springs from the left and top; `autoresize = W+BM` means there's an internal horizontal spring and a spring from the bottom.

To demonstrate autoresizing, I'll start with a view and two subviews, one stretched across the top, the other confined to the lower right (Figure 1-13):

```
let v1 = UIView(frame:CGRect(100, 111, 132, 194))
v1.backgroundColor = UIColor(red: 1, green: 0.4, blue: 1, alpha: 1)
let v2 = UIView(frame:CGRect(0, 0, 132, 10))
v2.backgroundColor = UIColor(red: 0.5, green: 1, blue: 0, alpha: 1)
let v1b = v1.bounds
let v3 = UIView(frame:CGRect(v1b.width-20, v1b.height-20, 20, 20))
v3.backgroundColor = UIColor(red: 1, green: 0, blue: 0, alpha: 1)
self.view.addSubview(v1)
v1.addSubview(v2)
v1.addSubview(v3)
```

To that example, I'll add code applying springs and struts to the two subviews to make them behave like the text field and the OK button I was hypothesizing earlier:

```
v2.autoresizingMask = .flexibleWidth
v3.autoresizingMask = [.flexibleTopMargin, .flexibleLeftMargin]
```

Now I'll resize the superview, bringing autoresizing into play; as you can see (Figure 1-14), the subviews remain pinned in their correct relative positions:

Figure 1-13. Before autoresizing

Figure 1-14. After autoresizing

```
v1.bounds.size.width += 40
v1.bounds.size.height -= 50
```

If autoresizing isn't sophisticated enough to achieve what you want, you have two choices:

- Combine it with manual layout in layoutSubviews. Autoresizing happens before layoutSubviews is called, so your layoutSubviews code is free to come marching in and tidy up whatever autoresizing didn't get quite right.

- Use autolayout. This is actually the same solution, because autolayout is in fact a way of injecting functionality into layoutSubviews. But using autolayout is a lot easier than writing your own layoutSubviews code!

Autolayout and Constraints

Autolayout is an opt-in technology, at the level of each individual view. You can use autoresizing and autolayout in different areas of the same interface; one sibling view can use autolayout while another sibling view does not, and a superview can use autolayout while some or all of its subviews do not. However, autolayout is implemented through the superview chain, so if a view uses autolayout, then automatically so do all its superviews; and if (as will almost certainly be the case) one of those views is the main view of a view controller, that view controller receives autolayout-related events.

But *how* does a view opt in to using autolayout? Simply by becoming involved with a constraint. Constraints are your way of telling the autolayout engine that you want it to perform layout on this view, as well as how you want the view laid out.

An autolayout constraint, or simply *constraint*, is an NSLayoutConstraint instance, and describes either the absolute width or height of a view, or else a *relationship* between an attribute of one view and an attribute of another view. In the latter case, the attributes don't have to be the same attribute, and the two views don't have to be siblings (subviews of the same superview) or parent and child (superview and subview) — the only requirement is that they share a common ancestor (a superview somewhere up the view hierarchy).

Here are the chief properties of an NSLayoutConstraint:

firstItem, firstAttribute, secondItem, secondAttribute
> The two views and their respective attributes (NSLayoutConstraint.Attribute) involved in this constraint. The possible attribute values are:
>
> - .width, .height
> - .top, .bottom
> - .left, .right, .leading, .trailing
> - .centerX, .centerY
> - .firstBaseline, .lastBaseline
>
> If the constraint is describing a view's absolute height or width, the secondItem will be nil and the secondAttribute will be .notAnAttribute.
>
> .firstBaseline applies primarily to multiline labels, and is some distance down from the top of the label (Chapter 10); .lastBaseline is some distance up from the bottom of the label.
>
> The meanings of the other attributes are intuitively obvious, except that you might wonder what .leading and .trailing mean: they are the international equivalent of .left and .right, automatically reversing their meaning on systems for which your app is localized and whose language is written right-to-left. The *entire* interface is automatically reversed on such systems — but that will work properly only if you've used .leading and .trailing constraints throughout the interface.

multiplier, constant
> These numbers will be applied to the second attribute's value to determine the first attribute's value. The second attribute's value is multiplied by the multiplier; the constant is added to that product; and the first attribute is set to the result. Basically, you're writing an equation $a_1 = ma_2 + c$, where a_1 and a_2 are

the two attributes, and *m* and *c* are the multiplier and the constant. In the degenerate case where the first attribute's value is to equal the second attribute's value, the multiplier will be 1 and the constant will be 0. If you're describing a view's width or height absolutely, the multiplier will be 1 and the constant will be the width or height value.

relation
> How the two attribute values are to be related to one another, as modified by the `multiplier` and the `constant`. This is the operator that goes in the spot where I put the equal sign in the equation in the preceding paragraph. Possible values are (NSLayoutConstraint.Relation):
>
> - `.equal`
> - `.lessThanOrEqual`
> - `.greaterThanOrEqual`

priority
> Priority values range from 1000 (required) down to 1, and certain standard behaviors have standard priorities. Constraints can have different priorities, determining the order in which they are applied. Starting in iOS 11, a priority is not a number but a UILayoutPriority struct wrapping the numeric value as its `rawValue`.

A constraint belongs to a view. A view can have many constraints: a UIView has a `constraints` property, along with these instance methods:

- `addConstraint(_:)`, `addConstraints(_:)`
- `removeConstraint(_:)`, `removeConstraints(_:)`

The question then is *which* view a given constraint should belong to. The answer is: the view that is closest up the view hierarchy from both views involved in the constraint. If possible, it should *be* one of those views. If the constraint dictates a view's absolute width, it belongs to that view; if it sets the top of a view in relation to the top of its superview, it belongs to that superview; if it aligns the tops of two sibling views, it belongs to their common superview.

However, you'll probably never call any of those methods! Starting in iOS 8, instead of adding a constraint to a particular view explicitly, you can *activate* the constraint. An activated constraint is *added to the correct view automatically*, relieving you from having to determine what view that would be. A constraint has an `isActive` property; you can set it to activate or deactivate a single constraint, plus it tells you whether a given constraint is part of the interface at this moment. There is also an NSLayout-Constraint class method `activate(_:)`, which takes an array of constraints, along with `deactivate(_:)`. Deactivating a constraint is like removing a subview: the constraint is removed from its view, and will go out of existence if you haven't retained it.

NSLayoutConstraint properties are read-only, except for `priority`, `constant`, and `isActive`. If you want to change anything else about an existing constraint, you must remove the constraint and replace it with a new one.

An NSLayoutConstraint also has a writable string `identifier` property. It can be set to any value you like, and can be useful for debugging or for finding a constraint later — so useful, in fact, that it might be good to have on hand an extension that lets you activate a constraint and set its identifier at the same time:

```
extension NSLayoutConstraint {
    func activate(withIdentifier id: String) {
        (self.identifier, self.isActive) = (id, true)
    }
}
```

(I owe that idea to Stack Overflow user Exquisitian; see *https://stackoverflow.com/a/ 57102973/341994*.)

 Once you are using explicit constraints to position and size a view, *do not set its frame* (or bounds and center); use constraints alone. Otherwise, when `layout-Subviews` is called, the view will jump back to where its constraints position it. (However, you may set a view's frame from *within* an implementation of `layout-Subviews`, and it is perfectly normal to do so.)

Implicit Autoresizing Constraints

The mechanism whereby individual views can opt in to autolayout can suddenly involve other views in autolayout, even though those other views were not using autolayout previously. Therefore, there needs to be a way, when such a view becomes involved in autolayout, to generate constraints for it — constraints that will determine that view's position and size identically to how its `frame` and `autoresizingMask` were determining them. The autolayout engine takes care of this for you: it reads the view's `frame` and `autoresizingMask` settings and translates them into *implicit* constraints (of class NSAutoresizingMaskLayoutConstraint). The autolayout engine treats a view in this special way only if the view has its `translatesAutoresizingMask-IntoConstraints` property set to `true` — which happens to be the default.

To demonstrate, I'll construct an example in two stages. In the first stage, I add to my interface, in code, a UILabel ("Hello") that *doesn't* use autolayout. I'll decide that this view's position is to be somewhere near the top right of the screen. To keep it in position near the top right, its `autoresizingMask` will be `[.flexibleLeft-Margin, .flexibleBottomMargin]`:

```
let lab1 = UILabel(frame:CGRect(270,20,42,22))
lab1.autoresizingMask = [.flexibleLeftMargin, .flexibleBottomMargin]
lab1.text = "Hello"
self.view.addSubview(lab1)
```

If we now rotate the device (or Simulator window), and the app rotates to compensate, the label stays correctly positioned near the top right corner by autoresizing.

Now I'll add a second label ("Howdy") that *does* use autolayout — and in particular, I'll attach it by a constraint to the first label (the meaning of this code will be made clear in subsequent sections; just accept it for now):

```
let lab2 = UILabel()
lab2.translatesAutoresizingMaskIntoConstraints = false
lab2.text = "Howdy"
self.view.addSubview(lab2)
NSLayoutConstraint.activate([
    lab2.topAnchor.constraint(
        equalTo: lab1.bottomAnchor, constant: 20),
    lab2.trailingAnchor.constraint(
        equalTo: self.view.trailingAnchor, constant: -20)
])
```

This causes the first label ("Hello") to be involved in autolayout. Therefore, the first label magically acquires four automatically generated implicit constraints of class NSAutoresizingMaskLayoutConstraint, such as to give the label the same size and position, and the same *behavior* when its superview is resized, that it had when it was configured by its `frame` and `autoresizingMask`:

```
<NSAutoresizingMaskLayoutConstraint H:[UILabel:'Hello']-(63)-|>
<NSAutoresizingMaskLayoutConstraint UILabel:'Hello'.minY == 20>
<NSAutoresizingMaskLayoutConstraint UILabel:'Hello'.width == 42>
<NSAutoresizingMaskLayoutConstraint UILabel:'Hello'.height == 22>
```

Recall that the original frame was (`270,20,42,22`). I'm on an iPhone 8 simulator, so the main view width is 375. I've simplified and rearranged the output, but what it says is that the label's right edge is 63 points from the main view's right (the label's original x value of 270 plus its `width` of 42 is 312, and the main view's `width` of 375 minus 312 is 63), its top is 20 points from the main view's top, and it is 42×22 in size.

But within this helpful automatic behavior lurks a trap. Suppose a view has acquired automatically generated implicit constraints, and suppose you then proceed to attach *further constraints* to this view, explicitly setting its position or size. There will then almost certainly be a *conflict* between your explicit constraints and the implicit constraints. The solution is to set the view's `translatesAutoresizingMaskInto-Constraints` property to `false`, so that the implicit constraints are *not* generated, and the view's *only* constraints are your explicit constraints.

The trouble is most likely to arise when you create a view *in code* and then position or size that view with constraints, *forgetting* that you also need to set its `translates-`

AutoresizingMaskIntoConstraints property to `false`. If that happens, you'll get a conflict between constraints. (To be honest, I usually *do* forget, and am reminded only when I *do* get a conflict between constraints.)

Creating Constraints in Code

We are now ready to write some code that creates constraints! I'll start by using the NSLayoutConstraint initializer:

- `init(item:attribute:relatedBy:toItem:attribute:multiplier:constant:)`

This initializer sets every property of the constraint, as I described them a moment ago — except the `priority`, which defaults to `.required` (1000), and the `identifier`, both of which can be set later if desired.

I'll generate the same views and subviews and layout behavior as in Figures 1-13 and 1-14, but using constraints. First, I'll create the views and add them to the interface. Observe that I don't bother to assign the subviews `v2` and `v3` explicit frames as I create them, because constraints will take care of positioning them. Also, I remember (for once) to set their `translatesAutoresizingMaskIntoConstraints` properties to `false`, so that they won't sprout additional implicit NSAutoresizingMaskLayout-Constraints:

```
let v1 = UIView(frame:CGRect(100, 111, 132, 194))
v1.backgroundColor = UIColor(red: 1, green: 0.4, blue: 1, alpha: 1)
let v2 = UIView()
v2.backgroundColor = UIColor(red: 0.5, green: 1, blue: 0, alpha: 1)
let v3 = UIView()
v3.backgroundColor = UIColor(red: 1, green: 0, blue: 0, alpha: 1)
self.view.addSubview(v1)
v1.addSubview(v2)
v1.addSubview(v3)
v2.translatesAutoresizingMaskIntoConstraints = false
v3.translatesAutoresizingMaskIntoConstraints = false
```

And here come the constraints; I'll add them to their views manually, just to show how it's done:

```
v1.addConstraint(
    NSLayoutConstraint(item: v2,
        attribute: .leading,
        relatedBy: .equal,
        toItem: v1,
        attribute: .leading,
        multiplier: 1, constant: 0)
)
v1.addConstraint(
    NSLayoutConstraint(item: v2,
        attribute: .trailing,
        relatedBy: .equal,
```

```
            toItem: v1,
            attribute: .trailing,
            multiplier: 1, constant: 0)
    )
    v1.addConstraint(
        NSLayoutConstraint(item: v2,
            attribute: .top,
            relatedBy: .equal,
            toItem: v1,
            attribute: .top,
            multiplier: 1, constant: 0)
    )
    v2.addConstraint(
        NSLayoutConstraint(item: v2,
            attribute: .height,
            relatedBy: .equal,
            toItem: nil,
            attribute: .notAnAttribute,
            multiplier: 1, constant: 10)
    )
    v3.addConstraint(
        NSLayoutConstraint(item: v3,
            attribute: .width,
            relatedBy: .equal,
            toItem: nil,
            attribute: .notAnAttribute,
            multiplier: 1, constant: 20)
    )
    v3.addConstraint(
        NSLayoutConstraint(item: v3,
            attribute: .height,
            relatedBy: .equal,
            toItem: nil,
            attribute: .notAnAttribute,
            multiplier: 1, constant: 20)
    )
    v1.addConstraint(
        NSLayoutConstraint(item: v3,
            attribute: .trailing,
            relatedBy: .equal,
            toItem: v1,
            attribute: .trailing,
            multiplier: 1, constant: 0)
    )
    v1.addConstraint(
        NSLayoutConstraint(item: v3,
            attribute: .bottom,
            relatedBy: .equal,
            toItem: v1,
            attribute: .bottom,
            multiplier: 1, constant: 0)
    )
```

Now, I know what you're thinking. You're thinking: "What are you, nuts? That is a boatload of code!" (Except that you probably used another four-letter word instead of "boat.") But that's something of an illusion. I'd argue that what we're doing here is actually *simpler* than the code with which we created Figure 1-13 using explicit frames and autoresizing.

After all, we merely create eight constraints in eight simple commands. (I've broken each command into multiple *lines*, but that's mere formatting.) They're verbose, but they are the same command repeated with different parameters, so creating them is simple. Moreover, our eight constraints determine the *position, size, and layout behavior* of our two subviews, so we're getting a lot of bang for our buck. Even more telling, these constraints are a far clearer expression of what's supposed to happen than setting a frame and `autoresizingMask`. The position of our subviews is described once and for all, both as they will initially appear and as they will appear if their superview is resized. And we don't have to use arbitrary math. Recall what we had to say before:

```
let v1b = v1.bounds
let v3 = UIView(frame:CGRect(v1b.width-20, v1b.height-20, 20, 20))
```

That business of subtracting the view's height and width from its superview's bounds height and width in order to position the view is confusing and error-prone. With constraints, we can speak the truth directly; our constraints say, plainly and simply, "v3 is 20 points wide and 20 points high and *flush with the bottom-right corner* of v1."

In addition, constraints can express things that autoresizing can't. Instead of applying an absolute height to v2, we could require that its height be exactly one-tenth of v1's height, regardless of how v1 is resized. To do that without autolayout, you'd have to implement `layoutSubviews` and enforce it manually, in code.

Anchor notation

The `NSLayoutConstraint(item:...)` initializer is rather verbose, though it has the virtue of singularity: one method can create any constraint. There's another way to do everything I just did, making exactly the same eight constraints and adding them to the same views, using a much more compact notation that takes the opposite approach: it concentrates on brevity but sacrifices singularity. Instead of focusing on the constraint, the compact notation focuses on the *attributes* to which the constraint relates. These attributes are expressed as *anchor* properties of a UIView:

- `widthAnchor`, `heightAnchor`
- `topAnchor`, `bottomAnchor`
- `leftAnchor`, `rightAnchor`, `leadingAnchor`, `trailingAnchor`
- `centerXAnchor`, `centerYAnchor`

- `firstBaselineAnchor`, `lastBaselineAnchor`

The anchor values are instances of NSLayoutAnchor subclasses. The constraint-forming methods are anchor instance methods. There are three possible relations — equal to, greater than or equal to, and less than or equal to — and the relationship might be with a constant or another anchor, yielding six combinations:

A constant alone

These methods are for an absolute width or height constraint:

- `constraint(equalToConstant:)`

- `constraint(greaterThanOrEqualToConstant:)`

- `constraint(lessThanOrEqualToConstant:)`

Another anchor

In a relationship with another anchor, we need both a constant and a multiplier. But for brevity you can omit the `multiplier:`, the `constant:`, or both. If the constant is omitted, it is `0`; if the multiplier is omitted, it is `1`:

- `constraint(equalTo:multiplier:constant:)`

- `constraint(greaterThanOrEqualTo:multiplier:constant:)`

- `constraint(lessThanOrEqualTo:multiplier:constant:)`

In iOS 10, a method was added that generates, not a constraint, but a new width or height anchor expressing the distance between two anchors; you can then set a view's width or height anchor in relation to that distance:

- `anchorWithOffset(to:)`

Starting in iOS 11, additional methods create a constraint based on a `constant` value provided by the runtime. This is helpful for getting the standard spacing between views, and is especially valuable when connecting text baselines vertically, because the system spacing will change according to the text size:

- `constraint(equalToSystemSpacingAfter:multiplier:)`

- `constraint(greaterThanOrEqualToSystemSpacingAfter:multiplier:)`

- `constraint(lessThanOrEqualToSystemSpacingAfter:multiplier:)`

- `constraint(equalToSystemSpacingBelow:multiplier:)`

- `constraint(greaterThanOrEqualToSystemSpacingBelow:multiplier:)`

- `constraint(lessThanOrEqualToSystemSpacingBelow:multiplier:)`

All of that may sound very elaborate when I describe it, but when you see it in action, you will appreciate immediately the benefit of this compact notation: it's easy to write (especially thanks to Xcode's code completion), easy to read, and easy to maintain.

Here we generate exactly the same constraints as in the preceding example; I'll call `activate` instead of adding each constraint to its view manually:

```
NSLayoutConstraint.activate([
    v2.leadingAnchor.constraint(equalTo:v1.leadingAnchor),
    v2.trailingAnchor.constraint(equalTo:v1.trailingAnchor),
    v2.topAnchor.constraint(equalTo:v1.topAnchor),
    v2.heightAnchor.constraint(equalToConstant:10),
    v3.widthAnchor.constraint(equalToConstant:20),
    v3.heightAnchor.constraint(equalToConstant:20),
    v3.trailingAnchor.constraint(equalTo:v1.trailingAnchor),
    v3.bottomAnchor.constraint(equalTo:v1.bottomAnchor)
])
```

That's eight constraints in eight lines of code.

Visual format notation

Another way to abbreviate your creation of constraints is to use a text-based shorthand called a *visual format*. This has the advantage of allowing you to describe multiple constraints simultaneously, and is appropriate particularly when you're arranging a series of views horizontally or vertically. I'll start with a simple example:

```
"V:|[v2(10)]"
```

In that expression, `V:` means that the vertical dimension is under discussion; the alternative is `H:`, which is also the default (so you can omit it). A view's name appears in square brackets, and a pipe (`|`) signifies the superview, so we're portraying v2's top edge as butting up against its superview's top edge. Numeric dimensions appear in parentheses, and a numeric dimension accompanying a view's name sets that dimension of that view, so we're also setting v2's height to 10.

To use a visual format, you have to provide a dictionary that maps the string name of each view mentioned by the visual format string to the actual view. The dictionary accompanying the preceding expression might be `["v2":v2]`.

Here, then, is yet another way of expressing the preceding examples, generating exactly the same eight constraints using four commands instead of eight, thanks to the visual format shorthand:

```
let d = ["v2":v2,"v3":v3]
NSLayoutConstraint.activate([
    NSLayoutConstraint.constraints(withVisualFormat:
        "H:|[v2]|", metrics: nil, views: d),
    NSLayoutConstraint.constraints(withVisualFormat:
        "V:|[v2(10)]", metrics: nil, views: d),
    NSLayoutConstraint.constraints(withVisualFormat:
```

```
        "H:[v3(20)]|", metrics: nil, views: d),
    NSLayoutConstraint.constraints(withVisualFormat:
        "V:[v3(20)]|", metrics: nil, views: d)
].flatMap{$0})
```

(The `constraints(withVisualFormat:...)` class method yields an array of constraints, so my literal array is an array of arrays of constraints. But `activate(_:)` expects an array of constraints, so I flatten my literal array.)

Here are some further things to know when generating constraints with the visual format syntax:

- The `metrics:` parameter is a dictionary with numeric values. This lets you use a name in the visual format string where a numeric value needs to go.

- The `options:` parameter, omitted in the preceding example, is a bitmask (NSLayoutConstraint.FormatOptions) chiefly allowing you to specify alignments to be applied to all the views mentioned in the visual format string.

- To specify the distance between two successive views, use hyphens surrounding the numeric value, like this: `"[v1]-20-[v2]"`. The numeric value may optionally be surrounded by parentheses.

- A numeric value in parentheses may be preceded by an equality or inequality operator, and may be followed by an at sign with a priority. Multiple numeric values, separated by comma, may appear in parentheses together, as in `"[v1(>=20@400,<=30)]"`.

For formal details of the visual format syntax, see the "Visual Format Syntax" appendix of Apple's *Auto Layout Guide* in the documentation archive.

The visual format syntax shows itself to best advantage when multiple views are laid out in relation to one another along the same dimension; in that situation, you can get many constraints generated by a single compact visual format string. However, it hasn't been updated for recent iOS versions, so there are some important types of constraint that visual format syntax can't express (such as pinning a view to the *safe area*, discussed later in this chapter).

Constraints as Objects

The examples so far have involved creating constraints and adding them directly to the interface — and then forgetting about them. But it is frequently useful to form constraints and keep them on hand for future use, typically in a property. A common use case is where you intend, at some future time, to change the interface in some radical way, such as by inserting or removing a view; you'll probably find it convenient to keep multiple sets of constraints on hand, each set being appropriate to a particular configuration of the interface. It is then trivial to swap constraints out of and into the interface along with views that they affect.

In this example, we create within our main view (self.view) three views, v1, v2, and v3, which are red, yellow, and blue rectangles respectively. For some reason, we will later want to remove the yellow view (v2) dynamically as the app runs, moving the blue view to where the yellow view was; and then, still later, we will want to insert the yellow view once again (Figure 1-15). So we have two alternating view configurations.

To prepare for this, we create *two* sets of constraints, one describing the positions of v1, v2, and v3 when all three are present, the other describing the positions of v1 and v3 when v2 is absent. For purposes of maintaining these sets of constraints, we have already prepared two properties, constraintsWith and constraintsWithout, initialized as empty arrays of NSLayoutConstraint. We will also need a strong reference to v2, so that it doesn't vanish when we remove it from the interface:

```
var v2 : UIView!
var constraintsWith = [NSLayoutConstraint]()
var constraintsWithout = [NSLayoutConstraint]()
```

Here's the code for creating the views:

```
let v1 = UIView()
v1.backgroundColor = .red
v1.translatesAutoresizingMaskIntoConstraints = false
let v2 = UIView()
v2.backgroundColor = .yellow
v2.translatesAutoresizingMaskIntoConstraints = false
let v3 = UIView()
v3.backgroundColor = .blue
v3.translatesAutoresizingMaskIntoConstraints = false
self.view.addSubview(v1)
self.view.addSubview(v2)
self.view.addSubview(v3)
self.v2 = v2 // retain
```

Now we create the constraints. In what follows, c1, c3, and c4 are in common to both situations (v2 is present or v2 is absent), so we simply activate them once and for all. The remaining constraints we store in two groups, one for each of the two situations:

```
// construct constraints
let c1 = NSLayoutConstraint.constraints(withVisualFormat:
    "H:|-(20)-[v(100)]", metrics: nil, views: ["v":v1])
let c2 = NSLayoutConstraint.constraints(withVisualFormat:
    "H:|-(20)-[v(100)]", metrics: nil, views: ["v":v2])
let c3 = NSLayoutConstraint.constraints(withVisualFormat:
    "H:|-(20)-[v(100)]", metrics: nil, views: ["v":v3])
let c4 = NSLayoutConstraint.constraints(withVisualFormat:
    "V:|-(100)-[v(20)]", metrics: nil, views: ["v":v1])
let c5with = NSLayoutConstraint.constraints(withVisualFormat:
    "V:[v1]-(20)-[v2(20)]-(20)-[v3(20)]", metrics: nil,
    views: ["v1":v1, "v2":v2, "v3":v3])
let c5without = NSLayoutConstraint.constraints(withVisualFormat:
    "V:[v1]-(20)-[v3(20)]", metrics: nil, views: ["v1":v1, "v3":v3])
```

Figure 1-15. Alternate sets of views and constraints

```
// apply common constraints
NSLayoutConstraint.activate([c1, c3, c4].flatMap{$0})
// first set of constraints (for when v2 is present)
self.constraintsWith.append(contentsOf:c2)
self.constraintsWith.append(contentsOf:c5with)
// second set of constraints (for when v2 is absent)
self.constraintsWithout.append(contentsOf:c5without)
```

Now we're ready to start alternating between `constraintsWith` and `constraints-Without`. We start with `v2` present, so it is `constraintsWith` that we initially make active:

```
// apply first set
NSLayoutConstraint.activate(self.constraintsWith)
```

All that preparation may seem extraordinarily elaborate, but the result is that when the time comes to swap `v2` out of or into the interface, it's trivial to swap the appropriate constraints at the same time:

```
func doSwap() {
    if self.v2.superview != nil {
        self.v2.removeFromSuperview()
        NSLayoutConstraint.deactivate(self.constraintsWith)
        NSLayoutConstraint.activate(self.constraintsWithout)
    } else {
        self.view.addSubview(v2)
        NSLayoutConstraint.deactivate(self.constraintsWithout)
        NSLayoutConstraint.activate(self.constraintsWith)
    }
}
```

In that code, I deactivate the old constraints before activating the new ones. Always proceed in that order; activating the new constraints with the old constraints still in force will cause a conflict (as I'll explain later in this chapter).

Margins and Guides

So far, I've been assuming that the anchor points of your constraints represent the literal edges and centers of views. Sometimes, however, you want a view to vend a set of secondary edges, with respect to which other views can be positioned. You might want subviews to keep a minimum distance from the edge of their superview, and the superview should be able to dictate what that minimum distance is. This notion of secondary edges is expressed in two different ways:

Edge insets

A view vends secondary edges as a UIEdgeInsets, a struct consisting of four floats representing inset values starting at the top and proceeding counterclockwise — top, left, bottom, right. This is useful when you need to interface with the secondary edges as numeric values — perhaps to set them or to perform manual layout based on them.

Layout guides

The UILayoutGuide class represents secondary edges as a kind of pseudoview. It has a frame (its `layoutFrame`) with respect to the view that vends it, but its important properties are its anchors, which are the same as for a view. This, obviously, is useful for autolayout.

Safe area

An important set of secondary edges (starting in iOS 11) is the *safe area*. This is a feature of a UIView, but it is imposed by the UIViewController that manages this view. One reason the safe area is needed is that the top and bottom of the interface are often occupied by a bar (status bar, navigation bar, toolbar, tab bar — see Chapter 12). Your layout of subviews will typically occupy the region *between* these bars. But that's not easy, because:

- A view controller's main view will typically extend vertically to the edges of the window *behind* those bars.
- The bars can come and go dynamically, and can change their heights. By default, in an iPhone app, the status bar will be present when the app is in portrait orientation, but will vanish when the app is in landscape orientation; similarly, a navigation bar is taller when the app is in portrait orientation than when the app is in landscape orientation.

Therefore, you need something else, other than the *literal* top and bottom of a view controller's main view, to which to anchor the vertical constraints that position its subviews — something that will *move* dynamically to reflect the current location of the bars. Otherwise, an interface that looks right under some circumstances will look wrong in others. Consider a view whose top is literally constrained to the top of the view controller's main view, which is its superview:

```
let arr = NSLayoutConstraint.constraints(withVisualFormat:
    "V:|-0-[v]", metrics: nil, views: ["v":v])
```

When the app is in landscape orientation, with the status bar removed by default, this view will be right up against the top of the screen, which is fine. But when the app is in portrait orientation, this view will *still* be right up against the top of the screen — which might look bad, because the status bar reappears and overlaps it.

To solve this problem, a UIViewController imposes the safe area on its main view, describing the region of the main view that is overlapped by the status bar and other bars. The top of the safe area matches the bottom of the lowest top bar, or the top of the main view if there is no top bar; the bottom of the safe area matches the top of the bottom bar, or the bottom of the main view if there is no bottom bar. The safe area changes as the situation changes — when the top or bottom bar changes its height, or vanishes entirely. On a device without a bezel, such as the iPhone X, the safe area is of even greater importance; its boundaries help keep your views away from the rounded corners of the screen, and prevent them from being interfered with by the sensors and the home indicator, both in portrait and in landscape.

In real life, therefore, you'll be particularly concerned to position subviews of a view controller's main view with respect to the main view's safe area. Your views constrained to the main view's safe area will avoid being overlapped by bars, and will move to track the edges of the main view's visible area. But *any* view — not just the view controller's main view — can participate in the safe area. When a view performs layout, it imposes the safe area on its own subviews, describing the region of each subview that is overlapped by its own safe area; so *every* view "knows" where the bars are. (There are some additional complexities that I'm omitting, because for practical purposes you probably won't encounter them.)

To retrieve a view's safe area as edge insets, fetch its `safeAreaInsets`. To retrieve a view's safe area as a layout guide, fetch its `safeAreaLayoutGuide`. You can learn that a subclassed view's safe area has changed by overriding `safeAreaInsetsDidChange`, or that a view controller's main view's safe area has changed by overriding the view controller's `viewSafeAreaInsetsDidChange`; in real life, however, using autolayout, you probably won't need that information — you'll just allow views pinned to a safe area layout guide to move as the safe area changes.

In this example, `v` is a view controller's main view, and `v1` is its subview; we construct a constraint between the top of `v1` and the top of the main view's safe area:

```
let c = v1.topAnchor.constraint(equalTo: v.safeAreaLayoutGuide.topAnchor)
```

A view controller can inset even further the safe area it imposes on its main view; set its `additionalSafeAreaInsets`. This, as the name implies, is added to the automatic safe area. It is a UIEdgeInsets. If you set a view controller's `additionalSafeAreaInsets` to a UIEdgeInsets with a top of 50, and if the status bar is showing and there is no other top bar, the default safe area top would be 20, so now it's 70. The `additionalSafeAreaInsets` is helpful if your main view has material at its edge that must always remain visible.

Margins

A view also has margins of its own. Unlike the safe area, which propagates down the view hierarchy from the view controller, you are free to set an individual view's margins. The idea is that a subview might be positioned with respect to its superview's margins, especially through an autolayout constraint. By default, a view has a margin of 8 on all four edges.

A view's margins are available as a UILayoutGuide through the UIView `layout-MarginsGuide` property. Here's a constraint between a subview's leading edge and its superview's leading margin:

```
let c = v.leadingAnchor.constraint(equalTo:
    self.view.layoutMarginsGuide.leadingAnchor)
```

In visual format syntax, a view pinned to its superview's edge using a single hyphen, with no explicit distance value, is interpreted as a constraint to the superview's margin:

```
let arr = NSLayoutConstraint.constraints(withVisualFormat:
    "H:|-[v]", metrics: nil, views: ["v":v])
```

The `layoutMarginsGuide` property is read-only. To allow you to set a view's margins, a UIView has a `layoutMargins` property, a writable UIEdgeInsets. Starting in iOS 11, Apple would prefer that you set the `directionalLayoutMargins` property instead; this has the feature that when your interface is reversed in a right-to-left system language for which your app is localized, its leading and trailing values behave correctly. It is expressed as an NSDirectionalEdgeInsets struct, whose properties are `top`, `leading`, `bottom`, and `trailing`.

Optionally, a view's layout margins can propagate down to its subview, in the following sense: a subview that overlaps its superview's margin may acquire the amount of overlap as a minimum margin of its own. To switch on this option, set the subview's `preservesSuperviewLayoutMargins` to `true`. Suppose we set the superview's `directionalLayoutMargins` to an NSDirectionalEdgeInsets with a `leading` value of 40. And suppose the subview is pinned 10 points from the superview's leading edge, so that it overlaps the superview's leading margin by 30 points. Then, if the subview's `preservesSuperviewLayoutMargins` is `true`, the subview's leading margin is 30.

By default, a view's margin values are treated as insets *from the safe area*. Suppose a view's top margin is 8. And suppose this view underlaps the entire status bar, acquiring a safe area top of 20. Then its *effective* top margin value is 28 — meaning that a subview whose top is pinned exactly to this view's top margin will appear 28 points below this view's top. If you don't like that behavior (perhaps because you have code that predates the existence of the safe area), you can switch it off by setting the view's `insetsLayoutMarginsFromSafeArea` property to `false`; now a top margin value of 8 means an effective top margin value of 8.

A view controller also has a `systemMinimumLayoutMargins` property; it imposes these margins on its main view as a minimum, meaning that you can increase the main view's margins beyond these limits, but an attempt to decrease a margin below them will fail silently. You can evade that restriction, however, by setting the view controller's `viewRespectsSystemMinimumLayoutMargins` property to `false`. The `systemMinimumLayoutMargins` default value is a top and bottom margin of 0 and side margins of 16 on a smaller device, with side margins of 20 on a larger device.

A second set of margins, a UIView's `readableContentGuide` (a UILayoutGuide), which you cannot change, enforces the idea that a subview consisting of text should not be allowed to grow as wide as an iPad in landscape, because that's too wide to read easily, especially if the text is small. By constraining such a subview horizontally to its superview's `readableContentGuide`, you ensure that that won't happen.

Custom layout guides

You can add your own custom UILayoutGuide objects to a view, for whatever purpose you like. They constitute a view's `layoutGuides` array, and are managed by calling `addLayoutGuide(_:)` or `removeLayoutGuide(_:)`. Each custom layout guide object must be configured entirely using constraints.

Why would you want to do that? Well, you can constrain a view to a UILayoutGuide, by means of its anchors. Since a UILayoutGuide is configured by constraints, and since other views can be constrained to it, it can participate in autolayout exactly as if it were a subview — but it is *not* a subview, and therefore it avoids all the overhead and complexity that a UIView would have.

Consider the question of how to *distribute views equally* within their superview. This is easy to arrange initially, but it is not obvious how to design evenly spaced views that will remain evenly spaced when their superview is resized. The problem is that constraints describe relationships between *views*, not between *constraints*; there is no way to constrain the spacing constraints between views to remain equal to one another automatically as the superview is resized.

You can, on the other hand, constrain the heights or widths of *views* to remain equal to one another. The traditional solution, therefore, is to resort to spacer views with their `isHidden` set to `true`. Suppose I have four views of equal heights that are to remain equally distributed vertically. Between them, I interpose three spacer views, also of equal heights. If we pin every view to the view below it, and the first and last view to the top and bottom of the superview, and *hide* the spacer views, they become the equal *spaces* between the visible views.

But spacer views are views; hidden or not, they add overhead with respect to drawing, memory, touch detection, and more. Custom UILayoutGuides solve the problem; they can serve the same purpose as spacer views, but they are *not* views.

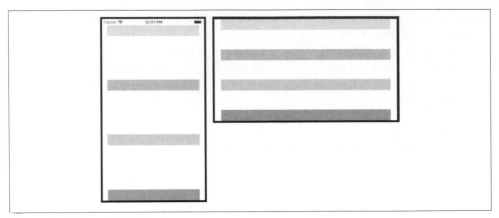

Figure 1-16. Equal distribution

I'll demonstrate. We have four views that are to remain equally distributed vertically. I constrain the left and right edges of the four views, their heights, and the top of the first view and the bottom of the last view. Now we want to set the vertical position of the two middle views such that they are always equidistant from their vertical neighbors (Figure 1-16).

To solve the problem, I introduce three UILayoutGuide objects between my real views. A custom UILayoutGuide object is added to a UIView, so I'll add mine to the view controller's main view. I then involve my three layout guides in the layout. Remember, they must be configured entirely using constraints! The four views are referenced through an array, views:

```
var guides = [UILayoutGuide]()
// one fewer guides than views ❶
for _ in views.dropLast() {
    let g = UILayoutGuide()
    self.view.addLayoutGuide(g)
    guides.append(g)
}
// guides leading and width are arbitrary ❷
let anc = self.view.leadingAnchor
for g in guides {
    g.leadingAnchor.constraint(equalTo:anc).isActive = true
    g.widthAnchor.constraint(equalToConstant:10).isActive = true
}
// guides top to previous view ❸
for (v,g) in zip(views.dropLast(), guides) {
    v.bottomAnchor.constraint(equalTo:g.topAnchor).isActive = true
}
// guides bottom to next view ❹
for (v,g) in zip(views.dropFirst(), guides) {
    v.topAnchor.constraint(equalTo:g.bottomAnchor).isActive = true
}
```

```
// guide heights equal to each other! ❺
let h = guides[0].heightAnchor
for g in guides.dropFirst() {
    g.heightAnchor.constraint(equalTo:h).isActive = true
}
```

❶ I create the layout guides and add them to the interface.

❷ I constrain the leading edges of the layout guides (arbitrarily, to the leading edge of the main view) and their widths (arbitrarily).

❸ I constrain each layout guide to the bottom of the view above it.

❹ I constrain each layout guide to the top of the view below it.

❺ Finally, our whole purpose is to distribute our views *equally*, so the heights of our layout guides must be *equal to one another*.

 In real life, if the problem is equal distribution, you are unlikely to use this technique directly, because you will use a UIStackView instead, and let the UIStackView generate all of that code for you — as I will explain a little later.

Constraint alignment

You can also change the location of your view's anchors themselves. Constraints are measured by default from a view's edges, but consider a view that draws, internally, a rectangle with a shadow; you probably want to pin other views to that drawn rectangle, not to the outside of the shadow.

To effect this, you can override your view's `alignmentRectInsets` property (or, more elaborately, its `alignmentRect(forFrame:)` and `frame(forAlignmentRect:)` methods). When you change a view's `alignmentRectInsets`, you are effectively changing where the view's edges are for purposes of *all* constraints involving those edges. If a view's alignment rect has a left inset of 30, then all constraints involving that view's `.leading` attribute or `leadingAnchor` are reckoned from that inset.

By the same token, you may want to be able to align your custom UIView with another view by their baselines. The assumption here is that your view has a subview containing text that itself has a baseline. Your custom view will return that subview in its implementation of `forFirstBaselineLayout` or `forLastBaselineLayout`.

Intrinsic Content Size

Certain built-in interface objects, when using autolayout, have an *inherent size* in one or both dimensions, dependent upon the object type and its content. Here are some examples:

- A UIButton has a standard height, and its width is determined by the length of its title.

- A UIImageView adopts the size of the image that it is displaying.

- A UILabel consisting of a single line of text adopts the size of the text that it is displaying.

This inherent size is the object's *intrinsic content size*. The intrinsic content size is used to generate constraints implicitly (of class NSContentSizeLayoutConstraint).

A change in the characteristics or content of a built-in interface object — a button's title, an image view's image, a label's text or font, and so forth — may cause its intrinsic content size to change. This, in turn, may alter your layout. You will want to configure your autolayout constraints so that your interface responds gracefully to such changes.

You do not have to supply explicit constraints configuring a dimension of a view whose intrinsic content size configures that dimension. But you might! And when you do, the tendency of an interface object to size itself to its intrinsic content size must not be allowed to conflict with its obedience to your explicit constraints. Therefore, the constraints generated from a view's intrinsic content size have a *lowered priority*, and come into force only if no constraint of a higher priority prevents them. The following methods allow you to access these priorities (the parameter is an NSLayoutConstraint.Axis, either `.horizontal` or `.vertical`):

`contentHuggingPriority(for:)`
> A view's resistance to growing larger than its intrinsic size in this dimension. In effect, there is an inequality constraint saying that the view's size in this dimension should be less than or equal to its intrinsic size. The default priority is usually `.defaultLow` (250), though some interface classes will default to a higher value if created in a nib.

`contentCompressionResistancePriority(for:)`
> A view's resistance to shrinking smaller than its intrinsic size in this dimension. In effect, there is an inequality constraint saying that the view's size in this dimension should be greater than or equal to its intrinsic size. The default priority is usually `.defaultHigh` (750).

Those methods are getters; there are corresponding setters, because you might need to change the priorities. Here are visual formats configuring two horizontally adjacent labels (`lab1` and `lab2`) to be pinned to the superview and to one another:

```
"V:|-20-[lab1]"
"V:|-20-[lab2]"
"H:|-20-[lab1]"
"H:[lab2]-20-|"
"H:[lab1(>=100)]-(>=20)-[lab2(>=100)]"
```

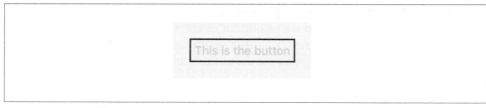

Figure 1-17. A self-sizing view

The inequalities ensure that as the superview becomes narrower or the text of the labels becomes longer, a reasonable amount of text will remain visible in both labels. At the same time, one label will be squeezed down to 100 points width, while the other label will be allowed to grow to fill the remaining horizontal space. The question is: which label is which? You need to answer that question. To do so, it suffices to give the two labels different compression resistance priorities; even a tiny difference will do:

```
let p = lab2.contentCompressionResistancePriority(for: .horizontal)
lab1.setContentCompressionResistancePriority(p+1, for: .horizontal)
```

You can supply an intrinsic size in your own custom UIView subclass by overriding `intrinsicContentSize`. Obviously you should do this only if your view's size somehow depends on its content. If you need the runtime to ask for your `intrinsicContentSize` again, because the contents have changed and the view needs to be laid out afresh, it's up to you to call your view's `invalidateIntrinsicContentSize` method.

Self-Sizing Views

So far, I have talked about layout (and autolayout in particular) as a way of solving the problem of what should happen to a superview's subviews when the superview is resized. However, autolayout also works in the opposite direction. If a superview's subviews determine their own size, they can also determine the size of the superview.

Consider this simple example. We have a plain vanilla UIView, which has as its sole subview a UIButton. And suppose this UIButton is pinned by constraints from all four edges to its superview, the plain vanilla UIView. Well, as I've already said, a UIButton under autolayout has an intrinsic size: its height is standard, and its width is dependent upon its title. So, all other things being equal, the size of the button is *determined*. Then, all other things being equal, the size of the plain vanilla view is *also* determined, *from the inside out*, by the size of the button, its subview. (See Figure 1-17; the inner rectangle with the black border is the button, and the outer rectangle is the plain vanilla UIView.)

What I mean by "all other things being equal" is simply that you don't determine the size of the plain vanilla superview in any *other* way. Let's say you pin the leading and top edges of the superview to *its* superview. Now we know the *position* of the superview. But we do not pin its trailing or bottom edges, and we don't give it a width or height constraint. You might say: Then the width and height of the superview are unknown! But not so. In this situation, the autolayout engine simply gets the width and height of the superview from the width and height of its subview, the button — because the width and height of the button *are* known, and there is a complete constraint relationship between the width and height of the button and the width and height of the superview.

I call a view such as our plain vanilla superview a *self-sizing view.* In effect, it has an intrinsic content size — not literally (we have not configured its `instrinsicContentSize`), but in the sense that it is, in fact, sized by its content. A self-sizing view's size does not have to be determined *solely* by its content; it is fine to give a self-sizing view a width constraint (or pin it on both sides) but allow its height to be determined by its content. If the superview is also pinned to its subview(s) horizontally to determine its width, that could result in a conflict between constraints — but in many cases it won't. Our plain vanilla superview can have its width determined by a hard-coded width constraint without causing a conflict; its subview is pinned to it horizontally, but its subview is a button whose width is determined by its intrinsic content size *at a lower priority* than the superview's width constraint, so the superview's width wins without a struggle (and the button subview is widened to match).

When a view is self-sizing based on the constraints of its subviews, you can ask it in code to size itself immediately in order to discover what its size *would* be if the autolayout engine were to perform layout at this moment. Send the view the `systemLayoutSizeFitting(_:)` message. The system will attempt to reach or at least approach the size you specify, at a very low priority. This call is relatively slow and expensive, because a temporary autolayout engine has to be created, set to work, and discarded. But sometimes that's the best way to get the information you need. Mostly likely you'll specify either `UIView.layoutFittingCompressedSize` or `UIView.layoutFittingExpandedSize`, depending on whether what you're after is the smallest or largest size the view can legally attain. There are a few situations where the iOS runtime actually does size a view that way (most notably with regard to UITableViewCells and UIBarButtonItems). I'll show an example in Chapter 7.

Stack Views

A stack view (UIStackView) is a kind of pseudoview whose job is to *generate constraints* for some or all of its subviews. These are its *arranged subviews.* In particular, a stack view solves the problem of providing constraints when subviews are to be configured linearly in a horizontal row or a vertical column. In practice, it turns out that many layouts can be expressed as an arrangement, possibly nested, of simple rows and columns of subviews. You are likely to resort to stack views to make your layout easier to construct and maintain.

You can supply a stack view with arranged subviews by calling its initializer `init(arrangedSubviews:)`. The arranged subviews become the stack view's `arrangedSubviews` read-only property. You can also manage the arranged subviews with these methods:

- `addArrangedSubview(_:)`
- `insertArrangedSubview(_:at:)`
- `removeArrangedSubview(_:)`

The `arrangedSubviews` array is different from, but is a subset of, the stack view's `subviews`. It's fine for the stack view to have subviews that are *not* arranged (for which you'll have to provide constraints yourself); on the other hand, if you set a view as an arranged subview and it is not already a subview, the stack view will adopt it as a subview at that moment.

The *order* of the `arrangedSubviews` is independent of the order of the `subviews`; the `subviews` order, you remember, determines the order in which the subviews are *drawn*, but the `arrangedSubviews` order determines how the stack view will *position* those subviews.

Using its properties, you configure the stack view to tell it *how* it should arrange its arranged subviews:

axis

> Which way should the arranged subviews be arranged? Your choices are (NSLayoutConstraint.Axis):
>
> - `.horizontal`
> - `.vertical`

alignment

> This describes how the arranged subviews should be laid out with respect to the *other* dimension. Your choices are (UIStackView.Alignment):
>
> - `.fill`
> - `.leading` (or `.top`)
> - `.center`
> - `.trailing` (or `.bottom`)
> - `.firstBaseline` or `.lastBaseline` (if the axis is `.horizontal`)

If the `axis` is `.vertical`, you can still involve the subviews' baselines in their spacing by setting the stack view's `isBaselineRelativeArrangement` to `true`.

distribution

How should the arranged subviews be positioned along the `axis`? This is why you are here! You're using a stack view because you want this positioning performed for you. Your choices are (UIStackView.Distribution):

.fill

The arranged subviews can have real size constraints or intrinsic content sizes along the arranged dimension. Using those sizes, the arranged subviews will fill the stack view from end to end. But there must be at least *one* view *without* a real size constraint, so that it can be resized to fill the space not taken up by the other views. If more than one view lacks a real size constraint, one of them must have a lowered priority for its content hugging (if stretching) or compression resistance (if squeezing) so that the stack view knows which view to resize.

.fillEqually

No view may have a real size constraint along the arranged dimension. The arranged subviews will be made the same size in the arranged dimension, so as to fill the stack view.

.fillProportionally

All arranged subviews *must* have an intrinsic content size and *no* real size constraint along the arranged dimension. The views will then fill the stack view, sized according to the *ratio* of their intrinsic content sizes.

.equalSpacing

The arranged subviews can have real size constraints or intrinsic content sizes along the arranged dimension. Using those sizes, the arranged subviews will fill the stack view from end to end with equal space between each adjacent pair.

.equalCentering

The arranged subviews can have real size constraints or intrinsic content sizes along the arranged dimension. Using those sizes, the arranged subviews will fill the stack view from end to end with equal distance between the centers of each adjacent pair.

The stack view's `spacing` property determines the spacing (or minimum spacing) between *all* the views. Starting in iOS 11, you can set the spacing for *individual* views by calling `setCustomSpacing(_:after:)`; if you need to turn individual spacing back off for a view, reverting to the overall `spacing` property value, set the custom spacing to `UIStackView.spacingUseDefault`. To impose the spacing that the system would normally impose, set the spacing to `UIStack-View.spacingUseSystem`.

`isLayoutMarginsRelativeArrangement`
> If `true`, the stack view's internal `layoutMargins` are involved in the positioning of its arranged subviews. If `false` (the default), the stack view's literal edges are used.

Do *not* manually add constraints positioning an arranged subview! Adding those constraints is precisely the job of the stack view. Your constraints will conflict with the constraints created by the stack view. On the other hand, you *must* constrain the stack view *itself*; otherwise, the layout engine has no idea what to do. Trying to use a stack view without constraining it is a common beginner mistake.

To illustrate, I'll rewrite the equal distribution code from earlier in this chapter (Figure 1-16). I have four views, with height constraints. I want to distribute them vertically in my main view. This time, I'll have a stack view do all the work for me:

```
// give the stack view arranged subviews
let sv = UIStackView(arrangedSubviews: views)
// configure the stack view
sv.axis = .vertical
sv.alignment = .fill
sv.distribution = .equalSpacing
// constrain the stack view
sv.translatesAutoresizingMaskIntoConstraints = false
self.view.addSubview(sv)
let marg = self.view.layoutMarginsGuide
let safe = self.view.safeAreaLayoutGuide
NSLayoutConstraint.activate([
    sv.topAnchor.constraint(equalTo:safe.topAnchor),
    sv.leadingAnchor.constraint(equalTo:marg.leadingAnchor),
    sv.trailingAnchor.constraint(equalTo:marg.trailingAnchor),
    sv.bottomAnchor.constraint(equalTo:self.view.bottomAnchor),
])
```

Inspecting the resulting constraints, you can see that the stack view is doing for us effectively just what we did earlier (generating UILayoutGuide objects and using them as spacers). But letting the stack view do it is a lot easier!

Another nice feature of UIStackView is that it responds intelligently to changes. Having configured things with the preceding code, if we were subsequently to make one of our arranged subviews invisible (by setting its `isHidden` to `true`), the stack view would respond by distributing the remaining subviews evenly, as if the hidden subview didn't exist. Similarly, we can change properties of the stack view itself in real time. Such flexibility can be very useful for making whole areas of your interface come and go and rearrange themselves at will.

A stack view, in certain configurations, can behave as a self-sizing view: its size, if not determined in any other way, in one or both dimensions, can be based on its subviews.

Internationalization

Your app's entire interface and its behavior are reversed when the app runs on a system for which the app is localized and whose language is right-to-left. Wherever you use leading and trailing constraints instead of left and right constraints, or if your constraints are generated by stack views or are constructed using the visual format language, your app's layout will participate in this reversal more or less automatically.

There may, however, be exceptions. Apple gives the example of a horizontal row of transport controls that mimic the buttons on a CD player: you wouldn't want the Rewind button and the Fast Forward button to be reversed just because the user's language reads right-to-left. Therefore, a UIView is endowed with a `semantic-ContentAttribute` property stating whether it should be flipped; the default is `.unspecified`, but a value of `.playback` or `.spatial` will prevent flipping, and you can also force an absolute direction with `.forceLeftToRight` or `.forceRightToLeft`. This property can also be set in the nib editor (using the Semantic pop-up menu in the Attributes inspector).

Interface directionality is a trait, a trait collection's `layoutDirection`; and a UIView has an `effectiveUserInterfaceLayoutDirection` property that reports the direction that it will use to lay out its contents. You can consult this property if you are constructing a view's subviews in code.

 You can test your app's right-to-left behavior easily by changing the scheme's Run option Application Language to "Right to Left Pseudolanguage."

Mistakes with Constraints

Creating constraints manually, as I've been doing so far in this chapter, is an invitation to make a mistake. Your totality of constraints constitute instructions for view layout, and it is all too easy, as soon as more than one or two views are involved, to generate faulty instructions. You can (and will) make two major kinds of mistake with constraints:

Conflict
    You have applied constraints that can't be satisfied simultaneously. This will be reported in the console (at great length).

Underdetermination (ambiguity)

A view uses autolayout, but you haven't supplied sufficient information to determine its size and position. This is a far more insidious problem, because nothing bad may seem to happen. If you're lucky, the view will at least fail to appear, or will appear in an undesirable place, alerting you to the problem.

Only `.required` constraints (priority 1000) can contribute to a conflict, as the runtime is free to ignore lower-priority constraints that it can't satisfy. Constraints with different priorities do not conflict with one another. Nonrequired constraints with the same priority can contribute to ambiguity.

Under normal circumstances, layout isn't performed until your code finishes running — and even then only if needed. Ambiguous layout isn't ambiguous until layout actually takes place; it is perfectly reasonable to cause an ambiguous layout temporarily, provided you resolve the ambiguity before `layoutSubviews` is called. On the other hand, a conflicting constraint conflicts the instant it is added. That's why, when replacing constraints in code, you should deactivate first and activate second, and not the other way round.

To illustrate, let's start by generating a conflict. In this example, we return to our small red square in the lower right corner of a big magenta square (Figure 1-13) and append a contradictory constraint:

```
let d = ["v2":v2,"v3":v3]
NSLayoutConstraint.activate([
    NSLayoutConstraint.constraints(withVisualFormat:
        "H:|[v2]|", metrics: nil, views: d),
    NSLayoutConstraint.constraints(withVisualFormat:
        "V:|[v2(10)]", metrics: nil, views: d),
    NSLayoutConstraint.constraints(withVisualFormat:
        "H:[v3(20)]|", metrics: nil, views: d),
    NSLayoutConstraint.constraints(withVisualFormat:
        "V:[v3(20)]|", metrics: nil, views: d),
    NSLayoutConstraint.constraints(withVisualFormat:
        "V:[v3(10)]|", metrics: nil, views: d) // *
].flatMap{$0})
```

The height of v3 can't be both 10 and 20. The runtime reports the conflict, and tells you which constraints are causing it:

```
Unable to simultaneously satisfy constraints. Probably at least one of the
constraints in the following list is one you don't want...

<NSLayoutConstraint:0x60008b6d0 UIView:0x7ff45e803.height == 20 (active)>,
<NSLayoutConstraint:0x60008bae0 UIView:0x7ff45e803.height == 10 (active)>
```

 Assigning a constraint (or a UILayoutGuide) an `identifier` string can make it easier to determine which constraint is which in a conflict report.

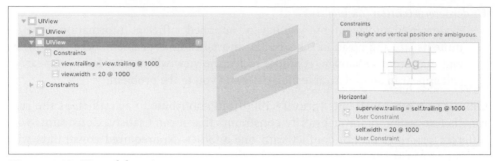

Figure 1-18. View debugging

Now we'll generate an ambiguity. Here, we neglect to give our small red square a height:

```
let d = ["v2":v2,"v3":v3]
NSLayoutConstraint.activate([
    NSLayoutConstraint.constraints(withVisualFormat:
        "H:|[v2]|", metrics: nil, views: d),
    NSLayoutConstraint.constraints(withVisualFormat:
        "V:|[v2(10)]", metrics: nil, views: d),
    NSLayoutConstraint.constraints(withVisualFormat:
        "H:[v3(20)]|", metrics: nil, views: d)
].flatMap{$0})
```

No console message alerts us to our mistake. Fortunately, v3 fails to appear in the interface, so we know something's wrong. *If your views fail to appear, suspect ambiguity.* In a less fortunate case, the view might appear, but (if we're lucky) in the wrong place. In a truly unfortunate case, the view might appear in the right place, but not consistently.

Suspecting ambiguity is one thing; tracking it down and proving it is another. Fortunately, the *view debugger* will report ambiguity instantly (Figure 1-18). With the app running, choose Debug → View Debugging → Capture View Hierarchy, or click the Debug View Hierarchy button in the debug bar. The exclamation mark in the Debug navigator, at the left, is telling us that this view (which does not appear in the canvas) has ambiguous layout; moreover, the Issue navigator, in the Runtime pane, tells us more explicitly, in words: "Height and vertical position are ambiguous for UIView."

Another useful trick is to pause in the debugger and engage in the following mystical conversation in the console:

```
(lldb) e -l objc -- [[UIApplication sharedApplication] windows][0]
(UIWindow *) $1 = ...
(lldb) e -l objc -O -- [$1 _autolayoutTrace]
```

The result is a graphical tree describing the view hierarchy and calling out any ambiguously laid out views:

```
•UIView:0x7f9fa36045c0
|   +UIView:0x7f9fa3604930
|   |   *UIView:0x7f9fa3604a90
|   |   *UIView:0x7f9fa3604e20- AMBIGUOUS LAYOUT
            for UIView:.minY{id: 33}, UIView:.Height{id: 34}
```

UIView also has a `hasAmbiguousLayout` property. I find it useful to set up a utility method that lets me check a view and all its subviews at any depth for ambiguity; see Appendix B.

To get a full list of the constraints responsible for positioning a particular view within its superview, log the results of calling the UIView instance method `constraints-AffectingLayout(for:)`. The parameter is an axis (NSLayoutConstraint.Axis), either `.horizontal` or `.vertical`. These constraints do not necessarily belong to this view (and the output doesn't tell you what view they do belong to). If a view doesn't participate in autolayout, the result will be an empty array. Again, a utility method can come in handy; see Appendix B.

Given the notions of conflict and ambiguity, it is easier to understand what priorities are for. Imagine that all constraints have been placed in boxes, where each box is a priority value, in descending order. Now pretend that we are the runtime, performing layout in obedience to these constraints. How do we proceed?

The first box (`.required`, 1000) contains all the required constraints, so we obey them first. (If they conflict, that's bad, and we report this in the log.) If there still isn't enough information to perform unambiguous layout given the required priorities alone, we pull the constraints out of the next box and try to obey them. If we can, consistently with what we've already done, fine; if we can't, or if ambiguity remains, we look in the *next* box — and so on.

For a box after the first, we don't care about obeying exactly the constraints it contains; if an ambiguity remains, we can use a lower-priority constraint value to give us something to aim at, resolving the ambiguity, without fully obeying the lower-priority constraint's desires. An inequality is an ambiguity, because an infinite number of values will satisfy it; a lower-priority equality can tell us what value to prefer, resolving the ambiguity, but there's no conflict even if we can't fully achieve that preferred value.

Configuring Layout in the Nib

The focus of the discussion so far has been on configuring layout in code. But that will often be unnecessary; instead, you'll set up your layout in the nib, using the nib editor. It would not be strictly true to say that you can do absolutely anything in the nib that you could do in code, but the nib editor is certainly a remarkably powerful way of configuring layout (and where it falls short, you can supplement it with code).

In the File inspector when a *.storyboard* or *.xib* file is selected, you can make two major choices related to layout, by way of checkboxes. The default is that these checkboxes are *checked*, and I recommend that you leave them that way:

Use Trait Variations
 If checked, various settings in the nib editor, such as the value of a constraint's `constant`, can be made to depend upon the environment's size classes at runtime; moreover, the modern repertoire of segues, such as popover and detail segues, springs to life.

Use Safe Area Layout Guides
 If checked, the safe area is present, and you can construct constraints pinned to it. By default, only a view controller's *main view's* safe area can have constraints pinned to it, but you can change that.

What you actually *see* in the nib editor canvas depends also on the checked menu items in the Editor → Canvas hierarchical menu (or use the Editor Options pop-up menu at the top right of the editor pane). If Layout Rectangles is unchecked, you won't see the outline of the safe area, though you can still construct constraints to it. If Constraints is unchecked, you won't see any constraints, though you can still construct them.

Autoresizing in the Nib

When you drag a view from the Library into the canvas, it uses autoresizing by default, and will continue to do so unless you involve it in autolayout by adding a constraint that affects it.

When editing a view that uses autoresizing, you can assign it springs and struts in the Size inspector. A solid line externally represents a strut; a solid line internally represents a spring. A helpful animation shows you the effect on your view's position and size as its superview is resized.

New in Xcode 11, in the nib editor an individual view has a Layout pop-up menu in the Size inspector allowing you specify its behavior with regard to constraints:

Automatic
 The default. The view's `translatesAutoresizingMaskIntoConstraints` is `true`, and you can position the view with autoresizing, until the view becomes involved in constraints, at which point its `translatesAutoresizingMaskInto-Constraints` becomes `false` and you will have to position and size this view entirely with constraints.

Translates Mask Into Constraints
 The view's `translatesAutoresizingMaskIntoConstraints` is `true`, and it will stay `true`. This view will resist becoming involved in constraints within the nib; it

Figure 1-19. Creating a constraint by Control-dragging

wants to use autoresizing only. You can't give it a width constraint or a constraint to its superview. You can involve the view in constraints from other views, as long as these would not cause a problem.

You can cause problems yourself by behaving irrationally; if a view starts out as Automatic and you give it constraints, and then you switch it to Translates Mask Into Constraints, you can readily create a conflict at runtime. Don't do that.

Creating a Constraint

The nib editor provides two primary ways to create a constraint:

Control-drag
> Control-drag from one view to another. A HUD (heads-up display) appears, listing constraints that you can create (Figure 1-19). Either view can be in the canvas or in the document outline. To create an internal width or height constraint, Control-drag from a view to itself.

> When you Control-drag within the canvas, the direction of the drag is used to winnow the options presented in the HUD: if you Control-drag horizontally within a view in the canvas, the HUD lists Width but not Height.

> While viewing the HUD, you might want to toggle the Option key to see some alternatives; this might make the difference between an edge or safe area constraint and a margin-based constraint. Holding the Shift key lets you create multiple constraints simultaneously.

Layout bar buttons
> Click the Align or Add New Constraints button at the right end of the layout bar below the canvas. These buttons summon little popover dialogs where you can choose multiple constraints to create (possibly for multiple views, if that's what you've selected beforehand) and provide them with numeric values (Figure 1-20). Constraints are not actually added until you click Add Constraints at the bottom!

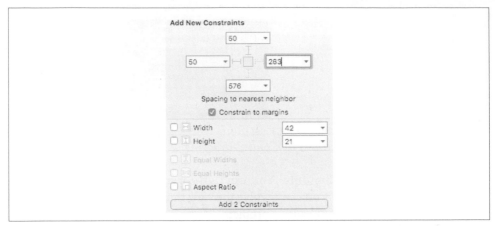

Figure 1-20. Creating constraints from the layout bar

 A constraint that you create in the nib does not have to be perfect immediately upon creation. You will subsequently be able to edit the constraint and configure it further, as I'll explain in the next section.

If you create constraints and then move or resize a view affected by those constraints, the constraints are *not* automatically changed. This means that the constraints no longer match the way the view is portrayed; if the constraints were now to position the view, they wouldn't put it where you've put it. The nib editor will alert you to this situation (a Misplaced Views issue), and can readily resolve it for you, but it won't change anything unless you explicitly ask it to.

There are additional view settings in the Size inspector:

- To set a view's layout margins explicitly, change the Layout Margins pop-up menu to Fixed (or better, to Language Directional).

- To make a view's layout margins behave as `readableContentGuide` margins, check Follow Readable Width.

- To allow construction of a constraint to the safe area of a view that isn't a view controller's main view, check its Safe Area Layout Guide.

Viewing and Editing Constraints

Constraints in the nib are full-fledged objects. They can be selected, edited, and deleted. Moreover, you can create an outlet to a constraint (and there are reasons why you might want to do so).

Constraints in the nib are visible in three places (Figure 1-21):

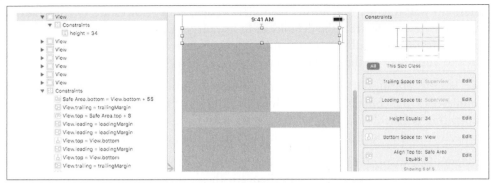

Figure 1-21. A view's constraints displayed in the nib

In the document outline
Constraints are listed in a special category, "Constraints," under the view to which they belong. (You'll have a much easier time distinguishing these constraints if you give your views meaningful labels!)

In the canvas
Constraints appear graphically as dimension lines when you select a view that they affect (unless you uncheck Editor → Canvas → Constraints).

In the Size inspector
When a view affected by constraints is selected, the Size inspector lists those constraints, along with a grid that displays the view's constraints graphically. Clicking a constraint in the grid filters the constraints listed below it.

When you select a constraint in the document outline or the canvas, or when you double-click a constraint in a view's Size inspector, you can view and edit that constraint's values in the Attributes or Size inspector. The inspector gives you access to almost all of a constraint's features: the anchors involved in the constraint (the First Item and Second Item pop-up menus), the relation between them, the constant and multiplier, and the priority. You can also set the identifier here (useful when debugging, as I mentioned earlier).

The First Item and Second Item pop-up menus may list alternative constraint types; a width constraint may be changed to a height constraint, for example. These pop-up menus may also list alternative *objects* to constrain to, such as other sibling views, the superview, and the safe area. Also, these pop-up menus may have a "Relative to margin" option, which you can check or uncheck to toggle between an edge-based and a margin-based constraint.

So if you accidentally created the wrong constraint, or if you weren't quite able to specify the desired constraint at creation time, editing will usually permit you to fix things. When you constrain a subview to the view controller's main view, the HUD offers no way to constrain to the main view's edge; your choices are to constrain to the main view's safe area (the default) or to its margin (if you hold Option). But having constrained the subview to the main view's safe area, you can then change Safe Area to Superview in the pop-up menu.

For simple editing of a constraint's constant, relation, priority, and multiplier, double-click the constraint in the canvas to summon a little popover dialog. When a constraint is listed in a view's Size inspector, double-click it to edit it in its own inspector, or click its Edit button to summon the little popover dialog.

A view's Size inspector also provides access to its content hugging and content compression resistance priority settings. Beneath these, there's an Intrinsic Size pop-up menu. The idea here is that your custom view might have an intrinsic size, but the nib editor doesn't know this, so it will report an ambiguity when you fail to provide (say) a width constraint that you know isn't actually needed; choose Placeholder to supply an intrinsic size and relieve the nib editor's worries.

In a constraint's Attributes or Size inspector, there is a Placeholder checkbox ("Remove at build time"). If you check this checkbox, the constraint you're editing *won't* be instantiated when the nib is loaded: in effect, you are deliberately generating ambiguous layout when the views and constraints are instantiated from the nib. You might do this because you want to simulate your layout in the nib editor, but you intend to provide a different constraint in code; perhaps you weren't quite able to describe this constraint in the nib, or the constraint depends upon circumstances that won't be known until runtime.

 Unfortunately, a custom UILayoutGuide can be created and configured only in code. If you want to configure a layout entirely in the nib editor, and if this configuration requires the use of spacer views and cannot be constructed by a UIStackView, you'll have to use spacer views — you cannot replace them with UILayoutGuide objects, because there are no UILayoutGuide objects in the nib editor.

Problems with Nib Constraints

I've already said that generating constraints manually, in code, is error-prone. But it isn't error-prone in the nib editor! The nib editor *knows* whether it contains problematic constraints. If a view is affected by any constraints, the Xcode nib editor will permit them to be ambiguous or conflicting, but it will also complain helpfully. You should pay attention to such complaints! The nib editor will bring the situation to your attention in various places:

In the canvas
    Constraints drawn in the canvas when you select a view that they affect use color coding to express their status:

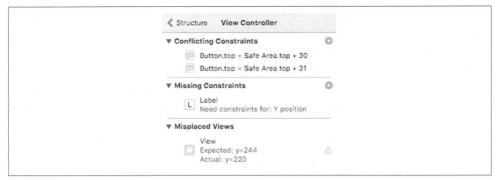

Figure 1-22. Layout issues in the document outline

Satisfactory constraints
Drawn in blue.

Problematic constraints
Drawn in red.

Misplacement constraints
Drawn in orange; these constraints are valid, but they are inconsistent with the frame you have imposed upon the view. I'll discuss misplaced views in the next paragraph.

In the document outline
If there are layout issues, the document outline displays a right arrow in a red or orange circle. Click it to see a detailed list of the issues (Figure 1-22). Hover the mouse over a title to see an Info button which you can click to learn more about the nature of this issue. The icons at the right are buttons: click one for a list of things the nib editor is offering to do to fix the issue for you. The chief issues are:

Conflicting Constraints
A conflict between constraints.

Missing Constraints
Ambiguous layout.

Misplaced Views
If you manually change the frame of a view that is affected by constraints (including its intrinsic size), then the canvas may be displaying that view differently from how it would really appear if the current constraints were obeyed. A Misplaced Views situation is also described in the canvas:

- The constraints in the canvas, drawn in orange, display the numeric *difference* between their values and the view's frame.

- A dotted outline in the canvas may show where the view *would* be drawn if the existing constraints were obeyed.

(You can turn off ambiguity checking for a particular view; use the Ambiguity pop-up menu in the view's Size inspector. This means you can omit a needed constraint and *not* be notified by the nib editor that there's a problem. You will need to generate the missing constraint in code, obviously, or you'll have ambiguous layout.)

Having warned you of problems with your layout, the nib editor also provides tools to fix them.

The Update Frames button in the layout bar (or Editor → Update Frames) changes the way the selected views or all views are drawn in the canvas, to show how things would really appear in the running app under the constraints as they stand. Alternatively, if you have resized a view with intrinsic size constraints, such as a button or a label, and you want it to resume the size it would have according to those intrinsic size constraints, select the view and choose Editor → Size to Fit Content.

 Be careful with Update Frames: if constraints are ambiguous, *this can cause a view to disappear.*

The Resolve Auto Layout Issues button in the layout bar (or the Editor → Resolve Auto Layout Issues hierarchical menu) proposes large-scale moves involving all the constraints affecting either selected views or all views:

Update Constraint Constants
Choose this menu item to change numerically all the existing constraints affecting a view to match the way the canvas is currently drawing the view's frame.

Add Missing Constraints
Create new constraints so that the view has sufficient constraints to describe its frame unambiguously. The added constraints correspond to the way the canvas is currently drawing the view's frame. This command may not do what you ultimately want; you should regard it as a starting point. After all, the nib editor can't read your mind! It doesn't know whether you think a certain view's width should be determined by an internal width constraint or by pinning it to the left and right of its superview; and it may generate alignment constraints with other views that you never intended.

Reset to Suggested Constraints
This is as if you chose Clear Constraints followed by Add Missing Constraints: it removes all constraints affecting the view, and replaces them with a complete set of automatically generated constraints describing the way the canvas is currently drawing the view's frame.

Clear Constraints
     Removes all constraints affecting the view.

Varying the Screen Size

The purpose of constraints will usually be to design a layout that responds to the possibility of the app launching on devices of different sizes, and perhaps subsequently being rotated. Imagining how this is going to work in real life is not always easy, and you may doubt that you are getting the constraints right as you configure them in the nib editor. Have no fear: Xcode is here to help.

There's a View As button at the lower left of the canvas. Click it to reveal (if they are not already showing) menus or buttons representing a variety of device types and orientations. Choose one, and the canvas's main views are resized accordingly. When that happens, the layout dictated by your constraints is obeyed immediately. So you can try out the effect of your constraints under different screen sizes right there in the canvas.

(This feature works only if the view controller's Simulated Size pop-up menu in the Size inspector says Fixed. If it says Freeform, the view won't be resized when you click a device type or orientation button.)

Conditional Interface Design

The View As button at the lower left of the canvas states the size classes for the currently chosen device and orientation, using a notation like this: wC hR. The w and h stand for "width" and "height," corresponding to the trait collection's .horizontalSizeClass and .verticalSizeClass respectively; the R and C stand for .regular and .compact.

The reason you're being given this information is that you might want the configuration of your constraints and views in the nib editor to be *conditional* upon the size classes that are in effect *at runtime*. You can arrange in the nib editor for your app's interface to detect the traitCollectionDidChange notification and respond to it:

- You can design your interface to rearrange itself when an iPhone app rotates to compensate for a change in device orientation.
- A single *.storyboard* or *.xib* file can be used to design the interface of a universal app, even if the iPad interface and the iPhone interface are quite different from one another.

The idea when constructing a conditional interface is that you design first for the most general case. When you've done that, and when you want to do something *different* for a *particular* size class situation, you'll describe that difference in the Attributes or Size inspector, or design that difference in the canvas:

In the Attributes or Size inspector

Look for a Plus symbol to the left of a value in the Attributes or Size inspector. This is a value that you can vary conditionally, depending on the environment's size class at runtime. The Plus symbol is a button! Click it to see a popover from which you can choose a specialized size class combination. When you do, that value now appears *twice*: once for the general case, and once for the specialized case which is marked using wC hR notation. You can now provide different values for those two cases.

In the canvas

Click the Vary for Traits button, to the right of the device types buttons (click View As if you don't see the Vary for Traits button). Two checkboxes appear, allowing you to specify that you want to match the width or height size class (or both) of the current size class. Any designing you now do in the canvas will be applied only to that width or height size class (or both), and the Attributes or Size inspector will be modified as needed.

I'll illustrate these approaches with a little tutorial. You'll need to have an example project on hand; make sure it's a universal app.

Size classes in the inspectors

Suppose we have a button in the canvas, and we want this button to have a yellow background *on iPad only*. (This is improbable but dramatic.) You can configure this directly in the Attributes inspector:

1. Select the button in the interface.

2. Switch to the Attributes inspector, and locate the Background pop-up menu in the View section of the inspector.

3. Click the Plus button to bring up a popover with pop-up menus for specifying size classes. An iPad has width (horizontal) size class Regular and height (vertical) size class Regular, so change the first two pop-up menus so that they both say Regular. Click Add Variation.

4. A second Background pop-up menu has appeared! It is marked wR hR. Change it to yellow (or any desired color).

The button now has a colored background on iPad but not on iPhone. To see that this is true, without running the app on different device types, use the View As button and the device buttons at the lower left of the canvas to switch between different screen sizes. When you click an iPad button, the button in the canvas has a yellow background. When you click an iPhone button, the button in the canvas has its default clear background.

Now that you know what the Plus button means, look over the Attributes and Size inspectors. Anything with a Plus button can be varied in accordance with the size class environment. A button's text can be a different font and size; this makes sense because you might want the text to be larger on an iPad. A button's Hidden checkbox can be different for different size classes, so that the button is invisible on some device types. And at the bottom of the Attributes inspector is the Installed checkbox; unchecking this for a particular size class combination causes the button to be entirely absent from the interface.

Size classes in the canvas

Suppose your interface has a button pinned to the top *left* of its superview. And suppose that, on iPad devices only, you want this button to be pinned to the top *right* of its superview. (Again, this is improbable but dramatic.) That means the button's leading constraint will exist only on iPhone devices, to be replaced by a trailing constraint on iPad devices. The constraints are different objects. The way to configure different objects for different size classes is to use the Vary for Traits button:

1. Among the device type buttons, click one of the iPhone buttons (furthest to the right). Configure the button so that it's pinned by its top and left to the top left of the main view.

2. Among the device type buttons, click one of the iPad buttons (furthest to the left). The size classes are now listed as wR hR.

3. Click Vary for Traits. In the little popover that appears, check *both* boxes: we want the change we are about to make to apply only when *both* the width size class *and* the height size class match our *current* size class (they should *both* be .regular). The entire layout bar becomes blue, to signify that we are operating in a special conditional design mode.

4. Make the desired change: Select the button in the interface; select the left constraint; delete the left constraint; slide the button to the right of the interface; Control-drag from the button to the right and create a new trailing constraint. If necessary, click the Update Frames button to make the orange Misplaced Views warning symbol go away.

5. Click Done Varying. The layout bar ceases to be blue.

We've created a conditional constraint. To see that this is true, click an iPhone device button and then click an iPad device button. As you do, the button in the interface jumps between the left and right sides of the interface. Its position depends upon the device type!

The inspectors for this button accord with the change we've just made. To see that this is true, click the button, select the trailing or leading constraint (depending on the device type), and look in the Attributes or Size inspector. The constraint has two Installed checkboxes, one for the general case and one for wR hR. Only one of these checkboxes is checked; the constraint is present in one case but not the other.

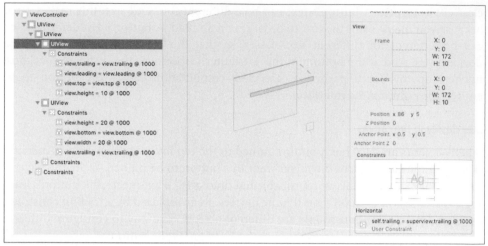

Figure 1-23. View debugging (again)

In the document outline, a constraint or view that is not installed for the current set of size classes is listed with a faded icon.

Xcode View Features

This section summarizes some miscellaneous view-related features of Xcode that are worth knowing about.

View Debugger

To enter the view debugger, choose Debug → View Debugging → Capture View Hierarchy, or click the Debug View Hierarchy button in the debug bar. The result is that your app's current view hierarchy is analyzed and displayed (Figure 1-23):

- On the left, in the Debug navigator, the views and their constraints are listed hierarchically. (View controllers are also listed as part of the hierarchy.)

- In the center, in the canvas, the views and their constraints are displayed graphically. The window starts out facing front, much as if you were looking at the screen with the app running; but if you swipe sideways a little in the canvas (or click the Orient to 3D button at the bottom of the canvas, or choose Editor → Orient to 3D), the window rotates and its subviews are displayed in front of it, in layers. You can adjust your perspective in various ways:

  - The slider at the lower left changes the distance between the layers.

  - The double-slider at the lower right lets you eliminate the display of views from the front or back of the layering order (or both).

- You can Option-double-click a view to focus on it, eliminating its superviews from the display. Double-click outside the view to exit focus mode.
- You can switch to wireframe mode.
- You can display constraints for the currently selected view.
- On the right, the Object inspector and the Size inspector tell you details about the currently selected object (view or constraint).

When a view is selected in the Debug navigator or in the canvas, the Size inspector lists its bounds and the constraints that determine those bounds. This, along with the layered graphical display of your views and constraints in the canvas, can help you ferret out the cause of any constraint-related difficulties.

Previewing Your Interface

When you're displaying the nib editor in Xcode, you're already seeing the results of your constraints in the current device size. You can change device size using the buttons or menu that appears when you click View As at the lower left. That same interface lets you toggle orientation and, new in Xcode 11, switch between light and dark mode.

For an even more realistic display, choose Editor → Preview (or choose Preview from the Editor Options pop-up menu). You'll see a preview of the currently selected view controller's view (or, in a *.xib* file, the top-level view).

At the bottom of each preview, a label tells you what device you're seeing, and a rotate button lets you toggle its orientation. At the lower left, a Plus button lets you add previews for different devices and device sizes, so you can view your interface on different devices *simultaneously*. The previews take account of constraints and conditional interface. At the lower right, a language pop-up menu lets you switch your app's text (buttons and labels) to another language for which you have localized your app, or to an artificial "double-length" language. To remove a previewed device, click to select it and press Delete.

Designable Views and Inspectable Properties

Your custom view can be drawn in the nib editor canvas and preview *even if it is configured in code*. To take advantage of this feature, you need a UIView subclass declared @IBDesignable. If an instance of this UIView subclass appears in the nib editor, then its self-configuration methods, such as willMove(toSuperview:), will be compiled and run as the nib editor prepares to portray your view. In addition, your view can implement the special method prepareForInterfaceBuilder to perform visual configurations aimed specifically at how it will be portrayed in the nib editor; in this way, you can portray in the nib editor a feature that your view will adopt *later* in the life of the app. If your view contains a UILabel that is created and configured

Figure 1-24. A designable view

empty but will eventually contain text, you could implement `prepareForInterface-Builder` to give the label some sample text to be displayed in the nib editor.

In Figure 1-24, I refactor a familiar example. Our view subclass gives itself a magenta background, along with two subviews, one across the top and the other at the lower right — all designed in code. The nib contains an instance of this view subclass. When the app runs, `willMove(toSuperview:)` will be called, the code will run, and the subviews will be present. But because `willMove(toSuperview:)` is also called by the nib editor, the subviews are displayed in the nib editor as well:

```
@IBDesignable class MyView: UIView {
    func configure() {
        self.backgroundColor = UIColor(red: 1, green: 0.4, blue: 1, alpha: 1)
        let v2 = UIView()
        v2.backgroundColor = UIColor(red: 0.5, green: 1, blue: 0, alpha: 1)
        let v3 = UIView()
        v3.backgroundColor = UIColor(red: 1, green: 0, blue: 0, alpha: 1)
        v2.translatesAutoresizingMaskIntoConstraints = false
        v3.translatesAutoresizingMaskIntoConstraints = false
        self.addSubview(v2)
        self.addSubview(v3)
        NSLayoutConstraint.activate([
            v2.leftAnchor.constraint(equalTo:self.leftAnchor),
            v2.rightAnchor.constraint(equalTo:self.rightAnchor),
            v2.topAnchor.constraint(equalTo:self.topAnchor),
            v2.heightAnchor.constraint(equalToConstant:20),
            v3.widthAnchor.constraint(equalToConstant:20),
            v3.heightAnchor.constraint(equalTo:v3.widthAnchor),
            v3.rightAnchor.constraint(equalTo:self.rightAnchor),
            v3.bottomAnchor.constraint(equalTo:self.bottomAnchor),
```

```
        ])
    }
    override func willMove(toSuperview newSuperview: UIView?) {
        self.configure()
    }
}
```

In addition, you can configure a custom view property directly in the nib editor. To do that, your UIView subclass needs a property that's declared @IBInspectable, and this property's type needs to be one of a limited list of inspectable property types (I'll tell you what they are in a moment). Now let's say there's an instance of this UIView subclass in the nib: that property will get a field of its own at the top of the view's Attributes inspector, where you can set the initial value of that property in the nib editor rather than its having to be set in code. (This feature is actually a convenient equivalent of setting a nib object's User Defined Runtime Attributes in the Identity inspector.)

The inspectable property types are: Bool, number, String, CGRect, CGPoint, CGSize, NSRange, UIColor, or UIImage. The property won't be displayed in the Attributes inspector unless its type is declared explicitly. You can assign a default value in code; the Attributes inspector won't portray this value as the default, but you can tell it to use the default by leaving the field empty (or, if you've entered a value, by deleting that value).

 An IBInspectable property's value, as set in the nib editor, is not applied until *after* init(coder:) and willMove(toSuperview:) have run. The earliest your code can retrieve this value at runtime is in awakeFromNib.

@IBDesignable and @IBInspectable are unrelated, but the former is aware of the latter. This means you can use an inspectable property to change the nib editor's display of your interface.

In this example, we use @IBDesignable and @IBInspectable to work around an annoying limitation of the nib editor. A UIView can draw its own border automatically, by setting its layer's borderWidth (Chapter 3). But this can be configured only in code. There's nothing in a view's Attributes inspector that lets you set a layer's borderWidth, and special layer configurations are not normally portrayed in the canvas. @IBDesignable and @IBInspectable to the rescue:

```
@IBDesignable class MyButton : UIButton {
    @IBInspectable var borderWidth : Int {
        set {
            self.layer.borderWidth = CGFloat(newValue)
        }
        get {
```

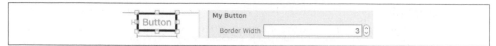

Figure 1-25. A designable view with an inspectable property

```
            return Int(self.layer.borderWidth)
        }
    }
}
```

The result is that, in the nib editor, our button's Attributes inspector has a Border Width custom property, and when we change the Border Width property setting, the button is redrawn with that border width (Figure 1-25). Moreover, we are setting this property in the nib, so when the app runs and the nib loads, the button really does have that border width in the running app.

Layout Events

This section summarizes three chief UIView events related to layout. These are events that you can receive and respond to by overriding them in your UIView subclass. You might want to do this in situations where layout is complex — when you need to supplement autoresizing or autolayout with manual layout in code, or when your layout configuration needs to change in response to changing conditions. (Closely related to these UIView events are some layout-related events you can receive and respond to in a UIViewController; I'll discuss them in Chapter 6.)

updateConstraints

If your interface involves autolayout and constraints, then updateConstraints is propagated *up* the hierarchy, starting at the deepest subview, when the runtime thinks your code might need an opportunity to configure constraints. You might override updateConstraints because you have a UIView subclass capable of altering its own constraints. If you do, you must finish up by calling super or the app will crash (with a helpful error message).

updateConstraints is called at launch time, but rarely after that unless you *cause* it to be called. You should never call updateConstraints directly. To trigger an immediate call to updateConstraints, send a view the updateConstraintsIf-Needed message. To force updateConstraints to be sent to a particular view, send it the setNeedsUpdateConstraints message.

traitCollectionDidChange(_:)

At launch time, and if the environment's trait collection changes thereafter, the traitCollectionDidChange(_:) message is propagated *down* the hierarchy of UITraitEnvironments. The incoming parameter is the *old* trait collection; to get the new trait collection, ask for self.traitCollection.

Earlier in this chapter I showed some code for swapping a view into or out of the interface together with the entire set of constraints laying out that interface. But I left open the matter of the conditions under which we wanted such swapping to occur; `traitCollectionDidChange` might be an appropriate moment, if the idea is to change the interface when the app rotates on an iPhone.

layoutSubviews

The `layoutSubviews` message is the moment when layout actually takes place. It is propagated *down* the hierarchy, starting at the top (typically the root view) and working down to the deepest subview. Layout can be triggered even if the trait collection didn't change; perhaps a constraint was changed, or the text of a label was changed, or a superview's size changed.

You can override `layoutSubviews` in a UIView subclass in order to take a hand in the layout process. If you're not using autolayout, `layoutSubviews` does nothing by default; `layoutSubviews` is your opportunity to perform manual layout after autoresizing has taken place. If you are using autolayout, you must call `super` or the app will crash (with a helpful error message).

You should never call `layoutSubviews` directly; to trigger an immediate call to `layoutSubviews`, send a view the `layoutIfNeeded` message (which may cause layout of the entire view tree, not only below but also above this view), or send `setNeedsLayout` to trigger a call to `layoutSubviews` later on, after your code finishes running, when layout would normally take place.

When you're using autolayout, what happens in `layoutSubviews`? The runtime, having examined and resolved all the constraints affecting this view's subviews, and having worked out values for their center and bounds, now simply assigns center and bounds values to them. In other words, `layoutSubviews` performs manual layout!

Knowing this, you might override `layoutSubviews` when you're using autolayout, in order to tweak the outcome. A typical structure is: first you call `super`, causing all the subviews to adopt their new frames; then you examine those frames; if you don't like the outcome, you can change things; and finally you call `super` *again*, to get a new layout outcome. As I mentioned earlier, setting a view's frame (or bounds or center) explicitly in `layoutSubviews` is perfectly fine, even if this view uses autolayout; that, after all, is what the autolayout engine itself is doing. Keep in mind, however, that you must *cooperate* with the autolayout engine. Do not call `setNeedsUpdateConstraints` — that moment has passed — and do not stray beyond the subviews *of this view*. (Disobeying those rules can cause your app to hang.)

Earlier in this chapter I showed some code for wrapping a view into part of the interface together with the entire set of constraints... laying out that interface itself; let's put the button of the conditions under which we wanted such wrapping to occur in the code. TestContentSizeChange might be an appropriate moment, if the idea is to change the interface when the app... shown on an iPhone...

CHAPTER 2
Drawing

The views illustrated in Chapter 1 were mostly colored rectangles; they had a
`backgroundColor` and no more. But that's not what a real iOS program looks like.
Everything the user sees is a UIView, and what the user sees is a lot more than a
bunch of colored rectangles. That's because the views that the user sees have *content*.
They contain *drawing*.

Many UIView subclasses, such as a UIButton or a UILabel, know how to draw themselves. Sooner or later, you're also going to want to do some drawing of your own.
You can prepare your drawing as an image file beforehand. You can draw an image
as your app runs, in code. You can display an image in a UIView subclass that knows
how to show an image, such as a UIImageView or a UIButton. A pure UIView is all
about drawing, and it leaves that drawing largely up to you; your code determines
what the view draws, and hence what it looks like in your interface.

This chapter discusses the mechanics of drawing. Don't be afraid to write drawing
code of your own! It isn't difficult, and it's often the best way to make your app look
the way you want it to. (I'll discuss how to draw text in Chapter 10.)

Images and Image Views

The basic general UIKit image class is UIImage. UIImage knows how to deal with
many standard image types, such as HEIC, TIFF, JPEG, GIF, and PNG. A UIImage
can be used wherever an image is to be displayed; it knows how to provide the image
data, and may be thought of loosely as wrapping the image data. It also provides supplementary information about its image, and lets you tweak certain aspects of the
image's behavior.

Where will the image data inside a UIImage come from? There are three main
sources:

- An image file previously stored on disk.

- An image that your app draws as it runs.

- Image data that your app downloads from the network.

The first two are what this chapter is about. Downloading image data is discussed in Chapter 23.

Image Files

UIImage can read a stored file, so if an image does not need to be created dynamically, but has already been created before your app runs, then drawing may be as simple as providing an image file as a resource inside your app itself. When an image file is to be included inside your app, iOS has a special affinity for PNG files, and you should prefer them whenever possible. (The converse operation, saving image data as an image file, is discussed in Chapter 22.)

A pre-existing image file in your app's bundle is most commonly obtained in code through the UIImage initializer `init(named:)`, which takes a string and returns a UIImage wrapped in an Optional, in case the image doesn't exist. This method looks in two places for the image:

Asset catalog
> We look in the asset catalog for an image set with the supplied name. The name is case-sensitive.

Top level of app bundle
> We look at the top level of the app's bundle for an image file with the supplied name. The name is case-sensitive and should include the file extension; if it doesn't, *.png* is assumed.

When calling `init(named:)`, an asset catalog is searched before the top level of the app's bundle. If there are multiple asset catalogs, they are all searched, but the search order is indeterminate, so avoid multiple image sets with the same name.

 The Image library lists images both in the asset catalog and at the app bundle's top level. Instead of calling `init(named:)`, which takes a literal string that you might type incorrectly, you can drag or double-click an image in the Image library to enter an *image literal* directly into your code. The resulting token represents a call to the UIImage initializer `init(imageLiteralResourceName:)`, and produces a UIImage, not an Optional.

With `init(named:)`, the image data may be cached in memory, and if you ask for the same image by calling `init(named:)` again later, the cached data may be supplied immediately. Caching is usually good, because decoding the image on disk into usable bitmap data is expensive.

Nevertheless, sometimes caching may not be what you want; if you know you're just going to fetch the image once and put it into the interface immediately, caching might represent an unnecessary strain on your app's memory. If so, there's another way: you can read an image file from your app bundle (not the asset catalog) directly and without caching, by calling `init(contentsOfFile:)`, which expects a pathname string. To obtain that pathname string, you can get a reference to your app's bundle with `Bundle.main`, and Bundle then provides instance methods for getting the pathname of a file within the bundle, such as `path(forResource:ofType:)`.

Hardware-related image variants

An image file can come in multiple variants for use on different hardware. When the image file is stored in the app bundle, these variants are distinguished through the use of special name suffixes:

High-resolution variants

On a device with a double-resolution screen, when an image is obtained by name from the app bundle, a file with the same name extended by `@2x`, if there is one, will be used automatically, with the resulting UIImage marked as double-resolution by assigning it a `scale` property value of `2.0`. Similarly, if there is a file with the same name extended by `@3x`, it will be used on a device with a triple-resolution screen, with a `scale` property value of `3.0`.

Double- and triple-resolution variants of an image file should have dimensions double and triple those of the base file. But thanks to the UIImage `scale` property, a high-resolution variant of an image has the same CGSize as the single-resolution image. On a high-resolution screen, your code and your interface continue to work without change, but your images look sharper.

This works for UIImage `init(named:)` and `init(contentsOfFile:)`. If there is a file called *pic.png* and a file called *pic@2x.png*, then on a device with a double-resolution screen, these methods will access *pic@2x.png* as a UIImage with a scale of `2.0`:

```
let im = UIImage(named:"pic") // uses pic@2x.png
if let path = Bundle.main.path(forResource: "pic", ofType: "png") {
    let im2 = UIImage(contentsOfFile:path) // uses pic@2x.png
}
```

Device type variants

A file with the same name extended by `~ipad` will automatically be used if the app is running natively on an iPad. You can use this in a universal app to supply different images automatically depending on whether the app runs on an iPhone (or iPod touch), on the one hand, or on an iPad, on the other. (This is true not just for images but for *any* resource obtained by name from the bundle. See Apple's *Resource Programming Guide* in the documentation archive.)

This works for UIImage `init(named:)` and Bundle `path(forResource:of-Type:)`. If there is a file called *pic.png* and a file called *pic~ipad.png*, then on an iPad, these methods will access *pic~ipad.png*:

```
let im = UIImage(named:"pic") // uses pic~ipad.png
let path = Bundle.main.path(
    forResource: "pic", ofType: "png") // uses pic~ipad.png
```

If possible, however, you will probably prefer to supply your image in an asset catalog rather than in the app bundle. This has the advantage, among other things, that you can forget all about those name suffix conventions! An asset catalog knows when to use an alternate image within an image set, not from its *name*, but from its *place* in the catalog:

- Put the single-, double-, and triple-resolution alternatives into the slots marked "1x," "2x," and "3x" respectively.

- For a distinct iPad variant of an image, check iPhone and iPad in the Attributes inspector for the image set, and separate slots for those device types will appear in the asset catalog.

- An image set in an asset catalog can make numerous further distinctions based on a device's processor type, wide color capabilities, and more.

Many of these distinctions are used not only by the runtime when the app runs, but also by the App Store when thinning your app for a specific target device.

Vector images

An image file in the asset catalog can be a vector-based PDF:

- If you switch the Scales pop-up menu to Single Scale and put the image into the single slot, it will be resized automatically for double or triple resolution, and because it's a vector image, the resizing will be sharp.

- If you switch the Scales pop-up menu to Individual and Single Scales and put the image also into the "1x" slot, and if you check Preserve Vector Data for this slot, the image will be resized sharply for *any* size, either when scaled automatically (by a UIImageView or other interface item), or when your code scales the image by redrawing it (as I'll describe later in this chapter).

New in Xcode 11 and iOS 13, the system supplies more than 1500 standard named SVG *symbol images* intended for use both as icons and in conjunction with text. To obtain one as a UIImage in code, call the UIImage initializer `init(systemName:)`. The symbol images are displayed along with their names in the SF Symbols app, available for download from Apple.

A few symbol images are so commonly used that they are vended directly as class properties of UIImage: `.add`, `.remove`, `.close`, `.actions`, `.checkmark`, and `.stroked-Checkmark`. In the nib editor, an interface object that accepts an image, such as a UIButton, lets you specify a symbol image by name using a pop-up menu.

Certain details of how a symbol image is drawn may be dictated through its `symbol-Configuration` (UIImage.SymbolConfiguration). You can supply this when you create the image, or you can change it by calling the UIImage instance methods `.withConfiguration(_:)` or `.applyingSymbolConfiguration(_:)`. Alternatively, you can attach a symbol configuration to the image view that displays the symbol image. Configurations can involve one of nine weights, one of three scales, a font or text style, and a point size, in various combinations; this is to facilitate association with text. I'll talk about that in detail in Chapter 10.

Asset catalogs and trait collections

An asset catalog can distinguish between variants of an asset intended for different trait collections ("Trait Collections" on page 27). The chief distinctions you might want to draw will involve size classes or user interface style (light and dark mode).

Consider an image that is to appear in different variants depending on the size class situation. In the Attributes inspector for your image set, use the Width Class and Height Class pop-up menus to specify which size class possibilities you want slots for. If we're on an iPhone with the app rotated to landscape orientation, and if there's both an Any Height and a Compact Height alternative in the image set, the Compact Height variant is used. These features are live as the app runs; if the app rotates from landscape to portrait, and there's both an Any height and a Compact height alternative in the image set, the Compact Height variant is *replaced* with the Any Height variant in your interface, there and then, *automatically*.

In the same way, an image can vary depending on whether the environment is in light mode or dark mode. To display the necessary slots, in the Attributes inspector, use the Appearance pop-up menu. If you choose Any, Dark, you'll get a slot for light or unspecified mode and a slot for dark mode, which is usually what you want. Again, a UIImage obtained from the asset catalog is live, and will switch *automatically* to the appropriate variant when the interface style changes. A named color defined in the asset catalog can make the same distinction, making it a dynamic color (as I described in Chapter 1).

If you need a specific trait collection variant of an image or named color in an asset catalog, and you know its name, you can call `init(named:in:compatibleWith:)`; the third parameter is the trait collection. But what if you *already* have this UIImage or UIColor and you *don't* know its name? For that matter, how does the interface in your running app, which *already* contains a UIImage or a UIColor, automatically change when the trait collection changes? This magic is baked into UIImage and UIColor.

Let's start with UIImage. When an image is obtained from an asset catalog through UIImage init(named:), its imageAsset property is a UIImageAsset that effectively points back into the asset catalog at the image set that it came from. Each image in the image set has a trait collection associated with it (its traitCollection). By calling the UIImageAsset method image(with:), passing a trait collection, you can ask an image's imageAsset for the image from the same image set appropriate to that trait collection.

A built-in interface object that displays an image, such as a UIImageView, is automatically trait collection–aware; it receives the traitCollectionDidChange(_:) message and responds accordingly. To demonstrate how this works under the hood, we can build a custom UIView with an image property that behaves the same way:

```
class MyView: UIView {
    var image : UIImage!
    override func traitCollectionDidChange(_ prevtc: UITraitCollection?) {
        super.traitCollectionDidChange(prevtc)
        self.setNeedsDisplay() // causes draw(_:) to be called
    }
    override func draw(_ rect: CGRect) {
        if var im = self.image {
            if let asset = self.image.imageAsset {
                im = asset.image(with:self.traitCollection)
            }
            im.draw(at:.zero)
        }
    }
}
```

The really interesting part is that no actual asset catalog is needed. You can treat images as trait-based alternatives for one another *without* using an asset catalog. You might do this because your code has constructed the images from scratch or has obtained them over the network while the app is running. The technique is to instantiate a UIImageAsset and then associate each image with a different trait collection by *registering* it with this same UIImageAsset. Here's an example:

```
let tcreg = UITraitCollection(verticalSizeClass: .regular)
let tccom = UITraitCollection(verticalSizeClass: .compact)
let moods = UIImageAsset()
let frowney = UIImage(named:"frowney")!
let smiley = UIImage(named:"smiley")!
moods.register(frowney, with: tcreg)
moods.register(smiley, with: tccom)
```

The amazing thing is that if we now display either frowney or smiley in a UIImage-View, we see the image associated with the environment's current vertical size class, and it automatically switches to the other image when the app changes orientation on an iPhone. Moreover, this works even though I didn't keep any persistent reference to `frowney`, `smiley`, or the UIImageAsset! (The reason is that the images are cached by the system and they maintain a strong reference to the UIImageAsset with which they are registered.)

UIColor works in a simpler way. There is no UIColorAsset class. A dynamic color is declared by calling `init(dynamicProvider:)`, whose parameter is a function that takes a trait collection and returns a color. The knowledge of the color corresponding to a trait collection is baked directly into the dynamic color, and you can extract it by calling `resolvedColor(with:)`, passing a trait collection.

Namespacing image files

When image files are numerous or need to be clumped into groups, the question arises of how to divide them into namespaces. Here are some possibilities:

Folder reference
> Instead of keeping images at the top level of your app bundle, you can keep them in a *folder* in the app bundle. This is easiest to maintain if you put a *folder reference* into your project; the folder itself is then copied into the app bundle at build time, along with all its contents. There are various ways to retrieve an image in such a folder:
>
> - Call UIImage `init(named:)` with the folder name and a forward slash in front of the image's name in the name string. If the folder is called *pix* and the image file is called *pic.png*, then the "name" of the image is `"pix/pic.png"`.
> - Call Bundle `path(forResource:ofType:inDirectory:)` to get the image file's path, followed by UIImage `init(contentsOfFile:)`.
> - Obtain the bundle path (`Bundle.main.bundlePath`) and use NSString pathname and FileManager methods to drill down to the desired file.

Asset catalog folder
> An asset catalog can provide virtual folders that function as namespaces. Suppose that an image set *myImage* is inside an asset catalog folder called *pix*; if you check Provides Namespace in the Attributes inspector for that folder, then the image can be accessed through UIImage `init(name:)` by the name `"pix/myImage"`.

Bundle
> A fuller form of `init(named:)` is `init(named:in:)`, where the second parameter is a bundle. This means you can keep images in a secondary bundle, such as a framework, and specify that bundle as a way of namespacing the image. This

approach works regardless of whether the image comes from an asset catalog or sits at the top level of the bundle.

Image files in the nib editor

Many built-in Cocoa interface objects will accept a UIImage as part of how they draw themselves; a UIButton can display an image, a UINavigationBar or a UITabBar can have a background image (Chapter 12), and so on. The image you want to supply will often come from an image file.

The nib editor stands ready to help you. The Attributes inspector of an interface object that can have an image will have a pop-up menu from which you can choose an image in your project — or, new in iOS 13, a built-in symbol image. Your project's images, as well as the built-in symbol images, are also listed in the Image library; from here, you can drag an image onto an interface object in the canvas, such as a button.

Image Views

When you want an image to appear in your interface, not inside a button or other interface object but purely as an image, you'll probably hand it to an image view — a UIImageView — which has the most knowledge and flexibility with regard to displaying images and is intended for this purpose. An image view is the displayer of images *par excellence*. In code, just set the image as the image view's `image`. In the nib editor, drag the image from the Image library onto an image view or set its image through the Image pop-up menu, or drag an image from the Image library directly into a plain UIView to get a UIImageView whose image is that image.

 New in iOS 13, an image view (or a UIButton, because its image is contained in an image view) can be configured to display a particular variant of any symbol image assigned to it by setting its `preferredSymbolConfiguration`; you can do that in code or in the nib editor.

A UIImageView can actually have *two* images, one assigned to its `image` property and the other assigned to its `highlightedImage` property; the value of the UIImageView's `isHighlighted` property dictates which of the two is displayed at any given moment. A UIImageView does not automatically highlight itself merely because the user taps it, the way a button does. However, there are certain situations where a UIImageView will respond to the highlighting of its surroundings; within a table view cell, for instance, a UIImageView will show its highlighted image when the cell is highlighted (Chapter 8).

A UIImageView is a UIView, so it can have a background color in addition to its image, it can have an alpha (transparency) value, and so forth (see Chapter 1). An image may have areas that are transparent, and a UIImageView will respect this, so an image of any shape can appear. A UIImageView without a background color is invisible except for its image, so the image simply appears in the interface, without the user being aware that it resides in a rectangular host. A UIImageView without an image and without a background color is invisible, so you could start with an empty UIImageView in the place where you will later need an image and subsequently assign the image in code. You can assign a new image to substitute one image for another, or set the image view's `image` property to `nil` to remove its image.

How a UIImageView draws its image depends upon the setting of its `contentMode` property (UIView.ContentMode); this property is actually inherited from UIView, and I'll discuss its more general purpose later in this chapter. `.scaleToFill` means the image's width and height are set to the width and height of the view, filling the view completely even if this alters the image's aspect ratio; `.center` means the image is drawn centered in the view without altering its size; and so on. Most commonly you'll use `.scaleAspectFit` or `.scaleAspectFill`; they both keep the image's aspect ratio while filling the image view. The difference is that `.scaleAspectFill` fills the image view in both dimensions, permitting some of the image to fall outside the image view. The best way to get a feel for the meanings of the various `contentMode` settings is to experiment with an image view in the nib editor: in the image view's Attributes inspector, change the Content Mode pop-up menu to see where and how the image draws itself.

You should also pay attention to a UIImageView's `clipsToBounds` property; if it is `false`, its image, even if it is larger than the image view and even if it is not scaled down by the `contentMode`, may be displayed in its entirety, extending beyond the image view itself.

When creating a UIImageView in code, you can take advantage of a convenience initializer, `init(image:)`. The default `contentMode` is `.scaleToFill`, but the image is not initially scaled; rather, *the image view itself is sized to match its image*. You will still probably need to position the UIImageView correctly in its superview. In this example, I'll put a picture of the planet Mars in the center of the app's interface (Figure 2-1; for the CGRect `center` property, see Appendix B):

```
let iv = UIImageView(image:UIImage(named:"Mars"))
self.view.addSubview(iv)
iv.center = iv.superview!.bounds.center
iv.frame = iv.frame.integral
```

What happens to the size of an existing UIImageView when you assign a new image to it depends on whether the image view is using autolayout. Under autolayout, the size of the image becomes the image view's `intrinsicContentSize`, so the image view *adopts the image's size* unless other constraints prevent.

Figure 2-1. Mars appears in my interface

An image view automatically acquires its `alignmentRectInsets` (see Chapter 1) from its image's `alignmentRectInsets`. If you're going to be aligning the image view to some other object using autolayout, you can attach appropriate `alignmentRect-Insets` to the image that the image view will display, and the image view will do the right thing. To do so in code, derive a new image by calling the original image's `with-AlignmentRectInsets(_:)` method; alternatively, you can set an image's `alignment-RectInsets` in the asset catalog (use the four Alignment fields).

Resizable Images

Certain interface contexts require an image that can be coherently resized to any desired proportions. A custom image that serves as the track of a slider or progress view (Chapter 12) must be able to fill a space of any length. Such an image is called a *resizable image.*

To make a resizable image in code, start with a normal image and call its `resizable-Image(withCapInsets:resizingMode:)` method. The `capInsets:` argument is a UIEdgeInsets, whose components represent distances inward from the edges of the image. In a context larger than the image, a resizable image can behave in one of two ways, depending on the `resizingMode:` value (UIImage.ResizingMode):

`.tile`
> The interior rectangle of the inset area is tiled (repeated) in the interior; each edge is formed by tiling the corresponding edge rectangle outside the inset area. The four corner rectangles outside the inset area are drawn unchanged.

`.stretch`
> The interior rectangle of the inset area is stretched *once* to fill the interior; each edge is formed by stretching the corresponding edge rectangle outside the inset area *once.* The four corner rectangles outside the inset area are drawn unchanged.

In these examples, assume that `self.iv` is a UIImageView with absolute height and width (so that it won't adopt the size of its image) and with a `contentMode` of `.scale-ToFill` (so that the image will exhibit resizing behavior). First, I'll illustrate tiling an entire image (Figure 2-2); note that the `capInsets:` is `.zero`, meaning no insets at all:

Figure 2-2. Tiling the entire image of Mars

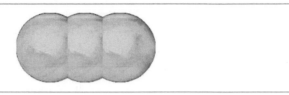

Figure 2-3. Tiling the interior of Mars

```
let mars = UIImage(named:"Mars")!
let marsTiled =
    mars.resizableImage(withCapInsets:.zero, resizingMode: .tile)
self.iv.image = marsTiled
```

Now we'll tile the interior of the image, changing the `capInsets:` argument from the previous code (Figure 2-3):

```
let marsTiled = mars.resizableImage(withCapInsets:
    UIEdgeInsets(
        top: mars.size.height / 4.0,
        left: mars.size.width / 4.0,
        bottom: mars.size.height / 4.0,
        right: mars.size.width / 4.0
    ), resizingMode: .tile)
```

Next, I'll illustrate stretching. We'll start by changing just the `resizingMode:` from the previous code (Figure 2-4):

```
let marsTiled = mars.resizableImage(withCapInsets:
    UIEdgeInsets(
        top: mars.size.height / 4.0,
        left: mars.size.width / 4.0,
        bottom: mars.size.height / 4.0,
        right: mars.size.width / 4.0
    ), resizingMode: .stretch)
```

A common stretching strategy is to make almost half the original image serve as a cap inset, leaving just a tiny rectangle in the center that must stretch to fill the entire interior of the resulting image (Figure 2-5):

Figure 2-4. Stretching the interior of Mars

Figure 2-5. Stretching a few pixels at the interior of Mars

Figure 2-6. Mars, stretched and clipped

```
let marsTiled = mars.resizableImage(withCapInsets:
    UIEdgeInsets(
        top: mars.size.height / 2.0 - 1,
        left: mars.size.width / 2.0 - 1,
        bottom: mars.size.height / 2.0 - 1,
        right: mars.size.width / 2.0 - 1
    ), resizingMode: .stretch)
```

In the preceding example, if the image view's `contentMode` is `.scaleAspectFill`, and if the image view's `clipsToBounds` is `true`, we get a sort of gradient effect, because the top and bottom of the stretched image are outside the image view and aren't drawn (Figure 2-6).

Alternatively, you can configure a resizable image in the asset catalog. It is often the case that a particular image will be used in your app chiefly as a resizable image, and always with the same `capInsets:` and `resizingMode:`, so it makes sense to configure this image once rather than having to repeat the same code.

To configure an image in an asset catalog as a resizable image, select the image and, in the Slicing section of the Attributes inspector, change the Slices pop-up menu to Horizontal, Vertical, or Horizontal and Vertical. When you do this, additional interface appears. You can specify the `resizingMode` with the Center pop-up menu. You

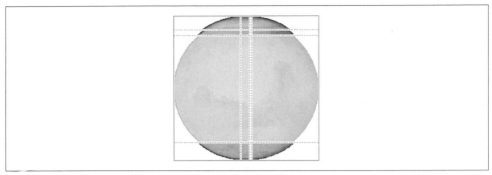

Figure 2-7. Mars, sliced in the asset catalog

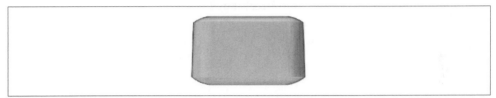

Figure 2-8. Mars, sliced and stretched

can work numerically, or click Show Slicing at the lower right of the canvas and work graphically.

This feature is even more powerful than `resizableImage(withCapInsets:resizing-Mode:)`. It lets you specify the end caps *separately* from the tiled or stretched region, with the rest of the image being sliced out. In Figure 2-7, the dark areas at the top left, top right, bottom left, and bottom right will be drawn as is; the narrow bands will be stretched, and the small rectangle at the top center will be stretched to fill most of the interior; but the rest of the image, the large central area covered by a sort of gauze curtain, will be omitted entirely. The result is shown in Figure 2-8.

Transparency Masks

Certain interface contexts, such as buttons and button-like interface objects, want to treat an image as a *transparency mask*, also known as a *template*. This means that the image color values are ignored, and only the transparency (alpha) values of each pixel matter. The image shown on the screen is formed by combining the image's transparency values with a single tint color.

The way an image will be treated is a property of the image, its `renderingMode`. This property is read-only; to change it in code, start with an image and generate a new image with a different rendering mode, by calling its `withRenderingMode(_:)` method.

The rendering mode values (UIImage.RenderingMode) are:

Figure 2-9. One image in two rendering modes

- `.automatic`
- `.alwaysOriginal`
- `.alwaysTemplate`

The default is `.automatic`, which means that the image is drawn normally except in those particular contexts that want to treat it as a transparency mask. With the other two rendering mode values, you can *force* an image to be drawn normally, even in a context that would usually treat it as a transparency mask, or you can *force* an image to be treated as a transparency mask, even in a context that would otherwise treat it normally.

To accompany this feature, iOS gives every UIView a `tintColor`, which will be used to tint any template images it contains. Moreover, this `tintColor` by default is inherited down the view hierarchy, and indeed throughout the entire app, starting with the window (Chapter 1). Assigning your app's main window a tint color is probably one of the few changes you'll make to the window; otherwise, your app adopts the system's blue tint color. (Alternatively, if you're using a main storyboard, set the Global Tint color in the File inspector.) Individual views can be assigned their own tint color, which is inherited by their subviews. Figure 2-9 shows two buttons displaying the same background image, one in normal rendering mode, the other in template rendering mode, in an app whose window tint color is red. (I'll say more about template images and `tintColor` in Chapter 12.)

You can assign an image a rendering mode in the asset catalog. Select the image set in the asset catalog, and use the Render As pop-up menu in the Attributes inspector to set the rendering mode to Default (`.automatic`), Original Image (`.alwaysOriginal`), or Template Image (`.alwaysTemplate`). This is an excellent approach whenever you have an image that you will use primarily in a specific rendering mode, because it saves you from having to remember to set that rendering mode in code every time you fetch the image. Instead, any time you call `init(named:)`, this image arrives with the rendering mode already set.

(The symbol images introduced in iOS 13 have no color of their own, so in effect they are *always* template images.)

Also new in iOS 13, a tint color can be applied to a UIImage directly; call `withTintColor(_:)` or `withTintColor(_:renderingMode:)`. This is useful particularly when you want to draw a symbol image or a template image in a context where there is no inherited tint color (such as a graphics context). Nonetheless, I find the behavior of these methods rather weird:

Original images become template images

If you apply `withTintColor` to an ordinary image, it is then treated as a template image — even if you also set the rendering mode to `.alwaysOriginal`.

Template images may ignore the assigned tint color

If you apply `withTintColor(_:)` to a template image — because it's a symbol image, or because you said `.alwaysTemplate`, or because we're in a context that treats an image as a transparency mask — then if you assign it into an view with a `tintColor` of its own, the tint color you specify is ignored! The view's tint color wins. If you want the tint color you specify to be obeyed, you must also set the rendering mode to `.alwaysOriginal`.

For example, the following code specifically sets a symbol image's tint color to red; nevertheless, what appears on the screen is a blue symbol image (because the default image view `tintColor` is blue):

```
let im = UIImage(systemName:"circle.fill")?.withTintColor(.red)
let iv = UIImageView(image:im)
self.view.addSubview(iv)
```

To get a red symbol image, you have to say this:

```
let im = UIImage(systemName:"circle.fill")?.withTintColor(.red,
    renderingMode: .alwaysOriginal) // *
let iv = UIImageView(image:im)
self.view.addSubview(iv)
```

Reversible Images

The entire interface is automatically reversed when your app runs on a system for which your app is localized if the system language is right-to-left. In general, this probably won't affect your images. The runtime assumes that you *don't* want images to be reversed when the interface is reversed, so its default behavior is to leave them alone.

Nevertheless, you *might* want an image to be reversed when the interface is reversed. Suppose you've drawn an arrow pointing in the direction from which new interface will arrive when the user taps a button. If the button pushes a view controller onto a navigation interface, that direction is from the right on a left-to-right system, but from the left on a right-to-left system. This image has directional meaning within the app's own interface; it needs to flip horizontally when the interface is reversed.

To make this possible in code, call the image's `imageFlippedForRightToLeftLayout-Direction` method and use the resulting image in your interface. On a left-to-right system, the normal image will be used; on a right-to-left system, a reversed variant of the image will be created and used automatically. You can override this behavior, even if the image is reversible, for a particular UIView displaying the image, such as a UIImageView, by setting that view's `semanticContentAttribute` to prevent mirroring.

You can make the same determination for an image in the asset catalog using the Direction pop-up menu (choose one of the Mirrors options). Moreover, the layout direction (as I mentioned in Chapter 1) is a trait, so you can have pairs of images to be used under left-to-right or right-to-left layout. The easy way to configure such pairs is to choose Both in the asset catalog's Direction pop-up menu; now there are left-to-right and right-to-left image slots where you can place your images. Alternatively, you can register the paired images with a UIImageAsset in code, as I demonstrated earlier in this chapter.

You can also force an image to be flipped horizontally without regard to layout direction or semantic content attribute by calling its `withHorizontallyFlipped-Orientation` method.

Graphics Contexts

Instead of plopping an image from an existing image file directly into your interface, you may want to create some drawing yourself, in code. To do so, you will need a *graphics context*. This is where the fun really begins!

A graphics context is basically a place you can draw. Conversely, you can't draw in code unless you've got a graphics context. There are several ways in which you might obtain a graphics context; these are the most common:

Cocoa creates the graphics context
> You subclass UIView and override `draw(_:)`. At the time your `draw(_:)` implementation is called, Cocoa has already created a graphics context and is asking you to draw into it, right now; whatever you draw is what the UIView will display.

Cocoa passes you a graphics context
> You subclass CALayer and override `draw(in:)`, or else you give a CALayer a delegate and implement the delegate's `draw(_:in:)`. The `in:` parameter is a graphics context. (Layers are discussed in Chapter 3.)

You create an image context
> The preceding two ways of getting a graphics context amount to drawing *on demand:* you slot your drawing code into the right place, and it is called whenever drawing needs to happen. The other major way to draw is just to make a UIImage yourself, once and for all. To create the graphics context that generates the image, you use a UIGraphicsImageRenderer.

Moreover, at any given moment there either is or is not a *current* graphics context:

- When UIView's `draw(_:)` is called, the UIView's drawing context is already the current graphics context.
- When CALayer's `draw(in:)` or its delegate's `draw(_:in:)` is called, the `in:` parameter is a graphics context, but it is *not* the current context. It's up to you to make it current if you need to.
- When you create an image context, that image context automatically becomes the current graphics context.

What beginners find most confusing about drawing is that there are two sets of tools for drawing, which take different attitudes toward the context in which they will draw. One set needs a current context; the other just needs a context:

UIKit

Various Cocoa classes know how to draw themselves; these include UIImage, NSString (for drawing text), UIBezierPath (for drawing shapes), and UIColor. Some of these classes provide convenience methods with limited abilities; others are extremely powerful. In many cases, UIKit will be all you'll need.

With UIKit, you can draw *only into the current context*. If there's already a current context, you just draw. But with CALayer, where you are handed a context as a parameter, if you want to use the UIKit convenience methods, you'll have to make that context the current context; you do this by calling `UIGraphicsPushContext(_:)` (and be sure to restore things with `UIGraphicsPopContext` later).

Core Graphics

This is the full drawing API. Core Graphics, often referred to as Quartz, or Quartz 2D, is the drawing system that underlies all iOS drawing; UIKit drawing is built on top of it. It is low-level and consists of C functions (though in Swift these are mostly "renamified" to look like method calls). There are a lot of them! This chapter will familiarize you with the fundamentals; for complete information, you'll want to study Apple's *Quartz 2D Programming Guide* in the documentation archive.

With Core Graphics, you must *specify a graphics context* (a CGContext) to draw into, explicitly, for each bit of your drawing. With CALayer, you are handed the context as a parameter, and that's the graphics context you want to draw into. But if there is already a current context, you have no reference to it until you call `UIGraphicsGetCurrentContext` to obtain it.

You don't have to use UIKit or Core Graphics *exclusively*. On the contrary, you can intermingle UIKit calls and Core Graphics calls in the same chunk of code to operate on the same graphics context. They merely represent two different ways of telling a graphics context what to do.

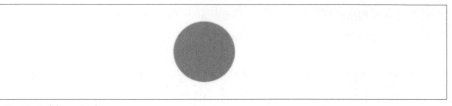

Figure 2-10. A blue circle

We have two sets of tools and three ways in which a context might be supplied; that makes six ways of drawing. I'll now demonstrate all six of them! To do so, I'll draw a blue circle (Figure 2-10). Without worrying just yet about the actual drawing commands, focus your attention on how the context is specified and on whether we're using UIKit or Core Graphics.

Drawing on Demand

There are four ways of drawing on demand, and I'll start with those. First, I'll implement a UIView subclass's `draw(_:)`, using UIKit to draw into the current context, which Cocoa has already prepared for me:

```
override func draw(_ rect: CGRect) {
    let p = UIBezierPath(ovalIn: CGRect(0,0,100,100))
    UIColor.blue.setFill()
    p.fill()
}
```

Now I'll do the same thing with Core Graphics; this will require that I first get a reference to the current context:

```
override func draw(_ rect: CGRect) {
    let con = UIGraphicsGetCurrentContext()!
    con.addEllipse(in:CGRect(0,0,100,100))
    con.setFillColor(UIColor.blue.cgColor)
    con.fillPath()
}
```

Next, I'll implement a CALayer delegate's `draw(_:in:)`. In this case, we're handed a reference to a context, but it isn't the current context. So I have to make it the current context in order to use UIKit (and I must remember to stop making it the current context when I'm done drawing):

```
override func draw(_ layer: CALayer, in con: CGContext) {
    UIGraphicsPushContext(con)
    let p = UIBezierPath(ovalIn: CGRect(0,0,100,100))
    UIColor.blue.setFill()
    p.fill()
    UIGraphicsPopContext()
}
```

To use Core Graphics in a CALayer delegate's `draw(_:in:)`, I simply keep referring to the context I was handed:

```
override func draw(_ layer: CALayer, in con: CGContext) {
    con.addEllipse(in:CGRect(0,0,100,100))
    con.setFillColor(UIColor.blue.cgColor)
    con.fillPath()
}
```

Drawing a UIImage

Now I'll make a UIImage of a blue circle. We can do this at any time (we don't need to wait for some particular method to be called) and in any class (we don't need to be in a UIView subclass).

To construct a UIImage in code, use a UIGraphicsImageRenderer. The basic technique is to create the renderer and call its `image` method to obtain the UIImage, handing it a function containing your drawing instructions.

In this example, I draw my image using UIKit:

```
let r = UIGraphicsImageRenderer(size:CGSize(100,100))
let im = r.image { _ in
    let p = UIBezierPath(ovalIn: CGRect(0,0,100,100))
    UIColor.blue.setFill()
    p.fill()
}
// im is the blue circle image, do something with it here ...
```

And here's the same thing using Core Graphics:

```
let r = UIGraphicsImageRenderer(size:CGSize(100,100))
let im = r.image { _ in
    let con = UIGraphicsGetCurrentContext()!
    con.addEllipse(in:CGRect(0,0,100,100))
    con.setFillColor(UIColor.blue.cgColor)
    con.fillPath()
}
// im is the blue circle image, do something with it here ...
```

In those examples, we're calling UIGraphicsImageRenderer's `init(size:)` and accepting its default configuration, which is usually what's wanted. To configure the image context further, call the UIGraphicsImageRendererFormat class method `default`, configure the format through its properties, and pass it to UIGraphicsImageRenderer's `init(size:format:)`. Those properties are:

opaque

> By default, `false`; the image context is transparent. If `true`, the image context is opaque and has a black background, and the resulting image has no transparency.

scale
> By default, the same as the scale of the main screen, `UIScreen.main.scale`. This means that the resolution of the resulting image will be correct for the device we're running on.

preferredRange
> The color gamut. Your choices are (UIGraphicsImageRendererFormat.Range):
>
> - `.standard`
> - `.extended`
> - `.automatic` (same as `.extended` if we're running on a device that supports "wide color")

A single parameter (ignored in the preceding examples) arrives into the UIGraphics-ImageRenderer's `image` function. It's a UIGraphicsImageRendererContext. This provides access to the configuring UIGraphicsImageRendererFormat (its `format`). It also lets you obtain the graphics context (its `cgContext`); you can alternatively get this by calling `UIGraphicsGetCurrentContext`, and the preceding code does so, for consistency with the other ways of drawing. In addition, the UIGraphicsImageRenderer-Context can hand you a copy of the image as drawn up to this point (its `currentImage`); also, it implements a few basic drawing commands of its own.

UIImage Drawing

A UIImage provides methods for drawing itself into the current context. We already know how to obtain a UIImage, and we already know how to obtain a graphics context and make it the current context, so we are ready to experiment with these methods.

Here, I'll make a UIImage consisting of two pictures of Mars side by side (Figure 2-11):

```
let mars = UIImage(named:"Mars")!
let sz = mars.size
let r = UIGraphicsImageRenderer(size:CGSize(sz.width*2, sz.height),
    format:mars.imageRendererFormat)
let im = r.image { _ in
    mars.draw(at:CGPoint(0,0))
    mars.draw(at:CGPoint(sz.width,0))
}
```

Observe that image scaling works perfectly in that example. If we have multiple resolution variants of our original Mars image, the correct one for the current device is used, and is assigned the correct `scale` value. The image context that we are drawing into also has the correct `scale` by default. And the resulting image `im` has the correct

Figure 2-11. Two images of Mars combined side by side

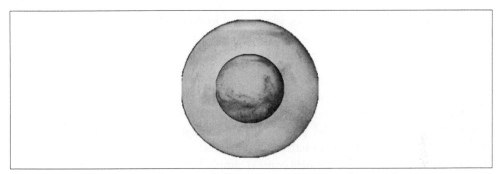

Figure 2-12. Two images of Mars in different sizes, composited

scale as well. Our code produces an image that looks correct on the current device, whatever its screen resolution may be.

 If your purpose in creating an image graphics context is to draw an existing UIImage into it, you can gain some efficiency by initializing the image renderer's format to the image's imageRendererFormat.

Additional UIImage methods let you scale an image into a desired rectangle as you draw (effectively resizing the image), and specify the compositing (blend) mode whereby the image should combine with whatever is already present. To illustrate, I'll create an image showing Mars centered in another image of Mars that's twice as large, using the .multiply blend mode (Figure 2-12):

```
let mars = UIImage(named:"Mars")!
let sz = mars.size
let r = UIGraphicsImageRenderer(size:CGSize(sz.width*2, sz.height*2),
    format:mars.imageRendererFormat)
let im = r.image { _ in
    mars.draw(in:CGRect(0,0,sz.width*2,sz.height*2))
    mars.draw(in:CGRect(sz.width/2.0, sz.height/2.0, sz.width, sz.height),
        blendMode: .multiply, alpha: 1.0)
}
```

Redrawing an image at a smaller size is of particular importance in iOS programming, because it is a waste of valuable memory to hand a UIImageView a large image and ask the image view to display it smaller. Some frameworks such as Image I/O (Chapter 22) and PhotoKit (Chapter 17) allow you to load a downsized image

Figure 2-13. Half the original image of Mars

thumbnail directly, but sometimes you'll need to downscale an image to fit within a given size yourself. For a general utility method that downsizes a UIImage to fit within a given CGSize, see Appendix B.

Sometimes, you may want to extract a smaller region of the original image — effectively cropping the image as you draw it. Unfortunately, there is no UIImage drawing method for specifying the source rectangle. You can work around this by creating a smaller graphics context and positioning the image drawing so that the desired region falls into it. There is no harm in doing this, and it's a perfectly standard strategy; what falls outside the graphics context simply isn't drawn.

To obtain an image of the right half of Mars, you can make a graphics context half the width of the `mars` image, and then draw `mars` shifted left, so that only its right half intersects the graphics context (Figure 2-13):

```
let mars = UIImage(named:"Mars")!
let sz = mars.size
let r = UIGraphicsImageRenderer(size:CGSize(sz.width/2.0, sz.height),
    format:mars.imageRendererFormat)
let im = r.image { _ in
    mars.draw(at:CGPoint(-sz.width/2.0,0))
}
```

A nice feature of UIGraphicsImageRenderer is that we can initialize it with a bounds instead of a size. Instead of drawing `mars` shifted left, we can achieve the same effect by drawing `mars` at `.zero` into a bounds that is shifted right:

```
let mars = UIImage(named:"Mars")!
let sz = mars.size
let r = UIGraphicsImageRenderer(
    bounds:CGRect(sz.width/2.0, 0, sz.width/2.0, sz.height),
    format:mars.imageRendererFormat)
let im = r.image { _ in
    mars.draw(at:.zero)
}
```

Vector images work like normal images. A PDF vector image in the asset catalog for which you have checked Preserve Vector Data will scale sharply when you call `draw(in:)`, and a symbol image always scales sharply:

```
let symbol = UIImage(systemName:"rhombus")!
let sz = CGSize(100,100)
let r = UIGraphicsImageRenderer(size:sz)
let im = r.image {_ in
    symbol.withTintColor(.purple).draw(in:CGRect(origin:.zero, size:sz))
}
```

The resulting rhombus is purple (because we gave the image a tint color before draw-ing it) and smoothly drawn at 100×100 (because it's a vector image). But of course, once you've drawn the vector image into a UIImage (like our im), *that* image is *not* a vector image, so it doesn't scale sharply.

It is better, however, not to do what I just did. You really should try not to call draw(in:) on a symbol image. Instead, generate a UIImage with a custom symbol configuration, specifying a point size, and call draw(at:), letting the symbol image size itself according to the point size you provided.

CGImage Drawing

The Core Graphics analog to UIImage is CGImage. In essence, a UIImage is (usually) a wrapper for a CGImage: the UIImage is bitmap image data plus scale, orientation, and other information, whereas the CGImage is the bare bitmap image data alone. The two are easily converted to one another: a UIImage has a cgImage property that accesses its Quartz image data, and you can make a UIImage from a CGImage using init(cgImage:) or init(cgImage:scale:orientation:).

A CGImage lets you create a new image cropped from a rectangular region of the original image, which you can't do with UIImage. (A CGImage has other powers a UIImage doesn't have; for instance, you can apply an image mask to a CGImage.) I'll demonstrate by splitting the image of Mars in half and drawing the two halves separately (Figure 2-14):

```
let mars = UIImage(named:"Mars")!
// extract each half as CGImage
let marsCG = mars.cgImage!
let sz = mars.size
let marsLeft = marsCG.cropping(to:
    CGRect(0,0,sz.width/2.0,sz.height))!
let marsRight = marsCG.cropping(to:
    CGRect(sz.width/2.0,0,sz.width/2.0,sz.height))!
let r = UIGraphicsImageRenderer(size: CGSize(sz.width*1.5, sz.height),
    format:mars.imageRendererFormat)
let im = r.image { ctx in
    let con = ctx.cgContext
    con.draw(marsLeft, in:
        CGRect(0,0,sz.width/2.0,sz.height))
    con.draw(marsRight, in:
        CGRect(sz.width,0,sz.width/2.0,sz.height))
}
```

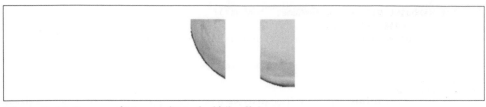

Figure 2-14. Image of Mars split in half (badly)

Well, *that* was a train wreck! In the first place, the drawing is upside-down. It isn't rotated; it's mirrored top to bottom, or, to use the technical term, *flipped*. This phenomenon can arise when you create a CGImage and then draw it, and is due to a mismatch in the native coordinate systems of the source and target contexts.

In the second place, we didn't split the image of Mars in half; we seem to have split it into quarters instead. The reason is that we're using a high-resolution device, and there is a high-resolution variant of our image file. When we call UIImage's init(named:), we get a UIImage that compensates for the increased size of a high-resolution image by setting its own `scale` property to match. But a CGImage doesn't have a `scale` property, and knows nothing of the fact that the image dimensions are increased! Therefore, on a high-resolution device, the CGImage that we extract from our Mars UIImage as `mars.cgImage` is larger (in each dimension) than `mars.size`, and all our calculations after that are wrong.

The simplest solution, when you drop down to the CGImage world to perform some transmutation, is to wrap the resulting CGImage in a UIImage and draw the UIImage *instead* of the CGImage. The UIImage can be formed in such a way as to compensate for scale — call init(cgImage:scale:orientation:) — and by drawing a UIImage instead of a CGImage, we avoid the flipping problem:

```
let mars = UIImage(named:"Mars")!
let sz = mars.size
let marsCG = mars.cgImage!
let szCG = CGSize(CGFloat(marsCG.width), CGFloat(marsCG.height))
let marsLeft =
    marsCG.cropping(to:
        CGRect(0,0,szCG.width/2.0,szCG.height))
let marsRight =
    marsCG.cropping(to:
        CGRect(szCG.width/2.0,0,szCG.width/2.0,szCG.height))
let r = UIGraphicsImageRenderer(size:CGSize(sz.width*1.5, sz.height),
    format:mars.imageRendererFormat)
let im = r.image { _ in
    UIImage(cgImage: marsLeft!,
        scale: mars.scale,
        orientation: mars.imageOrientation).draw(at:CGPoint(0,0))
```

```
UIImage(cgImage: marsRight!,
    scale: mars.scale,
    orientation: mars.imageOrientation).draw(at:CGPoint(sz.width,0))
}
```

Snapshots

An entire view — anything from a single button to your whole interface, complete with its contained hierarchy of views — can be drawn into the current graphics context by calling the UIView instance method drawHierarchy(in:afterScreen-Updates:). The result is a *snapshot* of the original view: it looks like the original view, but it's basically just a bitmap image of it, a lightweight visual duplicate.

 drawHierarchy(in:afterScreenUpdates:) is much faster than the CALayer method render(in:); nevertheless, the latter does still come in handy, as I'll show in Chapter 5.

An even faster way to obtain a snapshot of a view is to use the UIView (or UIScreen) instance method snapshotView(afterScreenUpdates:). The result is a UIView, not a UIImage; it's rather like a UIImageView that knows how to draw only one image, namely the snapshot. Such a snapshot view will typically be used as is, but you can enlarge its bounds and the snapshot image will stretch. If you want the stretched snapshot to behave like a resizable image, call resizableSnapshotView(from:after-ScreenUpdates:withCapInsets:) instead. It is perfectly reasonable to make a snapshot view from a snapshot view.

Snapshots are useful because of the dynamic nature of the iOS interface. You might place a snapshot of a view in your interface in front of the real view to hide what's happening, or use it during an animation to present the illusion of a view moving when in fact it's just a snapshot.

Here's an example from one of my apps. It's a card game, and its views portray cards. I want to animate the removal of all those cards from the board, flying away to an offscreen point. But I don't want to animate the views themselves! They need to stay put, to portray future cards. So I make a snapshot view of each of the card views; I then make the card views invisible, put the snapshot views in their place, and animate the snapshot views. This code will mean more to you after you've read Chapter 4, but the strategy is evident:

```
for v in views {
    let snapshot = v.snapshotView(afterScreenUpdates: false)!
    let snap = MySnapBehavior(item:snapshot, snapto:CGPoint(
        x: self.anim.referenceView!.bounds.midX,
        y: -self.anim.referenceView!.bounds.height)
    )
    self.snaps.append(snapshot) // keep a list so we can remove them later
    snapshot.frame = v.frame
```

```
        v.isHidden = true
        self.anim.referenceView!.addSubview(snapshot)
        self.anim.addBehavior(snap)
    }
```

CIFilter and CIImage

The "CI" in CIFilter and CIImage stands for Core Image, a technology for transforming images through mathematical filters. Core Image started life on the desktop (macOS), and when it was originally migrated into iOS 5, some of the filters available on the desktop were not available in iOS, presumably because they were then too intensive mathematically for a mobile device. Over the years, more and more macOS filters were added to the iOS repertoire, and now the two have complete parity: *all* macOS filters are available in iOS, and the two platforms have nearly identical APIs.

A filter is a CIFilter. There are more than 200 available filters; they fall naturally into several broad categories:

Patterns and gradients
> These filters create CIImages that can then be combined with other CIImages, such as a single color, a checkerboard, stripes, or a gradient.

Compositing
> These filters combine one image with another, using compositing blend modes familiar from image processing programs.

Color
> These filters adjust or otherwise modify the colors of an image. You can alter an image's saturation, hue, brightness, contrast, gamma and white point, exposure, shadows and highlights, and so on.

Geometric
> These filters perform basic geometric transformations on an image, such as scaling, rotation, and cropping.

Transformation
> These filters distort, blur, or stylize an image.

Transition
> These filters provide a frame of a transition between one image and another; by asking for frames in sequence, you can animate the transition (I'll demonstrate in Chapter 4).

Special purpose
> These filters perform highly specialized operations such as face detection and generation of barcodes.

A CIFilter is a set of instructions for generating a CIImage — the filter's *output image*. Moreover, most CIFilters operate on a CIImage — the filter's *input image*. So the output image of one filter can be the input image of another filter. In this way, filters can be *chained*. As you build a chain of filters, nothing actually happens; you're just configuring a sequence of instructions.

If the first CIFilter in the sequence needs an input image, you can get a CIImage from a CGImage with `init(cgImage:)`, or from a UIImage with `init(image:)`. When the last CIFilter in the sequence produces a CIImage, you can transform it into a bitmap drawing — a CGImage or a UIImage. In this way, you've transformed an image into another image, using CIImages and CIFilters as intermediaries. The final step, when you generate the bitmap drawing, is called *rendering* the image. When you render the image, the entire calculation described by the chain of filters is actually performed. Rendering the last CIImage in the sequence is the *only* calculation-intensive move.

 A common beginner mistake is trying to obtain a CIImage directly from a UIImage through the UIImage's `ciImage` property. In general, that's not going to work. That property does not transform a UIImage into a CIImage; it is applicable only to a UIImage that *already* wraps a CIImage, and most UIImages don't (they wrap a CGImage).

The basic use of a CIFilter is quite simple:

1. Obtain a CIFilter object. You can specify a CIFilter by its string name, by calling `init(name:)`; to learn the names, consult Apple's *Core Image Filter Reference* in the documentation archive, or call the CIFilter class method `filterNames(inCategories:)` with a `nil` argument. New in iOS 13, you can obtain a CIFilter object by calling a CIFilter convenience class method named after the string name:

   ```
   let filter = CIFilter(name: "CICheckerboardGenerator")!
   // or, new in iOS 13:
   let filter = CIFilter.checkerboardGenerator()
   ```

2. A filter has keys and values that determine its behavior. These are its *parameters*. You set them as desired. You can learn about a filter's parameters entirely in code, but typically you'll consult the documentation. To set a parameter, call `setValue(_:forKey:)`. New in iOS 13, you can set a convenience property of the CIFilter:

   ```
   filter.setValue(30, forKey: "inputWidth")
   // or, new in iOS 13:
   filter.width = 30
   ```

There are several variations on those steps:

- Instead of calling `setValue(_:forKey:)` repeatedly, you can call `setValuesFor-Keys(_:)` with a dictionary to set multiple parameters at once.

- Instead of obtaining the filter and then setting parameters, you can do both in a single move by calling `init(name:withInputParameters:)`.

- If a CIFilter requires an input CIImage, you can call `applying-Filter(_:parameters:)` on the CIImage to obtain the filter, set its parameters, and receive the output image, in a single move.

Now let's talk about how to render a CIImage. This, as I've said, is the only calculation-intensive move; it can be slow and expensive. There are three main ways:

With a CIContext

Create a CIContext by calling `init()` or `init(options:)`; this itself is expensive, so try to make just one CIContext and retain and reuse it. Then call the CIContext's `createCGImage(_:from:)`. The first parameter is the CIImage. The second parameter is a CGRect specifying the region of the CIImage to be rendered. A CIImage does not have a frame or bounds; its CGRect is its `extent`. The output is a CGImage.

With a UIImage

Create a UIImage wrapping the CIImage by calling `init(ciImage:)` or `init(ciImage:scale:orientation:)`. You then *draw* the UIImage into some graphics context; that is what causes the image to be rendered.

With a UIImageView

This is a shortcut for the preceding approach. Create a UIImage wrapping the CIImage and use it to set a UIImageView's `image`. The display of the image view causes the image to be rendered. In general, this approach works only on a device, though it might work in the simulator in Xcode 11.

 There are other ways of rendering a CIImage that have the advantage of being very fast and suitable for animated or rapid rendering. In particular, you could use Metal. But that's outside the scope of this book.

We're ready for an example! I'll start with an ordinary photo of myself (it's true I'm wearing a motorcycle helmet, but it's still ordinary) and create a circular vignette effect (Figure 2-15). I'll take advantage of the new iOS 13 convenience methods and properties; to bring these to life, we must `import CoreImage.CIFilterBuiltins`:

```
let moi = UIImage(named:"Moi")!
let moici = CIImage(image:moi)! ❶
let moiextent = moici.extent
let smaller = min(moiextent.width, moiextent.height)
let larger = max(moiextent.width, moiextent.height)
// first filter
let grad = CIFilter.radialGradient() ❷
```

Figure 2-15. A photo of me, vignetted

```
grad.center = moiextent.center
grad.radius0 = Float(smaller)/2.0 * 0.7
grad.radius1 = Float(larger)/2.0
let gradimage = grad.outputImage!
// second filter
let blend = CIFilter.blendWithMask()  ❸
blend.inputImage = moici
blend.maskImage = gradimage
let blendimage = blend.outputImage!
```

❶   From the image of me (`moi`), we derive a CIImage (`moici`).

❷   We use a CIFilter (`grad`) to form a radial gradient between the default colors of white and black.

❸   We use a second CIFilter (`blend`) to treat the radial gradient as a mask for blending between the photo of me and a default clear background: where the radial gradient is white (everything inside the gradient's inner radius) we see just me, and where the radial gradient is black (everything outside the gradient's outer radius) we see just the clear color, with a gradation in between, so that the image fades away in the circular band between the gradient's radii.

We have obtained the final CIImage in the chain (`blendimage`), and the processor has not yet performed any rendering. Now we want to generate the final bitmap and display it. Let's say we're going to display it as the `image` of a UIImageView `self.iv`. I'll demonstrate two of the ways of doing that.

First, the CIContext approach, `self.context` is a property initialized to a CIContext. The starred line is the actual rendering:

```
let moicg = self.context.createCGImage(blendimage, from: moiextent)! // *
self.iv.image = UIImage(cgImage: moicg)
```

Second, the UIImage drawing approach; the starred line is the actual rendering:

```
let r = UIGraphicsImageRenderer(size:moiextent.size)
self.iv.image = r.image { _ in
    UIImage(ciImage: blendimage).draw(in:moiextent) // *
}
```

A filter chain can be encapsulated into a single custom filter by subclassing CIFilter.
Your subclass just needs to override the `outputImage` property (and possibly other
methods such as `setDefaults`), with additional properties to make it key–value
coding compliant for any input keys. Here's our vignette filter as a simple CIFilter
subclass with two input keys; `inputImage` is the image to be vignetted, and `input-
Percentage` is a percentage (between 0 and 1) adjusting the gradient's inner radius:

```
class MyVignetteFilter : CIFilter {
    @objc var inputImage : CIImage?
    @objc var inputPercentage : NSNumber? = 1.0
    override var outputImage : CIImage? {
        return self.makeOutputImage()
    }
    private func makeOutputImage () -> CIImage? {
        guard let inputImage = self.inputImage else {return nil}
        guard let inputPercentage = self.inputPercentage else {return nil}
        let extent = inputImage.extent
        let smaller = min(extent.width, extent.height)
        let larger = max(extent.width, extent.height)
        let grad = CIFilter.radialGradient()
        grad.center = extent.center
        grad.radius0 = Float(smaller)/2.0 * inputPercentage.floatValue
        grad.radius1 = Float(larger)/2.0
        let gradimage = grad.outputImage!
        let blend = CIFilter.blendWithMask()
        blend.inputImage = self.inputImage
        blend.maskImage = gradimage
        return blend.outputImage
    }
}
```

And here's how to use our CIFilter subclass and display its output in a UIImageView:

```
let vig = MyVignetteFilter()
let moici = CIImage(image: UIImage(named:"Moi")!)!
vig.setValuesForKeys([
    "inputImage":moici,
    "inputPercentage":0.7
])
let outim = vig.outputImage!
let outimcg = self.context.createCGImage(outim, from: outim.extent)!
self.iv.image = UIImage(cgImage: outimcg)
```

CIImage is a powerful class in its own right, with many valuable convenience methods. You can apply a transform to a CIImage, crop it, and even apply a Gaussian blur
directly to it. Also, CIImage understands EXIF orientations and can use them to
reorient itself.

Blur and Vibrancy Views

Certain views on iOS, such as navigation bars and the control center, are translucent and display a blurred rendition of what's behind them. You can create similar effects using the UIVisualEffectView class.

A UIVisualEffectView is initialized by calling `init(effect:)`; the parameter is a UIVisualEffect. UIVisualEffect is an abstract superclass; the concrete subclasses are UIBlurEffect and UIVibrancyEffect. You'll use a visual effect view with a blur effect to blur what's behind it; then if you like you can add a visual effect with a vibrancy effect along with subviews. The vibrancy effect view goes inside the blur effect view's `contentView`. Any subviews of the vibrancy effect view go inside its `contentView`, and they will be treated as templates: all that matters is their opacity or transparency, as their color is replaced. Never give a UIVisualEffectView a direct subview!

UIBlurEffect is initialized by calling `init(style:)`. New in iOS 13, the styles are adaptive to light and dark user interface style, and are called *materials*. There are five of them (plus each material has two nonadaptive variants with `Light` or `Dark` appended to the name):

- `.systemUltraThinMaterial`
- `.systemThinMaterial`
- `.systemMaterial`
- `.systemThickMaterial`
- `.systemChromeMaterial`

UIVibrancyEffect is initialized by calling `init(blurEffect:style:)` (new in iOS 13). The first parameter will be the blur effect of the underlying UIVisualEffectView. The `style:` will be one of these:

- `.label`
- `.secondaryLabel`
- `.tertiaryLabel`
- `.quaternaryLabel`
- `.fill`
- `.secondaryFill`
- `.tertiaryFill`
- `.separator`

Here's an example of a blur effect view covering and blurring the interface (`self.view`), and containing a UILabel wrapped in a vibrancy effect view:

Figure 2-16. A blurred background and a vibrant label

```
let blurEffect = UIBlurEffect(style: .systemThinMaterial)
let blurView = UIVisualEffectView(effect: blurEffect)
blurView.frame = self.view.bounds
blurView.autoresizingMask = [.flexibleWidth, .flexibleHeight]
self.view.addSubview(blurView)
let vibEffect = UIVibrancyEffect(
    blurEffect: blurEffect, style: .label)
let vibView = UIVisualEffectView(effect:vibEffect)
let lab = UILabel()
lab.text = "Hello, world!"
lab.sizeToFit()
vibView.bounds = lab.bounds
vibView.center = self.view.bounds.center
vibView.autoresizingMask =
    [.flexibleTopMargin, .flexibleBottomMargin,
    .flexibleLeftMargin, .flexibleRightMargin]
blurView.contentView.addSubview(vibView)
vibView.contentView.addSubview(lab)
```

Figure 2-16 shows the result in light and dark mode.

Both a blur effect view and a blur effect view with an embedded vibrancy effect view are available as Library objects in the nib editor.

Drawing a UIView

Most of the examples of drawing so far in this chapter have produced UIImage objects. But, as I've already explained, a UIView itself provides a graphics context; whatever you draw into that graphics context will appear directly in that view. The technique here is to subclass UIView and implement the subclass's draw(_:) method. The result is that, from time to time, or whenever you send it the setNeedsDisplay message, your view's draw(_:) will be called. This is your subclass and your code, so you get to say how this view draws itself at that moment. Whatever drawing you do in draw(_:), that's what the interface will display.

When you override draw(_:), there will usually be no need to call super, since UIView's own implementation of draw(_:) does nothing. At the time that draw(_:) is called, the current graphics context has already been set to the view's own graphics context. You can use Core Graphics functions or UIKit convenience methods to draw into that context. I gave some basic examples earlier in this chapter ("Graphics Contexts" on page 96).

The need to draw in real time, on demand, surprises some beginners, who worry that drawing may be a time-consuming operation. This can indeed be a reasonable consideration, and where the same drawing will be used in many places in your interface, it may make sense to construct a UIImage instead, once, and then reuse that UIImage by drawing it in a view's draw(_:).

In general, though, you should not optimize prematurely. The code for a drawing operation may appear verbose and yet be extremely fast. Moreover, the iOS drawing system is efficient; it doesn't call draw(_:) unless it has to (or is told to, through a call to setNeedsDisplay), and once a view has drawn itself, the result is cached so that the cached drawing can be reused instead of repeating the drawing operation from scratch. (Apple refers to this cached drawing as the view's *bitmap backing store*.) You can readily satisfy yourself of this fact with some caveman debugging, logging in your draw(_:) implementation; you may be amazed to discover that your custom UIView's draw(_:) code is called only once in the entire lifetime of the app!

In fact, moving code to draw(_:) is commonly a way to *increase* efficiency. This is because it is more efficient for the drawing engine to render directly onto the screen than for it to render offscreen and then copy those pixels onto the screen.

Here are three important caveats with regard to UIView's draw(_:) method:

- Don't call draw(_:) yourself. If a view needs updating and you want its draw(_:) called, send the view the setNeedsDisplay message. This will cause draw(_:) to be called at the next proper moment.

- Don't override draw(_:) unless you are assured that this is legal. It is not legal to override draw(_:) in a subclass of UIImageView, for instance; you cannot combine your drawing with that of the UIImageView.

- Don't do anything in draw(_:) except draw. That sort of thing is a common beginner mistake. Other configurations, such as setting the view's background color, or adding subviews or sublayers, should be performed elsewhere, such as its initializer override.

Where drawing is extensive and can be compartmentalized into sections, you may be able to gain some additional efficiency by paying attention to the parameter passed into draw(_:). This parameter is a CGRect designating the region of the view's bounds that needs refreshing. Normally, this is the view's entire bounds; but if you call `setNeedsDisplay(_:)`, which takes a CGRect parameter, it will be the CGRect that you passed in as argument. You could respond by drawing only what goes into those bounds; but even if you don't, your drawing will be clipped to those bounds, so, while you may not spend less time drawing, the system will draw more efficiently.

When a custom UIView subclass has a `draw(_:)` implementation and you create an instance of this subclass in code, you may be surprised (and annoyed) to find that the view has a black background! This is a source of considerable confusion among beginners. The black background arises particularly when two things are true:

- The view's `backgroundColor` is `nil`.

- The view's `isOpaque` is `true`.

When a UIView is created in code with `init(frame:)`, by default both those things *are* true. If this issue arises for you and you want to get rid of the black background, override `init(frame:)` and have the view set its own `isOpaque` to `false`:

```
class MyView : UIView {
    override init(frame: CGRect) {
        super.init(frame:frame)
        self.isOpaque = false
    }
    required init?(coder: NSCoder) {
        fatalError("init(coder:) has not been implemented")
    }
}
```

With a UIView created in the nib, on the other hand, the black background problem doesn't arise. This is because the UIView's `backgroundColor` is not `nil`. The nib assigns it *some* actual background color, even if that color is `UIColor.clear`.

Graphics Context Commands

Whenever you draw, you are giving commands to the graphics context into which you are drawing. This is true regardless of whether you use UIKit methods or Core Graphics functions. Learning to draw is really a matter of understanding how a graphics context works. That's what this section is about.

Under the hood, Core Graphics commands to a graphics context are global C functions with names like `CGContextSetFillColor`; but Swift "renamification" recasts them as if a CGContext were a genuine object representing the graphics context, with the Core Graphics functions appearing as methods of the CGContext. Moreover, thanks to Swift overloading, multiple functions are collapsed into a single command; for example, `CGContextSetFillColor` and `CGContextSetFillColorWithColor` and `CGContextSetRGBFillColor` and `CGContextSetGrayFillColor` all become the same command, `setFillColor`.

Graphics Context Settings

As you draw in a graphics context, the drawing obeys the context's current settings. For this reason, the procedure is always to configure the context's settings first, and then draw. To draw a red line and then a blue line, you would first set the context's line color to red, and draw the first line; then you'd set the context's line color to blue, and draw the second line. To the eye, it appears that the redness and blueness are properties of the individual lines, but in fact, at the time you draw each line, line color is a feature of the entire graphics context.

A graphics context has, at every moment, a *state*, which is the sum total of all its current settings; the way a piece of drawing looks is the result of what the graphics context's state was at the moment that piece of drawing was performed. To help you manipulate entire states, the graphics context provides a *stack* for holding states. Every time you call `saveGState`, the context pushes the current state onto the stack; every time you call `restoreGState`, the context retrieves the state from the top of the stack (the state that was most recently pushed) and sets itself to that state. A common pattern is:

1. Call `saveGState`.
2. Manipulate the context's settings, changing its state.
3. Draw.
4. Call `restoreGState` to restore the state and the settings to what they were before you manipulated them.

You do not have to do this before *every* manipulation of a context's settings, because settings don't necessarily conflict with one another or with past settings. You can set the context's line color to red and then later to blue without any difficulty. But in certain situations you do want your manipulation of settings to be undoable, and I'll point out several such situations later in this chapter.

Many of the settings that constitute a graphics context's state, and that determine the behavior and appearance of drawing performed at that moment, are similar to those of any drawing application. Here are some of them, along with some of the commands that determine them (and some UIKit properties and methods that call them):

Line thickness and dash style
> `setLineWidth(_:)`, `setLineDash(phase:lengths:)`
> UIBezierPath `lineWidth`, `setLineDash(_:count:phase:)`

Line end-cap style and join style
> `setLineCap(_:)`, `setLineJoin(_:)`, `setMiterLimit(_:)`
> UIBezierPath `lineCapStyle`, `lineJoinStyle`, `miterLimit`

Line color or pattern
    setStrokeColor(_:), setStrokePattern(_:colorComponents:)
    UIColor setStroke

Fill color or pattern
    setFillColor(_:), setFillPattern(_:colorComponents:)
    UIColor setFill

Shadow
    setShadow(offset:blur:color:)

Overall transparency and compositing
    setAlpha(_:), setBlendMode(_:)

Anti-aliasing
    setShouldAntialias(_:)

Additional settings include:

Clipping area
    Drawing outside the clipping area is not physically drawn.

Transform (or "CTM," for "current transform matrix")
    Changes how points that you specify in subsequent drawing commands are mapped onto the physical space of the canvas.

Many of these settings will be illustrated by examples later in this chapter.

Paths and Shapes

By issuing a series of instructions for moving an imaginary pen, you construct a *path*, tracing it out from point to point. You must first tell the pen where to position itself, setting the current point; after that, you issue commands telling the pen how to trace out each subsequent piece of the path, one by one. Each new piece of the path starts by default at the current point; its end becomes the new current point.

A path can be compound, meaning that it consists of multiple independent pieces. A single path might consist of two separate closed shapes: say, a rectangle and a circle. When you call move(to:) in the *middle* of constructing a path, you pick up the imaginary pen and move it to a new location without tracing a segment, preparing to start an independent piece of the same path.

If you're worried, as you begin to trace out a path, that there might be an existing path and that your new path might be seen as a compound part of that existing path, you can call beginPath to specify that this is a different path; many of Apple's examples do this, but in practice I usually do not find it necessary.

Here are some path-drawing commands you're likely to give:

Position the current point
    `move(to:)`

Trace a line
    `addLine(to:)`, `addLines(between:)`

Trace a rectangle
    `addRect(_:)`, `addRects(_:)`

Trace an ellipse or circle
    `addEllipse(in:)`

Trace an arc
    `addArc(tangent1End:tangent2End:radius:)`

Trace a Bezier curve with one or two control points
    `addQuadCurve(to:control:)`, `addCurveTo(to:control1:control2:)`

Close the current path
    `closePath`. This appends a line from the last point of the path to the first point. There's no need to do this if you're about to fill the path, since it's done for you.

Note that a path, in and of itself, does *not* constitute drawing! First you provide a path; *then* you draw. Drawing can mean stroking the path or filling the path, or both. Again, this should be a familiar notion from certain drawing applications. The important thing is that stroking or filling a path *clears the path*. That path is now gone and we're ready to begin constructing a new path if desired:

Stroke or fill the current path (and clear the path)
    `strokePath`, `fillPath(using:)`, `drawPath`. Use `drawPath` if you want both to fill and to stroke the path in a single command, because if you merely stroke it first with `strokePath`, the path is cleared and you can no longer fill it. There are also some convenience functions that create a path from a CGRect or similar and stroke or fill it, in a single move:

- `stroke(_:)`, `strokeLineSegments(between:)`
- `fill(_:)`
- `strokeEllipse(in:)`
- `fillEllipse(in:)`

If a path needs to be reused or shared, you can encapsulate it as a CGPath. Like CGContext, CGPath and its mutable partner CGMutablePath are treated as class types under "renamification," and the global C functions that manipulate them are treated as methods. You can copy the graphics context's current path using the CGContext `path` method, or you can create a new CGMutablePath and construct the

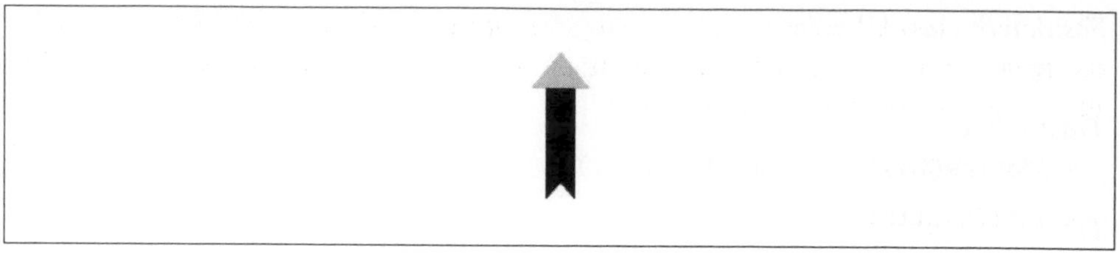

Figure 2-17. A simple path drawing

path using various functions, such as `move(to:transform:)` and `add-Line(to:transform:)`, that parallel the CGContext path-construction functions. Also, there are ways to create a path based on simple geometry or on an existing path:

- `init(rect:transform:)`
- `init(ellipseIn:transform:)`
- `init(roundedRect:cornerWidth:cornerHeight:transform:)`
- `copy(strokingWithWidth:lineCap:lineJoin:miterLimit:transform:)`
- `copy(dashingWithPhase:lengths:transform:)`
- `copy(using:)` (takes a pointer to a CGAffineTransform)

To illustrate the typical use of path-drawing commands, I'll generate the up-pointing arrow shown in Figure 2-17. This might not be the best way to create the arrow, and I'm deliberately avoiding use of the convenience functions, but it's clear and shows a nice basic variety of typical commands:

```
// obtain the current graphics context
let con = UIGraphicsGetCurrentContext()!
// draw a black (by default) vertical line, the shaft of the arrow
con.move(to:CGPoint(100, 100))
con.addLine(to:CGPoint(100, 19))
con.setLineWidth(20)
con.strokePath()
// draw a red triangle, the point of the arrow
con.setFillColor(UIColor.red.cgColor)
con.move(to:CGPoint(80, 25))
con.addLine(to:CGPoint(100, 0))
con.addLine(to:CGPoint(120, 25))
con.fillPath()
// snip a triangle out of the shaft by drawing in Clear blend mode
con.move(to:CGPoint(90, 101))
con.addLine(to:CGPoint(100, 90))
con.addLine(to:CGPoint(110, 101))
con.setBlendMode(.clear)
con.fillPath()
```

The UIKit class UIBezierPath is actually a wrapper for CGPath; the wrapped path is its `cgPath` property. It provides methods parallel to the CGContext and CGPath functions for constructing a path, such as:

- `init(rect:)`
- `init(ovalIn:)`
- `init(roundedRect:cornerRadius:)`
- `move(to:)`
- `addLine(to:)`
- `addArc(withCenter:radius:startAngle:endAngle:clockwise:)`
- `addQuadCurve(to:controlPoint:)`
- `addCurve(to:controlPoint1:controlPoint2:)`
- `close`

When you call the UIBezierPath instance methods `fill` or `stroke` or `fill(with:alpha:)` or `stroke(with:alpha:)`, the current graphics context settings are saved, the wrapped CGPath is made the current graphics context's path and stroked or filled, and the current graphics context settings are restored.

Using UIBezierPath together with UIColor, we could rewrite our arrow-drawing routine entirely with UIKit methods:

```
let p = UIBezierPath()
// shaft
p.move(to:CGPoint(100,100))
p.addLine(to:CGPoint(100, 19))
p.lineWidth = 20
p.stroke()
// point
UIColor.red.set()
p.removeAllPoints()
p.move(to:CGPoint(80,25))
p.addLine(to:CGPoint(100, 0))
p.addLine(to:CGPoint(120, 25))
p.fill()
// snip
p.removeAllPoints()
p.move(to:CGPoint(90,101))
p.addLine(to:CGPoint(100, 90))
p.addLine(to:CGPoint(110, 101))
p.fill(with:.clear, alpha:1.0)
```

There's no savings of code here over calling Core Graphics functions, so your choice of Core Graphics or UIKit is a matter of taste.

Clipping

A path can be used to mask out areas, protecting them from future drawing. This is called *clipping*. By default, a graphics context's clipping region is the entire graphics context, meaning that you can draw anywhere within the context.

The clipping area is a feature of the context as a whole, and any new clipping area is applied by intersecting it with the existing clipping area. To restore your clipping area to the default, call resetClip.

To illustrate, I'll rewrite the code that generated our original arrow (Figure 2-17) to use clipping instead of a blend mode to "punch out" the triangular notch in the tail of the arrow. This is a little tricky, because what we want to clip to is not the region inside the triangle but the region outside it. To express this, we'll use a compound path consisting of more than one closed area — the triangle, and the drawing area as a whole (which we can obtain as the context's boundingBoxOfClipPath).

Both when filling a compound path and when using it to express a clipping region, the system follows one of two rules:

Winding rule
> The fill or clipping area is denoted by an alternation in the direction (clockwise or counterclockwise) of the path demarcating each region.

Even-odd rule (EO)
> The fill or clipping area is denoted by a simple count of the paths demarcating each region.

Our situation is extremely simple, so it's easier to use the even-odd rule:

```
// obtain the current graphics context
let con = UIGraphicsGetCurrentContext()!
// punch triangular hole in context clipping region
con.move(to:CGPoint(90, 100))
con.addLine(to:CGPoint(100, 90))
con.addLine(to:CGPoint(110, 100))
con.closePath()
con.addRect(con.boundingBoxOfClipPath)
con.clip(using: .evenOdd)
// draw the vertical line
con.move(to:CGPoint(100, 100))
con.addLine(to:CGPoint(100, 19))
con.setLineWidth(20)
con.strokePath()
// draw the red triangle, the point of the arrow
con.setFillColor(UIColor.red.cgColor)
con.move(to:CGPoint(80, 25))
con.addLine(to:CGPoint(100, 0))
con.addLine(to:CGPoint(120, 25))
con.fillPath()
```

The UIBezierPath clipping commands are usesEvenOddFillRule and addClip.

Gradients

Gradients can range from the simple to the complex. A simple gradient (which is all I'll describe here) is determined by a color at one endpoint along with a color at the other endpoint, plus (optionally) colors at intermediate points; the gradient is then painted either linearly between two points or radially between two circles. You can't use a gradient as a path's fill color, but you can restrict a gradient to a path's shape by clipping, which will sometimes be good enough.

To illustrate, I'll redraw our arrow, using a linear gradient as the "shaft" of the arrow (Figure 2-18):

```
// obtain the current graphics context
let con = UIGraphicsGetCurrentContext()!
// punch triangular hole in context clipping region
con.move(to:CGPoint(10, 100))
con.addLine(to:CGPoint(20, 90))
con.addLine(to:CGPoint(30, 100))
con.closePath()
con.addRect(con.boundingBoxOfClipPath)
con.clip(using: .evenOdd)
// draw the vertical line, add its shape to the clipping region
con.move(to:CGPoint(20, 100))
con.addLine(to:CGPoint(20, 19))
con.setLineWidth(20)
con.replacePathWithStrokedPath()
con.clip()
// draw the gradient
let locs : [CGFloat] = [ 0.0, 0.5, 1.0 ]
let colors : [CGFloat] = [
    0.8, 0.4, // starting color, transparent light gray
    0.1, 0.5, // intermediate color, darker less transparent gray
    0.8, 0.4, // ending color, transparent light gray
]
let sp = CGColorSpaceCreateDeviceGray()
let grad = CGGradient(
    colorSpace:sp, colorComponents: colors, locations: locs, count: 3)!
con.drawLinearGradient(grad,
```

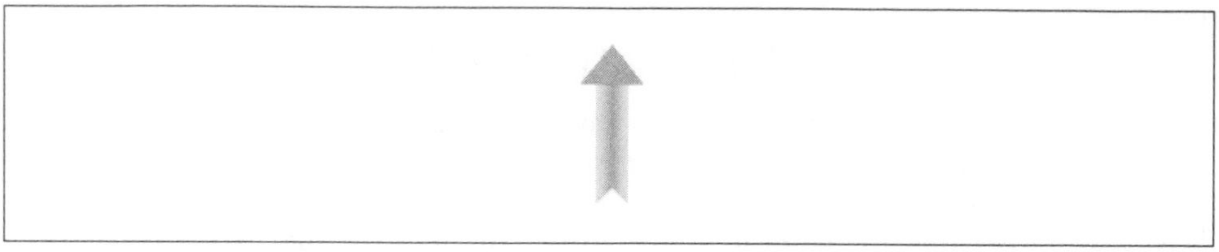

Figure 2-18. Drawing with a gradient

```
        start: CGPoint(89,0), end: CGPoint(111,0), options:[])
con.resetClip() // done clipping
// draw the red triangle, the point of the arrow
con.setFillColor(UIColor.red.cgColor)
con.move(to:CGPoint(80, 25))
con.addLine(to:CGPoint(100, 0))
con.addLine(to:CGPoint(120, 25))
con.fillPath()
```

The call to replacePathWithStrokedPath pretends to stroke the current path, using the current line width and other line-related context state settings, but then creates a new path representing the outside of that stroked path. Instead of a thick line we now have a rectangular region that we can use as the clip region.

We then create the gradient and paint it. The procedure is verbose but simple; everything is boilerplate. We describe the gradient as an array of locations on the continuum between one endpoint (0.0) and the other endpoint (1.0), along with the color components of the colors corresponding to each location; in this case, I want the gradient to be lighter at the edges and darker in the middle, so I use three locations, with the dark one at 0.5. We must also supply a color space; this will tell the gradient how to interpret our color components. Finally, we create the gradient and paint it into place.

(See also the discussion of gradient CIFilters earlier in this chapter. For yet another way to create a simple gradient, see the discussion of CAGradientLayer in the next chapter.)

Colors and Patterns

A color is a CGColor. CGColor is not difficult to work with, and can be converted to and from a UIColor through UIColor's init(cgColor:) and its cgColor property.

New in iOS 13, drawRect(_:) is called when the user interface style (light or dark) changes, and UITraitCollection.current is set for you, so any dynamic UIColors you use while drawing will be correct for the current interface style. But there's no such thing as a dynamic CGColor, so if you're using CGColor in some other situation, you might need to trigger a redraw manually. For an example, see "Interface Style" on page 29.

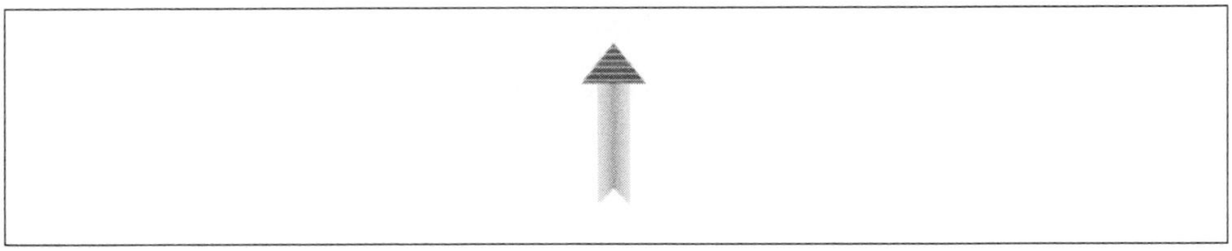

Figure 2-19. A patterned fill

A pattern is also a kind of color. You can create a pattern color and stroke or fill with it. The simplest way is to draw a minimal tile of the pattern into a UIImage and create the color by calling UIColor's init(patternImage:). To illustrate, I'll create a pattern of horizontal stripes and use it to paint the point of the arrow instead of a solid red color (Figure 2-19):

```
// create the pattern image tile
let r = UIGraphicsImageRenderer(size:CGSize(4,4))
let stripes = r.image { ctx in
    let imcon = ctx.cgContext
    imcon.setFillColor(UIColor.red.cgColor)
    imcon.fill(CGRect(0,0,4,4))
    imcon.setFillColor(UIColor.blue.cgColor)
    imcon.fill(CGRect(0,0,4,2))
}
// paint the point of the arrow with it
let stripesPattern = UIColor(patternImage:stripes)
stripesPattern.setFill()
let p = UIBezierPath()
p.move(to:CGPoint(80,25))
p.addLine(to:CGPoint(100,0))
p.addLine(to:CGPoint(120,25))
p.fill()
```

The Core Graphics equivalent, CGPattern, is considerably more powerful, but also much more elaborate:

```
con.saveGState()
let sp2 = CGColorSpace(patternBaseSpace:nil)!
con.setFillColorSpace(sp2)
let drawStripes : CGPatternDrawPatternCallback = { _, con in
    con.setFillColor(UIColor.red.cgColor)
    con.fill(CGRect(0,0,4,4))
    con.setFillColor(UIColor.blue.cgColor)
    con.fill(CGRect(0,0,4,2))
}
var callbacks = CGPatternCallbacks(
    version: 0, drawPattern: drawStripes, releaseInfo: nil)
let patt = CGPattern(info:nil, bounds: CGRect(0,0,4,4),
    matrix: .identity,
    xStep: 4, yStep: 4,
    tiling: .constantSpacingMinimalDistortion,
```

```
    isColored: true, callbacks: &callbacks)!
var alph : CGFloat = 1.0
con.setFillPattern(patt, colorComponents: &alph)
con.move(to:CGPoint(80, 25))
con.addLine(to:CGPoint(100, 0))
con.addLine(to:CGPoint(120, 25))
con.fillPath()
con.restoreGState()
```

To understand that code, it helps to read it backward. Everything revolves around the creation of patt using the CGPattern initializer. A pattern is a drawing in a rectangular "cell"; we have to state both the size of the cell (bounds:) and the spacing between origin points of cells (xStep:, yStep:). In this case, the cell is 4×4, and every cell exactly touches its neighbors both horizontally and vertically. We have to supply a transform to be applied to the cell (matrix:); in this case, we're not doing anything with this transform, so we supply the identity transform. We supply a tiling rule (tiling:). We have to state whether this is a color pattern or a stencil pattern; it's a color pattern, so isColored: is true. And we have to supply a pointer to a callback function that actually draws the pattern into its cell (callbacks:).

Except that that's *not* what we have to supply as the callbacks: argument. What we actually have to supply here is a pointer to a CGPatternCallbacks struct. This struct consists of a version: whose value is fixed at 0, along with pointers to *two* functions, the drawPattern: to draw the pattern into its cell, and the releaseInfo: called when the pattern is released. We're not specifying the second function here; it is for memory management, and we don't need it in this simple example.

As you can see, the actual pattern-drawing function (drawStripes) is very simple. The only tricky issue is that it must agree with the CGPattern as to the size of a cell, or the pattern won't come out the way you expect. We know in this case that the cell is 4×4. So we fill it with red, and then fill its lower half with blue. When these cells are tiled touching each other horizontally and vertically, we get the stripes that you see in Figure 2-19.

Having generated the CGPattern, we call the context's setFillPattern; instead of setting a fill color, we're setting a fill pattern, to be used the next time we fill a path (in this case, the triangular arrowhead). The colorComponents: parameter is a pointer to a CGFloat, so we have to set up the CGFloat itself beforehand.

The only thing left to explain is the first three lines of our code. It turns out that before you can call setFillPattern with a colored pattern, you have to set the context's fill color space to a pattern color space. If you neglect to do this, you'll get an error when you call setFillPattern. This means that the code as presented has left the graphics context in an undesirable state, with its fill color space set to a pattern color space. This would cause trouble if we were later to try to set the fill color to a normal color. The solution is to wrap the code in calls to `saveGState` and `restore-GState`.

You may have observed in Figure 2-19 that the stripes do not fit neatly inside the triangle of the arrowhead: the bottommost stripe is something like half a blue stripe. This is because a pattern is positioned not with respect to the shape you are filling (or stroking), but with respect to the graphics context as a whole. We could shift the pattern position by calling `setPatternPhase` before drawing.

Graphics Context Transforms

Just as a UIView can have a transform, so can a graphics context. Applying a transform to a graphics context has no effect on the drawing that's already in it; like other graphics context settings, it affects only the drawing that takes place after it is applied, altering the way the coordinates you provide are mapped onto the graphics context's area. A graphics context's transform is called its *CTM*, for "current transform matrix."

It is quite usual to take full advantage of a graphics context's CTM to save yourself from performing even simple calculations. You can multiply the current transform by any CGAffineTransform using `concatCTM`; there are also convenience functions for applying a translate, scale, or rotate transform to the current transform.

The base transform for a graphics context is already set for you when you obtain the context; that's how the system is able to map context drawing coordinates onto screen coordinates. Whatever transforms you apply are applied to the current transform, so the base transform remains in effect and drawing continues to work. You can return to the base transform after applying your own transforms by wrapping your code in calls to `saveGState` and `restoreGState`.

Here's an example. We have hitherto been drawing our upward-pointing arrow with code that knows how to place that arrow at only one location: the top left of its rectangle is hard-coded at `(80,0)`. This is silly. It makes the code hard to understand, as well as inflexible and difficult to reuse. Surely the sensible thing would be to draw the arrow at `(0,0)`, by subtracting 80 from all the x-values in our existing code. Now it is easy to draw the arrow at *any* position, simply by applying a translate transform beforehand, mapping `(0,0)` to the desired top-left corner of the arrow. To draw it at `(80,0)`, we would say:

```
con.translateBy(x:80, y:0)
// now draw the arrow at (0,0)
```

A rotate transform is particularly useful, allowing you to draw in a rotated orientation without any nasty trigonometry. It's a bit tricky because the point around which the rotation takes place is the origin. This is rarely what you want, so you have to apply a translate transform first, to map the origin to the point around which you

Figure 2-20. Drawing rotated

really want to rotate. But then, after rotating, in order to figure out where to draw, you will probably have to reverse your translate transform.

To illustrate, here's code to draw our arrow repeatedly at several angles, pivoting around the end of its tail (Figure 2-20). Since the arrow will be drawn multiple times, I'll start by encapsulating the drawing of the arrow as a UIImage. This is not merely to reduce repetition and make drawing more efficient; it's also because we want the entire arrow to pivot, including the pattern stripes, and this is the simplest way to achieve that:

```
lazy var arrow : UIImage = {
    let r = UIGraphicsImageRenderer(size:CGSize(40,100))
    return r.image { _ in
        self.arrowImage()
    }
}()
func arrowImage () {
    // obtain the current graphics context
    let con = UIGraphicsGetCurrentContext()!
    // draw the arrow into the graphics context
    // draw it at (0,0)! adjust all x-values by subtracting 80
    // ... actual code omitted ...
}
```

In our draw(_:) implementation, we draw the arrow image multiple times:

```
override func draw(_ rect: CGRect) {
    let con = UIGraphicsGetCurrentContext()!
    self.arrow.draw(at:CGPoint(0,0))
    for _ in 0..<3 {
        con.translateBy(x: 20, y: 100)
        con.rotate(by: 30 * .pi/180.0)
        con.translateBy(x: -20, y: -100)
        self.arrow.draw(at:CGPoint(0,0))
    }
}
```

Figure 2-21. Drawing with a shadow

Shadows

To add a shadow to a drawing, give the context a shadow value before drawing. The shadow position is expressed as a CGSize, where the positive direction for both values indicates down and to the right. The blur value is an open-ended positive number; Apple doesn't explain how the scale works, but experimentation shows that 12 is nice and blurry, 99 is so blurry as to be shapeless, and higher values become problematic.

Figure 2-21 shows the result of the same code that generated Figure 2-20, except that before we start drawing the arrow repeatedly, we give the context a shadow:

```
let con = UIGraphicsGetCurrentContext()!
con.setShadow(offset: CGSize(7, 7), blur: 12)
self.arrow.draw(at:CGPoint(0,0))
// ... and so on
```

It may not be evident from Figure 2-21, but we are adding a shadow each time we draw. This means the arrows are able to cast shadows on one another. Suppose, instead, that we want all the arrows to cast a single shadow collectively. The way to achieve this is with a *transparency layer*; this is basically a subcontext that accumulates all drawing and then adds the shadow. Our code for drawing the shadowed arrows now looks like this:

```
let con = UIGraphicsGetCurrentContext()!
con.setShadow(offset: CGSize(7, 7), blur: 12)
con.beginTransparencyLayer(auxiliaryInfo: nil)
self.arrow.draw(at:CGPoint(0,0))
for _ in 0..<3 {
    con.translateBy(x: 20, y: 100)
    con.rotate(by: 30 * .pi/180.0)
    con.translateBy(x: -20, y: -100)
    self.arrow.draw(at:CGPoint(0,0))
}
con.endTransparencyLayer()
```

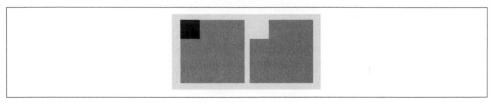

Figure 2-22. The very strange behavior of the clear function

Erasing

The CGContext `clear(_:)` function erases all existing drawing in a CGRect; combined with clipping, it can erase an area of any shape. The result can "punch a hole" through all existing drawing.

The behavior of `clear(_:)` depends on whether the context is transparent or opaque. This is particularly obvious and intuitive when drawing into an image context. If the image context is transparent, `clear(_:)` erases to transparent; otherwise it erases to black.

When drawing directly into a view, if the view's background color is `nil` or a color with even a tiny bit of transparency, the result of `clear(_:)` will appear to be transparent, punching a hole right through the view including its background color; if the background color is completely opaque, the result of `clear(_:)` will be black. This is because the view's background color determines whether the view's graphics context is transparent or opaque, so this is essentially the same behavior that I described in the preceding paragraph.

Figure 2-22 illustrates; the blue square on the left has been partly cut away to black, while the blue square on the right has been partly cut away to transparency. Yet these are instances of the same UIView subclass, drawn with exactly the same code! The UIView subclass's `draw(_:)` looks like this:

```
let con = UIGraphicsGetCurrentContext()!
con.setFillColor(UIColor.blue.cgColor)
con.fill(rect)
con.clear(CGRect(0,0,30,30))
```

The difference between the views in Figure 2-22 is that the `backgroundColor` of the first view is solid red with an alpha of 1, while the `backgroundColor` of the second view is solid red with an alpha of `0.99`. This difference is imperceptible to the eye — not to mention that the red color never appears, as it is covered with a blue fill! Nevertheless, it completely changes the effect of `clear(_:)`.

If you find this as confusing as I do, the simplest solution may be to drop down to the level of the view's `layer` and set its `isOpaque` property after setting the view's background color:

```
self.backgroundColor = .red
self.layer.isOpaque = false
```

That gives you a final and dependable say on the behavior of `clear(_:)`. If `layer.is-Opaque` is `false`, `clear(_:)` erases to transparency; if it is `true`, it erases to black.

Points and Pixels

A point is a dimensionless location described by an x-coordinate and a y-coordinate. When you draw in a graphics context, you specify the points at which to draw, and this works regardless of the device's resolution, because Core Graphics maps your drawing nicely onto the physical output using the base CTM and anti-aliasing. Therefore, throughout this chapter I've concerned myself with graphics context points, disregarding their relationship to screen pixels.

Nonetheless, pixels do exist. A pixel is a physical, integral, dimensioned unit of display in the real world. Whole-numbered points effectively lie between pixels, and this can matter if you're fussy, especially on a single-resolution device. If a vertical path with whole-number coordinates is stroked with a line width of 1, half the line falls on each side of the path, and the drawn line on the screen of a single-resolution device will seem to be 2 pixels wide (because the device can't illuminate half a pixel).

You may sometimes encounter the suggestion that if this effect is objectionable, you should try shifting the line's position by `0.5`, to center it in its pixels. This advice may appear to work, but it makes some simpleminded assumptions. A more sophisticated approach is to obtain the UIView's `contentScaleFactor` property. You can divide by this value to convert from pixels to points. Consider also that the most accurate way to draw a vertical or horizontal line is not to stroke a path but to fill a rectangle. This UIView subclass code will draw a perfect 1-pixel-wide vertical line on any device (`con` is the current graphics context):

```
con.fill(CGRect(100,0,1.0/self.contentScaleFactor,100))
```

Content Mode

A view that draws something within itself, as opposed to merely having a background color and subviews (as in the previous chapter), has *content*. This means that its `contentMode` property becomes important whenever the view is resized. As I mentioned earlier, the drawing system will avoid asking a view to redraw itself from scratch if possible; instead, it will use the cached result of the previous drawing operation (the bitmap backing store). If the view is resized, the system may simply stretch or shrink or reposition the cached drawing, if your `contentMode` setting instructs it to do so.

Figure 2-23. Automatic stretching of content

It's a little tricky to illustrate this point when the view's content is coming from draw(_:), because I have to arrange for the view to obtain its content from draw(_:) and then cause it to be resized without draw(_:) being called *again*. As the app starts up, I'll create an instance of a UIView subclass, MyView, that knows how to draw our arrow; then I'll use delayed performance to resize the instance after the window has shown and the interface has been initially displayed (for my delay function, see Appendix B):

```
delay(0.1) {
    mv.bounds.size.height *= 2 // mv is the MyView instance
}
```

We double the height of the view without causing draw(_:) to be called. The result is that the view's drawing appears at double its correct height. If our view's draw(_:) code is the same as the code that generated Figure 2-18, we get Figure 2-23.

Sooner or later, however, draw(_:) will be called, and the drawing will be refreshed in accordance with our code. Our code doesn't say to draw the arrow at a height that is relative to the height of the view's bounds; it draws the arrow at a fixed height. Therefore, the arrow will snap back to its original size.

A view's contentMode property should therefore usually be in agreement with how the view draws itself. Our draw(_:) code dictates the size and position of the arrow relative to the view's bounds origin, its top left; so we could set its contentMode to .topLeft. Alternatively, we could set it to .redraw; this will cause automatic scaling of the cached content to be turned off — instead, when the view is resized, its setNeedsDisplay method will be called, ultimately triggering draw(_:) to redraw the content.

CHAPTER 3

Layers

The tale told in Chapters 1 and 2 of how a UIView draws itself is only half the story. A UIView has a partner called its *layer*, a CALayer. A UIView does not actually draw itself onto the screen; it draws itself into its layer, and it is the layer that is portrayed on the screen. As I've already mentioned, a view is not redrawn frequently; instead, its drawing is cached, and the cached version of the drawing (the bitmap backing store) is used where possible. The cached version is, in fact, the layer. What I spoke of in Chapter 2 as the view's graphics context is actually the layer's graphics context.

This might seem to be a mere implementation detail, but layers are important and interesting in their own right. To understand layers is to understand views more deeply; layers extend the power of views:

Layers have properties that affect drawing
> Layers have drawing-related properties beyond those of a UIView. Because a layer is the recipient and presenter of a view's drawing, you can modify how a view is drawn on the screen by accessing the layer's properties. By reaching down to the level of its layer, you can make a view do things you can't do through UIView methods alone.

Layers can be combined within a single view
> A UIView's partner layer can contain additional layers. Since the purpose of layers is to draw, portraying visible material on the screen, this allows a UIView's drawing to be composited of multiple distinct pieces. This can make drawing easier, with the constituents of a drawing being treated as objects.

Layers are the basis of animation
> Animation allows you to add clarity, emphasis, and just plain coolness to your interface. Layers are made to be animated; the "CA" in "CALayer" stands for "Core Animation." Animation is the subject of Chapter 4.

Figure 3-1. A compass, composed of layers

Suppose we want to add a compass indicator to our app's interface. Figure 3-1 portrays a simple version of such a compass. It takes advantage of the arrow that we drew in Chapter 2; the arrow is drawn into a layer of its own. The other parts of the compass are layers too: the circle is a layer, and each of the cardinal point letters is a layer. The drawing is easy to assemble in code (and later in this chapter, that's exactly what we'll do); even more intriguing, the pieces can be repositioned and animated separately, so it's easy to rotate the arrow without moving the circle (and in Chapter 4, that's exactly what we'll do).

View and Layer

A UIView instance has an accompanying CALayer instance, accessible as the view's `layer` property. This layer has a special status: it is partnered with this view to embody all of the view's drawing. The layer has no corresponding `view` property, but the view is the layer's `delegate` (adopting CALayerDelegate). The documentation sometimes speaks of this layer as the view's *underlying layer*.

Because every view has an underlying layer, there is a tight integration between the two. The layer portrays all the view's drawing; if the view draws, it does so by contributing to the layer's drawing. The view is the layer's delegate. And the view's properties are often merely a convenience for accessing the layer's properties. When you set the view's `backgroundColor`, you are really setting the layer's `backgroundColor`, and if you set the layer's `backgroundColor` directly, the view's `backgroundColor` is set to match. Similarly, the view's `frame` is really the layer's `frame` and *vice versa*.

The view draws into its layer, and the layer caches that drawing; the layer can then be manipulated, changing the view's appearance, without necessarily asking the view to redraw itself. This is a source of great efficiency in the drawing system. It also explains such phenomena as the content stretching that we encountered in the last section of Chapter 2: when the view's bounds size changes, the drawing system, by default, simply stretches or repositions the cached layer image, until such time as the view is told to draw freshly, replacing the layer's content.

By default, when a UIView is instantiated, its layer is a plain vanilla CALayer. But that might not be what you want. Suppose you have declared a UIView subclass, and you want your subclass's underlying layer to be an instance of a CALayer subclass (built-in or your own). Then override your UIView subclass's `layerClass` class property to return that CALayer subclass.

That is how the compass in Figure 3-1 is created. We have a UIView subclass, CompassView, and a CALayer subclass, CompassLayer. Here is CompassView's implementation:

```
class CompassView : UIView {
    override class var layerClass : AnyClass {
        return CompassLayer.self
    }
}
```

When CompassView is instantiated, its underlying layer is a CompassLayer. In this example, there is no drawing in CompassView; its job — in this case, its *only* job — is to give CompassLayer a place in the visible interface, because a layer cannot appear without a view.

Layers and Sublayers

A layer can have sublayers, and a layer has at most one superlayer. We may say there is a *tree* of layers. This is similar and parallel to the tree of views (Chapter 1). In fact, so tight is the integration between a view and its underlying layer that these hierarchies are effectively the *same* hierarchy. Given a view and its underlying layer, that layer's superlayer is the view's superview's underlying layer, and that layer has as sublayers all the underlying layers of all the view's subviews. Indeed, because the layers are how the views actually get drawn, one might say that the view hierarchy really *is* a layer hierarchy (Figure 3-2).

At the same time, the layer hierarchy can go *beyond* the view hierarchy. A view has exactly one underlying layer, but a layer can have sublayers that are *not the underlying layers of any view*. So the hierarchy of layers that underlie views exactly matches the hierarchy of views, but the total layer tree may be a superset of that hierarchy. In Figure 3-3, we see the same view-and-layer hierarchy as in Figure 3-2, but two of the layers have additional sublayers that are theirs alone (that is, sublayers that are not any view's underlying layers).

From a visual standpoint, there may be nothing to distinguish a hierarchy of views from a hierarchy of layers. In Chapter 1 we drew three overlapping rectangles using

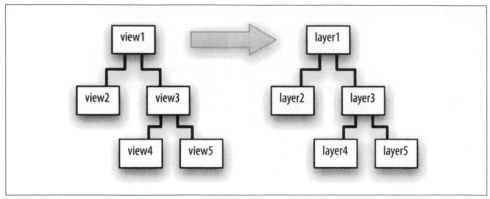

Figure 3-2. A hierarchy of views and the hierarchy of layers underlying it

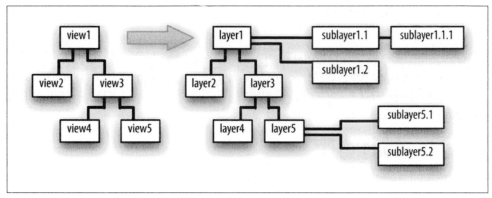

Figure 3-3. Layers that have sublayers of their own

a hierarchy of views (Figure 1-1). This code gives exactly the same visible display by manipulating layers (Figure 3-4):

```
let lay1 = CALayer()
lay1.backgroundColor = UIColor(red: 1, green: 0.4, blue: 1, alpha: 1).cgColor
lay1.frame = CGRect(113, 111, 132, 194)
self.view.layer.addSublayer(lay1)
let lay2 = CALayer()
lay2.backgroundColor = UIColor(red: 0.5, green: 1, blue: 0, alpha: 1).cgColor
lay2.frame = CGRect(41, 56, 132, 194)
lay1.addSublayer(lay2)
let lay3 = CALayer()
lay3.backgroundColor = UIColor(red: 1, green: 0, blue: 0, alpha: 1).cgColor
lay3.frame = CGRect(43, 197, 160, 230)
self.view.layer.addSublayer(lay3)
```

In Figure 3-4, Layer 1 and Layer 2 are siblings — they are sublayers of the main view's underlying layer — while Layer 3 is a sublayer of Layer 2. That's exactly parallel to the situation in Figure 1-1.

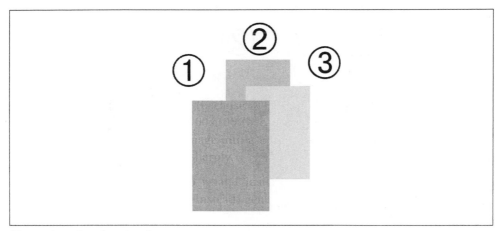

Figure 3-4. Overlapping layers

A view's subview's underlying layer is a sublayer of the view's underlying layer. Therefore, it can be positioned anywhere in the drawing order among any *other* sublayers the view may have. The fact that a view can be interspersed among layers is surprising to beginners. To illustrate, let's construct Figure 3-4 again, but between adding `lay2` and `lay3` to the interface, we'll add a subview:

```
// ...
lay1.addSublayer(lay2) // Layer 3
let iv = UIImageView(image:UIImage(named:"smiley"))
self.view.addSubview(iv) // Smiley view
iv.frame.origin = CGPoint(180,180)
let lay3 = CALayer() // Layer 1
// ...
```

The result is Figure 3-5. The smiley face (`iv`) was added to the interface before Layer 1 (`lay3`), so it appears behind it. The smiley face is a *view*, whereas Layer 1 is just a *layer*; so they are not siblings as views, since Layer 1 is not a view. But the smiley face is both a view and a layer; as layers, the smiley face and Layer 1 *are* siblings, since they have the same superlayer, namely the main view's layer. As siblings, either one can be made to appear in front of the other.

Whether a layer displays regions of its sublayers that lie outside that layer's own bounds depends upon the value of its `masksToBounds` property. This is parallel to a view's `clipsToBounds` property, and indeed, for a layer that is a view's underlying layer, they are the same thing. In Figures 3-4 and 3-5, the layers all have `clipsToBounds` set to `false` (the default); that's why Layer 3 is visible beyond the bounds of Layer 2, which is its superlayer.

Like a UIView, a CALayer has an `isHidden` property that can be set to take it and its sublayers out of the visible interface without actually removing it from its superlayer.

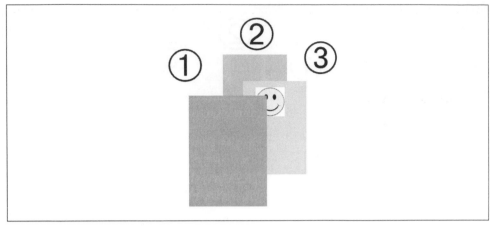

Figure 3-5. Overlapping layers and a view

Manipulating the Layer Hierarchy

Layers come with a full set of methods for reading and manipulating the layer hierarchy, parallel to the methods for reading and manipulating the view hierarchy. A layer has a `superlayer` property and a `sublayers` property, along with these methods:

- `addSublayer(_:)`
- `insertSublayer(_:at:)`
- `insertSublayer(_:below:)`, `insertSublayer(_:above:)`
- `replaceSublayer(_:with:)`
- `removeFromSuperlayer`

Unlike a view's `subviews` property, a layer's `sublayers` property is writable. You can give a layer multiple sublayers in a single move, by assigning to its `sublayers` property. To remove all of a layer's sublayers, set its `sublayers` property to `nil`.

Although a layer's sublayers have an order, reflected in the `sublayers` order and regulated with the methods I've just mentioned, this is not necessarily the same as their back-to-front drawing order. By default, it is, but a layer also has a `zPosition` property, a CGFloat, and this also determines drawing order. The rule is that all sublayers with the same `zPosition` are drawn in the order they are listed among their `sublayers` siblings, but lower `zPosition` siblings are drawn before higher `zPosition` siblings. (The default `zPosition` is `0.0`.)

Sometimes, the `zPosition` property is a more convenient way of dictating drawing order than sibling order is. If layers represent playing cards laid out in a solitaire game, it will likely be a lot easier and more flexible to determine how the cards overlap by setting their `zPosition` than by rearranging their sibling order.

Moreover, a subview's layer is itself just a layer, so you can rearrange the drawing order of subviews by setting the zPosition of their underlying layers! In our code constructing Figure 3-5, if we assign the image view's underlying layer a zPosition of 1, it is drawn in front of Layer 1:

```
self.view.addSubview(iv)
iv.layer.zPosition = 1
```

Positioning a Sublayer

Layer coordinate systems and positioning are similar to those of views. A layer's own internal coordinate system is expressed by its bounds, just like a view; its size is its bounds size, and its bounds origin is the internal coordinate at its top left.

A sublayer's position within its superlayer is not described by its center, like a view; a layer does not have a center. Instead, a sublayer's position within its superlayer is defined by a combination of *two* properties:

position
  A point expressed in the superlayer's coordinate system.

anchorPoint
  Where the position point is located, with respect to the layer's own bounds. It is a CGPoint describing a fraction (or multiple) of the layer's own bounds width and bounds height. (0.0,0.0) is the top left of the layer's bounds, and (1.0,1.0) is the bottom right of the layer's bounds.

Here's an analogy; I didn't make it up, but it's pretty apt. Think of the sublayer as pinned to its superlayer; then you have to say both where the pin passes through the sublayer (the anchorPoint) and where it passes through the superlayer (the position).

If the anchorPoint is (0.5,0.5) (the default), the position property works like a view's center property. A view's center is actually a special case of a layer's position. This is quite typical of the relationship between view properties and layer properties; the view properties are often a simpler — but less powerful — version of the layer properties.

A layer's position and anchorPoint are orthogonal (independent); changing one does not change the other. Therefore, changing either of them without changing the other changes where the layer is drawn within its superlayer.

In Figure 3-1, the most important point in the circle is its center; all the other objects need to be positioned with respect to it. Therefore, they all have the same position: the center of the circle. But they differ in their anchorPoint. The arrow's anchor-Point is (0.5,0.8), the middle of the shaft, near the tail. But the anchorPoint of a cardinal point letter is (0.5,3.0), well outside the letter's bounds, so as to place the letter near the edge of the circle.

A layer's frame is a purely derived property. When you get the frame, it is calculated from the bounds size along with the position and anchorPoint. When you set the frame, you set the bounds size and position. In general, you should regard the frame as a convenient façade and no more. Nevertheless, it is convenient! To position a sublayer so that it exactly overlaps its superlayer, you can just set the sublayer's frame to the superlayer's bounds.

 A layer created in code (as opposed to a view's underlying layer) has a frame and bounds of CGRect.zero and will not be visible on the screen even when you add it to a superlayer that is on the screen. Be sure to give your layer a nonzero width and height if you want to be able to see it! Creating a layer and adding it to a superlayer and then wondering why it isn't appearing in the interface is a common beginner error.

CALayer instance methods are provided for converting between the coordinate systems of layers within the same layer hierarchy; the first parameter can be a CGPoint or a CGRect, and the second parameter is another CALayer:

- convert(_:from:)
- convert(_:to:)

CAScrollLayer

If you're going to be moving a layer's bounds origin as a way of repositioning its sublayers *en masse*, you might like to make the layer a CAScrollLayer, a CALayer subclass that provides convenience methods for this sort of thing. (Despite the name, a CAScrollLayer provides no scrolling interface; the user can't scroll it by dragging.) By default, a CAScrollLayer's masksToBounds property is true, so that the CAScrollLayer acts like a window through which you see only what is within its bounds. (You can set its masksToBounds to false, but this would be an odd thing to do, as it somewhat defeats the purpose.)

To move the CAScrollLayer's bounds, you can talk either to it or to a sublayer (at any depth):

Talking to the CAScrollLayer
    Call this CAScrollLayer method:

scroll(to:)
        If the parameter is a CGPoint, changes the CAScrollLayer's bounds origin to that point. If the parameter is a CGRect, changes the CAScrollLayer's bounds origin minimally so that the given portion of the bounds rect is visible.

Talking to a sublayer

Call these CALayer methods on sublayers of the CAScrollLayer:

scroll(_:)

Changes the CAScrollLayer's bounds origin so that the given point *of the sublayer* is at the top left of the CAScrollLayer.

scrollRectToVisible(_:)

Changes the CAScrollLayer's bounds origin so that the given rect *of the sublayer's bounds* is within the CAScrollLayer's bounds area. You can also ask the sublayer for its visibleRect, the part of this sublayer now within the CAScrollLayer's bounds.

Layer and Delegate

A CALayer's delegate property is settable (to an instance of any class adopting CALayerDelegate). If a layer is *not* the underlying layer of a view, it can be useful to give it a delegate; you might do this in order to give another object a hand in the layer's layout or its drawing, both of which I'll discuss later. A layer's delegate can also participate in certain aspects of animation, as I'll explain in Chapter 4.

But be careful! Do *not*, under any circumstances, set the delegate of a layer that *is* the underlying layer of a UIView; and do *not* make a UIView the delegate of any layer other than its underlying layer. A UIView *must* be the delegate of its underlying layer; moreover, it must *not* be the delegate of any *other* layer. *Don't do anything to mess this up.* If you do, extremely bad things will happen; for instance, drawing will stop working correctly.

Layout of Layers

The view hierarchy is actually a layer hierarchy (Figure 3-2). The positioning of a view within its superview is actually the positioning of its layer within its superlayer (the superview's layer). A view can be repositioned and resized automatically in accordance with its autoresizingMask or through autolayout based on its constraints. So there is automatic layout of layers *if they are the underlying layers of views*. Otherwise, there is *no* automatic layout of layers in iOS; the only option for layout of layers that are not the underlying layers of views is manual layout that you perform in code.

When a layer needs layout, either because its bounds have changed or because you called setNeedsLayout, you can respond in either of two ways:

- The layer's layoutSublayers method is called; to respond, override layout-Sublayers in your CALayer subclass.

- Alternatively, implement `layoutSublayers(of:)` in the layer's delegate. (Remember, if the layer is a view's underlying layer, the view is its delegate.)

For your layer to do effective manual layout of its sublayers, you'll probably need a way to identify or refer to the sublayers. There is no layer equivalent of `viewWith-Tag(_:)`, so such identification and reference is entirely up to you. A CALayer does have a `name` property that you might misuse for your own purposes. Key–value coding can also be helpful here; layers implement key–value coding in a special way, discussed at the end of this chapter.

For a view's underlying layer, `layoutSublayers` or `layoutSublayers(of:)` is called after the view's `layoutSubviews`. Under autolayout, you must call `super` or else autolayout will break. Moreover, these methods may be called more than once during the course of autolayout; if you're looking for an automatically generated signal that it's time to do manual layout of sublayers, a view layout event might be a better choice (see "Layout Events" on page 78).

Drawing in a Layer

The simplest way to make something appear in a layer is through its `contents` property. This is parallel to the `image` in a UIImageView (Chapter 2). It is expected to be a CGImage (or `nil`, signifying no image). Here's how we might modify the code that generated Figure 3-5 in such a way as to generate the smiley face as a layer rather than a view:

```
let lay4 = CALayer()
let im = UIImage(named:"smiley")!
lay4.frame = CGRect(origin:CGPoint(180,180), size:im.size)
lay4.contents = im.cgImage
self.view.layer.addSublayer(lay4)
```

 Unfortunately, the CALayer `contents` property is typed as Any (wrapped in an Optional). That means you can assign *anything* to it. Setting a layer's `contents` to a UIImage, rather than a CGImage, will *fail silently* — the image doesn't appear, but there is no error either. This is absolutely maddening, and I wish I had a nickel for every time I've done it and then wasted hours figuring out why my layer isn't appearing.

There are also four methods that can be implemented to provide or draw a layer's content on demand, similar to a UIView's `draw(_:)`. A layer is very conservative about calling these methods (and you must not call any of them directly). When a layer *does* call these methods, I will say that the layer *redisplays itself*. Here is how a layer can be caused to redisplay itself:

- If the layer's `needsDisplayOnBoundsChange` property is `false` (the default), then the only way to cause the layer to redisplay itself is by calling `setNeedsDisplay` (or `setNeedsDisplay(_:)`, specifying a CGRect). Even this might not cause the layer to redisplay itself right away; if that's crucial, then you will also call `display-IfNeeded`.

- If the layer's `needsDisplayOnBoundsChange` property is `true`, then the layer will also redisplay itself when the layer's bounds change (rather like a view's `.redraw` content mode).

Here are the four methods that can be called when a layer redisplays itself; pick one to implement (don't try to combine them, you'll just confuse things):

`display` *in a subclass*
> Your CALayer subclass can override `display`. There's no graphics context at this point, so `display` is pretty much limited to setting the `contents` image.

`display(_:)` *in the delegate*
> You can set the CALayer's `delegate` property and implement `display(_:)` in the delegate. As with CALayer's `display`, there's no graphics context, so you'll just be setting the `contents` image.

`draw(in:)` *in a subclass*
> Your CALayer subclass can override `draw(in:)`. The parameter is a graphics context into which you can draw directly; it is *not* automatically made the current context.

`draw(_:in:)` *in the delegate*
> You can set the CALayer's `delegate` property and implement `draw(_:in:)` in the delegate. The second parameter is a graphics context into which you can draw directly; it is *not* automatically made the current context.

Assigning a layer a `contents` image and drawing directly into the layer are, in effect, mutually exclusive:

- If a layer's `contents` is assigned an image, this image is shown immediately and replaces whatever drawing may have been displayed in the layer.

- If a layer redisplays itself and `draw(in:)` or `draw(_:in:)` draws into the layer, the drawing replaces whatever image may have been displayed in the layer.

- If a layer redisplays itself and none of the four methods provides any content, the layer will be empty.

If a layer is a view's underlying layer, you usually won't use any of the four methods to draw into the layer: you'll use the view's `draw(_:)`. But you *can* use these methods if you really want to. In that case, you will probably want to implement `draw(_:)` anyway, leaving that implementation empty. The reason is that this causes the layer to redisplay itself at appropriate moments. When a view is sent `setNeedsDisplay` —

including when the view first appears — the view's underlying layer is also sent `set-NeedsDisplay`, *unless the view has no draw(_:) implementation* (because in that case, it is assumed that the view never needs redrawing). If you're drawing a view entirely by drawing to its underlying layer directly, and if you want the underlying layer to be redisplayed automatically when the view is told to redraw itself, you should implement `draw(_:)` to do nothing. (This technique has no effect on sublayers of the underlying layer.) These are legitimate (but unusual) techniques for drawing into a view:

- The view subclass implements an empty `draw(_:)`, along with either `displayLayer:` or `draw(_:in:)`.
- The view subclass implements an empty `draw(_:)` plus `layerClass`, to give the view a custom layer subclass — and the custom layer subclass implements either `display` or `draw(in:)`.

Drawing-Related Layer Properties

A layer has a scale, its `contentsScale`, which maps point distances in the layer's graphics context to pixel distances on the device. A layer that's managed by Cocoa, if it has contents, will adjust its `contentsScale` automatically as needed; if a view implements `draw(_:)`, then on a device with a double-resolution screen its underlying layer is assigned a `contentsScale` of 2. But a layer that you are creating and managing yourself has no such automatic behavior; it's up to you, if you plan to draw into the layer, to set its `contentsScale` appropriately. Content drawn into a layer with a `contentsScale` of 1 may appear pixellated or fuzzy on a high-resolution screen. And when you're starting with a UIImage and assigning its CGImage as a layer's `contents`, if there's a mismatch between the UIImage's `scale` and the layer's `contentsScale`, then the image may be displayed at the wrong size.

Three further layer properties strongly affect what the layer displays:

`backgroundColor`
>   Equivalent to a view's `backgroundColor` (and if this layer is a view's underlying layer, it *is* the view's `backgroundColor`). Changing the `backgroundColor` takes effect immediately. Think of the `backgroundColor` as separate from the layer's own drawing, and as painted *behind* the layer's own drawing.

`opacity`
>   Affects the overall apparent transparency of the layer. It is equivalent to a view's `alpha` (and if this layer is a view's underlying layer, it *is* the view's `alpha`). It affects the apparent transparency of the layer's sublayers as well. It affects the apparent transparency of the background color and the apparent transparency of

the layer's content separately (just as with a view's `alpha`). Changing the `opacity` property takes effect immediately.

`isOpaque`

Determines whether the layer's graphics context is opaque. An opaque graphics context is black; you can draw on top of that blackness, but the blackness is still there. A nonopaque graphics context is clear; where no drawing is, it is completely transparent.

Changing the `isOpaque` property has no effect until the layer redisplays itself. A view's underlying layer's `isOpaque` property is independent of the view's `isOpaque` property; they are unrelated and do entirely different things. But if the view implements `draw(_:)`, then setting the view's `backgroundColor` changes the layer's `isOpaque`! The latter becomes `true` if the new background color is opaque (alpha component of 1), and `false` otherwise. That's the reason behind the strange behavior of CGContext's `clear(_:)` method, described in Chapter 2.

 When drawing directly into a *layer*, the behavior of `clear(_:)` differs from what was described in Chapter 2 for drawing into a *view*: instead of punching a hole through the background color, it effectively paints with the layer's background color. This can have curious side effects, and I regard it as deeply weird.

Content Resizing and Positioning

A layer's content is stored (cached) as a bitmap which is then treated like an image:

- If the content came from setting the layer's `contents` property to an image, the cached content is that image; its size is the point size of the CGImage we started with.

- If the content came from drawing directly into the layer's graphics context, the cached content is the layer's entire graphics context; its size is the point size of the layer itself at the time the drawing was performed.

The layer's content is drawn in relation to the layer's bounds in accordance with various layer properties, which cause the cached content to be resized, repositioned, cropped, and so on, as it is displayed. The properties are:

`contentsGravity`

This property (CALayerContentsGravity) is parallel to a UIView's `contentMode` property, and describes how the content should be positioned or stretched in relation to the bounds. `.center` means the content is centered in the bounds without resizing; `.resize` (the default) means the content is sized to fit the bounds, even if this means distorting its aspect; and so forth.

For historical reasons, the terms bottom and top in the names of the contents-Gravity settings have the opposite of their expected meanings. Reverse them in your mind: when you mean the top, say .bottom; when you mean the top left, say .bottomLeft; and so on.

contentsRect

A CGRect expressing the proportion of the content that is to be displayed. The default is (0.0,0.0,1.0,1.0), meaning the entire content is displayed. The specified part of the content is sized and positioned in relation to the bounds in accordance with the contentsGravity. By setting the contentsRect, you can scale up part of the content to fill the bounds, or slide part of a larger image into view without redrawing or changing the contents image.

You can also use the contentsRect to scale down the content, by specifying a larger contentsRect such as (-0.5,-0.5,1.5,1.5); but any content pixels that touch the edge of the contentsRect will then be extended outward to the edge of the layer (to prevent this, make sure that the outermost pixels of the content are all empty).

contentsCenter

A CGRect, structured like contentsRect, expressing the central region of nine rectangular regions of the contentsRect that are variously allowed to stretch if the contentsGravity calls for stretching. The central region (the actual value of the contentsCenter) stretches in both directions. Of the other eight regions (inferred from the value you provide), the four corner regions don't stretch, and the four side regions stretch in one direction. (This should remind you of how a resizable image stretches; see Chapter 2.)

If a layer's content comes from drawing directly into its graphics context, then the layer's contentsGravity, of itself, has no effect, because the size of the graphics context, by definition, fits the size of the layer exactly; there is nothing to stretch or reposition. But the contentsGravity *will* have an effect on such a layer if its contentsRect is not (0.0,0.0,1.0,1.0), because now we're specifying a rectangle of some *other* size; the contentsGravity describes how to fit that rectangle into the layer.

Again, if a layer's content comes from drawing directly into its graphics context, then when the layer is resized, if the layer is asked to display itself again, the drawing is performed again, and once more the layer's content fits the size of the layer exactly. But if the layer's bounds are resized when needsDisplayOnBoundsChange is false, then the layer does *not* redisplay itself, so its cached content no longer fits the layer, and the contentsGravity matters.

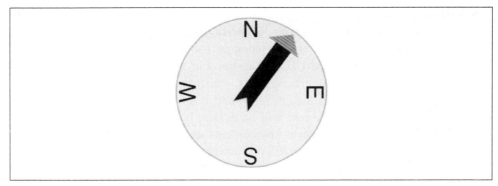

Figure 3-6. One way of resizing the compass arrow

By a judicious combination of settings, you can get the layer to perform some clever drawing for you that might be difficult to perform directly. Figure 3-6 shows the result of the following settings:

```
arrow.needsDisplayOnBoundsChange = false
arrow.contentsCenter = CGRect(0.0, 0.4, 1.0, 0.6)
arrow.contentsGravity = .resizeAspect
arrow.bounds = arrow.bounds.insetBy(dx: -20, dy: -20)
```

Because `needsDisplayOnBoundsChange` is `false`, the content is not redisplayed when the arrow's bounds are increased; instead, the cached content is used. The `contents-Gravity` setting tells us to resize proportionally; therefore, the arrow is both longer and wider than in Figure 3-1, but not in such a way as to distort its proportions. Notice that although the triangular arrowhead is wider, it is not longer; the increase in length is due entirely to the stretching of the arrow's shaft. That's because the `contentsCenter` region is within the shaft.

A layer's `masksToBounds` property has the same effect on its content that it has on its sublayers. If it is `false`, the whole content is displayed, even if that content (after taking account of the `contentsGravity` and `contentsRect`) is larger then the layer. If it is `true`, only the part of the content within the layer's bounds will be displayed.

 The value of a layer's bounds origin does not affect where its content is drawn. It affects only where its sublayers are drawn.

Layers that Draw Themselves

A few built-in CALayer subclasses provide some basic but helpful self-drawing ability:

CATextLayer

A CATextLayer has a `string` property, which can be an NSString or NSAttributedString (Chapter 10), along with other text formatting properties, somewhat like a simplified UILabel; it draws its `string`. The default text color, the `foregroundColor` property, is white, which is unlikely to be what you want. The text is different from the `contents` and is mutually exclusive with it: either the contents image or the text will be drawn, but not both, so in general you should not give a CATextLayer any contents image. In Figures 3-1 and 3-6, the cardinal point letters are CATextLayer instances.

CAShapeLayer

A CAShapeLayer has a `path` property, which is a CGPath. It fills or strokes this path, or both, depending on its `fillColor` and `strokeColor` values, and displays the result; the default is a `fillColor` of black and no `strokeColor`. It has properties for line thickness, dash style, end-cap style, and join style, similar to a graphics context; it also has the remarkable ability to draw only part of its path (`strokeStart` and `strokeEnd`), making it very easy to draw things like an arc of an ellipse. A CAShapeLayer may also have `contents`; the shape is displayed on top of the contents image, but there is no property permitting you to specify a compositing mode. In Figures 3-1 and 3-6, the background circle is a CAShapeLayer instance, stroked with gray and filled with a lighter, slightly transparent gray.

CAGradientLayer

A CAGradientLayer covers its background with a gradient, whose type (CAGradientLayerType) can be `.axial` (linear), `.radial`, or `.conic` (starting in iOS 12). It's an easy way to draw a gradient in your interface. The gradient is defined much as in the Core Graphics gradient example in Chapter 2, an array of locations and an array of corresponding colors, along with a start and end point. To clip the gradient's shape, you can add a mask to the CAGradientLayer (masks are discussed later in this chapter). A CAGradientLayer's `contents` are not displayed. Figure 3-7 shows our compass drawn with a linear CAGradientLayer behind it.

Transforms

The way a layer is drawn on the screen can be modified though a transform. This is not surprising, because a view can have a transform (see Chapter 1), and a view is drawn on the screen by its layer. You can treat a layer's transform as two-dimensional or as three-dimensional; with some additional preparation, you can even make a three-dimensional transform *look* three-dimensional (in a cartoony way).

Figure 3-7. A gradient drawn behind the compass

Affine Transforms

In the simplest case, when a transform is two-dimensional, you can access a layer's transform through the `affineTransform` method (and the corresponding setter, `setAffineTransform(_:)`). The value is a CGAffineTransform, familiar from Chapters 1 and 2.

A layer's `affineTransform` is analogous to a view's `transform`. For details, see "Transform" on page 20. The chief difference is that a view's `transform` is applied around its `center`, whereas a layer's transform is applied around the `anchorPoint`, which might not be at its center. (So the `anchorPoint` has a second purpose that I didn't tell you about when discussing it earlier.)

You now know everything needed to understand the code that generated Figure 3-7. In this code, `self` is the CompassLayer; it does no drawing of its own, but merely assembles and configures its sublayers. The four cardinal point letters are each drawn by a CATextLayer; they are drawn at the same coordinates, but they have different rotation transforms, and are anchored so that their rotation is centered at the center of the circle. For the arrow, CompassLayer adopts CALayerDelegate, makes itself the arrow layer's delegate, and calls `setNeedsDisplay` on the arrow layer; this causes `draw(_:in:)` to be called in CompassLayer (that code is just the same code we developed for drawing the arrow in Chapter 2, and is not repeated here). The arrow layer is positioned by an `anchorPoint` pinning its tail to the center of the circle, and rotated around that pin by a transform:

```
// the gradient
let g = CAGradientLayer()
g.contentsScale = UIScreen.main.scale
g.frame = self.bounds
g.colors = [
    UIColor.black.cgColor,
    UIColor.red.cgColor
]
```

```
g.locations = [0.0,1.0]
self.addSublayer(g)
// the circle
let circle = CAShapeLayer()
circle.contentsScale = UIScreen.main.scale
circle.lineWidth = 2.0
circle.fillColor = UIColor(red:0.9, green:0.95, blue:0.93, alpha:0.9).cgColor
circle.strokeColor = UIColor.gray.cgColor
let p = CGMutablePath()
p.addEllipse(in: self.bounds.insetBy(dx: 3, dy: 3))
circle.path = p
self.addSublayer(circle)
circle.bounds = self.bounds
circle.position = self.bounds.center
// the four cardinal points
let pts = "NESW"
for (ix,c) in pts.enumerated() {
    let t = CATextLayer()
    t.contentsScale = UIScreen.main.scale
    t.string = String(c)
    t.bounds = CGRect(0,0,40,40)
    t.position = circle.bounds.center
    let vert = circle.bounds.midY / t.bounds.height
    t.anchorPoint = CGPoint(0.5, vert)
    t.alignmentMode = .center
    t.foregroundColor = UIColor.black.cgColor
    t.setAffineTransform(
        CGAffineTransform(rotationAngle:CGFloat(ix) * .pi/2.0))
    circle.addSublayer(t)
}
// the arrow
let arrow = CALayer()
arrow.contentsScale = UIScreen.main.scale
arrow.bounds = CGRect(0, 0, 40, 100)
arrow.position = self.bounds.center
arrow.anchorPoint = CGPoint(0.5, 0.8)
arrow.delegate = self // we will draw the arrow in the delegate method
arrow.setAffineTransform(CGAffineTransform(rotationAngle:.pi/5.0))
self.addSublayer(arrow)
arrow.setNeedsDisplay() // draw, please
```

3D Transforms

A layer's affineTransform is merely a façade for accessing its transform. A layer's transform is a three-dimensional transform, a CATransform3D; when the layer is a view's underlying layer, this property is exposed at the level of the view through the view's transform3D. For details, see "Transform3D" on page 24. The chief difference is that a view's transform3D takes place around the view's center, whereas a layer's three-dimensional transform takes place around a three-dimensional extension of the `anchorPoint`, whose z-component is supplied by the `anchorPointZ` property. Most of the time, you'll probably leave the `anchorPointZ` at its default of `0.0`.

The following rotation flips a layer around its y-axis:

```
someLayer.transform = CATransform3DMakeRotation(.pi, 0, 1, 0)
```

What will we see after we do that? By default, the layer is considered double-sided, so when it is flipped to show its "back," what's drawn is an appropriately reversed version of the content of the layer (along with its sublayers, which by default are still drawn in front of the layer, but reversed and positioned in accordance with the layer's transformed coordinate system). But if the layer's `isDoubleSided` property is `false`, then when it is flipped to show its "back," the layer disappears (along with its sublayers); its "back" is transparent and empty.

Layers do not magically give you realistic three-dimensional rendering — for that you would use Metal, which is beyond the scope of this discussion. Layers are two-dimensional objects, and they are designed for speed and simplicity. But read on, because I'm about to talk about adding an illusion of depth.

Depth

There are two ways to place layers at different nominal depths with respect to their siblings:

- Through the z-component of their `position`, which is the `zPosition` property. (So the `zPosition` has a second purpose that I didn't tell you about earlier.)
- By applying a transform that translates the layer's position in the z-direction.

These two values, the z-component of a layer's position and the z-component of its translation transform, are related; in some sense, the `zPosition` is a shorthand for a translation transform in the z-direction. (If you provide both a `zPosition` and a z-direction translation, you can rapidly confuse yourself.)

In the real world, changing an object's `zPosition` would make it appear larger or smaller, as it is positioned closer or further away; but this, by default, is not the case in the world of layer drawing. There is no attempt to portray perspective; the layer planes are drawn at their actual size and flattened onto one another, with no illusion of distance. (This is called *orthographic projection*, and is the way blueprints are often drawn to display an object from one side.) If we want to portray a visual sense of depth using layers, we're going to need some additional techniques, as I shall now explain.

Sublayer transform

Here's a widely used trick for introducing a quality of perspective into the way layers are drawn: make them sublayers of a layer whose `sublayerTransform` property maps

Figure 3-8. A disappointing page-turn rotation

all points onto a "distant" plane. (This is probably just about the only thing the `sublayerTransform` property is ever used for.) Combined with orthographic projection, the effect is to apply one-point perspective to the drawing, so that things get perceptibly smaller in the negative z-direction.

Let's try applying a sort of "page-turn" rotation to our compass: we'll anchor it at its right side and then rotate it around the y-axis. Here, the sublayer we're rotating (accessed through a property, `rotationLayer`) is the gradient layer, and the circle and arrow are its sublayers so that they rotate with it:

```
self.rotationLayer.anchorPoint = CGPoint(1,0.5)
self.rotationLayer.position = CGPoint(self.bounds.maxX, self.bounds.midY)
self.rotationLayer.transform = CATransform3DMakeRotation(.pi/4.0, 0, 1, 0)
```

The results are disappointing (Figure 3-8); the compass looks more squashed than rotated. But now we'll also apply the distance-mapping transform. The superlayer here is `self`:

```
var transform = CATransform3DIdentity
transform.m34 = -1.0/1000.0
self.sublayerTransform = transform
```

The results (shown in Figure 3-9) are better, and you can experiment with values to replace `1000.0`; for an even more exaggerated effect, try `500.0`. Also, the `zPosition` of the `rotationLayer` will now affect how large it is.

Transform layers

Another way to draw layers with depth is to use CATransformLayer. This CALayer subclass doesn't do any drawing of its own; it is intended solely as a host for other layers. It has the remarkable feature that you can apply a transform to it and it will maintain the depth relationships among its own sublayers. In this example, how things look depends on whether or not `lay1` is a CATransformLayer:

Figure 3-9. A dramatic page-turn rotation

```
let lay2 = CALayer()
lay2.frame = f // some CGRect
lay2.backgroundColor = UIColor.blue.cgColor
lay1.addSublayer(lay2)
let lay3 = CALayer()
lay3.frame = f.offsetBy(dx: 20, dy: 30)
lay3.backgroundColor = UIColor.green.cgColor
lay3.zPosition = 10
lay1.addSublayer(lay3)
lay1.transform = CATransform3DMakeRotation(.pi, 0, 1, 0)
```

In that code, the superlayer lay1 has two sublayers, lay2 and lay3. The sublayers are added in that order, so lay3 is drawn in front of lay2. Then lay1 is flipped like a page being turned by setting its transform:

- If lay1 is a normal CALayer, the sublayer drawing order doesn't change; lay3 is *still* drawn in front of lay2, even after the transform is applied.

- If lay1 is a CATransformLayer, lay3 is drawn *behind* lay2 after the transform; they are both sublayers of lay1, so their depth relationship is maintained.

Figure 3-10 shows our page-turn rotation yet again, still with the sublayerTransform applied to self, but this time the only sublayer of self is a CATransformLayer:

```
var transform = CATransform3DIdentity
transform.m34 = -1.0/1000.0
self.sublayerTransform = transform
let master = CATransformLayer()
master.frame = self.bounds
self.addSublayer(master)
self.rotationLayer = master
```

The CATransformLayer, to which the page-turn transform is applied, holds the gradient layer, the circle layer, and the arrow layer. Those three layers are at different

Figure 3-10. Page-turn rotation applied to a CATransformLayer

depths (using different zPosition settings), and I've tried to emphasize the arrow's separation from the circle by adding a shadow (discussed in the next section):

```
circle.zPosition = 10
arrow.shadowOpacity = 1.0
arrow.shadowRadius = 10
arrow.zPosition = 20
```

You can see from its apparent offset that the circle layer floats in front of the gradient layer, but I wish you could see this page-turn as an animation, which makes the circle jump right out from the gradient as the rotation proceeds.

Even more remarkable, I've added a little white peg sticking through the arrow and running into the circle! It is a CAShapeLayer, rotated to be perpendicular to the CATransformLayer (I'll explain the rotation code later in this chapter):

```
let peg = CAShapeLayer()
peg.contentsScale = UIScreen.main.scale
peg.bounds = CGRect(0,0,3.5,50)
let p2 = CGMutablePath()
p2.addRect(peg.bounds)
peg.path = p2
peg.fillColor = UIColor(red:1.0, green:0.95, blue:1.0, alpha:0.95).cgColor
peg.anchorPoint = CGPoint(0.5,0.5)
peg.position = master.bounds.center
master.addSublayer(peg)
peg.setValue(Float.pi/2, forKeyPath:"transform.rotation.x")
peg.setValue(Float.pi/2, forKeyPath:"transform.rotation.z")
peg.zPosition = 15
```

In that code, the peg runs straight out of the circle toward the viewer, so it is initially seen end-on, and because a layer has no thickness, it is invisible. But as the

CATransformLayer pivots in our page-turn rotation, the peg maintains its orientation relative to the circle, and comes into view. In effect, the drawing portrays a 3D model constructed entirely out of layers!

There is, I think, a slight additional gain in realism if the same `sublayerTransform` is applied also to the CATransformLayer, but I have not done so here.

Further Layer Features

A CALayer has many additional properties that affect details of how it is drawn. Since these drawing details can be applied to a UIView's underlying layer, they are effectively view features as well.

Shadows

A CALayer can have a shadow, defined by its `shadowColor`, `shadowOpacity`, `shadowRadius`, and `shadowOffset` properties. To make the layer draw a shadow, set the `shadowOpacity` to a nonzero value. The shadow is normally based on the shape of the layer's nontransparent region, but deriving this shape can be calculation-intensive (so much so that in early versions of iOS, layer shadows weren't implemented). You can vastly improve performance by defining the shape yourself as a CGPath and assigning it to the layer's `shadowPath` property.

If a layer's `masksToBounds` is `true`, no part of its shadow lying outside its bounds is drawn. (This includes the underlying layer of a view whose `clipsToBounds` is `true`.) Wondering why the shadow isn't appearing for a layer that masks to its bounds is a common beginner mistake.

This in turn poses a puzzle. Suppose we have a view for which `clipsToBounds` *must* be `true`, but we want that view to cast a shadow anyway. How can we do that? Figure 3-11 shows an example. The kitten image is shown in an image view whose `contentMode` is `.scaleAspectFill`. The original kitten image is rectangular, not square; the scaled image is therefore *larger* than the image view. But we don't want the excess part of the image to be visible, so the image view's `clipsToBounds` is `true`. Yet we also want the image view to cast a shadow. How can that be done?

It *can't* be done. Figure 3-11 may *look* like that's what it's doing, but it isn't. It's a trick. There's another view that you don't see. It has the same `frame` as the image view, its background color is black, and it's behind the image view. Its `clipsToBounds` is `false`, and its layer has a shadow.

Figure 3-11. A clipping view with a shadow?

Borders and Rounded Corners

A CALayer can have a border (borderWidth, borderColor); the borderWidth is drawn inward from the bounds, potentially covering some of the content unless you compensate.

A CALayer's corners can be rounded, effectively bounding the layer with a rounded rectangle, by giving it a cornerRadius greater than zero. If the layer has a border, the border has rounded corners too. If the layer has a backgroundColor, that background is clipped to the shape of the rounded rectangle. If the layer's masksToBounds is true, the layer's content and its sublayers are clipped by the rounded corners.

Starting in iOS 11, you can round individual corners of a CALayer rather than having to round all four corners at once. To do so, set the layer's maskedCorners property to a CACornerMask, a bitmask whose values have these dreadful names:

- layerMinXMinYCorner
- layerMaxXMinYCorner
- layerMinXMaxYCorner
- layerMaxXMaxYCorner

Even if you set the maskedCorners, you won't see any corner rounding unless you also set the cornerRadius to a nonzero number.

Masks

A CALayer can have a mask. This is itself a layer, whose content must be provided somehow. The transparency of the mask's content in a particular spot becomes (all

Figure 3-12. A layer with a mask

other things being equal) the transparency of the layer at that spot. The mask's colors (hues) are irrelevant; only transparency matters. To position the mask, pretend it's a sublayer.

Figure 3-12 shows our arrow layer, with the gray circle layer behind it, and a mask applied to the arrow layer. The mask is silly, but it illustrates very well how masks work: it's an ellipse, with an opaque fill and a thick, semitransparent stroke. Here's the code that generates and applies the mask:

```
let mask = CAShapeLayer()
mask.frame = arrow.bounds
let path = CGMutablePath()
path.addEllipse(in: mask.bounds.insetBy(dx: 10, dy: 10))
mask.strokeColor = UIColor(white:0.0, alpha:0.5).cgColor
mask.lineWidth = 20
mask.path = path
arrow.mask = mask
```

Using a mask, we can do more generally what the `cornerRadius` and `masksToBounds` properties do. Here's a utility method that generates a CALayer suitable for use as a rounded rectangle mask:

```
func mask(size sz:CGSize, roundingCorners rad:CGFloat) -> CALayer {
    let rect = CGRect(origin:.zero, size:sz)
    let r = UIGraphicsImageRenderer(bounds:rect)
    let im = r.image { ctx in
        let con = ctx.cgContext
        con.setFillColor(UIColor(white:0, alpha:0).cgColor)
        con.fill(rect)
        con.setFillColor(UIColor(white:0, alpha:1).cgColor)
        let p = UIBezierPath(roundedRect:rect, cornerRadius:rad)
        p.fill()
    }
    let mask = CALayer()
    mask.frame = rect
    mask.contents = im.cgImage
    return mask
}
```

The CALayer returned from that method can be placed as a mask anywhere in a layer by adjusting its frame origin and assigning it as the layer's `mask`. The result is that all of that layer's content drawing and its sublayers (including, if this layer is a view's underlying layer, the view's subviews) are clipped to the rounded rectangle shape; everything outside that shape is not drawn.

A mask drawing can have values between opaque and transparent, and can mask to any shape. The transparent region doesn't have to be on the outside of the mask; you can use a mask that's opaque on the outside and transparent on the inside to "punch a hole" in a layer (or a view).

A mask is like a sublayer, in that there is no built-in mechanism for automatically resizing the mask as the layer is resized. If *you* don't resize the mask when the layer is resized, the mask *won't* be resized. A common beginner mistake is to apply a mask to a view's underlying layer before the view has been fully laid out; when the view *is* laid out, its size changes, but the mask's size doesn't, and now the mask doesn't "fit."

Alternatively, you can apply a mask as a view directly to another view through the *view's* mask property, rather than having to drop down to the level of layers. This is not functionally distinct from applying the mask view's layer to the view's layer — under the hood, in fact, it *is* applying the mask view's layer to the view's layer. Using a mask view does nothing directly to help with the problem of resizing the mask when the view's size changes; a mask view isn't a subview, so it is not subject to autoresizing or autolayout. On the other hand, if you resize a mask view manually, you can do so using view properties; that's very convenient if you're already resizing the view itself manually (such as when using view property animation, as discussed in the next chapter).

Layer Efficiency

By now, you're probably envisioning all sorts of compositing fun, with layers masking sublayers and laid semitransparently over other layers. There's nothing wrong with that, but when an iOS device is asked to shift its drawing from place to place, the movement may stutter because the device lacks the necessary computing power to composite repeatedly and rapidly. This sort of issue is likely to emerge particularly when your code performs an animation (Chapter 4) or when the user is able to animate drawing through touch, as when scrolling a table view (Chapter 8).

You may be able to detect these problems by eye, and you can quantify them on a device by using the Core Animation template in Instruments, which shows the frame rate achieved during animation. Also, the Simulator's Debug menu lets you summon colored overlays that provide clues as to possible sources of inefficient drawing that can lead to such problems; when running on a device, similar overlays are available by choosing from the hierarchical menu under Debug → View Debugging → Rendering.

Tricks like shadows and rounded corners and masks may be easy and fun, but in general, opaque drawing is most efficient. (Nonopaque drawing is what the Simulator marks when you check Debug → Color Blended Layers.) You may think that for some particular use case you *have* to do nonopaque drawing, but think again, because you might be wrong about that. If a layer will always be shown over a background consisting of a single color, you can give the layer its own background of that same color; when additional layer content is supplied, the visual effect will be the same as if that additional layer content were composited over a transparent background.

Another way to gain some efficiency is by "freezing" the entirety of the layer's drawing as a bitmap. In effect, you're drawing everything in the layer to a secondary cache and using the cache to draw to the screen. Copying from a cache is less efficient than drawing directly to the screen, but this inefficiency may be compensated for, if there's a deep or complex layer tree, by not having to composite that tree every time we render. To do this, set the layer's `shouldRasterize` to `true` and its `rasterizationScale` to some sensible value (probably `UIScreen.main.scale`). You can always turn rasterization off again by setting `shouldRasterize` to `false`, so it's easy to rasterize just before some massive or sluggish rearrangement of the screen and then unrasterize afterward.

In addition, there's a layer property `drawsAsynchronously`. The default is `false`. If set to `true`, the layer's graphics context accumulates drawing commands and obeys them later on a background thread; the drawing commands themselves run very quickly, because they are not being obeyed at the time you issue them. I haven't had occasion to use this, but presumably there could be situations where it keeps your app responsive when drawing would otherwise be time-consuming.

Layers and Key–Value Coding

All of a layer's properties are accessible through Cocoa key–value coding by way of keys with the same name as the property. These are two ways of doing the same thing:

```
layer.mask = mask
// or:
layer.setValue(mask, forKey: "mask")
```

In addition, CATransform3D and CGAffineTransform values can be expressed through key–value coding and key paths. Again, these are equivalent:

```
self.rotationLayer.transform = CATransform3DMakeRotation(.pi/4.0, 0, 1, 0)
// or:
self.rotationLayer.setValue(.pi/4.0, forKeyPath:"transform.rotation.y")
```

That notation is possible because CATransform3D is key–value coding compliant for a repertoire of keys and key paths. These are not properties; a CATransform3D doesn't have a `rotation` property. It doesn't have *any* properties, because it isn't even an object. You cannot say:

```
self.rotationLayer.transform.rotation.y = //... no, sorry
```
The transform key paths you'll use most often are:

- `"rotation.x"`, `"rotation.y"`, `"rotation.z"`
- `"rotation"` (same as `"rotation.z"`)
- `"scale.x"`, `"scale.y"`, `"scale.z"`
- `"translation.x"`, `"translation.y"`, `"translation.z"`
- `"translation"` (two-dimensional, a CGSize)

The Quartz Core framework also injects key–value coding compliance into CGPoint, CGSize, and CGRect, allowing you to use keys and key paths matching their struct component names. For a complete list of KVC compliant classes related to CALayer, along with the keys and key paths they implement, see "Core Animation Extensions to Key-Value Coding" in Apple's *Core Animation Programming Guide* in the documentation archive.

Moreover, you can treat a CALayer as a kind of dictionary, and get and set the value for *any* key. This means you can attach arbitrary information to an individual layer instance and retrieve it later. Earlier I mentioned that to apply manual layout to a layer's sublayers, you will need a way of identifying those sublayers. This feature could provide a way of doing that:

```
myLayer1.setValue("manny", forKey:"pepboy")
myLayer2.setValue("moe", forKey:"pepboy")
```

A layer doesn't have a `pepboy` property; the `"pepboy"` key is something I'm attaching to these layers arbitrarily. Now I can identify them later by getting the value of their respective `"pepboy"` keys.

Also, CALayer has a `defaultValue(forKey:)` class method; to implement it, you'll need to subclass and override. In the case of keys whose value you want to provide a default for, return that value; otherwise, return the value that comes from calling `super`. In this way, a key can have a non-`nil` value even if no value has ever been explicitly provided for that key.

The truth is that this feature, though delightful (and I often wish that all classes behaved like this), is not put there solely for your convenience and enjoyment. It's there to serve as the basis for animation, which is the subject of the next chapter.

CHAPTER 4

Animation

Animation is an attribute changing over time. This will typically be a visible attribute of something in the interface. The changing attribute might be positional: something moves or changes size, not jumping abruptly, but sliding smoothly. Other kinds of attribute can animate as well. A view's background color might change from red to green, not switching colors abruptly, but blending from one to the other. A view might change from opaque to transparent, not vanishing abruptly, but fading away.

Without help, most of us would find animation beyond our reach. There are just too many complications — complications of calculation, of timing, of screen refresh, of threading, and many more. Fortunately, help is provided. You don't perform an animation yourself; you describe it, you order it, and it is performed for you. You get *animation on demand*.

Asking for an animation can be as simple as setting a property value; under some circumstances, a single line of code will result in animation:

```
myLayer.backgroundColor = UIColor.red.cgColor // animate to red
```

Animation is easy because Apple wants to facilitate your use of it. Animation isn't just cool and fun; it clarifies that something is changing or responding. It is crucial to the character of the iOS interface.

One of my first apps was based on a macOS game in which the user clicks cards to select them. In the macOS version, a card was highlighted to show it was selected, and the computer would beep to indicate a click on an ineligible card. On iOS, these indications were insufficient: the highlighting felt weak, and you can't use a sound warning in an environment where the user might have the volume turned off or be listening to music. So in the iOS version, animation is the indicator for card selection (a selected card waggles eagerly) and for tapping on an ineligible card (the whole interface shudders, as if to shrug off the tap).

The purpose of this chapter is to explain the basics of animation itself; how you use it is another matter. Using animation effectively, especially in relation to touch (the subject of the next chapter), is a deep and complex subject involving psychology, biology, and other fields outside mere programming. Apple's own use of animation is deep and pervasive. It is used to make the interface feel live, fluid, responsive, intuitive, and natural. It helps to provide the user with a sense of what the user can do and is doing, of where the user is, of how things on the screen are related. Many WWDC videos go into depth about what Apple achieves with animation, and these can assist you in your own design.

Drawing, Animation, and Threading

Here's an interesting fact about how iOS draws to the screen: drawing doesn't actually take place at the time you give your drawing commands (Chapter 2). When you give a command that requires a view to be redrawn, the system remembers your command and marks the view as needing to be redrawn. Later, when all your code has run to completion and the system has, as it were, a free moment, then it redraws all views that need redrawing. Let's call this the *redraw moment*. (I'll explain what the redraw moment really is later in this chapter.)

Animation works the same way, and is part of the same process. When you ask for an animation to be performed, the animation doesn't start happening on the screen until the next redraw moment. (You can force an animation to start immediately, but this is unusual.)

Like a movie (especially an old-fashioned animated cartoon), an animation has "frames." An animated value does not change smoothly and continuously; it changes in small, individual increments that give the *illusion* of smooth, continuous change. This illusion works because the device itself undergoes periodic, rapid, more or less regular screen refreshes — a perpetual succession of redraw moments — and the incremental changes are made to fall between these refreshes. Apple calls the system component responsible for this the *animation server*.

Think of the "animation movie" as being interposed between the user and the "real" screen. While the animation lasts, this movie is superimposed onto the screen. When the animation is finished, the movie is removed, revealing the state of the "real" screen behind it. The user is unaware of all this, because (if you've done things correctly) at the time that it starts, the movie's first frame looks just like the state of the "real" screen at that moment, and at the time that it ends, the movie's last frame looks just like the state of the "real" screen at *that* moment.

When you animate a view's movement from position 1 to position 2, you can envision a typical sequence of events like this:

1. You reposition the view. The view is now set to position 2, but there has been no redraw moment, so it is still portrayed at position 1.

2. You order an animation of the view from position 1 to position 2.

3. The rest of your code runs to completion.

4. The redraw moment arrives. If there were no animation, the view would now suddenly be portrayed at position 2. But there *is* an animation, and so the "animation movie" appears. It starts with the view portrayed at position 1, so that is still what the user sees.

5. The animation proceeds, each "frame" portraying the view at intermediate positions between position 1 and position 2. (The documentation describes the animation as *in-flight.*)

6. The animation ends, portraying the view ending up at position 2.

7. The "animation movie" is removed, revealing the view indeed at position 2 — where you put it in the first step.

Realizing that the "animation movie" is different from what happens to the *real* view is key to configuring an animation correctly. A frequent complaint of beginners is that a position animation is performed as expected, but then, at the end, the view "jumps" to some other position. This happens because you set up the animation but failed to move the view to match its final position in the "animation movie"; when the "movie" is whipped away at the end of the animation, the real situation that's revealed doesn't match the last frame of the "movie," so the view appears to jump.

There isn't really an "animation movie" in front of the screen — but it's a good analogy, and the effect is much the same. To explain what's actually happening, I have to reveal something about layers that I omitted from Chapter 3. It is not a layer itself that is portrayed on the screen; it's a derived layer called the *presentation layer*. When you animate the change of a view's position or a layer's position from position 1 to position 2, its nominal position changes immediately; meanwhile, the presentation layer's position remains unchanged until the redraw moment, and then changes over time, and because that's what's actually drawn on the screen, that's what the user sees.

(A layer's presentation layer can be accessed through its `presentation` method — and the layer itself may be accessed through the presentation layer's `model` method. I'll give examples, in this chapter and the next, of situations where accessing the presentation layer is a useful thing to do.)

The animation server operates on an independent thread. You don't have to worry about that fact (thank heavens, because multithreading is generally rather tricky and complicated), but you can't ignore it either. Your code runs independently of and possibly simultaneously with the animation — that's what multithreading means — so communication between the animation and your code can require some planning.

Arranging for your code to be notified when an animation ends is a common need. Most of the animation APIs provide a way to set up such a notification. One use of an "animation ended" notification might be to chain animations together: one animation ends and then another begins, in sequence. Another use is to perform some sort of cleanup. A very frequent kind of cleanup has to do with handling of touches: what a touch means while an animation is in-flight might be quite different from what a touch means when no animation is taking place.

Since your code can run even after you've set up an animation, or might start running while an animation is in-flight, you need to be careful about setting up conflicting animations. Multiple animations can be set up (and performed) simultaneously, but an attempt to animate or change a property that's already in the middle of being animated may be incoherent. You'll want to take care not to let your animations step on each other's feet accidentally.

Outside forces can interrupt your animations. The user might send your app to the background, or an incoming phone call might arrive while an animation is in-flight. The system deals neatly with this situation by simply canceling all in-flight animations when an app is backgrounded; you've already arranged *before* the animation for your views to assume the final states they will have *after* the animation, so no harm is done — when your app resumes, everything is in the final state that you arranged beforehand. But if you wanted your app to resume an animation where it left off when it was interrupted, that would require some canny coding on your part.

Image View and Image Animation

UIImageView (Chapter 2) provides a form of animation so simple as to be scarcely deserving of the name; still, sometimes it might be all you need. You supply a UIImageView with an array of UIImages, as the value of its `animationImages` or `highlightedAnimationImages` property. This array represents the "frames" of a simple cartoon; when you send the `startAnimating` message, the images are displayed in turn, at a frame rate determined by the `animationDuration` property, repeating as many times as specified by the `animationRepeatCount` property (the default is 0, meaning to repeat forever), or until the `stopAnimating` message is received. Before and after the animation, the image view continues displaying its `image` (or `highlightedImage`).

Suppose we want an image of Mars to appear out of nowhere and flash three times on the screen. This might seem to require some sort of Timer-based solution, but it's far simpler to use an animating UIImageView:

```
let mars = UIImage(named: "Mars")!
let empty = UIGraphicsImageRenderer(size:mars.size).image {_ in}
let arr = [mars, empty, mars, empty, mars]
let iv = UIImageView(image:empty)
```

```
iv.frame.origin = CGPoint(100,100)
self.view.addSubview(iv)
iv.animationImages = arr
iv.animationDuration = 2
iv.animationRepeatCount = 1
iv.startAnimating()
```

You can combine UIImageView animation with other kinds of animation. You could flash the image of Mars while at the same time sliding the UIImageView rightward, using view animation as described in the next section.

UIImage provides a form of animation parallel to that of UIImageView: an image can itself be an *animated image.* Just as with UIImageView, this means that you've prepared multiple images that form a sequence serving as the "frames" of a simple cartoon. You can create an animated image with one of these UIImage class methods:

`animatedImage(with:duration:)`
> As with UIImageView's `animationImages`, you supply an array of UIImages. You also supply the duration for the whole animation.

`animatedImageNamed(_:duration:)`
> You supply the name of a single image file, as with `init(named:)`, with no file extension. The runtime appends `"0"` (or, if that fails, `"1"`) to the name you supply and makes *that* image file the first image in the animation sequence. Then it increments the appended number, gathering images and adding them to the sequence (until there are no more, or we reach `"1024"`).

`animatedResizableImageNamed(_:capInsets:resizingMode:duration:)`
> Combines an animated image with a resizable image (Chapter 2).

You do not tell an animated image to start animating, nor are you able to tell it how long you want the animation to repeat. Rather, an animated image is *always* animating, repeating its sequence once every `duration` seconds, so long as it appears in your interface; to control the animation, add the image to your interface or remove it from the interface, possibly exchanging it for a similar image that isn't animated.

An animated image can appear in the interface anywhere a UIImage can appear as a property of some interface object. In this example, I construct a sequence of red circles of different sizes, in code, and build an animated image which I then display in a UIButton:

```
var arr = [UIImage]()
let w : CGFloat = 18
for i in 0 ..< 6 {
    let r = UIGraphicsImageRenderer(size:CGSize(w,w))
    arr += [r.image { ctx in
        let con = ctx.cgContext
        con.setFillColor(UIColor.red.cgColor)
        let ii = CGFloat(i)
```

```
        con.addEllipse(in:CGRect(0+ii,0+ii,w-ii*2,w-ii*2))
        con.fillPath()
    }]
}
let im = UIImage.animatedImage(with:arr, duration:0.5)
b.setImage(im, for:.normal) // b is a button in the interface
```

 Images are memory hogs, and an array of images can cause your app to run completely out of memory. Confine your use of image view and image animation to a *few small images*.

View Animation

All animation is ultimately layer animation, which I'll discuss later in this chapter. However, for a limited range of properties, you can animate a UIView directly: these are its `alpha`, `bounds`, `center`, `frame`, `transform`, `transform3D`, and, if the view doesn't implement `draw(_:)`, its `backgroundColor` (Chapter 1). You can also animate a UIView's change of contents. In addition, the UIVisualEffectView `effect` property is animatable between `nil` and a UIBlurEffect (Chapter 2); and, starting in iOS 11, a view's underlying layer's `cornerRadius` (Chapter 3) is animatable under view animation as well. This list of animatable features, despite its brevity, will often prove quite sufficient.

A Brief History of View Animation

The view animation API has evolved historically by way of three distinct major stages:

Begin and commit
> Way back at the dawn of iOS time, a view animation was constructed imperatively using a sequence of UIView class methods. To use this API, you call `begin-Animations`, configure the animation, set an animatable property, and *commit* the animation by calling `commitAnimations`:
>
> ```
> UIView.beginAnimations(nil, context: nil)
> UIView.setAnimationDuration(1)
> self.v.backgroundColor = .red
> UIView.commitAnimations()
> ```

Block-based animation
> When Objective-C blocks were introduced in iOS 4, the entire operation of configuring a view animation was reduced to a single UIView class method, to which you pass a block in which you set an animatable property. In Swift, an Objective-C block is a function — usually an anonymous function. We can call this the *animations function*:

```
UIView.animate(withDuration:1) {
    self.v.backgroundColor = .red
}
```

Property animator

iOS 10 introduced a new object — a property animator (UIViewPropertyAnimator). It, too, receives an animations function in which you set an animatable property:

```
let anim = UIViewPropertyAnimator(duration: 1, curve: .linear) {
    self.v.backgroundColor = .red
}
anim.startAnimation()
```

Although begin-and-commit animation still exists, it is deprecated and you're unlikely to use it; block-based animation completely supersedes it. The property animator does *not* supersede block-based animation; rather, it supplements and expands it. There are certain kinds of animation (repeating animation, autoreversing animation, transition animation) where a property animator can't help you, and you'll go on using block-based animation. For the bulk of basic view animations, however, the property animator brings some valuable advantages — a full range of timing curves, multiple completion functions, and the ability to pause, resume, and reverse the animation, and to interact by touch with the animated view.

Property Animator Basics

The UIViewPropertyAnimator class adopts the UIViewImplicitlyAnimating protocol, which itself adopts the UIViewAnimating protocol:

UIViewAnimating protocol

A UIViewAnimating adopter can have its animation started, paused, and stopped:

- `startAnimation`
- `pauseAnimation`
- `stopAnimation(_:)`
- `finishAnimation(at:)`

Its `state` property reflects its current animation state (UIViewAnimatingState):

- `.inactive`
- `.active`
- `.stopped`

Its `isRunning` property distinguishes whether it is `.active` but paused.

UIViewAnimating also provides two settable properties:

`fractionComplete`
Essentially, the current "frame" of the animation.

`isReversed`
Determines whether the animation is running forward or backward.

UIViewImplicitlyAnimating protocol
A UIViewImplicitlyAnimating adopter can be given animations functions:

- `addAnimations(_:)`
- `addAnimations(_:delayFactor:)`

It can be given completion functions:

- `addCompletion(_:)`

UIViewImplicitlyAnimating also provides a `continueAnimation(withTiming-Parameters:durationFactor:)` method that allows a paused animation to be resumed with altered timing and duration; the `durationFactor` is the desired fraction of the animation's original duration, or zero to mean whatever remains of the original duration.

UIViewPropertyAnimator
UIViewPropertyAnimator's own methods consist solely of initializers; I'll discuss those later, when I talk about timing curves. It has some read-only properties describing how it was configured and started (such as its animation's `duration`), along with five settable properties:

`isInterruptible`
If `true` (the default), the animator can be paused or stopped.

`isUserInteractionEnabled`
If `true` (the default), animated views can be tapped midflight.

`scrubsLinearly`
If `true` (the default), then when the animator is paused, the animator's animation curve is temporarily replaced with a linear curve.

`isManualHitTestingEnabled`
If `true`, hit-testing is up to you; the default is `false`, meaning that the animator performs hit-testing on your behalf, which is usually what you want. (See Chapter 5 for more about hit-testing animated views.)

pausesOnCompletion

If `true`, then when the animation finishes, it does not revert to `.inactive`; the default is `false`.

As you can see, a property animator comes packed with power for controlling the animation after it starts. You can pause the animation in midflight, allow the user to manipulate the animation gesturally, resume the animation, reverse the animation, and much more. I'll illustrate those features in this and subsequent chapters.

In the simplest case, you'll just launch the animation and stand back, as I demonstrated earlier:

```
let anim = UIViewPropertyAnimator(duration: 1, curve: .linear) {
    self.v.backgroundColor = .red
}
anim.startAnimation()
```

In that code, the UIViewPropertyAnimator object `anim` is instantiated as a local variable, and we are not retaining it in a persistent property; yet the animation works because the animation server retains it. We *can* keep a persistent reference to the property animator if we're going to need it elsewhere, and I'll give examples later showing how that can be a useful thing to do.

When a property animator's animation is started, it transitions through state changes:

1. The animator starts life in the `.inactive` state with `isRunning` set to `false`.

2. When `startAnimation` is called, the animator enters the `.active` state with `isRunning` *still* set to `false` (paused).

3. The animator then immediately transitions to the `.active` state with `isRunning` set to `true`.

The "animation movie" starts running at the next redraw moment. Once the animation is set in motion, it continues to its finish and then passes through those same states in reverse:

1. The running animator was in the `.active` state with `isRunning` set to `true`.

2. When the animation finishes, the animator switches to `.active` with `isRunning` set to `false` (paused).

3. The animator then immediately transitions back to the `.inactive` state with `isRunning` set to `false`.

If you have set the animator's `pausesOnCompletion` to `true`, the final step is omitted; the animation pauses, *without* transitioning back to the `.inactive` state. Ultimately returning the animator to `.inactive` is then left up to you. To do that, you first send the animator the `stopAnimation(_:)` message, causing the animator to enter the special `.stopped` state. What happens next depends on the parameter you passed to `stopAnimation(_:)`; it's a Bool:

`stopAnimation(_:)` *parameter is* `false`
> You will ultimately call `finishAnimation(at:)`, after which the animator returns to `.inactive`.

`stopAnimation(_:)` *parameter is* `true`
> You want to dispense with `finishAnimation(at:)` and let the runtime clean up for you. The runtime will bring the animator back to `.inactive` immediately, without running any completion handlers.

It is a runtime error to let an animator go out of existence while paused (`.active` but `isRunning` is `false`) or stopped (`.stopped`). Your app will crash unceremoniously if you allow that to happen. If you pause an animator, you *must* eventually bring it back to the `.inactive` state in good order before the animator goes out of existence.

When the animator finishes and reverts to the `.inactive` state, it jettisons its animations. This means that the animator, if you've retained it, is reusable after finishing only if you supply new animations.

View Animation Basics

The most important elements of view animation are the animations function and the completion function:

Animations function
> Any change to an animatable view property made within an animations function will be animated.

Completion function
> The completion function lets us specify what should happen after the animation ends.

More than one animatable view property can be animated at the same time. Here, we animate simultaneous changes both in a view's color and in its position:

```
let anim = UIViewPropertyAnimator(duration: 1, curve: .linear) {
    self.v.backgroundColor = .red
    self.v.center.y += 100
}
anim.startAnimation()
```

More than one *view* can be animated at the same time. Suppose we want to replace a view in the view hierarchy with another view, not suddenly, but making the first view dissolve into the second. We start by placing the second view into the view hierarchy, with the same frame as the first view, but with an `alpha` of `0`, so that it is invisible.

Then we animate the change of the first view's `alpha` to 0 and the second view's `alpha` to 1. Finally, in the completion function, we remove the first view after the animation ends (invisibly, because its `alpha` ends at 0):

```
let v2 = UIView()
v2.backgroundColor = .black
v2.alpha = 0
v2.frame = self.v.frame
self.v.superview!.addSubview(v2)
let anim = UIViewPropertyAnimator(duration: 1, curve: .linear) {
    self.v.alpha = 0
    v2.alpha = 1
}
anim.addCompletion { _ in
    self.v.removeFromSuperview()
}
anim.startAnimation()
```

 Another way to remove a view from the view hierarchy with animation is to call the UIView class method `perform(_:on:options:animations:completion:)` with `.delete` as its first argument (this is, in fact, the only possible first argument). This causes the view to blur, shrink, and fade, and sends it `removeFromSuperview()` afterward.

Preventing animation

Code that isn't about animatable view properties can appear in an animations function with no problem. But we must be careful to keep any changes to animatable properties that we do *not* want animated out of the animations function. In the preceding example, in setting `v2.alpha` to 0, I just want to set it right now, instantly; I don't want that change to be animated. So I've put that line *outside* the animations function (and in particular, *before* it).

Sometimes, though, that's not so easy; perhaps, within the animations function, we must call a method that might perform unwanted animatable changes. The UIView class method `performWithoutAnimation(_:)` solves the problem; it goes inside an animations function, but whatever happens in *its* function is *not* animated. In this rather artificial example, the view jumps to its new position and then slowly turns red:

```
let anim = UIViewPropertyAnimator(duration: 1, curve: .linear) {
    self.v.backgroundColor = .red
    UIView.performWithoutAnimation {
        self.v.center.y += 100
    }
}
anim.startAnimation()
```

Conflicts and additive animations

The material inside an animations function (but not inside a `performWithout-Animation` function) *orders* the animation — that is, it gives instructions for what the animation will be when the redraw moment comes. If you change an animatable view property as part of the animation, you should *not* change that property again afterward; the results can be confusing, because there's a conflict with the animation you've already ordered. This code is essentially incoherent:

```
let anim = UIViewPropertyAnimator(duration: 2, curve: .linear) {
    self.v.center.y += 100
}
self.v.center.y += 300
anim.startAnimation()
```

What actually happens is that the view *jumps* 300 points down and then *animates* 100 points further down. That's probably not what you intended. After you've ordered an animatable view property to be animated inside an animations function, *don't change that view property's value again* until after the animation is over.

On the other hand, this code, while somewhat odd, nevertheless does a smooth single animation to a position 400 points further down:

```
let anim = UIViewPropertyAnimator(duration: 2, curve: .linear) {
    self.v.center.y += 100
    self.v.center.y += 300
}
anim.startAnimation()
```

That's because basic positional view animations are *additive* by default. This means that the second animation is run simultaneously with the first, and is blended with it.

To illustrate what it means for animations to be additive, let's take advantage of the fact that a property animator allows us to add a second animation that doesn't take effect until some amount of the first animation has elapsed:

```
let anim = UIViewPropertyAnimator(duration: 2, curve: .easeInOut) {
    self.v.center.y += 100
}
anim.addAnimations({
    self.v.center.x += 100
}, delayFactor: 0.5)
anim.startAnimation()
```

The `delayFactor:` of `0.5` means that the second animation will start halfway through the `duration`, which is 2 seconds. So the animated view heads straight downward for 1 second and then smoothly swoops off to the right while continuing down for another second, ending up 100 points down and 100 points to the right of where it started. The two animations might appear to conflict — they are both changing the center of our view, and they have different durations and therefore different speeds — but instead they blend together seamlessly.

An even stronger example is what happens when the two animations directly oppose one another:

```
let yorig = self.v.center.y
let anim = UIViewPropertyAnimator(duration: 2, curve: .easeInOut) {
    self.v.center.y += 100
}
anim.addAnimations({
    self.v.center.y = yorig
}, delayFactor: 0.5)
anim.startAnimation()
```

Amazingly, there's no conflict; instead, we get a smooth autoreversing animation. The animated view starts marching toward a point 100 points down from its original position, but at about the halfway point it smoothly — not abruptly or sharply — slows and reverses itself and returns to its original position.

View Animation Configuration

The details of how you configure a view animation differ depending on whether you're using a property animator or calling one of the UIView class methods. With a property animator, you configure the animator before telling it to start animating. With a UIView class method, on the other hand, everything has to be supplied in a single command, which both configures and orders the animation. The full form of the chief UIView class method is:

- `animate(withDuration:delay:options:animations:completion:)`

There are shortened versions of the same command; you can omit the `delay:` and `options:` parameters, and even the `completion:` parameter. But it's still the same command, and the configuration of the animation is effectively complete at this point.

Animations function

The animations function contains the commands that set animatable view properties:

- With a block-based UIView class method, you supply the animations function as the `animations:` parameter.
- With a property animator, the animations function is usually provided as the `animations:` argument when the property animator is instantiated. But you can add an animations function to a property animator after instantiating it; indeed, the `init(duration:timingParameters:)` initializer requires that you do this, as it lacks an `animations:` parameter. And you can do that more than once:

```
let anim = UIViewPropertyAnimator(duration: 1,
    timingParameters: UICubicTimingParameters(animationCurve:.linear))
anim.addAnimations {
    self.v.backgroundColor = .red
}
anim.addAnimations {
    self.v.center.y += 100
}
anim.startAnimation()
```

Completion function

A completion function contains commands that are to be executed when the animation finishes:

- With a UIView class method, you supply the completion function as the completion: parameter. It takes one parameter, a Bool reporting whether the animation finished.

- A property animator can have multiple completion functions, provided by calling addCompletion(_:). As with the animations functions, a property animator can be assigned more than one completion function; the completion functions are executed in the order in which they were added:

```
var anim = UIViewPropertyAnimator(duration: 1, curve: .linear) {
    self.v.backgroundColor = .red
    self.v.center.y += 100
}
anim.addCompletion {_ in
    print("hey")
}
anim.addCompletion {_ in
    print("ho")
}
anim.startAnimation() // animates, finishes, then prints "hey" and "ho"
```

A property animator's completion function takes one parameter, a UIViewAnimatingPosition reporting where the animation ended up: .end, .start, or .current. (I'll talk later about what those values mean.)

A property animator that is told to stop its animation with stopAnimation(_:) does *not* execute its completion functions at that time:

- If you called stopAnimation(false), the animator's completion functions are executed when you call finishAnimation(at:).

- If you called stopAnimation(true), the animator's completion functions are not executed at all.

Animation duration

The duration of an animation represents how long it takes (in seconds) to run from start to finish:

- With a block-based UIView class method, the animation duration is the `duration:` parameter.

- With a property animator, the animation duration is the `duration:` parameter when the property animator is initialized.

You can also think of the duration as the animation's speed. Obviously, if two views are told to move different distances in the same time, the one that must move further must move faster.

A duration of `0` doesn't really mean `0`. It means "use the default duration." This fact will be of interest later when we talk about nesting animations. Outside of a nested animation, the default is two-tenths of a second.

Animation delay

It is permitted to order the animation along with a delay before the animation goes into action. The default is no delay. A delay is *not* the same as applying the animation using delayed performance; the animation is applied immediately, but when it starts running it spins its wheels, with no visible change, until the delay time has elapsed:

- With a block-based UIView class method, the delay is the `delay:` parameter.

- To apply a delay to an animation with a property animator, call `start-Animation(afterDelay:)` instead of `startAnimation`.

Animation timing

Specifying a change in a value and a time over which it should be changed is insufficient to describe what should happen. Should we change at a constant rate the whole time? Should we change slowly at first and more quickly later? Questions like these are answered by *timing curves*. An animation's timing curve maps interpolated values to time:

- With a UIView class method, you get a choice of just four timing curves (supplied as part of the `options:` argument, as I'll explain in a moment).

- A property animator gives you very broad powers to configure the timing curve the way you want. This is such an important topic that I'll deal with it in a separate section later.

Animation options

In a UIView class method, the `options:` argument is a bitmask combining additional options. Here are some of the chief `options:` values (UIView.AnimationOptions) that you might wish to use:

Timing curve
> When supplied in this way, only four built-in timing curves are available. The term "ease" means that there is a gradual acceleration or deceleration between the animation's central speed and the zero speed at its start or end. Specify one at most:
>
> - `.curveEaseInOut` (the default)
> - `.curveEaseIn`
> - `.curveEaseOut`
> - `.curveLinear` (constant speed throughout)

`.repeat`
> If included, the animation will repeat indefinitely.

`.autoreverse`
> If included, the animation will run from start to finish (in the given duration time), and will then run from finish to start (also in the given duration time). The documentation's claim that you can autoreverse only if you also repeat is incorrect; you can use either or both (or neither).

When using `.autoreverse`, you will want to clean up at the end so that the view is back in its original position when the animation is over. To see what I mean, consider this code:

```
let opts : UIView.AnimationOptions = .autoreverse
let xorig = self.v.center.x
UIView.animate(withDuration:1, delay: 0, options: opts, animations: {
    self.v.center.x += 100
}, completion: nil)
```

The view animates 100 points to the right and then animates 100 points back to its original position — and then *jumps* 100 points *back to the right*. The reason is that the last actual value we assigned to the view's center x is 100 points to the right, so when the animation is over and the "animation movie" is whipped away, the view is revealed still sitting 100 points to the right. The solution is to move the view back to its original position in the completion function:

```
let opts : UIView.AnimationOptions = .autoreverse
let xorig = self.v.center.x
UIView.animate(withDuration:1, delay: 0, options: opts, animations: {
    self.v.center.x += 100
}, completion: { _ in
    self.v.center.x = xorig // *
})
```

There seems to be a major hole in the design of the block-based animation API; if you say .repeat, you must repeat indefinitely. What if your goal is to repeat a finite number of times? In the past, the solution was to resort to a command from the earliest generation of animation methods:

```
let opts : UIView.AnimationOptions = .autoreverse
let xorig = self.v.center.x
UIView.animate(withDuration:1, delay: 0, options: opts, animations: {
    UIView.setAnimationRepeatCount(3) // *
    self.v.center.x += 100
}, completion: { _ in
    self.v.center.x = xorig
})
```

New in iOS 13, the solution is to omit .autoreverse and .repeat from the animation options, and instead call another UIView class method, modifyAnimations(withRepeatCount:autoreverses:), inside the animations function, containing the actual animations:

```
let xorig = self.v.center.x
UIView.animate(withDuration:1, delay: 0, options: [], animations: {
    UIView.modifyAnimations(withRepeatCount: 3, autoreverses: true) {
        self.v.center.x += 100
    }
}, completion: { _ in
    self.v.center.x = xorig
})
```

There are also some options saying what should happen if we order an animation when another animation is already ordered or in-flight (so that we are effectively *nesting* animations):

.overrideInheritedDuration
> Prevents inheriting the duration from a surrounding or in-flight animation (the default is to inherit it).

.overrideInheritedCurve
> Prevents inheriting the timing curve from a surrounding or in-flight animation (the default is to inherit it).

`.beginFromCurrentState`

Suppose this animation animates a property already being animated by an animation that is previously ordered or in-flight. Starting this animation might cancel the previous animation, completing the requested change instantly. But with `.beginFromCurrentState`, this animation will use the presentation layer to decide where to start, and, if possible, will "blend" its animation with the previous animation. There is usually little need for `.beginFromCurrentState`, because simple view animations are additive by default; however, I'll demonstrate one possible use later in this chapter.

Timing Curves

A timing curve describes how an animation's speed should vary during the course of the animation. It does this by mapping the fraction of the animation's time that has elapsed (the x-axis) against the fraction of the animation's change that has occurred (the y-axis); its endpoints are therefore at (`0.0,0.0`) and (`1.0,1.0`), because at the beginning of the animation there has been no elapsed time and no change, and at the end of the animation all the time has elapsed and all the change has occurred. There are two kinds of timing curve: cubic Bézier curves and springing curves.

Cubic timing curves

A cubic Bézier curve is defined by its endpoints, where each endpoint needs only one Bézier control point to define the tangent to the curve. Because the curve's endpoints are known, defining the two control points is sufficient to describe the entire curve. That is, in fact, how a cubic timing curve is expressed.

The built-in ease-in-out timing function is defined by the two control points (`0.42,0.0`) and (`0.58,1.0`) — that is, it's a Bézier curve with one endpoint at (`0.0,0.0`), whose control point is (`0.42,0.0`), and the other endpoint at (`1.0,1.0`), whose control point is (`0.58,1.0`) (Figure 4-1).

With a UIView class method, you have a choice of four built-in timing curves; you specify one of them through the `options:` argument, as I've already explained.

With a property animator, you specify a timing curve as part of initialization. That's why I postponed telling you how to initialize a property animator until now. Here are three property animator initializers and how the timing curve is expressed:

`init(duration:curve:animations:)`

The `curve:` is a built-in timing curve, specified as a UIView.AnimationCurve enum. These are the same built-in timing curves as for a UIView class method:

- `.easeInOut`
- `.easeIn`

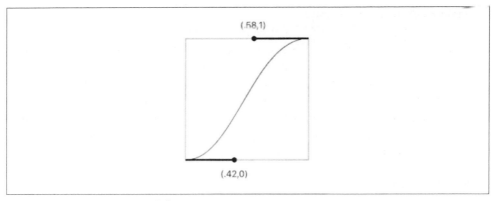

Figure 4-1. An ease-in-out Bézier curve

- `.easeOut`
- `.linear`

`init(duration:controlPoint1:controlPoint2:animations:)`
The timing curve is supplied as the two control points that define it.

`init(duration:timingParameters:)`
This is most general form of initializer; the other two are convenience initializers that call it. There's no `animations:` parameter, so you'll have to call `add-Animations` later to supply the animations function. The `timingParameters:` is an object adopting the UITimingCurveProvider protocol, which can be a UICubicTimingParameters instance or a UISpringTimingParameters instance (I'll talk about springing timing curves in a moment). The UICubicTimingParameters initializers are:

`init(animationCurve:)`
The value is one of the four built-in timing curves that I already mentioned, specified as a UIView.AnimationCurve enum.

`init()`
Provides a fifth built-in timing curve, used as the default for many built-in behaviors.

`init(controlPoint1:controlPoint2:)`
Defines the timing curve by its control points.

Defining a custom cubic timing curve is not difficult. Here's a cubic timing curve that eases in very slowly and finishes up all in a rush, whipping quickly into place after about two-thirds of the time has elapsed. I call this the "clunk" timing function:

```
anim = UIViewPropertyAnimator(
    duration: 1, timingParameters:
        UICubicTimingParameters(
            controlPoint1:CGPoint(0.9,0.1),
            controlPoint2:CGPoint(0.7,0.9)))
```

Springing timing curves

A springing timing curve is the solution to a physics problem whose initial conditions describe a mass attached to a stretched spring. The animation mimics releasing the spring and letting it rush toward and settle down at the destination value.

Springing timing curves are much more useful and widespread than you might suppose. A springing animation doesn't have to animate a view from place to place, and doesn't have to look particularly springy to be effective. A small initial spring velocity and a high damping gives a normal animation that wouldn't particularly remind anyone of a spring, but that does have a pleasingly rapid beginning and slow ending; many of Apple's own system animations are actually spring animations of that type (consider the way folders open in the home screen).

To use a springing timing curve with UIView block-based animation, you call a different class method:

- `animate(withDuration:delay:usingSpringWithDamping:initialSpring-Velocity:options:animations:completion:)`

You're supplying two parameters that vary the nature of the initial conditions, and hence the behavior of the animation over time:

Damping ratio
> The `damping:` parameter is a number between `0.0` and `1.0` that describes the amount of final oscillation. A value of `1.0` is *critically damped* and settles directly into place; lower values are *underdamped*. A value of `0.8` just barely overshoots and snaps back to the final value. A value of `0.1` waggles around the final value for a while before settling down.

Initial velocity
> The default is zero, and you'll usually leave it there. A nonzero initial velocity is useful particularly when converting from a gesture to an animation — that is, where the user is moving a view and releases it, and you want a springing animation to take over from there, starting out at the same velocity that the user was applying at the moment of release. Higher values cause greater overshoot, depending on the damping ratio. With a damping ratio of `0.3`, an initial velocity value of `1` overshoots a little and bounces about twice before settling into place, a value of `10` overshoots a bit further, and a value of `100` overshoots by more than twice the distance.

With a property animator, once again, you'll supply the timing curve as part of initialization:

`init(duration:dampingRatio:animations:)`
> The `dampingRatio:` argument is the same as the `damping:` in the UIView class method I just described. The initial velocity is zero.

`init(duration:timingParameters:)`
> This is the same initializer I discussed in connection with cubic timing curves. Recall that the `timingParameters:` is a UITimingCurveProvider; this can be a UISpringTimingParameters object, whose initializers are:

`init(dampingRatio:)`
> You supply a damping ratio, and the initial velocity is zero.

`init(dampingRatio:initialVelocity:)`
> The `initialVelocity:` is similar to the `initialSpringVelocity:` in the UIView class method I described a moment ago, except that it is a CGVector. Normally, only the x-component matters, in which case they are effectively the same thing; the y-component is considered only if what's being animated follows a two-dimensional path, as when you're changing both components of a view's `center`.

`init(mass:stiffness:damping:initialVelocity:)`
> A slightly different way of looking at the initial conditions. The overall `duration:` value is ignored; the actual duration will be calculated from the other parameters (and this calculated duration can be discovered by reading the resulting property animator's `duration`). The first three parameters are in proportion to one another. A high `mass:` can cause a vast overshoot. A low `stiffness:` or a low `damping:` can result in a long settle-down time. The mass is usually quite small, while the stiffness and damping are usually quite large.

`init()`
> The default spring animation; it is quite heavily damped, and settles into place in about half a second. The overall `duration:` value is ignored. In terms of the previous initializer, the `mass:` is 3, the `stiffness:` is 1000, the `damping:` is 500, and the `initialVelocity:` is (0,0).

Canceling a View Animation

Once a view animation is in-flight, how can you cancel it? And what should "cancel" mean in the first place? This is one of the key areas where a property animator shows off its special powers. To illustrate why, I'll start by showing what you have to do to cancel a block-based animation.

Canceling a block-based animation

Imagine a simple unidirectional positional animation, with a long duration so that we can interrupt it in midflight. To facilitate the explanation, I'll conserve both the view's original position and its final position in properties:

```
self.pOrig = self.v.center
self.pFinal = self.v.center
self.pFinal.x += 100
UIView.animateWithDuration(4, animations: {
    self.v.center = self.pFinal
})
```

We have a button that we can tap during that animation, and this button is supposed to cancel the animation. How can we do that?

One possibility is to reach down to the CALayer level and call `removeAllAnimations`:

```
self.v.layer.removeAllAnimations()
```

That has the advantage of simplicity, but the effect is jarring: the "animation movie" is whipped away instantly, "jumping" the view to its final position, effectively doing what the system does automatically when the app goes into the background.

So let's try to devise a more subtle form of cancellation: the view should *hurry* to its final position. This is a case where the additive nature of animations actually gets in our way. We cannot merely impose another animation that moves the view to its final position with a short duration, because this doesn't cancel the existing animation. Therefore, we must remove the first animation manually. We already know how to do that: call `removeAllAnimations`. But we also know that if we do that, the view will jump to its final position; we want it to remain, for the moment, at its current position — meaning *the animation's* current position. But where on earth is that?

To find out, we have to ask the view's *presentation layer* where it currently is. We reposition the view at the location of its presentation layer, and *then* remove the animation, and *then* perform the final "hurry home" animation:

```
self.v.layer.position = self.v.layer.presentation()!.position
self.v.layer.removeAllAnimations()
UIView.animate(withDuration:0.1) {
    self.v.center = self.pFinal
}
```

Another alternative is that cancellation means hurrying the view back to its *original* position. In that case, animate the view's `center` to its original position instead of its destination position:

```
self.v.layer.position = self.v.layer.presentation()!.position
self.v.layer.removeAllAnimations()
UIView.animate(withDuration:0.1) {
    self.v.center = self.pOrig
}
```

Yet another possibility is that cancellation means just *stopping* wherever we happen to be. In that case, omit the final animation:

```
self.v.layer.position = self.v.layer.presentation()!.position
self.v.layer.removeAllAnimations()
```

Canceling a property animator's animation

Now I'll show how do those things with a property animator. We don't have to reach down to the level of the layer. We don't call `removeAllAnimations`. We don't query the presentation layer. We don't have to memorize the start position or the end position. The property animator does all of that for us!

For the sake of ease and generality, let's hold the animator in an instance property where all of our code can see it. Here's how it is configured:

```
self.anim = UIViewPropertyAnimator(
    duration: 4, timingParameters: UICubicTimingParameters())
self.anim.addAnimations {
    self.v.center.x += 100
}
self.anim.startAnimation()
```

Here's how to cancel the animation by hurrying home to its end:

```
self.anim.pauseAnimation()
self.anim.continueAnimation(withTimingParameters: nil, durationFactor: 0.1)
```

We first *pause* the animation, because otherwise we can't make changes to it. But the animation does not visibly pause, because we resume at once with a modification of the original animation, which is smoothly blended into the existing animation. The short `durationFactor:` is the "hurry" part; we want a much shorter duration than our animation's original duration. We don't have to tell the animator where to animate to; in the absence of any other commands, it animates to its original destination. The `nil` value for the `timingParameters:` tells the animation to use the existing timing curve.

What about canceling the animation by hurrying home to its beginning? It's exactly the same, except that we reverse the animation.

```
self.anim.pauseAnimation()
self.anim.isReversed = true
self.anim.continueAnimation(withTimingParameters: nil, durationFactor: 0.1)
```

Again, we don't have to tell the animator where to animate to; it knows where we started, and reversing means to go there.

Using the same technique, we could interrupt the animation and hurry to anywhere we like — by adding another animations function before continuing. Here, cancellation causes us to rush right off the screen:

```
self.anim.pauseAnimation()
self.anim.addAnimations {
    self.v.center = CGPoint(-200,-200)
}
self.anim.continueAnimation(withTimingParameters: nil, durationFactor: 0.1)
```

What about canceling the animation by stopping wherever we are? Just stop the animation:

```
self.anim.stopAnimation(false)
self.anim.finishAnimation(at: .current)
```

Recall that the `false` argument means: "Please allow me to call `finish-Animation(at:)`." We want to call `finishAnimation(at:)` in order to specify where the view should end up when the "animation movie" is removed. By passing in `.current`, we state that we want the animated view to end up right where it is now. If we were to pass in `.start` or `.end`, the view would *jump* to that position (if it weren't there already).

We can now understand the incoming parameter in the completion function! It is the position where we ended up:

- If the animation finished by proceeding to its end, the completion function parameter is `.end`.
- If we reversed the animation and it finished by proceeding back to its start, as in our second cancellation example, the parameter is `.start`.
- If we called `finishAnimation(at:)`, the parameter is the `at:` argument we specified in the call.

Canceling a repeating animation

Suppose that the animation we want to cancel is an infinitely repeating autoreversing animation. It will presumably be created with the UIView class method:

```
self.pOrig = self.v.center
let opts : UIView.AnimationOptions = [.autoreverse, .repeat]
UIView.animate(withDuration:1, delay: 0, options: opts, animations: {
    self.v.center.x += 100
})
```

Let's say our idea of cancellation is to have the animated view hurry back to its original position; that is why we have saved the original position as an instance property.

This is a situation where the `.beginFromCurrentState` option is useful! That's because a repeating animation is *not* additive with a further animation. It is therefore sufficient simply to impose the "hurry" animation on top of the existing repeating animation, because it contradicts the repeating animation and therefore also cancels it. The `.beginFromCurrentState` option prevents the view from jumping momentarily to the "final" position, 100 points to the right, to which we set it when we initiated the repeating animation:

```
let opts : UIView.AnimationOptions = .beginFromCurrentState
UIView.animate(withDuration:0.1, delay:0, options:opts, animations: {
    self.v.center = self.pOrig
})
```

Frozen View Animation

Another important feature of a property animator is that its animation can be *frozen*. We already know that the animation can be paused — or never even started. A frozen animation is simply left in this state. It can be started or resumed at any time subsequently; or we can keep the animation frozen, but move it to a different "frame" of the animation by setting its `fractionComplete`, controlling the frozen animation manually.

In this simple example, we have in the interface a slider (a UISlider) and a small red square view. As the user slides the slider from left to right, the red view follows along — and gradually turns green, depending how far the user slides the slider. If the user slides the slider all the way to the right, the view is at the right and is fully green. If the user slides the slider all the way back to the left, the view is at the left and is fully red. To the user, this doesn't look like it involves any animation; it looks like the view just obeys the slider. But in fact a frozen animation is the way accomplish it.

The property animator is configured with an animation moving the view all the way to right and turning it all the way green. But the animation is never started:

```
self.anim = UIViewPropertyAnimator(duration: 1, curve: .easeInOut) {
    self.v.center.x = self.pTarget.x
    self.v.backgroundColor = .green()
}
```

The slider, whenever the user moves it, simply changes the animator's `fractionComplete` to match its own percentage:

```
self.anim.fractionComplete = CGFloat(slider.value)
```

Apple refers to this technique of manually moving a frozen animation back and forth from frame to frame as *scrubbing*. A common use case is that the user will touch and move the animated view itself. This will come in handy in connection with interactive view controller transitions in Chapter 6.

In that example, I deliberately set the timing curve to `.easeInOut` in order to illustrate the real purpose of the `scrubsLinearly` property. You would think that a nonlinear timing curve would affect the relationship between the position of the slider and the position of the view: with an `.easeInOut` timing curve, the view would arrive at the far right before the slider does. But that doesn't happen, because a nonrunning animation switches its timing curve to `.linear` *automatically* for as long as it is nonrunning. The purpose of the `scrubsLinearly` property, whose default property is `true`, is to allow you to turn *off* that behavior by setting it to `false` on the rare occasions when this might be desirable.

Custom Animatable View Properties

By default, as I explained earlier, only a few basic view properties are animatable through view animation. Changing some other view property in an animations function won't animate anything. But you can define a custom view property that *can* be animated in an animations function, provided the custom view property itself changes an animatable view property.

Imagine a UIView subclass, MyView, which has a Bool `swing` property. All this does is reposition the view: when `swing` is set to `true`, the view's `center` x-coordinate is increased by 100; when `swing` is set to `false`, it is decreased by 100. A view's `center` is animatable, so the `swing` property *itself* can be animatable.

The trick (suggested by an Apple WWDC 2014 video) is to implement MyView's `swing` setter with a zero-duration animation:

```
class MyView : UIView {
    var swing : Bool = false {
        didSet {
            var p = self.center
            p.x = self.swing ? p.x + 100 : p.x - 100
            UIView.animate(withDuration:0) {
                self.center = p
            }
        }
    }
}
```

If we now change a MyView's `swing` directly, the view jumps to its new position; there is no animation. But if an animations function changes the `swing` property, the `swing` setter's animation inherits the duration of the surrounding animations function — because such inheritance is, as I mentioned earlier, the default. So the change in position is animated, with the specified duration:

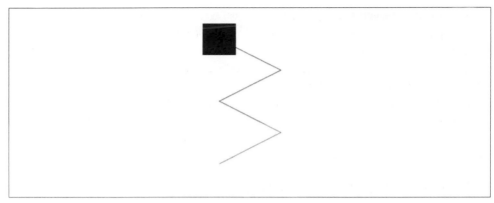

Figure 4-2. A zig-zag animation

```
let anim = UIViewPropertyAnimator(duration: 1, curve: .easeInOut) {
    self.v.swing.toggle()
}
anim.startAnimation()
```

Keyframe View Animation

A view animation can be described as a set of keyframes. This means that, instead of a simple beginning and end point, you specify multiple *stages* in the animation and those stages are joined together for you. This can be useful as a way of chaining animations together, or as a way of defining a complex animation that can't be described as a single change of value.

To create a keyframe animation, you call this UIView class method:

• `animateKeyframes(withDuration:delay:options:animations:completion:)`

It takes an animations function, and inside that function you call this UIView class method multiple times to specify each stage:

• `addKeyframe(withRelativeStartTime:relativeDuration:animations:)`

Each keyframe's start time and duration is between 0 and 1, *relative to the animation as a whole*. (Giving a keyframe's start time and duration in seconds is a common beginner mistake.)

To illustrate, I'll oscillate a view back and forth horizontally while moving it down the screen vertically, forming a zig-zag (Figure 4-2):

```
var p = self.v.center
let dur = 0.25
var start = 0.0
let dx : CGFloat = 100
let dy : CGFloat = 50
var dir : CGFloat = 1
```

```
UIView.animateKeyframes(withDuration:4, delay: 0, animations: {
    UIView.addKeyframe(withRelativeStartTime:start,
        relativeDuration: dur) {
            p.x += dx*dir; p.y += dy
            self.v.center = p
    }
    start += dur; dir *= -1
    UIView.addKeyframe(withRelativeStartTime:start,
        relativeDuration: dur) {
            p.x += dx*dir; p.y += dy
            self.v.center = p
    }
    start += dur; dir *= -1
    UIView.addKeyframe(withRelativeStartTime:start,
        relativeDuration: dur) {
            p.x += dx*dir; p.y += dy
            self.v.center = p
    }
    start += dur; dir *= -1
    UIView.addKeyframe(withRelativeStartTime:start,
        relativeDuration: dur) {
            p.x += dx*dir; p.y += dy
            self.v.center = p
    }
})
```

In that code, there are four keyframes, evenly spaced: each is 0.25 in duration (one-fourth of the whole animation) and each starts 0.25 later than the previous one (as soon as the previous one ends). In each keyframe, the view's center x-coordinate increases or decreases by 100, alternately, while its center y-coordinate keeps increasing by 50.

The keyframe values are points in space and time; the actual animation interpolates between them. How this interpolation is done depends upon the options: parameter (omitted in the preceding code). Several UIView.KeyframeAnimationOptions values have names that start with calculationMode; pick one. The default is .calculation-ModeLinear. In our example, this means that the path followed by the view is a sharp zig-zag; the view seems to bounce off invisible walls at the right and left. But if our choice is .calculationModeCubic, our view describes a smooth S-curve, starting at the view's initial position and ending at the last keyframe point, and passing through the three other keyframe points like the maxima and minima of a sine wave.

Because my keyframes are perfectly even, I could achieve the same effects by using .calculationModePaced or .calculationModeCubicPaced, respectively. The paced options ignore the relative start time and relative duration values of the keyframes; you might as well pass 0 for all of them. Instead, they divide up the times and durations evenly, exactly as my code has done.

Finally, `.calculationModeDiscrete` means that the changed animatable properties don't animate: the animation jumps to each keyframe.

The outer animations function can contain other changes to animatable view properties, as long as they don't conflict with the `addKeyframe` animations; these are animated over the total duration:

```
UIView.animateKeyframes(withDuration:4, delay: 0, animations: {
    self.v.alpha = 0
    // ...
```

The result is that as the view zigzags back and forth down the screen, it also gradually fades away.

It is legal and meaningful, although the documentation fails to make this clear, to supply a timing curve as part of the `options:` argument. If you don't do that, the default is `.curveEaseInOut`, which may not be what you want. Unfortunately Swift's obsessive-compulsive attitude toward data types resists folding a UIView.Animation-Options timing curve directly into a value that is typed as a UIView.Keyframe-AnimationOptions; so you have to trick the compiler into letting you do it. Here's how to combine `.calculationModeLinear` with `.curveLinear`:

```
var opts : UIView.KeyframeAnimationOptions = .calculationModeLinear
let opt2 : UIView.AnimationOptions = .curveLinear
opts.insert(UIView.KeyframeAnimationOptions(rawValue:opt2.rawValue))
```

That's two different senses of `linear`! The first means that the path described by the moving view is a sequence of straight lines. The second means that the moving view's speed along that path is steady.

You might want to pause or reverse a keyframe view animation by way of a property animator. To do so, nest your call to `UIView.animateKeyframes...` inside the property animator's animations function. The property animator's duration and timing curve are then inherited, so this is another way to dictate the keyframe animation's timing.

The power and utility of keyframe animations often goes unappreciated by beginners. Keyframes do not have to be sequential, nor do they all have to involve the same property. They can be used to coordinate different animations; they are a good way to chain animations, or to overlap animations. In this example, our view animates slowly to the right, and changes color suddenly *in the middle* of its movement:

```
let anim = UIViewPropertyAnimator(
    duration: 4, timingParameters: UICubicTimingParameters())
anim.addAnimations {
    UIView.animateKeyframes(withDuration: 0, delay: 0, animations: {
        UIView.addKeyframe(withRelativeStartTime: 0,
            relativeDuration: 1) {
                self.v.center.x += 100
```

```
        }
        UIView.addKeyframe(withRelativeStartTime: 0.5,
            relativeDuration: 0.25) {
                self.v.backgroundColor = .red
        }
    })
  }
  anim.startAnimation()
```

There are other ways to arrange the same outward effect, but this way, the entire animation is placed under the control of a single property animator, and is easy to pause, scrub, reverse, and so on.

Transitions

A *transition* is an animation that emphasizes a view's change of content. Transitions are ordered using one of two UIView class methods:

- `transition(with:duration:options:animations:completion:)`
- `transition(from:to:duration:options:completion:)`

The transition animation types are expressed as part of the `options:` bitmask:

- `.transitionFlipFromLeft`, `.transitionFlipFromRight`
- `.transitionCurlUp`, `.transitionCurlDown`
- `.transitionFlipFromBottom`, `.transitionFlipFromTop`
- `.transitionCrossDissolve`

Transitioning one view

`transition(with:...)` takes one UIView parameter, and performs the transition animation on that view. In this example, a UIImageView containing an image of Mars flips over as its image changes to a smiley face; it looks as if the image view were two-sided, with Mars on one side and the smiley face on the other:

```
let opts : UIView.AnimationOptions = .transitionFlipFromLeft
UIView.transition(with:self.iv, duration: 0.8, options: opts, animations: {
    self.iv.image = UIImage(named:"Smiley")
})
```

In that example, I've put the content change inside the animations function. That's conventional but misleading; the truth is that if all that's changing is the content, *nothing* needs to go into the animations function. The change of content can be anywhere, before or even after this entire line of code. It's the flip that's being animated. You might use the animations function here to order additional animations, such as a change in a view's center.

You can do the same sort of thing with a custom view that does its own drawing. Let's say that I have a UIView subclass, MyView, that draws either a rectangle or an ellipse depending on the value of its Bool `reverse` property:

```
class MyView : UIView {
    var reverse = false
    override func draw(_ rect: CGRect) {
        let f = self.bounds.insetBy(dx: 10, dy: 10)
        let con = UIGraphicsGetCurrentContext()!
        if self.reverse {
            con.strokeEllipse(in:f)
        }
        else {
            con.stroke(f)
        }
    }
}
```

This code flips a MyView instance while changing its drawing from a rectangle to an ellipse or *vice versa*:

```
let opts : UIView.AnimationOptions = .transitionFlipFromLeft
self.v.reverse.toggle()
UIView.transition(with:self.v, duration: 1, options: opts, animations: {
    self.v.setNeedsDisplay()
})
```

By default, if a view has subviews whose layout changes as part of a transition animation, that change in layout is *not* animated: the layout changes directly to its final appearance when the transition ends. If you want to display a subview of the transitioning view being animated as it assumes its final state, include `.allowAnimated-Content` in the `options:` bitmask.

Transitioning two views and their superview

`transition(from:to:...)` takes two UIView parameters; the first view is *replaced* by the second, while *their superview* undergoes the transition animation. There are two possible configurations, depending on the `options:` you provide:

Remove one subview, add the other

If `.showHideTransitionViews` is *not* one of the `options:`, then the second subview is not in the view hierarchy when we start; the transition removes the first subview from its superview and adds the second subview to that same superview.

Hide one subview, show the other

If `.showHideTransitionViews` *is* one of the `options:`, then both subviews are in the view hierarchy when we start; the `isHidden` of the first is `false`, the `isHidden` of the second is `true`, and the transition reverses those values.

In this example, a label `self.lab` is already in the interface. The animation causes the superview of `self.lab` to flip over, while at the same time a different label, `lab2`, is substituted for the existing label:

```
let lab2 = UILabel(frame:self.lab.frame)
lab2.text = self.lab.text == "Hello" ? "Howdy" : "Hello"
lab2.sizeToFit()
UIView.transition(from:self.lab, to: lab2,
    duration: 0.8, options: .transitionFlipFromLeft) { _ in
        self.lab = lab2
}
```

It's up to you to make sure beforehand that the second view has the desired position, so that it will appear in the right place in its superview.

Transitions are another handy but probably underutilized iOS animation feature. Earlier, I demonstrated how to replace one view with another by adding the second view, animating the `alpha` values of both views, and removing the first view in the completion function. That's a common technique for implementing a dissolve, but calling `transition(from:to:...)` with a `.transitionCrossDissolve` animation is simpler and does the same thing.

Implicit Layer Animation

All animation is ultimately layer animation. Up to now, we've been talking about view animation, which uses layer animation under the hood. Now we're going to talk about how to animate a layer directly.

Amazingly, animating a layer can be as simple as setting a layer property. A change in what the documentation calls an *animatable property* of a CALayer is *automatically* interpreted as a request to animate that change. In other words, animation of layer property changes is the default! Multiple property changes are considered part of the same animation. This mechanism is called *implicit animation*.

In Chapter 3 we constructed a compass out of layers. Suppose we have created that interface, and that we have a reference to the arrow layer (`arrow`). If we rotate the arrow layer by changing its `transform` property, *the arrow rotation is animated*:

```
arrow.transform = CATransform3DRotate(arrow.transform, .pi/4.0, 0, 0, 1)
```

You may be wondering: if implicit animation is the default, why didn't we notice it happening in any of the layer examples in Chapter 3? It's because there are two common situations where implicit layer animation *doesn't* happen:

Underlying layer
> Implicit layer animation doesn't operate on a UIView's underlying layer. You *can* animate a UIView's underlying layer directly, but you must use explicit layer animation (discussed later in this chapter).

During layer tree preparation

Implicit layer animation doesn't affect a layer as it is being created, configured, and added to the interface. Implicit animation comes into play when you change an animatable property of a layer that is *already* present in the interface.

Animatable Layer Properties

CALayer properties listed in the documentation as animatable are `anchorPoint` and `anchorPointZ`, `backgroundColor`, `borderColor`, `borderWidth`, `bounds`, `contents`, `contentsCenter`, `contentsRect`, `cornerRadius`, `isDoubleSided`, `isHidden`, `masksTo-Bounds`, `opacity`, `position` and `zPosition`, `rasterizationScale` and `should-Rasterize`, `shadowColor`, `shadowOffset`, `shadowOpacity`, `shadowRadius`, and `sublayerTransform` and `transform`.

In addition, a CAShapeLayer's `path`, `strokeStart`, `strokeEnd`, `fillColor`, `stroke-Color`, `lineWidth`, `lineDashPhase`, and `miterLimit` are animatable; so are a CAText-Layer's `fontSize` and `foregroundColor`, and a CAGradientLayer's `colors`, `locations`, and `endPoint`.

Basically, a property is animatable because there's some sensible way to interpolate the intermediate values between one value and another. The nature of the animation attached to each property is therefore generally just what you would intuitively expect. When you change a layer's `isHidden` property, it fades out of view (or into view). When you change a layer's `contents`, the old contents are dissolved into the new contents. And so forth.

 A layer's `cornerRadius` is animatable by explicit layer animation, or by view animation, but not by implicit layer animation.

Animation Transactions

Animation operates with respect to a *transaction* (a CATransaction), which collects all animation requests and hands them over to the animation server in a single batch. Every animation request takes place in the context of some transaction. You can make this explicit by wrapping your animation requests in calls to the CATransaction class methods `begin` and `commit`; the result is a *transaction block*. Additionally, there is always an *implicit transaction* surrounding your code, and you can operate on this implicit transaction without any `begin` and `commit`.

To modify the characteristics of an implicit animation, you modify the transaction that surrounds it. Typically, you'll use these CATransaction class methods:

`setAnimationDuration(_:)`
The duration of the animation.

setAnimationTimingFunction(_:)
> A CAMediaTimingFunction; layer timing functions are discussed in the next section.

setDisableActions(_:)
> Toggles implicit animations for this transaction.

setCompletionBlock(_:)
> A function (taking no parameters) to be called when the animation ends; it is called even if no animation is triggered during this transaction.

flush()
> Pauses subsequent code until the current transaction has finished.

CATransaction also implements key–value coding to allow you to set and retrieve a value for an arbitrary key, similar to CALayer.

By nesting transaction blocks, you can apply different animation characteristics to different elements of an animation. You can also use transaction commands outside of any transaction block to modify the implicit transaction. In our previous example, we could slow down the animation of the arrow like this:

```
CATransaction.setAnimationDuration(0.8)
arrow.transform = CATransform3DRotate(arrow.transform, .pi/4.0, 0, 0, 1)
```

An important use of transactions is to turn implicit animation *off*. This is valuable because implicit animation is the default, and can be unwanted (and a performance drag). To turn off implicit animation, call setDisableActions(true). There are other ways to turn off implicit animation (discussed later in this chapter), but this is the simplest.

setCompletionBlock(_:) establishes a completion function that signals the end, not only of the implicit layer property animations you yourself have ordered as part of this transaction, but of *all* animations ordered during this transaction, including Cocoa's own animations. It's a way to be notified when any and all animations come to an end.

The flush method can solve the problem of implicit animation not working during preparation of the layer tree. This attempt to add a layer and make it appear by growing from a point doesn't animate:

```
// ... create and configure lay ...
lay.bounds.size = .zero
self.view.layer.addSublayer(lay)
CATransaction.setAnimationDuration(2)
lay.bounds.size = CGSize(100,100) // no animation
```

But this does animate:

```
// ... create and configure lay ...
lay.bounds.size = .zero
self.view.layer.addSublayer(lay)
CATransaction.flush() // *
CATransaction.setAnimationDuration(2)
lay.bounds.size = CGSize(100,100) // animation
```

A better alternative, perhaps, would be to use explicit layer animation (discussed in the next section) rather than implicit layer animation.

And now for a revelation. The "redraw moment" that I've spoken of earlier is actually the end of the current transaction:

- You set a view's background color; the displayed color of the background is changed when the transaction ends.

- You call setNeedsDisplay; draw(_:) is called when the transaction ends.

- You call setNeedsLayout; layout happens when the transaction ends.

- You order an animation; the animation starts when the transaction ends.

What's really happening is this. Your code runs within an implicit transaction. Your code comes to an end, and the transaction commits itself. It is then, as part of the transaction commit procedure, that the screen is updated: first layout, then drawing, then obedience to layer property changes, then the start of any animations. The animation server then continues operating on a background thread; it has kept a reference to the transaction, and calls its completion function, if any, when the animations are over.

 An explicit transaction block that orders an animation to a layer, if the block is *not preceded by any other changes to the layer*, can cause animation to begin immediately when the CATransaction class method commit is called, without waiting for the redraw moment, while your code continues running. In my experience, this can cause trouble (animation delegate messages cannot arrive, and the presentation layer can't be queried properly) and should be avoided.

Media Timing Functions

The CATransaction class method setAnimationTimingFunction(_:) takes as its parameter a media timing function (CAMediaTimingFunction). This is the Core Animation way of describing the same cubic Bézier timing curves I discussed earlier.

To specify a built-in timing curve, call the CAMediaTimingFunction initializer init(name:) with one of these parameters (CAMediaTimingFunctionName):

- .linear

- .easeIn

- .easeOut

- .easeInEaseOut

- .default

To define your own timing curve, supply the coordinates of the two Bézier control points by calling init(controlPoints:). Here we define the "clunk" timing curve and apply it to the rotation of the compass arrow:

```
let clunk = CAMediaTimingFunction(controlPoints: 0.9, 0.1, 0.7, 0.9)
CATransaction.setAnimationTimingFunction(clunk)
arrow.transform = CATransform3DRotate(arrow.transform, .pi/4.0, 0, 0, 1)
```

Core Animation

Core Animation is the fundamental underlying iOS animation technology. View animation and implicit layer animation are both merely convenient façades for Core Animation. Core Animation is *explicit layer animation*.

Core Animation is vastly more powerful than simple implicit layer animation. Also, it works on a view's underlying layer, so it's the only way to apply full-on layer property animation to a view, letting you transcend the limited repertoire of animatable view properties. On the other hand, animating a view's underlying layer with Core Animation is layer animation, not view animation, so you don't get any automatic layout of that view's subviews; that can be a reason for preferring view animation.

CABasicAnimation and Its Inheritance

The simplest way to animate a property with Core Animation is with a CABasic-Animation object. CABasicAnimation derives much of its power through its inheritance, so I'll describe that inheritance along with CABasicAnimation itself. You will readily see that all the property animation features we have met already are embodied in a CABasicAnimation instance:

CAAnimation
CAAnimation is an abstract class, meaning that you'll only ever use a subclass of it. Some of CAAnimation's powers come from its implementation of the CAMediaTiming protocol.

delegate
An adopter of the CAAnimationDelegate protocol. The delegate messages are:

- animationDidStart(_:)

- animationDidStop(_:finished:)

A CAAnimation instance *retains its delegate*; this is very unusual behavior and can cause trouble if you're not conscious of it (as I know all too well from experience). Alternatively, don't set a delegate; to make your code run after the animation ends, call the CATransaction class method set-CompletionBlock(_:) before configuring the animation.

duration, timingFunction

The length of the animation, and its timing function (a CAMediaTiming-Function). A duration of 0 (the default) means 0.25 seconds unless overridden by the transaction.

autoreverses, repeatCount, repeatDuration

For an infinite repeatCount, use Float.greatestFiniteMagnitude. The repeatDuration property is a different way to govern repetition, specifying how long the repetition should continue rather than how many repetitions should occur; don't specify both a repeatCount and a repeatDuration.

beginTime

The delay before the animation starts. To delay an animation with respect to now, call CACurrentMediaTime and add the desired delay in seconds. The delay does not eat into the animation's duration.

timeOffset

A shift in the animation's overall timing; looked at another way, specifies the starting frame of the "animation movie," which is treated as a loop. An animation with a duration of 8 and a time offset of 4 plays its second half followed by its first half.

CAAnimation, along with all its subclasses, implements key–value coding to allow you to set and retrieve a value for an arbitrary key, similar to CALayer (Chapter 3) and CATransaction.

CAPropertyAnimation

CAPropertyAnimation is a subclass of CAAnimation. It too is abstract, and adds the following:

keyPath

The all-important string specifying the CALayer key that is to be animated. Recall from Chapter 3 that CALayer properties are accessible through KVC keys; now we are using those keys! The convenience initializer init(key-Path:) creates the instance and assigns it a keyPath.

isAdditive

If true, the values supplied by the animation are added to the current presentation layer value.

isCumulative

> If `true`, a repeating animation starts each repetition where the previous repetition ended rather than jumping back to the start value.

valueFunction

> Converts a simple scalar value that you supply into a transform.

 There is no animatable CALayer key called `"frame"`. To animate a layer's frame using explicit layer animation, if both its `position` and `bounds` are to change, you must animate both. Similarly, you cannot use explicit layer animation to animate a layer's `affineTransform` property, because `affineTransform` is not a property (it's a pair of convenience methods); you must animate its `transform` instead. Attempting to form an animation with a key path of `"frame"` or `"affineTransform"` is a common beginner error.

CABasicAnimation

CABasicAnimation is a subclass (not abstract!) of CAPropertyAnimation. It adds the following:

fromValue, toValue

> The starting and ending values for the animation. These values must be Objective-C objects, so numbers and structs will have to be wrapped accordingly, using NSNumber and NSValue; fortunately, Swift will automatically take care of this for you. If neither `fromValue` nor `toValue` is provided, the former and current values of the property are used. If just one of them is provided, the other uses the current value of the property.

byValue

> Expresses one of the endpoint values as a *difference* from the other rather than in absolute terms. So you would supply a `byValue` instead of a `fromValue` or instead of a `toValue`, and the actual `fromValue` or `toValue` would be calculated for you by subtraction or addition with respect to the other value. If you supply *only* a `byValue`, the `fromValue` is the property's current value.

Using a CABasicAnimation

Having constructed and configured a CABasicAnimation, the way you order it to be performed is to *add it to a layer*. This is done with the CALayer instance method `add(_:forKey:)`. (I'll discuss the purpose of the `forKey:` parameter later; it's fine to ignore it and use `nil`, as I do in the examples that follow.)

But there's a slight twist. A CAAnimation is *merely* an animation; all it does is describe the hoops that the presentation layer is to jump through, the "animation movie" that is to be presented. It has no effect on the layer *itself*. If you naïvely create a CABasicAnimation and add it to a layer with add(_:forKey:), the animation happens and then the "animation movie" is whipped away to reveal the layer sitting there in exactly the same state as before. It is up to *you* to change the layer to match what the animation *will* ultimately portray. The converse, of course, is that you *don't* have to change the layer if it *doesn't* change as a result of the animation.

To ensure good results, start by taking a plodding, formulaic approach to the use of CABasicAnimation, like this:

1. Capture the start and end values for the layer property you're going to change, because you're likely to need these values in what follows.

2. Change the layer property to its end value, first calling setDisable-Actions(true) if necessary to prevent implicit animation.

3. Construct the explicit animation, using the start and end values you captured earlier, and with its keyPath corresponding to the layer property you just changed.

4. Add the explicit animation to the layer. An explicit animation is *copied* when it is added to a layer, and the copy added to the layer is immutable, so the animation must be configured beforehand.

Here's how you'd use this approach to animate our compass arrow rotation:

```
// capture the start and end values
let startValue = arrow.transform
let endValue = CATransform3DRotate(startValue, .pi/4.0, 0, 0, 1)
// change the layer, without implicit animation
CATransaction.setDisableActions(true)
arrow.transform = endValue
// construct the explicit animation
let anim = CABasicAnimation(keyPath:#keyPath(CALayer.transform))
anim.duration = 0.8
let clunk = CAMediaTimingFunction(controlPoints:0.9, 0.1, 0.7, 0.9)
anim.timingFunction = clunk
anim.fromValue = startValue
anim.toValue = endValue
// ask for the explicit animation
arrow.add(anim, forKey:nil)
```

Once you're comfortable with the full form, you will find that in many cases it can be condensed. When the fromValue and toValue are not set, the former and current values of the property are used automatically. (This magic is possible because, at the time the CABasicAnimation is added to the layer, the presentation layer still has the former value of the property, while the layer itself has the new value — and so the CABasicAnimation is able to retrieve them.) In our example, therefore, there is no need to set the fromValue and toValue, and no need to capture the start and end values beforehand. We can also omit disabling implicit animations, perhaps because the explicit animation of the transform cancels the implicit animation for us. Here's the condensed version:

```
arrow.transform = CATransform3DRotate(arrow.transform, .pi/4.0, 0, 0, 1)
let anim = CABasicAnimation(keyPath:#keyPath(CALayer.transform))
anim.duration = 0.8
let clunk = CAMediaTimingFunction(controlPoints:0.9, 0.1, 0.7, 0.9)
anim.timingFunction = clunk
arrow.add(anim, forKey:nil)
```

There's no need to change the layer if it doesn't change as a result of the animation. Let's make the compass arrow appear to vibrate rapidly, without ultimately changing its current orientation. To do this, we'll waggle it back and forth, using a repeated animation, between slightly clockwise from its current position and slightly counterclockwise from its current position. The "animation movie" neither starts nor stops at the current position of the arrow, but for this animation it doesn't matter, because it all happens so quickly as to appear natural:

```
// capture the start and end values
let nowValue = arrow.transform
let startValue = CATransform3DRotate(nowValue, .pi/40.0, 0, 0, 1)
let endValue = CATransform3DRotate(nowValue, -.pi/40.0, 0, 0, 1)
// construct the explicit animation
let anim = CABasicAnimation(keyPath:#keyPath(CALayer.transform))
anim.duration = 0.05
anim.timingFunction = CAMediaTimingFunction(name:.linear)
anim.repeatCount = 3
anim.autoreverses = true
anim.fromValue = startValue
anim.toValue = endValue
// ask for the explicit animation
arrow.add(anim, forKey:nil)
```

That code, too, can be shortened considerably from its full form. We can avoid calculating the new rotation values based on the arrow's current transform by setting our animation's isAdditive property to true; the animation's property values are then added to the existing property value for us (they are relative, not absolute). For a transform, "added" means "matrix-multiplied," so we can describe the waggle without any reference to the arrow's current rotation. Moreover, because our rotation is so simple (around a cardinal axis), we can take advantage of CAProperty-Animation's valueFunction; the animation's property values can then be simple scalars (in this case, angles), because the valueFunction tells the animation to interpret them as rotations around the z-axis:

```
let anim = CABasicAnimation(keyPath:#keyPath(CALayer.transform))
anim.duration = 0.05
anim.timingFunction = CAMediaTimingFunction(name:.linear)
anim.repeatCount = 3
anim.autoreverses = true
anim.isAdditive = true
```

```
anim.valueFunction = CAValueFunction(name:.rotateZ)
anim.fromValue = Float.pi/40
anim.toValue = -Float.pi/40
arrow.add(anim, forKey:nil)
```

 Instead of using a valueFunction, we could have set the animation's key path to "transform.rotation.z" to achieve the same effect. Apple advises against this, though, as it can result in mathematical trouble when there is more than one rotation.

Let's return once more to our arrow "clunk" rotation for another implementation, this time using the isAdditive and valueFunction properties. We set the arrow layer to its final transform at the outset, so when the time comes to configure the animation, its toValue, in isAdditive terms, will be 0; the fromValue will be its current value expressed *negatively*, like this:

```
let rot = CGFloat.pi/4.0
CATransaction.setDisableActions(true)
arrow.transform = CATransform3DRotate(arrow.transform, rot, 0, 0, 1)
// construct animation additively
let anim = CABasicAnimation(keyPath:#keyPath(CALayer.transform))
anim.duration = 0.8
let clunk = CAMediaTimingFunction(controlPoints:0.9, 0.1, 0.7, 0.9)
anim.timingFunction = clunk
anim.fromValue = -rot
anim.toValue = 0
anim.isAdditive = true
anim.valueFunction = CAValueFunction(name:.rotateZ)
arrow.add(anim, forKey:nil)
```

That is an interesting way of describing the animation; in effect, it expresses the animation in reverse, regarding the final position as correct and the current position as an aberration to be corrected. It also happens to be how additive view animations are rewritten behind the scenes, and explains their behavior.

Springing Animation

Springing animation is exposed at the Core Animation level through the CASpring-Animation class (a CABasicAnimation subclass). Its properties are the same as the parameters of the fullest form of the UISpringTimingParameters initializer, except that its initialVelocity is a CGFloat, not a CGVector. The duration is ignored, but don't omit it. The actual duration calculated from your specifications can be extracted as the settlingDuration property:

```
CATransaction.setDisableActions(true)
self.v.layer.position.y += 100
let anim = CASpringAnimation(keyPath: #keyPath(CALayer.position))
anim.damping = 0.7
anim.initialVelocity = 20
```

```
anim.mass = 0.04
anim.stiffness = 4
anim.duration = 1 // ignored, but you need to supply something
self.v.layer.add(anim, forKey: nil)
```

Keyframe Animation

Keyframe animation (CAKeyframeAnimation) is an alternative to basic animation (CABasicAnimation); they are both subclasses of CAPropertyAnimation, and they are used in similar ways. The difference is that you need to tell the keyframe animation what the keyframes are. In the simplest case, you can just set its `values` array. This tells the animation its starting value, its ending value, and some specific values through which it should pass on the way between them.

Here's a new version of our animation for waggling the compass arrow, expressing it as a keyframe animation. The stages include the start and end states along with eight alternating waggles in between, with the degree of waggle becoming progressively smaller:

```
var values = [0.0]
let directions = sequence(first:1) {$0 * -1}
let bases = stride(from: 20, to: 60, by: 5)
for (base, dir) in zip(bases, directions) {
    values.append(Double(dir) * .pi / Double(base))
}
values.append(0.0)
let anim = CAKeyframeAnimation(keyPath:#keyPath(CALayer.transform))
anim.values = values
anim.isAdditive = true
anim.valueFunction = CAValueFunction(name: .rotateZ)
arrow.add(anim, forKey:nil)
```

Here are some CAKeyframeAnimation properties:

`values`

> The array of values that the animation is to adopt, including the starting and ending value.

`timingFunctions`

> An array of timing functions, one for each stage of the animation (this array will be one element shorter than the `values` array).

`keyTimes`

> An array of times to accompany the array of values, defining when each value should be reached. The times start at 0 and are expressed as increasing fractions of 1, ending at 1.

calculationMode

Describes how the `values` are treated to create *all* the values through which the animation must pass (CAAnimationCalculationMode):

.linear

The default. A simple straight-line interpolation from value to value.

.cubic

Constructs a single smooth curve passing through all the values (and additional advanced properties, `tensionValues`, `continuityValues`, and `biasValues`, allow you to refine the curve).

.paced, .cubicPaced

The timing functions and key times are ignored, and the velocity is made constant through the whole animation.

.discrete

No interpolation: we jump directly to each value at the corresponding key time.

path

When you're animating a property whose values are pairs of floats (CGPoints), this is an alternative way of describing the values; instead of a `values` array, which must be interpolated to arrive at the intermediate values along the way, you supply the entire interpolation as a single CGPath. The points used to define the path are the keyframe values, so you can still apply timing functions and key times. If you're animating a position, the `rotationMode` property lets you ask the animated object to rotate so as to remain perpendicular to the path.

In this example, the `values` array is a sequence of five images (`self.images`) to be presented successively and repeatedly in a layer's `contents`, like the frames in a movie; the effect is similar to image animation, discussed earlier in this chapter:

```
let anim = CAKeyframeAnimation(keyPath:#keyPath(CALayer.contents))
anim.values = self.images.map {$0.cgImage!}
anim.keyTimes = [0.0, 0.25, 0.5, 0.75, 1.0]
anim.calculationMode = .discrete
anim.duration = 1.5
anim.repeatCount = .greatestFiniteMagnitude
self.sprite.add(anim, forKey:nil) // sprite is a CALayer
```

Making a Property Animatable

So far, we've been animating built-in animatable properties. If you define your own property on a CALayer subclass, you can easily make that property animatable through a CAPropertyAnimation. Here we animate the increase or decrease in a

CALayer subclass property called `thickness`, using essentially the pattern for explicit animation that we've already developed:

```
let lay = self.v.layer as! MyLayer
let cur = lay.thickness
let val : CGFloat = cur == 10 ? 0 : 10
lay.thickness = val
let ba = CABasicAnimation(keyPath:#keyPath(MyLayer.thickness))
ba.fromValue = cur
lay.add(ba, forKey:nil)
```

To make our layer responsive to such a command, it needs a `thickness` property (obviously), and it must return `true` from the class method `needsDisplay(forKey:)` for this property:

```
class MyLayer : CALayer {
    @objc var thickness : CGFloat = 0
    override class func needsDisplay(forKey key: String) -> Bool {
        if key == #keyPath(thickness) {
            return true
        }
        return super.needsDisplay(forKey:key)
    }
}
```

Returning `true` from `needsDisplay(forKey:)` causes this layer to be redisplayed repeatedly as the `thickness` property changes. So if we want to *see* the animation, this layer also needs to draw itself in some way that depends on the `thickness` property. Here, I'll implement the layer's `draw(in:)` to make `thickness` the thickness of the black border around a red rectangle:

```
override func draw(in con: CGContext) {
    let r = self.bounds.insetBy(dx:20, dy:20)
    con.setFillColor(UIColor.red.cgColor)
    con.fill(r)
    con.setLineWidth(self.thickness)
    con.stroke(r)
}
```

At every frame of the animation, `draw(in:)` is called, and because the `thickness` value differs at each step, the rectangle's border appears animated.

We have made MyLayer's `thickness` property animatable when using explicit layer animation, but it would be even cooler to make it animatable when using implicit layer animation (that is, when setting `lay.thickness` directly). Later in this chapter, I'll show how to do that.

No law says that we *have* to draw. Consider layer animation more abstractly as a way of getting the runtime to calculate and send us a series of *timed interpolated values*. Those values arrive through the runtime repeatedly calling our draw(in:), but we are free to use them however we like.

Grouped Animations

A grouped animation (CAAnimationGroup) combines multiple animations — its animations, an array of animations — into a single animation. By delaying and timing the various component animations, complex effects can be achieved.

A CAAnimationGroup is a CAAnimation subclass, so it has a duration and other animation features. Think of the CAAnimationGroup as the parent, and its animations as its children. The children *inherit* default property values from their parent. If you don't set a child's duration explicitly, for instance, it will inherit the parent's duration.

Let's use a grouped animation to construct a sequence where the compass arrow rotates and then waggles. This requires very little modification of code we've already written. We express the first animation in its full form, with explicit fromValue and toValue. We postpone the second animation using its beginTime property; notice that we express this in relative terms, as a number of seconds into the parent's duration, not with respect to CACurrentMediaTime. Finally, we set the overall parent duration to the sum of the child durations, so that it can embrace both of them (failing to do this, and then wondering why some child animations never occur, is a common beginner error):

```
// capture current value, set final value
let rot = .pi/4.0
CATransaction.setDisableActions(true)
let current = arrow.value(forKeyPath:"transform.rotation.z") as! Double
arrow.setValue(current + rot, forKeyPath:"transform.rotation.z")
// first animation (rotate and clunk)
let anim1 = CABasicAnimation(keyPath:#keyPath(CALayer.transform))
anim1.duration = 0.8
let clunk = CAMediaTimingFunction(controlPoints:0.9, 0.1, 0.7, 0.9)
anim1.timingFunction = clunk
anim1.fromValue = current
anim1.toValue = current + rot
anim1.valueFunction = CAValueFunction(name:.rotateZ)
// second animation (waggle)
var values = [0.0]
let directions = sequence(first:1) {$0 * -1}
let bases = stride(from: 20, to: 60, by: 5)
for (base, dir) in zip(bases, directions) {
    values.append(Double(dir) * .pi / Double(base))
}
values.append(0.0)
```

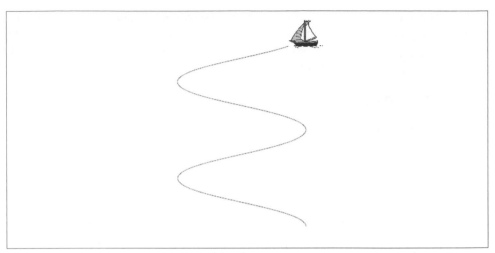

Figure 4-3. A boat and the course she'll sail

```
let anim2 = CAKeyframeAnimation(keyPath:#keyPath(CALayer.transform))
anim2.values = values
anim2.duration = 0.25
anim2.isAdditive = true
anim2.beginTime = anim1.duration - 0.1
anim2.valueFunction = CAValueFunction(name: .rotateZ)
// group
let group = CAAnimationGroup()
group.animations = [anim1, anim2]
group.duration = anim1.duration + anim2.duration
arrow.add(group, forKey:nil)
```

In that example, I grouped two animations that animated the *same* property *sequentially*. Now let's do the opposite: we'll group some animations that animate *different* properties *simultaneously*.

I have a small view (`self.v`), located near the top-right corner of the screen, whose layer contents are a picture of a sailboat facing to the left. I'll "sail" the boat in a curving path, both down the screen and left and right across the screen, like an extended letter "S" (Figure 4-3). Each time the boat comes to a vertex of the curve, changing direction across the screen, I'll flip the boat so that it faces the way it's about to move. At the same time, I'll constantly rock the boat, so that it always appears to be pitching a little on the waves.

Here's the first animation, the movement of the boat (its `position`) along its curving path. It illustrates the use of a CAKeyframeAnimation with a CGPath; once we've calculated the path, we know the final position of the boat, and we set it so the boat won't jump back to the start afterward. The `calculationMode` of `.paced` ensures an even speed over the whole path. We don't set an explicit duration because we want to adopt the duration of the group:

```
let h : CGFloat = 200
let v : CGFloat = 75
let path = CGMutablePath()
var leftright : CGFloat = 1
var next : CGPoint = self.v.layer.position
var pos : CGPoint
path.move(to:CGPoint(next.x, next.y))
for _ in 0 ..< 4 {
    pos = next
    leftright *= -1
    next = CGPoint(pos.x+h*leftright, pos.y+v)
    path.addCurve(to:CGPoint(next.x, next.y),
        control1: CGPoint(pos.x, pos.y+30),
        control2: CGPoint(next.x, next.y-30))
}
CATransaction.setDisableActions(true)
self.v.layer.position = next
let anim1 = CAKeyframeAnimation(keyPath:#keyPath(CALayer.position))
anim1.path = path
anim1.calculationMode = .paced
```

Here's the second animation, the reversal of the direction the boat is facing. This is simply a rotation around the y-axis. It's another CAKeyframeAnimation, but we make no attempt at visually animating this reversal: the calculationMode is .discrete, so that the boat image reversal is a sudden change, as in our earlier "sprite" example. There is one less value than the number of points in our first animation's path, and the first animation has an even speed, so the reversals take place at each curve apex with no further effort on our part. (If the pacing were more complicated, we could give both the first and the second animation identical keyTimes arrays, to coordinate them.) Once again, we don't set an explicit duration:

```
let revs = [0.0, .pi, 0.0, .pi]
let anim2 = CAKeyframeAnimation(keyPath:#keyPath(CALayer.transform))
anim2.values = revs
anim2.valueFunction = CAValueFunction(name:.rotateY)
anim2.calculationMode = .discrete
```

Here's the third animation, the rocking of the boat. It has a short duration, and repeats indefinitely:

```
let pitches = [0.0, .pi/60,0, 0.0, -.pi/60,0, 0.0]
let anim3 = CAKeyframeAnimation(keyPath:#keyPath(CALayer.transform))
anim3.values = pitches
anim3.repeatCount = .greatestFiniteMagnitude
anim3.duration = 0.5
anim3.isAdditive = true
anim3.valueFunction = CAValueFunction(name:.rotateZ)
```

Finally, we combine the three animations, assigning the group an explicit duration that will be adopted by the first two animations:

```
let group = CAAnimationGroup()
group.animations = [anim1, anim2, anim3]
group.duration = 8
self.v.layer.add(group, forKey:nil)
```

Here are some further CAAnimation properties (from the CAMediaTiming protocol) that come into play especially when animations are grouped:

speed
> The ratio between a child's timescale and the parent's timescale. If a parent and child have the same duration, but the child's speed is 1.5, the child's animation runs one-and-a-half times as fast as the parent.

fillMode
> Suppose the child animation begins after the parent animation, or ends before the parent animation, or both. What should happen to the appearance of the property being animated, outside the child animation's boundaries? The answer depends on the child's fillMode (CAMediaTimingFillMode):

> .removed
> > The child animation is removed, revealing the layer property at its actual current value whenever the child is not running.

> .forwards
> > The final presentation layer value of the child animation remains afterward.

> .backwards
> > The initial presentation layer value of the child animation appears right from the start.

> .both
> > Combines the previous two.

Freezing an Animation

An animation can be frozen using Core Animation at the level of the animation or of the layer, with an effect similar to what we did with a property animator earlier.

This feature depends upon the fact that the CAMediaTiming protocol is adopted by CALayer. CAMediaTiming properties of a layer affect the behavior of any animation attached to that layer. The speed property effectively changes the animation's duration: a speed of 2 means that a 10-second animation plays in 5 seconds, and a speed of 0 means the animation is frozen. When the animation is frozen, the timeOffset property dictates what frame of the animation is displayed.

To illustrate, let's explore the animatable `path` property of a CAShapeLayer. Consider a layer that can display a rectangle or an ellipse *or any of the intermediate shapes between them.* I can't imagine what the notion of an intermediate shape between a rectangle or an ellipse may mean, let alone how to draw such an intermediate shape; but thanks to frozen animations, I don't have to. Here, I'll construct the CAShapeLayer, add it to the interface, give it an animation from a rectangle to an ellipse, and keep a reference to it as a property:

```
let shape = CAShapeLayer()
shape.frame = v.bounds
v.layer.addSublayer(shape)
shape.fillColor = UIColor.clear.cgColor
shape.strokeColor = UIColor.red.cgColor
let path = CGPath(rect:shape.bounds, transform:nil)
shape.path = path
let path2 = CGPath(ellipseIn:shape.bounds, transform:nil)
let ba = CABasicAnimation(keyPath:#keyPath(CAShapeLayer.path))
ba.duration = 1
ba.fromValue = path
ba.toValue = path2
shape.speed = 0
shape.timeOffset = 0
shape.add(ba, forKey: nil)
self.shape = shape
```

I've added the animation to the layer, but I've also set the layer's `speed` to 0, so no animation takes place; the rectangle is displayed and that's all. As in my earlier example, there's a UISlider in the interface. I'll respond to the user changing the value of the slider by setting the frame of the animation:

```
self.shape.timeOffset = Double(slider.value)
```

Transitions

A layer transition is an animation involving two "copies" of a single layer, in which the second "copy" appears to replace the first. It is described by an instance of CATransition (a CAAnimation subclass), which has these chief properties specifying the animation:

`type`
> Your choices are (CATransitionType):

> - `.fade`
> - `.moveIn`
> - `.push`
> - `.reveal`

Figure 4-4. A push transition

subtype

> If the `type` is not `.fade`, your choices are (CATransitionSubtype):
>
> - `.fromRight`
> - `.fromLeft`
> - `.fromTop`
> - `.fromBottom`

 For historical reasons, the terms `bottom` and `top` in the names of the `subtype` settings have the opposite of their expected meanings. Reverse them in your mind: when you mean the top, say `.fromBottom`.

Consider first what happens when we perform a layer transition without changing anything else about the layer:

```
let t = CATransition()
t.type = .push
t.subtype = .fromBottom
t.duration = 2
lay.add(t, forKey: nil)
```

The entire layer exits moving down from its original place while fading away, and another copy of the very same layer enters moving down from above while fading in. If, at the same time, we change something about the layer's contents, then the old contents will appear to exit downward while the new contents appear to enter from above:

```
// ... configure the transition as before ...
CATransaction.setDisableActions(true)
lay.contents = UIImage(named: "Smiley")!.cgImage
lay.add(t, forKey: nil)
```

Typically, the layer that is to be transitioned will be inside a superlayer that has the same size and whose `masksToBounds` is `true`. This confines the visible transition to the bounds of the layer itself. (Otherwise, the entering and exiting versions of the layer are visible outside the layer.) In Figure 4-4, which shows a smiley face pushing an image of Mars out of the layer, I've emphasized this arrangement by giving the superlayer a border as well.

A transition on a superlayer can happen simultaneously with animation of a sublayer. The animation will be seen to occur on the second "copy" of the layer as it moves into position. This is analogous to the `.allowAnimatedContent` option for a view animation.

Animations List

To understand how CALayer's `add(_:forKey:)` actually works (and what the "key" is), you need to know about a layer's *animations list*.

An animation is an object (a CAAnimation) that modifies how a layer is drawn. It does this merely by being attached to the layer; the layer's drawing mechanism does the rest. A layer maintains a list of animations that are currently in force. To add an animation to this list, you call `add(_:forKey:)`. When the time comes to draw itself, the layer looks through its animations list and draws itself in accordance with whatever animations it finds there. (The list of things the layer must do in order to draw itself is sometimes referred to by the documentation as the *render tree*.) The order in which animations were added to the list is the order in which they are applied.

The animations list behaves somewhat like a dictionary. An animation has a key — the `forKey:` parameter in `add(_:forKey:)`. If an animation with a certain key is added to the list when an animation with that key is already in the list, the one that is already in the list is removed. So *only one animation with a given key* can be in the list at a time; I call this the *exclusivity rule*.

The exclusivity rule explains why ordering an animation can sometimes cancel an animation already ordered or in-flight: the two animations had the same key, so the first one was removed. (Additive view animations affecting the same property work around this limitation by giving the additional animations a *different key name* — for example, `"position"` and `"position-2"`.)

Unlike a dictionary, the animations list will also accept an animation with *no key* — the key is `nil`. Animations with a `nil` key are *not* subject to the exclusivity rule; there can be more than one animation in the list with no key.

The `forKey:` parameter in `add(_:forKey:)` is *not a property name*. It *could* be a property name, but it can be any arbitrary value. Its purpose is to enforce the exclusivity rule. It does *not* have any meaning with regard to what property a CAProperty-Animation animates; that is the job of the animation's `keyPath`. (Apple's use of the term "key" in `add(_:forKey:)` is misleading; I wish they had named this method something like `add(_:identifier:)`.)

Nevertheless, a relationship between the "key" in `add(_:forKey:)` and the `keyPath` of a CAPropertyAnimation does exist: if a CAPropertyAnimation's `keyPath` is `nil` at the time that it is added to a layer with `add(_:forKey:)`, that `keyPath` is set to the value of the `forKey:` parameter! Therefore you can *misuse* the `forKey:` parameter in `add(_:forKey:)` as a way of specifying what `keyPath` an animation animates — and implicit layer animation crucially depends on this fact.

 Many Core Animation examples *do* misuse `forKey:` in just that way, supplying `nil` as the animation's `keyPath` and specifying the property to be animated as the "key" in `add(_:forKey:)`. This is *wrong!* Set the animation's `keyPath` explicitly.

You can use the exclusivity rule to your own advantage, to keep your code from stepping on its own feet. Some code of yours might add an animation to the list using a certain key; then later, some other code might come along and correct this, removing that animation and replacing it with another. By using the same key, the second code is easily able to override the first: "You may have been given some other animation with this key, but throw it away; play this one instead."

In some cases, the key you supply is ignored and a different key is substituted. In particular, the key with which a CATransition is added to the list is always `"transition"` — and so there can be only one transition animation in the list.

You can think of an animation in a layer's animations list as being the "animation movie" I spoke of at the start of this chapter. As long as an animation is in the list, the movie is present, either waiting to be played or actually playing. An animation that has finished playing is, in general, pointless; the animation should now be removed from the list, as its presence serves no purpose and it imposes an extra burden on the render tree. Therefore, an animation has an `isRemovedOnCompletion` property, which defaults to `true`: when the "movie" is over, the animation removes itself from the list.

 Many Core Animation examples set `isRemovedOnCompletion` to `false` and set the animation's `fillMode` to `.forwards` or `.both` as a lazy way of preventing a property from jumping back to its initial value when the animation ends. This is *wrong!* An animation needs to be removed when it is completed; the `fillMode` is intended for use with a child animation within a grouped animation. To prevent jumping at the end of the animation, set the animated property value to match the final frame of the animation.

You can't access the entire animations list directly. You can access the key names of the animations in the list, with `animationKeys`; and you can obtain or remove an animation with a certain key, with `animation(forKey:)` and `removeAnimation(forKey:)`; but animations with a `nil` key are inaccessible. You can remove all animations, including animations with a `nil` key, using `removeAllAnimations`. When your app is suspended, `removeAllAnimations` is called on all layers for you; that is why it is possible to suspend an app coherently in the middle of an animation.

If an animation is in-flight when you remove it from the animations list, it will stop; but that doesn't happen until the next redraw moment. If you need an animation to be removed immediately, you might be able to make that happen by wrapping the `remove` call in an explicit transaction block.

Actions

For the sake of completeness, I will explain how implicit animation really works — that is, how implicit animation is turned into explicit animation behind the scenes. The basis of implicit animation is the *action mechanism*. Your code can hook into the action mechanism to *change* the behavior of implicit animation in interesting ways. Feel free to skip this section if you don't want to get into the under-the-hood nitty-gritty of implicit animation.

What an Action Is

An *action* is an object that adopts the CAAction protocol. This means simply that it implements `run(forKey:object:arguments:)`. The action object could do *anything* in response to this message. The notion of an action is completely general. The only built-in class that adopts the CAAction protocol happens to be CAAnimation, but in fact the action object doesn't have to be an animation — it doesn't even have to perform an animation.

You would never send `run(forKey:object:arguments:)` to an object directly. Rather, this message is sent to an action object for you, as the basis of implicit animation. The `key` is the property that was set, and the `object` is the layer whose property was set.

What an animation does when it receives `run(forKey:object:arguments:)` is to assume that the `object:` is a layer, and to add itself to that layer's animations list. For an animation, receiving the `run(forKey:object:arguments:)` message is like being told: "Play yourself!"

Recall that if an animation's `keyPath` is `nil`, the key by which the animation is assigned to a layer's animations list is used as the `keyPath`. When an animation is sent `run(forKey:object:arguments:)`, it calls `add(_:forKey:)` to add itself to the layer's animation's list, *using the name of the property as the key*. The animation's `keyPath` for an implicit layer animation is usually `nil`, so the animation's `keyPath` winds up being set to the same key! That is how the property that you set ends up being the property that is animated.

Action Search

Now we know what a CAAction is. But what's the connection between a CALayer and a CAAction? It all starts with the CALayer instance method `action(forKey:)`. The following events cause a layer's `action(forKey:)` method to be called:

- A CALayer property is set, directly or using setValue(_:forKey:). For most built-in properties, the layer's response is to call action(forKey:), passing along the name of the property as the key. Certain properties get special treatment:
  - Setting a layer's frame property sets its position and bounds and calls action(forKey:) for the "position" and "bounds" keys.
  - Calling a layer's setAffineTransform(_:) method sets its transform and calls action(forKey:) for the "transform" key.
  - You can configure a custom property to call action(forKey:) by designating it as @NSManaged, as I'll demonstrate later in this chapter.
- The layer is sent setValue(_:forKey:) with a key that is *not* a property, because CALayer's setValue(_:forUndefinedKey:), by default, calls action(forKey:).
- Various other miscellaneous types of event take place, such as the layer being added to the interface. I'll give some examples later.

All of that presupposes that CATransaction.disableActions() is false. If CATransaction.setDisableActions(true) has been called, it *prevents* the action(forKey:) message from being sent, and that's the end of the story: there can be no implicit animation in this transaction.

Very well, but let's say that a layer's action(forKey:) *is* called. The layer now embarks upon an elaborate search for an action object (a CAAction) to which it can send the run(forKey:object:arguments:) message. This is the *action search*.

At each stage of the action search, the following rules are obeyed regarding what is returned from that stage of the search:

An action object
> If an action object is produced, that is the end of the search. The action mechanism sends that action object the run(forKey:object:arguments:) message; if this an animation, the animation responds by adding itself to the layer's animations list.

NSNull()
> If NSNull() is produced, that is the end of the search. There will be no implicit animation; NSNull() means, "Do nothing and stop searching."

nil
> If nil is produced, the search continues to the next stage.

The action search proceeds by stages:

1. The layer's action(forKey:) might terminate the search before it even starts. The layer will do this if it is the underlying layer of a view, or if the layer is not part of a window's layer hierarchy; there should be no implicit animation, so the

whole mechanism is nipped in the bud. (This stage is special in that a returned value of `nil` ends the search and no animation takes place.)

2. If the layer has a delegate that implements `action(for:forKey:)`, that message is sent to the delegate, with this layer as the first parameter and the property name as the key. If an action object or `NSNull()` is returned, the search ends.

3. The layer has a property called `actions`, which is a dictionary. If there is an entry in this dictionary with the given key, that value is used, and the search ends.

4. The layer has a property called `style`, which is a dictionary. If there is an entry in this dictionary with the key `actions`, it is assumed to be a dictionary; if this `actions` dictionary has an entry with the given key, that value is used, and the search ends. Otherwise, if there is an entry in the `style` dictionary called `style`, the same search is performed within it, and so on recursively until either an `actions` entry with the given key is found (the search ends) or there are no more `style` entries (the search continues).

   (If the `style` dictionary sounds profoundly weird, that's because it is profoundly weird. It is actually a special case of a larger, separate mechanism, which is also profoundly weird, having to do not with actions, but with a CALayer's implementation of KVC. When you call `value(forKey:)` on a layer, if the key is undefined by the layer itself, the `style` dictionary is consulted. I have never written or seen code that uses this mechanism for anything.)

5. The layer's class is sent `defaultAction(forKey:)`, with the property name as the key. If an action object or `NSNull()` is returned, the search ends.

6. If the search reaches this last stage, a default animation is supplied, as appropriate. For a property animation, this is a plain vanilla CABasicAnimation.

Hooking Into the Action Search

You can affect the action search at any of its various stages to modify what happens when the search is triggered. This is where the fun begins!

You can turn off implicit animation just for a particular property. One way would be to return `nil` from `action(forKey:)` itself, in a CALayer subclass. Here's the code for a CALayer subclass that doesn't have implicit animation for its `position` property:

```
override func action(forKey key: String) -> CAAction? {
    if key == #keyPath(position) {
        return nil
    }
    return super.action(forKey:key)
}
```

For more precise control, we can take advantage of the fact that a CALayer acts like a dictionary, allowing us to set an arbitrary key's value. We'll embed a switch in our CALayer subclass that we can use to turn implicit `position` animation on and off:

```
override func action(forKey key: String) -> CAAction? {
    if key == #keyPath(position) {
        if self.value(forKey:"suppressPositionAnimation") != nil {
            return nil
        }
    }
    return super.action(forKey:key)
}
```

To turn off implicit `position` animation for an instance of this layer, we set its `"suppressPositionAnimation"` key to a non-`nil` value:

```
layer.setValue(true, forKey:"suppressPositionAnimation")
```

Another possibility is to intervene at some stage of the search to produce an action object of your own. You would then be affecting how implicit animation behaves. Let's say we want a certain layer's duration for an implicit `position` animation to be 5 seconds. We can achieve this with a minimally configured animation, like this:

```
let ba = CABasicAnimation()
ba.duration = 5
```

The idea now is to situate this animation where it will be produced by the action search for the `"position"` key. We could, for instance, put it into the layer's `actions` dictionary:

```
layer.actions = ["position": ba]
```

The only property of this animation that we have set is its duration; that setting, however, is final. Although animation properties that you don't set can be set through CATransaction, in the usual manner for implicit property animation, animation properties that you *do* set *can't* be overridden through CATransaction. When we set this layer's `position`, if an implicit animation results, its duration is 5 seconds, even if we try to change it through CATransaction:

```
CATransaction.setAnimationDuration(1.5) // won't work
layer.position = CGPoint(100,100) // animated, takes 5 seconds
```

Storing an animation in the `actions` dictionary is a somewhat inflexible way to hook into the action search. If we have to write our animation beforehand, we know nothing about the layer's starting and ending values for the changed property. A much more powerful approach is to make our action object a custom CAAction object — because in that case, it will be sent `run(forKey:...)`, and we can construct and run an animation *now*, when we are in direct contact with the layer to be animated. Here's a barebones version of such an object:

```
class MyAction : NSObject, CAAction {
    func run(forKey event: String, object anObject: Any,
        arguments dict: [AnyHashable : Any]?) {
            let anim = CABasicAnimation(keyPath: event)
            anim.duration = 5
            let lay = anObject as! CALayer
            let newP = lay.value(forKey:event)
            let oldP = lay.presentation()!.value(forKey:event)
            lay.add(anim, forKey:nil)
    }
}
```

A MyAction instance might then be the action object that we store in the `actions` dictionary:

```
layer.actions = ["position": MyAction()]
```

Our custom CAAction object, MyAction, doesn't do anything very interesting — but it could. That's the point. As the code demonstrates, we have access to the name of the animated property (`event`), the old value of that property (from the layer's presentation layer), and the new value of that property (from the layer itself). That's enough information to build a complete animation from the ground up and add it to the layer.

Here's a modification of our MyAction object that creates and runs a keyframe animation that "waggles" as it goes from the start value to the end value:

```
class MyWagglePositionAction : NSObject, CAAction {
    func run(forKey event: String, object anObject: Any,
        arguments dict: [AnyHashable : Any]?) {
            let lay = anObject as! CALayer
            let newP = lay.value(forKey:event) as! CGPoint
            let oldP = lay.presentation()!.value(forKey:event) as! CGPoint
            let d = sqrt(pow(oldP.x - newP.x, 2) + pow(oldP.y - newP.y, 2))
            let r = Double(d/3.0)
            let theta = Double(atan2(newP.y - oldP.y, newP.x - oldP.x))
            let wag = 10 * .pi/180.0
            let p1 = CGPoint(
                oldP.x + CGFloat(r*cos(theta+wag)),
                oldP.y + CGFloat(r*sin(theta+wag)))
            let p2 = CGPoint(
                oldP.x + CGFloat(r*2*cos(theta-wag)),
                oldP.y + CGFloat(r*2*sin(theta-wag)))
            let anim = CAKeyframeAnimation(keyPath: event)
            anim.values = [oldP,p1,p2,newP]
            anim.calculationMode = .cubic
            lay.add(anim, forKey:nil)
    }
}
```

By adding this CAAction object to a layer's `actions` dictionary under the `"position"` key, we have created a CALayer that waggles when its `position` property is set. Our

CAAction doesn't set the animation's `duration`, so our own call to CATransaction's `setAnimationDuration(_:)` works. The power of this mechanism is simply staggering. We can modify *any* layer in this way — even one that doesn't belong to us. (And we don't actually have to add an animation to the layer; we are free to interpret the setting of this property however we like!)

Instead of modifying a layer's `actions` dictionary, we could hook into the action search by setting the layer's delegate to an instance that responds to `action(for:forKey:)`. The delegate can behave differently depending on what key this is (and even what *layer* this is). Here's an implementation that does exactly what the `actions` dictionary did — it returns an instance of our custom CAAction object, so that setting the layer's position waggles it into place:

```
func action(for layer: CALayer, forKey key: String) -> CAAction? {
    if key == #keyPath(CALayer.position) {
        return MyWagglePositionAction()
    }
}
```

Finally, I'll demonstrate overriding `defaultAction(forKey:)`. This code would go into a CALayer subclass; setting this layer's `contents` will automatically trigger a push transition from the left:

```
override class func defaultAction(forKey key: String) -> CAAction? {
    if key == #keyPath(contents) {
        let tr = CATransition()
        tr.type = .push
        tr.subtype = .fromLeft
        return tr
    }
    return super.defaultAction(forKey:key)
}
```

 Both the delegate's `action(for:forKey:)` and the subclass's `defaultAction(forKey:)` are declared as returning a `CAAction`. Therefore, to return `NSNull()` from your implementation of one of these methods, you'll need to cast it to `CAAction` to quiet the compiler; you're lying (NSNull does not adopt CAAction), but it doesn't matter.

Making a Custom Property Implicitly Animatable

Earlier in this chapter, we made a custom layer's `thickness` property animatable through explicit layer animation. Now that we know how implicit layer animation works, we can make our layer's `thickness` property animatable through implicit animation as well. We will then be able to animate our layer's thickness with code like this:

```
let lay = self.v.layer as! MyLayer
let cur = lay.thickness
let val : CGFloat = cur == 10 ? 0 : 10
lay.thickness = val // implicit animation
```

We have already implemented `needsDisplay(forKey:)` to return `true` for the "thickness" key, and we have provided an appropriate `draw(in:)` implementation. Now we'll add two further pieces of the puzzle. As we now know, to make our MyLayer class respond to direct setting of a property, we need to hook into the action search and return a CAAction. The obvious place to do this is in the layer itself, at the very start of the action search, in an `action(forKey:)` implementation:

```
override func action(forKey key: String) -> CAAction? {
    if key == #keyPath(thickness) {
        let ba = CABasicAnimation(keyPath: key)
        ba.fromValue = self.presentation()!.value(forKey:key)
        return ba
    }
    return super.action(forKey:key)
}
```

Finally, we must declare MyLayer's `thickness` property `@NSManaged`. Otherwise, `action(forKey:)` won't be called in the first place and the action search will never happen:

```
class MyLayer : CALayer {
    @NSManaged var thickness : CGFloat
    // ...
}
```

 The `@NSManaged` declaration invites Cocoa to generate and dynamically inject getter and setter accessors into our layer class; it is the equivalent of Objective-C's `@dynamic` (and is completely different from Swift's `dynamic`).

Nonproperty Actions

An action search is triggered when a layer is added to a superlayer (key `"onOrderIn"`) and when a layer's sublayers are changed by adding or removing a sublayer (key `"sublayers"`).

In this example, we use our layer's delegate so that when our layer is added to a superlayer, it will "pop" into view:

```
let layer = CALayer()
// ... configure layer here ...
layer.delegate = self
self.view.layer.addSublayer(layer)
```

In the layer's delegate (`self`), we implement the actual animation as a group animation, fading the layer quickly in from an opacity of 0 and at the same time scaling its transform to make it momentarily appear a little larger:

```
func action(for layer: CALayer, forKey key: String) -> CAAction? {
    if key == "onOrderIn" {
        let anim1 = CABasicAnimation(keyPath:#keyPath(CALayer.opacity))
        anim1.fromValue = 0.0
        anim1.toValue = layer.opacity
        let anim2 = CABasicAnimation(keyPath:#keyPath(CALayer.transform))
        anim2.toValue = CATransform3DScale(layer.transform, 1.2, 1.2, 1.0)
        anim2.autoreverses = true
        anim2.duration = 0.1
        let group = CAAnimationGroup()
        group.animations = [anim1, anim2]
        group.duration = 0.2
        return group
    }
}
```

The documentation says that when a layer is removed from a superlayer, an action is sought under the key `"onOrderOut"`. This is true but useless, because by the time the action is sought, the layer has already been removed from the superlayer, so returning an animation has no visible effect. A possible workaround is to trigger the animation in some other way (and remove the layer afterward, if desired). To illustrate, let's implement an arbitrary key `"farewell"` so that it shrinks and fades the layer and then removes it from its superlayer:

```
layer.delegate = self
layer.setValue("", forKey:"farewell")
```

The supplier of the action object — in this case, the layer's delegate — returns the shrink-and-fade animation; it also sets itself as that animation's delegate, and removes the layer when the animation ends:

```
func action(for layer: CALayer, forKey key: String) -> CAAction? {
    if key == "farewell" {
        let anim1 = CABasicAnimation(keyPath:#keyPath(CALayer.opacity))
        anim1.fromValue = layer.opacity
        anim1.toValue = 0.0
        let anim2 = CABasicAnimation(keyPath:#keyPath(CALayer.transform))
        anim2.toValue = CATransform3DScale(layer.transform, 0.1, 0.1, 1.0)
        let group = CAAnimationGroup()
        group.animations = [anim1, anim2]
        group.duration = 0.2
        group.delegate = self
        group.setValue(layer, forKey:"remove")
        layer.opacity = 0
        return group
    }
}
```

```
func animationDidStop(_ anim: CAAnimation, finished flag: Bool) {
    if let layer = anim.value(forKey:"remove") as? CALayer {
        layer.removeFromSuperlayer()
    }
}
```

Emitter Layers

Emitter layers (CAEmitterLayer) are, to some extent, on a par with animated images: once you've set up an emitter layer, it just sits there animating all by itself. The nature of this animation is rather narrow: an emitter layer emits particles, which are CAEmitterCell instances. But by clever setting of the properties of an emitter layer and its emitter cells, you can achieve some astonishing effects. Moreover, the animation is itself animatable using Core Animation.

Here are some basic properties of a CAEmitterCell:

contents, contentsRect
> These are modeled after the eponymous CALayer properties, although CAEmitterCell is not a CALayer subclass; so, respectively, an image (a CGImage) and a CGRect specifying a region of that image. They define the image that a cell will portray.

birthrate, lifetime
> How many cells per second should be emitted, and how many seconds each cell should live before vanishing, respectively.

velocity
> The speed at which a cell moves. The unit of measurement is not documented; perhaps it's points per second.

emissionLatitude, emissionLongitude
> The angle at which the cell is emitted from the emitter, as a variation from the perpendicular. Longitude is an angle within the plane; latitude is an angle out of the plane.

Here's some code to create a very elementary emitter cell:

```
// make a gray circle image
let r = UIGraphicsImageRenderer(size:CGSize(10,10))
let im = r.image {
    ctx in let con = ctx.cgContext
    con.addEllipse(in:CGRect(0,0,10,10))
    con.setFillColor(UIColor.gray.cgColor)
    con.fillPath()
}
// make a cell with that image
let cell = CAEmitterCell()
cell.contentsScale = UIScreen.main.scale
```

```
cell.birthRate = 5
cell.lifetime = 1
cell.velocity = 100
cell.contents = im.cgImage
```

The result is that little gray circles should be emitted slowly and steadily, five per second, each one vanishing in one second. Now we need an emitter layer from which these circles are to be emitted. Here are some basic CAEmitterLayer properties (beyond those it inherits from CALayer); these define an imaginary object, an emitter, that will be producing the emitter cells:

emitterPosition
: The point at which the emitter should be located, in superlayer coordinates. You can optionally add a third dimension to this point, emitterZPosition.

emitterSize
: The size of the emitter.

emitterShape
: The shape of the emitter. The dimensions of the shape depend on the emitter's size; the cuboid shape depends also on a third size dimension, emitterDepth. Your choices are (CAEmitterLayerEmitterShape):

- .point
- .line
- .rectangle
- .cuboid
- .circle
- .sphere

emitterMode
: The region of the shape from which cells should be emitted. Your choices are (CAEmitterLayerEmitterMode):

- .points
- .outline
- .surface
- .volume

Let's start with the simplest possible case, a single point emitter:

```
let emit = CAEmitterLayer()
emit.emitterPosition = CGPoint(30,100)
emit.emitterShape = .point
emit.emitterMode = .points
```

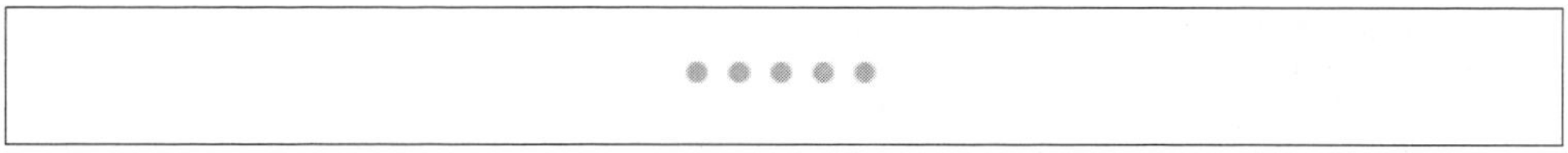

Figure 4-5. A really boring emitter layer

We tell the emitter what types of cell to emit by assigning those cells to its `emitter-Cells` property (an array of CAEmitterCell). We then add the emitter to our interface, and presto, it starts emitting:

```
emit.emitterCells = [cell]
self.view.layer.addSublayer(emit)
```

The result is a constant stream of gray circles emitted from the point (`30.0,100.0`), each circle marching steadily to the right and vanishing after one second (Figure 4-5).

Now that we've succeeded in creating a boring emitter layer, we can start to vary some parameters. The `emissionRange` defines a cone in which cells will be emitted; if we increase the `birthRate` and widen the `emissionRange`, we get something that looks like a stream shooting from a water hose:

```
cell.birthRate = 100
cell.lifetime = 1.5
cell.velocity = 100
cell.emissionRange = .pi/5.0
```

In addition, as the cell moves, it can be made to accelerate (or decelerate) in each dimension, using its `xAcceleration`, `yAcceleration`, and `zAcceleration` properties. Here, we turn the stream into a falling cascade, like a waterfall coming from the left:

```
cell.xAcceleration = -40
cell.yAcceleration = 200
```

All aspects of cell behavior can be made to vary randomly, using the following CAEmitterCell properties:

`lifetimeRange`, `velocityRange`
> How much the lifetime and velocity values are allowed to vary randomly for different cells.

`scale`
`scaleRange`, `scaleSpeed`
> The scale alters the size of the cell; the range and speed determine how far and how rapidly this size alteration is allowed to change over the lifetime of each cell.

`spin`
`spinRange`
> The spin is a rotational speed (in radians per second); its range determines how far this speed is allowed to change over the lifetime of each cell.

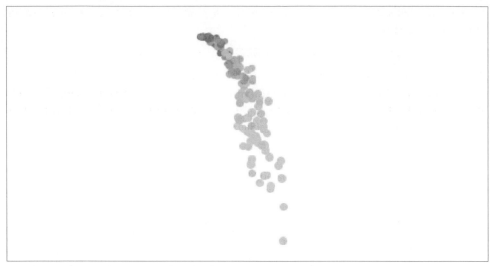

Figure 4-6. An emitter layer that makes a sort of waterfall

`color`
`redRange, greenRange, blueRange, alphaRange`
`redSpeed, greenSpeed, blueSpeed, alphaSpeed`
> The color is painted in accordance with the opacity of the cell's contents image; it combines with the image's color, so if we want the color stated here to appear in full purity, our contents image should use only white. The range and speed determine how far and how rapidly each color component is to change.

Here we add some variation so that the circles behave a little more independently of one another. Some live longer than others, some come out of the emitter faster than others. And they all start out a shade of blue, but change to a shade of green about halfway through the stream (Figure 4-6):

```
cell.lifetimeRange = 0.4
cell.velocityRange = 20
cell.scaleRange = 0.2
cell.scaleSpeed = 0.2
cell.color = UIColor.blue.cgColor
cell.greenRange = 0.5
cell.greenSpeed = 0.75
```

Once the emitter layer is in place and animating, you can change its parameters and the parameters of its emitter cells through key–value coding on the emitter layer. You can access the emitter cells through the emitter layer's `"emitterCells"` key path; to specify a cell type, use its `name` property (which you'll have to have assigned earlier) as the next piece of the key path. Suppose we've set `cell.name` to `"circle"`; now we'll change the cell's greenSpeed so that each cell changes from blue to green much earlier in its lifetime:

```
emit.setValue(3.0, forKeyPath:"emitterCells.circle.greenSpeed")
```

The significance of this is that such changes can themselves be animated! Here, we'll attach to the emitter layer a repeating animation that causes our cell's greenSpeed to move slowly back and forth between two values. The result is that the stream varies, over time, between being mostly blue and mostly green:

```
let key = "emitterCells.circle.greenSpeed"
let ba = CABasicAnimation(keyPath:key)
ba.fromValue = -1.0
ba.toValue = 3.0
ba.duration = 4
ba.autoreverses = true
ba.repeatCount = .greatestFiniteMagnitude
emit.add(ba, forKey:nil)
```

A CAEmitterCell can itself function as an emitter — that is, it can have cells of its own. Both CAEmitterLayer and CAEmitterCell conform to the CAMediaTiming protocol, and their beginTime and duration properties can be used to govern their times of operation, much as in a grouped animation. This code causes our existing waterfall to spray tiny droplets in the region of the "nozzle" (the emitter):

```
let cell2 = CAEmitterCell()
cell.emitterCells = [cell2]
cell2.contents = im.cgImage
cell2.emissionRange = .pi
cell2.birthRate = 200
cell2.lifetime = 0.4
cell2.velocity = 200
cell2.scale = 0.2
cell2.beginTime = 0.04
cell2.duration = 0.2
```

But if we change the beginTime to be larger (hence later), the tiny droplets happen near the bottom of the cascade. We must also increase the duration, or stop setting it altogether, since if the duration is less than the beginTime, no emission takes place at all (Figure 4-7):

```
cell2.beginTime = 1.4
cell2.duration = 0.4
```

We can also alter the picture by changing the behavior of the emitter itself. This change turns the emitter into a line, so that our cascade becomes broader (more like Niagara Falls):

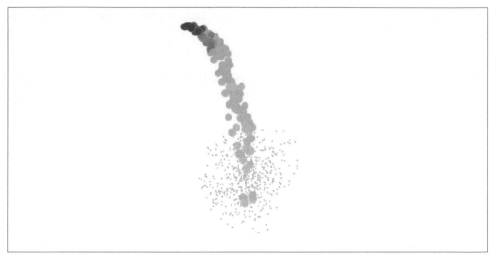

Figure 4-7. The waterfall makes a kind of splash

```
emit.emitterPosition = CGPoint(100,25)
emit.emitterSize = CGSize(100,100)
emit.emitterShape = .line
emit.emitterMode = .outline
cell.emissionLongitude = 3 * .pi/4
```

There's more to know about emitter layers and emitter cells, but at this point you know enough to understand Apple's sample code simulating such things as fire and smoke and pyrotechnics, and you can explore further on your own.

CIFilter Transitions

Core Image filters (Chapter 2) include transitions. You supply two images and a frame time between 0 and 1; the filter supplies the corresponding frame of a one-second animation transitioning from the first image to the second. Figure 4-8 shows the frame at frame time 0.75 for a starburst transition from a solid red image to a photo of me. (You don't see the photo of me, because this transition, by default, "explodes" the first image to white first, and then quickly fades to the second image.)

Animating a Core Image transition filter is up to us. We need a way of rapidly calling the same method repeatedly; in that method, we'll request and draw each frame of the transition. This could be a job for a Timer, but a better way is to use a *display link* (CADisplayLink), a form of timer that's linked directly to the refreshing of the display (hence the name). The display refresh rate is hardware-dependent, but is typically every sixtieth of a second or faster; UIScreen.maximumFramesPerSecond will tell you the nominal value, and the nominal time between refreshes is the display link's duration.

Figure 4-8. Midway through a starburst transition

 For the smoothest display of a Core Image transition filter animation with the least strain on the device's CPU, you would use Metal. But that's outside the scope of this book.

Like a timer, the display link calls a designated method of ours every time it fires. We can slow the rate of calls by setting the display link's `preferredFramesPerSecond`. We can learn the exact time when the display link last fired by querying its `timestamp`, and that's the best way to decide what frame needs displaying now.

In this example, I'll display the animation in a view's layer. We initialize ahead of time, in properties, everything we'll need later to obtain an output image for a given frame of the transition — the CIFilter, the image's `extent`, and the CIContext. We also have a `timestamp` property, which we initialize as well:

```
let moi = CIImage(image:UIImage(named:"moi")!)!
self.moiextent = moi.extent
let tran = CIFilter.flashTransition()
tran.inputImage = CIImage(color: CIColor(color:.red))
tran.targetImage = moi
tran.center = self.moiextent.center
self.tran = tran
self.timestamp = 0.0 // signal that we are starting
self.context = CIContext()
```

We create the display link, setting it to call into our `nextFrame` method, and start it going by adding it to the main run loop, which retains it:

```
let link = CADisplayLink(target:self, selector:#selector(self.nextFrame))
link.add(to:.main, forMode:.default)
```

Our `nextFrame(_:)` method is called with the display link as parameter (`sender`). We store the initial `timestamp` in our property, and use the difference between that and each successive `timestamp` value to calculate our desired frame. We ask the filter for the corresponding image and display it. When the frame value exceeds 1, the animation is over and we invalidate the display link (just like a repeating timer), which releases it from the run loop:

```
let scale = 1.0
@objc func nextFrame(_ sender:CADisplayLink) {
    if self.timestamp < 0.01 { // pick up and store first timestamp
        self.timestamp = sender.timestamp
        self.frame = 0.0
    } else { // calculate frame
        self.frame = (sender.timestamp - self.timestamp) * scale
    }
    sender.isPaused = true // defend against frame loss
    self.tran.setValue(self.frame, forKey:"inputTime")
    let moi = self.context.createCGImage(
        tran.outputImage!, from:self.moiextent)
    CATransaction.setDisableActions(true)
    self.v.layer.contents = moi
    if self.frame > 1.0 {
        sender.invalidate()
    }
    sender.isPaused = false
}
```

I have surrounded the time-consuming calculation and drawing of the image with calls to the display link's `isPaused` property, in case the calculation time exceeds the time between screen refreshes; perhaps this isn't necessary, but it can't hurt. Our animation occupies one second; changing that value is merely a matter of multiplying by a different `scale` value when we set our `frame` property.

UIKit Dynamics

UIKit dynamics comprises a suite of classes supplying a convenient API for animating views in a manner reminiscent of real-world physical behavior. Views can be subjected to gravity, collisions, bouncing, and transient forces, with effects that would otherwise be difficult to achieve.

UIKit dynamics should not be treated as a game engine. It is deliberately quite cartoony and simple, animating only the position (`center`) and rotation transform of views within a flat two-dimensional space. UIKit dynamics relies on CADisplayLink, and the calculation of each frame takes place on the main thread (not on the animation server's background thread). There's no "animation movie" and no distinct presentation layer; the views really are being repositioned in real time. UIKit Dynamics is not intended for extended use; it is a way of momentarily emphasizing or clarifying functional transformations of your interface.

The Dynamics Stack

Implementing UIKit dynamics involves configuring a "stack" of three things:

A dynamic animator

A dynamic animator, a UIDynamicAnimator instance, is the ruler of the physics world you are creating. It has a reference view, whose bounds define the coordinate system of the animator's world. A view to be animated must be a subview of the reference view (though it does not have to be within the reference view's bounds). Retaining the animator is up to you, typically with an instance property. It's fine for an animator to sit empty until you need it; an animator whose world is empty (or at rest) is not running, and occupies no processor time.

A behavior

A UIDynamicBehavior is a rule describing how a view should behave. You'll typically use a built-in subclass, such as UIGravityBehavior or UICollisionBehavior. You configure the behavior and add it to the animator; an animator has methods and properties for managing its behaviors, such as `addBehavior(_:)`, `behaviors`, `removeBehavior(_:)`, and `removeAllBehaviors`. Even if an animation is already in progress, a behavior's configuration can be changed and behaviors can be added to and removed from the animator.

An item

An item is any object that implements the UIDynamicItem protocol. A UIView is such an object! You add a UIView (one that's a subview of your animator's reference view) to a behavior (one that belongs to that animator) — and at that moment, the view comes under the influence of that behavior. If this behavior is one that causes motion, and if no other behaviors prevent, the view will now move (the animator is running).

Some behaviors can accept multiple items, and have methods and properties such as `addItem(_:)`, `items`, and `removeItem(_:)`. Others can have just one or two items and must be initialized with these from the outset.

A UIDynamicItemGroup is a way of combining multiple items to form a single item. Its only property is its `items`. You apply behaviors to the resulting grouped item, not to the subitems that it comprises. Those subitems maintain their physical relationship to one another. For purposes of collisions, the boundaries of the individual subitems are respected.

That's sufficient to get started, so let's try it! First I'll create my animator and store it in a property:

```
self.anim = UIDynamicAnimator(referenceView: self.view)
```

Now I'll cause an existing subview of `self.view` (a UIImageView, `self.iv`, displaying the planet Mars) to drop off the screen, under the influence of gravity. I create a UIGravityBehavior, add it to the animator, and add `self.iv` to it:

```
let grav = UIGravityBehavior()
self.anim.addBehavior(grav)
grav.addItem(self.iv)
```

As a result, `self.iv` comes under the influence of gravity and is now animated downward off the screen. (A UIGravityBehavior object has properties configuring the strength and direction of gravity, but I've left them here at their defaults.)

An immediate concern is that our view falls forever. This is a serious waste of memory and processing power. If we no longer need the view after it has left the screen, we should take it out of the influence of UIKit dynamics by removing it from any behaviors to which it belongs (and we can also remove it from its superview). One way to do this is by removing from the animator any behaviors that are no longer needed. In our simple example, where the animator's entire world contains just this one item, it will be sufficient to call `removeAllBehaviors`.

But how will we know when the view is off the screen? A UIDynamicBehavior can be assigned an `action` function, which is called repeatedly as the animator drives the animation. I'll configure our gravity behavior's `action` function to check whether `self.iv` is still within the bounds of the reference view, by calling the animator's `items(in:)` method. Actually, `items(in:)` returns an array of UIDynamicItem, but I want an array of UIView, so I have a UIDynamicAnimator extension that will cast down safely:

```
extension UIDynamicAnimator {
    func views(in rect: CGRect) -> [UIView] {
        let nsitems = self.items(in: rect) as NSArray
        return nsitems.compactMap {$0 as? UIView}
    }
}
```

Here's my first attempt:

```
grav.action = {
    let items = self.anim.views(in:self.view.bounds)
    let ix = items.firstIndex(of:self.iv)
    if ix == nil {
        self.anim.removeAllBehaviors()
        self.iv.removeFromSuperview()
    }
}
```

This works in the sense that, after the image view leaves the screen, the image view is removed from the window and the animation stops. Unfortunately, there is also a memory leak: neither the image view nor the gravity behavior has been released. One solution is, in `grav.action`, to set `self.anim` (the animator property) to `nil`, breaking the retain cycle. This is a perfectly appropriate solution if, as here, we no longer need the animator for anything; a UIDynamicAnimator is a lightweight object and can very reasonably come into existence only for as long as we need to run an animation. Another possibility is to use delayed performance; even a delay of 0 solves the problem, presumably because the behavior's `action` function is no longer running at the time we remove the behavior:

```
grav.action = {
    let items = self.anim.views(in:self.view.bounds)
    let ix = items.firstIndex(of:self.iv)
    if ix == nil {
        delay(0) {
            self.anim.removeAllBehaviors()
            self.iv.removeFromSuperview()
        }
    }
}
```

Now let's add some further behaviors. If falling straight down is too boring, we can add a UIPushBehavior to apply a slight rightward impulse to the view as it begins to fall:

```
let push = UIPushBehavior(items:[self.iv], mode:.instantaneous)
push.pushDirection = CGVector(1,0)
self.anim.addBehavior(push)
```

The view now falls in a parabola to the right. Next, let's add a UICollisionBehavior to make our view strike the "floor" of the screen:

```
let coll = UICollisionBehavior()
coll.collisionMode = .boundaries
coll.collisionDelegate = self
let b = self.view.bounds
coll.addBoundary(withIdentifier:"floor" as NSString,
    from:CGPoint(b.minX, b.maxY), to:CGPoint(b.maxX, b.maxY))
self.anim.addBehavior(coll)
coll.addItem(self.iv)
```

The view now falls in a parabola onto the floor of the screen, bounces a tiny bit, and comes to rest. It would be nice if the view bounced a bit more. Characteristics internal to a dynamic item's physics, such as bounciness (`elasticity`), are configured by assigning it to a UIDynamicItemBehavior:

```
let bounce = UIDynamicItemBehavior()
bounce.elasticity = 0.8
self.anim.addBehavior(bounce)
bounce.addItem(self.iv)
```

Our view now bounces higher; nevertheless, when it hits the floor, it stops moving to the right, so it just bounces repeatedly, less and less, and ends up at rest on the floor. I'd prefer that, after it bounces, it should roll to the right, so that it eventually leaves the screen. Part of the problem here is that, in the mind of the physics engine, our view, even though it displays a round image, is itself *not* round. We can change that.

We'll have to subclass our view class (UIImageView) and make sure our view is an instance of this subclass:

```
class MyImageView : UIImageView {
    override var collisionBoundsType: UIDynamicItemCollisionBoundsType {
        return .ellipse
    }
}
```

Our image view now has the ability to roll. The effect is quite realistic: the image itself appears to roll to the right after it bounces. But it isn't rolling very fast (because we didn't initially push it very hard). To remedy that, I'll add some rotational velocity as part of the first bounce. A UICollisionBehavior has a delegate to which it sends messages when a collision occurs. I'll make `self` the collision behavior's delegate, and when the delegate message arrives, I'll add rotational velocity to the existing dynamic item bounce behavior, so that our view starts spinning clockwise:

```
func collisionBehavior(_ behavior: UICollisionBehavior,
    beganContactFor item: UIDynamicItem,
    withBoundaryIdentifier identifier: NSCopying?,
    at p: CGPoint) {
        // look for the dynamic item behavior
        let b = self.anim.behaviors
        if let bounce = (b.compactMap {$0 as? UIDynamicItemBehavior}).first {
            let v = bounce.angularVelocity(for:item)
            if v <= 6 {
                bounce.addAngularVelocity(6, for:item)
            }
        }
}
```

The view now falls in a parabola to the right, strikes the floor, spins clockwise, and bounces off the floor and continues bouncing its way off the right side of the screen.

Custom Behaviors

You will commonly find yourself composing a complex behavior out of a combination of several built-in UIDynamicBehavior subclass instances. It might make sense to express that combination as a single custom UIDynamicBehavior subclass.

To illustrate, I'll turn the behavior from the previous section into a custom subclass of UIDynamicBehavior. Let's call it MyDropBounceAndRollBehavior. Now we can apply this behavior to our view, `self.iv`, very simply:

```
self.anim.addBehavior(MyDropBounceAndRollBehavior(view:self.iv))
```

All the work is now done by the MyDropBounceAndRollBehavior instance. I've designed it to affect just one view, so its initializer looks like this:

```
let v : UIView
init(view v:UIView) {
    self.v = v
    super.init()
}
```

A UIDynamicBehavior can receive a reference to its dynamic animator just before being added to it, by implementing `willMove(to:)`, and can refer to it subsequently as `self.dynamicAnimator`. To incorporate actual behaviors into itself, our custom UIDynamicBehavior subclass creates and configures each behavior and calls `add-ChildBehavior(_:)`; it can refer to the array of its child behaviors as `self.child-Behaviors`. When our custom behavior is added to or removed from the dynamic animator, the effect is the same as if its child behaviors themselves were added or removed.

Here is the rest of MyDropBounceAndRollBehavior. Our precautions in the gravity behavior's action function so as not to cause a retain cycle are simpler than before; it suffices to designate `self` as an unowned reference and remove `self` from the animator explicitly:

```
override func willMove(to anim: UIDynamicAnimator?) {
    guard let anim = anim else { return }
    let sup = self.v.superview!
    let b = sup.bounds
    let grav = UIGravityBehavior()
    grav.action = { [unowned self] in
        let items = anim.views(in: b)
        if items.firstIndex(of:self.v) == nil {
            anim.removeBehavior(self)
            self.v.removeFromSuperview()
        }
    }
    self.addChildBehavior(grav)
    grav.addItem(self.v)
    let push = UIPushBehavior(items:[self.v], mode:.instantaneous)
    push.pushDirection = CGVector(1,0)
    self.addChildBehavior(push)
    let coll = UICollisionBehavior()
    coll.collisionMode = .boundaries
    coll.collisionDelegate = self
    coll.addBoundary(withIdentifier:"floor" as NSString,
        from: CGPoint(b.minX, b.maxY), to:CGPoint(b.maxX, b.maxY))
    self.addChildBehavior(coll)
    coll.addItem(self.v)
    let bounce = UIDynamicItemBehavior()
    bounce.elasticity = 0.8
    self.addChildBehavior(bounce)
    bounce.addItem(self.v)
}
func collisionBehavior(_ behavior: UICollisionBehavior,
```

```
    beganContactFor item: UIDynamicItem,
    withBoundaryIdentifier identifier: NSCopying?,
    at p: CGPoint) {
        // look for the dynamic item behavior
        let b = self.childBehaviors
        if let bounce = (b.compactMap {$0 as? UIDynamicItemBehavior}).first {
            let v = bounce.angularVelocity(for:item)
            if v <= 6 {
                bounce.addAngularVelocity(6, for:item)
            }
        }
    }
}
```

Animator and Behaviors

Here are some further UIDynamicAnimator methods and properties:

delegate

> The delegate (UIDynamicAnimatorDelegate) is sent messages `dynamicAnimator-DidPause(_:)` and `dynamicAnimatorWillResume(_:)`. The animator is paused when it has nothing to do: it has no dynamic items, or all its dynamic items are at rest.

isRunning

> If `true`, the animator is not paused; some dynamic item is being animated.

elapsedTime

> The total time during which this animator has been running since it first started running. The `elapsedTime` does not increase while the animator is paused, nor is it reset. You might use this in a delegate method or `action` method to decide that the animation is over.

updateItem(usingCurrentState:)

> Once a dynamic item has come under the influence of the animator, the animator is responsible for positioning that dynamic item. If your code manually changes the dynamic item's position or other relevant attributes, call this method so that the animator can take account of those changes.

 You can turn on a display that reveals visually what the animator is doing, showing its attachment lines and so forth; assuming that `self.anim` refers to the dynamic animator, you would say:

```
self.anim.perform(Selector(("setDebugEnabled:")), with:true)
```

UIDynamicItemBehavior

A UIDynamicItemBehavior doesn't apply any force or velocity; it is a way of endowing items with internal physical characteristics that will affect how they respond to other dynamic behaviors. Here are some of them:

density
> Changes the impulse-resisting mass in relation to size. When we speak of an item's mass, we mean a combination of its size and its density.

elasticity
> The item's tendency to bounce on collision.

friction
> The item's tendency to be slowed by sliding past another item.

isAnchored
> An anchored item is not affected by forces that would make an item move; it remains stationary. This can give you something with friction and elasticity off of which you can bounce and slide other items.

resistance, angularResistance, allowsRotation
> The item's tendency to come to rest unless forces are actively applied. allowsRotation can prevent the item from acquiring any angular velocity at all.

charge
> Meaningful only with respect to magnetic and electric fields, which I'll get to in a moment.

addLinearVelocity(_:for:), linearVelocity(for:)
addAngularVelocity(_:for:), angularVelocity(for:)
> Methods for tweaking linear and angular velocity.

UIGravityBehavior

UIGravityBehavior imposes an acceleration on its dynamic items. By default, this acceleration is downward with a magnitude of 1 (arbitrarily defined as 1000 points per second per second). You can customize gravity by changing its gravityDirection (a CGVector) or its angle and magnitude.

UIFieldBehavior

UIFieldBehavior is a generalization of UIGravityBehavior. A field affects any of its items for as long as they are within its area of influence, as described by these properties:

position
> The center of the field's effective area of influence, in reference view coordinates. The default position is CGPoint.zero, the reference view's top left corner.

region
> The shape of the field's effective area of influence; a UIRegion. The default is that the region is infinite, but you can limit it to a circle by its radius or to a rectangle by its size. More complex region shapes can be achieved by taking the union, intersection, or difference of two regions, or the inverse of a region.

strength
> The magnitude of the field. It can be negative to reverse the directionality of the field's forces.

falloff
> Defines a change in strength proportional to the distance from the center.

minimumRadius
> Specifies a central circle within which there is no field effect.

direction, smoothness, animationSpeed
> Applicable only to those built-in field types that define them.

The built-in field types are obtained by calling a class factory method:

linearGravityField(direction:)
> Like UIGravityBehavior. Accelerates the item in the direction of a vector that you supply, proportionally to its mass, the length of the vector, and the strength of the field. The vector is the field's direction, and can be changed.

velocityField(direction:)
> Like UIGravityBehavior, but it doesn't apply an acceleration (a force) — instead, it applies a constant velocity.

radialGravityField(position:)
> Like a point-oriented version of UIGravityBehavior. Accelerates the item toward, or pushes it away from, the field's designated central point (its position).

springField
> Behaves as if there were a spring stretching from the item to the center, so that the item oscillates back and forth across the center until it settles there.

electricField
> Behaves like an electric field emanating from the center. The default strength and falloff are both 1. If you set the falloff to 0, then a negatively charged item, all other things being equal, will oscillate endlessly across the center.

`magneticField`
> Behaves like a magnetic field emanating from the center. A moving charged item's path is bent away from the center.

`vortexField`
> Accelerates the item sideways with respect to the center.

`dragField`
> Reduces the item's speed.

`noiseField(smoothness:animationSpeed:)`
> Adds random disturbance to the position of the item. The `smoothness` is between 0 (noisy) and 1 (smooth). The `animationSpeed` is how many times per second the field should change randomly. Both can be changed in real time.

`turbulenceField(smoothness:animationSpeed:)`
> Like a noise field, but takes the item's velocity into account.

Think of a field as an infinite grid of CGVectors, with the potential to affect the speed and direction (that is, the velocity) of an item within its borders; at every instant of time the vector applicable to a particular item can be recalculated. You can write a custom field by calling the UIFieldBehavior class method `field(evaluationBlock:)` with a function that takes the item's position, velocity, mass, and charge, along with the animator's elapsed time, and returns a CGVector.

In this (silly) example, we create a delayed drag field: for the first quarter second it does nothing, but then it suddenly switches on and applies the brakes to its items, bringing them to a standstill if they don't already have enough velocity to escape the region's boundaries:

```
let b = UIFieldBehavior.field {
    (beh, pt, v, m, c, t) -> CGVector in
    if t > 0.25 {
        return CGVector(-v.dx, -v.dy)
    }
    return CGVector(0,0)
}
```

The evaluation function receives the behavior itself as a parameter, so it can consult the behavior's properties in real time. You can define your own properties by subclassing UIFieldBehavior. If you're going to do that, you might as well also define your own class factory method to configure and return the custom field. To illustrate, I'll turn the hard-coded `0.25` delay from the previous example into an instance property:

```
class MyDelayedFieldBehavior : UIFieldBehavior {
    var delay = 0.0
    class func dragField(delay del:Double) -> Self {
        let f = self.field {
            (beh, pt, v, m, c, t) -> CGVector in
            if t > (beh as! MyDelayedFieldBehavior).delay {
                return CGVector(-v.dx, -v.dy)
            }
            return CGVector(0,0)
        }
        f.delay = del
        return f
    }
}
```

Here's an example of creating and configuring our delayed drag field:

```
let b = MyDelayedFieldBehavior.dragField(delay:0.95)
b.region = UIRegion(size: self.view.bounds.size)
b.position = self.view.bounds.center
b.addItem(v)
self.anim.addBehavior(b)
```

UIPushBehavior

UIPushBehavior applies a force either instantaneously or continuously (`mode`), the latter constituting an acceleration. How this force affects an object depends in part upon the object's mass. The effect of a push behavior can be toggled with the `active` property; an instantaneous push is repeated each time the `active` property is set to `true`.

To configure a push behavior, set its `pushDirection` or its `angle` and `magnitude`. In addition, a push may be applied at an offset from the center of an item. This will apply an additional angular acceleration. In my earlier example, I could have started the view spinning clockwise by means of its initial push, like this:

```
push.setTargetOffsetFromCenter(
    UIOffset(horizontal:0, vertical:-200), for: self.iv)
```

UICollisionBehavior

UICollisionBehavior watches for collisions either between items belonging to this same behavior or between an item and a boundary (`mode`). One collision behavior can have multiple items and multiple boundaries. A boundary may be described as a line between two points or as a UIBezierPath, or you can turn the reference view's bounds into boundaries (`setTranslatesReferenceBoundsIntoBoundary(with:)`). Boundaries that you create can have an identifier. The `collisionDelegate` (UICollision-BehaviorDelegate) is called when a collision begins and again when it ends.

How a given collision affects the item(s) involved depends on the physical characteristics of the item(s), which may be configured through a UIDynamicItemBehavior.

A dynamic item, such as a UIView, can have a customized collision boundary, rather than its collision boundary being merely the edges of its frame. You can have a rectangle dictated by the frame, an ellipse dictated by the frame, or a custom shape — a convex counterclockwise simple closed UIBezierPath. The relevant properties, collisionBoundsType and (for a custom shape) collisionBoundingPath, are readonly, so you will have to subclass, as I did in my earlier example.

UISnapBehavior

UISnapBehavior causes one item to snap to one point as if pulled by a spring. Its damping describes how much the item should oscillate as its settles into that point. This is a very simple behavior: the snap occurs immediately when the behavior is added to the animator, and there's no notification when it's over.

The snap behavior's snapPoint is a settable property. Having performed a snap, you can subsequently change the snapPoint and cause another snap to take place.

UIAttachmentBehavior

UIAttachmentBehavior attaches an item to another item or to a point in the reference view, depending on how you initialize it:

- init(item:attachedTo:)
- init(item:attachedToAnchor:)

The attachment point is, by default, the item's center; to change that, there's a different pair of initializers:

- init(item:offsetFromCenter:attachedTo:offsetFromCenter:)
- init(item:offsetFromCenter:attachedToAnchor:)

The attaching medium's physics are governed by the behavior's length, frequency, and damping. If the frequency is 0 (the default), the attachment is like a bar; otherwise, and especially if the damping is very small, it is like a spring.

If the attachment is to another item, that item might move. If the attachment is to an anchor, you can move the anchorPoint. When that happens, this item moves too, in accordance with the physics of the attaching medium. An anchorPoint is particularly useful for implementing a draggable view within an animator world, as I'll demonstrate in the next chapter.

There are several more varieties of attachment:

Limit attachment

A limit attachment is created with this class method:

- `limitAttachment(with:offsetFromCenter:attachedTo:offsetFrom-`
  `Center:)`

It's like a rope running between two items. Each item can move freely and independently until the `length` is reached, at which point the moving item drags the other item along.

Fixed attachment

A fixed attachment is created with this class method:

- `fixedAttachment(with:attachedTo:attachmentAnchor:)`

It's as if there are two rods; each rod has an item at one end, with the other ends of the rods being welded together at the anchor point. If one item moves, it must remain at a fixed distance from the anchor, and will tend to rotate around it while pulling it along, at the same time making the other item rotate around the anchor.

Pin attachment

A pin attachment is created with this class method:

- `pinAttachment(with:attachedTo:attachmentAnchor:)`

A pin attachment is like a fixed attachment, but instead of the rods being welded together, they are hinged together. Each item is free to rotate around the anchor point, at a fixed distance from it, *independently*, subject to the pin attachment's `frictionTorque` which injects resistance into the hinge.

Sliding attachment

A sliding attachment can involve one or two items, and is created with one of these class methods:

- `slidingAttachment(with:attachmentAnchor:axisOfTranslation:)`
- `slidingAttachment(with:attachedTo:attachmentAnchor:axisOf-`
  `Translation:)`

Imagine a channel running through the anchor point, its direction defined by the axis of translation (a CGVector). Then an item is attached to a rod whose other end slots into that channel and is free to slide up and down it, but whose angle relative to the channel is fixed by its initial definition (given the item's position, the anchor's position, and the channel axis) and cannot change.

The channel is infinite by default, but you can add end caps that define the limits of sliding. To do so, you specify the attachment's `attachmentRange`; this is a

UIFloatRange, which has a minimum and a maximum. The anchor point is 0, and you are defining the minimum and maximum with respect to that; a float range (-100.0,100.0) provides freedom of movement up to 100 points away from the initial anchor point. It may take some experimentation to discover whether the end cap along a given direction of the channel is the minimum or the maximum.

If there is one item, the anchor is fixed. If there are two items, they can slide independently, and the anchor is free to follow along if one of the items pulls it.

Here's an example of a sliding attachment. We start with a black square and a red square, sitting on the same horizontal, and attached to an anchor midway between them:

```
// first view
let v = UIView(frame:CGRect(0,0,50,50))
v.backgroundColor = .black
self.view.addSubview(v)
// second view
let v2 = UIView(frame:CGRect(200,0,50,50))
v2.backgroundColor = .red
self.view.addSubview(v2)
// sliding attachment
let a = UIAttachmentBehavior.slidingAttachment(with:v,
    attachedTo: v2, attachmentAnchor: CGPoint(125,25),
    axisOfTranslation: CGVector(0,1))
a.attachmentRange = UIFloatRange(minimum: -200, maximum: 200)
self.anim.addBehavior(a)
```

The axis through the anchor point is vertical, and we have permitted a maximum of 200. We now apply a slight vertical downward push to the black square:

```
let p = UIPushBehavior(items: [v], mode: .continuous)
p.pushDirection = CGVector(0,0.05)
self.anim.addBehavior(p)
```

The black square moves slowly vertically downward, with its rod sliding down the channel, until its rod hits the maximum end cap at 200. At that point, the anchor breaks free and begins to move, dragging the red square with it, the two of them continuing downward and slowly rotating round their connection of two rods and the channel.

Motion Effects

A view can respond in real time to the way the user tilts the device. Typically, the view's response will be to shift its position slightly. This is used in various parts of the interface, to give a sense of the interface's being layered (parallax). When an alert is present, if the user tilts the device, the alert shifts its position; the effect is a subtle suggestion that the alert is floating slightly in front of everything else on the screen.

Your own views can behave in the same way. A view will respond to shifts in the position of the device if it has one or more motion effects (UIMotionEffect), provided the user has not turned off motion effects in the device's Accessibility settings. A view's motion effects are managed with methods `addMotionEffect(_:)` and `remove-MotionEffect(_:)`, and the `motionEffects` property.

The UIMotionEffect class is abstract. The chief subclass provided is UIInterpolating-MotionEffect. Every UIInterpolatingMotionEffect has a single key path, which uses key–value coding to specify the property of its view that it affects. It also has a type, specifying which axis of the device's tilting (horizontal tilt or vertical tilt) is to affect this property. Finally, it has a maximum and minimum relative value, the furthest distance that the affected property of the view is to be permitted to wander from its actual value as the user tilts the device.

Related motion effects should be combined into a UIMotionEffectGroup (a UIMotionEffect subclass), and the group added to the view:

```
let m1 = UIInterpolatingMotionEffect(
    keyPath:"center.x", type:.tiltAlongHorizontalAxis)
m1.maximumRelativeValue = 10.0
m1.minimumRelativeValue = -10.0
let m2 = UIInterpolatingMotionEffect(
    keyPath:"center.y", type:.tiltAlongVerticalAxis)
m2.maximumRelativeValue = 10.0
m2.minimumRelativeValue = -10.0
let g = UIMotionEffectGroup()
g.motionEffects = [m1,m2]
v.addMotionEffect(g)
```

You can write your own UIMotionEffect subclass by implementing a single method, `keyPathsAndRelativeValues(forViewerOffset:)`, but this will rarely be necessary.

Animation and Layout

As I've already explained, layout ultimately takes place at the end of a CATransaction, when `layoutSubviews` is sent down the view hierarchy and autolayout constraints are obeyed. It turns out that the layout performed at this moment can be animated! To make that happen, order an animation of `layoutIfNeeded`:

```
UIView.animate(withDuration: 0.5) {
    self.layoutIfNeeded()
}
```

That code means: when layout takes place at the end of this transaction, all changes in the size or position of views should be performed, not instantly, but over a period of half a second.

Animating layout can be useful when you're trying to mediate between animation and autolayout. You may not have thought of these two things as needing mediation, but they do: they are, in fact, diametrically opposed to one another. As part of an animation, you may be changing a view's frame (or bounds, or center). You're really not supposed to do that when you're using autolayout. If you do, an animation may not work correctly — or it may appear to work at first, before any layout has happened, but then there can be undesirable side effects when layout *does* happen.

The reason, as I explained in Chapter 1, is that when layout takes place under autolayout, what matters are a view's constraints. If the constraints affecting a view don't resolve to the size and position that the view has at the moment of layout, the view will jump as the constraints are obeyed. That is almost certainly not what you want.

To persuade yourself that this can be a problem, just animate a view's position and then ask for immediate layout, like this:

```
UIView.animateWithDuration(1, animations:{
    self.v.center.x += 100
}, completion: { _ in
    self.v.superview!.setNeedsLayout()
    self.v.superview!.layoutIfNeeded()
})
```

If we're using autolayout, the view slides to the right and then jumps back to the left. This is bad. It's up to us to keep the constraints synchronized with the reality, so that when layout comes along in the natural course of things, our views don't jump into undesirable states.

One option is to revise the violated constraints to match the new reality. If we've planned far ahead, we may have armed ourselves in advance with a reference to those constraints; in that case, our code can now remove and replace them — or, if the only thing that needs changing is the `constant` value of a constraint, we can change that value in place. Otherwise, discovering what constraints are now violated, and getting a reference to them, is not at all easy.

But there's a better way. Instead of performing the animation first and then revising the constraints, we can change the constraints first and then animate layout. (Again, this assumes that we have a reference to the constraints in question.) If we are animating a view (`self.v`) 100 points rightward, and if we have a reference (`con`) to the constraint whose `constant` positions that view horizontally, we would say:

```
con.constant += 100
UIView.animate(withDuration:1) {
    self.v.superview!.layoutIfNeeded()
}
```

This technique is not limited to a simple change of `constant`. You can overhaul the constraints quite dramatically and still animate the resulting change of layout. In this example, I animate a view (`self.v`) from one side of its superview (`self.view`) to the other by removing its leading constraint and replacing it with a trailing constraint:

```
let c = self.oldConstraint.constant
NSLayoutConstraint.deactivate([self.oldConstraint])
let newConstraint = v.trailingAnchor.constraint(
    equalTo:self.view.layoutMarginsGuide.trailingAnchor, constant:-c)
NSLayoutConstraint.activate([newConstraint])
UIView.animate(withDuration:0.4) {
    self.v.superview!.layoutIfNeeded()
}
```

Another possibility is to use a snapshot of the original view (Chapter 1). Add the snapshot temporarily to the interface — without using autolayout, and perhaps hiding the original view — and animate the snapshot:

```
let snap = self.v.snapshotView(afterScreenUpdates:false)!
snap.frame = self.v.frame
self.v.superview!.addSubview(snap)
self.v.isHidden = true
UIView.animate(withDuration:1) {
    snap.center.x += 100
}
```

That works because the snapshot view is not under the influence of autolayout, so it stays where we put it even if layout takes place. But if we need to remove the snapshot view and reveal the real view, then the real view's constraints will probably still have to be revised.

Yet another approach is to animate the view's `transform` instead of the view itself:

```
UIView.animate(withDuration:1) {
    self.v.transform = CGAffineTransform(translationX: 100, y: 0)
}
```

That's extremely robust, but of course it works only if the animation *can* be expressed as a transform, and it leaves open the question of how long we want a transformed view to remain lying around in our interface.

CHAPTER 5

Touches

[Winifred the Woebegone illustrates hit-testing:] Hey nonny nonny, is it you? — Hey nonny nonny nonny no! — Hey nonny nonny, is it you? *— Hey nonny nonny nonny* no!

—Marshall Barer,
Once Upon a Mattress

A *touch* is an instance of the user putting a finger on the screen. The system and the hardware, working together, know *when* a finger contacts the screen and *where* it is. A finger is fat, but its location is cleverly reduced to a single point.

A UIResponder is a potential recipient of touches. A UIView is a UIResponder and is the *visible* recipient of touches. There are other UIResponder subclasses, but none of them is visible on the screen. The user *sees* a view by virtue of its underlying layer; the user *touches* a view by virtue of the fact that it is a UIResponder.

A touch is represented as an object (a UITouch instance) that is bundled up in an envelope (a UIEvent) that the system delivers to your app. It is then up to your app to deliver the envelope to the appropriate UIView. In the vast majority of cases, this will happen automatically the way you expect, and you will respond to a touch by way of the view in which the touch occurred.

Most built-in interface views deal with these low-level UITouch deliveries for you. They analyze and reduce the touches, and then notify your code at a higher level — you hear about functionality and intention rather than raw touches:

- A UIButton reports that it was tapped.
- A UITextField reports that its text changed.
- A UITableView reports that the user selected a cell.
- A UIScrollView, when dragged, reports that it scrolled; when pinched outward, it reports that it zoomed.

Nevertheless, it is useful to know how to respond to touches yourself, so that you can implement your own touchable views, and so that you understand what Cocoa's built-in views are actually doing.

In this chapter, I'll start by discussing touch detection and response by views (and other UIResponders) at their lowest level. Then I'll proceed to describe the higher-level, more practical mechanism that you'll use most of the time — gesture recognizers, which categorize touches into gesture types for you. Finally, I'll deconstruct the touch-delivery architecture whereby touches are reported to your views in the first place.

Touch Events and Views

Imagine a screen that the user is not touching at all: the screen is "finger-free." Now the user touches the screen with one or more fingers. From that moment until the time the screen is once again finger-free, all touches and finger movements together constitute what Apple calls a single *multitouch sequence*.

The system reports to your app, during a given multitouch sequence, every change in finger configuration, so that your app can figure out what the user is doing. Every such report is a UIEvent. In fact, every report having to do with the same multitouch sequence is *the same UIEvent instance*, arriving repeatedly, each time there's a change in finger configuration.

Every UIEvent reporting a change in the user's finger configuration contains one or more UITouch objects. Each UITouch object corresponds to a single finger; conversely, every finger touching the screen is represented in the UIEvent by a UITouch object. Once a UITouch instance has been created to represent a finger that has touched the screen, *the same UITouch instance* is used to represent that finger throughout this multitouch sequence until the finger leaves the screen.

Now, it might sound as if the system, during a multitouch sequence, constantly has to bombard the app with huge numbers of reports. But that's not really true. The system needs to report only *changes* in the finger configuration. For a given UITouch object (representing, remember, a specific finger), only four things can happen. These are called *touch phases*, and are described by a UITouch instance's `phase` property (UITouch.Phase):

`.began`
> The finger touched the screen for the first time; this UITouch instance has just been created. This is always the first phase, and arrives only once.

`.moved`
> The finger moved upon the screen.

`.stationary`

> The finger remained on the screen without moving. Why is it necessary to report this? Well, remember, once a UITouch instance has been created, it must be present every time the UIEvent for this multitouch sequence arrives. So if the UIEvent arrives because something *else* happened (e.g., a new finger touched the screen), the UIEvent must report what *this* finger has been doing, even if it has been doing nothing.

`.ended`

> The finger left the screen. Like `.began`, this phase arrives only once. The UITouch instance will now be destroyed and will no longer appear in UIEvents for this multitouch sequence.

Those four phases are sufficient to describe everything that a finger can do. Actually, there is one more possible phase:

`.cancelled`

> The system has aborted this multitouch sequence because something interrupted it. What might interrupt a multitouch sequence? There are many possibilities. Perhaps the user clicked the Home button or the screen lock button in the middle of the sequence. A local notification alert may have appeared (Chapter 13); on an iPhone, a call may have come in. And as we shall see, a gesture recognizer recognizing its gesture may also trigger touch cancellation. If you're dealing with touches yourself, you cannot afford to ignore touch cancellations; they are your opportunity to get things into a coherent state when the sequence is interrupted.

When a UITouch first appears (`.began`), your app works out which UIView it is associated with. (I'll give full details, later in this chapter, as to how it does that.) This view is then set as the touch's `view` property, and *remains* so; from then on, this UITouch is *always* associated with this view (until that finger leaves the screen).

The UITouches that constitute a UIEvent might be associated with different views. Accordingly, one and the same UIEvent is distributed to *all the views of all the UITouches it contains*. Conversely, if a view is sent a UIEvent, it's because that UIEvent contains at least one UITouch whose `view` is this view.

If every UITouch in a UIEvent associated with a certain UIView has the phase `.stationary`, that UIEvent is *not* sent to that UIView. There's no point, because as far as that view is concerned, nothing happened.

 Do not retain a reference to a UITouch or UIEvent object over time; it is mutable and doesn't belong to you. If you want to save touch information, extract and save the information, not the touch itself.

Receiving Touches

A UIResponder, and therefore a UIView, has four *touch methods* corresponding to the four UITouch phases that require UIEvent delivery. A UIEvent is delivered to a view by calling one of these methods:

touchesBegan(_:with:)
> A finger touched the screen, creating a UITouch.

touchesMoved(_:with:)
> A finger previously reported to this view with touchesBegan(_:with:) has moved. (On a device with 3D touch, "moved" might mean a change of pressure rather than location.)

touchesEnded(_:with:)
> A finger previously reported to this view with touchesBegan(_:with:) has left the screen.

touchesCancelled(_:with:)
> We are bailing out on a finger previously reported to this view with touchesBegan(_:with:).

The parameters of the touch methods are:

The relevant touches
> These are the event's touches whose phase corresponds to the name of the method and (normally) whose view is this view. They arrive as a Set. If there is only one touch in the set, or if any touch in the set will do, you can retrieve it with first (a set is unordered, so *which* element is first is arbitrary).

The event
> This is the UIEvent instance. It contains its touches as a Set, which you can retrieve with the allTouches message. This means *all* the event's touches, including but not necessarily limited to those in the first parameter; there might be touches in a different phase or intended for some other view. You can call touches(for:) to ask for the set of touches associated with a particular view or window.

When we say that a certain view *is receiving a touch*, that is a shorthand expression meaning that it is being sent a UIEvent containing this UITouch, over and over, by calling one of its touch methods, corresponding to the phase this touch is in, from the time the touch is created until the time it is destroyed.

A UITouch has some useful methods and properties:

`location(in:)`, `previousLocation(in:)`

The current and previous location of this touch with respect to the coordinate system of a given view. The view you'll be interested in will often be `self` or `self.superview`; supply `nil` to get the location with respect to the window. The previous location will be of interest only if the phase is `.moved`.

`timestamp`

When the touch last changed. A touch is timestamped when it is created (`.began`) and each time it moves (`.moved`). There can be a delay between the occurrence of a physical touch and the delivery of the corresponding UITouch; to learn about the timing of touches, consult the timestamp, not the clock.

`tapCount`

If two touches are in roughly the same place in quick succession, and the first one is brief, the second one may be characterized as a repeat of the first. They are different touch objects, but the second will be assigned a `tapCount` one larger than the previous one. The default is 1, so if a touch's `tapCount` is 3, then this is the third tap in quick succession in roughly the same spot.

`view`

The view with which this touch is associated.

`majorRadius`, `majorRadiusTolerance`

Respectively, the radius of the touch (approximately half its size) and the uncertainty of that measurement, in points.

A UITouch carries some additional information that may be useful if the touch arrived through an Apple Pencil rather than a finger, such as how the pencil is oriented.

Here are some additional UIEvent properties:

`type`

This will be `UIEvent.EventType.touches`. There are other event types, but you're not going to receive any of them this way.

`timestamp`

When the event occurred.

You can reduce the latency between the user's touches and your app's rendering to the screen. On certain devices, the touch detection rate is doubled or even quadrupled, and you can ask for the extra touches. On all devices, a few future touches may be predicted, and you can ask for these. Such features would be useful particularly in a drawing app.

Restricting Touches

A number of UIView properties restrict the delivery of touches to particular views:

isUserInteractionEnabled
> If set to `false`, this view (along with its subviews) is excluded from receiving touches. Touches on this view or one of its subviews fall through to a view behind it.

alpha
> If set to `0.0` (or extremely close to it), this view (along with its subviews) is excluded from receiving touches. Touches on this view or one of its subviews fall through to a view behind it.

isHidden
> If set to `true`, this view (along with its subviews) is excluded from receiving touches. This makes sense, since from the user's standpoint, the view and its subviews are not even present.

isMultipleTouchEnabled
> If set to `false`, this view never receives more than one touch simultaneously; once it receives a touch, it doesn't receive any other touches until the first touch has ended.

isExclusiveTouch
> A view whose `isExclusiveTouch` is `true` receives a touch only if no other views in the same window have touches associated with them; conversely, once a view whose `isExclusiveTouch` is `true` has received a touch, then while that touch exists, no other view in the same window receives any touches. (This is the only one of these properties that can't be set in the nib editor.)

A view can receive touches and yet be completely invisible because its background color is `.clear`. So this is an *invisible touchable view.* You can configure an invisible touchable view so that touches on this view do *not* fall through to the views behind it; that can be a useful trick. Later I'll give an example of an invisible touchable view that lets some touches fall through but not others.

If a superview's `clipsToBounds` is `false`, then a subview that is outside the bounds of the superview is *visible.* But any part of a subview that is outside the bounds of its superview *cannot be touched.* So you can end up unintentionally with a view that is visible but partially or totally untouchable. That's very confusing to your users, and might be confusing to you! Getting yourself into this situation, and then wondering why your view isn't responding normally to touches, is a common beginner mistake. This behavior has to do with how hit-testing works; later in this chapter, I'll explain that, along with a way of changing it.

Interpreting Touches

Once you receive calls in your touch methods, what do those touches *mean?* Sometimes they don't mean anything special; the raw touches are all you need. In a drawing program, you might want to know quite literally what the user's finger is doing and no more, and the touch methods will tell you. Most of the time, however, the user's touches *do* have meaning, and you will want to *interpret* those touches. What is the user doing? What are the user's intentions?

Thanks to gesture recognizers (discussed later in this chapter), in most cases you won't have to interpret touches at all; you'll let a gesture recognizer do most of that work. Even so, it is beneficial to be conversant with the nature of touch interpretation; this will help you use, subclass, and create gesture recognizers. Furthermore, not every touch sequence can be codified through a gesture recognizer; sometimes, directly interpreting touches is the best approach.

To figure out what's going on as touches are received by a view, your code must essentially function as a kind of state machine. You'll receive various touch method calls, and your response will depend in part upon what happened previously, so you'll have to record somehow, probably in instance properties, whatever information you'll need subsequently in order to decide what to do when the *next* touch method is called. Such an architecture can make writing and maintaining touch-analysis code quite tricky.

To illustrate the business of interpreting touches, we'll start with a view that can be dragged with the user's finger. For simplicity, I'll assume that this view receives only a single touch at a time. (This assumption is easy to enforce by setting the view's isMultipleTouchEnabled to false, which is the default.)

The trick to making a view follow the user's finger is to realize that a view is positioned by its center, which is in superview coordinates, but the user's finger might not be at the center of the view. So at every stage of the drag we must change the view's center by the change in the user's finger position in superview coordinates:

```
override func touchesMoved(_ touches: Set<UITouch>, with e: UIEvent?) {
    let t = touches.first!
    let loc = t.location(in:self.superview)
    let oldP = t.previousLocation(in:self.superview)
    let deltaX = loc.x - oldP.x
    let deltaY = loc.y - oldP.y
    var c = self.center
    c.x += deltaX
    c.y += deltaY
    self.center = c
}
```

Next, let's add a restriction that the view can be dragged only vertically or horizontally. All we have to do is hold one coordinate steady; but which coordinate? Everything seems to depend on what the user does initially. So we'll do a one-time test the first time we receive touchesMoved(_:with:). Now we're maintaining two Bool state properties, self.decided and self.horiz:

```
override func touchesBegan(_ touches: Set<UITouch>, with e: UIEvent?) {
    self.decided = false
}
override func touchesMoved(_ touches: Set<UITouch>, with e: UIEvent?) {
    let t = touches.first!
    if !self.decided {
        self.decided = true
        let then = t.previousLocation(in:self)
        let now = t.location(in:self)
        let deltaX = abs(then.x - now.x)
        let deltaY = abs(then.y - now.y)
        self.horiz = deltaX >= deltaY
    }
    let loc = t.location(in:self.superview)
    let oldP = t.previousLocation(in:self.superview)
    let deltaX = loc.x - oldP.x
    let deltaY = loc.y - oldP.y
    var c = self.center
    if self.horiz {
        c.x += deltaX
    } else {
        c.y += deltaY
    }
    self.center = c
}
```

Look at how things are trending. We are maintaining multiple state properties, which we are managing across multiple methods, and our touch method implementation is divided into branches that depend on the state of our state machine. Our state machine is very simple, but already our code is becoming difficult to read and to maintain — and things will only become more messy as we try to make our view's behavior more sophisticated.

Another area in which manual touch handling can rapidly prove overwhelming is when it comes to distinguishing between different gestures that the user might perform on a view. Imagine a view that distinguishes between a finger tapping briefly and a finger remaining down for a longer time. We can't know how long a tap is until it's over, so we must wait until then before deciding; once again, this requires maintaining state in a property (self.time):

```
override func touchesBegan(_ touches: Set<UITouch>, with e: UIEvent?) {
    self.time = touches.first!.timestamp
}
override func touchesEnded(_ touches: Set<UITouch>, with e: UIEvent?) {
```

```
        let diff = e!.timestamp - self.time
        if (diff < 0.4) {
            print("short")
        } else {
            print("long")
        }
    }
```

A similar challenge is distinguishing between a single tap and a double tap. The UITouch `tapCount` property already makes this distinction, but that, by itself, is not enough to help us react differently to the two. Having received a tap whose `tapCount` is 1, we must wait long enough (using delayed performance) to give a second tap a chance to arrive. This is unfortunate, because it means that if the user intends a single tap, some time will elapse before anything happens in response to it. But there's nothing we can readily do about that.

Distributing our various tasks correctly is tricky. We *know* when we have a double tap as early as `touchesBegan(_:with:)`, but we *respond* to the double tap in `touches-Ended(_:with:)`. Therefore, we use a property (`self.single`) to communicate between the two. We don't start our delayed response to a single tap until `touches-Ended(_:with:)`, because what matters is the time between the taps as a whole, not between the starts of the taps:

```
override func touchesBegan(_ touches: Set<UITouch>, with e: UIEvent?) {
    let ct = touches.first!.tapCount
    switch ct {
    case 2:
        self.single = false
    default: break
    }
}
override func touchesEnded(_ touches: Set<UITouch>, with e: UIEvent?) {
    let ct = touches.first!.tapCount
    switch ct {
    case 1:
        self.single = true
        delay(0.3) {
            if self.single { // no second tap intervened
                print("single tap")
            }
        }
    case 2:
        print("double tap")
    default: break
    }
}
```

As if that code weren't confusing enough, let's now consider combining our detection for a single or double tap with our earlier code for dragging a view horizontally or vertically. This is to be a view that can detect four kinds of gesture: a single tap, a double tap, a horizontal drag, and a vertical drag. We must include the code for all possibilities and make sure they don't interfere with each other. The result is horrifying — a forced join between two already complicated sets of code, along with an additional pair of state properties (`self.drag`, `self.decidedTapOrDrag`) to track the decision between the tap gestures on the one hand and the drag gestures on the other:

```swift
override func touchesBegan(_ touches: Set<UITouch>, with e: UIEvent?) {
    // be undecided
    self.decidedTapOrDrag = false
    // prepare for a tap
    let ct = touches.first!.tapCount
    switch ct {
    case 2:
        self.single = false
        self.decidedTapOrDrag = true
        self.drag = false
        return
    default: break
    }
    // prepare for a drag
    self.decidedDirection = false
}
override func touchesMoved(_ touches: Set<UITouch>, with e: UIEvent?) {
    if self.decidedTapOrDrag && !self.drag {return}
    self.superview!.bringSubviewToFront(self)
    let t = touches.first!
    self.decidedTapOrDrag = true
    self.drag = true
    if !self.decidedDirection {
        self.decidedDirection = true
        let then = t.previousLocation(in:self)
        let now = t.location(in:self)
        let deltaX = abs(then.x - now.x)
        let deltaY = abs(then.y - now.y)
        self.horiz = deltaX >= deltaY
    }
    let loc = t.location(in:self.superview)
    let oldP = t.previousLocation(in:self.superview)
    let deltaX = loc.x - oldP.x
    let deltaY = loc.y - oldP.y
    var c = self.center
    if self.horiz {
        c.x += deltaX
    } else {
        c.y += deltaY
    }
    self.center = c
}
override func touchesEnded(_ touches: Set<UITouch>, with e: UIEvent?) {
    if !self.decidedTapOrDrag || !self.drag {
        // end for a tap
        let ct = touches.first!.tapCount
```

```
            switch ct {
            case 1:
                self.single = true
                delay(0.3) {
                    if self.single {
                        print("single tap")
                    }
                }
            case 2:
                print("double tap")
            default: break
            }
        }
    }
```

That code seems to work, but it's hard to say whether it covers all possibilities coherently; it's barely legible and the logic borders on the mysterious. This is the kind of situation for which gesture recognizers were devised.

Gesture Recognizers

Writing and maintaining a state machine that interprets touches across a combination of three or four touch methods is hard enough when a view confines itself to expecting only one kind of gesture, such as dragging. It becomes even more involved when a view wants to accept and respond differently to different kinds of gesture. Furthermore, many types of gesture are conventional and standard; it seems insane to require every developer, independently, to devise a way of responding to what is, in effect, a universal vocabulary.

The solution is gesture recognizers, which standardize common gestures and allow the code for different gestures to be separated and encapsulated into different objects. And thanks to gesture recognizers, it is unnecessary to subclass UIView merely in order to implement touch interpretation.

Gesture Recognizer Classes

A *gesture recognizer* (a subclass of UIGestureRecognizer) is an object whose job is to detect that a multitouch sequence equates to one particular type of gesture. It is attached to a UIView. The gesture recognizers attached to a view are its gesture-Recognizers; this property is settable (and might be nil). You can also manage gesture recognizers individually with these methods:

- addGestureRecognizer(_:)

- removeGestureRecognizer(_:)

A UIGestureRecognizer implements the four touch methods, but it is not a responder (a UIResponder), so it does not participate in the responder chain. If, however, a new touch is going to be delivered to a view, it is also associated with and delivered to that view's gesture recognizers if it has any, *and* to that view's *superview's* gesture recognizers if *it* has any, and so on up the view hierarchy. So the place of a gesture recognizer in the view hierarchy matters, even though it isn't part of the responder chain.

UITouch and UIEvent provide complementary ways of learning how touches and gesture recognizers are associated:

- UITouch's `gestureRecognizers` lists the gesture recognizers that are currently handling this touch.

- UIEvent's `touches(for:)` can take a gesture recognizer parameter; it then lists the touches that are currently being handled by that gesture recognizer.

Each gesture recognizer maintains its own state as touch events arrive, building up evidence as to what kind of gesture this is. When one of them decides that it has recognized its own particular type of gesture, it emits either a single message (a finger has tapped) or a series of messages (a finger is moving); the distinction here is between a *discrete* and a *continuous* gesture.

What message a gesture recognizer emits, and what object it sends that message to, is configured through a target–action dispatch table attached to the gesture recognizer. A gesture recognizer is rather like a UIControl in this regard; indeed, one might say that a gesture recognizer simplifies the touch handling of *any* view to be like that of a control. The difference is that one control may report several different control events, whereas each gesture recognizer reports only one gesture type, with different gestures being reported by different gesture recognizers.

UIGestureRecognizer itself is abstract, providing methods and properties to its subclasses. Among these are:

`init(target:action:)`
> The designated initializer. The gesture recognizer will signal that something has happened by sending the action message to the target. Further target–action pairs may be added with `addTarget(_:action:)` and removed with `removeTarget(_:action:)`.
>
> Two forms of `action:` selector are possible: either there is no parameter, or there is a single parameter which will be the gesture recognizer. Most commonly, you'll use the second form, so that the target can identify, query, and communicate with the gesture recognizer.

`numberOfTouches`
> How many touches the gesture recognizer is tracking. In general, this is the number of fingers the user must employ to make the gesture that this gesture recognizer is interested in. The touches themselves are inaccessible by way of the gesture recognizer.

`location(ofTouch:in:)`

The first parameter is an index number (smaller than `numberOfTouches`) identifying the touch. The second parameter is the view whose coordinate system you want to use.

`isEnabled`

A convenient way to turn a gesture recognizer off without having to remove it from its view.

`state, view`

I'll discuss state later on. The `view` is the view to which this gesture recognizer is attached; it is an Optional.

Built-in UIGestureRecognizer subclasses are provided for six common gesture types: tap, pinch (inward or outward), pan (drag), swipe, rotate, and long press. Each embodies properties and methods likely to be needed for each type of gesture, either in order to *configure* the gesture recognizer beforehand or in order to query it as to the *status* of an ongoing gesture:

UITapGestureRecognizer (discrete)

Configuration: `numberOfTapsRequired`, `numberOfTouchesRequired` ("touches" means simultaneous fingers).

UIPinchGestureRecognizer (continuous)

Two fingers moving toward or away from each other. Status: `scale`, `velocity`.

UIRotationGestureRecognizer (continuous)

Two fingers moving round a common center. Status: `rotation`, `velocity`.

UISwipeGestureRecognizer (discrete)

A straight-line movement in one of the four cardinal directions. Configuration: `direction` (meaning permitted directions, a bitmask), `numberOfTouches-Required`.

UIPanGestureRecognizer (continuous)

Dragging. Configuration: `minimumNumberOfTouches`, `maximumNumberOfTouches`. Status: `translation(in:)`, `setTranslation(_:in:)`, `velocity(in:)`; the coordinate system of the specified view is used.

UIScreenEdgePanGestureRecognizer

A UIPanGestureRecognizer subclass. It recognizes a pan gesture that starts at an edge of the screen. It adds a configuration property, `edges`, a UIRectEdge; despite the name (and the documentation), this must be set to a single edge.

UILongPressGestureRecognizer (continuous)

Configuration: `numberOfTapsRequired`, `numberOfTouchesRequired`, `minimum-PressDuration`, `allowableMovement`. The `numberOfTapsRequired` is the count of taps *before* the tap that stays down, so it can be 0 (the default). The `allowableMovement` setting lets you compensate for the fact that the user's finger is unlikely to remain steady during an extended press: we need to provide some limit before deciding that this gesture is, say, a drag, and not a long press after all. On the other hand, once the long press is recognized, the finger is permitted to drag as part of the long press gesture.

UIGestureRecognizer also provides a `location(in:)` method. This is a single point, even if there are multiple touches. The subclasses implement this variously. Typically, the location is where the touch is if there's a single touch, but it's a sort of midpoint ("centroid") if there are multiple touches.

We already know enough to implement, using a gesture recognizer, a view that responds to a single tap, or a view that responds to a double tap. Here's code (probably from our view controller's `viewDidLoad`) that implements a view (`self.v`) that responds to a single tap by calling our `singleTap` method:

```
let t = UITapGestureRecognizer(target:self, action:#selector(singleTap))
self.v.addGestureRecognizer(t)
```

And here's code that implements a view (`self.v2`) that responds to a double tap by calling our `doubleTap` method:

```
let t = UITapGestureRecognizer(target:self, action:#selector(doubleTap))
t.numberOfTapsRequired = 2
self.v2.addGestureRecognizer(t)
```

For a continuous gesture like dragging, we need to know both when the gesture is in progress and when the gesture ends. This brings us to the subject of a gesture recognizer's state.

A gesture recognizer implements a notion of *states* (the `state` property, UIGestureRecognizer.State); it passes through these states in a definite progression. The gesture recognizer remains in the `.possible` state until it can make a decision one way or the other as to whether this is in fact the correct gesture. The documentation neatly lays out the possible progressions:

Wrong gesture

`.possible` → `.failed`. No action message is sent.

Discrete gesture (like a tap), recognized

`.possible` → `.ended`. One action message is sent, when the state changes to `.ended`.

Continuous gesture (like a drag), recognized

.possible → .began → .changed (repeatedly) → .ended. Action messages are sent once for .began, as many times as necessary for .changed, and once for .ended.

Continuous gesture, recognized but later cancelled

.possible → .began → .changed (repeatedly) → .cancelled. Action messages are sent once for .began, as many times as necessary for .changed, and once for .cancelled.

The same action message arrives at the same target every time, so the action method must differentiate by asking about the gesture recognizer's state. The usual implementation involves a switch statement.

To illustrate, we will implement, using a gesture recognizer, a view that lets itself be dragged around in any direction by a single finger. Our maintenance of state is greatly simplified, because a UIPanGestureRecognizer maintains a delta (translation) for us. This delta, available using translation(in:), is reckoned from the touch's initial position. We don't even need to record the view's original center, because we can call setTranslation(_:in:) to reset the UIPanGestureRecognizer's delta every time:

```
func viewDidLoad {
    super.viewDidLoad()
    let p = UIPanGestureRecognizer(target:self, action:#selector(dragging))
    self.v.addGestureRecognizer(p)
}
@objc func dragging(_ p : UIPanGestureRecognizer) {
    let v = p.view!
    switch p.state {
    case .began, .changed:
        let delta = p.translation(in:v.superview)
        var c = v.center
        c.x += delta.x; c.y += delta.y
        v.center = c
        p.setTranslation(.zero, in: v.superview)
    default: break
    }
}
```

To illustrate the use of a UIPanGestureRecognizer's velocity(in:), let's imagine a view that the user can drag, but which then springs back to where it was. We can express "springs back" with a spring animation (Chapter 4). We'll just add an .ended case to our dragging(_:) method (dest is the original center of our view v):

```
case .ended, .cancelled:
    let anim = UIViewPropertyAnimator(
        duration: 0.4,
        timingParameters: UISpringTimingParameters(
```

```
        dampingRatio: 0.6,
        initialVelocity: .zero))
anim.addAnimations {
    v.center = dest
}
anim.startAnimation()
```

That's good, but it would be more realistic if the view had some momentum at the moment the user lets go of it. If the user drags the view quickly away from its home and releases it, the view should keep moving a little in the same direction before springing back into place. That's what the spring animation's `initialVelocity:` parameter is for! We can easily find out what the view's velocity is, at the moment the user releases it, by asking the gesture recognizer:

```
let vel = p.velocity(in: v.superview!)
```

Unfortunately, we cannot use this value directly as the spring animation's `initial-Velocity`; there's a type impedance mismatch. The view's velocity is expressed as a CGPoint measured in points per second; but the spring's `initialVelocity` is expressed as a CGVector measured as a proportion of the distance to be traveled over the course of the animation. Fortunately, the conversion is easy:

```
case .ended, .cancelled:
    let vel = p.velocity(in: v.superview!)
    let c = v.center
    let distx = abs(c.x - dest.x)
    let disty = abs(c.y - dest.y)
    let anim = UIViewPropertyAnimator(
        duration: 0.4,
        timingParameters: UISpringTimingParameters(
            dampingRatio: 0.6,
            initialVelocity: CGVector(vel.x/distx, vel.y/disty)))
    anim.addAnimations {
        v.center = dest
    }
    anim.startAnimation()
```

A pan gesture recognizer can be used also to make a view draggable under the influence of a UIDynamicAnimator (Chapter 4). The strategy here is that the view is attached to one or more anchor points through a UIAttachmentBehavior; as the user drags, we move the anchor point(s), and the view follows. In this example, I set up the whole UIKit dynamics "stack" of objects as the gesture begins, anchoring the view at the point where the touch is; then I move the anchor point to stay with the touch. Instance properties `self.anim` and `self.att` store the UIDynamicAnimator and the UIAttachmentBehavior, respectively; `self.view` is our view's superview, and is the animator's reference view:

```
@objc func dragging(_ p: UIPanGestureRecognizer) {
    switch p.state {
    case .began:
        self.anim = UIDynamicAnimator(referenceView:self.view)
        let loc = p.location(ofTouch:0, in:p.view)
        let cen = p.view!.bounds.center
        let off = UIOffset(horizontal: loc.x-cen.x, vertical: loc.y-cen.y)
        let anchor = p.location(ofTouch:0, in:self.view)
        let att = UIAttachmentBehavior(item:p.view!,
            offsetFromCenter:off, attachedToAnchor:anchor)
        self.anim.addBehavior(att)
        self.att = att
    case .changed:
        self.att.anchorPoint = p.location(ofTouch:0, in: self.view)
    default:
        self.anim = nil
    }
}
```

The outcome is that the view both moves and rotates in response to dragging, like a plate being pulled about on a table by a single finger.

By adding behaviors to the dynamic animator, we can limit further what the view is permitted to do as it is being dragged by its anchor. Imagine a view that can be lifted vertically and dropped, but cannot be moved horizontally. As I demonstrated earlier, you can prevent horizontal dragging through the implementation of your response to touch events (and later in this chapter, I'll show how to do this by subclassing UIPan-GestureRecognizer). But the same sort of limitation can be imposed by way of the underlying physics of the world in which the view exists, perhaps with a sliding attachment.

Gesture Recognizer Conflicts

A view can have more than one gesture recognizer associated with it. This isn't a matter merely of multiple recognizers attached to a single view; as I have said, if a view is touched, not only its own gesture recognizers but also any gesture recognizers attached to views further up the view hierarchy are in play simultaneously. I like to think of a view as surrounded by a *swarm* of gesture recognizers — its own, and those of its superview, and so on. (In reality, it is a *touch* that has a swarm of gesture recognizers; that's why a UITouch has a `gestureRecognizers` property, in the plural.)

The superview gesture recognizer swarm comes as a surprise to beginners, but it makes sense, because without it, certain gestures would be impossible. Imagine a pair of views, each of which the user can tap individually, but which the user can also touch simultaneously (one finger on each view) to rotate them together around their mutual centroid. Neither view can detect the rotation *qua* rotation, because neither view receives both touches; only the superview can detect it, so the fact that the views themselves respond to touches must not prevent the superview's gesture recognizer from operating.

The question naturally arises, then, of what happens when multiple gesture recognizers are in play. There is a conflict between these gesture recognizers, each trying to recognize the current multitouch sequence as its own appropriate gesture. How will it be resolved?

The rule is simple. In general, by default, once a gesture recognizer succeeds in recognizing its gesture, any *other* gesture recognizers associated with its touches are *forced into the* `.failed` *state*, and whatever touches were associated with those gesture recognizers are no longer sent to them; in effect, the first gesture recognizer in a swarm that recognizes its gesture owns the gesture (and its touches) from then on.

In many cases, this "first past the post" behavior, on its own, will yield exactly the desired behavior. We can add both our single tap UITapGestureRecognizer and our UIPanGestureRecognizer to a view and everything will just work; dragging works, and single tap works:

```
let t = UITapGestureRecognizer(target:self, action:#selector(singleTap))
self.v.addGestureRecognizer(t)
let p = UIPanGestureRecognizer(target: self, action: #selector(dragging))
self.v.addGestureRecognizer(p)
```

You can take a hand in how conflicts are resolved, and sometimes you will need to do so. What happens if we add a double tap gesture recognizer and a single tap gesture recognizer to the same view? Double tap works, but without preventing the single tap from working: on a double tap, *both* the single tap action method *and* the double tap action method are called.

If that isn't what we want, we don't have to use delayed performance, as we did earlier. Instead, we can create a *dependency* between one gesture recognizer and another. One way to do that is with the UIGestureRecognizer `require(toFail:)` method. This method is rather badly named; it doesn't mean "force this other recognizer to fail," but rather, "you can't succeed unless this other recognizer has failed." It tells its recipient to suspend judgment about whether this is its gesture until some *other* gesture recognizer (the parameter) has had a chance to decide whether this is *its* gesture. In the case of the single tap gesture recognizer and the double tap gesture recognizer, we want the single tap gesture to suspend judgment until the double tap gesture recognizer can decide whether this is a double tap:

```
let t2 = UITapGestureRecognizer(target:self, action:#selector(doubleTap))
t2.numberOfTapsRequired = 2
self.v.addGestureRecognizer(t2)
let t1 = UITapGestureRecognizer(target:self, action:#selector(singleTap))
t1.require(toFail:t2) // *
self.v.addGestureRecognizer(t1)
```

Another conflict that can arise is between a gesture recognizer and a view that already knows how to respond to the same gesture, such as a UIControl. This problem pops up particularly when the gesture recognizer belongs to the UIControl's superview. The UIControl's mere presence does not "block" the superview's gesture recognizer from recognizing a gesture on the UIControl, even if it is a UIControl that responds autonomously to touches. Your window's root view might have a UITapGesture-Recognizer attached to it (perhaps because you want to be able to recognize taps on the background); if there is also a UIButton within that view, how is the tap gesture recognizer to ignore a tap on the button?

The UIView instance method `gestureRecognizerShouldBegin(_:)` solves the problem. It is called automatically; to modify its behavior, use a custom UIView subclass and override it. Its parameter is a gesture recognizer belonging to this view or to a view further up the view hierarchy. That gesture recognizer has recognized its gesture as taking place in this view; but by returning `false`, the view can tell the gesture recognizer to bow out and do nothing, not sending any action messages, and permitting this view to respond to the touch as if the gesture recognizer weren't there.

For example, a UIButton could return `false` for a single tap UITapGesture-Recognizer; a single tap on the button would then trigger the button's action message and not the gesture recognizer's action message. And in fact a UIButton, by default, *does* return `false` for a single tap UITapGestureRecognizer whose view is not the UIButton itself.

Other built-in controls may also implement `gestureRecognizerShouldBegin(_:)` in such a way as to prevent accidental interaction with a gesture recognizer; the documentation says that a UISlider implements it in such a way that a UISwipeGesture-Recognizer won't prevent the user from sliding the "thumb," and there may be other cases that aren't documented explicitly. Naturally, you can take advantage of this feature in your own UIView subclasses as well.

There are additional ways of resolving possible gesture recognizer conflicts through a gesture recognizer's delegate or with a gesture recognizer subclass.

Gesture Recognizer Delegate

A gesture recognizer can have a delegate (UIGestureRecognizerDelegate), which can perform two types of task: blocking operation and mediating conflict.

These delegate methods can *block a gesture recognizer's operation*.

`gestureRecognizerShouldBegin(_:)`
    Sent to the delegate before the gesture recognizer passes out of the `.possible` state; return `false` to force the gesture recognizer to proceed to the `.failed` state. This happens *after* `gestureRecognizerShouldBegin(_:)` has been sent to

the view in which the touch took place; that view must not have returned `false`, or we wouldn't have reached this stage.

gestureRecognizer(_:shouldReceive:)
> Sent to the delegate before a touch is sent to the gesture recognizer's touches-Began(_:with:) method; return `false` to prevent that touch from ever being sent to the gesture recognizer.

These delegate methods can *mediate gesture recognition conflict*:

gestureRecognizer(_:shouldRecognizeSimultaneouslyWith:)
> Sent when a gesture recognizer, having recognized its gesture, is about to force another gesture recognizer to fail, to the delegates of *both* gesture recognizers. Return `true` to prevent that failure, allowing both gesture recognizers to operate simultaneously.

gestureRecognizer(_:shouldRequireFailureOf:)
gestureRecognizer(_:shouldBeRequiredToFailBy:)
> Sent very early in the life of a gesture, when all gesture recognizers in a view's swarm are still in the `.possible` state, to the delegates of *all* of them, pairing the gesture recognizer whose delegate this is with each of the other gesture recognizers in the swarm. Return `true` to prioritize between this pair of gesture recognizers, saying that one cannot succeed until the other has first failed. In essence, these delegate methods turn the decision made once and permanently in `require(toFail:)` into a live decision that can be made freshly every time a gesture occurs.

As an example, we will use delegate messages to combine a UILongPressGesture-Recognizer and a UIPanGestureRecognizer. The user must perform a tap-and-a-half (tap, then tap and hold) to "get the view's attention," which we will indicate by a pulsing animation on the view; then and only then, the user can drag the view.

The UIPanGestureRecognizer's action method will take care of the drag, using the code shown earlier in this chapter. The UILongPressGestureRecognizer's action method will take care of starting and stopping the animation:

```
@objc func longPress(_ lp:UILongPressGestureRecognizer) {
    switch lp.state {
    case .began:
        let anim = CABasicAnimation(keyPath: #keyPath(CALayer.transform))
        anim.toValue = CATransform3DMakeScale(1.1, 1.1, 1)
        anim.fromValue = CATransform3DIdentity
        anim.repeatCount = .greatestFiniteMagnitude
        anim.autoreverses = true
        lp.view!.layer.add(anim, forKey:nil)
    case .ended, .cancelled:
```

```
            lp.view!.layer.removeAllAnimations()
        default: break
        }
    }
```

As we created our gesture recognizers, we kept a reference to the UILongPress-GestureRecognizer (`self.longPresser`). We also made ourself the UIPanGesture-Recognizer's delegate, so we will receive delegate messages. If the UIPanGestureRecognizer tries to declare success while the UILongPressGesture-Recognizer's state is `.failed` or still at `.possible`, we prevent it. If the UILongPress-GestureRecognizer succeeds, we permit the UIPanGestureRecognizer to operate as well:

```
func gestureRecognizerShouldBegin(_ g: UIGestureRecognizer) -> Bool {
    switch self.longPresser.state {
    case .possible, .failed:
        return false
    default:
        return true
    }
}
func gestureRecognizer(_ g: UIGestureRecognizer,
    shouldRecognizeSimultaneouslyWith g2: UIGestureRecognizer) -> Bool {
        return true
}
```

The result is that the view can be dragged only while it is pulsing; in effect, what we've done is to compensate, using delegate methods, for the fact that UIGesture-Recognizer has no `require(toSucceed:)` method.

Subclassing Gesture Recognizers

To subclass UIGestureRecognizer or a built-in gesture recognizer subclass:

- You'll need to `import UIKit.UIGestureRecognizerSubclass`. This allows you to set a gesture recognizer's `state` property (which is otherwise read-only), and exposes declarations for the methods you may need to override.

- Override any relevant touch methods (as if the gesture recognizer were a UIResponder); if you're subclassing a built-in gesture recognizer subclass, you will almost certainly call `super` so as to take advantage of the built-in behavior. In overriding touch methods, try to think like a gesture recognizer: as these methods are called, the gesture recognizer is setting its state, and you must participate coherently in that process.

To illustrate, we will subclass UIPanGestureRecognizer so as to implement a view that can be moved only horizontally or vertically. Our strategy will be to make *two* UIPanGestureRecognizer subclasses — one that allows only horizontal movement, and another that allows only vertical movement. They will make their recognition decisions in a mutually exclusive manner, so we can attach an instance of each to the same view. This encapsulates the decision-making logic in a gorgeously object-oriented way — a far cry from the spaghetti code we wrote earlier to do this same task.

I will show only the code for the horizontal drag gesture recognizer, because the vertical recognizer is symmetrically identical. We maintain just one property, `self.origLoc`, which we will use once to determine whether the user's initial movement is horizontal. We override `touchesBegan(_:with:)` to set our property with the first touch's location:

```
override func touchesBegan(_ touches: Set<UITouch>, with e: UIEvent) {
    self.origLoc = touches.first!.location(in:self.view!.superview)
    super.touchesBegan(touches, with:e)
}
```

We then override `touchesMoved(_:with:)`; all the recognition logic is here. This method will be called for the first time with the state still at `.possible`. At that moment, we look to see if the user's movement is more horizontal than vertical. If it isn't, we set the state to `.failed`. But if it is, we just step back and let the superclass do its thing:

```
override func touchesMoved(_ touches: Set<UITouch>, with e: UIEvent) {
    if self.state == .possible {
        let loc = touches.first!.location(in:self.view!.superview)
        let deltaX = abs(loc.x - self.origLoc.x)
        let deltaY = abs(loc.y - self.origLoc.y)
        if deltaY >= deltaX {
            self.state = .failed
        }
    }
    super.touchesMoved(touches, with:e)
}
```

If this gesture recognizer is attached to a view, we now have a view that moves only if the user's initial gesture is horizontal. But that isn't the entirety of what we want; we want a view that moves only horizontally. To implement that, we'll override `translation(in:)` so that our gesture recognizer lies to its client about where the user's finger is:

```
override func translation(in view: UIView?) -> CGPoint {
    var proposedTranslation = super.translation(in:view)
    proposedTranslation.y = 0
    return proposedTranslation
}
```

That example was simple, because we subclassed a fully functional built-in UIGestureRecognizer subclass. If you were to write your own UIGestureRecognizer subclass entirely from scratch, there would be more work to do:

Touch methods

You should definitely implement all four touch methods. Their job, at a minimum, is to advance the gesture recognizer through the canonical progression of its states. When the first touch arrives at a gesture recognizer, its state will be `.possible`; you never explicitly set the recognizer's state to `.possible` yourself. As soon as you know this can't be our gesture, you set the state to `.failed`. (Apple says that a gesture recognizer should "fail early, fail often.") If the gesture gets past all the failure tests, you set the state instead either to `.ended` (for a discrete gesture) or to `.began` (for a continuous gesture); if `.began`, then you might set it to `.changed`, and ultimately you must set it to `.ended`. Don't concern yourself with the sending of action messages; they will be sent automatically at the appropriate moments.

`reset` *method*

You should also probably implement `reset`. This is called after you reach the end of the progression of states to notify you that the gesture recognizer's state is about to be set back to `.possible`; it is your chance to return your state machine to its starting configuration. This is important because your gesture recognizer might stop receiving touches without notice. Just because it gets a `touches-Began(_:with:)` call for a particular touch doesn't mean it will ever get `touches-Ended(_:with:)` for that touch. If your gesture recognizer fails to recognize its gesture, either because it declares failure or because it is still in the `.possible` state when another gesture recognizer recognizes, it won't get any more touch method calls for any of the touches that were being sent to it. `reset` is the one reliable signal that it's time to clean up and get ready to receive the beginning of another possible gesture.

You can incorporate delegate-like behavior into a gesture recognizer subclass, by overriding the following methods:

- `canPrevent(_:)`
- `canBePrevented(by:)`
- `shouldRequireFailure(of:)`
- `shouldBeRequiredToFail(by:)`

The `prevent` methods are similar to the delegate `shouldBegin` method, and the `fail` methods are similar to the delegate `fail` methods. By implementing them, you can mediate gesture recognizer conflict at the class level. The built-in gesture recognizer subclasses already do this; that is why a single tap UITapGestureRecognizer does not, by recognizing its gesture, cause the failure of a double tap UITapGestureRecognizer.

You can also, in a gesture recognizer subclass, send `ignore(_:for:)` directly to a gesture recognizer (typically to `self`) to ignore a specific touch of a specific event. This has the same effect as the delegate method `gestureRecognizer(_:shouldReceive:)` returning `false`, blocking all future delivery of that touch to the gesture recognizer. You might use this to ignore a new touch that arrives when you're in the middle of an already recognized gesture.

Gesture Recognizers in the Nib

Instead of instantiating a gesture recognizer in code, you can create and configure it in a *.xib* or *.storyboard* file. In the nib editor, drag a gesture recognizer from the Library onto a view; the gesture recognizer becomes a top-level nib object, and the view's `gestureRecognizers` outlet is connected to the gesture recognizer. (You can add more than one gesture recognizer to a view in the nib: the view's `gesture-Recognizers` property is an array, and its `gestureRecognizers` outlet is an outlet collection.) The gesture recognizer is a full-fledged nib object, so you can make an outlet to it. A view retains its gesture recognizers, so there will usually be no need for additional memory management on a gesture recognizer instantiated from a nib.

The gesture recognizer's properties are configurable in the Attributes inspector, and the gesture recognizer has a `delegate` outlet. To configure a gesture recognizer's target–action pair in the nib editor, treat it like a UIControl's control event. The action method's signature should be marked `@IBAction`, and it should take a single parameter, which will be a reference to the gesture recognizer. You can form the action in any of the same ways as for a control action. A gesture recognizer can have multiple target–action pairs, but only one target–action pair can be configured for a gesture recognizer using the nib editor.

3D Touch Press Gesture

On a device with 3D touch, you can treat pressing as a kind of gesture. It isn't formally a gesture; there is, unfortunately, no 3D touch press gesture recognizer. Nevertheless, your code can detect a 3D touch press, responding dynamically to the degree of force being applied.

The simplest approach is to use the UIPreviewInteraction class. You initialize a UIPreviewInteraction object with the view in which pressing is to be detected, retain the UIPreviewInteraction object, and assign it a delegate (adopting the UIPreview-InteractionDelegate protocol). The delegate is sent these messages, starting when the user begins to apply force within the view:

`previewInteractionShouldBegin(_:)`
> Optional. Return `false` to ignore this press gesture. Among other things, this method might query the UIPreviewInteraction's `view` and `location(in:)` to decide how to proceed.

```
previewInteraction(_:didUpdatePreviewTransition:ended:)
```
The amount of applied force has changed. The amount of force is reported (in the second parameter) as a value between 0 and 1. When 1 is reached, `ended:` is also `true`, and the device vibrates.

```
previewInteraction(_:didUpdateCommitTransition:ended:)
```
Optional. Behaves exactly like the previous method. If implemented, the gesture has two stages, increasing from 0 to 1 and reported by the *previous* delegate method, and then increasing *again* from 0 to 1 and reported by *this* method.

```
previewInteractionDidCancel(_:)
```
The user has backed off the gesture completely before reaching a full press (or the touch was cancelled for some other reason).

To illustrate, imagine a sort of Whack-a-Mole game where the user is to remove views by 3D pressing each one. (In real life, there would also need to be a way to play the game on a device that lacks 3D touch.) As the user presses, we'll apply a scale transform to the view, increasing its apparent size in proportion to the amount of force, while at the same time fading the view away by decreasing its opacity; if the user reaches a full press, we'll remove the view completely.

We'll implement this in the simplest possible way. The code will all go into the pressable view itself. When the view is added to its superview, it creates and configures the UIPreviewInteraction object, storing it in an instance property (`self.prev`):

```
override func didMoveToSuperview() {
    self.prev = UIPreviewInteraction(view: self)
    self.prev.delegate = self
}
```

As force reports arrive, we'll increase the view's scale transform and decrease its opacity accordingly:

```
func previewInteraction(_ : UIPreviewInteraction,
    didUpdatePreviewTransition prog: CGFloat,
    ended: Bool) {
        let scale = prog + 1
        self.transform = CGAffineTransform(scaleX: scale, y: scale)
        let alph = ((1-prog)*0.6) + 0.3
        self.alpha = alph
        if ended { // device vibrates
            self.removeFromSuperview()
        }
}
```

The view now expands and explodes off the screen with a satisfying pop ("haptic feedback") as the user presses on it. If the user backs off the gesture completely, we'll remove the transform and restore our opacity:

```
func previewInteractionDidCancel(_ : UIPreviewInteraction) {
    self.transform = .identity
    self.alpha = 1
}
```

Alternatively, we might use a property animator, taking advantage of its ability to manage a "frozen" animation ("Frozen View Animation" on page 183). Here's a rewrite in which a property animator is used (held in an instance property, self.anim):

```
func makeAnimator() {
    self.anim = UIViewPropertyAnimator(duration: 1, curve: .linear) {
        [unowned self] in
        self.alpha = 0.3
        self.transform = CGAffineTransform(scaleX: 2, y: 2)
    }
}
override func didMoveToSuperview() {
    self.prev = UIPreviewInteraction(view: self)
    self.prev.delegate = self
    self.makeAnimator()
}
func previewInteractionDidCancel(_ : UIPreviewInteraction) {
    self.anim.pauseAnimation()
    self.anim.isReversed = true
    self.anim.addCompletion { _ in self.makeAnimator() }
    self.anim.continueAnimation(
        withTimingParameters: nil, durationFactor: 0.01)
}
func previewInteraction(_ : UIPreviewInteraction,
    didUpdatePreviewTransition prog: CGFloat,
    ended: Bool) {
        self.anim.fractionComplete = min(max(prog, 0.05), 0.95)
        if ended {
            self.anim.stopAnimation(false)
            self.anim.finishAnimation(at: .end)
            self.removeFromSuperview()
        }
}
```

Touch Delivery

Here's the full standard procedure by which a touch is delivered to views and gesture recognizers:

- When a new touch appears, the application performs hit-testing to determine the view that was touched. This view will be permanently associated with this touch, and is called, appropriately, the *hit-test view*. The logic of ignoring a view in response to its isUserInteractionEnabled, isHidden, and alpha properties is implemented by denying this view the ability to become the hit-test view.

- When the touch situation changes, the application calls its own `sendEvent(_:)`, which in turn calls the window's `sendEvent(_:)`. The window delivers each of an event's touches by calling the appropriate touch method(s):

  - As a touch first appears, the logic of obedience to `isMultipleTouchEnabled` and `isExclusiveTouch` is considered. If permitted by that logic:

    ○ The touch is delivered to the hit-test view's swarm of gesture recognizers.

    ○ The touch is delivered to the hit-test view itself.

  - If a gesture is recognized by a gesture recognizer, then for any touch associated with this gesture recognizer:

    ○ `touchesCancelled(_:for:)` is sent to the touch's view, and the touch is no longer delivered to its view.

    ○ If the touch was associated with any other gesture recognizer, that gesture recognizer is forced to fail.

  - If a gesture recognizer fails, either because it declares failure or because it is forced to fail, its touches are no longer delivered to it, but (except as already specified) they continue to be delivered to their view.

The rest of this chapter discusses the details of touch delivery. As you'll see, nearly every bit of the standard procedure can be customized to some extent.

Hit-Testing

Hit-testing is the determination of what view the user touched. View hit-testing uses the UIView instance method `hitTest(_:with:)`, whose first parameter is the CGPoint of interest. It returns either a view (the hit-test view) or `nil`. The idea is to find the frontmost view containing the touch point.

The first thing a view's `hitTest(_:with:)` does is to implement the logic of touch restrictions exclusive to a view. If the view's `isUserInteractionEnabled` is `false`, or its `isHidden` is `true`, or its `alpha` is close to `0.0`, it immediately returns `nil`, meaning that neither it nor any of its subviews can be the hit-test view. Observe that these restrictions do not, of themselves, exclude a view from being hit-tested; on the contrary, they operate precisely by affecting a view's hit-test result.

(Hit-testing knows nothing about `isMultipleTouchEnabled`, which involves multiple touches, or `isExclusiveTouch`, which involves multiple views. The logic of obedience to these properties is implemented at a later stage of the story.)

If the view has not returned `nil` for any of those reasons, the `hitTest(_:with:)` method proceeds by an elegant recursive algorithm:

1. A view's `hitTest(_:with:)` first calls the same method on its own subviews, if it has any, because a subview is considered to be in front of its superview. The subviews are queried in front-to-back order (Chapter 1), so if two sibling views overlap, the one in front reports the hit first.

2. If, as a view hit-tests its subviews, any of those subviews responds by returning a view, it stops querying its subviews and immediately returns the view that was returned to it. In this way, the very first view to declare itself the hit-test view percolates all the way to the top of the call chain and *is* the hit-test view.

3. If, on the other hand, a view has no subviews, or if all of its subviews return `nil` (indicating that neither they nor their subviews was hit), then the view calls `point(inside:with:)` on itself:

   - If this call reveals that the touch was inside this view, the view returns itself, and so this view *is* the hit-test view, as I just explained.

   - Otherwise this view returns `nil` and the search continues.

No problem arises if a view being hit-tested has a transform, because `point(inside:with:)` takes the transform into account. That's why a rotated button continues to work correctly.

Performing Hit-Testing

You can perform hit-testing yourself at any moment where it might prove useful. In calling `hitTest(_:with:)`, supply a point *in the coordinates of the view to which the message is sent*. The second parameter is supposed to be a UIEvent, but it can be `nil` if you have no event.

Suppose we have a superview with two UIImageView subviews. We want to detect a tap in either UIImageView, but we want to handle this *at the level of the superview*. We can attach a UITapGestureRecognizer to the superview, but then the gesture recognizer's `view` is the superview, so how will we know which subview, if any, the tap was in?

First, ensure that `isUserInteractionEnabled` is `true` for both UIImageViews. UIImageView is one of the few built-in view classes where this property is `false` by default, and a view whose `isUserInteractionEnabled` is `false` won't normally be the result of a call to `hitTest(_:with:)`. Then, when our gesture recognizer's action method is called, we can perform hit-testing to determine where the tap was:

```
// g is the gesture recognizer
let p = g.location(ofTouch:0, in: g.view)
let v = g.view?.hitTest(p, with: nil)
if let v = v as? UIImageView { // ...
```

Hit-Test Munging

You can override hitTest(_:with:) in a UIView subclass, to alter its results during touch delivery, customizing the touch delivery mechanism. I call this *hit-test munging*. Hit-test munging can be used selectively as a way of turning user interaction on or off in an area of the interface. In this way, some unusual effects can be achieved. I'll give a couple of examples and leave the other possibilities to your imagination.

Suppose we want to permit the touching of subviews outside the bounds of their superview. As I mentioned earlier, if a view's clipsToBounds is false, a paradox arises: the user can *see* the regions of its subviews that are outside its bounds, but can't *touch* them. This behavior can be changed by a view that overrides hitTest(_:with:):

```swift
override func hitTest(_ point: CGPoint, with e: UIEvent?) -> UIView? {
    if let result = super.hitTest(point, with:e) {
        return result
    }
    for sub in self.subviews.reversed() {
        let pt = self.convert(point, to:sub)
        if let result = sub.hitTest(pt, with:e) {
            return result
        }
    }
    return nil
}
```

In this next example, we implement a pass-through view. The idea is that only one object in our interface should be touchable; everything else should behave as if isUserInteractionEnabled were false. In a complex interface, actually cycling through all our subviews and toggling isUserInteractionEnabled might be too much trouble. As a shortcut, we place an invisible view in front of the entire interface and use hit-test munging so that only one view behind it (self.passthruView) is touchable. In effect, this is a view that is (selectively) touchable even though the user can't see it:

```swift
class MyView: UIView {
    weak var passthruView : UIView?
    override func hitTest(_ point: CGPoint, with e: UIEvent?) -> UIView? {
        if let pv = self.passthruView {
            let pt = pv.convert(point, from: self)
            if pv.point(inside: pt, with: e) {
                return nil
            }
        }
        return super.hitTest(point, with: e)
    }
}
```

Hit-Testing for Layers

Layers do *not* receive touches. A touch is reported to a view, not a layer. A layer, except insofar as it is a view's underlying layer and gets touch reporting because of its view, is completely untouchable; from the point of view of touches and touch reporting, it's as if the layer weren't on the screen at all. No matter where a layer may appear to be, a touch falls through the layer to whatever view is behind it.

In the case of a layer that is a view's underlying layer, you don't need layer hit-testing, because you've got view hit-testing. The layer is the view's drawing; where it appears is where the view is. So a touch in that layer is equivalent to a touch in its view. Indeed, one might say (and it is often said) that this is what views are actually for: to provide layers with touchability.

Nevertheless, hit-testing for layers is possible. It doesn't happen automatically, as part of sendEvent(_:) or anything else; it's up to you. It's just a convenient way of finding out which layer *would* receive a touch at a point, if layers *did* receive touches. To hit-test layers, call hitTest(_:) on a layer, with a point *in superlayer coordinates*. Layer hit-testing knows nothing of the restrictions on touch delivery; it just reports on every sublayer, even one whose view has isUserInteractionEnabled set to false.

The only layers on which you'd need special hit-testing would presumably be layers that are not themselves any view's underlying layer. Still, all layers are part of the layer hierarchy and can participate in layer hit-testing. So the most comprehensive way to hit-test layers is to start with the topmost layer, the window's layer. In this example, we subclass UIWindow and override its hitTest(_:with:) so as to get layer hit-testing every time there is view hit-testing:

```
override func hitTest(_ point: CGPoint, with e: UIEvent?) -> UIView? {
    let lay = self.layer.hitTest(point)
    // ... possibly do something with that information
    return super.hitTest(point, with:e)
}
```

In that code, self is the window, which is a special case. In general, you'll have to convert to superlayer coordinates. I'll demonstrate in the next example.

Let's return to the CompassView developed in Chapter 3, in which all the parts of the compass are layers; we want to know whether the user tapped on the arrow layer, and if so, we'll rotate the arrow. For simplicity, we've given the CompassView a UITap-GestureRecognizer, and this is its action method, in the CompassView itself. We convert to our superview's coordinates, because these are also our layer's superlayer coordinates:

```
@objc func tapped(_ t:UITapGestureRecognizer) {
    let p = t.location(ofTouch:0, in: self.superview)
    let hitLayer = self.layer.hitTest(p)
    if let arrow = (self.layer as? CompassLayer)?.arrow {
```

```
        if hitLayer == arrow { // respond to touch
            arrow.transform = CATransform3DRotate(
                arrow.transform, .pi/4.0, 0, 0, 1)
        }
    }
}
```

Hit-Testing for Drawings

The preceding example (letting the user tap on the compass arrow) does work, but we might complain that it is reporting a hit on the arrow layer even if the hit misses the *drawing* of the arrow. That's true for view hit-testing as well. A hit is reported if we are within the view or layer as a whole; hit-testing knows nothing of drawing, transparent areas, and so forth.

If you know how the region is drawn and can reproduce the edge of that drawing as a CGPath, you can call contains(_:using:transform:) to test whether a point is inside it. So, in our compass layer, we could override hitTest(_:) along these lines:

```
override func hitTest(_ p: CGPoint) -> CALayer? {
    var lay = super.hitTest(p)
    if lay == self.arrow {
        let pt = self.arrow.convert(p, from:self.superlayer)
        let path = CGMutablePath()
        path.addRect(CGRect(10,20,20,80))
        path.move(to:CGPoint(0, 25))
        path.addLine(to:CGPoint(20, 0))
        path.addLine(to:CGPoint(40, 25))
        path.closeSubpath()
        if !path.contains(pt, using: .winding) {
            lay = nil
        }
    }
    return lay
}
```

Alternatively, it might be the case that if a pixel of the drawing is transparent, it's outside the drawn region, so that it suffices to detect whether the tapped pixel is transparent. Unfortunately, there's no built-in way to ask a drawing (or a view, or a layer) for the color of a pixel. Instead, you have to make a *bitmap graphics context* and copy the drawing into it, and then ask the bitmap for the color of a pixel. If you can reproduce the content as an image, and all you care about is transparency, you can make a one-pixel alpha-only bitmap, draw the image in such a way that the pixel you want to test is the pixel drawn into the bitmap, and examine the transparency of the resulting pixel. In this example, im is our UIImage and point is the coordinates of the pixel we want to test:

```
let info = CGImageAlphaInfo.alphaOnly.rawValue
let pixel = UnsafeMutablePointer<UInt8>.allocate(capacity:1)
defer {
    pixel.deinitialize(count: 1)
    pixel.deallocate()
}
pixel[0] = 0
let sp = CGColorSpaceCreateDeviceGray()
let context = CGContext(data: pixel,
    width: 1, height: 1, bitsPerComponent: 8, bytesPerRow: 1,
    space: sp, bitmapInfo: info)!
UIGraphicsPushContext(context)
im.draw(at:CGPoint(-point.x, -point.y))
UIGraphicsPopContext()
let p = pixel[0]
let alpha = Double(p)/255.0
let transparent = alpha < 0.01
```

There may not be a one-to-one relationship between the pixels of the underlying drawing and the points of the drawing as portrayed on the screen. (Perhaps the drawing is stretched.) In many cases, the CALayer method render(in:) can be helpful here. This method allows you to copy a layer's actual drawing into a graphics context of your choice. If that context is an image context (Chapter 2), you can use the resulting image as im in the preceding code.

Hit-Testing During Animation

Making a view touchable by the user while it is being animated is a tricky business, because the view may not be located where the user sees it. Recall (from Chapter 4) that the animation is just an "animation movie" — what the user sees is the *presentation layer*. The view itself, which the user is trying to touch, is at the location of the *model layer*. If user interaction is allowed during an animation that moves a view from one place to another, and if the user taps where the animated view appears to be, the tap might mysteriously fail because the actual view is elsewhere; conversely, the user might accidentally tap where the view actually is, and the tap will hit the animated view even though it appears to be elsewhere.

For this reason, view animation ordered through a UIView class method, by default, turns off touchability of a view while it is being animated — though you can override that with .allowUserInteraction in the options: argument.

If you're not using a property animator, you can make an animated view touchable if you really want to, but it takes some work: you have to *hit-test the presentation layer*. In this simple example, we implement hit-test munging in the view being animated:

```
override func hitTest(_ point: CGPoint, with e: UIEvent?) -> UIView? {
    let pres = self.layer.presentation()!
    let suppt = self.convert(point, to: self.superview!)
    let prespt = self.superview!.layer.convert(suppt, to: pres)
    return super.hitTest(prespt, with: e)
}
```

That works, but the animated view, as Apple puts it in the WWDC 2011 videos, "swallows the touch." Suppose the view in motion is a button. Although our hit-test munging makes it possible for the user to tap the button as it is being animated, and although the user sees the button highlight in response, the button's action message is not sent in response to this highlighting if the animation is in-flight when the tap takes place. This behavior seems unfortunate, though it's generally possible to work around it (perhaps with a gesture recognizer).

A property animator makes things far simpler. By default, a property animator's isUserInteractionEnabled is true. That means the animated view *is* touchable. As long as you don't also set the property animator's isManualHitTestingEnabled to true, the property animator will hit-test the animated view's presentation layer for you. (If you *do* set isManualHitTestingEnabled to true, the job of hit-testing is turned back over to you; you might want to do this in complicated situations where the property animator's hit-test munging isn't sufficient.) Moreover, the animated view *doesn't* "swallow the touch."

So, to animate a button that remains tappable while the animation is in-flight, just animate the button:

```
let goal : CGPoint = // whatever
let anim = UIViewPropertyAnimator(duration: 10, curve: .linear) {
    self.button.center = goal // button can be tapped while moving
}
anim.startAnimation()
```

By combining the power of a property animator to make its animated view touchable with its power to make its animation interruptible, we can make a view alternate between being animated and being manipulated by the user. To illustrate, I'll extend the preceding example. The view is slowly animating its way toward the goal position. But at any time, the user can grab it and drag it around, during which time the animation is interrupted. As soon as the user releases the view, the animation resumes: the view continues on its way toward the goal position.

In order to be draggable, the view has a UIPanGestureRecognizer. The property animator is now retained in an instance property (self.anim) so that the gesture recognizer's action method can access it; we have a method that creates the property animator (you'll see in a moment what the factor: parameter is for):

```
func configAnimator(factor:Double = 1) {
    self.anim = UIViewPropertyAnimator(
        duration: 10 * factor, curve: .linear) {
            self.button.center = self.goal
    }
}
```

All the work takes place in the gesture recognizer's action method; as usual, we have a switch statement that tests the gesture recognizer's `state`. In the `.began` case, we interrupt the animation so that dragging can happen:

```
case .began:
    if self.anim.state == .active {
        self.anim.stopAnimation(true)
    }
    fallthrough
```

The `.changed` case is our usual code for making a view draggable:

```
case .changed:
    let delta = p.translation(in:v.superview)
    var c = v.center
    c.x += delta.x; c.y += delta.y
    v.center = c
    p.setTranslation(.zero, in: v.superview)
```

The `.ended` case is the really interesting part. Our aim is to resume animating the view from wherever it is now toward the `goal`. In my opinion, this feels most natural if the *speed* at which the view moves remains the same. The ratio between durations is the ratio between the distance of the view's *original* position from the `goal` and its *current* distance from the goal:

```
case .ended:
    // how far are we from the goal relative to original distance?
    func pyth(_ pt1:CGPoint, _ pt2:CGPoint) -> CGFloat {
        return hypot(pt1.x - pt2.x, pt1.y - pt2.y)
    }
    let origd = pyth(self.oldButtonCenter, self.goal)
    let curd = pyth(v.center, self.goal)
    let factor = curd/origd
    self.configAnimator(factor:Double(factor))
    self.anim.startAnimation()
```

Initial Touch Event Delivery

Whenever the multitouch situation changes, an event containing all touches is handed to the UIApplication instance by calling its sendEvent(_:), and the UIApplication in turn hands it to the UIWindow by calling *its* sendEvent(_:). The UIWindow then performs the complicated logic of examining, for every touch, the hit-test view and its superviews and their gesture recognizers, and deciding which of them should be sent a touch method call.

You can override `sendEvent(_:)` in a subclass of UIWindow or UIApplication. These are delicate and crucial maneuvers, however, and you wouldn't want to lame your application by interfering with them. Moreover, it is unlikely, nowadays, that you would need to resort to such measures. A typical use case before the advent of gesture recognizers was that you needed to detect touches directed to an object of some built-in interface class that you couldn't subclass; but gesture recognizers exist now, and solve the problem nicely.

Gesture Recognizer and View

When a touch first appears and is delivered to a gesture recognizer, it is *also* delivered to its hit-test view, the same touch method being called on both.

This is the most reasonable approach, as it means that touch interpretation by a view isn't jettisoned just because gesture recognizers are in the picture. Later on in the multitouch sequence, if all the gesture recognizers in a view's swarm declare failure to recognize their gesture, that view's internal touch interpretation continues as if gesture recognizers had never been invented. Moreover, touches and gestures are two different things; sometimes you want to respond to both. In one of my apps, where the user can tap cards, each card has a single tap gesture recognizer and a double tap gesture recognizer, but it also responds directly to `touchesBegan(_:with:)` by reducing its own opacity, and to `touchesEnded(_:with:)` and `touches-Cancelled(_:with:)` by restoring its opacity. The result is that the user always sees *some* feedback when touching a card, *instantly*, regardless of what the gesture turns out to be.

Later, if a gesture recognizer in a view's swarm recognizes its gesture, that view is sent `touchesCancelled(_:with:)` for any touches that went to that gesture recognizer and were hit-tested to that view, and subsequently the view *no longer receives those touches*. This behavior can be changed by setting a gesture recognizer's `cancels-TouchesInView` property to `false`; if you were to do that for every gesture recognizer in a view's swarm, the view would receive touch events more or less as if no gesture recognizers were in the picture.

If a gesture recognizer happens to be ignoring a touch — perhaps it was told to do so with `ignore(_:for:)` — then `touchesCancelled(_:with:)` *won't* be sent to the view for that touch when that gesture recognizer recognizes its gesture. A touch ignored by a gesture recognizer effectively falls through to the view, as if the gesture recognizer didn't exist.

Gesture recognizers can also *delay* the delivery of some touch methods to a view, by means of these properties:

delaysTouchesEnded

If true (the default), then when a touch reaches .ended and the gesture recognizer's touchesEnded(_:with:) is called, if the gesture recognizer is still allowing touches to be delivered to the view because its state is still .possible, it doesn't deliver this touch until it has resolved the gesture. When it does, either it will recognize the gesture, in which case the view will have touchesCancelled(_:with:) called instead (as already explained), or it will declare failure and *now* the view will have touchesEnded(_:with:) called.

The reason for this behavior is most obvious with a gesture where multiple taps are required. Consider a double tap gesture recognizer. The first tap ends, but this is insufficient for the gesture recognizer to declare success or failure, so it withholds that touchesEnded(_:with:) from the view. If there is a second tap, the gesture recognizer will succeed and send touchesCancelled(_:with:) to the view — but it can't do that if the view has already been sent touches-Ended(_:with:)! So it was right to withhold touchesEnded(_:with:) in the first place.

delaysTouchesBegan

If true, we delay the *entire* suite of touch methods from being called on a view. Again, this delay would be until the gesture recognizer can resolve the gesture: either it will recognize it, in which case the view will have touches-Cancelled(_:with:) called, or it will declare failure, in which case the view will receive touchesBegan(_:with:) plus any further touch method calls that were withheld — except that it will receive *at most* one touchesMoved(_:with:) call, the last one, because if a lot of these were withheld, to queue them all up and send them all at once now would be insane.

When touches are delayed and then delivered, what's delivered is the original touch with the original event, which still have their original timestamps. Because of the delay, these timestamps may differ significantly from now. As I've already said, analysis that is concerned with timing of touches should consult the timestamp, not the clock.

Touch Exclusion Logic

It is up to the UIWindow's sendEvent(_:) to implement the logic of isMultiple-TouchEnabled and isExclusiveTouch:

isMultipleTouchEnabled

If a new touch is hit-tested to a view whose isMultipleTouchEnabled is false and that already has an existing touch hit-tested to it, then sendEvent(_:) never delivers the new touch to that view. But that touch *is* delivered to the view's swarm of gesture recognizers; in other words, gesture recognizers are *not* affected by the existence of the `isMultipleTouchEnabled` property.

`isExclusiveTouch`

If there's an `isExclusiveTouch` view in the window, then `sendEvent(_:)` must decide whether a particular touch should be delivered, in accordance with the meaning of `isExclusiveTouch`, which I described earlier. If a touch is not delivered to a view because of `isExclusiveTouch` restrictions, it is *not* delivered to its swarm of gesture recognizers either; in other words, gesture recognizers *are* affected by the existence of the `isExclusiveTouch` property.

To illustrate, suppose you have two views with touch handling, and their common superview has a pinch gesture recognizer. Normally, if you touch both views simultaneously and pinch, the pinch gesture recognizer recognizes. But if both views are marked `isExclusiveTouch`, the pinch gesture recognizer does *not* recognize.

Gesture Recognition Logic

When a gesture recognizer recognizes its gesture, everything changes. As we've already seen, the touches for this gesture recognizer are sent to their hit-test views as a `touchesCancelled(_:with:)` message, and then no longer arrive at those views (unless the gesture recognizer's `cancelsTouchesInView` is `false`). Moreover, all other gesture recognizers pending with regard to these touches are made to fail, and then are no longer sent the touches they were receiving either.

If the very same event might cause more than one gesture recognizer to recognize, there's an algorithm for picking the one that will succeed and make the others fail: a gesture recognizer lower down the view hierarchy (closer to the hit-test view) prevails over one higher up the hierarchy, and a gesture recognizer more recently added to its view prevails over one less recently added.

There are various ways to modify this "first past the post" behavior:

Dependency order

Certain methods institute a dependency order, causing a gesture recognizer to be put on hold when it tries to transition from the `.possible` state to the `.began` (continuous) or `.ended` (discrete) state; only if a certain other gesture recognizer fails is this one permitted to perform that transition:

- `require(toFail:)`
  sent to a gesture recognizer

- `shouldRequireFailure(of:)`
  in a subclass

- shouldBeRequiredToFail(by:)
  in a subclass

- gestureRecognizer(_:shouldRequireFailureOf:)
  in the delegate

- gestureRecognizer(_:shouldBeRequiredToFailBy:)
  in the delegate

The first of those methods sets up a permanent relationship between two gesture recognizers, and cannot be undone; but the others are sent every time a gesture starts in a view whose swarm includes both gesture recognizers, and the result is applied only on this occasion.

The delegate methods work together as follows. For each pair of gesture recognizers in the hit-test view's swarm, the members of that pair are arranged in a fixed order (as I've already described). The first of the pair is sent shouldRequire and then shouldBeRequired, and then the second of the pair is sent should-Require and then shouldBeRequired. But if any of those four methods returns true, the relationship between that pair is settled and we proceed immediately to the next pair.

(Apple says that in a dependency like this, the gesture recognizer that fails first is not sent reset, and won't receive any touches, until the second finishes its state sequence and is sent reset, so that they resume recognizing together.)

Success into failure

Certain methods, by returning false, turn success into failure; at the moment when a gesture recognizer is about to declare that it recognizes its gesture, transitioning from the .possible state to the .began (continuous) or .ended (discrete) state, it is forced to fail instead:

- gestureRecognizerShouldBegin(_:)
  in a view

- gestureRecognizerShouldBegin(_:)
  in the delegate

Simultaneous recognition

Certain methods ensure that when a gesture recognizer succeeds, some other gesture recognizer is *not* forced to fail:

- gestureRecognizer(_:shouldRecognizeSimultaneouslyWith:)
  in the delegate

- canPrevent(_:)
  in a subclass

- `canBePrevented(by:)`
  in a subclass

In the subclass methods, `prevent` means "by succeeding, you force failure upon this other," and `bePrevented` means "by succeeding, this other forces failure on you." They work together as follows. `canPrevent` is called first; if it returns `false`, that's the end of the story for that gesture recognizer, and `canPrevent` is called on the other gesture recognizer. But if `canPrevent` returns `true` when it is first called, the other gesture recognizer is sent `canBePrevented`. If it returns `true`, that's the end of the story; if it returns `false`, the process starts over the other way round, sending `canPrevent` to the second gesture recognizer, and so forth. In this way, conflicting answers are resolved without the device exploding: prevention is regarded as exceptional (even though it is in fact the norm) and will happen only if it is acquiesced to by everyone involved.

Interface

This part of the book describes view controllers, the major building blocks of an app's interface and functionality, along with the views provided by the UIKit framework:

- Chapter 6 is about view controllers, the basis of an iOS app's architecture. View controllers manage interface and respond to user actions. Most of your app's code will be in a view controller.

- Chapter 7 is about scroll views, which let the user slide and zoom the interface.

- Chapter 8 explains table views and collection views, which are scroll views for navigating through data.

- Chapter 9 is about popovers, split views, iPad multitasking, drag and drop, and multiple windows on iPad.

- Chapter 10 describes how text is presented in an iOS app's interface.

- Chapter 11 explains how to put a web browser inside your app.

- Chapter 12 describes all the remaining built-in UIKit interface objects.

- Chapter 13 is about various forms of modal dialog that can appear in front of an app's interface.

PART II

interface

CHAPTER 6

View Controllers

An iOS app's interface is dynamic, and with good reason. The entire interface has to fit into a single display consisting of a single window, which in the case of the iPhone can be forbiddingly tiny. The solution is to change the interface. In response to some event — typically a user action — a new view, possibly with an elaborate hierarchy of subviews, replaces or covers the previous interface.

For this to work, regions of interface material — often the entire contents of the screen — must come and go in an agile fashion that is understandable to the user. There will typically be a logical, structural, and functional relationship between the view that was showing and the view that replaces or covers it. This relationship will need to be maintained behind the scenes, in your code.

The relationship between views also needs to be indicated to the user. Multiple views may be pure alternatives or siblings of one another, or one view may be a temporary replacement for another, or views may be like successive pages of a book. Animation is often used to emphasize and clarify these relationships as one view is superseded by another. Navigational interface and a vivid, suggestive gestural vocabulary give the user an ability to control what's seen and an understanding of the possible options: a tab bar whose buttons summon alternate views, a back button or a swipe gesture for returning to a previously visited view, a tap on an interface element to dive deeper into a conceptual world, a Done or Cancel button to escape from a settings screen, and so forth.

In Cocoa apps, the management of this dynamic interface is performed through view controllers. A *view controller* is an instance of UIViewController. Actually, it will be an instance of a UIViewController *subclass*; UIViewController is designed to be subclassed. You might write your own UIViewController subclass; you might use a built-in subclass such as UINavigationController or UITabBarController; or you might subclass a built-in subclass such as UITableViewController (Chapter 8).

A view controller manages a view together with that view's subviews, their subviews, and so on. The single superview at the top of that hierarchy is the view controller's *main view*, or simply its *view*; the view controller's `view` property points to it. A view controller's main view has no explicit pointer to the view controller that manages it, but a view controller is a UIResponder and is in the responder chain just above its view, so it is its view's `next` responder.

View Controller Responsibilities

For a view controller to be useful, its view must somehow *get into the visible interface*; a view controller is usually responsible for that, but typically *not* the view controller whose view this is — rather, this will be some view controller whose view is *already* in the interface. In many cases, that will happen automatically (I'll talk more about that in the next section), but you can participate in the process, and for some view controllers you may have to do the work yourself. A view that comes may also eventually go, and the view controller responsible for putting a view into the interface will usually be responsible also for removing it.

A view controller will typically provide *animation* of the interface as a view comes or goes. Built-in view controller subclasses, and built-in ways of summoning or removing a view controller and its view, come with built-in animations. We are all familiar with tapping something to make new interface slide in from the side of the screen, and then later tapping a back button to make that interface slide back out again. Whoever is responsible for getting a view controller's view into the interface is also responsible for providing the animation.

The most powerful view controller is the *top-level view controller*. This might be a fullscreen presented view controller, as I'll explain later in this chapter; but most of the time it will be your app's *root view controller*. This is the view controller managing the *root view*, the view that sits at the top of the entire view hierarchy, as the one and only direct subview of the window, acting as the superview for the rest of the app's interface (Chapter 1). The root view controller attains this lofty position because `UIApplicationMain`, or your code, puts it there, instantiating it and assigning it to the window's `rootViewController` property. The window responds by taking the view controller's main view, giving it the correct frame (resizing it if necessary), and making it its own subview ("How an App Launches" on page 4).

The top-level view controller bears ultimate responsibility for some important decisions about the behavior of your app:

Manipulation of the status bar
> The status bar is actually a secondary window belonging to the runtime. The runtime consults the top-level view controller as to whether the status bar should be present and, if so, whether its text should be light or dark.

Rotation of the interface

> The user can rotate the device, and you might like the interface to rotate in response, to compensate. The runtime consults the top-level view controller about whether to permit such rotation.

Above and beyond all this, view controllers are typically the heart of any app, by virtue of their role in the app's overall architecture. Views give the user something to tap, and they display data for the user to see; the logic of determining, at any given moment, *what* views are shown, *what* data those views display, and *what* the response to the user's gestures should be, is usually vested in a view controller.

View Controller Hierarchy

There is always one root view controller, along with its view, the root view. There may also be other view controllers, each of which has its own main view. Those other view controllers are *subordinate* to the root view controller. There are two subordination relationships between view controllers:

Parentage (containment)

> A view controller can *contain* another view controller. The containing view controller is the *parent* of the contained view controller; the contained view controller is a *child* of the containing view controller. A containment relationship between two view controllers is reflected in their views: the child view controller's view, if it is in the interface at all, is a *subview* (at some depth) of the parent view controller's view.
>
> The parent view controller is responsible for getting a child view controller's view into the interface, by making it a subview of its own view, and (if necessary) for removing it later. Introduction of a view, removal of a view, and replacement of one view with another often involve a parent view controller managing its children and their views.

Presentation (modal)

> A view controller can *present* another view controller. The first view controller is the *presenting* view controller of the second; the second view controller is the *presented* view controller of the first. The second view controller's view replaces or covers, completely or partially, the first view controller's view.
>
> The name of this mechanism, and of the relationship between the view controllers, has evolved over time. In iOS 4 and before, the presented view controller was called a *modal view controller*, and its view was a *modal view*; there is an analogy here to the desktop, where a window is modal if it sits in front of, and denies the user access to, the rest of the interface until it is explicitly dismissed. The terms *presented view controller* and *presented view* are more recent and more

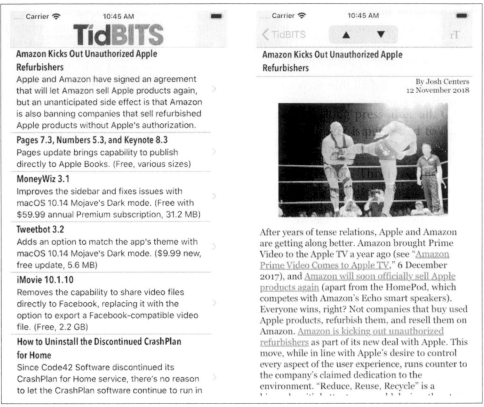

Figure 6-1. The TidBITS News app

general, but the historical term "modal" still appears in the documentation and in the API.

Here's an example of a parent view controller and a child view controller — the familiar navigation interface, where the user taps something and new interface slides in from the side, replacing the current interface. Figure 6-1 shows the TidBITS News app displaying a list of story headlines and summaries (on the left). The user taps an entry in the list, and the whole list slides away to one side, and the text of that story slides in from the other side (on the right).

The list and the story are both child view controllers. The parent view controller is a UINavigationController, which manipulates the views of its children to bring about this animated change of the interface. The parent view controller (the navigation controller) stays put, and so does its own view, which functions as a fixed superview within which all this view-swapping takes place.

Here's an example of a presenting view controller and a presented view controller. Figure 6-2 shows the Zotz! app's settings screen (on the left). The user can edit a

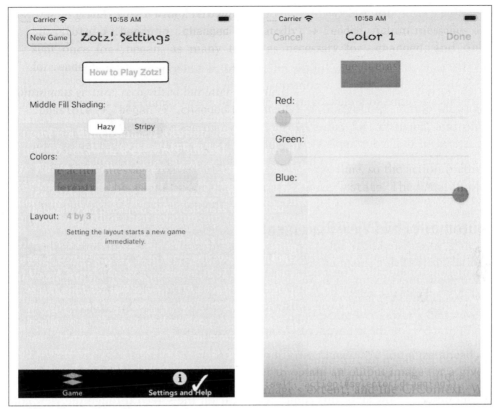

Figure 6-2. The Zotz! app

color by tapping a color swatch; a new screen then slides up from the bottom, offering three color sliders (on the right). The color editing interface is modal; it is being presented from the settings screen. The color editing interface has a Cancel button and a Done button, clearly implying that this is a place where the user must make a decision and can do nothing else until the decision is made. (But as I'll explain later, that isn't the only use of a presented view controller.)

There is a *hierarchy of view controllers*. It starts with the root view controller, which is the *only* nonsubordinate view controller. Every other view controller, if its view is to appear in the interface, *must* be a subordinate view controller. It can be a *child* view controller of some parent view controller; or it can be a *presented* view controller of some presenting view controller. And those are the only possibilities!

There is also a *hierarchy of views*. And there is a well-defined relationship between the view controller hierarchy and the view hierarchy:

- For a parent view controller and child view controller, the child's view, if present in the interface, must be a *subview* of the parent's view.

- For a presenting view controller and presented view controller, the presented view controller's view either *replaces* or *covers* (partially or completely) the presenting view controller's view.

In this way, the actual views of the interface form a hierarchy dictated by *and parallel to* some portion of the view controller hierarchy: *every* view visible in the interface owes its presence to a view controller's view, either because it *is* a view controller's view, or because it's a *subview* of a view controller's view.

It is *crucial* that your app's view controller hierarchy and view hierarchy be structured coherently, in the way I have just described, at every moment of your app's lifetime. If your app behaves as a good Cocoa citizen, they will be — as I will now illustrate.

Automatic Child View Placement

The placement of a view controller's view into the view hierarchy will often be performed automatically. You might never need to put a UIViewController's view into the view hierarchy yourself. You'll manipulate view controllers; their hierarchy and their built-in functionality will construct and manage the view hierarchy for you.

In Figure 6-1, on the left, we see two interface elements:

- The navigation bar, containing the TidBITS logo.
- The list of stories, which is actually a UITableView.

I will describe how all of this comes to appear on the screen through the view controller hierarchy and the view hierarchy. The relationship between view controllers and views is diagrammed in Figure 6-3. In the diagram, notice the word "automatic" in the two large right-pointing arrows associating a view controller with its view; this tells you how the view controller's view became part of the view hierarchy:

Root view controller
  The window's root view controller is a UINavigationController:

  - The UINavigationController's view is the window's sole immediate subview (the root view). That happened *automatically*, by virtue of the UINavigationController being the window's `rootViewController`.
  - The navigation bar is a subview of that view.

Child view controller
  The UINavigationController has a child UIViewController (a parent–child relationship). The child is a custom UIViewController subclass, which I've called MasterViewController:

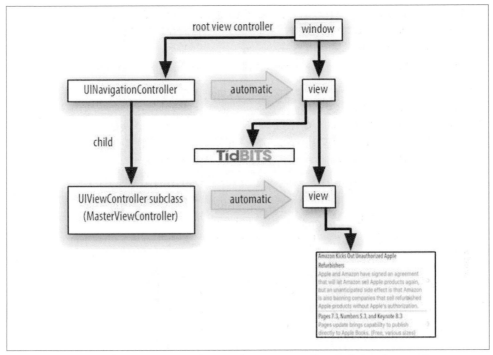

Figure 6-3. The TidBITS News app's initial view controller and view hierarchy

- MasterViewController's view is the UITableView, and it is *another* subview of the UINavigationController's view. That happened *automatically*, by virtue of the MasterViewController being the UINavigationController's child.

Manual Child View Placement

Sometimes, you'll write your own parent view controller class. In that case, *you* will be doing the kind of work that the UINavigationController was doing in that example, so you will need to put a child view controller's view into the interface *manually*, as a subview (at some depth) of the parent view controller's view.

I'll illustrate with another app of mine (Figure 6-4). The interface displays a flashcard containing information about a Latin word, along with a toolbar (the dark area at the bottom) where the user can tap an icon to choose additional functionality.

The app actually contains over a thousand of these Latin words, and I want the user to be able to navigate between flashcards to see the next or previous word; there is an excellent built-in UIViewController subclass for this purpose, the UIPageViewController. But the toolbar at the bottom stays put, so the toolbar can't be inside the UIPageViewController's view. How is this going to work?

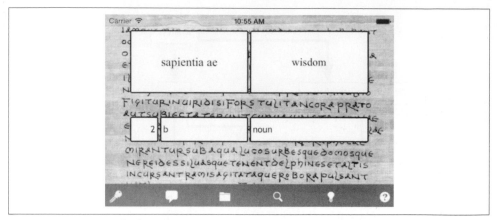

Figure 6-4. A Latin flashcard app

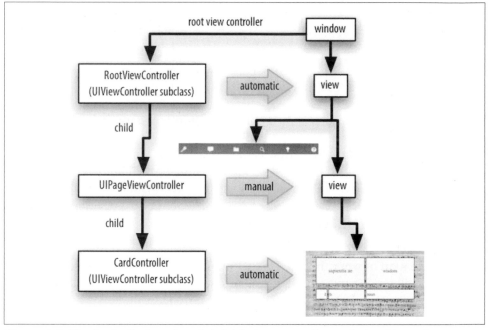

Figure 6-5. The Latin flashcard app's initial view controller and view hierarchy

Again, I will describe how the interface comes to appear on the screen through the view controller hierarchy and the view hierarchy. The relationships are diagrammed in Figure 6-5:

Root view controller

The window's root view controller is my own UIViewController subclass, called RootViewController:

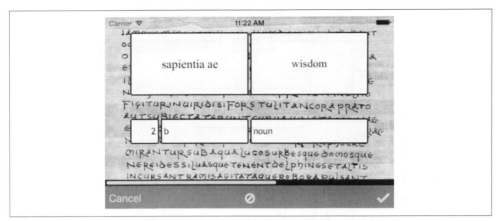

Figure 6-6. The Latin flashcard app, in drill mode

- RootViewController's view becomes the window's subview (the root view) *automatically*, by virtue of the RootViewController being the window's `root-ViewController`.
- The toolbar is a subview of RootViewController's view.

Child view controller
In order for the UIPageViewController's view to appear in the interface, since it is not the root view controller, it *must* be some view controller's child. My Root-ViewController is the only possible parent, so it must function as a custom parent view controller, with the UIPageViewController as its child. So I have made that happen, and therefore:

- I myself have had to put the UIPageViewController's view *manually* as a subview into my RootViewController's view.

Child view controller
I hand the UIPageViewController, as its child, an instance of another custom UIViewController subclass, called CardController (representing a flashcard):

- The UIPageViewController displays the CardController's view as a subview of its own view *automatically*.

Presented View Placement

My Latin flashcard app has a second mode, where the user is drilled on a subset of the cards in random order; the interface looks very much like the first mode's interface (Figure 6-6), but it behaves completely differently.

In reality, this is a presented view controller. The relationship between view controllers and views is diagrammed in Figure 6-7:

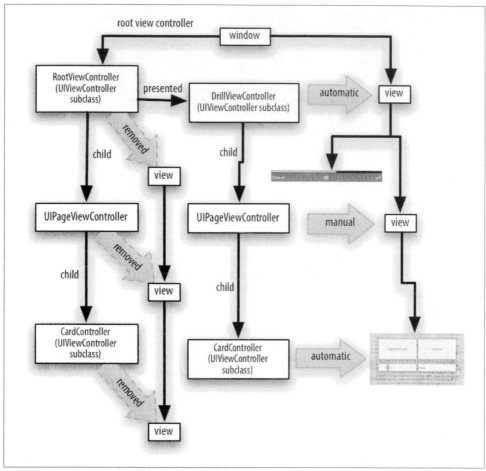

Figure 6-7. The Latin flashcard app's drill mode view controller and view hierarchy

Presented view controller

I have a UIViewController subclass called DrillViewController; it is structured very much like RootViewController. When the user is in drill mode, a DrillView-Controller is *presented* by the RootViewController. This means that the Drill-ViewController's interface takes over the screen *automatically:*

- The DrillViewController's view, with its whole subview hierarchy, including the views of the DrillViewController's children in the view controller hierarchy, *replaces* the RootViewController's view and *its* whole subview hierarchy.

Presenting view controller

The RootViewController is still the window's `rootViewController`, and its hierarchy of child view controllers remains in place while the DrillViewController is being presented. But:

- The RootViewController's view and its subviews are not in the interface.
- They will be returned to the interface automatically when we leave drill mode (because the presented DrillViewController is dismissed), and the situation will look like Figure 6-5 once again.

Ensuring a Coherent Hierarchy

For any app that you write, for every moment in the lifetime of that app, you should be able to construct a diagram showing the hierarchy of view controllers and charting how each view controller's view fits into the view hierarchy. The diagram should be similar to mine! The view hierarchy should run in neat parallel with the view controller hierarchy; there should be no crossed wires or orphan views. Every view controller's view should be placed *automatically* into the view hierarchy, *except* in the following two situations:

- You have created a custom parent view controller, and this view controller is its child ("Container View Controllers" on page 375).
- You're doing a custom transition animation ("Custom Transition" on page 350).

You can *see* the view controller hierarchy in schematic form by pausing in the debugger and giving this incantation:

```
(lldb) e -l objc -O -- [UIViewController _printHierarchy]
```

If I give that command when my Latin flashcard app is in the state shown in Figure 6-4, the output looks like this (omitting some of the information):

```
<JS_Latin_Vocab_iPhone_3.RootViewController ... >
   | <UIPageViewController ... >
   |    | <JS_Latin_Vocab_iPhone_3.CardController ... >
```

The analysis accords with mine: The window's root view controller is my RootViewController, which has a child UIPageViewController, which has a child CardController.

Another way to inspect the view controller hierarchy is the view debugger (Figure 6-8). This provides even more information. The view controller hierarchy is displayed with circular icons; interleaved with those, the corresponding view hierarchy is displayed with square icons.

Together, the view controller hierarchy and the view hierarchy constitute the bulk of the *responder chain*. What you're really doing by following the rules is ensuring a coherent responder chain.

Figure 6-8. The view debugger displays the view controller hierarchy

View Controller Creation

A view controller is an instance like any other, and it is *created* like any other instance — by instantiating its class. You might perform this instantiation in code; in that case, you'll also initialize and configure the instance as needed. Here's an example from one of my own apps:

```
let llc = LessonListController(terms: self.terms)
let nav = UINavigationController(rootViewController: llc)
```

In that example:

- LessonListController is my own UIViewController subclass, so I have called its designated initializer, which I myself have defined.

- UINavigationController is a built-in UIViewController subclass, and I have called one of its convenience initializers.

Once a view controller comes into existence, it must be *retained* so that it will persist. That will happen automatically when the view controller is assigned a place in the view controller hierarchy:

- A view controller assigned as a window's rootViewController is retained by the *window*.

- A view controller assigned as another view controller's child is retained by the *parent* view controller.

- A presented view controller is retained by the *presenting* view controller.

The retaining view controller then takes ownership, and will release the other view controller in good order if and when it is no longer needed.

Here's an example, from one of my apps, of view controllers being instantiated and then retained through their insertion into the view controller hierarchy:

```
let llc = LessonListController(terms: self.terms) ❶❷
let nav = UINavigationController(rootViewController: llc) ❸
self.present(nav, animated: true) ❹
```

That's the same code I showed a moment ago, extended by one line. It comes from a view controller class called RootViewController. Here's how view controller creation and memory management works in those three lines:

❶ The current view controller, `self`, is a RootViewController instance. It is already the window's `rootViewController`, and is retained by the window.

❷ I instantiate LessonListController.

❸ I instantiate UINavigationController, and I assign the LessonListController instance to the UINavigationController instance as its child; the navigation controller retains the LessonListController instance and takes ownership of it.

❹ I present the UINavigationController instance on `self`, the RootViewController instance; the RootViewController instance is the presenting view controller, and it retains and takes ownership of the UINavigationController instance as its presented view controller.

Whenever you instantiate a view controller, you should ask yourself who will be retaining it. Everything works fine if you do things correctly, but it is possible to do things incorrectly. If you're not careful, you might put a view controller's view into the interface while permitting the view controller itself to go out of existence. If that happens, the view will mysteriously fail to perform its intended functionality, because that functionality is embodied in the view controller, which no longer exists. (Yes, I've made this mistake.)

How a View Controller Obtains Its View

When it first comes into existence, a view controller *has no view*. A view is a relatively heavyweight object, involving interface elements that can entail a significant amount of memory. Therefore, a view controller postpones obtaining its view until it is first asked for the value of its `view` property. At that moment, if its `view` property is `nil`, the view controller sets about obtaining its view. (We say that a view controller loads its view *lazily*.) Typically, this happens because the time has come to put the view controller's view into the interface.

In working with a newly instantiated view controller, be careful not to refer to its `view` property if you don't need to, as that can cause the view controller to obtain its view prematurely. (As usual, I speak from experience.) To learn whether a view controller *has* a view without causing it to *load* its view, consult its `isViewLoaded` property. You can also refer to a view controller's view safely, without loading it, as its `viewIfLoaded` (an Optional).

As soon as a view controller has its view, its `viewDidLoad` method is called. If this view controller is an instance of your own UIViewController subclass, `viewDidLoad` is your opportunity to modify the contents of this view — to populate it with subviews, to tweak the subviews it already has, and so forth — as well as to perform other initializations of the view controller and its properties. `viewDidLoad` is generally regarded as a valuable place to put initialization code, because it is one of the *earliest* events in the life of the view controller instance, and it is called only *once* in the instance's lifetime.

When `viewDidLoad` is called, the view controller's `view` property is pointing to the view, so it is safe to refer to `self.view`. Bear in mind that the view may not yet be part of the interface! In fact, it almost certainly is not. (To confirm this, check whether `self.view.window` is `nil`.) You cannot necessarily rely on the *dimensions* of the view at this point to be the dimensions that the view will assume when it becomes visible in the interface. Performing dimension-dependent customizations prematurely in `viewDidLoad` is a common beginner mistake, and I'll talk about that in detail later in this chapter.

Before `viewDidLoad` is called, the view controller must *obtain* its view. The question of where and how the view controller will get its view is often crucial. In some cases, to be sure, you won't care about this. In particular, when a view controller is an instance of a built-in UIViewController subclass such as UINavigationController or UITabBarController, its view is out of your hands; you might never have cause to refer to this view over the entire course of your app's lifetime, and you simply trust that the view controller will generate its view somehow. But when the view controller is an instance of your own subclass of UIViewController, and when you yourself will design or modify its view, it becomes essential to understand the process whereby a view controller gets its view.

This process is not difficult to understand. It is rather elaborate, because there are multiple possibilities, but it is *not magic*. Nevertheless it probably causes beginners more confusion than any other aspect of Cocoa programming. The main alternatives are:

- The view may be instantiated in the view controller's own code, manually.
- The view may be created as an empty generic UIView, automatically.
- The view may be loaded from a nib file.

To demonstrate, we'll need a view controller that we instantiate manually. For the sake of simplicity, I'll use the window's `rootViewController`.

To follow along hands-on, start with a clean project created from the Single View App template. The template includes a storyboard and a UIViewController subclass called ViewController, but we're going to ignore both of those, behaving as if the storyboard didn't exist. Instead, we'll have a class called RootViewController; in code, at launch, we'll instantiate it and make that instance the window's root view controller (see "App Without a Storyboard" on page 6). When you launch the project, you'll know that the root view controller has obtained its view, because you'll *see* it.

Manual View

To supply a UIViewController's view manually, in code, override its `loadView` method. Your job here is to obtain an instance of UIView (or a subclass of UIView) — typically by instantiating it directly — and *assign it to* `self.view`. You must *not* call `super` (for reasons that I'll make clear later on).

Let's try it:

1. We need a UIViewController subclass, so choose File → New → File; specify iOS → Source → Cocoa Touch Class. Click Next.
2. Name the class RootViewController, and specify that it is to be a UIViewController subclass. Uncheck "Also create XIB file" (if it happens to be checked). Click Next.
3. Confirm that we're saving into the appropriate folder and group, and that these files will be part of the app target. Click Create.

We now have a RootViewController class, and we proceed to edit its code. In *RootViewController.swift*, we'll implement `loadView`. To convince ourselves that the example is working correctly, we'll give the view that we create manually an identifiable color, and we'll put some interface inside it, namely a "Hello, World" label:

```
override func loadView() {
    let v = UIView()
    v.backgroundColor = .green
    self.view = v // *
    let label = UILabel()
    v.addSubview(label)
    label.text = "Hello, World!"
    label.autoresizingMask = [
        .flexibleTopMargin,
        .flexibleLeftMargin,
        .flexibleBottomMargin,
        .flexibleRightMargin]
    label.sizeToFit()
    label.center = v.bounds.center
    label.frame = label.frame.integral
}
```

The starred line is the key: we made a view and we assigned it to `self.view`. To see that that code works, we need to instantiate RootViewController and place that instance into our view controller hierarchy. Edit *SceneDelegate.swift* to look like this:

```
import UIKit
class SceneDelegate: UIResponder, UIWindowSceneDelegate {
    var window: UIWindow?
    func scene(_ scene: UIScene,
            willConnectTo session: UISceneSession,
            options connectionOptions: UIScene.ConnectionOptions) {
        if let windowScene = scene as? UIWindowScene {
            self.window = UIWindow(windowScene: windowScene)
            let rvc = RootViewController() // *
            self.window!.rootViewController = rvc // *
            self.window!.backgroundColor = .white
            self.window!.makeKeyAndVisible()
        }
    }
}
```

Again, the starred lines are the key: we instantiate RootViewController and make that instance the window's root view controller. Build and run the app. Sure enough, there's our green background and our "Hello, world" label!

When we created our view controller's view (`self.view`), we never gave it a reasonable frame. This is because we are relying on someone else to frame the view appropriately. In this case, the "someone else" is the window. When its `rootViewController` property is set to a view controller, it responds by giving the view controller's view a frame and putting it into the window as a subview, making it the root view.

In general, it is the responsibility of whoever puts a view controller's view into the interface to give the view the correct frame — and this will never be the view controller itself (although under some circumstances the view controller can express a preference in this regard). Indeed, the size of a view controller's view may be changed as it is placed into the interface, and you must keep that possibility in mind as you design your view controller's view and its subviews. (That's why, in the preceding code, I used autoresizing to keep the label centered in the view, no matter how the view may be resized.)

Generic Automatic View

We should distinguish between *creating* a view and *populating* it. The preceding example fails to draw this distinction. The lines that create our RootViewController's view are merely these:

```
let v = UIView()
self.view = v
```

Everything else configures and populates the view, turning it green and putting a label into it. A more appropriate place to populate a view controller's view is its `view-DidLoad` implementation, which, as I've already mentioned, is called after the view exists and can be referred to as `self.view`. We could therefore rewrite the preceding example like this (just for fun, I'll use autolayout this time):

```
override func loadView() {
    let v = UIView()
    self.view = v
}
override func viewDidLoad() {
    super.viewDidLoad()
    let v = self.view!
    v.backgroundColor = .green
    let label = UILabel()
    v.addSubview(label)
    label.text = "Hello, World!"
    label.translatesAutoresizingMaskIntoConstraints = false
    NSLayoutConstraint.activate([
        label.centerXAnchor.constraint(equalTo:v.centerXAnchor),
        label.centerYAnchor.constraint(equalTo:v.centerYAnchor)
    ])
}
```

But if we're going to do that, we can go even further and remove our implementation of `loadView` entirely! It turns out that if you *don't* implement `loadView`, and if no view is supplied in any other way, then UIViewController's default implementation of `loadView` will do *exactly* what we are doing: it creates a generic UIView object and assigns it to `self.view`. If we needed our view controller's view to be a particular UIView subclass, that wouldn't be acceptable; but in this case, our view controller's view *is* a generic UIView object, so it *is* acceptable.

Comment out or delete the entire `loadView` implementation from the preceding code, and build and run the app; our example still works!

View in a Separate Nib

In the preceding examples, we supplied and designed our view controller's view in code. That works, but of course we're missing out on the convenience of configuring and populating the view by designing it graphically in Xcode's nib editor. So now let's see how a view controller can obtain its view, ready-made, from a nib file.

To make this work, the nib file must be properly configured in accordance with the demands of the nib-loading mechanism. The view controller instance will already have been created. It will load the nib, *setting itself as the nib's owner*. The nib must be prepared for this situation:

- The owner object must have the same class as the view controller. This will also cause the owner object to have a `view` outlet.

- The owner object's `view` outlet must point to the view object in the nib.

The consequence is that when the view controller loads the nib, the view instantiated from the nib is assigned to the view controller's `view` property automatically.

Let's try it with a *.xib* file. In a *.xib* file, the owner object is the File's Owner proxy object. We can use the example we've already developed, with our RootView-Controller class. Delete the implementation of `loadView` (if you haven't already) and `viewDidLoad` from *RootViewController.swift*, because we want the view to come from a nib and we're going to populate it in the nib. Then:

1. Choose File → New → File and specify iOS → User Interface → View. This will be a *.xib* file containing a UIView object. Click Next.

2. Name the file *MyNib* (meaning *MyNib.xib*). Confirm the appropriate folder and group, and make sure that the file will be part of the app target. Click Create.

3. Edit *MyNib.xib*. Prepare it in the way I described a moment ago:

    a. Select the File's Owner object; in the Identity inspector, set its class to Root-ViewController. As a result, the File's Owner now has a `view` outlet.

    b. Connect the File's Owner `view` outlet to the View object.

4. Design the view. To make it clear that this is not the same view we were creating previously, perhaps you should give the view a red background color (in the Attributes inspector). Drag a UILabel into the middle of the view and give it some text, such as "Hello, World!"

When our RootViewController instance wants its view, we want it to load the *MyNib* nib. To make it do that, we must associate this nib with our RootViewController instance. Recall these two lines in *SceneDelegate.swift*:

```
let rvc = RootViewController()
self.window!.rootViewController = rvc
```

We're going to change the first of those two lines. A UIViewController has a `nibName` property that tells it what nib, if any, it should load to obtain its view. But we are not allowed to set the `nibName` property of `rvc`; it is read-only, meaning that only Root-ViewController can set its own `nibName`. Instead, as we instantiate the view controller, we use the designated initializer, `init(nibName:bundle:)`, like this:

```
let rvc = RootViewController(nibName:"MyNib", bundle:nil)
self.window!.rootViewController = rvc
```

(The `nil` argument to the `bundle:` parameter specifies the main bundle, which is almost always what you want.) The result is that RootViewController *does* set its own `nibName` to `"MyNib"`, and obtains its view by locating that nib file and loading it.

To prove that this works, build and run. The red background appears! Our view controller's view is being obtained by loading it from the nib.

The eponymous nib

Now I'm going to describe a shortcut, based on the *name* of the nib. It turns out that if the nib name passed to `init(nibName:bundle:)` is `nil`, a nib will be sought automatically *with the same name as the view controller's class*. Moreover, UIView-Controller's `init()` turns out to be a convenience initializer: it actually calls `init(nibName:bundle:)`, passing `nil` for both arguments.

This means that we can return to using `init()` to initialize the view controller, provided that the nib file's name *matches the name* of the view controller class. Let's try it:

1. Rename *MyNib.xib* to *RootViewController.xib*.

2. Change the code that instantiates and initializes our RootViewController back to what it was before:

    ```
    let rvc = RootViewController()
    self.window!.rootViewController = rvc
    ```

Build and run. It works!

There's an additional aspect to that shortcut. It seems ridiculous that we should end up with a nib that has "Controller" in its name merely because our view controller, as is so often the case, has "Controller" in *its* name. A nib, after all, is not a controller. It turns out that the runtime, in looking for a view controller's corresponding nib, will in fact try stripping "Controller" off the end of the view controller class's name. We can name our nib file *RootView.xib* instead of *RootViewController.xib*, and it will *still* be properly associated with our RootViewController instance.

Automatic XIB file creation

When we created our UIViewController subclass, RootViewController, we saw in the Xcode dialog a checkbox offering to create an eponymous *.xib* file at the same time: "Also create XIB file." We deliberately unchecked it. We are now in a position to understand what happens if we check that checkbox:

- Xcode creates *RootViewController.swift* and *RootViewController.xib*.

- Xcode configures *RootViewController.xib*:

    - The File's Owner's class is set to the view controller's class, RootView-Controller.

    - The File's Owner's `view` outlet is hooked up to the view.

The view controller and *.xib* file are ready for use together: you instantiate the view controller with a `nil` nib name, and it gets its view from the eponymous nib. (The *.xib* file created by Xcode in response to checking "Also create XIB file" does *not* have "Controller" stripped off the end of its name; you can rename it manually later if the default name bothers you.)

Summary

We can now summarize the sequence whereby a view controller's view is obtained. It turns out that the entire process is driven by loadView:

1. When the view controller first decides that it needs its view, loadView is *always* called:

    - If we override loadView, we supply and set the view in code, and we do *not* call super. Therefore, the process of seeking a view comes to an end.

    - If we *don't* override loadView, UIViewController's built-in default implementation of loadView takes over, and performs the rest of the process.

2. UIViewController's default implementation of loadView looks for a nib:

    - If the view controller's nibName property is not nil, a nib with that name is sought, and the process comes to an end.

    - If the view controller's nibName property *is* nil, then:

        1. An eponymous nib is sought. If it is found, it is loaded and the process comes to an end.

        2. If the view controller's name ends in "Controller," an eponymous nib without the "Controller" is sought. If it is found, it is loaded and the process comes to an end.

3. If we reach this point, UIViewController's default implementation of loadView creates a generic UIView.

If things go wrong during that process, at best the wrong view might appear; at worst the app might crash. Typically a crash happens because the view controller tries to obtain its view by loading a nib, but it fails, because:

- A nibName is specified but there is no such nib.

- A nib is found but the nib itself is not correctly configured: the file's owner is not of the right class, or its view outlet is not set.

How Storyboards Work

Up to this point, in explaining where a view controller comes from and how it gets its view, I've been ignoring the existence of storyboards. That's not because storyboards work differently from what I've been describing; it's because storyboards work *the same way* as what I've been describing.

First of all, what *is* a storyboard? It's actually a collection of nib files, along with some ancillary information about them (stored in an *Info.plist* file). And what's a nib file? It's just a set of instructions for creating and configuring instances. When a nib is loaded during the running of the app, those instructions are obeyed and the instances are created and configured. The instances in question will mostly be UIView instances; the advantage of a nib as a way of making view instances is that you get to design those views graphically, as in a drawing program, instead of having to describe them in code. But it is also legal for a nib object to be a view controller. So it is possible to store the instructions for creating and configuring a view controller in a nib file, and to obtain the actual view controller instance at runtime by loading the nib.

Storyboards contain *scenes*. Each scene consists of a view controller. Each view controller goes into a nib file. When the app runs, if an instance of that view controller is needed, that nib is loaded — and so that view controller's class is instantiated and the instance is configured. That answers the question about where the view controller comes from.

And how does this view controller get its view? Well, it *can* get its view in any of the ways I've just finished describing, but usually it will use the third way: it will get its view from a nib. By default, a storyboard scene contains *two* things: a view controller *and its main view.* The view controller goes into a nib file, and its main view goes into *another* nib file. This second nib file configures the view, its subviews, and any other top-level objects such as gesture recognizers. The view nib has a special name, such as *01J-lp-oVM-view-Ze5-6b-2t3.nib*, so that the view controller can find it later. And the view nib is correctly configured: its File's Owner class is the view controller's class, with its view outlet hooked to the view. When the view controller has been instantiated and needs its view, it loads the corresponding view nib.

As a result of this architecture, a storyboard has all the memory management advantages of nib files: none of these nib files are loaded until the instances that they contain are needed, and they can be loaded multiple times to give additional instances of the same nib objects. At the same time, you get the convenience of being able, through the nib editor, to see and edit a lot of your app's interface simultaneously in one place.

How a Storyboard View Controller Nib is Loaded

A storyboard is first and foremost a source of view controller instances. In fact, you can set up your app in such a way that a storyboard is the source of *every* view controller that your app will ever instantiate; what's more, you can usually configure the storyboard in such a way that every view controller your app will ever need will be instantiated *automatically* at exactly the moment it is needed.

To instantiate a view controller from a storyboard, we must load a view controller nib from that storyboard. The process therefore starts with a reference to the storyboard. You can get a reference to a storyboard chiefly in one of two ways:

- Through the storyboard's name, by calling the UIStoryboard initializer `init(name:bundle:)`.

- Through the `storyboard` property of a view controller that has already been instantiated from that storyboard.

When a view controller needs to be instantiated from a storyboard, its nib can be loaded in one of four main ways:

Initial view controller

One view controller in the storyboard may be designated the storyboard's *initial view controller* (also called its *entry point*). To instantiate that view controller, call this UIStoryboard instance method:

- `instantiateInitialViewController`

The view controller instance is returned, or `nil` if the storyboard has no initial view controller.

By identifier

A view controller in a storyboard may be assigned an arbitrary string identifier; this is its Storyboard ID in the Identity inspector. To instantiate that view controller, call this UIStoryboard instance method:

- `instantiateViewController(withIdentifier:)`

The view controller instance is returned, or you'll crash if the storyboard has no such view controller.

By relationship

A parent view controller in a storyboard may have immediate children, such as a UINavigationController and its initial child view controller. The nib editor will show a *relationship* connection between them. When the parent is instantiated (the source of the relationship), the initial children (the destination of the relationship) are *automatically* instantiated at the same time.

By a triggered segue

A view controller in a storyboard may be the source of a *segue* whose destination is a child or presented view controller. When the segue is triggered and performed, it *automatically* instantiates the destination view controller.

How a Storyboard View Nib is Loaded

When a view controller is instantiated from its storyboard nib, it has no view, because (as we know) view controller views are loaded lazily. Sooner or later, the view controller will probably want its view (typically because it is time to put that view into the interface). How will it get it?

The view nib, as I already mentioned, has been assigned a special name, such as *01J-lp-oVM-view-Ze5-6b-2t3.nib*. It turns out that the view controller, in *its* nib, was handed that same special name: its `nibName` property was set to the name of the view nib. So when the view controller wants its view, it loads it in the normal way! Its `nibName` is not `nil`, so it looks for a nib by that name — and finds it. The nib is loaded and the view becomes the view controller's `view`.

Alternatively, it is possible (though not common), in the nib editor, to select the view inside a view controller in a storyboard and *delete* it. That view controller then will *not* have a corresponding view nib in the storyboard, and will have to obtain its view in some *other* way:

- Through an implementation of `loadView` in the corresponding class's code.
- By loading an eponymous nib that you supply as a *.xib* file.
- As a generic UIView created automatically.

View Resizing

It's important to be prepared for the possibility that your view controller's main view will be resized. This might happen because:

- The view is put into the interface.
- The app rotates.
- The surrounding interface changes; for example, a navigation bar gets taller or shorter, appears or disappears.
- The window itself is resized in the iPad multitasking interface.

You'll want to use layout to help your app cope with all this resizing. Autolayout is likely to be your most important ally (Chapter 1). If your code also needs to take a hand in responding to a change in the view controller's view size, that code will probably go into the view controller itself. A view controller has properties and receives events connected to the resizing of its view, so it can respond when resizing takes place, and can even help dictate the arrangement of the interface if needed.

View Size in the Nib Editor

When you design your interface in the nib editor, there are various settings for specifying the size of a view controller's main view:

The View As button at the lower left of the canvas
> You can specify that you want all view controller main views displayed at the size of a particular device, along with an orientation.

The Simulated Metrics pop-up menus in the Attributes inspector
> You can adjust for the presence or absence of interface elements that can affect layout (status bar, top bar, bottom bar).

The Simulated Size pop-up menu in the Size inspector
> By choosing Freeform, you can display a view controller's view at *any* size.

But that's just a way of *displaying* the view. It tells you nothing about the size that the view will be *when the app runs*. There's a wide range of possible sizes that the view may assume when the app runs on different devices, in different orientations, and with different surroundings. No single device size, orientation, or metrics can reflect all of these.

If you design the interface only for the size you see in the nib editor, you can get a rude surprise when you actually run the app and the view appears at some *other* size! Failing to take account of this possibility is a common beginner mistake. Be sure to design your app's interface to be coherent at *any* size it may actually assume. Use every tool at your disposal, including building and running on every simulator, to ensure this.

Bars and Underlapping

A view controller's view will often have to adapt to the presence of bars at the top and bottom of the screen:

The status bar
> The status bar is transparent, so that the region of a view behind it is visible through it. The root view, and any other fullscreen view, must occupy the *entire window*, including the status bar area. The top of the view will be behind the status bar, underlapping it and visible through it; a view behind the status bar can't be touched. You'll want to design your view so that interface objects that the user needs to see or touch are not covered by the status bar.

Top and bottom bars
> Top and bottom bars may be displayed by a navigation controller (navigation bar, toolbar) or tab bar controller (tab bar). Your view controller's view may

extend *behind* a bar, underlapping it. You'll want to design your view so that top and bottom bars don't conceal any of your view's important interface.

Safe area

The status bar may be present or absent. Top and bottom bars may be present or absent, and, if present, their height can change. How will your interface cope with such changes? The primary coping mechanism is the view controller's *safe area* (see "Safe area" on page 48). The top and bottom of the safe area move automatically at runtime to reflect the view's environment.

Here's how the safe area top is determined:

- If there is a status bar and no top bar, the safe area top is at the bottom of the status bar.
- If there is a top bar, the safe area top is at the bottom of the top bar.
- If there is no top bar and no status bar, the safe area top is at the top of the view.

Here's how the safe area bottom is determined:

- If there is a bottom bar, the safe area bottom is at the top of the bottom bar.
- If there is no bottom bar, the safe area bottom is at the bottom of the view.

(On a device without a bezel, the safe area top and bottom will take account of the "notch" and home indicator, so they might not be at the top and bottom of the view.)

The easiest way to involve the safe area in your view layout is through autolayout and constraints. A view vends the safe area as its `safeAreaLayoutGuide`. Typically, the view whose `safeAreaLayoutGuide` you'll be interested in is the view controller's main view. By constraining a subview to the `topAnchor` or `bottomAnchor` of the `safeArea-LayoutGuide`, you guarantee that the subview will move when the top or bottom of the safe area changes. Such constraints are easy to form in the nib editor — they are the default when you form a constraint from a subview to the main view.

Status bar

The status bar can be present or absent. The default behavior is that it is present, except in landscape orientation on an iPhone, where it is absent. If the status bar is present, its background is transparent and it contains text; that text can be light or dark, so as to show up against whatever is behind the status bar. The default behavior (new in iOS 13) is that the text color responds so as to contrast with the user interface style (light mode or dark mode).

The top-level view controller — which is usually the root view controller — gets a say in this behavior. Your UIViewController subclass, if an instance of it is the top-level view controller, can exercise this power by overriding these properties:

`preferredStatusBarStyle`

Your choices (UIStatusBarStyle) are:

`.default`

New in iOS 13, this means automatic in response to the user interface style. If the interface is in dark mode, the text will be light; if the interface is in light mode, the text will be dark.

`.lightContent`

The text will be light.

`.darkContent`

The text will be dark. New in iOS 13; previously, the `.default` setting gave this effect.

`prefersStatusBarHidden`

A value of `true` makes the status bar invisible; a value of `false` makes the status bar visible, even in landscape orientation on an iPhone.

Your override will be a computed variable with a getter function; your getter can return the result of a call to `super` to get the default behavior.

Even if your view controller is *not* the top-level view controller, those properties might *still* be consulted and obeyed, because your view controller might be the child of a parent that *is* the top-level view controller but *delegates* the decision-making power to one of its children, through an override of these properties:

`childForStatusBarStyle`
`childForStatusBarHidden`

Used to delegate the decision on the status bar style or visibility to a child view controller's `preferredStatusBarStyle` or `prefersStatusBarHidden`.

A tab bar controller is a case in point. It implements those properties to allow its selected child (the child view controller whose view is currently being displayed) to decide the status bar style and visibility.

You are not in charge of when status bar–related properties are consulted, but you can provide a nudge: if the situation has changed and one of those properties would now give a different answer, call `setNeedsStatusBarAppearanceUpdate` on your view controller.

If you call `setNeedsStatusBarAppearanceUpdate` and the status bar style or visibility changes, the change will be sudden. If you prefer to animate the change over time, call `setNeedsStatusBarAppearanceUpdate` inside an animations function. If the visibility changes, the nature of the animation is set by your view controller's override of preferredStatusBarUpdateAnimation; the value you return (UIStatusBar-Animation) can be .fade, .slide, or .none.

When you change the visibility of the status bar, the top of the safe area may move up or down. If your main view has subviews with constraints to the safe area's top anchor, those subviews will move. By default, the user will see this movement as a jump. If you prefer that the movement of the subviews should be animated, animate the change in layout by calling layoutIfNeeded on your view ("Animation and Layout" on page 240). If you are also animating the change in the status bar's visibility, you'll do that in the same animations function in which you call setNeedsStatusBar-AppearanceUpdate. In this example, a button's action method toggles the visibility of the status bar with smooth animation:

```
var hide = false
override var prefersStatusBarHidden : Bool {
    return self.hide
}
@IBAction func doButton(_ sender: Any) {
    self.hide.toggle()
    UIView.animate(withDuration:0.4) {
        self.setNeedsStatusBarAppearanceUpdate()
        self.view.layoutIfNeeded()
    }
}
```

New in iOS 13, if you want to know the current state of the status bar, you should ask the window scene's status bar manager (UIStatusBarManager). It has properties statusBarFrame, isStatusBarHidden, and statusBarStyle (always reported as .darkContent or .lightContent). This works even if your app doesn't explicitly support window scenes, because there is always an implicit window scene:

```
if let sbman = self.view.window?.windowScene?.statusBarManager {
    let isHidden = sbman.isStatusBarHidden
    // ...
}
```

Extended layout

If a view controller is the child of a navigation controller or tab bar controller, you can govern whether its view underlaps a top bar (navigation bar) or bottom bar (toolbar, tab bar) with these UIViewController properties:

edgesForExtendedLayout
    A UIRectEdge governing what bars this view controller's view is permitted to underlap:

.all
    A top bar or a bottom bar. The default.

`.top`
> Top bars only.

`.bottom`
> Bottom bars only.

`.none`
> This view controller's view won't underlap top and bottom bars.

`extendedLayoutIncludesOpaqueBars`
> Top and bottom bars can be translucent or not, according to the value of their `isTranslucent` property. If a view controller's `extendedLayoutIncludesOpaque-Bars` property is `true`, then if its `edgesForExtendedLayout` permits underlapping of bars, those bars will be underlapped even if their `isTranslucent` is `false`. The default is `false`, meaning that *only* translucent bars are underlapped.

Resizing and Layout Events

A view controller receives *resizing events* that notify it of changes related to the main view being resized:

`willTransition(to:with:)` *(UIContentContainer protocol)*
> Sent when the view controller's *trait collection* is about to change. This can happen for many reasons, but one possibility is a size change that causes the size classes to change, such as the app rotating 90 degrees on an iPhone. The first parameter is the *new* trait collection (a UITraitCollection). The old trait collection is still available as `self.traitCollection`. If you override this method, call `super`.

`viewWillTransition(to:with:)` *(UIContentContainer protocol)*
> Sent when the main view's *size* is about to change. The app might be about to undergo rotation, or the user might be widening or narrowing the window under iPad multitasking (see Chapter 9). The first parameter is the *new* size (a CGSize). The old size is still available as `self.view.bounds.size`. If you override this method, call `super`.

`traitCollectionDidChange(_:)` *(UITraitEnvironment protocol)*
> Sent after the trait collection changes. The parameter is the *old* trait collection; the new trait collection is available as `self.traitCollection`. If you override this method, call `super` *first* before doing anything else. (New in iOS 13, `trait-CollectionDidChange(_:)` is *not* sent when your app launches or when a view controller's view is first added to the interface.)

Do not do anything time-consuming or irrelevant in the resizing events! These events can arrive multiple times in quick succession when the app (or scene) goes into the background, so that the runtime can obtain screenshots in both orientations and in both user interface styles (light and dark mode).

The `with:` parameter in the first two methods is a *transition coordinator* (UIViewControllerTransitionCoordinator). If we're getting these events because rotation is about to take place, we can hook into the rotation animation by calling this method of the coordinator:

`animate(alongsideTransition:completion:)`
> The first parameter is an animations function; animations we supply here will be performed in coordination with the rotation animation. The second parameter is an optional completion function to be executed when the rotation animation is over.

If you need to know what the rotation is, as a CGAffineTransform, that is the coordinator's `targetTransform`. Here's a useful trick in case you need to keep a view (`self.v`) oriented the same way with respect to the *device* regardless of how the interface rotates:

```
self.v.transform =
    coordinator.targetTransform.inverted().concatenating(self.v.transform)
```

In addition, a UIViewController receives *layout events* related to the layout of its view (and compare "Layout Events" on page 78 for the corresponding UIView events):

`updateViewConstraints`
> The view is about to be told to update its constraints (`updateConstraints`), including at application launch. If you override this method, call `super`.

`viewWillLayoutSubviews`
`viewDidLayoutSubviews`
> These events surround the moment when the view is sent `layoutSubviews`, including at application launch. They are important and useful events, but they can arrive more often than you might expect, so don't do any work that you don't have to.

Layout events can be a more reliable way to detect a size change than the resizing events. There are many circumstances, such as the showing and hiding of a navigation bar that isn't underlapped, under which your view can be resized *without* a size change being reported, and you don't necessarily get any resizing event when your view is added to the interface, or at launch, even though it probably is resized at that moment. (I regard this as a flaw in the view controller event architecture.) But under those same circumstances you'll always get layout events.

Rotation

Your app can rotate, moving its top to correspond to a different edge of the device's screen. Your view controller will be intimately concerned with rotation of the app.

 A Simulator window can automatically rotate if the orientation of the app changes. Choose Hardware → Rotate Device Automatically to toggle this setting. Your choice applies to all Simulator windows.

Uses of Rotation

There are two complementary uses of rotation:

Compensatory rotation
> The app rotates to compensate for the orientation of the device, so that the interface appears right way up with respect to how the user is holding the device.

Forced rotation
> The app rotates when a particular view appears in the interface, or when the app launches, to indicate that the user needs to reorient the device in order to view the interface the right way up. This is typically because the interface has been specifically designed, in view of the fact that the screen is not square, to appear in just one orientation (portrait or landscape).

In the case of the iPhone, no law says that your app has to perform compensatory rotation. Most of my iPhone apps do not do so. My view controller views often look best in just one orientation (either just portrait or just landscape), and they stubbornly stay there regardless of how the user holds the device.

Some of those same apps may have some view controller views that look best in portrait and others that look best in landscape. In that case, I have no compunction about forcing the user to rotate the device differently depending on what view is being displayed. This is reasonable, because the iPhone has a natural right way up, and because it is small and easily reoriented 90 degrees with a twist of the user's wrist.

On the other hand, Apple thinks of an iPad as having no natural top, and would prefer iPad apps to rotate to at least two opposed orientations (such as both landscape orientations), and preferably to all four possible orientations, so that the user isn't restricted as to how the device is held.

Allowing a single interface to rotate between two orientations that are 90 degrees apart is tricky, because its dimensions must change — roughly speaking, its height and width are transposed — and this may require a change of layout, perhaps with quite substantial alterations, such as removal or addition of part of the interface. A good example is the behavior of Apple's Mail app on the iPad: in landscape, the master pane and the detail pane appear side by side, but in portrait, the master pane is removed and must be summoned as a temporary overlay on top of the detail pane (explained in Chapter 9).

Permitting Compensatory Rotation

By default, when you create an Xcode project, the app will perform compensatory rotation in response to the user's rotation of the device. For an iPhone app, this means that the app can appear with its top at the top or either side of the device. For an iPad app, it means that the app can assume any of the four orientations.

If the default behavior isn't what you want, it is up to you to change it. There are three levels at which you can make changes:

The app's Info.plist
The app itself, in its *Info.plist*, declares once and for all every orientation the interface will ever be permitted to assume. It does this under the "Supported interface orientations" key, UISupportedInterfaceOrientations. For a universal app, this is supplemented by "Supported interface orientations (iPad)," UISupportedInterfaceOrientations~ipad. These keys can be set through checkboxes when you edit the app target, in the General tab.

The app delegate's application(_:supportedInterfaceOrientationsFor:)
This method, if implemented, returns a bitmask listing every orientation the interface is permitted to assume at that moment. This list *overrides* the *Info.plist* settings. In this way, the app delegate can do dynamically what the *Info.plist* can do only statically. This method is called at least once every time the device rotates.

The top-level view controller's supportedInterfaceOrientations
The top-level view controller — that is, the root view controller, or a view controller presented fullscreen — may override the supportedInterfaceOrientations property, returning a bitmask listing every orientation that the interface is permitted to assume at that moment. New in iOS 13, if both the app delegate and the view controller participate in this decision, the view controller wins outright. (In iOS 12 and before, their contributions must intersect or the app will crash.)

The top-level view controller can also override shouldAutorotate. This is a Bool, and the default is true. It is consulted at least once every time the device rotates; if it returns false, that's the end of the matter — supportedInterfaceOrientations is not consulted and the interface does not perform compensatory rotation.

Built-in parent view controllers, when they are the top-level view controller, do *not* automatically consult their children about rotation. If your view controller is a child view controller of a UITabBarController or a UINavigationController, it has no direct say in how the app rotates. Those parent view controllers, however, do consult their *delegates* about rotation, as I'll explain later.

You can call the UIViewController class method `attemptRotationToDevice-Orientation` to prompt the runtime to do immediately what it would do if the user were to rotate the device, namely to walk the three levels I've just described and, if the results permit rotation of the interface to match the current device orientation, to rotate the interface at that moment. This would be useful if, say, your view controller had previously returned `false` from `shouldAutorotate`, but is now for some reason prepared to return `true` and wants to be asked again, immediately.

The bitmask you return from `application(_:supportedInterfaceOrientations-For:)` or `supportedInterfaceOrientations` is a UIInterfaceOrientationMask. It may be one of these values, or multiple values combined:

- `.portrait`
- `.landscapeLeft`
- `.landscapeRight`
- `.portraitUpsideDown`
- `.landscape` (a combination of `.left` and `.right`)
- `.all` (a combination of `.portrait`, `.upsideDown`, `.left`, and `.right`)
- `.allButUpsideDown` (a combination of `.portrait`, `.left`, and `.right`)

For example:

```
override var supportedInterfaceOrientations : UIInterfaceOrientationMask {
    return .portrait
}
```

If your code needs to know the current physical orientation of the *device* (as opposed to the current orientation of the interface), it is `UIDevice.current.orientation`. Possible values (UIDeviceOrientation) are `.unknown`, `.portrait`, and so on. The `orientation` also has two convenient properties, `isPortrait` and `isLandscape`, that return a Bool.

 On iPad, if your app permits all four orientations, and if it doesn't opt out of iPad multitasking, then `supportedInterfaceOrientations` and `should-Autorotate` are *never* consulted, because the answer is known in advance: compensatory rotation is always performed.

Initial Orientation

I've talked about how to determine what orientations your app can support in the course of its lifetime; but what about its *initial* orientation, the very first orientation your app will assume when it launches? In general, an app will launch directly into whatever permitted orientation is closest to the device's current orientation at launch time; this makes sense and is generally what you expect.

There can be a complication when the orientation in which the device is held would have been legal, but the initial root view controller rules it out. Suppose the device is held in portrait, and the *Info.plist* permits all orientations, but the root view controller's supportedInterfaceOrientations is set to return .landscape. Then the app starts to launch into portrait, realizes its mistake, and finishes launching in landscape. On the iPhone, this entails a kind of semirotation: willTransition(to:with:) is sent to report a trait collection change, but oddly there is *no size change*.

To work around that problem, here's a trick that I use. Let's say that my app needs *eventually* to be able to rotate to portrait, so I need to permit all orientations, but its *initial* root view controller must appear only in landscape. In my *Info.plist*, I permit *only* landscape; that way, my app launches directly into landscape, no matter how the device is oriented. But in my app delegate's application(_:supportedInterface-OrientationsFor:), I return .all; that way, my app can rotate *subsequently* to portrait if it needs to.

Detecting Rotation

On the whole, you are unlikely to want to detect rotation *per se*. You are more likely to want to respond to a change of size classes, or a change of layout; you'll use a trait collection event or a layout event. If you really do need to detect that rotation is taking place, even on an iPad, the best way is through the size change event will-Transition(to:with:). Size changes can happen for other reasons, so to determine that this really was a rotation, compare the orientation of the interface before and after the transition; new in iOS 13, you can find out the interface orientation by asking the window scene:

```
override func viewWillTransition(to size: CGSize,
    with coordinator: UIViewControllerTransitionCoordinator) {
        super.viewWillTransition(to:size, with: coordinator)
        let before = self.view.window?.windowScene?.interfaceOrientation
        coordinator.animate(alongsideTransition: nil) { _ in
            let after = self.view.window?.windowScene?.interfaceOrientation
            if before != after {
                // we rotated
            }
        }
}
```

The `interfaceOrientation` is a UIInterfaceOrientation; possible values are .portrait and so on. Two convenient `interfaceOrientation` properties, isLandscape and isPortrait, return a Bool.

View Controller Manual Layout

What if a view controller wants to participate directly, in code, in the layout of its main view's subviews? A view controller's view can be resized, both as the view is first put into the interface and later as the app runs and is rotated. Where should your view controller's layout code be placed in order to behave coherently in the face of these potential size changes?

Initial Manual Layout

There is a natural temptation to perform initial layout-related tasks in `viewDidLoad`. This method is extraordinarily convenient. It is guaranteed to be called exactly once very early in the life of the view controller; the view controller has its view, and if it got that view from a nib, properties connected to outlets from that nib have been set. This seems like the perfect place for initializations. But initialization and layout are not the same thing.

At the time `viewDidLoad` is called, the view controller's view has been loaded, but it has *not* yet been inserted into the interface, the view has *not* been fully resized for the first time, and initial layout has *not* yet taken place. You cannot do anything here that depends upon knowing the dimensions of the view controller's view or any other nib-loaded view — for the simple reason that you do *not* know them. Performing layout-related tasks in `viewDidLoad` and then wondering why things are sized or positioned incorrectly is a common beginner mistake.

Imagine that our view controller is the child of a navigation controller, and that our view controller does *not* underlap top and bottom bars. And suppose we wish, in code, before our view controller's view appears, to create a label and place it in the lower left corner of our main view. This code looks as if it should do that:

```
override func viewDidLoad() {
    super.viewDidLoad()
    let lab = UILabel()
    lab.text = "Hello"
    lab.sizeToFit()
    lab.frame.origin.y = self.view.bounds.height - lab.frame.height // *
    self.view.addSubview(lab)
}
```

The app launches, our main view appears — and there's no label. Where did it go? The view debugger reveals the answer: it's below the bottom of the screen. `viewDid-Load` runs *before* the main view is resized. The starred line calculates the label's `frame.origin.y` based on our main view's `bounds.height`, and *then* the main view's `bounds.height` changes, so the calculation is wrong. `viewDidLoad` is *too soon.*

The natural place to put that sort of code is an event related to resizing and layout of the main view — such as `viewWillLayoutSubviews`. But we need to be careful, because `viewWillLayoutSubviews` may be called many times over the life of our view controller. We can *position* our label in `viewWillLayoutSubviews` each time it is called, and indeed that's probably a good thing to do, because it takes care of repositioning the label when the main view's size changes on rotation; but we don't want to *create* our label more than once. A neat solution is to create the view (once) in `viewDidLoad` and position it (whenever layout is needed) in `viewWillLayoutSubviews`:

```
var lab : UILabel!
override func viewDidLoad() {
    super.viewDidLoad()
    self.lab = UILabel()
    self.lab.text = "Hello"
    self.lab.sizeToFit()
    self.view.addSubview(lab)
}
override func viewWillLayoutSubviews() {
    self.lab.frame.origin.y = self.view.bounds.height - self.lab.frame.height
}
```

If possible, you shouldn't do manual layout in the first place. You can create and insert this label in `viewDidLoad` and configure it for future layout by giving it autolayout constraints:

```
override func viewDidLoad() {
    let lab = UILabel()
    lab.text = "Hello"
    self.view.addSubview(lab)
    lab.translatesAutoresizingMaskIntoConstraints = false
    NSLayoutConstraint.activate([
        lab.leadingAnchor.constraint(equalTo: self.view.leadingAnchor),
        lab.bottomAnchor.constraint(equalTo: self.view.bottomAnchor)
    ])
}
```

That is *not* a case of doing manual layout in `viewDidLoad`. The constraints are not layout; they are instructions as to how this view should be sized and positioned by the runtime when layout does happen. (Autoresizing would work fine here too.)

Manual Layout During Rotation

The same principles apply to manual layout later in the life of the app. Let's say that rotation is taking place, and we want to respond by changing the layout in some way. Again, `viewWillLayoutSubviews` is an excellent place to do that:

Order of events

By the time layout occurs, all the *other* initial conditions are already in place. If the trait collection needed to change, it *has* changed. If our main view needed to be resized, it *has* been resized.

Animation

Rotation of the interface is animated. If the layout is changing in response to rotation, we want the change to be animated in coordination with the rotation animation. If we perform our changes in a `layoutSubviews` event, it *will* be animated during rotation! This, in effect, is because the runtime has animated a call to `layoutIfNeeded` before the rotation starts ("Animation and Layout" on page 240).

Let's say I have a large green rectangle that should occupy the left one-third of the interface, but only when we are in landscape orientation (the main view's width is larger than its height) and only when we are in a `.regular` horizontal size class. This rectangle should come and go in a smooth animated fashion; let's decide to have it appear from, or vanish off to, the left of the interface.

I can manage all of that entirely by means of manual layout. As in the previous example, I'll distribute responsibilities between `viewDidLoad` (creating the view) and `viewWillLayoutSubviews` (positioning the view):

```
var greenView : UIView!
override func viewDidLoad() {
    super.viewDidLoad()
    self.greenView = UIView()
    self.greenView.backgroundColor = .green
    self.view.addSubview(self.greenView)
}
override func viewWillLayoutSubviews() {
    func greenViewShouldAppear() -> Bool {
        let tc = self.traitCollection
        let sz = self.view.bounds.size
        if tc.horizontalSizeClass == .regular {
            if sz.width > sz.height {
                return true
            }
        }
        return false
    }
    if greenViewShouldAppear() {
        self.greenView.frame = CGRect(0, 0,
            self.view.bounds.width/3.0, self.view.bounds.height
        )
    } else {
        self.greenView.frame = CGRect(
            -self.view.bounds.width/3.0, 0,
```

```
                self.view.bounds.width/3.0, self.view.bounds.height
            )
        }
    }
```

This is a very handy technique. If a view is under the influence of autolayout and we change its constraints instead of its frame in `viewWillLayoutSubviews`, the change in layout is *still* animated in coordination with a rotation animation!

Presented View Controller

Back when the only iOS device was an iPhone, a presented view controller was called a *modal* view controller. Under that original architecture, when a view controller is *presented*, the root view controller remains in place, but the root view controller's view is taken out of the interface and the modal view controller's view is used instead (Figure 6-7). There is usually a general sense that this replacement is temporary; eventually, the presented view controller will be *dismissed*. The presented interface will then be removed and the original interface will be restored.

Presented view controllers have evolved since the early days, particularly with regard to how their views relate to the existing interface. Instead of replacing the entire interface, a presented view controller's view can:

- Replace a *subview* within the existing interface.
- Cover the existing interface completely or partially, *without* removing any existing interface.

For the most part, the "modal" characterization still applies. A presented view controller's view generally blocks access to the "real" view, and the user must work there until it is removed and the "real" view is visible again.

The color picker view in my Zotz! app (Figure 6-2) is modal in that sense. It is an interface that says, "You are now configuring a color, and that's all you can do; change the color or cancel, or you'll be stuck here forever." The user can't get out of this view without tapping Cancel or Done, and the view that the user was previously using is visible as a blur behind this view, waiting for the user to return to it.

Presentation and Dismissal

The key methods for presenting and dismissing a view controller are:

`present(_:animated:completion:)`
> To make a view controller present another view controller, you send the first view controller this message, handing it the second view controller, which you will probably instantiate for this purpose. The first view controller will typically be `self`.

We now have two view controllers that stand in the relationship of being one another's `presentingViewController` and `presentedViewController` respectively. The presented view controller is retained, and its view replaces or covers the presenting view controller's view in the interface.

`dismiss(animated:completion:)`
The "presented" state of affairs persists until the presenting view controller is sent this message. The presented view controller's view is then removed from the interface, the original interface is restored, and the presented view controller is released; it will thereupon typically go out of existence.

As the view of the presented view controller appears, and again when it is dismissed, there's an option for animation to be performed as the transition takes place (the `animated:` argument, a Bool). The `completion:` parameter, which can be `nil`, lets you supply a function to be run after the transition (including the animation) has finished.

View controller relationships during presentation

The presenting view controller (the presented view controller's `presentingView-Controller`) is not necessarily the same view controller to which you sent `present(_:animated:completion:)`. It will help if we distinguish *three* roles that view controllers can play in presenting a view controller:

Presented view controller
The first argument to `present(_:animated:completion:)`.

Original presenter
The view controller to which `present(_:animated:completion:)` was sent. Apple sometimes refers to this view controller as the *source*; "original presenter" is my own term.

The presented view controller is set as the original presenter's `presentedView-Controller`.

Presenting view controller
The view controller whose view is replaced or covered by the presented view controller's view. By default, it is the view controller that was the top-level view controller prior to the presentation. It might not be the same as the original presenter.

This view controller is set as the presented view controller's `presentingView-Controller`. The presented view controller is set as the presenting view controller's `presentedViewController`. (This means that the presented view controller might be the `presentedViewController` of two different view controllers.)

When you want to dismiss a presented view controller, you can send `dismiss(animated:completion:)` to *any* of those three objects; the runtime will use the linkages between them to transmit the necessary messages up the chain on your behalf to the `presentingViewController`.

You can test whether a view controller's `presentedViewController` or `presenting-ViewController` is `nil` to learn whether presentation is occurring. A view controller whose `presentingViewController` is `nil` is not a presented view controller at this moment.

A view controller can present only one view controller at a time. If you send `present(_:animated:completion:)` to a view controller whose `presentedView-Controller` isn't `nil`, nothing will happen and the completion function is not called (and you'll get a warning from the runtime). A presented view controller can itself present a view controller, though, so there can be a chain of presented view controllers.

If you send `dismiss(animated:completion:)` to a view controller in the middle of a presentation chain — a view controller that has both a `presentingViewController` and a `presentedViewController` — then its `presentedViewController` is dismissed.

If you send `dismiss(animated:completion:)` to a view controller whose `presented-ViewController` is `nil` and that has no `presentingViewController`, nothing will happen (not even a warning in the console), and the completion function is not called.

Manual view controller presentation

To illustrate, let's make one view controller present another, by calling `present(_:animated:completion:)`. (I'll talk later about how to arrange things in a storyboard with a modal segue so that `present(_:animated:completion:)` is called for you.)

Start with an iPhone project made from the Single View App template. It contains one view controller class, called ViewController. We'll need a second view controller class:

1. Choose File → New → File and specify iOS → Source → Cocoa Touch Class. Click Next.
2. Name the class SecondViewController, make it a subclass of UIViewController, and check the XIB checkbox so that we can design this view controller's view in the nib editor. Click Next.
3. Confirm the folder, group, and app target membership, and click Create.

4. Edit *SecondViewController.xib*, and do something there to make the view distinctive, so that you'll recognize it when it appears; you might give it a red background color.

5. In *ViewController.swift*, give ViewController an action method that instantiates SecondViewController and presents it:

```
@IBAction func doPresent(_ sender: Any) {
    let svc = SecondViewController()
    svc.modalPresentationStyle = .fullScreen
    self.present(svc, animated:true)
}
```

6. Edit *Main.storyboard* and add a button to the ViewController's main view. Make an action connecting that button's Touch Up Inside control event to ViewController's doPresent.

Run the project. In ViewController's view, tap the button. SecondViewController's view slides into place over ViewController's view. We've presented a view controller!

In our lust for instant gratification, we have neglected to provide a way to dismiss the presented view controller. If you'd like to do that:

1. In *SecondViewController.swift*, give SecondViewController an action method that dismisses SecondViewController:

```
@IBAction func doDismiss(_ sender: Any) {
    self.presentingViewController?.dismiss(animated:true)
}
```

2. Edit *SecondViewController.xib* and add a button to SecondViewController's view. Connect that button to SecondViewController's doDismiss.

Run the project. You can now alternate between ViewController's view and SecondViewController's view, presenting and dismissing in turn. Go ahead and play for a while with your exciting new app; I'll wait.

Configuring a Presentation

This section describes some configurable aspects of how a view controller's view behaves as the view controller is presented.

Transition style

When a view controller is presented and later when it is dismissed, a simple animation of its view can be performed, according to whether the animated: parameter of the corresponding method is true. The animation type is the presented view controller's *modal transition style*. To choose an animation type, set the presented view controller's `modalTransitionStyle` property prior to the presentation. This value can be set in code or in the nib editor. Your choices (UIModalTransitionStyle) are:

`.coverVertical` *(the default)*
> The view slides up from the bottom on presentation and down on dismissal. The definition of "bottom" depends on the orientation of the device and the orientations the view controllers support.

`.flipHorizontal`
> The view flips on the vertical axis. If this is a `.fullScreen` or `.currentContext` presentation (as I'll describe in the next section), the presenting and presented views behave like the front and back of a piece of paper. The "vertical axis" is the device's long axis, regardless of the app's orientation.

`.crossDissolve`
> The views effectively remain stationary, and one fades into the other.

 A fourth option, `.partialCurl`, is completely unusable in iOS 13 and should be avoided.

Alternatively, instead of a built-in modal transition style, you can substitute your own custom transition animation, as I'll explain later in this chapter.

Presentation style

When a view controller is presented, its view appears. Where that view is placed is determined by the presented view controller's *modal presentation style*. To choose a presentation style, set the presented view controller's `modalPresentationStyle` property prior to the presentation. This value can be set in code or in the nib editor. Your choices (UIModalPresentationStyle) are:

`.fullScreen`
> The presented view controller covers the entire screen. The presenting view controller is the top-level view controller, and its view — meaning the entire interface — is replaced. This was the default before iOS 13.

`.overFullScreen`
> Similar to `.fullScreen`, but the presenting view controller's view is *not* replaced; instead, it stays where it is, possibly being visible during the transition, and remaining visible behind the presented view controller's view if the latter has some transparency.

`.pageSheet`
> New in iOS 13, this is the default and its appearance is different from earlier systems. On the iPad it is smaller than the screen. On the iPhone in portrait

(`.compact` horizontal size class), it covers the screen but leaves a gap at the top, while the existing interface shrinks a little behind it. (It can look like that on the iPad too if the dynamic text size is very large.) On the iPhone in landscape (`.compact` vertical size class), indistinguishable from `.overFullScreen`.

`.formSheet`

On the iPad, similar to `.pageSheet` but smaller (and it has a `.compact` horizontal size class). As the name implies, this is intended to allow the user to fill out a form (Apple describes this as "gathering structured information from the user"). On the iPhone, indistinguishable from `.pageSheet`.

`.currentContext`

The presenting view controller can be *any* view controller, such as a child view controller. The presented view controller's view replaces the presenting view controller's view, which may have been occupying only a portion of the screen. I'll explain later how to specify the presenting view controller.

`.overCurrentContext`

Like `.currentContext`, but the presented view controller's view covers the presenting view controller's view rather than replacing it. This will often be a better choice than `.currentContext`, because some subviews don't behave well when automatically removed from their superview and restored later.

`.automatic`

New in iOS 13. Okay, I lied when I said that `.pageSheet` is the default in iOS 13. *This* is the default! You'll rarely need to set it explicitly. In general it resolves to `.pageSheet`, but it also allows certain built-in view controllers to choose their own presentation style. In the storyboard, the Automatic presentation style is backward-compatible, resolving to `.fullScreen` on iOS 12 and before.

Alternatively, instead of a built-in modal presentation style, you can create your own custom transition that places the presented view controller's view anywhere you like, as I'll explain later in this chapter.

User dismissal of a sheet

New in iOS 13, by default, a sheet (page sheet or form sheet) can be dismissed by dragging down (except on an iPhone in landscape where it is treated as if it were `.fullScreen`).

To prevent this, set the presented view controller's `isModalInPresentation` to `true`; the user will still be able to drag the sheet down, but it will snap back into place instead of being dismissed. To detect this gesture, use the *presentation controller delegate*. (I'll talk later about what the presentation controller is.) Set the presented view

---

controller's `presentationController?.delegate` to an object adopting the UIAdaptivePresentationControllerDelegate protocol and implement this delegate method:

`presentationControllerDidAttemptToDismiss(_:)`
> Called when the user attempts to drag a page sheet down but is prevented from doing so. The idea is that you might put up some interface explaining *why* the user can't dismiss the sheet this way.

Instead of setting `isModalInPresentation` permanently, you can make the same decision in real time in a different presentation controller delegate method:

`presentationControllerShouldDismiss(_:)`
> If you return `false`, it is as if you had momentarily set `isModalInPresentation` to `true`: the user is attempting to drag down and failing to dismiss, so `presentationControllerDidAttemptToDismiss(_:)` is called immediately.

If `isModalInPresentation` is not `true` and `presentationControllerShouldDismiss(_:)` does not return `false`, the user's drag can succeed in dismissing the presented view controller. To let you detect what's happening, there are two more presentation controller delegate methods:

`presentationControllerWillDismiss(_:)`
> The user is starting to drag down. This does *not* necessarily mean that the user will complete the drag gesture; the user might release the sheet, in which case it will pop back into place and won't be dismissed. The idea is that you might want to coordinate some change of interface with the dismissal gesture (by means of the presented view controller's `transitionCoordinator`, as I'll explain later).

`presentationControllerDidDismiss(_:)`
> The user has completed the drag gesture and the sheet has been dismissed.

You don't get any delegate event when you dismiss the sheet in code with `dismiss(animated:completion:)`, because you already know that the sheet is being dismissed.

 The drag gesture is implemented by a UIPanGestureRecognizer further up the view hierarchy. If you need to immobilize the presented view so that it doesn't move in response to the user's gesture, implement `gestureRecognizerShouldBegin` (in a view subclass or a gesture recognizer delegate) to return `false`.

Current context presentation

When the presented view controller's `modalPresentationStyle` is `.currentContext` or `.overCurrentContext`, a decision has to be made by the runtime as to what view controller should be the presenting view controller. This will determine what view will be replaced or covered by the presented view controller's view. The decision involves another UIViewController property, `definesPresentationContext` (a Bool), and possibly still *another* UIViewController property, `providesPresentation-ContextTransitionStyle`:

1. Starting with the original presenter — that is, the view controller to which `present(_:animated:completion:)` was sent — we (the runtime) walk up the chain of parent view controllers, looking for one whose `definesPresentation-Context` property is `true`.

    *   If we *don't* find one, the search has failed. Things work as if the presented view controller's `modalPresentationStyle` were `.automatic`, and we don't proceed to the next step.

    *   If we *do* find one, that's the one — it will be the `presentingView-Controller`, and its view will be replaced or covered by the presented view controller's view — and we do proceed to the next step.

2. If we get here, we have found a `presentingViewController` whose `defines-PresentationContext` property is `true`. We now look to see if its `provides-PresentationContextTransitionStyle` property is *also* `true`. If so, *that* view controller's `modalTransitionStyle` is used for this transition animation, rather than the presented view controller's `modalTransitionStyle`.

To illustrate, I need a parent–child view controller arrangement to work with. This chapter hasn't yet discussed any parent view controllers in detail, but the simplest is UITabBarController, which I discuss in the next section, and it's easy to create a working app with a UITabBarController-based interface, so that's the example I'll use:

1. Start with the Tabbed App template. It provides three view controllers — the UITabBarController and two children, FirstViewController and SecondView-Controller.

2. As in the previous example, I want us to create and present the presented view controller manually, rather than letting the storyboard do it automatically; so make a new view controller class with an accompanying *.xib* file, to use as a presented view controller — call it ExtraViewController.

3. In *ExtraViewController.xib*, give the view a distinctive background color, so you'll recognize it when it appears.

4. In the storyboard, put a button in the First View Controller view (First Scene), and connect it to an action method in *FirstViewController.swift* that summons the new view controller as a presented view controller:

    ```
    @IBAction func doPresent(_ sender: Any) {
        let vc = ExtraViewController()
        self.present(vc, animated: true)
    }
    ```

Run the project and tap the button. In iOS 13, we get the default `.pageSheet` presentation style. The presenting view controller is the root view controller, which is the UITabBarController. The entire interface, including the tab bar, is covered by the presented view controller's view.

Now change the code to look like this:

```
@IBAction func doPresent(_ sender: Any) {
    let vc = ExtraViewController()
    self.definesPresentationContext = true // *
    vc.modalPresentationStyle = .currentContext // *
    self.present(vc, animated: true)
}
```

Run the project and tap the button. The presented view controller's view replaces the first view controller's view, while the tab bar remains visible. That's because the presented view controller's `modalPresentationStyle` is `.currentContext`, and `definesPresentationContext` is `true` in FirstViewController. The search for a context stops in FirstViewController, which becomes the presenting view controller — meaning that the presented view replaces FirstViewController's view instead of the root view.

We can also override the presented view controller's transition animation through the `modalTransitionStyle` property of the presenting view controller:

```
@IBAction func doPresent(_ sender: Any) {
    let vc = ExtraViewController()
    self.definesPresentationContext = true
    self.providesPresentationContextTransitionStyle = true // *
    self.modalTransitionStyle = .flipHorizontal // *
    vc.modalPresentationStyle = .currentContext
    self.present(vc, animated: true)
}
```

Because the presenting view controller's `providesPresentationContextTransitionStyle` is `true`, the transition uses the `.flipHorizontal` animation belonging to the presenting view controller, rather than the default `.coverVertical` animation of the presented view controller.

Configuration in the nib editor

Most of what I've described so far can be configured in a *.storyboard* or *.xib* file. A view controller's Attributes inspector lets you set its transition style and presentation style, as well as `definesPresentationContext` and `providesPresentationContextTransitionStyle`.

If you're using a storyboard, you can configure one view controller to present another view controller by connecting them with a Present Modally segue; to do the presentation, you trigger the segue (or give the user a way to trigger it) instead of calling `present(_:animated:completion:)`. The segue's Attributes inspector lets you set the presentation style and transition style (and whether there is to be animation). Dismissal is a little more involved; either you must dismiss the presented view controller in code, by calling `dismiss(animated:completion:)`, or you must use an unwind segue. I'll discuss triggered segues and unwind segues in detail later in this chapter.

Communication with a Presented View Controller

In real life, the original presenter will probably have information to impart to the presented view controller as the latter is created and presented, and the presented view controller will probably want to pass information back to the original presenter as it is dismissed. Knowing how to arrange this exchange of information can be very important.

Passing information from the original presenter to the presented view controller is usually easy, because the original presenter typically has a reference to the presented view controller before the latter's view appears in the interface. Suppose the presented view controller has a public `data` property. Then the original presenter can easily set this property as it instantiates the presented view controller:

```
@IBAction func doPresent(_ sender: Any) {
    let svc = SecondViewController()
    svc.data = "This is very important data!" // *
    self.present(svc, animated:true)
}
```

You might even give the presented view controller a designated initializer that accepts — and requires — the data that it needs to do its job, so that whoever creates it *must* pass it that data.

If you're using a storyboard and a Present Modally segue, things are a bit different. In the original presenter, you typically implement `prepare(for:sender:)` as a moment when the original presenter and the presented view controller will meet, and the former can hand across any needed data. New in iOS 13, you can have the segue call an `@IBSegueAction` method in the original presenter, to accomplish the same thing a bit more cleanly. I'll give more details later in this chapter.

Passing information back from the presented view controller to the original presenter is a more interesting problem. The presented view controller will need to know who the original presenter is, but it doesn't automatically have a reference to it (the original presenter, remember, is not necessarily the same as the `presentingViewController`). Moreover, the presented view controller will need to know the signature of some method, implemented by the original presenter, that it can call in order to hand over the information — and this needs to work regardless of the original presenter's class.

The standard solution is to use *delegation*:

1. The presented view controller defines a *protocol* declaring a method that it wants to call before it is dismissed.

2. The presented view controller provides a means whereby it can be handed a reference to an object conforming to this protocol. Think of that reference as the presented view controller's *delegate*. Very often, this will be a property — perhaps called `delegate` — typed *as the protocol*. Such a property should probably be weak, since an object usually has no business retaining its delegate.

3. The original presenter *conforms* to this protocol: it declares adoption of the protocol, and it implements the required method.

4. As the original presenter creates and configures the presented view controller, it hands the presented view controller a reference to itself, in its role as adopter of the protocol, by *assigning itself as the delegate* of the presented view controller.

5. As the presented view controller is dismissed, it looks to see if it has a delegate. If so, it calls the required method on that delegate, passing it the associated information.

This sounds elaborate, but with practice you'll find yourself able to implement it very quickly. To illustrate, suppose that (as in our earlier example) the root view controller, ViewController, presents SecondViewController. Then our code in *SecondViewController.swift* would look like this:

```
protocol SecondViewControllerDelegate : class {
    func accept(data:Any)
}
class SecondViewController : UIViewController {
    var data : Any?
    weak var delegate : SecondViewControllerDelegate?
    @IBAction func doDismiss(_ sender: Any) {
        self.delegate?.accept(data:"Even more important data!")
        self.presentingViewController?.dismiss(animated:true)
    }
}
```

It is now ViewController's job to adopt the SecondViewControllerDelegate protocol, and to set itself as the SecondViewController's delegate. If it does so, then when the delegate method is called, ViewController will be handed the data:

```
class ViewController : UIViewController, SecondViewControllerDelegate {
    @IBAction func doPresent(_ sender: Any) {
        let svc = SecondViewController()
        svc.data = "This is very important data!"
        svc.delegate = self // *
        self.present(svc, animated:true)
    }
```

```
    func accept(data:Any) {
        // do something with data here
    }
}
```

New in iOS 13, there's a problem: the presented view controller can be dismissed by the user dragging down the view. That won't cause doDismiss to be called, and SecondViewController won't call the delegate method. We need a way for the presented view controller to hear about its own dismissal *no matter how* that dismissal is triggered.

A good solution is to override the UIViewController method viewWillDisappear (discussed later in this chapter). There is more than one reason why viewWill-Disappear might be called; we can ensure that this really is the moment of our own dismissal by consulting isBeingDismissed. Here's how SecondViewController would look now:

```
protocol SecondViewControllerDelegate : class {
    func accept(data:Any)
}
class SecondViewController : UIViewController {
    var data : Any?
    weak var delegate : SecondViewControllerDelegate?
    @IBAction func doDismiss(_ sender: Any) {
        self.presentingViewController?.dismiss(animated:true)
    }
    override func viewDidDisappear(_ animated: Bool) {
        super.viewDidDisappear(animated)
        if self.isBeingDismissed {
            self.delegate?.accept(data:"Even more important data!")
        }
    }
}
```

Adaptive Presentation

When a view controller is about to appear with a modalPresentationStyle of .page-Sheet or .formSheet, you get a second opportunity to change its effective modal-PresentationStyle, and even to substitute a different view controller, based on the current trait collection environment. This is called *adaptive presentation*. The idea is that your presented view controller might appear one way for certain trait collections and another way for others — on an iPad as opposed to an iPhone, for instance.

The adaptations you can perform in iOS 13 are:

- You can adapt .pageSheet or .formSheet to .fullScreen or .overFullScreen.

- You can adapt .pageSheet to .formSheet; this will make a visible difference only on an iPad.

(It isn't illegal to try to perform another adaptation, but it isn't going to work either.)

To implement adaptive presentation, use the presentation controller delegate: set the presented view controller's `presentationController?.delegate` to an object adopting the UIAdaptivePresentationControllerDelegate protocol, *before* presenting the view controller. When you *do* present the view controller, but before its view actually appears, the delegate is sent these messages:

`adaptivePresentationStyle(for:traitCollection:)`
> The first parameter is the presentation controller, and its `presentationStyle` is the `modalPresentationStyle` it proposes to use. Return a different modal presentation style to use instead (or `.none` if you don't want to change the presentation style).

`presentationController(_:willPresentWithAdaptiveStyle:transition-Coordinator:)`
> Called just before the presentation takes place. If the `adaptiveStyle:` is `.none`, adaptive presentation is *not* going to take place.

`presentationController(_:viewControllerForAdaptivePresentationStyle:)`
> Called only if adaptive presentation *is* going to take place. The first parameter is the presentation controller, and its `presentedViewController` is the view controller it proposes to present. Return a different view controller to present instead (or `nil` to keep the current presented view controller).

Here's how to present a view controller as a `.pageSheet` on iPad but as `.overFullScreen` on iPhone:

```
extension ViewController : UIAdaptivePresentationControllerDelegate {
    @IBAction func doPresent(_ sender: Any) {
        let svc = SecondViewController()
        svc.modalPresentationStyle = .pageSheet
        svc.presentationController!.delegate = self // *
        self.present(svc, animated:true)
    }
    func adaptivePresentationStyle(for controller: UIPresentationController,
        traitCollection: UITraitCollection) -> UIModalPresentationStyle {
            if traitCollection.horizontalSizeClass == .compact ||
                traitCollection.verticalSizeClass == .compact {
                    return .overFullScreen
            }
            return .none // don't adapt
    }
}
```

Now let's extend that example by presenting one view controller on iPad but a different view controller on iPhone; this method won't be called when `adaptivePresentationStyle` returns `.none`, so it affects iPhone only:

```
extension ViewController : UIAdaptivePresentationControllerDelegate {
    func presentationController(_ controller: UIPresentationController,
        viewControllerForAdaptivePresentationStyle: UIModalPresentationStyle)
        -> UIViewController? {
            let newvc = ThirdViewController()
            return newvc
    }
}
```

In real life, of course, when substituting a different view controller, you might need to configure it before returning it, doing things like giving it data or setting its delegate. A common scenario is to return the *same* view controller wrapped in a navigation controller; I'll illustrate in Chapter 9.

Presentation, Rotation, and the Status Bar

A `.fullScreen` presented view controller, even though it is not the root view controller, is the *top-level view controller*, and acquires some of the same mighty powers as if it *were* the root view controller:

- Its `supportedInterfaceOrientations` and `shouldAutorotate` are honored; this view controller gets to limit your app's legal orientations.

- Its `prefersStatusBarHidden` and `preferredStatusBarStyle` are honored; this view controller gets to dictate the appearance of the status bar.

When you present a view controller whose `modalPresentationStyle` is `.fullScreen`, if its `supportedInterfaceOrientations` do not include the app's current orientation, the app's orientation *will rotate*, as the presented view appears, to an orientation that the presented view controller supports — and the same thing will be true in reverse when the presented view controller is dismissed. This is the *only* officially sanctioned way to perform *forced rotation* (as I called it earlier in this chapter).

 On an iPad, if your app permits all four orientations and does not opt out of iPad multitasking, its view controllers' `supportedInterfaceOrientations` are not even consulted, so forced rotation doesn't work.

The presented view controller's `supportedInterfaceOrientations` bitmask might permit multiple possible orientations. The view controller may then also wish to specify which of those multiple orientations it should have *initially* when it is presented. To do so, override `preferredInterfaceOrientationForPresentation`; this property is consulted before `supportedInterfaceOrientations`, and its value is a single UIInterfaceOrientation (*not* a bitmask).

When a view controller is presented, if its presentation style is *not* `.fullScreen`, a question arises of whether its status bar properties (`prefersStatusBarHidden` and `preferredStatusBarStyle`) should be consulted. By default, the answer is no, because this view controller is not the top-level view controller. To make the answer be yes, set this view controller's `modalPresentationCapturesStatusBarAppearance` to `true`.

Tab Bar Controller

A *tab bar* (UITabBar, see also Chapter 12) is a horizontal bar containing tab bar items. A tab bar item (UITabBarItem) displays, by default, an image and a title. The title usually appears *beside* the image; on an iPhone in portrait orientation, the title appears *below* the image. At all times, exactly one of a tab bar's items is selected (highlighted); when the user taps an item, it becomes the selected item.

If there are too many items to fit on a tab bar, the excess items are subsumed into a final More item. When the user taps the More item, a list of the excess items appears, and the user can select one; the user can also be permitted to edit the tab bar, determining which items appear in the tab bar itself and which ones spill over into the More list.

A tab bar is an independent interface object, but it is nearly always used in conjunction with a *tab bar controller* (UITabBarController, a subclass of UIViewController) to form a *tab bar interface*. The tab bar controller displays the tab bar at the bottom of its own view. From the user's standpoint, the tab bar items correspond to views; when the user selects a tab bar item, the corresponding view appears, filling the remainder of the space. The user is employing the tab bar to choose an entire area of your app's functionality.

In reality, the UITabBarController is a parent view controller; you give it child view controllers, which the tab bar controller then contains. Tapping a tab bar item changes which child view controller is currently selected, and the view that appears is that child view controller's view.

Familiar examples of a tab bar interface on the iPhone are Apple's Clock app and Music app.

You can get a reference to the tab bar controller's tab bar through its `tabBar` property. In general, you won't need this. When using a UITabBarController, you do not interact (as a programmer) with the tab bar itself; you don't create it or set its items. You provide the UITabBarController with children, and it does the rest; when the UITabBarController's view is displayed, there's the tab bar along with the view of the selected item. You can, however, customize the *look* of the tab bar (see Chapter 12 for details).

Tab Bar Items

For each view controller you assign as a tab bar controller's child, you'll need to create and configure the tab bar item that will appear as its representative in the tab bar.

This tab bar item will be your child view controller's `tabBarItem`, a UITabBarItem; this is a subclass of UIBarItem, an abstract class that provides some of its most important properties, such as `title`, `image`, and `isEnabled`.

There are two ways to make a tab bar item:

By borrowing it from the system
> Instantiate UITabBarItem using `init(tabBarSystemItem:tag:)`, and assign the instance to your child view controller's `tabBarItem`. Consult the documentation for the list of available system items. You can't customize a system tab bar item's title; you must accept the title the system hands you.

By making your own
> Instantiate UITabBarItem using `init(title:image:tag:)` and assign the instance to your child view controller's `tabBarItem`. Alternatively, use the view controller's existing `tabBarItem` and set its `image` and `title`. Instead of setting the `title` of the `tabBarItem`, you can set the `title` property of the view controller itself; doing this automatically sets the `title` of its current `tabBarItem` (unless the tab bar item is a system tab bar item), though the converse is not true.
>
> You can also add a separate `selectedImage` later, or by initializing with `init(title:image:selectedImage:)`. The `selectedImage` will be displayed in place of the normal `image` when this tab bar item is selected in the tab bar.

The `image` (and `selectedImage`) for a tab bar item should be a 30×30 PNG, or a vector image (see Chapter 2). Apple prefers you to use a vector image, and new in iOS 13 the vast repertoire of standard symbol images is available. By default, the image will be treated as a transparency mask (a template). You can instead display the image as is, and not as a transparency mask, by deriving an image whose rendering mode is `.alwaysOriginal`.

A tab bar controller automatically reduces the height of its tab bar when the vertical size class is `.compact` (an iPhone in landscape orientation, except for a big iPhone). If the image is not a vector image, you will have to cope with the possibility that the tab bar item will be displayed at reduced size when the tab bar's height is reduced. The solution is to set the tab bar item's `landscapeImagePhone` to a 20×20 PNG; it will be used when the vertical size class is `.compact`.

 A tab bar item's `selectedImage` is not used in a `.compact` vertical size class environment if it also has a separate `landscapeImagePhone`. I regard this as a bug.

Other ways in which you can customize the look of a tab bar item are discussed in Chapter 12.

Configuring a Tab Bar Controller

Basic configuration of a tab bar controller is simple: just hand it the view controllers that will be its children. To do so, collect those view controllers into an array and set the UITabBarController's `viewControllers` property to that array. The view controllers in the array are now the tab bar controller's child view controllers; the tab bar controller is the `parent` of the view controllers in the array. The tab bar controller is also the `tabBarController` of the view controllers in the array and of all their children; a child view controller at any depth can learn that it is contained by a tab bar controller and can get a reference to that tab bar controller. The tab bar controller retains the array, and the array retains the child view controllers.

Here's a simple example from one of my apps, in which I construct a tab bar interface in code; the tab bar controller later becomes the window's root view controller:

```
let vc1 = GameBoardController()
let sc = SettingsController()
let vc2 = UINavigationController(rootViewController:sc)
let tabBarController = UITabBarController()
tabBarController.viewControllers = [vc1, vc2]
tabBarController.selectedIndex = 0
tabBarController.delegate = self
```

A tab bar controller's tab bar displays the `tabBarItem` of each child view controller. The order of the tab bar items is the order of the view controllers in the tab bar controller's `viewControllers` array. A child view controller will probably want to configure its `tabBarItem` property early in its lifetime, so that the `tabBarItem` is ready by the time the view controller is handed as a child to the tab bar controller. `viewDidLoad` is *not* early enough! That's because the view controllers (other than the initially selected view controller) have no view when the tab bar controller initially appears. It is common to implement an initializer for this purpose.

Here's an example from the same app as the previous code (in the GameBoardController class):

```
init() {
    super.init(nibName:nil, bundle:nil)
    // tab bar configuration
    self.tabBarItem.image = UIImage(named: "game")
    self.title = "Game"
}
```

If you change the tab bar controller's view controllers array later in its lifetime and you want the corresponding change in the tab bar's display of its items to be animated, call `setViewControllers(_:animated:)`.

To ask the tab bar controller which tab bar item the user has selected, you can couch your query in terms of the child view controller (`selectedViewController`) or by index number in the array (`selectedIndex`). You can also *set* those properties to switch between displayed child view controllers programmatically. If you don't do that before the tab bar controller appears, then initially the first tab bar item will be selected by default.

 You can supply a view animation when a tab bar controller's selected tab item changes and one child view controller's view is replaced by another, as I'll explain later in this chapter.

You can also set the UITabBarController's delegate (adopting UITabBarController-Delegate). The delegate gets messages allowing it to prevent a given tab bar item from being selected, and notifying it when a tab bar item is selected and when the user is customizing the tab bar from the More item.

If a tab bar controller is the top-level view controller, it determines your app's compensatory rotation behavior. To take a hand in that determination without having to subclass UITabBarController, make one of your objects the tab bar controller's delegate and implement these methods, as needed:

- `tabBarControllerSupportedInterfaceOrientations(_:)`
- `tabBarControllerPreferredInterfaceOrientationForPresentation(_:)`

A top-level tab bar controller also determines your app's status bar appearance. However, a tab bar controller implements `childForStatusBarStyle` and `childForStatus-BarHidden` so that the actual decision is relegated to the child view controller whose view is currently being displayed: the child's `preferredStatusBarStyle` and `prefers-StatusBarHidden` are consulted and obeyed.

If the tab bar contains few enough items that it doesn't need a More item, there won't be one, and the tab bar won't be user-customizable. If there *is* a More item, you can exclude some tab bar items from being customizable by setting the `customizable-ViewControllers` property to an array that lacks them; setting this property to `nil` means that the user can see the More list but can't rearrange the items. Setting the `viewControllers` property sets the `customizableViewControllers` property to the same value, so if you're going to set the `customizableViewControllers` property, do it *after* setting the `viewControllers` property. The `moreNavigationController` property can be compared with the `selectedViewController` property to learn whether the user is currently viewing the More list.

You can configure a UITabBarController in a storyboard. The UITabBarController's contained view controllers can be set directly — there will be a "view controllers" relationship between the tab bar controller and each of its children — and the contained view controllers will be instantiated together with the tab bar controller. Moreover, each contained view controller has a Tab Bar Item; you can select this and set many aspects of the `tabBarItem`, such as its system item or its title, image, selected image, and tag, directly in the nib editor. (If a view controller in a nib doesn't have a Tab Bar Item and you want to configure this view controller for use in a tab bar interface, drag a Tab Bar Item from the Library onto the view controller.) To start a project with a main storyboard that has a UITabBarController as its initial view controller, begin with the Tabbed App template.

 You will rarely if ever have a need to subclass UITabBar. If you do, and if you want to use an instance of your subclass as a tab bar controller's tab bar, you'll have to create the tab bar controller in a storyboard. A tab bar controller configured in a storyboard can have a custom tab bar subclass, but a tab bar controller created in code, as far as I can tell, cannot.

Navigation Controller

A *navigation bar* (UINavigationBar, see also Chapter 12) is a horizontal bar displaying, in its simplest form, a center title and a right button. When the user taps the right button, the navigation bar animates, sliding its interface out to the left and replacing it with a new interface that enters from the right. The new interface displays a back button at the left side, and a new center title — and possibly a new right button. The user can tap the back button to go back to the first interface, which slides in from the left; or, if there's a right button in the second interface, the user can tap it to go further forward to a third interface, which slides in from the right.

The successive interfaces of a navigation bar behave like a stack. In fact, a navigation bar does represent an actual stack — an internal stack of *navigation items* (UINavigationItem). It starts out with one navigation item: the *root item* or *bottom item* of the stack. Since there is initially just one navigation item, it is also initially the *top item* of the stack (the navigation bar's topItem). The navigation bar's interface is always representing whatever its top item is at that moment. When the user taps a right button, a new navigation item is *pushed* onto the stack; it becomes the top item, and its interface is seen. When the user taps a back button, the top item is *popped* off the stack, and the navigation item that was previously beneath it in the stack — the *back item* (the navigation bar's backItem) — becomes the top item, and its interface is seen.

A navigation bar is an independent interface object, but it is most commonly used in conjunction with a *navigation controller* (UINavigationController, a subclass of UIViewController) to form a *navigation interface.* Just as there is a stack of navigation items in the navigation bar, there is a stack of view controllers in the navigation controller. These view controllers are the navigation controller's children, and each navigation item belongs to a view controller — it is a view controller's navigationItem.

The navigation controller performs automatic coordination of the navigation bar and the overall interface. Whenever a view controller comes to the top of the navigation controller's stack, its view is displayed in the interface; at the same time, its navigationItem is pushed onto the top of the navigation bar's stack, and is displayed in the navigation bar as its top item. Moreover, the animation in the navigation bar is reinforced by animation of the interface as a whole: by default, a view controller's view slides into the main interface from the side just as its navigation item slides into the navigation bar from the same side.

 You can substitute a different view animation when a view controller is pushed onto or popped off a navigation controller's stack, as I'll explain later in this chapter.

With a navigation controller, your code can control the overall navigation. So you can let the user navigate in any way that suits the interface. There is only one back item, and the back button in the navigation bar is a standard convention telling the user what it is and providing a way to navigate to it by tapping, so you'll usually display the back button. But for letting the user push a new view controller, instead of a right button in the navigation bar, there might be something the user taps inside the main interface, such as a listing in a table view. (Figure 6-1 is a navigation interface that works this way.) Your app can decide in real time, in response to the user's tap, what the next view controller should be; typically, you won't even create the next view controller until the user asks to navigate to it. The navigation interface becomes a *master–detail interface*.

You can get a reference to the navigation controller's navigation bar through its navigationBar property. In general, you won't need this. When using a UINavigationController, you do not interact (as a programmer) with the navigation bar itself; you don't create it or manipulate its navigation items. You provide the UINavigationController with children, and it does the rest, handing each child view controller's navigationItem to the navigation bar for display and showing the child view controller's view each time navigation occurs. You can, however, customize the *look* of the navigation bar (see Chapter 12 for details).

A navigation interface may optionally display a *toolbar* at the bottom. A toolbar (UIToolbar) is a horizontal view displaying a row of toolbar items. A toolbar item may provide information, or it may be something the user can tap. A tapped item is not selected, as in a tab bar; rather, it represents the initiation of an action, like a button. You can get a reference to a UINavigationController's toolbar through its toolbar property. The look of the toolbar can be customized (Chapter 12). In a navigation interface, the contents of the toolbar are determined automatically by the view controller that is currently the top item in the stack: they are its toolbarItems.

A familiar example of a navigation interface is Apple's Settings app on the iPhone. The Mail app on the iPhone is a navigation interface that includes a toolbar.

A toolbar can be used independently, and often is. An independent toolbar, not in a navigation interface, may appear at the top on an iPad, where it plays something of the role that the menu bar plays on the desktop; but it typically appears at the bottom on an iPhone (Figure 6-4 has a toolbar at the bottom). If you need a top bar on the iPhone, you might put a view controller inside a navigation controller even if no actual navigation is going to take place, just for the convenience of the navigation bar with its title and buttons at the top of the screen.

Bar Button Items

The items in a UIToolbar or a UINavigationBar are *bar button items* — UIBarButtonItem, a subclass of UIBarItem. A bar button item comes in one of two broadly different flavors:

Basic bar button item
   The bar button item behaves like a simple button.

Custom view
   The bar button item has no inherent behavior, but has (and displays) a custom-View.

UIBarItem is not a UIView subclass. A basic bar button item is button-like, but it has no frame, no UIView touch handling, and so forth. But a UIBarButtonItem's custom-View, if it has one, *is* a UIView, so you can display any sort of view in a toolbar or navigation bar, and that view can have subviews, touch handling, and so on.

Let's start with the basic bar button item (no custom view). A bar button item, like a tab bar item, inherits from UIBarItem the title, image, and isEnabled properties. The title text color, by default, comes from the bar button item's tintColor, which may be inherited from the bar itself or from higher up the view hierarchy. Assigning an image removes the title. The image should usually be quite small; Apple recommends 22×22. By default, it will be treated as a transparency mask (a template): the hue of its pixels will be ignored, and the transparency of its pixels will be combined with the bar button item's tint color. You can instead display an image as is, and not as a transparency mask, by deriving an image whose rendering mode is .always-Original (see Chapter 2).

A basic bar button item has a style property (UIBarButtonItem.Style); this will usually be .plain. The alternative, .done, causes the title to be bold. You can further refine the title font and style. In addition, a bar button item can have a background image; this will typically be a small resizable image, and can be used to provide a border. Full details appear in Chapter 12.

A bar button item also has target and action properties. These facilitate its button-like behavior: tapping a bar button item calls the action method on the target, so you can handle the tap in some object that makes sense for your architecture, such as the view controller.

There are three ways to make a bar button item:

By borrowing it from the system
> Make a UIBarButtonItem with `init(barButtonSystemItem:target:action:)`. Consult the documentation for the list of available system items; they are not the same as for a tab bar item. You can't assign a title or change the image. (But you can change the tint color or assign a background image.)

By making your own basic bar button item
> Make a UIBarButtonItem with `init(title:style:target:action:)` or with `init(image:style:target:action:)`. New in iOS 13, the repertoire of standard symbol images is available.
>
> Also, `init(image:landscapeImagePhone:style:target: action:)` lets you specify a second image for use when the vertical size class is `.compact`, because the bar's height might be smaller in this situation.

By making a custom view bar button item
> Make a UIBarButtonItem with `init(customView:)`, supplying a UIView that the bar button item is to display. The bar button item has no action and target; the UIView itself must somehow implement button behavior if that's what you want. For instance, the `customView` might be a UISegmentedControl, but then it is the UISegmentedControl's target and action that give it button behavior.
>
> Your custom view can and should use autolayout internally. Provide sufficient constraints to size the view from the inside out; otherwise, it may have no size (and might be invisible).

Bar button items in a toolbar are horizontally positioned automatically by the system. You can't control their position precisely, but you can provide hints. You can give a bar button item an absolute `width`, and you can incorporate spacers into the toolbar; these are created with `init(barButtonSystemItem:target:action:)`, but they have no visible appearance, and cannot be tapped. Place `.flexibleSpace` system items between the visible items to distribute the visible items equally across the width of the toolbar. There is also a `.fixedSpace` system item whose `width` lets you insert a space of defined size.

Navigation Items and Toolbar Items

What appears in a navigation bar (UINavigationBar) depends upon the navigation items (UINavigationItem) in its stack. In a navigation interface, the navigation controller will manage the navigation bar's stack for you; your job is to configure the `navigationItem` of each child view controller. The UINavigationItem properties are (see also Chapter 12):

`title`
`titleView`

> The `title` is a string. Setting a view controller's `title` property sets the `title` of its `navigationItem` automatically, and is usually the best approach. The `title-View` can be any kind of UIView, and can implement further UIView functionality such as touchability.
>
> In iOS 10 and before, the `title` and the `titleView` are displayed in the same spot — the center of the navigation bar. So there can be only one: if there is a `titleView`, it is shown instead of the `title`. Starting in iOS 11, the `title` may be shown at the *bottom* of the navigation bar, in which case both the `title` and the `titleView` can appear; I'll explain more about that in a moment.
>
> As with a custom view, the `titleView` should use autolayout internally, with sufficient constraints to size the view from the inside out.

`prompt`

> An optional string to appear centered above everything else in the navigation bar. The navigation bar's height will be increased to accommodate it.

`rightBarButtonItem` *or* `rightBarButtonItems`

> A bar button item or, respectively, an array of bar button items to appear at the right side of the navigation bar; the first item in the array will be rightmost.

`backBarButtonItem`

> When a view controller is pushed on top of this view controller, the navigation bar will display at its left a button pointing to the left, whose title is *this* view controller's `title`. That button is *this* view controller's navigation item's `backBar-ButtonItem`. In other words, the back button displayed in the navigation bar belongs, not to the top item (the `navigationItem` of the current view controller), but to the back item (the `navigationItem` of the view controller that is one level down in the stack).
>
> Most of the time, the default behavior is the behavior you'll want, and you'll leave the back button alone. If you wish, though, you can customize the back button by setting a view controller's `navigationItem.backBarButtonItem` so that it contains an image, or a title differing from the view controller's `title`. The best technique is to provide a new UIBarButtonItem whose target and action are `nil`; the runtime will add a correct target and action, so as to create a working back button. Here's how to create a back button with a custom image instead of a title:

```
let b = UIBarButtonItem(
    image:UIImage(named:"files"), style:.plain, target:nil, action:nil)
self.navigationItem.backBarButtonItem = b
```

A Bool property, `hidesBackButton`, allows the top navigation item to suppress display of the back button. If you set this to `true`, you'll probably want to provide some other means of letting the user navigate back.

The visible indication that the back button *is* a back button is a chevron (the *back indicator*) that's separate from the button itself. This chevron can also be customized, but it's a feature of the navigation bar, not the bar button item. (I'll give an example in Chapter 12.)

`leftBarButtonItem` *or* `leftBarButtonItems`

A bar button item or, respectively, an array of bar button items to appear at the left side of the navigation bar; the first item in the array will be leftmost. The `leftItemsSupplementBackButton` property, if set to `true`, allows both the back button and one or more left bar button items to appear.

Starting in iOS 11, a navigation bar can adopt an increased height in order to display the top item's `title` in a large font *below* the bar button items. This is a navigation bar feature, its `prefersLargeTitles` property. In order to accommodate the possibility that different view controllers will have different preferences in this regard, a navigation item has a `largeTitleDisplayMode`, which may be one of the following:

`.always`

The navigation item's `title` is displayed large if the navigation bar's `prefersLargeTitles` is `true`.

`.never`

The navigation item's `title` is *not* displayed large.

`.automatic`

The navigation item's `title` display is the same as the `title` display of the back item — that is, of the navigation item preceding this one in the navigation bar's stack. This is the default. The idea is that all navigation items pushed onto a navigation bar will display their titles in the same way, until a pushed navigation item declares `.always` or `.never`.

The navigation controller may grow or shrink its navigation bar to display or hide the large title as the contents of its view are scrolled — yet another reason why a nimble interface based on autolayout and the safe area is crucial.

 New in iOS 13, a navigation bar with a large title is transparent by default. I'll talk in Chapter 12 about how to change that.

A view controller's `navigationItem` is not just something to be prepared before that view controller is pushed onto a navigation controller's stack; it is *live*. You can change its properties while its interface is being displayed in the navigation bar. In one of my apps, we play music from the user's library using interface in the navigation bar. The `titleView` is a progress view (UIProgressView, Chapter 12) that needs updating every second to reflect the playback position in the current song, and the right bar button should be either the system Play button or the system Pause button, depending on whether we are paused or playing. So I have a timer that periodically checks the state of the music player (`self.mp`); we access the progress view and the right bar button by way of `self.navigationItem`:

```
// change the progress view
let prog = self.navigationItem.titleView!.subviews[0] as! UIProgressView
if let item = self.nowPlayingItem {
    let current = self.mp.currentPlaybackTime
    let total = item.playbackDuration
    prog.progress = Float(current / total)
} else {
    prog.progress = 0
}
// change the bar button
let whichButton : UIBarButtonItem.SystemItem? = {
    switch self.mp.currentPlaybackRate {
    case 0..<0.1:
        return .play
    case 0.1...1.0:
        return .pause
    default:
        return nil
    }
}()
if let which = whichButton {
    let bb = UIBarButtonItem(barButtonSystemItem: which,
        target: self, action: #selector(doPlayPause))
    self.navigationItem.rightBarButtonItem = bb
}
```

Each view controller to be pushed onto the navigation controller's stack is responsible also for supplying the items to appear in the navigation interface's toolbar, if there is one: set the view controller's `toolbarItems` property to an array of UIBarButton-Item instances. You can change the toolbar items even while the view controller's view and current `toolbarItems` are showing, optionally with animation, by sending `setToolbarItems(_:animated:)` to the view controller.

Configuring a Navigation Controller

You configure a navigation controller by manipulating its stack of view controllers. This stack is the navigation controller's `viewControllers` array property, though you will rarely need to manipulate that property directly.

The view controllers in a navigation controller's `viewControllers` array are the navigation controller's child view controllers; the navigation controller is the `parent` of the view controllers in the array. The navigation controller is also the `navigationController` of the view controllers in the array and of all their children; a child view controller at any depth can learn that it is contained by a navigation controller and can get a reference to that navigation controller. The navigation controller retains the array, and the array retains the child view controllers.

The normal way to manipulate a navigation controller's stack is by pushing or popping one view controller at a time. When the navigation controller is instantiated, it is usually initialized with `init(rootViewController:)`; this is a convenience method that assigns the navigation controller a single initial child view controller, the root view controller that goes at the bottom of the stack:

```
let fvc = FirstViewController()
let nav = UINavigationController(rootViewController:fvc)
```

Instead of `init(rootViewController:)`, you might choose to create the navigation controller with `init(navigationBarClass:toolbarClass:)` in order to set a custom subclass of UINavigationBar or UIToolbar. If you do that, you'll have to set the navigation controller's root view controller separately.

You can also set the UINavigationController's delegate (adopting UINavigationControllerDelegate). The delegate receives messages before and after a child view controller's view is shown.

If a navigation controller is the top-level view controller, it determines your app's compensatory rotation behavior. To take a hand in that determination without having to subclass UINavigationController, make one of your objects the navigation controller's delegate and implement these methods, as needed:

- `navigationControllerSupportedInterfaceOrientations(_:)`
- `navigationControllerPreferredInterfaceOrientationForPresentation(_:)`

But don't try to use those methods to implement forced rotation between one view controller and the next as it is pushed onto the stack. That isn't going to work. The way to implement forced rotation is to use a fullscreen presented view controller, as I explained earlier.

A top-level navigation controller also determines your app's status bar visibility. However, a navigation controller implements `childForStatusBarHidden` so that the actual decision is relegated to the child view controller whose view is currently being displayed: the child's `prefersStatusBarHidden` is consulted and obeyed. On a device without a bezel, such as the iPhone X, the status bar cannot be hidden if the navigation bar is present.

Determining the status bar *style* (light or dark content) is more complicated:

The navigation bar is hidden

If the navigation bar is hidden but the status bar is showing, then your view controller's `preferredStatusBarStyle` override gets to determine the status bar style. That's because the navigation controller's `childForStatusBarStyle` points to the child view controller whose view is currently being displayed.

The navigation bar is showing

If the navigation bar is showing, the navigation controller does not relegate the decision to its child view controller. Instead, the status bar content color depends on the navigation bar's `barStyle` — the status bar content is dark if the navigation bar style is `.default`, and light if the navigation bar style is `.black`.

New in iOS 13, that works only if the navigation bar doesn't display a large title, and only if you don't use the new UIBarAppearance properties (Chapter 12); Apple probably expects you to leave the status bar style alone and let it respond automatically to the user interface style (light or dark mode). Just don't make your navigation bar so dark in light mode that dark status bar content isn't legible in front of it.

A navigation controller will typically appear on the screen initially containing just its root view controller and displaying its root view controller's view, with no back button (because there is nowhere to go back to). Subsequently, when the user asks to navigate to a new view, you create the next view controller and push it onto the stack by calling `pushViewController(_:animated:)` on the navigation controller. The navigation controller performs the animation, and displays the new view controller's view:

```
let svc = SecondViewController()
self.navigationController!.pushViewController(svc, animated: true)
```

The command for going back is `popViewController(animated:)`, but you might never need to call it yourself, as the runtime will call it for you when the user taps the back button. When a view controller is popped from the stack, the `viewControllers` array removes and releases the view controller, which is usually permitted to go out of existence at that point.

(There's a second way to push a view controller onto the navigation controller's stack, without referring to the navigation controller: `show(_:sender:)`. This method *pushes* the view controller if we are in a navigation interface, but otherwise *presents* it as a presented view controller. I'll talk more about that in Chapter 9.)

Instead of tapping the back button, the user can go back by dragging a pushed view controller's view from the left edge of the screen. This is actually a way of calling `pop-ViewController(animated:)`, with the difference that the animation is interactive. The UINavigationController uses a UIScreenEdgePanGestureRecognizer to detect and track the user's gesture. You can obtain a reference to this gesture recognizer as the navigation controller's `interactivePopGestureRecognizer`; you can disable the gesture recognizer to prevent this way of going back, or you can mediate between your own gesture recognizers and this one (see Chapter 5).

You can manipulate the stack more directly if you wish. You can call `popView-Controller(animated:)` explicitly; to pop multiple items so as to leave a particular view controller at the top of the stack, call `popToViewController(_:animated:)`, or to pop all the items down to the root view controller, call `popToRootView-Controller(animated:)`. All of these methods return the popped view controller (or view controllers, as an array) in case you want to do something with them. To set the entire stack at once, call `setViewControllers(_:animated:)`. You can access the stack through the `viewControllers` property. Manipulating the stack directly is the only way, for instance, to remove or insert a view controller in the middle of the stack.

 If a view controller needs a signal that it is being popped, override `viewWill-Disappear` and see if `self.isMovingFromParent` is `true`.

The view controller at the top of the stack is the `topViewController`; the view controller whose view is displayed is the `visibleViewController`. Those will normally be the same, but they needn't be, as the `topViewController` might present a view controller, in which case the presented view controller will be the `visibleView-Controller`. Other view controllers can be accessed through the `viewControllers` array by index number. The root view controller is at index 0; if the array's `count` is c, the back view controller (the one whose `navigationItem.backBarButtonItem` is currently displayed in the navigation bar) is at index `c-2`.

The `topViewController` may need to communicate with the next view controller as the latter is pushed onto the stack, or with the back view controller as it itself is popped off the stack. The problem is parallel to that of communication between an original presenter and a presented view controller, which I discussed earlier in this chapter ("Communication with a Presented View Controller" on page 330), so I won't say more about it here.

A child view controller will probably want to configure its `navigationItem` early in its lifetime, so as to be ready for display in the navigation bar by the time the view controller is handed as a child to the navigation controller. Apple warns (in the UIViewController class reference, under `navigationItem`) that `loadView` and `viewDidLoad` are not appropriate places to do this, because the circumstances under which the view is needed are not related to the circumstances under which the navigation item is needed. Apple's own code examples routinely violate this warning, but it is probably best to override a view controller initializer for this purpose.

A navigation controller's navigation bar is accessible as its `navigationBar`, and can be hidden and shown with `setNavigationBarHidden(_:animated:)`. (It is possible, though not common, to maintain and manipulate a navigation stack through a navigation controller whose navigation bar never appears.) Its toolbar is accessible as its `toolbar`, and can be hidden and shown with `setToolbarHidden(_:animated:)`.

A view controller also has the power to specify that its ancestor's bottom bar (a navigation controller's toolbar, or a tab bar controller's tab bar) should be hidden as this view controller is pushed onto a navigation controller's stack. To do so, set the view controller's `hidesBottomBarWhenPushed` property to `true`. The trick is that you must do this very early, before the view loads; the view controller's initializer is a good place. The bottom bar remains hidden from the time this view controller is pushed to the time it is popped, even if other view controllers are pushed and popped on top of it in the meantime.

A navigation controller can perform automatic hiding and showing of its navigation bar (and, if normally shown, its toolbar) in response to various situations, as configured by properties:

When tapped

If the navigation controller's `hidesBarsOnTap` is `true`, a tap that falls through the top view controller's view is taken as a signal to toggle bar visibility. The relevant gesture recognizer is the navigation controller's `barHideOnTapGestureRecognizer`.

When swiped

If the navigation controller's `hidesBarsOnSwipe` is `true`, an upward or downward swipe respectively hides or shows the bars. The relevant gesture recognizer is the navigation controller's `barHideOnSwipeGestureRecognizer`.

In landscape

If the navigation controller's `hidesBarsWhenVerticallyCompact` is `true`, bars are automatically hidden when the app rotates to landscape on the iPhone (and `hidesBarsOnTap` is treated as `true`, so the bars can be shown again by tapping).

When the user is typing

> If the navigation controller's `hidesBarsWhenKeyboardAppears` is `true`, bars are automatically hidden when the virtual keyboard appears (see Chapter 10).

In the nib editor, you can configure a UINavigationController and any view controller that is to serve in a navigation interface. In the Attributes inspector, use a navigation controller's Bar Visibility and Hide Bars checkboxes to determine the presence of the navigation bar and toolbar. The navigation bar and toolbar are themselves subviews of the navigation controller, and you can configure them with the Attributes inspector as well. A navigation bar has a Prefers Large Titles checkbox. A navigation controller's root view controller can be specified; in a storyboard, there will be a "root view controller" relationship between the navigation controller and its root view controller. The root view controller is automatically instantiated together with the navigation controller.

A view controller in the nib editor has a Navigation Item where you can specify its title, its prompt, and the text of its back button. A navigation item has a Large Title pop-up menu, where you can set its `largeTitleDisplayMode`. You can drag Bar Button Items into a view controller's navigation bar in the canvas to set the left buttons and right buttons of its `navigationItem`. Moreover, the Navigation Item has outlets, one of which permits you to set its `titleView`. Similarly, you can give a view controller Bar Button Items that will appear in the toolbar. (If a view controller in a nib doesn't have a Navigation Item and you want to configure this view controller for use in a navigation interface, drag a Navigation Item from the Library onto the view controller.)

To start an iPhone project with a main storyboard that has a UINavigationController as its initial view controller, begin with the Master–Detail App template. Alternatively, start with the Single View App template, select the existing view controller, and choose Editor → Embed In → Navigation Controller (or choose Navigation Controller from the Embed button at the lower right of the canvas). A view controller to be subsequently pushed onto the navigation stack can be configured in the storyboard as the destination of a push segue; I'll talk more about that later in this chapter.

Custom Transition

You can customize the transitions when these built-in view controllers change views:

Tab bar controller

> When a tab bar controller changes which of its child view controllers is selected, by default there is no view animation; you can add a custom animation.

Navigation controller

> When a navigation controller pushes or pops a child view controller, by default there is a sideways sliding view animation; you can replace this with a custom animation.

Presented view controller

> When a view controller is presented or dismissed, there is a limited set of built-in view animations (`modalTransitionStyle`); you can substitute a custom animation. Moreover, you can customize the ultimate size and position of the presented view, and how the presenting view is seen behind it; you can also provide ancillary views that remain during the presentation.

Given the extensive animation resources of iOS (see Chapter 4), this is an excellent chance for you to provide your app with variety, distinction, and clarity. The view of a child view controller pushed onto a navigation controller's stack needn't arrive sliding from the side; it can expand by zooming from the middle of the screen, drop from above and fall into place with a bounce, snap into place like a spring, or whatever else you can dream up. A familiar example is Apple's Calendar app, which transitions from a year to a month, in a navigation controller, by zooming in.

A custom transition animation can optionally be *interactive*: instead of tapping and causing an animation to take place, the user performs an extended gesture and gradually summons the new view to supersede the old one. A familiar example is the Photos app, which lets the user pinch a photo, in a navigation controller, to pop to the album containing it.

A custom transition animation can optionally be *interruptible*. You can provide a way for the user to pause the animation, possibly interact with the animated view by means of a gesture, and then resume (or cancel) the animation.

Noninteractive Custom Transition Animation

In the base case, you provide a custom animation that is *not* interactive. Configuring your custom animation requires three steps:

1. Before the transition begins, you give the view controller in charge of the transition a delegate.

2. As the transition begins, the delegate will be asked for an *animation controller*. You will return a reference to some object adopting the UIViewController-AnimatedTransitioning protocol (or `nil` to specify that the default animation, if any, should be used).

   The delegate (configured in step 1) and the animation controller (returned in step 2) are often the same object, and in my examples they will be; but they don't have to be. The animation controller can be any object, possibly a dedicated lightweight object instantiated just to govern this transition. The animation controller needn't even be the same object every time step 2 happens; we could readily return a different animation controller, depending on the circumstances, or `nil` to specify the default transition.

3. The animation controller will be sent these messages:

   `transitionDuration(using:)`
   The animation controller must return the duration of the custom animation.

   `animateTransition(using:)`
   The animation controller should perform the animation.

   `interruptibleAnimator(using:)`
   Optional; if implemented, the animation controller should return an object adopting the UIViewImplicitlyAnimating protocol, which may be a property animator.

   `animationEnded(_:)`
   Optional; if implemented, the animation controller may perform cleanup following the animation.

I like to use a property animator to govern the animation; it will need to be accessible from multiple methods, so it must live in an instance property. I like to type this instance property as `UIViewImplicitlyAnimating?`; that way, I can use `nil` to indicate that the property animator doesn't exist. Here's what the four animation controller methods will need to do:

`transitionDuration(using:)`
We'll return the property animator's animation duration.

`animateTransition(using:)`
We'll call `interruptibleAnimator(using:)` to obtain the property animator, and we'll tell the property animator to start animating.

`interruptibleAnimator(using:)`
This is where all the real work happens. We're being asked for the property animator. There is a danger that we will be called multiple times during the animation, so if the property animator already exists in our instance property, we simply return it; if it doesn't exist, we create and configure it and assign it to our instance property, and *then* return it.

`animationEnded(_:)`
We'll clean up any instance properties; at a minimum, we'll set our property animator instance property to `nil`.

The heart of the matter is what `interruptibleAnimator(using:)` does to configure the property animator and its animation. In general, a custom transition animation works like this:

1. The `using:` parameter is the *transition context* (adopting the UIViewController-ContextTransitioning protocol). By querying the transition context, you can obtain:

    - The *container view*, an already existing view within which all the action is to take place.

    - The outgoing and incoming view controllers.

    - The outgoing and incoming views. These are probably the main views of the outgoing and incoming view controllers, but you should obtain the views directly from the transition context, just in case they aren't. The outgoing view is already inside the container view.

    - The initial `frame` of the outgoing view, and the ultimate `frame` where the incoming view must end up.

2. Having gathered this information, your mission is:

    a. Put the incoming view into the container view.

    b. Animate that view so as to end up at its correct ultimate `frame`. (You may also animate the outgoing view if you wish.)

3. When the animation ends, your completion function *must* call the transition context's `completeTransition` to tell it that the animation is over. In response, the outgoing view is removed automatically, and the animation comes to an end (and our `animationEnded` will be called).

I'll illustrate with the transition between two child view controllers of a tab bar controller, when the user taps a different tab bar item. By default, this transition isn't animated; one view just replaces the other. A possible custom animation is that the new view controller's view should slide in from one side while the old view controller's view should slide out the other side. The direction of the slide should depend on whether the index of the new view controller is greater or less than that of the old view controller. Let's implement that.

For simplicity, I'll do all the work in a single custom class called Animator:

```
class Animator : NSObject {
    var anim : UIViewImplicitlyAnimating?
    unowned var tbc : UITabBarController
    init(tabBarController tbc: UITabBarController) {
        self.tbc = tbc
    }
}
```

I'll keep an Animator instance as a property of some stable object, such as the app delegate or scene delegate. The tab bar controller is in charge of the transition, so the first step is to make the Animator its delegate:

```
if let tbc = self.window?.rootViewController as? UITabBarController {
    self.animator = Animator(tabBarController: tbc)
    tbc.delegate = self.animator
}
```

As the UITabBarControllerDelegate, the Animator will be sent a message whenever the tab bar controller is about to change view controllers. That message is:

- `tabBarController(_:animationControllerForTransitionFrom:to:)`

The second step is to implement that method. We must return an animation controller, namely, some object implementing UIViewControllerAnimatedTransitioning. I'll return `self`:

```
extension Animator : UITabBarControllerDelegate {
    func tabBarController(_ tabBarController: UITabBarController,
        animationControllerForTransitionFrom fromVC: UIViewController,
        to toVC: UIViewController) -> UIViewControllerAnimatedTransitioning? {
            return self
    }
}
```

The third step is to implement the animation controller (UIViewControllerAnimated-Transitioning). I'll start with stubs for the four methods we're going to write:

```
extension Animator : UIViewControllerAnimatedTransitioning {
    func transitionDuration(using ctx: UIViewControllerContextTransitioning?)
        -> TimeInterval {
            // ...
    }
    func animateTransition(using ctx: UIViewControllerContextTransitioning) {
        // ...
    }
    func interruptibleAnimator(using ctx: UIViewControllerContextTransitioning)
        -> UIViewImplicitlyAnimating {
            // ...
    }
    func animationEnded(_ transitionCompleted: Bool) {
        // ...
    }
}
```

Our `transitionDuration` must reveal in advance the duration of our animation:

```
func transitionDuration(using ctx: UIViewControllerContextTransitioning?)
    -> TimeInterval {
        return 0.4
}
```

Our `animateTransition` simply calls `interruptibleAnimator` to obtain the property animator, and tells it to animate:

```
func animateTransition(using ctx: UIViewControllerContextTransitioning) {
    let anim = self.interruptibleAnimator(using: ctx)
    anim.startAnimation()
}
```

The workhorse is `interruptibleAnimator`. If the property animator already exists, we unwrap it and return it, and that's all:

```
func interruptibleAnimator(using ctx: UIViewControllerContextTransitioning)
    -> UIViewImplicitlyAnimating {
        if self.anim != nil {
            return self.anim!
        }
        // ...
}
```

If we haven't returned, we need to construct the property animator. First, we thoroughly query the transition context `ctx` about the parameters of this animation:

```
let vc1 = ctx.viewController(forKey:.from)!
let vc2 = ctx.viewController(forKey:.to)!
let con = ctx.containerView
let r1start = ctx.initialFrame(for:vc1)
let r2end = ctx.finalFrame(for:vc2)
let v1 = ctx.view(forKey:.from)!
let v2 = ctx.view(forKey:.to)!
```

Now we can prepare for our intended animation. In this case, we are sliding the views, so we need to decide the final frame of the outgoing view and the initial frame of the incoming view. We are sliding the views sideways, so those frames should be positioned sideways from the initial frame of the outgoing view and the final frame of the incoming view, which the transition context has just given us. *Which* side they go on depends upon the relative place of these view controllers among the children of the tab bar controller:

```
let ix1 = self.tbc.viewControllers!.firstIndex(of:vc1)!
let ix2 = self.tbc.viewControllers!.firstIndex(of:vc2)!
let dir : CGFloat = ix1 < ix2 ? 1 : -1
var r1end = r1start
r1end.origin.x -= r1end.size.width * dir
var r2start = r2end
r2start.origin.x += r2start.size.width * dir
```

Now we're ready for the animations function. We put the second view controller's view into the container view at its initial frame, and animate our views:

```
    v2.frame = r2start
    con.addSubview(v2)
    let anim = UIViewPropertyAnimator(duration: 0.4, curve: .linear) {
        v1.frame = r1end
        v2.frame = r2end
    }
```

We must not neglect to supply the completion function that calls `complete-Transition`:

```
    anim.addCompletion { _ in
        ctx.completeTransition(true)
    }
```

Our property animator is ready! We retain it in our `self.anim` property, and we also return it:

```
    self.anim = anim
    return anim
```

That completes `interruptibleAnimator`. Finally, our `animationEnded` cleans up by destroying the property animator:

```
    func animationEnded(_ transitionCompleted: Bool) {
        self.anim = nil
    }
```

That's all there is to it. Our example animation wasn't very complex, but an animation needn't be complex to be interesting, significant, and helpful to the user; I use this animation in my own apps, and I think it enlivens and clarifies the transition.

One possibility that I didn't illustrate in my example is that you are free to introduce additional views temporarily into the container view during the course of the animation; you'll probably want to remove them in the completion function. You might use this to make some interface object appear to migrate from one view controller's view into the other (in reality you'd probably use a snapshot view; see Chapter 1).

Interactive Custom Transition Animation

With an interactive custom transition animation, the idea is that we track something the user is doing, typically by means of a gesture recognizer (see Chapter 5), and perform the "frames" of the transition in response.

To make a custom transition animation interactive, you supply, in addition to the animation controller, an *interaction controller*. This is an object adopting the UIViewControllerInteractiveTransitioning protocol. Again, this object needn't be the same as the animation controller, but it often is, and in my examples it will be. The runtime calls the interaction controller's `startInteractiveTransition(_:)` *instead* of the animation controller's `animateTransition(using:)`.

Configuring your custom animation requires the following steps:

1. Before the transition begins, you give the view controller in charge of the transition a delegate.

2. You'll need a gesture recognizer that tracks the interactive gesture. When the gesture recognizer recognizes, make it trigger the transition to the new view controller.

3. As the transition begins, the delegate will be asked for an animation controller. You will return a UIViewControllerAnimatedTransitioning object.

4. The delegate will also be asked for an interaction controller. You will return a UIViewControllerInteractiveTransitioning object (or `nil` to prevent the transition from being interactive). This object implements `startInteractive-Transition(_:)`.

5. The gesture recognizer continues by repeatedly calling `updateInteractive-Transition(_:)` on the transition context, as well as managing the frames of the animation.

6. Sooner or later the gesture will end. At this point, decide whether to declare the transition completed or cancelled, and finish the animation accordingly. A typical approach is to say that if the user performed more than half the full gesture, that constitutes completion; otherwise, it constitutes cancellation.

7. The animation is now completed, and its completion function is called. You *must* call the transition context's `finishInteractiveTransition` or `cancel-InteractiveTransition`, and then call its `completeTransition(_:)` with an argument stating whether the transition was finished or cancelled.

8. Finally, `animationEnded` is called, and you can clean up.

(You may be asking: why is it necessary to keep talking to the transition context throughout the process? The reason is that the animation might have a component separate from what you're doing, such as the change in the appearance of the navigation bar during a navigation controller push or pop transition. The transition context, in order to coordinate that animation with the interactive gesture and with your animation, needs to be kept abreast of where things are throughout the course of the interaction.)

I'll describe how to make an interactive version of the tab bar controller transition animation that we developed in the previous section. The user will be able to drag from the edge of the screen to bring the tab bar controller's adjacent view controller in from the right or from the left.

In the previous section, I cleverly planned ahead for this section. Almost all the code from the previous section can be left as is! I'll build on that code, in such a way that the same custom transition animation can be *either* noninteractive (the user taps a tab bar item) *or* interactive (the user drags from one edge).

In my Animator object, I'm going to need two more instance properties, in addition to `anim` and `tvc`:

```
var anim : UIViewImplicitlyAnimating?
unowned var tbc : UITabBarController
weak var context : UIViewControllerContextTransitioning?
var interacting = false
```

The `interacting` property will be used as a signal that our transition is to be interactive. The `context` property is needed because the gesture recognizer's action method is going to need access to the transition context. (Sharing the transition context through a property may seem ugly, but the elegant alternatives would make the example more complicated, so we'll just do it this way.)

To track the user's gesture, I'll put a pair of UIScreenEdgePanGestureRecognizers into the interface. The gesture recognizers are attached to the tab bar controller's view (`tbc.view`), as this will remain constant while the views of its view controllers are sliding across the screen. In the Animator's initializer, I create the gesture recognizers and make the Animator their delegate, so I can dictate which of them is applicable to the current situation:

```
init(tabBarController tbc: UITabBarController) {
    self.tbc = tbc
    super.init()
    let sep = UIScreenEdgePanGestureRecognizer(
        target:self, action:#selector(pan))
    sep.edges = UIRectEdge.right
    tbc.view.addGestureRecognizer(sep)
    sep.delegate = self
    let sep2 = UIScreenEdgePanGestureRecognizer(
        target:self, action:#selector(pan))
    sep2.edges = UIRectEdge.left
    tbc.view.addGestureRecognizer(sep2)
    sep2.delegate = self
}
```

Acting as the delegate of the two gesture recognizers, we prevent either pan gesture recognizer from operating unless there is another child of the tab bar controller available on that side of the current child:

```
extension Animator : UIGestureRecognizerDelegate {
    func gestureRecognizerShouldBegin(_ g: UIGestureRecognizer) -> Bool {
        let ix = self.tbc.selectedIndex
        return
            (g as! UIScreenEdgePanGestureRecognizer).edges == .right ?
                ix < self.tbc.viewControllers!.count - 1 : ix > 0
    }
}
```

If the gesture recognizer action method pan is called, our interactive transition animation is to take place. I'll break down the discussion according to the gesture recognizer's states. In .begin, I raise the self.interacting flag and trigger the transition by setting the tab bar controller's selectedIndex:

```
@objc func pan(_ g:UIScreenEdgePanGestureRecognizer) {
    switch g.state {
    case .begin:
        self.interacting = true
        if g.edges == .right {
            self.tbc.selectedIndex = self.tbc.selectedIndex + 1
        } else {
            self.tbc.selectedIndex = self.tbc.selectedIndex - 1
        }
    // ...
    }
}
```

The transition begins. We are asked for our animation controller and our transition controller. We will supply a transition controller only if the self.interacting flag was raised; if the self.interacting flag is *not* raised, the user tapped a tab bar item and we are back in the preceding example:

```
extension AppDelegate: UITabBarControllerDelegate {
    func tabBarController(_ tabBarController: UITabBarController,
        animationControllerForTransitionFrom fromVC: UIViewController,
        to toVC: UIViewController) -> UIViewControllerAnimatedTransitioning? {
            return self
    }
    func tabBarController(_ tabBarController: UITabBarController,
        interactionControllerFor ac: UIViewControllerAnimatedTransitioning)
        -> UIViewControllerInteractiveTransitioning? {
            return self.interacting ? self : nil
    }
}
```

As a UIViewControllerInteractiveTransitioning adopter, our startInteractive-Transition(_:) is called instead of animateTransition(using:). Our animate-Transition(using:) is still in place, and still does the same job it did in the previous section. So we call it to obtain the property animator, and set the property animator instance property. But we do *not* tell the property animator to animate! We are interactive; we intend to manage the "frames" of the animation ourselves (see "Frozen View Animation" on page 183). We also set the UIViewControllerContextTransitioning property, so that the gesture recognizer's action method can access it:

```
extension AppDelegate : UIViewControllerInteractiveTransitioning {
    func startInteractiveTransition(_ ctx:UIViewControllerContextTransitioning){
        self.anim = self.interruptibleAnimator(using: ctx)
        self.context = ctx
    }
}
```

The user's gesture proceeds, and we are now back in the gesture recognizer's action method, in the .changed state. We calculate the completed percentage of the gesture, and update both the property animator's "frame" and the transition context:

```
case .changed:
    let v = g.view!
    let delta = g.translation(in:v)
    let percent = abs(delta.x/v.bounds.size.width)
    self.anim?.fractionComplete = percent
    self.context?.updateInteractiveTransition(percent)
```

Ultimately, the user's gesture ends. Our goal now is to "hurry" to the start of the animation or the end of the animation, depending on how far the user got through the gesture. With a property animator, that's really easy (see "Canceling a View Animation" on page 179):

```
case .ended:
    let anim = self.anim as! UIViewPropertyAnimator
    anim.pauseAnimation()
    if anim.fractionComplete < 0.5 {
        anim.isReversed = true
    }
    anim.continueAnimation(
        withTimingParameters:
        UICubicTimingParameters(animationCurve:.linear),
        durationFactor: 0.2)
```

The animation comes to an end, and the completion function that we gave our property animator in interruptibleAnimator is called. This is the one place in our interruptibleAnimator that needs to be a little different from the preceding example; we must send different messages to the transition context, depending on whether we finished at the end or reversed to the start:

```
anim.addCompletion { finish in
    if finish == .end {
        ctx.finishInteractiveTransition()
        ctx.completeTransition(true)
    } else {
        ctx.cancelInteractiveTransition()
        ctx.completeTransition(false)
    }
}
```

Finally, our animationEnded is called, and we clean up our instance properties:

```
func animationEnded(_ transitionCompleted: Bool) {
    self.interacting = false
    self.anim = nil
}
```

Another variation would be to make the custom transition animation interruptible. Again, this is straightforward thanks to the existence of property animators. While a view is in the middle of being animated, the property animator implements touchability of the animated view, and allows you to pause the animation. The user can be permitted to do such things as grab the animated view in the middle of the animation and move it around with the animation paused, and the animation can then resume when the user lets go of the view (as I demonstrated in "Hit-Testing During Animation" on page 274). You could equally incorporate these features into a custom transition animation.

You can also use a UIPreviewInteraction ("3D Touch Press Gesture" on page 266) to drive a view controller custom transition animation through 3D touch. In that case, the user's press is the gesture, and what advances the interactive custom transition animation is the UIPreviewInteraction and its delegate methods, rather than a gesture recognizer and its action method.

Custom Presented View Controller Transition

With a presented view controller transition, you can customize not only the *animation* but also the final *position* of the presented view. Moreover, you can introduce ancillary views which *remain in the scene* while the presented view is presented, and are not removed until after dismissal is complete; for instance, if the presented view is smaller than the presenting view and covers it only partially, you might add a dimming view between them, to darken the presenting view (just as a `.formSheet` presentation does).

There is no existing view to serve as the container view; therefore, when the presentation starts, the runtime constructs the container view and inserts it into the interface, leaving it there while the view remains presented. In the case of a `.fullScreen` presentation, the runtime also rips the presenting view out of the interface and inserts it into the container view, in case you want to animate it as well. For other styles of presentation, the container view is in front of the presenting view.

The work of customizing a presentation is distributed between *two* objects:

The animation controller
  The animation controller should be responsible for only the animation, the movement of the presented view into its final position.

The custom presentation controller

The determination of the presented view's final position is the job of the presentation controller. The presentation controller is also responsible for inserting any extra views, such as a dimming view, into the container view; Apple says that the animation controller animates the content, while the presentation controller animates the "chrome."

This distribution of responsibilities may sound rather elaborate, but in fact the opposite is true: it greatly simplifies things, because if you don't need one kind of customization you can omit it:

- If you supply an animation controller and no custom presentation controller, you dictate the animation, but the presented view will end up wherever the modal presentation style puts it.

- If you supply a custom presentation controller and no animation controller, a default modal transition style animation will be performed, but the presented view will end up at the position your custom presentation controller dictates.

Customizing the animation

I'll start with a situation where we don't use the presentation controller: all we want to do is customize the animation part of a built-in presentation style. The steps are almost completely parallel to how we customized a tab bar controller animation:

1. Give the presented view controller a delegate. This means that you set the presented view controller's `transitioningDelegate` property to an object adopting the UIViewControllerTransitioningDelegate protocol.

2. The delegate will be asked for an animation controller, and will return an object adopting the UIViewControllerAnimatedTransitioning protocol. Unlike a tab bar controller or navigation controller, a presented view controller's view undergoes *two* animations — the presentation and the dismissal — and therefore the delegate is asked *separately* for controllers:

   - `animationController(forPresented:presenting:source:)`
   - `interactionControllerForPresentation(using:)`
   - `animationController(forDismissed:)`
   - `interactionControllerForDismissal(using:)`

   You are free to customize just one animation, leaving the other at the default by not providing a controller for it.

3. The animation controller will implement its four methods as usual — `transitionDuration`, `animateTransition`, `interruptibleAnimator`, and `animationEnded`.

To illustrate, let's say we're running on an iPad, and we want to present a view using the `.formSheet` presentation style. But instead of using any of the built-in animation types (transition styles), we'll have the presented view appear to grow from the middle of the screen.

The only mildly tricky step is the first one. The `transitioningDelegate` must be set very early in the presented view controller's life — before the presentation begins. But the presented view controller doesn't exist before the presentation begins. The most reliable solution is for the presented view controller to assign its own delegate in its own initializer:

```
required init?(coder: NSCoder) {
    super.init(coder:coder)
    self.transitioningDelegate = self
}
```

The presentation begins, and we're on to the second step. The transitioning delegate (UIViewControllerTransitioningDelegate) is asked for an animation controller; here, I'll have it supply `self` once again, and I'll do this only for the presentation, leaving the dismissal to use the default animation (and I'm not making this example interactive, so I don't implement the `interactionController` methods):

```
func animationController(forPresented presented: UIViewController,
    presenting: UIViewController, source: UIViewController)
    -> UIViewControllerAnimatedTransitioning? {
        return self
}
```

The third step is that the animation controller (UIViewControllerAnimatedTransitioning) is called upon to implement the animation. Our implementations of `transitionDuration`, `animateTransition`, and `animationEnded` are the usual boilerplate, so I'll show only `interruptibleAnimator`, which configures the property animator; observe that we don't care about the `.from` view controller (its view isn't even in the container view):

```
func interruptibleAnimator(using ctx: UIViewControllerContextTransitioning)
    -> UIViewImplicitlyAnimating {
        if self.anim != nil {
            return self.anim!
        }
        let vc2 = ctx.viewController(forKey:.to)
        let con = ctx.containerView
        let r2end = ctx.finalFrame(for:vc2!)
        let v2 = ctx.view(forKey:.to)!
        v2.frame = r2end
        v2.transform = CGAffineTransform(scaleX: 0.1, y: 0.1)
        v2.alpha = 0
        con.addSubview(v2)
        let anim = UIViewPropertyAnimator(duration: 0.4, curve: .linear) {
            v2.alpha = 1
```

```
            v2.transform = .identity
        }
        anim.addCompletion { _ in
            ctx.completeTransition(true)
        }
        self.anim = anim
        return anim
    }
```

If we wish to customize both animation and dismissal using the same animation con-troller, there is a complication: the roles of the view controllers are reversed in the mind of the transition context. On presentation, the presented view controller is the .to view controller, but on dismissal, it is the .from view controller. For a presen-tation that isn't .fullScreen, the unused view is nil, so you can distinguish the cases by structuring your code like this:

```
let v1 = ctx.view(forKey:.from)
let v2 = ctx.view(forKey:.to)
if let v2 = v2 { // presenting
    // ...
} else if let v1 = v1 { // dismissing
    // ...
}
```

Customizing the presentation

Now let's involve the presentation controller: we will customize the final frame of the presented view controller's view, and we'll even add some "chrome" to the presenta-tion. This will require some additional steps:

1. In addition to setting the presented view controller's transitioningDelegate, you set its modalPresentationStyle to .custom.

2. The result of the preceding step is that the delegate (the adopter of UIViewCon-trollerTransitioningDelegate) is sent an additional message:

   • presentationController(forPresented:presenting:source:)

   Your mission is to return an instance of a *custom UIPresentationController sub-class*. This will then be the presented view controller's presentation controller from the time presentation begins to the time dismissal ends. You create this instance by calling (directly or indirectly) the designated initializer:

   • init(presentedViewController:presenting:)

3. By means of appropriate overrides in the UIPresentationController subclass, you participate in the presentation, dictating the presented view's final position (frameOfPresentedViewInContainerView) and adding "chrome" to the presen-tation as desired.

The UIPresentationController has properties pointing to the `presentingView-Controller` as well the `presentedViewController` and the `presentedView`, plus the `presentationStyle` set by the presented view controller. It also obtains the `containerView`, which it subsequently communicates to the animation controller's transition context. It has some methods and properties that can be overridden in the subclass; you only need to override the ones that require customization for your particular implementation:

`frameOfPresentedViewInContainerView`
> The final position of the presented view. The animation controller, if there is one, will receive this from the transition context's `finalFrame(for:)` method.

`presentationTransitionWillBegin`
`presentationTransitionDidEnd`
`dismissalTransitionWillBegin`
`dismissalTransitionDidEnd`
> Use these events as signals to add or remove "chrome" (extra views) to the container view.

`containerViewWillLayoutSubviews`
`containerViewDidLayoutSubviews`
> Use these layout events as signals to update the "chrome" views if needed.

A presentation controller is not a view controller, but UIPresentationController adopts some protocols that UIViewController adopts, and gets the same resizing-related messages that a UIViewController gets, as I described earlier in this chapter. It adopts UITraitEnvironment, meaning that it has a `traitCollection` and participates in the trait collection inheritance hierarchy, and receives the `traitCollectionDidChange(_:)` message. It also adopts UIContentContainer, meaning that it receives `willTransition(to:with:)` and `viewWillTransition(to:with:)`.

I'll expand the preceding example to implement a custom presentation style that looks like a `.formSheet` *even on an iPhone*. The first step is to set the presentation style to `.custom` when we set the transitioning delegate:

```
required init?(coder: NSCoder) {
    super.init(coder:coder)
    self.transitioningDelegate = self
    self.modalPresentationStyle = .custom // *
}
```

The result (step two) is that this extra UIViewControllerTransitioningDelegate method is called so that we can provide a custom presentation controller:

```
func presentationController(forPresented presented: UIViewController,
    presenting: UIViewController?, source: UIViewController)
    -> UIPresentationController? {
        let pc = MyPresentationController(
            presentedViewController: presented, presenting: presenting)
        return pc
}
```

Everything else happens in the implementation of our UIPresentationController sub-class (named MyPresentationController). To make the presentation look like an iPad .formSheet, we inset the presented view's frame:

```
override var frameOfPresentedViewInContainerView : CGRect {
    return super.frameOfPresentedViewInContainerView.insetBy(dx:40, dy:40)
}
```

We could actually stop at this point! The presented view now appears in the correct position. Unfortunately, the presenting view is appearing undimmed behind it. Let's add dimming, by inserting a translucent dimming view into the container view, being careful to deal with the possibility of subsequent rotation:

```
override func presentationTransitionWillBegin() {
    let con = self.containerView!
    let shadow = UIView(frame:con.bounds)
    shadow.backgroundColor = UIColor(white:0, alpha:0.4)
    con.insertSubview(shadow, at: 0)
    shadow.autoresizingMask = [.flexibleWidth, .flexibleHeight]
}
```

Again, this works perfectly, but now I don't like what happens when the presented view is dismissed: the dimming view vanishes suddenly at the end of the dismissal. I'd rather have the dimming view fade out, and I'd like it to fade out *in coordination with the dismissal animation*. The way to arrange that is through the object vended by the presented view controller's transitionCoordinator property (a UIViewController-TransitionCoordinator); in particular, we can call its animate(alongside-Transition:completion:) method to add our own animation:

```
override func dismissalTransitionWillBegin() {
    let con = self.containerView!
    let shadow = con.subviews[0]
    if let tc = self.presentedViewController.transitionCoordinator {
        tc.animate(alongsideTransition: { _ in
            shadow.alpha = 0
        })
    }
}
```

Once again, we could stop at this point. But I'd like to add a further refinement. A .formSheet view has rounded corners. I'd like to make our presented view look the same way:

```
override var presentedView : UIView? {
    let v = super.presentedView!
    v.layer.cornerRadius = 6
    v.layer.masksToBounds = true
    return v
}
```

Finally, for completeness, it would be nice, during presentation, to dim the appearance of any button titles and other tinted interface elements visible through the dimming view, to emphasize that they are disabled:

```
override func presentationTransitionDidEnd(_ completed: Bool) {
    let vc = self.presentingViewController
    let v = vc.view
    v?.tintAdjustmentMode = .dimmed
}
override func dismissalTransitionDidEnd(_ completed: Bool) {
    let vc = self.presentingViewController
    let v = vc.view
    v?.tintAdjustmentMode = .automatic
}
```

Transition Coordinator

In the previous section, I mentioned that a view controller has a transition-Coordinator, which is typed as a UIViewControllerTransitionCoordinator. A view controller's transitionCoordinator exists only during a transition between view controllers, such as presentation or pushing. Its actual class is of no importance; UIViewControllerTransitionCoordinator is a protocol. This protocol, in turn, conforms to the UIViewControllerTransitionCoordinatorContext protocol, just like a transition context; indeed, it is a kind of wrapper around the transition context.

A view controller can use its transitionCoordinator to find out about the transition it is currently involved in. Moreover, as I've already said, it can take advantage of animate(alongsideTransition:completion:) to add animation of its view's internal interface as part of a transition animation. This works equally for a custom animation or a built-in animation; in fact, the point is that the view controller can behave agnostically with regard to how its own view is being animated.

In this example, a presented view controller animates part of its interface into place as the animation proceeds (whatever that animation may be):

```
override func viewWillAppear(_ animated: Bool) {
    super.viewWillAppear(animated)
    if let tc = self.transitionCoordinator {
        tc.animate(alongsideTransition:{ _ in
            self.buttonTopConstraint.constant += 200
```

```
                self.view.layoutIfNeeded()
            })
        }
    }
```

Here, a `.pageSheet` presented view controller fades out its subviews as the user drags down the view to dismiss it:

```
func presentationControllerWillDismiss(_ pc: UIPresentationController) {
    if let tc = pc.presentedViewController.transitionCoordinator {
        tc.animate(alongsideTransition: {_ in
            for v in pc.presentedViewController.view.subviews {
                v.alpha = 0
            }
        })
    }
}
```

The transition coordinator implements an additional method that might be of occasional interest:

`notifyWhenInteractionChanges(_:)`

> The argument you pass is a function to be called; the transition context is the function's parameter. Your function is called whenever the transition changes between being interactive and being noninteractive; this might be because the interactive transition was cancelled.

In this example, a navigation controller has pushed a view controller, and now the user is popping it interactively (using the default drag-from-the-left-edge gesture). If the user cancels, the back view controller can hear about it, like this:

```
override func viewWillAppear(_ animated: Bool) {
    super.viewWillAppear(animated)
    let tc = self.transitionCoordinator
    tc?.notifyWhenInteractionChanges { ctx in
        if ctx.isCancelled {
            // ...
        }
    }
}
```

 I have not found any occasion when the child of a tab bar controller has a non-nil transition coordinator — even though you may have given the tab bar controller's transition a custom animation. I regard this as a bug.

Page View Controller

A page view controller (UIPageViewController) is like a book that can be viewed one page at a time. The user, by a gesture, can navigate in one direction or the other to see the next or the previous page, successively — like turning the pages of a book.

A page view controller only *seems* to have multiple pages. In reality, it has only the one page that the user is looking at. That page is the view of its one child view controller. The page view controller navigates to another page by releasing its existing child view controller and replacing it with another. This is a very efficient architecture: it makes no difference whether the page view controller lets the user page through three pages or ten thousand pages, because each page is created in real time, on demand, and exists only as long as the user is looking at it.

The page view controller's children are its `viewControllers`. In general, there will be at most one of them (though there is a rarely used configuration in which a page view controller can have two pages at a time, as I'll explain in a moment). The page view controller is its current child's `parent`.

Preparing a Page View Controller

To create a UIPageViewController in code, use its designated initializer:

- `init(transitionStyle:navigationOrientation:options:)`

Here's what the parameters mean:

`transitionStyle:`
> The animation type during navigation (UIPageViewController.TransitionStyle). Your choices are:
>
> - `.pageCurl`
> - `.scroll` (sliding)

`navigationOrientation:`
> The direction of navigation (UIPageViewController.NavigationOrientation). Your choices are:
>
> - `.horizontal`
> - `.vertical`

`options:`
> A dictionary. Possible keys are (UIPageViewController.OptionsKey):
>
> `.spineLocation`
>> If you're using the `.pageCurl` transition style, this is the position of the pivot line around which those page curl transitions rotate. The value (UIPageViewController.SpineLocation) is one of the following:
>>
>> - `.min` (left or top)
>> - `.mid` (middle; in this configuration there are *two* children, and *two* pages are shown at once)

- `.max` (right or bottom)

`.interPageSpacing`
> If you're using the `.scroll` transition style, this is the spacing between successive pages, visible as a gap during the transition (the default is 0).

You configure the page view controller's initial content by handing it its initial child view controller(s). You do that by calling this method:

- `setViewControllers(_:direction:animated:completion:)`

Here's what the parameters mean:

`viewControllers:`
> An array of one view controller — unless you're using the `.pageCurl` transition style and the `.mid` spine location, in which case it's an array of two view controllers.

`direction:`
> The animation direction (UIPageViewController.NavigationDirection). This probably won't matter when you're assigning the page view controller its initial content, as you are not likely to want any animation. Possible values are:
>
> - `.forward`
> - `.backward`

`animated:`, `completion:`
> A Bool and a completion function.

To allow the user to page through the page view controller, you assign the page view controller a `dataSource`, which should conform to the UIPageViewControllerData-Source protocol. The `dataSource` is told whenever the user starts to change pages, and should respond by immediately providing another view controller whose view will constitute the new page. Typically, the data source will create this view controller on the spot.

Here's a minimal example. Each page in the page view controller is to portray an image of a named Pep Boy. The first question is where the pages will come from. My data model consists of an array (`self.pep`) of the string names of the three Pep Boys:

```
let pep : [String] = ["Manny", "Moe", "Jack"]
```

To match these, I have three eponymous image files (`manny`, `moe`, and `jack`), portraying each Pep Boy. I've also got a UIViewController subclass called Pep, capable of displaying a Pep Boy's image in an image view. I initialize a Pep object with its designated initializer `init(pepBoy:)`, supplying the name of a Pep Boy from the array; the Pep object sets its own `boy` property:

```
init(pepBoy boy:String) {
    self.boy = boy
    super.init(nibName: nil, bundle: nil)
}
```

Pep's `viewDidLoad` fetches the corresponding image and assigns it as the image of a UIImageView within its own view:

```
override func viewDidLoad() {
    super.viewDidLoad()
    self.pic.image = UIImage(named:self.boy.lowercased())
}
```

At any given moment, our page view controller is to have one Pep instance as its child; its current page will portray a Pep Boy. Here's how I create the page view controller itself (in my app delegate or scene delegate):

```
// make a page view controller
let pvc = UIPageViewController(
    transitionStyle: .scroll, navigationOrientation: .horizontal)
// give it an initial page
let page = Pep(pepBoy: self.pep[0])
pvc.setViewControllers([page], direction: .forward, animated: false)
// give it a data source
pvc.dataSource = self
// put its view into the interface
self.window!.rootViewController = pvc
```

That's sufficient to show the first page, but I haven't yet explained how to allow the user to navigate to a new page! That's the job of the data source, as I'll describe in the next section.

The page view controller is a UIViewController, and its view must get into the interface by standard means. You can make the page view controller the window's `root-ViewController`, as I do here; you can make it a presented view controller; you can make it a child view controller of a tab bar controller or a navigation controller. If you want the page view controller's view to be a subview of a custom view controller's view, the custom view controller must be configured as a container view controller, as I'll describe later in this chapter.

Page View Controller Navigation

We now have a page view controller's view in our interface, itself containing and displaying the view of the one Pep view controller that is its child. In theory, we have *three* pages, because we have three Pep Boys and their images — but the page view controller knows about only one of them.

You don't supply (or even create) another page until the page view controller asks for it by calling one of these data source methods:

- `pageViewController(_:viewControllerAfter:)`
- `pageViewController(_:viewControllerBefore:)`

The job of those methods is to return the requested successive view controller — or `nil`, to signify that there is no further page in this direction. Your strategy for doing that will depend on how your model maintains the data. My data, as you'll recall, is an array of unique strings:

```
let pep : [String] = ["Manny", "Moe", "Jack"]
```

And a Pep view controller has one of those strings as its boy property. So all I have to do is start with the current Pep view controller's boy and find the previous name or the next name in the array:

```
func pageViewController(_ pvc: UIPageViewController,
    viewControllerAfter vc: UIViewController) -> UIViewController? {
        let boy = (vc as! Pep).boy
        let ix = self.pep.firstIndex(of:boy)! + 1
        if ix >= self.pep.count {
            return nil
        }
        return Pep(pepBoy: self.pep[ix])
}
func pageViewController(_ pvc: UIPageViewController,
    viewControllerBefore vc: UIViewController) -> UIViewController? {
        let boy = (vc as! Pep).boy
        let ix = self.pep.firstIndex(of:boy)! - 1
        if ix < 0 {
            return nil
        }
        return Pep(pepBoy: self.pep[ix])
}
```

We now have a working page view controller! The user, with a sliding gesture, can page through it, one page at a time. When the user reaches the first page or the last page, it is impossible to go further in that direction.

 A `.scroll` style page view controller may cache some of its view controllers in advance. Therefore you should make no assumptions about *when* these data source methods will be called. If you need to be notified when the user is actually turning the page, use the delegate (which I'll describe later), not the data source.

You can also, at any time, call `setViewControllers` to change programmatically what page is being displayed, possibly with animation. In this way, you can "jump" to a page other than a successive page (something that the user cannot do with a gesture).

Page indicator

If you're using the `.scroll` transition style, the page view controller can optionally display a page indicator (a UIPageControl, see Chapter 12). The user can look at this to get a sense of what page we're on, and can tap to the left or right of it to navigate. To get the page indicator, you must implement two more data source methods; they are consulted in response to `setViewControllers`. We called that method initially to configure the page view controller; if we never call it again (because the user simply keeps navigating to the next or previous page), these data source methods won't be called again either, because they don't need to be: the page view controller will keep track of the current index on its own:

```
func presentationCount(for pvc: UIPageViewController) -> Int {
    return self.pep.count
}
func presentationIndex(for pvc: UIPageViewController) -> Int {
    let page = pvc.viewControllers![0] as! Pep
    let boy = page.boy
    return self.pep.firstIndex(of:boy)!
}
```

Unfortunately, the page view controller's page indicator by default has white dots and a clear background, so it is invisible in front of a white background. You'll want to customize it to change that. There is no direct access to it, so it's simplest to use the appearance proxy (Chapter 12):

```
let proxy = UIPageControl.appearance()
proxy.pageIndicatorTintColor = UIColor.red.withAlphaComponent(0.6)
proxy.currentPageIndicatorTintColor = .red
proxy.backgroundColor = .yellow
```

Navigation gestures

If you've assigned the page view controller the `.pageCurl` transition style, the user can navigate by tapping at either edge of the view or by dragging across the view. These gestures are detected through two gesture recognizers, which you can access through the page view controller's `gestureRecognizers` property. The documentation suggests that you might change where the user can tap or drag, by attaching those gesture recognizers to a different view, and other customizations are possible as well. In this code, I change the behavior of a `.pageCurl` page view controller (`pvc`) so that the user must double tap to request navigation:

```
for g in pvc.gestureRecognizers {
    if let g = g as? UITapGestureRecognizer {
        g.numberOfTapsRequired = 2
    }
}
```

Of course you are also free to add to the user's stock of gestures for requesting navigation. You can supply any controls or gesture recognizers that make sense for your app, and respond by calling setViewControllers. Suppose you're using the .scroll transition style; by default, there's no tap gesture recognizer, so the user can't tap to request navigation (unless there's also a page control). Let's change that. I've added invisible views at either edge of my Pep view controller's view, with tap gesture recognizers attached. When the user taps, the tap gesture recognizer fires, and the action method posts a notification whose object is the tap gesture recognizer:

```
@IBAction func tap (_ sender: UIGestureRecognizer?) {
    NotificationCenter.default.post(name:Pep.tap, object: sender)
}
```

In the app delegate, I have registered to receive this notification. When it arrives, I use the tap gesture recognizer's view's tag to learn which view was tapped; I then navigate accordingly (pvc is the page view controller):

```
NotificationCenter.default.addObserver(
    forName:Pep.tap, object: nil, queue: .main) { n in
        let g = n.object as! UIGestureRecognizer
        let which = g.view!.tag
        let vc0 = pvc.viewControllers![0]
        guard let vc = (which == 0 ?
            self.pageViewController(pvc, viewControllerBefore: vc0) :
            self.pageViewController(pvc, viewControllerAfter: vc0))
            else {return}
        let dir : UIPageViewController.NavigationDirection =
            which == 0 ? .reverse : .forward
        pvc.view.isUserInteractionEnabled = false
        pvc.setViewControllers([vc], direction: dir, animated: true) { _ in
            pvc.view.isUserInteractionEnabled = true
        }
    }
}
```

In that code, I turn off user interaction when the page animation starts and turn it back on when the animation ends. Otherwise we can crash (or get into an incoherent state) if the user taps during the animation.

Other Page View Controller Configurations

It is possible to assign a page view controller a delegate (UIPageViewController-Delegate), which gets an event when the user starts turning the page and when the user finishes turning the page, and can change the spine location dynamically in response to a change in device orientation. As with a tab bar controller's delegate or a navigation controller's delegate, a page view controller's delegate also gets messages allowing it to specify the page view controller's app rotation policy, so there's no need to subclass UIPageViewController solely for that purpose.

One further bit of configuration applicable to a `.pageCurl` page view controller is the `isDoubleSided` property. If it is `true`, the next page occupies the back of the previous page. The default is `false`, unless the spine is in the middle, in which case it's `true` and can't be changed. Your only option here, therefore, is to set it to `true` when the spine isn't in the middle, and in that case the back of each page would be a sort of throwaway page, glimpsed by the user during the page curl animation.

A page view controller in a storyboard lets you configure its transition style, navigation orientation, page spacing, spine location, and `isDoubleSided` property. (It also has delegate and data source outlets, but you're not allowed to connect them to other view controllers, because you can't draw an outlet from one scene to another in a storyboard.) It has no child view controller relationship, so you can't set the page view controller's initial child view controller in the storyboard; you'll have to complete the page view controller's initial configuration in code.

Container View Controllers

UITabBarController, UINavigationController, and UIPageViewController are all built-in *parent view controllers*: you hand them a child view controller and they do all the work, retaining that child view controller and putting its view into the interface inside their own view. What if you wanted your own view controller to do the same sort of thing?

Your UIViewController subclass can act as a *custom* parent view controller, managing child view controllers and putting their views into the interface. Your view controller becomes a *container view controller*. It does what the built-in parent view controllers do, except that *you* get to specify the details — what it means for a view controller to be a child of this kind of parent view controller, how many children it has, which of its children's views appear in the interface and where they appear, and so on. A container view controller can also participate actively in the business of trait collection inheritance and view resizing.

An example appears in Figure 6-4 — and the construction of that interface is charted in Figure 6-5. We have a page view controller, but it is not the root view controller, and its view does not occupy the entire interface. How is that achieved? It is *not* achieved by simply grabbing the page view controller's view and plopping it into the interface. You must *never* do that.

To put a view controller's view into the interface manually, you *must* have a container view controller, and it must *follow certain rules*. The container view controller must act as a well-behaved parent view controller. If another view controller is formally made its child, then the parent is permitted — as long it follows the rules — to put that child view controller's view into the interface as a subview of its own view.

Adding and Removing Children

A view controller has a `children` array; that's what gives it the power to be a parent. But you must not directly manipulate this array. A child view controller needs to receive certain definite events at particular moments:

- As it becomes a child view controller
- As its view is added to and removed from the interface
- As it ceases to be a child view controller

Therefore, to act as a parent view controller, your UIViewController subclass must fulfill certain responsibilities:

Adding a child
    When a view controller is to *become your view controller's child*, your view controller must do these things, in this order:

1. Send `addChild(_:)` to itself, with the child as argument. The child is automatically added to your `children` array and is retained.

2. Get the child view controller's view into the interface (as a subview of your view controller's view), if that's what adding a child view controller means.

3. Send `didMove(toParent:)` to the child view controller, with your view controller as argument.

Removing a child
    When a view controller is to *cease being your view controller's child*, your view controller must do these things, in this order:

1. Send `willMove(toParent:)` to the child, with a `nil` argument.

2. Remove the child view controller's view from the interface.

3. Send `removeFromParent` to the child. The child is automatically removed from your `children` array and is released.

That little dance ensures that a child view controller will always receive `willMove(toParent:)` followed by `didMove(toParent:)`. But you don't actually send both those messages explicitly:

- `addChild(_:)` sends `willMove(toParent:)` for you *automatically*.
- `removeFromParent` sends `didMove(toParent:)` for you *automatically*.

In each case, therefore, you *do* send explicitly the *other* message, the one that adding or removing a child view controller *doesn't* send for you — and of course you must send it so that everything happens in the correct order.

When you do this dance correctly, the proper parent–child relationship results: the container view controller can refer to its children as its `children`, and any child has a reference to the parent as its `parent`. If you don't do it correctly, all sorts of bad things can happen; in a worst-case scenario, the child view controller won't even survive, and its view won't work correctly, because the view controller was never properly retained as part of the view controller hierarchy (see "View Controller Hierarchy" on page 287). So do the dance correctly!

The initial child view controller

Example 6-1 provides a schematic approach for how to obtain an initial child view controller and put its view into the interface. (Alternatively, a storyboard can do this work for you, with no code, as I'll explain later in this chapter.)

Example 6-1. Adding an initial child view controller

```
let vc = // whatever; this is the initial child view controller
self.addChild(vc) // "will" called for us
// insert view into interface between "will" and "did"
self.view.addSubview(vc.view)
vc.view.frame = // whatever, or use constraints
// when we call add, we must call "did" afterward
vc.didMove(toParent: self)
```

In many cases, that's all you'll need. You have a parent view controller and a child view controller, and they are paired *permanently*, for the lifetime of the parent. That's how Figure 6-4 behaves: RootViewController has the UIPageViewController as its child, and the page view controller's view as its own view's subview, for the entire lifetime of the app.

To illustrate, I'll use the same page view controller that I used in my earlier examples, the one that displays Pep Boys; but this time, its view won't occupy the entire interface. My window's root view controller, in its `viewDidLoad`, will create and configure the page view controller as its child. Note how I perform the dance:

```
let pep : [String] = ["Manny", "Moe", "Jack"]
override func viewDidLoad() {
    super.viewDidLoad()
    let pvc = UIPageViewController(
        transitionStyle: .scroll, navigationOrientation: .horizontal)
    pvc.dataSource = self
    self.addChild(pvc) // dance, step 1
    self.view.addSubview(pvc.view) // dance, step 2
    // ... configure frame or constraints here ...
    pvc.didMove(toParent: self) // dance, step 3
    let page = Pep(pepBoy: self.pep[0])
    pvc.setViewControllers([page], direction: .forward, animated: false)
}
```

Replacing a child view controller

It is also possible to *replace* one child view controller's view in the interface with another (comparable to how UITabBarController behaves when a different tab bar item is selected). The simplest way is with this parent view controller instance method:

- `transition(from:to:duration:options:animations:completion:)`

That method manages the stages in good order, adding the view of one child view controller (`to:`) to the interface before the transition and removing the view of the other child view controller (`from:`) from the interface after the transition, and seeing to it that the child view controllers receive lifetime events (such as `viewWill-Appear(_:)`) at the right moment. Here's what the last three arguments are for:

`options:`
> A bitmask (UIView.AnimationOptions) comprising the same possible options that apply to any view transition (see "Transitions" on page 188).

`animations:`
> An animations function. This may be used for animating views other than the two views being managed by the transition animation specified in the `options:` argument; alternatively, if none of the built-in transition animations is suitable, you can animate the transitioning views yourself here (they are both in the interface when the animations function is called).

`completion:`
> A completion function. This will be important if the transition involves the removal or addition of a child view controller. At the time when you call `transition`, both view controllers must be children of the parent view controller; so if you're going to remove one of the view controllers as a child, you'll do it in the completion function. Similarly, if you owe a new child view controller a `did-Move(toParent:)` call, you'll use the completion function to fulfill that debt.

Here's an example. To keep things simple, suppose that our view controller has just one child view controller at a time, and displays the view of that child view controller within its own view. So let's say that when our view controller is handed a new child view controller, it substitutes that new child view controller for the old child view controller, and replaces the old child view controller's view with the new child view controller's view in the interface. Here's code that does that correctly; the view controllers are `fromvc` and `tovc`:

```
// we have already been handed the new view controller
// set up the new view controller's view's frame
tovc.view.frame = // ... whatever
// must have both as children before we can transition between them
self.addChild(tovc) // "will" called for us
```

```
    // when we call remove, we must call "will" (with nil) beforehand
    fromvc.willMove(toParent: nil)
    // then perform the transition
    self.transition(
        from:fromvc, to:tovc,
        duration:0.4, options:.transitionFlipFromLeft,
        animations:nil) { _ in
            // when we call add, we must call "did" afterward
            tovc.didMove(toParent: self)
            fromvc.removeFromParent() // "did" called for us
    }
```

If we're using constraints to position the new child view controller's view, where will
we set up those constraints? Before you call transition... is too soon, as the new
child view controller's view is not yet in the interface. The completion function is too
late: if the view is added with no constraints, it will have no initial size or position, so
the animation will be performed and then the view will suddenly seem to pop into
existence as we provide its constraints. The animations function turns out to be a
very good place:

```
    // must have both as children before we can transition between them
    self.addChild(tovc) // "will" called for us
    // when we call remove, we must call "will" (with nil) beforehand
    fromvc.willMove(toParent: nil)
    // then perform the transition
    self.transition(
        from:fromvc, to:tovc,
        duration:0.4, options:.transitionFlipFromLeft,
        animations: {
            tovc.view.translatesAutoresizingMaskIntoConstraints = false
            // ... configure tovc.view constraints here ...
        }) { _ in
            // when we call add, we must call "did" afterward
            tovc.didMove(toParent: self)
            fromvc.removeFromParent() // "did" called for us
    }
```

If the built-in transition animations are unsuitable, you can omit the options: argument and provide your own animation in the animations function, at which time
both views are in the interface. In this example, I animate a substitute view (an image
view showing a snapshot of tovc.view) to grow from the top left corner; then I configure the real view's constraints and remove the substitute:

```
    // tovc.view.frame is already set
    let r = UIGraphicsImageRenderer(size:tovc.view.bounds.size)
    let im = r.image { ctx in
        tovc.view.layer.render(in:ctx.cgContext)
    }
    let iv = UIImageView(image:im)
    iv.frame = .zero
    self.view.addSubview(iv)
```

```
tovc.view.alpha = 0 // hide the real view
// must have both as children before we can transition between them
self.addChild(tovc) // "will" called for us
// when we call remove, we must call "will" (with nil) beforehand
fromvc.willMove(toParent: nil)
// then perform the transition
self.transition(
    from:fromvc, to:tovc,
    duration:0.4, // no options:
    animations: {
        iv.frame = tovc.view.frame // animate bounds change
        // ... configure tovc.view constraints here ...
    }) { _ in
        tovc.view.alpha = 1
        iv.removeFromSuperview()
        // when we call add, we must call "did" afterward
        tovc.didMove(toParent: self)
        fromvc.removeFromParent() // "did" called for us
    }
}
```

Status Bar, Traits, and Resizing

A parent view controller, instead of dictating the status bar appearance through its own implementation of preferredStatusBarStyle or prefersStatusBarHidden, can defer the responsibility to one of its children, by overriding these properties:

- childForStatusBarStyle

- childForStatusBarHidden

That's what a UITabBarController does (as I've already mentioned). Your custom parent view controller can do the same thing.

A container view controller also participates in trait collection inheritance. In fact, you might insert a container view controller into your view controller hierarchy just to take advantage of this feature. A parent view controller has the amazing ability to lie to a child view controller about the environment, thanks to this method:

- setOverrideTraitCollection(_:forChild:)

The first parameter is a UITraitCollection that will be combined with the inherited trait collection and communicated to the specified child.

Why would you want to lie to a child view controller about its environment? Well, imagine that we're writing an iPad app, and we have a view controller whose view can appear either fullscreen or as a small subview of a parent view controller's main view. The view's interface might need to be different when it appears in the smaller size. You could configure that difference using size classes (conditional constraints) in the nib editor, with one interface for a .regular horizontal size class (iPad) and another interface for a .compact horizontal size class (iPhone). Then, when the view is to appear in its smaller size, we lie to its view controller and tell it that the horizontal size class *is* `.compact`:

```
let vc = // the view controller we're going to use as a child
self.addChild(vc) // "will" called for us
let tc = UITraitCollection(horizontalSizeClass: .compact)
self.setOverrideTraitCollection(tc, forChild: vc) // heh heh
vc.view.frame = // whatever
self.view.addSubview(vc.view)
vc.didMove(toParent: self)
```

UIPresentationController has a similar power, through its `overrideTrait-Collection` property, allowing it to lie to its presented view controller about the inherited trait collection. That is how a `.formSheet` presented view controller comes to have a `.compact` horizontal size class even on an iPad.

 New in iOS 13, if your only reason for overriding the trait collection is to affect the user interface style (light or dark), you can set the `.overrideUserInterface-Style` of a view controller or view instead.

A parent view controller sets the size of a child view controller's view. A child view controller, however, can express a preference as to what size it would like its view to be, by setting its own `preferredContentSize` property. The chief purpose of this property is to be consulted by a parent view controller when this view controller is its child. It is a preference and no more; no law says that the parent must consult the child, or that the parent must obey the child's preference.

If a view controller's `preferredContentSize` is set while it is already a child view controller, the runtime automatically communicates this fact to the parent view controller by calling this UIContentContainer method:

- `preferredContentSizeDidChange(forChildContentContainer:)`

The parent view controller may implement this method to consult the child's `preferredContentSize`, and may change the child's view's size in response if it so chooses.

A parent view controller, as an adopter of the UIContentContainer protocol, is also responsible for communicating to its children that their sizes are changing and what their new sizes will be. It is the parent view controller's duty to implement this method:

`size(forChildContentContainer:withParentContainerSize:)`
Should be implemented to return each child view controller's correct size at any moment.

Failure to implement this method will cause the child view controller to be handed the wrong size in its viewWillTransition(to:with:) — it will be given the *parent's* new size rather than its own new size!

If your parent view controller implements viewWillTransition(to:with:), it should call super so that viewWillTransition(to:with:) will be passed down to its children. This works even if your implementation is explicitly changing the size of a child view controller, provided you have implemented size(forChildContent-Container:withParentContainerSize:) to return the new size.

Previews and Context Menus

New in iOS 13, you can permit the user to summon a preview along with a menu by long pressing on a view. The preview can be a view controller's view, and a possible response when the user taps the preview is to transition to that view controller. So the user can preview the new view controller *without* actually transitioning to it, and then optionally can *perform* the transition.

(That's the sequence of actions known in iOS 12 and before as *peek and pop*. But peek and pop was available only on devices with 3D touch, whereas this new iOS 13 mechanism is available on any device.)

Everything starts with a UIContextMenuInteraction and its delegate (UIContext-MenuInteractionDelegate). You add the interaction to a view, and a special long press gesture recognizer is installed for you. When the user long presses the view, this delegate method is called:

- contextMenuInteraction(_:configurationForMenuAtLocation:)

Your job is to create a UIContextMenuConfiguration, configure it, and return it. Both the preview and the menu are optional:

- If you supply a menu but no preview, the view that the user long presses is used as a preview.
- If you supply a preview but no menu, just the preview is displayed.
- If you return nil, nothing happens.

To demonstrate, imagine that I have a root view controller whose view contains three buttons titled Manny, Moe, and Jack. I also have a Pep view controller whose initializer takes the name of a Pep Boy, and whose view displays an image of that Pep Boy. Let's permit the user to long press one of the buttons to summon the corresponding Pep view controller as a preview.

In the root view controller's viewDidLoad, I'll install the long press gesture recognizer on the superview of the three buttons:

```
self.buttonSuperview.addInteraction(UIContextMenuInteraction(delegate:self))
```

When the user long presses a button, I'm asked for a UIContextMenuConfiguration. I start by looking to see which button the user is long pressing; if none, I return nil and nothing further happens. If we get past that point, the user has long pressed one of the buttons; I'll use the button's title to initialize a Pep view controller and present it as a preview:

```
func contextMenuInteraction(_ inter: UIContextMenuInteraction,
    configurationForMenuAtLocation loc: CGPoint)
    -> UIContextMenuConfiguration? {
        guard let button = inter.view?.hitTest(loc, with:nil) as? UIButton
            else {return nil}
        let boy = button.currentTitle!
        let config = UIContextMenuConfiguration(
            identifier: button.tag as NSNumber, previewProvider: {
                let pep = Pep(pepBoy: boy)
                pep.preferredContentSize = CGSize(width: 240, height: 300)
                return pep
            }
        )
        return config
}
```

That's all there is to it! We don't have to supply a preferredContentSize for the view controller, but the preview may be too large otherwise. We also don't have to supply an identifier: for the menu configuration; I'll explain now why I did that.

Currently, when the user long presses a button, all three buttons and their superview pop out of the background before the preview is shown — because their superview is the view that I attached the UIContextMenuInteraction to. That isn't quite the effect I want: I want just the button the user is pressing to pop out. To specify what view should pop out, we implement another delegate method:

- contextMenuInteraction(_:previewForHighlightingMenuWith-
  Configuration:)

Our job is to return a UITargetedPreview, which is basically a snapshot of a view along with a location where it should appear. This can be a view already in the interface, in which case the location is already known. I've marked the three buttons with tag values so that I can identify a button; I know the tag of the button that the user is pressing, because I cleverly set it as the UIContextMenuConfiguration's identifier:

```
func contextMenuInteraction(_ inter: UIContextMenuInteraction,
    previewForHighlightingMenuWithConfiguration
    config: UIContextMenuConfiguration) -> UITargetedPreview? {
        if let tag = config.identifier as? Int {
            if let button = self.buttonSuperview.viewWithTag(tag) {
                return UITargetedPreview(view: button)
```

```
            }
        }
        return nil
    }
```

If the context menu configuration has a menu but no preview view controller, then the targeted preview also becomes the preview that is displayed along with the menu. But our context menu configuration does have a preview view controller. So the button pops out of the background as the user presses it, and then fades away as the Pep view controller's view is displayed.

Finally, to make it possible for the user to tap the preview to dismiss it, we implement this delegate method:

- `contextMenuInteraction(_:willPerformPreviewActionForMenu-`
  `With:animator:)`

The object that arrives as the `animator:` parameter accepts an animation function and a completion function, and hands us the preview's view controller if there is one. I'll perform the full transition to that view controller in the completion function:

```
func contextMenuInteraction(_ inter: UIContextMenuInteraction,
    willPerformPreviewActionForMenuWith config: UIContextMenuConfiguration,
    animator: UIContextMenuInteractionCommitAnimating) {
        if let vc = animator.previewViewController as? Pep {
            animator.preferredCommitStyle = .pop
            animator.addCompletion {
                self.present(vc, animated: true) // or whatever
            }
        }
    }
```

If we want to display a menu, we supply a function as the third parameter to the UIContextMenuConfiguration initializer. Its job is to return a UIMenu. This will be the *main* UIMenu, which typically will have no title and will itself act as a wrapper for its menu *elements*. Menu elements are effectively menu items; they are visible and tappable, and can have a title and an image. They are of two types:

UIAction
    A UIAction has a `handler:` function. When the user taps it, the entire menu interface (including the preview) is dismissed and the `handler:` function runs.

UIMenu
    A UIMenu (other than the main menu) looks like a UIAction, but it also has menu elements of its own, which the user does not see at first. When the user taps the UIMenu, the entire menu vanishes and is replaced by the elements of this UIMenu. In this way, you can create a menu with hierarchical levels.

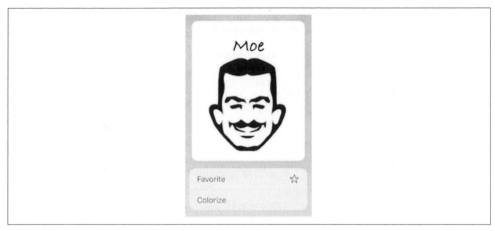

Figure 6-9. A context menu and preview

As an example of a simple UIAction, I'll create a Favorites menu item. The user can tap this to make the currently previewed Pep Boy the favorite. The user's current favorite is stored in the user defaults. If this Pep Boy is already the user's favorite, the menu item has a filled star; otherwise it has an empty star:

```
let favKey = "favoritePepBoy"
let fav = UserDefaults.standard.string(forKey:favKey)
let star = boy == fav ? "star.fill" : "star"
let im = UIImage(systemName: star)
let favorite = UIAction(title: "Favorite", image: im) { _ in
    UserDefaults.standard.set(boy, forKey:favKey)
}
```

Here's a hierarchical UIMenu. I'll pretend that the user can colorize the current Pep Boy in a choice of red, green, or blue; I have no actual colorization functionality, so I'll just print to the console for purposes of the example:

```
let red = UIAction(title: "Red") {action in
    print ("coloring", boy, action.title.lowercased())
}
let green = UIAction(title: "Green") {action in
    print ("coloring", boy, action.title.lowercased())
}
let blue = UIAction(title: "Blue") {action in
    print ("coloring", boy, action.title.lowercased())
}
let color = UIMenu(title: "Colorize", children: [red,green,blue])
```

I'll rewrite our UIContextMenuConfiguration so that a menu will be displayed along with the preview image (Figure 6-9). I'll mark where the UIAction and UIMenu are created, but I've already shown you that code so I'll omit it here:

```
func contextMenuInteraction(_ inter: UIContextMenuInteraction,
    configurationForMenuAtLocation loc: CGPoint)
    -> UIContextMenuConfiguration? {
        guard let button = inter.view?.hitTest(loc, with: nil) as? UIButton
            else {return nil}
        let boy = button.currentTitle!
        // ... create the UIAction ...
        let favorite = // ...
        }
        // ... create the UIMenu ...
        let color = // ...
        let config = UIContextMenuConfiguration(
            identifier: button.tag as NSNumber,
            previewProvider: {
                let pep = Pep(pepBoy: boy)
                pep.preferredContentSize = CGSize(width: 240, height: 300)
                return pep
            }
        ) { _ in
            return UIMenu(title: "", children: [favorite, color])
        }
        return config
}
```

Storyboards

A storyboard is a way of *automatically* creating view controllers and performing the kind of coherent view controller management and transitions that I've described throughout this chapter. A storyboard doesn't necessarily reduce the amount of code you'll have to write, but it does clarify the relationships between your view controllers over the course of your app's lifetime. Instead of having to hunt around in your code to see which class creates which view controller and when, you can view and manage the chain of view controller creation graphically in the nib editor.

A storyboard is a collection of view controller nibs, which are displayed as its scenes. Each view controller is instantiated from its own nib, as needed, and will then obtain its view, as needed — typically from a view nib that you've configured in the same scene by editing the view controller's view. I described this in "How Storyboards Work" on page 304. As I explained there, a view controller may be instantiated from a storyboard *automatically* in various ways:

Initial view controller
    If your app (or window scene) has a main storyboard, as specified in the *Info.plist*, that storyboard's initial view controller will be instantiated and assigned as the window's `rootViewController` *automatically* as the app launches. To specify that a view controller is a storyboard's initial view controller, check the "Is Initial View Controller" checkbox in its Attributes inspector. This will cause any existing initial view controller to lose its initial view controller

status. The initial view controller is distinguished graphically in the canvas by an arrow pointing to it from the left, and in the document outline by the presence of the Storyboard Entry Point.

Relationship

Two built-in parent view controllers can specify their children directly in the storyboard, setting their `viewControllers` array:

- UITabBarController can specify multiple children (its "view controllers").
- UINavigationController can specify its single initial child (its "root view controller").

To add a view controller as a child to one of those parent view controller types, Control-drag from the parent view controller to the child view controller; in the little HUD that appears, choose the appropriate listing under Relationship Segue. The result is a *relationship* whose source is the parent and whose destination is the child. The destination view controller will be instantiated *automatically* when the source view controller is instantiated, and will be assigned into its `view-Controllers` array, making it a child and retaining it.

Triggered segue

A triggered segue configures a *future* situation, when, while the app is running, the segue will somehow be *triggered*. At that time, one view controller that already exists (the source) will cause the instantiation of another view controller (the destination), bringing the latter into existence *automatically*. Two types of triggered segue are particularly common (their names in the nib editor depend on whether the "Use Trait Variations" checkbox is checked in the File inspector):

Show (formerly Push)

The future view controller will be *pushed* onto the stack of the navigation controller of which the existing view controller is already a child.

The name Show comes from the `show(_:sender:)` method, which pushes a view controller onto the parent navigation controller if there is one, but behaves adaptively if there is not (I'll talk more about that in Chapter 9). A Show segue from a view controller that is *not* a navigation controller's child will *present* the future view controller rather than pushing it, as there is no navigation stack to push onto. Setting up a Show segue without a navigation controller and then wondering why there is no push is a common beginner mistake.

Present Modally (formerly Modal)

The future view controller will be a *presented* view controller (and the existing view controller will be its original presenter).

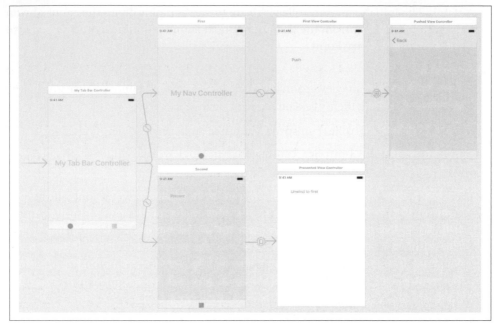

Figure 6-10. The storyboard of an app

A triggered segue may emanate from the source view controller itself, and is then a *manual* segue; it must be triggered in code, using the segue's identifier. Alternatively, it can emanate from something in the source view controller's view that the user can interact with — a gesture recognizer, or a tappable view such as a button or a table view cell — and is then an *action* segue, meaning that the segue will be triggered *automatically*, bringing the destination view controller into existence, when a tap or other gesture occurs.

To create a triggered segue, Control-drag from the tappable object in the first view controller, or from the first view controller itself, to the second view controller. In the little HUD that appears, choose the type of segue you want. If you dragged from the view controller, this will be a manual segue; if you dragged from a tappable object, it will be an action segue.

Figure 6-10 shows the storyboard of a small test app. The initial view controller (at the left) is a tab bar controller. It will be instantiated automatically when the app launches. Through two "view controllers" relationships, it has two children, which will both be instantiated automatically together with the tab bar controller:

- The tab bar controller's first child (upper row) is a navigation controller, which itself, through a "root view controller" relationship, has one child, which will also be instantiated automatically and will be placed at the bottom of the navigation controller's stack when the navigation controller is instantiated.

- That child has a triggered Show segue to *another* view controller, giving it the ability in the future to create that view controller and *push* it onto the navigation controller's stack.

- The tab bar controller's second child (lower row) has a triggered Present Modally segue to another view controller, giving it the ability in the future to create that view controller and *present* it.

It is also possible to instantiate a view controller from a storyboard *manually*, in code. That way, you are still creating the view controller instance on demand, but you also get the convenience of designing its view in the nib editor, and the instance comes with the segues that emanate from it in the storyboard.

Your code can instantiate a view controller manually from a storyboard by calling one of these methods:

- `instantiateInitialViewController`

- `instantiateViewController(withIdentifier:)`

The `identifier:` in the second method is a string that must match the Storyboard ID in the Identity inspector of some view controller in the storyboard (or you'll crash).

New in iOS 13, each of those methods has a variant that takes a function whose parameter is an NSCoder and that returns a view controller. Your function must call `init(coder:)`, using that same NSCoder as the argument. You might prefer these variants, for two reasons:

- Your function can call a custom initializer that does other things besides calling `init(coder:)`, and it can perform additional configurations on the view controller that's being instantiated.

- These methods are generics, so the return type is your view controller's type, rather than a plain UIViewController that you then have to cast down.

To illustrate, here's a rewrite of an earlier example ("App Without a Storyboard" on page 6) where we used a condition in our `scene(_:willConnectTo:options:)` implementation in order to decide at launch time what the window's root view controller should be. In the case where the user has not yet logged in, when we call `instantiateViewController(identifier:)`, we'll take advantage of the new iOS 13 variant that takes a function:

```
self.window = UIWindow(windowScene: windowScene)
let userHasLoggedIn : Bool = // ...
let sb = UIStoryboard(name: "Main", bundle: nil)
if userHasLoggedIn {
    let vc = sb.instantiateViewController(identifier: "UserHasLoggedIn")
    self.window!.rootViewController = vc
} else {
```

```
        let lvc = sb.instantiateViewController(identifier: "LoginScreen") { // *
            LoginViewController(coder:$0, message:"You need to log in first.")
        }
        // could perform further initializations here
        self.window!.rootViewController = lvc
    }
    self.window!.makeKeyAndVisible()
```

The idea here is that LoginViewController has an initializer `init(coder:message:)`, and we are able to call that initializer while loading this view controller from the storyboard. Moreover, we can perform further configuration of the view controller without casting it down; `lvc` is already typed, not as a vanilla UIViewController, but as LoginViewController. None of that was possible before iOS 13.

Triggered Segues

A triggered segue is a true segue (as opposed to a relationship, which isn't). The most common types are Show (Push) and Present Modally (Modal). A segue is a full-fledged object, an instance of UIStoryboardSegue, and it can be configured in the nib editor through its Attributes inspector. However, it is not instantiated by the loading of a nib, and it cannot be pointed to by an outlet. Rather, it will be instantiated *when the segue is triggered*, at which time its designated initializer will be called, namely `init(identifier:source:destination:)`.

A segue's `source` and `destination` are the two view controllers between which it runs. The segue is directional, so the source and destination are clearly distinguished. The source view controller is the one that will exist already, before the segue is triggered; the destination view controller will be instantiated when the segue is triggered, along with the segue itself.

A segue's `identifier` is a string. You can set this string for a segue in a storyboard in the Attributes inspector; that's useful when you want to trigger the segue manually in code (you'll specify it by means of its identifier), or when you have code that can receive a segue as parameter and you need to distinguish which segue this is.

Triggered segue behavior

The default behavior of a segue when it is triggered is exactly the behavior of the corresponding manual transition described earlier in this chapter:

Show (Push)
> The segue is going to call `pushViewController(_:animated:)` (if we are in a navigation interface). To set `animated:` to `false`, uncheck the Animates checkbox in the Attributes inspector.

Present Modally (Modal)

The segue is going to call `present(_:animated:completion:)`. To set `animated:` to `false`, uncheck the Animates checkbox in the Attributes inspector. Other presentation options, such as the modal presentation style and the modal transition style, can be set in Attributes inspector either for the destination view controller or for the segue; the segue settings take precedence.

You can further customize a triggered segue's behavior by providing your own UIStoryboardSegue subclass. The key thing is that you must implement your custom segue's `perform` method, which will be called after the segue is triggered and instantiated, to do the actual transition from one view controller to another.

If this is a push segue or a modal segue, it already knows how to do the transition; therefore, in the Attributes inspector for the segue, you specify your UIStoryboardSegue subclass, and in that subclass, you call `super` in your `perform` implementation.

Let's say that you want to add a custom transition animation to a modal segue. You can do this by writing a segue class that makes itself the destination view controller's transitioning delegate in its `perform` implementation before calling `super`:

```
class MyCoolSegue: UIStoryboardSegue {
    override func perform() {
        let dest = self.destination
        dest.modalPresentationStyle = .custom
        dest.transitioningDelegate = self
        super.perform()
    }
}
extension MyCoolSegue: UIViewControllerTransitioningDelegate {
    func animationController(forPresented presented: UIViewController,
        presenting: UIViewController,
        source: UIViewController) -> UIViewControllerAnimatedTransitioning? {
            return self
    }
    // ...
}
extension MyCoolSegue: UIViewControllerAnimatedTransitioning {
    func transitionDuration(using ctx: UIViewControllerContextTransitioning?)
        -> TimeInterval {
            return 0.8
    }
    // ...
}
```

The rest is then exactly as in "Custom Presented View Controller Transition" on page 361. MyCoolSegue is the UIViewControllerTransitioningDelegate, so its `animation-Controller(forPresented:...)` will be called. MyCoolSegue is also the UIViewControllerAnimatedTransitioning object, so its `transitionDuration` and so forth will be called. In short, we are now off to the races with a custom presented view controller transition, with all the code living inside MyCoolSegue — a pleasant encapsulation of functionality.

You can also create a *completely* custom segue. To do so, in the HUD when you Control-drag to create the segue, ask for a Custom segue, and then, in the Attributes inspector, specify your UIStoryboardSegue subclass. Again, you must override `perform`, but now you *don't* call `super` — the *whole transition* is up to you! Your `perform` implementation can access the segue's `identifier`, `source`, and `destination` properties. The `destination` view controller has already been instantiated, but that's all; it is entirely up to your code to make this view controller either a child view controller or a presented view controller, and to cause its view to appear in the interface.

How a segue is triggered

A triggered segue will be triggered in one of two ways:

Through a user gesture
> If a segue emanates from a gesture recognizer or from a tappable view, it is an *action segue*, meaning that it will be triggered automatically when the tap or other gesture occurs.
>
> Your source view controller class can prevent an action segue from being triggered. To do so, override this method:
>
> `shouldPerformSegue(withIdentifier:sender:)`
>> Sent when an action segue is about to be triggered. Returns a Bool (and the default is `true`), so if you don't want this segue triggered on this occasion, return `false`.

In code
> If a segue emanates from a view controller as a whole, it is a *manual segue*, and triggering it is up to your code. Send this message to the source view controller:
>
> `performSegue(withIdentifier:sender:)`
>> Triggers a segue whose source is this view controller. The segue will need an identifier in the storyboard so that you can specify it here! `shouldPerform-Segue(withIdentifier:sender:)` will *not* be called, because if you didn't want the segue triggered, you wouldn't have called `performSegue` in the first place.

An action segue with an identifier can be treated as a manual segue: that is, you can trigger it by calling `performSegue`, doing in code what the user could have done by tapping.

View controller communication

When a segue is triggered, the destination view controller is instantiated automatically; your code does not instantiate it. This raises a crucial question: how are you going to communicate between the source view controller and the destination view controller? This, you'll remember, was the subject of an earlier section of this chapter ("Communication with a Presented View Controller" on page 330), where I used this code as an example:

```
let svc = SecondViewController()
svc.data = "This is very important data!"
svc.delegate = self
self.present(svc, animated:true)
```

In that code, the first view controller creates the second view controller, and therefore has a reference to it at that moment — so it has an opportunity to communicate with it, passing along some data to it, and setting itself as its delegate, before presenting it. With a modal segue, however, the second view controller is instantiated for you, and the segue itself is going to call `present(_:animated:completion:)`. So when and how will the first view controller be able to set `svc.data` and set itself as `svc`'s delegate?

Prior to iOS 13, the solution is for the source view controller to override `prepare(for:sender:)`. After a segue has instantiated the destination view controller but before the segue is actually performed, the source view controller's `prepare(for:sender:)` is called. The first parameter is the segue, and the segue has a reference to the destination view controller — so this is the moment when the source view controller and the destination view controller meet! The source view controller can now perform configurations on the destination view controller, hand it data, and so forth. The source view controller can work out which segue is being triggered by examining the segue's `identifier` and `destination` properties, and the `sender` is the interface object that was tapped to trigger the segue (or, if `performSegue(with-Identifier:sender:)` was called in code, whatever object was supplied as the `sender:` argument):

```
override func prepare(for segue: UIStoryboardSegue, sender: Any?) {
    if segue.identifier == "second" {
        let svc = segue.destination as! SecondViewController
        svc.data = "This is very important data!"
        svc.delegate = self
    }
}
```

That solves the communication problem, but in a clumsy way. The fact is that `prepare(for:sender:)` is a blunt instrument:

- The `destination` arrives typed as a plain UIViewController, and it is up to your code to know its actual type and cast it down before configuring it.

- The destination view controller is instantiated for you, by calling `init(coder:)`. That means you can't call a custom initializer; in `prepare(for:sender:)`, you can only set properties after initialization is over.

- If more than one segue emanates from a view controller, they are all bottlenecked through the same `prepare(for:sender:)` implementation, which devolves into an ugly series of conditions to distinguish them.

New in iOS 13, there's an elegant alternative architecture. In the source view controller, you implement a method marked `@IBSegueAction`, with this signature:

```
@IBSegueAction
func f(coder:NSCoder, sender:Any?, ident:String?) -> UIViewController? {
```

The method name is up to you; so are the external parameter names. The third parameter, or the second and third parameters, may be omitted. The second parameter is just like the `sender:` in `prepare(for:sender:)`. The third parameter is the segue's `identifier`. The result type can be a specific UIViewController subclass. It doesn't have to be an Optional; if it is, and if you return `nil`, everything proceeds as if this IBSegueAction method didn't exist.

To arrange for an IBSegueAction method to be called, you create an action connection in the storyboard *from the segue* to this method. (Technically, this is an *instantiation action*.) When the IBSegueAction method is called, the segue has been triggered. You must now instantiate the correct class of view controller by directly or indirectly calling `init(coder:)` with the `coder` that was passed to you, and *return* that view controller instance (or `nil` if the return type is an Optional).

To illustrate, I'll rewrite the preceding code. Let's give SecondViewController an initializer that accepts the `data` it needs to do its work:

```
init(coder:NSCoder, data:Any) {
    self.data = data
    super.init(coder:coder)!
}
```

Here's an IBSegueAction method that calls that initializer:

```
@IBSegueAction func config(coder:NSCoder) -> SecondViewController { ❶
    let svc = SecondViewController( ❷
        coder:coder, data:"This is very important data!") { ❸
    svc.delegate = self ❹
    return svc
}
```

❶ We can give our IBSegueAction method any name we like. We can give the parameters any external names we like. We can omit the second and third parameters. We can specify a particular view controller class as the return type, and it doesn't have to be an Optional.

❷ We have to know the class of the segue's destination view controller, so that we can instantiate it. If we instantiate a view controller that is not of the right class, we'll crash at runtime. But we can configure the storyboard so that only one segue ever calls this IBSegueAction method, and so we can be confident about its destination without checking its `identifier`.

❸ We are able to call a custom initializer, something that a segue on its own could not have done. Our custom initializer *must* call `init(coder:)` with the same coder we received as our first parameter; otherwise, we'll crash at runtime.

❹ We are able to perform additional customizations, just as we would have done in `prepare(for:sender:)`. But there is no need to cast down first!

Even if you use the IBSegueAction mechanism, `prepare(for:sender:)` will still be called afterward if you've implemented it. Nevertheless, you might end up never implementing `prepare(for:sender:)` at all! Instead, you might rely entirely on the IBSegueAction mechanism.

Container Views and Embed Segues

The only parent view controllers for which you can create relationship segues specifying their children in a storyboard are the built-in UITabBarController and UINavigationController. That's because the nib editor understands how they work. If you write your own custom container view controller ("Container View Controllers" on page 375), the nib editor doesn't even know that your view controller *is* a container view controller, so it can't be the source of a relationship segue.

Nevertheless, you can perform some initial parent–child configuration of your custom container view controller in a storyboard, if your situation conforms to these assumptions:

- Your parent view controller will have one initial child view controller.
- You want the child view controller's view placed somewhere in the parent view controller's view.

To configure your parent view controller in a storyboard, drag a Container View object from the Library into the parent view controller's view in the canvas. The result is a view, together with an *embed segue* leading from it to an additional child view controller. You can then specify the child view controller's correct class in its Identity inspector. Alternatively, delete the child view controller, Control-drag from the container view to some *other* view controller, and specify an Embed segue in the HUD.

The container view is not only a way of generating the embed segue, but also a way of specifying where you want the child view controller's view to go. When an embed segue is triggered, the destination view controller is instantiated and made the source view controller's child, and its view becomes the container view's subview, with its frame matching the container view's bounds. The entire child-addition dance is performed correctly and automatically for you: `addChild(_:)` is called, the child's view is put into the interface, and `didMove(toParent:)` is called.

If the frame of the container view is going to change during the lifetime of the app, you're probably going to want the frame of the embedded child view controller's view to change with it. In the child view controller scene, use its view's Size inspector to set the Layout pop-up menu to Translates Mask Into Constraints, and give the view autoresizing struts externally on all four sides. (This may have been done for you by default when you created the container view.)

An embed segue is a triggered segue. It can have an identifier, and the standard messages are sent to the source view controller when the segue is triggered. At the same time, it has this similarity to a relationship: when the source (parent) view controller is instantiated, the runtime wants to trigger the segue automatically, instantiating the child view controller and embedding its view in the container view *now*. If that isn't what you want, override `shouldPerformSegue(withIdentifier:sender:)` in the parent view controller to return `false` for this segue, and call `performSegue(withIdentifier:sender:)` later when you *do* want the child view controller instantiated.

The parent view controller is sent `prepare(for:sender:)` before the child's view loads. At this time, the child has not yet been added to the parent's `children` array. If you allow the segue to be triggered when the parent view controller is instantiated, then by the time the parent's `viewDidLoad` is called, the child's `viewDidLoad` has already been called, the child has already been added to the parent's `children`, and the child's view is already inside the parent's view.

If, as the app runs, you subsequently want to replace the child view controller's view with another child view controller's view in the interface, you can call `transition(from:to:duration:options:animations:completion:)` as I described earlier in this chapter; sizing the new view and configuring it so that it is pinned to the container view will be up to you. (If you really want to, you can arrange this in the storyboard by means of a custom segue.)

Storyboard References

A storyboard reference is a *placeholder* for a specific view controller. Instead of a large and complicated network of segues running all over your storyboard, possibly crisscrossing in confusing ways, you can effectively *jump* through the storyboard reference to the actual destination view controller. Add a storyboard reference to the canvas of the storyboard. When you create a segue, you can Control-drag to the storyboard reference.

To specify what view controller a storyboard reference stands for, you need to perform two steps:

1. Select the view controller and, in the Identity inspector, give it a Storyboard ID.

2. Select the storyboard reference and, in the Attributes inspector, enter that same Storyboard ID as its Referenced ID.

But wait — there's more! The referenced view controller doesn't even have to be in the same storyboard as the storyboard reference. You can use a storyboard reference to jump to a view controller in *a different storyboard*. This allows you to organize your app's interface into multiple storyboards.

To configure a storyboard reference to refer to a view controller in a different storyboard, use the Storyboard pop-up menu in its Attributes inspector. The rule is that if you specify the Storyboard but not the Referenced ID, the storyboard reference stands for the target storyboard's initial view controller. But it is better to specify *both* the Storyboard *and* the Referenced ID.

Unwind Segues

Here's an interesting puzzle: Storyboards and segues would appear to be useful only half the time, because segues are asymmetrical. There is a push segue but no pop segue. There is a present modally segue but no dismiss segue.

The reason, in a nutshell, is that a triggered segue cannot "go back." A triggered segue *instantiates* the destination view controller; it creates a new view controller instance. But when dismissing a presented view controller or popping a pushed view controller, we don't need any *new* view controller instances. We want to return, somehow, to an *existing* instance of a view controller.

Beginners sometimes make a triggered segue from view controller A to view controller B, and then try to express the notion "go back" by making *another* triggered segue from view controller B to view controller A. The result is a vicious cycle of segues, with presentation piled on presentation, or push piled on push, one view controller instantiated on top of another on top of another. *Don't do that.* (Unfortunately, the nib editor doesn't alert you to this mistake.)

The solution is an *unwind segue*. An unwind segue *does* let you express the notion "go back" in a storyboard. Basically, it lets you jump to any view controller that is already instantiated further up your view controller hierarchy, destroying the source view controller and any intervening view controllers in good order.

Creating an unwind segue

Before you can create an unwind segue, you must implement an *unwind method* in the class of some view controller represented in the storyboard. This should be a

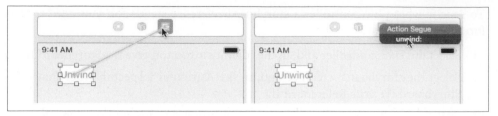

Figure 6-11. Creating an unwind segue

method marked @IBAction as a hint to the storyboard editor, and taking a single parameter, a UIStoryboardSegue. You can name it unwind if you like, but the name doesn't really matter:

```
@IBAction func unwind(_ seg: UIStoryboardSegue) {
    // ...
}
```

Think of this method as a marker, specifying that the view controller in which it appears can be the destination for an unwind segue. It is, in fact, a little more than a marker: it will also be called when the segue is triggered. But its marker functionality is much more important — so much so that, in many cases, you won't give this method any code at all. Its *presence* is what matters.

Now you can create an unwind segue. Doing so involves the use of the Exit proxy object that appears in every scene of a storyboard. This is what the Exit proxy is for! Control-drag from the view controller you want to go back *from* (for a manual segue), or from something like a button in that view controller's view (for an action segue), connecting it to the Exit proxy object *in the same scene* (Figure 6-11). A little HUD appears, listing all the known unwind methods (similar to how action methods are listed in the HUD when you connect a button to its target). Click the name of the unwind method you want. You have now made an unwind segue, bound to that unwind method.

How an unwind segue works

When an unwind segue is *triggered*:

1. If this is an action segue, the source view controller's shouldPerformSegue(with-Identifier:sender:) is called — just as for a normal segue. This is your chance to forestall the whole process by returning false.

2. The name of the unwind method to which the unwind segue is bound is *only* a name. The unwind segue's actual destination view controller is unknown! Therefore, the runtime now starts walking up the view controller hierarchy looking for a destination view controller. The first view controller it finds that *implements* the unwind method will, by default, be the destination view controller.

Assume now that the destination view controller has been found. Then the runtime proceeds to *perform* the segue:

1. The source view controller's `prepare(for:sender:)` is called with the segue as the first parameter — just as for a normal segue. The two view controllers are now in contact (because the other view controller is the segue's `destination`). This is an opportunity for the source view controller to hand information to the destination view controller before being destroyed! An unwind segue is an alternative to delegation in this regard.

2. The destination view controller's unwind method is called. Its parameter is the segue. The two view controllers are now in contact *again* (because the other view controller is the segue's `source`). It is perfectly reasonable for the unwind method body to be empty; its real purpose is to mark this view controller as the destination view controller.

3. The source view controller is *destroyed* along with any intervening view controllers up to (but not including) the destination view controller, in good order. We have "gone back" to the destination view controller.

In general, that's all you need to know about unwind segues.

Now I'll go back and explain in detail *how* the destination view controller is found, and *how* the segue is actually performed. This is partly out of sheer interest — they are both devilishly clever — and partly in case you need to customize the process. You can skip the discussion if the technical details aren't of interest.

How the destination view controller is found

The process of locating the destination view controller starts by walking *up* the view controller hierarchy. Every view controller has either a `parent` or a `presentingViewController`, so the next view controller up the hierarchy is that view controller — though it might also be necessary to walk back *down* the hierarchy, to a child (at some depth) of one of the parents we encounter:

1. At each step up the view controller hierarchy, the runtime sends this view controller the following event:

   - `allowedChildrenForUnwinding(from:)`

   This view controller's job is to supply an *array of its own direct children*. The array can be empty, but it must be an array. To help form this array, the view controller calls this method:

   - `childContaining(_:)`

   This tells the view controller which of its own children is, or is the ultimate parent of, the source view controller. We don't want to go down *that* branch of the view hierarchy; that's the branch we just came *up*. So this view controller *subtracts* that view controller from the array of its own child view controllers, and returns the resulting array.

2. There are two possible kinds of result from the previous step (the value returned from `allowedChildren...`):

There are children
> If the previous step yielded an array with one or more child view controllers in it, the runtime performs step 1 on all of them (stopping if it finds the destination), going *down* the view hierarchy.

There are no children
> If, on the other hand, the previous step yielded an *empty* array, the runtime asks *this same* view controller the following question:
>
> - `canPerformUnwindSegueAction(_:from:sender:)`

The default implementation of this method is simply to call `responds(to:)` on `self`, asking whether this view controller contains an implementation of the unwind method we're looking for. The result is a Bool. If it is `true`, we *stop. This is the destination view controller.* If it is `false`, we continue with the search *up* the view controller hierarchy, finding the next view controller and performing step 1 again.

The recursive application of this algorithm will eventually arrive at an existing view controller instance with an implementation of the unwind method if there is one.

How an unwind segue is performed

The way an unwind segue is performed is just as ingenious as how the destination is found. During the walk in search of the destination view controller, the runtime *remembers* the walk. There's a *path* of view controllers between the source and the destination, and the runtime walks that path:

- If it encounters a *presented* view controller on the path, the runtime calls `dismiss(animated:completion:)` on the presenting view controller.

- If it encounters a *parent* view controller on the path, the runtime tells it to `unwind(for:towards:)`.

The second parameter of `unwind(for:towards:)` is the *direct child* of this parent view controller leading down the branch where the destination lives. This child might or might not *be* the destination, but that's no concern of this parent view controller. Its job is merely to *get us onto that branch*, whatever that may mean for this kind of parent view controller.

If this procedure (called *incremental unwind*) is followed correctly, we will in fact end up at the destination, releasing in good order all intervening view controllers that need to be released.

Unwind segue customization

Knowing how an unwind segue works, you can see how to intervene in and customize the process:

- In a custom view controller that contains an implementation of the unwind method, you might implement `canPerformUnwindSegueAction(_:from:withSender:)` to return `false` instead of `true` so that it doesn't become the destination on this occasion.

- In a custom parent view controller, you might implement `allowedChildrenForUnwinding(from:)`. In all probability, your implementation will consist simply of listing your `children`, calling `childContaining(_:)` to find out which of your children is or contains the source, subtracting that child from the array, and returning the array — just as the built-in parent view controllers do.

- In a custom container view controller, you might implement `unwind(for:towards:)`. The second parameter is one of your current children; you will do whatever it means for this parent view controller to make this the currently displayed child.

In `allowedChildrenForUnwinding(from:)` and `childContaining(_:)`, the parameter is not a UIStoryboardSegue. It's an instance of a special value class called UIStoryboardUnwindSegueSource, which has no other job than to communicate, in these two methods, the essential information about the unwind segue needed to make a decision. It has a `source`, a `sender`, and an `unwindAction` (the Selector specified when forming the unwind segue).

 Do *not* override `childContaining(_:)`. It knows more than you do; you wouldn't want to interfere with its operation.

View Controller Lifetime Events

As views come and go, driven by view controllers and the actions of the user, events arrive that give your view controller the opportunity to respond to the various stages of its own existence and the management of its view. By overriding these methods, your UIViewController subclass can perform appropriate tasks at appropriate moments:

`viewDidLoad`
> The view controller has obtained its view (as explained earlier in this chapter); `self.view` exists, and if obtaining the view involved loading a nib, outlets have been hooked up. This does *not* mean that the view is in the interface or that it has been given its correct size. You should call `super` in your implementation, just in case a superclass has work to do in *its* implementation.

`willTransition(to:with:)`
`viewWillTransition(to:with:)`
`traitCollectionDidChange(_:)`
> The view controller's view is being resized or the trait environment is changing, or both (as explained earlier in this chapter). Your implementation of these methods should call `super`.

`updateViewConstraints`
`viewWillLayoutSubviews`
`viewDidLayoutSubviews`
> The view is receiving `updateConstraints` and `layoutSubviews` events (as explained earlier in this chapter). Your implementation of `updateView-Constraints` should call `super`.

`willMove(toParent:)`
`didMove(toParent:)`
> The view controller is being added or removed as a child of another view controller (as explained earlier in this chapter). Your implementation of these methods should call `super`.

`viewWillAppear(_:)`
`viewDidAppear(_:)`
`viewWillDisappear(_:)`
`viewDidDisappear(_:)`
> The view is being added to or removed from the interface. This includes being supplanted by another view controller's view or being restored through the removal of another view controller's view. A view that has appeared is in the window; it is part of your app's active view hierarchy. A view that has disappeared is not in the window; its `window` is `nil`. Your implementation of these methods should call `super`.
>
> To distinguish more precisely *why* your view is appearing or disappearing, consult any of these properties of the view controller:
>
> - `isBeingPresented`
> - `isBeingDismissed`

- isMovingtoParent

- isMovingFromParent

Order of Events

To get a sense for when view controller lifetime events arrive, it helps to examine some specific scenarios in which they normally occur. Consider a UIViewController being pushed onto the stack of a navigation controller. It receives, in this order, the following messages:

1. `willMove(toParent:)`

2. `viewWillAppear(_:)`

3. `viewWillLayoutSubviews`

4. `viewDidLayoutSubviews`

5. `viewDidAppear(_:)`

6. `didMove(toParent:)`

When this same UIViewController is popped off the stack of the navigation controller, it receives, in this order, the following messages:

1. `willMove(toParent:)` (with parameter `nil`)

2. `viewWillDisappear(_:)`

3. `viewDidDisappear(_:)`

4. `didMove(toParent:)` (with parameter `nil`)

Disappearance, as I mentioned a moment ago, can happen because another view controller's view supplants this view controller's view. Consider a UIViewController functioning as the top (and visible) view controller of a navigation controller. When another view controller is pushed on top of it, the first view controller gets these messages:

1. `viewWillDisappear(_:)`

2. `viewDidDisappear(_:)`

The converse is also true. When a view controller is popped from a navigation controller, the view controller that was below it in the stack (the back view controller) receives these messages:

1. `viewWillAppear(_:)`

2. `viewDidAppear(_:)`

Appear and Disappear Events

The `appear` and `disappear` events are particularly appropriate for making sure that a view controller's view reflects your app's underlying data each time it appears. These methods are useful also when something must be true exactly so long as a view is in the interface. A repeating Timer that must be running while a view is present might be started in the view controller's `viewDidAppear(_:)` and stopped in its `viewWill-Disappear(_:)`. (This architecture also allows you to avoid the retain cycle that could result if you waited to invalidate the timer in a `deinit` that might otherwise never arrive.)

Changes to the interface performed in `viewDidAppear(_:)` or `viewWill-Disappear(_:)` may be visible to the user as they occur. If that's not what you want, use the other member of the pair. In a certain view containing a long scrollable text, I want the scroll position to be the same when the user returns to this view as it was when the user left it, so I save the scroll position in `viewWillDisappear(_:)` and restore it in `viewWillAppear(_:)` — not `viewDidAppear(_:)`, where the user might see the scroll position jump.

The `appear` events are not layout events. Don't make any assumptions about whether your views have achieved their correct size just because the view is appearing — even if those assumptions seem to be correct. To respond when layout is taking place, implement layout events.

A view does not disappear if a presented view controller's view merely covers it rather than supplanting it. A view controller that presents another view controller as a sheet (`.pageSheet` or `.formSheet`) gets no lifetime events during presentation and dismissal. Sheet presentation is the default in iOS 13, so your older code may need to be revised.

A view does not disappear merely because the app is backgrounded and suspended. That fact sometimes surprises beginners, and has important implications for how you save data in case the app is terminated in the background. You cannot rely solely on a `disappear` event for saving data that the app will need the next time it launches; if you are to cover every case, you may need to ensure that your data-saving code also runs in response to a lifetime event sent to your app delegate or scene delegate (see Appendix A).

 Sometimes a `will` event arrives without the corresponding `did` event. A case in point is when an interactive transition animation begins and is cancelled. I regard this as a bug.

Event Forwarding to a Child View Controller

A custom container view controller must effectively send `willMove(toParent:)` and `didMove(toParent:)` to its children manually, and it will do so if you perform the dance correctly when your view controller acquires or loses a child view controller (see "Container View Controllers" on page 375).

A custom container view controller must forward resizing events to its children. This will happen automatically if you call `super` in your implementation of the `will-Transition` methods.

The `appear` and `disappear` events are normally passed along automatically. However, you can take charge by overriding this property:

`shouldAutomaticallyForwardAppearanceMethods`
> If you override this property to return `false`, you are responsible for seeing that the four `appear` and `disappear` methods are called on your view controller's children. You do *not* do this by calling these methods directly. The reason is that you have no access to the correct moment for sending them. Instead, you call these two methods on your child view controller:

`beginAppearanceTransition(_:animated:)`
`endAppearanceTransition`
> > The first parameter of the first method is a Bool saying whether this view controller's view is about to appear (`true`) or disappear (`false`).

Here's an example of the kind of thing you'll have to do in the `appear` methods if your `shouldAutomaticallyForwardAppearanceMethods` is `false`:

```
override func viewWillAppear(_ animated: Bool) {
    super.viewWillAppear(animated)
    let child = // whatever
    if child.isViewLoaded && child.view.superview != nil {
        child.beginAppearanceTransition(true, animated: true)
    }
}
override func viewDidAppear(_ animated: Bool) {
    super.viewDidAppear(animated)
    let child = // whatever
    if child.isViewLoaded && child.view.superview != nil {
        child.endAppearanceTransition()
    }
}
```

The `disappear` methods will be similar, except that the first argument for `begin-AppearanceTransition` is `false`.

When your custom container view controller swaps one child for another in the interface, you should *not* call the UIViewController `transition...` method if your shouldAutomaticallyForwardAppearanceMethods is `false`. Instead, you perform the transition animation directly, calling `beginAppearanceTransition(_:animated:)` and `endAppearanceTransition` yourself. A minimal correct implementation might involve a UIView `transition...` animation class method ("Transitions" on page 188). Here's an example; I've put asterisks to call attention to the additional method calls that forward the `appear` and `disappear` events to the children (`fromvc` and `tovc`):

```
self.addChild(tovc) // "will" called for us
fromvc.willMove(toParent: nil)
fromvc.beginAppearanceTransition(false, animated:true) // *
tovc.beginAppearanceTransition(true, animated:true) // *
UIView.transition(
    from:fromvc.view, to:tovc.view,
    duration:0.4, options:.transitionFlipFromLeft) {_ in
        tovc.endAppearanceTransition() // *
        fromvc.endAppearanceTransition() // *
        tovc.didMove(toParent: self)
        fromvc.removeFromParent()
}
```

View Controller Memory Management

Memory is at a premium on a mobile device, so you want to minimize your app's use of memory. Your motivations are partly altruistic and partly selfish. While your app is running, other apps are suspended in the background; you want to keep your memory usage as low as possible so that those other apps have room to remain suspended and the user can readily switch to them from your app. You also want to prevent your own app from being terminated! If your app is backgrounded and suspended while using a lot of memory, it may be terminated in the background when memory runs short. If your app uses an inordinate amount of memory while in the foreground, it may be summarily killed before the user's very eyes.

One strategy for avoiding using too much memory is to release any memory-hogging objects you're retaining if they are not needed at this moment. Because a view controller is the basis of so much of your application's architecture, it is likely to be a place where you'll concern yourself with releasing unneeded memory.

One of your view controller's most memory-intensive objects is its view. Fortunately, the iOS runtime manages a view controller's view's memory for you. If a view controller's view is not in the interface, it can be temporarily dispensed with. In such a situation, if memory is getting tight, then even though the view controller itself persists, and even though it retains its actual view, the runtime may release the view's backing store (the cached bitmap representing the view's drawn contents). The view will then be redrawn when and if it is to be shown again later.

Your view controller should override this method so that it can receive an event when memory runs low:

didReceiveMemoryWarning

> Sent to a view controller to advise it of a low-memory situation. It is preceded by a call to the app delegate's applicationDidReceiveMemoryWarning, together with a UIApplication.didReceiveMemoryWarningNotification posted to any registered objects. You are invited to respond by releasing any data that you can do without. Do not release data that you can't readily and quickly recreate! The documentation advises that you should call super.

To test the behavior of your app under low-memory circumstances, run your app in the Simulator and choose Hardware → Simulate Memory Warning. I don't believe this has any actual effect on memory, but a memory warning of sufficient severity is sent to your app, so you can see the results of triggering your low-memory response code.

Another approach, which works also on a device, is to call an undocumented method. First, define a dummy protocol to make the selector legal:

```
@objc protocol Dummy {
    func _performMemoryWarning()
}
```

Now you can send that selector to the shared application:

```
UIApplication.shared.perform(#selector(Dummy._performMemoryWarning))
```

(Be sure to remove that code when it is no longer needed for testing, as the App Store won't accept it.)

There are no hard and fast rules about what might be occupying your app's memory unnecessarily. Use the Allocations template in Instruments to find out! When multiple view controllers exist simultaneously, interface objects and data in a view controller whose view is not currently visible are obvious candidates for purging when memory is tight. You might also discover that you are retaining large objects that you don't really need. It will come as no surprise that the most common source of accidental memory bloat is images; a retained array of images, or an image that is much larger than the size at which it needs to be displayed in the interface, can waste a lot of memory and should always be avoided.

Lazy Loading

If you're going to release data in didReceiveMemoryWarning, you must concern yourself with how you're going to get it back. A simple and reliable mechanism is *lazy loading* — a getter that reconstructs or fetches the data if it is nil.

Suppose we have a property `myBigData` which might be a big piece of data. We make this a computed property, storing the real data in a private property (I'll call it `_myBig-Data`). Our computed property's setter simply writes through to the private property. In `didReceiveMemoryWarning`, we write `myBigData` out as a file (Chapter 22) and set `myBigData` to `nil`, which sets `_myBigData` to `nil` as well, releasing the big data from memory. The getter for `myBigData` implements lazy loading: if we try to get `myBig-Data` when `_myBigData` is `nil`, we attempt to fetch the data from the file — and if we succeed, we delete the file (to prevent stale data):

```swift
private let fnam = "myBigData"
private var _myBigData : Data! = nil
var myBigData : Data! {
    set (newdata) { self._myBigData = newdata }
    get {
        if _myBigData == nil {
            let fm = FileManager.default
            let f = fm.temporaryDirectory.appendingPathComponent(self.fnam)
            if let d = try? Data(contentsOf:f) {
                self._myBigData = d
                do {
                    try fm.removeItem(at:f)
                } catch {
                    print("Couldn't remove temp file")
                }
            }
        }
        return self._myBigData
    }
}
func saveAndReleaseMyBigData() {
    if let myBigData = self.myBigData {
        let fm = FileManager.default
        let f = fm.temporaryDirectory.appendingPathComponent(self.fnam)
        if let _ = try? myBigData.write(to:f) {
            self.myBigData = nil
        }
    }
}
override func didReceiveMemoryWarning() {
    super.didReceiveMemoryWarning()
    self.saveAndReleaseMyBigData()
}
```

NSCache, NSPurgeableData, and Memory-Mapping

When your big data can be reconstructed from scratch on demand, you can take advantage of the built-in NSCache class, which is like a dictionary with the ability to clear out its own entries automatically under memory pressure. As in the previous example, a computed property can be used as a façade:

```
    private let _cache = NSCache<NSString, NSData>()
    var cachedData : Data {
        let key = "somekey" as NSString
        if let olddata = self._cache.object(forKey:key) {
            return olddata as Data
        }
        let newdata = // ... recreate data ...
        self._cache.setObject(newdata as NSData, forKey: key)
        return newdata
    }
```

Another built-in class that knows how to clear itself out is NSPurgeableData. It is a subclass of NSMutableData. To signal that the data should be discarded, send your object `discardContentIfPossible`. Wrap any access to data in calls to `beginContent-Access` and `endContentAccess`; the former returns a Bool to indicate whether the data was accessible. The tricky part is getting those access calls right; when you create an NSPurgeableData, you must send it an unbalanced `endContentAccess` to make its content discardable:

```
    private var _purgeable = NSPurgeableData()
    var purgeabledata : Data {
        if self._purgeable.beginContentAccess() && self._purgeable.length > 0 {
            let result = self._purgeable.copy() as! Data
            self._purgeable.endContentAccess()
            return result
        } else {
            let data = // ... recreate data ...
            self._purgeable = NSPurgeableData(data:data)
            self._purgeable.endContentAccess()
            return data
        }
    }
```

(For more about NSCache and NSPurgeableData, see the "Caching and Purgeable Memory" chapter of Apple's *Memory Usage Performance Guidelines* in the documentation archive.)

At an even lower level, you can store your data as a file (in some reasonable location such the Caches directory) and read it using the Data initializer `init(contentsOf-URL:options:)` with an `options:` argument `.alwaysMapped`. This creates a memory-mapped data object, which has the remarkable feature that it isn't considered to belong to your memory at all; the system has no hesitation in clearing it from RAM, because it is backed through the virtual memory system by the file, and will be read back into memory automatically when you next access it. This is suitable only for large immutable data, because small data might fragment a virtual memory page.

Background Memory Usage

You will also wish to concern yourself with releasing memory when your app is about to be suspended. If your app has been backgrounded and suspended and the system later discovers it is running short of memory, it will go hunting through the suspended apps, looking for memory hogs that it can kill in order to free up that memory. If the system decides that your suspended app is a memory hog, it isn't politely going to wake your app and send it a memory warning; it's just going to terminate your app in its sleep. The time to be concerned about releasing memory, therefore, is *before* the app is suspended. You'll probably want your view controller to be registered to receive a notification from the application or scene that we are about to go into the background. The arrival of this notification is an opportunity to release any easily restored memory-hogging objects, such as `myBigData` in the previous example:

```
var didAppearInitially = false
override func viewDidAppear(_ animated: Bool) {
    super.viewDidAppear(animated)
    if !didAppearInitially {
        didAppearInitially = true
        NotificationCenter.default.addObserver(self,
            selector: #selector(backgrounding),
            name: UIScene.didEnterBackgroundNotification,
            object: self.view.window?.windowScene)
    }
}
@objc func backgrounding(_ n:Notification) {
    self.saveAndReleaseMyBigData()
}
```

In real life, we should be returning from our `backgrounding` method as quickly as possible; the way to do that is to get onto a background thread and call `begin-BackgroundTask` (see Chapter 24).

 A nice feature of NSCache is that it evicts its objects automatically when your app goes into the background.

CHAPTER 7

Scroll Views

A scroll view (UIScrollView) is a view whose content is larger than its bounds. To reveal a desired area, the user can scroll the content by dragging, or you can reposition the content in code. The scroll view functions as a limited window on a larger world of content.

A scroll view isn't magic; it takes advantage of ordinary UIView features (Chapter 1). The content is simply the scroll view's subviews. When the scroll view scrolls, what's really changing is the scroll view's own bounds origin; the subviews are positioned with respect to the bounds origin, so they move with it. The scroll view's clipsTo-Bounds is true, so any content positioned within the scroll view is visible and any content positioned outside it is not.

A scroll view has the following specialized abilities:

- It knows how to shift its bounds origin in response to the user's gestures.
- It provides scroll indicators whose size and position give the user a clue as to the content's size and position.
- It can enforce paging, whereby the user can scroll only by a fixed amount.
- It supports zooming, so that the user can resize the content with a pinch gesture.
- It provides delegate methods so that your code knows how the user is scrolling and zooming.

Content Size

How *far* should a scroll view scroll? Clearly, that depends on how much *content* it has. The scroll view already knows how far it should be allowed to slide its subviews downward and rightward: the limit is reached when the scroll view's bounds origin is

`CGPoint.zero`. What the scroll view *needs* to know is how far it should be allowed to slide its subviews upward and leftward. That is the scroll view's *content size* — its `contentSize` property.

The scroll view uses its `contentSize`, in combination with its own bounds size, to set the limits on how large its bounds origin can become. It may be helpful to think of the scroll view's scrollable content as the rectangle defined by `CGRect(origin:.zero, size:contentSize)`; this is the rectangle that the user can inspect by scrolling. If a dimension of the `contentSize` isn't larger than the same dimension of the scroll view's own bounds, the content won't be scrollable in that dimension: there is nothing to scroll, as the entire scrollable content is already showing.

The default is that the `contentSize` is `.zero` — meaning that the scroll view *isn't scrollable*. To get a working scroll view, therefore, it will be crucial to set its `content-Size` correctly. You can do this directly, in code; or, if you're using autolayout, the `contentSize` can be calculated for you based on the autolayout constraints of the scroll view's subviews (as I'll demonstrate in a moment).

How big should a scroll view's content size be? Clearly that depends on the size of its subviews. Typically, you'll want the content size to be just large enough to embrace all the subviews: they, after all, are the content the user needs to be able to see. You'll likely want to set the content size correctly at the outset. You can subsequently alter a scroll view's content (subviews) or `contentSize`, or both, dynamically as the app runs; in and of themselves, they are independent.

A `contentSize` that has been set manually, in code, does not change just because the scroll view's bounds change; you might not want the `contentSize` to change in response to rotation, but if you do, you will need to change it manually, in code, *again*. On the other hand, if a scroll view's content size is set automatically using autolayout based on the scroll view's subviews, then if the content size embraces those subviews it will continue to do so when the app orientation changes.

Creating a Scroll View in Code

Let's start by creating a scroll view, providing it with subviews, and making those subviews viewable by scrolling, entirely in code. There are two ways to set the `contentSize`, so I'll demonstrate each of them in turn.

Manual Content Size

In the first instance, let's not use autolayout at all. Our project is based on the Single View App template, with a single view controller class, ViewController. In View-Controller's `viewDidLoad`, I'll create the scroll view to fill the main view, and populate it with a vertical column of 30 UILabels whose text contains a sequential number so that we can see where we are when we scroll:

```
let sv = UIScrollView(frame: self.view.bounds)
sv.autoresizingMask = [.flexibleWidth, .flexibleHeight]
self.view.addSubview(sv)
sv.backgroundColor = .white
var y : CGFloat = 10
for i in 0 ..< 30 {
    let lab = UILabel()
    lab.text = "This is label \(i+1)"
    lab.sizeToFit()
    lab.frame.origin = CGPoint(10,y)
    sv.addSubview(lab)
    y += lab.bounds.size.height + 10
}
var sz = sv.bounds.size
sz.height = y
sv.contentSize = sz // *
```

The crucial move is the last line, where we tell the scroll view how large its `content-Size` is to be. Our `sz.height` accommodates all the labels, but `sz.width` matches the scroll view's width; the scroll view will be scrollable vertically but not horizontally (a common scenario).

There is no rule about the order in which you perform the two operations of setting the `contentSize` and populating the scroll view with subviews. In that example, we set the `contentSize` afterward because it is more convenient to track the heights of the subviews as we add them than to calculate their total height in advance.

Automatic Content Size with Autolayout

With autolayout, things are different. Under autolayout, a scroll view interprets the constraints of its immediate subviews in a special way. Constraints between a scroll view and its direct subviews are *not* a way of positioning the subviews relative to the scroll view (as they would be if the superview were an ordinary UIView). Rather, they are a way of describing the scroll view's `contentSize` *from the inside out*.

To see this, let's rewrite the preceding example to use autolayout. The scroll view and its subviews have their `translatesAutoresizingMaskIntoConstraints` set to false, and we're giving them explicit constraints:

```
let sv = UIScrollView()
sv.backgroundColor = .white
sv.translatesAutoresizingMaskIntoConstraints = false
self.view.addSubview(sv)
NSLayoutConstraint.activate([
    sv.topAnchor.constraint(equalTo:self.view.topAnchor),
    sv.bottomAnchor.constraint(equalTo:self.view.bottomAnchor),
    sv.leadingAnchor.constraint(equalTo:self.view.leadingAnchor),
```

```
        sv.trailingAnchor.constraint(equalTo:self.view.trailingAnchor),
    ])
    var previousLab : UILabel? = nil
    for i in 0 ..< 30 {
        let lab = UILabel()
        // lab.backgroundColor = .red
        lab.translatesAutoresizingMaskIntoConstraints = false
        lab.text = "This is label \(i+1)"
        sv.addSubview(lab)
        lab.leadingAnchor.constraint(
            equalTo: sv.leadingAnchor, constant: 10).isActive = true
        lab.topAnchor.constraint(
            // first one, pin to top; all others, pin to previous
            equalTo: previousLab?.bottomAnchor ?? sv.topAnchor,
            constant: 10).isActive = true
        previousLab = lab
    }
```

The labels are correctly positioned relative to one another, but the scroll view isn't scrollable. Moreover, setting the contentSize manually doesn't help; it has no effect!

Why is that? It's because we're using autolayout, so we must generate the content-Size by means of constraints between the scroll view and its immediate subviews. We've almost done that, but not quite. We are *missing a constraint*. We have to add one more constraint, showing the scroll view what the height of its contentSize should be:

```
    sv.bottomAnchor.constraint(
        equalTo: previousLab!.bottomAnchor, constant: 10).isActive = true
```

The constraints of the scroll view's subviews now describe the contentSize height: the top label is pinned to the top of the scroll view, the next one is pinned to the one above it, and so on — *and the bottom one is pinned to the bottom of the scroll view*. Consequently, the runtime calculates the contentSize height from the inside out as the sum of all the vertical constraints (including the intrinsic heights of the labels), and the scroll view is vertically scrollable to show all the labels.

We should also provide a contentSize width; here, I'll add a trailing constraint from the bottom label, which will be narrower than the scroll view, so we won't actually scroll horizontally:

```
    previousLab!.trailingAnchor.constraint(
        equalTo:sv.trailingAnchor).isActive = true
```

Scroll View Layout Guides

Starting in iOS 11, there's another way to determine a scroll view's content size. A UIScrollView has a contentLayoutGuide. If we give the content layout guide a width constraint or a height constraint, we determine the contentSize directly. If we pin the scroll view's subviews to the content layout guide, we determine the `contentSize` from the inside out; this is clearer than pinning the subviews to the scroll view itself. I'll rewrite the preceding example to use the `contentLayoutGuide`:

```
let sv = UIScrollView()
sv.backgroundColor = .white
sv.translatesAutoresizingMaskIntoConstraints = false
self.view.addSubview(sv)
NSLayoutConstraint.activate([
    sv.topAnchor.constraint(equalTo:self.view.topAnchor),
    sv.bottomAnchor.constraint(equalTo:self.view.bottomAnchor),
    sv.leadingAnchor.constraint(equalTo:self.view.leadingAnchor),
    sv.trailingAnchor.constraint(equalTo:self.view.trailingAnchor),
])
let svclg = sv.contentLayoutGuide // *
var previousLab : UILabel? = nil
for i in 0 ..< 30 {
    let lab = UILabel()
    // lab.backgroundColor = .red
    lab.translatesAutoresizingMaskIntoConstraints = false
    lab.text = "This is label \(i+1)"
    sv.addSubview(lab)
    lab.leadingAnchor.constraint(
        equalTo: svclg.leadingAnchor,
        constant: 10).isActive = true
    lab.topAnchor.constraint(
        // first one, pin to top; all others, pin to previous
        equalTo: previousLab?.bottomAnchor ?? svclg.topAnchor,
        constant: 10).isActive = true
    previousLab = lab
}
svclg.bottomAnchor.constraint(
    equalTo: previousLab!.bottomAnchor, constant: 10).isActive = true
svclg.widthAnchor.constraint(equalToConstant:0).isActive = true // *
```

The last line demonstrates that we can set the content layout guide's height or width constraint *directly* to determine that dimension of the content size. Thanks to the content layout guide, I'm able to set the content size width directly to zero, which states precisely what I mean: don't scroll horizontally.

Also starting in iOS 11, there's a second UIScrollView property, its `frameLayout-Guide`, which is pinned to the scroll view's frame. This gives us an even better way to state that the scroll view should not scroll horizontally, by making the content layout guide width the same as the frame layout guide width:

```
let svflg = sv.frameLayoutGuide
svclg.widthAnchor.constraint(equalTo:svflg.widthAnchor).isActive = true
```

Using a Content View

A commonly used arrangement is to give a scroll view just *one* immediate subview; all other views inside the scroll view are subviews of this single immediate subview of the scroll view, which is often called the *content view*. The content view is usually a generic UIView; the user won't even know it's there. It has no purpose other than to contain the other subviews — and to help determine the scroll view's content size. The idea is that the scroll view's contentSize should exactly match the dimensions of the content view. There are two ways to achieve that, depending on whether we want to set the content size manually or using autolayout:

- Set the content view's translatesAutoresizingMaskIntoConstraints to true, and set the scroll view's contentSize manually to the size of the content view.

- Set the content view's translatesAutoresizingMaskIntoConstraints to false, set its size with constraints, and pin its edges with constraints to the scroll view's content layout guide. If all four of those edge constraints have a constant of 0, the scroll view's contentSize will be the same as the size of the content view.

This arrangement works independently of whether the content view's own subviews are positioned explicitly by their frames or using constraints, so there are four possible combinations:

No constraints
> The content view is sized by its frame, its contents are positioned by their frames, and the scroll view's contentSize is set explicitly.

Content view constraints
> The content view is sized by its own height and width constraints, and its edges are pinned to the content layout guide to set the scroll view's content size.

Content view and content constraints
> The content view is sized from the inside out by the constraints of its subviews, and its edges are pinned to the content layout guide to set the scroll view's content size.

Content constraints only
> The content view is sized by its frame, and the scroll view's contentSize is set explicitly; but the content view's subviews are positioned using constraints. (This option is rather far-fetched, but I list it for the sake of completeness.)

I'll illustrate by rewriting the previous example to use a content view (v) in each of those ways. All four possible combinations start the same way:

```
let sv = UIScrollView()
sv.backgroundColor = .white
sv.translatesAutoresizingMaskIntoConstraints = false
self.view.addSubview(sv)
NSLayoutConstraint.activate([
    sv.topAnchor.constraint(equalTo:self.view.topAnchor),
    sv.bottomAnchor.constraint(equalTo:self.view.bottomAnchor),
    sv.leadingAnchor.constraint(equalTo:self.view.leadingAnchor),
    sv.trailingAnchor.constraint(equalTo:self.view.trailingAnchor),
])
let v = UIView() // content view!
sv.addSubview(v)
```

The differences lie in what happens next. The first combination is that no constraints are used, and the scroll view's content size is set explicitly. It's very like the first example in this chapter, except that the labels are added to the content view, not to the scroll view. The content view's height is a little taller than the bottom of the lowest label, and its width is a little wider than the widest label, so it neatly contains all the labels:

```
var y : CGFloat = 10
var maxw : CGFloat = 0
for i in 0 ..< 30 {
    let lab = UILabel()
    lab.text = "This is label \(i+1)"
    lab.sizeToFit()
    lab.frame.origin = CGPoint(10,y)
    v.addSubview(lab)
    y += lab.bounds.size.height + 10
    maxw = max(maxw, lab.frame.maxX + 10)
}
// set content view frame and content size explicitly
v.frame = CGRect(0,0,maxw,y)
sv.contentSize = v.frame.size
```

The second combination is that the content view is sized by explicit width and height constraints, and its edges are pinned by constraints to the scroll view's content layout guide to give the scroll view a content size:

```
var y : CGFloat = 10
var maxw : CGFloat = 0
for i in 0 ..< 30 {
    let lab = UILabel()
    lab.text = "This is label \(i+1)"
    lab.sizeToFit()
    lab.frame.origin = CGPoint(10,y)
    v.addSubview(lab)
    y += lab.bounds.size.height + 10
    maxw = max(maxw, lab.frame.maxX + 10)
}
// set content view width, height, and edge constraints
// content size is calculated for us
```

```
v.translatesAutoresizingMaskIntoConstraints = false
let svclg = sv.contentLayoutGuide
NSLayoutConstraint.activate([
    v.widthAnchor.constraint(equalToConstant:maxw),
    v.heightAnchor.constraint(equalToConstant:y),
    svclg.topAnchor.constraint(equalTo:v.topAnchor),
    svclg.bottomAnchor.constraint(equalTo:v.bottomAnchor),
    svclg.leadingAnchor.constraint(equalTo:v.leadingAnchor),
    svclg.trailingAnchor.constraint(equalTo:v.trailingAnchor),
])
```

The third combination is that the content view is self-sizing based on constraints from its subviews ("Self-Sizing Views" on page 55), and the content view's edges are pinned by constraints to the scroll view's content layout guide. In a very real sense, the scroll view gets its content size *from the labels*. This is similar to the second example in this chapter, except that the labels are added to the content view:

```
var previousLab : UILabel? = nil
for i in 0 ..< 30 {
    let lab = UILabel()
    // lab.backgroundColor = .red
    lab.translatesAutoresizingMaskIntoConstraints = false
    lab.text = "This is label \(i+1)"
    v.addSubview(lab)
    lab.leadingAnchor.constraint(
        equalTo: v.leadingAnchor,
        constant: 10).isActive = true
    lab.topAnchor.constraint(
        // first one, pin to top; all others, pin to previous
        equalTo: previousLab?.bottomAnchor ?? v.topAnchor,
        constant: 10).isActive = true
    previousLab = lab
}
// last one, pin to bottom, this dictates content size height
v.bottomAnchor.constraint(
    equalTo: previousLab!.bottomAnchor, constant: 10).isActive = true
// need to do something about width
v.trailingAnchor.constraint(
    equalTo: previousLab!.trailingAnchor, constant: 10).isActive = true
// pin content view to scroll view, sized by its subview constraints
// content size is calculated for us
v.translatesAutoresizingMaskIntoConstraints = false
let svclg = sv.contentLayoutGuide
NSLayoutConstraint.activate([
    svclg.topAnchor.constraint(equalTo:v.topAnchor),
    svclg.bottomAnchor.constraint(equalTo:v.bottomAnchor),
    svclg.leadingAnchor.constraint(equalTo:v.leadingAnchor),
    svclg.trailingAnchor.constraint(equalTo:v.trailingAnchor),
])
```

The fourth (and somewhat improbable) combination is that the content view's subviews are positioned using constraints, but we set the content view's frame and the scroll view's content size explicitly. How can we derive the content view size from the constraints of its subviews? By calling `systemLayoutSizeFitting(_:)` to perform layout for us:

```
var previousLab : UILabel? = nil
for i in 0 ..< 30 {
    let lab = UILabel()
    // lab.backgroundColor = .red
    lab.translatesAutoresizingMaskIntoConstraints = false
    lab.text = "This is label \(i+1)"
    v.addSubview(lab)
    lab.leadingAnchor.constraint(
        equalTo: v.leadingAnchor,
        constant: 10).isActive = true
    lab.topAnchor.constraint(
        // first one, pin to top; all others, pin to previous
        equalTo: previousLab?.bottomAnchor ?? v.topAnchor,
        constant: 10).isActive = true
    previousLab = lab
}
// last one, pin to bottom, this dictates content size height!
v.bottomAnchor.constraint(
    equalTo: previousLab!.bottomAnchor, constant: 10).isActive = true
// need to do something about width
v.trailingAnchor.constraint(
    equalTo: previousLab!.trailingAnchor, constant: 10).isActive = true
// autolayout helps us learn the consequences of those constraints
let minsz = v.systemLayoutSizeFitting(UIView.layoutFittingCompressedSize)
// set content view frame and content size explicitly
v.frame = CGRect(origin:.zero, size:minsz)
sv.contentSize = minsz
```

Scroll View in a Nib

A UIScrollView object is available in the nib editor's Library, so you can drag it into a view in the canvas and give it subviews. Alternatively, you can wrap existing views in the canvas in a UIScrollView as an afterthought: to do so, select the views and choose Editor → Embed In → Scroll View (or choose Scroll View from the Embed button at the lower right of the canvas).

New in Xcode 11, a scroll view's content layout guide and frame layout guide are present in the nib editor (if you don't see them, check Content Layout Guides in the Size inspector); using a content view, you can configure a scroll view in the nib editor much as you'd configure it in code.

While designing the scroll view's subviews initially, you might need to make the view controller's main view large enough to accommodate them. To do so, set the view controller's Simulated Size pop-up menu in its Size inspector to Freeform; now you can change the main view's size. But that might not be necessary, because once you've

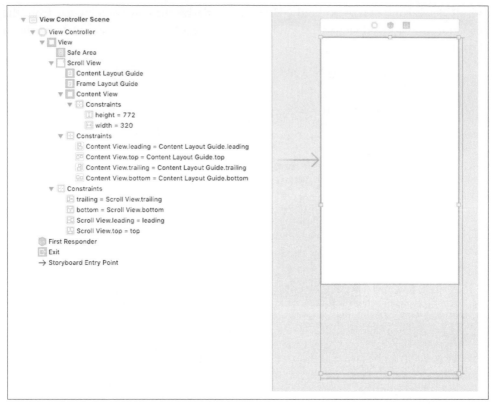

Figure 7-1. A scroll view in the nib editor

provided sufficient constraint information, the scroll view is scrollable directly in the nib editor (new in Xcode 11).

The nib editor understands how scroll view configuration works, and will alert you with a warning (about the "scrollable content size") until you've provided enough constraints to determine unambiguously the scroll view's `contentSize`.

Figure 7-1 shows a scroll view whose content size is configured *manually* in the nib editor. There is no way to enter content size information for a scroll view in the Attributes or Size inspector; the scroll view has a content layout guide, but you can't apply width and height constraints to it directly. (I regard that as a bug.) So I've used a content view as an intermediary. The content view is the scroll view's subview; it has explicit width and height constraints and is pinned with zero-constant constraints to the scroll view's content layout guide. The width and height constraint constants of the content view are 320 and 772 respectively, so this is saying that the scroll view's `contentSize` should be (320,772).

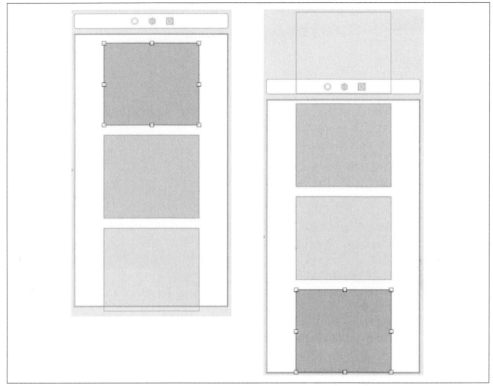

Figure 7-2. Designing a scroll view's contents

We can now proceed to populate the content view with subviews. Purely for demonstration purposes, I'll use four plain vanilla UIViews, and I won't use autolayout. I can design the first three views directly, because they fit within the main view (Figure 7-2, left). But what about the last view? The scroll view's content size is determined, so I can scroll the scroll view directly in the nib editor; once the bottom of the content view is within the main view, I can add the fourth view (Figure 7-2, right).

Instead of dictating the scroll view's content size numerically with explicit width and height constraints on the content view, you can apply constraints to the content view from its subviews and let those subviews size the content view from the inside out, setting the scroll view's `contentSize` as a result. In Figure 7-3, the subviews have explicit height and width constraints and are pinned to one another and to the top and bottom of the content view, and the content view is pinned to the scroll view's content layout guide, so the scroll view is scrollable to view all of the subviews. Moreover, I've given the subviews zero-constant leading and trailing constraints to the content view, and I've centered the content view horizontally within the scroll view's frame layout guide; the result is that the subviews are centered horizontally on any screen size.

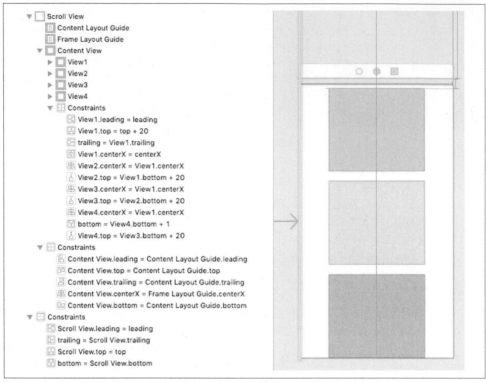

Figure 7-3. A scroll view whose content is sized by its subviews

(Strictly speaking, I suppose the content view in that example is unnecessary; we could pin the scroll view's subviews directly to its content layout guide.)

Content Inset

The content inset of a scroll view is a margin space around its content. In effect, it changes where the content stops when the scroll view is scrolled all the way to its extreme limit.

The main reason why this is important is that a scroll view will typically underlap other interface. In the app with 30 labels that we created at the start of this chapter, the scroll view occupies the entirety of the view controller's main view — and the view controller's main view underlaps the status bar. That means that the top of the scroll view underlaps the status bar. And *that* means that at launch time, and whenever the scroll view's content is scrolled all the way down, the first label, which is now as far down as it can go, is partly hidden by the text of the status bar.

You might say: Well, don't do that! Don't let the scroll view underlap the status bar in the first place; pin the top of the scroll view to the bottom of the status bar. But that isn't necessarily what we want; and in any case, the problem is not where the top of the scroll view is, but where the top of its *content* is considered to be. When the content is being scrolled *upward*, it's fine for that content to pass behind the status bar! The problem is what happens when the content is moved *downward* as far as it can go. Its content top shouldn't stop at the top of the scroll view; the stopping point should be further down, at the *bottom* of the status bar. The scroll view's content inset solves the problem, positioning the top of the scroll view's content lower than the top of the scroll view, by the amount that the scroll view underlaps the status bar.

But it's more complicated than that. The content inset needs to be *live*. After all, the status bar can come and go. The top of the scroll view's content should be further down than the top of the scroll view itself when the iPhone is in portrait orientation and the status bar is present; but when the iPhone is in landscape orientation and the status bar vanishes, the content inset needs to be adjusted so that the top of the content will be identical to the top of the scroll view.

And of course the status bar isn't the only kind of top bar; there's also the navigation bar, which can come and go as well, and can change its height. Plus there are bottom bars, which can *also* come and go, and can change *their* heights. The runtime would like your view to underlap those bars. With a scroll view, this looks cool, because the scroll view's contents are visible in a blurry way through the translucent bar; but clearly the top and bottom values of the scroll view's content inset need to be adjusted so that the scrolling limits stay between the top bar and the bottom bar, even as these bars can come and go and change their heights.

The boundaries I'm describing here, as has no doubt already occurred to you, are the boundaries of the safe area ("Safe area" on page 48). If a scroll view would simply adjust its content inset automatically to correspond to the safe area, its content would scroll in exactly the right way so as to be visible regardless of how any bars are underlapped. And that in fact is exactly what *does* happen by default.

A scroll view knows where the top and bottom bars are because the safe area is propagated down the view hierarchy, and it knows how to adjust its content inset to correspond to the safe area. It will do that in accordance with its `contentInset-AdjustmentBehavior` property (UIScrollView.ContentInsetAdjustmentBehavior):

`.always`
: The content is inset to match the safe area.

`.never`
: The content is not inset to match the safe area.

`.scrollableAxes`
: The content is inset to match the safe area only for a dimension in which the scroll view is scrollable.

`.automatic`
> Similar to `scrollableAxes`, but is also backward compatible. In iOS 10 and before, a view controller had an `automaticallyAdjustsScrollViewInsets` property (now deprecated); `.automatic` means that the scroll view can respond to that as well.

The default `contentInsetAdjustmentBehavior` is `.automatic` — which means that your scroll view will probably adjust its content inset appropriately with no work on your part!

To find out numerically how the scroll view has set its content inset, consult its `adjustedContentInset` property. Suppose we're in a navigation interface, where the scroll view coincides with the view controller's main view and underlaps the top bars. Suppose further that the navigation bar doesn't have a large title. Then in portrait orientation on an iPhone, the status bar and the navigation bar together add 64 points of height to the top of the safe area. So if the scroll view's content inset adjustment behavior isn't `.never`, its `adjustedContentInset` is `(64.0,0.0,0.0,0.0)`.

A scroll view also has a `contentInset` property, which will usually be `.zero`. If you set it to some other value, that value is applied *additively* to increase the `adjusted-ContentInset`. In the navigation interface scenario from the preceding paragraph, if we also set the scroll view's `contentInset` to a UIEdgeInsets whose `top:` is `30`, then the `adjustedContentInset` will have a `top` value of `94`, and there will be an additional 30-point gap between the top of the content and the bottom of the navigation bar when the content is scrolled all the way down.

 New in iOS 13, if a navigation bar has a large title, then as the scroll view's content is scrolled downward and the large title appears, the navigation bar becomes transparent by default, revealing the scroll view behind it. This shouldn't make any appreciable difference, because *ex hypothesi* the entire content of the scroll view is already scrolled down past the bottom of the navigation bar, so the navigation bar won't overlap that content.

Scrolling

For the most part, the purpose of a scroll view will be to let the user scroll. Here are some scroll view properties that affect the user experience with regard to scrolling:

`isScrollEnabled`
> If `false`, the user can't scroll, but you can still scroll in code (as explained later in this section). You could put a UIScrollView to various creative purposes other than letting the user scroll; scrolling in code to a different region of the content might be a way of replacing one piece of interface by another, possibly with animation.

scrollsToTop
> If `true` (the default), and assuming scrolling is enabled, the user can tap on the status bar as a way of making the scroll view scroll its content to the top (that is, the content moves all the way down). You can override this setting dynamically through the scroll view's delegate, discussed later in this chapter.

bounces
> If `true` (the default), then when the user scrolls to a limit of the content, it is possible to scroll somewhat further (possibly revealing the scroll view's `background-Color` behind the content, if a subview was covering it); the content then snaps back into place when the user releases it. Otherwise, the user experiences the limit as a sudden inability to scroll further in that direction.

alwaysBounceVertical
alwaysBounceHorizontal
> If `true`, and assuming that `bounces` is `true`, then even if the `contentSize` in the given dimension isn't larger than the scroll view (so that no scrolling is actually possible in that dimension), the user can scroll somewhat and the content then snaps back into place when the user releases it. Otherwise, the user experiences a simple inability to scroll in this dimension.

isDirectionalLockEnabled
> If `true`, and if scrolling is possible in both dimensions (even if only because `alwaysBounce` is `true`), then the user, having begun to scroll in one dimension, can't scroll in the other dimension without ending the gesture and starting over. In other words, the user is constrained to scroll vertically or horizontally but not both at once.

decelerationRate
> The rate at which scrolling is damped out, and the content comes to a stop, after the user's gesture ends. As convenient examples, standard constants are provided (UIScrollView.DecelerationRate):
>
> - `.normal` (0.998)
> - `.fast` (0.99)
>
> Lower values mean faster damping; experimentation suggests that values lower than 0.5 are viable but barely distinguishable from one another. You can effectively override this value dynamically through the scroll view's delegate, discussed later in this chapter.

`showsHorizontalScrollIndicator`
`showsVerticalScrollIndicator`
> The scroll indicators are bars that appear only while the user is scrolling in a scrollable dimension (where the content is larger than the scroll view); they indicate both the size of the content in that dimension and the user's position within it. The default is `true` for both.
>
> Because the user cannot see the scroll indicators except when actively scrolling, there is normally no indication that the view is scrollable. I regard this as somewhat unfortunate, because it makes the possibility of scrolling less discoverable; I'd prefer an option to make the scroll indicators constantly visible. Apple suggests that you call `flashScrollIndicators` when the scroll view appears, to make the scroll indicators visible momentarily.

`indicatorStyle`
> The way the scroll indicators are drawn. Your choices (UIScrollView.Indicator-Style) are `.black`, `.white`, and `.default`; new in iOS 13, `.default` responds to the user interface style (light or dark mode), contrasting with a system background color.

 The scroll indicators are subviews of the scroll view (they are actually UIImage-Views). Do not assume that the subviews you add to a UIScrollView are its only subviews!

Scrolling in Code

You can scroll in code, and you can do so even if the user can't scroll. The content moves to the position you specify, with no bouncing and no exposure of the scroll indicators. You can specify the new position in two ways:

`scrollRectToVisible(_:animated:)`
> Adjusts the content so that the specified CGRect of the content is within the scroll view's bounds. This is imprecise, because you're not saying exactly what the resulting scroll position will be, but sometimes guaranteeing the visibility of a certain portion of the content is exactly what you're after.

`contentOffset`
> A property signifying the point (CGPoint) of the content that is located at the scroll view's top left (effectively the same thing as the scroll view's bounds origin). Setting it changes the current scroll position, or call `setContent-Offset(_:animated:)` to set the `contentOffset` with animation. The values normally go up from `(0.0,0.0)` until the limit dictated by the `contentSize` and the scroll view's own bounds size is reached.

The `adjustedContentInset` (discussed in the previous section) can affect the meaning of the `contentOffset`. Recall the scenario where the scroll view underlaps the status bar and a navigation bar and acquires an `adjustedContentInset` with a top of 64. Then when the scroll view's content is scrolled all the way down, the `contentOffset` is not (0.0,0.0) but (0.0,-64.0). The (0.0,0.0) point is the top of the content rect, which is located at the bottom of the navigation bar; the point at the top left of the scroll view itself is 64 points above that.

That fact manifests itself particularly when *you* want to scroll, in code. If you scroll by setting the `contentOffset`, you need to subtract the corresponding `adjustedContentInset` value. Staying with our scroll view that underlaps a navigation bar, if your goal is to scroll the scroll view so that the top of its content is visible, you do *not* say this (the scroll view is `self.sv`):

```
self.sv.contentOffset.y = 0
```

Instead, you say this:

```
self.sv.contentOffset.y = -self.sv.adjustedContentInset.top
```

Paging

If its `isPagingEnabled` property is `true`, the scroll view doesn't let the user scroll freely; instead, the content is considered to consist of equal-sized sections. The user can scroll only in such a way as to move to a different section. The size of a section is set automatically to the size of the scroll view's bounds. The sections are the scroll view's *pages*. This is a *paging* scroll view.

When the user stops dragging, a paging scroll view gently snaps automatically to the nearest whole page. Let's say that a paging scroll view scrolls only horizontally, and that its subviews are image views showing photos, sized to match the scroll view's bounds:

- If the user drags horizontally to the left to a point where *less* than half of the next photo to the right is visible, and raises the dragging finger, the paging scroll view snaps its content back to the right until the entire first photo is visible again.

- If the user drags horizontally to the left to a point where *more* than half of the next photo to the right is visible, and raises the dragging finger, the paging scroll view snaps its content further to the left until the entire second photo is visible.

The usual arrangement is that a paging scroll view is as large, or nearly as large, in its scrollable dimension, as the window. Under this arrangement, it is impossible for the user to move the content more than a single page in any direction with a single gesture; the size of the page is the size of the scroll view's bounds, so the user will run out of surface area to drag on before being able to move the content the distance of a page and a half, which is what would be needed to make the scroll view skip a page.

Another possibility is for the paging scroll view to be slightly *larger* than the window in its scrollable dimension. This allows each page's content to fill the scroll view while also providing gaps between the pages, visible when the user starts to scroll. The user is still able to move from page to page, because it is still possible to drag more than half a new page into view.

When the user raises the dragging finger, the scroll view's action in adjusting its content is considered to be *decelerating*, and the scroll view's delegate (discussed in more detail later in this chapter) will receive `scrollViewWillBeginDecelerating(_:)`, followed by `scrollViewDidEndDecelerating(_:)` when the scroll view's content has stopped moving and a full page is showing. These messages can be used to detect efficiently that the page may have changed.

Using the delegate methods, a paging scroll view can be coordinated with a UIPage-Control (Chapter 12). In this example, a page control (`self.pager`) is updated whenever the user causes a horizontally scrollable scroll view (`self.sv`) to display a different page:

```
func scrollViewDidEndDecelerating(_ scrollView: UIScrollView) {
    let x = self.sv.contentOffset.x
    let w = self.sv.bounds.size.width
    self.pager.currentPage = Int(x/w)
}
```

Conversely, we can scroll the scroll view to a new page manually when the user taps the page control:

```
@IBAction func userDidPage(_ sender: Any) {
    let p = self.pager.currentPage
    let w = self.sv.bounds.size.width
    self.sv.setContentOffset(CGPoint(CGFloat(p)*w,0), animated:true)
}
```

A useful interface is a paging scroll view where you supply pages dynamically as the user scrolls. In this way, you can display a huge number of pages without having to put them all into the scroll view at once. In fact, a scrolling UIPageViewController (Chapter 6) implements exactly that interface! Its `.interPageSpacing` options key even provides the gap between pages that I mentioned earlier.

A compromise between a UIPageViewController and a completely preconfigured paging scroll view is a scroll view whose `contentSize` can accommodate all pages, but whose actual page content is supplied lazily. The only pages that have to be present at all times are the page visible to the user and the two pages adjacent to it on either side, so that there is no delay in displaying a new page's content when the user starts to scroll. (This approach is exemplified by Apple's PageControl sample code.)

Tiling

Suppose we have some finite but really big content that we want to display in a scroll view, such as a very large image that the user can inspect piecemeal by scrolling. To hold the entire image in memory may be onerous or impossible. One solution to this kind of problem is *tiling*.

The idea behind tiling is that there's no need to hold the entire image in memory; all we need at any given moment is the part of the image visible to the user right now. Mentally, divide the content rectangle into a matrix of rectangles; these rectangles are the tiles. In reality, divide the huge image into corresponding rectangles. Then whenever the user scrolls, we look to see whether part of any empty tile has become visible, and if so, we supply its content. At the same time, we can release the content of all tiles that are completely offscreen. At any given moment, only the tiles that are showing have content. There is some latency associated with this approach (the user scrolls, then any newly visible empty tiles are filled in), but we will have to live with that.

There is actually a built-in CALayer subclass for helping us implement tiling — CATiledLayer. Its `tileSize` property sets the dimensions of a tile. The usual approach to using CATiledLayer is to implement `draw(_:)` in a UIView whose underlying layer is the CATiledLayer; under that arrangement, the host view's `draw(_:)` is called every time a new tile is needed, and its parameter is the rect of the tile we are to draw.

The `tileSize` may need to be adjusted for the screen resolution. On a double-resolution device, the CATiledLayer's `contentsScale` will be doubled, and the tiles will be half the size that we ask for. If that isn't acceptable, we can double the `tileSize` dimensions.

To illustrate, I'll use as my tiles a few of the "CuriousFrog" images already created for us as part of Apple's own PhotoScroller sample code. The images have names of the form *CuriousFrog_500_x_y.png*, where *x* and *y* are integers corresponding to the picture's position within the matrix. The images are 256×256 pixels; for this example, I've selected a 3×3 matrix of images.

We will give our scroll view (`self.sv`) one subview, a UIView subclass (called Tiled-View) that exists purely to give our CATiledLayer a place to live. `TILESIZE` is defined as 256, to match the image dimensions:

```
override func viewDidLoad() {
    let f = CGRect(0,0,3*TILESIZE,3*TILESIZE)
    let content = TiledView(frame:f)
    let tsz = TILESIZE * content.layer.contentsScale
    (content.layer as! CATiledLayer).tileSize = CGSize(tsz, tsz)
```

```
        self.sv.addSubview(content)
        self.sv.contentSize = f.size
        self.content = content
    }
```

Here's the code for TiledView. As Apple's sample code points out, we must fetch images with init(contentsOfFile:) in order to avoid the automatic caching behavior of init(named:) — after all, we're going to all this trouble exactly to avoid using more memory than we have to:

```
override class var layerClass : AnyClass {
    return CATiledLayer.self
}
override func draw(_ r: CGRect) {
    let tile = r
    let x = Int(tile.origin.x/TILESIZE)
    let y = Int(tile.origin.y/TILESIZE)
    let tileName = String(format:"CuriousFrog_500_\(x+3)_\(y)")
    let path = Bundle.main.path(forResource: tileName, ofType:"png")!
    let image = UIImage(contentsOfFile:path)!
    image.draw(at:CGPoint(CGFloat(x)*TILESIZE,CGFloat(y)*TILESIZE))
}
```

In this configuration, our TiledView's drawRect is called *on a background thread*. This is unusual, but it shouldn't cause any trouble as long as you confine yourself to standard thread-safe activities. Fortunately, fetching the tile image and drawing it *are* thread-safe.

There is no special call for invalidating an offscreen tile. You're just supposed to trust that the CATiledLayer will eventually clear offscreen tiles if needed in order to conserve memory.

CATiledLayer has a class method fadeDuration that dictates the duration of the animation that fades a new tile into view. You can create a CATiledLayer subclass and override this method to return a value different from the default (0.25), but this is probably not worth doing, as the default value is a good one. Returning a smaller value won't make tiles appear faster; it just replaces the nice fade-in with an annoying flash.

Zooming

To implement zooming of a scroll view's content, you set the scroll view's minimum-ZoomScale and maximumZoomScale so that at least one of them isn't 1 (the default). You also implement viewForZooming(in:) in the scroll view's delegate to tell the scroll view which of its subviews is to be the scalable view. The scroll view then zooms by applying a scale transform to this subview. The amount of that transform is the scroll view's zoomScale property.

Typically, you'll want the scroll view's entire content to be scalable, so you'll have one direct subview of the scroll view that acts as the scalable view, and anything else inside the scroll view will be a subview of the scalable view, so as to be scaled together with it. This is another reason for arranging your scroll view's subviews inside a single content view, as I suggested earlier.

To illustrate, we can start with any of the four content view–based versions of our scroll view containing 30 labels from earlier in this chapter ("Using a Content View" on page 416). I called the content view v. Now we add these lines:

```
v.tag = 999
sv.minimumZoomScale = 1.0
sv.maximumZoomScale = 2.0
sv.delegate = self
```

We have assigned a tag to the view that is to be scaled, so that we can refer to it later. We have set the scale limits for the scroll view. And we have made ourselves the scroll view's delegate. Now all we have to do is implement viewForZooming(in:) to return the scalable view:

```
func viewForZooming(in scrollView: UIScrollView) -> UIView? {
    return scrollView.viewWithTag(999)
}
```

This works: the scroll view now responds to pinch gestures by scaling! Recall that in our 30 labels example, the scroll view is not scrollable horizontally. Nevertheless, in this scenario, the width of the content view matters, because when it is scaled up, including during the act of zooming, the user will be able to scroll to see any part of it. So a good policy would be for the content view to embrace its content quite tightly.

The user can actually scale considerably beyond the limits we set in both directions; in that case, when the gesture ends, the scale snaps back to the limit value. If we wish to confine scaling strictly to our defined limits, we can set the scroll view's bounces-Zoom to false; when the user reaches a limit, scaling will simply stop.

If the minimumZoomScale is less than 1, then when the scalable view becomes smaller than the scroll view, it is pinned to the scroll view's top left. If you don't like this, you can change it by subclassing UIScrollView and overriding layoutSubviews, or by implementing the scroll view delegate method scrollViewDidZoom(_:). Here's a simple example (drawn from a WWDC 2010 video) demonstrating an override of layoutSubviews that keeps the scalable view centered in either dimension whenever it is smaller than the scroll view in that dimension:

```
override func layoutSubviews() {
    super.layoutSubviews()
    if let v = self.delegate?.viewForZooming?(in:self) {
        let svw = self.bounds.width
        let svh = self.bounds.height
        let vw = v.frame.width
```

```
            let vh = v.frame.height
            var f = v.frame
            if vw < svw {
                f.origin.x = (svw - vw) / 2.0
            } else {
                f.origin.x = 0
            }
            if vh < svh {
                f.origin.y = (svh - vh) / 2.0
            } else {
                f.origin.y = 0
            }
            v.frame = f
        }
    }
```

Zooming is, in reality, the application of a scale transform to the scalable view. This has two important consequences that can surprise you if you're unprepared:

The `frame` *of the scalable view*
The frame of the scalable view is scaled to match the current `zoomScale`. This follows as a natural consequence of applying a scale transform to the scalable view.

The `contentSize` *of the scroll view*
The scroll view is concerned to make scrolling continue to work correctly: the limits as the user scrolls should continue to match the limits of the content, and commands like `scrollRectToVisible(_:animated:)` should continue to work the same way for the same values. Therefore, the scroll view automatically scales its own `contentSize` to match the current `zoomScale`.

Zooming Programmatically

To zoom programmatically, you have two choices:

`zoomTo(_:animated:)`
Zooms so that the given rectangle of the content occupies as much as possible of the scroll view's bounds. The `contentOffset` is automatically adjusted to keep the content occupying the entire scroll view.

`setZoomScale(_:animated:)`
Zooms in terms of scale value. The `contentOffset` is automatically adjusted to keep the current center centered, with the content occupying the entire scroll view.

In this example, I implement double tapping as a zoom gesture. In my action method for the double tap UITapGestureRecognizer attached to the scalable view, a double tap means to zoom to maximum scale, minimum scale, or actual size, depending on the current scale value:

```
@IBAction func tapped(_ tap : UIGestureRecognizer) {
    let v = tap.view!
    let sv = v.superview as! UIScrollView
    if sv.zoomScale < 1 {
        sv.setZoomScale(1, animated:true)
        let pt = CGPoint((v.bounds.width - sv.bounds.width)/2.0,0)
        sv.setContentOffset(pt, animated:false)
    }
    else if sv.zoomScale < sv.maximumZoomScale {
        sv.setZoomScale(sv.maximumZoomScale, animated:true)
    }
    else {
        sv.setZoomScale(sv.minimumZoomScale, animated:true)
    }
}
```

Zooming with Detail

Sometimes, you may want more from zooming than the mere application of a scale transform to the scaled view. The scaled view's drawing is cached beforehand into its layer, so when we zoom in, the bits of the resulting bitmap are drawn larger. This means that a zoomed-in scroll view's content may be fuzzy (pixellated). You might prefer the content to be redrawn more sharply at its new size.

(On a high-resolution device, this might not be an issue. If the user is allowed to zoom only up to double scale, you can draw at double scale right from the start; the results will look good at single scale, because the screen has high resolution, as well as at double scale, because that's the scale you drew at.)

One solution is to take advantage of a CATiledLayer feature that I didn't mention earlier. It turns out that CATiledLayer is aware not only of scrolling but also of scaling: you can configure it to ask for tiles to be drawn when the layer is scaled to a new order of magnitude. When your drawing routine is called, the graphics context itself has already been scaled by a transform.

In the case of an image into which the user is to be permitted to zoom deeply, you might be forearmed with multiple tile sets constituting the image, each set having double the tile size of the previous set (as in Apple's PhotoScroller example). In other cases, you may not need tiles at all; you'll just draw again, at the new resolution.

Besides its tileSize, you'll need to set two additional CATiledLayer properties:

levelsOfDetail
> The number of different resolutions at which you want to redraw, where each level has twice the resolution of the previous level.

levelsOfDetailBias
> The number of levels of detail that are *larger* than single size (1x).

Those two properties work together. To illustrate, suppose we specify two levels of detail. Then we can ask to redraw when zooming to double size (2x) and when zooming back to single size (1x). But that isn't the *only* thing two levels of detail might mean; to complete the meaning, we need to set the `levelsOfDetailBias`. If `levelsOfDetail` is 2, then if we want to redraw when zooming to 2x and when zooming back to 1x, the `levelsOfDetailBias` needs to be 1, because one of those levels is larger than 1x. If we were to leave `levelsOfDetailBias` at 0, the default, we would be saying we want to redraw when zooming to 0.5x and back to 1x — we have two levels of detail but neither is larger than 1x, so one must be smaller than 1x.

The CATiledLayer will ask for a redraw at a higher resolution as soon as the view's size becomes larger than the previous resolution. In other words, if there are two levels of detail with a bias of 1, the layer will be redrawn at 2x as soon as it is zoomed even a little bit larger than 1x. This is an excellent approach, because although a level of detail would look blurry if scaled up, it looks pretty good scaled down.

Let's say I have a TiledView that hosts a CATiledLayer, in which I intend to draw an image. I haven't broken the image into tiles, because the maximum size at which the user can view it isn't prohibitively large; the original image happens to be 838×958, and can be held in memory easily. Rather, I'm using a CATiledLayer in order to take advantage of its ability to change resolutions automatically. The image will be drawn initially at less than quarter-size (namely 208×238), and we will permit the user to zoom in to the full size of the image. If the user never zooms in to view the image larger than the initial display, we will be saving a considerable amount of memory; if the user does zoom in, that will cost us more memory, but we have determined that this won't be prohibitive.

The CATiledLayer is configured like this:

```
let scale = lay.contentsScale
lay.tileSize = CGSize(208*scale,238*scale)
lay.levelsOfDetail = 3
lay.levelsOfDetailBias = 2
```

The `tileSize` has been adjusted for screen resolution, so the result is:

- As originally displayed at 208×238, there is one tile and we can draw our image at quarter size.

- If the user zooms in, to show the image larger than its originally displayed size, there will be 4 tiles and we can draw our image at half size.

- If the user zooms in still further, to show the image larger than double its originally displayed size (416×476), there will be 16 tiles and we can draw our image at full size, which will continue to look good as the user zooms all the way in to the full size of the original image.

We don't need to draw each tile individually. Each time we're called upon to draw a tile, we'll draw the entire image into the TiledView's bounds; whatever falls outside the requested tile will be clipped out and won't be drawn.

Here's my TiledView's draw(_:) implementation. I have an Optional UIImage property currentImage, initialized to nil, and a CGSize property currentSize initialized to .zero. Each time draw(_:) is called, I compare the tile size (the incoming rect parameter's size) to currentSize. If it's different, I know that we've changed by one level of detail and we need a new version of currentImage, so I create the new version of currentImage at a scale appropriate to this level of detail. Finally, I draw currentImage into the TiledView's bounds:

```
override func drawRect(rect: CGRect) {
    let (lay, bounds) = DispatchQueue.main.sync {
        return (self.layer as! CATiledLayer, self.bounds)
    }
    let oldSize = self.currentSize
    if !oldSize.equalTo(rect.size) {
        // make a new size
        self.currentSize = rect.size
        // make a new image
        let tr = UIGraphicsGetCurrentContext()!.ctm
        let sc = tr.a/lay.contentsScale
        let scale = sc/4.0
        let path = Bundle.main.path(
            forResource: "earthFromSaturn", ofType:"png")!
        let im = UIImage(contentsOfFile:path)!
        let sz = CGSize(im.size.width * scale, im.size.height * scale)
        let f = UIGraphicsImageRendererFormat.default()
        f.opaque = true; f.scale = 1 // *
        let r = UIGraphicsImageRenderer(size: sz, format: f)
        self.currentImage = r.image { _ in
            im.draw(in:CGRect(origin:.zero, size:sz))
        }
    }
    self.currentImage?.draw(in:bounds)
}
```

(The DispatchQueue.main.sync call at the start initializes my local variables lay and bounds on the main thread, even though drawRect is called on a background thread; see Chapter 24.)

An alternative approach (from a WWDC 2011 video) is to make yourself the scroll view's delegate so that you get an event when the zoom ends, and then change the scalable view's contentScaleFactor to match the current zoom scale, compensating for the high-resolution screen at the same time:

```
func scrollViewDidEndZooming(_ scrollView: UIScrollView,
    with view: UIView?, atScale scale: CGFloat) {
        if let view = view {
            scrollView.bounces = self.oldBounces
            view.contentScaleFactor = scale * UIScreen.main.scale // *
        }
    }
}
```

In response, the scalable view's `draw(_:)` will be called, and its `rect` parameter will be the CGRect to draw into. The view may appear fuzzy for a while as the user zooms in, but when the user stops zooming, the view is redrawn sharply. That approach comes with a caveat: you mustn't overdo it. If the zoom scale, screen resolution, and scalable view size are high, you will be asking for a very large graphics context, which could cause your app to use too much memory.

For more about displaying a large image in a zoomable scroll view, see Apple's Large Image Downsizing example.

Scroll View Delegate

The scroll view's delegate (adopting the UIScrollViewDelegate protocol) receives messages that let you track in great detail what the scroll view is up to:

`scrollViewDidScroll(_:)`
> If you scroll in code without animation, you will receive this message *once* afterward. If the user scrolls, either by dragging or with the scroll-to-top feature, or if you scroll in code with animation, you will receive this message *repeatedly* throughout the scroll, including during the time the scroll view is decelerating after the user's finger has lifted; there are other delegate messages that tell you, in those cases, when the scroll has finally ended.

`scrollViewDidEndScrollingAnimation(_:)`
> If you scroll in code with animation, you will receive this message afterward, when the animation ends.

`scrollViewWillBeginDragging(_:)`
`scrollViewWillEndDragging(_:withVelocity:targetContentOffset:)`
`scrollViewDidEndDragging(_:willDecelerate:)`
> If the user scrolls by dragging, you will receive these messages at the start and end of the user's finger movement. If the user brings the scroll view to a stop before lifting the finger, `willDecelerate` is `false` and the scroll is over. If the user lets go of the scroll view while the finger is moving, or when paging is turned on, `willDecelerate` is `true` and we proceed to the delegate messages reporting deceleration.

The purpose of `scrollViewWillEndDragging` is to let you customize the outcome of the content's deceleration. The third argument is a pointer to a CGPoint; you can use it to set a different CGPoint, specifying the `contentOffset` value the scroll view should have when the deceleration is over. By taking the `velocity:` into account, you can allow the user to "fling" the scroll view with momentum before it comes to a halt.

`scrollViewWillBeginDecelerating(_:)`
`scrollViewDidEndDecelerating(_:)`

Sent once each after `scrollViewDidEndDragging(_:willDecelerate:)` arrives with a value of `true`. When `scrollViewDidEndDecelerating(_:)` arrives, the scroll is over.

`scrollViewShouldScrollToTop(_:)`
`scrollViewDidScrollToTop(_:)`

These have to do with the feature where the user can tap the status bar to scroll the scroll view's content to its top. You won't get either of them if `scrollsToTop` is `false`, because the scroll-to-top feature is turned off. The first lets you prevent the user from scrolling to the top on this occasion even if `scrollsToTop` is `true`. The second tells you that the user has employed this feature and the scroll is over.

If you wanted to do something after a scroll ends completely regardless of how the scroll was performed, you'd need to implement multiple delegate methods:

- `scrollViewDidEndDragging(_:willDecelerate:)` in case the user drags and stops (`willDecelerate` is `false`).
- `scrollViewDidEndDecelerating(_:)` in case the user drags and the scroll continues afterward.
- `scrollViewDidScrollToTop(_:)` in case the user uses the scroll-to-top feature.
- `scrollViewDidEndScrollingAnimation(_:)` in case you scroll with animation.

In addition, the scroll view has read-only properties reporting its state:

`isTracking`
The user has touched the scroll view, but the scroll view hasn't decided whether this is a scroll or some kind of tap.

`isDragging`
The user is dragging to scroll.

`isDecelerating`
The user has scrolled and has lifted the finger, and the scroll is continuing.

There are also three delegate messages that report zooming:

`scrollViewWillBeginZooming(_:with:)`

If the user zooms or you zoom in code, you will receive this message as the zoom begins.

`scrollViewDidZoom(_:)`

If you zoom in code, even with animation, you will receive this message *once*. If the user zooms, you will receive this message *repeatedly* as the zoom proceeds. (You will probably also receive `scrollViewDidScroll(_:)`, possibly many times, as the zoom proceeds.)

`scrollViewDidEndZooming(_:with:atScale:)`

If the user zooms or you zoom in code, you will receive this message after the last `scrollViewDidZoom(_:)`.

In addition, the scroll view has read-only properties reporting its state during a zoom:

`isZooming`

The scroll view is zooming. It is possible for `isDragging` to be true at the same time.

`isZoomBouncing`

The scroll view's `bouncesZoom` is `true`, and now it *is* bouncing: it was zoomed beyond its minimum or maximum limit, and now it is returning automatically to that limit. As far as I can tell, you'll get only one `scrollViewDidZoom(_:)` while the scroll view is in this state.

The delegate also receives `scrollViewDidChangeAdjustedContentInset(_:)` when the adjusted content inset changes. This is matched by a method `adjustedContent-InsetDidChange` that can be overridden in a UIScrollView subclass.

Scroll View Touches

Since the early days of iOS, improvements in UIScrollView's internal implementation have eliminated most of the worry once associated with touches inside a scroll view. A scroll view will interpret a drag or a pinch as a command to scroll or zoom, and any other gesture will fall through to the subviews; buttons and similar interface objects inside a scroll view work just fine.

You can even put a scroll view inside a scroll view, and this can be a useful thing to do, in contexts where you might not think of it at first. Apple's PhotoScroller example, based on principles discussed in a delightful WWDC 2010 video, is an app where a single photo fills the screen: you can page-scroll from one photo to the next, and you can zoom into the current photo with a pinch gesture. This is implemented as a scroll view inside a scroll view: the outer scroll view is for paging between images, and the inner scroll view contains the current image and is for zooming (and for scrolling to different parts of the zoomed-in image). Similarly, a WWDC 2013 video deconstructs the iOS 7 lock screen in terms of scroll views embedded in scroll views.

Gesture recognizers (Chapter 5) have also greatly simplified the task of adding custom gestures to a scroll view. For instance, some older code in Apple's documentation, showing how to implement a double tap to zoom in and a two-finger tap to zoom out, used old-fashioned touch handling; but this is no longer necessary. Simply attach to your scroll view's scalable subview any gesture recognizers for these sorts of gesture, and they will mediate automatically among the possibilities.

In the past, making something inside a scroll view draggable required setting the scroll view's `canCancelContentTouches` property to `false`. (The reason for the name is that the scroll view, when it realizes that a gesture is a drag or pinch gesture, normally sends `touchesCancelled(_:with:)` to a subview tracking touches, so that the scroll view and not the subview will be affected.) But unless you're implementing old-fashioned direct touch handling, you probably won't have to concern yourself with this. Regardless of how `canCancelContentTouches` is set, a draggable control, such as a UISlider, remains draggable inside a scroll view.

Here's an example of a draggable object inside a scroll view implemented through a gesture recognizer. Suppose we have an image of a map, larger than the screen, and we want the user to be able to scroll it in the normal way to see any part of the map, but we also want the user to be able to drag a flag into a new location on the map. We'll put the map image in an image view and wrap the image view in a scroll view, with the scroll view's `contentSize` the same as the map image view's size. The flag is a small image view; it's another subview of the scroll view, and it has a UIPan-GestureRecognizer. The pan gesture recognizer's action method allows the flag to be dragged, exactly as described in Chapter 5:

```
@IBAction func dragging (_ p: UIPanGestureRecognizer) {
    let v = p.view!
    switch p.state {
    case .began, .changed:
        let delta = p.translation(in:v.superview!)
        v.center.x += delta.x
        v.center.y += delta.y
        p.setTranslation(.zero, in: v.superview)
    default: break
    }
}
```

The user can now drag the map or the flag (Figure 7-4). Dragging the map brings the flag along with it, but dragging the flag doesn't move the map.

An interesting addition to that example would be to implement *autoscrolling*, meaning that the scroll view scrolls itself when the user drags the flag close to its edge.

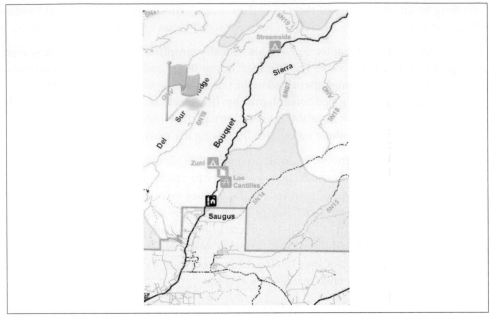

Figure 7-4. A scrollable map with a draggable flag

This, too, is greatly simplified by gesture recognizers; in fact, we can add autoscrolling code directly to the `dragging(_:)` action method:

```
@IBAction func dragging (_ p: UIPanGestureRecognizer) {
    let v = p.view!
    switch p.state {
    case .began, .changed:
        let delta = p.translation(in:v.superview!)
        v.center.x += delta.x
        v.center.y += delta.y
        p.setTranslation(.zero, in: v.superview)
        // autoscroll
        let sv = self.sv!
        let loc = p.location(in:sv)
        let f = sv.bounds
        var off = sv.contentOffset
        let sz = sv.contentSize
        var c = v.center
        // to the right
        if loc.x > f.maxX - 30 {
            let margin = sz.width - sv.bounds.maxX
            if margin > 6 {
                off.x += 5
                sv.contentOffset = off
                c.x += 5
                v.center = c
                self.keepDragging(p)
```

```
                    }
                }
                // to the left
                if loc.x < f.origin.x + 30 {
                    let margin = off.x
                    if margin > 6 {
                        // ...
                    }
                }
                // to the bottom
                if loc.y > f.maxY - 30 {
                    let margin = sz.height - sv.bounds.maxY
                    if margin > 6 {
                        // ...
                    }
                }
                // to the top
                if loc.y < f.origin.y + 30 {
                    let margin = off.y
                    if margin > 6 {
                        // ...
                    }
                }
            }
        default: break
        }
    }
    func keepDragging (_ p: UIPanGestureRecognizer) {
        let del = 0.1
        delay(del) {
            self.dragging(p)
        }
    }
}
```

The `delay` in `keepDragging` (see Appendix B), combined with the change in offset, determines the speed of autoscrolling. The material omitted in the second, third, and fourth cases is obviously parallel to the first case, and is left as an exercise for the reader.

A scroll view's touch handling is itself based on gesture recognizers attached to the scroll view, and these are available to your code through the scroll view's `panGesture-Recognizer` and `pinchGestureRecognizer` properties. This means that if you want to customize a scroll view's touch handling, it's easy to add more gesture recognizers and mediate between them and the gesture recognizers already attached to the scroll view.

To illustrate, I'll build on the previous example. Suppose we want the flag to start out offscreen, and we'd like the user to be able to summon it with a rightward swipe. We can attach a UISwipeGestureRecognizer to our scroll view, but it will never recognize its gesture because the scroll view's own pan gesture recognizer will recognize first.

But we have access to the scroll view's pan gesture recognizer, so we can compel it to yield to our swipe gesture recognizer by sending it `require(toFail:)`:

```
self.sv.panGestureRecognizer.require(toFail:self.swipe)
```

The UISwipeGestureRecognizer can now recognize a rightward swipe. The flag has been waiting invisibly offscreen; in the gesture recognizer's action method, we position the flag just off to the top left of the scroll view's visible content and animate it onto the screen. We then disable the swipe gesture recognizer; its work is done:

```swift
@IBAction func swiped (_ g: UISwipeGestureRecognizer) {
    let sv = self.sv!
    let p = sv.contentOffset
    self.flag.frame.origin = p
    self.flag.frame.origin.x -= self.flag.bounds.width
    self.flag.isHidden = false
    UIView.animate(withDuration:0.25) {
        self.flag.frame.origin.x = p.x
        // thanks for the flag, now stop operating altogether
        g.isEnabled = false
    }
}
```

Floating Scroll View Subviews

A scroll view's subview will appear to "float" over the scroll view if it remains stationary while the rest of the scroll view's content is being scrolled.

Before autolayout, this sort of thing was rather tricky to arrange; you had to use a delegate event to respond to every change in the scroll view's bounds origin by shifting the "floating" view's position to compensate, so as to appear to remain fixed. With autolayout, an easy solution is to set up constraints pinning the subview to something *outside* the scroll view. Even better, the scroll view itself provides a `frameLayoutGuide`; pin a subview to that, to make the subview stand still while the scroll view scrolls.

In this example, the image view is a subview of the scroll view that doesn't move during scrolling:

```swift
let iv = UIImageView(image:UIImage(named:"smiley"))
iv.translatesAutoresizingMaskIntoConstraints = false
self.sv.addSubview(iv)
let svflg = self.sv.frameLayoutGuide
NSLayoutConstraint.activate([
    iv.rightAnchor.constraint(equalTo:svflg.rightAnchor, constant: -5),
    iv.topAnchor.constraint(equalTo:svflg.topAnchor, constant: 25)
])
```

Scroll View Performance

Several times in earlier chapters I've mentioned performance problems and ways to increase drawing efficiency. The likeliest place to encounter such issues is in connection with a scroll view. As a scroll view scrolls, views must be drawn very rapidly as they appear on the screen. If the drawing system can't keep up with the speed of the scroll, the scrolling will visibly stutter.

Performance testing and optimization is a big subject, so I can't tell you exactly what to do if you encounter stuttering while scrolling. But certain general suggestions, mostly extracted from a really great WWDC 2010 video, should come in handy (and see also "Layer Efficiency" on page 156, some of which I'm repeating here):

- Everything that can be opaque should be opaque: don't force the drawing system to composite transparency, and remember to tell it that an opaque view or layer *is* opaque by setting its isOpaque property to true. If you really must composite transparency, keep the size of the nonopaque regions to a minimum.

- If you're drawing shadows, don't make the drawing system calculate the shadow shape for a layer: supply a shadowPath, or use Core Graphics to create the shadow with a drawing. Similarly, avoid making the drawing system composite the shadow as a transparency against another layer; if the background layer is white, your opaque drawing can itself include a shadow already drawn on a white background.

- Don't make the drawing system scale images for you; supply the images at the target size for the correct resolution.

- Coalesce layers (including views). The fewer layers constitute the render tree, the less work the drawing system has to do in order to render them.

- In a pinch, you can just eliminate massive swatches of the rendering operation by setting a layer's shouldRasterize to true. You could do this when scrolling starts and then set it back to false when scrolling ends.

Apple's documentation also says that setting a view's clearsContextBeforeDrawing to false may make a difference. I can't confirm or deny this; it may be true, but I haven't encountered a case that positively proves it.

Xcode provides tools that will help you detect inefficiencies in the drawing system. In the Simulator, the Debug menu shows you blended layers (where transparency is being composited) and images that are being copied, misaligned, or rendered off-screen, and the Xcode Debug → View Debugging → Rendering hierarchical menu provides even more options. On a device, the Core Animation template of Instruments tracks the frame rate for you, allowing you to measure performance objectively while scrolling.

CHAPTER 8

Table Views and Collection Views

I'm gonna ask you the three big questions. — Go ahead. — Who made you? — You did. —
Who owns the biggest piece of you? — You do. — What would happen if I dropped you? —
I'd go right down the drain.
—Dialogue by Garson Kanin
and Ruth Gordon,
Pat and Mike

A table view (UITableView) is a vertically scrolling UIScrollView (Chapter 7) containing a single column of rectangular cells. Each cell is a UITableViewCell, a UIView subclass. A table view has three main purposes:

Information
> The cells constitute a list, which will often be text. The cells are usually quite small, in order to maximize the quantity appearing on the screen at once, so the information may be condensed, truncated, or summarized.

Choice
> The cells may represent choices. The user chooses by tapping a cell, which selects the cell; the app responds appropriately to that choice.

Navigation
> The response to the user's choosing a cell might be navigation to another interface.

An extremely common configuration is a *master–detail interface*, a navigation interface where the master view is a table view (Chapter 6): the user taps a table view cell to navigate to the details about that cell. This is one reason why the information in a table view cell can be a summary: to see the full information, the user can ask for the detail view. Figure 6-1 is an example.

In addition to its column of cells, a table view can have a number of other features:

- A table can include a header view at the top and a footer view at the bottom.

- The cells can be clumped into sections. Each section can have a header and a footer, which may explain the section and tell the user where we are within the table.

- If the table has sections, a section index can be provided as an overlay column of abbreviated section titles, which the user can tap or drag to jump to the start of a section; this makes a long table tractable.

- Tables can be editable: the user can be permitted to insert, delete, and reorder cells, and to edit information within a cell.

- Cells can have actions: the user can swipe a cell sideways to reveal buttons that act in relation to that cell.

- Cells can have menus: the user can long press a cell to pop up a menu with tappable menu items.

- A table can have a grouped format, where the cells are embedded into a common background that includes the section header and footer information. This format is often used for clumping small numbers of related cells, with explanations provided by the headers and footers.

Table view cells themselves can be extremely flexible. Some basic cell formats are provided, such as a text label along with a small image view, but you are free to design your own cell as you would any other view. There are also some standard interface items that are commonly used in a cell, such as a checkmark to indicate selection, or a right-pointing chevron to indicate that tapping the cell navigates to a detail view.

Figure 8-1 shows a familiar table view: Apple's Music app. Each table cell displays a song's name and artist, in truncated form; the user can tap to play the song. The table is divided into sections; as the user scrolls, the current section header stays pinned to the top of the table view.

Figure 8-2 shows a familiar grouped table: Apple's Settings app. It's a master–detail interface. The master view has sections, but they aren't labeled with headers: they merely clump related topics. The detail view sometimes has just a single cell per section, using section headers and footers to explain what that cell does.

It would be difficult to overstate the importance of table views. An iOS app without a table view somewhere in its interface would be a rare thing, especially on the small iPhone screen. Indeed, table views are key to the small screen's viability. I've written apps consisting entirely of table views.

It is not uncommon to use a table view even in situations that have nothing particularly table-like about them, simply because it is so convenient. In one of my apps I want the user to be able to choose between three levels of difficulty and two sets of images. In a desktop application I'd probably use radio buttons; but there are no

Figure 8-1. A familiar table view

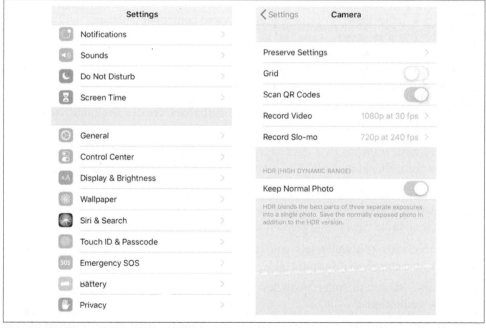

Figure 8-2. A familiar grouped table

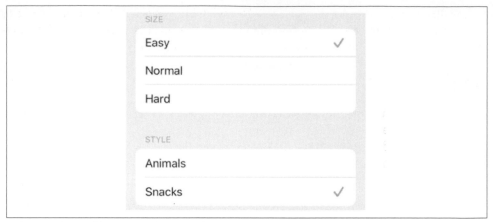

Figure 8-3. A table view as an interface for choosing options

radio buttons among the standard iOS interface objects. Instead, I use a grouped table view so small that it doesn't even scroll. This gives me section headers, tappable cells, and a checkmark indicating the current choice (Figure 8-3).

Table View Controller

In the examples throughout this chapter, I'll use a table view controller in conjunction with a table view. This is a built-in view controller subclass, UITableViewController, whose main view is a table view. You're not obliged to use a UITableViewController with every table view — it doesn't do anything that you couldn't do yourself by other means — but it is certainly convenient. Here are some features of a table view controller:

- UITableViewController's `init(style:)` initializer creates the table view with a plain or grouped format.
- Every table view needs a data source and a delegate (as I'll explain later); a table view controller is its table view's data source and delegate by default.
- The table view is the table view controller's `tableView`. It is also the table view controller's `view`, but the `tableView` property is typed as a UITableView, so you can send table view messages to it without casting down.
- A table view controller lets you configure the layout and content of an entire table in a storyboard (a static table).
- A table view controller provides interface for automatic toggling of its table view's edit mode.

A table view controller is so convenient, in fact, that it might make sense to use one with *every* table view. Suppose a table view is to be a subview of some view controller's main view. That could be a "loose" table view. But it might be better to make the view controller a custom container view controller with a table view controller as its child ("Container View Controllers" on page 375).

Table View Cells

A table view's structure and contents are generally not configured in advance. Rather, you supply the table view with a data source and a delegate (which will often be the same object), and the table view turns to these in real time, as the app runs, whenever it needs a piece of information about its own structure and contents.

This architecture (which might surprise beginners) is part of a brilliant strategy to conserve resources. Imagine a long table consisting of thousands of rows. It must appear to consist of thousands of cells as the user scrolls. But a cell is a UIView; to maintain thousands of cells internally would put a terrible strain on memory. Therefore, the table typically maintains only as many cells as are showing simultaneously at any one moment. As the user scrolls to reveal new cells, those cells are created on the spot; meanwhile, the cells that have been scrolled out of view are permitted to die.

That's ingenious, but wouldn't it be even cleverer if, instead of letting a cell die as it scrolls *out* of view, we whisked it around to the other end and reused it as one of the cells being scrolled *into* view? Yes, and in fact that's exactly what you're supposed to do. You do it by assigning each cell a *reuse identifier*.

As cells with a given reuse identifier are scrolled out of view, the table view maintains a bunch of them in a pile. As a cell is about to be scrolled into view, you ask the table view for a cell from that pile, specifying the pile by means of the reuse identifier. The table view hands an old used cell back to you, and now you can configure it as the cell that is about to be scrolled into view. Cells are *reused* to minimize not only the number of actual cells in existence at any one moment but the number of actual cells *ever created*. A table of 1000 rows might very well never need to create more than about a dozen cells *over the entire lifetime of the app!*

To facilitate this architecture, your code must be prepared, on demand, to supply the table with pieces of requested data. Of these, the most important is the cell to be slotted into a given position. A position in the table is specified by means of an index path (IndexPath), used here to combine a section number with a row number; it is often referred to as a *row* of the table. Your data source object may at any moment be sent the message `tableView(_:cellForRowAt:)`, and you must respond by returning the UITableViewCell to be displayed at that row of the table. And you must return it *fast*: the user is scrolling *now*, so the table needs that cell *now*.

Built-In Cell Styles

A simple way to obtain a table view cell is to start with one of the four built-in table view cell styles. A cell using a built-in style is created by calling `init(style:reuseIdentifier:)`. The `reuseIdentifier:` is what allows cells previously assigned to rows that are no longer showing to be reused for cells that are; it will usually be the same for all cells in a table. Your choices of cell style (UITableViewCell.CellStyle) are:

`.default`
> The cell has a UILabel (its `textLabel`), with an optional UIImageView (its `imageView`) at the left. If there is no image, the label occupies the width of the cell.

`.value1`
> The cell has two UILabels (its `textLabel` and its `detailTextLabel`) side by side, with an optional UIImageView (its `imageView`) at the left. The first label is left-aligned; the second label is right-aligned. If the first label's text is too long, the second label won't appear.

`.value2`
> The cell has two UILabels (its `textLabel` and its `detailTextLabel`) side by side. No UIImageView will appear. The first label is right-aligned; the second label is left-aligned. The label sizes are fixed, and the text of either will be truncated if it's too long.

`.subtitle`
> The cell has two UILabels (its `textLabel` and its `detailTextLabel`), one above the other, with an optional UIImageView (its `imageView`) at the left.

To experiment with the built-in cell styles, do this:

1. Start with the Single View App template.

2. We're going to ignore the storyboard ("App Without a Storyboard" on page 6). So we need a class to serve as our root view controller. Choose File → New → File and specify iOS → Source → Cocoa Touch Class. Click Next.

3. Make this class a UITableViewController subclass called RootViewController. The XIB checkbox should be *checked*; Xcode will create an eponymous *.xib* file containing a table view, correctly configured with its File's Owner as our RootViewController class. Click Next.

4. Make sure you're saving into the correct folder and group, and that the app target is checked. Click Create.

5. Rewrite SceneDelegate's `scene(_:willConnectTo:options:)` to make our RootViewController the window's `rootViewController`:

```
    if let windowScene = scene as? UIWindowScene {
        self.window = UIWindow(windowScene: windowScene)
        self.window!.rootViewController = RootViewController()
        self.window!.backgroundColor = .white
        self.window!.makeKeyAndVisible()
    }
```

6. Now modify the RootViewController class (which comes with a lot of templated code), as in Example 8-1.

Example 8-1. Basic table data source schema

```
let cellID = "Cell"
override func numberOfSections(in tableView: UITableView) -> Int {
    return 1 ❶
}
override func tableView(_ tableView: UITableView,
    numberOfRowsInSection section: Int) -> Int {
        return 20 ❷
}
override func tableView(_ tableView: UITableView,
    cellForRowAt indexPath: IndexPath) -> UITableViewCell {
        var cell : UITableViewCell! = tableView.dequeueReusableCell(
            withIdentifier: self.cellID) ❸
        if cell == nil {
            cell = UITableViewCell(style:.default,
                reuseIdentifier: self.cellID) ❹
            cell.textLabel!.textColor = .red ❺
        }
        cell.textLabel!.text = "Hello there! \(indexPath.row)" ❻
        return cell
}
```

The key parts of the code are:

❶ Our table will have one section.

❷ Our table will consist of 20 rows. Having multiple rows will give us a sense of how our cell looks when placed among other cells.

❸ In tableView(_:cellForRowAt:), you should *always* start by asking the table view for a reusable cell. Here, we will receive either an already existing reused cell or nil.

❹ If we received nil, we create the cell from scratch, ourselves. This is where you specify the built-in table view cell style you want to experiment with.

Figure 8-4. The world's simplest table

❺ At this point in the code you can modify characteristics of the cell (`cell`) that are to be the same for *every* cell of the table. For the moment, I've symbolized this by assuming that every cell's text is to be the same color.

❻ We now have the cell to be used for *this* row of the table, so at this point in the code you can modify features of the cell (`cell`) that are unique to this row. I've symbolized this by appending the row number to the text of each row.

Run the app to see the world's simplest table (Figure 8-4).

Now you can experiment with your cell's appearance by tweaking the code and running the app. Feel free to try different built-in cell styles in the place where we are now specifying `.default`.

Label features

Our built-in cell style's `textLabel` is a UILabel, so further flexibility within each built-in style comes from the flexibility of a label. Not everything can be customized, because after you return the cell some further configuration takes place, which may override your settings; for instance, the size and position of the cell's subviews are not up to you. (I'll explain, a little later, how to get around that.) But you get a remarkable degree of freedom. Here are a few basic UILabel properties for you to play with now, and I'll talk much more about UILabels in Chapter 10:

`text`
> The string shown in the label.

`textColor`, `highlightedTextColor`
> The color of the text. The `highlightedTextColor` applies when the cell is highlighted or selected (tap on a cell to select it).

`textAlignment`
> How the text is aligned; some possible choices (NSTextAlignment) are `.left`, `.center`, and `.right`.

numberOfLines

> The maximum number of lines of text to appear in the label. Text that is long but permitted to wrap, or that contains explicit linefeed characters, can appear completely in the label if the label is tall enough and the number of permitted lines is sufficient. 0 means there's no maximum; the default is 1.

font

> The label's font. You could reduce the font size as a way of fitting more text into the label. A font name includes its style:
>
> ```
> cell.textLabel!.font = UIFont(name:"Helvetica-Bold", size:12.0)
> ```

shadowColor, shadowOffset

> The text shadow. Adding a little shadow can increase clarity and emphasis for large text.

Image view features

You can also assign the image view (cell.imageView) an image. The frame of the image view can't be changed, but you can inset its apparent size by supplying a smaller image and setting the image view's contentMode to .center. It's a good idea in any case, for performance reasons, to supply images at their drawn size and resolution rather than making image views scale them down for you (see "UIImage Drawing" on page 100).

Cell features

The cell itself also has some properties you can play with:

accessoryType

> A built-in type (UITableViewCell.AccessoryType) of accessory view, which appears at the cell's right end:
>
> ```
> cell.accessoryType = .disclosureIndicator
> ```

accessoryView

> Your own UIView, which appears at the cell's right end (overriding the accessoryType):
>
> ```
> let b = UIButton(type:.system)
> b.setTitle("Tap Me", for:.normal)
> b.sizeToFit()
> // ... add action and target here ...
> cell.accessoryView = b
> ```

indentationLevel, indentationWidth

> These properties give the cell a left margin, useful for suggesting a hierarchy among cells. You can also set a cell's indentation level in real time, with respect

to the table row into which it is slotted, by implementing the delegate's `table-View(_:indentationLevelForRowAt:)` method.

`separatorInset`

This property affects both the drawing of the separator between cells and the indentation of content of the built-in cell styles. A UIEdgeInsets; only the left and right insets matter. The default is a left inset of 15, but the built-in table view cell styles may shift it to match the left layout margin of the root view (16 or 20).

`selectionStyle`

How the background looks when the cell is selected (UITableViewCell.Selection-Style). The default is solid gray (`.default`), or you can choose `.none`. Solid colors of cell subviews can obscure the default gray.

`backgroundColor`
`backgroundView`
`selectedBackgroundView`

What's behind everything else drawn in the cell. Solid colors of cell subviews can obscure any of these. The `selectedBackgroundView` is drawn in front of the `backgroundView` (if any) when the cell is selected, and will appear instead of whatever the `selectionStyle` dictates. The `backgroundColor` is behind the `backgroundView`. There is no need to set the frame of the `backgroundView` and `selectedBackgroundView`; they will be resized automatically to fit the cell.

`multipleSelectionBackgroundView`

If the table's `allowsMultipleSelection` or `allowsMultipleSelectionDuring-Editing` is `true`, used instead of the `selectedBackgroundView` when the cell is selected.

In this example, we set the cell's `backgroundView` to display an image with some transparency at the outside edges, so that the `backgroundColor` shows behind it, and we set the `selectedBackgroundView` to an almost transparent blue rectangle, to darken that image when the cell is selected (Figure 8-5):

```
cell.textLabel!.textColor = .white
let v = UIImageView() // no need to set frame
v.contentMode = .scaleToFill
v.image = UIImage(named:"linen")
cell.backgroundView = v
let v2 = UIView() // no need to set frame
v2.backgroundColor = UIColor.blue.withAlphaComponent(0.2)
cell.selectedBackgroundView = v2
cell.backgroundColor = .red
```

Figure 8-5. A cell with an image background

If those features are to be true of every cell ever displayed in the table, then that code should go in the spot numbered 5 in Example 8-1; it would be wasteful to do the same thing all over again when an existing cell is reused.

Table view features

Finally, here are a few properties of the table view itself worth playing with:

rowHeight
> The height of every cell. Taller cells may accommodate more information. You can also change this value in the nib editor; the table view's row height appears in the Size inspector. With a built-in cell style, the cell's subviews have their autoresizing set so as to compensate correctly. You can also set a cell's height in real time by implementing the delegate's tableView(_:heightForRowAt:) method, so that a table's cells may differ from one another in height (more about that later in this chapter).

separatorStyle, separatorColor
> These can also be set in the nib. Separator styles (UITableViewCell.Separator-Style) are .none and .singleLine.

separatorInset, separatorInsetReference
> These can also be set in the nib. The table view's separatorInset is adopted by individual cells that don't have their own explicit separatorInset; to put it another way, the table view's separatorInset is the default, but a cell can override it.
>
> The separatorInsetReference (introduced in iOS 11) determines how the separator inset is understood, either .fromCellEdges or .fromAutomaticReference (meaning from the margins). The default is .fromCellEdges.

backgroundColor, backgroundView
> What's behind all the cells of the table; this may be seen if the cells have transparency, or if the user scrolls the cells beyond their limit. The backgroundView is drawn on top of the backgroundColor.

`tableHeaderView`, `tableFooterView`

> Views to be shown before the first row and after the last row, respectively, as part of the table's scrolling content. You must dictate their heights explicitly, by setting their frame or bounds height; their widths will be dynamically resized to fit the table. You can allow the user to interact with these views (and their subviews); for example, a view can be (or can contain) a UIButton.
>
> You can alter a table header or footer view dynamically during the lifetime of the app; if you change its height, you must set the corresponding table view property afresh to notify the table view of what has happened.

`insetsContentViewsToSafeArea`

> The cell's contents, such as its `textLabel`, are inside an unseen view called the `contentView`; those contents are positioned with respect to the content view's bounds. If this property is `true` (the default), the safe area insets will inset the frame of the content view; that's significant in landscape on an iPhone without a bezel, such as the iPhone X. (The `backgroundColor` and `backgroundView` are *not* inset by the safe area insets.)

`cellLayoutMarginsFollowReadableWidth`

> If this property is `true`, the content view margins will be inset on a wide screen (such as an iPad in landscape) to prevent text content from becoming overly wide. Starting in iOS 12, the default is `false`.

Registering a Cell Class

In Example 8-1, I used this method to obtain the reusable cell:

- `dequeueReusableCell(withIdentifier:)`

But there's a better way:

- `dequeueReusableCell(withIdentifier:for:)`

The *outward* difference is that the second method has a second parameter — an IndexPath. But that's mere boilerplate; you received an index path as the last parameter of `tableView(_:cellForRowAt:)`, and you'll just pass it along as the second parameter here. The *functional* difference is very dramatic:

The result is never `nil`

> Unlike `dequeueReusableCell(withIdentifier:)`, the value returned by `dequeueReusableCell(withIdentifier:for:)` is never `nil` (in Swift, it isn't an Optional). If there is a free reusable cell with the given identifier, it is returned. If there isn't, a new one is created for you, automatically. Step 4 of Example 8-1 can be eliminated!

The cell size is known earlier

Unlike `dequeueReusableCell(withIdentifier:)`, the cell returned by `dequeue-ReusableCell(withIdentifier:for:)` has its final bounds. That's possible because you've passed the index path as an argument, so the runtime knows this cell's ultimate destination within the table, and has already consulted the table's `rowHeight` or the delegate's `tableView(_:heightForRowAt:)`. This can make laying out the cell's contents much easier.

The identifier is consistent

A danger with `dequeueReusableCell(withIdentifier:)` is that you may accidentally pass an incorrect reuse identifier and end up not reusing cells. With `dequeueReusableCell(withIdentifier:for:)`, that can't happen (for reasons that I will now explain).

Those are powerful advantages, and for that reason I suggest always using `dequeue-ReusableCell(withIdentifier:for:)`. This will mean that Example 8-1 is wrong and will have to be modified; in a moment, that's just what I'll do. But first we need to talk about some more implications of using `dequeueReusableCell(with-Identifier:for:)`.

Let's go back to the first advantage of `dequeueReusableCell(withIdentifier:for:)` — if there isn't a reusable cell with the given identifier, *the table view will create the cell;* you never instantiate the cell yourself. But how does the table view know how to do that? You have to tell it in advance, associating the reuse identifier with the correct means of instantiation. There are three possibilities:

Provide a class

You *register* a class with the table view, associating that class with the reuse identifier. The table view will instantiate that class.

Provide a nib

You *register* a .xib file with the table view, associating that nib with the reuse identifier. The table view will load the nib to instantiate the cell.

Provide a storyboard

If you're getting the cell from a storyboard, you *don't* register anything with the table view; instead, you associate the cell in the storyboard with the reuse identifier by entering that reuse identifier in the Identifier field of the cell's Attributes inspector. The table view will instantiate the cell from the storyboard.

In my examples so far, we're not using a storyboard (I'll discuss that approach later). So let's use the first approach: we'll *register a class* with the table view. To do so, before we call `dequeueReusableCell(withIdentifier:for:)` for the first time, we call `register(_:forCellReuseIdentifier:)`, where the first parameter is the UITableViewCell class or a subclass thereof. That will associate this class with our reuse identifier. It will also add a measure of safety, because henceforth if we pass a bad identifier into `dequeueReusableCell(withIdentifier:for:)`, the app will crash (with a helpful log message); we are forcing ourselves to reuse cells properly.

This is a very elegant mechanism. It also raises some new questions:

When should I register with the table view?

Do it early, before the table view starts generating cells; `viewDidLoad` is a good place:

```
let cellID = "Cell"
override func viewDidLoad() {
    super.viewDidLoad()
    self.tableView.register(
        UITableViewCell.self, forCellReuseIdentifier: self.cellID)
}
```

How do I specify a built-in table view cell style?

We are no longer calling `init(style:reuseIdentifier:)`, so where do we make our choice of built-in cell style? The default cell style is `.default`, so if that's what you wanted, the problem is solved. Otherwise, subclass UITableViewCell and register the subclass; in the subclass, override `init(style:reuseIdentifier:)` to substitute the cell style you're after (passing along the reuse identifier you were handed).

Suppose we want the `.subtitle` style. Let's call our UITableViewCell subclass MyCell. So we now specify `MyCell.self` in our call to `register(_:forCell-ReuseIdentifier:)`. MyCell's initializer looks like this:

```
override init(style: UITableViewCell.CellStyle,
    reuseIdentifier: String?) {
        super.init(style:.subtitle, reuseIdentifier: reuseIdentifier)
}
```

How do I know whether the returned cell is new or reused?

Good question! `dequeueReusableCell(withIdentifier:for:)` never returns `nil`, so we need some *other* way to distinguish between configurations that are to apply once and for all to a *new cell* (step 5 of Example 8-1) and configurations that differ for *each row* (step 6). It's up to you, when performing one-time configuration on a cell, to give that cell some distinguishing mark that you can look for later to determine whether a cell requires one-time configuration.

Suppose every cell is to have a two-line text label. Then there is no point configuring the text label of *every* cell returned by `dequeueReusableCell(with-Identifier:for:)` to have two lines; the reused cells have already been configured. But how will we know which cells need their text label to be configured? It's easy: they are the ones whose text label *hasn't* been configured:

```
override func tableView(_ tableView: UITableView,
    cellForRowAt indexPath: IndexPath) -> UITableViewCell {
        let cell = tableView.dequeueReusableCell(
            withIdentifier: self.cellID, for: indexPath) as! MyCell
        if cell.textLabel!.numberOfLines != 2 { // not configured!
            cell.textLabel!.numberOfLines = 2
            // other one-time configurations here ...
        }
        cell.textLabel!.text = // ...
        // other individual configurations here ...
        return cell
}
```

We are now ready to rewrite Example 8-1 to use `dequeueReusableCell(with-Identifier:for:)`. The result is Example 8-2.

Example 8-2. Basic table data source schema, revised

```
let cellID = "Cell"
override func viewDidLoad() {
    super.viewDidLoad()
    self.tableView.register(
        UITableViewCell.self, forCellReuseIdentifier: self.cellID) ❶
}
override func numberOfSections(in tableView: UITableView) -> Int {
    return 1 ❷
}
override func tableView(_ tableView: UITableView,
    numberOfRowsInSection section: Int) -> Int {
        return 20 ❸
}
override func tableView(_ tableView: UITableView,
    cellForRowAt indexPath: IndexPath) -> UITableViewCell {
        let cell = tableView.dequeueReusableCell(
            withIdentifier: self.cellID, for: indexPath) ❹
        if cell.textLabel!.numberOfLines != 2 { ❺
            cell.textLabel!.numberOfLines = 2
            // ... other universal configurations here ...
        }
        cell.textLabel!.text = "Hello there! \(indexPath.row)" ❻
        // ... other individual configurations here ...
        return cell
}
```

❶ Register the cell identifier with the table view. No law requires that this be done in viewDidLoad, but it's a good place because it's called once, early. (This step *must be omitted* if the cell is to come from a storyboard, as I'll explain later.)

❷ Give the number of sections our table is to have.

❸ Give the number of rows each section is to have.

❹ Call `dequeueReusableCell(withIdentifier:for:)` to obtain a cell for this reuse identifier, passing along the incoming index path. If the registered cell class is a UITableViewCell subclass, you'll probably need to cast down here; this is a situation where a forced downcast is justified, because if the cast fails something is very wrong and we can't proceed.

❺ If there are configurations to be performed that are the same for *every* cell, look to see whether *this* cell has already been configured. If not, configure it.

❻ Modify features of the cell that are *unique to this row*, and return the cell.

Custom Cells

In real life it is unusual to rest content with the built-in cell styles. They give the beginner a leg up in getting started with table views, but there is nothing sacred about them, and soon you'll surely want to transcend them, putting yourself in charge of how a table's cells look and what subviews they contain. You want a *custom cell*.

Keep in mind, as you design your custom cell, that the cell has a `contentView` property, which is one of its subviews; things like the `accessoryView` are outside the `contentView`, but all *your* custom subviews must be subviews of the `contentView`. This allows the cell to continue working correctly.

 As long as you never speak of the cell's `textLabel`, `detailTextLabel`, or `image-View`, they are never created or inserted into the cell. You don't need to remove them if you don't want to use them.

I'll illustrate four possible approaches to customizing the contents of a cell:

- Start with a built-in cell style, but supply a UITableViewCell subclass and override `layoutSubviews` to alter the frames of the built-in subviews.
- In `tableView(_:cellForRowAt:)`, add subviews to each cell's `contentView` as the cell is created.
- Design the cell in a nib, and load that nib in `tableView(_:cellForRowAt:)` each time a cell needs to be created.
- Design the cell in a storyboard.

Overriding a cell's subview layout

You can't directly change the frame of a built-in cell style subview in `table-View(_:cellForRowAt:)`, because the cell's `layoutSubviews` comes along later and overrides your changes. The workaround is to override the cell's `layoutSubviews`!

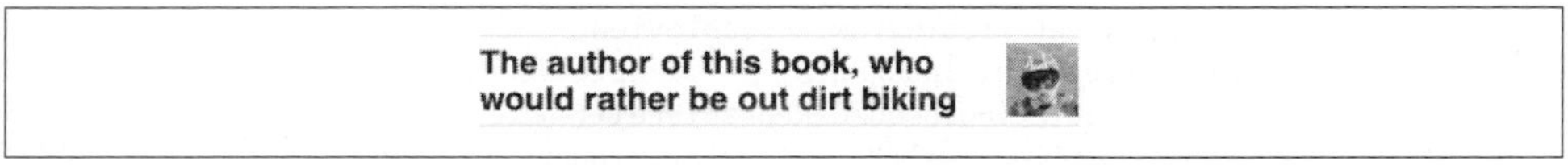

<table>
<tr><td>The author of this book, who
would rather be out dirt biking</td><td></td></tr>
</table>

Figure 8-6. A cell with its label and image view swapped

This is a straightforward solution if your main objection to a built-in style is the frame of an existing subview.

To illustrate, let's modify a .default cell so that the image is at the right end instead of the left end (Figure 8-6). We'll make a UITableViewCell subclass called MyCell; here is MyCell's layoutSubviews:

```
override func layoutSubviews() {
    super.layoutSubviews()
    let cvb = self.contentView.bounds
    let imf = self.imageView!.frame
    self.imageView!.frame.origin.x = cvb.size.width - imf.size.width - 15
    self.textLabel!.frame.origin.x = 15
}
```

We must also make sure to *use* MyCell as our cell type:

```
self.tableView.register(MyCell.self, forCellReuseIdentifier: self.cellID)
```

Adding subviews in code

Instead of modifying the existing default subviews, you can add completely new views to each UITableViewCell's content view. The best place to do this in code is tableView(_:cellForRowAt:). Here are some things to keep in mind:

- The new views must be added when we configure a brand new cell — but not when we reuse a cell, because a reused cell already has them. (Adding multiple copies of the same subview repeatedly, as the cell is reused, is a common beginner mistake.)

- We must never send addSubview(_:) to the cell itself — only to its contentView (or some subview thereof).

- We should assign the new views an appropriate autoresizingMask or constraints, because the cell's content view might be resized.

- Each new view needs a way to be identified and referred to elsewhere. A tag is a simple solution.

I'll rewrite the previous example to use this technique. We don't need a UITableViewCell subclass; the registered cell class can be UITableViewCell itself. If this is a new cell, we add the subviews, position them, and assign them tags. If this is a reused cell, we *don't* add the subviews — the cell already has them! Either way, we then use the tags to refer to the subviews:

```
override func tableView(_ tableView: UITableView,
    cellForRowAt indexPath: IndexPath) -> UITableViewCell {
        let cell = tableView.dequeueReusableCell(
            withIdentifier: self.cellID, for: indexPath)
        if cell.viewWithTag(1) == nil { // no subviews! add them
            let iv = UIImageView(); iv.tag = 1
            cell.contentView.addSubview(iv)
            let lab = UILabel(); lab.tag = 2
            cell.contentView.addSubview(lab)
            // ... position the subviews ...
        }
        // can refer to subviews by their tags
        let lab = cell.viewWithTag(2) as! UILabel
        let iv = cell.viewWithTag(1) as! UIImageView
        // ...
        return cell
}
```

Designing a cell in a nib

We can avoid the verbosity of the previous code by designing the cell in a nib. We start by creating a *.xib* file that will consist, in effect, solely of this one cell; then we design the cell:

1. In Xcode, create the *.xib* file by specifying iOS → User Interface → View. Let's call it *MyCell.xib*.

2. Edit *MyCell.xib*. In the nib editor, delete the existing View and replace it with a Table View Cell from the Library.

   The cell's design window shows a standard-sized cell; you can resize it as desired, but the actual size of the cell in the interface will be dictated by the table view's width and its rowHeight (or the delegate's response to tableView(_:heightFor-RowAt:)). The cell already has a contentView, and any subviews you add will be inside that; do not subvert that arrangement.

3. You can choose a built-in table view cell style in the Style pop-up menu of the Attributes inspector, which gives you the default subviews, locked in their standard positions. But if you set the Style pop-up menu to Custom, you start with a blank slate; let's do that.

4. Design the cell! Let's implement, from scratch, the same subviews we've already implemented in the preceding two examples: a UILabel on the left side of the cell, and a UIImageView on the right side. Just as when adding subviews in code, we should set each subview's autoresizing behavior or constraints, and *give each subview a tag*, so that later, in tableView(_:cellForRowAt:), we'll be able to refer to the label and the image view using viewWithTag(_:), exactly as in the previous example.

The only remaining question is how to load the cell from the nib. It's simple! When we register with the table view, which we're currently doing in `viewDidLoad`, when we call `register(_:forCellReuseIdentifier:)`, we supply a nib instead of a class. To specify the nib, call UINib's initializer `init(nibName:bundle:)`, like this:

```
self.tableView.register(
    UINib(nibName:"MyCell", bundle:nil), forCellReuseIdentifier:self.cellID)
```

That's all there is to it. In `tableView(_:cellForRowAt:)`, when we call `dequeue-ReusableCell(withIdentifier:for:)`, if the table has no free reusable cell already in existence, the nib will automatically be loaded and the cell will be instantiated from it and returned to us.

You may wonder how that's possible, when we haven't specified a File's Owner class or added an outlet from the File's Owner to the cell in the nib. The answer is that the nib conforms to a specific format. The UINib instance method `instantiate(with-Owner:options:)` can load a nib with a `nil` owner, and it returns an array of the nib's instantiated top-level objects. A nib registered with the table view is expected to have exactly one top-level object, and that top-level object is expected to be a UITableViewCell; the cell can easily be extracted from the resulting array, as it is the array's only element. Our nib meets those expectations!

 The nib *must* conform to this format: it must have *exactly* one top-level object, a UITableViewCell. Unfortunately, this means that some configurations are difficult or impossible in the nib. A cell's `backgroundView` cannot be configured in the nib, because this would require the presence of a second top-level nib object. The simplest workaround is to add the `backgroundView` in code.

The advantages of this approach should be immediately obvious. The subviews can now be designed in the nib editor, and code that was creating and configuring each subview can be deleted. All code that sizes and positions our subviews can be removed; we can specify the constraints in the nib editor. If we were configuring the label — assigning it a font, a line break mode, a `numberOfLines` — all of that code can be removed; we can specify those things in the nib editor.

But we can go further. In `tableView(_:cellForRowAt:)`, we are still referring to the cell's subviews by way of `viewWithTag(_:)`. There's nothing wrong with that, but perhaps you'd prefer to use names. Now that we're designing the cell in a nib, that's easy. Provide a UITableViewCell subclass with outlet properties, and configure the nib file accordingly:

1. Create a UITableViewCell subclass — let's call it MyCell — and declare two outlet properties:

```
class MyCell : UITableViewCell {
    @IBOutlet var theLabel : UILabel!
    @IBOutlet var theImageView : UIImageView!
}
```

That is the *entirety* of MyCell's code; it exists solely so that we can create these outlets.

2. Edit the table view cell nib *MyCell.xib*. Change the class of the cell (in the Identity inspector) to MyCell, and connect the outlets from the cell to the respective subviews.

The result is that in our implementation of `tableView(_:cellForRowAt:)`, once we've typed the cell as a MyCell, the compiler will let us use the property names to access the subviews:

```
let cell = tableView.dequeueReusableCell(
    withIdentifier: self.cellID, for: indexPath) as! MyCell // *
let lab = cell.theLabel // *
let iv = cell.theImageView // *
// ... configure lab and iv ...
```

Designing a cell in a storyboard

If your table view is instantiated from a storyboard, then along with all the ways of obtaining and designing its cells that I've already described, there is an additional option. You can have the table view obtain its cells *from the storyboard itself*. This means you can also *design* the cell in the storyboard.

Let's experiment with this way of obtaining and designing a cell:

1. Start with a project based on the Single View App template.

2. In the project, create a file for a UITableViewController subclass called Root-ViewController, *without* a corresponding *.xib* file.

3. In the storyboard, delete the View Controller scene. Drag a Table View Controller into the empty canvas, and set its class to RootViewController. Make sure it's the initial view controller.

4. The table view controller in the storyboard comes with a table view. In the story-board, select that table view, and, in the Attributes inspector, set the Content pop-up menu to Dynamic Prototypes, and set the number of Prototype Cells to 1 (those are the defaults).

The table view in the storyboard now contains a single table view cell with a content view. You can do in this cell exactly what we were doing before when designing a table view cell in a *.xib* file! I like being able to refer to my custom cell subviews with property names, so we'll use a table view cell subclass with outlets. Our procedure is just like what we did in the previous example:

1. In code, declare a UITableViewCell subclass — let's call it MyCell — with two outlet properties:

```
class MyCell : UITableViewCell {
    @IBOutlet var theLabel : UILabel!
    @IBOutlet var theImageView : UIImageView!
}
```

2. In the storyboard, select the table view's prototype cell and change its class in the Identity inspector to MyCell.

3. Drag a label and an image view into the prototype cell, position and configure them as desired, and connect the outlets from the cell to the respective subviews.

So far, so good; but there is one crucial question I have not yet answered: how will you tell the table view to get its cells from the storyboard? The answer is: by *not* calling `register(_:forCellReuseIdentifier:)`! Instead, when you call `dequeueReusableCell(withIdentifier:for:)`, you supply an identifier that matches the *prototype cell's identifier* in the storyboard:

1. If you are calling `register(_:forCellReuseIdentifier:)` in RootView-Controller's code, *delete that line.*

2. In the storyboard, select the prototype cell. In the Attributes inspector, enter `Cell` (or whatever the string value of `self.cellID` is) in the Identifier field.

Now RootViewController's `tableView(_:cellForRowAt:)` works exactly as it did in the previous example:

```
let cell = tableView.dequeueReusableCell(
    withIdentifier: self.cellID, for: indexPath) as! MyCell
let lab = cell.theLabel
let iv = cell.theImageView
```

When your UITableViewController is to get its cells from the UITableView-Controller scene in the storyboard, there are several ways to go wrong. These are all common beginner mistakes:

Wrong view controller class
    In the storyboard, make sure that your UITableViewController's class, in the Identity inspector, matches the class of your UITableViewController subclass in code. If you get this wrong, none of your table view controller code will run.

Wrong cell identifier
    In the storyboard, make sure that the prototype cell identifier matches the reuse identifier in your code's `dequeueReusableCell(withIdentifier:for:)` call. If you get this wrong, your app will crash (with a helpful message in the console).

Wrong cell class

In the storyboard, make sure that your prototype cell's class, in the Identity inspector, is the class you expect to receive from `dequeueReusableCell(with-Identifier:for:)`. If you get this wrong, your app will crash when the cell can't be cast down.

Wrong registration

In your table view controller code, make sure you do *not* call `register(_:for-CellReuseIdentifier:)`. If you do call it, you will be telling the runtime *not* to get the cell from the storyboard. If you get this wrong by registering a nib, then (if you're lucky) your app will crash (with a helpful message in the console). If you get it wrong by registering a class, your cells might be mysteriously empty and your app might even crash when you access outlets that have never been connected.

Table View Data

The structure and content of the actual data portrayed in a table view comes from the *data source*, an object pointed to by the table view's `dataSource` property and adopting the UITableViewDataSource protocol. The data source is the heart and soul of the table. What surprises beginners is that the data source operates not by *setting* the table view's structure and content, but by *responding on demand*. The data source, *qua* data source, consists of a set of methods that the table view will call whenever it needs information; in effect, the table view will ask your data source some questions. This architecture has important consequences for how you write your code, which can be summarized by these simple guidelines:

Be ready

Your data source cannot know *when* or *how often* any of these methods will be called, so it must be prepared to answer *any question at any time*.

Be fast

The table view is asking for data in real time; the user is probably scrolling through the table *right now*. So you mustn't gum up the works; you must be ready to supply responses as fast as possible.

Be consistent

There are multiple data source methods, and you cannot know *which* one will be called at a given moment. So you must make sure your responses are mutually consistent at *any* moment. A common beginner error is forgetting to take into account, in your data source methods, the possibility that the data might not yet be ready.

Another source of confusion for beginners is that methods are rather oddly distributed between the data source and the *delegate*, an object pointed to by the table view's `delegate` property and adopting the UITableViewDelegate protocol; in some cases, one may seem to be doing the job of the other. This is not usually a cause of any real difficulty, because the object serving as data source might also be the object serving as delegate. Nevertheless, it is rather inconvenient when you're consulting the documentation; you'll probably want to keep the data source and delegate documentation pages open simultaneously as you work.

 When you're using a table view controller with a corresponding table view in the storyboard (or in a *.xib* file created at the same time), the table view controller comes to you already configured as both the table view's data source and the table view's delegate. Creating a table view in some other way, and then forgetting to set its `dataSource` and `delegate`, is a common beginner mistake.

The Three Big Questions

Pretend now that you are the data source. Like Katherine Hepburn in *Pat and Mike*, the basis of your success is your ability, at any time, to answer the Three Big Questions; you must know the answers and be able to recite them at any moment:

How many sections does this table have?
The table will call `numberOfSections(in:)`; respond with an integer. In theory you can sometimes omit this method, as the default response is 1, which is often correct. However, I never omit it; for one thing, returning 0 is a good way to say that you've no data yet, and will prevent the table view from asking any other questions.

How many rows does this section have?
The table will call `tableView(_:numberOfRowsInSection:)`. The table supplies a section number — the first section is numbered 0 — and you respond with an integer. In a table with only one section there is probably no need to examine the incoming section number.

What cell goes in this row of this section?
The table will call `tableView(_:cellForRowAt:)`. The index path is expressed as an IndexPath; UITableView extends IndexPath to add two read-only properties — `section` and `row`. Using these, you extract the requested section number and row number, and return a fully configured UITableViewCell, ready for display in the table view. The first row of a section is numbered 0. I have already explained how to obtain the cell in the first place, by calling `dequeueReusableCell(withIdentifier:for:)` (see Example 8-2).

How you're going to fulfill these obligations depends on your data model and what your table is trying to portray. You can acquire and store and arrange your data whenever and however you like. The important thing is that you're going to be receiving an IndexPath specifying a section and a row, and you need to be able to lay your hands on the data corresponding to that slot *now* and configure the cell *now*. So construct your model, and your algorithm for consulting it in the Three Big Questions, in such a way that the data source can access any requested piece of data instantly.

Suppose our table is to list the names of the Pep Boys. Our table has only one section, so our data model can be very simple — an array of string names (`self.pep`). We're using a UITableViewController, and it is the table view's data source. So our code might look like this:

```
let pep = ["Manny", "Moe", "Jack"]
override func numberOfSections(in tableView: UITableView) -> Int {
    return 1
}
override func tableView(_ tableView: UITableView,
    numberOfRowsInSection section: Int) -> Int {
        return self.pep.count
}
override func tableView(_ tableView: UITableView,
    cellForRowAt indexPath: IndexPath) -> UITableViewCell {
        let cell = tableView.dequeueReusableCell(
            withIdentifier: self.cellID, for: indexPath)
        cell.textLabel!.text = pep[indexPath.row]
        return cell
}
```

At this point you may be feeling some exasperation. You want to object: "But that's trivial!" Exactly so! Your access to the data model *should* be trivial. That's the sign of a data model that's well designed for access by your table view's data source. Your implementation of `tableView(_:cellForRowAt:)` might have some interesting work to do in order to configure the *form* of the cell, but accessing the actual *data* should be simple and boring.

Above all, your data source methods must be *fast*. In particular, when `tableView(_:cellForRowAt:)` is called, the user is probably scrolling; you have only a few milliseconds to supply a cell, or else that scrolling will stutter. And the runtime itself is competing with you for those milliseconds, because even after you provide the cell, the runtime must perform layout and drawing on it, which are relatively expensive operations. You may be able to speed up layout and drawing by paying attention to the suggestions in the last section of Chapter 7. You may be able to obtain the data in advance of `tableView(_:cellForRowAt:)` by implementing *prefetching* in your data source. If that's not sufficient, you may have to skip portraying this data in the table, supply a placeholder, and insert the data into the table later. I'll give an example in Chapter 23.

There are two other ways to supply a table view with data; I'll discuss them later in this chapter:

- If the table view's entire structure and contents are known beforehand and won't change, you can design it in a storyboard as a *static* table and omit the Three Big Questions. See "Cell Choice and Static Tables" on page 491.

- New in iOS 13, you can use a *diffable data source* to hold the data and answer the Three Big Questions for you. This is useful especially when the table view's structure and contents can change before the user's eyes. See "Table View Diffable Data Source" on page 502.

Reusing Cells

An important goal of `tableView(_:cellForRowAt:)` is to conserve resources by reusing cells. As I've already explained, once a cell's row is no longer visible on the screen, that cell can be slotted into a row that *is* visible — with its portrayed data appropriately modified, of course! — so that only a few more than the number of simultaneously visible cells will ever need to be instantiated.

A table view is ready to implement this strategy for you; all you have to do is call `dequeueReusableCell(withIdentifier:for:)`. For any given identifier, you'll be handed either a newly minted cell or a reused cell that previously appeared in the table view but is now no longer needed because it has scrolled out of view.

To prove to yourself the efficiency of the cell-caching architecture, do something to differentiate newly instantiated cells from reused cells, and keep track of the newly instantiated cells, like this:

```
override func numberOfSections(in tableView: UITableView) -> Int {
    return 1
}
override func tableView(_ tableView: UITableView,
    numberOfRowsInSection section: Int) -> Int {
        return 1000 // make a lot of rows this time!
}
var cells = 0
override func tableView(_ tableView: UITableView,
    cellForRowAt indexPath: IndexPath) -> UITableViewCell {
    let cell = tableView.dequeueReusableCell(
        withIdentifier: self.cellID, for: indexPath) as! MyCell
    let lab = cell.theLabel!
    lab.text = "Row \(indexPath.row) of section \(indexPath.section)"
    if lab.tag != 999 {
        lab.tag = 999
```

```
        self.cells += 1; print("New cell \(self.cells)")
    }
    return cell
}
```

When we run this code and scroll through the table, every cell is numbered correctly, so there appear to be 1000 cells. But the console messages show that only about a dozen distinct cells are ever actually created.

Be certain that *your* table view code passes that test, and that you are truly reusing cells! Fortunately, one of the benefits of calling `dequeueReusableCell(with-Identifier:for:)` is that it forces you to supply a valid reuse identifier. But it is still possible to subvert the architecture of cell reuse.

(For instance, you might obtain a cell in some improper way, such as instantiating it directly every time `tableView(_:cellForRowAt:)` is called; I have even seen beginners call `dequeueReusableCell(withIdentifier:for:)`, only to throw away that cell and instantiate a fresh cell manually in the next line. Don't do that!)

Forgetting that cells are reused is the *single most common beginner mistake* associated with table views. Typically, everything in the table may look fine at first, but then when the table view is scrolled, incorrect values or incorrect interface will appear in some of the cells. The reason is that the cell you are configuring for a particular row in `tableView(_:cellForRowAt:)` (step 6 in Example 8-2) may already have been configured for some other row. Therefore you must configure *everything* about the cell that might need configuring, with your logic covering *every* possible case, making *no assumptions* about the prior state of the cell. Otherwise, the cell may retain unwanted state from its previous use in a different row.

As usual, I learned that lesson the hard way. (I was a beginner once!) In the TidBITS News app, there was a little loudspeaker icon that should appear in a given cell in the master view's table view only if a recording was associated with this article. So I initially wrote this code:

```
if item.enclosures != nil && item.enclosures.count > 0 {
    cell.speaker.isHidden = false
}
```

At first, everything seemed to be fine; but after scrolling the table view up and down a few times, I ended up with a loudspeaker icon in just about every cell! Do you see why? Once you start scrolling, your cells are likely to be reused. Based on my code, a reused cell will *always* have a visible loudspeaker icon if, in a previous usage, that cell has *ever* had a visible loudspeaker icon!

The solution was to rewrite the logic to *cover all possibilities completely*, like this:

```
cell.speaker.isHidden =
    !(item.enclosures != nil && item.enclosures.count > 0)
```

You do get a sort of second bite of the cherry: there's a delegate method, `table-View(_:willDisplay:forRowAt:)`, that is called for every cell just before it appears in the table. This is absolutely the last minute to configure a cell. But don't misuse this method. You're functioning as the delegate here, not the data source; you may set the final details of the cell's appearance, but you shouldn't be consulting the data model at this point. It is of great importance that you not do anything even slightly time-consuming in `tableView(_:willDisplay:forRowAt:)`; the cell is literally just milliseconds away from appearing in the interface.

An additional delegate method is `tableView(_:didEndDisplaying:forRowAt:)`. This tells you that the cell no longer appears in the interface and has become free for reuse. You could take advantage of this to tear down any resource-heavy customization of the cell or simply to prepare it somehow for subsequent future reuse.

The table view can maintain more than one cache of reusable cells; this could be useful if your table view contains more than one type of cell (where the meaning of "type of cell" is pretty much up to you). This is why you must *name* each cache by attaching a reuse identifier string to each cell. All the examples in this chapter (and in this book, and in fact in every UITableView I've ever created) use just one cache and just one identifier, but there can be more than one. If you're using a storyboard as a source of cells, there would then need to be more than one prototype cell.

Table View Sections

Your table data may be grouped into multiple sections. Here are some reasons why you might do that:

- You want to clump the table cells into groups in the table view.
- You want to display section headers (or footers, or both) in the table view.
- You want to make navigation of the table view easier through an index.
- You want to facilitate rearranging entire portions of the table view contents.

A table that is to have sections may require some planning in the construction and architecture of its data model. In order to answer the Three Big Questions, you need to know immediately how many sections your data has and how many rows a given section has; then, given a section number and a row number, you need to be able to fetch the data for that row. Clearly a simple array of individual row data, like the array of strings listing the names of the Pep Boys in our earlier example, is not going to be sufficient.

A section-based data structure typically needs two levels. A standard minimal approach is an array of sections, each section containing an array of row data, as shown in Example 8-3.

Example 8-3. Section-based data

```
struct Row {
    // properties pertaining to each row
}
struct Section {
    // properties pertaining to each section
    var rowData : [Row]
}
var sections = [Section]() // data model
```

Now the Three Big Questions are easy to answer. The number of sections is `self.sections.count`. The number of rows in the section numbered `section` is `self.sections[section].rowData.count`. And your implementation of `table-View(_:cellForRowAt:)` can index into the section with `indexPath.section`, and from there into the row data with `indexPath.row`:

```
let data = self.sections[indexPath.section].rowData[indexPath.row]
```

The details will depend on the exact nature of your data and what you want to portray in your table. You will very likely want a section-based table view to have section headers, so I'll talk about that before giving an example.

Section Headers and Footers

A section header or footer appears between the cells, before the first row of a section or after the last row of a section, respectively. In a nongrouped table, a section header or footer detaches itself while the user scrolls the table, pinning itself to the top or bottom of the table view and floating over the scrolled rows, giving the user a clue, at every moment, as to where we are within the table. Also, a section header or footer can contain custom views, so it's a place where you might put additional information, or even functional interface, such as a button the user can tap.

 Don't confuse the section headers and footers with the header and footer of the table as a whole. The latter are properties of the table view itself, its `tableHeaderView` and `tableFooterView`, discussed earlier in this chapter. The table header view appears only when the table is scrolled all the way down; the table footer view appears only when the table is scrolled all the way up.

The number of sections is determined by your reply to the first Big Question, `numberOfSections(in:)`. For each section, the table view will consult your data source and delegate to learn whether this section has a header or a footer, or both, or neither (the default).

A section header or footer in the table view will usually be a UITableViewHeaderFooterView. This is a UIView subclass intended specifically for this purpose; much like a table view cell, it is reusable. It has the following properties:

`textLabel`
A label (UILabel) for displaying the text of the header or footer.

`detailTextLabel`
This label, if you set its text, appears only in a grouped style table.

`contentView`
A subview of the header or footer, to which you can add custom subviews.

`backgroundView`
Any view you want to assign. The `contentView` is in front of the `background-View`. The `contentView` has a clear background by default, so the `background-View` shows through.

If the `backgroundView` is `nil` (the default), the header or footer view will supply its own background view whose `backgroundColor` is derived (in some unspecified way) from the table's `backgroundColor`.

 Don't set a UITableViewHeaderFooterView's `backgroundColor`; instead, give it a `backgroundView` and set that view's `backgroundColor`.

There are two ways in which you can supply a header or footer. You can use both, but it will be less confusing if you pick just one:

Header or footer title string
You implement one or both of these data source methods:

- `tableView(_:titleForHeaderInSection:)`
- `tableView(_:titleForFooterInSection:)`

Return `nil` to indicate that the given section has no header (or footer). The header or footer view itself is a UITableViewHeaderFooterView, and is reused automatically. The string you supply becomes the view's `textLabel.text`.

(In a grouped style table, the string's capitalization may be changed. To avoid that, use the second way of supplying the header or footer.)

Header or footer view
You implement one or both of these delegate methods:

- `tableView(_:viewForHeaderInSection:)`
- `tableView( ;viewForFootei InSection:)`

The view you supply is used as the entire header or footer and is automatically resized to the table's width and the section header or footer height. (I'll discuss in a moment how the height is determined.)

It would be great to be able to design a table view section header (or footer) view in the nib editor — but you can't. That's because of a massive shortcoming in Xcode: The nib editor's Library doesn't include a UITableViewHeaderFooterView!

The irony is that there's a UITableView method that *would* allow you to do this *if* the Library included a UITableViewHeaderFooterView. In theory, you can call `register(_:forHeaderFooterViewReuseIdentifier:)` to register a nib instead of a class, just as with a UITableViewCell. But without a UITableViewHeaderFooterView in the nib, you can never call that method; it is useless.

Some popular "solutions" attempt to circumvent this shortcoming by misusing a UITableViewCell prototype as a header, or by putting a UIView in a nib and setting its class in the Identity inspector to be UITableViewHeaderFooterView. Those don't work; don't try them. Until Apple fixes this bug, you *can't* design a header or footer view in a nib and that's that. A viable workaround is: Design an ordinary UIView in a nib. Implement the `viewFor` delegate method to load that nib, obtain the view, and insert it inside a UITableViewHeaderFooterView's `contentView`.

When you implement `viewFor...`, you are not required to return a UITableView-HeaderFooterView, but you should do so. The procedure is much like making a cell reusable:

1. You register beforehand with the table view by calling `register(_:forHeader-FooterViewReuseIdentifier:)` with the UITableViewHeaderFooterView class or a subclass.

2. To obtain the reusable view, call `dequeueReusableHeaderFooterView(with-Identifier:)` on the table view; the result will be either a newly instantiated view or a reused view.

3. You can then configure this view as desired. You can set its `textLabel.text`; you can give its `contentView` custom subviews. In the latter case, use autoresizing or constraints to ensure that the subviews will be positioned and sized appropriately when the view itself is resized.

In addition, these delegate methods permit you to perform final configurations on your header or footer views:

```
tableView(_:willDisplayHeaderView:forSection:)
tableView(_:willDisplayFooterView:forSection:)
```
    You can perform further configurations here, if desired. If you generated the default UITableViewHeaderFooterView by implementing `titleFor...`, you can

tweak it here. These delegate methods are matched by `didEndDisplaying` methods.

The runtime resizes your header or footer before displaying it. Its width will be the table view's width; its height will be the table view's `sectionHeaderHeight` or `sectionFooterHeight` unless you implement one of these delegate methods to say otherwise:

```
tableView(_:heightForHeaderInSection:)
tableView(_:heightForFooterInSection:)
```
> Returning 0 (or failing to dictate the height at all) hides the header or footer.
>
> Returning `UITableView.automaticDimension` means 0 if `titleFor...` returns `nil` or the empty string (or isn't implemented); otherwise, it means the table view's `sectionHeaderHeight` or `sectionFooterHeight`.

 Starting in iOS 11, you can size a section header or footer from the inside out, using autolayout constraints. I'll talk about that later in this chapter.

A header or footer view in a nongrouped table is in front of the table's cells. Moreover, when a header or footer view is not pinned to the top or bottom of the table view, there is a transparent gap behind it. You'll want to take that into account when designing your header or footer view.

Table View Section Example

Here's a simple example to illustrate a table view with sections. Suppose we intend to display the names of all 50 U.S. states in alphabetical order as the rows of a table view, and that we wish to divide the table into sections according to the first letter of each state's name. We'll have section headers, each consisting of a single letter of the alphabet; the cells of each section will list the names of the states that start with that letter.

Let's adapt the sectioned data scheme from Example 8-3 to our use case. The only section-related property we need is the name of the section; the only thing we intend to display in our table view cells is the name of the state, so the row data for each cell can be a String:

```
struct Section {
    var sectionName : String
    var rowData : [String]
}
var sections : [Section]() // data model
```

Let's say I have the alphabetized list of state names as a text file, which starts like this:

```
Alabama
Alaska
Arizona
Arkansas
California
Colorado
Connecticut
Delaware
...
```

I'll prepare the data model by loading the text file and parsing it into a Section array:

```
override func viewDidLoad() {
    super.viewDidLoad()
    let s = try! String(
        contentsOfFile: Bundle.main.path(
            forResource: "states", ofType: "txt")!)
    let states = s.components(separatedBy:"\n")
    let d = Dictionary(grouping: states) {String($0.prefix(1))}
    self.sections = Array(d).sorted{$0.key < $1.key}.map {
        Section(sectionName: $0.key, rowData: $0.value)
    }
    // ...
}
```

The value of this preparatory dance is evident when we are bombarded with questions from the table view about cells and headers; supplying the answers is trivial, just as it should be:

```
override func numberOfSections(in tableView: UITableView) -> Int {
    return self.sections.count
}
override func tableView(_ tableView: UITableView,
    numberOfRowsInSection section: Int) -> Int {
        return self.sections[section].rowData.count
}
override func tableView(_ tableView: UITableView,
    cellForRowAt indexPath: IndexPath) -> UITableViewCell {
        let cell = tableView.dequeueReusableCell(
            withIdentifier: self.cellID, for: indexPath)
        let s = self.sections[indexPath.section].rowData[indexPath.row]
        cell.textLabel!.text = s
        return cell
}
override func tableView(_ tableView: UITableView,
    titleForHeaderInSection section: Int) -> String? {
        return self.sections[section].sectionName
}
```

Let's modify that example to illustrate creation of a custom header view with `tableView(_:viewForHeaderInSection:)`. I register my header identifier in `viewDidLoad`:

```
let headerID = "Header"
override func viewDidLoad() {
    super.viewDidLoad()
    // ...
    self.tableView.register(UITableViewHeaderFooterView.self,
        forHeaderFooterViewReuseIdentifier: self.headerID)
}
```

We delete `tableView(_:titleForHeaderInSection:)` and implement `table-View(_:viewForHeaderInSection:)`. For completely new views, I'll place my own label inside the `contentView` and give it some basic configuration; then I'll perform individual configuration on all views, new or reused:

```
override func tableView(_ tableView: UITableView,
    viewForHeaderInSection section: Int) -> UIView? {
        let h = tableView.dequeueReusableHeaderFooterView(
            withIdentifier: self.headerID)!
        if h.viewWithTag(1) == nil {
            h.backgroundView = UIView()
            h.backgroundView?.backgroundColor = .black
            let lab = UILabel()
            lab.tag = 1
            lab.font = UIFont(name:"Georgia-Bold", size:22)
            lab.textColor = .green
            lab.backgroundColor = .clear
            h.contentView.addSubview(lab)
            // ... add constraints ...
        }
        let lab = h.contentView.viewWithTag(1) as! UILabel
        lab.text = self.sections[section].sectionName
        return h
}
```

Section Index

If your table view has the plain style, you can add an index down the side of the table, where the user can tap or drag to jump to the start of a section — helpful for navigating long tables. To generate the index, implement the data source method `section-IndexTitles(for:)`, returning an array of string titles to appear as entries in the index.

For our list of state names, that's trivial, just as it should be:

```
override func sectionIndexTitles(for tv: UITableView) -> [String]? {
    return self.sections.map{$0.sectionName}
}
```

The index can appear even if there are no section headers. It will appear only if the number of rows exceeds the table view's `sectionIndexMinimumDisplayRowCount` property value; the default is 0, so the index is always displayed by default. You will want the index entries to be short — preferably just one character — because each cell's content view will shrink to compensate, so you're sacrificing some cell real estate.

You can modify three table view properties that affect the index's appearance:

`sectionIndexColor`
The index text color.

`sectionIndexBackgroundColor`
The index background color. I advise giving the index some background color, because otherwise the index distorts the colors of what's behind it in a distracting way.

`sectionIndexTrackingBackgroundColor`
The index background color while the user's finger is sliding over it. By default, it's the same as the `sectionIndexBackgroundColor`.

Normally, there will be a one-to-one correspondence between the index entries and the sections; when the user taps an index entry, the table jumps to the start of the corresponding section. But under certain circumstances you may want to customize this correspondence. Suppose there are 100 sections, but there isn't room to display 100 index entries comfortably on the iPhone. The index will automatically curtail itself, omitting some index entries and inserting bullets to suggest the omission, but you might prefer to take charge of the situation.

To do so, supply a shorter index, and implement the data source method `table-View(_:sectionForSectionIndexTitle:at:)`, returning the number of the section to jump to. You are told both the title and the index number of the section index listing that the user chose, so you can use whichever is convenient.

 If the table view has a section index, its scroll indicators will never appear.

Variable Row Heights

Most tables have rows that are all the same height, as set by the table view's `row-Height`. It is possible, though, for different rows to have different heights. You can see an example in the TidBITS News app (Figure 6-1).

Back when I first wrote my TidBITS News and Albumen apps for iOS 4, variable row heights were possible but virtually unheard-of; I knew of no other app that was using them, and Apple provided no guidance, so I had to invent my own technique by trial and error. There were three main challenges:

Measurement
> *What* should the height of a given row be?

Timing
> *When* should the determination of each row's height be made?

Layout
> How should the *subviews* of each cell be configured for its individual height?

Over the years since then, implementing variable row heights has become considerably easier. In iOS 6, with the advent of autolayout, both measurement and layout became much simpler. In iOS 7, new table view properties made it possible to improve the timing. Then iOS 8 permitted variable row heights to be implemented *automatically*, without your having to worry about any of these problems. Starting in iOS 11, section header and footer heights can be implemented automatically as well.

I will briefly describe, in historical order, four different techniques that I have used over the years in my own apps. Perhaps you won't use any of the first three, because the automatic row heights feature makes them unnecessary; nevertheless, a basic understanding of them will give you an appreciation of what the fourth approach is doing for you. Besides, in my experience, the automatic row heights feature can be slow; for efficiency and speed, you might want to revert to one of the earlier techniques.

Manual Row Height Measurement

In its earliest incarnation, my variable row heights technique depends on the delegate's `tableView(_:heightForRowAt:)`. Whatever height I return for a given row, that's the height that the cell at that row will be given.

The timing is interesting. Before our `tableView(_:cellForRowAt:)` is called for even *one* row, we are sent `tableView(_:heightForRowAt:)` for *every* row. In preparation for this situation, I start with an array of Optional CGFloats stored in a property, `self.rowHeights`. (Assume, for simplicity, that the table has just one section, so that the row number can serve directly as an index into the array.) Initially, all the values in the array are `nil`. Once the real values have been filled in, the array can be used to supply a requested height instantly.

To calculate the cell heights, I have a utility method, `setUpCell(_:for:)`. It takes a cell and an index path, lays out the cell using the actual data for that row, and returns (as a CGFloat) the height required for the cell to accommodate that layout.

(Before the days of autolayout, doing the actual work of measurement in `setUpCell(_:for:)` was laborious; I had to lay out the cell manually, assigning a frame to each subview, one by one. The main challenge was dealing with labels whose text, and therefore height, could vary from row to row. I'll spare you the gory details!)

When the delegate's `tableView(_:heightForRowAt:)` is called, either this is the very first time it has been called or it isn't. So either we've already constructed `self.row-Heights` or we haven't. If we haven't, we construct it now, by immediately calling the `setUpCell(_:for:)` utility method for *every row* and storing each resulting height in `self.rowHeights`. The cell that I'm passing to `setUpCell(_:for:)` isn't going into the table; it's just a dummy copy of the cell, to give me something to configure and work out the resulting cell height. From now on, I'm ready to answer `table-View(_:heightForRowAt:)` for *any* row, *immediately* — all I have to do is return the appropriate value from the `self.rowHeights` array:

```
override func tableView(_ tableView: UITableView,
    heightForRowAt indexPath: IndexPath) -> CGFloat {
    let ix = indexPath.row
    if self.rowHeights[ix] == nil {
        let objects = UINib(nibName: "MyCell", bundle: nil)
            .instantiate(withOwner: nil)
        let cell = objects.first as! UITableViewCell
        for ix in 0..<self.rowHeights.count {
            let indexPath = IndexPath(row: ix, section: 0)
            let h = self.setUpCell(cell, for: indexPath)
            self.rowHeights[ix] = h
        }
    }
    return self.rowHeights[ix]!
}
```

My `setUpCell(_:for:)` utility is also called by `tableView(_:cellForRowAt:)`, but now I'm laying out the *real* cell — and ignoring the returned height value:

```
override func tableView(_ tableView: UITableView,
    cellForRowAt indexPath: IndexPath) -> UITableViewCell {
    let cell = tableView.dequeueReusableCell(
        withIdentifier: self.cellID, for: indexPath)
    self.setUpCell(cell, for:indexPath)
    return cell
}
```

Measurement and Layout with Constraints

With autolayout in the picture, constraints are of great assistance. They obviously perform layout of each cell for us, because that's what constraints do. But they can also perform measurement of the height of each cell. If constraints ultimately pin every subview to the `contentView` in such a way as to size the `contentView` height unambiguously *from the inside out*, then we simply call `systemLayoutSize-Fitting(_:)` on the `contentView` to learn the resulting height of the cell.

My `setUpCell(_:for:)` no longer needs to perform any layout, calculate any heights, or return a value; I hand it a reference to a cell, it puts the data into the cell, and now I can do whatever I like with that cell. If this is the model cell being used for measurement in `tableView(_:heightForRowAt:)`, I call `systemLayoutSizeFitting(_:)` to get the height:

```swift
override func tableView(_ tableView: UITableView,
    heightForRowAt indexPath: IndexPath) -> CGFloat {
        let ix = indexPath.row
        if self.rowHeights[ix] == nil {
            let objects = UINib(nibName: "MyCell", bundle: nil)
                .instantiate(withOwner: nil)
            let cell = objects.first as! UITableViewCell
            for ix in 0..<self.rowHeights.count {
                let indexPath = IndexPath(row: ix, section: 0)
                self.setUpCell(cell, for: indexPath)
                let v = cell.contentView                    // *
                let sz = v.systemLayoutSizeFitting(
                    UIView.layoutFittingCompressedSize)  // *
                self.rowHeights[ix] = sz.height
            }
        }
        return self.rowHeights[ix]!
}
```

If this is the real cell generated by dequeuing in `tableView(_:cellForRowAt:)`, I simply set up the cell and return it, as before.

Estimated Height

In iOS 7, three new table view properties were introduced:

- `estimatedRowHeight`
- `estimatedSectionHeaderHeight`
- `estimatedSectionFooterHeight`

To accompany those, there are also three table view delegate methods:

- `tableView(_:estimatedHeightForRowAt:)`
- `tableView(_:estimatedHeightForHeaderInSection:)`
- `tableView(_:estimatedHeightForFooterInSection:)`

The idea here is to reduce the amount of time spent calculating row heights at the outset. If you supply an estimated row height, then when `tableView(_:heightForRowAt:)` is called repeatedly before the table is displayed, it is called *only for the visible cells* of the table; for the remaining cells, the *estimated* height is used. The runtime obtains enough information to lay out the entire table very quickly: the only real heights you have to provide up front are those of the initially visible rows. The downside is that this layout is only an approximation, and will have to be corrected later: as new rows are scrolled into view, tableView(_:heightForRowAt:) will be called for those new rows, and the layout of the whole table will be revised accordingly.

In my implementation, the estimated height is set in viewDidLoad (it can alternatively be set in the nib editor):

```
self.tableView.estimatedRowHeight = 75
```

Now in my tableView(_:heightForRowAt:) implementation, when I find that a requested height value in self.rowHeights is nil, I don't fill in *all* the values of self.rowHeights — I fill in *just that one height.* It's simply a matter of removing the for loop:

```
override func tableView(_ tableView: UITableView,
    heightForRowAt indexPath: IndexPath) -> CGFloat {
        let ix = indexPath.row
        if self.rowHeights[ix] == nil {
            let objects = UINib(nibName: "MyCell", bundle: nil)
                .instantiate(withOwner: nil)
            let cell = objects.first as! UITableViewCell
            let indexPath = IndexPath(row: ix, section: 0)
            self.setUpCell(cell, for: indexPath)
            let v = cell.contentView
            let sz = v.systemLayoutSizeFitting(
                UIView.layoutFittingCompressedSize)
            self.rowHeights[ix] = sz.height
        }
        return self.rowHeights[ix]!
}
```

Automatic Row Height

Starting in iOS 8, a completely automatic calculation of variable row heights was introduced. This, in effect, does behind the scenes what I'm doing in table-View(_:heightForRowAt:) in the preceding code: it relies upon autolayout to calculate a cell's height from the inside out based on the constraints of its subviews, and it performs that calculation and caches a row's height the first time it is needed, before it appears on the screen.

To use the automatic row height mechanism, all you have to do is to set the table view's estimatedRowHeight — and *don't* implement tableView(_:heightForRow-At:). In some cases, it may be necessary to set the table view's row height to UITable-View.automaticDimension as well (again, this can be configured in the nib editor instead):

```
self.tableView.rowHeight = UITableView.automaticDimension
self.tableView.estimatedRowHeight = 75
```

Once I've done that, I can adopt this approach in my app just by deleting my `table-View(_:heightForRowAt:)` implementation entirely!

Starting in iOS 11, you don't even have to supply an `estimatedRowHeight`; it can be `UITableView.automaticDimension` as well. Basically, the rule is that if the `rowHeight` is `UITableView.automaticDimension`, then as long as the `estimatedRowHeight` isn't 0, you'll get automatic row heights:

```
self.tableView.rowHeight = UITableView.automaticDimension
self.tableView.estimatedRowHeight = UITableView.automaticDimension
```

Also starting in iOS 11, section headers and footers participate in the same variable height mechanism. If the table view's `sectionHeaderHeight` and `estimatedSection-HeaderHeight` are both `UITableView.automaticDimension`, the headers will have their heights determined by autolayout from the inside out.

New in Xcode 11, if you design a cell or header (or footer) prototype in the nib editor using autolayout, then once there are sufficient internal constraints to dictate the height, the prototype *in the nib editor* will be sized to that height. It's only a simulation — the real row height will be calculated at runtime — but it's better than in Xcode 10 and before, where the size of the prototype cell in the nib editor was completely meaningless.

I have said that adopting automatic row heights allows you to delete your implementation of the `height` delegate method, such as `tableView(_:heightForRowAt:)`. But you don't *have* to delete it, and you don't have to adopt automatic height calculation for *every* row. Whatever your table view's `height` settings may be, you can still override them for *individual* rows, headers, or footers with a `height` delegate method, so long as the `estimatedRowHeight` isn't 0:

- If `tableView(_:heightForRowAt:)` returns `UITableView.automaticDimension`, you'll get automatic determination of this row's height, even if the table view's `rowHeight` is absolute.
- If `tableView(_:heightForRowAt:)` returns an absolute height, that height will be used for this row, even if the table view's `rowHeight` is `UITableView.automatic-Dimension`.

You still have to provide an absolute height for the table view's `tableHeaderView` and `tableFooterView`, by setting its bounds or frame height; its height is not determined for you by means of internal constraints. (I regard this as a bug.)

The automatic row height mechanism is particularly well suited to cells containing UILabels whose height will depend upon their text contents, because the label provides that height in its `intrinsicContentSize`. If you want to use the automatic row height mechanism in conjunction with a *custom* UIView subclass whose height can vary, you should make your view behave like a label! Don't set your view's height constraint directly; instead, have your UIView subclass override `intrinsicContent-Size`, and set some property on which that override depends:

```
class MyView : UIView {
    var internalHeight : CGFloat = 200 {
        didSet {
            self.invalidateIntrinsicContentSize()
        }
    }
    override var intrinsicContentSize: CGSize {
        return CGSize(width:300, height:self.internalHeight)
    }
}
```

Obviously, taking advantage of the automatic row height mechanism is very easy: but easy does not necessarily mean best. There is also a question of performance. The four techniques I've outlined here run not only from oldest to newest but also from fastest to slowest. Manual layout is faster than calling `systemLayoutSize-Fitting(_:)`, and calculating the heights of all rows up front, though it may cause a longer pause initially, makes scrolling faster for the user because no row heights have to be calculated while scrolling. You will have to measure and decide which approach is most suitable.

Also, I said earlier that the cell returned to you from `dequeueReusableCell(with-Identifier:for:)` in your implementation of `tableView(_:cellForRowAt:)` already has its final size. But if you use automatic row heights, that's not true, because automatic calculation of a cell's height can't take place until after the cell exists! Any code that relies on the cell having its final size in `tableView(_:cellForRowAt:)` will break when you switch to automatic row heights. You can probably work around this by moving that code to `tableView(_:willDisplay:forRowAt:)`, where the final cell size has definitely been achieved.

 If you implement `tableView(_:heightForRowAt:)`, don't make any assumptions about how many times or how often it will be called. It can be called multiple times in succession for the same row. Your implementation needs to be as fast and efficient as possible; if it involves work, cache the results so as not to waste time doing the same work twice.

Table View Selection

One of the chief purposes of your table view is likely to be to let the user select a cell by tapping it. Selection of a cell involves a change of state. A table view cell has a normal state, a highlighted state (according to its `isHighlighted` property), and a selected state (according to its `isSelected` property). You can change these states directly, optionally with animation, by calling `setHighlighted(_:animated:)` or `set-Selected(_:animated:)` on the cell; but you don't want to act behind the table's back, so you are more likely to manage selection through the table view, letting the table view manage and track the state of its cells.

Although selection and highlighting are different states, selection implies highlighting. When a cell is selected, it propagates the highlighted state down through its subviews by setting each subview's isHighlighted property if it has one. That is why a UILabel's highlightedTextColor applies when the cell is selected. Similarly, a UIImageView (such as the cell's imageView) can have a highlightedImage that is shown when the cell is selected.

By default, being selected will mean that the cell is redrawn with a gray background view, but you can change this at the individual cell level, as I've already explained: you can change the cell's selectionStyle or, for full customization, set its selected-BackgroundView (or multipleSelectionBackgroundView).

 In iOS 12 and earlier, a selected cell changes the background color of the content view and all its subviews to .clear, exposing the selectedBackgroundView or the default gray. In iOS 13, that no longer happens; a cell with an opaque contentView background color might give the user no indication that it is selected.

The user can tap a cell to select it if you have not set the table view's allows-Selection property to false. You can also permit the user to select multiple cells; to do so, set the table view's allowsMultipleSelection property to true. If the user taps an already selected cell, by default it stays selected if the table doesn't allow multiple selection, but it is deselected if the table does allow multiple selection.

Managing Cell Selection

Your code can learn and manage the selection through these UITableView properties and instance methods:

indexPathForSelectedRow
indexPathsForSelectedRows

> These read-only properties report the currently selected row(s), or nil if there is no selection.
>
> Don't accidentally examine the wrong property! Asking for indexPathFor-SelectedRow when the table view allows multiple selection gives a result that will have you scratching your head in confusion. (As usual, I speak from experience.)

selectRow(at:animated:scrollPosition:)
> The animation involves fading in the selection, but the user may not see this unless the selected row is already visible.

The last parameter dictates whether and how the table view should scroll to reveal the newly selected row; your choices (UITableView.ScrollPosition) are .top, .middle, .bottom, and .none. For the first three options, the table view scrolls (with animation, if the second parameter is true) so that the selected row is at the specified position among the visible cells. For .none, the table view does not scroll; if the selected row is not already visible, it does not become visible.

deselectRow(at:animated:)

Deselects the given row (if it is selected); the optional animation involves fading out the selection. No automatic scrolling takes place.

To deselect *all* currently selected rows, call selectRow(at:...) with a nil index path.

Selection is preserved when a selected cell is scrolled off the screen; the row is still reported as selected, and the cell will still appear selected when it is scrolled back on screen.

Responding to Cell Selection

Response to user selection is through these table view delegate methods:

- tableView(_:shouldHighlightRowAt:)
- tableView(_:didHighlightRowAt:)
- tableView(_:didUnhighlightRowAt:)
- tableView(_:willSelectRowAt:)
- tableView(_:didSelectRowAt:)
- tableView(_:willDeselectRowAt:)
- tableView(_:didDeselectRowAt:)

The delegate method you'll be most interested in with regard to selection is table-View(_:didSelectRowAt:). This is your signal that the user has selected a cell! Your response will depend upon the purpose of this table view and what selection is supposed to mean.

Despite their names, the two will methods are actually should methods and expect a return value:

- Return nil to prevent the selection (or deselection) from taking place.
- Return the same index path to permit the selection (or deselection), or a different index path to cause a different cell to be selected (or deselected).

The highlight methods arrive first, so you can return false from table-View(_:shouldHighlightRowAt:) to prevent a cell from being selected. When the user taps a cell and willSelect is called, then if this table view permits only single cell selection, willDeselect will be called subsequently for any previously selected cells.

Here's an example of implementing tableView(_:willSelectRowAt:). When allowsSelection is true and allowsMultipleSelection is not, the default behavior is that if the user taps an already selected row, the selection does not change. We can alter this so that tapping a selected row deselects it:

```
override func tableView(_ tableView: UITableView,
    willSelectRowAt indexPath: IndexPath) -> IndexPath? {
        if tableView.indexPathForSelectedRow == indexPath {
            tableView.deselectRow(at:indexPath, animated:false)
            return nil
        }
        return indexPath
}
```

A cell's highlighted state and its selected state are, in fact, two different states, even though the user doesn't know the difference between them: whether the cell is highlighted or selected, the cell's subviews are highlighted and the selectedBackground-View appears. There are two different states because the user might touch a cell in two different ways:

The user touches and scrolls
> The cell is *highlighted, then unhighlighted*; the user sees the flash of the selected-BackgroundView and the highlighted subviews, until the table begins to scroll and the cell returns to normal.

The user touches and lifts the finger
> The cell is *highlighted, then selected*; the user sees the selectedBackgroundView and highlighted subviews appear and remain. There is actually a moment in the sequence where the cell has been highlighted and then unhighlighted and not yet selected, but the user doesn't see any momentary unhighlighting of the cell, because no redraw moment occurs (see Chapter 4).

Navigation from a Table View

A common response to user selection is navigation. A master–detail architecture is typical: the table view lists things the user can see in more detail, and a tap displays the detailed view of the tapped thing. On the iPhone, very often the table view will be in a navigation interface, and you will respond to user selection by creating the detail view and pushing it onto the navigation controller's stack.

Here's the code from my Albumen app that navigates from the list of albums to the list of songs in the album that the user has tapped:

```
    override func tableView(_ tableView: UITableView,
        didSelectRowAt indexPath: IndexPath) {
            let t = TracksViewController(
                mediaItemCollection: self.albums[indexPath.row])
            self.navigationController!.pushViewController(t, animated: true)
    }
```

In a storyboard, when you draw a segue from a UITableViewCell, you are given a choice of two segue triggers: Selection Segue and Accessory Action. If you create a selection segue, the segue will be triggered *automatically* when the user selects a cell; in this way, you can arrange to push or present another view controller in response to cell selection without code.

 Do not create a selection segue and *also* implement tableView(_:didSelectRow-At:) so as to perform a transition (such as calling performSegue). This is a common beginner mistake, and can have confusing consequences because you're trying to perform two transitions simultaneously when the user taps a cell.

If you're using a UITableViewController, then by default, whenever the table view appears, the selection is cleared automatically in viewWillAppear(_:), and the scroll indicators are flashed in viewDidAppear(_:). You can prevent the automatic clearing of the selection by setting the table view controller's clearsSelectionOnViewWill-Appear to false. You can get a nice effect by implementing deselection in viewDid-Appear(_:) instead: when the user returns to the table, the row remains momentarily selected before it deselects itself.

By convention, if selecting a table view cell causes navigation, the cell should be given an accessoryType (UITableViewCell.AccessoryType) of .disclosureIndicator. This is a plain gray right-pointing chevron at the right end of the cell. The chevron itself doesn't respond to user interaction; it is not a button, but rather a visual cue that the user can tap the cell to learn more.

Two additional accessoryType settings *are* buttons:

.detailButton
    Drawn as a letter "i" in a circle.

.detailDisclosureButton
    Drawn like .detailButton, along with a disclosure indicator chevron to its right.

To respond to the tapping of a detail button, implement the table view delegate's tableView(_:accessoryButtonTappedForRowWith:). Alternatively, in a storyboard, you can Control-drag a connection from a cell and choose an Accessory Action segue. A common convention is that selecting the cell as a whole does one thing and tapping the detail button does something else. In Apple's Phone app, tapping a contact's listing in the Recents table places a call to that contact, but tapping the detail button navigates to that contact's detail view.

Table View Scrolling and Layout

A UITableView is a UIScrollView, so everything you already know about scroll views is applicable (Chapter 7). In addition, a table view supplies two convenience methods for scrolling in code:

- `scrollToRow(at:at:animated:)`
- `scrollToNearestSelectedRow(at:animated:)`

One of the parameters is a scroll position, like the `scrollPosition` parameter for `selectRow`, discussed earlier in this chapter.

The following UITableView methods mediate between the table's bounds coordinates on the one hand and table structure on the other:

- `indexPathForRow(at:)`
- `indexPathsForRows(in:)`
- `rect(forSection:)`
- `rectForRow(at:)`
- `rectForFooter(inSection:)`
- `rectForHeader(inSection:)`

The table view's own table header view and table footer view are its direct subviews, so their positions within the table's bounds are given by their frames.

If you want to receive UIScrollView delegate messages from the table view, implement them in the table view's delegate. The table view's delegate *is* its scroll view delegate; there is no need to set a scroll view delegate explicitly or adopt UIScrollViewDelegate formally, because UITableViewDelegate conforms to UIScrollViewDelegate.

Refreshing a Table View

If you want a table view's contents to change, you first change the underlying data and then inform the table view that the data have changed. This causes the table view to refresh itself; basically, you're requesting that the Three Big Questions be asked all over again. At first blush, this seems inefficient; but it isn't. Remember, in a table that caches reusable cells, there are no cells of interest other than those actually showing in the table at this moment. Having worked out the layout of the table through the section header and footer heights and row heights, the table has to regenerate only those cells that are actually visible.

You can cause the table data to be refreshed using any of several methods:

`reloadData`

> The table view will ask the Three Big Questions all over again, including heights of rows and section headers and footers, and the index, much as when the table view first appears.

`reloadRows(at:with:)`

> The first parameter is an array of index paths. The table view will ask the Three Big Questions all over again, including heights, but not index entries. Cells are requested only for visible cells among those you specify.

`reloadSections(_:with:)`

> The first parameter is an IndexSet. The table view will ask the Three Big Questions all over again, including heights of rows and section headers and footers, and the index. Cells, headers, and footers are requested only for visible elements of the sections you specify.

The latter two methods can perform animations that cue the user as to what's changing. For the `with:` argument, you'll specify what animation you want by passing one of the following (UITableView.RowAnimation):

`.fade`

> The old fades into the new.

`.right`, `.left`, `.top`, `.bottom`

> The old slides out in the stated direction, and is replaced from the opposite direction.

`.middle`

> Hard to describe; it's a sort of venetian blind effect on each cell individually.

`.automatic`

> The table view just "does the right thing." This is especially useful for grouped style tables, because if you pick the wrong animation, the display can look very funny as it proceeds.

`.none`

> No animation.

If all you need is to refresh the index, call `reloadSectionIndexTitles`; this calls the data source's `sectionIndexTitles(for:)`.

 Calling a `reload` method deselects any affected cells; calling `reloadData` deselects *all* selected cells. Calling `reloadData`, and then calling `indexPathForSelectedRow` and wondering what happened to the selection, is a common beginner mistake.

Call `reloadData` whenever the model data has changed and you want to alert the table view to that fact. The usual scenario in my own apps is that the data may take time to assemble or prepare.

My Albumen app consists of a table view controller whose table view lists the albums in the user's music library. Gathering that data takes time. Therefore I must instantiate the table view controller *first* and gather the data *later*, because if we pause to gather the data *before* instantiating the table view controller, the app will take too long to launch — the delay will be perceptible, and we might even crash (because iOS forbids long launch times). Therefore the data properties that will be used to populate the table view are all Optionals; they are set to `nil` until the data are gathered, at which time they are assigned their "real" values:

```
class RootViewController : UITableViewController {
    var albums : [MPMediaItemCollection]?
    override func tableView(_ tableView: UITableView,
        numberOfRowsInSection section: Int) -> Int {
            return self.albums?.count ?? 0
    }
    // ...
}
```

When the app launches and the table view appears, the table view turns to the table view controller and asks the Three Big Questions. My implementation of `table-View(_:numberOfRowsInSection:)` sees that `albums` is `nil` and returns 0 — and so the table is initially empty. Meanwhile, the data are being gathered. After gathering the data, I call `reloadData` tell my table view to ask the Three Big Questions *again*. This time, `albums` is *not* `nil`, but rather consists of actual data — and this time, `table-View(_:numberOfRowsInSection:)` returns the `count` of the `albums` array, and `table-View(_:cellForRowAt:)` is called to populate the table.

Cell Choice and Static Tables

As a further example of using `reloadData`, I'll implement the interface shown in Figure 8-3. The idea here is to give the user a choice among cells, where a section of a table effectively functions as an iOS equivalent of macOS radio buttons, with an `accessoryType` of `.checkmark` to indicate the current choice. My table view has a grouped style (it looks particularly nice with the `.insetGrouped` style, new in iOS 13), and consists of two sections. The first section, with a "Size" header, has three mutually exclusive choices: "Easy," "Normal," or "Hard." The second section, with a "Style" header, has two choices: "Animals" or "Snacks."

This table's entire contents, except for the checkmark, are known beforehand and won't change. It is, in effect, a *static* table. If we're using a UITableViewController subclass instantiated from a storyboard, the nib editor lets us design a static table, including the headers and the cells *and their content*, directly in the storyboard. Select

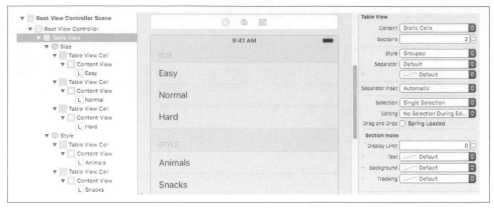

Figure 8-7. Designing a static table in the storyboard editor

the table and set its Content pop-up menu in the Attributes inspector to Static Cells to make the table editable in this way (Figure 8-7).

When you're using a static table, you are still free to implement table view data source and delegate methods, provided you cooperate with what the static table is already doing for you. This is useful when you'll have relevant information at run-time that you don't have while designing the storyboard. You can implement `table-View(_:cellForRowAt:)`, but your implementation must not dequeue a cell explicitly; instead, obtain the cell by calling `super`. Now you can add runtime modifications to the cell.

I'll add the checkmarks to our static table by implementing `tableView(_:cellForRow-At:)` to set the cell's `accessoryType`. Note the call to `super`, as well as the call to `tableView(_:titleForHeaderInSection:)` to learn the title of the current section. The user defaults will store the current choice in each of the two categories; in both cases, the key is the section title and the value is the label text of the chosen cell:

```
override func tableView(_ tv: UITableView,
    cellForRowAt ix: IndexPath) -> UITableViewCell {
        let cell = super.tableView(tv, cellForRowAt:ix)
        let ud = UserDefaults.standard
        cell.accessoryType = .none
        if let title = self.tableView(
            tv, titleForHeaderInSection:ix.section) {
                if let label = ud.object(forKey:title) as? String {
                    if label == cell.textLabel!.text {
                        cell.accessoryType = .checkmark
                    }
                }
        }
        return cell
}
```

The position of the checkmark needs to change in response to the user tapping a cell. When the user taps a cell, the cell is selected. I want the user to see that selection momentarily, as feedback, but then I want to deselect, adjusting the checkmarks so that that cell is the only one checked in its section. In `tableView(_:didSelectRow-At:)`, I set the user defaults, and then I reload the table view's data. This removes the selection and causes `tableView(_:cellForRowAt:)` to be called to adjust the checkmarks:

```
override func tableView(_ tv: UITableView, didSelectRowAt ix: IndexPath) {
    let ud = UserDefaults.standard
    let setting = tv.cellForRow(at:ix)!.textLabel!.text
    let header = self.tableView(tv, titleForHeaderInSection:ix.section)!
    ud.setValue(setting, forKey:header)
    tv.reloadData()
}
```

Direct Access to Cells

It is also possible to access and alter a table's individual cells directly. This can be a lightweight approach to refreshing the table, plus you can supply your own animation within the cell as it alters its appearance. But don't forget that the cells are not the data! If you change the content of a cell manually, make sure that you have *also* changed the model corresponding to it, so that the row will appear correctly if its data is reloaded later. Do *not* change the display of a table cell directly *without* also changing the underlying data! The "source of truth" for a table view is the data, not the transient appearance of the cells. Be sure to design your data model and your implementation of `tableView(_:cellForRowAt:)` to accommodate any real-time changes you'll need to make.

When accessing a cell directly, you'll probably want to check first that the cell is visible within the table view's bounds; nonvisible cells don't really exist (except as potential cells waiting in the reuse cache), and there's no point changing them manually, as they'll be configured in accordance with the data model when they are scrolled into view, through the usual call to `tableView(_:cellForRowAt:)`.

Here are some UITableView properties and methods that mediate between cells, rows, and visibility:

`visibleCells`
    An array of the cells actually showing within the table's bounds.

`indexPathsForVisibleRows`
    An array of the rows actually showing within the table's bounds.

`cellForRow(at:)`
> Returns a UITableViewCell if the table is maintaining a cell for the given row (typically because this is a visible row); otherwise, returns nil.

`indexPath(for:)`
> Given a cell obtained from the table view, returns the row into which it is slotted.

By the same token, you can get access to the views constituting headers and footers, by calling `headerView(forSection:)` or `footerView(forSection:)`. You should assume that if a section is returned by `indexPathsForVisibleRows`, its header or footer might be visible.

Refresh Control

If you want to grant the user some interface for requesting that a table view be refreshed, you might like to use a UIRefreshControl. You aren't required to use this; it's just Apple's attempt to provide a standard interface.

To give a table view a refresh control, assign a UIRefreshControl to the table view's `refreshControl` property; this property is actually inherited from UIScrollView. You can also configure this in the nib editor through a table view controller's Refreshing pop-up menu in the Attributes inspector.

To request a refresh, the user scrolls the table view downward to display the refresh control and holds long enough to indicate that this scrolling is deliberate. The refresh control then acknowledges visually that it is refreshing, and remains visible until refreshing is complete.

The refresh control is normally displayed at the top of the scrolling part of the table view. Starting in iOS 11, if we're in a navigation interface (UINavigationController) with a navigation bar that displays large titles, the refresh control appears *in the navigation bar*, which stretches to accommodate it when visible; for this to work properly, it is *crucial* that the table view should underlap the navigation bar.

A refresh control is a control (UIControl, Chapter 12), and you will want to hook its Value Changed event to an action method; you can do that in the nib editor by making an action connection, or you can do it in code:

```
self.tableView.refreshControl = UIRefreshControl()
self.tableView.refreshControl!.addTarget(
    self, action: #selector(doRefresh), for: .valueChanged)
```

Once a refresh control's action message has fired, the control remains visible and indicates by animation (similar to an activity indicator) that it is refreshing, until you send it the `endRefreshing` message:

```
@IBAction func doRefresh(_ sender: Any) {
    // ...
    (sender as! UIRefreshControl).endRefreshing()
}
```

You can initiate a refresh animation in code with `beginRefreshing`, but this does not fire the action message. It also doesn't display the refresh control; to display it, scroll the table view:

```
self.refreshControl!.sizeToFit()
let top = self.tableView.adjustedContentInset.top
let y = self.refreshControl!.frame.maxY + top
self.tableView.setContentOffset(CGPoint(0, -y), animated:true)
self.refreshControl!.beginRefreshing()
self.doRefresh(self.refreshControl!)
```

(The `sizeToFit` call works around a bug where the refresh control may otherwise report its own frame height as less than 1 point.)

A refresh control also has these properties:

`isRefreshing` *(read-only)*
:   Whether the refresh control is refreshing.

`tintColor`
:   The refresh control's color. It is *not* inherited from the view hierarchy (I regard this as a bug).

`attributedTitle`
:   Styled text displayed below the refresh control's activity indicator. On attributed strings, see Chapter 10.

`backgroundColor` *(inherited from UIView)*
:   If you give a table view controller's `refreshControl` a background color, that color completely covers the table view's own background when the refresh control is revealed.

The `attributedTitle` sometimes fails to appear unless the refresh control has a background color (I regard this as a bug); on the other hand, a refresh control background color that's different from the table view's own background can ruin the entire look of the refresh control. A good compromise is to give the table view and the refresh control the same background color.

Editing a Table View

A table view cell has a normal state and an editing state, according to its `isEditing` property. The editing state (or *edit mode*) is typically indicated visually by one or more of the following:

Editing controls
>At least one editing control will usually appear, such as a Minus button (for deletion) at the left side.

Shrinkage
>The content of the cell will usually shrink to allow room for an editing control. If there is no editing control, you can prevent a cell shifting its left end rightward in edit mode with the delegate's `tableView(_:shouldIndentWhileEditingRowAt:)`.

Changing accessory view
>The cell's accessory view will change automatically in accordance with its `editingAccessoryType` or `editingAccessoryView`. If you assign neither, so that they are `nil`, the cell's existing accessory view will vanish when in edit mode.

You could set a cell's `isEditing` property directly, but you don't want to act behind the table's back, so you are more likely to let the table view manage editability. Table view editability is controlled through the table view's `isEditing` property, usually by sending the table the `setEditing(_:animated:)` message. The table responds by changing the edit mode of its cells.

Toggling a Table View's Edit Mode

Putting the table into edit mode is usually left up to the user. A typical interface would be an Edit button that the user can tap. In a navigation interface, we might have our view controller supply the button as a bar button item in the navigation bar:

```
let b = UIBarButtonItem(barButtonSystemItem: .edit,
    target: self, action: #selector(doEdit))
self.navigationItem.rightBarButtonItem = b
```

Our action method will be responsible for putting the table into edit mode, so in its simplest form it might look like this:

```
@objc func doEdit(_ sender: Any) {
    self.tableView.setEditing(true, animated:true)
}
```

But now we face the problem of getting *out* of edit mode. The standard interface is that the Edit button replaces itself with a Done button; the same button, either Edit or Done, now switches the table view into or out of edit mode:

```
@objc func doEdit(_ sender: Any) {
    var which : UIBarButtonItem.SystemItem
    if !self.tableView.isEditing {
        self.tableView.setEditing(true, animated:true)
        which = .done
    } else {
        self.tableView.setEditing(false, animated:true)
        which = .edit
```

```
    }
    let b = UIBarButtonItem(barButtonSystemItem: which,
        target: self, action: #selector(doEdit))
    self.navigationItem.rightBarButtonItem = b
}
```

But it turns out that all of that is completely unnecessary; if we want standard behavior, it's already implemented for us! A UIViewController has an `editButtonItem` property, which vends a bar button item that does precisely what we need:

- It calls the UIViewController's `setEditing(_:animated:)` when tapped.
- It tracks the UIViewController's `isEditing` property, and changes its own title accordingly (Edit or Done).

Moreover, UITableViewController's implementation of `setEditing(_:animated:)` is to call `setEditing(_:animated:)` on its table view. So if we're using a UITableViewController, we get all of the desired behavior for free, just by retrieving the `editButtonItem` and inserting the resulting button into our interface:

```
    self.navigationItem.rightBarButtonItem = self.editButtonItem
```

When the table view enters edit mode, it consults its data source and delegate about the editability of individual rows:

`tableView(_:canEditRowAt:)` *to the data source*
: The default is `true`. The data source can return `false` to prevent the given row from entering edit mode.

`tableView(_:editingStyleForRowAt:)` *to the delegate*
: Each standard editing style corresponds to a control that will appear in the cell. The choices (UITableViewCell.EditingStyle) are:

   `.delete`
   : The cell shows a Minus button at its left end. The user can tap this to summon a Delete button, which the user can then tap to confirm the deletion. This is the default.

   `.insert`
   : The cell shows a Plus button at its left end; this is usually taken to be an insert button.

   `.none`
   : No editing control appears.

If the user taps an insert button (the Plus button) or a delete button (the Delete button that appears after the user taps the Minus button), the data source is sent the `tableView(_:commit:forRowAt:)` message. That's where the actual insertion or deletion needs to happen. I'll talk more about that in a moment.

Edit Mode and Selection

When a table view is in edit mode, a cell can be selected by the user if the table view's `allowsSelectionDuringEditing` is `true`. (The default is `false`.)

If both `allowsSelectionDuringEditing` and `allowsMultipleSelectionDuring-Editing` are `true`, the user can select multiple cells when the table view is in edit mode. In that case, `tableView(_:editingStyleForRowAt:)` is ignored; neither a Minus button nor a Plus button will appear at the left end of any cell. Instead, a cell shows an empty circle at its left end, which will be filled with a checkmark if the cell is selected.

The empty circle and checkmark can be suppressed for an individual cell if `table-View(_:canEditRowAt:)` for that cell returns `false`. The user can still select a cell for which the empty circle is suppressed, unless selection for that cell is *also* suppressed by `tableView(_:willSelectRowAt:)`.

New in iOS 13, if multiple selection during editing is enabled, the user can select multiple cells with a gesture, panning across cells with two fingers, when the table view is in edit mode. Moreover, a delegate method lets the user perform multiple selection with this panning gesture even if the table view is *not* in edit mode:

`tableView(_:shouldBeginMultipleSelectionInteractionAt:)`
> Consulted only if both `allowsSelectionDuringEditing` and `allowsMultiple-SelectionDuringEditing` are `true`, and when the table view is not in edit mode. Return `true` to permit multiple selection with the panning gesture. The default is `false`. If `true`, then as the gesture begins, the table enters edit mode and the circles appear.
>
> (If the table view controller's `editButtonItem` is displayed, it does *not* change modes automatically at that moment; I regard that as a bug. You can work around it by calling `self.setEditing(true, animated: true)` before returning `true`.)

Two more delegate methods, also new in iOS 13, report that the user is changing a multiple selection:

`tableView(_:didBeginMultipleSelectionInteractionAt:)`
`tableViewDidEndMultipleSelectionInteraction(_:)`
> Sent at the beginning and end, respectively, of a change in a multiple selection. This might be due to a multiple selection gesture or to tapping rows individually.

Changing a Table View's Structure

When you want to alter the structure of the table before the user's eyes, you can call one or more of the following UITableView methods:

- `insertRows(at:with:)`
- `deleteRows(at:with:)`
- `insertSections(_:with:)`
- `deleteSections(_:with:)`
- `moveSection(_:toSection:)`
- `moveRow(at:to:)`

The `with:` parameters are row animations that are effectively the same ones discussed earlier in connection with refreshing table data. For an insertion, `.left` means to slide in from the left, and for a deletion it means to slide out to the left. The two `move` methods provide animation with no provision for customizing it.

Before you change the table with these commands, you *must* first change the data model, so that when the changes are over, the table view can coherently refresh itself. Before you delete a row, you must first remove from the model the datum that it represents — and so on, for any structural change. Coordinating between the state of the data model and the state of the table view can be tricky. The runtime will alert you with error messages if you do it incorrectly.

A further difficulty arises when multiple changes are to be made in a single move. If you were to delete row 1 of a certain section and then row 2 of the same section, you might reasonably worry that the notion "row 2" would have changed its meaning after row 1 is removed, so that you might need to delete row 1 twice, or change the order of your deletions.

To help with this problem, there's a UITableView instance method, `performBatch-Updates(_:completion:)`. When you issue *any* commands that alter a table view's structure, you should do so inside a call to that method! It takes two functions, similar to an animation: the first function contains the commands and their animations, and the second function is a completion function that will be called after the animations have finished.

Combining multiple commands into a single batch update ensures that those commands are coherent. When there are multiple commands, the batch reorders them for you and interprets them correctly:

- If you perform insertions and deletions, the deletions are performed first.
- If you perform multiple deletions, they are performed in reverse index order, and the indexes refer to the state of the table *before* the deletions.
- If you perform insertions, they are performed in ascending index order, and the indexes refer to the state of the table *after* the deletions.

- If you perform moves, they are decomposed into deletions and insertions; the source index refers to the state of the table *before* the deletions, while the destination index refers to the state of the table *after* the deletions.

(A batch update can also include `reloadRows` and `reloadSections` commands — but not `reloadData`.)

But the help that `performBatchUpdates` gives you does *not* apply to the commands with which you alter your data model. When you alter the data model, *you* need to behave like the batch update engine! Otherwise you can crash, or wind up with your data model in an incoherent state.

Deleting a Cell

The simplest case of editing a table view's structure is deletion of a single cell. In effect, deletion of cells is the default, because:

- If you don't implement `tableView(_:canEditRowAt:)`, the default for all rows is that they are editable.
- If you don't implement `tableView(_:editingStyleForRowAt:)`, the default editing style for all rows is `.delete`.

What you *do* need to implement is `tableView(_:commit:forRowAt:)`. You then get two features automatically:

Minus button and Delete button
 If the table view is in edit mode, all editable cells get a Minus button at the left end, and if the user taps it, the cell displays a Delete button at the right end. If the user taps the Delete button, `tableView(_:commit:forRowAt:)` is called with the `.delete` action.

Swipe-to-delete
 All editable cells permit swipe-to-delete when the table view is *not* in edit mode. The user can swipe left on a cell and the Delete button appears; if the user taps the Delete button, or if the user keeps swiping left, `tableView(_:commit:forRow-At:)` is called with the `.delete` action.

You can customize the Delete button's title with the table view delegate method `tableView(_:titleForDeleteConfirmationButtonForRowAt:)`.

Let's modify our table of state names so that the user can delete any cell. All we have to do is implement `tableView(_:commit:forRowAt:)` to get swipe-to-delete. In that implementation, we proceed in two stages. First, we remove the deleted row — from the data and then from the table. Second, if the deletion of that row emptied a section, we remove the deleted section — from the data and then from the table:

```
override func tableView(_ tableView: UITableView,
    commit editingStyle: UITableViewCell.EditingStyle,
    forRowAt ip: IndexPath) {
        switch editingStyle {
        case .delete:
            tableView.performBatchUpdates({
                self.sections[ip.section].rowData.remove(at:ip.row)
                tableView.deleteRows(at:[ip], with: .automatic)
                if self.sections[ip.section].rowData.count == 0 {
                    self.sections.remove(at:ip.section)
                    tableView.deleteSections(
                        IndexSet(integer: ip.section), with:.fade)
                }
            })
        default: break
        }
}
```

We can also allow the user to delete a row when the table view is in edit mode. All we have to do is provide the user with a way to get the table view *into* edit mode! If the table view is managed by a table view controller in a navigation interface, we can simply supply the built-in Edit button:

```
self.navigationItem.rightBarButtonItem = self.editButtonItem
```

The user can now tap the Edit button to put the table view into edit mode, tap a row's Minus button to reveal the Delete button, and tap the Delete button to delete the row.

An interesting question is how to turn swipe-to-delete *off* while still allowing the user to delete rows when the table view is in edit mode. We get swipe-to-delete "for free" by virtue of our having supplied an implementation of `tableView(_:commit:forRow-At:)`, and we cannot remove that implementation — we need it so that when the user taps the Minus button and the Delete button in edit mode, deletion actually occurs. One solution is to make all rows noneditable unless the table view is already in edit mode:

```
override func tableView(_ tableView: UITableView,
    editingStyleForRowAt indexPath: IndexPath)
    -> UITableViewCell.EditingStyle {
        return tableView.isEditing ? .delete : .none
}
```

Deleting Multiple Cells

Now let's talk about deletion of multiple cells. A reasonable interface would be to allow the user to perform multiple selection and then delete the selected cells. If we allow multiple selection in edit mode, or if we permit two-finger panning to perform multiple selection, we get the circles that are filled with checkmarks as the user selects cells — but we don't get any Minus editing controls, so there will have to be a Delete button elsewhere to act upon the current selection.

What should that button do? We can easily learn the index paths of the selected rows. Using those index paths, we'll delete the corresponding rows — from the data and then from the table. Now we'll look to see if any sections in the data model are empty. If they are, we'll delete those sections — from the data and then from the table.

If we do all that in a `performBatchUpdates` call, we don't have to worry about the order in which we delete rows and sections from the table view. But we *do* have to worry about the order in which we delete items from our data model!

Suppose a section's `rowData` has four elements and the selected rows include that section's row 0 and row 3. If we delete element 0 and then element 3, we'll crash — because after deleting element 0, there is no longer an element 3. Similarly, if we want to delete sections 1 and 2, and we start by deleting `self.sections[1]`, the section we were calling 2 has become the new `self.sections[1]`; if we delete `self.sections[2]`, either we'll crash (if there aren't enough sections) or we'll delete the wrong section. The solution is to ensure that all deletions are performed in reverse index order, higher elements first:

```
guard let sel = self.tableView.indexPathsForSelectedRows else {return}
self.tableView.performBatchUpdates({
    for ip in sel.sorted().reversed() { // *
        self.sections[ip.section].rowData.remove(at:ip.row)
    }
    self.tableView.deleteRows(at:sel, with: .automatic)
    let secs = self.sections.indices.filter {
        self.sections[$0].rowData.count == 0
    }
    for sec in secs.reversed() { // *
        self.sections.remove(at:sec)
    }
    self.tableView.deleteSections(IndexSet(secs), with: .fade)
})
```

Table View Diffable Data Source

Even a fairly simple structural rearrangement of a table view, such as deleting multiple rows, is beset with pitfalls, as the preceding example demonstrates. We have to call `performBatchUpdates`; we have to delete from the data model before deleting physical rows or sections from the table view; and we have to be careful about the order of operations when changing the data model. If the desired rearrangement is more elaborate, involving both deletions and insertions or moving rows from place to place, the complexity increases. The procedures are delicate and tedious; the code is difficult to write and difficult to read.

That's the motivation behind an alternative data source architecture, new in iOS 13 — the *diffable data source*.

In this architecture, the data source is a special class of object that maintains a special relationship with the table view. You don't have to answer the Three Big Questions; you don't have to query your data. Instead, you supply the data, and the data source automatically feeds it to the table view for you. And when you *change* the data in your data source, the data source knows the difference between the new data and the old data — hence the term *diffable* — and *automatically* performs the corresponding changes in the table view, with appropriate animations!

For this to work, the data — both section data and row data — must be Hashable. This allows the data to be queried efficiently. And that means that each piece of section data and each piece of row data must be *unique*. Hashable implies Equatable; two pieces of data that are equal to one another will be seen as the same piece of data, and cannot go into two different rows or two different sections.

(For this reason, the diffable data source is considered to contain, not actual data, but *identifiers*, called the *section identifiers* and the *item identifiers*. Both a table view and a collection view can have a diffable data source; so a diffable data source uses the term *item* rather than *row,* because that's the term a collection view uses.)

In practice, this will not prove to be much of a restriction. Making your section data and row data types Hashable will probably be easy. If your data type is a struct, most likely either it is Hashable already or you can make it Hashable just by declaring conformance to Hashable.

The only difficulty arises if there is a danger of duplication. Suppose your row data is just a name, which is a String. And suppose the strings for two different rows might be the same. Then a mere String cannot be your row data type, because values for different rows need to be unique. Instead, turn your data into a struct that associates the string with a unique identifier, and base your conformance to Equatable and Hashable on that identifier:

```
struct RowData : Hashable {
    let name : String
    let uid = UUID()
    static func ==(lhs:RowData, rhs:RowData) -> Bool {
        return lhs.uid == rhs.uid
    }
    func hash(into hasher: inout Hasher) {
        hasher.combine(uid)
    }
}
```

The diffable data source architecture revolves around two objects: a *data source* (a UITableViewDiffableDataSource) and a *snapshot* (an NSDiffableDataSourceSnapshot). These are generic types, parameterized on the section identifier type and the item identifier type. The data source has a reference to the table view, and it keeps the table view updated with its data. But its data is immutable; you cannot directly set it or change it. Instead, when you want to alter the data source's data, either to populate it initially or to change it, you create a snapshot and *apply* the snapshot to the data source (and you then let the snapshot go out of existence). The data source can calculate the difference between its existing data and the snapshot's data, and can make the table view animate that change.

A question that arises when you use a diffable data source is where the "real" data will live:

Separately
> You maintain the data separately (probably in an instance property). You structure the data in any way that's convenient and appropriate. Each time you want to change what the table view displays, you construct a snapshot based on the data and apply it to the data source.

In the data source itself
> There is no data instance property other than the data source itself. To change the table's data, you obtain a snapshot from the data source, change it, and apply it to the data source.

I prefer the second approach wherever possible; after all, the data source is going to store internally whatever data we hand it, so why bother storing another version of the same data elsewhere? Nevertheless, sometimes the first approach will be better — as when the data might at any time be updated automatically through some independent or asynchronous mechanism.

Populating a Diffable Data Source

To populate a table view with a diffable data source requires two steps:

1. Initialize a UITableViewDiffableDataSource instance with your table view; in response, the table view's `dataSource` is set automatically to this instance. Retain the instance, typically as an instance property.

2. Create an NSDiffableDataSourceSnapshot and feed it your section and row data (the section identifiers and item identifiers). Apply the snapshot to the data source. You can now release the snapshot; it has done its work.

Let's rewrite our table of state names to use a diffable data source. Keep in mind that there are no longer any Three Big Questions! We may have a UITableView-Controller, but it is not the table view's data source and it does not implement any data source methods. The diffable data source is going to be the table view's data source.

We have, as you remember, an alphabetized list of state names as a text file. Previously, we prepared the data model in `viewDidLoad` by parsing that text file into an instance property called `self.sections`, which is an array of Section structs. Now we don't need `self.sections`, and we don't need any Section struct! Instead, we have an instance property I'll call `self.datasource`, which is a UITableViewDiffableData-Source.

I'm going to describe the two steps in reverse order. So pretend for now that `self.datasource` has already been declared and initialized; I'll return to that in a moment.

Our section data is a letter of the alphabet, and our row data consists of just the name of a state. Both the letters and the state names are unique, and they are Strings, a Hashable type. So the data source's parameterized types can be simply `<String, String>`.

Here's how we previously parsed the text file into an array of Section objects:

```
let s = try! String(
    contentsOfFile: Bundle.main.path(
        forResource: "states", ofType: "txt")!)
let states = s.components(separatedBy:"\n")
let d = Dictionary(grouping: states) {String($0.prefix(1))}
self.sections = Array(d).sorted{$0.key < $1.key}.map { // *
    Section(sectionName: $0.key, rowData: $0.value)
}
```

We now remove the last statement, where we assign into `self.sections`. Instead, we create an NSDiffableDataSourceSnapshot and parse the text file into that. We then apply the snapshot to `self.datasource`:

```
let sections = Array(d).sorted{$0.key < $1.key} // *
var snap = NSDiffableDataSourceSnapshot<String,String>()
for section in sections {
    snap.appendSections([section.0])
    snap.appendItems(section.1)
}
self.datasource.apply(snap, animatingDifferences: false)
```

The structure of that code is typical. We are giving the data source its initial data, so we start with an empty snapshot. We then append a section and its items, then another section and its items, and so on. There is a method `appendItems(_:to-Section:)`, but we don't have to use it here, because there's a convenient shortcut: when we call `appendItems`, those items are appended to the most recently appended section.

Finally, we apply the snapshot to the data source. The apply method takes three parameters, two of which can be omitted:

- `apply(_:animatingDifferences:completion:)`

If we don't set `animatingDifferences:` to `false`, we'll get animation. But we don't want any animation here, as the table view is about to appear for the first time and we want it simply to appear populated.

Now I'll go back and write the declaration for `self.datasource`. The initializer for UITableViewDiffableDataSource takes two parameters: the table view, and a function. I'll start by writing the declaration without the function body. I'll make `datasource` a `lazy` instance property so that its initializer can legally refer to the table view, which is also an instance property:

```
lazy var datasource =
    UITableViewDiffableDataSource(tableView:self.tableView) {
        // ...
}
```

What goes into the anonymous function body? Basically, the function must do what `tableView(_:cellForRowAt:)` would do: it must dequeue, populate, and return a cell. The function receives the same two parameters as `tableView(_:cellForRowAt:)` — the table view and an index path. But it also receives a third parameter — the data for this row! There is no need to use the index path to look up the cell data in an array; the index path is needed only to dequeue the cell:

```
lazy var datasource =
    UITableViewDiffableDataSource(tableView:self.tableView) { tv, ip, s in
        let cell =
            tv.dequeueReusableCell(withIdentifier: self.cellID, for: ip)
        cell.textLabel!.text = s
        return cell
}
```

That is sufficient to make our table view display a list of state names! But the list is not visibly divided into sections; it has no section headers. How we generate section headers depends on whether we want to call `tableView(_:titleForHeaderIn-Section:)` or `tableView(_:viewForHeaderInSection:)`.

Previously, we were using `tableView(_:viewForHeaderInSection:)`; let's go on using it. It's a delegate method. Our table view's data source has changed, but its delegate has not. If the UITableViewController was the table view's delegate, it can *still* be the table view's delegate. And the code remains almost exactly the same as before. Here's how it looked previously:

```
override func tableView(_ tableView: UITableView,
    viewForHeaderInSection section: Int) -> UIView? {
        let h = tableView.dequeueReusableHeaderFooterView(
            withIdentifier: self.headerID)!
        // ...
```

```
            let lab = h.contentView.viewWithTag(1) as! UILabel
            lab.text = self.sections[section].sectionName // *
            return h
    }
```

Only the starred line needs to change. It refers to `self.sections`, the Section array. There is no longer any `self.sections`! The data lives inside `self.datasource`. To access it, we ask `self.datasource` for a snapshot; now we can interrogate the data:

```
        lab.text = self.datasource.snapshot().sectionIdentifiers[section]
```

In that line, we're working around an impedance mismatch. The diffable data source and the snapshot can access identifiers in terms of the identifier itself — that's why identifiers are unique and Hashable. But `tableView(_:viewForHeaderInSection:)` knows nothing of that; it provides a section *number*. So we end up indexing into the section identifier array, much as we would have done before diffable data sources existed.

Subclassing a Diffable Data Source

When you're using a diffable data source, the table view's `dataSource` is now a UITableViewDiffableDataSource. This means that any UITableViewDataSource functionality not implemented automatically by the UITableViewDiffableDataSource must be implemented explicitly by subclassing. Our `self.datasource` instance property must now be an instance of the subclass, which I'll call MyDataSource.

If we want a section index down the side of our table view, we need to override the relevant data source methods in a subclass:

```
    class MyDataSource : UITableViewDiffableDataSource<String,String> {
        override func sectionIndexTitles(for tv: UITableView) -> [String]? {
            let snap = self.snapshot()
            return snap.sectionIdentifiers
        }
        override func tableView(_ tableView: UITableView,
            sectionForSectionIndexTitle title: String, at index: Int) -> Int {
                let snap = self.snapshot()
                return snap.indexOfSection(title) ?? 0
        }
    }
```

Similarly, if we want the table cells to be editable when the table view enters edit mode, we must explicitly enable editability in our subclass:

```
    override func tableView(_ tableView: UITableView,
        canEditRowAt indexPath: IndexPath) -> Bool {
            return true
    }
```

And if we wanted to supply header titles rather than header views, `table-View(_:titleForHeaderInSection:)` is a data source method, not a delegate method, and we'd need to implement it in the subclass.

Changing a Diffable Data Source

The real power of diffable data sources emerges when we alter the data source and the corresponding changes in the table view are performed and animated for us. To illustrate, let's implement deletion of multiple rows of the table view. We do *not* call `performBatchUpdates`! We do *not* call `deleteRows(at:with:)` or `delete-Sections(_:with:)`! We just change the snapshot and apply it, and both the data and the table view are updated for us — with animation of the table view changes.

 The magic ability of the diffable data source to deduce how a new snapshot differs from the old one and to express that through animated changes in the table view comes from the CollectionDifference struct and the `difference(from:)` and `applying` Array instance methods, which are new in iOS 13. In all probability you won't use these explicitly in your own code.

To illustrate, let's say we have permitted the user to select multiple rows while the table view is in edit mode, and we have supplied a Delete button that the user can tap to delete the selected rows. Now we are going to implement the Delete button's action method.

If the user deletes all the rows of a section, we also want to delete that section. All the work takes place in the snapshot, so it will be useful to extend NSDiffableDataSource-Snapshot to enforce that rule:

```
extension NSDiffableDataSourceSnapshot {
    mutating func deleteWithSections(_ items : [ItemIdentifierType]) {
        self.deleteItems(items)
        let empties = self.sectionIdentifiers.filter {
            self.numberOfItems(inSection: $0) == 0
        }
        self.deleteSections(empties)
    }
}
```

Our Delete button obtains a snapshot from the data source, gathers the item identifiers for the selected rows, calls that method, and applies the snapshot:

```
guard let sel = self.tableView.indexPathsForSelectedRows else {return}
let rowids = sel.map {
    self.datasource.itemIdentifier(for: $0)
}.compactMap {$0}
var snap = self.datasource.snapshot()
snap.deleteWithSections(rowids)
self.datasource.apply(snap)
```

That's all there is to it! Once again, we're working around an impedance mismatch: the table view describes the selected rows in terms of their index paths, but the snapshot wants lists of item identifiers and section identifiers. Luckily, the data source provides methods such as `itemIdentifier(for:)` to convert between index paths and identifiers. And the resulting code is far simpler and more robust than what we were previously doing in `performBatchUpdates`. We just change the data and the table view changes to match, automatically, with animation. The animation looks particularly nice, I think, if we set the data source's default animation beforehand:

```
self.datasource.defaultRowAnimation = .left
```

Pros and Cons of the Diffable Data Source

Should you adopt a diffable data source for your table view? Or should you stick with the old-style Three Big Questions data source? Here are some arguments in favor of the diffable data source:

Less code
> The Three Big Questions are eliminated. You still have to write code equivalent to the third Big Question, but it is nicely encapsulated in the function you supply to the data source initializer, and the actual data for each row arrives directly into the function as a parameter.

No custom data model storage
> There may be no need to devise a structure for your data model and store it in an instance property, because the diffable data source stores the data for you.

Easy data modification
> It's easy to insert, delete, or move data items or sections directly in a snapshot and keep those changes synchronized with the table view by applying the snapshot to the data source.

In other respects, a diffable data source may feel like a step backward:

Separation of data source from delegate
> You might have to subclass UITableViewDiffableDataSource and override data source methods there, rather than implementing those methods in the same class as the delegate. This separation of the data source from the delegate is somewhat unfortunate, and you might have to implement more data source methods than you would with a Three Big Questions data source.

Impedance mismatch
> The table view thinks in terms of cells and index paths, and the UITableViewDataSource and UITableViewDelegate methods are couched in those terms. But the diffable data source thinks in terms of unique identifiers, so you may end up converting back and forth. Conversion isn't difficult, but it can feel inelegant.

No `performBatchUpdates`
> With a diffable data source, calling `performBatchUpdates` is illegal. But certain techniques involving animated layout (described later in this chapter) depend upon calling `performBatchUpdates`.

More Table View Editing

This section describes some further types of change you can permit the user to perform in a table view.

Rearranging Cells

When a table view is in edit mode, it can display a reordering control at the right end of each cell. The user can drag this to rearrange the cells:

- To make the reordering control appear, the data source must implement `tableView(_:moveRowAt:to:)`. That method will be called when the user does rearrange cells, and you should respond by rearranging the data model to match.

- To suppress the reordering control for an individual row, implement the data source method `tableView(_:canMoveRowAt:)`.

- To limit where a particular row can be moved to, implement the delegate method `tableView(_:targetIndexPathForMoveFromRowAt:toProposedIndexPath:)`.

To illustrate, let's permit the user to rearrange cells within the table of U.S. states. Let's decide that rows can be rearranged only within their section; the user can reverse the order of Kansas and Kentucky, but can't drag either Kansas or Kentucky outside of the K section. Since a one-row section can't be rearranged, we'll suppress the reordering control when a cell is the only one in its section.

For simplicity, I'll assume the data model is our old-fashioned `self.sections` instance property, an array of Section where each Section has a `rowData` property that's an array of state names. To make the reordering controls spring to life when the table view is in edit mode, we have to implement `tableView(_:moveRowAt:to:)`. We're going to guarantee that a row can't move out of its section, so all we have to do is rearrange the `rowData` within the section to match what the user did:

```
override func tableView(_ tableView: UITableView,
    moveRowAt srcip: IndexPath, to destip: IndexPath) {
        let sec = srcip.section
        let srcrow = srcip.row
        let destrow = destip.row
        self.sections[sec].rowData.swapAt(srcrow, destrow)
}
```

We prevent the reordering control from appearing if the section has only one row:

Figure 8-8. A simple phone directory app

```
override func tableView(_ tableView: UITableView,
    canMoveRowAt ip: IndexPath) -> Bool {
        return self.sections[ip.section].rowData.count > 1
}
```

We prevent the user from dragging a row out of its section, by substituting the source index path for the destination index path unless they are in the same section; if the user drops the cell in a different section, it snaps back into its original place:

```
override func tableView(_ tableView: UITableView,
    targetIndexPathForMoveFromRowAt srcip: IndexPath,
    toProposedIndexPath destip: IndexPath) -> IndexPath {
        if destip.section != srcip.section {
            return srcip
        }
        return destip
}
```

Editable Content in Cells

A cell might have content that the user can edit directly, such as a UISwitch that the user can switch on or off (Chapter 12), or a UITextField where the user can change the text (Chapter 10). As in the previous example, the user changes the view, and you must update the model accordingly. But now there's no magic data source method to tell us what's happening. *You* need to arrange to hear that the user has made a change in a row of the table view, and you need to know *which* row the user changed so that you can reflect that change back into the data model.

To illustrate, imagine an app that maintains a list of names and phone numbers. The data are displayed as a grouped style table, and they become editable when the user taps the Edit button (Figure 8-8).

The table displays just one name but can display multiple phone numbers, so my data model looks like this:

```
var name = ""
var numbers = [String]()
```

We don't need an editing control at the left end of a cell when it's being edited:

```
override func tableView(_ tableView: UITableView,
    editingStyleForRowAt indexPath: IndexPath)
    -> UITableViewCell.EditingStyle {
        return .none
}
```

A UITextField is editable if its `isEnabled` is true. To tie this to the cell's `isEditing` state, I'll use a custom UITableViewCell class called MyCell with a single UITextField connected to an outlet property called `textField`:

```
class MyCell : UITableViewCell {
    @IBOutlet weak var textField : UITextField!
    override func didTransition(to state: UITableViewCell.StateMask) {
        self.textField.isEnabled = state.contains(.showingEditControl)
        super.didTransition(to:state)
    }
}
```

How will we hear that the user is editing a text field? One obvious way is to be the text field's delegate (adopting the UITextFieldDelegate protocol; I'll talk more about that in Chapter 10). We can conveniently set that up when we configure the cell:

```
override func tableView(_ tableView: UITableView,
    cellForRowAt indexPath: IndexPath) -> UITableViewCell {
        let cell = tableView.dequeueReusableCell(
            withIdentifier: self.cellID, for: indexPath) as! MyCell
        switch indexPath.section {
        case 0:
            cell.textField.text = self.name
        case 1:
            cell.textField.text = self.numbers[indexPath.row]
            cell.textField.keyboardType = .numbersAndPunctuation
        default: break
        }
        cell.textField.delegate = self // *
        return cell
}
```

Acting as the text field's delegate, we are responsible for implementing the Return button in the keyboard to dismiss the keyboard; we can do so by implementing `text-FieldShouldReturn(_:)`:

```
func textFieldShouldReturn(_ textField: UITextField) -> Bool {
    textField.endEditing(true)
    return false
}
```

Still acting as the text field's delegate, we can hear that the user has changed the text field's text, by implementing `textFieldDidEndEditing(_:)`:

```
func textFieldDidEndEditing(_ textField: UITextField) {
    // ???
}
```

Now we face a fundamental challenge. We know which text field this is, because it arrives as the parameter to the delegate method. But we don't know the index path of the cell containing this text field! And we need to know that in order to update the data model correctly.

There are various solutions to this problem, usually involving the text field's `tag` or some custom property. But the approach I favor is this: The table view knows what index path corresponds to this cell, and the cell is a superview of the text field, so I just walk up the view hierarchy from the text field to the cell. It is then trivial to update the model:

```
func textFieldDidEndEditing(_ textField: UITextField) {
    var v : UIView? = textField
    repeat { v = v?.superview } while !(v is UITableViewCell)
    if let cell = v as? MyCell {
        if let ip = self.tableView.indexPath(for:cell) {
            let s = cell.textField.text ?? ""
            switch ip.section {
            case 0: self.name = s
            case 1: self.numbers[ip.row] = s
            default: break
            }
        }
    }
}
```

Expandable Cell

A useful trick is to animate a change in the height of one or more cells by performing an empty batch operation:

```
self.tableView.performBatchUpdates(nil)
```

This causes the section and row *structure* of the table to be asked for, along with calculation of all heights, but no *views* are requested; the table view is laid out freshly without reloading any cells. But if any heights have changed since the last time the table view was laid out, the change in height is animated!

Apple's Calendar app is an example. When you're editing an event and you tap on the Starts or Ends date, a space opens up just below that row of the table, revealing a date picker. In reality, the date picker is in its own table view cell. It was there all along, but you couldn't see it because the cell had zero height and its `clipsToBounds` is `true`. When you tap on the Starts or Ends date, `performBatchUpdates` is called.

This causes `tableView(_:heightForRowAt:)` to be called, and a different answer is given for the height of this cell. The cell expands to reveal the date picker. (A cell that behaves this way is sometimes called an *accordion* cell.)

We can get the same effect using code along these lines:

```
var showDatePicker = false
func toggleDatePickerCell() {
    self.showDatePicker.toggle()
    self.tableView.performBatchUpdates(nil)
}
func tableView(_ tableView: UITableView,
    heightForRowAt indexPath: IndexPath) -> CGFloat {
        if indexPath == datePickerPath {
            return self.showDatePicker ? 200 : 0
        }
        return tableView.rowHeight
}
```

Table View Swipe Action Buttons

We've already seen that you can swipe a cell sideways to reveal a Delete button. You can customize that interface, introducing additional buttons that the user can reveal by swiping a cell sideways. That's how Apple's Mail app works: the user can swipe a message listing left to reveal three buttons, or swipe right to reveal one button, and can tap a button to perform an action on that message.

Starting in iOS 11, Apple provides an API that allows your app to have the same kind of interface as the Mail app. For each row of the table view, you specify *swipe actions;* these are buttons that can appear at the right or left (leading or trailing) end of the cell when the user swipes sideways. There are two delegate methods that you can implement:

- `tableView(_:leadingSwipeActionsConfigurationForRowAt:)`
- `tableView(_:trailingSwipeActionsConfigurationForRowAt:)`

Your job here is to return a UISwipeActionsConfiguration object (or `nil`), which wraps an array of UIContextualAction objects; a UIContextualAction is a button, initialized with a style (`.normal` or `.destructive`), a title, and an action function that will be called when the action is to be executed. The title can be `nil`, because you might set the UIContextualAction's `image` instead. Here's a simple example, where we implement a Delete button with a trash-can icon, along with a blue Mark button; the user can swipe left to see them:

```
override func tableView(_ tableView: UITableView,
    trailingSwipeActionsConfigurationForRowAt ip: IndexPath)
    -> UISwipeActionsConfiguration? {
        let d = UIContextualAction(style: .destructive, title: nil) {
```

```
            action, view, completion in
            tableView.performBatchUpdates({
                self.sections[ip.section].rowData.remove(at:ip.row)
                tableView.deleteRows(at:[ip], with: .automatic)
                if self.sections[ip.section].rowData.count == 0 {
                    self.sections.remove(at:ip.section)
                    tableView.deleteSections(
                        IndexSet(integer: ip.section), with:.fade)
                }
            })
            completion(true)
        }
        d.image = UIGraphicsImageRenderer(size:CGSize(30,30)).image { _ in
            UIImage(named:"trash")?.draw(in: CGRect(0,0,30,30))
        }
        let m = UIContextualAction(style: .normal, title: "Mark") {
            action, view, completion in
            print("Mark") // in real life, do something here
            completion(true)
        }
        m.backgroundColor = .blue
        let config = UISwipeActionsConfiguration(actions: [d,m])
        return config
    }
```

The code for the first button (d) comes directly from the `.delete` case of the `table-View(_:commit:forRowAt:)` implementation we developed earlier. In fact, if the table view is in edit mode with a Minus button and the user taps the Minus button, the custom contextual actions are revealed; they have replaced the default Delete button! So if you use a trailing swipe action, you probably won't need to implement `table-View(_:commit:forRowAt:)` at all.

The action function receives as its parameters the UIContextualAction itself, the view (which you probably won't need), and a completion function. You *must* call this completion function, with a Bool argument, to signal that the action is over and the swiped cell should slide back into place.

The `actions` for the UISwipeActionsConfiguration object are supplied in order, starting at the far end of the cell. A UISwipeActionsConfiguration object has one additional property, a Bool called `performsFirstActionWithFullSwipe`. If this is `true`, the user can keep swiping to perform the first action; if `false`, the user must swipe to reveal the button and then tap the button. The default is `true` for trailing actions, `false` for leading actions.

Table View Menus

You can permit the user to summon a menu by long pressing on a table view cell. In iOS 12 and before, this menu was managed through the UIMenuController class, and the menu was similar to what appears above a text field when you double tap or long press within the text (saying Copy, Paste, Select, and so forth). New in iOS 13, it's the same UIContextMenuConfiguration architecture that I discussed earlier ("Previews and Context Menus" on page 382). With a table view, you don't need to add a UIContextMenuInteraction or declare a delegate; instead, the table view is ready for the user to long press on a cell, and the delegate is the table view's delegate. The key method is:

- `tableView(_:contextMenuConfigurationForRowAt:point:)`

You return a UIContextMenuConfiguration instance (or `nil` to opt out on this occasion). The second parameter is the index path for the cell the user is pressing.

Here's a minimal example where we allow the user to summon a Copy context menu item by long pressing a cell. Presume this is our table view listing U.S. states, and we want the user to be able to copy the name of a state:

```
override func tableView(_ tableView: UITableView,
    contextMenuConfigurationForRowAt ip: IndexPath, point: CGPoint)
    -> UIContextMenuConfiguration? {
        let config = UIContextMenuConfiguration(
            identifier:nil, previewProvider: nil) { _ in
                let action = UIAction(title: "Copy") { _ in
                    let state = self.sections[ip.section].rowData[ip.row]
                    UIPasteboard.general.string = state
                }
                let menu = UIMenu(title: "", children: [action])
                return menu
        }
        return config
}
```

The user can now long press a cell to summon a menu consisting of single menu item labeled "Copy." If the user taps that item, the name of the corresponding state is copied onto the pasteboard.

There are three additional delegate methods, similar to the UIContextMenuInteractionDelegate methods I discussed earlier:

- `tableView(_:previewForHighlightingContextMenuWithConfiguration:)`
- `tableView(_:previewForDismissingContextMenuWithConfiguration:)`
- `tableView(_:willPerformPreviewActionForMenuWith:)`

If you don't supply a preview, the entire cell is used as a preview. If you return a subview of the cell as the UITargetedPreview in `previewForHighlighting`, it looks best if you return the same subview in `previewForDismissing`.

For all three of these delegate methods, you'll likely want to know what cell the user is pressing. But no incoming parameter tells you that; all you get is the UIContextMenu-

Configuration. One solution is to use the index path (or, if you're using a diffable data source, a unique item identifier) as the `identifier:` when you initialize the configuration; then, in these delegate methods, you can ask the configuration for its `identifier`. Another possibility might be to subclass UIContextMenuConfiguration and give the subclass properties that carry any needed data into the delegate methods.

Table View Searching

A common need is to make a table view searchable, typically through a search field (a UISearchBar; see Chapter 12). A standard interface for listing the results of such a search is itself a table view. The interface should respond to what the user types in the search field by changing what appears in the list of results. To help you, there's a UIViewController subclass, UISearchController.

UISearchController has nothing to do, *per se*, with table views! It's completely agnostic about what is being searched and about the form in which the results are presented. Still, using a table view to present the results of searching a table view is a common interface, so this is a good place to introduce UISearchController.

Configuring a Search Controller

A UISearchController is a view controller; it provides an interface containing a search bar and the results of the search. The search controller vends its search bar, and you'll put that search bar into your initial interface. When the user taps in the search bar to begin searching, the search controller will take over the screen. And that's basically *all* the search controller does. It knows nothing about doing any actual searching or about showing the user the results of the search. All of that is up to you. You provide two things:

Search results controller
> The search results controller is your view controller that shows the user the results of the search. The UISearchController will display the search results controller's view, but what happens in that view is up to you.

Search results updater
> The search results updater is the search controller's conduit to you; basically, it's a kind of delegate. The search results controller will be repeatedly informing you that the user has edited the text in the search field; in response, you'll perform the actual search and update the results.

Here's what's going to happen:

- When the time comes to display search results (because the user has tapped inside the search bar in your initial interface), the search controller will present itself as a presented view controller, displaying the same search bar, with the search results controller's view embedded inside its own view.

• When the user edits in the search bar, the search controller will notify the search results updater.

• When the user taps the search bar's Cancel button, the search controller will dismiss itself.

The minimalistic nature of the search controller's behavior is exactly the source of its power and flexibility, because it leaves you free to manage the details of what searching means and what displaying search results means.

Here are the general steps for configuring a UISearchController (and I'll talk about exceptions in subsequent sections):

1. Instantiate a view controller whose job will be to display the results of the search. This is the search results controller. (In this discussion, the search results controller will be a UITableViewController, but no law requires this.)

2. Instantiate UISearchController, calling the designated initializer, `init(search-ResultsController:)`, with the search results controller as argument. *Retain the search controller.* The search controller will retain the search results controller as a child view controller.

3. Assign to the search controller's `searchResultsUpdater` an object to be notified when the search results change. This is the search results updater. It must adopt the UISearchResultsUpdating protocol, which means that it implements one method: `updateSearchResults(for:)`. Often, the search results updater will be the search results controller, but no law requires this.

4. Acquire the search controller's `searchBar` and put it into the interface.

A UISearchController has just a few other properties you might want to configure:

`obscuresBackgroundDuringPresentation`
Whether a "dimming view" should appear behind the search controller's own view. Defaults to `true`, but there are situations where it needs to be set to `false` (as I'll demonstrate later).

`hidesNavigationBarDuringPresentation`
Whether a navigation bar, if present, should be hidden. Defaults to `true`, but there are situations where it needs to be set to `false` (as I'll demonstrate later).

A UISearchController has its own ideas about when it wants to show the search bar's scope bar if it has one, the search bar's Cancel button, and the search results controller's view. New in iOS 13, that automatic behavior is governed by three properties:

- `automaticallyShowsCancelButton`

- `automaticallyShowsScopeBar`

- `automaticallyShowsSearchResultsController`

If you set any of the corresponding properties — the search bar's `showsCancel-Button`, the search bar's `showsScopeBar`, or the search controller's `showsSearchResultsController` — that `automaticallyShows` property is set to `false` and control of that property is turned over to you.

A UISearchController can also be assigned a real delegate (UISearchControllerDelegate), which is notified before and after presentation and dismissal. The delegate works in one of two ways:

`presentSearchController(_:)`
> If you implement this method, then you are expected to present the search controller yourself, by calling `present(_:animated:completion:)`. In that case, the other delegate methods are *not* called.

`willPresentSearchController(_:)`
`didPresentSearchController(_:)`
`willDismissSearchController(_:)`
`didDismissSearchController(_:)`
> Called only if you didn't implement `presentSearchController(_:)`.

Using a Search Controller

I'll demonstrate several variations on the theme of using a search controller to make a table view searchable. In these examples, the searchable table view will be (you guessed it) the list of U.S. states, with sections and an index, developed earlier in this chapter. Searching will mean finding the search text within the text displayed in the single label in each of the table view's cells — that is, we will search the state names.

Minimal search results table

Let's start with the simplest possible case. We will have two table view controllers — one managing the original table view, the other managing the search results table view. I propose to make the search results table view as minimal as possible, a rock-bottom table view with `.default` style cells, where each search result will be the `text` of a cell's `textLabel` (Figure 8-9).

In the original table's UITableViewController, I configure the UISearchController, in accordance with the steps that I described earlier. I have a property, `self.searcher`, waiting to retain the search controller. I also have a second UITableViewController subclass, boringly named SearchResultsController, whose job will be to obtain and

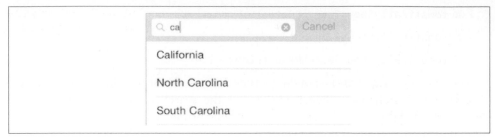

Figure 8-9. Searching a table

present the search results. In `viewDidLoad`, I instantiate SearchResultsController, create and configure the UISearchController, and put the search controller's search bar into the interface as the table view's header view (and scroll to hide that search bar initially, a common convention):

```
let src = SearchResultsController(data: self.sections)
let searcher = UISearchController(searchResultsController: src)
self.searcher = searcher
searcher.searchResultsUpdater = src
let b = searcher.searchBar
b.autocapitalizationType = .none
self.tableView.tableHeaderView = b
self.tableView.reloadData()
self.tableView.scrollToRow(
    at:IndexPath(row: 0, section: 0), at:.top, animated:false)
```

 Adding the search bar as the table view's header view has an odd side effect: it causes the table view's background color to be covered by an ugly gray color, visible above the search bar when the user scrolls down. The official workaround is to assign the table view a `backgroundView` with the desired color.

Now we turn to SearchResultsController. It's a table view controller. I'm not using sections in the SearchResultsController's table, so as I receive the searchable data, I flatten it to a simple array:

```
var originalData : [String]
var filteredData = [String]()
init(data:[RootViewController.Section]) {
    self.originalData = data.map{$0.rowData}.flatMap{$0}
    super.init(nibName: nil, bundle: nil)
}
```

What I display in the table view is not `self.originalData` but a *different* array, `self.filteredData`. This is initially empty, because there are no search results until the user starts typing in the search field. So how does our search results table go from being empty to displaying any search results? SearchResultsController is also the `searchResultsUpdater` of our UISearchController. It adopts the UISearchResults-Updating protocol, so it implements `updateSearchResults(for:)`, which will be called each time the user changes the text of the search bar. This method simply uses the current text of the search controller's `searchBar` to filter `self.originalData` into `self.filteredData`, and reloads the table view:

```
func updateSearchResults(for searchController: UISearchController) {
    let sb = searchController.searchBar
    let target = sb.text!
    self.filteredData = self.originalData.filter { s in
        let found = s.range(of:target, options: .caseInsensitive)
        return (found != nil)
    }
    self.tableView.reloadData()
}
```

That's all! Of course, it's an artificially simple example; in real life you would presumably want to allow the user to *do* something with the search results, perhaps by tapping on a cell in the search results table.

Using a diffable data source instead of a Three Big Questions data source is a nice way to animate the results table as the user types in the search bar. Now there's no need for a `filteredData` instance property; we simply filter the original data into a snapshot and apply it:

```
func updateSearchResults(for searchController: UISearchController) {
    let sb = searchController.searchBar
    let target = sb.text!
    var snap = NSDiffableDataSourceSnapshot<Int,String>()
    snap.appendSections([0])
    snap.appendItems(self.originalData.filter { s in
        let found = s.range(of:target, options: .caseInsensitive)
        return (found != nil)
    })
    self.datasource.apply(snap)
}
```

Search bar in navigation bar

In a navigation interface, you can put the UISearchController's search bar into the navigation bar. Starting in iOS 11, Apple seems to prefer that interface over putting it into the table view's header view, and facilitates it through a UINavigationItem property: instead of finding a place for the search bar in the navigation bar yourself — as its `titleView`, for instance — you set the `searchController` of your view controller's `navigationItem` directly to your UISearchController instance. When you do that, you don't need to retain the search controller; the navigation item will retain it for you:

```
let src = SearchResultsController(data: self.sections)
let searcher = UISearchController(searchResultsController: src)
searcher.searchResultsUpdater = src
self.navigationItem.searchController = searcher // *
```

Nothing else needs to change; our search results controller just keeps right on working.

The consequences of this arrangement are:

- The navigation bar stretches to accommodate the search bar, which appears *below* everything else in the navigation bar; the search bar makes no inroads on the space used by the title and the bar button items.

- If the navigation bar's prefersLargeTitles is true, the interface still works just fine, with the search bar displayed below the large title if there is one.

- If the navigation item's hidesSearchBarWhenScrolling property is true, the navigation bar expands and contracts to reveal or hide the search bar as the user scrolls.

- You can decide whether the overall navigation bar should remain present when the search controller's view is being presented, by setting the search controller's hidesNavigationBarDuringPresentation. The default is true, which means that the navigation bar shrinks to show just the search bar at the top during the search.

- The search bar can have scope buttons! Set the search bar's scopeButtonTitles as desired. By default, the scope buttons will appear when the search controller presents its view.

I'll demonstrate the use of scope buttons. Let's say we've configured this search bar with two scope buttons:

```
let b = searcher.searchBar
b.scopeButtonTitles = ["Contains", "Starts With"]
```

We must take account of the currently selected scope button whenever we set self.filteredData. New in iOS 13, updateSearchResults is called when the user changes the selected scope button, so its implementation is simple:

```
func updateSearchResults(for sc: UISearchController) {
    if let target = sc.searchBar.text {
        let selectedIndex = sc.searchBar.selectedScopeButtonIndex
        self.filteredData = self.originalData.filter { s in
            var options = String.CompareOptions.caseInsensitive
            if selectedIndex == 1 { // 1 means "starts with"
                options.insert(.anchored)
            }
            let found = s.range(of:target, options: options)
            return (found != nil)
        }
        self.tableView.reloadData()
    }
}
```

No search results controller

You can also use a search controller *without* a search results controller. Instead, you can present the search results *in the original table view*.

To configure our search controller, we pass `nil` as its `searchResultsController` and set the original table view controller as the `searchResultsUpdater`. We must also set the search controller's `obscuresBackgroundDuringPresentation` to `false`; this allows the original table view to remain *visible and touchable* behind the search controller's view:

```
let searcher = UISearchController(searchResultsController:nil) // *
self.searcher = searcher
searcher.obscuresBackgroundDuringPresentation = false // *
searcher.searchResultsUpdater = self
searcher.delegate = self
```

We have also made ourselves the search controller's delegate, because we might need to distinguish whether we're in the middle of a search or not. We have a Bool property, `self.searching`, that acts as a flag; we raise and lower the flag when searching begins and ends. We also create a copy of our data model whenever we're about to start searching; the reason for that will be clear in a moment:

```
func willPresentSearchController(_ searchController: UISearchController) {
    self.originalSections = self.sections // keep copy of original data
    self.searching = true
}
func willDismissSearchController(_ searchController: UISearchController) {
    self.searching = false
}
```

Our table view data source and delegate methods don't need to change unless there's a difference in the interface depending on whether or not we're searching. Let's say we want to remove the index while searching is in progress:

```
override func sectionIndexTitlesForTableView(tableView: UITableView)
    -> [String]? {
        return self.searching ? nil : self.sections.map{$0.sectionName}
}
```

All that remains is to implement `updateSearchResults(for:)`. Similar to our search results controller, whenever we're doing a search we're going to filter `self.original-Sections` into `self.sections` based on the search bar text:

```
func updateSearchResults(for searchController: UISearchController) {
    let sb = searchController.searchBar
    let target = sb.text!
    if target == "" {
        self.sections = self.originalSections
    } else {
        self.sections = self.originalSections.reduce(into:[Section]()) {
```

```
            acc, sec in
            let rowData = sec.rowData.filter {
                $0.range(of:target, options: .caseInsensitive) != nil
            }
            if rowData.count > 0 {
                acc.append(Section(
                    sectionName: sec.sectionName, rowData: rowData))
            }
        }
    }
    self.tableView.reloadData()
}
```

Collection Views

A collection view (UICollectionView) is a UIScrollView that generalizes the notion of a table view. Where a table view has *rows*, a collection view has *items*. (UICollection-View extends IndexPath so that you can refer to its `item` property instead of its `row` property, though in fact they are interchangeable.) If you mentally substitute for items for rows, you'll find that, knowing about table views, you know a great deal about collection views already:

- The items are portrayed by reusable cells. These are UICollectionViewCell instances. If the collection view is instantiated from a storyboard, you can get reusable cells from the storyboard; otherwise, you'll register a class or nib with the collection view.

- A collection view can clump its items into sections.

- A collection view has a data source (UICollectionViewDataSource) and a delegate (UICollectionViewDelegate), and it's going to ask the data source Three Big Questions:

  - `numberOfSections(in:)`

  - `collectionView(_:numberOfItemsInSection:)`

  - `collectionView(_:cellForItemAt:)`

  Alternatively, new in iOS 13, you can use a UICollectionViewDiffableData-Source.

- To answer the third Big Question, your data source will obtain a reusable cell by dequeuing it from the collection view:

  - `dequeueReusableCell(withReuseIdentifier:for:)`

- A collection view allows the user to select a cell, or multiple cells. The delegate is notified of highlighting and selection.

- Your code can rearrange the cells, inserting, moving, and deleting cells or entire sections, with animation.

- If the delegate permits, the user can long press a cell to produce a menu, or to rearrange the cells by dragging.

- You can scroll your collection view in code by calling `scrollTo-Item(at:at:animated:)`. The collection view's delegate is its scroll view delegate (and UICollectionViewDelegate conforms to UIScrollViewDelegate).

- A collection view can have a refresh control.

- You can manage your UICollectionView through a UICollectionViewController.

A collection view section can have a header and footer, but the collection view itself does not call them that; instead, it generalizes its subview types into cells, on the one hand, and *supplementary views*, on the other. A supplementary view is just a UICollectionReusableView, which is UICollectionViewCell's superclass. A supplementary view is associated with a *kind*, an arbitrary string that categorizes it however you like; you can have a header as one kind, a footer as another kind, and anything else you can imagine. Having made that mental substitution, you can see that supplementary views behave quite similarly to section header or footer views in a table view:

- Supplementary views are reusable.

- You are asked for a supplementary view in a data source method (*not* a delegate method):
    - `collectionView(_:viewForSupplementaryElementOfKind:at:)`

- In that method, your data source will obtain a reusable supplementary view by dequeuing it from the collection view:
    - `dequeueReusableSupplementaryView(ofKind:withReuseIdentifier:for:)`

Here are some small differences between a table view and a collection view:

- A collection view has no edit mode (nor has a collection view cell).

- A collection view has no section index.

The *big* difference between a table view and a collection view is how the collection view lays out its elements (cells and supplementary views). A table view lays out its cells in just one way: a vertically scrolling column, where the cell widths are the width of the table view, their heights are dictated by the table view or the delegate, and the cells are touching one another. A collection view has no such rules. In fact, a collection view doesn't lay out its elements at all! That job is left to another object — a *collection view layout*.

A collection view layout is an instance of a UICollectionViewLayout subclass. It is responsible for the overall layout of the collection view that owns it. It does this by answering some Big Questions of its own, posed by the collection view; the most important are these:

`collectionViewContentSize`
> How big is the entire content? The collection view needs to know this, because it is a scroll view (Chapter 7), and this will be the content size of the scrollable material that it will display.

`layoutAttributesForElements(in:)`
> Where are the elements to be positioned within the content rectangle? The layout attributes, as I'll explain in more detail in a moment, are bundles of positional information.

To answer these questions, the collection view layout needs to ask the collection view some questions as well. It will want to know the collection view's bounds; also, it will probably call such methods as `numberOfSections` and `numberOfItems(inSection:)`, and the collection view, in turn, will get the answers to those questions from its data source.

The collection view layout can assign the elements any positions it likes, and the collection view will faithfully draw them in those positions within its content rectangle. That seems very open-ended, and indeed it is. To get you started, there are two built-in UICollectionViewLayout subclasses:

- UICollectionViewFlowLayout
- UICollectionViewCompositionalLayout (new in iOS 13)

UICollectionViewFlowLayout arranges its cells in something like a grid. The grid can be scrolled either horizontally or vertically, but not both, so it's a series of rows or columns. Through properties and a delegate protocol of its own (UICollectionView-DelegateFlowLayout), the UICollectionViewFlowLayout instance lets you provide instructions about how big the cells are and how they should be spaced. It defines two supplementary view kinds to let you give each section a header and a footer.

Figure 8-10 shows a collection view, laid out with a flow layout, from my Latin flashcard app. This interface lists the chapters and lessons into which the flashcards are divided, and allows the user to jump to a desired lesson by tapping it. Previously, I was using a table view to present this list; when collection views were introduced (in iOS 6), I adopted one for this interface, and you can see why. Instead of a lesson item like "1a" occupying an entire row that stretches the whole width of a table, it's just a little rectangle; in landscape orientation, the flow layout fits about half a dozen of these rectangles into a line for me. So a collection view is a much more compact and appropriate way to present this interface than a table view.

If UICollectionViewFlowLayout doesn't quite meet your needs, you can subclass it. Alternatively, you can subclass UICollectionViewLayout itself to create a layout from

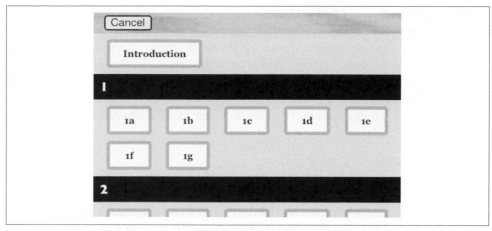

Figure 8-10. A collection view in my Latin flashcard app

scratch. New in iOS 13, there's a third possibility: you can use a UICollectionView-CompositionalLayout. This is a powerful and flexible layout that does all the heavy lifting for you; it can do everything a flow layout can do, and much more.

Collection View Classes

Here's a conceptual overview of the main classes associated with UICollectionView; I don't recite all the properties and methods of each class, because you can gather them from the documentation:

UICollectionViewController
A UIViewController subclass. Like a table view controller, UICollectionView-Controller is convenient if a UICollectionView is to be a view controller's view, but using it is not required. It is the delegate and data source of its collection-View by default. The designated initializer requires you to supply a collection view layout instance, which will be assigned to the collection view as its layout. In the nib editor, there is a Collection View Controller nib object, which comes with a collection view.

UICollectionView
A UIScrollView subclass. Its capabilities are parallel to those of a UITableView, as I outlined in the preceding section. It has a backgroundColor (because it's a view) and optionally a backgroundView in front of that. Its designated initializer requires you to supply a collection view layout instance, which will be its collectionViewLayout. In the nib editor, there is a Collection View nib object, which comes with a Collection View Flow Layout by default; you can change the collection view layout class with the Layout pop-up menu in the Attributes inspector.

UICollectionViewLayoutAttributes

A value class (a bunch of properties) tying together an element's `indexPath` with the specifications for how and where it should be drawn. These specifications are reminiscent of view or layer properties, with names like `frame`, `center`, `size`, `transform`, and so forth. Layout attributes objects function as the mediators between the collection view layout and the collection view; they are what the collection view layout passes to the collection view to tell it where all the elements of the view should go.

UICollectionViewCell

An extremely minimal view class. It has an `isHighlighted` property and an `isSelected` property. It has a `contentView`, a `selectedBackgroundView`, a `backgroundView`, and of course (since it's a view) a `backgroundColor`, layered in that order, just like a table view cell; everything else is up to you. If you start with a collection view in a storyboard, you get prototype cells, which you obtain by dequeuing. Otherwise, you obtain cells through registration and dequeuing.

UICollectionReusableView

The superclass of UICollectionViewCell — so it is even more minimal! This is the class of supplementary views such as headers and footers. If you're using a flow layout in a storyboard, you are given header and footer prototype views, which you obtain by dequeuing; otherwise, you obtain reusable views through registration and dequeuing.

UICollectionViewLayout

The layout workhorse class for a collection view. A collection view cannot exist without a collection view layout instance! As I've already said, the collection view layout knows how much room all the subviews occupy, and supplies the `collectionViewContentSize` that sets the `contentSize` of the collection view, *qua* scroll view. In addition, the collection view layout must answer questions from the collection view, by supplying a UICollectionViewLayoutAttributes object, or an array of such objects, saying where and how elements should be drawn. These questions come in two categories:

Static attributes

The collection view wants to know the layout attributes of an element (an item or supplementary view), specified by the element's index path, or of all elements within a given rect.

Dynamic attributes

The collection view is inserting or removing elements. It asks for the layout attributes that an element, specified by index path, should have as insertion begins or removal ends. The collection view can animate between the element's static attributes and these dynamic attributes. If an element's dynamic layout attributes `alpha` is 0 as removal ends, the element will appear to fade away as it is removed.

The collection view also notifies the collection view layout of pending changes through some methods whose names start with `prepare` and `finalize`. This is another way for the collection view layout to participate in animations, or to perform other kinds of preparation and cleanup.

UICollectionViewLayout is an abstract class; to use it, you must subclass it, or start with a built-in subclass, either UICollectionViewFlowLayout or (new in iOS 13) UICollectionViewCompositionalLayout.

Flow Layout

UICollectionViewFlowLayout is a concrete subclass of UICollectionViewLayout. It lays out items in a grid that can be scrolled either horizontally or vertically, and it defines two supplementary element types to serve as the header and footer of a section. A collection view in the nib editor has a Layout pop-up menu that lets you choose a Flow layout, and you can configure the flow layout in the Size inspector; in a storyboard, you can even add and design a header and a footer.

A flow layout has the following configurable properties:

- `scrollDirection`, either `.vertical` or `.horizontal`
- `sectionInset` (the margins for a section); starting in iOS 11, the `sectionInset-Reference` property lets you specify where the inset is measured from (`.fromContentInset`, `.fromLayoutMargins`, or `.fromSafeArea`)
- `itemSize`, along with `minimumLineSpacing` (spacing in the scroll direction) and `minimumInteritemSpacing` (spacing in the other direction)
- `headerReferenceSize`, `footerReferenceSize`
- `sectionHeadersPinToVisibleBounds`, `sectionFootersPinToVisibleBounds`; if true, they cause the headers and footers to behave like table view section headers and footers when the user scrolls

At a minimum, if you want to see any section headers, you must assign the flow layout a `headerReferenceSize`, because the default is `.zero`. Otherwise, you get initial defaults that will at least allow you to see something immediately, such as an `itemSize` of (50.0,50.0) along with reasonable default spacing between items and rows (or columns).

UICollectionViewFlowLayout also defines a delegate protocol of its own, UICollectionViewDelegateFlowLayout. The flow layout automatically treats the collection view's delegate as its own delegate. The section margins, item size, item spacing, line spacing, and header and footer size can be set for individual sections, cells, and supplementary views through this delegate.

 You must explicitly declare that the collection view's delegate adopts the UICollectionViewDelegateFlowLayout protocol. Otherwise, your flow layout delegate methods won't be called.

To illustrate, here's how the view shown in Figure 8-10 is created. I have a UICollectionViewController subclass, LessonListController. Every collection view must have a collection view layout, so LessonListController's designated initializer initializes itself with a UICollectionViewFlowLayout:

```
init(terms data:[Term]) {
    // ... other self-initializations here ...
    let layout = UICollectionViewFlowLayout()
    super.init(collectionViewLayout:layout)
}
```

In `viewDidLoad`, we give the flow layout its hints about the sizes of the margins, cells, and headers, as well as registering for cell and header reusability:

```
let headerID = "LessonHeader"
let cellID = "LessonCell"
override func viewDidLoad() {
    super.viewDidLoad()
    let layout = self.collectionView.collectionViewLayout
        as! UICollectionViewFlowLayout
    layout.sectionInset = UIEdgeInsets(top:10, left:20, bottom:10, right:20)
    layout.headerReferenceSize = CGSize(0,40)
    layout.itemSize = CGSize(70,45)
    self.collectionView.register(
        UINib(nibName: self.cellID, bundle: nil),
        forCellWithReuseIdentifier: self.cellID)
    self.collectionView.register(
        UICollectionReusableView.self,
        forSupplementaryViewOfKind: UICollectionView.elementKindSectionHeader,
        withReuseIdentifier: self.headerID)
    self.collectionView.backgroundColor = .myGolden
    self.collectionView.contentInsetAdjustmentBehavior = .always
}
```

My data model is just like the model for the table of U.S. states I've been using throughout this chapter. (What are the chances of *that*?) The difference is that my `rowData`, instead of being an array of Strings, is an array of Terms. (Term is basically a custom value class.) The first two of the Three Big Questions are extremely familiar:

```
override func numberOfSections(
    in collectionView: UICollectionView) -> Int {
        return self.sections.count
}
```

```
override func collectionView(_ collectionView: UICollectionView,
    numberOfItemsInSection section: Int) -> Int {
        return self.sections[section].rowData.count
}
```

The third of the Three Big Questions creates and configures the cells. In a *.xib* file, I've designed the cell with a single subview, a UILabel with tag 1; if the text of that label is still "Label", the cell has come freshly minted from the nib and needs further initial configuration. Among other things, I assign each new cell a selected-BackgroundView and give the label a highlightedTextColor, to get an automatic indication of selection:

```
override func collectionView(_ collectionView: UICollectionView,
    cellForItemAt indexPath: IndexPath) -> UICollectionViewCell {
        let cell = collectionView.dequeueReusableCell(
            withReuseIdentifier: self.cellID, for: indexPath)
        let lab = cell.viewWithTag(1) as! UILabel
        if lab.text == "Label" {
            lab.highlightedTextColor = .white
            cell.backgroundColor = .myPaler
            cell.layer.borderColor = UIColor.brown.cgColor
            cell.layer.borderWidth = 5
            cell.layer.cornerRadius = 5
            let v = UIView()
            v.backgroundColor = UIColor.blue.withAlphaComponent(0.8)
            cell.selectedBackgroundView = v
        }
        let term = self.sections[indexPath.section].rowData[indexPath.item]
        lab.text = term.lesson + term.sectionFirstWord
        return cell
}
```

The data source is also asked for the supplementary element views; in my case, these are the section headers. I configure the header entirely in code. Again I distinguish between newly minted views and reused views; the latter will already have a single subview, a UILabel:

```
override func collectionView(_ collectionView: UICollectionView,
    viewForSupplementaryElementOfKind kind: String,
    at indexPath: IndexPath) -> UICollectionReusableView {
        let v = collectionView.dequeueReusableSupplementaryView(
            ofKind: kind,
            withReuseIdentifier: self.headerID, for: indexPath)
        if v.subviews.count == 0 {
            let lab = UILabel(frame:CGRect(10,0,100,40))
            lab.font = UIFont(name:"GillSans-Bold", size:20)
            lab.backgroundColor = .clear
            v.addSubview(lab)
            v.backgroundColor = .black
            lab.textColor = .myPaler
        }
```

```
        let lab = v.subviews[0] as! UILabel
        lab.text = self.sections[indexPath.section].sectionName
        return v
    }
```

As you can see from Figure 8-10, the first section is treated specially — it has no header, and its cell is wider. I take care of that with two UICollectionViewDelegate-FlowLayout methods:

```
func collectionView(_ collectionView: UICollectionView,
    layout lay: UICollectionViewLayout,
    sizeForItemAt indexPath: IndexPath) -> CGSize {
        var sz = (lay as! UICollectionViewFlowLayout).itemSize
        if indexPath.section == 0 {
            sz.width = 150
        }
        return sz
}
func collectionView(_ collectionView: UICollectionView,
    layout lay: UICollectionViewLayout,
    referenceSizeForHeaderInSection section: Int) -> CGSize {
        var sz = (lay as! UICollectionViewFlowLayout).headerReferenceSize
        if section == 0 {
            sz.height = 0
        }
        return sz
}
```

When the user taps a cell, I hear about it through the delegate method `collection-View(_:didSelectItemAt:)` and respond accordingly. And that's the entire code for managing this collection view!

Compositional Layout

New in iOS 13, there's another concrete UICollectionViewLayout subclass, UICollectionViewCompositionalLayout. It can do everything UICollectionViewFlowLayout can do; even more important, it can achieve layouts that previously required you to write a custom UICollectionViewLayout subclass from scratch.

You construct a compositional layout by building up a description from the smallest element to the largest (hence the term *compositional*). The elements are:

item (NSCollectionLayoutItem)
    In effect, a cell.

group (NSCollectionLayoutGroup)
    A single unidimensional set of items, either horizontal or vertical. Think of it as a single row or column. In most layouts, a group will run along the other axis from

the layout's scrolling direction. If a layout scrolls vertically, a group will typically be horizontal and will represent one row of cells.

section (NSCollectionLayoutSection)
A section repeats a group. If a group is a row, a section may contain many rows. Your data may have one or more sections. Sections can be laid out differently from one another.

layout (UICollectionViewCompositionalLayout)
The object that will actually be handed to the collection view as its layout.

Size, Count, Spacing, and Insets

As you construct a compositional layout, you must specify the *size* of a section's group, the *size* of an item in the group, and the *count* of items per group. These are the most important determinants of how the cells will be laid out in the section; further refinements are provided through various spacing and inset properties.

Size is specified using the NSCollectionLayoutSize initializer `init(widthDimension:heightDimension:)`. A dimension is an NSCollectionLayoutDimension, which has four class methods:

`absolute`
A definite number of points.

`fractionalWidth`
`fractionalHeight`
A proportion, between 0 and 1, of the container. For an item, the container is the group. For a group, the container is the collection view bounds. These are just numbers, so it is legal for the `heightDimension:` to be a `fractionalWidth` and *vice versa.*

`estimated`
A number of points, but you are inviting the layout engine to measure cells using internal autolayout constraints to determine the actual value. A common situation is that one dimension of a size is fixed while the other is estimated.

A group is instantiated using the `horizontal` or `vertical` class method. You supply parameters in two different ways:

`horizontal(layoutSize:subitems:)`
`vertical(layoutSize:subitems:)`
The group repeats one or more item types, as many per group as will fit. Suppose the `subitems:` consists of two item types, one wide and one narrow; then the layout will alternate wide item with narrow item, filling a group before going on to the next group.

```
horizontal(layoutSize:subitem:count:)
vertical(layoutSize:subitem:count:)
```
The group repeats a single item type, a fixed number of times per group. The items will be equally sized, possibly overriding the item's own size in that dimension. For instance, you can specify that there should be exactly three equally sized items per group.

Apple's own examples illustrate some basic combinations of item size, group size, and item count; these are all vertically scrolling collection views, so a group is a row:

- The item has width dimension fractional width 1 and height dimension fractional height 1. The group has width dimension fractional width 1 and height dimension absolute 44, and the `subitems:` initializer is used. So each row is as wide as the collection view and 44 points tall, with one item per row, filling the row. It looks like a table view.

- Like the previous layout, but the group's `subitem:count:` initializer is used with a `count:` of 2. There are exactly two cells per row and they have equal widths; the item's `layoutSize:` width dimension is effectively ignored.

- The item has width dimension fractional width `0.2` and height dimension fractional height 1. The group has width dimension 1 and height dimension fractional *width* `0.2`, and the `subitems:` initializer is used. So an item's width is one-fifth the width of the collection view, and a row's height is that same value — and an item's height fills it, resulting in a grid of square cells, five per row.

Further size refinements are applied through spacing and insets properties of the item, group, and section:

Item `edgeSpacing`
An NSLayoutEdgeSpacing object with `leading:`, `top:`, `trailing:`, and `bottom:` parameters. A parameter is either `nil` or an NSCollectionLayoutSpacing object, instantiated through a class function, either `flexible` or `fixed`. For instance, in a vertically scrolling layout whose group uses the `subitems:` initializer, if there is room for only one cell per group, then a `leading:` and `trailing:` spacing of `.flexible(0)` will center the cell horizontally.

Group `interItemSpacing`
The distance between items within the group. This is also an NSCollectionLayoutSpacing, so it can be `flexible`, causing the items to be spaced out equally and justified at both extremes.

Section `interGroupSpacing`
A CGFloat determining absolutely the distance between rows (or columns) in the section.

Layout `interSectionSpacing`

> A CGFloat. A property, not of the layout itself, but of its `configuration`, a UICollectionViewCompositionalLayoutConfiguration (a value class). The configuration is also how you specify the layout's `scrollDirection`; the default is `.vertical`, so if that's what you want, and if you don't need to set the section spacing, you might not need a layout configuration.

Item, group, or section `contentInsets`

> An NSDirectionalEdgeInsets (Chapter 1). Content insets are applied *after* the sizing and layout have been worked out. In Apple's example of a grid with 5 square cells per row, if a positive `contentInsets` is applied to the item, there are *still* five cells per row, each in a square area, but a cell itself is inset within that square area. (Any `contentInsets` along an `estimated` dimension are ignored.)

You now know almost enough to achieve the layout shown in Figure 8-10 as a compositional layout! I haven't talked yet about section headers, and the first section's single item needs to be wider than all other items; but if we concentrate on just the items of the remaining sections, we can construct the layout like this:

```
private static func prepareLayout() -> UICollectionViewLayout {
    let itemSize = NSCollectionLayoutSize(
        widthDimension: .absolute(70),
        heightDimension: .fractionalHeight(1))
    let item = NSCollectionLayoutItem(layoutSize: itemSize)
    let groupSize = NSCollectionLayoutSize(
        widthDimension: .fractionalWidth(1),
        heightDimension: .absolute(45))
    let group = NSCollectionLayoutGroup.horizontal(
        layoutSize: groupSize, subitems: [item])
    group.interItemSpacing = .flexible(10)
    group.contentInsets = NSDirectionalEdgeInsets(
        top: 0, leading: 20, bottom: 0, trailing: 20)
    let section = NSCollectionLayoutSection(group: group)
    let vSpace = CGFloat(10)
    section.contentInsets = NSDirectionalEdgeInsets(
        top: vSpace, leading: 0, bottom: vSpace, trailing: 0)
    section.interGroupSpacing = vSpace
    let layout = UICollectionViewCompositionalLayout(section: section)
    return layout
}
```

Here's how that compositional layout mimics the flow layout shown in Figure 8-10:

Flow behavior

> The compositional layout behaves like a flow layout because the group uses the `subitems:` initializer, meaning that a row consists of as many cells as will fit, along with `.flexible` spacing to cause the cells to be justified at the leading and trailing edges with equal spacing between them.

Cell size

In the flow layout, we set an `itemSize` of `CGSize(70,45)`. In the compositional layout, an item has width dimension absolute `70` and height dimension fractional height `1`, while the group has width dimension fractional width `1` and height dimension absolute `45`.

Margins

The flow layout has a `sectionInset` with a UIEdgeInsets value (`10.0,20.0,10.0,20.0`). In the compositional layout, horizontally, each group has leading and trailing margins; vertically, each section has top and bottom margins along with spacing between the rows.

Supplementary Items

In a compositional layout, supplementary items come in two main categories:

NSCollectionLayoutSupplementaryItem

An item or group's `supplementaryItems`. An item's supplementary items must be declared in the item initializer; a group has a settable `supplementaryItems` property.

It is initialized with `init(layoutSize:elementKind:containerAnchor:item-Anchor:)`. The `elementKind:` is an arbitrary string. The anchors are NSCollectionLayoutAnchor objects; the item anchor is optional. An anchor has `edges` (an NSDirectionalRectEdge) along with an optional `absoluteOffset` or `fractional-Offset`, which is a CGPoint. An NSDirectionalRectEdge is an option set consisting of `.top`, `.trailing`, `.leading`, and `.bottom`. A supplementary item also has a `zIndex` for front-to-back layering.

Apple's example of an item's supplementary item has edges `[.top, .trailing]` and a `fractionalOffset` of `CGPoint(x:0.5,y:-0.5)`. That's a badge centered at the top right corner.

NSCollectionLayoutBoundarySupplementaryItem

(An NSCollectionLayoutSupplementaryItem subclass.) A section or layout's `boundarySupplementaryItems`. A section has a settable `boundarySupplementary-Items` property; you supply a layout's boundary supplementary items as part of its `configuration`.

It has an `alignment` which is an NSRectAlignment, along with a possible `absoluteOffset`. The NSRectAlignment is an enum specifying a single edge or corner: `.top`, `.topLeading`, `.leading`, and so on; a header in a vertically scrolling layout would be attached to the section's `.top`. If the supplementary item's `extendsBoundary` is `true` (the default), it lies *outside* what would otherwise be the layout size of its container. There is also a `pinToVisibleBounds` property so that a section header or footer can behave like a table header or footer.

We are now ready to add section headers to the Latin LessonListController example! As we construct the section, we insert these lines:

```
let headerSize = NSCollectionLayoutSize(
    widthDimension: .fractionalWidth(1),
    heightDimension: .absolute(40))
let header = NSCollectionLayoutBoundarySupplementaryItem(
    layoutSize: headerSize, elementKind: "header", alignment: .top)
section.boundarySupplementaryItems = [header]
```

I've used an arbitrary `elementKind:` string `"header"`. Its significance is that I use the same string to register the reusable view class with the collection view:

```
self.collectionView!.register(
    UICollectionReusableView.self,
    forSupplementaryViewOfKind: "header",
    withReuseIdentifier:self.headerID)
```

Our implementation of `collectionView(_:viewForSupplementaryElementOf-Kind:at:)` is called, and section headers now appear in the layout! Our compositional layout now looks almost identical to the original flow layout in Figure 8-10. Only the first section is wrong; I'll deal with that now.

Multiple Section Layouts

In the layout shown in Figure 8-10, the first section needs to be special. It should have no section header, and its single cell needs to be wider than the subsequent cells. With a flow layout, we took care of these differences with two UICollectionView-DelegateFlowLayout methods. With a compositional layout, we handle section differences by changing the layout initialization slightly. Currently, we have this:

```
let itemSize = NSCollectionLayoutSize( // ...
// ...
let section = NSCollectionLayoutSection(group: group)
// ...
let layout = UICollectionViewCompositionalLayout(section: section)
return layout
```

We change it to this:

```
let layout = UICollectionViewCompositionalLayout { index, env in
    let itemSize = NSCollectionLayoutSize( // ...
    // ...
    let section = NSCollectionLayoutSection(group: group)
    // ...
    return section
}
return layout
```

That initializer defines a layout along with a *section provider* function that is fed the index number of every section and returns a section. So the section we construct can differ depending on the index number! The starred comments mark the lines where we behave differently; if this is the first section, an item is 150 points wide instead of 70 points wide, and we don't attach the `header`:

```
let layout = UICollectionViewCompositionalLayout { index, env in
    let itemSize = NSCollectionLayoutSize(
        widthDimension: .absolute(index == 0 ? 150 : 70), // *
        heightDimension: .fractionalHeight(1))
    // ...
    let section = NSCollectionLayoutSection(group: group)
    // ...
    let header = NSCollectionLayoutBoundarySupplementaryItem(
        layoutSize: headerSize, elementKind: "header", alignment: .top)
    if index != 0 { // *
        section.boundarySupplementaryItems = [header]
    }
    return section
}
return layout
```

The second parameter in the section provider function (`env`) is an NSCollection-LayoutEnvironment object, a value class consisting of two properties:

`container`
> An NSCollectionLayoutContainer telling us the `contentSize` and `content-Insets` of the overall layout.

`traitCollection`
> The current UITraitCollection for this view.

Using this information, you can make your layout differ depending on the size or orientation of the view. Apple's example is a grid of cells with five cells per row, unless the view is wider than a certain amount, in which case it becomes ten cells per row.

Other Compositional Layout Features

This section describes some further compositional layout features.

Manual cell layout

So far, we've been sizing our cells (items) by initializing a group with the `.horizontal` or `.vertical` class functions and giving an item a `layoutSize`. But there's another way. You initialize the group with the `.custom` class function. You supply an *item provider* function: it receives an NSCollectionLayoutEnvironment (whose `container` reports the content size and content insets of this group), and returns an array of NSCollectionLayoutGroupCustomItem objects. This is a value

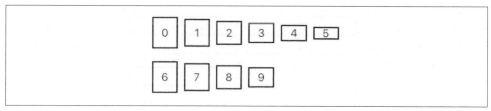

Figure 8-11. Manual cell layout

class consisting of a `frame` and an optional `zIndex`. You are now in complete charge of how many cells this group contains and what their frames should be.

In this example, the height of each cell in the row is a little smaller than that of the preceding cell; a new row starts when there are too many cells or the cell height becomes vanishingly small (Figure 8-11):

```swift
let group = NSCollectionLayoutGroup.custom(layoutSize: sz) { env in
    var items = [NSCollectionLayoutGroupCustomItem]()
    let w = CGFloat(40)
    var frame = CGRect(0, 0, w, env.container.contentSize.height)
    while true {
        items.append(NSCollectionLayoutGroupCustomItem(frame: frame))
        frame.origin.x += w + 10
        frame.size.height -= 6; frame.origin.y += 3
        if frame.size.height < 20 {
            return items
        }
        if frame.maxX > env.container.contentSize.width {
            return items
        }
    }
}
```

Nested groups

A group is an item (NSCollectionLayoutGroup is a subclass of NSCollectionLayout-Item). This means that a group can contain a group. A nested group can have a different orientation (horizontal or vertical) from its container group.

In this example, the section's group is a horizontal group composed of two vertical groups of two items. The result is that items are clumped into blocks of four, in the order upper left, lower left, upper right, lower right (Figure 8-12):

```swift
let itemSize = NSCollectionLayoutSize(
    widthDimension: .fractionalWidth(1),
    heightDimension: .fractionalHeight(0.5))
let item = NSCollectionLayoutItem(layoutSize: itemSize)
let vgroupSize = NSCollectionLayoutSize(
    widthDimension: .fractionalWidth(0.48),
    heightDimension: .absolute(60))
```

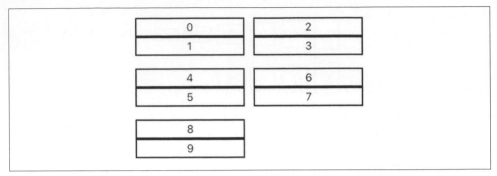

Figure 8-12. Nested groups

```
let vgroup = NSCollectionLayoutGroup.vertical(
    layoutSize: vgroupSize, subitems: [item])
let hgroupSize = NSCollectionLayoutSize(
    widthDimension: .fractionalWidth(1),
    heightDimension: .absolute(60))
let hgroup = NSCollectionLayoutGroup.horizontal(
    layoutSize: hgroupSize, subitems: [vgroup])
hgroup.interItemSpacing = .flexible(1)
let section = NSCollectionLayoutSection(group: hgroup)
```

Orthogonal scrolling

A section has an `orthogonalScrollingBehavior` property, a UICollectionLayout-SectionOrthogonalScrollingBehavior enum. By default, this is `.none`. If you change it to anything else, the section's groups are arranged in a *single* row (or column) along the other axis from the layout's scrolling direction, and the section is *scrollable* so that the user can view all the items. For instance, if the layout scrolls vertically, a scrolling section lines up all its groups in a single horizontal row, which scrolls horizontally. It's like having a collection view inside a collection view, scrolling at right angles to it.

The scrolling behavior values are:

`continuous`
Normal unrestricted scrolling.

`continuousGroupLeadingBoundary`
Normal unrestricted scrolling, but comes to rest with the leading edge of a group at the leading edge of the collection view.

`paging`
The user can scroll only one collection view width at a time.

`groupPaging`
The user can scroll only one group at a time.

```
groupPagingCentered
```
The user can scroll only one group at a time, and a group comes to rest centered in the collection view.

Collection View Diffable Data Source

A collection view's data source can be a diffable data source (UICollectionViewDiffableDataSource). It works similarly to a table view's diffable data source ("Table View Diffable Data Source" on page 502), but there are some extra requirements (and failure to fulfill them will result in a crash at runtime):

- Any calls to the collection view's `register(_:forCellWithReuseIdentifier:)` or `register(_:forSupplementaryViewOfKind:)` must take place *before* an initial snapshot is applied to the data source.

- If any supplementary views are to be displayed, the diffable data source's `supplementaryViewProvider` property must be set *before* an initial snapshot of data is applied to the data source. Basically, this function replaces the data source method `collectionView(_:viewForSupplementaryElementOfKind:at:)`, and must do the same work that that method would have done. Its parameters are the collection view, the supplementary view kind (a string), and the index path, and it returns a UICollectionReusableView that has been dequeued from the collection view.

To illustrate, I'll create a simple collection view (with a flow layout) based on the Three Big Questions; then I'll convert it to use a diffable data source. This will be a collection view version of the table view displaying the names of the U.S. states in sections, and the conversion will be exactly parallel to what I did earlier in "Populating a Diffable Data Source" on page 504.

First I'll construct the Three Big Questions version of my collection view. The data model initially will be our familiar array of Section objects:

```
struct Section {
    var sectionName : String
    var itemData : [String]
}
var sections : [Section]()
```

When the view loads (`viewDidLoad`), we parse the text file of state names into the `self.sections` array as usual:

```
let s = try! String(
    contentsOfFile: Bundle.main.path(
        forResource: "states", ofType: "txt")!)
let states = s.components(separatedBy:"\n")
```

```
let d = Dictionary(grouping: states) {String($0.prefix(1))}
self.sections = Array(d).sorted{$0.key < $1.key}.map {
    Section(sectionName: $0.key, itemData: $0.value)
}
```

We register our cell and header types; our cell is a UICollectionViewCell subclass called Cell, designed in a nib called *Cell.xib,* with a `lab` outlet to a UILabel:

```
self.collectionView.register(UINib(nibName:"Cell", bundle:nil),
    forCellWithReuseIdentifier: self.cellID)
self.collectionView.register(UICollectionReusableView.self,
    forSupplementaryViewOfKind:UICollectionView.elementKindSectionHeader,
    withReuseIdentifier: self.headerID)
```

We also configure the flow layout (I won't bother showing that code). Now for the data source methods. Here are the Three Big Questions:

```
override func numberOfSections(
    in collectionView: UICollectionView) -> Int {
        return self.sections.count
}
override func collectionView(_ collectionView: UICollectionView,
    numberOfItemsInSection section: Int) -> Int {
        return self.sections[section].itemData.count
}
override func collectionView(_ collectionView: UICollectionView,
    cellForItemAt indexPath: IndexPath) -> UICollectionViewCell {
        let cell = collectionView.dequeueReusableCell(
            withReuseIdentifier: self.cellID, for: indexPath) as! Cell
        // ...
        cell.lab.text =
            self.sections[indexPath.section].itemData[indexPath.row]
        return cell
}
```

And here's how we provide the header views:

```
override func collectionView(_ collectionView: UICollectionView,
    viewForSupplementaryElementOfKind kind: String,
    at indexPath: IndexPath) -> UICollectionReusableView {
        let v = collectionView.dequeueReusableSupplementaryView(
            ofKind: kind, withReuseIdentifier: self.headerID, for: indexPath)
        if v.subviews.count == 0 {
            let lab = UILabel()
            v.addSubview(lab)
            // ...
        }
        let lab = v.subviews[0] as! UILabel
        lab.text = self.sections[indexPath.section].sectionName
        return v
}
```

That's a working collection view; now I'll convert it to use a diffable data source.

We delete the Section struct and the `sections` instance property. Instead, we have a diffable data source instance property. I'll make this an Optional initialized to `nil`:

```
var datasource : UICollectionViewDiffableDataSource<String,String>! = nil
```

In `viewDidLoad`, we do things in a definite order — registration, instantiation, and population:

```
// registration ❶
self.collectionView.register(UINib(nibName:"Cell", bundle:nil),
    forCellWithReuseIdentifier: self.cellID)
self.collectionView.register(UICollectionReusableView.self,
    forSupplementaryViewOfKind:UICollectionView.elementKindSectionHeader,
    withReuseIdentifier: self.headerID)
// instantiation ❷
self.datasource = UICollectionViewDiffableDataSource<String,String>(
    collectionView:self.collectionView) { cv,ip,s in
        return self.makeCell(cv,ip,s) // *
}
self.datasource.supplementaryViewProvider = { cv,kind,ip in
    return self.makeSupplementaryView(cv,kind,ip) // *
}
// population ❸
// ...
self.datasource.apply(snap, animatingDifferences: false)
```

❶ We *register* our cell and supplementary view.

❷ We *instantiate* the diffable data source and configure it with two functions, one for producing cells, and one for producing supplementary views. I've coded speculatively, postponing the actual code of those functions by moving them into instance methods.

❸ We *populate* the diffable data source with data. This part is identical to how we populated the table view diffable data source with the same data, so I've omitted it (except for the last line).

Now I'll write the two functions from step 2, which I called `makeCell` and `make-SupplementaryView`. These are effectively the same as what we were already doing in our data source methods!

`makeCell` replaces `collectionView(_:cellForItemAt:)`, and does the same thing, except that we receive the actual data from the diffable data source:

```
func makeCell(_ collectionView:UICollectionView,
    _ indexPath:IndexPath, _ s:String) -> UICollectionViewCell {
        let cell = collectionView.dequeueReusableCell(
            withReuseIdentifier: self.cellID, for: indexPath) as! Cell
```

```
        // ...
        cell.lab.text = s // *
        return cell
    }
```

makeSupplementaryView replaces collectionView(_:viewForSupplementary-
ElementOfKind:at:), and does the same thing, except that we look up the data in the
diffable data source:

```
    func makeSupplementaryView(_ collectionView:UICollectionView,
        _ kind:String, _ indexPath:IndexPath) -> UICollectionReusableView {
        let v = collectionView.dequeueReusableSupplementaryView(
            ofKind: kind, withReuseIdentifier: self.headerID, for: indexPath)
        if v.subviews.count == 0 {
            let lab = UILabel()
            v.addSubview(lab)
            // ...
        }
        let lab = v.subviews[0] as! UILabel
        let snap = self.datasource.snapshot() // *
        lab.text = snap.sectionIdentifiers[indexPath.section] // *
        return v
    }
```

Basic Cell Manipulation

This section describes some basic manipulations you can perform on collection view
cells.

Selecting Cells

A collection view has a notion of cell selection, similar to a table view:

- A collection view has allowsSelection and allowsMultipleSelection properties; if these are not false, the user can tap a cell to select it.

- A collection view has an indexPathsForSelectedItems property, along with
  methods for selecting and deselecting an item.

- A cell has an isSelected property and a selectedBackgroundView property.

- The delegate has a full complement of should and did methods for highlighting
  and unhighlighting, selecting and deselecting. When the user taps to select a cell,
  the cell highlights, unhighlights, and selects (though the user is unaware of this,
  as a highlighted cell and a selected cell look the same).

- New in iOS 13, the delegate also has three multipleSelectionInteraction
  methods for when the user pans with two fingers to perform multiple selection;
  unlike a table view, a collection view has no notion of edit mode to complicate

matters. You can permit multiple selection by gesture even if the collection view's `allowsMultipleSelection` is `false`.

As with a table view, you can indicate selection visually with subviews that respond to highlighting and the `selectedBackgroundView` property. Earlier in this chapter, I configured a cell containing a label like this:

```
lab.highlightedTextColor = .white
cell.backgroundColor = .myPaler
let v = UIView()
v.backgroundColor = UIColor.blue.withAlphaComponent(0.8)
cell.selectedBackgroundView = v
```

Deleting Cells

Unlike table views, collection views don't provide any standard interface for allowing the user to delete cells. You are free to display a UICollectionViewController's `edit-ButtonItem`, and when the user taps it, the collection view controller's `set-Editing(_:animated:)` is called; but the interface does not automatically change in response, and neither a collection view nor a collection view cell has an `isEditing` property. Providing interface that lets the user express a desire to delete a cell is left completely up to you.

Deleting cells is a lot simpler if you're using a diffable data source. With a Three Big Questions data source, you have to alter the data, being careful about the order of operations, and then call `performBatchUpdates` to remove items and sections from the collection view. With a diffable data source, you just manipulate a snapshot and apply it.

Suppose we have a diffable data source, and the user has selected multiple cells and has tapped a Delete button; I want to respond by deleting the selected cells, along with any sections that are now empty. Unsurprisingly, the code for doing that is almost exactly the same as what we developed earlier for doing this in a table view ("Changing a Diffable Data Source" on page 508):

```
guard let sel = self.collectionView.indexPathsForSelectedItems,
    sel.count > 0 else {return}
let rowids = sel.map {
    self.datasource.itemIdentifier(for: $0)
}.compactMap {$0}
var snap = self.datasource.snapshot()
snap.deleteWithSections(rowids) // implemented in an extension
self.datasource.apply(snap)
```

Menu Handling

Menu handling is completely parallel to a table view. In iOS 13, you'll probably want to use the new context menu interface based on UIMenu and UIAction. Here's some code that lets the user long press a cell to produce a Copy menu item; as usual, I have a collection view displaying U.S. state names, and the name of the long pressed cell's state is copied to the clipboard if the user taps Copy:

```
override func collectionView(_ collectionView: UICollectionView,
    contextMenuConfigurationForItemAt indexPath: IndexPath,
    point: CGPoint) -> UIContextMenuConfiguration? {
        let config = UIContextMenuConfiguration(
            identifier:nil, previewProvider: nil) { _ in
                let action = UIAction(title: "Copy") { _ in
                    let d = self.datasource
                    if let state = d.itemIdentifier(for: indexPath) {
                        UIPasteboard.general.string = state
                        print("copied", state)
                    }
                }
                let menu = UIMenu(title: "", children: [action])
                return menu
            }
        return config
}
```

 Menus don't play very well with selection, because the long pressed cell visibly highlights first, after which the long press gesture recognizer recognizes, unhighlights the cell, and produces the menu.

Rearranging Cells

You can permit the user to rearrange cells by dragging them. If you're using a collection view controller, it supplies a gesture recognizer ready to respond to the user's long press gesture followed by a drag. (This is incompatible with a menu, because the menu long press gesture recognizer recognizes first.)

To permit the drag to proceed, you implement two data source methods:

collectionView(_:canMoveItemAt:)
    Return true to allow this item to be moved.

collectionView(_:moveItemAt:to:)
    The item has been moved to a new index path. Update the data model, and reload cells as needed.

You can also limit where the user can drag with this delegate method:

collectionView(_:targetIndexPathForMoveFromItemAt:toProposedIndexPath:)
    Return either the proposed index path or some other index path. To prevent the drag entirely, return the original index path (the second parameter).

If you're using a diffable data source, you'll have to subclass UICollectionView-DiffableDataSource and implement the data source methods in the subclass.

In this example, we're using a diffable data source, and we permit the user to rearrange items within a section but not to drag an item outside its section. The data source methods, implemented in a diffable data source subclass, are similar to the table view example from earlier in this chapter:

```
override func collectionView(_ collectionView: UICollectionView,
    canMoveItemAt indexPath: IndexPath) -> Bool {
        return true
}
override func collectionView(_ cv: UICollectionView,
    moveItemAt source: IndexPath, to dest: IndexPath) {
        let srcid = self.itemIdentifier(for: source)!
        let destid = self.itemIdentifier(for: dest)!
        var snap = self.snapshot()
        if dest.item > source.item {
            snap.moveItem(srcid, afterItem: destid)
        } else {
            snap.moveItem(srcid, beforeItem: destid)
        }
        self.apply(snap, animatingDifferences:false)
}
```

The delegate method prevents the move if the drag crosses a section boundary:

```
override func collectionView(_ collectionView: UICollectionView,
    targetIndexPathForMoveFromItemAt orig: IndexPath,
    toProposedIndexPath prop: IndexPath) -> IndexPath {
        if orig.section != prop.section {
            return orig
        }
        return prop
}
```

If you prefer to provide your own gesture recognizer, then if you're using a collection view controller, set its installsStandardGestureForInteractiveMovement to false. Your gesture recognizer action method will need to call these collection view methods to keep the collection view apprised of what's happening (and the data source and delegate methods will then be called appropriately):

- beginInteractiveMovementForItem(at:)
- updateInteractiveMovementTargetPosition(_:)
- endInteractiveMovement
- cancelInteractiveMovement

Figure 8-13. A carousel layout

Custom Collection View Layouts

It is possible that neither a flow layout nor a compositional layout does quite what you want, and that you'll want to tweak its behavior or even write your own UICollectionViewLayout subclass. The topic is a very large one, but getting started is not difficult; this section explores the basics.

Tweaking a Layout

Both UICollectionViewFlowLayout and UICollectionViewCompositionalLayout constitute powerful starting points, so it may be that all you need is to tweak what they already do. To illustrate, I'll use an example from a WWDC 2012 video.

Suppose we have a horizontally scrolling collection view as wide as the screen and 128 points tall. Centered vertically in this collection view is a horizontal series of single square cells 75 points on a side, spaced fairly well apart. About three cells fit on the screen; the user can scroll horizontally to see more cells.

Our goal is to modify the behavior of the collection view such that as the user scrolls horizontally, the currently central cell is emphasized. As a cell approaches the horizontal center of the screen, it grows, and as it moves away from the horizontal center, it returns to its normal size. This sort of interface is commonly referred to as a *carousel* (Figure 8-13).

Flow layout subclass

We can easily configure our collection view with a flow layout:

```
lay.itemSize = CGSize(width: 75, height: 75)
lay.minimumLineSpacing = 65
```

To achieve our "carousel" tweak, we subclass UICollectionViewFlowLayout and set our collection view's `collectionViewLayout` to an instance of the subclass. In the subclass, we override the method that describes how each cell should be laid out, namely `layoutAttributesForElements(in:)`.

The parameter of the `layoutAttributesForElements(in:)` method is a CGRect, and the method returns an array of UICollectionViewLayoutAttributes objects describing all the subviews of the collection view within that CGRect. The properties of each attributes object are the `indexPath` identifying the view, along with the `frame`, `center`, `size`, `transform`, `transform3D`, and `zIndex` that it should have. All of these properties are basically correct already in the default implementation, so we can call `super` and make modifications as necessary. All we have to do is to change the `transform3D` when this cell is near the center of the screen.

A layout has a `collectionView` property, which we can use to work out the collection view's visible bounds and the horizontal center of those bounds. Having called `super`, we have the array of attributes objects that the method would return. We copy the attribute objects (that's crucial) and examine the `frame` and `center` of each one in turn. If it isn't within the visible bounds, or if it isn't a cell, or if it isn't sufficiently close to the horizontal center of the screen, there's nothing more to do. Otherwise, we change the `transform3D` in proportion to the distance of the `center` from the collection view's horizontal center, and substitute the copy for the original. Finally, we return the whole array of copies:

```
override func layoutAttributesForElements(in rect: CGRect)
    -> [UICollectionViewLayoutAttributes]? {
        guard let cv = self.collectionView else { return nil }
        let r = CGRect(origin:cv.contentOffset, size:cv.bounds.size)
        let arr = super.layoutAttributesForElements(in: rect)!
        return arr.map { atts in
            let atts = atts.copy() as! UICollectionViewLayoutAttributes
            if atts.representedElementCategory == .cell {
                if atts.frame.intersects(r) {
                    let d = abs(r.midX - atts.center.x)
                    let act = CGFloat(70)
                    let nd = d/act
                    if d < act {
                        let scale = 1 + 0.5*(1-(abs(nd)))
                        let t = CATransform3DMakeScale(scale,scale,1)
                        atts.transform3D = t
                    }
                }
            }
            return atts
        }
}
```

We also override another method:

```
override func shouldInvalidateLayout(
    forBoundsChange newBounds: CGRect) -> Bool {
        return true
}
```

This override ensures that the collection view will ask for layout repeatedly as the user scrolls. Our flow layout subclass is complete!

Compositional layout invalidation handler

Exactly the same overrides work if we are using a compositional layout instead of a flow layout, and we could do the same thing by subclassing UICollectionViewCompositionalLayout. But there's no need for that! It turns out that a compositional layout provides a hook method that lets us modify the attributes of visible items directly.

To do so, we set the section's `visibleItemsInvalidationHandler` to a function that takes three parameters:

- An array of NSCollectionLayoutVisibleItems. These are just like UICollectionViewLayoutAttributes objects, except that you can set their properties directly. Moreover, the array contains only objects representing those collection view subviews that are actually visible at the moment.
- A CGPoint representing the collection view's current scrolling offset.
- The NSCollectionLayoutEnvironment.

Here's a compositional layout that looks and behaves like our tweaked flow layout:

```
let itemSize = NSCollectionLayoutSize(
    widthDimension: .fractionalWidth(1),
    heightDimension: .absolute(75))
let item = NSCollectionLayoutItem(layoutSize: itemSize)
item.edgeSpacing = NSCollectionLayoutEdgeSpacing(
    leading: nil, top: .flexible(0),
    trailing: nil, bottom: .flexible(0))
let groupSize = NSCollectionLayoutSize(
    widthDimension: .absolute(75),
    heightDimension: .fractionalHeight(1))
let group = NSCollectionLayoutGroup.vertical(
    layoutSize: groupSize, subitems: [item])
let section = NSCollectionLayoutSection(group: group)
section.interGroupSpacing = 65
section.contentInsets = NSDirectionalEdgeInsets(
    top: 0, leading: 75, bottom: 0, trailing: 75)
section.visibleItemsInvalidationHandler = { items, offset, env in
    let r = CGRect(origin:offset, size:env.container.contentSize)
    let cells = items.filter {$0.representedElementCategory == .cell}
    for item in cells {
        let d = abs(r.midX - item.center.x)
        let act = CGFloat(70)
        let nd = d/act
        if d < act {
            let scale = 1 + 0.5*(1-(abs(nd)))
            let t = CATransform3DMakeScale(scale,scale,1)
            item.transform3D = t
        }
    }
}
```

```
let config = UICollectionViewCompositionalLayoutConfiguration()
config.scrollDirection = .horizontal
let layout = UICollectionViewCompositionalLayout(
    section: section, configuration:config)
```

Collection View Layout Subclass

For total freedom, you can subclass UICollectionViewLayout itself. The WWDC 2012 videos demonstrate a UICollectionViewLayout subclass that arranges its cells in a circle; the WWDC 2013 videos demonstrate a UICollectionViewLayout subclass that piles its cells into a single stack in the center of the collection view, like a deck of cards seen from above. For my example, I'll write a simple collection view layout that ignores sections and presents all cells as a plain grid of squares. This is unnecessary now that compositional layouts exist, but it demonstrates nicely the basics of writing a layout from scratch.

In my UICollectionViewLayout subclass, called MyLayout, the big questions I will need to answer are collectionViewContentSize and layoutAttributesFor-Elements(in:). To answer them, I'll calculate the entire layout of my grid beforehand. The prepare method is the perfect place to do this; it is called every time something about the collection view or its data changes. I'll calculate the grid of cells and express their positions as an array of UICollectionViewLayoutAttributes objects; I'll store that information in a property self.atts, which is a dictionary keyed by index path so that I can retrieve a given layout attributes object by its index path quickly. I'll also store the size of the grid in a property self.sz:

```
override func prepare() {
    let sections = self.collectionView.numberOfSections
    // work out cell size based on bounds size
    let sz = self.collectionView!.bounds.size
    let width = sz.width
    let shortside = (width/100).rounded(.down)
    let side = width/shortside
    // generate attributes for all cells
    var (x,y) = (0,0)
    var atts = [UICollectionViewLayoutAttributes]()
    for i in 0 ..< sections {
        let jj = self.collectionView!.numberOfItems(inSection:i)
        for j in 0 ..< jj {
            let att = UICollectionViewLayoutAttributes(
                forCellWith: IndexPath(item:j, section:i))
            att.frame = CGRect(CGFloat(x)*side,CGFloat(y)*side,side,side)
            atts += [att]
            x += 1
            if CGFloat(x) >= shortside {
                x = 0; y += 1
            }
        }
    }
}
```

```
        for att in atts {
            self.atts[att.indexPath] = att
        }
        let fluff = (x == 0) ? 0 : 1
        self.sz = CGSize(width, CGFloat(y+fluff) * side)
    }
```

It is now trivial to implement collectionViewContentSize, layoutAttributesFor-Elements(in:), and layoutAttributesForItem(at:). I'll just fetch the requested information from the sz or atts property:

```
override var collectionViewContentSize : CGSize {
    return self.sz
}
override func layoutAttributesForElements(in rect: CGRect)
    -> [UICollectionViewLayoutAttributes]? {
        return Array(self.atts.values)
}
override func layoutAttributesForItem(at indexPath: IndexPath)
    -> UICollectionViewLayoutAttributes? {
        return self.atts[indexPath]
}
```

Finally, I want to implement shouldInvalidateLayout(forBoundsChange:) to return true, so that if the interface is rotated, my prepare method will be called again to recalculate the grid. There's a potential source of inefficiency here, though: the user scrolling the collection view counts as a bounds change as well. Therefore, I return false unless the bounds size has changed:

```
var oldBoundsSize = CGSize.zero
override func shouldInvalidateLayout(forBoundsChange newBounds: CGRect)
    -> Bool {
        let ok = newBounds.size != self.oldBoundsSize
        if ok {
            self.oldBoundsSize = newBounds.size
        }
        return ok
}
```

Decoration Views

A *decoration view* is a third type of collection view subview, on a par with cells and supplementary views. The difference is that it is implemented entirely by the collection view layout. You register a decoration view class (or nib) with the layout — not with the collection view. A collection view will faithfully draw a decoration view imposed by the collection view layout, but none of the methods and properties of a collection view, its data source, or its delegate involve decoration views. There is no support for letting the user select a decoration view or reposition a decoration view.

There aren't even any collection view methods for finding out what decoration views exist or where they are located.

A flow layout comes with no built-in support for adding a decoration view, but a compositional layout does. It is of class NSCollectionLayoutDecorationItem (an NSCollectionLayoutItem subclass), and represents just one kind of decoration, a background behind a section. So there's a single class function, background, which takes an elementKind, and you set the section's decorationItems. There must be a corresponding UICollectionReusableView (or a nib containing such a view) registered with the layout.

As a simple example, I'll put a pale blue background behind each section of a compositional layout. Here's my view class:

```
class Deco : UICollectionReusableView {
    override init(frame: CGRect) {
        super.init(frame: frame)
        self.backgroundColor = UIColor.blue.withAlphaComponent(0.1)
    }
    required init?(coder: NSCoder) {
        fatalError("init(coder:) has not been implemented")
    }
}
```

Here's how I register that class with the layout when I configure the collection view:

```
let layout = self.createLayout()
layout.register(Deco.self, forDecorationViewOfKind: "background")
self.collectionView.collectionViewLayout = layout
```

And here's how the decoration view is added to the section (in createLayout):

```
let deco = NSCollectionLayoutDecorationItem.background(
    elementKind: "background")
deco.contentInsets = NSDirectionalEdgeInsets(
    top: 5, leading: 5, bottom: 5, trailing: 5)
section.decorationItems = [deco]
```

You can also implement a decoration view in a layout subclass that you write, and you are free to define any desired mechanism for allowing a user of this collection view layout to customize your decoration views. You implement layoutAttributes-ForDecorationView(ofKind:at:) to return a UICollectionViewLayoutAttributes object that positions the UICollectionReusableView. To construct this object, you call init(forDecorationViewOfKind:with:) and configure its properties. Finally, you implement layoutAttributesForElements(in·) such that the result of layout-AttributesForDecorationView(ofKind:at:) is included in the returned array.

Switching Layouts

An astonishing feature of a collection view is that its collection view layout object can be swapped out on the fly. You can substitute one collection view layout for another, by calling `setCollectionViewLayout(_:animated:completion:)`. The data hasn't changed, and the collection view can identify each element uniquely and persistently, so it responds by moving every element from its position according to the old layout to its position according to the new layout — and, if the `animated:` argument is `true`, it does this *with animation!* The elements are seen to rearrange themselves, as if by magic.

This animated change of layout can even be driven interactively in response to a user gesture. You call `startInteractiveTransition(to:completion:)` on the collection view, and a special layout object is returned — a UICollectionViewTransitionLayout instance (or a subclass thereof; to make it a subclass, you need to have implemented `collectionView(_:transitionLayoutForOldLayout:newLayout:)` in your collection view delegate). This transition layout is temporarily made the collection view's layout, and your job is then to keep it apprised of the transition's progress (through its `transitionProgress` property) and ultimately to call `finishInteractive-Transition` or `cancelInteractiveTransition` on the collection view.

Furthermore, when one collection view controller is pushed on top of another in a navigation interface, the runtime will do exactly the same thing for you, as a custom view controller transition. To arrange this, the first collection view controller's `use-LayoutToLayoutNavigationTransitions` property must be `false` and the second collection view controller's `useLayoutToLayoutNavigationTransitions` property must be `true`. The result is that when the second collection view controller is pushed onto the navigation controller, *the collection view remains in place*, and the collection view layout specified by the second collection view controller is substituted for the collection view's existing collection view layout, with animation of the elements as they adopt their new positions.

During the transition, as the second collection view controller is pushed onto the navigation stack, the two collection view controllers share the same collection view, and the collection view's data source and delegate remain the first view controller. After the transition is complete, however, the collection view's delegate becomes the *second* view controller, even though its data source is still the *first* view controller. I find this profoundly weird; why does the runtime change who the delegate is, and why would I want the delegate to be different from the data source? I solve the problem by resetting the delegate in the second view controller, like this:

```
override func viewDidAppear(_ animated: Bool) {
    super.viewDidAppear(animated)
    let oldDelegate = self.collectionView.delegate
    DispatchQueue.main.async {
        self.collectionView.delegate = oldDelegate
    }
}
```

Collection Views and UIKit Dynamics

The UICollectionViewLayoutAttributes class adopts the UIDynamicItem protocol (see Chapter 4). This means that collection view elements can be animated under UIKit dynamics. The world of the animator here is not a superview but the collection view layout itself:

- Instead of `init(referenceView:)`, you'll create the UIDynamicAnimator by calling `init(collectionViewLayout:)`.

- When adding an item to a UIDynamicBehavior, instead of being a UIView, the item is a UICollectionViewLayoutAttributes object.

But there's a tricky bit. On every frame of its animation, the UIDynamicAnimator is going to change the layout attributes of some items — but the collection view knows nothing of that! It still wants to draw those items in accordance with the collection view layout's `layoutAttributesForElements(in:)`. We need to make the collection view modify its `layoutAttributesForElements(in:)` so as to obtain those layout attributes from the UIDynamicAnimator. There are some helpful UIDynamicAnimator convenience methods:

`layoutAttributesForCell(at:)`
`layoutAttributesForSupplementaryView(ofKind:at:)`
   The layout attributes for the requested item, in accordance with where the animator wants to put them — or `nil` if the specified item is not being animated.

How will we hook into the layout's `layoutAttributesForElements(in:)`? In iOS 12 and before, you'd need a custom subclass of UICollectionViewLayout so that you could override `layoutAttributesForElements(in:)`. New in iOS 13, if you're using a compositional layout, you can use the section's `visibleItemsInvalidation-Handler`.

In this example, I'm using a compositional layout to arrange the collection view's cells in a grid. I'll animate the visible cells to fall off the screen with random rates and random rotation. As usual, I have an Optional UIDynamicAnimator instance property called `self.anim`:

```
let layout = cv.collectionViewLayout
let anim = UIDynamicAnimator(collectionViewLayout: layout)
var atts = [UICollectionViewLayoutAttributes]()
for ip in cv.indexPathsForVisibleItems {
    if let att = cv.layoutAttributesForItem(at: ip) {
        let beh = UIDynamicItemBehavior(items:[att])
        beh.resistance = CGFloat.random(in: 0.2...6)
        beh.addAngularVelocity(CGFloat.random(in: -2...2), for: att)
        anim.addBehavior(beh)
        atts.append(att)
    }
}
let grav = UIGravityBehavior(items: atts)
grav.action = {
    let items = anim.items(in: self.collectionView.bounds)
    if items.count == 0 {
        anim.removeAllBehaviors()
        self.anim = nil
    }
}
anim.addBehavior(grav)
self.anim = anim
```

We run that code, and nothing appears to happen. But something *is* happening: the
animator runs, and it stops as expected when all the cells are off the screen. The trouble is that the cells drawn by the collection view are not moving! This is where the
visibleItemsInvalidationHandler comes in, when we construct our compositional
layout:

```
let section = NSCollectionLayoutSection(group: group)
section.visibleItemsInvalidationHandler = { items, offset, env in
    if let anim = self.anim {
        for item in items {
            if let atts = anim.layoutAttributesForCell(at:item.indexPath) {
                item.center = atts.center
                item.transform3D = atts.transform3D
            }
        }
    }
}
```

While the animator is running, the invalidation handler is called on every frame. We
cycle through the NSCollectionLayoutVisibleItem objects (items), replacing their
center and transform3D values with those provided by the animator. The cells now
visibly fall off the screen when the animator runs.

iPad Interface

This chapter discusses some iOS interface features that differ between the iPad and the iPhone:

Popovers and split views
> Popovers and split views were exclusive to the iPad when they were introduced in iOS 3.2. Starting in iOS 8, they became available also on the iPhone, where they typically adapt, appearing in an altered form more appropriate to the smaller screen.

iPad multitasking
> iPad multitasking, introduced in iOS 9, is an interface confined to the iPad, where two apps can occupy the screen simultaneously.

Drag and drop
> Drag and drop was introduced in iOS 11 primarily to allow the user to drag from one app to another in an iPad multitasking interface. It can also be used within a single app, even on the iPhone.

Multiple windows
> New in iOS 13, an app can display multiple windows on the iPad.

Popovers

A *popover* is a temporary view layered in front of the main interface. It is usually associated, through a sort of arrow, with a view in the main interface, such as the button that the user tapped to summon the popover. It might be effectively modal, preventing the user from working in the rest of the interface; alternatively, it might vanish if the user taps outside it.

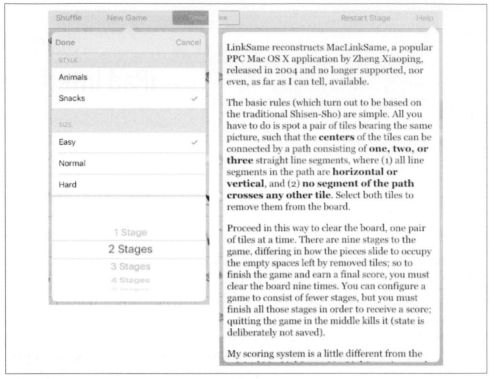

Figure 9-1. Two popovers

Popovers bring to the larger iPad the smaller, more lightweight flavor of the iPhone. In my LinkSame app, both the settings view (where the user configures the game) and the help view (which describes how to play the game) are popovers (Figure 9-1). On the iPhone, such a view might occupy the entire screen; we'd navigate to it, and the user would later have to navigate back to the main interface. But with the larger iPad screen, neither view is large enough, or important enough, to occupy the entire screen exclusively. A popover is the perfect solution. Our view is small and secondary; the user summons it temporarily, works with it, and then dismisses it, while the main interface continues to occupy the rest of the screen.

A popover is actually a form of presented view controller — a presented view controller with a `modalPresentationStyle` of `.popover` (which I didn't tell you about in Chapter 6). There's a guideline that a maximum of one popover at a time should be shown; a view controller can't have more than one presented view controller at a time, so the guideline is enforced automatically.

Like a sheet presented view controller, a popover can adapt, depending on the size class environment. The default adaptation of a popover on the iPhone depends on what system we're running on:

iOS 12 and before

The default adaptation on the iPhone is `.fullScreen`.

iOS 13

New in iOS 13, the default adaptation on the iPhone is `.formSheet`. This is indistinguishable from `.pageSheet`, meaning that it leaves a gap at the top in portrait, but behaves like `.overFullScreen` in landscape.

But you don't have to accept the default; you can customize how the popover adapts. It can appear on the iPhone as `.fullScreen` even in portrait; it can even appear as a popover. I'll explain later how to make it do that.

 A popover presented view controller that appears as a popover has a `.compact` horizontal size class, even on an iPad.

To display a popover, you're going to present a view controller. Before that presentation takes place, you'll turn this into a popover presentation by setting the view controller's `modalPresentationStyle` to `.popover`:

```
let vc = MyViewController()
vc.modalPresentationStyle = .popover
self.present(vc, animated: true)
```

But that code is insufficient. In fact, it will crash at runtime when the popover is presented! The reason is that some further configuration of the popover is required before it appears.

To configure a popover, you'll talk to its *presentation controller*. Setting the view controller's `modalPresentationStyle` to `.popover`, as in the preceding code, causes its `presentationController` to become a UIPopoverPresentationController (a UIPresentationController subclass); that is the object you need to talk to. The popover view controller's `popoverPresentationController` property points to that UIPopoverPresentationController (or to `nil`).

In general, it is permissible to perform your configurations just *after* telling your view controller to present the popover, because even though you have ordered the presentation, it hasn't actually started yet. This is a common pattern:

```
let vc = MyViewController()
vc.modalPresentationStyle = .popover
self.present(vc, animated: true)
if let pop = vc.popoverPresentationController {
    // ... configure pop here ...
}
```

Arrow Source and Direction

At a minimum, the popover presentation controller needs to know where its arrow should point. You'll specify this by setting one of the following:

barButtonItem

> A bar button item in the interface, with which the popover should be associated. The popover's arrow will point to this bar button item. Typically, this will be the bar button item that was tapped in order to summon the popover (as in Figure 9-1).

sourceView, sourceRect

> A UIView in the interface, along with a CGRect *in that view's coordinate system*, with which the popover should be associated. The popover's arrow will point to this rect. Typically, the sourceView will be the view that was tapped in order to summon the popover, and the sourceRect will be that view's bounds.

Here's a minimal popover presentation that works without crashing; the popover is summoned by tapping a UIButton in the interface, and this is that button's action method:

```
@IBAction func doButton(_ sender: Any) {
    let vc = MyViewController()
    vc.modalPresentationStyle = .popover
    self.present(vc, animated: true)
    if let pop = vc.popoverPresentationController {
        let v = sender as! UIView
        pop.sourceView = v
        pop.sourceRect = v.bounds
    }
}
```

In addition to the arrow source, you can set the desired arrow direction, as the popover presentation controller's permittedArrowDirections. This is a bitmask with possible values .up, .down, .left, and .right. The default is .any, comprising all four bitmask values; that will usually be what you want.

Popover Size

You can specify the desired size of the popover view. This information is provided through the presented view controller's preferredContentSize. Recall (from Chapter 6) that a view controller can use its preferredContentSize to communicate to its container view controller, *qua* UIContentContainer, the size that it would like to be. The popover presentation controller is a presentation controller (UIPresentationController), which is also a UIContentContainer; it will consult the presented view controller's preferredContentSize and will try, within limits, to respect it. The presentation of the popover won't fail if you don't supply a size for the popover, but you probably will want to supply one, as the default is unlikely to be desirable.

Who will set the presented view controller's preferredContentSize, and when? It's up to you. The presented view controller might set its own preferredContentSize; its viewDidLoad is a reasonable place, or, if the view controller is instantiated from a nib, the nib editor provides Content Size fields in the Attributes inspector. Alternatively, you can set the presented view controller's preferredContentSize when you configure the popover presentation controller:

```
if let pop = vc.popoverPresentationController {
    let v = sender as! UIView
    pop.sourceView = v
    pop.sourceRect = v.bounds
    vc.preferredContentSize = CGSize(200,500) // *
}
```

It is possible to change the presented view controller's preferredContentSize while the popover is showing. The popover presentation controller will hear about this (through the preferredContentSizeDidChange mechanism discussed in Chapter 6), and may respond by changing the popover's size, with animation.

The popover presentation controller's canOverlapSourceViewRect can be set to true to permit the popover to cover the source view if space becomes tight while attempting to comply with the preferredContentSize. The default is false.

You can also set the popover presentation controller's popoverLayoutMargins as a way of encouraging the popover to maintain some distance from the edges of the presenting view controller's view. (This property was broken starting about iOS 8, but works correctly in iOS 13.)

Popover Appearance

By default, a popover presentation controller bases the arrow color on the color of the presented view controller's view. Alternatively, you can set the popover presentation controller's backgroundColor; this sets the arrow color as well. But in iOS 13 the presented view controller's own view color will override this, unless it is .clear or nil.

For full control, you can customize the entire outside of the popover — that is, the "frame" surrounding the content, *including* the arrow. To do so, you set the UIPopoverPresentationController's popoverBackgroundViewClass to your own subclass of UIPopoverBackgroundView (a UIView subclass). You then implement the UIPopoverBackgroundView's draw(_:) method to draw the arrow and the frame. The size of the arrow is dictated by your implementation of the arrowHeight property. The thickness of the frame is dictated by your implementation of the contentViewInsets property.

Figure 9-2. A very silly popover

A very silly example is shown in Figure 9-2. Here's how that result was achieved. I start by implementing five inherited members that we are required to override, along with our initializer:

```
class MyPopoverBackgroundView : UIPopoverBackgroundView {
    override class func arrowBase() -> CGFloat { return 20 }
    override class func arrowHeight() -> CGFloat { return 20 }
    override class func contentViewInsets() -> UIEdgeInsets {
        return UIEdgeInsets(top: 20, left: 20, bottom: 20, right: 20)
    }
    // we are required to implement these, even trivially
    var arrOff : CGFloat
    var arrDir : UIPopoverArrowDirection
    override var arrowDirection : UIPopoverArrowDirection {
        get { return self.arrDir }
        set { self.arrDir = newValue }
    }
    override var arrowOffset : CGFloat {
        get { return self.arrOff }
        set { self.arrOff = newValue }
    }
    override init(frame:CGRect) {
        self.arrOff = 0
        self.arrDir = .any
        super.init(frame:frame)
        self.isOpaque = false
    }
    // ...
}
```

Now I'll implement `draw(_:)`. Its job is to draw the frame and the arrow. This can be a bit tricky, because we need to draw differently depending on the arrow direction (which we can learn from the UIPopoverBackgroundView's `arrowDirection` property). I'll simplify by assuming that the arrow direction will always be `.up`.

I'll start with the frame. I divide the view's overall rect into two areas, the arrow area on top and the frame area on the bottom, and I draw the frame into the bottom area as a resizable image (Chapter 2):

```
override func draw(_ rect: CGRect) {
    let linOrig = UIImage(named: "linen.png")!
    let capw = linOrig.size.width / 2.0 - 1
    let caph = linOrig.size.height / 2.0 - 1
    let lin = linOrig.resizableImage(
        withCapInsets:
            UIEdgeInsets(top: caph, left: capw, bottom: caph, right: capw),
        resizingMode:.tile)
    let arrowHeight = Self.arrowHeight()
    let arrowBase = Self.arrowBase()
    // ... draw arrow here ...
    let (_,body) = rect.divided(atDistance: arrowHeight, from: .minYEdge)
    lin.draw(in:body)
}
```

Our next task is to fill in the blank left by the "draw arrow here" comment in the preceding code. We don't actually have to do that; we could quite legally stop at this point. Our popover would then have no arrow, but that's no disaster; many developers dislike the arrow and seek a way to remove it, and this constitutes a legal way. But let's continue by drawing the arrow.

My arrow will consist simply of a texture-filled isosceles triangle, with an excess base rectangle joining it to the frame. The runtime has set the `arrowOffset` property to tell us where to draw the arrow: this offset measures the positive distance between the center of the view's edge and the center of the arrow. However, the runtime will have no hesitation in setting the `arrowOffset` all the way at the edge of the view, or even beyond its bounds (in which case it won't be drawn); to prevent this, I impose a maximum offset limit:

```
let con = UIGraphicsGetCurrentContext()!
con.saveGState()
// clamp offset
var propX = self.arrowOffset
let limit : CGFloat = 22.0
let maxX = rect.size.width/2.0 - limit
propX = min(max(propX, limit), maxX)
// draw!
con.translateBy(x: rect.size.width/2.0 + propX - arrowBase/2.0, y: 0)
con.move(to:CGPoint(0, arrowHeight))
con.addLine(to:CGPoint(arrowBase / 2.0, 0))
con.addLine(to:CGPoint(arrowBase, arrowHeight))
```

```
con.closePath()
con.addRect(CGRect(0,arrowHeight,arrowBase,15))
con.clip()
lin.draw(at:CGPoint(-40,-40))
con.restoreGState()
```

Passthrough Views

When you're configuring your popover, you'll want to plan ahead for how the popover is to be dismissed. The default behavior is that the user can tap anywhere *outside* the popover to dismiss it, but it can be modified through two properties:

UIPopoverPresentationController's `passthroughViews` *property*
An array of views in the interface behind the popover; the user can interact normally with these views while the popover is showing, and the popover will *not* be dismissed.

UIViewController's `isModalInPresentation` *property*
(New in iOS 13, replacing `isModalInPopover`, which is deprecated.) If this is `true` for the presented view controller (or for its current child view controller, as in a tab bar interface or navigation interface), then if the user taps outside the popover, the popover is *not* dismissed. The default is `false`. The user can still interact with any of the `passthroughViews`, even if `isModalInPresentation` is `true`.

If you've set the presented view controller's `isModalInPresentation` to `true`, you've removed the user's ability to dismiss the popover by tapping outside it. You would then presumably provide some *other* way of letting the user dismiss the popover — typically, a button *inside* the popover which the user can tap in order to call `dismiss(animated:completion:)`.

Surprisingly, if a popover is summoned by the user tapping a UIBarButton item in a toolbar, other UIBarButtonItems in that toolbar are automatically turned into passthrough views! This means that, while the popover is showing, the user can tap any other button in the toolbar. I regard this as a bug; working around it is remarkably difficult. If you set the popover presentation controller's `passthroughViews` too soon, your setting is overridden by the runtime. The best place is the presentation's completion function:

```
self.present(vc, animated: true) {
    vc.popoverPresentationController?.passthroughViews = nil
}
```

Popover Presentation, Dismissal, and Delegate

A popover is a form of presented view controller. To show a popover, you'll call `present(_:animated:completion:)`. If you want to dismiss a popover in code, you'll call `dismiss(animated:completion:)`.

Messages to the popover presentation controller's delegate (UIPopoverPresentation-ControllerDelegate) provide further information and control. Typically, you'll set the delegate in the same place you're performing the other configurations:

```
if let pop = vc.popoverPresentationController {
    // ... other configurations go here ...
    pop.delegate = self
}
```

The most commonly used delegate methods are:

`prepareForPopoverPresentation(_:)`
> The popover is being presented. This is another opportunity to perform initial configurations, such as what interface object the arrow points to. (But this method is still called too early for you to work around the `passthroughViews` issue I discussed a moment ago.)

`presentationControllerShouldDismiss(_:)`
> (New in iOS 13, replacing `popoverPresentationControllerShouldDismiss-Popover(_:)`, which is deprecated.) The user is dismissing the popover by tapping outside it. Return `false` to prevent dismissal. *Not* called when you dismiss the popover in code.

`presentationControllerWillDismiss(_:)`
> (New in iOS 13.) The user has dismissed the popover by tapping outside it. The popover is still on the screen. *Not* called when you dismiss the popover in code.

`presentationControllerDidDismiss(_:)`
> (New in iOS 13, replacing `popoverPresentationControllerDidDismiss-Popover(_:)`, which is deprecated.) The user has dismissed the popover by tapping outside it. The popover is gone from the screen and dismissal is complete, even though the popover presentation controller still exists. *Not* called when you dismiss the popover in code.

`popoverPresentationController(_:willRepositionPopoverTo:in:)`
> The popover's `sourceView` is involved in new layout activity. This might be because the interface is rotating. The `to:` and `in:` parameters are mutable pointers to the popover's `sourceRect` and `sourceView` respectively, so you can change the attachment of the arrow through their `pointee` properties.

The delegate methods provide the popover presentation controller as parameter, and if necessary you can use it to identify the popover more precisely; the view controller being presented is the popover presentation controller's `presentedViewController`. The delegate `dismiss` methods make up for the fact that, when the user dismisses the popover, you don't have the sort of direct information and control that you would get if *you* had dismissed the popover by calling `dismiss(animated:completion:)` with a completion function.

If a popover can be dismissed *both* by tapping outside the popover *and* by tapping an interface item that calls `dismiss(animated:completion:)`, you may have to duplicate some code in order to cover all cases. Consider the first popover shown in Figure 9-1. It has a Done button and a Cancel button; the idea here is that the user sets up a desired game configuration and then, while dismissing the popover, either saves it (Done) or doesn't (Cancel). But what if the user taps outside the popover? I interpret that as cancellation. If the Cancel button's action function does any work besides dismissing the popover, my `presentationControllerDidDismiss(_:)` implementation will have to do the same thing.

Adaptive Popovers

A popover is a presented view controller, so it's *adaptive* (see "Adaptive Presentation" on page 332). By default, on an iPhone, the `.popover` modal presentation style will adapt as `.formSheet`, which is identical in appearance to `.pageSheet`, the default for a presented view controller on an iPhone; and so with no extra code you'll get something eminently sensible on both types of device.

But sometimes the default is not quite what you want. A case in point appears in Figure 9-1. The popover on the right, containing our help info, has no internal button for dismissal. It doesn't need one on the iPad, because the user can dismiss the popover by tapping outside it. But this is a universal app. On the iPhone, the popover will adapt to `.formSheet`. In landscape on the iPhone, a `.formSheet` presentation appears as fullscreen — and the user will have *no way to dismiss* this view controller! Clearly, we need a Done button that appears inside the presented view controller's view — but only on the iPhone.

To achieve this, we can take advantage of UIPresentationController delegate methods. The popover presentation controller *is* a UIPresentationController, and its delegate (UIPopoverPresentationControllerDelegate) *is* a UIPresentationController delegate (UIAdaptivePresentationControllerDelegate). Set the presentation controller's delegate *before* calling `present(_:animated:completion:)`; otherwise, the adaptive presentation delegate methods won't be called:

```
let vc = MyViewController()
vc.modalPresentationStyle = .popover
if let pop = vc.popoverPresentationController {
    pop.delegate = self // *
}
self.present(vc, animated: true)
```

We'll implement the delegate method `presentationController(_:viewController-ForAdaptivePresentationStyle:)` to substitute a different view controller. The substitute view controller can be the original view controller wrapped in a UINavigationController! If we also give our original view controller a `navigation-Item` with a working Done button, the problem is solved:

```
func presentationController(_ controller: UIPresentationController,
    viewControllerForAdaptivePresentationStyle
    style: UIModalPresentationStyle) -> UIViewController? {
        let vc = controller.presentedViewController
        let nav = UINavigationController(rootViewController: vc)
        let b = UIBarButtonItem(barButtonSystemItem: .done,
            target: self, action: #selector(dismissHelp))
        vc.navigationItem.rightBarButtonItem = b
        return nav
}
@objc func dismissHelp(_ sender: Any) {
    self.dismiss(animated:true)
}
```

The outcome is that in a situation where we don't adapt (such as an iPad) we get an ordinary popover; otherwise, we get a presented view controller that can be dismissed with a Done button in a navigation bar.

You can also implement the delegate method `adaptivePresentation-Style(for:traitCollection:)`. You might use this to return something other than a sheet in a `.compact` size class environment. One possibility is to return `.none`, in which case the presented view controller will be a popover *even on iPhone*:

```
func adaptivePresentationStyle(for controller: UIPresentationController,
    traitCollection: UITraitCollection) -> UIModalPresentationStyle {
        return .none
}
```

Popover Segues

If you're using a storyboard (with Use Trait Variations checked), you can configure a popover presentation with little or no code. Draw (Control-drag) a segue from a button or view controller that is to *summon* the popover to a view controller that is to *be* the popover, and specify Present As Popover as the segue type. The result is a *popover segue*.

The segue, as it is triggered, configures the presentation just as you would configure it in code. It instantiates and initializes the presented view controller, sets its modal presentation style to `.popover`, and presents it. The `sourceView`, `barButtonItem`, and `permittedArrowDirections` can be set in the segue's Attributes inspector. You can also set the passthrough views in the nib editor — but not in such a way as to override the unwanted bar button item behavior I discussed earlier.

To perform additional configurations in code, implement `prepare(for:sender:)`. At the time `prepare(for:sender:)` is called, the `popoverPresentationController` of the segue's `destination` view controller exists, but the presentation has not yet begun, so you can successfully set the popover presentation controller's delegate here if desired:

```
override func prepare(for segue: UIStoryboardSegue, sender: Any?) {
    if segue.identifier == "MyPopover" {
        let dest = segue.destination
        if let pop = dest.popoverPresentationController {
            pop.delegate = self
        }
    }
}
```

The popover version of an unwind segue is dismissal of the popover, and so both presentation and dismissal can be managed through the storyboard. A further possibility is to specify a custom segue class (as I explained in Chapter 6).

 Unfortunately, a popover triggered through a popover segue has some major flaws. It might not point its arrow correctly at its source view; in fact, under some circumstances it covers the source view. The popover can't be configured in the segue's IBSegueAction, because the popover presentation controller doesn't yet exist. Also, it's hard to avoid the bug where bar button items are passthrough views by default (because there's no good moment to set the `passthroughViews` to `nil`). Therefore I recommend avoiding popover segues altogether.

Popover Presenting a View Controller

A popover can present a view controller internally; you'll specify a `modalPresentationStyle` of `.currentContext` or `.overCurrentContext`, because otherwise the presented view will appear over the entire screen (see Chapter 6).

What happens when the user taps outside a popover that is currently presenting a view controller's view internally? Unfortunately, different systems behave differently. Here's a sample:

iOS 7 and before
    Nothing happens.

iOS 8.1
    The entire popover, including the internal presented view controller, is dismissed.

iOS 8.3
    The internal presented view controller is dismissed, while the popover remains.

iOS 9 and later
    Like iOS 8.1.

In my opinion, the iOS 7 behavior was correct. Presented view controllers are supposed to be modal. They don't spontaneously dismiss themselves because the user taps elsewhere; there has to be some internal interface, such as a Done button or a Cancel button, that the user must tap in order to dismiss the view controller and proceed. You can restore the iOS 7 behavior by implementing the delegate method `presentationControllerShouldDismiss(_:)` to prevent dismissal if the popover is itself presenting a view controller:

```
func presentationControllerShouldDismiss(
    _ pc: UIPresentationController) -> Bool {
        return pc.presentedViewController.presentedViewController == nil
}
```

Split Views

A *split view* involves two views belonging to two view controllers. The view controllers are the children of a parent view controller, a *split view controller* (UISplitViewController). The child view controllers are the split view controller's `viewControllers`. A UIViewController that is a child, at any depth, of a UISplitViewController has a reference to the UISplitViewController through its `splitViewController` property.

The chief purpose of a split view controller is to implement a master–detail architecture. The first view is the master view, and is usually a list, such as a table view. The user taps an item of that list to specify what should appear in the second view, which is the detail view. We may speak of the two children of the split view controller as the *master* view controller and the *detail* view controller. Officially, they are the *primary* and *secondary* view controllers.

The split view controller is *adaptive*, meaning that, by default, the implementation appears differently depending on whether we're running on an iPad or an iPhone:

Split view on the iPhone
    The master–detail architecture is expressed as a navigation interface. The user sees one view at a time. The master view occupies the screen; the user taps an item in the master view; the detail view replaces the master view.

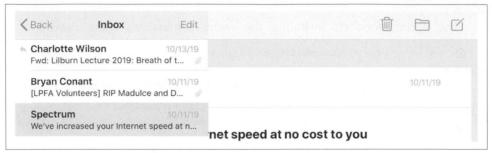

Figure 9-3. A familiar split view interface

Split view on the iPad

Both views are displayed simultaneously. Usually, the master view is narrower, roughly the width of a typical iPhone. The user taps an item in the master view; the detail view responds by changing its contents.

In landscape orientation on the iPad, the master view and the detail view appear side by side. In portrait orientation on the iPad, there are two possible arrangements:

Side by side

The two views appear side by side as in landscape orientation. Apple's Settings app is an example.

Overlay

The detail view appears alone, with an option to summon the master view from the side as an overlay, either by tapping a bar button item or by swiping from the edge of the screen. Apple's Mail app is an example (Figure 9-3).

Xcode's Master–Detail App template will give you an adaptive UISplitView-Controller instantiated from the storyboard, with no work on your part. To understand how that works, let's start by constructing and configuring a split view controller entirely in code. We'll get it working on the iPad before proceeding to the iPhone version. Then we'll return to consideration of the storyboard template.

Expanded Split View Controller (iPad)

For reasons that will be clear later, a split view controller on the iPad is called an *expanded* split view controller. An expanded split view controller has two child view controllers simultaneously.

In this example, our master view (owned by MasterViewController) will be a table view listing the names of the three Pep Boys. Our detail view (owned by DetailView-Controller) will contain a single label displaying the name of the Pep Boy selected in the master view.

Our first cut at writing MasterViewController simply displays the table view:

```swift
class MasterViewController: UITableViewController {
    let model = ["Manny", "Moe", "Jack"]
    let cellID = "Cell"
    override func viewDidLoad() {
        super.viewDidLoad()
        self.tableView.register(UITableViewCell.self,
            forCellReuseIdentifier: self.cellID)
    }
    override func numberOfSections(in tableView: UITableView) -> Int {
        return 1
    }
    override func tableView(_ tableView: UITableView,
        numberOfRowsInSection section: Int) -> Int {
            return model.count
    }
    override func tableView(_ tableView: UITableView,
        cellForRowAt indexPath: IndexPath) -> UITableViewCell {
            let cell = tableView.dequeueReusableCell(
                withIdentifier: self.cellID, for: indexPath)
            cell.textLabel!.text = model[indexPath.row]
            return cell
    }
}
```

DetailViewController, in its `viewDidLoad` implementation, puts the label (`self.lab`) into the interface; it also has a public boy string property whose value appears in the label. We are deliberately agnostic about the order of events; our interface works correctly regardless of whether boy is set before or after `viewDidLoad` is called:

```swift
class DetailViewController: UIViewController {
    var lab : UILabel!
    var boy : String = "" {
        didSet {
            if self.lab != nil {
                self.lab.text = self.boy
            }
        }
    }
    override func viewDidLoad() {
        super.viewDidLoad()
        self.view.backgroundColor = .white
        let lab = UILabel()
        lab.translatesAutoresizingMaskIntoConstraints = false
        self.view.addSubview(lab)
        NSLayoutConstraint.activate([
            lab.topAnchor.constraint(
                equalTo: self.view.safeAreaLayoutGuide.topAnchor,
                constant: 100),
            lab.centerXAnchor.constraint(
                equalTo: self.view.centerXAnchor)
```

```
        ])
        self.lab = lab
        self.lab.text = self.boy
    }
}
```

Our app delegate (or, in iOS 13, our scene delegate) constructs the interface by creating a UISplitViewController, giving it its two initial children, and putting its view into the window:

```
let svc = UISplitViewController()
svc.viewControllers =
    [MasterViewController(style:.plain), DetailViewController()]
self.window!.rootViewController = svc
self.window!.backgroundColor = .white
self.window!.makeKeyAndVisible()
```

The result certainly *looks* like a split view interface. In landscape orientation, the two views appear side by side; in portrait orientation, the detail view appears alone, but the master view can be summoned by swiping from the edge of the screen, and it can be dismissed by tapping outside it.

However, the app doesn't yet *do* anything! In particular, when we tap on a Pep Boy's name in the master view, the detail view doesn't change. Let's add that code (to MasterViewController):

```
override func tableView(_ tableView: UITableView,
    didSelectRowAt indexPath: IndexPath) {
        let detail = DetailViewController()
        detail.boy = model[indexPath.row]
        self.showDetailViewController(detail, sender: self) // *
}
```

The starred line is the key to the entire implementation of the master–detail architecture. Despite being sent to `self`, the call to `showDetailViewController(_:sender:)` actually walks up the view controller hierarchy until it arrives at the split view controller. (The mechanism of this walk is quite interesting of itself; I'll discuss it later.) The split view controller responds by making the `detail` view controller its second child, replacing the existing detail view and causing the selected Pep Boy's name to appear in the interface.

Things are going very well, but our app still doesn't look like a standard master–detail view interface. The usual thing is that both the master view and the detail view should contain a navigation bar. The detail view in portrait orientation can then display in its navigation bar a left button that summons the master view, so that the user doesn't have to know about the swipe gesture. This button is vended by the UISplitView-Controller, through its `displayModeButtonItem` property. To construct the interface properly, we need to change our scene delegate code so that the split view controller's children are navigation controllers:

```
let svc = UISplitViewController()
let master = MasterViewController(style:.plain)
master.title = "Pep" // *
let nav1 = UINavigationController(rootViewController:master) // *
let detail = DetailViewController()
let nav2 = UINavigationController(rootViewController:detail) // *
svc.viewControllers = [nav1, nav2] // *
self.window!.rootViewController = svc
let b = svc.displayModeButtonItem // *
detail.navigationItem.leftBarButtonItem = b // *
detail.navigationItem.leftItemsSupplementBackButton = true // *
```

Having made that adjustment, we must also adjust our MasterViewController code. Consider what will happen when the user taps a Pep Boy name in the master view. At the moment, we are making a new DetailViewController and making it the split view controller's second child. That is now wrong; we must make a new UINavigation-Controller instead, with a new DetailViewController as its child. And this new DetailViewController doesn't have the displayModeButtonItem as its leftBarButton-Item, so we have to add it:

```
override func tableView(_ tableView: UITableView,
    didSelectRowAt indexPath: IndexPath) {
        let detail = DetailViewController()
        detail.boy = model[indexPath.row]
        let b = self.splitViewController?.displayModeButtonItem
        detail.navigationItem.leftBarButtonItem = b // *
        detail.navigationItem.leftItemsSupplementBackButton = true // *
        let nav = UINavigationController(rootViewController: detail) // *
        self.showDetailViewController(nav, sender: self)
}
```

When the app is in portrait orientation, showing just the detail view, the display-ModeButtonItem summons the master view. When the app is in landscape orientation with the two views displayed side by side, the displayModeButtonItem automatically hides itself. Our iPad split view implementation is complete!

Collapsed Split View Controller (iPhone)

As I've said, a split view controller is adaptive. We can see this if we now launch our existing app on the iPhone: astoundingly, it works almost perfectly. There's a navigation interface. Tapping a Pep Boy's name in the master view pushes the new detail view controller onto the navigation stack, with its view displaying that name. The detail view's navigation bar has a back button that pops the detail view controller and returns us to the master view.

The only thing that isn't quite right is that the app launches with the detail view showing, rather than the master view. To fix that, we first add a line to our scene delegate launch code, to assign a delegate (UISplitViewControllerDelegate) to the UISplitViewController:

```
let svc = UISplitViewController()
svc.delegate = self // *
```

We then implement one delegate method:

```
func splitViewController(_ svc: UISplitViewController,
    collapseSecondary vc2: UIViewController,
    onto vc1: UIViewController) -> Bool {
        return true
}
```

That's all; on the iPhone, the app now behaves correctly!

To understand what that delegate method does, you need to know more about how the split view controller works. It adopts one of two states: it is either collapsed or expanded, in accordance with its `isCollapsed` property. This distinction corresponds to whether or not the environment's trait collection has a `.compact` horizontal size class: if so, the split view controller collapses. This means that the split view controller collapses as it launches on an iPhone.

An expanded split view controller has *two* child view controllers simultaneously. But a collapsed split view controller has only *one* child view controller. So when the app launches on the iPhone and the split view controller collapses, it must remove one child view controller. But which one? To find out, the split view controller *asks its delegate* how to proceed. In particular, it calls these delegate methods:

`primaryViewController(forCollapsing:)`
> The collapsed split view controller will have only one child view controller. *What* view controller should this be? By default, it will be the current *first* view controller, but you can implement this method to return a different answer.

`splitViewController(_:collapseSecondary:onto:)`
> The collapsing split view controller is proposing to remove its *second* view controller, leaving its *first* view controller as its only child view controller. Return `true` to permit this to happen.
>
> If this method returns `false` (the default), the split view controller sends `collapseSecondaryViewController(_:for:)` to the *first* view controller. What happens to the second view controller is now up to the first view controller.

Our first view controller is a UINavigationController, which has a built-in response to `collapseSecondaryViewController(_:for:)`. By default, it wants to push the specified secondary view controller onto its own stack. But if we let it do that, we end up launching with the detail view showing on the iPhone, as we've already seen. Therefore, we implement `splitViewController(_:collapseSecondary:onto:)` to return `true`. That permits the split view controller to remove its second view controller, and we end up launching with the master view showing on the iPhone.

As on the iPad, the call to `showDetailViewController(_:sender:)`, when the user taps a row of the master table view, is the heart of the interface's functionality. The key here is that the interface responds in two different ways, depending on whether the split view controller is expanded or collapsed:

On the iPad (expanded)
> The new view controller becomes the split view controller's second (detail) view controller, and the detail view, already visible in the interface, is replaced.

On the iPhone (collapsed)
> There is just one child view controller; it is a navigation controller, and the new view controller is pushed onto its stack.

 On an iPhone, we are pushing a UINavigationController onto a UINavigation-Controller's stack. This is an odd thing to do, and is possible only thanks to some internal voodoo. Don't do it in any other context!

Expanding Split View Controller (Big iPhone)

A "big" iPhone (currently the iPhone 6/7/8 Plus, iPhone XR, iPhone XS Max, iPhone 11, and iPhone 11 Pro Max) is a hybrid: it's horizontally compact in portrait orientation, but *not* in landscape orientation. In effect, the split view controller thinks it's on an iPhone when the app is in portrait, but it thinks it has been magically moved over to an iPad when the app rotates to landscape. The split view controller *alternates* between `isCollapsed` being `true` and `false` on a single device. In portrait, the split view displays a single navigation interface, with the master view controller at its root, like an iPhone. In landscape, the master and detail views are displayed side by side, like an iPad.

When the app, running on a big iPhone, rotates to portrait, or if it launches into portrait, the split view controller collapses, going through the very same procedure I just described for an iPhone. When it rotates to landscape, it performs the opposite of collapsing — namely, *expanding*.

As the split view controller expands, it has the inverse of the problem it has when it collapses. A collapsed split view controller has just *one* child view controller, but an expanded split view controller has *two* child view controllers. What view controllers should they be? To find out, the split view controller *asks its delegate* how to proceed:

`primaryViewController(forExpanding:)`
> What view controller should be the expanded view controller's *first* child view controller? By default, it will be the *current* child view controller, but you can implement this method to return a different answer.

```
splitViewController(_:separateSecondaryFrom:)
```
What view controller should be the expanded split view controller's *second* child view controller? Implement this method to return that view controller.

If you don't implement this method, or if you return `nil`, the split view controller sends `separateSecondaryViewController(for:)` to the *first* view controller. That method, in turn, returns a view controller, or `nil`:

- If it returns a view controller, the split view controller makes that view controller its second view controller.

- If it returns `nil`, the split view controller uses the view controller that was *previously* its second view controller.

The default response of a plain vanilla UIViewController to `separateSecondary-ViewController(for:)` is to return `nil`. But a UINavigationController, if it has two children (a root view controller and a pushed view controller), pops its `top-ViewController` off the navigation stack and returns the popped view controller.

When our app is rotated from portrait to landscape, exactly the right thing now happens, with no further coding on our part: if the navigation controller has pushed a DetailViewController onto its stack, it now pops it and hands it to the split view controller, which displays its view as the detail view!

On a big iPhone in landscape, the `displayModeButtonItem` is present (whereas it disappears automatically on an iPad in landscape). Instead of appearing as a "back" chevron, it's an "expand" symbol (two arrows pointing away from each other). When the user taps it, the master view is hidden and the detail view occupies the entire screen — and the `displayModeButtonItem` changes to a chevron. Tapping the chevron toggles back the other way: the master view is shown again.

So, is our split view interface finished? Not quite! There is one remaining problem. Suppose we're in landscape (`.regular` horizontal size class) and the user is looking at the *detail* view controller. Now the user rotates to portrait (`.compact` horizontal size class). The split view controller collapses. Without extra precautions, we'll end up displaying the *master* view controller — because we went to the trouble of arranging that, back when we thought the only way to collapse was to *launch* into a `.compact` horizontal size class:

```
func splitViewController(_ svc: UISplitViewController,
    collapseSecondary vc2: UIViewController,
    onto vc1: UIViewController) -> Bool {
        return true
}
```

The result is that the user's place in the application has been lost. I think we can solve this satisfactorily simply by having the split view controller's delegate keep track of whether the user has *ever* chosen to see a detail view. I'll use an instance property, `self.detailChosen`. When the user taps a row of the master view list to navigate to the detail view, we emit a notification:

```
static let detailChosen = Notification.Name("detailChosen")
override func tableView(_ tableView: UITableView,
    didSelectRowAt indexPath: IndexPath) {
        // ... as before ...
        NotificationCenter.default.post(name:Self.detailChosen, object:self)
}
```

The split view controller's delegate has registered to receive that notification, and sets `detailChosen` to `true` in response:

```
NotificationCenter.default.addObserver(
    forName: MasterViewController.detailChosen,
    object: nil, queue: nil) { _ in
        self.detailChosen = true
}
```

When the split view controller collapses, the split view controller's delegate uses that instance property to decide what to do — that is, whether to display the master view controller or the detail view controller:

```
func splitViewController(_ svc: UISplitViewController,
    collapseSecondary vc2: UIViewController,
    onto vc1: UIViewController) -> Bool {
        if let nav = vc2 as? UINavigationController,
            nav.topViewController is DetailViewController,
            self.detailChosen {
                return false
        }
        return true
}
```

Customizing a Split View Controller

Here are some properties of a UISplitViewController that allow it to be customized:

`primaryEdge`
> Which side the primary view appears on. Your choices (UISplitView-Controller.PrimaryEdge) are `.leading` and `.trailing`.

`presentsWithGesture`
> A Bool. If `false`, the screen edge swipe gesture that shows the master view in portrait orientation on an iPad is disabled. The default is `true`.

`preferredDisplayMode`
> The display mode describes how an expanded split view controller's primary view is displayed. Set this property to change the current display mode of an

expanded split view controller programmatically, or set it to `.automatic` to allow the display mode to adopt its default value. To learn the actual display mode being used, ask for the current `displayMode`.

An expanded split view controller has three possible display modes (UISplitView-Controller.DisplayMode):

`.allVisible`
> The two views are shown side by side.

`.primaryHidden`
> The primary view is not present.

`.primaryOverlay`
> The primary view is shown as a temporary overlay in front of the secondary view.

The default automatic behaviors are:

iPad in landscape
> The `displayModeButtonItem` is hidden, and the display mode is `.allVisible`.

iPad in portrait
> The `displayModeButtonItem` is shown, and the display mode toggles between `.primaryHidden` and `.primaryOverlay`.

Big iPhone in landscape
> The `displayModeButtonItem` is shown, and the display mode toggles between `.primaryHidden` and `.allVisible`.

`preferredPrimaryColumnWidthFraction`
> Sets the master view width in `.allVisible` and `.primaryOverlay` display modes, as a percentage of the whole split view (between 0 and 1). Your setting may have no effect unless you also constrain the width limits absolutely through the `minimumPrimaryColumnWidth` and `maximumPrimaryColumnWidth` properties. To specify the default width, use `UISplitViewController.automaticDimension`. To learn the actual width being used, ask for the current `primaryColumnWidth`.

You can also track and govern the display mode with these delegate methods:

`splitViewController(_:willChangeTo:)`
> The `displayMode` of an expanded split view controller is about to change, meaning that its first view controller's view will be shown or hidden. You might want to alter the interface somehow in response.

`targetDisplayModeForAction(in:)`
Called whenever something happens that might affect the display mode, such as:

- The split view controller is showing for the first time.
- The interface is rotating.
- The user summons or dismisses the primary view.

Return a display mode to specify what the user's tapping the `displayModeButton-Item` should subsequently do (and, by extension, how the button is portrayed), or `.automatic` to accept what the split view controller would normally do.

Here's an example of setting the `preferredDisplayMode` from one of my own apps. The master view is a UITableView; when the user selects a row of the table, if we're on an iPad with the master view shown as an overlay, then in addition to setting the detail view controller, I slide the master view out of the way so that the entire detail view is visible:

```
override func tableView(_ tableView: UITableView,
    didSelectRowAt indexPath: IndexPath) {
        // ...
        if let svc = self.splitViewController {
            if !svc.isCollapsed {
                if svc.displayMode == .primaryOverlay {
                    UIView.animate(withDuration: 0.3, animations: {
                        svc.preferredDisplayMode = .primaryHidden
                    }) { _ in
                        svc.preferredDisplayMode = .automatic
                    }
                }
            }
        }
}
```

After collapsing or expanding, a UISplitViewController emits the `UIView-Controller.showDetailTargetDidChangeNotification`.

If a split view controller is the top-level view controller, it determines your app's compensatory rotation behavior. To take a hand in that determination without having to subclass UISplitViewController, make one of your objects the split view controller's delegate and implement these methods, as needed:

- `splitViewControllerSupportedInterfaceOrientations(_:)`
- `splitViewControllerPreferredInterfaceOrientationForPresentation(_:)`

A split view controller does not relegate decisions about the status bar appearance to its children. To hide the status bar when a split view controller is the root view controller, you might have to subclass UISplitViewController; alternatively, you could wrap the split view controller in a custom container view controller, as I describe later in this chapter.

Split View Controller in a Storyboard

I've shown how to construct a working split view controller interface in code. But how does a split view controller interface constructed in the storyboard work? In just the same way! Not only does it have the same *structure* that we constructed in code; it uses effectively the same *code* that we used to make our split view controller interface behave correctly.

To see this, make a new project from the Master–Detail App template and study the storyboard that it provides. The storyboard starts with a split view controller, already configured (Figure 9-4):

- The split view controller has two relationships, "master view controller" and "detail view controller," specifying its two children. Those two children are both navigation controllers.

- The first navigation controller has a "root view controller" relationship to a MasterViewController, which is a UITableViewController.

- The second navigation controller has a "root view controller" relationship to a DetailViewController.

- The prototype table view cell in the master table view has an action segue — a Show Detail segue whose destination is the detail navigation controller. A Show Detail segue, when triggered, calls showDetailViewController(_:sender:) — and you already know what *that* does.

The displayModeButtonItem has to be added; that's done in code, in the scene delegate's implementation of scene(_:willConnectTo:options:). The code obtains a reference to the split view controller and to the detail view controller, and creates and configures the displayModeButtonItem:

```
guard let splitViewController =
    window.rootViewController as? UISplitViewController
        else { return }
guard let navigationController =
    splitViewController.viewControllers.last as? UINavigationController
        else { return }
navigationController.topViewController?.navigationItem.leftBarButtonItem =
    splitViewController.displayModeButtonItem
```

The displayModeButtonItem must also be managed when the Show Detail segue is triggered. That's done in code, in the master view controller:

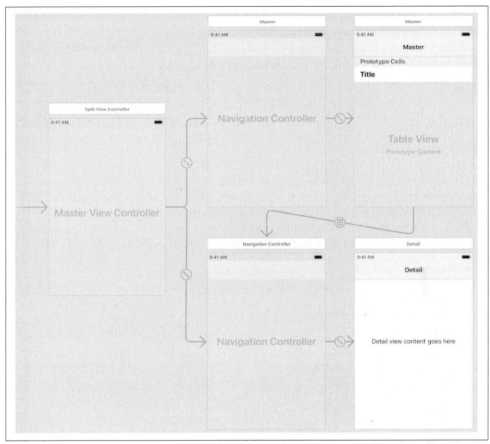

Figure 9-4. How the storyboard configures a split view interface

```
override func prepare(for segue: UIStoryboardSegue, sender: Any?) {
    if segue.identifier == "showDetail" {
        if let indexPath = tableView.indexPathForSelectedRow {
            let controller =
                (segue.destination as! UINavigationController)
                    .topViewController as! DetailViewController
            controller.navigationItem.leftBarButtonItem =
                splitViewController?.displayModeButtonItem
            controller.navigationItem.leftItemsSupplementBackButton = true
            // ... also pass data to controller ...
        }
    }
}
```

In addition, the template code sets the scene delegate as the split view controller's delegate, and implements `splitViewController(_:collapseSecondary:onto:)`.

So the Master–Detail App template, apart from instantiating the view controllers from the storyboard, ends up doing in code almost everything we did when we created the view controllers in code. So what advantage is there in instantiating the split view controller and its child view controllers from the storyboard? Not much, in my opinion. In fact, the Master–Detail App template is arguably *worse* than the code we wrote earlier; the template code is verbose and opaque, because the architecture has been constructed automatically, behind the code's back, and the code must now scramble to get references to the various view controllers.

Setting the Collapsed State

Suppose you want side-by-side display of the two child view controllers' views in landscape *even on an iPhone*. How would you arrange that? The problem here is that we need to control the value of the split view controller's isCollapsed property — but we can't just set it directly, because this property is read-only.

The split view controller decides its own expanded or collapsed state depending on the environment — in particular, on whether the current trait collection's horizontal size class is .compact. We need, therefore, to *lie to the split view controller* about its trait collection environment, effectively making it believe that it's on an iPad even though it's really on an iPhone.

We can do that by interposing our own custom container view controller above the split view controller in the view controller hierarchy — typically, as the split view controller's direct parent. We can then send this container view controller the set-OverrideTraitCollection(_:forChild:) message, causing it to pass the trait collection of our choosing down the view controller hierarchy to the split view controller.

In this example, our container view controller is the app's root view controller; its child is a split view controller. The split view controller's view completely occupies the container view controller's view. The container's own view is never seen; the container view controller exists *solely* in order to manage the split view controller. Early in the life of the app, the container view controller configures the split view controller and lies to it about the environment:

```
var didInitialSetup = false
override func viewWillLayoutSubviews() {
    if !self.didInitialSetup {
        self.didInitialSetup = true
        let svc = self.children[0] as! UISplitViewController
        svc.preferredDisplayMode = .allVisible
        svc.preferredPrimaryColumnWidthFraction = 0.5
        svc.maximumPrimaryColumnWidth = 500
        let traits = UITraitCollection(traitsFrom: [
            UITraitCollection(horizontalSizeClass: .regular)
        ])
```

```
        self.setOverrideTraitCollection(traits,
            forChild: svc)
    }
}
```

The result is that the split view controller displays both its children's views side by side, both in portrait and landscape, like the Settings app on the iPad, *even on the iPhone*.

Another use of this same trick, based on Apple's AdaptivePhotos sample code, is to make a small iPhone behave more like a big iPhone, with a `.regular` horizontal size class in landscape (the split view controller expands) but a `.compact` horizontal size class in portrait (the split view controller collapses):

```
override func viewWillTransition(to size: CGSize,
    with coordinator: UIViewControllerTransitionCoordinator) {
        let svc = self.children[0] as! UISplitViewController
        if size.width > size.height {
            let traits = UITraitCollection(traitsFrom: [
                UITraitCollection(horizontalSizeClass: .regular)
            ])
            self.setOverrideTraitCollection(traits,
                forChild: svc)
        } else {
            self.setOverrideTraitCollection(nil,
                forChild: svc)
        }
        super.viewWillTransition(to: size, with: coordinator)
}
```

View Controller Message Percolation

At the heart of the split view controller master–detail architecture is the `showDetail-ViewController(_:sender:)` method. As I mentioned earlier, my code sends this message to `self` (the master view controller), but it is actually the split view controller that responds. How is that possible? The answer is that this message *percolates up* the view controller hierarchy to the split view controller.

Only two built-in UIViewController methods are implemented to behave in this way: `show(_:sender:)` and `showDetailViewController(_:sender:)`. Underlying this behavior is a *general* architecture for percolating a message up the view controller hierarchy, which I will now describe.

The heart of the message-percolation architecture is the method `targetView-Controller(forAction:sender:)`, where the `action:` parameter is the selector for the method we're inquiring about. This method, using some deep introspective voodoo, looks to see whether the view controller to which the message was sent *overrides the UIViewController implementation* of the method in question. If so, it returns `self`; if not, it effectively recurses *up* the view controller hierarchy, returning the result of calling the same method with the same parameters on its parent view controller or presenting view controller — or nil if no view controller is ultimately returned to it. (A view controller subclass that *does* override the method in question but does *not* want to be the target view controller can implement the UIResponder method `canPerformAction(_:withSender:)` to return `false`.)

So `show(_:sender:)` and `showDetailViewController(_:sender:)` are implemented to call `targetViewController(forAction:sender:)`. If this call returns a target, they send themselves to that target. If it *doesn't* return a target, they call `present(_:animated:completion:)` as a kind of fallback.

The reason for the percolation architecture is that it allows `show(_:sender:)` and `showDetailViewController(_:sender:)` to work *differently* depending on how the view controller to which they are originally sent is situated in the view controller hierarchy. Two built-in UIViewController subclasses, UINavigationController and UISplitViewController, override one or both of these methods, and if they are *further up the view controller hierarchy* than the view controller on which these methods are called, they will take charge of what happens:

UINavigationController `show(_:sender:)`
> UINavigationController implements `show(_:sender:)` to call `pushViewController(_:animated:)`. That explains the dual behavior of `show(_:sender:)` — everything depends on whether or not we're in a navigation interface:

> *In a navigation interface*
>> If you send `show(_:sender:)` to a view controller whose parent is a UINavigationController, it is the navigation controller's implementation that will be called, meaning that the parameter view controller is *pushed* onto the stack.

> *Not in a navigation interface*
>> If you send `show(_:sender:)` to a view controller *without* a parent that overrides this method, it can't find a target, so it executes its fallback, meaning that the parameter view controller is *presented*.

UISplitViewController `showDetailViewController(_:sender:)`
> UISplitViewController implements `showDetailViewController(_:sender:)` as follows. First, it calls the delegate method `splitViewController(_:showDetail:sender:)`; if the delegate returns `true`, UISplitViewController does nothing (and in that case, *you* would be responsible for getting the parameter view controller's view into the interface). Otherwise:

If the split view controller is expanded

> The split view controller replaces its second child view controller with the parameter view controller.

If the split view controller is collapsed

> If the split view controller's first (and only) child view controller is a UINavigationController, it sends `show(_:sender:)` to it — and the navigation controller responds by pushing the parameter view controller onto its own stack.
>
> If not, the split view controller calls `present(_:animated:completion:)`.

UISplitViewController `show(_:sender:)`

> UISplitViewController implements `show(_:sender:)` as follows. First, it calls the delegate method `splitViewController(_:show:sender:)`; if the delegate returns `true`, UISplitViewController does nothing (and that case, *you* would be responsible for getting the parameter view controller's view into the interface). Otherwise:

If the split view controller is expanded

> If the `sender:` is the split view controller's first view controller, the split view controller replaces the *first* view controller with the parameter view controller.
>
> If not, it replaces its *second* view controller with the parameter view controller.

If the split view controller is collapsed

> The split view controller calls `present(_:animated:completion:)`.

Now that you understand the percolation mechanism, perhaps you'd like to know whether your own custom methods can participate in it. They can! Extend UIViewController to implement your method such that it calls `targetViewController(for-Action:sender:)` on `self` and sends the action method to the target if there is one:

```
extension UIViewController {
    @objc func showHide(_ sender: Any) {
        if let target = self.targetViewController(
            forAction:#selector(showHide), sender: sender) {
                target.showHide(self)
        }
    }
}
```

In that example, I don't know what any particular UIViewController subclass's override of `showHide(_:)` may do, and I don't care! What matters is that if `showHide(_:)` is sent to a view controller that *doesn't* override it, it will percolate up the view

Figure 9-5. Slideover multitasking mode and splitscreen multitasking mode

controller hierarchy until we find a view controller that *does* override it, and it is *that override* that will be called.

iPad Multitasking

Current iPad models can perform a kind of multitasking where the windows of *two different apps* can appear *simultaneously*. There are two multitasking modes (Figure 9-5):

Slideover
> One app appears in a narrow format in front of the other, occupying roughly one-third of the screen's width. The rear app continues to occupy the full width of the screen. On older iPad models, the rear app is deactivated and covered by a dimming view, and the user cannot interact with it without dismissing the front app. On all iPad models capable of running iOS 13, the rear app remains active and the user can interact with either app.

Splitscreen
> The two apps appear side by side and are both active simultaneously; the user can interact with either app. One of the two apps can occupy roughly one-third of the screen's width; in landscape orientation, the apps can also divide the screen's width equally. Splitscreen multitasking mode is not available on some older iPad models; it is available on all iPad models capable of running iOS 13.

Your iPad or universal app, by default, will participate in iPad multitasking if your *Info.plist* permits all four orientations. If you would like to opt out of participation in iPad multitasking, set the *Info.plist* key UIRequiresFullScreen to YES; you can do that conveniently while editing the app target by checking Requires Full Screen in the General tab. But Apple warns that this option is slated to be removed; multitasking will be a requirement.

If your app participates in iPad multitasking, its size can change from occupying the device's entire screen to a narrower size. This, in turn, may be accompanied by a change in the trait collection. If your app appears in narrow format (because it is occupying roughly one-third of the screen, in slideover or splitscreen mode), then even though it's on an iPad, it will have a `.compact` horizontal size class. If your app occupies half the screen in splitscreen mode, it *might* have a `.compact` horizontal size class, depending on how large this iPad's screen is and what orientation the iPad is in. So your app can be toggled between a `.compact` horizontal size class and a `.regular` horizontal size class, and it must be prepared to cope with that change.

When your app changes size because of multitasking, your view controller will receive events to signal what's happening (see "Resizing and Layout Events" on page 312); the application or scene (or both) may be *inactive* at the time these events arrive:

- Your view controller will receive `viewWillTransition(to:with:)` to report the *size* change.

- If the size change also involves a transition from one horizontal size class to another, then your view controller will also receive `willTransition(to:with:)` and `traitCollectionDidChange(_:)` to report the *trait collection* change.

The good news is that, if your app is a universal app, it is probably prepared *already* to respond coherently to these events, and might well be able to participate in iPad multitasking with no significant change. Your code should already be thinking in terms of size classes, not device type. A view controller on an iPad can have a `.compact` horizontal size class quite apart from iPad multitasking (it might be a popover or form sheet presented view controller), so your code is already prepared for that possibility. And your view controllers will adapt to a size class change in real time:

- If a view controller is a presented view controller, then if the size transition involves a trait collection transition, the view controller will adapt, there and then. An iPad popover will transform into a sheet before the user's eyes as the app transitions from a `.regular` horizontal size class to `.compact` (and you can take a hand in how the presented view controller adapts by functioning as the presentation controller's delegate).

- In a split view controller interface, the split view controller will collapse and expand before the user's eyes as the app transitions from a `.regular` horizontal size class to `.compact` and back again. This is no different from the ability of a split view controller to collapse and expand when a big iPhone is rotated, and the same precautions will take care of it satisfactorily.

Here are some of the likely challenges you'll face in adapting your app to cope with iPad multitasking:

Size ratio

The variety of *absolute* sizes that your app's interface might assume under iPad multitasking is unlikely to raise any new concerns. If this is a universal app, then you are *already* taking care of a wide range of possible sizes through size classes and autolayout, and you probably won't have to do anything new to cover these new sizes. But there's a large possible range of *ratios* between the longer and shorter dimensions of your window's size. On a large iPad Pro, the window can go from a roughly square `1.04` height-to-width ratio all the way up to a very tall and narrow `3.6` height-to-width ratio. Designing an interface that looks decent and can be operated correctly under such widely variable size ratios can be tricky.

Window bounds and screen bounds

Under iPad multitasking, you can't assume that window bounds are screen bounds (see "Window Coordinates and Screen Coordinates" on page 26). What actually changes when your app is resized is the size of its *window*. Under iPad multitasking, your app's window bounds can be different from screen bounds. Moreover, if your app appears on the right, its window origin is shifted to the right; this changes the relationship between a view's position in window coordinates and its position in screen coordinates. You probably weren't using screen coordinates for anything anyway, but if you were, your code will need to change.

Resource sharing

An important implication of iPad multitasking is that your app may effectively be frontmost *at the same time* as some other app. This means that the other app can be using both the processor (especially the main thread) and memory at a time when your app is not suspended. For this to work, all apps participating in iPad multitasking need to be on good behavior, adhering to best practices with regard to threading (see Chapter 24) and memory usage (see "View Controller Memory Management" on page 406).

Drag and Drop

Drag and drop, introduced in iOS 11, allows the user to drag something from one app into another; it can also be used within a single app. What the user appears to drag is a view, but what is actually communicated to the target app is data. Drag and drop is effectively a visual form of copy and paste — with this important difference:

Copy and paste uses a clipboard

Typically, copy and paste starts by copying the actual data to be communicated onto a clipboard. The data sits in the clipboard, ready to paste anywhere. The data in the clipboard can be pasted multiple times in multiple places.

Drag and drop uses a promise

  With drag and drop between apps, no actual data is carried around during the drag. The data might be large; it might take time to acquire. What's carried is effectively a promise to supply a certain type of data on request; that promise isn't fulfilled until the drop takes place. Only the drop target can receive the data.

Drag and Drop Architecture

From an app's point of view, drag and drop operates at the level of individual views. The user performs a set sequence of actions:

1. The user long presses on a view; if this is a view from which dragging is possible (a *drag source*), a visible avatar — a *preview* — appears under the user's finger.

2. The user may then start dragging the preview.

3. The user drags the preview over some other view, possibly in a different app; if this is a view on which dropping is possible (a *drop destination*), the preview is badged to indicate this.

4. If the user releases the preview over a drop destination, the preview disappears, and the actual data is communicated from the source to the destination. (If the user releases the preview when it is *not* badged, the drag and drop is cancelled and no data is communicated.)

To prepare for drag and drop, therefore, your app will need either a drag source view or a drop destination view (or both):

Configuring a drag source view

  To configure a view so that dragging from it is possible, you create a UIDragInteraction object and attach it to that view. You don't subclass UIDragInteraction; rather, you give it a *delegate* (adopting the UIDragInteractionDelegate protocol). From your app's standpoint, it is this delegate that does all the work if the user actually tries to perform a drag from the source view.

Configuring a drop destination view

  To configure a view so that dropping onto it is possible, you create a UIDropInteraction object and attach it to that view. You don't subclass UIDropInteraction; rather, you give it a *delegate* (adopting the UIDropInteractionDelegate protocol). From your app's standpoint, it is this delegate that does all the work if the user actually tries to drop onto the destination view.

Drag and drop needs to operate between apps and outside of any app; it is a system-level technology. Between the start of the drag and the ultimate drop, the user, moving the preview, is interacting with the runtime — not the source app or the destination app. The preview being dragged doesn't belong to either app. In a sense, while dragging, the user isn't "in" any app at all; by the same token, while dragging, the user is not prevented from interacting with your app.

The runtime sends messages to the drag interaction delegate or the drop interaction delegate, as appropriate, at the start and end of the drag and drop. In those messages, the runtime presents two different faces:

- To the drag interaction delegate, it presents a UIDragSession object (a UIDrag-DropSession subclass).
- To the drop interaction delegate, it presents a UIDropSession object (another UIDragDropSession subclass).

More than one piece of data can be supplied through a single drag and drop session. The data itself is accessed through a nest of envelopes. Here's how the session is initially configured by the drag interaction delegate:

1. At the heart of each envelope is a single NSItemProvider representing a single piece of data.
2. Each item provider is wrapped in a UIDragItem.
3. The drag items are attached to the drag session.

At the other end of the process, the drop interaction delegate reverses the procedure:

1. The drop session contains drag items.
2. Each drag item contains a single NSItemProvider.
3. Each item provider is the conduit for fetching the corresponding piece of data.

Basic Drag and Drop

You now know enough for an example! I'll talk through a basic drag and drop operation. In my example, the source view will be a simple color swatch; it vends a color. The destination view will receive that color as the session's data. The source view and the destination view could be in two different apps, but the architecture is completely general, so they could be in the same app — it makes no difference.

The drag source view

The drag source view (which I'm calling `dragView`) can be configured like this:

```
@IBOutlet weak var dragView: UIView!
override func viewDidLoad() {
    super.viewDidLoad()
    let dragger = UIDragInteraction(delegate: self)
    self.dragView.addInteraction(dragger)
}
```

The user long presses on the source view, and the UIDragInteraction detects this. (If you think this makes a UIDragInteraction rather like a gesture recognizer, you're exactly right; in fact, adding a drag interaction to a view installs *four* gesture recognizers on that view.) The drag interaction turns to its delegate (UIDragInteractionDelegate) to find out what to do. A UIDragInteractionDelegate has just one required method, and this is it:

```
func dragInteraction(_ interaction: UIDragInteraction,
    itemsForBeginning session: UIDragSession) -> [UIDragItem] {
        let ip = NSItemProvider(object:UIColor.red)
        let di = UIDragItem(itemProvider: ip)
        return [di]
}
```

The drag delegate's `dragInteraction(_:itemsForBeginning:)` must return an array of drag items. If the array is empty, that's the end of the story; there will be no drag. In our case, we want to permit the drag. Our data is very simple, so we just package it up inside an item provider, pop the item provider into a drag item, and return an array consisting of that drag item.

The user now sees the preview and can drag it. The source effectively retires from the story. So much for the source view!

You may be wondering: where did the preview come from? We didn't supply a custom preview, so the system takes a snapshot of the drag source view, enlarges it slightly, makes it somewhat transparent, and uses that as the draggable preview. For our color swatch example, that might be perfectly acceptable.

The drop destination view

The drop destination view (which I'm calling `dropView`) can be configured in a manner remarkably similar to how we configured the source view:

```
@IBOutlet weak var dropView: UIView!
override func viewDidLoad() {
    super.viewDidLoad()
    let dropper = UIDropInteraction(delegate: self)
    self.dropView.addInteraction(dropper)
}
```

A drop interaction delegate has no required methods, but nothing is going to happen unless we implement this method:

```
func dropInteraction(_ interaction: UIDropInteraction,
    sessionDidUpdate session: UIDropSession) -> UIDropProposal {
        return UIDropProposal(operation: .copy)
}
```

In `dropInteraction(_:sessionDidUpdate:)`, our job is to return a UIDropProposal. This will be initialized with a UIDropOperation that will usually be `.cancel` or .copy. If it's .cancel, the user won't see any feedback while dragging over this view, and if the user drops onto this view, nothing will happen (the entire operation will be cancelled). If it's .copy, the preview is badged with a Plus sign while the user is dragging over this view, and if the user drops onto this view, we can be notified of this and can proceed to ask for the data.

In our implementation of dropInteraction(_:sessionDidUpdate:), we have expressed a willingness to accept a drop regardless of what sort of data is associated with this session. Let's refine that. If what we accept is a color, we should base our response on whether any of the session's item providers promise us color data. We can query the item providers individually, or we can ask the session itself:

```
func dropInteraction(_ interaction: UIDropInteraction,
    sessionDidUpdate session: UIDropSession) -> UIDropProposal {
        let op : UIDropOperation =
            session.canLoadObjects(ofClass: UIColor.self) ? .copy : .cancel
        return UIDropProposal(operation:op)
}
```

Finally, let's say the drop actually occurs on the destination view. The drop interaction delegate's opportunity to obtain the data is its implementation of drop-Interaction(_:performDrop:). In this method, there are two ways to ask for the data. The simple way is to ask the session itself:

```
func dropInteraction(_ interaction: UIDropInteraction,
    performDrop session: UIDropSession) {
        session.loadObjects(ofClass: UIColor.self) { colors in
            if let color = colors[0] as? UIColor {
                // do something with color here
            }
        }
}
```

The more elaborate way is to get a reference to an item provider and ask the item provider to load the data:

```
func dropInteraction(_ interaction: UIDropInteraction,
    performDrop session: UIDropSession) {
        for item in session.items {
            let ip = item.itemProvider
            ip.loadObject(ofClass: UIColor.self) { (color, error) in
                if let color = color as? UIColor {
                    // do something with color here
                }
            }
        }
}
```

There's an important difference between those two approaches:

`loadObjects(ofClass:)`

When calling the session's `loadObjects(ofClass:)`, the completion function is called on the *main* thread.

`loadObject(ofClass:)`

When calling an item provider's `loadObject(ofClass:)`, the completion function is called on a *background* thread.

If you use the second way and you intend to update or otherwise communicate with the interface, you'll need to step out to the main thread (see Chapter 24); I'll show an example later in this chapter.

Item Providers

It's no coincidence that my color swatch example in the preceding section uses a UIColor as the data passed through the drag and drop session. UIColor implements two key protocols, NSItemProviderWriting and NSItemProviderReading. That's why my code was able to make two important method calls:

The drag source and `init(object:)`

At the drag source end of things, I was able to construct my item provider by calling NSItemProvider's initializer `init(object:)`. That's because UIColor adopts the NSItemProviderWriting protocol; the parameter of `init(object:)` must be an instance of an NSItemProviderWriting adopter.

The drop destination and `loadObject(ofClass:)`

At the drop destination end of things, I was able to get the data from my item provider by calling `loadObject(ofClass:)`. That's because UIColor adopts the NSItemProviderReading protocol; the parameter of `loadObject(ofClass:)` must be an NSItemProviderReading adopter.

Other common classes that adopt these protocols include NSString, UIImage, NSURL, MKMapItem, and CNContact. But what if your data's class isn't one of those? Then adopt those protocols in *your* class!

To illustrate, I'll create a Person class and then configure it so that Person data can be passed through drag and drop. Here's the basic Person class:

```
final class Person : NSObject, Codable {
    let firstName: String
    let lastName: String
    init(firstName:String, lastName.String) {
        self.firstName = firstName
        self.lastName = lastName
        super.init()
    }
    override var description : String {
        return self.firstName + " " + self.lastName
```

```
        }
        enum MyError : Error { case oops }
        static let personUTI = "neuburg.matt.person"
    }
```

It turns out that the only kind of data that can actually pass through a drag and drop session is a Data object. Therefore, I'm going to need a way to serialize a Person as Data to pass it from the source to the destination. That's why my Person class adopts the Codable protocol, which makes serialization trivial (Chapter 22). I also supply a simple Error type, to use as a signal if things go wrong. Finally, there is no standard UTI (universal type identifier) for my Person type, so I've made one up.

NSItemProviderWriting

Now I'll make it possible to call NSItemProvider's init(object:) when the object: is a Person. To do so, I adopt NSItemProviderWriting, which has two required members:

```
extension Person : NSItemProviderWriting {
    static var writableTypeIdentifiersForItemProvider = [personUTI] ❶
    func loadData(withTypeIdentifier typeid: String,
        forItemProviderCompletionHandler
        ch: @escaping (Data?, Error?) -> Void) -> Progress? { ❷
            switch typeid {
            case Self.personUTI:
                do {
                    ch(try PropertyListEncoder().encode(self), nil)
                } catch {
                    ch(nil, error)
                }
            default: ch(nil, MyError.oops)
            }
            return nil
    }
}
```

❶ The `writableTypeIdentifiersForItemProvider` property lists type identifiers for the various representations in which we are willing to supply our data. At the moment, I'm willing to supply a Person only as a Person.

❷ `loadData(withTypeIdentifier:forItemProviderCompletionHandler:)` will be called when a drop destination asks for our data. The drop has occurred, and our Person object, originally passed into NSItemProvider's init(object:), is going to package itself up as a Data object. That's easy, because Person is Codable. There are no existing conventions for the format in which a Person is coded as Data, so I use a property list. Whatever happens, I make sure to *call the completion function* — either I pass in a Data object as the first parameter, or I pass in an Error object as the second parameter. That's crucial!

Our data doesn't take any time to generate, so I'm returning `nil` from the `loadData` method. If our data were time-consuming to supply, we might wish to return a Progress object with the fetching of our data tied to the updating of that object. I'll talk more about the purpose of the Progress object later.

NSItemProviderReading

Next I'll make it possible to call NSItemProvider's `loadObject(ofClass:)` when the `class:` is `Person.self`. To do so, I adopt NSItemProviderReading, which has two required members:

```
extension Person : NSItemProviderReading {
    static var readableTypeIdentifiersForItemProvider = [personUTI] ❶
    static func object(withItemProviderData data: Data,
        typeIdentifier typeid: String) throws -> Self { ❷
            switch typeid {
            case personUTI:
                do {
                    let p = try PropertyListDecoder().decode(self, from: data)
                    return p
                } catch {
                    throw error
                }
            default: throw MyError.oops
            }
    }
}
```

Everything I'm doing to implement NSItemProviderReading complements what I did to implement NSItemProviderWriting:

❶ The `readableTypeIdentifiersForItemProvider` property lists type identifiers for any representations that we know how to transform into a Person. At the moment, we do this only for an actual Person.

❷ When `object(withItemProviderData:typeIdentifier:)` is called with the Person type identifier, this means that a Person object is arriving at the destination, packaged up as a Data object. Our job is to extract it and return it. Well, we know how it has been encoded; it's a property list! So we decode it and return it. If anything goes wrong, we throw an error instead.

The upshot is that drag and drop of a Person object now works perfectly within our app, if we drop on a view whose UIDropInteractionDelegate expects a Person object.

Vending additional representations

What if we want a Person to be draggable from our app to some other app? It's unlikely that another app will know about our Person class. Or what if we want a Person to be draggable within our app to a view that expects some other kind of data?

So far, our `writableTypeIdentifiersForItemProvider` property declares just one UTI, signifying that we dispense a Person object. But we can add other UTIs, signifying that we provide alternate representations of a Person. Let's decide to vend a Person as text:

```
static var writableTypeIdentifiersForItemProvider =
    [personUTI, kUTTypeUTF8PlainText as String]
```

(The constant `kUTTypeUTF8PlainText`, along with other UTI names, can be found in the Mobile Core Services framework; you'll need to `import MobileCoreServices`.)

Now we need to supplement our implementation of `loadData(withType-Identifier:forItemProviderCompletionHandler:)` to take account of the possibility that we may be called by someone who is expecting a String instead of a Person. What string shall we provide? How about a string rendering of the Person's name? It happens that our `description` property is ready and willing to provide that. And there's a simple standard way to wrap a UTF-8 string as Data: just call `data(using: .utf8)`. So all we have to do is add this case to our switch statement:

```
case kUTTypeUTF8PlainText as NSString as String:
    ch(self.description.data(using: .utf8)!, nil)
```

The result is that if a Person is dragged and dropped onto a view that expects a string to be dropped on it, the Person's name is provided as the data. A UITextField is such a view; if a Person is dragged and dropped onto a text field, the Person's name is inserted into the text field!

Receiving additional representations

We can also extend our implementation of the NSItemProviderReading protocol in a similar way. Here, our app contains a view that expects a Person to be dropped onto it, and we want it to have the ability to accept data of some other kind. Suppose the user drags a String and drops it onto our view. A String is not a Person, but perhaps this String is in fact a person's name. We could make a Person from that String.

To make that possible, we add a UTI to our `readableTypeIdentifiersForItem-Provider` property, signifying that we can derive a Person from text:

```
static var readableTypeIdentifiersForItemProvider =
    [personUTI, kUTTypeUTF8PlainText as String]
```

To go with that, we add a case to the switch statement in our `object(withItem-ProviderData:typeIdentifier:)` implementation. We pull the String out of the

Data object, parse it in a crude way into a first and last name, and create a Person object:

```
case kUTTypeUTF8PlainText as NSString as String:
    if let s = String(data: data, encoding: .utf8) {
        let arr = s.split(separator:" ")
        let first = arr.dropLast().joined(separator: " ")
        let last = arr.last ?? ""
        return self.init(firstName: first, lastName: String(last))
    }
    throw MyError.oops
```

The result is that if the string `"Matt Neuburg"` is dragged onto a view that expects a Person object, the drop is accepted, because our Person type has signified that it knows how to turn a string into a Person, and the result of the drop is a Person with first name `"Matt"` and last name `"Neuburg"`.

Slow Data Delivery

Pretend that you are the drop interaction delegate, and you are now asking for the data in your implementation of `dropInteraction(_:performDrop:)`. Whether you call the session's `loadObjects(ofClass:)` or an item provider's `loadObject(ofClass:)`, your completion function is called *asynchronously* when the data arrives. This could take some considerable time, depending on the circumstances. (See Appendix C for more about what "asynchronous" means.)

Therefore, by default, if things take too long, the runtime puts up a dialog tracking the overall progress of data delivery and allowing the user to cancel it. If you like, you can replace the runtime's dialog with your own progress interface. (If you intend to do that, set the drop session's `progressIndicatorStyle` to `.none`, to suppress the default dialog — and make sure that your interface gives the user a way to cancel.)

You can stay informed about the supplying of the data through a Progress object (Chapter 12). A Progress object has `fractionCompleted` and `isFinished` properties that you can track through key–value observing in order to update your interface; you can also cancel the loading process by telling the Progress object to `cancel`. There are two ways to get such an object:

- The session vends an overall Progress object as its `progress` property.
- An individual item provider's `loadObject` method can return a Progress object tracking the delivery of its own data.

Even if you rely on the runtime's default progress dialog, there can be a disconcerting effect of blankness when all the apparent action comes to an end without any data to display. You can discover this situation by implementing your drop interaction delegate's `dropInteraction(_:concludeDrop:)` method. When that method is called, all visible activity in the interface has stopped. If you discover here that the drop session's `progress.isFinished` is `false`, then depending on the nature of your interface, you might need to provide some sort of temporary view, to show the user that something has happened, until the actual data arrives.

Additional Delegate Methods

Additional UIDragInteractionDelegate and UIDropInteractionDelegate methods allow the delegate to dress up the drag or drop process in more detail:

Drag interaction delegate
> Drag interaction delegate methods let the delegate supply drag items, provide a preview, restrict the type of drag permitted, animate along with the start of the drag, and hear about each stage of the entire session.

Drop interaction delegate
> Drop interaction delegate methods let the delegate signify willingness to accept the drop, track the user's finger dragging over the view, and, when an actual drop takes place, provide a preview, perform an animation, and request the associated data.

Here are some examples; for full details, consult the documentation.

Custom drag preview

The drag interaction delegate can supply a preview to replace the snapshot of its view. Let's modify our earlier color swatch example to illustrate. Our color swatch is red; it will create a label containing the word "RED" and provide that as the preview.

The trick is that we have to say where this label should initially appear. To do that, we create a UIDragPreviewTarget, which specifies a container view in the interface to which our preview will be added as a subview, along with a center for the preview in that view's coordinate system. This view will be removed from the container when the user either fails to initiate the drag or does in fact start dragging; in the latter case, it will be replaced by a snapshot. Then we combine our preview with that target as a UITargetedDragPreview. In this case, we want the center of the label under the user's finger; we can find out from the session where the user's finger is:

```
func dragInteraction(_ interaction: UIDragInteraction,
    previewForLifting item: UIDragItem, session: UIDragSession)
    -> UITargetedDragPreview? {
        let lab = UILabel()
        lab.text = "RED"
        lab.textAlignment = .center
        lab.textColor = .red
        lab.layer.borderWidth = 1
        lab.layer.cornerRadius = 10
        lab.sizeToFit()
        lab.frame = lab.frame.insetBy(dx: -10, dy: -10)
```

```
            let v = interaction.view!
            let ptrLoc = session.location(in: v)
            let targ = UIDragPreviewTarget(container: v, center: ptrLoc)
            let params = UIDragPreviewParameters()
            params.backgroundColor = .white
            return UITargetedDragPreview(view: lab,
                parameters: params, target: targ)
    }
```

In addition to a view and a target, a UITargetedDragPreview is initialized with a
UIDragPreviewParameters object. In the preceding code, I used the UIDragPreview-
Parameters object to make the preview's background white, just to give it a role in the
example. Another useful possibility is to set the UIDragPreviewParameters visible-
Path property, supplying a clipping path, in case you want the preview to be a snap-
shot of a certain subregion of the source view.

The drag interaction delegate can also *change* the preview in the course of the drag.
To do so, it will set the drag item's previewProvider to a function returning a
UIDragPreview (which has no target, because it has no relationship to the app's
interface). If the drag interaction delegate does this in, say, drag-
Interaction(_:itemsForBeginning:), the previewProvider function won't be
called until the drag begins, so the user will see the lifting preview first, and will see
the previewProvider preview after the drag starts. Another strategy is to implement
dragInteraction(_:sessionDidMove:) and set the previewProvider there; the preview will change at that moment. But dragInteraction(_:sessionDidMove:) is
called repeatedly, so be careful not to set the same drag item's previewProvider to
the same function over and over.

In addition, the drag interaction delegate can set a cancel preview, with drag-
Interaction(_:previewForCancelling:withDefault:). This is used if the user
begins to drag the preview but then releases it while not over a drop destination. A
nice effect is to keep the existing drag preview (accessible through the third parameter) but retarget it to say where it should fall to as it vanishes; and in fact UITargeted-
DragPreview has a retargetedPreview(with:) method for this very purpose.
Furthermore, the UIDragPreviewTarget initializer lets you supply a transform:
parameter that will be applied over the course of the animation as the preview falls.

The drop interaction delegate, too, can provide a preview to replace the dragged preview when the drop animation occurs; it works just like the cancel preview.

Additional animation

The drag interaction delegate can make the source view perform some sort of animation along with the runtime's initial animated display of the preview. In this example,
I'll fade the color swatch slightly:

```
func dragInteraction(_ interaction: UIDragInteraction,
    willAnimateLiftWith anim: UIDragAnimating, session: UIDragSession) {
        if let v = interaction.view {
            anim.addAnimations {
                v.alpha = 0.5
            }
        }
}
```

I could have supplied a completion function by calling `addCompletion`, but I didn't, so the color swatch stays faded throughout the drag. Clearly, I don't want it to stay faded forever; when the drag ends, I'll be called back again, and I'll restore the swatch's `alpha` then:

```
func dragInteraction(_ interaction: UIDragInteraction,
    session: UIDragSession, willEndWith operation: UIDropOperation) {
        if let v = interaction.view {
            UIView.animate(withDuration:0.3) {
                v.alpha = 1
            }
        }
}
```

 The animations you pass with `addAnimations` are applied *before* the runtime takes its snapshot to form the default preview. Therefore, the results of those animations appear *in* the default preview. To avoid that, supply your own preview.

The drop interaction delegate gets a corresponding message, `dropInteraction(_:item:willAnimateDropWith:)`. By retargeting the drop preview and performing its own animations alongside the drop, the drop interaction delegate can create some vivid effects.

Flocking

If a source view's drag interaction delegate implements `dragInteraction(_:itemsForAddingTo:withTouchAt:)`, and if that implementation returns a nonempty array of drag items, then the user can tap on this source view *while already dragging a preview*, as a way of adding *more* drag items to the existing session. Apple refers to this as *flocking*.

If you permit flocking, be careful of unintended consequences. If the user can tap a source view to get flocking *once* during a drag, the user can tap the *same* source view to get flocking *again* during that drag. This will result in the session effectively carrying multiple copies of the same data, which is probably not what you want. You can solve this problem by examining the session's current drag items to make sure you're not adding another drag item whose item provider refers to the same data.

Table Views and Collection Views

Table views and collection views get a special implementation of drag and drop, focusing on their cells. There is no need to supply a UIDragInteraction or UIDrop-Interaction; instead, simply give the table view or collection view an appropriate delegate:

UITableView

> The delegate properties are:
>
> - `dragDelegate` (UITableViewDragDelegate)
> - `dropDelegate` (UITableViewDropDelegate)

UICollectionView

> The delegate properties are:
>
> - `dragDelegate` (UICollectionViewDragDelegate)
> - `dropDelegate` (UICollectionViewDropDelegate)

The methods of these delegates are generally analogous to, but simpler than, those of UIDragInteractionDelegate and UIDropInteractionDelegate. I'll discuss some table view drag and drop delegate methods; collection views work very similarly.

Table view dragging

To illustrate dragging, let's return to the table of U.S. states developed in Chapter 8, and make it possible to drag a cell and drop it on a view that expects text. Our text will be, appropriately enough, the name of the state. The implementation is trivial. First, in some early event such as `viewDidLoad`, we give our table view a drag delegate:

```
self.tableView.dragDelegate = self
```

Then, acting as drag delegate, we implement the only required method, `table-View(_:itemsForBeginning:at:)`. There's nothing new or surprising about our implementation:

```
func tableView(_ tableView: UITableView,
    itemsForBeginning session: UIDragSession,
    at indexPath: IndexPath) -> [UIDragItem] {
        let s = self.sections[indexPath.section].rowData[indexPath.row]
        let ip = NSItemProvider(object:s as NSString)
        let di = UIDragItem(itemProvider: ip)
        return [di]
    }
```

That's all we have to do! It is now possible to long press on a cell to get a drag preview snapshotting the cell, and that preview can be dropped on any drop target that expects text.

Table view dropping

Now let's do the converse: we'll make it possible to drop on a table. Imagine that I have a table of person names, whose underlying model is an array containing a single Section whose rowData is an array of Person. I want the user to be able to drop a Person onto the table view; in response, I'll insert that person into the data, and I'll insert a cell representing that person into the table. We give our table view a drop delegate:

```
self.tableView.dropDelegate = self
```

Acting as the drop delegate, I implement two delegate methods. First, I implement tableView(_:dropSessionDidUpdate:withDestinationIndexPath:) to determine, as the user's finger passes over the table view, whether the drop should be possible. The destination index path might be nil, indicating that the user's finger is not over a row of the table. Also, the dragged data might not be something that can generate a Person. In either case, I return the .cancel operation. Otherwise, I return the .copy operation to badge the dragged preview and permit the drop:

```swift
func tableView(_ tableView: UITableView,
    dropSessionDidUpdate session: UIDropSession,
    withDestinationIndexPath ip: IndexPath?) -> UITableViewDropProposal {
        if ip == nil {
            return UITableViewDropProposal(operation: .cancel)
        }
        if !session.canLoadObjects(ofClass: Person.self) {
            return UITableViewDropProposal(operation: .cancel)
        }
        return UITableViewDropProposal(operation: .copy,
            intent: .insertAtDestinationIndexPath)
}
```

In the UITableViewDropProposal initializer, the intent: argument (UITableView-DropProposal.Intent) tells the table view how to animate as the user's finger hovers over it:

.insertAtDestinationIndexPath
> For when the drop would insert rows; the table view opens a gap between rows under the user's finger.

.insertIntoDestinationIndexPath
> For when the drop would not insert rows; the row under the user's finger highlights, suggesting that the dropped material will be incorporated into that row in some way.

.automatic
> A combination of the previous two, depending on precisely where the user's finger is.

```
.unspecified
```
The table doesn't respond while the user's finger is over it.

Next, I implement the required `tableView(_:performDropWith:)` method. The drop is now happening; we need to retrieve the incoming data and update the table. The second parameter is a UITableViewDropCoordinator; everything we need to know about what's happening, such as the index path and the session, is available through the coordinator:

```
func tableView(_ tableView: UITableView,
    performDropWith coord: UITableViewDropCoordinator) {
        if let ip = coord.destinationIndexPath {
            coord.session.loadObjects(ofClass: Person.self) { persons in
                for person in (persons as! [Person]).reversed() {
                    tableView.performBatchUpdates({
                        self.sections[ip.section].rowData.insert(
                            person, at: ip.row)
                        tableView.insertRows(at: [ip], with: .none)
                    })
                }
            }
        }
}
```

Time-consuming table view drop data delivery

The preceding example works, but we are not updating the table until the data arrives. We are skirting the issue of what will happen if the data takes time to arrive. The drop happens, and we should insert a row *right now* — that is, *before* asking for the data. But at that moment, we obviously don't yet have the data! So either we must freeze the interface while we wait for the data to arrive, which sounds like very bad interface, or we must update the table with data that we don't yet have, which sounds like a metaphysical impossibility.

The solution is to use a *placeholder cell* for each new row while we wait for its data. The technique is best understood through an example. I'll use the item provider to fetch the data this time:

```
func tableView(_ tableView: UITableView,
    performDropWith coord: UITableViewDropCoordinator) {
        guard let ip = coord.destinationIndexPath else {return}
        for item in coord.items {
            let item = item.dragItem
            guard item.itemProvider.canLoadObject(ofClass: Person.self)
                else {continue}
            let ph = UITableViewDropPlaceholder( ❶
                insertionIndexPath: ip,
                reuseIdentifier: self.cellID,
                rowHeight: self.tableView.rowHeight)
            ph.cellUpdateHandler = { cell in ❷
```

```
            cell.textLabel?.text = ""
        }
        let con = coord.drop(item, to: ph) ❸
        item.itemProvider.loadObject(ofClass: Person.self) { p, e in ❹
            DispatchQueue.main.async { ❺
                guard let p = p as? Person else { ❻
                    con.deletePlaceholder(); return
                }
                con.commitInsertion(dataSourceUpdates: {ip in ❼
                    tableView.performBatchUpdates({
                        self.sections[ip.section].rowData.insert(
                            p, at: ip.row)
                    })
                })
            }
        }
    }
}
```

For each drag item capable of providing a Person object, this is what we do:

❶   We make a UITableViewDropPlaceholder, supplying our cell's `reuseIdentifier` so that the table view can dequeue a cell for us to use as a placeholder cell.

❷   We set the placeholder's `cellUpdateHandler` to a function that will be called to configure the placeholder cell. In my simple table, we're using a basic default cell with a `textLabel` that normally displays the full name of a Person; for the place-holder cell, the `textLabel` should be blank.

❸   We call the coordinator's `drop(_:to:)` with the placeholder, to perform the drop animation and create the placeholder cell; a context object (UITableViewDrop-PlaceholderContext) is returned. The placeholder cell is now visible in the table. The important thing is that the table view knows that this is not a real cell! For purposes of all data source and delegate methods, it will behave as if the cell didn't exist. In particular, it won't call `tableView(_:cellForRowAt:)` for this cell; the cell is static and is already completely configured by the `cellUpdateHandler` function we supplied earlier.

❹   Now, at long last, we call `loadObject(ofClass:)` to ask for the actual data!

❺   Eventually, we are called with the data on a background thread. We step out to the main thread, because we're about to talk to the interface.

❻   If we didn't get the expected data, the placeholder cell is no longer needed, and we remove it by calling the context object's `deletePlaceholder`.

❼ If we reach this point, we've got data! We call the context object's `commit-Insertion(dataSourceUpdates:)` with a function that updates *the model only*. As a result, `tableView(_:cellForRowAt:)` is called to supply the real cell, which quietly replaces the placeholder cell in good order.

While your table view contains placeholders, the table view's `hasUncommitted-Updates` is `true`. Use that property as a flag to prevent your other code from calling `reloadData` on the table view, which would cause the placeholders to be lost and the entire table view update process to get out of whack.

Table view drop animations

In step 3 of the preceding example, we gave the UITableViewDropCoordinator a drop animation command to create the placeholder cell. This command must be given outside of the `loadObject` completion function, because the drop is about to happen *now*, so the animation must replace the default drop animation *now*, not at some asynchronous future time. The drop coordinator obeys four drop animation commands:

`drop(_:to:)`
  The second parameter is a UITableViewDropPlaceholder.

`drop(_:intoRowAt:rect:)`
  Animates the drop preview into the cell at the specified row, to the frame specified in that cell's bounds coordinates.

`drop(_:to:)`
  Animates the drop preview *anywhere*. The second parameter is a UIDragPreview-Target combining a container and a center in the container's bounds coordinates.

`drop(_:toRowAt:)`
  Snapshots the cell at the given row, replaces the drop preview with that snapshot, and animates the snapshot to fit the cell. This is useful under a very limited set of circumstances:

  • You want to give the impression that the drop *replaces* the contents of a cell.

  • The drag and drop must be *local* (see later in this chapter), so that the model can be updated with the new data and the row can be reloaded *before* the snapshot is taken.

Spring Loading

Spring loading is an effect similar to what happens on an iOS device's home screen when the user goes into "jiggly mode" and then drags an app's icon over a folder: the folder highlights, then flashes several times, then opens. In this way, the user can open the folder as part of the drag, and can then continue the drag, dropping the icon inside the opened folder.

You can use spring loading in an analogous way. Suppose there's a button in your interface that the user can tap to transition to a presented view controller. You can make that button be spring loaded, so that the user, in the middle of a drag, can hover over that button to make it perform that transition — and can then drop on something inside the newly presented view.

To make a button be spring loaded, set its `isSpringLoaded` property to `true`, and call its `addInteraction(_:)` method with a UISpringLoadedInteraction object. That object's initializer takes a function to be performed when the spring loaded interaction actually fires; the button's normal control event action function, which fires in response to the button being tapped, does *not* fire as a result of spring loading, though of course you can make the spring loaded interaction function fire it:

```
self.button.isSpringLoaded = true
self.button.addInteraction(UISpringLoadedInteraction() { int, con in
    let vc = // some view controller
    // ... other preparations ...
    self.present(vc, animated: true)
})
```

In the spring loaded interaction function, the second parameter (`con` in the preceding code) is a UISpringLoadedInteractionContext object providing information about the interaction. It reports the location of the drag, and it has a `state` describing how the view is currently responding. The first parameter (`int`) is the UISpringLoaded-Interaction itself.

A fuller form of initializer lets you give the UISpringLoadedInteraction object two further properties:

An interaction behavior
    A UISpringLoadedInteractionBehavior, to which you can attach two functions — one to be called when the interaction wants permission to proceed, the other to be called when the interaction has finished.

An interaction effect
    A UISpringLoadedInteractionEffect, to which you can attach a function to be called every time the interaction's state changes.

Spring loading is available for buttons and button-like interface objects such as bar button items and tab bar items, as well as for UIAlertController (Chapter 13), where the spring loading is applied to the alert's buttons. It is also supported by table views and collection views, where it applies to the cells; if turned on, it can be turned off for individual cells by delegate methods:

- `tableView(_:shouldSpringLoadRowAt:with:)`
- `collectionView(_:shouldSpringLoadItemAt:with:)`

iPhone and Local Drag and Drop

By default, a UIDragInteraction comes into existence with its `isEnabled` property set to `false` on an iPhone. To bring dragging to life on an iPhone, set that property to `true`. Similarly, table views and collection views have a `dragInteractionEnabled` property that you'll need to set explicitly to `true` on an iPhone if you want dragging to work.

There's no iPad multitasking interface on the iPhone, so the only drag and drop your app will be capable of will be *local* drag and drop, within the app itself.

On an iPad, local drag and drop is always *possible*, of course, but you can also *restrict* a drag originating in your app to remain local to the app by implementing the drag interaction delegate method `dragInteraction(_:sessionIsRestrictedToDragging-Application:)` to return `true`. That situation can subsequently be detected by reading the session's `isRestrictedToDraggingApplication` property.

A drag that is dropped within the same app can provide the drop destination with more information, and more directly, than the same drag can provide to another app. We no longer have to pipe the data asynchronously through the session by means of a Data object; instead (or in addition), we can use these properties:

UIDragItem `localObject`
> The drag item can carry actual data with it, or a reference to an object that can provide the data, in its `localObject` property, and the drop interaction delegate can read this value directly, in real time, on the main thread — but only in the same app. If you try to read the `localObject` in an app different from the one where the drag originated, it will be `nil`.

UIDragSession `localContext`
> The drag session can maintain state, in its `localContext` property, and the drop interaction delegate can read this value directly, in real time, on the main thread, by way of the drop session's `localDragSession` — but only in the same app. If you try to read the `localDragSession` in an app different from the one where the drag originated, it will be `nil`.

Table and collection view `sourceIndexPath`
> If drag and drop takes place within a table view or collection view, the UITableViewDropItem or UICollectionViewDropItem has a `sourceIndexPath` revealing where the drag started. If you try to read the `sourceIndexPath` in an app different from the one where the drag originated, it will be `nil`.

Multiple Windows

New in iOS 13, your app running on an iPad with iPad multitasking can have more than one window. The idea is that once there are two windows on a single app, the user can arrange them with multitasking so as to see two things at once. Apple's own apps illustrate this: using multiple windows, you can see simultaneously two contacts in the Contacts app, two maps in the Maps app, two tabs in Safari, and so on. Sometimes you can also drag something from one window to another.

There are various ways to make a new window in an app that supports this feature. The user can long press on an app's icon, choose Show All Windows (to enter what Apple calls App Exposé), and tap the Plus button, or drag the app's icon from the Dock onto its own window. Some apps also provide an internal means of generating a new window, such as tapping a button, or dragging something to the side of the screen. In Apple's Maps app, a marked location can be dragged to the side of the screen to become a new window.

Your app might wish to participate in this architecture if the user might benefit from it. To opt in, in the Application Scene Manifest entry in your *Info.plist*, switch "Enable Multiple Windows" to YES.

The Window Architecture

Here are the classes and objects involved in the window architecture:

Scene
> The app's *scenes* are instances of UIWindowScene, a UIScene subclass. Each scene can be in the foreground or in the background, activated or deactivated.

Window
> Each UIWindowScene owns a *window*. Actually, a window scene can have multiple windows (its `windows`), but only one of these is what you would think of as *your* app's window, holding your view controllers and your app's interface. The window is created with a `windowScene` and maintains a reference to it.

Session
> Every scene has associated with it one *session*. This is a UISceneSession. The scene and the session have pointers to one another. The reason for this pairing is that a session can persist even if its scene has been *disconnected* in the background to save memory. The snapshots in the app switcher interface belong to scene sessions; there may or may not be a connected scene associated with a snapshot.

Delegate

Your live link to a scene is the scene's *delegate,* a UIResponder adopting the UIWindowSceneDelegate protocol. In the app templates, this is an instance of the SceneDelegate class. It gets events when the scene is connected to or disconnected from its session, and when its activation or foreground state changes. In the app templates, the scene delegate also has a `window` property that retains the window.

You're going to want to know how to get references to the pieces of that architecture. Here are some common approaches:

From the scene delegate

All the scene delegate events come with a reference to the scene.

From the application

The shared application has references to all sessions as its `openSessions`, and to all scenes that are connected to sessions as its `connectedScenes`, and to all windows as its `windows`, so you can get a needed reference from the top down.

From a view controller

A view controller has no direct reference to any part of the architecture. But it has a `view`, which (if it is in the interface) has a `window`, which has a `windowScene`, which has a `session`, so you can chain together a needed reference from the bottom up.

Scene Creation

At launch time and whenever a new window is created, the runtime creates these objects in this order:

1. The scene session
2. The scene configuration
3. The window scene
4. The scene delegate
5. The window

The *scene configuration* is a value class (UISceneConfiguration) containing instructions for instantiating the window scene and the scene delegate. It is the object described in the *Info.plist* by the "Scene Configuration" entry in the "Application Scene Manifest." This is an array of "Application Session Role" entries, each of which is a dictionary uniting a "Configuration Name" and a "Delegate Class Name" (the name of the class that is to be instantiated as the scene delegate), along with an optional "Storyboard Name." (You can also include the "Class Name" if you want the scene's class to be a custom subclass of UIWindowScene; but this is unlikely.)

Early in the window creation process, the runtime may turn to your app delegate and call `application(_:configurationForConnecting:options:)` if it exists. This is your chance to construct or modify the scene configuration *in code*. Here's an implementation that does the same thing that the default *Info.plist* "Scene Configuration" entry does; in fact, if you have this implementation, you can delete the "Scene Configuration" entry from the *Info.plist* altogether:

```
func application(_ application: UIApplication,
    configurationForConnecting connectingSceneSession: UISceneSession,
    options: UIScene.ConnectionOptions) -> UISceneConfiguration {
        let config = UISceneConfiguration(
            name: "Default Configuration", sessionRole: .windowApplication)
        config.delegateClass = SceneDelegate.self
        config.storyboard = UIStoryboard(name: "Main", bundle: nil)
        return config
}
```

It's perfectly possible that you'll have just one scene configuration, described in the *Info.plist*. So why might you implement `application(_:configurationFor-Connecting:options:)` at all? Well, if you have several window types and your implementation of the SceneDelegate class threatens to become overly complex, you might use a different scene configuration to specify a different scene delegate class for a certain window type. To know whether you need to do that on any particular call, you'd look at the incoming `options`. It's a value class that tells you why this window is being created. I'll talk more about that later.

When a window closes, its scene session can persist, identified by its `persistentIdentifier`, in order to be reused when the window is created again. This persistence is the basis of scene saving and restoration, which I'll discuss later; it operates even between runs of your app. When a window is created with a scene session that has survived from earlier, you *won't* get a call to `application(_:configurationForConnecting:options:)` — even if the app is launching from scratch — because the configuration for this scene session is already known.

The next important event your code receives during the window creation process is the scene delegate's `scene(_:willConnectTo:options:)`. At this point, if this scene uses a storyboard, the window has already been created and assigned to the scene delegate's `window` property, and it has a `rootViewController` instantiated from the storyboard's initial view controller — and if you do nothing, the window will be made visible for you. But if the scene doesn't use a storyboard, or if you want to substitute a different window class or a different root view controller, this is your chance to do so (see "App Without a Storyboard" on page 6).

Window Creation and Closing

If the user asks directly within your app to create a new window — by tapping a New Window button in your interface, for instance — you can call this UIApplication method to create the window:

- `requestSceneSessionActivation(_:userActivity:options:errorHandler:)`

If the first parameter (the session) is `nil`, a new window is created.

The most important parameter is the `userActivity`. This is an NSUserActivity object that will arrive into the `options` parameter of `application(_:configurationFor-Connecting:options:)` and `scene(_:willConnectTo:options:)`, in that parameter's `userActivities` property. Your code will examine this to learn what sort of window this is to be in order to configure things appropriately. So the NSUserActivity object is a kind of message to yourself. By setting its `activityType` and its `userInfo` (a dictionary), you can encode the needed information into that message.

Suppose my app's root view controller allows the user to display any of the three Pep Boys, and has a button the user can tap to open a new window for editing the current Pep Boy (whatever "editing" may mean for this app). Clearly the NSUserActivity object needs to say which Pep Boy is current. Let's say that this information is stored in an instance property, `self.pepName`. Here's a possible implementation:

```
let opts = UIScene.ActivationRequestOptions()
opts.requestingScene = self.view.window?.windowScene
let act = NSUserActivity(activityType:
    PepEditorViewController.newEditorActivityType)
let key = PepEditorViewController.whichPepBoyWeAreEditing
act.userInfo = [key: self.pepName]
UIApplication.shared.requestSceneSessionActivation(
    nil, userActivity: act, options: opts, errorHandler: nil)
```

So now there are two reasons why a new window might be created in my app, and my `scene(_:willConnectTo:options:)` needs to behave differently depending on why *this* window is being created. On the one hand, we might be launching, or the user may have requested a new window from the App Exposé interface; in that case, I should just allow my window to be populated with the normal root view controller. On the other hand, the user may have tapped the button asking to edit the current Pep Boy; in that case, I should instantiate the editing view controller, populate it with the information about what Pep Boy to display, and set it as the window's root view controller.

And how will I distinguish those two cases? By looking for the NSUserActivity that I provided in my call to `requestSceneSessionActivation`:

```
var pepName = ""
let key = PepEditorViewController.whichPepBoyWeAreEditing
let type = PepEditorViewController.newEditorActivityType
if let act = connectionOptions.userActivities.first(where: {
    $0.activityType == type
}) {
    if let pep = act.userInfo?[key] as? String {
        pepName = pep
    }
}
if !pepName.isEmpty {
    let s = scene.session.configuration.storyboard!
    let peped = s.instantiateViewController(identifier: "pepEditor")
        as! PepEditorViewController
    peped.pepName = pepName
    self.window?.rootViewController = peped
}
// ... and otherwise, do nothing ...
```

Subsequently, PepEditorViewController's `viewDidLoad` comes along and configures the actual interface based on which Pep Boy it finds in its `pepName` property.

Closing a window is even simpler. You call this UIApplication method:

- `requestSceneSessionDestruction(_:options:errorHandler:)`

The `options` should specify the animation as the window vanishes. Your choices are (UIWindowScene.DismissalAnimation):

- `.standard`

- `.commit` (the user was asked whether to save something, and said yes)

- `.decline` (the user was asked whether to save something, and said no)

Here's an example of a Close Window button implementation:

```
guard let session = self.view.window?.windowScene?.session else {return}
let opts = UIWindowSceneDestructionRequestOptions()
opts.windowDismissalAnimation = .standard
UIApplication.shared.requestSceneSessionDestruction(
    session, options: opts, errorHandler: nil)
```

State Saving and Restoration

While a window session persists, its scene might be disconnected and destroyed in the background. When the user taps that window session's snapshot in the app switcher, a new window will be created, and you'll need to recreate the entire view controller hierarchy and state to populate it.

For this purpose, a session maintains a `stateRestorationActivity` property, which is an NSUserActivity. You are supposed to use this for state saving and restoration:

State saving

When the scene is backgrounded, the scene delegate is asked what the value of the `stateRestorationActivity` property should be. Your job is to supply an NSUserActivity populated with all the information needed later to restore state for this scene's window.

State restoration

When the same session recreates its window and your scene delegate's `scene(_:willConnectTo:options:)` is called, the session gives back this NSUser-Activity in its `stateRestorationActivity` property. (This works even if the app was completely terminated in the background.) Your job is to extract the NSUserActivity and recreate the window's contents.

Unfortunately, Apple provides very little guidance on *how* to perform these tasks. I'll describe a strategy that might be useful.

How state is saved

An NSUserActivity works in a special way with a UIResponder. A UIResponder has a `userActivity` property. When a UIResponder's `userActivity` actually holds an NSUserActivity, that NSUserActivity is "saved" automatically as needed by the runtime, by calling the responder's implementation of `updateUserActivityState(_:)`, which can write into the NSUserActivity's `userInfo`. If multiple responders share the same NSUserActivity instance, they *all* get an opportunity to write into the same NSUserActivity's `userInfo`. The state-saving mechanism takes advantage of this architecture:

- A UIScene, by virtue of being a UIResponder, has a `userActivity` property, which can hold an NSUserActivity and cause it to persist for the lifetime of the scene.

- From time to time, and especially when the scene goes into the background, the scene delegate method `stateRestorationActivity(for:)` is called. It should simply return the scene's `userActivity`.

- When `stateRestorationActivity(for:)` returns an NSUserActivity, all responders that are holding that NSUserActivity in their `userActivity` property are automatically sent an `updateUserActivityState(_:)` event with that NSUser-Activity as the parameter, and can contribute to its `userInfo`.

- The session will then keep that NSUserActivity as its expression of saved state, and will supply it in its `stateRestorationActivity` property at restoration time.

An implementation might look like this. The scene delegate either creates the scene's `userActivity` or passes the received restoration activity into it, and returns that as its own user activity:

```
func scene(_ scene: UIScene, willConnectTo session: UISceneSession,
    options connectionOptions: UIScene.ConnectionOptions) {
        guard let scene = scene as? UIWindowScene else { return }
        scene.userActivity =
            session.stateRestorationActivity ??
            NSUserActivity(activityType: "com.neuburg.mw.restoration")
}
func stateRestorationActivity(for scene: UIScene) -> NSUserActivity? {
    return scene.userActivity
}
```

Every view controller should use its own `viewDidAppear(_:)` to share that user activity object. That way, its own `updateUserActivityState(_:)` will be called automatically when we go into the background, and it has a chance to contribute to the global pool of the `userInfo`:

```
override func viewDidAppear(_ animated: Bool) {
    super.viewDidAppear(animated)
    self.userActivity = self.view.window?.windowScene?.userActivity
}
// called automatically at saving time
override func updateUserActivityState(_ activity: NSUserActivity) {
    super.updateUserActivityState(activity)
    // gather info into `info`
    activity.addUserInfoEntries(from: info)
}
```

That's all! If every view controller does that, then every view controller that is alive at the time we go into background gets a chance to contribute to the user info of the shared user activity object, and so every view controller's state can be saved. Later, that same user activity object will return if the window needs to be recreated.

How to restore state

Suppose now that the window *does* later need to be recreated. The scene delegate observes that an NSUserActivity object is present in the session's `stateRestoration-Activity`. Now what?

I've devised a strategy that mimics the state saving mechanism in reverse. The runtime gives us no help with this so we have to do everything ourselves:

- The scene delegate should copy the `userInfo` out of the session's `state-RestorationActivity` immediately. That's because the `userInfo` may soon be deleted through subsequent calls to `updateUserActivityState`.

- Every view controller should have a property to hold the restoration `userInfo` dictionary. Let's call it `restorationInfo`, typed as `[AnyHashable:Any]?`.

- The scene delegate is responsible for assigning the `userInfo` dictionary into the root view controller's `restorationInfo` property. The root view controller is then responsible for recreating its child view controller if it has one (it will know whether to do this by looking in the `restorationInfo`), and for assigning the same dictionary into *its* `restorationInfo` property — and so on, for *every* view controller that needs to be restored. Each view controller's `restorationInfo` is set before its own `viewDidLoad` is called, so it can proceed to configure itself and then create the next view controller in the chain if there is one.

- In its own `viewDidAppear`, every view controller should set its own `restoration-Info` back to `nil`, to ensure that it doesn't attempt to "restore" any subsequent view controllers that it may create.

Here's a simple example. Our root view controller can display any of the three Pep Boys in a child UIPageViewController, and the user can change which Pep Boy is being displayed. (This is in fact the same app described in "Container View Controllers" on page 375.) Now let's say we go into the background. We need to record which Pep Boy is being displayed, so that the same Pep Boy can be displayed if the window is destroyed and has to be recreated later. As I explained earlier, we can ensure that by our implementation of `updateUserActivityState`:

```
override func viewDidAppear(_ animated: Bool) {
    super.viewDidAppear(animated)
    self.userActivity = self.view.window?.windowScene?.userActivity
    self.restorationInfo = nil
}
override func updateUserActivityState(_ activity: NSUserActivity) {
    super.updateUserActivityState(activity)
    let boy = // string representing currently showing Pep Boy
    let key = Self.currentPepBoyRestorationKey
    activity.addUserInfoEntries(from: [key:boy])
}
```

We go into the background, the scene gets disconnected, and later the user asks to see this scene again. The window is created, and the scene delegate's `scene(_:will-ConnectTo:options:)` is called; it sets the root view controller's `restorationInfo`:

```
func scene(_ scene: UIScene,
    willConnectTo session: UISceneSession,
    options connectionOptions: UIScene.ConnectionOptions) {
        guard let scene = scene as? UIWindowScene else { return }
        scene.userActivity =
            session.stateRestorationActivity ??
            NSUserActivity(activityType: "com.neuburg.my.restoration")
        if let rvc = window?.rootViewController as? RootViewController {
            rvc.restorationInfo = scene.userActivity?.userInfo // *
        }
}
```

The root view controller's `viewDidLoad` is now called. It sees that it has a `restorationInfo`, so it configures itself based on that:

```
override func viewDidLoad() {
    super.viewDidLoad()
    let info = self.restorationInfo
    var page = Pep(pepBoy: self.pep[0]) // default
    let key = Self.currentPepBoyRestorationKey
    if let boy = info?[key] as? String {
        page = Pep(pepBoy:boy)
    }
    // ... display the Pep view controller as a child ...
}
```

The story becomes longer if there are more view controllers in the hierarchy, but it doesn't become more complicated. It's just a matter of every view controller storing sufficient information, in the common NSUserActivity object's `userInfo`, so that it can restore itself later if necessary.

Further Multiple Window Considerations

Adopting multiple windows is not simple. Here are some further considerations to be aware of (and there are many other details you'll want to look into on your own).

Drag and drop

Drag and drop works just as described earlier in this chapter, except for one thing: what if you want the user to be able to drag something to the edge of the screen in order to create a new window? In that case, call `registerObject(_:visibility:)` on the UIDragItem's NSItemProvider, with the first parameter being (you guess it) an NSUserActivity. This NSUserActivity's `activityType` must be listed in your *Info.plist* under the `NSUserActivityTypes` key; that allows the drag to pass out of your app into the system and back into your app as a call to create a new window. In the call to your scene delegate's `scene(_:willConnectTo:options:)`, the same NSUserActivity will arrive in the `userActivities` of the `options` parameter, and you can detect this and configure the new window, just as I described earlier.

Data sharing

The relationship between your data and your interface becomes more complicated when there are multiple windows, because more than one window might hold an instance of the very same view controller. No individual view controller instance can be used as the "source of truth" for the app's data. Instead, the data will need to be stored in some persistent central location. When the user (or some other outside force) makes a change in the data, you'll need to send that information up to the persistent central data model, and the central data model will then need to send that information back down (probably by means of a notification or a similar publish-and-subscribe mechanism) to all instances of that view controller, each of which will update its view's interface accordingly.

The session has a `userInfo` object of its own. You can use this for any purpose you like, including storing data to be preserved in case the window is opened later. It can also be used as a global repository of data among view controllers within this window, as an alternative to the app's user defaults.

If a scene is in the foreground when its interface is updated, the interface will change before the user's eyes. If the scene is in the background, the user can't see it, but you *still* might want to change the interface so that the app switcher snapshot is updated. To do so, call the UIApplication method `requestSceneSessionRefresh(_:)`.

Memory management

When a scene is about to be disconnected from its session, and the window and scene delegate are about to be released, the scene delegate is sent `sceneDidDisconnect(_:)`. If there is data to be preserved, this is a key moment to preserve it. If the scene was maintaining any scratch files or other independently persistent objects, this is a key moment to delete them.

A scene session has a `persistentIdentifier`, a unique string that persists for the lifetime of the session, even if the app is terminated and relaunched, even across restarts of the device. This can help you associate saved data with the session to which it belongs.

CHAPTER 10

Text

Drawing text into your app's interface is one of the most complex and powerful things that iOS does for you. But iOS also shields you from much of that complexity; all you need is some text to draw, and possibly an interface object to draw it for you.

Text to appear in your app's interface will be an NSString (bridged from Swift String) or an NSAttributedString. NSAttributedString adds text styling to an NSString, including runs of different character styles, along with paragraph-level features such as alignment, line spacing, and margins.

To make your NSString or NSAttributedString appear in the interface, you can hand it to an interface object that knows how to draw it, or you can draw it into a graphics context yourself:

Text-drawing interface objects
Interface objects that know how to draw an NSString or NSAttributedString are:

UILabel
Displays text, possibly consisting of multiple lines; neither scrollable nor editable.

UITextField
Displays a single line of editable text.

UITextView
Displays multiline text; can be scrollable and editable.

Self-drawing text
Both NSString and NSAttributedString have methods for drawing themselves into any graphics context.

Deep under the hood, all text drawing is performed through a low-level technology with a C API called Core Text. At a higher level, iOS provides Text Kit, a middle-level technology lying on top of Core Text. UITextView is largely just a lightweight wrapper around Text Kit, and Text Kit can also draw directly into a graphics context. By working with Text Kit, you can readily do all sorts of useful text-drawing tricks without having to sweat your way through Core Text.

(Another way of drawing text is to use a web view, a scrollable view displaying rendered HTML. A web view can also display various additional document types, such as PDF, RTF, and *.doc*. Web views draw their text using a somewhat different technology, and are discussed in Chapter 11. For display of PDFs, see also the discussion of PDF Kit in Chapter 22.)

Fonts and Font Descriptors

There are two ways of specifying a font: as a UIFont suitable for use with strings, attributed strings, and UIKit interface objects; or as a CTFont suitable for Core Text. You're unlikely to use CTFont; I'll focus exclusively on UIFont.

To describe a UIFont in terms of its features, and to perform transformations between fonts, you use UIFontDescriptor; you can convert both ways between UIFont and UIFontDescriptor. The Core Text analog is CTFontDescriptor, which is toll-free bridged to UIFontDescriptor so that you can cast between them (and this bridging can be used to convert between UIFont and CTFont).

Fonts

A font (UIFont) is a simple object. You specify a font by its name and size by calling the UIFont initializer `init(name:size:)`, and you can transform a font to the same font in a different size by calling the `withSize(_:)` instance method. UIFont also provides some properties for learning a font's various metrics, such as its `lineHeight` and `capHeight`.

To ask for a font by name, you have to *know* the font's name. Every font variant (bold, italic, and so on) counts as a different font, and font variants are clumped into families. UIFont has class methods that tell you the names of the families and the names of the fonts within them. To learn, in the console, the name of every built-in font, you would say:

```
UIFont.familyNames.forEach {
    UIFont.fontNames(forFamilyName:$0).forEach {print($0)}}
```

When calling `init(name:size:)`, you can specify a font by its family name or by its font name (technically, its PostScript name). For example, `"Avenir"` is a family name; the plain font within that family is `"Avenir-Book"`. Either of those is legal as the `name:` argument. The initializer is failable, so you'll know if you've specified the font incorrectly — you'll get `nil`.

System font

The system font, used by default for things like UILabel text and UIButton titles, can be obtained by calling the UIFont class method `systemFont(ofSize:weight:)`. A UIFont class property such as `buttonFontSize` will give you the standard size. Possible weights, in order from lightest to heaviest, are (UIFont.Weight):

- `.ultraLight`
- `.thin`
- `.light`
- `.regular`
- `.medium`
- `.semibold`
- `.bold`
- `.heavy`
- `.black`

Starting in iOS 9, the system font (which was formerly Helvetica) is San Francisco, and comes in all of those weights, except at sizes smaller than 20 points, where the extreme ultralight, thin, and black are missing. A variant of the system font whose digits are monospaced can be obtained by calling `monospacedDigitSystemFont(ofSize:weight:)`. I'll talk later about how to obtain additional variants.

Dynamic type

If you have text for the user to read or edit — in a UILabel, a UITextField, or a UITextView (all discussed later in this chapter) — you are encouraged to take advantage of *dynamic type*. If a font is linked to dynamic type, then:

Text size is up to the user
> The user specifies a size preference using a slider in the Settings app. Additional larger sizes may be enabled under Accessibility. Possible sizes (UIContentSize-Category) are:
>
> - `.unspecified`
> - `.extraSmall`
> - `.small`
> - `.medium`

- `.large`
- `.extraLarge`
- `.extraExtraLarge`
- `.extraExtraExtraLarge`
- `.accessibilityMedium`
- `.accessibilityLarge`
- `.accessibilityExtraLarge`
- `.accessibilityExtraExtraLarge`
- `.accessibilityExtraExtraExtraLarge`

You specify a role

You specify a dynamic type font in terms of the *role* it is to play in your layout. The size and weight are determined for you by the system, based on the user's text size preference. Possible roles that you can specify (UIFont.TextStyle) are:

- `.largeTitle`
- `.title1`
- `.title2`
- `.title3`
- `.headline`
- `.subheadline`
- `.body`
- `.callout`
- `.footnote`
- `.caption1`
- `.caption2`

You'll probably want to experiment with specifying various roles for your individual pieces of text, to see which looks appropriate in context. (In Figure 6-1, the headlines are `.subheadline` and the blurbs are `.caption1`.)

When dynamic type was first introduced, in iOS 7, it wasn't actually dynamic. The user could change the preferred text size, but responding to that change, by refreshing the fonts of your interface objects, was left up to you. But starting in iOS 10, you can set the `adjustsFontForContentSizeCategory` property of your UILabel, UIText-Field, or UITextView to `true` (in code or in the nib editor); if this interface object uses dynamic type, it will then respond *automatically* if the user changes the text size preference in the Settings app.

One way to make your text use dynamic type is to specify a dynamic type font supplied by the system. To do that in the nib editor, summon the font popover and, in the Font pop-up menu, choose one of the Text Style menu items. To do the same thing in code, call the UIFont class method `preferredFont(forTextStyle:)`:

```
self.label.font = UIFont.preferredFont(forTextStyle: .headline)
self.label.adjustsFontForContentSizeCategory = true
```

The font, in that case, is effectively the system font in another guise. But you might prefer to use some other font. Starting in iOS 11, there's an easy way to do that: instantiate a UIFontMetrics object by calling `init(forTextStyle:)` (or use the `default` class property, which corresponds to the `.body` text style); then call `scaledFont(for:)` with your base font. To illustrate, I'll convert an existing label to respond to the user's dynamic text size preference, even though its font is *not* the system font:

```
let f = self.label2.font
self.label2.font = UIFontMetrics(forTextStyle: .caption1).scaledFont(for: f)
self.label2.adjustsFontForContentSizeCategory = true
```

Adoption of dynamic type means that your interface must now respond to the possibility that text will grow and shrink, with interface objects changing size in response. Obviously, autolayout can be a big help here (Chapter 1). A standard vertical spacing constraint between labels, from the upper label's last baseline to the lower label's first baseline, will respond to dynamic text size preference changes. You can configure this in the nib editor, or in code by calling `constraint(equalToSystemSpacingBelow:multiplier:)`. If the distance you want is not identically the standard system spacing, set the constraint's `multiplier`.

Sometimes, more radical adjustments of the overall layout may be needed, especially when we get into the five very large `.accessibility` text sizes. You'll have to respond to text size changes in code in order to make those adjustments. To do so, implement `traitCollectionDidChange(_:)`. The text size preference is reported through the trait collection's `preferredContentSizeCategory`. UIContentSizeCategory overloads the comparison operators so that you can determine easily whether one size is larger than another; also, the `isAccessibilityCategory` property tells you whether this size is one of the `.accessibility` text sizes. To help you scale actual numeric values, the UIFontMetrics instance method `scaledValue(for:)` adjusts a CGFloat with respect to the user's current text size preferences.

 To test your app's response to changes in the user's dynamic text size preference, click the Environment Overrides button in the project window's debug bar to summon a popover where you can use the Text switch and slider. This feature is new in Xcode 11 and iOS 13.

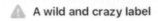

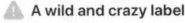

Figure 10-1. A dynamic text label with a symbol image

Symbol Images and Text

The built-in symbol images, new in iOS 13 (Chapter 2), are intended for use in conjunction with text. That is why a symbol configuration (UIImage.SymbolConfiguration) is constructed in terms of text features such as font, weight, and point size. If you derive the symbol configuration from the characteristics of the text with which it is to be associated, it will harmonize with that text.

Symbol configurations also work with dynamic text. Set up the symbol configuration in terms of a dynamic text style, and the symbol image will respond automatically when the user changes the text size preference in the Settings app, changing its own size just like text.

A symbol image configuration also has a scale: .default, .small, .medium, or .large. This is so that the image size can be adjusted relative to any associated text without breaking the harmonization between them.

A typical arrangement is that the symbol image is in a UIImageView while the text is in a label. If you have configured them so that their their size and weight harmonize, they will also align correctly with one another if they are aligned by their vertical centers. (If you have a multiline label and you prefer that the image should be aligned with the first line of the label, align them by their first baselines instead.)

Figure 10-1 demonstrates how an image view and label can resize themselves together in response to a change in the user's text size preference. The label's font is the .headline text style. The image view displays a symbol image, and its symbol configuration has the .headline text style with a .large scale for emphasis. The label and image view are aligned by their horizontal centers. Thanks to autolayout, the image view changes size in response to the image's size while the label maintains a fixed horizontal spacing from it. No code was involved in preparing this example; everything was configured in the nib editor.

Font Descriptors

A font descriptor (UIFontDescriptor, toll-free bridged to Core Text's CTFontDescriptor) describes a font in terms of its features. You can then use those features

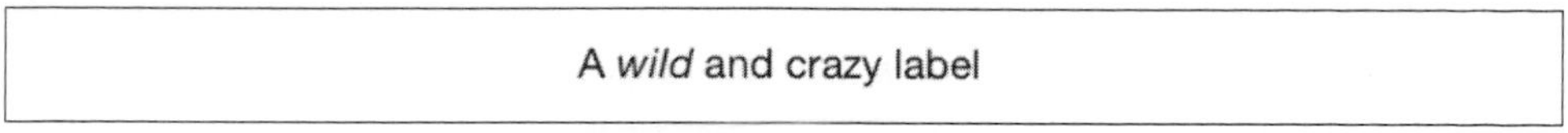

```
A wild and crazy label
```

Figure 10-2. A dynamic type font with an italic variant

to convert between font descriptors, and ultimately to derive a new font. Given a font descriptor `desc`, you can ask for a corresponding italic font descriptor like this:

```
let desc2 = desc.withSymbolicTraits(.traitItalic)
```

If `desc` was originally a descriptor for Avenir-Book 15, `desc2` is now a descriptor for Avenir-BookOblique 15. However, it is not the *font* Avenir-BookOblique 15; a font descriptor is not a font. The question is how to get from a font to a corresponding font descriptor, and *vice versa:*

To convert from a font to a font descriptor

Ask for the font's `fontDescriptor` property. Alternatively, you can obtain a font descriptor directly just as you would obtain a font, by calling its initializer `init(name:size:)` or its class method `preferredFontDescriptor(withTextStyle:)`.

To convert from a font descriptor to a font

Call the UIFont initializer `init(descriptor:size:)`, typically supplying a size of 0 to signify that the size should not change. This can be slow, because the entire font collection must be searched; so don't do it in speed-sensitive situations.

This will be a common pattern in your code, as you convert from font to font descriptor to perform some transformation, and then back to font:

```
let f = UIFont(name: "Avenir", size: 15)!
let desc = f.fontDescriptor
let desc2 = desc.withSymbolicTraits(.traitItalic)
let f2 = UIFont(descriptor: desc2!, size: 0) // Avenir-BookOblique 15
```

The same technique is useful for obtaining styled variants of the dynamic type fonts. Here I prepare to form an NSAttributedString whose font is mostly `UIFont.TextStyle.body`, but with one italicized word (Figure 10-2):

```
let body = UIFontDescriptor.preferredFontDescriptor(withTextStyle:.body)
let emphasis = body.withSymbolicTraits(.traitItalic)!
let fbody = UIFont(descriptor: body, size: 0)
let femphasis = UIFont(descriptor: emphasis, size: 0)
```

New in iOS 13, using the same technique, you can obtain alternative variants of the system font. These are referred to as *system designs*. The designs are (UIFontDescriptor.SystemDesign):

- `.default`
- `.rounded`

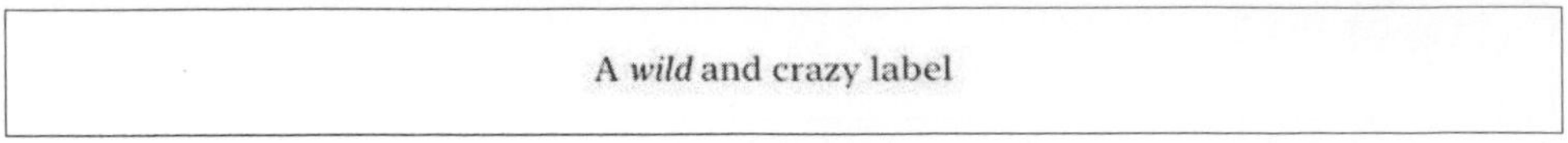

Figure 10-3. A dynamic type font with a serif design

- .serif

- .monospaced

To access a system design font, start with a dynamic type font descriptor and call withDesign(_:). To illustrate, I'll modify the previous code; now my fonts have a serif, because they come from the .serif system design (Figure 10-3):

```
var body = UIFontDescriptor.preferredFontDescriptor(withTextStyle:.body)
if let desc = body.withDesign(.serif) { // *
    body = desc
}
let emphasis = body.withSymbolicTraits(.traitItalic)!
let fbody = UIFont(descriptor: body, size: 0)
let femphasis = UIFont(descriptor: emphasis, size: 0)
```

Exploring font features

You can explore a font's features by way of a UIFontDescriptor. Some features are available directly as properties, such as postscriptName and symbolicTraits. The symbolicTraits is expressed as a bitmask:

```
let f = UIFont(name: "GillSans-BoldItalic", size: 20)!
let d = f.fontDescriptor
let traits = d.symbolicTraits
let isItalic = traits.contains(.traitItalic) // true
let isBold = traits.contains(.traitBold) // true
```

For other types of information, call object(forKey:) with a UIFont-Descriptor.AttributeName as the key:

```
let f = UIFont(name: "GillSans-BoldItalic", size: 20)!
let d = f.fontDescriptor
let vis = d.object(forKey:.visibleName)!
// Gill Sans Bold Italic
```

Accessing typographical variants

Another use of font descriptors is to access typographical variants of a font. To do so, you construct a dictionary whose keys (UIFontDescriptor.FeatureKey) specify two pieces of information: the feature type (.featureIdentifier) and the feature selector (.typeIdentifer). I'll obtain a variant of the Didot font that draws its minuscules as small caps (Figure 10-4):

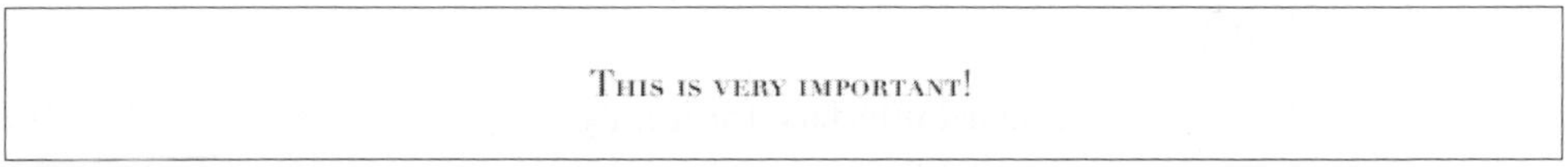

Figure 10-4. A small caps font variant

```
let desc = UIFontDescriptor(name:"Didot", size:18)
let d = [
    UIFontDescriptor.FeatureKey.featureIdentifier: kLowerCaseType,
    UIFontDescriptor.FeatureKey.typeIdentifier: kLowerCaseSmallCapsSelector
]
let desc2 = desc.addingAttributes([.featureSettings:[d]])
let f = UIFont(descriptor: desc2, size: 0)
```

(Typographical identifier constants such as `kLowerCaseSmallCapsSelector` come from the Core Text header *SFNTLayoutTypes.h*.)

The system (and dynamic type) font can also portray small caps; in fact, it can do this in two different ways: in addition to `kLowerCaseType` and `kLowerCaseSmallCaps-Selector`, where lowercase characters are shown as small caps, it implements `kUpper-CaseType` and `kUpperCaseSmallCapsSelector`, where uppercase characters are shown as small caps.

Another system (and dynamic type) font feature is an alternative set of glyph forms designed for legibility, with a type of `kStylisticAlternativesType`. If the selector is `kStylisticAltOneOnSelector`, the 6 and 9 glyphs have straight tails. If the selector is `kStylisticAltSixOnSelector`, certain letters also have special distinguishing shapes, such as the lowercase "l" (ell) which has a curved bottom, to distinguish it from capital "I" which has a top and bottom bar.

How are you supposed to discover what typographical variants a particular font supports? In code, you have to drop down to the level of Core Text:

```
let desc = UIFontDescriptor(name: "Didot", size: 20) as CTFontDescriptor
let f = CTFontCreateWithFontDescriptor(desc,0,nil)
let arr = CTFontCopyFeatures(f)
```

The resulting array of dictionaries includes entries [`CTFeatureTypeIdentifier:37`], which is `kLowerCaseType`, and [`CTFeatureSelectorIdentifier:1`], which is `kLower-CaseSmallCapsSelector`.

A more practical (and fun) approach to exploring a font's typographical variants is to obtain a copy of the font on the desktop, install it, launch TextEdit, choose Format → Font → Show Fonts, select the font, and open the Typography panel, exposing the font's various features. Now you can experiment on selected text.

Choosing a Font

New in iOS 13, there's a standard interface for letting the user pick a font. This is the UIFontPickerViewController. To use it, create a configuration (UIFontPickerViewController.Configuration) and set its properties as desired, and initialize the picker with the configuration. Then assign the picker a delegate and present the picker as a presented view controller.

Configuration properties are:

`displayUsingSystemFont`
> The default is `false`, meaning that each font name is shown in that font. If `true`, all font names are shown in a system font.

`includeFaces`
> The default is `false`, meaning that only font families are listed. If `true`, a listed font family comprising multiple fonts can reveal the names of those fonts, and the user can choose a specific font.

`filteredTraits`
> Symbolic traits to which the listed fonts should be limited. This is a bitmask, so you can combine multiple font family classes and features. Only fonts matching one or more of those traits will be listed.

`filteredLanguagesPredicate`
> A language predicate formed with the class method `filterPredicate(for-FilteredLanguages:)`. Only fonts appropriate to that language will be listed.

The delegate (UIFontPickerViewControllerDelegate) can implement two methods:

`fontPickerViewControllerDidCancel(_:)`
> Called when the user cancels using the Cancel button (but not when the user manually swipes the presented view down to dismiss it).

`fontPickerViewControllerDidPickFont(_:)`
> The user has tapped on a font listing and the picker has been dismissed. You should ask the picker for its `selectedFontDescriptor`. This might be the descriptor for a font family or (if the configuration's `includeFaces` is `true`) for a font name.

Adding Fonts

You are not limited to the fonts that are built in by default as part of the system. There are ways to obtain additional fonts.

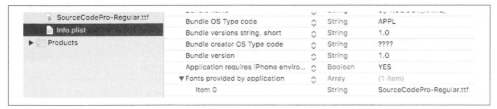

Figure 10-5. Embedding a font in an app bundle

Fonts in the app bundle

A font included at the top level of your app bundle will be loaded at launch time and available to your app if your *Info.plist* lists it under the "Fonts provided by application" key (`UIAppFonts`).

Figure 10-5 shows a font included in the app bundle, along with the *Info.plist* entry that lists it. Observe that what you're listing here is the name of the font *file*.

Downloadable Apple fonts

All macOS fonts are available for download from Apple's servers; you can obtain and start using one while your app is running.

To download a font in real time, you'll have to specify the font as a font descriptor and drop down to the level of Core Text (`import CoreText`) to call `CTFont‐DescriptorMatchFontDescriptorsWithProgressHandler`. It takes a function which is called repeatedly at every stage of the download process; it will be called on a background thread, so if you want to use the downloaded font immediately in the interface, you must step out to the main thread (see Chapter 24).

I'll attempt to use Nanum Brush Script as my UILabel's font; if it isn't installed, I'll attempt to download it and *then* use it as my UILabel's font. I've inserted a lot of unnecessary logging to mark the stages of the download process:

```
let name = "NanumBrush"
let size : CGFloat = 24
let f : UIFont! = UIFont(name:name, size:size)
if f != nil {
    self.lab.font = f
    print("already installed")
    return
}
print("attempting to download font")
let desc = UIFontDescriptor(name:name, size:size)
CTFontDescriptorMatchFontDescriptorsWithProgressHandler(
    [desc] as CFArray, nil, { state, prog in
        switch state {
        case .didBegin:
            NSLog("%@", "matching did begin")
```

```
                case .willBeginDownloading:
                    NSLog("%@", "downloading will begin")
                case .downloading:
                    let d = prog as NSDictionary
                    let key = kCTFontDescriptorMatchingPercentage
                    let cur = d[key]
                    if let cur = cur as? NSNumber {
                        NSLog("progress: %@%%", cur)
                    }
                case .didFinishDownloading:
                    NSLog("%@", "downloading did finish")
                case .didFailWithError:
                    NSLog("%@", "downloading failed")
                case .didFinish:
                    NSLog("%@", "matching did finish")
                    DispatchQueue.main.async {
                        let f : UIFont! = UIFont(name:name, size:size)
                        if f != nil {
                            NSLog("%@", "got the font!")
                            self.lab.font = f
                        }
                    }
                default:break
                }
                return true
    })
```

Installed fonts

The preceding ways of adding fonts make those fonts available within your app but nowhere else. New in iOS 13, apps can install fonts to be made available system-wide. Apple calls an app that does this a *font provider* app, and it calls fonts provided in this way *installed* fonts (as opposed to the built-in fonts that come with the system). A font provider app can include its fonts at the top level of the app bundle or in the asset catalog as on-demand resources (see "On-Demand Resources" on page 1081).

To act as a font provider requires a special entitlement; in the Signing & Capabilities tab of the target editor, choose the Fonts capability and check "Install Fonts." The fonts must be approved by Apple during the app review process. The user has the final say, so an attempt to install a font will cause the system to put up a dialog asking for the user's approval, and fonts installed by a font provider app can be deleted in the Settings app (under General → Fonts); if the user deletes a font provider app, all the fonts it provides are deleted as well.

Just as installing a font system-wide is a special privilege, so is using a font installed in this way. An app that wants access to fonts installed by a font provider app requires the same entitlement as a font provider, except that you check "Use Installed Fonts." An app that uses installed fonts needs to be aware that the user can install or remove fonts at any time; a notification lets you know when the list has changed.

Installing fonts and using installed fonts in code involves talking to Core Text (`import CoreText`) using a C API. As a simple demonstration, I'll use the app from the start of this section, where I included the SourceCodePro font in my app bundle. I'll act as a font provider and attempt to install that font for use system-wide:

```
if let url = Bundle.main.url(
    forResource: "SourceCodePro-Regular", withExtension: "ttf") {
        let urls = [url] as CFArray
        CTFontManagerRegisterFontURLs(urls, .persistent, true) { errs, ok in
            // ... user is asked for permission to install ...
            return true
        }
}
```

To act as a user of that font, I can also use a C API; if I know the descriptor of the font I want to use, I can call `CTFontManagerRequestFonts`. Moreover, because my app has the "Use Installed Fonts" entitlement, UIFontPickerViewController will include installed fonts in its list, and if the user picks one, that font will be available to my app immediately without any further action on my part.

For more information, look at the *CTFontManager.h* header (and Apple has a WWDC 2019 video on this topic).

Attributed Strings

Styled text, possibly consisting of multiple style runs with different font, size, color, and other text features in different parts of the text, is expressed as an *attributed string* (NSAttributedString and its mutable subclass, NSMutableAttributedString). An NSAttributedString consists of an NSString (its `string`) plus the attributes, applied in ranges. If the string "one red word" is blue except for the word "red" which is red, and if these are the only changes over the course of the string, then there are three distinct style runs — everything before the word "red," the word "red" itself, and everything after the word "red." Nevertheless, we can apply the attributes in two steps, first making the whole string blue, and then making the word "red" red, just as you would expect.

Attributed String Attributes

The attributes applied to a range of an attributed string are described in dictionaries. Each possible attribute has a predefined name, used as a key in these dictionaries; here are some of the most important attributes (NSAttributedString.Key):

.font
    A UIFont. The default is Helvetica 12 (*not* San Francisco, the system font).

`.foregroundColor`

The text color, a UIColor.

`.backgroundColor`

The color *behind* the text, a UIColor. You could use this to highlight a word.

`.ligature`

An NSNumber wrapping 0 or 1, expressing whether or not you want ligatures used. Some fonts, such as Didot, have ligatures that are on by default.

`.kern`

An NSNumber wrapping the floating-point amount of kerning. A negative value brings a glyph closer to the following glyph; a positive value adds space between them.

`.strikethroughStyle`
`.underlineStyle`

An NSNumber wrapping one of these values (NSUnderlineStyle, an option set) describing the line weight:

- `.none`

- `.single`

- `.double`

- `.thick`

In addition, you may specify a line pattern; the line pattern settings have names that start with `pattern`, such as `.patternDot`, `.patternDash`, and so on. Also, you may specify `.byWord`; if you do not, then if the underline or strikethrough range spans multiple words, the whitespace between the words will be underlined or struck through.

`.strikethroughColor`
`.underlineColor`

A UIColor. If not defined, the foreground color is used.

`.strokeWidth`

An NSNumber wrapping a Float. The stroke width is peculiarly coded. If it's positive, then the text glyphs are stroked but not filled, giving an outline effect, and the foreground color is used unless a separate stroke color is defined. If it's negative, then its absolute value is the width of the stroke, and the glyphs are both filled (with the foreground color) and stroked (with the stroke color).

`.strokeColor`

The stroke color, a UIColor.

`.shadow`

    An NSShadow object. An NSShadow is just a value class, combining a `shadow-Offset`, `shadowColor`, and `shadowBlurRadius`.

`.textEffect`

    An NSAttributedString.TextEffectStyle. The only text effect style you can specify is `.letterpressStyle`.

`.attachment`

    An NSTextAttachment object. A text attachment is basically an inline image. I'll discuss text attachments later on.

`.link`

    A URL. This may give the style range a default appearance, such as color and underlining, but you can override this by adding attributes to the same style range. In a noneditable, selectable UITextView, the link is tappable to go to the URL (as I'll explain later in this chapter).

`.baselineOffset`
`.obliqueness`
`.expansion`

    An NSNumber wrapping a Float.

`.paragraphStyle`

    An NSParagraphStyle object. This is basically just a value class, assembling text features that apply properly to paragraphs as a whole, not merely to characters. Here are its most important properties:

- `alignment` (NSTextAlignment)
  - `.left`
  - `.center`
  - `.right`
  - `.justified`
  - `.natural` (left-aligned or right-aligned depending on the localization; a right-to-left language will be right-aligned)
- `lineBreakMode` (NSLineBreakMode)
  - `.byWordWrapping`
  - `.byCharWrapping`
  - `.byClipping`
  - `.byTruncatingHead`

- .byTruncatingTail
- .byTruncatingMiddle

- firstLineHeadIndent, headIndent (left margin), tailIndent (right margin)
- lineHeightMultiple, maximumLineHeight, minimumLineHeight
- lineSpacing
- paragraphSpacing, paragraphSpacingBefore
- hyphenationFactor (0 or 1)
- defaultTabInterval, tabStops (the tab stops are an array of NSTextTab objects; I'll give an example in a moment)
- allowsDefaultTighteningForTruncation (if true, permits some negative kerning to be applied automatically to a truncating paragraph if this would prevent truncation)

To construct an NSAttributedString, you can call init(string:attributes:) if the entire string has the same attributes; otherwise, you'll use its mutable subclass NSMutableAttributedString, which lets you set attributes over a range.

To construct an NSParagraphStyle, you'll use its mutable subclass NSMutable-ParagraphStyle. You should apply a paragraph style to the *first character* of a paragraph; that dictates how the whole paragraph is rendered. (Applying a paragraph style to a character other than the first character of a paragraph can cause the paragraph style to be ignored.)

Both NSAttributedString and NSParagraphStyle come with default values for all attributes, so you only have to set the attributes you care about. However, Apple says that explicitly supplying a font, foreground color, and paragraph style makes attributed strings more efficient. Also, new in iOS 13, the default foreground color, coloring the text black, won't behave properly in dark mode; the adaptable text color is .label.

Making an Attributed String

We now know enough for an example! I'll draw my attributed strings in a disabled (noninteractive) UITextView; its background is white, but its superview's background is gray, so you can see the text view's bounds relative to the text. (Ignore the text's vertical positioning, which is configured independently as a feature of the text view itself.)

First, two words of my attributed string are made extra-bold by stroking in a different color. I start by dictating the entire string and the overall style of the text; then I apply the special style to the two stroked words (Figure 10-6):

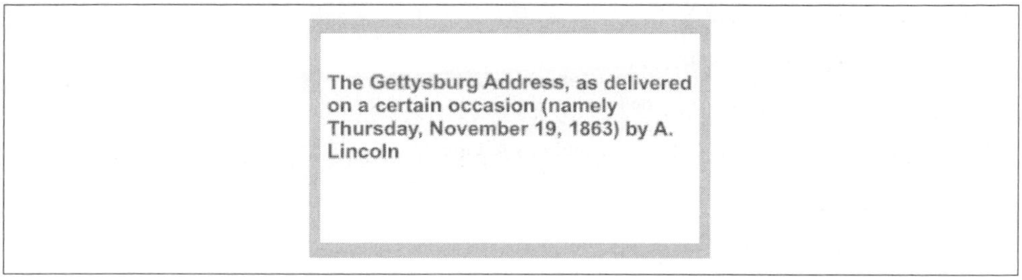

Figure 10-6. An attributed string

```
let s1 = """
    The Gettysburg Address, as delivered on a certain occasion \
    (namely Thursday, November 19, 1863) by A. Lincoln
    """
let content = NSMutableAttributedString(string:s1, attributes:[
    .font: UIFont(name:"Arial-BoldMT", size:15)!,
    .foregroundColor: UIColor(red:0.251, green:0.000, blue:0.502, alpha:1)
])
let r = (content.string as NSString).range(of:"Gettysburg Address")
content.addAttributes([
    .strokeColor: UIColor.red,
    .strokeWidth: -2.0
], range: r)
self.tv.attributedText = content
```

Carrying on from the previous code, I'll also make the whole paragraph centered and indented from the edges of the text view. To do so, I create a paragraph style and apply it to the first character. Note how the margins are dictated: the `tailIndent` is negative, to bring the right margin leftward, and the `firstLineHeadIndent` must be set separately, as the `headIndent` does not automatically apply to the first line (Figure 10-7):

```
let para = NSMutableParagraphStyle()
para.headIndent = 10
para.firstLineHeadIndent = 10
para.tailIndent = -10
para.lineBreakMode = .byWordWrapping
para.alignment = .center
para.paragraphSpacing = 15
content.addAttribute(
    .paragraphStyle,
    value:para, range:NSMakeRange(0,1))
self.tv.attributedText = content
```

Next, I'll enlarge the first character of a paragraph. I assign the first character a larger font size, I expand its width slightly, and I reduce its kerning (Figure 10-8):

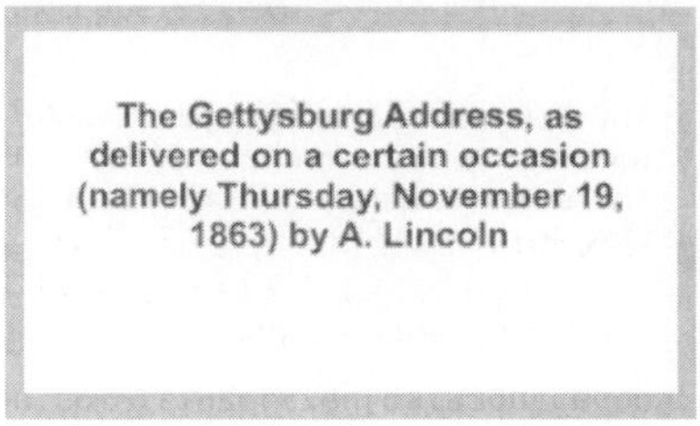

Figure 10-7. An attributed string with a paragraph style

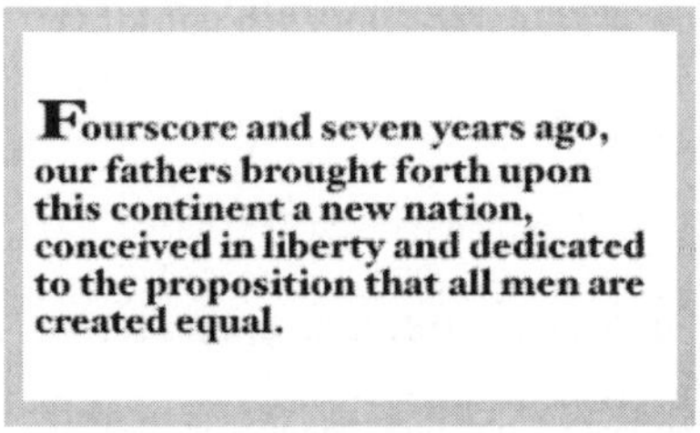

Figure 10-8. An attributed string with an expanded first character

```
let s2 = """
    Fourscore and seven years ago, our fathers brought forth \
    upon this continent a new nation, conceived in liberty and \
    dedicated to the proposition that all men are created equal.
    """
content2 = NSMutableAttributedString(string:s2, attributes: [
    .font: UIFont(name:"HoeflerText-Black", size:16)!
])
content2.addAttributes([
    .font: UIFont(name:"HoeflerText-Black", size:24)!,
    .expansion: 0.3,
    .kern: -4
], range:NSMakeRange(0,1))
self.tv.attributedText = content2
```

Carrying on from the previous code, I'll once again construct a paragraph style and add it to the first character. My paragraph style illustrates full justification and automatic hyphenation (Figure 10-9):

```
content2.addAttribute(.paragraphStyle,
    value:lend { (para:NSMutableParagraphStyle) in
        para.headIndent = 10
        para.firstLineHeadIndent = 10
        para.tailIndent = -10
        para.lineBreakMode = .byWordWrapping
        para.alignment = .justified
```

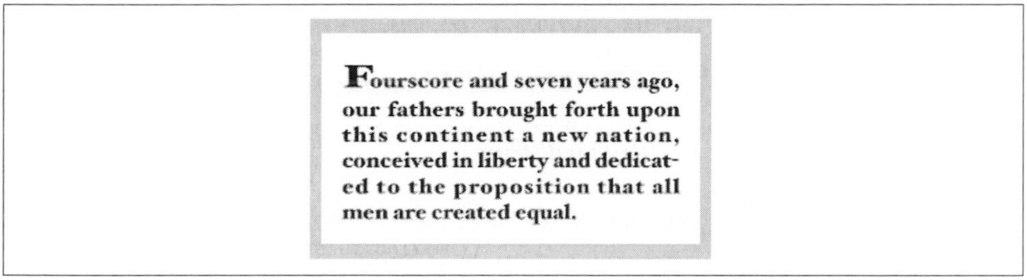

Figure 10-9. An attributed string with justification and autohyphenation

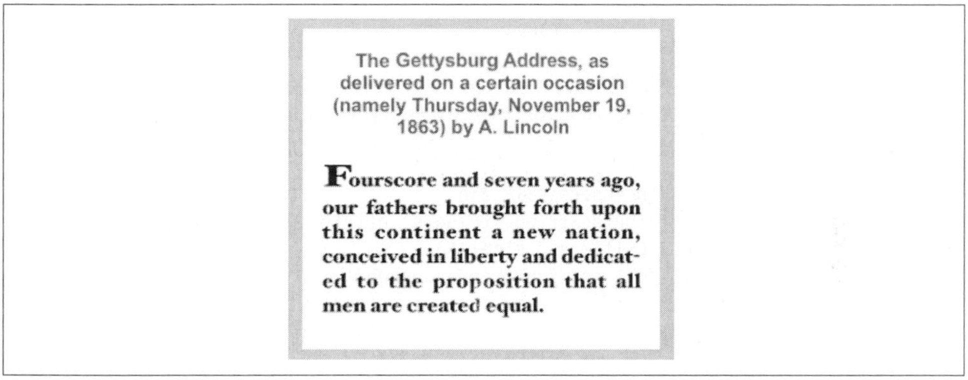

Figure 10-10. A single attributed string comprising differently styled paragraphs

```
            para.lineHeightMultiple = 1.2
            para.hyphenationFactor = 1.0
        }, range:NSMakeRange(0,1))
    self.tv.attributedText = content2
```

 When working temporarily with a value class such as NSMutableParagraphStyle, it feels clunky to be forced to instantiate the class and configure the instance before using it for the one and only time. So I've written a little Swift generic function, `lend` (see Appendix B), that lets me do all that in an anonymous function at the point where the value class is actually used.

Now we come to the Really Amazing Part. I can make a *single* attributed string consisting of *both* paragraphs, and a single text view can portray it (Figure 10-10):

```
    let end = content.length
    content.replaceCharacters(in:NSMakeRange(end, 0), with:"\n")
    content.append(content2)
    self.tv.attributedText = content
```

Tab stops

A tab stop is an NSTextTab, a value class whose initializer lets you set its `location` (points from the left edge) and `alignment`.

Figure 10-11. Tab stops in an attributed string

The initializer also lets you include an options: dictionary whose key (NSText-Tab.OptionKey) is .columnTerminators, as a way of setting the tab stop's column terminator characters. A common use is to create a decimal tab stop, for aligning currency values at their decimal point. You can obtain a value appropriate to a given locale by calling NSTextTab's class method columnTerminators(for:).

Here's a demonstration (Figure 10-11); I have deliberately omitted the last digit from the second currency value, to prove that the tab stop really is aligning the numbers at their decimal points:

```
let s = "Onions\t$2.34\nPeppers\t$15.2\n"
let mas = NSMutableAttributedString(string:s, attributes:[
    .font:UIFont(name:"GillSans", size:15)!,
    .paragraphStyle:lend { (p:NSMutableParagraphStyle) in
        let terms = NSTextTab.columnTerminators(for:Locale.current)
        let tab = NSTextTab(textAlignment:.right, location:170,
            options:[.columnTerminators:terms])
        p.tabStops = [tab]
        p.firstLineHeadIndent = 20
    }
])
self.tv.attributedText = mas
```

The tabStops array can also be modified by calling addTabStop(_:) or removeTab-Stop(_:) on the paragraph style. Note that a paragraph style comes with some default tab stops.

Text attachments

A text attachment is basically an inline image. To make one, you need an instance of NSTextAttachment initialized with image data; the easiest way is to start with a UIImage and assign it directly to the NSTextAttachment's image property. You must also give the NSTextAttachment a nonzero bounds; the image will be scaled to the size of the bounds you provide, and a .zero origin places the image on the text baseline.

A text attachment is attached to an NSAttributedString using the .attachment key; the text attachment itself is the value. The range to which this attribute is applied must consist of a special nonprinting character whose UTF-16 codepoint is NSText-Attachment.character (0xFFFC). The simplest way to arrange that is to call the NSAttributedString initializer init(attachment:); you hand it an attachment, and it

Figure 10-12. Text attachments in an attributed string

hands you an attributed string consisting of the NSTextAttachment character with
its `.attachment` attribute set to that text attachment. You can then insert this attributed string into your own attributed string at the point where you want the image to
appear.

To illustrate, I'll add an image of onions and an image of peppers just after the words
"Onions" and "Peppers" in the attributed string (`mas`) that I created in the previous
example (Figure 10-12):

```
let onions = // ... get image ...
let peppers = // ... get image ...
let onionatt = NSTextAttachment()
onionatt.image = onions
onionatt.bounds = CGRect(0,-5,onions.size.width,onions.size.height)
let onionattchar = NSAttributedString(attachment:onionatt)
let pepperatt = NSTextAttachment()
pepperatt.image = peppers
pepperatt.bounds = CGRect(0,-1,peppers.size.width,peppers.size.height)
let pepperattchar = NSAttributedString(attachment:pepperatt)
let r = (mas.string as NSString).range(of:"Onions")
mas.insert(onionattchar, at:(r.location + r.length))
let r2 = (mas.string as NSString).range(of:"Peppers")
mas.insert(pepperattchar, at:(r2.location + r2.length))
self.tv.attributedText = mas
```

New in iOS 13, you might want to use a built-in symbol image as a text attachment.
To do so, do *not* create the NSTextAttachment object and then assign the symbol to
its `image` property; instead, use the new initializer `init(image:)`. This causes the
symbol image's configuration, including its point size and baseline offset, to be set
automatically to harmonize with the surrounding text. If you want the symbol image
to pick up its tint color from the foreground color of the surrounding text, specify
an `.alwaysOriginal` rendering mode:

```
let checkim = UIImage(systemName:"checkmark.circle")!
    .withRenderingMode(.alwaysOriginal)
let check = NSTextAttachment(image:checkim) // *
let checkchar = NSAttributedString(attachment:check)
let index = // ...
mas.insert(checkchar, at:index)
```

Other ways to create an attributed string

The nib editor provides an ingenious interface for letting you construct attributed strings wherever built-in interface objects (such as UILabel or UITextView) accept them as a property; it's not perfect, though, and isn't suitable for lengthy or complex text.

It is also possible to import an attributed string from text in some other standard format, such as HTML or RTF. (There are also corresponding export methods.) To import, get the target text into a Data object and call `init(data:options:document-Attributes:)`; alternatively, start with a file and call `init(url:options:document-Attributes:)`. The `options:` allow you to specify the source text's format. Here we read an RTF file from the app bundle as an attributed string and show it in a text view (`self.tv`):

```
let url = Bundle.main.url(forResource: "test", withExtension: "rtf")!
let opts : [NSAttributedString.DocumentReadingOptionKey : Any] =
    [.documentType : NSAttributedString.DocumentType.rtf]
let s = try! NSAttributedString(
    url: url, options: opts, documentAttributes: nil)
self.tv.attributedText = s
```

Modifying and Querying an Attributed String

We can coherently modify just the character content of a mutable attributed string by calling `replaceCharacters(in:with:)`, which takes an NSRange and a substitute string. This method can do two different kinds of thing, depending whether the range has zero length:

Replacement
> If the range has *nonzero* length, we're *replacing* characters. The replacement characters all take on the attributes of the *first replaced* character.

Insertion
> If the range has *zero* length, we're *inserting* characters. The inserted characters all take on the attributes of the character *preceding* the insertion — except that, if we insert at the *start*, there is no preceding character, so the inserted characters take on the attributes of the character *following* the insertion.

You can query an attributed string about the attributes applied to a single character, asking either about all attributes at once with `attributes(at:effectiveRange:)`, or about a particular attribute by name with `attribute(_:at:effectiveRange:)`. The `effectiveRange:` argument is a pointer to an NSRange variable, which will be set by indirection to the range over which the same attribute value, or set of attribute values, applies.

In this example, we ask about the last character of our `content` attributed string:

```
var range : NSRange = NSMakeRange(0,0)
let d = content.attributes(at:content.length-1, effectiveRange:&range)
```

After that, `range` is {111,175}, and d is:

```
[__C.NSAttributedStringKey(_rawValue: NSFont):
    <UICTFont: 0x7ff533904ae0>
        font-family: "HoeflerText-Black";
        font-weight: bold;
        font-style: normal;
        font-size: 16.00pt]
```

So now we know that the last character's `.font` attribute is Hoefler Text 16, and that that attribute is applied over a stretch of 175 characters starting at character 111.

Because style runs are something of an artifice, the `effectiveRange` might not be what you would think of as the *entire* style run. The methods with `longestEffective-Range:` parameters work out the entire style run range for you; but this comes at the cost of some efficiency, and in practice you typically won't need this information anyway, because you're cycling through ranges — so that speed, even at the cost of *more* iterations, matters more than getting the longest effective range on *every* iteration.

In this example, I start with the `content` attributed string and change all the size 15 material to Arial Bold 20. I don't care whether I'm handed longest effective ranges (and my code explicitly says so); I just want to cycle efficiently:

```
content.enumerateAttribute(.font,
    in:NSMakeRange(0,content.length),
    options:.longestEffectiveRangeNotRequired) { value, range, stop in
        let font = value as! UIFont
        if font.pointSize == 15 {
            content.addAttribute(.font,
                value:UIFont(name: "Arial-BoldMT", size:20)!,
                range:range)
        }
    }
```

Custom Attributes

You are permitted to apply your own custom attributes to a stretch of text in an attributed string. Your attributes won't directly affect how the string is drawn, because the text engine doesn't know what to make of them; but it doesn't object to them either. In this way, you can mark a stretch of text invisibly for your own future use.

In this example, I have a UILabel whose text includes a date. Every so often, I want to replace the date by the current date. The problem is that when the moment comes to replace the date, I don't know where it is: I know neither its length nor the length of the text that precedes it. The solution is to use an attributed string where the date part is marked with a custom attribute.

My custom attribute is defined by extending NSAttributedString.Key:

```
extension NSAttributedString.Key {
    static let myDate = NSAttributedString.Key("myDate")
}
```

I've applied this attribute to the date part of my label's attributed text, with an arbitrary value of 1. Now I can readily find the date again later, because the text engine will tell me where it is:

```
let mas = NSMutableAttributedString(
    attributedString: self.lab.attributedText!)
mas.enumerateAttribute(.myDate, in: NSMakeRange(0, mas.length)) {
    value, r, stop in
    if let value = value as? Int, value == 1 {
        mas.replaceCharacters(in: r, with: Date().description)
        stop.pointee = true
    }
}
self.lab.attributedText = mas
```

Drawing and Measuring an Attributed String

You can draw an attributed string yourself, rather than having a built-in interface object do it for you; and sometimes this will prove to be the most reliable approach. An NSString can be drawn into a rect with draw(in:withAttributes:) and related methods; an NSAttributedString can be drawn with draw(at:), draw(in:), and draw(with:options:context:).

Here, I draw an attributed string (content) into an image graphics context and extract the image, which might then be displayed by an image view:

```
let rect = CGRect(0,0,280,250)
let r = UIGraphicsImageRenderer(size:rect.size)
let im = r.image { ctx in
    UIColor.white.setFill()
    ctx.cgContext.fill(rect)
    content.draw(in:rect)
}
```

Similarly, you can draw an attributed string directly in a UIView's draw(_:) override. Imagine that we have a UIView subclass called StringDrawer that has an attributed-Text property; the idea is that we just assign an attributed string to that property and the StringDrawer redraws itself:

```
self.drawer.attributedText = content
```

And here's StringDrawer:

```
class StringDrawer : UIView {
    @NSCopying var attributedText : NSAttributedString! {
        didSet {
            self.setNeedsDisplay()
        }
    }
    override func draw(_ rect: CGRect) {
        let r = rect.offsetBy(dx: 0, dy: 2)
        let opts : NSStringDrawingOptions = .usesLineFragmentOrigin
        self.attributedText.draw(with:r, options: opts, context: context)
    }
}
```

The .usesLineFragmentOrigin option is crucial here. Without it, the string is drawn with its *baseline* at the rect origin (so that it appears *above* that rect), and it doesn't wrap. The rule is that .usesLineFragmentOrigin is the implicit default for simple draw(in:), but for draw(with:options:context:) you must specify it explicitly.

NSAttributedString also provides methods to *measure* an attributed string, such as boundingRect(with:options:context:). As before, the .usesLineFragmentOrigin option is crucial; without it, the measured text doesn't wrap and the returned height will be very small. The documentation warns that the returned height can be fractional and that you should round up to an integer if the height of a view is going to depend on this result.

The context: parameter of methods such as draw(with:options:context:) lets you supply an instance of NSStringDrawingContext, a simple value class whose total-Bounds property tells you where you just drew.

 The documentation lists additional features of NSStringDrawingContext, such as its minimumScaleFactor; but these appear to be nonfunctional.

Labels

A label (UILabel) is a simple built-in interface object for displaying text. I listed some of its chief properties in Chapter 8 ("Built-In Cell Styles" on page 450).

If you're displaying a plain NSString in a label, by way of the label's text property, then you are likely also to set the label's font, textColor, and textAlignment properties, and possibly its shadowColor and shadowOffset properties. The label's text can have an alternate highlightedTextColor, to be used when its isHighlighted property is true, as when the label is in a selected cell of a table view.

On the other hand, if you're using an NSAttributedString, then you'll set just the label's attributedText property and let the attributes dictate things like color, alignment, and shadow. In general, if your intention is to display text in a single font, size, color, and alignment, you probably won't bother with `attributedText`; but if you *do* set the `attributedText`, you should make it your *only* way of dictating text style features. Those other UILabel properties do mostly work when you have set the `attributedText`, but they're going to change the attributes of your *entire* attributed string, with results that you might not intend. Setting the `text` of a UILabel that has `attributedText` will effectively override the attributes.

 The `highlightedTextColor` property affects the `attributedText` only if the latter is the same color as the `textColor`.

Number of Lines

A UILabel's `numberOfLines` property is extremely important. Together with the label's line breaking behavior and resizing behavior, it determines how much of the text will appear. The default is `1` — a single line — which can come as a surprise. To make a label display more than one line of text, you must explicitly set its `numberOf-Lines` to a value greater than 1, or to `0` to indicate that there is to be no maximum.

Line break characters in a label's text are honored. In a single-line label, you won't see whatever follows the first line break character.

Wrapping and Truncation

UILabel line breaking (wrapping) and truncation behavior, which applies to both single-line and multiline labels, is determined by the `lineBreakMode` (of the label or the attributed string). The options (NSLineBreakMode) are those that I listed earlier in discussing NSParagraphStyle, but their *behavior* within a label needs to be described:

`.byClipping`
Lines break at word-end, but the *last* line can continue past its boundary, even if this leaves a character showing only partially.

`.byWordWrapping`
Lines break at word-end, but if this is a single-line label, indistinguishable from `.byClipping`.

`.byCharWrapping`
Lines break in midword in order to maximize the number of characters in each line.

```
.byTruncatingHead
.byTruncatingMiddle
.byTruncatingTail
```
> Lines break at word-end; if the text is too long for the label, then the *last* line displays an ellipsis at the start, middle, or end of the line respectively, and text is omitted at the point of the ellipsis.
>
> The `allowsDefaultTighteningForTruncation` property, if `true`, permits some negative kerning to be applied automatically to a `truncating` label if this would prevent truncation.

A UILabel's line break behavior is *not* the same as what happens when an NSAttributedString draws itself into a graphics context:

- The default line break mode for an NSAttributedString's NSParagraphStyle is `.byWordWrapping`, but the default line break mode for a new label is `.byTruncatingTail`.

- An NSAttributedString whose NSParagraphStyle's `lineBreakMode` doesn't have `wrapping` in its name *doesn't wrap* when it draws itself (it consists of a single line), but a multiline UILabel *always* wraps, regardless of its line break mode.

Fitting Label and Text

If a label is too small for its text, the entire text won't show. If a label is too big for its text, the text is vertically centered in the label, with space above and below. Either of those might be undesirable; you might prefer the label to *fit* its text.

If you're not using autolayout, in most simple cases `sizeToFit` will do the right thing; I believe that behind the scenes it is calling `boundingRect(with:options:context:)`.

If you're using autolayout, a label will correctly configure its own `intrinsicContentSize` automatically, based on its contents — and therefore, all other things being equal, the label will size itself to fit its contents *with no code at all*. Every time you reconfigure the label in a way that affects its contents (setting its text, changing its font, setting its attributed text, and so forth), the label *automatically* invalidates and recalculates its intrinsic content size and resizes itself to fit. There are two general cases to consider:

Short single-line label
> You might give the label no width or height constraints; you'll constrain its position, but you'll let the label's `intrinsicContentSize` provide both the label's width and its height.

Multiline label

Most likely, you'll want to dictate the label's width, while letting the label's height change automatically to accommodate its contents. There are two ways to do this:

Set the label's internal width constraint

This is appropriate particularly when the label's width is to remain fixed ever after.

Set the label's `preferredMaxLayoutWidth`

This property is a hint to help the label's calculation of its `intrinsicContentSize`. It is the width at which the label, as its contents increase, will stop growing horizontally to accommodate those contents, and start growing vertically instead.

Consider a label whose top, left, and right edges are pinned to its superview, while its height is free to change based on its `intrinsicContentSize`. Presume also that the superview's width can change, possibly due to rotation, changing the width of the label. Then the label's height will always perfectly fit its contents, provided that, after every width change, the label's `preferredMaxLayoutWidth` is adjusted *to match its current width*.

How can we make that happen? It's easy. It turns out that if we simply set the label's `preferredMaxLayoutWidth` to 0, that will be taken as a signal that the label should change its `preferredMaxLayoutWidth` to match its width *automatically* whenever its width changes. Moreover, that happens to be the default `preferredMaxLayoutWidth` value! (In the nib editor, at the top of a label's Size inspector, when the Explicit checkbox is unchecked and the Desired Width field says "Automatic," that means the label's `preferredMaxLayoutWidth` is 0; again, this is the default.) So a label in this configuration will *always* fit its contents, with no effort on your part.

Instead of letting a label grow, you can permit its text font size to shrink if this would allow more of the text to fit. How the text is repositioned when the font size shrinks is determined by the label's `baselineAdjustment` property. For this feature to operate, *all* of the following conditions must be met:

- The label's `adjustsFontSizeToFitWidth` property must be `true`.
- The label's `minimumScaleFactor` must be less than `1.0`.
- The label's size must be limited.
- *Either* this must be a single-line label (`numberOfLines` is 1) *or* the line break mode (of the label or the attributed string) must *not* have `wrapping` in its name.

Customized Label Drawing

Methods that you can override in a subclass to modify a label's drawing are draw-Text(in:) and textRect(forBounds:limitedToNumberOfLines:). This is the code for a UILabel subclass that outlines the label with a black rectangle and puts a five-point inset around the label's contents:

```
class BoundedLabel: UILabel {
    override func awakeFromNib() {
        super.awakeFromNib()
        self.layer.borderWidth = 2.0
        self.layer.cornerRadius = 3.0
    }
    override func drawText(in rect: CGRect) {
        super.drawText(in: rect.insetBy(dx: 5, dy: 5).integral)
    }
}
```

 A CATextLayer (Chapter 3) is like a lightweight, layer-level version of a UILabel. If the width of the layer is insufficient to display the entire string, we can get truncation behavior with the truncationMode property. If the isWrapped property is set to true, the string will wrap. We can also set the alignment with the alignmentMode property. And its string property can be an NSAttributedString.

Text Fields

A text field (UITextField) is for brief user text entry. It portrays just a single line of text; any line break characters in its text are treated as spaces. It has many of the same properties as a label. You can provide it with a plain NSString, setting its text, font, textColor, and textAlignment, or provide it with an attributed string, setting its attributedText. You can learn (and set) a text field's overall text attributes as an attributes dictionary through its defaultTextAttributes property.

UITextField adopts the UITextInput protocol, which itself adopts the UIKeyInput protocol. These protocols endow a text field with methods for such things as obtaining the text field's current selection and inserting text at the current selection. I'll give examples later in this section.

Under autolayout, a text field's intrinsicContentSize will attempt to set its width to fit its contents; if its width is fixed, you can set its adjustsFontSizeToFitWidth and minimumFontSize properties to allow the text size to shrink somewhat.

Text that is too long for the text field is displayed with an ellipsis at the end. To change the position of the ellipsis, assign the text field an attributed string with different truncation behavior, such as .byTruncatingHead. When long text is being edited, the ellipsis is removed and the text shifts to show the insertion point.

Regardless of whether you originally supplied a plain string or an attributed string, if the text field's `allowsEditingTextAttributes` property is `true`, the user, when editing in the text field, can summon a menu toggling the selected text's bold, italics, or underline features.

A text field has a `placeholder` property, which is the text that appears faded within the text field when it has no text (its `text` or `attributedText` has been set to `nil`, or the user has removed all the text); the idea is that you can use this to suggest to the user what the text field is for. It has a styled text alternative, `attributedPlaceholder`.

If a text field's `clearsOnBeginEditing` property is `true`, it automatically deletes its existing text (and displays the placeholder) when editing begins within it. If a text field's `clearsOnInsertion` property is `true`, then when editing begins within it, the text remains, but is invisibly selected, and will be replaced by the user's typing.

A text field's border drawing is determined by its `borderStyle` property. Your options (UITextField.BorderStyle) are:

`.none`
> No border.

`.line`
> A plain black rectangle.

`.bezel`
> A gray rectangle, where the top and left sides have a very slight, thin shadow.

`.roundedRect`
> A larger rectangle with slightly rounded corners and a flat, faded gray color.

You can supply a background image (`background`) — though it is ignored if the `borderStyle` is `.roundedRect`. If you combine a background image with a `borderStyle` of `.none`, or if the image has no transparency so that it covers the existing border, you get to draw your own border. The image is automatically resized, and you will probably want to supply a resizable image. A second image (`disabledBackground`) can be displayed when the text field's `isEnabled` property, inherited from UIControl, is `false`. The user can't interact with a disabled text field, but without a `disabledBackground` image, the user may lack a sufficient visual clue to this fact. You can't set the `disabledBackground` unless you have also set the `background`.

A text field may contain one or two ancillary overlay views, its `leftView` and `rightView`, and possibly a Clear button (a gray circle with a white X). The automatic visibility of each of these is determined by the `leftViewMode`, `rightViewMode`, and `clearButtonMode`, respectively. The view mode values (UITextField.ViewMode) are:

`.never`

The view never appears.

`.whileEditing`

A Clear button appears if there is text in the field and the user is editing. A left or right view appears if the user is editing, even if there is no text in the field.

`.unlessEditing`

A Clear button appears if there is text in the field and the user is not editing. A left or right view appears if the user is not editing, or if the user is editing but there is no text in the field.

`.always`

A Clear button appears if there is text in the field. A left or right view always appears.

Depending on what sort of view you use, your `leftView` and `rightView` may have to be sized manually (possibly using internal constraints) so as not to overwhelm the text view contents. If a right view and a Clear button appear at the same time, the right view may cover the Clear button unless you reposition it.

The positions and sizes of *any* of the components of the text field can be set in relation to the text field's bounds by overriding the appropriate method in a subclass:

- `clearButtonRect(forBounds:)`
- `leftViewRect(forBounds:)`
- `rightViewRect(forBounds:)`
- `borderRect(forBounds:)`
- `textRect(forBounds:)`
- `placeholderRect(forBounds:)`
- `editingRect(forBounds:)`

You should make no assumptions about when or how frequently these methods will be called; the same method might be called several times in quick succession. (Also, these methods should all be called with a parameter that is the bounds of the text field, but some are sometimes called with a 100×100 bounds; this feels like a bug.)

You can also override in a subclass the methods `drawText(in:)` and `draw-Placeholder(in:)`. You should either draw the specified text or call `super` to draw it; if you do neither, the text won't appear. Both these methods are called with a parameter whose size is the dimensions of the text field's text area, but whose origin is `.zero`. In effect what you've got is a graphics context for just the text area; any drawing you do outside the given rectangle will be clipped.

Summoning and Dismissing the Keyboard

The presence or absence of the virtual keyboard is intimately tied to a text field's editing state. They both have to do with the text field's status as the *first responder*:

- When a text field is first responder, it is being edited and the keyboard is present.

- When a text field is no longer first responder, it is no longer being edited, and if no other text field (or text view) becomes first responder, the keyboard is not present. The keyboard is not dismissed if one text field takes over first responder status from another.

When the user taps in a text field, by default it *is* first responder, and so the keyboard appears *automatically* if it was not already present. You can also control the presence or absence of the keyboard *in code*, together with a text field's editing state, by way of the text field's first responder status:

Becoming first responder
> To make the insertion point appear within a text field and to cause the keyboard to appear, you send `becomeFirstResponder` to that text field.

Resigning first responder
> To make a text field stop being edited and to cause the keyboard to disappear, you send `resignFirstResponder` to that text field. (Actually, `resignFirstResponder` returns a Bool, because a responder might return `false` to indicate that for some reason it refuses to obey this command.)
>
> Alternatively, call the UIView `endEditing(_:)` method on the first responder *or any superview* (including the window) to ask or compel the first responder to resign first responder status.

The `endEditing(_:)` method is useful particularly because there may be times when you want to dismiss the keyboard without knowing who the first responder is. You can't send `resignFirstResponder` if you don't know who to send it to. And, amazingly, there is no simple way to learn what view is first responder!

 In a view presented in the `.formSheet` modal presentation style on the iPad (Chapter 6), the keyboard, by default, does *not* disappear when a text field resigns first responder status. This is presumably because a form sheet is intended primarily for text input, so the keyboard is felt as accompanying the form as a whole, not individual text fields. Optionally, you can prevent this exceptional behavior: in your UIViewController subclass, override `disablesAutomaticKeyboardDismissal` to return `false`.

Once the user has tapped in a text field and the keyboard has automatically appeared, how is the user supposed to get rid of it? On the iPad, the keyboard may contain a button that dismisses the keyboard. Otherwise, this is an oddly tricky issue. You would think that the Return key in the keyboard would dismiss the keyboard, since you can't enter a Return character in a text field; but, of itself, it doesn't.

One solution is to be the text field's delegate and to implement a text field delegate method, `textFieldShouldReturn(_:)`. When the user taps the Return key in the keyboard, we hear about it through this method, and we receive a reference to the text field; we can respond by telling the text field to resign its first responder status, which dismisses the keyboard:

```
func textFieldShouldReturn(_ tf: UITextField) -> Bool {
    tf.resignFirstResponder()
    return false
}
```

Certain virtual keyboards lack a Return key. In that case, you'll need some other way to allow the user to dismiss the keyboard, such as a button elsewhere in the interface. If there's a scroll view in the interface, you can set its `keyboardDismissMode` to provide a way of letting the user dismiss the keyboard. The options (UIScroll-View.KeyboardDismissMode) are:

`.none`
> The default; if the keyboard doesn't contain a button that lets the user dismiss it, we must use code to dismiss it.

`.interactive`
> The user can dismiss the keyboard by dragging it down.

`.onDrag`
> The keyboard dismisses itself if the user scrolls the scroll view.

A scroll view with a `keyboardDismissMode` that isn't `.none` also calls `resignFirstResponder` on the text field when it dismisses the keyboard.

Keyboard Covers Text Field

The keyboard, having appeared from offscreen, occupies on the iPhone a position "docked" at the bottom of the screen. This may cover the text field in which the user wants to type, even if it is first responder.

This is not likely to be a major issue on the iPad, because the user has ways of moving the keyboard. New in iOS 13, the user has a choice of three ways to unmoor the text field from its "docked" position at the bottom of the screen:

Undock
> The keyboard moves up slightly while continuing to occupy the full width of the screen; the user can drag it up and down.

Split
> The keyboard becomes smaller and splits into two separate parts pinned to opposite edges of the screen; the user can drag them up and down together.

Floating
> The keyboard becomes even smaller and looks like an iPhone keyboard, less than half the width of the screen; the user can drag it anywhere.

So on the iPad your interface probably won't need to compensate for the keyboard, because the user can move the keyboard instead.

You'll typically want to reveal the text field on the iPhone so as to ensure that it is not covered by the keyboard. To help with this, you can register for keyboard-related notifications:

- `UIResponder.keyboardWillShowNotification`
- `UIResponder.keyboardDidShowNotification`
- `UIResponder.keyboardWillHideNotification`
- `UIResponder.keyboardDidHideNotification`

Those notifications all have to do with the docked position of the keyboard. On the iPhone, keyboard docking and keyboard visibility are equivalent: the keyboard is visible if and only if it is docked.

Two additional notifications are sent *both* when the keyboard enters and leaves the screen *and* (on the iPad) when the user drags it, splits or unsplits it, and docks or undocks it:

- `UIResponder.keyboardWillChangeFrameNotification`
- `UIResponder.keyboardDidChangeFrameNotification`

On the iPad, where the user can undock the keyboard, the keyboard is said to show if it is being docked, whether that's because it is appearing from offscreen or because the user is docking it, and it is said to hide if it is being undocked, whether that's because it is moving offscreen or because the user is undocking it. If the keyboard is already undocked and the user moves it around the screen, or if the keyboard appears into or disappears from an undocked configuration, you get *only* changeFrame notifications.

The most important situations to respond to on the iPhone are those corresponding to the willShow and willHide notifications, when the keyboard is attaining or leaving its docked position at the bottom of the screen. You might think that it would also be necessary to handle the changeFrame notification, in case the keyboard changes its height — as when the user switches from the text keyboard to the emoji keyboard on the iPhone. But the willShow notification is sent in that situation too.

Each notification's `userInfo` dictionary contains information describing what the keyboard will do or has done, under these keys:

- `UIResponder.keyboardFrameBeginUserInfoKey`

- `UIResponder.keyboardFrameEndUserInfoKey`

- `UIResponder.keyboardAnimationDurationUserInfoKey`

- `UIResponder.keyboardAnimationCurveUserInfoKey`

When you receive a `willShow` notification, you can look at the user info's `UIResponder.keyboardFrameEndUserInfoKey` to learn what position the keyboard is moving to. It is an NSValue wrapping a CGRect *in screen coordinates*. By converting the coordinate system as appropriate, you can compare the keyboard's new frame with the frame of your interface items. If the keyboard's new frame intersects a text field's frame (in the same coordinates), the keyboard is going to cover that text field. You're going to want to take evasive maneuvers.

A natural-looking approach is to slide the entire interface upward as the keyboard appears, just enough to expose the text field being edited above the top of the keyboard. The simplest way to do that is for the entire interface to be inside a scroll view — which is, after all, a view that knows how to slide its contents. This scroll view need not be ordinarily scrollable by the user; in fact, the user may be completely unaware of its existence. But *after* the keyboard appears, the scroll view *should* be scrollable by the user, so that the user can inspect the entire interface at will, even while the keyboard is covering part of it. We can ensure that by adjusting the scroll view's `content-Inset`.

This behavior is in fact implemented automatically by a UITableViewController. When a text field inside a table cell is first responder, the table view controller adjusts the `bottom` of the table view's `adjustedContentInset` to compensate for the keyboard. The result is that the entire table view content is available within the space between the top of the table view and the top of the keyboard.

Moreover, a scroll view has two additional bits of built-in behavior that will help us:

- It scrolls automatically to reveal the first responder. This will make it easy for us to expose the text field being edited.

- It has, as I already mentioned, a `keyboardDismissMode`, which can give us an additional way to allow the user to dismiss the keyboard.

Let's imitate UITableViewController's behavior with a scroll view containing text fields. In particular, our interface consists of a scroll view containing a content view; the content view contains several text fields.

In `viewDidLoad`, we register for keyboard notifications:

```
NotificationCenter.default.addObserver(self,
    selector: #selector(keyboardShow),
    name: UIResponder.keyboardWillShowNotification, object: nil)
NotificationCenter.default.addObserver(self,
    selector: #selector(keyboardHide),
    name: UIResponder.keyboardWillHideNotification, object: nil)
```

We are the delegate of any text fields, so that we can hear about it when the user taps the Return key in the keyboard. We use that as a signal to dismiss the keyboard, as I suggested earlier:

```
func textFieldShouldReturn(_ tf: UITextField) -> Bool {
    tf.resignFirstResponder()
    return false
}
```

It will help to have on hand a utility function that works out the geometry based on the notification's userInfo dictionary and the bounds of the view we're concerned with (which will be the scroll view). If the keyboard wasn't within the view's bounds and now it will be, it is entering; if it was within the view's bounds and now it won't be, it is exiting. We return that information, along with the keyboard's frame in the view's bounds coordinates:

```
enum KeyboardState {
    case unknown
    case entering
    case exiting
}
func keyboardState(for d:[AnyHashable:Any], in v:UIView?)
    -> (KeyboardState, CGRect?) {
        var rold = d[UIResponder.keyboardFrameBeginUserInfoKey] as! CGRect
        var rnew = d[UIResponder.keyboardFrameEndUserInfoKey] as! CGRect
        var ks : KeyboardState = .unknown
        var newRect : CGRect? = nil
        if let v = v {
            let co = UIScreen.main.coordinateSpace
            rold = co.convert(rold, to:v)
            rnew = co.convert(rnew, to:v)
            newRect = rnew
            if !rold.intersects(v.bounds) && rnew.intersects(v.bounds) {
                ks = .entering
            }
            if rold.intersects(v.bounds) && !rnew.intersects(v.bounds) {
                ks = .exiting
            }
        }
        return (ks, newRect)
}
```

When we get a willShow notification, we first check whether the keyboard is about to enter our scroll view's bounds; if so, we store the scroll view's current content offset, content inset, and scroll indicator insets. Then we alter the scroll view's insets appropriately, allowing the scroll view itself to scroll the first responder into view if needed:

```
@objc func keyboardShow(_ n:Notification) {
    let d = n.userInfo!
    let (state, rnew) = keyboardState(for:d, in:self.scrollView)
    if state == .entering {
        self.oldContentInset = self.scrollView.contentInset
        self.oldIndicatorInset = self.scrollView.scrollIndicatorInsets
        self.oldOffset = self.scrollView.contentOffset
    }
    if let rnew = rnew {
        let h = rnew.intersection(self.scrollView.bounds).height
        self.scrollView.contentInset.bottom = h
        self.scrollView.scrollIndicatorInsets.bottom = h
    }
}
```

When the keyboard hides, we reverse the process, restoring the saved values:

```
@objc func keyboardHide(_ n:Notification) {
    let d = n.userInfo!
    let (state, _) = keyboardState(for:d, in:self.scrollView)
    if state == .exiting {
        self.scrollView.contentOffset = self.oldOffset
        self.scrollView.scrollIndicatorInsets = self.oldIndicatorInset
        self.scrollView.contentInset = self.oldContentInset
    }
}
```

Behind the scenes, we are inside an animations function at the time that our notifications arrive. This means that our changes to the scroll view are nicely animated in coordination with the keyboard appearing and disappearing.

Under iPad multitasking (Chapter 9), your app can receive keyboard show and hide notifications if *another* app summons or dismisses the keyboard. This makes sense because the keyboard is, after all, covering your app. You can distinguish whether your app was responsible for summoning the keyboard by examining the show notification userInfo dictionary's UIResponder.keyboardIsLocalUserInfoKey; but in general you probably won't have to, provided you handle keyboard notifications coherently in the first place.

Text Field Delegate and Control Event Messages

As editing begins and proceeds in a text field, various messages are sent to the text field's delegate, adopting the UITextFieldDelegate protocol. Some of these messages are also available as notifications. Using them, you can customize the text field's behavior during editing:

`textFieldShouldBeginEditing(_:)`
Return `false` to prevent the text field from becoming first responder.

`textFieldDidBeginEditing(_:)`
`UITextField.textDidBeginEditingNotification`
The text field has become first responder.

`textFieldShouldClear(_:)`
Return `false` to prevent the operation of the Clear button or of automatic clearing on entry (`clearsOnBeginEditing`). This event is *not* sent when the text is cleared because `clearsOnInsertion` is `true`, presumably because the user is not clearing the text but rather changing it.

`textFieldShouldReturn(_:)`
The user has tapped the Return button in the keyboard. We have already seen that this can be used as a signal to dismiss the keyboard.

`textFieldDidChangeSelection(_:)`
(New in iOS 13.) The text field selection has changed. This happens any time the position of the insertion point or the selection changes for any reason, so this delegate message reports almost any editing action. Merely typing a character changes the selection, because the insertion point position is now greater by one character.

`textField(_:shouldChangeCharactersIn:replacementString:)`
`UITextField.textDidChangeNotification`
The notification is a signal that the user *has* edited the text, but the delegate method is your chance to *interfere* with the user's editing *before* it takes effect. You can return `false` to prevent the proposed change; if you're going to do that, you can replace the user's edit with your own, by changing the text field's text directly (there is no circularity, as this delegate method is not called when you do that).

In this example, the user can enter only lowercase characters (the `insertText` method comes from the UIKeyInput protocol, which UITextField adopts):

```
func textField(_ textField: UITextField,
    shouldChangeCharactersIn range: NSRange,
    replacementString string: String) -> Bool {
        if string.isEmpty { // backspace
            return true
        }
        let lc = string.lowercased()
        textField.insertText(lc)
        return false
}
```

As the example shows, you can distinguish whether the user is typing or pasting, on the one hand, or backspacing or cutting, on the other; in the latter case, the replacement string will be empty. You are *not* notified when the user changes text styling through the Bold, Italics, or Underline menu items.

`textFieldShouldEndEditing(_:)`
Return `false` to prevent the text field from resigning first responder (even if you just sent `resignFirstResponder` to it). You might do this because the text is invalid or unacceptable in some way. The user will not know why the text field is refusing to end editing, so the usual thing is to put up an alert (Chapter 13) explaining the problem.

`textFieldDidEndEditing(_:)`
`UITextField.textDidEndEditingNotification`
The text field has resigned first responder. See "Editable Content in Cells" on page 511 for an example of using the delegate method to fetch the text field's current text and store it in the model.

A text field is a control (UIControl; see also Chapter 12). That means you can attach a target–action pair to any of the events that it reports in order to receive a message when that event occurs. Of the various control event messages emitted by a text field, the two most useful (in my experience) are:

Editing Changed (`.editingChanged`*)*
Sent after the user performs any editing. If your goal is to respond to changes, rather than to forestall them, this is a better way than the delegate method `text-Field(_:shouldChangeCharactersIn:replacementString:)`, because it arrives at the right moment, namely *after* the change has occurred, and because it can detect attributes changes, which the delegate method can't do.

Did End on Exit (`.editingDidEndOnExit`*)*
Sent when the user taps the Return button in the text field's keyboard. Surprisingly, if this control event is configured to trigger an action message, the keyboard is dismissed *automatically* — even if the action method does nothing. In fact, the action method doesn't even have to exist! The action can be `nil`-targeted. There is no penalty for implementing a `nil`-targeted action that walks up the responder chain without finding a method that handles it.

In this example, I create a UITextField subclass that *automatically dismisses itself* when the user taps Return:

```
@objc protocol Dummy {
    func dummy(_ sender: Any)
}
class MyTextField: UITextField {
    required init?(coder: NSCoder) {
```

```
        super.init(coder:coder)
        self.addTarget(nil,
            action:#selector(Dummy.dummy), for:.editingDidEndOnExit)
    }
}
```

You can configure the same thing in the nib editor. Edit the First Responder proxy object in the Attributes inspector, adding a new First Responder Action; call it dummy:. Now hook the Did End on Exit event of the text field to the dummy: action of the First Responder proxy object.

Text Field Menu

When the user double taps or long presses in a text field, a menu appears. It contains menu items such as Select, Select All, Paste, Copy, Cut, and Replace; which menu items appear depends on the circumstances. Many of the selectors for these standard menu items are listed in the UIResponderStandardEditActions protocol. Commonly used standard actions are:

- cut(_:)
- copy(_:)
- select(_:)
- selectAll(_:)
- paste(_:)
- delete(_:)
- toggleBoldface(_:)
- toggleItalics(_:)
- toggleUnderline(_:)

Some other menu items are known only through their Objective-C selectors:

- _promptForReplace:
- _define:
- _showTextStyleOptions:

The menu can be customized; this involves setting the shared UIMenuController object's menuItems property to an array of UIMenuItem instances representing the menu items that may appear in addition to those that the system puts there.

Actions for menu items are nil-targeted, so they percolate up the responder chain. You can implement a menu item's action anywhere up the responder chain; if you do this for a standard menu item at a point in the responder chain before the system receives it, you can interfere with and customize what it does. You govern the presence or absence of a menu item by implementing the UIResponder method `can-PerformAction(_:withSender:)` in the responder chain.

To illustrate, we'll devise a text field whose menu includes our own menu item, Expand. I'm imagining a text field where the user can select a U.S. state's two-letter abbreviation (such as "CA") and can then summon the menu and tap Expand to replace it with the state's full name (such as "California"). I'll implement this in a UITextField subclass called MyTextField, in order to guarantee that the Expand menu item will be available when an instance of this subclass is first responder, but at no other time.

At some moment before the user taps in an instance of MyTextField (such as our view controller's `viewDidLoad`), we modify the global menu:

```
let mi = UIMenuItem(title:"Expand", action:#selector(MyTextField.expand))
let mc = UIMenuController.shared
mc.menuItems = [mi]
```

The text field subclass has a property, `self.list`, which has been set to a dictionary whose keys are state name abbreviations and whose values are the corresponding state names. A utility function looks up an abbreviation in the dictionary:

```
func state(for abbrev:String) -> String? {
    return self.list[abbrev.uppercased()]
}
```

We implement `canPerformAction(_:withSender:)` to govern the contents of the menu. Let's presume that we want our Expand menu item to be present only if the selection consists of a two-letter state abbreviation. UITextField conforms to the UITextInput protocol, which lets us learn the selected text:

```
override func canPerformAction(_ action: Selector,
    withSender sender: Any?) -> Bool {
        if action == #selector(expand) {
            if let r = self.selectedTextRange, let s = self.text(in:r) {
                return (s.count == 2 && self.state(for:s) != nil)
            }
        }
        return super.canPerformAction(action, withSender:sender)
}
```

When the user chooses the Expand menu item, the `expand` message is sent up the responder chain. We catch it in our UITextField subclass and obey it by replacing the selected text with the corresponding state name:

```
@objc func expand(_ sender: Any) {
    if let r = self.selectedTextRange, let s = self.text(in:r) {
        if let ss = self.state(for:s) {
            self.replace(r, withText:ss)
        }
    }
}
```

We can also implement the selector for, and modify the behavior of, any of the standard menu items. Here, I'll implement `copy(_:)` and modify its behavior. First we call `super` to get standard copying behavior; then we modify what's now on the pasteboard:

```
override func copy(_ sender: Any?) {
    super.copy(sender)
    let pb = UIPasteboard.general
    if let s = pb.string {
        let ss = // ... alter s here ...
        pb.string = ss
    }
}
```

Drag and Drop

A text field implements drag and drop (Chapter 9) by way of the UITextDraggable and UITextDroppable protocols. By default, a text field's text is draggable (even on iPhone, new in iOS 13), but you can set the `isEnabled` property of its `textDrag-Interaction` to change that. If a text field's text is draggable, then by default its dragged text can be dropped within the same text field.

To customize a text field's drag and drop behavior, provide a `textDragDelegate` (UITextDragDelegate) or `textDropDelegate` (UITextDropDelegate) and implement any of their various methods. You can change the drag preview, change the drag items, and so forth. To turn a text field's droppability on or off depending on some condition, give it a `textDropDelegate` and implement `textDroppable-View(_:proposalForDrop:)` to return an appropriate UITextDropProposal.

Keyboard and Input Configuration

There are various ways to configure the virtual keyboard that appears when a text field becomes first responder. This configuration is performed through properties, not of the keyboard, but of the text field.

Text input traits

A UITextField adopts the UITextInputTraits protocol. This protocol's properties customize physical features and behaviors of the keyboard, as well as the text field's response to input (and these properties can also be set in the nib editor):

- Set the `keyboardType` to choose one of many alternate built-in keyboard layouts. For instance, set it to `.numberPad` to make the virtual keyboard for this text field consist of digits.

  Setting the keyboard type does *not* prevent the user from entering certain characters into this text field. On an iPhone, even with a `.numberPad` keyboard type, the user can paste letters or type them with an external keyboard; on an iPad, the user can switch the `.numberPad` keyboard to show letters. To limit what characters can be entered into a text field, use the `textField(_:shouldChange-CharactersIn:replacementString:)` delegate method that I described earlier.

- Set the `returnKeyType` to determine the text of the Return key (if the keyboard is of a type that has one).

- Give the keyboard a dark or light shade (`keyboardAppearance`).

- Turn off autocapitalization or autocorrection (`autocapitalizationType`, `autocorrectionType`).

- Use or don't use smart quotes, smart dashes, and smart spaces during insertion and deletion (`smartQuotesType`, `smartDashesType`, `smartInsertDeleteType`).

- Make the Return key disable itself if the text field has no content (`enablesReturn-KeyAutomatically`).

- Make the text field a password field (`secureTextEntry`).

- Set the `textContentType` to assist the system in making semantically appropriate spelling and autofill suggestions.

Accessory view

You can attach an accessory view to the top of the keyboard by setting the text field's `inputAccessoryView`. For instance, an accessory view containing a button can serve as a way to let the user dismiss keyboards whose type has no Return key, such as `.numberPad`, `.phonePad`, and `.decimalPad`.

Figure 10-13 shows a `.phonePad` keyboard. It has no Return key, so we've added a Done button in its accessory view. The accessory view itself is designed in a view *.xib* file. We (the view controller) are the text field's delegate; when the text field becomes first responder, we configure the keyboard:

```
func textFieldDidBeginEditing(_ tf: UITextField) {
    self.currentField = tf // keep track of first responder
    let arr =
        UINib(nibName:"AccessoryView", bundle:nil).instantiate(withOwner:nil)
    let accessoryView = arr[0] as! UIView
    let b = accessoryView.subviews[0] as! UIButton
    b.addTarget(self, action:#selector(doNextButton), for:.touchUpInside)
    let b2 = accessoryView.subviews[1] as! UIButton
```

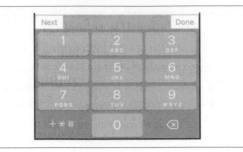

Figure 10-13. A phonePad keyboard with an accessory view

```
    b2.addTarget(self, action:#selector(doDone), for:.touchUpInside)
    tf.inputAccessoryView = accessoryView
    tf.keyboardAppearance = .dark
    tf.keyboardType = .phonePad
}
```

When the Done button is tapped, we dismiss the keyboard:

```
@objc func doDone(_ sender: Any) {
    self.currentField = nil
    self.view.endEditing(false)
}
```

The Next button lets the user navigate to the next text field. I have an array property (`self.textFields`) populated with references to all the text fields in the interface. My `textFieldDidBeginEditing` implementation stores a reference to the current text field in a property (`self.currentField`), because in order to determine the *next* text field, I need to know which one is *this* text field:

```
@objc func doNextButton(_ sender: Any) {
    var ix = self.textFields.firstIndex(of:self.currentField)!
    ix = (ix + 1) % self.textFields.count
    let v = self.textFields[ix]
    v.becomeFirstResponder()
}
```

Input view

Going even further, you can replace the system keyboard entirely with a view of your own creation. This is done by setting the text field's `inputView`. For best results, the custom view should be a UIInputView, and ideally it should be the `inputView` (and `view`) of a UIInputViewController. The input view controller needs to be retained, but not as a child view controller in the view controller hierarchy; the keyboard is not one of your app's views, but is layered by the system in front of your app. The input view's contents might imitate a standard system keyboard, or may consist of any interface you like.

An input view controller, used in this way, is also the key to supplying *other* apps with a keyboard. See the "Custom Keyboard" chapter of Apple's *App Extension Programming Guide* in the documentation archive.

To illustrate, I'll implement a standard beginner example: I'll replace a text field's keyboard with a UIPickerView. Here's the input view controller, MyPickerVC. Its viewDidLoad puts the UIPickerView into the inputView and positions it with auto-layout constraints:

```
class MyPickerVC : UIInputViewController {
    override func viewDidLoad() {
        let iv = self.inputView!
        iv.translatesAutoresizingMaskIntoConstraints = false
        let p = UIPickerView()
        p.delegate = self
        p.dataSource = self
        iv.addSubview(p)
        p.translatesAutoresizingMaskIntoConstraints = false
        NSLayoutConstraint.activate([
            p.topAnchor.constraint(equalTo: iv.topAnchor),
            p.bottomAnchor.constraint(equalTo: iv.bottomAnchor),
            p.leadingAnchor.constraint(equalTo: iv.leadingAnchor),
            p.trailingAnchor.constraint(equalTo: iv.trailingAnchor),
        ])
    }
}
extension MyPickerVC : UIPickerViewDelegate, UIPickerViewDataSource {
    // ...
}
```

The text field itself is configured in our main view controller:

```
class ViewController: UIViewController {
    @IBOutlet weak var tf: UITextField!
    let pvc = MyPickerVC()
    override func viewDidLoad() {
        super.viewDidLoad()
        self.tf.inputView = self.pvc.inputView
    }
}
```

It is also possible to use an input view controller to manage a text field's inputAccessoryView. To do that, you set the text field's inputAccessoryViewController instead of its inputAccessoryView. To do *that*, you have to subclass UITextField to give it a writable inputAccessoryViewController (because this property, as inherited from UIResponder, is read-only):

```
class MyTextField : UITextField {
    var _iavc : UIInputViewController?
    override var inputAccessoryViewController: UIInputViewController? {
        get {
            return self._iavc
```

```
        }
        set {
            self._iavc = newValue
        }
    }
}
```

Let's use that feature to give the user a way to dismiss the "keyboard" consisting entirely of a UIPickerView. We'll attach a Done button as the text field's accessory input view and manage it with another input view controller, MyDoneButtonVC. I'll configure the button much as I configured the picker view, by putting it into the input view controller's inputView:

```
class MyDoneButtonVC : UIInputViewController {
    weak var delegate : UIViewController?
    override func viewDidLoad() {
        let iv = self.inputView!
        iv.translatesAutoresizingMaskIntoConstraints = false
        iv.allowsSelfSizing = true // crucial
        let b = UIButton(type: .system)
        b.tintColor = .black
        b.setTitle("Done", for: .normal)
        b.sizeToFit()
        b.addTarget(self, action: #selector(doDone), for: .touchUpInside)
        b.backgroundColor = UIColor.lightGray
        iv.addSubview(b)
        b.translatesAutoresizingMaskIntoConstraints = false
        NSLayoutConstraint.activate([
            b.topAnchor.constraint(equalTo: iv.topAnchor),
            b.bottomAnchor.constraint(equalTo: iv.bottomAnchor),
            b.leadingAnchor.constraint(equalTo: iv.leadingAnchor),
            b.trailingAnchor.constraint(equalTo: iv.trailingAnchor),
        ])
    }
    @objc func doDone() {
        if let del = self.delegate {
            (del as AnyObject).doDone?()
        }
    }
}
```

Now our main view controller configures the text field like this:

```
class ViewController: UIViewController {
    @IBOutlet weak var tf: UITextField!
    let pvc = MyPickerVC()
    let mdbvc = MyDoneButtonVC()
    override func viewDidLoad() {
        super.viewDidLoad()
        self.tf.inputView = self.pvc.inputView
```

```
            (self.tf as! MyTextField).inputAccessoryViewController = self.mdbvc
            self.mdbvc.delegate = self
        }
    }
```

When the Done button is tapped, MyDoneButtonVC's doDone method is called. It, in turn, calls the doDone method of its delegate, if there is one. Its delegate is our original ViewController, which can implement doDone to set the text of the text field and dismiss the keyboard.

An important advantage of using an input view controller is that it is a view controller. Despite not being part of the app's view controller hierarchy, it is sent standard view controller messages such as viewDidLayoutSubviews and traitCollectionDidChange, allowing you to respond coherently to rotation and other changes.

Input view without a text field

With only a slight modification, you can use the techniques described in the preceding section to present a custom input view to the user *without* the user editing any text field. Suppose we have a label in our interface; we can allow the user to tap a button to summon our custom input view and use that input to change the text of the label. (See Figure 10-14; as usual, my example revolves around letting the user specify one of the Pep Boys.)

The trick here is that the relevant UITextField properties and methods are all inherited from UIResponder — and a UIViewController is a UIResponder. All we have to do is override our view controller's canBecomeFirstResponder to return true, and then call its becomeFirstResponder — just like a text field. If the view controller has overridden inputView, our custom input view will appear as the virtual keyboard. If the view controller has overridden inputAccessoryView or inputAccessoryViewController, the accessory view will be attached to that keyboard.

Here's an implementation of that scenario. Normally, our view controller's canBecomeFirstResponder returns false, so that the input view won't appear. But when the user taps the button in our interface, we switch to returning true and call becomeFirstResponder. Presto, the input view appears along with the accessory view, because we've also overridden inputView and inputAccessoryViewController. When the user taps the Done button in the accessory view, we update the label and dismiss the keyboard:

```
    class ViewController: UIViewController {
        @IBOutlet weak var lab: UILabel!
        let pvc = MyPickerVC()
        let mdbvc = MyDoneButtonVC()
        override func viewDidLoad() {
            super.viewDidLoad()
            self.mdbvc.delegate = self // for dismissal
```

Figure 10-14. Editing a label with a custom input view

```
    }
    var showKeyboard = false
    override var canBecomeFirstResponder: Bool {
        return showKeyboard
    }
    override var inputView: UIView? {
        return self.pvc.inputView
    }
    override var inputAccessoryViewController: UIInputViewController? {
        return self.mdbvc
    }
    @IBAction func doPickBoy(_ sender: Any) { // button in the interface
        self.showKeyboard = true
        self.becomeFirstResponder()
    }
    @objc func doDone() { // user tapped Done button in accessory view
        self.lab.text = pvc.currentPep // update label
        self.resignFirstResponder() // dismiss keyboard
        self.showKeyboard = false
    }
}
```

Shortcuts bar

On the iPad, the shortcuts bar appears along with spelling suggestions at the top of the keyboard. You can customize it by adding bar button items.

The shortcuts bar is the text field's `inputAssistantItem` (inherited from UIResponder), and it has `leadingBarButtonGroups` and `trailingBarButtonGroups`. A button group is a UIBarButtonItemGroup, an array of UIBarButtonItems along with an optional `representativeItem` to be shown if there isn't room for the whole array; if the representative item has no target–action pair, tapping it will summon a popover containing the actual group.

In this example, we add a Camera bar button item to the right (trailing) side of the shortcuts bar for our text field (`self.tf`):

```
let bbi = UIBarButtonItem(
    barButtonSystemItem: .camera, target: self, action: #selector(doCamera))
let group = UIBarButtonItemGroup(
    barButtonItems: [bbi], representativeItem: nil)
let shortcuts = self.tf.inputAssistantItem
shortcuts.trailingBarButtonGroups.append(group)
```

Keyboard language

Suppose your app performs a Russian dictionary lookup. It would be nice to be able to force the keyboard to appear as Russian in conjunction with your text field. But you can't. You can't access the Russian keyboard unless the user has explicitly enabled it; and even if the user *has* explicitly enabled it, your text field can only express a preference as to the language in which the keyboard initially appears. To do so, override your view controller's `textInputMode` property along these lines:

```
override var textInputMode: UITextInputMode? {
    for tim in UITextInputMode.activeInputModes {
        if tim.primaryLanguage == "ru-RU" {
            return tim
        }
    }
    return super.textInputMode
}
```

Another keyboard language–related property is `textInputContextIdentifier`. You can use this to ensure that the runtime remembers the language to which the keyboard was set the last time each text field was edited. To do so, override `textInput-ContextIdentifier` in your view controller as a computed variable whose getter fetches the value of a stored variable, and set that stored variable to some appropriate unique value whenever the editing context changes, whatever that may mean for your app.

Text Views

A text view (UITextView) is a scroll view subclass (UIScrollView); it is *not* a control. It displays multiline text, possibly scrollable, possibly editable. Many of its properties are similar to those of a text field:

- A text view has `text`, `font`, `textColor`, and `textAlignment` properties.
- A text view has `attributedText`, `allowsEditingTextAttributes`, and `typing-Attributes` properties, as well as `clearsOnInsertion`.

- An editable text view governs its keyboard just as a text field does: when it is first responder, it is being edited and shows the keyboard, and it adopts the UIText-Input protocol and has `inputView` and `inputAccessoryView` properties.

- A text view's menu works the same way as a text field's.

- A text view implements drag and drop similarly to a text field.

A text view can be editable or not, according to its `isEditable` property. You can do things with a noneditable text view that you can't do otherwise, as I'll explain later. A text field can be selectable without being editable, if its `isEditable` property is `false` but its `isSelectable` property is `true`; in that case, the user can select text and copy it.

A text view is a scroll view, so everything you know about scroll views applies (see Chapter 7). It can be scrollable (by the user) or not. Its `contentSize` is maintained for you automatically as the text changes, so as to contain the text exactly; if the text view is scrollable, the user can see any of its text. The text view's delegate (UITextView-Delegate) is its scroll view delegate (UIScrollViewDelegate). A text view has a `scroll-RangeToVisible(_:)` method so that you can scroll in terms of a range of its text.

A text view provides information about, and control of, its selection: it has a `selectedRange` property which you can get and set.

A text view's delegate messages (UITextViewDelegate) and notifications are similar to those of a text field. The following delegate methods and notifications should have a familiar ring:

- `textViewShouldBeginEditing(_:)`

- `textViewDidBeginEditing(_:)`
  `UITextView.textDidBeginEditingNotification`

- `textViewShouldEndEditing(_:)`

- `textViewDidEndEditing(_:)`
  `UITextView.textDidEndEditingNotification`

- `textView(_:shouldChangeTextIn:replacementText:)`

- `textViewDidChange(_:)`
  `UITextView.textDidChangeNotification`

Links, Text Attachments, and Data

A link is a stretch of attributed text to which the `.link` attribute has been applied. The default appearance of links in a text view is determined by the text view's `link-TextAttributes`. By default, this is a bluish color with no underline, but you can change it. Alternatively, you can apply any desired attributes to the individual links in the text view's `attributedText`; in that case, set the text view's `linkTextAttributes` to an empty dictionary to prevent it from overriding the individual link attributes.

The user can tap on a link, or on a text attachment, if the text view is selectable but not editable. The text view's delegate can then decide how to respond to the tap:

`textView(_:shouldInteractWith:in:interaction:)`
> The third parameter is a range. The last parameter tells you what the user is doing (UITextItemInteraction):
>
> - `.invokeDefaultAction` means tap.
> - `.presentActions` means long press.
> - `.preview` means 3D touch, but (new in iOS 13) it won't occur.
>
> This method comes in two forms:
>
> *The second parameter is a URL*
> > The user is interacting with a link. The default is `true`.
>
> *The second parameter is an NSTextAttachment*
> > The user is interacting with an inline image. The default is `false`.

Return `true` to get a default response. By returning `false`, you can substitute your own response, effectively treating the link or image as a button. Default responses when the second parameter is a URL are:

`.invokeDefaultAction`
> The URL is opened in Safari.

`.presentActions`
> A UIMenu (new in iOS 13) is presented, with menu items Open, Add to Reading List, Copy, and Share.

Default responses when the second parameter is a text attachment are:

`.invokeDefaultAction`
> Nothing happens.

`.presentActions`
> A UIMenu is presented, with menu items Copy Image and Save to Camera Roll.

A text view also has a `dataDetectorTypes` property; if the text view is selectable but not editable, this allows text of these types, specified as a UIDataDetectorTypes bitmask (and presumably located using NSDataDetector), to be treated as tappable links.

`textView(_:shouldInteractWith:in:interaction:)` will catch these taps as well; the second parameter will be a URL, but it won't necessarily be much use to you. You can distinguish a phone number through the URL's scheme (it will be "tel"), and the rest of the URL is the phone number; but other types will be more or less opaque (the scheme is "x-apple-data-detectors"). More important, you have the range, so you can obtain the tapped text. You can return true for the default response, or return false and substitute your own response. Some common UIDataDetectorTypes are:

.phoneNumber
    Default responses are:

    .invokeDefaultAction
        An alert is presented, with an option to call the number.

    .presentActions
        A UIMenu presented, with menu items Call, FaceTime, Send Message, Add to Contacts, and Copy.

.address
    Default responses are:

    .invokeDefaultAction
        The address is looked up in the Maps app.

    .presentActions
        A UIMenu is presented, with menu items Get Directions, Open in Maps, Add to Contacts, and Copy Address, and a preview displaying a map showing the address if possible.

.calendarEvent
    Default responses are:

    .invokeDefaultAction
        An action sheet is presented, with menu items Create Event, Create Reminder, Show in Calendar, and Copy Event.

    .presentActions
        A UIMenu is presented, with the same menu items as the default action, along with a preview showing the relevant time in the user's Calendar.

(There are three more data detector types: .shipmentTrackingNumber, .flightNumber, and .lookupSuggestion.)

 In my tests, returning false from your textView(_:shouldInteractWith:in:interaction:) implementation does not always prevent the default response in iOS 13. I regard this as a bug.

Self-Sizing Text View

On some occasions, you may want a *self-sizing* text view — that is, a text view that adjusts its height automatically to embrace the amount of text it contains.

The simplest approach, under autolayout, is to prevent the text view from scrolling by setting its `isScrollEnabled` to `false`. The text view now has an intrinsic content size and will behave just like a label ("Fitting Label and Text" on page 645). Pin the top and sides of the text view, and the bottom will shift automatically to accommodate the content as the user types. In effect, you've made a cross between a label (there are multiple lines and the height adjusts to fit the text) and a text field (the user can edit).

To put a limit on how tall a self-sizing text view can grow, keep track of the height of its `contentSize` (perhaps in `viewDidLayoutSubviews`) and, if it gets too big, set the text view's `isScrollEnabled` to `true` and constrain its height.

Text View and Keyboard

The fact that a text view is a scroll view comes in handy when the keyboard partially covers a text view. The text view usually dominates the screen, and you can respond to the keyboard partially covering it by adjusting the text view's `contentInset` and `scrollIndicatorInsets`, exactly as we did earlier in this chapter with a scroll view containing a text field ("Keyboard Covers Text Field" on page 651). There is no need to worry about the text view's `contentOffset`; the text view will scroll as needed to reveal the insertion point as the keyboard shows, and will scroll itself correctly as the keyboard hides.

How is the keyboard to be dismissed? The Return key is meaningful for character entry, so you won't want to use it to dismiss the keyboard. On the iPad, there is usually a separate button in the keyboard that dismisses the keyboard, solving the problem; on the iPhone there might be no such button.

On the iPhone, the interface might consist of a text view and the keyboard, which is *always* showing. Instead of dismissing the keyboard, the user dismisses the entire interface. In Apple's Mail app on the iPhone, when the user is composing a message, the keyboard is present; if the user taps Cancel or Send, the mail composition interface is dismissed and so is the keyboard.

Alternatively, you can provide interface for dismissing the keyboard explicitly. In Apple's Notes app, when a note is being edited, the keyboard is present and a Done button appears; the user taps the Done button to dismiss the keyboard. If there's no good place to put a Done button in the interface, you could attach an accessory view to the keyboard itself, as I did in an earlier example.

Also, being a scroll view, a text view has a `keyboardDismissMode`. By setting this to `.interactive` or `.onDrag`, you can permit the user to hide the keyboard by scrolling or dragging. Apple does that in both the Mail app and the Notes app.

Text Kit

Text Kit comes originally from macOS, where you may already be more familiar with it than you realize. Much of the text-editing "magic" of Xcode itself is due to Text Kit; and the TextEdit app is just a thin wrapper around Text Kit. Text Kit comprises a small group of classes that are responsible for drawing text; simply put, they turn an NSAttributedString into graphics. You can take advantage of Text Kit to modify text drawing in ways that were once possible only by dipping down to the low-level C-based world of Core Text.

Text Kit has three chief classes: NSTextStorage, NSLayoutManager, and NSTextContainer. Instances of these three classes join to form a "stack" of objects that allow Text Kit to operate. In the minimal and most common case, a text storage has a layout manager, and a layout manager has a text container, forming the "stack."

Here's what the three chief Text Kit classes do:

NSTextStorage
> A subclass of NSMutableAttributedString. It is, or holds, the underlying text. It has one or more layout managers, and notifies them when the text changes.
>
> By subclassing and delegation (NSTextStorageDelegate), a text storage's behavior can be modified so that it applies attributes in a custom fashion.

NSLayoutManager
> This is the master text drawing class. It has one or more text containers, and is owned by a text storage. It draws the text storage's text into the boundaries defined by the text container(s).
>
> A layout manager can have a delegate (NSLayoutManagerDelegate), and can be subclassed. This, as you may well imagine, is a powerful and sophisticated class.

NSTextContainer
> Owned by a layout manager; helps that layout manager by defining the region in which the text is to be laid out. It does this in three primary ways:
>
> *Size*
>> The text container's top left is the origin for the text layout coordinate system, and the text will be laid out within the text container's rectangle.

Exclusion paths
> The exclusionPaths property consists of UIBezierPath objects within which no text is to be drawn.

Subclassing
> By subclassing, you can place each chunk of text drawing anywhere at all (except inside an exclusion path).

Text View and Text Kit

A UITextView provides direct access to the underlying Text Kit engine. It has the following Text Kit–related properties:

textContainer
> The text view's text container (an NSTextContainer instance). UITextView's designated initializer is init(frame:textContainer:); the textContainer: can be nil to get a default text container, or you can supply your own custom text container.

textContainerInset
> The margins of the text container, designating the area within the contentSize rectangle in which the text as a whole is drawn. Changing this value changes the margins immediately, causing the text to be freshly laid out. The default is a top and bottom of 8.

layoutManager
> The text view's layout manager (an NSLayoutManager instance).

textStorage
> The text view's text storage (an NSTextStorage instance).

When you initialize a text view with a custom text container, you hand it the entire "stack" of Text Kit instances, the stack is retained, and the text view is operative. The simplest case might look like this:

```
let r = // ... frame for the new text view
let lm = NSLayoutManager()
let ts = NSTextStorage()
ts.addLayoutManager(lm)
let tc = NSTextContainer(size:CGSize(r.width, .greatestFiniteMagnitude))
lm.addTextContainer(tc)
let tv = UITextView(frame:r, textContainer:tc)
```

Text Container

An NSTextContainer has a size, within which the text will be drawn.

In a text view, by default, the text container's width is the width of the text view, while its height is effectively infinite, allowing the drawing of the text to grow vertically but not horizontally beyond the bounds of the text view, and making it possible to scroll the text vertically.

NSTextContainer also has `heightTracksTextView` and `widthTracksTextView` properties, causing the text container to be resized to match changes in the size of the text view — if the text view is resized because of interface rotation, for instance. By default, as you might expect, `widthTracksTextView` is `true`, while `heightTracksText-View` is `false`: the text fills the width of the text view, and is laid out freshly if the text view's width changes, but its height remains effectively infinite. The text view itself configures its own `contentSize` so that the user can scroll just to the bottom of the existing text.

When you change a text view's `textContainerInset`, it modifies its text container's size as necessary. In the default configuration, this means that it modifies the text container's width; the top and bottom insets are implemented through the text container's position within the content rect. Within the text container, additional side margins are imposed by the text container's `lineFragmentPadding`; the default is 5, but you can change it.

If the text view's `isScrollEnabled` is `false`, then by default its text container's `heightTracksTextView` and `widthTracksTextView` are both `true`, and the text container size is adjusted so that the text fills the text view. In that case, you can also set the text container's `lineBreakMode`. This works like the line break mode of a UILabel: for instance, if the line break mode is `.byTruncatingTail`, then the last line has an ellipsis at the end (if the text is too long for the text view). You can also set the text container's `maximumNumberOfLines`, which is like a UILabel's `numberOfLines`. In effect, you've turned the text view into a label!

But a nonscrolling text view isn't *just* a label, because you've got access to the Text Kit stack that backs it. For example, you can apply exclusion paths to the text container. Figure 10-15 shows a case in point. The text wraps in longer and longer lines, and then in shorter and shorter lines, because there's an exclusion path on the right side of the text container that's a rectangle with a large V-shaped indentation.

In Figure 10-15, the text view (`self.tv`) is initially configured in the view controller's `viewDidLoad`:

```
self.tv.attributedText = // ...
self.tv.textContainerInset =
    UIEdgeInsets(top: 20, left: 20, bottom: 20, right: 0)
self.tv.isScrollEnabled = false
```

The exclusion path is then drawn and applied in `viewDidLayoutSubviews`:

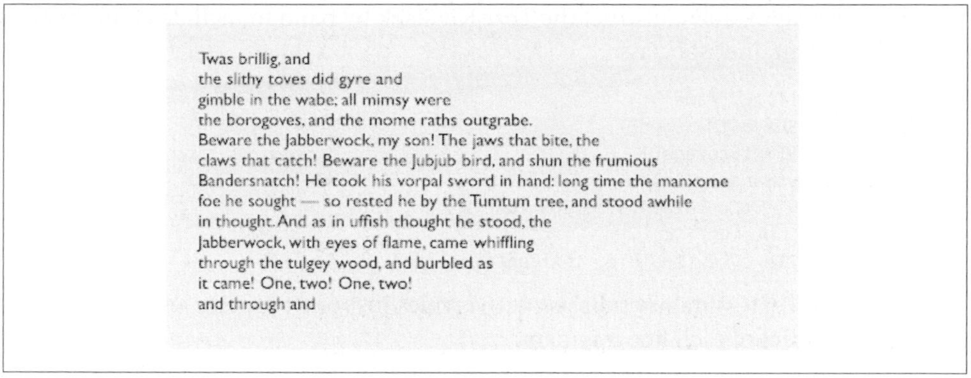

Figure 10-15. A text view with an exclusion path

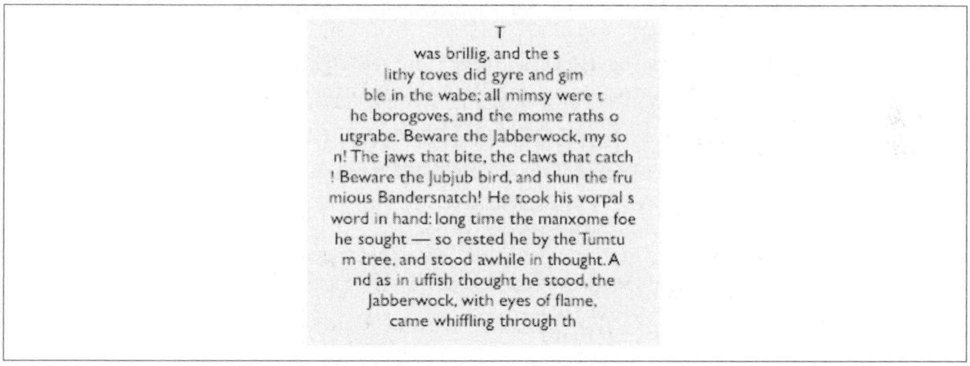

Figure 10-16. A text view with a subclassed text container

```
override func viewDidLayoutSubviews() {
    let sz = self.tv.textContainer.size
    let p = UIBezierPath()
    p.move(to: CGPoint(sz.width/4.0,0))
    p.addLine(to: CGPoint(sz.width,0))
    p.addLine(to: CGPoint(sz.width,sz.height))
    p.addLine(to: CGPoint(sz.width/4.0,sz.height))
    p.addLine(to: CGPoint(sz.width,sz.height/2.0))
    p.close()
    self.tv.textContainer.exclusionPaths = [p]
}
```

You can also subclass NSTextContainer to modify the rectangle in which the layout manager wants to position a piece of text. (Each piece of text is actually a line fragment; I'll explain in the next section what a line fragment is.) In Figure 10-16, the text is inside a circle.

To achieve the layout shown in Figure 10-16, I set the attributed string's line break mode to .byCharWrapping (to bring the right edge of each line as close as possible to the circular shape), and construct the Text Kit stack by hand to include an instance of my NSTextContainer subclass:

```
let r = self.tv.frame
let lm = NSLayoutManager()
let ts = NSTextStorage()
ts.addLayoutManager(lm)
let tc = MyTextContainer(size:CGSize(r.width, r.height))
lm.addTextContainer(tc)
let tv = UITextView(frame:r, textContainer:tc)
```

Here's my NSTextContainer subclass; it overrides just one property and one method, to dictate the rect of each line fragment:

```
class MyTextContainer : NSTextContainer {
    override var isSimpleRectangularTextContainer : Bool { return false }
    override func lineFragmentRect(forProposedRect proposedRect: CGRect,
        at characterIndex: Int,
        writingDirection baseWritingDirection: NSWritingDirection,
        remaining remainingRect: UnsafeMutablePointer<CGRect>?) -> CGRect {
            var result = super.lineFragmentRect(
                forProposedRect:proposedRect, at:characterIndex,
                writingDirection:baseWritingDirection,
                remaining:remainingRect)
            let r = self.size.height / 2.0
            // convert initial y so that circle is centered at origin
            let y = r - result.origin.y
            let theta = asin(y/r)
            let x = r * cos(theta)
            // convert resulting x from circle centered at origin
            let offset = self.size.width / 2.0 - r
            result.origin.x = r-x+offset
            result.size.width = 2*x
            return result
    }
}
```

Alternative Text Kit Stack Architectures

The default Text Kit stack consists of one text storage, which has one layout manager, which has one text container. But a text storage can have multiple layout managers, and a layout manager can have multiple text containers. What's that all about?

Multiple text containers

If one layout manager has multiple text containers, the overflow from each text container is drawn in the next one. In Figure 10-17, there are two text views; the text has filled the first text view, and has then continued by flowing into and filling the second text view. As far as I can tell, the text views can't be made editable in this

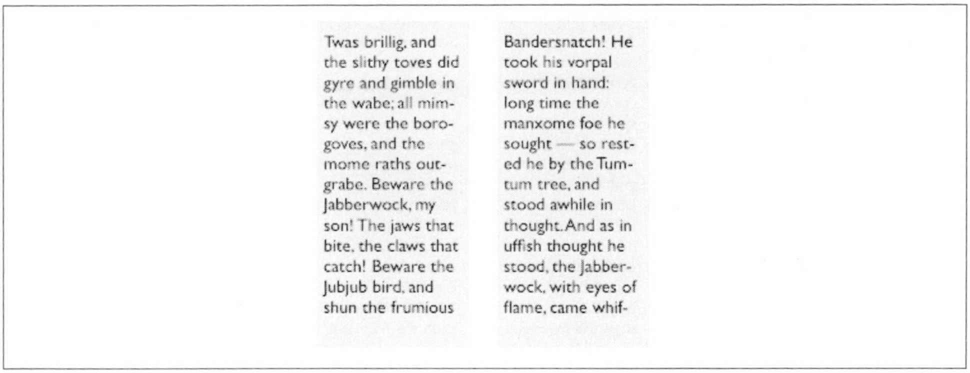

Figure 10-17. A layout manager with two text containers

configuration; but clearly this is a way to achieve a multicolumn or multipage layout, or you could use text views of different sizes for a magazine-style layout.

It is possible to achieve that arrangement by disconnecting the layout managers of existing text views from their text containers and rebuilding the stack from below. In this example, though, I'll build the entire stack by hand:

```
let r = // frame
let r2 = // frame
let mas = // content
let ts1 = NSTextStorage(attributedString:mas)
let lm1 = NSLayoutManager()
ts1.addLayoutManager(lm1)
let tc1 = NSTextContainer(size:r.size)
lm1.addTextContainer(tc1)
let tv = UITextView(frame:r, textContainer:tc1)
let tc2 = NSTextContainer(size:r2.size)
lm1.addTextContainer(tc2)
let tv2 = UITextView(frame:r2, textContainer:tc2)
```

Multiple layout managers

If one text storage has multiple layout managers, then each layout manager is laying out the same text. In Figure 10-18, there are two text views displaying the same text. The remarkable thing is that if you edit one text view, the other changes to match. (That's how Xcode lets you edit the same code file in different windows, tabs, or panes.)

Again, this arrangement is probably best achieved by building the entire text stack by hand:

```
let r = // frame
let r2 = // frame
let mas = // content
let ts1 = NSTextStorage(attributedString:mas)
```

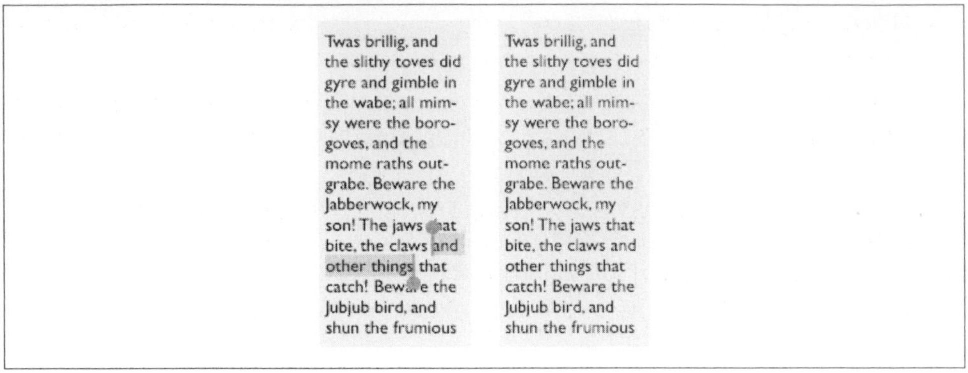

Figure 10-18. A text storage with two layout managers

```
let lm1 = NSLayoutManager()
ts1.addLayoutManager(lm1)
let lm2 = NSLayoutManager()
ts1.addLayoutManager(lm2)
let tc1 = NSTextContainer(size:r.size)
let tc2 = NSTextContainer(size:r2.size)
lm1.addTextContainer(tc1)
lm2.addTextContainer(tc2)
let tv = UITextView(frame:r, textContainer:tc1)
let tv2 = UITextView(frame:r2, textContainer:tc2)
```

Layout Manager

The first thing to know about a layout manager is the geometry in which it thinks. To envision a layout manager's geometrical world, think in terms of glyphs and line fragments:

Glyph
> The drawn analog of a character. The correspondence is not one-to-one; multiple glyphs can correspond to one character, and multiple characters can correspond to one glyph. The layout manager's job is to translate the characters into glyphs, get those glyphs from a font, and draw them.

Line fragment
> A rectangle in which glyphs are drawn, one after another. (The reason it's a line *fragment*, and not simply a line, is that a line might be interrupted by the text container's exclusion paths.)

A glyph has a location in terms of the line fragment into which it is drawn. A line fragment's coordinates are in terms of the text container. The layout manager can convert between these coordinate systems, and between text and glyphs:

- Given a range of text in the text storage, the layout manager knows where the corresponding glyphs are drawn in the text container.

- Conversely, given a location in the text container, the layout manager knows what glyph is drawn there and what range of text in the text storage that glyph represents.

What's missing from that geometry is what, if anything, the text container corresponds to in the real world. A text container is not, itself, a real rectangle in the real world; it's just a class that tells the layout manager a size to draw into. Making that rectangle meaningful for drawing purposes is up to some *other* class outside the Text Kit stack.

A UITextView is a case in point. It has a text container, which it shares with a layout manager. The text view knows how its own content is scrolled and how the rectangle represented by its text container is inset within that scrolling content. The layout manager doesn't know anything about that; it sees the text container as a purely theoretical rectangular boundary. Only when the layout manager actually draws does it make contact with the real world of some graphics context — and it must be told, on those occasions, how the text container's rectangle is offset within that graphics context.

Layout geometry of a text view

Consider a text view scrolled so as to place some word at the top left of its visible bounds. I'll use the layout manager to learn what word it is.

I can ask the layout manager what character or glyph corresponds to a certain point in the text container, but what point should I ask about? Translating from the real world to text container coordinates is up to me; I must take into account both the scroll position of the text view's content and the inset of the text container within that content:

```
let off = self.tv.contentOffset
let top = self.tv.textContainerInset.top
let left = self.tv.textContainerInset.left
var tctopleft = CGPoint(off.x - left, off.y - top)
```

Now I'm speaking in text container coordinates, which are layout manager coordinates. One possibility is then to ask directly for the index (in the text storage's string) of the corresponding character:

```
let ixx = self.tv.layoutManager.characterIndex(for:tctopleft,
    in:self.tv.textContainer,
    fractionOfDistanceBetweenInsertionPoints:nil)
```

That, however, does not give quite the results one might intuitively expect. If *any* of a word is poking down from above into the visible area of the text view, that is the word whose first character is returned. I think we intuitively expect, if a word isn't fully visible, that the answer should be the word that starts the *next* line, which *is* fully visible. So I'll modify that code in a simpleminded way. I'll obtain the index of the *glyph* at my initial point; from this, I can derive the rect of the line fragment containing it. If that line fragment is not at least three-quarters visible, I'll add one line fragment height to the starting point and derive the glyph index again. Then I'll convert the glyph index to a character range:

```
var ix = self.tv.layoutManager.glyphIndex(for:tctopleft,
    in:self.tv.textContainer, fractionOfDistanceThroughGlyph:nil)
let frag = self.tv.layoutManager.lineFragmentRect(
    forGlyphAt:ix, effectiveRange:nil)
if tctopleft.y > frag.origin.y + 0.5*frag.size.height {
    tctopleft.y += frag.size.height
    ix = self.tv.layoutManager.glyphIndex(for:tctopleft,
        in:self.tv.textContainer, fractionOfDistanceThroughGlyph:nil)
}
let charRange = self.tv.layoutManager.characterRange(
    forGlyphRange: NSMakeRange(ix,0), actualGlyphRange:nil)
```

Finally, I'll use NLTokenizer (import NaturalLanguage) to get the range of the entire word to which this character belongs:

```
let tokenizer = NLTokenizer(unit: .word)
tokenizer.setLanguage(.english)
let text = self.tv.text!
tokenizer.string = text
let range = NSMakeRange(charRange.location, 100)
let words = tokenizer.tokens(for: Range(range, in:text)!)
if let word = words.first {
    print(text[word])
}
```

Clearly, the same sort of technique could be used to formulate a custom response to a tap — answering the question, "What word did the user just tap on?"

Layout manager drawing

By subclassing NSLayoutManager (and by implementing its delegate), many powerful effects can be achieved. As a simple example, I'll carry on from the preceding code by drawing a rectangular outline around the word we just located. To make this possible, I have an NSLayoutManager subclass, MyLayoutManager, an instance of which is built into the Text Kit stack for this text view. MyLayoutManager has a public NSRange property, wordRange. Having worked out what word I want to outline, I set the layout manager's wordRange and invalidate its drawing of that word, to force a redraw:

```
let range = NSRange(word, in:text)
let lm = self.tv.layoutManager as! MyLayoutManager
lm.wordRange = range
lm.invalidateDisplay(forCharacterRange:range)
```

In MyLayoutManager, I've overridden the method that draws the background behind glyphs, `drawBackground(forGlyphRange:at:)`. At the moment this method is called, there is already a graphics context, so all we have to do is draw.

First, I call `super`. Then, if the range of glyphs to be drawn includes the glyphs for the range of characters in `self.wordRange`, I ask for the rect of the bounding box of those glyphs, and stroke it to form the rectangle. As I mentioned earlier, the bounding box is in text container coordinates, but now we're drawing in the real world, so I have to compensate by offsetting the drawn rectangle by the same amount that the text container is supposed to be offset in the real world; fortunately, the text view tells us (through the `origin:` parameter) what that offset is:

```
override func drawBackground(forGlyphRange glyphsToShow: NSRange,
    at origin: CGPoint) {
        super.drawBackground(forGlyphRange:glyphsToShow, at:origin)
        if self.wordRange.length == 0 {
            return
        }
        var range = self.glyphRange(forCharacterRange:self.wordRange,
            actualCharacterRange:nil)
        range = NSIntersectionRange(glyphsToShow, range)
        if range.length == 0 {
            return
        }
        if let tc = self.textContainer(forGlyphAt:range.location,
            effectiveRange:nil, withoutAdditionalLayout:true) {
                var r = self.boundingRect(forGlyphRange:range, in:tc)
                r.origin.x += origin.x
                r.origin.y += origin.y
                let c = UIGraphicsGetCurrentContext()!
                c.saveGState()
                c.setStrokeColor(UIColor.black.cgColor)
                c.setLineWidth(1.0)
                c.stroke(r)
                c.restoreGState()
        }
}
```

Text Kit Without a Text View

UITextView is the only built-in iOS class that has a Text Kit stack to which you are given programmatic access. But that doesn't mean it's the only place where you can draw with Text Kit! You can draw with Text Kit *anywhere you can draw* — that is, in any graphics context (Chapter 2). When you do so, you should always call both `drawBackground(forGlyphRange:at:)` (the method I overrode in the previous example) and `drawGlyphs(forGlyphRange:at:)`, in that order. The `at:` argument is the point where you consider the text container's origin to be within the current graphics context.

To illustrate, I'll change the implementation of the StringDrawer class that I described earlier in this chapter. Previously, StringDrawer's draw(_:) implementation told the attributed string (`self.attributedText`) to draw itself:

```
override func draw(_ rect: CGRect) {
    let r = rect.offsetBy(dx: 0, dy: 2)
    let opts : NSStringDrawingOptions = .usesLineFragmentOrigin
    self.attributedText.draw(with:r, options: opts, context: context)
}
```

Instead, I'll construct the Text Kit stack and tell its layout manager to draw the text:

```
override func draw(_ rect: CGRect) {
    let lm = NSLayoutManager()
    let ts = NSTextStorage(attributedString:self.attributedText)
    ts.addLayoutManager(lm)
    let tc = NSTextContainer(size:rect.size)
    lm.addTextContainer(tc)
    tc.lineFragmentPadding = 0
    let r = lm.glyphRange(for:tc)
    lm.drawBackground(forGlyphRange:r, at:CGPoint(0,2))
    lm.drawGlyphs(forGlyphRange: r, at:CGPoint(0,2))
}
```

Building the entire Text Kit stack by hand may seem like overkill for that simple example, but imagine what *else* I could do now that I have access to the entire Text Kit stack! I can use properties, subclassing, delegation, and alternative stack architectures to achieve customizations and effects that, before Text Kit was migrated to iOS, were difficult or impossible to achieve without dipping down to the level of Core Text.

The two-column display of U.S. state names on the iPad shown in Figure 10-19 was a Core Text example in early editions of this book, requiring 50 or 60 lines of elaborate C code, complicated by the necessity of flipping the context to prevent the text from being drawn upside-down. Nowadays, it can be achieved easily through Text Kit — effectively just by reusing code from earlier examples in this chapter.

We can also make the display of state names interactive, with the name of the tapped state briefly outlined with a rectangle (Figure 10-20). When I implemented this using Core Text in earlier editions of the book, it was insanely difficult, not least because we had to keep track of all the line fragment rectangles ourselves. But it's easy with Text Kit, because the layout manager knows all the answers.

We have a UIView subclass, StyledText. In its layoutSubviews, it creates the Text Kit stack — a layout manager with two text containers, to achieve the two-column layout — and stores the whole stack, along with the rects at which the two text containers are to be drawn, in properties:

ALABAMA	MONTANA
ALASKA	NEBRASKA
ARIZONA	NEVADA
ARKANSAS	NEW HAMPSHIRE
CALIFORNIA	NEW JERSEY
COLORADO	NEW MEXICO
CONNECTICUT	NEW YORK
DELAWARE	NORTH CAROLINA
FLORIDA	NORTH DAKOTA
GEORGIA	OHIO
HAWAII	OKLAHOMA
IDAHO	OREGON
ILLINOIS	PENNSYLVANIA
INDIANA	RHODE ISLAND
IOWA	SOUTH CAROLINA
KANSAS	SOUTH DAKOTA
KENTUCKY	TENNESSEE
LOUISIANA	TEXAS
MAINE	UTAH
MARYLAND	VERMONT
MASSACHUSETTS	VIRGINIA
MICHIGAN	WASHINGTON
MINNESOTA	WEST VIRGINIA
MISSISSIPPI	WISCONSIN
MISSOURI	WYOMING

Figure 10-19. Two-column text in small caps

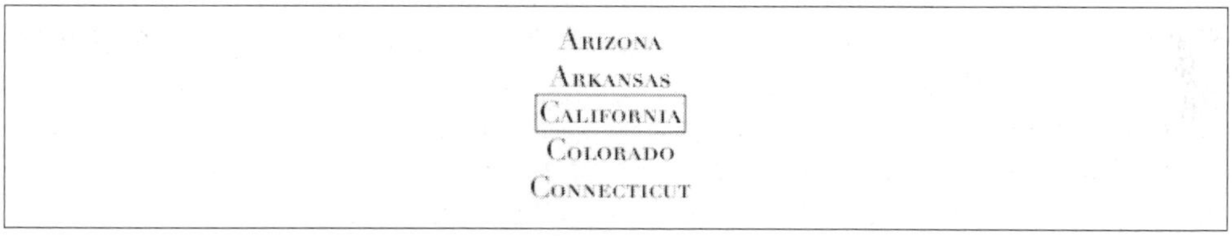

ARIZONA
ARKANSAS
CALIFORNIA
COLORADO
CONNECTICUT

Figure 10-20. The user has tapped on California

```
override func layoutSubviews() {
    super.layoutSubviews()
    var r1 = self.bounds
    r1.origin.y += 2 // a little top space
    r1.size.width /= 2.0 // column 1
    var r2 = r1
    r2.origin.x += r2.size.width // column 2
    let lm = MyLayoutManager()
    let ts = NSTextStorage(attributedString:self.text)
    ts.addLayoutManager(lm)
    let tc = NSTextContainer(size:r1.size)
    lm.addTextContainer(tc)
```

```
        let tc2 = NSTextContainer(size:r2.size)
        lm.addTextContainer(tc2)
        self.lm = lm; self.ts = ts; self.tc = tc; self.tc2 = tc2
        self.r1 = r1; self.r2 = r2
    }
```

Our `draw(_:)` is just like the previous example, except that we have two text containers to draw:

```
override func draw(_ rect: CGRect) {
    let range1 = self.lm.glyphRange(for:self.tc)
    self.lm.drawBackground(forGlyphRange:range1, at: self.r1.origin)
    self.lm.drawGlyphs(forGlyphRange:range1, at: self.r1.origin)
    let range2 = self.lm.glyphRange(for:self.tc2)
    self.lm.drawBackground(forGlyphRange:range2, at: self.r2.origin)
    self.lm.drawGlyphs(forGlyphRange:range2, at: self.r2.origin)
}
```

So much for drawing the text! We now have Figure 10-19.

On to Figure 10-20. When the user taps on our view, a tap gesture recognizer's action method is called. We are using the same layout manager subclass developed in the preceding section of this chapter: it draws a rectangle around the glyphs corresponding to the characters of its `wordRange` property. All we have to do in order to make the flashing rectangle around the tapped word is work out what that range is, set our layout manager's `wordRange` property and redraw ourselves, and then (after a short delay) set the `wordRange` property back to a zero range and redraw ourselves again to remove the rectangle.

We start by working out which column the user tapped in; this tells us which text container it is, and what the tapped point is in text container coordinates (`g` is the tap gesture recognizer):

```
var p = g.location(in:self)
var tc = self.tc!
if !self.r1.contains(p) {
    tc = self.tc2!
    p.x -= self.r1.size.width
}
```

Now we can ask the layout manager what glyph the user tapped on, and hence the whole range of glyphs within the line fragment the user tapped in. If the user tapped to the left of the first glyph or to the right of the last glyph, no word was tapped, and we return:

```
var f : CGFloat = 0
let ix =
    self.lm.glyphIndex(for:p, in:tc, fractionOfDistanceThroughGlyph:&f)
var glyphRange : NSRange = NSMakeRange(0,0)
self.lm.lineFragmentRect(forGlyphAt:ix, effectiveRange:&glyphRange)
if ix == glyphRange.location && f == 0.0 {
```

```
        return
    }
    if ix == glyphRange.location + glyphRange.length - 1 && f == 1.0 {
        return
    }
```

If the last glyph of the line fragment is a whitespace glyph, we don't want to include it in our rectangle, so we subtract it from the end of our range. Then we're ready to convert to a character range, and we can learn the name of the state that the user tapped on:

```
func lastCharIsControl () -> Bool {
    let lastCharRange = glyphRange.location + glyphRange.length - 1
    let property = self.lm.propertyForGlyph(at:lastCharRange)
    return property.contains(.controlCharacter)
}
while lastCharIsControl() {
    glyphRange.length -= 1
}
let characterRange =
    self.lm.characterRange(forGlyphRange:glyphRange, actualGlyphRange:nil)
let s = self.text.string
if let r = Range(characterRange, in:s) {
    let stateName = s[r]
    print("you tapped \(stateName)")
}
```

Finally, we flash the rectangle around the state name by setting and resetting the word-Range property of the subclassed layout manager:

```
let lm = self.lm as! MyLayoutManager
lm.wordRange = characterRange
self.setNeedsDisplay()
delay(0.3) {
    lm.wordRange = NSMakeRange(0, 0)
    self.setNeedsDisplay()
}
```

CHAPTER 11

Web Views

A web view is a web browser, which is a powerful thing: it knows how to fetch resources through the internet, and it can render HTML and CSS, and can respond to Java-Script. It is a network communication device, as well as an interactive layout, animation, and media display engine.

In a web view, links and other ancillary resources work automatically. If your web view's HTML refers to an image, the web view will fetch it and display it. If the user taps on a link, the web view will fetch that content and display it; if the link is to some sort of media (a sound or video file), the web view will allow the user to play it.

A web view can also display some other types of content commonly encountered as internet resources. It can display PDF files, as well as documents in such formats as *.rtf*, Microsoft Word (*.doc* and *.docx*), and Pages. (A Pages file that is actually a bundle must be compressed to form a single *.pages.zip* resource.)

 A web view should also be able to display *.rtfd* files, but this feature is not working properly; Apple suggests that you convert to an attributed string as I described in Chapter 10 (specifying a document type of NSRTFDTextDocument-Type), or use a QLPreviewController (Chapter 22).

The loading and rendering of a web view's content takes time, and may involve networking. Your app's interface, however, is not blocked or frozen while the content is loading. On the contrary, your interface remains accessible and operative. The web view, in fetching and rendering a web page and its linked components, is doing something quite complex, involving both threading and network interaction — I'll have a lot more to say about this in Chapters 23 and 24 — but it shields you from this complexity, and it operates in the background, off the main thread. Your own interaction with the web view stays on the main thread and is straightforward. You ask the web view to load some content; then you sit back and let it worry about the details.

iOS 9 introduced App Transport Security. Your app, by default, cannot load external URLs that are not secure (`https:`). You can turn off this restriction completely or in part in your *Info.plist*. See Chapter 23 for details.

WKWebView

WKWebView is part of the WebKit framework (`import WebKit`). The designated initializer is `init(frame:configuration:)`. The second parameter, `configuration:`, is a WKWebViewConfiguration. You can create a configuration beforehand:

```
let config = WKWebViewConfiguration()
// ... configure config here ...
let wv = WKWebView(frame: rect, configuration:config)
```

Alternatively, you can modify the web view's configuration later, through its `configuration` property. Either way, you'll probably want to perform configurations before the web view has a chance to load any content, because some settings will affect *how* it loads or renders that content. Here are some of the more important WKWebViewConfiguration properties:

`suppressesIncrementalRendering`
> If `true`, the web view's visible content doesn't change until all linked renderable resources (such as images) have finished loading. The default is `false`.

`allowsInlineMediaPlayback`
> If `true`, linked media are played inside the web page. The default is `false` (the fullscreen player is used).

`mediaTypesRequiringUserActionForPlayback`
> Types of media that *won't* start playing automatically, without a user gesture. A bitmask (WKAudiovisualMediaTypes) with possible values `.audio`, `.video`, and `.all`.

`allowsPictureInPictureMediaPlayback`
> See Chapter 15 for a discussion of picture-in-picture playback.

`dataDetectorTypes`
> Types of content that may be transformed automatically into tappable links. Similar to a text view's data detectors (Chapter 10).

`websiteDataStore`
> A WKWebsiteDataStore. By supplying a data store, you get control over stored resources. Its `httpCookieStore` is a WKHTTPCookieStore where you can examine, add, and remove cookies.

preferences

A WKPreferences object. This is a value class embodying four properties:

- `minimumFontSize`
- `javaScriptEnabled`
- `javaScriptCanOpenWindowsAutomatically`
- `isFraudulentWebsiteWarningEnabled` (new in iOS 13)

`userContentController`

A WKUserContentController object. This is how you can inject JavaScript into a web page and communicate between your code and the web page's content. I'll give an example later. Also, you can give the `userContentController` a rule list (WKContentRuleList) that filters the web view's content.

A WKWebView is not a scroll view, but it *has* a scroll view (`scrollView`). You can use this to scroll the web view's content programmatically and to respond as the scroll view's delegate when the user scrolls, plus you can get references to the scroll view's gesture recognizers and add gesture recognizers of your own.

You can take a snapshot of a web view's content by calling `take-Snapshot(with:completionHandler:)`. The snapshot image is passed into the completion function as a UIImage.

In the nib editor, the Objects library contains a WKWebView object that you can drag into your interface as you design it; you might need to link to the WebKit framework manually (in the app target's Link Binary With Libraries build phase) to prevent the app from crashing as the nib loads. Many WKWebViewConfiguration and WKPreferences properties can be configured in the nib editor as well.

Web View Content

You can supply a web view with content using one of four methods, depending on the content's type:

A URLRequest

Form a URLRequest from a URL and call `load(_:)`. The URLRequest initializer is `init(url:cachePolicy:timeoutInterval:)`, but the second and third parameters are optional and will often be omitted. Additional URLRequest configuration includes such properties as `allowsExpensiveNetworkAccess` (see Chapter 23):

```
let url = URL(string: "https://www.apple.com")!
let req = URLRequest(url: url)
// could set req.allowsExpensiveNetworkAccess here
self.wv.load(req)
```

A local file

Obtain a local file URL and call `loadFileURL(_:allowingReadAccessTo:)`. The second parameter effectively sandboxes the web view into a single file or directory. In this example from one of my apps, the HTML file *zotzhelp.html* refers to images in the same directory as itself:

```
let url = Bundle.main.url(
    forResource: "zotzhelp", withExtension: "html")!
view.loadFileURL(url, allowingReadAccessTo: url)
```

An HTML string

Prepare a string consisting of valid HTML, and call `loadHTMLString(_:base-URL:)`. The `baseURL:` specifies how partial URLs in your HTML are to be resolved (as when the HTML refers to resources in your app bundle). Starting with an HTML string is useful particularly when you want to construct your HTML programmatically or make changes to it before handing it to the web view. In this example from the TidBITS News app, my HTML consists of two strings: a wrapper with the usual `<html>` tags, and the body content derived from an RSS feed. I assemble them and hand the resulting string to my web view for display:

```
let templatepath = Bundle.main.path(
    forResource: "htmlTemplate", ofType:"txt")!
let base = URL(fileURLWithPath:templatepath)
var s = try! String(contentsOfFile:templatepath)
let ss = // actual body content for this page
s = s.replacingOccurrences(of:"<content>", with:ss)
self.wv.loadHTMLString(s, baseURL:base)
```

A Data object

Call `load(_:MIMEType:characterEncodingName:baseURL:)`. This is useful particularly when the content has itself arrived from the network, as the parameters correspond to the properties of a URLResponse. This example will be more meaningful to you after you've read Chapter 23:

```
let sess = URLSession.shared
let url = URL(string:"https://www.someplace.net/someImage.jpg")!
let task = sess.dataTask(with: url) { data, response, err in
    if let response = response,
        let mime = response.mimeType,
        let enc = response.textEncodingName,
        let data = data {
            self.wv.load(data, mimeType: mime,
                characterEncodingName: enc, baseURL: url)
    }
}
```

All four methods return a WKNavigation object, but I ignored it in my examples. If you like, you can capture it to identify an individual page-loading operation, as I'll explain later.

Tracking Changes in a Web View

A WKWebView has properties that can be tracked with key–value observing, such as:

- isLoading
- estimatedProgress
- url
- title

You can observe these properties to be notified as a web page loads or changes.

To illustrate, I'll give the user feedback while a page is loading by displaying an activity indicator (Chapter 12). I'll start by putting the activity indicator in the center of my web view and keeping a reference to it:

```
let act = UIActivityIndicatorView(style:.large)
act.backgroundColor = UIColor(white:0.1, alpha:0.5)
act.color = .white
self.wv.addSubview(act)
act.translatesAutoresizingMaskIntoConstraints = false
NSLayoutConstraint.activate([
    act.centerXAnchor.constraint(equalTo:wv.centerXAnchor),
    act.centerYAnchor.constraint(equalTo:wv.centerYAnchor)
])
self.activity = act
```

Now I observe the web view's isLoading property (self.obs is a Set instance property). When the web view starts loading or stops loading, I'm notified, so I can show or hide the activity view:

```
let ob = self.wv.observe(\.isLoading, options:.new) {[unowned self] wv,ch in
    if let val = ch.newValue {
        if val {
            self.activity.startAnimating()
        } else {
            self.activity.stopAnimating()
        }
    }
}
self.obs.insert(ob)
```

Web View Navigation

A WKWebView maintains a back and forward list of the URLs to which the user has navigated. The list is its `backForwardList`, a WKBackForwardList, which is a collection of read-only properties (and one method):

- `currentItem`
- `backItem`
- `forwardItem`
- `item(at:)`

Each item in the list is a WKBackForwardItem, a simple value class basically consisting of a `url` and a `title`.

A WKWebView responds to `goBack`, `goForward` and `go(to:)`, so you can tell it in code to navigate the list. Its properties `canGoBack` and `canGoForward` are key–value observable; typically you would use that fact to enable or disable a Back and Forward button in your interface in response to the list changing.

A WKWebView also has a settable property, `allowsBackForwardNavigation-Gestures`. The default is `false`; if `true`, the user can swipe sideways to go back and forward in the list. This property can also be set in the nib editor.

To prevent or reroute navigation that the user tries to perform by tapping links, set yourself as the WKWebView's `navigationDelegate` (WKNavigationDelegate) and implement `webView(_:decidePolicyFor:decisionHandler:)`, where the `for:` parameter is a WKNavigationAction that you can examine to help make your decision. Among other things, its `request` property is the URLRequest we are proposing to perform — look at its `url` to see where we are proposing to go — along with a `navigationType`, which will be one of the following (WKNavigationType):

- `.linkActivated`
- `.backForward`
- `.reload`
- `.formSubmitted`
- `.formResubmitted`
- `.other`

You are also handed a `decisionHandler` function which you *must* call with a WKNavigationActionPolicy argument — either `.cancel` or `.allow`.

In this example, I permit navigation in the most general case — otherwise nothing would ever appear in my web view! — but if the user taps a link, I forbid it and show that URL in Mobile Safari instead:

```
func webView(_ webView: WKWebView,
    decidePolicyFor navigationAction: WKNavigationAction,
    decisionHandler: @escaping (WKNavigationActionPolicy) -> Void) {
        if navigationAction.navigationType == .linkActivated {
            if let url = navigationAction.request.url {
                UIApplication.shared.open(url)
                decisionHandler(.cancel)
                return
            }
        }
        decisionHandler(.allow)
}
```

New in iOS 13, a web view has a *content mode* (WKWebpagePreferences.Content-Mode), determining how the web view represents itself as a browser to the server:

`.desktop`
> The default on an iPad when the web view is fullscreen. Web sites will appear in their desktop version.

`.mobile`
> The default on an iPhone, or on the iPad when the web view is not fullscreen (perhaps it's in a popover, or we're doing iPad multitasking). Web sites will appear in their mobile version.

To access desktop mode in a WKWebView, you'll need to set the configuration's `applicationNameForUserAgent` property to a desktop browser's user agent string, such as `"Version/13.0.1 Safari/605.1.15"`. You can set this in the nib editor.

If you want to change the content mode for a particular web page during navigation, implement `webView(_:decidePolicyFor:preferences:decisionHandler:)`. The third parameter is a WKWebpagePreferences object, a simple value class with just one property — its `preferredContentMode`. Set this property to `.desktop` or `.mobile`, and pass the WKWebpagePreferences object into the `decisionHandler` call as the second argument.

Several other WKNavigationDelegate methods can notify you as a page loads (or fails to load). Under normal circumstances, you'll receive them in this order:

- `webView(_:didStartProvisionalNavigation:)`
- `webView(_:didCommit:)`
- `webView(_:didFinish:)`

Those delegate methods, and all navigation commands, including the four ways of loading your web view with initial content, supply a WKNavigation object. You can use this in an equality comparison to determine whether the navigations referred to in different methods are the same navigation (roughly speaking, the same page-loading operation). New in iOS 13, this object also has an `effectiveContentMode` property that tells you the current content mode (`.desktop` or `.mobile`).

Communicating with a Web Page

Your code can pass JavaScript messages into and out of a WKWebView's web page, allowing you to change the page's contents or respond to changes within it, even while it is being displayed.

Communicating into a web page

To send a message into an *already loaded* WKWebView web page, call `evaluateJava-Script(_:completionHandler:)`. Your JavaScript runs within the context of the web page.

In this example, the user is able to decrease the size of the text in the web page. We have prepared some JavaScript that generates a `<style>` element containing CSS that sets the `font-size` for the page's `<body>` in accordance with a property, `self.fontsize`:

```
var fontsize = 18
var cssrule : String {
    return """
    var s = document.createElement('style');
    s.textContent = 'body { font-size: \(self.fontsize)px; }';
    document.documentElement.appendChild(s);
    """
}
```

When the user taps a button, we decrement `self.fontsize`, construct that Java-Script, and send it to the web page:

```
func doDecreaseSize (_ sender: Any) {
    self.fontsize -= 1
    if self.fontsize < 10 {
        self.fontsize = 20
    }
    let s = self.cssrule
    self.wv.evaluateJavaScript(s)
}
```

That's clever, but we have not done anything about setting the web page's *initial* `font-size`. Let's fix that.

A WKWebView allows us to inject JavaScript into the web page *at the time it is loaded*. To do so, we use the `userContentController` of the WKWebView's configuration. We create a WKUserScript, specifying the JavaScript it contains, along with an `injectionTime` which can be either before (`.documentStart`) or after (`.documentEnd`) a page's content has loaded. In this case, we want it to be before; otherwise, the user will see the font size change suddenly:

```
let script = WKUserScript(source: self.cssrule,
    injectionTime: .atDocumentStart, forMainFrameOnly: true)
let config = self.wv.configuration
config.userContentController.addUserScript(script)
```

Communicating out of a web page

To communicate out of a web page, you need first to install a message handler to receive the communication. Again, this involves the `userContentController`. You call `add(_:name:)`, where the first argument is an object that must implement the WKScriptMessageHandler protocol, so that its `userContentController(_:didReceive:)` method can be called later:

```
let config = self.wv.configuration
config.userContentController.add(self, name: "playbutton")
```

We have just installed a `playbutton` message handler. This means that the DOM for our web page now contains an element, among its `window.webkit.messageHandlers`, called `playbutton`. A message handler sends its message when it receives a `postMessage()` function call. The WKScriptMessageHandler (`self` in this example) will get a call to its `userContentController(_:didReceive:)` method if JavaScript inside the web page sends `postMessage()` to the `window.webkit.messageHandlers.playbutton` object.

To make that actually happen, I've put an `<img>` tag into my web page's HTML, defining an image that will act as a tappable button:

```
<img src="listen.png"
  onclick="window.webkit.messageHandlers.playbutton.postMessage('play')">
```

When the user taps that image, the message is posted, and so my code runs and I can respond:

```
func userContentController(_ userContentController: WKUserContentController,
    didReceive message: WKScriptMessage) {
        if message.name == "playbutton" {
            if let body = message.body as? String {
                if body == "play" {
                    // ... do stuff here ...
```

```
                }
            }
        }
    }
```

There's just one little problem: that code causes a retain cycle. The reason is that a WKUserContentController leaks, and it retains the WKScriptMessageHandler, which in this case is `self` — and so `self` will never be deallocated. But `self` is the view controller, so that's very bad. My solution is to create an intermediate trampoline object that can be harmlessly retained, and that has a weak reference to `self`:

```
class MyMessageHandler : NSObject, WKScriptMessageHandler {
    weak var delegate : WKScriptMessageHandler?
    init(delegate:WKScriptMessageHandler) {
        self.delegate = delegate
        super.init()
    }
    func userContentController(_ ucc: WKUserContentController,
        didReceive message: WKScriptMessage) {
            self.delegate?.userContentController(ucc, didReceive: message)
    }
}
```

Now when I add myself as a script message handler, I do it by way of the trampoline object:

```
let config = self.wv.configuration
let handler = MyMessageHandler(delegate:self)
config.userContentController.add(handler, name: "playbutton")
```

Now that I've broken the retain cycle, my own `deinit` is called, and I can release the offending objects:

```
deinit {
    let ucc = self.wv.configuration.userContentController
    ucc.removeAllUserScripts()
    ucc.removeScriptMessageHandler(forName:"playbutton")
}
```

JavaScript alerts

If a web page tries to put up a JavaScript alert, nothing will happen in your app unless you assign the WKWebView a `uiDelegate`, an object adopting the WKUIDelegate protocol, and implement these methods:

`webView(_:runJavaScriptAlertPanelWithMessage:initiatedByFrame:completion-Handler:)`
    Called by JavaScript `alert`.

```
webView(_:runJavaScriptConfirmPanelWithMessage:initiatedByFrame:
completionHandler:)
```
    Called by JavaScript `confirm`.

```
webView(_:runJavaScriptTextInputPanelWithPrompt:defaultText:initiatedBy-
Frame:completionHandler:)
```
    Called by JavaScript `prompt`.

Your implementation should put up an appropriate alert (UIAlertController, see Chapter 13) and call the completion function when it is dismissed. Here's a minimal implementation for the `alert` method:

```swift
func webView(_ webView: WKWebView,
    runJavaScriptAlertPanelWithMessage message: String,
    initiatedByFrame frame: WKFrameInfo,
    completionHandler: @escaping () -> Void) {
        let host = frame.request.url?.host
        let alert = UIAlertController(title: host, message: message,
            preferredStyle: .alert)
        alert.addAction(UIAlertAction(title: "OK", style: .default) { _ in
            completionHandler()
        })
        self.present(alert, animated:true)
}
```

Similarly, if a web page's JavaScript calls `window.open`, implement this method:

- `webView(_:createWebViewWith:for:windowFeatures:)`

Your implementation can return `nil`, or else create a new WKWebView, get it into the interface, and return it.

Custom Schemes

Starting in iOS 11, you can feed data into a web page by implementing a custom URL scheme. When the web page asks for the data by way of the scheme, the WKWeb-View turns to your code to supply the data.

Let's say I have an MP3 file called `"theme"` in my app's asset catalog, and I want the user to be able to play it through an `<audio>` tag in my web page. I've invented a custom scheme that signals to my app that we want this audio data, and my web page's `<source>` tag asks for its data using that scheme:

```swift
weak var wv: WKWebView!
let sch = "neuburg-custom-scheme-demo-audio" // custom scheme
override func viewDidLoad() {
    super.viewDidLoad()
    let config = WKWebViewConfiguration()
    // ... configure the web view ...
    let r = // ... CGRect for web view frame ...
```

```
        let wv = WKWebView(frame: r, configuration: config)
        self.view.addSubview(wv)
        self.wv = wv
        let s = """
        <!DOCTYPE html><html><head>
        <meta name="viewport" content="initial-scale=1.0, user-scalable=no" />
        </head><body>
        <p>Here you go:</p>
        <audio controls>
        <source src="\(sch)://theme" />
        </audio>
        </body></html>
        """
        self.wv.loadHTMLString(s, baseURL: nil)
    }
```

Now let's fill in the missing code, where we configure the web view to accept sch as a custom scheme:

```
let sh = SchemeHandler()
sh.sch = self.sch
config.setURLSchemeHandler(sh, forURLScheme: self.sch)
```

The call to setURLSchemeHandler requires that we provide an object that adopts the WKURLSchemeHandler protocol. That object cannot be self, or we'll get ourselves into a retain cycle (similar to the problem we had with WKScriptMessageHandler earlier); so I'm configuring and passing a custom SchemeHandler helper object instead.

The WKURLSchemeHandler protocol methods are where the action is. When the web page wants data with our custom scheme, it calls our SchemeHandler's web-View(_:start:) method. The second parameter is a WKURLSchemeTask that operates as our gateway back to the web view. Its request property contains the URLRequest from the web page. We must call the WKURLSchemeTask's methods, first supplying a URLResponse, then handing it the data, then telling it that we've finished:

```
class SchemeHandler : NSObject, WKURLSchemeHandler {
    var sch : String?
    func webView(_ webView: WKWebView, start task: WKURLSchemeTask) {
        if let url = task.request.url,
            let sch = self.sch,
            url.scheme == sch,
            let host = url.host,
            let theme = NSDataAsset(name:host) {
                let data = theme.data
                let resp = URLResponse(url: url, mimeType: "audio/mpeg",
                    expectedContentLength: data.count,
                    textEncodingName: nil)
                task.didReceive(resp)
                task.didReceive(data)
```

```
                task.didFinish()
        } else {
            task.didFailWithError(NSError(domain: "oops", code: 0))
        }
    }
    func webView(_ webView: WKWebView, stop task: WKURLSchemeTask) {
        print("stop")
    }
}
```

The outcome is that the audio controls appear in our web page, and when the user taps the Play button, what plays is the MP3 file from the app's asset catalog.

 This feature works only if we create the web view ourselves, in code, using the init(frame:configuration:) initializer, with the WKWebViewConfiguration object prepared beforehand. So we can't use a custom scheme with a web view instantiated from a nib. I regard this limitation as a bug.

Web View Previews and Context Menus

As I described earlier ("Previews and Context Menus" on page 382), 3D touch peek and pop is superseded in iOS 13 by the use of a long press to summon a preview with a context menu. If a WKWebView's allowsLinkPreview property is true, the user can long press on a link to summon a preview of the linked page, along with default menu items Open Link, Add to Reading List, Copy Link, Share, and Hide Link Previews. (This property can be set in the nib editor.)

The default response to the user tapping on the preview is to open the link in Safari. This mechanism does *not* pass through your navigation delegate's implementation of webView(_:decidePolicyFor:decisionHandler:). Instead, if you wish to customize your app's response to the user previewing links, you can implement methods in your uiDelegate (WKUIDelegate) that are parallel to the UIContextMenuInteraction-Delegate methods:

webView(_:contextMenuConfigurationForElement:completionHandler:)
> The element: is a WKContextMenuElementInfo, which is merely a value class carrying a single property, the linkURL for the link that the user is pressing on. Your job is to call the completionHandler with one of these as argument:
>
> - A fully configured UIContextMenuConfiguration created by calling the initializer init(identifier:previewProvider:actionProvider:). If you supply an action provider function, the incoming parameter is an array of the default UIActions, so you can keep any or all of those as menu items if you want to.
>
> - nil to permit the default behavior.

- An empty UIContextMenuConfiguration (no preview provider, no action provider) to prevent anything from happening.

`webView(_:contextMenuWillPresentForElement:)`
   The context menu is about to appear.

`webView(_:contextMenuForElement:willCommitWithAnimator:)`
   The user has tapped the preview. You might add a completion handler to the animator to perform a view controller transition.

`webView(_:contextMenuDidEndForElement:)`
   The preview and menu have been dismissed, no matter how.

Safari View Controller

A Safari view controller (SFSafariViewController) embeds the Mobile Safari interface in a separate process inside your app. It provides the user with a browser interface familiar from Mobile Safari itself. In a toolbar, which can be shown or hidden by scrolling, there are Back and Forward buttons, a Share button including standard Safari features such as Add Bookmark and Add to Reading List, and a Safari button that lets the user load the same page in the real Safari app. In a navigation bar, which can be shrunk or grown by scrolling, are a read-only URL field, a Text button where the user can change the text size, enter Reader view, and configure site settings, plus a Refresh button, along with a Done button. The user has access to autofill and to Safari cookies with no intervention by your app.

The idea, according to Apple, is that when you want to present internal HTML content, such as an HTML string, you'll use a WKWebView, but when you really want to allow the user to access the web, you'll use a Safari view controller. In this way, you are saved from the trouble of trying to build a full-fledged web browser yourself.

To use a Safari view controller (`import SafariServices`), create the SFSafariViewController, initialize it with a URL, and present it:

```
let svc = SFSafariViewController(url: url)
self.present(svc, animated: true)
```

In this example, we interfere (as a WKWebView's `navigationDelegate`) with the user tapping on a link in our web view, so that the linked page is displayed in an SFSafariViewController within our app:

```
func webView(_ webView: WKWebView,
    decidePolicyFor navigationAction: WKNavigationAction,
    decisionHandler: @escaping (WKNavigationActionPolicy) -> Void) {
        if navigationAction.navigationType == .linkActivated {
            if let url = navigationAction.request.url {
                let svc = SFSafariViewController(url: url)
                self.present(svc, animated: true)
```

```
                decisionHandler(.cancel)
                return
            }
        }
        decisionHandler(.allow)
    }
```

When the user taps the Done button in the navigation bar, the Safari view controller is dismissed. You can change the title of the Done button; to do so, set the Safari view controller's `dismissButtonStyle` to `.done`, `.close`, or `.cancel`.

You can set the color of the Safari view controller's navigation bar (`preferredBar-TintColor`) and bar button items (`preferredControlTintColor`). This allows the look of the view to harmonize with the rest of your app.

You can configure a Safari view controller by creating an SFSafariView-Controller.Configuration object and passing it to the Safari view controller through its initializer `init(url:configuration:)`. Using the configuration object, you can prevent the Safari view controller's top and bottom bars from collapsing when the user scrolls; to do so, set its `barCollapsingEnabled` property to `false`.

You can make yourself the Safari view controller's delegate (SFSafariViewController-Delegate) and implement any of these methods:

`safariViewController(_:didCompleteInitialLoad:)`
`safariViewControllerDidFinish(_:)`
> Called on presentation and dismissal of the Safari view controller, respectively.

`func safariViewController(_:initialLoadDidRedirectTo:)`
> Reports that the Safari view controller's initial web page differs from the URL you originally provided, because redirection occurred.

`safariViewController(_:activityItemsFor:title:)`
> Allows you to supply your own Share button items; I'll explain what activity items are in Chapter 13.

`safariViewController(_:excludedActivityTypesFor:title:)`
> In a sense, the converse of the preceding: allows you to eliminate unwanted activity types from the Share button.

Developing Web View Content

Before designing the HTML to be displayed in a web view, you might want to read up on the brand of HTML native to the mobile WebKit rendering engine. There are certain limitations; mobile WebKit doesn't use plug-ins such as Flash, and it imposes limits on the size of resources (such as images) that it can display. On the plus side, WebKit is in the vanguard of the march toward HTML5 and CSS3, and has many special capabilities suited for display on a mobile device. For documentation and other resources, see Apple's Safari Dev Center.

A good place to start is the *Safari Web Content Guide* (in the documentation archive). It contains links to other relevant documentation, such as the *Safari CSS Visual Effects Guide*, which describes some things you can do with WebKit's implementation of CSS3 (like animations), and the *Safari HTML5 Audio and Video Guide*, which describes WebKit's audio and video player support.

If nothing else, you'll want to be aware of one important aspect of web page content — the *viewport*. This is typically set through a `<meta>` tag in the `<head>` area:

```
<meta name="viewport" content="initial-scale=1.0, user-scalable=no">
```

Without that line, or something similar, a web page may be laid out incorrectly when it is rendered: your content may appear tiny (because it is being rendered as if the screen were large), or it may be too wide for the view, forcing the user to scroll horizontally to read it. The viewport's `user-scalable` attribute can be treated as `yes` by setting the WKWebViewConfiguration's `ignoresViewportScaleLimits` to `true`.

Another important section of the *Safari Web Content Guide* describes how you can use a `media` attribute in the `<link>` tag that loads your CSS to load different CSS depending on what kind of device your app is running on (also known as a *responsive* web page); you might have one CSS file that lays out your web view's content on an iPhone, and another that lays it out on an iPad.

Inspecting, debugging, and experimenting with web view content is greatly eased by the Web Inspector, built into Safari on the desktop. It can see a web view in your app running on a device or the Simulator, and lets you analyze every aspect of how it works. You can hover the mouse over a web page element in the Web Inspector to highlight the rendering of that element in the running app. Moreover, the Web Inspector lets you change your web view's content in real time, with many helpful features such as CSS autocompletion.

JavaScript and the document object model (*DOM*) are also extremely powerful. Event listeners allow JavaScript code to respond directly to touch and gesture events, so that the user can interact with elements of a web page much as if they were iOS-native touchable views; it can also take advantage of Core Location and Core Motion facilities to respond to where the user is on earth and how the device is positioned (see Chapter 21). Additional helpful documentation includes Apple's *WebKit DOM Programming Topics* and the WebKit JS framework reference page.

CHAPTER 12

Controls and Other Views

This chapter discusses all UIView subclasses provided by UIKit that haven't been discussed already. It's remarkable how few of them there are; UIKit exhibits a notable economy of means in this regard.

Additional UIView subclasses, as well as UIViewController subclasses that create interface, are provided by other frameworks. There will be examples in Part III.

UIActivityIndicatorView

An activity indicator (UIActivityIndicatorView) appears as the spokes of a small wheel. You set the spokes spinning with `startAnimating`, giving the user a sense that some time-consuming process is taking place. You stop the spinning with `stopAnimating`. If the activity indicator's `hidesWhenStopped` is `true` (the default), it is visible only while spinning.

An activity indicator comes in a `style`; if it is created in code, you'll set its style with `init(style:)`. Your choices (UIActivityIndicatorView.Style) are:

- `.large`
- `.medium`

(Those styles are new in iOS 13, replacing the older `.whiteLarge`, `.white`, and `gray`.)

An activity indicator has a standard size, which depends on its style. Changing its size in code changes the size of the view, but not the size of the spokes. For bigger spokes, you can resort to a scale transform.

You can assign an activity indicator a `color`; this overrides the default gray color of the spokes. An activity indicator is a UIView, so you can also set its `background-`

Figure 12-1. A large activity indicator

Color; a nice effect is to give an activity indicator a contrasting background color and to round its corners by way of the view's layer (Figure 12-1).

Here's some code from a UITableViewCell subclass in one of my apps. In this app, it takes some time, after the user taps a cell to select it, for me to construct the next view and navigate to it; to cover the delay, I show a spinning activity indicator in the center of the cell while it's selected:

```
override func setSelected(_ selected: Bool, animated: Bool) {
    if selected {
        let v = UIActivityIndicatorView(style:.large)
        v.color = .yellow
        v.backgroundColor = UIColor(white:0.2, alpha:0.6)
        v.layer.cornerRadius = 10
        v.frame = v.frame.insetBy(dx: -10, dy: -10)
        v.center = self.contentView.convert(self.bounds.center, from: self)
        v.tag = 1001
        self.contentView.addSubview(v)
        v.startAnimating()
    } else {
        self.viewWithTag(1001)?.removeFromSuperview()
    }
    super.setSelected(selected, animated: animated)
}
```

If activity involves the network, you might want to set the UIApplication's isNetwork-ActivityIndicatorVisible to true. This displays a small spinning activity indicator in the status bar. The indicator is not reflecting actual network activity; if it's visible, it's spinning. Be sure to set it back to false when the activity is over.

An activity indicator is simple and standard, but you can't change the way it's drawn. One obvious alternative would be a UIImageView with an animated image, as described in Chapter 4. Another solution is a CAReplicatorLayer, a layer that makes multiple copies of its sublayer; by animating the sublayer, you animate the copies. This is a very common approach (in fact, it wouldn't surprise me to learn that UIActivityIndicatorView is implemented using CAReplicatorLayer). Here's an example:

```
let lay = CAReplicatorLayer()
lay.frame = CGRect(0,0,100,20)
let bar = CALayer()
bar.frame = CGRect(0,0,10,20)
bar.backgroundColor = UIColor.red.cgColor
```

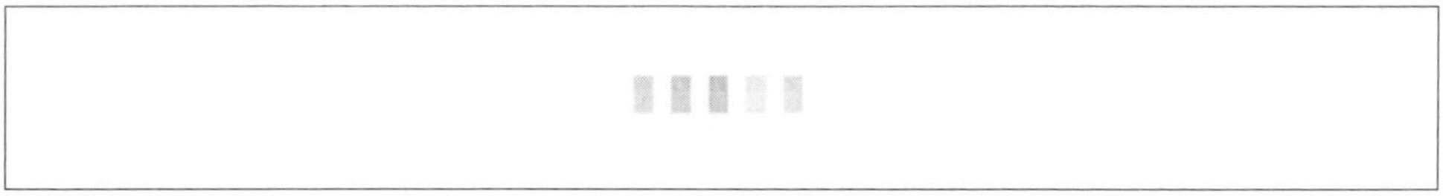

Figure 12-2. A custom activity indicator

```
lay.addSublayer(bar)
lay.instanceCount = 5
lay.instanceTransform = CATransform3DMakeTranslation(20, 0, 0)
let anim = CABasicAnimation(keyPath: #keyPath(CALayer.opacity))
anim.fromValue = 1.0
anim.toValue = 0.2
anim.duration = 1
anim.repeatCount = .greatestFiniteMagnitude
bar.add(anim, forKey: nil)
lay.instanceDelay = anim.duration / Double(lay.instanceCount)
self.view.layer.addSublayer(lay)
// ... give the replicator layer a position ...
```

Our single red vertical bar (bar) is replicated to make five red vertical bars. We repeatedly fade the bar from opaque to transparent, but because we've set the replicator layer's instanceDelay, the replicated bars fade in sequence, so that the darkest bar appears to be marching repeatedly to the right (Figure 12-2).

UIProgressView

A progress view (UIProgressView) is a "thermometer" graphically displaying a percentage. This may be a static percentage, or it might represent a time-consuming process whose percentage of completion is known (if the percentage of completion is unknown, you're more likely to use an activity indicator). In one of my apps, I use a progress view to show how many cards are left in the deck; in another of my apps, I use a progress view to show the current position within the song being played by the built-in music player.

A progress view comes in a style, its progressViewStyle; if the progress view is created in code, you'll set its style with init(progressViewStyle:). Your choices (UIProgressView.Style) are:

- .default
- .bar

A .bar progress view is intended for use in a UIBarButtonItem, as the title view of a navigation item, and so on. Both styles draw the thermometer extremely thin — just 2 pixels and 3 pixels, respectively. Figure 12-3 shows a .default progress view. Changing a progress view's frame height directly has no visible effect on how the thermometer is drawn. Under autolayout, to make a thicker thermometer, supply a

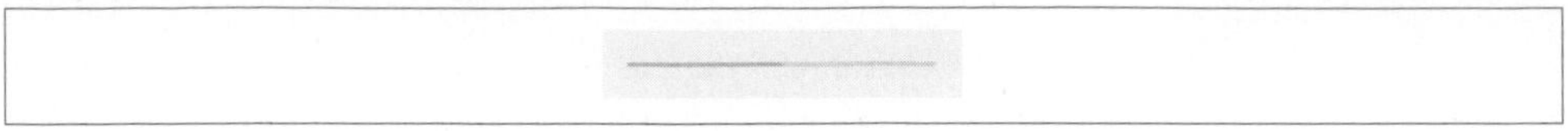

Figure 12-3. A progress view

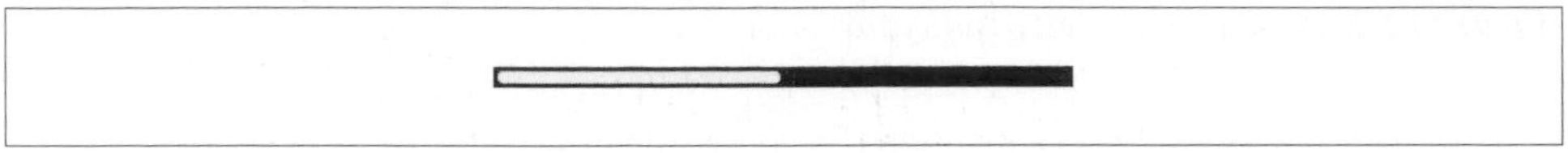

Figure 12-4. A thicker progress view using a custom progress image

height constraint with a larger value, overriding the intrinsic content height. Alternatively, subclass UIProgressView and override sizeThatFits(_:).

The fullness of the thermometer is the progress view's progress property. This is a value between 0 and 1, inclusive; you'll usually do some elementary arithmetic to convert from the value you're reflecting to a value within that range. It is also a Float; in Swift, you may have to coerce explicitly. A change in progress value can be animated by calling setProgress(_:animated:). This progress view reflects the number of cards remaining in a deck of 52 cards:

```
let r = self.deck.cards.count
self.prog.setProgress(Float(r)/52, animated: true)
```

The default color of the filled portion of a progress view is the tintColor (which may be inherited from higher up the view hierarchy). The default color for the unfilled portion is gray for a .default progress view and transparent for a .bar progress view. You can customize the colors; set the progress view's progressTintColor and trackTintColor, respectively. This can also be done in the nib editor.

Alternatively, you can customize the image used to draw the filled portion of the progress view (its progressImage), along with the image used to draw the unfilled portion (its trackImage). This can also be done in the nib editor. Each image must be stretched to the length of the filled or unfilled area, so you'll want to use a resizable image. Be sure to give the progress view sufficient height, as I explained earlier, to accommodate your images. Here's a simple example from one of my apps (Figure 12-4):

```
let r = UIGraphicsImageRenderer(size:CGSize(10,10))
var trackim : UIImage?
let im = r.image { ctx in
    let con = ctx.cgContext
    // track
    con.setFillColor(UIColor.black.cgColor)
    con.fill(CGRect(0,0,10,10))
    trackim = ctx.currentImage
    // progress
    con.setFillColor(UIColor.yellow.cgColor)
    con.fillEllipse(in: CGRect(2,2,6,6))
```

Figure 12-5. A circular custom progress view

```
    }
    self.prog.trackImage = trackim?.resizableImage(
        withCapInsets:UIEdgeInsets(top: 4, left: 4, bottom: 4, right: 4),
        resizingMode:.stretch)
    self.prog.progressImage = im.resizableImage(
        withCapInsets:UIEdgeInsets(top: 4, left: 4, bottom: 4, right: 4),
        resizingMode:.stretch)
```

Progress View Alternatives

For maximum flexibility, you can design your own UIView subclass that behaves like a thermometer. It doesn't have to *look* like a thermometer! A common interface (as in Apple's App Store app during a download) is to draw the arc of a circle. This effect is easily achieved by setting the strokeEnd of a CAShapeLayer with a circular path. Here's a UIButton subclass that implements it (Figure 12-5):

```
class MyCircularProgressButton : UIButton {
    var progress : Float = 0 {
        didSet {
            self.shapelayer?.strokeEnd = CGFloat(self.progress)
        }
    }
    private weak var shapelayer : CAShapeLayer?
    override func layoutSubviews() {
        super.layoutSubviews()
        guard self.shapelayer == nil else {return}
        let layer = CAShapeLayer()
        layer.frame = self.bounds
        layer.lineWidth = 2
        layer.fillColor = nil
        layer.strokeColor = UIColor.red.cgColor
        let b = UIBezierPath(ovalIn: self.bounds.insetBy(dx: 3, dy: 3))
        layer.path = b.cgPath
        layer.strokeStart = 0
        layer.strokeEnd = 0
        layer.setAffineTransform(CGAffineTransform(rotationAngle: -.pi/2.0))
        self.layer.addSublayer(layer)
        self.shapelayer = layer
    }
}
```

The Progress Class

A progress view has an `observedProgress` property that you can set to a Progress object. Progress is a Foundation class that abstracts the notion of task progress: it has a `totalUnitCount` property and a `completedUnitCount` property, and their ratio generates its `fractionCompleted`, which is read-only and observable with KVO.

If you assign a Progress object to a progress view's `observedProgress` property and configure and update it, the progress view will *automatically* use the changes in the Progress object's `fractionCompleted` to update its own `progress`. That's useful because you might already have a time-consuming process that maintains and vends its own Progress object. (For a case in point, see "Slow Data Delivery" on page 597.)

How should your progress view's `observedProgress` be related to the Progress object vended by the time-consuming process? There are two possibilities:

- In simple cases, you might assign the process's Progress object *directly* to your progress view's `observedProgress`.

- Alternatively, you can configure your progress view's `observedProgress` as the *parent* of the process's Progress object.

When Progress objects stand in a parent–child relationship, the progress of an operation reported to the child automatically forms an appropriate fraction of the progress reported by the parent; this allows a single Progress object, acting as the ultimate parent, to conglomerate the progress of several individual operations. There are two ways to put two Progress objects into a parent–child relationship:

Explicit parent
> Call the parent's `addChild(_:withPendingUnitCount:)` method. Alternatively, create the child by initializing it with reference to the parent, by calling `init(totalUnitCount:parent:pendingUnitCount:)`.

Implicit parent
> This approach uses the notion of the *current* Progress object. The rule is that while a Progress object is current, any new Progress objects will become its child automatically. The whole procedure comes down to doing things in the right order:
>
> 1. Tell the prospective parent Progress object to `becomeCurrent(withPendingUnitCount:)`.
>
> 2. Create the child Progress object without an explicit parent, by calling `init(totalUnitCount:)`. As if by magic, it becomes the other Progress object's child (because the other Progress object is current).

3. Tell the parent to `resignCurrent`. This balances the earlier `become-Current(withPendingUnitCount:)` and completes the configuration.

UIPickerView

A picker view (UIPickerView) displays selectable choices using a rotating drum metaphor. Its default height is adaptive — 162 in an environment with a `.compact` vertical size class (an iPhone in landscape orientation) and 216 otherwise — but you are free to set its height to something else. Its width is generally up to you.

Each drum, or column, is called a *component*. Your code configures the UIPickerView's content through its data source (UIPickerViewDataSource) and delegate (UIPickerViewDelegate), which are usually the same object. Your data source and delegate must answer some Big Questions similar to those posed by a UITableView (Chapter 8):

`numberOfComponents(in:)`
How many components (drums) does this picker view have?

`pickerView(_:numberOfRowsInComponent:)`
How many rows does this component have? The first component is numbered 0.

`pickerView(_:titleForRow:forComponent:)`
`pickerView(_:attributedTitleForRow:forComponent:)`
`pickerView(_:viewForRow:forComponent:reusing:)`
What should this row of this component display? The first row is numbered 0. You can supply a simple string, an attributed string (Chapter 10), or an entire view such as a UILabel; but you should supply every row of every component the same way.

 In `pickerView(_:viewForRow:forComponent:reusing:)`, the `reusing:` parameter, if not `nil`, is supposed to be a view that you supplied for a row now no longer visible, giving you a chance to reuse it, much as cells are reused in a table view. In actual fact, the `reusing:` parameter is *always* `nil`. Views don't leak — they go out of existence in good order when they are no longer visible — but they aren't reused. I regard this as a bug.

Here's the code for a UIPickerView (Figure 12-6) that displays the names of the 50 U.S. states, stored in an array (`self.states`). We implement `pickerView(_:viewForRow:forComponent:reusing:)` just because it's the most interesting case; as our views, we supply UILabel instances. The `view` parameter is always `nil`, so we ignore it and make a new UILabel every time we're called. The state names appear centered because the labels are centered within the picker view:

Figure 12-6. A picker view

```swift
func numberOfComponents(in pickerView: UIPickerView) -> Int {
    return 1
}
func pickerView(_ pickerView: UIPickerView,
    numberOfRowsInComponent component: Int) -> Int {
        return self.states.count
}
func pickerView(_ pickerView: UIPickerView,
    viewForRow row: Int,
    forComponent component: Int,
    reusing view: UIView?) -> UIView {
        let lab = UILabel()
        lab.text = self.states[row]
        lab.backgroundColor = .clear
        lab.sizeToFit()
        return lab
}
```

The delegate may further configure the UIPickerView's physical appearance by means of these methods:

- `pickerView(_:rowHeightForComponent:)`
- `pickerView(_:widthForComponent:)`

The delegate may implement `pickerView(_:didSelectRow:inComponent:)`, so as to be notified each time the user spins a drum to a new position. You can also query the picker view directly by sending it `selectedRow(inComponent:)`.

You can set the value to which any drum is turned by calling `selectRow(_:inComponent:animated:)`. Other handy picker view methods allow you to request that the data be reloaded, and there are properties and methods to query the picker view's structure:

- `reloadComponent(_:)`
- `reloadAllComponents`
- `numberOfComponents`

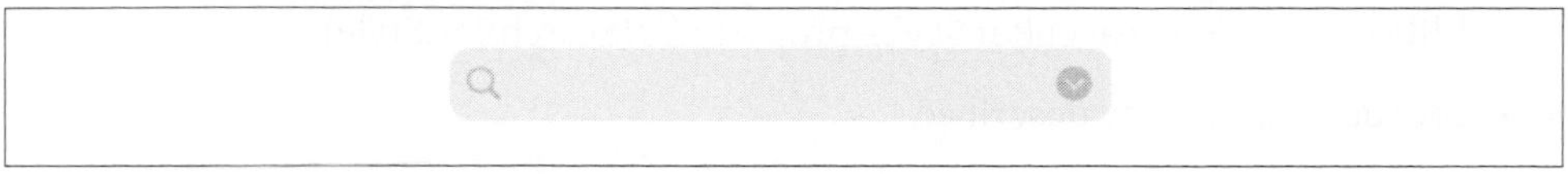

Figure 12-7. A search bar with a search results button

- `numberOfRows(inComponent:)`
- `view(forRow:forComponent:)`

By implementing `pickerView(_:didSelectRow:inComponent:)` and calling `reload-Component(_:)`, you can make a picker view where the values displayed by one drum depend dynamically on what is selected in another. One can imagine extending our U.S. states example to include a second drum listing major cities in each state; when the user switches to a different state in the first drum, a different set of major cities appears in the second drum.

UISearchBar

A search bar (UISearchBar) is essentially a wrapper for a text field; it has a text field as one of its subviews. It is displayed by default as a rounded rectangle containing a magnifying glass icon, where the user can enter text (Figure 12-7). It does not, of itself, do any searching or display the results of a search; a common interface involves displaying the results of a search in a table view, and the UISearchController class makes this easy to do (see Chapter 8).

A search bar's current text is its `text` property. It can have a `placeholder`, which appears when there is no text. A `prompt` can be displayed above the search bar to explain its purpose. Delegate methods (UISearchBarDelegate) notify you of editing events; for their use, compare the text field and text view delegate methods discussed in Chapter 10:

- `searchBarShouldBeginEditing(_:)`
- `searchBarTextDidBeginEditing(_:)`
- `searchBar(_:textDidChange:)`
- `searchBar(_:shouldChangeTextIn:replacementText:)`
- `searchBarShouldEndEditing(_:)`
- `searchBarTextDidEndEditing(_:)`

A search bar has a `barStyle` (UIBarStyle):

- `.default`, in iOS 12 and before, a flat light gray background and a white search field; in iOS 13, a white background and a light gray search field
- `.black`, a black background and a black search field

In addition, there's a `searchBarStyle` property (UISearchBar.Style):

- `.default`, as already described
- `.prominent`, identical to `.default`
- `.minimal`, transparent background without a border

Alternatively, you can set a search bar's `barTintColor` to change its background color; if the bar style is `.black`, the `barTintColor` will also tint the search field itself. The `tintColor` property, meanwhile, whose value may be inherited from higher up the view hierarchy, governs the color of search bar components such as the Cancel button title and the flashing insertion cursor.

A search bar can also have a custom `backgroundImage`; this will be treated as a resizable image. The `backgroundImage` overrides all other ways of determining the background, and the search bar's `backgroundColor`, if any, appears behind it — though under some circumstances, if the search bar's `isTranslucent` is `false`, the `barTintColor` may appear behind it instead.

The search field area where the user enters text can be offset with respect to its background, using the `searchFieldBackgroundPositionAdjustment` property; you might do this if you had enlarged the search bar's height and wanted to position the search field within that height. The text can be offset within the search field with the `searchTextPositionAdjustment` property.

You can also replace the image of the search field itself; this is the image that is normally a rounded rectangle. To do so, call `setSearchFieldBackgroundImage(_:for:)`. The second parameter is a UIControl.State; the possible states are `.normal` and `.disabled`. But a search bar has no disabled state; the state here refers to the search field, which is a text field and *can* be disabled. Before iOS 13, there was no official access to this text field; you had to cycle through the search bar's subviews recursively to find it (for `subviews(ofType:)`, see Appendix B):

```
if let tf = self.sb.subviews(ofType: UITextField.self).first {
    tf.isEnabled = false
}
```

New in iOS 13, the search field is exposed through the search bar's `searchTextField` property:

```
self.sb.searchTextField.isEnabled = false
```

The search field image will be drawn vertically centered in front of the background and behind the contents of the search field (such as the text); its width will be adjusted for you, but it is up to you choose an appropriate height, and to ensure an appropriate background color so that the user can read the text.

A search bar displays an internal cancel button automatically (normally an X in a circle) if there is text in the search field. Internally, at its right end, a search bar may display a search results button (`showsSearchResultsButton`), which may be selected or not (`isSearchResultsButtonSelected`), or a bookmark button (`showsBookmark-Button`); if you ask to display both, you'll get the search results button. These buttons vanish if text is entered in the search bar so that the cancel button can be displayed. There is also an option to display a Cancel button externally (`showsCancelButton`, or call `setShowsCancelButton(_:animated:)`). The internal cancel button works automatically to remove whatever text is in the field; the other buttons do nothing, but delegate methods notify you when they are tapped:

- `searchBarResultsListButtonClicked(_:)`
- `searchBarBookmarkButtonClicked(_:)`
- `searchBarCancelButtonClicked(_:)`

You can customize the images used for the search icon (a magnifying glass, by default) and any of the internal right icons (the internal cancel button, the search results button, and the bookmark button) with `setImage(_:for:state:)`; about 20×20 seems to be a good size. The icon in question (the `for:` parameter) is specified using one of these values (UISearchBar.Icon):

- `.search`
- `.clear` (the internal cancel button)
- `.bookmark`
- `.resultsList`

The documentation says that the possible `state:` values are `.normal` and `.disabled`, but this is wrong; the choices are `.normal` and `.highlighted`. The highlighted image appears while the user taps on the icon (except for the search icon, which isn't a button). If you don't supply a normal image, the default image is used; if you supply a normal image but no highlighted image, the normal image is used for both. Setting `isSearchResultsButtonSelected` to `true` reverses the search results button's behavior: it displays the highlighted image, but when the user taps it, it displays the normal image. To change an icon's location, call `setPositionAdjustment(_:for:)`.

It may appear that there is no way to customize the external Cancel button, but in fact, although you've no official direct access to it through the search bar, you can customize it using the UIBarButtonItem appearance proxy, as discussed later in this chapter.

A search bar may also display scope buttons. These are intended to let the user alter the meaning of the search; precisely how you use them is up to you. To make the scope buttons appear, use the `showsScopeBar` property. The actual button titles are

Figure 12-8. A horrible search bar

the `scopeButtonTitles` property; the currently selected scope button is the `selected-ScopeButtonIndex` property. The delegate is notified when the user taps a different scope button:

- `searchBar(_:selectedScopeButtonIndexDidChange:)`

The overall look of the scope bar can be heavily customized, using these properties and methods:

`scopeBarBackgroundImage`
> The scope bar background. It will be stretched or tiled as needed.

`setScopeBarButtonBackgroundImage(_:for:)`
> Sets the background of the smaller area constituting the actual buttons; the states (the `for:` parameter) are `.normal` and `.selected`. You should supply a resizable image; if you don't, the image will be made resizable for you, but you might not like the way the runtime decides what region of the image will be stretched behind each button.

`setScopeBarButtonDividerImage(_:forLeftSegmentState:rightSegmentState:)`
> The dividers between the buttons are normally vertical lines, but you can customize them with this method. A full complement of dividers consists of three images, one when the buttons on both sides of the divider are normal (unselected) and one each when a button on one side or the other is selected; if you supply an image for just one state combination, it is used for the other two state combinations. The height of the divider image is adjusted for you, but the width is not; you'll normally use an image just a few pixels wide.

`setScopeBarButtonTitleTextAttributes(_:for:)`
> The text attributes of the titles of the scope buttons. The attributes are specified like the attributes dictionary of an NSAttributedString (Chapter 10).

By combining the various customization possibilities, a completely unrecognizable search bar of inconceivable ugliness can easily be achieved (Figure 12-8). Let's be careful out there.

The problem of allowing the keyboard to appear without covering the search bar is exactly as for a text field (Chapter 10). Text input properties of the search bar configure its keyboard and typing behavior like a text field as well. When the user taps the Search key in the keyboard, the delegate is notified, and it is then up to you to dismiss the keyboard (`resignFirstResponder`) and perform the search:

- `searchBarSearchButtonClicked(_:)`

New in iOS 13, a search bar's text field's class is public: it is a UISearchTextField, a UITextField subclass that lets you display *search tokens* (UISearchToken). A search token is initialized with text (and possibly an image) and is displayed as a rounded-rectangle cartouche; you should also set its `representedObject` so you know what the search token signifies. The user can select and delete an entire token, unless you set the field's `allowsDeletingTokens` to `false`. Each search token is a single-length "character," and any search tokens in the search field must precede any actual text; if you try to put a search token anywhere else, you'll crash. The field's `textualRange` tells you what part of the field consists of real text.

A search bar can be embedded in a toolbar or navigation bar as a bar button item's custom view, or in a navigation bar as a `titleView`. A common configuration is a UISearchController's search bar in a navigation bar; see the discussion of the UINavigationItem `searchController` property in Chapter 8. Alternatively, a UISearchBar can *itself* function as a top bar, without being inside any other bar. In that case, you'll want the search bar's height to be extended automatically under the status bar; I'll explain later in this chapter how to arrange that.

UIControl

UIControl is a subclass of UIView whose chief purpose is to be the superclass of several further built-in classes (controls) and to endow them with common behavior.

The most important thing that controls have in common is that they automatically track and analyze touch events (Chapter 5) and report them to your code as significant control events by way of action messages. Each control implements some subset of the possible control events. The control events (UIControl.Event) are:

- `.touchDown`
- `.touchDownRepeat`
- `.touchDragInside`
- `.touchDragOutside`
- `.touchDragEnter`
- `.touchDragExit`
- `.touchUpInside`

- `.touchUpOutside`
- `.touchCancel`
- `.valueChanged`
- `.editingDidBegin`
- `.editingChanged`
- `.editingDidEnd`
- `.editingDidEndOnExit`
- `.allTouchEvents`
- `.allEditingEvents`
- `.allEvents`

The control events also have informal names that are visible in the Connections inspector when you're editing a nib. I'll mostly use the informal names in the next couple of paragraphs.

Control events fall roughly into three groups:

- The user has touched the screen (Touch Down, Touch Drag Inside, Touch Up Inside, etc.).
- The user has edited text (Editing Did Begin, Editing Changed, etc.).
- The user has changed the control's value (Value Changed).

Apple's documentation is rather coy about which controls normally emit actions for which control events, so here's a list obtained through experimentation:

UIButton
  All Touch events

UIDatePicker
  Value Changed

UIPageControl
  All Touch events, Value Changed

UIRefreshControl
  Value Changed

UISegmentedControl
  Value Changed

UISlider
  All Touch events, Value Changed

Touch Inside and Touch Outside

There is no explicit Touch Down Inside event, because *any* sequence of Touch events begins with Touch Down, which *must* be inside the control. If it weren't, this sequence of touches would not belong to this control, and there would be no control events at all!

There is some virtual leeway as to where the "outside" of a control is. When the user taps within a control and starts dragging, the Inside events are triggered even after the drag moves outside the control's bounds. But after a certain distance from the control is exceeded, an invisible boundary is crossed, Touch Drag Exit is triggered, and now Outside events are reported until the drag crosses back within the invisible boundary, at which point Touch Drag Enter is triggered and the Inside events are reported again. In the case of a UIButton, the crossing of this invisible boundary is exactly when the button automatically unhighlights (as the drag exits); to catch a legitimate button press, you probably want to consider only Touch Up Inside.

For other controls, there may be some slight complications. A UISwitch will unhighlight when a drag reaches a certain distance from it, but the touch is still considered legitimate and can still change the UISwitch's value; therefore, when the user's finger leaves the screen, the UISwitch reports a Touch Up Inside event, even while reporting Touch Drag Outside events.

UISwitch
  All Touch events, Value Changed

UIStepper
  All Touch events, Value Changed

UITextField
  All Touch events except the Up events, and all Editing events (see Chapter 10 for details)

UIControl (generic)
  All Touch events

A control also has a *primary* control event called `.primaryActionTriggered`, presumably to save you from having to remember what the primary control event is. The primary control event is Value Changed for all controls except for UIButton, where it is Touch Up Inside, and UITextField, where it is Did End On Exit.

For each control event that you want to hear about, you attach to the control one or more target–action pairs. You can do this in the nib editor or in code. For any given control, each control event and its target–action pairs form a dispatch table. These methods and properties permit you to manipulate and query the dispatch table:

- `addTarget(_:action:for:)`
- `removeTarget(_:action:for:)`
- `actions(forTarget:forControlEvent:)`
- `allTargets`
- `allControlEvents` (a bitmask of control events with at least one target–action pair attached)

An action method (the method that will be called on the target when the control event occurs) may adopt any of three signatures, whose parameters are:

- The control and the UIEvent
- The control only
- No parameters

The second signature is by far the most common. It's unlikely that you'd want to dispense altogether with the parameter telling you which control sent the control event. It's equally unlikely that you'd want to examine the original UIEvent that triggered this control event, since control events deliberately shield you from dealing with the nitty-gritty of touches. (I suppose you might, on rare occasions, have some reason to examine the UIEvent's `timestamp`.)

When a control event occurs, the control consults its dispatch table, finds all the target–action pairs associated with that control event, and reports the control event by sending each action message to the corresponding target.

 The action messaging mechanism is actually more complex than I've just stated. The UIControl does not really send the action message directly; rather, it tells the shared application to send it. When a control wants to send an action message reporting a control event, it calls its own `sendAction(_:to:for:)` method. This in turn calls the shared application instance's `sendAction(_:to:from:for:)`, which actually sends the specified action message to the specified target. In theory, you could call or override either of these methods to customize this aspect of the message-sending architecture, but it is extremely unlikely that you would do so.

To make a control emit its action message(s) corresponding to a particular control event right now, in code, call its `sendActions(for:)` method (which is never called automatically by the runtime). Suppose you tell a UISwitch programmatically to change its setting from Off to On. This doesn't cause the switch to report a control event, as it would if the *user* had slid the switch from Off to On; if you wanted it to do so, you could use `sendActions(for:)`, like this:

```
self.sw.setOn(true, animated: true)
self.sw.sendActions(for: .valueChanged)
```

You might also use `sendActions(for:)` in a subclass to customize the circumstances under which a control reports control events. I'll give an example later in this chapter.

A control has `isEnabled`, `isSelected`, and `isHighlighted` properties; any of these can be `true` or `false` independently of the others. Together, they correspond to the control's `state`, a bitmask of three possible values (UIControl.State):

- `.highlighted` (`isHighlighted` is `true`)
- `.disabled` (`isEnabled` is `false`)
- `.selected` (`isSelected` is `true`)

A fourth state, `.normal`, corresponds to a zero `state` bitmask, meaning that `isEnabled` is `true` and that `isSelected` and `isHighlighted` are both `false`.

A control that is not enabled does not respond to user interaction. Whether the control also portrays itself differently, to cue the user to this fact, depends upon the control. A disabled UISwitch is faded, but a rounded rect text field, by default, gives the user no obvious cue that it is disabled. The visual nature of control selection and highlighting, too, depends on the control. Neither highlighting nor selection make any difference to the appearance of a UISwitch, but a highlighted UIButton usually looks quite different from a normal UIButton.

A control has `contentHorizontalAlignment` and `contentVerticalAlignment` properties. These matter only if the control has content that can be aligned. You are most likely to use them in connection with a UIButton to position its title and internal image (I'll say more about that later in this chapter).

A text field (UITextField) is a control; see Chapter 10. A refresh control (UIRefreshControl) is a control; see Chapter 8. The remaining controls are covered here, and then I'll give a simple example of writing your own custom control.

UISwitch

A switch (UISwitch, Figure 12-9) portrays a Bool value: it looks like a sliding switch, and its `isOn` property is either `true` or `false`. The user can slide or tap to toggle the switch's setting. When the user changes the switch's setting, the switch reports a Value Changed control event. To change the `isOn` property's value with accompanying animation, call `setOn(_:animated:)`.

A switch has only one size; any attempt to set its size will be ignored. You can customize a switch's appearance by setting these properties:

onTintColor
     The color of the track when the switch is at the On setting.

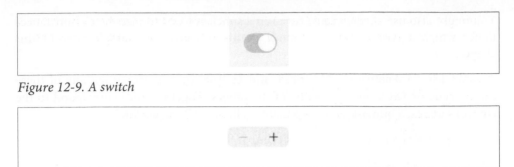

Figure 12-9. A switch

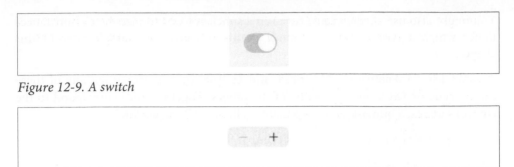

Figure 12-10. A stepper

`thumbTintColor`
> The color of the slidable button.

`tintColor`
> The color of the outline when the switch is at the Off setting.

There is no `offTintColor` property. A switch's track when the switch is at the Off setting is a translucent gray, and its color can't be customized. I regard this as a bug. Merely changing the switch's `backgroundColor` is not a successful workaround, because the background color shows outside the switch's outline. New in iOS 13, a hacky workaround is to locate the switch's subview that draws its filled shape when the switch is off, and change *its* background color:

```
self.sw.subviews[0].subviews[0].backgroundColor = .green
```

 The UISwitch properties `onImage` and `offImage`, added in iOS 6 after much clamoring (and hacking) by developers, have no effect in iOS 7 and later.

UIStepper

A stepper (UIStepper, Figure 12-10) looks like two buttons side by side, one labeled (by default) with a minus sign, the other with a plus sign. The user can tap or hold a button, and can slide a finger from one button to the other as part of the same interaction with the stepper.

The stepper maintains a numeric value, which is its `value`; this is what the user is manipulating with the stepper's buttons, incrementing or decrementing it by 1. Each time the user increments or decrements the value, it changes by the stepper's `stepValue`. If the `minimumValue` or `maximumValue` is reached, the user can go no further in that direction, and to show this, the corresponding button is disabled — unless the stepper's `wraps` property is `true`, in which case the value goes beyond the maximum by starting again at the minimum, and *vice versa*.

As the user changes the stepper's `value`, a Value Changed control event is reported. Portraying the numeric value itself is up to you; you might use a label or (as here) a progress view:

```
@IBAction func doStep(_ sender: Any) {
    let step = sender as! UIStepper
    self.prog.setProgress(
        Float(step.value / (step.maximumValue - step.minimumValue)),
        animated:true)
}
```

If a stepper's `isContinuous` is `true` (the default), a long touch on one of the buttons will update the value repeatedly; the updates start slowly and get faster. If the stepper's `autorepeat` is `false`, the updated value is not reported as a Value Changed control event until the entire interaction with the stepper ends; the default is `true`.

A stepper has only one size; any attempt to set its size will be ignored. But most other aspects of the appearance of a stepper can be customized. The color of the outline and the button captions is the stepper's `tintColor`, which may be inherited from further up the view hierarchy. You can also dictate the images that constitute the stepper's structure with these methods:

- `setDecrementImage(_:for:)`
- `setIncrementImage(_:for:)`
- `setDividerImage(_:forLeftSegmentState:rightSegmentState:)`
- `setBackgroundImage(_:for:)`

The images work similarly to a search bar's scope bar (described earlier in this chapter). The background images should probably be resizable; they are stretched behind both buttons, half the image being seen as the background of each button. If the button is disabled (because we've reached the value's limit in that direction), it displays the `.disabled` background image; otherwise, it displays the `.normal` background image, except that it displays the `.highlighted` background image while the user is tapping it. You'll probably want to provide all three background images if you're going to provide any; the default is used if a state's background image is `nil`. You'll probably want to provide three divider images as well, to cover the three combinations of one or neither segment being highlighted. The increment and decrement images, replacing the default minus and plus signs, are composited on top of the background image; they are treated as template images, colored by the `tintColor`, unless you explicitly provide an `.alwaysOriginal` image. If you provide only a `.normal` image, it will be adjusted automatically for the other two states. Figure 12-11 shows a customized stepper.

Figure 12-11. A customized stepper

UIPageControl

A page control (UIPageControl) is a row of dots; each dot is called a *page*, because it is intended to be used in conjunction with some other interface that portrays something analogous to pages, such as a UIScrollView with its `isPagingEnabled` set to `true`. Coordinating the page control with this other interface is usually up to you; see Chapter 7 for an example. A UIPageViewController in scroll style can optionally display a page control that's automatically coordinated with its content (Chapter 6).

The number of dots is the page control's `numberOfPages`. To learn the minimum bounds size required to accommodate a given number of dots, call `size(forNumberOfPages:)`. You can make the page control wider than the dots to increase the target region on which the user can tap. The user can tap to one side or the other of the current page's dot to increment or decrement the current page; the page control then reports a Value Changed control event.

The dot colors differentiate the current page, the page control's `currentPage`, from the others; by default, the current page is portrayed as a solid dot, while the others are slightly transparent. You can customize a page control's `pageIndicatorTintColor` (the color of the dots in general) and `currentPageIndicatorTintColor` (the color of the current page's dot); you will almost certainly want to do this, as the default dot color is white, which under normal circumstances may be hard to see.

It is possible to set a page control's `backgroundColor`; you might do this to show the user the tappable area, or to make the dots more clearly visible by contrast.

If a page control's `hidesForSinglePage` is `true`, the page control becomes invisible when its `numberOfPages` changes to 1.

If a page control's `defersCurrentPageDisplay` is `true`, then when the user taps to increment or decrement the page control's value, the display of the current page is not changed. A Value Changed control event is reported, but it is up to your code to handle this action and call `updateCurrentPageDisplay`. A case in point might be if the user's changing the current page triggers an animation, and you don't want the current page dot to change until the animation ends.

UIDatePicker

A date picker (UIDatePicker) looks like a UIPickerView (discussed earlier in this chapter), but it is not a UIPickerView subclass; it uses a UIPickerView to draw itself, but it provides no official access to that picker view. Its purpose is to express the notion of a date and time, taking care of the calendrical and numerical complexities so that you don't have to. When the user changes its setting, the date picker reports a Value Changed control event.

A UIDatePicker has one of four modes (`datePickerMode`), determining how it is drawn (UIDatePicker.Mode):

`.time`
> The date picker displays a time; for example, it has an hour component and a minutes component.

`.date`
> The date picker displays a date; for example, it has a month component, a day component, and a year component.

`.dateAndTime`
> The date picker displays a date and time; for example, it has a component showing day of the week, month, and day, plus an hour component and a minutes component.

`.countDownTimer`
> The date picker displays a number of hours and minutes; for example, it has an hours component and a minutes component.

Exactly what components a date picker displays, and what values they contain, depends by default upon the user's preferences in the Settings app (General → Language & Region → Region). A U.S. time displays an hour numbered 1 through 12 plus minutes and AM or PM, but a British time displays an hour numbered 1 through 24 plus minutes. If the user changes the region format in the Settings app, the date picker's display will change immediately.

A date picker has `calendar` and `timeZone` properties, respectively a Calendar and a TimeZone; these are `nil` by default, meaning that the date picker responds to the user's system settings. You can also change these values manually; if you live in California and you set a date picker's `timeZone` to GMT, the displayed time is shifted forward by 8 hours, so that 11 AM is displayed as 7 PM (if it is winter).

The minutes component, if there is one, defaults to showing every minute, but you can change this with the `minuteInterval` property. The maximum value is 30, in which case the minutes component values are 0 and 30. An attempt to set the `minuteInterval` to a value that doesn't divide evenly into 60 will be silently ignored.

The date represented by a date picker (unless its mode is `.countDownTimer`) is its `date` property, a Date. The default date is now, at the time the date picker is instantiated. For a `.date` date picker, the time by default is 12 AM (midnight), local time; for a `.time` date picker, the date by default is today. The internal value is reckoned in the local time zone, so it may be different from the displayed value, if you have changed the date picker's `timeZone`.

The maximum and minimum values enabled in the date picker are determined by its `maximumDate` and `minimumDate` properties. Values outside this range may appear, but they will be disabled and the user won't be able to choose one (the date picker will snap back so that its value stays within range). There isn't really any practical limit on the range that a date picker can display, because displayed values are appended dynamically as the user spins the "drums." In this example, we set the initial minimum and maximum dates of a date picker (dp) to the beginning and end of 1954. We also set the actual `date`, so that the date picker will be set initially to a value within the minimum–maximum range:

```
dp.datePickerMode = .date
var dc = DateComponents(year:1954, month:1, day:1)
let c = Calendar(identifier:.gregorian)
let d1 = c.date(from: dc)!
dp.minimumDate = d1
dp.date = d1
dc.year = 1955
let d2 = c.date(from: dc)!
dp.maximumDate = d2
```

The value displayed in a `.countDownTimer` date picker is its `countDownDuration`; this is a TimeInterval, which is a Double representing a number of seconds, even though the minimum interval displayed is a minute. A `.countDownTimer` date picker does not actually do any counting down! You are expected to count down in some other way, and to use some other interface to display the countdown. The Timer tab of Apple's Clock app shows a typical interface; the user configures a picker view to set the `countDownDuration` initially, but once the counting starts, the picker view is hidden and a label displays the remaining time.

 Don't change the `timeZone` of a `.countDownTimer` date picker; if you do, the displayed value will be shifted, and you will confuse the heck out of yourself (and your users). Don't set the `maximumDate` and `minimumDate` properties values for a `.countDownTimer` date picker; if you do, you might cause a crash with an out-of-range exception. A nasty bug makes the Value Changed event from a `.count-DownTimer` date picker unreliable (especially just after the app launches, and whenever the user has tried to set the timer to zero). The workaround is not to rely on the Value Changed event; you might provide a button in the interface that the user can tap to make your code read the date picker's `countDown-Duration`.

UISlider

A slider (UISlider) is an expression of a continuously settable value (its value, a Float) between some minimum and maximum (its minimumValue and maximumValue; they are 0 and 1 by default). It is portrayed as an object, the *thumb*, positioned along a *track*. As the user changes the thumb's position, the slider reports a Value Changed control event; it may do this continuously as the user presses and drags the thumb (if the slider's isContinuous is true, the default) or only when the user releases the thumb (if isContinuous is false). While the user is pressing on the thumb, the slider is in the .highlighted state. To change a slider's value with animation of the thumb, call setValue(_:animated:) *in an animations function.*

A commonly expressed desire is to modify a slider's behavior so that if the user taps on its track, the slider moves to the spot where the user tapped. Unfortunately, a slider does not, of itself, respond to taps on its track; no control event is reported. Still, with a gesture recognizer, most things are possible; here's the action method for a UITapGestureRecognizer attached to a UISlider:

```
@objc func tapped(_ g:UIGestureRecognizer) {
    let s = g.view as! UISlider
    if s.isHighlighted {
        return // tap on thumb, let slider deal with it
    }
    let pt = g.location(in:s)
    let track = s.trackRect(forBounds: s.bounds)
    if !track.insetBy(dx: 0, dy: -10).contains(pt) {
        return // not on track, forget it
    }
    let percentage = pt.x / s.bounds.size.width
    let delta = Float(percentage) * (s.maximumValue - s.minimumValue)
    let value = s.minimumValue + delta
    delay(0.1) {
        UIView.animate(withDuration: 0.15) {
            s.setValue(value, animated:true) // animate sliding the thumb
        }
    }
}
```

A slider's tintColor (which may be inherited from further up the view hierarchy) determines the color of the track to the left of the thumb. You can change the color of the two parts of the track with the minimumTrackTintColor and maximumTrackTint-Color properties. You can change the color of the thumb with the thumbTintColor property.

The images at the ends of the track are the slider's minimumValueImage and maximum-ValueImage, and they are nil by default. If you set them to actual images (which can also be done in the nib editor), the slider will attempt to position them within its own

Figure 12-12. Repositioning a slider's images and track

Figure 12-13. Replacing a slider's thumb

bounds, shrinking the drawing of the track to compensate. You can change that behavior by overriding these methods in a subclass:

- `minimumValueImageRect(forBounds:)`
- `maximumValueImageRect(forBounds:)`
- `trackRect(forBounds:)`

The bounds passed in are the slider's bounds. In this example (Figure 12-12), we expand the track width to the full width of the slider, and draw the images outside the slider's bounds. The images are still visible, because the slider does not clip its subviews to its bounds. In the figure, I've given the slider a background color so you can see how the track and images are related to its bounds:

```
override func maximumValueImageRect(forBounds bounds: CGRect) -> CGRect {
    return super.maximumValueImageRect(
        forBounds:bounds).offsetBy(dx: 31, dy: 0)
}
override func minimumValueImageRect(forBounds bounds: CGRect) -> CGRect {
    return super.minimumValueImageRect(
        forBounds: bounds).offsetBy(dx: -31, dy: 0)
}
override func trackRect(forBounds bounds: CGRect) -> CGRect {
    var result = super.trackRect(forBounds: bounds)
    result.origin.x = 0
    result.size.width = bounds.size.width
    return result
}
```

The thumb is also an image, and you set it with `setThumbImage(_:for:)`. There are two chiefly relevant states, `.normal` and `.highlighted`. If you supply images for both, the thumb will change automatically while the user is dragging it. By default, the image will be centered in the track at the point represented by the slider's current value; you can shift this position by overriding `thumbRect(forBounds:track-Rect:value:)` in a subclass. In this example, the image is repositioned slightly upward (Figure 12-13):

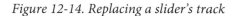

Figure 12-14. Replacing a slider's track

```
override func thumbRect(forBounds bounds: CGRect,
    trackRect rect: CGRect, value: Float) -> CGRect {
        return super.thumbRect(forBounds: bounds,
            trackRect: rect, value: value).offsetBy(dx: 0, dy: -7)
}
```

Enlarging or offsetting a slider's thumb can mislead the user as to the area where it can be touched to drag it. The slider, not the thumb, is the touchable UIControl; only the part of the thumb that intersects the slider's bounds will be draggable. The user may try to drag the part of the thumb that is drawn outside the slider's bounds, and will fail (and be confused). One solution is to increase the slider's height; if you're using autolayout, you can add an explicit height constraint in the nib editor, or override `intrinsicContentSize` in code (Chapter 1). Another solution is to subclass and use hit-test munging (Chapter 5):

```
override func hitTest(_ point: CGPoint, with e: UIEvent?) -> UIView? {
    let tr = self.trackRect(forBounds: self.bounds)
    if tr.contains(point) { return self }
    let r = self.thumbRect(
        forBounds: self.bounds, trackRect: tr, value: self.value)
    if r.contains(point) { return self }
    return nil
}
```

The track is two images, one appearing to the left of the thumb, the other to its right. They are set with `setMinimumTrackImage(_:for:)` and `setMaximumTrackImage(_:for:)`. If you supply images both for `.normal` state and for `.highlighted` state, the images will change while the user is dragging the thumb. The images should be resizable, because that's how the slider cleverly makes it look like the user is dragging the thumb along a single static track. In reality, there are two images; as the user drags the thumb, one image grows horizontally and the other shrinks horizontally. For the left track image, the right end will be hidden under the thumb; for the right track image, the left end will be hidden under the thumb. Figure 12-14 shows a track derived from a single 15×15 image of a circular object (a coin):

```
let coinEnd = UIImage(named:"coin")!.resizableImage(withCapInsets:
    UIEdgeInsets(top: 0, left: 7, bottom: 0, right: 7), resizingMode: .stretch)
self.setMinimumTrackImage(coinEnd, for:.normal)
self.setMaximumTrackImage(coinEnd, for:.normal)
```

Figure 12-15. A segmented control

UISegmentedControl

A segmented control (UISegmentedControl, Figure 12-15) is a row of tappable segments; a segment is rather like a button. The user taps a segment to select it, choosing among options. New in iOS 13, the selected segment is indicated by a rounded rectangle overlay. The behavior of this overlay depends on the segmented control's isMomentary property:

isMomentary *is* false
> The default. Tapping a segment causes the overlay to slide over to cover that segment, where it remains.

isMomentary *is* true
> When a segment is tapped, the overlay appears momentarily and then vanishes, so that there is no visible indication that any segment is selected. Internally, the tapped segment remains the selected segment.

The selected segment can be set and retrieved with the selectedSegmentIndex property; when you set it in code, the selected segment remains visibly selected, even for an isMomentary segmented control. A selectedSegmentIndex value of UISegmented-Control.noSegment means no segment is selected; in iOS 13, the overlay won't disappear unless you also call setNeedsLayout on the segmented control (this feels like a bug). When the user taps a segment that isn't already visibly selected, the segmented control reports a Value Changed event.

A segment can be individually enabled or disabled with setEnabled(_:forSegment-At:), and its enabled state can be retrieved with isEnabledForSegment(at:). A disabled segment, by default, is drawn faded; the user can't tap it, but it can still be selected in code.

New in iOS 13, the background color of the selection overlay is dictated by the segmented control's selectedSegmentTintColor.

A segment has either a title or an image; when one is set, the other becomes nil. The methods for setting and fetching the title and image for existing segments are:

- setTitle(_:forSegmentAt:), titleForSegment(at:)
- setImage(_:forSegmentAt:), imageForSegment(at:)

An image is treated as a template image unless you explicitly provide an `.always-Original` image. A template image or a title gets its default color from the effective tint color. New in iOS 13, the effective tint color is *not* the segmented control's `tint-Color`; the `tintColor` does nothing (I regard this as a bug). The default effective tint color in iOS 13 is `.label`, and the way to change it (tinting both titles and images) is to call the segmented control's `setTitleTextAttributes(_:for:)` with a different `.foregroundColor`:

```
self.seg.setTitleTextAttributes([
    .foregroundColor: UIColor.red
], for: .normal)
```

If you're creating the segmented control in code, configure the segments with `init(items:)`, which takes an array, each item being either a string or an image:

```
let seg = UISegmentedControl(items:
    [UIImage(named:"one")!.withRenderingMode(.alwaysOriginal), "Two"])
```

Methods for managing segments dynamically are:

- `insertSegment(withTitle:at:animated:)`
- `insertSegment(with:at:animated:)` (the first parameter is a UIImage)
- `removeSegment(at:animated:)`
- `removeAllSegments`

The number of segments can be retrieved with the read-only `numberOfSegments` property.

If the segmented control's `apportionsSegmentWidthsByContent` property is `false`, segment sizes will be made equal to one another; if it is `true`, each segment's width will be sized individually to fit its content. Alternatively, you can set a segment's width explicitly with `setWidth(_:forSegmentAt:)`; setting a segment's width to `0` means that this segment is to be sized automatically.

A segmented control has a standard height; if you're using autolayout, you can change the height through constraints or by overriding `intrinsicContentSize` — or by setting its background image, as I'll describe in a moment. A segmented control's height does *not* automatically increase to accommodate a segment image that's too tall; instead, the image's height is squashed to fit the segmented control's height.

To change the position of the content (title or image) within a segment, call `set-ContentOffset(_:forSegmentAt:)`.

Further methods for customizing a segmented control's appearance are parallel to those for setting the look of a stepper or the scope bar portion of a search bar:

Figure 12-16. A segmented control, customized

- setBackgroundImage(_:for:barMetrics:)

- setDividerImage(_:forLeftSegmentState:rightSegmentState:barMetrics:)

- setContentPositionAdjustment(_:forSegmentType:barMetrics:)

I'll talk later about what the barMetrics: is ("Bar Metrics" on page 740); you'll usually pass .default. The segmentType: parameter is needed because, by default, the segments at the two extremes have rounded ends (and, if a segment is the lone segment, both its ends are rounded); the argument (UISegmentedControl.Segment) lets you distinguish among the possibilities:

- .any

- .left

- .center

- .right

- .alone

As I mentioned a moment ago, setting a background image changes the segmented control's height. New in iOS 13, it also removes the selection overlay, leaving it up to you to indicate selection by supplying different background images for the .normal and .selected states (Figure 12-16):

```
let sz = CGSize(100,60)
let linen = UIImage(named:"linen")!
let im = UIGraphicsImageRenderer(size:sz).image {_ in
    linen.draw(in:CGRect(origin: .zero, size: sz))
    }.resizableImage(withCapInsets:
        UIEdgeInsets(top: 0,left: 10,bottom: 0,right: 10),
        resizingMode: .stretch)
self.seg.setBackgroundImage(im, for:.normal, barMetrics: .default)
let im2 = UIGraphicsImageRenderer(size:sz).image {ctx in
    let r = CGRect(origin: .zero, size: sz)
    ctx.cgContext.setFillColor(UIColor.blue.withAlphaComponent(0.1).cgColor)
    ctx.cgContext.fill(r)
    linen.draw(in: r, blendMode: .destinationAtop, alpha: 1)
    }.resizableImage(withCapInsets:
        UIEdgeInsets(top: 0,left: 10,bottom: 0,right: 10),
        resizingMode: .stretch)
self.seg.setBackgroundImage(im2, for:.selected, barMetrics: .default)
```

UIButton

A button (UIButton) is a fundamental tappable control, which may contain a title, an internal image (referred to simply as the button's "image"), and a background image:

Title

> Along with the title, you can add a title color and a title shadow color — or you can supply an attributed title, dictating these features and more in a single value through an NSAttributedString (Chapter 10).

Image

> The button can have both a title and an image, provided the image is small enough, in which case the image is shown to the left of the title by default; if the image is too large, the title won't appear.

> New in iOS 13, a button can have a preferred symbol configuration, in case the internal image is a symbol image. This is similar to the UIImageView preferred symbol configuration: you apply it to the button and it is applied to the symbol image for you. If the button has both a symbol image and a title, and if the title font is not the default, matching the symbol configuration to the title is up to you.

Background image

> The background image size will always match the button's bounds (technically, its `backgroundRect(forBounds:)`). Either it will resize the button to match its own size or it will stretch to match the button size. This is different from the behavior of the internal image, which might be sized down if the button is too small for it, but will never be sized up larger than its own actual size.

These features can vary depending on the button's current state, which may be either `.normal` or any combination of one or more of the other states — `.highlighted`, `.selected`, and `.disabled`. In this way, a state change, whether automatic (the button is highlighted while the user is tapping it) or programmatically imposed, can of itself alter a button's appearance. Therefore, you do not simply set them as properties; instead, you have to specify a corresponding state — or multiple states, using a bitmask:

- `setTitle(_:for:)`
- `setTitleColor(_:for:)`
- `setTitleShadowColor(_:for:)`
- `setAttributedTitle(_:for:)`
- `setImage(_:for:)`

- `setBackgroundImage(_:for:)`

- `setPreferredSymbolConfiguration(_:forImageIn:)`

Similarly, when getting these button features, you must either specify a single state you're interested in or ask about the feature as currently displayed:

- `title(for:)`, `currentTitle`

- `titleColor(for:)`, `currentTitleColor`

- `titleShadowColor(for:)`, `currentTitleShadowColor`

- `attributedTitle(for:)`, `currentAttributedTitle`

- `image(for:)`, `currentImage`

- `backgroundImage(for:)`, `currentBackgroundImage`

- `preferredSymbolConfigurationForImage(in:)`
  `currentPreferredSymbolConfiguration`

When configuring these features with the `set` methods (or in the nib editor), if you don't specify a feature for a particular state, or if the button adopts more than one state at once, an internal heuristic is used to determine what to display. I can't describe all possible combinations, but here are some general observations:

- If you specify a feature for a particular state (highlighted, selected, or disabled), and the button is in *only* that state, that feature will be used.

- If you *don't* specify a feature for a particular state (highlighted, selected, or disabled), and the button is in *only* that state, the normal version of that feature will be used as fallback. (That's why many examples earlier in this book have assigned a title for `.normal` only; that's sufficient to give the button a title in every state.)

- Combinations of states often cause the button to fall back on the feature for normal state. If a button is both highlighted and selected, the button will display its normal title, even if it has a highlighted title, a selected title, or both.

Some of the `set` methods may be animated, and this can have unpleasant side effects. Preventing the animation can be tricky. A workaround that seems reliable is to ask for layout without animation, like this:

```
self.button.setAttributedTitle(t, for: .normal) // t is an attributed string
UIView.performWithoutAnimation {
    self.button.layoutIfNeeded()
}
```

A button has a type, and the initializer is `init(type:)`. The types (UIButton.Button-Type) are:

`.system`

> If you don't provide an attributed title with an explicit color, the title text appears in the button's `tintColor`, which may be inherited from further up the view hierarchy; when the button is tapped, the title text color momentarily changes to a color derived from what's behind it (which might be the button's `backgroundColor`). The image is treated as a template image, colored by the `tintColor`, unless you explicitly provide an `.alwaysOriginal` image; when the button is tapped, the image (even if it isn't a template image) is momentarily tinted to a color derived from what's behind it.
>
> New in iOS 13, in the special case where you want a `.system` button consisting of a symbol image and nothing else, you can use a convenience class factory method, `systemButton(with:target:action:)`, where the first parameter is intended to be a symbol image.

`.custom`

> There's no automatic coloring of the title or the image, and the image is a normal image by default.

`.detailDisclosure, .infoLight, .infoDark, .contactAdd`

> System buttons whose image is set automatically to a standard image. The first three are an "i" in a circle, and are indistinguishable from one another in iOS 13. `.contactAdd` is a Plus in a circle.

`.close`

> New in iOS 13. A system button that has a dark gray "x" (the `"xmark"` symbol image) as its image and a light gray filled circle as its background image, both unaffected by the tint color. You probably should not add a title, as that would deform the filled circle.

There is no built-in button type with an outline (border), comparable to the Rounded Rect style of iOS 6 and before. You can provide an outline by some simple manipulation of the button's layer, or by constructing a background image (as in Figure 12-19).

A UIButton has some properties determining how it draws its images in various states, which can save you the trouble of specifying different images for different states:

`showsTouchWhenHighlighted`

> If `true`, then the button projects a circular white glow when highlighted. If the button has an internal image, the glow is centered behind it. This feature is suitable particularly if the button image is small and circular. If the button has no internal image, the glow is centered at the button's center. The glow is drawn on top of the background image or color, if any.

`adjustsImageWhenHighlighted`

> In a `.custom` button, if this property is `true` (the default), then if there is no separate highlighted image (and if `showsTouchWhenHighlighted` is `false`), the normal image is darkened when the button is highlighted. This applies equally to the internal image and the background image. (A `.system` button is already tinting its highlighted image, so this property doesn't apply.)

`adjustsImageWhenDisabled`

> If `true`, then if there is no separate disabled image, the normal image is shaded when the button is disabled. This applies equally to the internal image and the background image. The default is `true` for a `.custom` button and `false` for a `.system` button.

A button has a natural size in relation to its contents. If you're using autolayout, the button can adopt that size automatically as its `intrinsicContentSize`, and you can modify the way it does this by overriding `intrinsicContentSize` in a subclass or by applying explicit constraints. If you're not using autolayout and you create a button in code, send it `sizeToFit` or give it an explicit size; otherwise, the button may have size `.zero`, making it invisible. Creating a zero-size button and then wondering why the button isn't visible in the interface is a common beginner mistake.

The title is displayed in a UILabel (Chapter 10), and the label features of the title can be accessed through the button's `titleLabel`. Beginners often wonder how to make a button's title consist of more than one line; the answer is obvious, once you remember that the title is displayed in a label: set the button's `titleLabel.numberOfLines`. In general, the label's properties may be set, provided they do not conflict with existing UIButton features. You can use the label to set the title's `font` and `shadowOffset`; but the title's text, color, and shadow color should be set using the appropriate button methods specifying a button state. If the title is given a shadow in this way, then the button's `reversesTitleShadowWhenHighlighted` property also applies: if `true`, the `shadowOffset` values are replaced with their additive inverses when the button is highlighted. But the modern way to do that sort of thing is through the button's attributed title.

The internal image is drawn by a UIImageView (Chapter 2), whose features can be accessed through the button's `imageView`. For instance, you can change the internal image view's `alpha` to make the image more transparent.

The internal position of the image and title as a whole are governed by the button's `contentVerticalAlignment` and `contentHorizontalAlignment` (inherited from UIControl). You can also tweak the position of the image and title, together or separately, by setting the button's `contentEdgeInsets`, `titleEdgeInsets`, or `imageEdgeInsets`. Increasing an inset component increases that margin; a positive `top` component makes the distance between that object and the top of the button larger

Figure 12-17. A customized button

than normal (where "normal" is where the object would be according to the alignment settings). The `titleEdgeInsets` or `imageEdgeInsets` values are added to the overall `contentEdgeInsets` values. For instance, you could make the internal image appear to the right of the title by decreasing the left `titleEdgeInsets` and increasing the left `imageEdgeInsets`.

Four methods also let you customize a button's positioning of its elements by overriding them in a subclass:

- `titleRect(forContentRect:)`
- `imageRect(forContentRect:)`
- `contentRect(forBounds:)`
- `backgroundRect(forBounds:)`

Those methods are called whenever the button is redrawn, including every time it changes state. The content rect is the area in which the title and image are placed. By default, the content rect and the background rect are the same.

Here's an example of a customized button (Figure 12-17). In a UIButton subclass, we increase the button's `intrinsicContentSize` to give it larger margins around its content (for `withDelta`, see Appendix B), and we configure the background rect to shrink the button slightly when highlighted as a way of providing feedback when the user taps the button:

```
override var intrinsicContentSize : CGSize {
    return super.intrinsicContentSize.withDelta(dw:25, dh: 20)
}
override func backgroundRect(forBounds bounds: CGRect) -> CGRect {
    var result = super.backgroundRect(forBounds:bounds)
    if self.isHighlighted {
        result = result.insetBy(dx: 3, dy: 3)
    }
    return result
}
```

The button, which is a `.custom` button, is assigned an internal image and a background image from the same resizable image, along with attributed titles for the `.normal` and `.highlighted` states. The internal image glows when highlighted, thanks to `adjustsImageWhenHighlighted`.

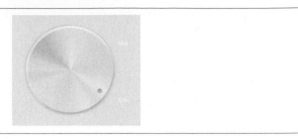

Figure 12-18. A custom control

Custom Controls

If you create your own UIControl subclass, you automatically get the built-in Touch events; in addition, there are several methods that you can override in order to customize touch tracking, along with properties that tell you whether touch tracking is going on:

- beginTracking(_:with:)
- continueTracking(_:with:)
- endTracking(_:with:)
- cancelTracking(with:)
- isTracking
- isTouchInside

The main reason for using a custom UIControl subclass — rather than, say, a UIView subclass and gesture recognizers — would probably be to obtain the convenience of control events. Also, the touch-tracking methods, though not as high-level as gesture recognizers, are at least a level up from the UIResponder touch methods (Chapter 5): they track a single touch, and both beginTracking and continueTracking return a Bool, giving you a chance to stop tracking the current touch.

To illustrate, we'll build a simplified knob control (Figure 12-18). The control starts life at its minimum position, with an internal angle value of 0; it can be rotated clockwise with a single finger as far as its maximum position, with an internal angle value of 5 (radians). The words "Min" and "Max" appearing in the interface are actually labels; the control just draws the knob, and to rotate it we'll apply a rotation transform.

Our control is a UIControl subclass, MyKnob. It has a public CGFloat angle property, and there's a private CGFloat property self.initialAngle that we'll use internally during rotation. Because a UIControl is a UIView, it can draw itself, which it does with an image file included in our app bundle:

```
override func draw(_ rect: CGRect) {
    UIImage(named:"knob")!.draw(in: rect)
}
```

We'll need a utility function for transforming a touch's Cartesian coordinates into polar coordinates, giving us the angle to be applied as a rotation to the view:

```
func pToA (_ t:UITouch) -> CGFloat {
    let loc = t.location(in: self)
    let c = self.bounds.center
    return atan2(loc.y - c.y, loc.x - c.x)
}
```

Now we're ready to override the tracking methods. beginTracking simply notes down the angle of the initial touch location. continueTracking uses the difference between the current touch location's angle and the initial touch location's angle to apply a transform to the view, and updates the angle property. endTracking triggers the Value Changed control event. So our first draft looks like this:

```
override func beginTracking(_ t: UITouch, with _: UIEvent?) -> Bool {
    self.initialAngle = pToA(t)
    return true
}
override func continueTracking(_ t: UITouch, with _: UIEvent?) -> Bool {
    let ang = pToA(t) - self.initialAngle
    let absoluteAngle = self.angle + ang
    self.transform = self.transform.rotated(by: ang)
    self.angle = absoluteAngle
    return true
}
override func endTracking(_: UITouch?, with _: UIEvent?) {
    self.sendActions(for: .valueChanged)
}
```

That works: we can put a MyKnob into the interface and hook up its Value Changed control event (this can be done in the nib editor), and sure enough, when we run the app, we can rotate the knob and, when our finger lifts from the knob, the Value Changed action method is called.

However, our class needs modification. When the angle is set programmatically, we should respond by rotating the knob; at the same time, we need to clamp the incoming value to the allowable minimum or maximum:

```
var angle : CGFloat = 0 {
    didSet {
        self.angle = min(max(self.angle, 0), 5) // clamp
        self.transform = CGAffineTransform(rotationAngle: self.angle)
    }
}
```

Now we should revise continueTracking. We no longer need to perform the rotation, since setting the angle will do that for us. On the other hand, we do need to clamp the gesture when the minimum or maximum rotation is exceeded. My solution is simply to stop tracking; in that case, endTracking will never be called, so we also need to trigger the Value Changed control event. Also, it might be nice to give the programmer the option to have the Value Changed control event reported continuously as continueTracking is called repeatedly; so we'll add a public isContinuous Bool property and obey it:

```
override func continueTracking(_ t: UITouch, with _: UIEvent?) -> Bool {
    let ang = pToA(t) - self.initialAngle
    let absoluteAngle = self.angle + ang
    switch absoluteAngle {
    case -CGFloat.greatestFiniteMagnitude...0:
        self.angle = 0
        self.sendActions(for: .valueChanged)
        return false
    case 5...CGFloat.greatestFiniteMagnitude:
        self.angle = 5
        self.sendActions(for: .valueChanged)
        return false
    default:
        self.angle = absoluteAngle
        if self.isContinuous {
            self.sendActions(for: .valueChanged)
        }
        return true
    }
}
```

Bars

There are three bar types:

UINavigationBar
 A navigation bar should appear only at the top of the screen. It is usually used in conjunction with a UINavigationController.

UIToolbar
 A toolbar may appear at the bottom or at the top of the screen, though the bottom is more common. It is usually used in conjunction with a UINavigation-Controller, where it appears at the bottom.

UITabBar
 A tab bar should appear only at the bottom of the screen. It is usually used in conjunction with a UITabBarController.

This section summarizes the facts about the three bar types and the items that populate them.

Bar Position

If a bar is to occupy the top of the screen, its apparent height should be increased to underlap the transparent status bar. This is taken care of for you in the case of a UINavigationBar owned by a UINavigationController; otherwise, it's up to you. The mechanism for doing that involves the notion of a *bar position*. The UIBarPositioning protocol is adopted by the bars that can go at the top of the screen, namely UINavigationBar and UIToolbar — along with UISearchBar, because it can be used independently as a top bar. This protocol defines one property, `barPosition`, whose possible values (UIBarPosition) are:

- `.any`
- `.bottom`
- `.top`
- `.topAttached`

But `barPosition` is read-only, so how are you supposed to set it? Use the bar's delegate! The delegate protocols UINavigationBarDelegate, UIToolbarDelegate, and UISearchBarDelegate all conform to UIBarPositioningDelegate, which defines one method, `position(for:)`. This provides a way for a bar's delegate to dictate the bar's `barPosition`. In this example, we have a "loose" navigation bar that's not owned by a navigation controller:

```
class ViewController: UIViewController, UINavigationBarDelegate {
    @IBOutlet weak var navbar: UINavigationBar!
    override func viewDidLoad() {
        super.viewDidLoad()
        self.navbar.delegate = self
    }
    func position(for bar: UIBarPositioning) -> UIBarPosition {
        return .topAttached
    }
}
```

The bar's apparent height will be extended upward so as to underlap the status bar if the bar's delegate returns `.topAttached` from its implementation of `position(for:)`. To get the final position right, the bar's top should also have a zero-constant constraint to the safe area layout guide's top.

Similarly, a toolbar or tab bar whose bottom has a zero-constant constraint to the safe area layout guide bottom will have its apparent height extended downward behind the home indicator on an iPhone without a bezel.

I say that a bar's *apparent* height is extended, because in fact its height remains untouched. It is *drawn* extended, and this drawing is visible because the bar's `clipsToBounds` is `false`. For this reason (and others), you should not set a bar's `clipsToBounds` to `true`.

Bar Metrics

Bars are almost always used in conjunction with standard parent view controllers, UINavigationController and UITabBarController. These parent view controllers will change the height of the bar in a `.compact` horizontal size class environment, depending on the vertical size class (reflecting the app's orientation), either `.regular` or `.compact`.

For this reason, some methods for setting features of a bar or a bar button item (or a view that might be used in a bar, such as a segmented control) take a *bar metrics* parameter — because you might want those features to vary depending on the automatic height applied to the bar. Possible bar metrics values are (UIBarMetrics):

- `.default`
- `.compact`
- `.defaultPrompt`
- `.compactPrompt`

The `compact` metrics apply in a `.compact` vertical size class environment. The `prompt` metrics apply to a bar whose height is extended downward to accommodate prompt text (and to a search bar whose scope buttons are showing). But in general you'll probably just supply `.default`; the feature you are configuring will then be set for *all* bar metrics that you don't specify separately.

Bar and Item Appearance

A problem with bar metrics is that it doesn't distinguish sufficiently amongst the possible bar configurations. For instance, a navigation controller's navigation bar can be extended downward in order to display a large title — and in iOS 13, it then takes on a special look (the bar becomes transparent). Similarly, a tab bar controller's tab bar on an iPhone in portrait orientation draws its tab bar items with the title under the image rather than beside it.

New in iOS 13, therefore, a hierarchy of *appearances* is introduced. Each bar type has various appearance properties (UIBarAppearance); when you customize the bar, you do so by customizing a particular bar appearance. Moreover, a bar appearance has various bar item appearances, so that you can dictate certain common features of bar button items belonging to that kind of bar. And to complete the picture, each bar item appearance comes in different flavors corresponding to the bar item's state. Here's a hierarchical outline of the various bar and bar item appearance properties:

UINavigationBar

A navigation bar has three bar appearances with three item appearances:

- `standardAppearance`, `compactAppearance`, `scrollEdgeAppearance` (UINavigationBarAppearance, a UIBarAppearance subclass)

  - `buttonAppearance`, `backButtonAppearance`, `doneButtonAppearance` (UIBarButtonItemAppearance)

    - `normal`, `disabled`, `highlighted` (UIBarButtonItemStateAppearance)

UIToolbar

A toolbar has two bar appearances with two item appearances:

- `standardAppearance`, `compactAppearance` (UIToolbarAppearance, a UIBarAppearance subclass)

  - `buttonAppearance`, `doneButtonAppearance` (UIBarButtonItemAppearance)

    - `normal`, `disabled`, `highlighted` (UIBarButtonItemStateAppearance)

UITabBar

A tab bar has one bar appearance with three item appearances:

- `standardAppearance` (UITabBarAppearance, a UIBarAppearance subclass)

  - `stackedLayoutAppearance`, `inlineLayoutAppearance`, `compactInline-LayoutAppearance` (UITabBarItemAppearance)

    - `normal`, `disabled`, `highlighted` (UITabBarItemStateAppearance)

A bar's standard appearance always exists, but the others don't (they are Optionals and are `nil` by default). If a bar has no compact appearance, the standard appearance is used. You can create a bar appearance or item appearance and assign it to an appearance property; the state appearance properties are read-only, so you just set their properties as desired.

This architecture may seem elaborate, but in fact it makes customizing bars much simpler and clearer than before, because the actual properties of the various appearance objects are simple and direct, and your customization code is easy to read and understand, as subsequent examples will show.

Bar Background and Shadow

The default bar background in iOS 13 is a blur of whatever is behind the bar, whitish in light mode and blackish in dark mode (`.systemChromeMaterial`) — except that a navigation bar, when extended to show the large title, is completely transparent with no blur. To override those defaults, use these properties of the appropriate bar appearance (UIBarAppearance):

`backgroundColor`
    A UIColor that occupies the entire bar.

`backgroundImage`
`backgroundImageContentMode`
    A UIImage that appears in front of the background color, along with the content mode for drawing it. The default content mode is `.scaleToFill`, which is probably what you want. You can supply a resizable image if you like. If the image is a template image, its color is the bar's `tintColor` by default.

`backgroundEffect`
    A UIBlurEffect. If the background color is not opaque, and if the background image has some nonopaque pixels or does not completely fill the bar, content behind the bar will be visible; this property determines how that content will be blurred to get the standard translucent effect. The default is `.systemChrome-Material`, which is probably what you want. `nil` means no blur.

To illustrate, I'll configure a navigation bar to adopt three different colors depending on its configuration; the so-called `scrollEdgeAppearance` is used when the navigation bar is extended to show the large title:

```
let bar = self.navigationController!.navigationBar
bar.prefersLargeTitles = true
let app = UINavigationBarAppearance()
app.backgroundColor = UIColor.red.withAlphaComponent(0.2)
bar.standardAppearance = app
app.backgroundColor = UIColor.blue.withAlphaComponent(0.2)
bar.compactAppearance = app
app.backgroundColor = UIColor.orange.withAlphaComponent(0.2)
bar.scrollEdgeAppearance = app
```

If I hadn't set the `compactAppearance`, a compact navigation bar would be red (using the `standardAppearance`), but I *must* set the `scrollEdgeAppearance` if I don't want the large title navigation bar to be transparent.

By default, a bar (except for the transparent large title navigation bar) casts a thin gray-tinted shadow upon whatever is behind it, at its bottom edge if it is a top bar, at its top edge if it is a bottom bar. To change the shadow, use these properties of the appropriate bar appearance:

shadowImage

> If nil, the default shadow is used. If you supply an image, it should probably be very small, just one or two pixels in height and one pixel in width; the image will be tiled to the width of the bar.

shadowColor

> If there is no shadow image, this color tints the default shadow. If there is an image and it is a template image, this color tints it. If there is an image and it is *not* a template image, the shadow color is ignored. If both the shadowImage and the shadowColor are nil, the bar will have no shadow.

As a shortcut, three convenience methods on UIBarAppearance are provided for setting a bar appearance's background properties:

configureWithDefaultBackground

> The background has the .systemChromeMaterial blur effect and the default shadow.

configureWithOpaqueBackground

> The background has the system background color and the default shadow.

configureWithTransparentBackground

> All properties are nil. There is no background color, no blur, and no shadow.

 The old isTranslucent bar property is not needed in iOS 13 and should probably be avoided. The default is true and you should leave it there. Setting it to false accomplishes nothing useful and can have unwanted side effects.

Bar Button Items

You don't add subviews to a bar. Instead, you populate the bar with *bar items*. For a navigation bar or toolbar, these will be bar button items (UIBarButtonItem, a subclass of UIBarItem). A bar button item is not a UIView, but you can still put an arbitrary view into a bar, because a bar button item can contain a custom view.

A bar button item may be instantiated with any of five methods:

- init(barButtonSystemItem:target:action:)
- init(title:style:target:action:)
- init(image:style:target:action:)
- init(image:landscapeImagePhone:style:target:action:)
- init(customView:)

The style: options (UIBarButtonItem.Style) are .plain and .done; the difference is that .done title text is bold. No bar button item style supplies an outline (border).

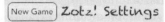

Figure 12-19. A bar button item with a border

(The .bordered style is deprecated, and its appearance is identical to .plain.) If you want an outline, you have to supply it yourself; for the left bar button item in the settings view of my Zotz! app (Figure 12-19), I use a custom view that's a UIButton with a background image.

The image is not resized for you; roughly 24×24 is a reasonable size. If you provide both an image and a landscapeImagePhone, the latter is used when the bar is compact (on an iPhone in landscape orientation — hence the name). New in iOS 13, if the image is a symbol image, there is no need for a separate landscapeImagePhone, because the scale of the symbol image configuration is adjusted automatically. A bar button item's image is treated by default as a template image, unless you explicitly provide an .alwaysOriginal image.

A bar button item's tintColor property tints the title text or template image of the button; it is inherited from the tintColor of the bar, or you can override it for an individual bar button item.

A bar button item inherits from UIBarItem the ability to adjust the image position with imageInsets (and landscapeImagePhoneInsets), plus the isEnabled and tag properties.

You can set a bar button item's width property, but if the bar button item has a custom view, you can and should size the view from the inside out using autolayout constraints.

You can also give a bar button item a background image, and you can adjust the background image's position. In addition, you can apply text attributes to the bar button item's title, and you can adjust the title's position. There are two ways to do these things: you can do them to *individual* bar button items, or you can apply them to a bar's bar button items *as a whole,* by way of the bar's appearance.

 New in iOS 13, a bar buttom item's background image is resized horizontally to fit the bar button item, *but not vertically* (unless this is a system button). This is a major change from iOS 12, where the background image is resized in both dimensions; it can break your existing interface, and I regard it as a bug.

Individual bar button item settings

Here are the UIBarButtonItem methods for customizing the title and background image of an individual bar button item. Some of these methods take a parameter that's a UIControl.State (.normal, .highlighted, and so forth). Some of them take a

UIBarMetrics parameter (.default, .compact, and so forth). Some take both. Confusingly, the for: parameter, if there is no separate barMetrics: parameter, is sometimes a UIControl.State and sometimes a UIBarMetrics (this is an unfortunate consequence of Swift 3 "renamification"). The backButton methods apply only if the bar button item is being used as a back button item in a navigation bar (as I'll describe in the next section):

Applying an attributes dictionary to a bar button item's title

- setTitleTextAttributes(_:for:)

- setTitlePositionAdjustment(_:for:)

- setBackButtonTitlePositionAdjustment(_:for:)

Giving a bar button item a background image

- setBackgroundImage(_:for:barMetrics:)

- setBackgroundImage(_:for:style:barMetrics:)

- setBackButtonBackgroundImage(_:for:barMetrics:)

- setBackgroundVerticalPositionAdjustment(_:for:)

- setBackButtonBackgroundVerticalPositionAdjustment(_:for:)

Appearance bar button item settings

The appearance methods (UIBarButtonItemStateAppearance) are:

- titleTextAttributes

- titlePositionAdjustment

- backgroundImage

- backgroundImagePositionAdjustment

They are useful particularly when you want to configure features of all (or most) of a bar's bar button items at once. You usually *do* want to do that, because uniformity is generally desirable; and if there's an exception, you can override the general appearance property settings with the individual setting methods.

Let's say I want every bar button item in my navigation bar to have a white background normally and a yellow background while the user is tapping it:

```
let bar = self.navigationController!.navigationBar
let r = UIGraphicsImageRenderer(size: CGSize(40,30))
let im = r.image { ctx in
    let con = ctx.cgContext
    con.setFillColor(UIColor.white.cgColor)
    ctx.fill(CGRect(0,0,40,30))
}
bar.standardAppearance.buttonAppearance.normal.backgroundImage = im
```

```
let im2 = r.image { ctx in
    let con = ctx.cgContext
    con.setFillColor(UIColor.yellow.cgColor)
    ctx.fill(CGRect(0,0,40,30))
}
bar.standardAppearance.buttonAppearance.highlighted.backgroundImage = im2
```

That code exemplifies how neatly we can express ourselves, thanks to the hierarchical organization of the appearance properties. If we want a different variant for a different bar configuration, we specify a different *bar* appearance; for example, if we want a smaller image height when the bar is compact, we set the bar's `compactAppearance` instead of its `standardAppearance`. If we want a different variant for a different type of bar button item, we specify a different *item* appearance; for example, if we don't want these settings to apply to the back button, we give the back button an empty (not `nil`!) image:

```
let none = UIImage()
bar.standardAppearance.backButtonAppearance.normal.backgroundImage = none
```

Navigation Bar

A navigation bar (UINavigationBar) is populated by navigation items (UINavigation-Item). The UINavigationBar maintains a stack; UINavigationItems are pushed onto and popped off of this stack. The UINavigationItem that is currently topmost in the stack (the UINavigationBar's `topItem`), in combination with the UINavigationItem just beneath it in the stack (the UINavigationBar's `backItem`), determines what appears in the navigation bar:

`title, titleView`

> The `title` (string) or `titleView` (UIView) of the `topItem` appears in the center of the navigation bar. You can and should size the `titleView` from the inside out using autolayout constraints.

`largeTitleDisplayMode`

> Whether the navigation bar's large title can be displayed; possible values are `.always`, `.never`, or `.automatic` (meaning inherited from further down the stack). The large title will not be displayed if this property is `.never`, or the navigation bar is compact, or the navigation bar's `prefersLargeTitles` is `false`. If the top view controller's main view is or contains a UIScrollView, the large title, if displayed, collapses as it is scrolled upward.

`prompt`

> The `prompt` (string) appears at the top of the navigation bar, whose height increases to accommodate it.

Figure 12-20. A back button animating to the left

`rightBarButtonItem`, `rightBarButtonItems`
`leftBarButtonItem`, `leftBarButtonItems`

> The `rightBarButtonItem` and `leftBarButtonItem` appear at the right and left ends of the navigation bar. A UINavigationItem can have multiple right bar button items and multiple left bar button items; its `rightBarButtonItems` and `leftBarButtonItems` properties are arrays (of bar button items). The bar button items are displayed from the outside in: that is, the first item in the `leftBarButtonItems` is leftmost, while the first item in the `rightBarButtonItems` is rightmost. If there are multiple buttons on a side, the `rightBarButtonItem` is the first item of the `rightBarButtonItems` array, and the `leftBarButtonItem` is the first item of the `leftBarButtonItems` array.

`backBarButtonItem`

> The `backBarButtonItem` of the `backItem` appears at the left end of the navigation bar. It is automatically configured so that, when tapped, the `topItem` is popped off the stack. Even if the `backItem` has no `backBarButtonItem`, there is *still* a back button at the left end of the navigation bar, taking its title from the `title` of the `backItem`.

> The back button can be suppressed, if:

> - The `topItem` has its `hidesBackButton` set to `true`.
> - The `topItem` has a `leftBarButtonItem`. But if the `topItem` has its `leftItemsSupplementBackButton` set to `true`, it can have both a `leftBarButtonItem` and a back button.

The indication that the back button *is* a back button is supplied by the navigation bar's `backIndicatorImage`, which by default is a left-pointing chevron appearing to the left of the back button. You can customize this image; the image that you supply is treated as a template image by default. You must also supply a `backIndicatorTransitionMaskImage`. The purpose of the mask image is to indicate the region where the back button should disappear as it slides out to the left when a new navigation item is pushed onto the stack. In Figure 12-20, the back button title, which is sliding out to the left, is visible to the right of the chevron but not to the left of the chevron; that's because on the left side of the chevron it is masked out.

New in iOS 13, we can and should perform this setting through a UINavigationBarAppearance property, by calling `setBackIndicatorImage(_:transitionMaskImage:)`. But there's a bug: this method uses the image as the mask and the mask as the image! So we have to swap them to compensate. (Try it both ways, in case Apple fixes the bug by the time you read this.) In this example, I replace the chevron with a left-pointing triangle (a symbol image):

```
let sz = CGSize(20,20)
let arrow = UIImage(systemName:"arrowtriangle.left")!
let indic =
    UIGraphicsImageRenderer(size:sz).image { ctx in
        arrow.draw(in:CGRect(0,0,20,20)) // indicator is arrow
}
let indicmask =
    UIGraphicsImageRenderer(size:sz).image { ctx in
        ctx.fill(CGRect(0,0,20,20)) // mask is entire image
    }
// but it's backward! so reverse them
bar.standardAppearance.setBackIndicatorImage(
    indicmask, transitionMaskImage: indic)
```

You can configure the attributes dictionary for the title by setting the navigation bar's titleTextAttributes, and you can shift the title's position through the title-PositionAdjustment. You can configure the large title's attributes dictionary by setting the navigation bar's largeTitleTextAttributes. New in iOS 13, these are all UINavigationBarAppearance properties. Here's how my Zotz! app configures the title shown in Figure 12-19:

```
bar.standardAppearance.titleTextAttributes = [
    .font: UIFont(name:"Chalkduster", size:20)!,
    .foregroundColor: UIColor.black
]
```

New in iOS 13, a view controller's navigationItem, like a UINavigationBar, has standardAppearance, compactAppearance, and scrollEdgeAppearance properties. Using these, different view controllers can configure the navigation bar differently, depending on which one is currently the navigation controller's topViewController.

Toolbar

A toolbar (UIToolbar, Figure 12-21) displays a row of UIBarButtonItems, which are its items. The items are displayed from left to right in the order in which they appear in the items array. You can set the items with animation by calling set-Items(_:animated:). The items within the toolbar are positioned automatically; you can intervene in this positioning by using the system bar button items .flexible-Space and .fixedSpace, along with the UIBarButtonItem width property.

When a toolbar is used as part a navigation interface (a UINavigationController's toolbar), its items are set by each child view controller through its toolbarItems property. To change the items before the user's eyes, call setToolbar-Items(_:animated:).

Figure 12-21. A toolbar

New in iOS 13, to configure all of the toolbar's bar button items uniformly, use the `buttonAppearance` (or `doneButtonAppearance`) of the toolbar's `standardAppearance` or `compactAppearance`.

Tab Bar

A tab bar (UITabBar) displays tab bar items (UITabBarItem), its `items`, each consisting of a title and an image. To change the items with animation, call `setItems(_:animated:)`. If, as will usually be the case, the tab bar is owned by a UITabBarController, the tab bar items are the `tabBarItem` properties of the tab bar controller's children, and you manipulate them with the tab bar controller's `viewControllers` and by calling `setViewControllers(_:animated:)`.

The tab bar maintains a current selection among its items, its `selectedItem`, which is a UITabBarItem, not an index number; you can set it in code, or the user can set it by tapping on a tab bar item. When the user changes the selection, `tabBar(_:didSelect:)` is sent to the delegate (UITabBarDelegate). With a UITabBarController, the tab bar controller is the delegate, and you'll use its `selectedViewController` or `selectedIndex`, along with its delegate (UITabBarControllerDelegate).

You get very little control over how the tab bar items are laid out, and even then only when the tab bar items are "stacked," meaning that the icon appears above the title (only on an iPhone in portrait orientation):

Item positioning
> New in iOS 13, this can be set through the tab bar's `standardAppearance`, using the UITabBarAppearance `stackedItemPositioning` property. There are three possible values (UITabBar.ItemPositioning):

> `.centered`
>> The items are crowded together at the center.

> `.fill`
>> The items are spaced out evenly.

> `.automatic`
>> On the iPhone, the same as `.fill`. (On the iPad, the same as `.centered`; but tab bar items are never stacked on the iPad nowadays, so this appears to be a dead letter.)

Item spacing

In iOS 13, the standard appearance's `stackedItemSpacing`. The space between items, if the positioning is `.centered`. For the default space, specify 0.

Item width

In iOS 13, the standard appearance's `stackedItemWidth`. The width of the items, if the positioning is `.centered`. For the default width, specify 0.

Here's an example:

```
let tb = self.tabBarController!.tabBar
let tbapp = UITabBarAppearance()
tbapp.stackedItemPositioning = .centered
tbapp.stackedItemSpacing = 0
tbapp.stackedItemWidth = 35
tb.standardAppearance = tbapp
```

You can set an image to be drawn behind the selected tab bar item to indicate that it's selected; it is the tab bar's `selectionIndicatorImage`. The documentation claims that in iOS 13 you can set the `selectionIndicatorImage`, along with the `selection-IndicatorTintColor`, through the tab bar's `standardAppearance`; but in my tests this is not working.

A UITabBarItem is created with one of these methods:

- `init(tabBarSystemItem:tag:)`
- `init(title:image:tag:)`
- `init(title:image:selectedImage:)`

UITabBarItem is a subclass of UIBarItem, so in addition to its `title` and `image` it inherits the ability to adjust the image position with `imageInsets`, plus the `isEnabled` and `tag` properties. The UITabBarItem itself adds the `selectedImage` property; this image replaces the `image` when this item is selected.

You can assign a tab bar item an alternate `landscapeImagePhone` (inherited from UIBarItem) to be used on the iPhone in landscape orientation. However, doing so disables the `selectedImage`; I regard that as a bug. The best workaround is to supply the `image` only, as a vector image or symbol image (Chapter 2).

A tab bar item's image is treated, by default, as a template image, tinted with the tab bar's `tintColor` when selected and with its `unselectedItemTintColor` otherwise. New in iOS 13, you can use the UITabBarAppearance `iconColor` property instead:

```
let app = UITabBarAppearance()
app.stackedLayoutAppearance.normal.iconColor = .red
app.stackedLayoutAppearance.selected.iconColor = .green
tb.standardAppearance = app
```

Figure 12-22. A tab bar

A tab bar item's title is also tinted when selected, by default, with the the tab bar's `tintColor`.

Getting full control of a tab bar item's title color and other text attributes is not easy. In theory, you should be able to call `setTitleTextAttributes(_:for:)`, inherited from UIBarItem, setting a color for `.normal` and a color for `.selected`:

```
let f = UIFont(name: "Georgia", size: 13)!
self.tabBarItem.setTitleTextAttributes(
    [.font:f, .foregroundColor:UIColor.red], for: .normal)
self.tabBarItem.setTitleTextAttributes(
    [.font:f, .foregroundColor:UIColor.green], for: .selected)
```

The trouble is that in iOS 13 the `.normal` color is ignored. I regard that as a bug. You can work around it by setting the tab bar's `unselectedItemTintColor`:

```
self.tabBarController?.tabBar.unselectedItemTintColor = .red
```

But that's too broad a brush; what if you wanted to set the `.normal` title color of different tab bar items to different colors?

Here's another problem. In theory, you should be able to set the `titleText-Attributes` for a tab bar's items by way of the tab bar's `standardAppearance`, like this:

```
let app = UITabBarAppearance()
app.stackedLayoutAppearance.normal.titleTextAttributes = [
    .font:UIFont(name:"Avenir-Heavy", size:14)!,
    .foregroundColor:UIColor.black
]
self.tabBarController?.tabBar.standardAppearance = app
```

Unfortunately, that causes the tab bar item titles to be truncated. That's a clear bug, and I have not found a workaround.

New in iOS 13, a tab bar item has a `standardAppearance` property. Using this, different view controllers can configure the tab bar differently, depending on which one's tab bar item is currently selected. (But you can't use it to work around the tab bar `standardAppearance` bugs.)

Figure 12-22 is an example of a customized tab bar, I've set the tab bar's selection indicator image (the checkmark), the icon color (golden when selected), and the text attributes of the tab bar items (green when selected).

Figure 12-23. Automatically generated More list

The user can be permitted to alter the contents of the tab bar, setting its tab bar items from among a larger repertoire of tab bar items. When used in conjunction with a UITabBarController, the customization interface is provided automatically. If there are a lot of items, a More item is present as the last item in the tab bar; the user can tap this to access the remaining items through a table view. In this table view, the user can select any of the excess items to navigate to the corresponding view, or switch to the customization interface by tapping the Edit button. Figure 12-23 shows how a More list looks by default.

The way this works is that the automatically provided More item corresponds to a UINavigationController with a root view controller whose `view` is a UITableView. You have access to this navigation controller as the UITabBarController's `more-NavigationController`, and therefore you can customize its appearance to some extent.

Tint Color

Both UIView and UIBarButtonItem have a `tintColor` property. This property has a remarkable built-in feature: its value, if not set explicitly (or if set to `nil`), is inherited from its superview. (UIBarButtonItems don't have a superview, because they aren't views; but for purposes of this feature, pretend that they are views, and that the containing bar is their superview.)

The idea is to simplify the task of giving your app a consistent overall appearance. Many built-in interface objects use the `tintColor` for some aspect of their appearance, as I've already described. If a `.system` button's `tintColor` is red, either because you've set it directly or because it has inherited that color from higher up the view hierarchy, it will have red title text by default.

The inheritance architecture works exactly the way you would expect:

Superviews and subviews
> When you set the `tintColor` of a view, that value is inherited by all subviews of that view. The ultimate superview is the window; you can set the `tintColor` of

your UIWindow instance, and its value will be inherited by *every* view that ever appears in your interface.

Overriding

The inherited `tintColor` can be overridden by setting a view's `tintColor` explicitly. You can set the `tintColor` of a view partway down the view hierarchy so that it and all its subviews have a different `tintColor` from the rest of the interface. In this way, you might subtly suggest that the user has entered a different world.

Propagation

If you change the `tintColor` of a view, the change immediately propagates down the hierarchy of its subviews — except, of course, that a view whose `tintColor` has been explicitly set to a color of its own is unaffected, along with its subviews.

Whenever a view's `tintColor` changes, including when its `tintColor` is initially set at launch time, and including when *you* set it in code, this view and all its affected subviews are sent the `tintColorDidChange` message. A subview whose `tintColor` has been explicitly set to a color of its own is *not* sent the `tintColorDidChange` message merely because its superview's `tintColor` changes; that's because the subview's own `tintColor` *didn't* change.

When you ask a view for its `tintColor`, what you get is the `tintColor` of the view itself, if its own `tintColor` has been explicitly set to a color, or else the `tintColor` inherited from higher up the view hierarchy. In this way, you can always learn what the *effective* tint color of a view is.

A UIView also has a `tintAdjustmentMode`. Under certain circumstances, such as the summoning of an alert (Chapter 13) or a popover (Chapter 9), the system will set the `tintAdjustmentMode` of the view at the top of the view hierarchy to `.dimmed`. This causes the `tintColor` to change to a variety of gray. The idea is that the tinting of the background should become monochrome, emphasizing the primacy of the view that occupies the foreground (the alert or popover). See "Custom Presented View Controller Transition" on page 361 for an example of my own code making this change.

By default, a change in the `tintAdjustmentMode` propagates all the way down the view hierarchy, changing *all* `tintAdjustmentMode` values and *all* `tintColor` values — and sending *all* subviews the `tintColorDidChange` message. When the foreground view goes away, the system will set the topmost view's `tintAdjustmentMode` to `.normal`, and that change, too, will propagate down the hierarchy.

This propagation behavior is governed by the `tintAdjustmentMode` of the subviews. The default `tintAdjustmentMode` value is `.automatic`, meaning that you want this view's `tintAdjustmentMode` to adopt its superview's `tintAdjustmentMode` automatically. When you ask for a view's `tintAdjustmentMode`, what you get is just like what you get for `tintColor` — you're told the *effective* tint adjustment mode (`.normal` or `.dimmed`) inherited from up the view hierarchy.

If, on the other hand, you set a view's `tintAdjustmentMode` *explicitly* to `.normal` or `.dimmed`, this tells the system that you want to be left in charge of the `tint-AdjustmentMode` for this part of the hierarchy, preventing automatic propagation. To turn automatic propagation back on, set the `tintAdjustmentMode` back to `.automatic`.

Appearance Proxy

When you want to customize the look of an interface object, instead of sending a message to the object itself, you can send that message to an *appearance proxy* for that object's class. The appearance proxy then passes that same message along to the actual *future* instances of that class. You'll usually configure your appearance proxies once very early in the lifetime of the app, and never again. The app delegate's `application(_:didFinishLaunchingWithOptions:)`, before the window has been displayed, is the obvious place to do this, because your code runs before *any* instances of *any* interface objects are created, and affects *all* of them.

This architecture, like the `tintColor` that I discussed in the previous section, helps you give your app a consistent appearance with a minimum of code. Also, the appearance proxy sometimes allows customization of interface objects that you have no official way to refer to directly (such as a search bar's external Cancel button).

There are four class methods for obtaining an appearance proxy:

`appearance`
> Returns a general appearance proxy for the receiver class. The method you call on the appearance proxy will be applied generally to future instances of this class.

`appearance(for:)`
> The parameter is a *trait collection*. The method you call on the appearance proxy will be applied to future instances of the receiver class when the environment matches the specified trait collection.

`appearance(whenContainedInInstancesOf:)`
> The argument is an *array of classes*, arranged in order of containment from inner to outer. The method you call on the appearance proxy will be applied only to instances of the receiver class that are actually contained in the way you describe. The notion of what "contained" means is deliberately left vague; basically, it works the way you intuitively expect it to work.

`appearance(for:whenContainedInInstancesOf:)`
> A combination of the preceding two.

When configuring appearance proxy objects, *specificity trumps generality*. You could call `appearance` to say what should happen for *most* instances of some class, and call the other methods to say what should happen instead for *certain* instances of that class. Similarly, longer `whenContainedInInstancesOf:` chains are more specific than shorter ones.

Here's some code from my Latin flashcard app (`myGolden` and `myPaler` are class properties defined by an extension on UIColor):

```
UIBarButtonItem.appearance().tintColor = .myGolden ❶
UIBarButtonItem.appearance(
    whenContainedInInstancesOf: [UIToolbar.self])
        .tintColor = .myPaler ❷
UIBarButtonItem.appearance(
    whenContainedInInstancesOf: [UIToolbar.self, DrillViewController.self])
        .tintColor = .myGolden ❸
```

That means:

❶ In general, bar button items should be tinted golden.

❷ But bar button items in a toolbar are an exception: they should be tinted paler.

❸ But bar button items in the toolbar in DrillViewController's view are an exception to the exception: they should be tinted golden.

Sometimes, in order to express sufficient specificity, I find myself defining subclasses for no other purpose than to refer to them when obtaining an appearance proxy. Here's some more code from my Latin flashcard app:

```
let app = UINavigationBarAppearance()
app.backgroundImage = marble
UINavigationBar.appearance().compactAppearance = app
let app2 = UINavigationBarAppearance()
app2.titleTextAttributes = [.foregroundColor: UIColor.white]
app2.backgroundColor = .black
BlackNavigationBar.appearance().compactAppearance = app2
```

In that code, BlackNavigationBar is a UINavigationBar subclass that does nothing whatever. Its sole purpose is to tag one navigation bar in my interface so that I can refer to it in that code! As a result, I'm able to say, in effect, "All navigation bars in this app should have `marble` as their background image, except for the one BlackNavigationBar."

(That code also demonstrates that the new iOS 13 bar appearance properties can themselves be applied to a class appearance proxy.)

The ultimate in specificity is to customize the look of an instance directly. If you set one particular UIBarButtonItem's `tintColor` property, then setting the tint color by way of a UIBarButtonItem appearance proxy will have no effect on that particular bar button item.

Not every message that can be sent to an instance of a class can be sent to that class's appearance proxy. Unfortunately, the compiler can't help you here; illegal code like this will compile, but will probably crash at runtime:

```
UIBarButtonItem.appearance().action = #selector(configureAppearance)
```

The problem is not that UIBarButtonItem has no `action` property; on the contrary, that code compiles because it *does* have an `action` property! But that property is not one that you can set by way of the appearance proxy, and the mistake isn't caught until that line executes and the runtime tries to configure an actual UIBarButtonItem.

When in doubt, look at the class documentation; there should be a section that lists the properties and methods applicable to the appearance proxy for this class. The UINavigationBar class documentation has a section called "Customizing the Bar Appearance," the UIBarButtonItem class documentation has a section called "Customizing Appearance," and so forth.

To define your own appearance-compliant property, declare that property `@objc dynamic` in your UIView subclass.

CHAPTER 13

Modal Dialogs

A modal dialog demands attention; while it is present, the user can do nothing other than work within it or dismiss it. This chapter discusses various forms of modal dialog:

- Within your app, you can show alerts and action sheets. An *alert* is basically a message, possibly with an opportunity for text entry, and some buttons. An *action sheet* is effectively a column of buttons.

- You can provide a sort of action sheet even when your app is not frontmost (or even running) by allowing the user to summon *quick actions* — also known as *shortcut items* — by long pressing on your app's icon.

- A *local notification* is an alert that the system presents on your app's behalf, even when your app isn't frontmost.

- A *today widget* is interface that appears in the screen that the user sees by swiping sideways in the lock screen or home screen. Your app can provide a today widget by means of a today extension. Your today widget can also appear as a quick action.

- An *activity view* is typically summoned by the user from a Share button. It displays possible courses of external and internal action (activities), such as handing off data to another app, or processing data within your app. Your app can also provide activities that *other* apps can display in *their* activity views, through an action extension or share extension.

Alerts and Action Sheets

Alerts and action sheets are both forms of presented view controller (Chapter 6). They are managed through the UIAlertController class, a UIViewController subclass. To show an alert or an action sheet is a three-step process:

1. Instantiate UIAlertController with `init(title:message:preferredStyle:)`. The `title:` and `message:` are large and small descriptive text to appear at the top of the dialog. The `preferredStyle:` argument (UIAlertController.Style) will be either `.alert` or `.actionSheet`.

2. Configure the dialog by calling `addAction(_:)` on the UIAlertController as many times as needed. An action is a UIAlertAction, which basically means it's a button to appear in the dialog, along with a function to be executed when the button is tapped; to create one, call `init(title:style:handler:)`. Possible `style:` values are (UIAlertAction.Style):

   - `.default`
   - `.cancel`
   - `.destructive`

   An alert may also have text fields (I'll talk about that in a moment).

3. Call `present(_:animated:completion:)` to present the UIAlertController.

The dialog is automatically dismissed when the user taps any button.

Alerts

An alert (UIAlertController style `.alert`) pops up unexpectedly in the middle of the screen, with an elaborate animation, and may be thought of as an attention-getting interruption. It contains a title, a message, and some number of buttons, one of which may be the cancel button, meaning that it does nothing but dismiss the alert. In addition, an alert may contain one or two text fields.

Alerts are minimal, and intentionally so: they are meant for simple, quick interactions or display of information. Often there is only a cancel button, the primary purpose of the alert being to show the user the message ("You won the game!"); additional buttons may be used to give the user a choice of how to proceed ("You won the game; would you like to play another?" "Cancel," "Play Another," "Replay").

Figure 13-1 shows a basic alert, illustrating the title, the message, and the three button styles: `.destructive`, `.default`, and `.cancel` respectively. Here's the code that generated it:

```
let alert = UIAlertController(title: "Not So Fast!",
    message: """
    Do you really want to do this \
    tremendously destructive thing?
    """,
    preferredStyle: .alert)
func handler(_ act:UIAlertAction) {
    print("User tapped \(act.title as Any)")
}
```

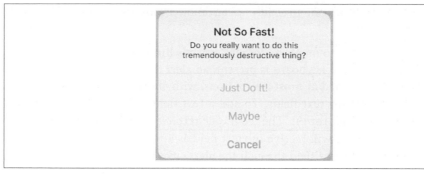

Figure 13-1. An alert

```
alert.addAction(UIAlertAction(title: "Cancel",
    style: .cancel, handler: handler))
alert.addAction(UIAlertAction(title: "Just Do It!",
    style: .destructive, handler: handler))
alert.addAction(UIAlertAction(title: "Maybe",
    style: .default, handler: handler))
self.present(alert, animated: true)
```

In Figure 13-1, the `.destructive` button appears first and the `.cancel` button appears last, without regard to the order in which they were added with `addAction`. The order in which the `.default` buttons were added, on the other hand, will be the order of the buttons themselves. If no `.cancel` button is added, the last `.default` button will be displayed as a `.cancel` button.

You can also designate an action as the alert's `preferredAction`. This appears to boldify the title of that button. Suppose I append this to the preceding code:

```
alert.preferredAction = alert.actions[2]
```

The order of the `actions` array is the order in which we added actions, so the preferred action is now the Maybe button. The order isn't changed — the Maybe button still appears second — but the bold styling is removed from the Cancel button and placed on the Maybe button instead.

The dialog is dismissed automatically when the user taps a button. If you don't want to respond to the tap of a particular button, you can supply `nil` as the `handler:` argument (or omit it altogether), but the dialog will still be dismissed. In the preceding code, I've provided a minimal `handler:` function, just to show what one looks like. As the example demonstrates, the function receives the original UIAlertAction as a parameter, and can examine it as desired. The function can also access the alert controller itself, provided the alert controller is in scope at the point where the `handler:` function is defined (which will usually be the case). My example code assigns the same function to all three buttons, but more often you'll give each button its own individual `handler:` function, probably as an anonymous function using trailing closure syntax.

Text fields may be added to an alert. Because space is limited on the smaller iPhone screen, especially when the keyboard is present, an alert that is to contain a text field should probably be assigned at most two buttons, with short titles such as "OK" and "Cancel," and at most two text fields. To add a text field to an alert, call `addText-Field(configurationHandler:)`. The `configurationHandler:` function is called *before* the alert appears; it will receive the text field as a parameter. Button `handler:` functions can access the text field through the alert's `textFields` property, which is an array.

In this example, the user is invited to enter a number in a text field. When the text field is added, its `configurationHandler:` function configures the keyboard. If the alert is dismissed with the OK button, the OK button's `handler:` function reads the text from the text field:

```
let alert = UIAlertController(title: "Enter a number:",
    message: nil, preferredStyle: .alert)
alert.addTextField { tf in
    tf.keyboardType = .numberPad
}
func handler(_ act:UIAlertAction) {
    let tf = alert.textFields![0]
    // ... can read tf.text here ...
}
alert.addAction(UIAlertAction(title: "Cancel", style: .cancel))
alert.addAction(UIAlertAction(title: "OK",
    style: .default, handler: handler))
self.present(alert, animated: true)
```

A puzzle arises as to how to prevent the user from dismissing the alert if the text fields are not acceptably filled in. The alert will be dismissed if the user taps a button, and no button `handler:` function can prevent this. The solution is to *disable* the relevant buttons until the text fields are satisfactory. A UIAlertAction has an `isEnabled` property for this very purpose. I'll modify the preceding example so that the OK button is disabled initially:

```
alert.addAction(UIAlertAction(title: "Cancel", style: .cancel))
alert.addAction(UIAlertAction(title: "OK",
    style: .default, handler: handler))
alert.actions[1].isEnabled = false
self.present(alert, animated: true)
```

But this raises a new puzzle: how will the OK button ever be enabled? The text field can have a delegate or a control event target–action pair (Chapter 10), and so we can hear about the user typing in it. I'll modify the example again so that I'm notified as the user edits the text field:

```
alert.addTextField { tf in
    tf.keyboardType = .numberPad
    tf.addTarget(self,
        action: #selector(self.textChanged), for: .editingChanged)
}
```

Our `textChanged` method will now be called when the user edits, but this raises a further puzzle: how will this method, which receives a reference to the text field, get a reference to the OK button in the alert in order to enable it? My approach is to work my way up the responder chain from the text field to the alert controller. Here, I enable the OK button if and only if the text field contains some text:

```
@objc func textChanged(_ sender: Any) {
    let tf = sender as! UITextField
    var resp : UIResponder? = tf
    while !(resp is UIAlertController) { resp = resp?.next }
    let alert = resp as? UIAlertController
    alert?.actions[1].isEnabled = (tf.text != "")
}
```

But there is a hole in our implementation, because a user with a hardware keyboard can still enter nondigits and can still press Return to dismiss the alert even when the text field is empty. To prevent *that*, we also give the text field a delegate (in the `handler:` function for `alert.addTextField`) and implement the appropriate delegate methods:

```
func textField(_ textField: UITextField,
    shouldChangeCharactersIn range: NSRange,
    replacementString string: String) -> Bool {
        if string.isEmpty { return true }
        if Int(string) == nil { return false }
        return true
}
func textFieldShouldReturn(_ textField: UITextField) -> Bool {
    return textField.text != ""
}
```

Action Sheets

An action sheet (UIAlertController style `.actionSheet`) may be considered the iOS equivalent of a menu; it consists primarily of buttons. On the iPhone, it slides up from the bottom of the screen; on the iPad, it appears as a popover.

Where an alert is an interruption, an action sheet is a crossroads: it presents courses of action between which the user is to choose. In Apple's Messages app, the edit button summons an action sheet whose buttons are Select Messages, Edit Name and Photo, and Cancel. An action sheet is often used to give the user a second chance before taking a possibly destructive action. In Apple's Photos app, asking to delete a photo brings up an action sheet whose buttons are Delete Photo and Cancel; in

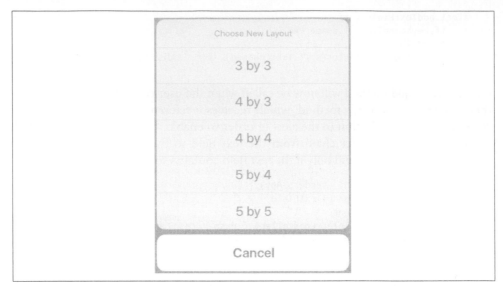

Figure 13-2. An action sheet on the iPhone

Apple's Calendar app, starting to create a new event and then canceling brings up an action sheet whose buttons are Discard Changes and Keep Editing.

Figure 13-2 shows a basic action sheet on the iPhone. It was constructed with the following code:

```
let action = UIAlertController(
    title: "Choose New Layout", message: nil, preferredStyle: .actionSheet)
action.addAction(UIAlertAction(title: "Cancel", style: .cancel))
func handler(_ act:UIAlertAction) {
    // ... do something here with act.title ...
}
for s in ["3 by 3", "4 by 3", "4 by 4", "5 by 4", "5 by 5"] {
    action.addAction(UIAlertAction(title: s,
        style: .default, handler: handler))
}
self.present(action, animated: true)
```

On the iPad, an action sheet wants to be a popover. This means that a UIPopover-PresentationController will take charge of it. It is incumbent upon you to provide something for the popover's arrow to point to (as explained in Chapter 9) or you'll crash at runtime:

```
self.present(action, animated: true)
if let pop = action.popoverPresentationController {
    let v = sender as! UIView
    pop.sourceView = v
    pop.sourceRect = v.bounds
}
```

Figure 13-3. A presented view behaving like an alert

The cancel button for a popover action sheet on the iPad is suppressed, because the user can dismiss the popover by tapping outside it. On the iPhone, too, where the cancel button is displayed, the user can *still* dismiss the action sheet by tapping outside it. When the user does that, the cancel button's handler: function will be called, just as if the user had tapped the cancel button — even if the cancel button is not displayed.

Alert Alternatives

Alerts and action sheets are deliberately limited, inflexible, and inappropriate to any but the simplest cases. Their interface can contain title text, buttons, and (for an alert) one or two text fields, and that's all. What if you wanted more interface than that?

Some developers have hacked into their alerts or action sheets in an attempt to force them to be more customizable. *This is wrong*, and in any case there is no need for such extremes. These are just presented view controllers, and if you don't like what they contain, you can make your own presented view controller with its own customized view. If you also want that view to look and behave like an alert or an action sheet, then make it so!

As I have shown ("Custom Presented View Controller Transition" on page 361), it is easy to create a small presented view that looks and behaves quite like an alert or action sheet, floating in front of the main interface and darkening everything behind it — the difference being that this is an ordinary view controller's view, belonging entirely to you, so that you can populate it with any interface you like (Figure 13-3).

But a presented view controller doesn't have to look like an alert in order to have the same effect. A popover is virtually a secondary window, and can be truly modal. The popovers in Figure 9-1 are effectively modal dialogs. A presented view controller on an iPad can use the .formSheet presentation style, which is effectively a dialog window smaller than the screen. On the iPhone, *any* presented view is essentially a modal dialog, and can replace an alert or action sheet. In Apple's Mail app, when reading a mail message, the action button in iOS 12 and earlier summons an action sheet letting the user reply to the current message, forward it, or print it; in iOS 13,

Apple wanted to add many more options, so now that button summons a custom presented view controller instead of an action sheet.

Quick Actions

Quick actions are essentially a column of buttons summoned when the user long presses on your app's icon. They should represent convenient ways of accessing functionality that the user could equally have performed from within your app.

Quick actions are of two kinds:

Static quick actions
> Static quick actions are described in your app's *Info.plist*. The system can present them even if your app isn't running — indeed, even if your app has *never* run — because it can read your app's *Info.plist*.

Dynamic quick actions
> Dynamic quick actions are configured in code. This means that they are not available until your app's code has actually run. Your code can alter and remove dynamic quick actions, but it cannot affect your app's static quick actions.

When the user taps a quick action, your app is brought to the front (launching it if necessary) and a delegate method is called. In iOS 12 and before, this was an app delegate method; in iOS 13 with window scene support, it is a scene delegate method. You'll be handed a UIApplicationShortcutItem describing the button the user tapped; now you can respond as appropriate.

A UIApplicationShortcutItem is just a value class, embodying five properties describing the button that will appear in the interface. Those five properties have analogs in the *Info.plist*, so that you can configure your static quick actions. The *Info.plist* UIApplicationShortcutItems entry is an array of dictionaries, one for each quick action, each containing the properties and values you wish to set.

The UIApplicationShortcutItem properties and corresponding *Info.plist* keys are:

`type`
`UIApplicationShortcutItemType`
> An arbitrary string. You can use this string in your delegate method to distinguish which button was tapped. Required.

`localizedTitle`
`UIApplicationShortcutItemTitle`
> The button title; a string. Required.

localizedSubtitle
UIApplicationShortcutItemSubtitle
> The button subtitle; a string. Optional.

icon
UIApplicationShortcutItemIconType
UIApplicationShortcutItemIconFile
> An icon to appear in the button. Optional, but it's good to supply some icon, because if you don't, you'll get an ugly filled circle by default. When forming a UIApplicationShortcutItem in code, you'll supply a UIApplicationShortcutIcon object as its icon property. UIApplicationShortcutIcon has four initializers:

> init(type:)
> > A UIApplicationShortcutIcon.IconType. This is an enum of about 30 cases, each representing a built-in standard image, such as .time (a clock icon).

> init(templateImageName:)
> > Works like UIImage's init(named:). The image will be treated as a template image. Apple says that the image should be 35×35, though a larger image will be scaled down appropriately.

> init(systemImageName:)
> > New in iOS 13. Works like UIImage's init(systemName:). The image should be a symbol image.

> init(contact:)
> > A CNContact (see Chapter 18). The icon will be based on the contact's picture or initials.

> In the *Info.plist*, you may use either the IconType key or the IconFile key. The value for the IconType key is the Objective-C name of a UIApplicationShortcutIcon.IconType case, such as UIApplicationShortcutIconTypeTime. The value for the IconFile key is the name of an image file in your app, suitable for use with UIImage(named:).

userInfo
UIApplicationShortcutItemUserInfo
> An optional dictionary of additional information, whose usage is completely up to you.

To illustrate, imagine that our app's purpose is to remind the user periodically to go get a cup of coffee. Figure 13-4 shows a quick actions menu of three items generated when the user long presses our app's icon. The first two items are static items, generated by our settings in the *Info.plist*, which is shown in Figure 13-5.

Figure 13-4. Quick actions

▼ UIApplicationShortcutItems	Array	(2 items)
▼ Item 0	Dictionary	(5 items)
UIApplicationShortcutItemIconFile	String	cup
UIApplicationShortcutItemSubtitle	String	In 5 minutes...
UIApplicationShortcutItemTitle	String	Coffee Reminder
UIApplicationShortcutItemType	String	coffee.schedule
▼ UIApplicationShortcutItemUserInfo	Dictionary	(1 item)
time	Number	5
▼ Item 1	Dictionary	(5 items)
UIApplicationShortcutItemIconFile	String	cup
UIApplicationShortcutItemSubtitle	String	In 15 minutes...
UIApplicationShortcutItemTitle	String	Coffee Reminder
UIApplicationShortcutItemType	String	coffee.schedule
▼ UIApplicationShortcutItemUserInfo	Dictionary	(1 item)
time	Number	15

Figure 13-5. Static quick actions in the Info.plist

The third quick action item in Figure 13-4 is a dynamic item. The idea is that our app lets the user set a time interval as a favorite default interval. We cannot know what this favorite interval will be until the app runs and the user sets it; that's why this item is dynamic. Here's the code that generates it; all we have to do is set our shared UIApplication object's shortcutItems property:

```
let subtitle = "In 1 hour..." // or whatever
let time = 60 // or whatever
let item = UIApplicationShortcutItem(type: "coffee.schedule",
    localizedTitle: "Coffee Reminder", localizedSubtitle: subtitle,
    icon: UIApplicationShortcutIcon(templateImageName: "cup"),
    userInfo: ["time":time as NSNumber])
UIApplication.shared.shortcutItems = [item]
```

Both in the *Info.plist* static quick actions and in this dynamic quick action, I've configured the userInfo so that when I receive this UIApplicationShortcutItem in my delegate method, I can look at the value of its "time" key to find out what time interval the user specified.

So now let's say the user taps one of the quick action buttons. Our delegate method is called! If our app is already running, this will be the scene delegate's window-

Scene(_:performActionFor:completionHandler:) method. In our response, we are supposed to finish by calling the completionHandler, passing a Bool to indicate success or failure; but in fact I see no difference in behavior regardless of whether we pass true or false, or even if we omit to call the completionHandler entirely:

```
func windowScene(_ windowScene: UIWindowScene,
    performActionFor shortcutItem: UIApplicationShortcutItem,
    completionHandler: @escaping (Bool) -> Void) {
        if shortcutItem.type == "coffee.schedule" {
            if let d = shortcutItem.userInfo {
                if let time = d["time"] as? Int {
                    // ... do something with time ...
                    completionHandler(true)
                }
            }
        }
        completionHandler(false)
}
```

If our app is launched from scratch by the user tapping a quick action button, windowScene(_:performActionFor:completionHandler:) is *not* called. Instead, we have to implement scene(_:willConnectTo:options:) and check whether the options: parameter's shortcutItem isn't nil:

```
func scene(_ scene: UIScene,
    willConnectTo session: UISceneSession,
    options connectionOptions: UIScene.ConnectionOptions) {
        if let shortcutItem = connectionOptions.shortcutItem {
            if shortcutItem.type == "coffee.schedule" {
                if let d = shortcutItem.userInfo {
                    if let time = d["time"] as? Int {
                        // ... do something with time ...
                    }
                }
            }
        }
}
```

New in iOS 13, if your app supports multiple windows on iPad, the runtime needs a way to know *which* window scene's delegate to call. To answer that question, use your UIScene's activationConditions: set it to a UISceneActivationConditions object whose canActivateForTargetContentIdentifierPredicate and prefersToActivateForTargetContentIdentifierPredicate properties specify appropriate predicates. The targetContentIdentifier in question is a property of UIApplicationShortcutItem; it's just a string, such as "myShortcutIdentifier". The predicate's self *is* the incoming targetContentIdentifier string, so the predicate will be something like this:

```
let pred = NSPredicate(format: "self == 'myShortcutIdentifier'")
```

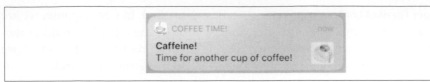

Figure 13-6. A local notification

 Apple has not explained how to specify a symbol image or a target content identifier for a static UIApplicationShortcutItem defined in the *Info.plist*.

Local Notifications

A local notification (Figure 13-6) is an alert to the user that can appear even if your app is not frontmost — indeed, even if your app is not running. Your app does not present a local notification; the system does. You instruct the system as to when the notification should *fire*, and then you just stand back and let the system deal with it. (The notification *can* appear even when your app *is* frontmost; but even then it is the system that is presenting it on your behalf.)

Notification alerts can appear in any of these venues:

- On the lock screen.
- In the notification center; this is the interface that appears when the user swipes down from the top screen edge.
- As a banner at the top of the screen.

A local notification, as it fires, can do other things:

- It can play a sound.
- It can cause a badge number to appear on, or to be removed from, your app's icon.

Taken together, those five possibilities constitute your app's *delivery options* for local notifications. The user, in the Settings app, can veto any of the delivery options for your app's local notifications, and can even turn off your app's local notifications entirely. The user can also do just the opposite, turning on delivery options that were previously turned off. A user who permits your notifications to appear as a banner also gets to choose between a *temporary* banner, which vanishes spontaneously after displaying itself briefly, and a *persistent* banner, which remains until the user dismisses it.

The user can also, upon receipt of a notification from your app, summon a Manage Notifications dialog, where a Deliver Quietly button limits your app's notifications to appear only in the notification center; there is also a Turn Off button that suppresses them entirely (Figure 13-7). Other user settings can affect notification delivery as

Figure 13-7. The user manages your app's notifications

well; for instance, the user turning on Do Not Disturb has the same effect as choosing Deliver Quietly.

The user can interact with local notification alerts in some rudimentary ways. At a minimum, a local notification alert can be tapped as a way for the user to summon your app, bringing it to the front if it is backgrounded, and launching it if it isn't running. This response to the notification is its *default action*. In the lock screen or notification center, the user can slide the notification to reveal standard buttons such as Clear (to close the alert), Manage (to bring up the dialog shown in Figure 13-7), and Open (to summon your app).

The user can also elect to *view* the notification. Depending on the circumstances, the user might slide the notification sideways to reveal the View button and tap it, or drag it downward, or long press it. This produces the notification's *secondary interface*, which you get to design.

You can add *custom actions*, in the form of buttons to appear in the secondary interface. A local notification can also carry an *attachment*, which may be an image, a sound file, or a video; in the secondary interface, if the attachment is an image, the image is displayed, and if the attachment is audio or video, interface is provided for playing it.

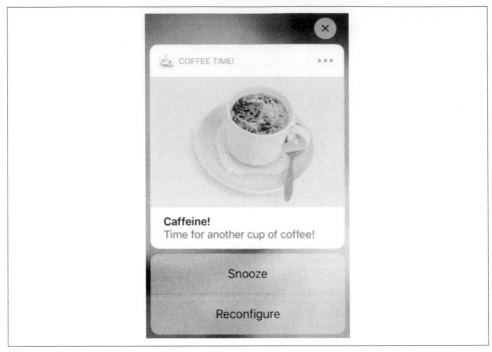

Figure 13-8. Local notification secondary interface

In Figure 13-6, the little image at the right of the alert is the thumbnail of an image attachment. In Figure 13-8, the user has summoned the alert's secondary interface, displaying the image as well as two custom action buttons.

But wait, there's more! You can modify the secondary interface still further by writing a *notification content extension*. This lets you design the interior of the secondary interface however you like. Figure 13-9 shows an example; I've replaced the default title and body with a caption in my own font, and I've shown the attachment image in a smaller size.

Use of a local notification involves several steps:

1. Your app must obtain *authorization* for notifications.

2. You might register a notification *category*.

3. Your app creates and *schedules* the local notification, handing it over to the system.

4. Your app is prepared to hear about the user *responding* to the notification after it fires.

I'll describe this sequence one step at a time; then I'll talk about writing a notification content extension.

Figure 13-9. Local notification with custom secondary interface

You'll need to import the User Notifications framework (`import User-Notifications`). Most of your activity will ultimately involve the user notification center, a singleton UNUserNotificationCenter instance available by calling `UNUser-NotificationCenter.current()`.

Authorization for Local Notifications

You have a choice of two strategies for obtaining initial authorization for your app's notifications:

Full authorization

> This form of authorization, broadly speaking, has been around since iOS 8. Before trying to schedule any local notifications, you ask the system to present a one-time authorization alert on your behalf. The user must choose between granting and denying authorization to your app (Figure 13-10, on the left). An app that gains full authorization in this way is eligible initially for all delivery options.

Provisional authorization

> This form of authorization was introduced in iOS 12. With *no* explicit user authorization, you can be *automatically* authorized for "quiet" delivery: your notifications can appear in the notification center *only*, with no sound and no icon badging. In the notification center, your notification is accompanied by options to keep or turn off your app's notifications (Figure 13-10, on the right). If the user ignores this choice, "quiet" delivery of your app's notifications will continue. If the user taps Keep, an action sheet lets the user grant your app full authorization.

Figure 13-10. Two ways of requesting user authorization

Which strategy should you choose? Full authorization, if you can obtain it, gives your notifications the widest range of possible venues immediately; but it can be hard to obtain. Who of us hasn't seen that alert (Figure 13-10, on the left) and wondered: "What's *that* all about?" If you're like me, you instinctively tap Don't Allow and move on. The idea of provisional authorization is that the user, having seen your notifications in the notification center, and having understood what they are for, might then grant full authorization. But whatever sort of authorization you obtain initially is just that — initial authorization. The user, at any time, can return to the Settings app and increase or decrease the powers of your local notifications.

Whichever strategy you decide on, your first step before scheduling any local notifications should be to find out whether we are already authorized. To do so, call the user notification center's `getNotificationSettings` method. It returns a UNNotificationSettings object asynchronously; examine the `authorizationStatus` property of that object. The possibilities are (UNAuthorizationStatus):

`.denied`
> The user has explicitly disallowed all notifications from your app. There may be no point scheduling any local notifications, as they will not fire unless the user's settings are changed. (You might put up an alert begging the user to switch to the Settings app and authorize your app's notifications.)

`.authorized`
> You have full authorization. Go ahead and schedule a local notification.

`.provisional`
> You have provisional authorization. Go ahead and schedule a local notification.

`.notDetermined`
> This is the really interesting case — the moment when you're going to try to get authorization! You should immediately send `requestAuthorization(options:)` to the user notification center. A Bool is returned asynchronously, telling you

whether authorization was granted. The `options:` argument is a UNAuthorizationOptions object, an option set that can include any of the following:

`.badge`
`.sound`
`.alert`

> The maximum range of abilities you want your app to have. `.badge` means you might want your app's icon to be badged with a number when a notification fires. `.sound` means you might want a sound to play when a notification fires. `.alert` means you might want a notification alert to be presented when a notification fires. Be sure to include all choices that might be needed for any of your app's notifications, as you won't get another chance! For instance, if you don't include `.badge`, the switch that lets the user turn on badges for your app's notifications will never even appear in Settings.

`.provideAppNotificationSettings`

> I'll discuss this more in a moment.

`.provisional`

> You are opting for provisional authorization.

If your UNAuthorizationOptions *doesn't* include `.provisional`, your call to `requestAuthorization(options:)` when the authorization status is `.notDetermined` will cause the authorization alert to appear (Figure 13-10, on the left), and the user must make a choice on the spot. The outcome of that choice is the Bool that is returned from the call to `requestAuthorization(options:)`. If it *does* include `.provisional`, that alert will *never* appear, and you will be granted provisional authorization immediately — the Bool will be `true`.

Both `getNotificationSettings` and `requestAuthorization(options:)` return their results *asynchronously* (see Appendix C) and possibly on a background thread (Chapter 24). This means that you cannot simply follow a call to `getNotificationSettings` with a call to `requestAuthorization(options:)`; if you do, `requestAuthorization(options:)` will run *before* `getNotificationSettings` has a chance to return its UNNotificationSettings object! Instead, you must *nest* the calls by means of their completion functions, like this:

```
let center = UNUserNotificationCenter.current()
center.getNotificationSettings { settings in
    switch settings.authorizationStatus {
    case .denied: break // or beg for authorization
    case .authorized, .provisional: break // or schedule a notification
    case .notDetermined:
        center.requestAuthorization(options:[.alert, .sound]) { ok, err in
            if let err = err {
                return // could do something with the error information
```

```
            }
            if ok {
                // authorized; could schedule a notification
            }
        }
    }
    @unknown default: fatalError()
}
```

The parameter that arrives in your `getNotificationSettings` completion function (`settings` in the preceding code) is a UNNotificationSettings object. This object describes your app's notification settings in the Settings app as they are configured at this moment. That information might be of interest at any time, especially because the user can change those settings. In addition to its `authorizationStatus`, a UNNotificationSettings object has the following properties:

`soundSetting`
`badgeSetting`
`alertSetting`
`notificationCenterSetting`
`lockScreenSetting`
> How the user has configured the notification settings for your app. A UNNotificationSetting:
>
> - `.enabled`
> - `.disabled`
> - `.notSupported`

`alertStyle`
> How the user has configured the alert style setting for your app. A UNAlertStyle:
>
> - `.banner`
> - `.alert`
> - `.none`

`showPreviewsSetting`
> How the user has configured previews for your app. I'll discuss the implications of this setting later. A UNShowPreviewsSetting:
>
> - `.always`
> - `.whenAuthenticated`
> - `.never`

```
providesAppNotificationSettings
```
This depends on whether your app included `.provideAppNotification-Settings` when requesting authorization. I'll explain that later, when I talk about the user notification center delegate.

Notification Categories

A notification category is a somewhat nebulous entity, embracing a miscellany of possible settings to be associated with individual notifications. You register any desired categories with the user notification center; each category has an arbitrary string identifier. Later, when you create a notification, you associate it with a previously registered category by means of that string identifier.

Categories have grown over the years to embrace more and more settings, so a category (UNNotificationCategory) now has three initializers with increasingly more parameters. The fullest form is:

- `init(identifier:actions:intentIdentifiers:hiddenPreviewsBody-Placeholder:categorySummaryFormat:options:)`

The `identifier:` is how a subsequent notification will be matched to this category. I'll talk about the other parameters later (except for `intentIdentifiers:`; it has to do with SiriKit, which is not covered in this book).

To bring a category into force, you register it with the user notification center by calling `setNotificationCategories`. The parameter is an array of categories:

```
let cat1 = UNNotificationCategory(identifier: /* ... */)
let cat2 = UNNotificationCategory(identifier: /* ... */)
let cat3 = UNNotificationCategory(identifier: /* ... */)
let center = UNUserNotificationCenter.current()
center.setNotificationCategories([cat1, cat2, cat3])
```

There are no category management commands, in the sense of adding or removing individual categories. But the categories are maintained as a Set, so it does no harm to register the same identical category multiple times. Moreover, there is a command that allows you to *get* categories; you can retrieve the existing categories, add a category to the list, and set the categories again:

```
let center = UNUserNotificationCenter.current()
center.getNotificationCategories { cats in
    var cats = cats
    let newcat = UNNotificationCategory(identifier: /* ... */)
    cats.insert(newcat)
    center.setNotificationCategories(cats)
}
```

You might use a notification category for any of the following purposes:

- You want your notification's secondary interface to display custom actions.

- You want your app to be notified when the user dismisses your notification.

- You want to customize the text of your notification when the user has suppressed previews.

- You want to customize the text that summarizes your notifications when they are grouped.

I'll talk now about the first three of those uses, leaving grouped notifications for later.

Custom actions

Custom actions are basically buttons that appear in a notification's secondary interface (Figure 13-8). Before iOS 12, the only way to get these was through a notification category. Starting in iOS 12, you can create custom actions in a notification context extension, so you don't need to use a category for this unless your notification has no corresponding notification context extension.

A custom action is a UNNotificationAction, a value class whose initializer is:

- `init(identifier:title:options:)`

The `identifier:` is an arbitrary string; you might use it later to distinguish which button was tapped. The `title:` is the text to appear in the button. The `options:` are a UNNotificationActionOptions bitmask; here are the options and what they mean if you include them:

`.foreground`
Tapping this button summons your app to the foreground. Otherwise, this button will call your app in the background; your app will be given just enough time to respond and will then be suspended.

`.destructive`
This button will be marked in the interface as dangerous (by being displayed in red).

`.authenticationRequired`
If this is not a `.foreground` button, then if the user's device requires authentication (such as a passcode) to go beyond the lock screen, tapping this button in the lock screen will also require authentication. The idea is to prevent performance of this action from the lock screen without the user explicitly unlocking it.

Alternatively, an action can be a text field where the user can type and then tap a button to send the text to your app. This is a UNTextInputNotificationAction, a UNNotificationAction subclass. Its initializer is:

- `init(identifier:title:options:textInputButtonTitle:textInput-Placeholder:)`

Having created your actions, initialize your UNNotificationCategory with the actions in an array as the `actions:` argument. I'll explain how your app responds to the tapping of a custom action button later, when I talk about the user notification center delegate (and custom content extensions).

Dismiss action

The user can dismiss your local notification (removing it from the notification center) without interacting with it in any other way that might cause your app to get an event — without tapping it to summon your app (the default action) and without tapping a custom action button. Normally, when that happens, your app will get no event at all, so you won't even know that the user has seen the notification.

However, you can change that. In the UNNotificationCategory initializer, the `options:` parameter is a UNNotificationCategoryOptions, an option set. Include `.customDismissAction` if you want your code to get an event under those circumstances. I'll explain how your app gets this event later, when I talk about the user notification center delegate.

Previews

Notifications can pop up unexpectedly, including on the lock screen. So the user might prefer, in the interests of privacy, to suppress the notification's text when the alert initially appears. The text would then be visible only in the notification's secondary interface. The text in a local notification alert when it initially appears is called the *preview* of the notification.

In the Settings app, the user has three choices about when previews should be permitted to appear: always, when the phone is unlocked (to prevent the previews on the lock screen only), and never.

By default, if previews are turned off, the title and subtitle of the notification are suppressed, and the body text is replaced by a placeholder — the word "Notification." Instead of "Notification," you can supply your own placeholder. In the UNNotificationCategory initializer, set the `hiddenPreviewsBodyPlaceholder:` argument to the desired placeholder.

If your notification's title and subtitle contain no sensitive information, you can cause them to appear even if previews are turned off. To do so, include the UNNotificationCategoryOptions `.hiddenPreviewsShowTitle` and `.hiddenPreviewsShowSubtitle` in the `options:` argument when you initialize your UNNotificationCategory.

Scheduling a Local Notification

To schedule a notification, you create a UNNotificationRequest, by calling its designated initializer:

- `init(identifier:content:trigger:)`

You then tell the user notification center to `add(_:)` this notification to its internal list of scheduled notifications.

The `identifier:` is an arbitrary string. You might use this later on to distinguish which notification this is. And it lets you prevent clutter. If you schedule a notification when a previous notification with the same identifier is already scheduled, the previous notification is deleted; if a notification fires (is delivered) when a previous notification with the same identifier is already sitting in the notification center, the previous notification is deleted.

The `content:` is the heart and soul of this individual notification — what it is to display, what information it carries, and so forth. It is sometimes referred to as the *payload* of the notification. It is a UNNotificationContent object, but that class is immutable; in order to *form* the payload, you'll start by instantiating its mutable subclass, UNMutableNotificationContent. You will then assign values to as many of its properties as you like. Those properties are:

`title`, `subtitle`, `body`
> Text visible in the notification alert.

`attachments`
> UNNotificationAttachment objects. An attachment is created by calling its designated initializer:
>
> - `init(identifier:url:options:)`
>
> The `identifier:` is an arbitrary string. The `url:` is the attachment itself; it must be a file URL pointing to an image file, an audio file, or a video file on disk. The file must be fairly small, because the system, in order to present it on your behalf in the notification's interface after the notification fires some time in the future, is going to *copy* it off to a private secure area of its own.

`sound`
> A sound (UNNotificationSound) to be played when the notification fires. You can specify a sound file in your app bundle by name (UNNotificationSound-Name), or call `default` to specify the default sound:
>
> ```
> content.sound =
>     UNNotificationSound(named: UNNotificationSoundName("test.aif"))
> ```

---

badge

A number to appear on your app's icon after this notification fires. Specify `0` to remove an existing badge. (You can also set or remove your app's icon badge at any time by means of the shared application's `applicationIconBadgeNumber`.)

categoryIdentifier

The identifier string of a previously registered category. This is how your local notification will be associated with the settings you've applied to that category.

userInfo

An arbitrary dictionary, to carry extra information you'll retrieve later.

threadIdentifier

A string; notification alerts with the same thread identifier are grouped together physically in the lock screen and notification center. I'll talk more about that later.

launchImageName

Your app might be launched from scratch by the user tapping this notification's alert. Suppose that when this happens, you're going to configure your app so that it appears differently from how it normally launches. You might want the momentary launch screen, shown while your app starts up, to correspond to that different interface. This is how you specify the alternative launch image to be used in that situation.

The `trigger:` parameter tells the system how to know when it's time for this notification to fire. It will be expressed as a subclass of UNNotificationTrigger:

UNTimeIntervalNotificationTrigger

Fires starting a certain number of seconds from now, possibly repeating every time that number of seconds elapses. The initializer is:

- `init(timeInterval:repeats:)`

UNCalendarNotificationTrigger

Fires at a certain date-time, expressed using DateComponents, possibly repeating when the same DateComponents occurs again. For instance, if you use the Date-Components to express nine o'clock in the morning, without regard to date, then the trigger, if repeating, would be nine o'clock *every* morning. The initializer is:

- `init(dateMatching:repeats:)`

UNLocationNotificationTrigger

Fires when the user enters or leaves a certain geographical region. I'll discuss this further in Chapter 21.

As an example, here's the code that generated Figure 13-6:

```
let interval = // ... whatever ...
let trigger = UNTimeIntervalNotificationTrigger(
    timeInterval: interval, repeats: false)
let content = UNMutableNotificationContent()
content.title = "Caffeine!"
content.body = "Time for another cup of coffee!"
content.sound = UNNotificationSound.default
content.categoryIdentifier = self.categoryIdentifier
let url = Bundle.main.url(forResource: "cup2", withExtension: "jpg")!
if let att = try? UNNotificationAttachment(
    identifier: "cup", url: url, options:nil) {
        content.attachments = [att]
}
let req = UNNotificationRequest(
    identifier: "coffeeNotification", content: content, trigger: trigger)
let center = UNUserNotificationCenter.current()
center.add(req)
```

Hearing About a Local Notification

In order to hear about your scheduled local notification after it fires, you need to configure some object to be the user notification center's `delegate`, adopting the UNUserNotificationCenterDelegate protocol. You'll want to do this very early in your app's lifetime, because you might need to be sent a delegate message immediately upon launching; `application(_:didFinishLaunchingWithOptions:)` is a good place. The user notification center delegate might be the app delegate itself, or it might be some helper object that the app delegate creates and retains:

```
func application(_ application: UIApplication,
    didFinishLaunchingWithOptions launchOptions:
    [UIApplication.LaunchOptionsKey : Any]?) -> Bool {
        let center = UNUserNotificationCenter.current()
        center.delegate = self // or whatever
        return true
}
```

The UNUserNotificationCenterDelegate protocol consists of three optional methods. All three of them provide you with a UNNotification object containing the fire `date` and your original `request` (UNNotificationRequest). You can identify the local notification, and you can extract information from it, such as an attachment or the `userInfo` dictionary. Here are the delegate methods:

`userNotificationCenter(_:willPresent:withCompletionHandler:)`
This method is called only if your app is frontmost when your local notification fires. By default, when that happens, the notification's entire user interface is suppressed: no sound is played, no banner appears, no notification is added to the notification center or the lock screen. This method lets *you* know that the notification fired, but the *user* has no way of knowing. The idea is that your app

itself, as it is already frontmost, might inform the user of whatever the user needs to know.

However, you can opt to let the system do what it would have done if your app had *not* been frontmost. You are handed a completion function; you *must* call it, with some combination of UNNotificationPresentationOptions values — `.alert`, `.sound`, and `.badge` — or an empty option set, if you want the default behavior. Here's an example where we tell the runtime to present the local notification alert within our app:

```
func userNotificationCenter(_ center: UNUserNotificationCenter,
    willPresent notification: UNNotification,
    withCompletionHandler completionHandler:
    @escaping (UNNotificationPresentationOptions) -> ()) {
        completionHandler([.sound, .alert])
}
```

`userNotificationCenter(_:didReceive:withCompletionHandler:)`
Called when the user interacts with your local notification alert. The second parameter is a UNNotificationResponse, consisting of two properties. One, the `notification`, is the UNNotification object. The other, the `actionIdentifier`, is a string telling you what the user did; there are three possibilities:

`UNNotificationDefaultActionIdentifier`
The user performed the default action, tapping the alert or the Open button to summon your app.

`UNNotificationDismissActionIdentifier`
The user dismissed the local notification alert. You won't hear about this (and this method won't be called) unless you specified the `.customDismiss-Action` option for this notification's category.

A custom action identifier string
The user tapped a custom action button, and this is its `identifier`.

If the custom action was a text input action, then the UNNotificationResponse will be a subclass, UNTextInputNotificationResponse, which has an additional `userText` property. You'll cast down safely and retrieve the `userText`:

```
if let textresponse = response as? UNTextInputNotificationResponse {
    let text = textresponse.userText
    // ...
}
```

You are handed a completion function, which you *must* call when you're done. You must be quick, because it may be that you are being awakened momentarily in the background, and your code is running on the main thread. Here's an example where the user has tapped a custom action button; I use a background task (Chapter 24) and my delay utility (Appendix B) so as to return immediately before proceeding to obey the button:

```
func userNotificationCenter(_ center: UNUserNotificationCenter,
    didReceive response: UNNotificationResponse,
    withCompletionHandler completionHandler: @escaping () -> ()) {
        let id = response.actionIdentifier
        if id == "snooze" {
            var id = UIBackgroundTaskIdentifier.invalid
            id = UIApplication.shared.beginBackgroundTask {
                UIApplication.shared.endBackgroundTask(id)
            }
            delay(0.1) {
                self.createNotification()
                UIApplication.shared.endBackgroundTask(id)
            }
        }
        completionHandler()
}
```

If the user tapped on your notification alert (the default action), your app is activated and, if necessary, launched from scratch. New in iOS 13, if your app with window scene support is launched from scratch or if the notification is routed to a scene that was previously disconnected, your scene delegate's scene(_:will-ConnectTo:options:) is called with the notificationResponse in its options: parameter. As with a shortcut item, you can set your notification request content's targetContentIdentifier to specify which scene the notification should be routed to. In any case, userNotificationCenter(_:didReceive:with-CompletionHandler:) is still called.

userNotificationCenter(_:openSettingsFor:)

When you requested authorization, you may have included the .provideApp-NotificationSettings option. Doing so constitutes a promise that your app provides its own *internal interface* for letting the user manage notifications-related settings. In response, the runtime provides on your behalf a special app notification settings button in appropriate places like the Settings app. The user has now tapped that button, and you should immediately display that interface.

How might you use this feature? Well, suppose your app has several clearly distinct categories of notification; you might want to allow the user to elect to turn notifications on or off for a particular category. Your app provides interface for letting the user do that, and the button in the Settings app provides a direct pathway to that interface. The idea is that permitting the user to perform fine-grained notification management will reduce clutter in the user's interface and might increase the chances that the user will allow your app to continue sending notifications.

Figure 13-11. A local notification group

Figure 13-12. Customizing a group summary

Grouped Notifications

In iOS 12 and later, grouping of notifications by app is the default (though, as usual, the user can turn it off). So you do not need to set the `threadIdentifier` of a notification request's payload (UNMutableNotificationContent) merely in order to group your notifications in the lock screen and the notification center. Rather, the purpose of the `threadIdentifier` is so that, if you have multiple notification types, you can use different `threadIdentifier` values to subdivide your app's group into multiple groups.

Another way to tweak your grouped notifications is to change the summary text that labels each group. In Figure 13-11, the summary text "2 more notifications" is generated automatically. It might be nice to customize it, depending on what sort of thing my notifications represent. For example, I might like to describe these notifications as "reminders." That's the purpose of the `categorySummaryFormat:` parameter of the UNNotificationCategory initializer.

The `categorySummaryFormat:` is a format string. At a minimum, it will contain a `"%u"` format specifier where the count is to go, such as `"%u more reminders"` (Figure 13-12).

When you create the payload for your notification, you can supply a `summaryArgument` string. By default, the summary text will then incorporate this as the sender or source of the notification; if the `summaryArgument` for three notifications is `"Matt"`, the summary text will say "2 more notifications from Matt." To customize that, my `categorySummaryFormat` string would need to contain a `"%@"` format specifier where the summary argument is to go, such as `"%u more reminders from %@"`.

(Rarely, an app might also include a `summaryArgumentCount` in the payload. This is to cover the special case where a single notification represents more than one of whatever is represented. In the summary text, the count will be sum of the `summaryArgumentCount` values of the grouped notifications, rather than just the count of the grouped notifications.)

Managing Notifications

The user notification center is introspectable. It vends two lists of notifications: those that have been scheduled but have not yet fired, and those that have fired but have not yet been removed from the user's notification center:

Scheduled notifications

These are the methods for managing scheduled notifications:

- `getPendingNotificationRequests(completionHandler:)`
- `removePendingNotificationRequests(withIdentifiers:)`
- `removeAllPendingNotificationRequests`

You can examine the list of scheduled notifications, and you can remove a notification from the list to cancel it; that also means you can effectively reschedule a notification (by removing it, copying it with any desired alterations, and adding the resulting notification).

Delivered notifications

These are the methods for managing delivered notifications:

- `getDeliveredNotifications(completionHandler:)`
- `removeDeliveredNotifications(withIdentifiers:)`
- `removeAllDeliveredNotifications`

By judicious removal of notifications from this list, you can keep the user's notification center trimmed. You might prefer that only your most recently delivered notification should appear in the notification center. You can even modify the text of a delivered notification, so that the notification will be up-to-date when the user gets around to dealing with it; to do so, you add a notification whose identifier is the same as that of an existing notification.

 Canceling a repeating local notification is up to your code; if you don't provide a way of doing that, then if the user wants to prevent the notification from recurring, the only recourse may be to delete your app.

Notification Content Extensions

You can customize what appears in your notification's secondary interface. To do so, you write a *notification content extension*. This is a target, separate from your app target, because the system needs to access it outside your app, possibly when your app isn't even running.

To add a notification content extension to your app, create a new target and specify iOS → Application Extension → Notification Content Extension. The template gives you a good start on your extension. You have a storyboard with a single scene, and the code for a corresponding view controller. The code file imports both the User Notifications framework and the User Notifications UI framework, and the view controller adopts the UNNotificationContentExtension protocol.

The view controller code contains a stub implementation of the `didReceive(_:)` method, which is the only required method. The parameter is a UNNotification whose `request` is your original UNNotificationRequest; you can examine this and extract information from it as you configure your interface. If you want to extract an attachment, you'll have to wrap your access in calls to these URL methods:

- `startAccessingSecurityScopedResource`
- `stopAccessingSecurityScopedResource`

The only other thing your view controller really needs to do is to set its own `preferredContentSize` to the desired dimensions of the custom interface. Alternatively, you can use autolayout to size the interface from the inside out.

To illustrate, here's how the custom interface in Figure 13-9 was attained. The interface consists of a label and an image view. The image view is to contain the image attachment from the local notification, so I extract the image from the attachment and set it as the image view's image. I find that the interface doesn't reliably appear unless we also call `setNeedsLayout` at the end:

```
override func viewDidLoad() {
    super.viewDidLoad()
    self.preferredContentSize = CGSize(320, 80)
}
func didReceive(_ notification: UNNotification) {
    let req = notification.request
    let content = req.content
    let atts = content.attachments
    if let att = atts.first, att.identifier == "cup" {
        if att.url.startAccessingSecurityScopedResource() {
            if let data = try? Data(contentsOf: att.url) {
                self.imageView.image = UIImage(data: data)
            }
            att.url.stopAccessingSecurityScopedResource()
```

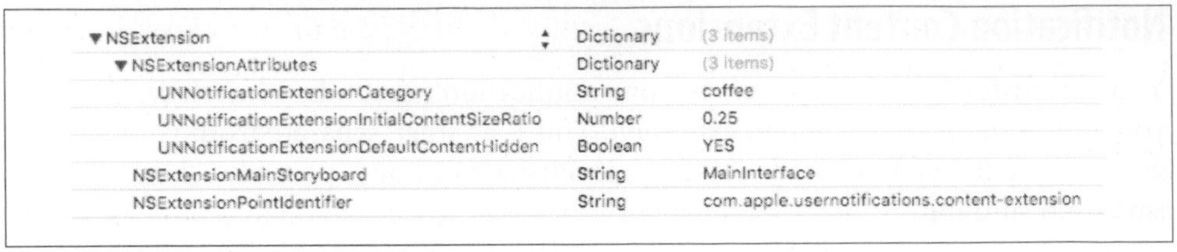

▼ NSExtension		Dictionary	(3 items)
	▼ NSExtensionAttributes	Dictionary	(3 items)
	UNNotificationExtensionCategory	String	coffee
	UNNotificationExtensionInitialContentSizeRatio	Number	0.25
	UNNotificationExtensionDefaultContentHidden	Boolean	YES
	NSExtensionMainStoryboard	String	MainInterface
	NSExtensionPointIdentifier	String	com.apple.usernotifications.content-extension

Figure 13-13. A content extension's Info.plist

```
            }
        }
        self.view.setNeedsLayout()
    }
```

The template also includes an *Info.plist* for your extension. You will need to modify it by configuring these keys:

UNNotificationExtensionCategory

A string corresponding to the categoryIdentifier of the local notification(s) to which this custom secondary interface is to be applied. This is how the runtime knows to associate this notification content extension with this notification! There does *not* have to be an actual category with this identifier.

UNNotificationExtensionInitialContentSizeRatio

A number representing the width of your custom interface divided by its height. This doesn't have to be perfect — and indeed it probably can't be, since you don't know the actual width of the screen on which this interface will be displayed — but the idea is to give the system a rough idea of the size as it prepares to display the custom interface.

UNNotificationExtensionDefaultContentHidden

Optional. A Boolean. Set to YES if you want to eliminate the default display of the local notification's title, subtitle, and body from the custom interface.

UNNotificationExtensionOverridesDefaultTitle

Optional. A Boolean. Set to YES if you want to replace the default display of your app's name at the top of the interface (where it says "Coffee Time!" in Figure 13-9) with a title of your own choosing. To determine that title, set your view controller's title property in your didReceive(_:) implementation.

Figure 13-13 shows the relevant part of the *Info.plist* for my content extension.

Action button management

Your secondary interface may include custom action buttons. If the user taps one of these, your user notification center delegate's userNotificationCenter(_:did-Receive:withCompletionHandler:) is called, as I described earlier. However, your notification content extension view controller can intervene in this mechanism by implementing `didReceive(_:completionHandler:)`. This is different from `did-Receive(_:)`! The parameter is a UNNotificationResponse, not a UNNotification, and there's a second parameter, the completion function.

What you do in your implementation of `didReceive(_:completionHandler:)` is up to you. You might respond by changing the interface in some way. When you've finished doing whatever you came to do, the runtime needs to know how to proceed; you tell it by calling the completion function with one of these responses (UNNotificationContentExtensionResponseOption):

`.doNotDismiss`
> The local notification alert remains in place, still displaying the custom secondary interface.

`.dismiss`
> The alert is dismissed.

`.dismissAndForwardAction`
> The alert is dismissed and the action is passed along to your user notification center delegate's `userNotificationCenter(_:didReceive:withCompletion-Handler:)`.

Even if you tell the completion function to dismiss the alert, you can *still* modify the interface, delaying the call to the completion function so that the user has time to see the change.

Your notification content extension view controller can create and remove custom actions on the fly, in code. Your view controller inherits the UIViewController `extensionContext` property, which is an NSExtensionContext object. Its `notificationActions` property is an array of UNNotificationAction. A UNNotificationAction is an action button! This array therefore initially consists of whatever action buttons you configured in your category — and any changes you make to it will immediately be reflected by the action buttons the user sees.

This means you don't have to create your custom actions in your category configuration in the first place! Creating custom action buttons in your category configuration allows you to have custom buttons *without* a notification content extension. But if you have a notification content extension, you can create the custom actions in the view controller's `didReceive(_:completionHandler:)` instead.

Interface interaction

Prior to iOS 12, a custom secondary interface (the notification content extension view controller's main view) is *not interactive*. If the user taps it, nothing happens — except that the notification's default action is performed, which means that the notification is dismissed and your app is summoned. The exception is that the runtime can add a tappable play/pause button for you; this is useful if your custom interface contains video or audio material. Three UNNotificationContentExtension properties can be overridden to dictate that the play/pause button should appear and where it should go, and two methods can be implemented to hear when the user taps the play/pause button.

Starting in iOS 12, the view controller's main view *can* be interactive. This is an opt-in feature: under the `NSExtensionAttributes` in the *Info.plist*, add the `UNNotificationExtensionUserInteractionEnabled` Boolean key and set its value to YES. Now the entire mechanism for user interaction springs to life. For instance, your interface can contain a button; if you've configured its action in the storyboard to call a method in your view controller, the user can tap the button to call that method.

Making your content extension view interactive in this way means that the user can no longer tap in the view to trigger the notification's default action, dismissing the notification and summoning your app. Therefore, there is a way for your *code* to trigger the notification's default action: tell the extension context to `perform-NotificationDefaultAction`. In your app, the user notification center delegate's `userNotificationCenter(_:didReceive:withCompletionHandler:)` will be called with the `UNNotificationDefaultActionIdentifier`, as you would expect.

You can also dismiss the notification *without* summoning your app: tell the extension context to `dismissNotificationContentExtension`. In that case, `userNotificationCenter(_:didReceive:withCompletionHandler:)` is *not* called, even if you have registered for the `.customDismissAction` (I regard that as a bug).

Today Extensions

The interface that appears when the user swipes sideways in the lock screen, the home screen, or the notification center is the *today list*. (New in iOS 13, the user can elect to have the today list appear on the left side of the home screen.) Here, apps can contribute *today widgets* — informative bits of interface. Apple's Weather app posts the local temperature here, in a widget that the user can tap to open the Weather app itself (Figure 13-14).

Your app, too, can provide a widget to appear here. To make that happen, you give your app a *today extension*. Your app vends the extension, and the user has the option of adding it to the today list (Figure 13-15).

To add a today extension to your app, create a new target and specify iOS → Application Extension → Today Extension. The template gives you a good start on your extension. You have a storyboard with a single scene, and the code for a corresponding view controller that adopts the NCWidgetProviding protocol. You might need to

Figure 13-14. A built-in today extension

Figure 13-15. A custom today extension

edit the extension's *Info.plist* to set the "Bundle display name" entry — this is the title that will appear above your extension.

Design your extension's interface in the storyboard provided. To size your extension's height, provide sufficient constraints to determine the full height of the interface from the inside out, or set your view controller's `preferredContentSize`.

Each time your today extension's interface is about to appear, your today extension view controller is given an opportunity to update its interface, through its implementation of the NCWidgetProviding method `widgetPerformUpdate(completion-Handler:)`. Be sure to finish up by calling the `completionHandler`, handing it an NCUpdateResult, which will be `.newData`, `.noData`, or `.failed`. Time-consuming work should be performed off the main thread (see Chapter 24):

```
func widgetPerformUpdate(completionHandler:
    @escaping (NCUpdateResult) -> ()) {
        // ... do stuff quickly ...
        completionHandler(.newData)
}
```

Communication back to your app can be a little tricky. In Figure 13-15, two buttons invite the user to set up a reminder notification; I've implemented these to open our CoffeeTime app by calling `open(_:completionHandler:)` — a method of the view controller's `extensionContext`, not the shared application, which is not available from here:

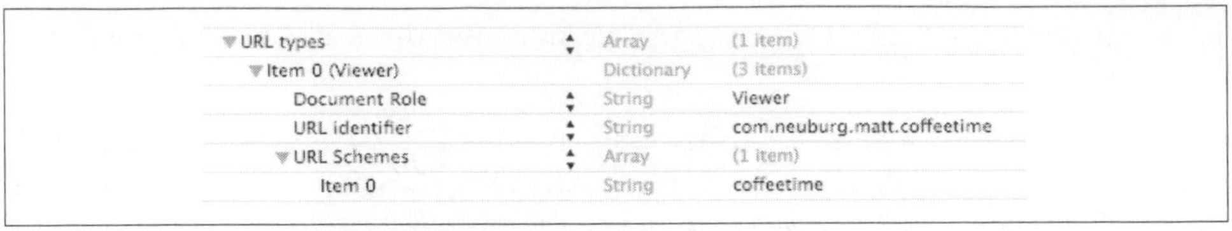

URL types		Array	(1 item)
▼ Item 0 (Viewer)		Dictionary	(3 items)
Document Role		String	Viewer
URL identifier		String	com.neuburg.matt.coffeetime
▼ URL Schemes		Array	(1 item)
Item 0		String	coffeetime

Figure 13-16. A custom URL declaration

```swift
@IBAction func doButton(_ sender: Any) {
    let v = sender as! UIView
    var comp = URLComponents()
    comp.scheme = "coffeetime"
    comp.host = String(v.tag) // button's tag is number of minutes
    if let url = comp.url {
        self.extensionContext?.open(url)
    }
}
```

The CoffeeTime app receives this message because I've given it three things:

A custom URL scheme

The `coffeetime` scheme is declared in the app's *Info.plist* (Figure 13-16).

An implementation of `scene(_:openURLContexts:)`

In the scene delegate, I've implemented this method to analyze the URL when it arrives. (In iOS 12 and before, this would be `application(_:open:options:)` in the app delegate.) I've coded the original URL so that its `host` is actually the number of minutes specified in the tapped button's title. By retrieving that value, I can respond appropriately (presumably by scheduling a local notification for that number of minutes from now):

```swift
func scene(_ scene: UIScene,
    openURLContexts URLContexts: Set<UIOpenURLContext>) {
        guard let url = URLContexts.first?.url else { return }
        let scheme = url.scheme
        let host = url.host
        if scheme == "coffeetime" {
            if let host = host, let min = Int(host) {
                print("got \(min) from our today extension")
            }
        }
}
```

An implementation of `scene(_:willConnectTo:options:)`

If our app is not running when the message is sent from the today extension, `scene(_:openURLContexts:)` will *not* be called. Instead, our scene delegate's implementation of `scene(_:willConnectTo:options:)` must look in the `urlContexts` property of the `options:` parameter, discover the URL there, and respond.

A today extension's widget interface can have two heights: compact and expanded. If you take advantage of this feature, your widget will have a Show More or Show Less button (similar to the Weather app's widget, Figure 13-14). To do so:

1. Run this code early in the life of your view controller, probably in its `viewDid-Load` implementation:

   ```
   self.extensionContext?.widgetLargestAvailableDisplayMode = .expanded
   ```

2. Implement `widgetActiveDisplayModeDidChange(_:withMaximumSize:)`. The first parameter is an NCWidgetDisplayMode, either `.compact` or `.expanded`. The idea is that you would respond by changing your view controller's `preferred-ContentSize` to the smaller or larger size, respectively.

If your app has a today extension, the today extension widget is displayed *automatically* when the user performs the long press gesture that summons quick actions ("Quick Actions" on page 764). The widget can be interactive (as ours is), so you might be able to use it *instead* of quick action buttons.

Activity Views

An activity view is the view belonging to a UIActivityViewController, typically appearing when the user taps a Share button. To display it, you start with one or more pieces of data, such as a string or an image, that you want the user to have the option of sharing or working with. The activity view, when it appears, will then contain a menu item or app icon for every activity (UIActivity) that can work with this type of data. The user may tap one of these to send the data to the activity, and is then perhaps shown additional interface belonging to the provider of the chosen activity.

Figure 13-17 shows an activity view from Mobile Safari. There's a row displaying the icons of some apps that provide applicable built-in system-wide activities; this is followed by menu items representing activities provided internally by Safari itself. When you present an activity view within your app, you can add menu items for activities provided internally by *your* app. Moreover, your app can provide system-wide activities that are available when *any* app presents an activity view; these come in two forms:

Share extensions

A *share extension* is represented as an app icon in the upper row of an activity view. Share extensions are for apps that can accept information into themselves, either for storage, such as Notes and Reminders, or for sending out to a server, such as Twitter and Facebook.

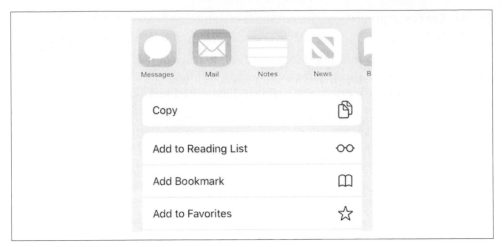

Figure 13-17. An activity view

Action extensions
> An *action extension* is represented among the menu items of an activity view. Action extensions offer to perform some kind of manipulation on the data provided by the host app.

I'll describe how to present an activity view and how to construct an activity that's internal to your app. Then I'll give an example of writing an action extension, and finally an example of writing a share extension.

Presenting an Activity View

You will typically want to present an activity view in response to the user tapping a Share button in your app. To do so:

1. Instantiate UIActivityViewController. The initializer you'll be calling is:

   • `init(activityItems:applicationActivities:)`

   The `activityItems:` argument is an array of objects to be shared or operated on, such as string or image objects. Presumably these are objects associated somehow with the interface the user is looking at right now.

2. Set the activity view controller's `completionWithItemsHandler` property to a function that will be called when the user's interaction with the activity interface has finished.

3. Present the activity view controller, as a presented view controller; on the iPad, it will be a popover, so you'll also configure the popover presentation controller. The presented view will be dismissed automatically when the user cancels or chooses an activity.

Here's an example:

```
let url = Bundle.main.url(forResource:"sunglasses", withExtension:"png")!
let things : [Any] = ["This is a cool picture", url]
let avc = UIActivityViewController(
    activityItems:things, applicationActivities:nil)
avc.completionWithItemsHandler = { type, ok, items, err in
    // ...
}
self.present(avc, animated:true)
if let pop = avc.popoverPresentationController {
    let v = sender as! UIView
    pop.sourceView = v
    pop.sourceRect = v.bounds
}
```

The activity view is populated automatically with known system-wide activities that can handle any of the types of data you provided as the `activityItems:` argument. These activities represent UIActivity types (UIActivity.ActivityType):

- `.postToFacebook`
- `.postToTwitter`
- `.postToWeibo`
- `.message`
- `.mail`
- `.print`
- `.copyToPasteboard`
- `.assignToContact`
- `.saveToCameraRoll`
- `.addToReadingList`
- `.postToFlickr`
- `.postToVimeo`
- `.postToTencentWeibo`
- `.airDrop`
- `.openInIBooks`
- `.markupAsPDF`

Consult the UIActivity class documentation to learn what types of activity item each of these activities can handle. For instance, the `.mail` activity will accept a string, an image, or a file (such as an image file) designated by a URL; it will present a mail composition interface with the activity item(s) in the body.

Since the default is to include all the system-wide activities that can handle the provided data, if you *don't* want a certain system-wide activity included in the activity view, you must exclude it explicitly. You do this by setting the UIActivityView-Controller's `excludedActivityTypes` property to an array of activity type constants.

 Apps other than Messages, Mail, and Books have no corresponding UIActivity type, because they are implemented as share extensions; it is up to the *user* to include or exclude them.

In the UIActivityViewController initializer `init(activityItems:application-Activities:)`, if you would prefer that an element of the `activityItems:` array should be an object that will supply the data instead of the data itself, make it an object that adopts the UIActivityItemSource protocol. Typically, this object will be `self` (the view controller in charge of all this code). Here's a minimal, artificial example:

```
extension ViewController : UIActivityItemSource {
    func activityViewControllerPlaceholderItem(
        _ activityViewController: UIActivityViewController) -> Any {
            return ""
    }
    func activityViewController(
        _ activityViewController: UIActivityViewController,
        itemForActivityType activityType: UIActivity.ActivityType?) -> Any? {
            return "Coolness"
    }
}
```

The first method provides a placeholder that exemplifies the type of data that will be returned; the second method returns the actual data. The second method can return different data depending on the activity type that the user chose; in this way, you could provide one string to Notes and another string to Mail.

The UIActivitySource protocol also answers a commonly asked question about how to get the Mail activity to populate the mail composition form with a default subject:

```
extension ViewController : UIActivityItemSource {
    // ...
    func activityViewController(
        _ activityViewController: UIActivityViewController,
        subjectForActivityType activityType: UIActivity.ActivityType?)
        -> String {
            return "This is cool"
    }
}
```

If your `activityItems:` data is time-consuming to provide, substitute an instance of a UIActivityItemProvider subclass:

```
let avc = UIActivityViewController(
    activityItems:[MyProvider(placeholderItem: "")],
    applicationActivities:nil)
```

The `placeholderItem:` in the initializer signals the type of data that this UIActivity-
ItemProvider object will actually provide. Your UIActivityItemProvider subclass
should override the `item` property to return the actual object. This property will be
consulted on a background thread, and UIActivityItemProvider is itself an Operation
subclass (see Chapter 24).

Custom Activities

The purpose of the `applicationActivities:` parameter of `init(activity-
Items:applicationActivities:)` is for you to list any additional activities imple-
mented internally by your own app. These will appear as menu items when your app
presents an activity view. Each activity will be an instance of one of your own UIActivity subclasses.

To illustrate, I'll create a minimal (and nonsensical) activity called Be Cool that
accepts string activity items. It is a UIActivity subclass called MyCoolActivity. So, to
include Be Cool among the choices presented to the user by a UIActivityView-
Controller, I'd say:

```
let things : [Any] = ["This is a cool picture", url]
let avc = UIActivityViewController(
    activityItems:things, applicationActivities:[MyCoolActivity()])
```

Now let's implement MyCoolActivity. It has an array property called `items`, for reasons that will be apparent in a moment. We need to arm ourselves with an image to
represent this activity in the activity view; this will be treated as a template image and
will be scaled down automatically. Here's the preparatory part of the implementation
of MyCoolActivity:

```
var items : [Any]?
var image : UIImage
override init() {
    // ... construct self.image ...
    super.init()
}
override class var activityCategory : UIActivity.ActivityCategory {
    return .action // the default
}
override var activityType : UIActivity.ActivityType {
    return UIActivity.ActivityType("com.neuburg.matt.coolActivity")
}
override var activityTitle : String? {
    return "Be Cool"
}
override var activityImage : UIImage? {
```

Figure 13-18. Our activity appears in our activity view

```
    return self.image
}
override func canPerform(withActivityItems activityItems: [Any]) -> Bool {
    for obj in activityItems {
        if obj is String {
            return true
        }
    }
    return false
}
override func prepare(withActivityItems activityItems: [Any]) {
    self.items = activityItems
}
```

If we return `true` from `canPerform(withActivityItems:)`, then a menu item for this activity with title Be Cool and displaying our `activityImage` will appear in the activity view (Figure 13-18).

If the user taps our menu item, `prepare(withActivityItems:)` will be called. We retain the `activityItems` into our `items` property, because they won't be arriving again when we are actually told to perform the activity.

The next step is that we *are* told to perform the activity. To do so, we implement one of these:

`perform` *method*

    We immediately perform the activity directly, using the activity items we've already retained. If the activity is time-consuming, it should be performed on a background thread (Chapter 24) so that we can return immediately; the activity view interface will be taken down and the user will be able to go on interacting with the app.

`activityViewController` *property*

    We have further interface that we'd like to show the user as part of the activity, so we provide an instance of a UIViewController subclass. The activity view mechanism will present this view controller for us; it is not our job to present or dismiss it. (Nevertheless, we may present or dismiss dependent interface. If our view controller is a navigation controller with a custom root view controller, we might push another view controller onto its stack while the user is interacting with the activity.)

No matter which of these two methods we implement, we *must* eventually call this activity instance's `activityDidFinish(_:)`. This is the signal to the activity view mechanism that the activity is over. If the activity view mechanism is still presenting any interface, it will be taken down, and the argument we supply here, a Bool signifying whether the activity completed successfully, will be passed into the function we supplied earlier as the activity view controller's `completionWithItemsHandler`:

```
override func perform() {
    // ... do something with self.items here ...
    self.activityDidFinish(true)
}
```

If the UIActivity is providing a view controller as its `activityViewController`, it will want to hand that view controller a reference to `self` beforehand, so that the view controller can call the activity's `activityDidFinish(_:)` when the time comes.

Suppose our activity involves letting the user draw a mustache on a photo of someone. Our view controller will provide interface for doing that, including some way of letting the user signal completion, such as a Cancel button and a Done button. When the user taps either of those, we'll do whatever else is necessary (such as saving the altered photo somewhere if the user tapped Done) and then call `activityDid-Finish(_:)`. We could implement the `activityViewController` property like this:

```
override var activityViewController : UIViewController? {
    let mvc = MustacheViewController(activity: self, items: self.items!)
    return mvc
}
```

And then MustacheViewController would have code like this:

```
weak var activity : UIActivity?
var items: [Any]
init(activity:UIActivity, items:[Any]) {
    self.activity = activity
    self.items = items
    super.init(nibName: "MustacheViewController", bundle: nil)
}
// ... other stuff ...
@IBAction func doCancel(_ sender: Any) {
    self.activity?.activityDidFinish(false)
}
@IBAction func doDone(_ sender: Any) {
    self.activity?.activityDidFinish(true)
}
```

Note that MustacheViewController's reference to the UIActivity (`self.activity`) is weak; otherwise, a retain cycle ensues.

Our `activityViewController` is displayed as a presented view controller. In iOS 13, this is a sheet that the user can dismiss by dragging down. If the user does that, the right thing happens automatically: `activityDidFinish` is called for us with an argument of `false`.

 The purpose of the SFSafariViewController delegate method `safariView-Controller(_:activityItemsFor:title:)` (Chapter 11) is now clear. This view controller's view appears inside your app, but it isn't your view controller, its Share button is not your button, and the activity view that it presents is not your activity view. Therefore, you need some other way to add custom UIActivity items to that activity view; to do so, implement this method.

Action Extensions

Your app's activity can appear among the menu items when some *other* app displays an activity view. To make that happen, you write an action extension. A single app can provide multiple action extensions.

To write an action extension, start with the appropriate target template, iOS → Application Extension → Action Extension. There are two kinds of action extension, with or without an interface; you'll make your choice in the second pane as you create the target.

In the *Info.plist*, in addition to setting the bundle name, which will appear below the activity's icon in the activity view, you'll need to specify what types of data this activity accepts as its operands. In the `NSExtensionActivationRule` dictionary, you'll provide one or more keys, such as:

- `NSExtensionActivationSupportsFileWithMaxCount`
- `NSExtensionActivationSupportsImageWithMaxCount`
- `NSExtensionActivationSupportsMovieWithMaxCount`
- `NSExtensionActivationSupportsText`
- `NSExtensionActivationSupportsWebURLWithMaxCount`

For the full list, see the "Action Extension Keys" section of Apple's *Information Property List Key Reference*. It is also possible to declare in a more sophisticated way what types of data your activity accepts, by writing an NSPredicate string as the value of the `NSExtensionActivationRule` key. Figure 13-19 shows the relevant part of the *Info.plist* for an action extension that accepts one text object.

To supply the image that will appear in the menu item for your activity, add an asset catalog to the action extension target and create an iOS app icon in the asset catalog. The icon will be treated as a template image.

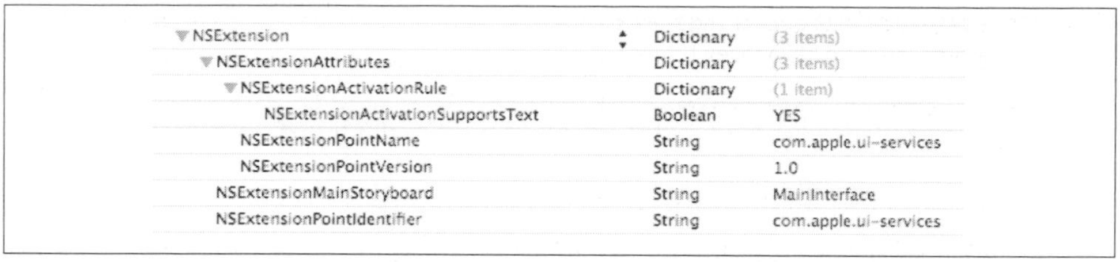

NSExtension		Dictionary	(3 items)
▼ NSExtensionAttributes		Dictionary	(3 items)
▼ NSExtensionActivationRule		Dictionary	(1 item)
NSExtensionActivationSupportsText		Boolean	YES
NSExtensionPointName		String	com.apple.ui-services
NSExtensionPointVersion		String	1.0
NSExtensionMainStoryboard		String	MainInterface
NSExtensionPointIdentifier		String	com.apple.ui-services

Figure 13-19. An action extension Info.plist

How to Debug an Extension

An extension doesn't run in your process, so breakpoints and logging are ineffective. Here is a simple technique that solves the problem.

Your project contains multiple schemes — one for your host app, and one each for any extensions it contains. Build and run the host app, to copy it onto the destination (a simulator or device). Now switch the Scheme pop-up menu in the Xcode window toolbar to your extension, and run it. A dialog appears asking what app to run. Select your host app and click Run.

Your host app will run; proceed to summon your extension and exercise it. What you're debugging is the extension, and all debugging features will work as expected.

I'll describe how to implement an action extension with an interface. This, in effect, is your chance to inject an entire presented view controller into another app! As an example, our extension accepts a string that might be the two-letter abbreviation of one of the U.S. states, and if it is, it provides the name of the state.

The template provides a storyboard with one scene, along with the code for a corresponding UIViewController subclass called ActionViewController. I'll give the interface a Cancel button, a Done button (`self.doneButton`), and a label (`self.lab`). I'll also declare two Optional string properties to hold our data, `self.orig` (the incoming string) and `self.expansion` (the state name, if any). Finally, `self.list` will be a dictionary whose keys are state name abbreviations and whose values are the corresponding state names; that information comes from a text file in the action extension bundle:

```
let list : [String:String] = {
    let path = Bundle.main.url(forResource:"abbrevs", withExtension:"txt")!
    // ... load the text file as a string, parse into dictionary (result)
    return result
}()
```

I have a little utility method that looks up a string in that dictionary:

```
func state(for abbrev:String) -> String? {
    return self.list[abbrev]
}
```

Our view controller's `viewDidLoad` starts by preparing the interface:

```
override func viewDidLoad() {
    super.viewDidLoad()
    self.doneButton.isEnabled = false
    self.lab.text = "No expansion available."
    // ...
}
```

We turn next to the data from the host app, which is supposed to be a string that might be a state abbreviation. It arrives by way of the view controller `extension-Context` property, which is an NSExtensionContext (wrapped in an Optional). Think of this as a holding a nest of envelopes that we must examine and open:

- The NSExtensionContext's `inputItems` is an array of NSExtensionItem objects.
- An NSExtensionItem has an `attachments` array of NSItemProvider objects.
- An NSItemProvider vends items, each of which represents the data in a particular format. In particular:
  - We can *ask* whether an NSItemProvider has an item of a particular type, by calling `hasItemConformingToTypeIdentifier(_:)`.
  - We can *retrieve* the item of a particular type, by calling `loadItem(forType-Identifier:options:completionHandler:)`. The item may be vended lazily, and can take time to prepare and provide; so we proceed in the `completion-Handler:` function to receive the item and do something with it.

We are expecting only one item, so it will be provided by the first NSItemProvider inside the first NSExtensionItem. So my first move is to look inside that envelope and make sure it contains a string:

```
if self.extensionContext == nil {
    return
}
let items = self.extensionContext!.inputItems
let desiredType = kUTTypePlainText as String
guard let extensionItem = items[0] as? NSExtensionItem
    else {return}
guard let provider = extensionItem.attachments?.first
    else {return}
guard provider.hasItemConformingToTypeIdentifier(self.desiredType)
    else {return}
```

If we've gotten this far, there's a string in that envelope, and we're now ready to retrieve it and see if it is the abbreviation of a state. If it is, I'll enable the Done button and offer to place the abbreviation on the clipboard if the user taps that button:

```
provider.loadItem(forTypeIdentifier: desiredType) { item, err in
    DispatchQueue.main.async {
        if let orig = (item as? String)?.uppercased() {
            self.orig = orig
            if let exp = self.state(for:orig) {
                self.expansion = exp
                self.lab.text = """
                    Can expand \(orig) to \(exp).
                    Tap Done to place on clipboard.
                    """
                self.doneButton.isEnabled = true
            }
        }
    }
}
```

All that remains is to implement the action methods for the Cancel and Done buttons. They must both call this method of the extension context:

• `completeRequest(returningItems:completionHandler:)`

That call is the signal that our interface should be taken down. The only difference
between the two buttons is that the Done button puts the expanded state name onto
the clipboard:

```
@IBAction func cancel(_ sender: Any) {
    self.extensionContext?.completeRequest(returningItems: nil)
}
@IBAction func done(_ sender: Any) {
    UIPasteboard.general.string = self.expansion!
    self.extensionContext?.completeRequest(returningItems: nil)
}
```

Share Extensions

Your app can appear in the row of app icons when some *other* app displays an activity view. To make that happen, you write a share extension. A share extension is similar to an action extension, but instead of processing the data it receives, it is expected
to deposit that data somehow, such as storing it or posting it to a server. Your app
can provide at most one share extension.

The user, after tapping your app's icon in the activity view, is given an opportunity to
interact further with the data before completing the share operation, possibly modifying it or canceling altogether. To make this possible, the Share Extension template,
when you create the target (iOS → Application Extension → Share Extension), will
give you a storyboard and a view controller. This view controller can be one of
two types:

Figure 13-20. A share extension

An SLComposeServiceViewController
> The SLComposeServiceViewController provides a standard interface for displaying editable text in a UITextView along with a possible preview, plus user-configurable option buttons, along with a Cancel button and a Post button.

A plain view controller subclass
> If you opt for a plain view controller subclass, then designing its interface, including providing a way to dismiss it, will be up to you.

Whichever form of interface you elect to use, your way of dismissing it will be this familiar-looking incantation:

```
self.extensionContext?.completeRequest(returningItems:nil)
```

I'll describe the basics of working with an SLComposeServiceViewController. Its view contains a text view that is already populated with the text passed along from the host app when the view appears, so there's very little more for you to do; you can add a preview view and option buttons, and that's just about all. Figure 13-20 shows my share extension, summoned from within the Notes app; the text of the note has been copied automatically into the SLComposeServiceViewController's text view.

An option button displays a title string and a value string. When tapped, it will typically summon interface where the user can change the value string. My SLCompose-ServiceViewController implements an option button, visible in Figure 13-20. It's a Size button, whose value can be Large, Medium, or Small. (I have no idea what this choice is supposed to signify for my app; it's only an example!) I'll explain how I did that.

To create the configuration option, I override the SLComposeServiceViewController `configurationItems` method to return an array of one SLComposeSheetConfigurationItem. Its `title` and `value` are displayed in the button. Its `tapHandler` will be called when the button is tapped. Typically, you'll create a view controller and push it into the interface with pushConfigurationViewController:

```
weak var config : SLComposeSheetConfigurationItem?
var selectedText = "Large" {
    didSet {
        self.config?.value = self.selectedText
    }
}
override func configurationItems() -> [Any]! {
    let c = SLComposeSheetConfigurationItem()!
    c.title = "Size"
    c.value = self.selectedText
    c.tapHandler = { [unowned self] in
        let tvc = TableViewController(style: .grouped)
        tvc.selectedSize = self.selectedText
        tvc.delegate = self
        self.pushConfigurationViewController(tvc)
    }
    self.config = c
    return [c]
}
```

My TableViewController is a UITableViewController subclass. Its table view displays three rows whose cells are labeled Large, Medium, and Small, along with a checkmark (compare the table view described in "Cell Choice and Static Tables" on page 491). The tricky part is that I need a way to communicate with this table view controller: I need to tell it what the configuration item's value is now, and I need to hear from it what the user chooses in the table view. So I've given the table view controller a property (selectedSize) where I can deposit the configuration item's value, and I've declared a delegate protocol so that the table view controller can set the selected-Text of the SLComposeServiceViewController. This is the relevant portion of my TableViewController class:

```
protocol SizeDelegate : class {
    var selectedText : String {get set}
}
class TableViewController: UITableViewController {
    var selectedSize : String?
    weak var delegate : SizeDelegate?
    override func tableView(_ tableView: UITableView,
        didSelectRowAt indexPath: IndexPath) {
            let cell = tableView.cellForRow(at:indexPath)!
            let s = cell.textLabel!.text!
            self.selectedSize = s
            self.delegate?.selectedText = s
            tableView.reloadData()
    }
    // ...
}
```

The navigation interface is provided for me, so I don't have to do anything about popping the table view controller: the user will do that by tapping the Back button after choosing a size. In my `configurationItems` implementation, I cleverly kept a reference to my configuration item as `self.config`. When the user chooses from the table view, its `tableView(_:didSelectRowAt:)` sets my `selectedText`, and my `selectedText` setter observer promptly changes the `value` of the configuration item to whatever the user chose.

The user, when finished interacting with the share extension interface, will tap one of the provided buttons, either Cancel or Post. The Cancel button is handled automatically: the interface is dismissed. The Post button is hooked automatically to my `did-SelectPost` implementation, where I fetch the text from my own `contentText` property, do something with it, and dismiss the interface:

```
override func didSelectPost() {
    let s = self.contentText
    // ... do something with it ...
    self.extensionContext?.completeRequest(returningItems:nil)
}
```

If the material provided from the host app were more elaborate, I would pull it out of `self.extensionContext` in the same way as for an action extension. If there were networking to do at this point, I would initiate a background URLSession (as I'll explain in Chapter 23).

There is no official way, as far as I can tell, to change the title or appearance of the Cancel and Post buttons. Apps that show different buttons, such as Reminders and Notes, are either not using SLComposeServiceViewController or are using a technique available only to Apple. I was able to change my Post button to a Save button like this:

```
override func viewDidLayoutSubviews() {
    super.viewDidLayoutSubviews()
    self.navigationController?.navigationBar.topItem?
        .rightBarButtonItem?.title = "Save"
}
```

But whether that's legal, and whether it will keep working on future systems, is anybody's guess.

Some Frameworks

This part of the book gets you started on some of Cocoa's specialized frameworks:

- Chapter 14 talks about playing sound.
- Chapter 15 talks about playing video and introduces the powerful AV Foundation framework.
- Chapter 16 is about how to access the user's music library.
- Chapter 17 is about how to access the user's photo library, and discusses using the device's camera.
- Chapter 18 is about how to access the user's contacts.
- Chapter 19 is about how to access the user's calendars and reminders.
- Chapter 20 explains how to display and customize a map, how to show the user's current location, and how to convert between a location and an address.
- Chapter 21 is about the sensors that tell your app where the device is located and how it is oriented.

Some Frameworks

CHAPTER 14

Audio

iOS provides various technologies that allow your app to produce, record, and process sound. The topic is a large one, so I'll concentrate on the basics. Suggestions for further exploration appear at the end of this chapter.

None of the classes discussed in this chapter provides any transport interface within your app — that is, interface for allowing the user to stop and start playback of sound. If you want transport interface, here are some options:

- You can create your own interface.
- You can associate the built-in "remote control" buttons with your app, as I'll explain in this chapter.
- A web view (Chapter 11) supports the HTML5 `<audio>` tag; this can be a simple, lightweight way to play audio and to allow the user to control playback (including use of AirPlay).
- You could treat the sound as a movie and use the interface-providing classes that I'll discuss in Chapter 15; this can also be a good way to play a sound file located remotely over the internet.

System Sounds

The simplest form of sound is *system sound*, which is the iOS equivalent of the basic computer "beep." This is implemented through System Sound Services, part of the Audio Toolbox framework; you'll need to `import AudioToolbox`. The API for playing a system sound comes in two forms — the old form, and a new form that was introduced in iOS 9.

The old form involves calling one of two C functions, which behave very similarly to one another:

```
AudioServicesPlayAlertSound
```
On an iPhone, may also vibrate the device, depending on the user's settings.

```
AudioServicesPlaySystemSound
```
On an iPhone, there won't be an accompanying vibration, but you can elect to have this "sound" *be* a device vibration (by passing kSystemSoundID_Vibrate as the name of the "sound").

The sound file to be played needs to be an uncompressed AIFF or WAV file (or an Apple CAF file wrapping one of those). To hand the sound to these functions, you'll need a SystemSoundID, which you obtain by calling AudioServicesCreateSystem-SoundID with a URL that points to a sound file. In this example, the sound file is in our app bundle:

```
let sndurl = Bundle.main.url(forResource:"test", withExtension: "aif")!
var snd : SystemSoundID = 0
AudioServicesCreateSystemSoundID(sndurl as CFURL, &snd)
AudioServicesPlaySystemSound(snd)
```

That code works — we hear the sound — but there's a problem: we have failed to exercise proper memory management. We need to call AudioServicesDispose-SystemSoundID to release our SystemSoundID. But when shall we do this? Audio-ServicesPlaySystemSound executes *asynchronously*. So the solution can't be to call AudioServicesDisposeSystemSoundID in the next line, because this would release our sound just as it is about to start playing, resulting in silence:

```
let sndurl = Bundle.main.url(forResource:"test", withExtension: "aif")!
var snd : SystemSoundID = 0
AudioServicesCreateSystemSoundID(sndurl as CFURL, &snd)
AudioServicesPlaySystemSound(snd)
AudioServicesDisposeSystemSoundID(snd) // oops, no sound!
```

The correct approach is to implement a *sound completion function* to be called when the sound has finished playing. The sound completion function is specified by calling AudioServicesAddSystemSoundCompletion. It must be supplied as a C pointer-to-function, but Swift lets you pass a global or local Swift function (including an anonymous function) where a C pointer-to-function is expected. So our code now looks like this:

```
let sndurl = Bundle.main.url(forResource:"test", withExtension: "aif")!
var snd : SystemSoundID = 0
AudioServicesCreateSystemSoundID(sndurl as CFURL, &snd)
AudioServicesAddSystemSoundCompletion(snd, nil, nil, { snd, _ in
    AudioServicesRemoveSystemSoundCompletion(snd)
    AudioServicesDisposeSystemSoundID(snd)
}, nil)
AudioServicesPlaySystemSound(snd)
```

Note that when we are about to release the sound, we first release the sound completion function itself.

Now for the new form. The new calls take *two* parameters: a SystemSoundID and a completion function. The completion function takes no parameters; we can still refer to the SystemSoundID in order to dispose of its memory, because it is in scope. Here, we'll call `AudioServicesPlaySystemSoundWithCompletion` instead of `AudioServicesPlaySystemSound`; we no longer need to call `AudioServicesRemoveSystemSoundCompletion`, because we never called `AudioServicesAddSystemSoundCompletion`:

```
let sndurl = Bundle.main.url(forResource:"test", withExtension: "aif")!
var snd : SystemSoundID = 0
AudioServicesCreateSystemSoundID(sndurl as CFURL, &snd)
AudioServicesPlaySystemSoundWithCompletion(snd) {
    AudioServicesDisposeSystemSoundID(snd)
}
```

Audio Session

Audio on the device — *all* audio belonging to *all* apps and processes — is controlled and mediated by the *media services daemon*. This daemon must juggle many demands; your app is just one of many clamoring for its attention and cooperation. As a result, your app's audio can be affected and even overruled by other apps and external factors.

Your communication with the audio services daemon is conducted through an *audio session*, which is a singleton AVAudioSession instance created automatically as your app launches. This is part of the AV Foundation framework; you'll need to `import AVFoundation`. You'll refer to your app's AVAudioSession by way of the class method `sharedInstance`.

Category

Your app, if it is going to be producing sound, needs to specify a *policy* regarding that sound and tell the media services daemon about it. This policy will answer such questions as:

- Should your app's sound be stopped when the screen is locked?
- If other sound is being produced (as when the Music app is playing a song in the background), should your app stop that sound or be layered on top of it?

To declare your audio session's policy, you'll set its *category* (AVAudioSession.Category) by calling `setCategory(_:mode:options:)`. I'll explain later about the `mode:` and `options:`; the `options:` parameter may be omitted, and if you have no mode, you can use a mode of `.default`. Your app needn't set just one category for all time; different activities or stages in the lifetime of your app might require that the category should change.

The basic policies for audio playback are:

Ambient (`.ambient`*)*
>   Your app's audio plays even while another app is playing audio, and is stopped by the phone's Silent switch and screen locking.

Solo Ambient (`.soloAmbient`*, the default)*
>   Your app stops any audio being played by other apps, and is stopped by the phone's Silent switch and screen locking.

Playback (`.playback`*)*
>   Your app stops any audio being played by other apps, and is *not* stopped by the Silent switch. It is stopped by screen locking, unless it is also configured to play in the background (as explained later in this chapter).

Audio session category options (the `options:` parameter, AVAudioSession.Category-Options) allow you to modify the playback policies:

Mixable audio (`.mixWithOthers`*)*
>   You can override the Playback policy so as to allow other apps to continue playing audio. Your sound is then said to be *mixable*. Mixability can also affect you in the other direction: another app's mixable audio can continue to play even when your app's Playback policy is *not* mixable.

Mixable except for speech (`.interruptSpokenAudioAndMixWithOthers`*)*
>   Similar to `.mixWithOthers`, but although you are willing to mix with background music, you are electing to stop background speech. An app's audio is marked as speech by setting its audio session mode to `.spokenAudio`.

Ducking audio (`.duckOthers`*)*
>   You can override a policy that allows other audio to play, so as to *duck* (diminish the volume of) that other audio. Ducking is a form of mixing.

Activation and Deactivation

Your audio session policy is not in effect unless your audio session is also *active*. By default, it isn't. Asserting your audio session policy is done by a combination of configuring the audio session and activating the audio session. To activate your audio session, you call `setActive(true)`.

The question is *when* to call `setActive(true)`. This depends on whether you need your audio session to be active all the time or only when you are producing sound. In many cases, it will be best not to activate your audio session until just before you really need it, that is, when you are starting to produce sound. But let's take a very simple case where our sounds are always occasional, intermittent, and nonessential. We want sound from other apps, such as the Music app, to be allowed to continue playing when the user launches or switches to our app. That's the Ambient policy. Our policy will never vary, and it doesn't stop other audio, so we might as well set our app's category and activate it at launch time:

```
func application(_ application: UIApplication,
    didFinishLaunchingWithOptions launchOptions:
    [UIApplication.LaunchOptionsKey : Any]?) -> Bool {
        let sess = AVAudioSession.sharedInstance()
        try? sess.setCategory(.ambient, mode:.default)
        try? sess.setActive(true)
        return true
}
```

It is also possible to call setActive(false), deactivating your audio session. There are various reasons why you might deactivate (and perhaps reactivate) your audio session over the lifetime of your app.

One possible reason is that you want to *change* something about your audio session policy. Certain changes in your audio session category and options don't take effect unless you deactivate the existing policy and activate the new policy. Ducking is a good example; I'll demonstrate in the next section.

Another reason for deactivating your audio session is that you have stopped playing sound; you no longer need to hog the device's audio, and you want to yield to other apps that were stopped by your audio session policy, so that they can resume playing. You can even send a message to other apps as you do this, by supplying the .notify-OthersOnDeactivation option in a call to setActive(_:options:), like this:

```
let sess = AVAudioSession.sharedInstance()
try? sess.setActive(false, options: .notifyOthersOnDeactivation)
```

 Apple suggests that you might want to register for AVAudioSession.media-ServicesWereResetNotification. If this notification arrives, the media services daemon was somehow hosed. In this situation, you should basically start from scratch, configuring your category and activating your audio session, as well as resetting and recreating any audio-related objects.

Ducking

As an example of deactivating and activating your audio session, I'll describe how to implement ducking.

Presume that we have configured and activated an Ambient category audio session, as described in the preceding sections. This category permits other audio to continue playing. Now let's say we do sometimes play a sound, but it's brief and doesn't require other sound to stop entirely — but we'd like other audio to be quieter momentarily while we're playing our sound. That's ducking!

Background sound is not ducked automatically just because we play a sound of our own. It is up to *us* to duck the background sound as we start to play our sound, and to stop ducking when our sound ends. We do this by changing our Ambient category to use or not to use the .duckOthers option. To make such a change, the most reliable approach is three steps:

1. Deactivate our audio session.

2. Reconfigure our audio session category with a changed set of options.

3. Activate our audio session.

So, just before we play our sound, we duck any other sound by adding .duckOthers to the options on our Ambient category:

```
let sess = AVAudioSession.sharedInstance()
try? sess.setActive(false)
let opts = sess.categoryOptions.union(.duckOthers)
try? sess.setCategory(sess.category, mode: sess.mode, options: opts)
try? sess.setActive(true)
```

When our sound finishes playing, we unduck any other sound by removing .duck-Others from the options on our category:

```
let sess = AVAudioSession.sharedInstance()
try? sess.setActive(false)
let opts = sess.categoryOptions.subtracting(.duckOthers)
try? sess.setCategory(sess.category, mode: sess.mode, options:opts)
try? sess.setActive(true)
```

Interruptions

Management of your audio session is complicated by the fact that it can be *interrupted*. On an iPhone, a phone call can arrive or an alarm can go off. Or another app might assert its audio session over yours, possibly because your app went into the background and the other app came into the foreground. Under certain circumstances, merely going into the background will interrupt your audio session.

When your audio session is interrupted, *it is deactivated*. That means you need to know when the interruption ends, so that you can reactivate your audio session. In order to know that, you will need to register for the AVAudioSession.interruption-Notification. You should do this as early as possible, perhaps at launch time.

The AVAudioSession.interruptionNotification can arrive either because an interruption begins or because it ends. To learn whether the interruption began or ended, you'll examine the AVAudioSessionInterruptionTypeKey entry in the notification's userInfo dictionary; this will be a UInt encoding an AVAudioSession.Interruption-Type, either `.began` or `.ended`.

When an interruption to your audio session begins, your audio has already paused and your audio session has been deactivated. If your app contains interface for playing and pausing, you might change a Pause button to a Play button. But apart from this there's no particular work for you to do. When the interruption ends, on the other hand, activating your audio session and possibly resuming playback of your audio might be up to you:

```
NotificationCenter.default.addObserver(forName:
    AVAudioSession.interruptionNotification, object: nil, queue: nil) { n in
        let why = n.userInfo![AVAudioSessionInterruptionTypeKey] as! UInt
        let type = AVAudioSession.InterruptionType(rawValue: why)!
        switch type {
        case .began:
            // update interface if needed
        case .ended:
            try? AVAudioSession.sharedInstance().setActive(true)
            // update interface if needed
            // resume playback?
        @unknown default: fatalError()
        }
}
```

The notification telling you that the interruption is over can include a message from some other app that interrupted you and has now deactivated its audio session. The other app sends that message by deactivating its audio session along with the `.notify-OthersOnDeactivation` option, as I demonstrated earlier. You'll receive the message in the userInfo dictionary's AVAudioSessionInterruptionOptionKey entry; its value will be a UInt encoding an AVAudioSession.InterruptionOptions, which might be `.shouldResume`:

```
guard let opt = n.userInfo![AVAudioSessionInterruptionOptionKey] as? UInt
    else {return}
if AVAudioSession.InterruptionOptions(rawValue:opt).contains(.shouldResume) {
    // resume playback
}
```

Secondary Audio

Apple draws a fine-grained distinction between two types of audio, primary audio and secondary audio. Apple's example is a game app, where intermittent sound effects are the primary audio, while an ongoing underlying soundtrack is the secondary audio. The idea is that the user might be playing a song in the background (from the Music app, for instance), and that your app would therefore suppress its own secondary audio while continuing to produce its primary audio, allowing the user's chosen Music track to function as the soundtrack behind your game's sound effects.

At key moments, such as when your app is activated or when you're thinking of producing secondary audio, you should check your audio session's secondaryAudio-ShouldBeSilencedHint property. If it is true, don't play your secondary audio.

It is also possible, under certain circumstances, that the secondaryAudioShouldBe-SilencedHint will go from false to true while your app is frontmost. An example is when your app is frontmost with an .ambient audio session and the user brings up the control center and uses the Play button to resume the current Music app song. There may be no interruption of your audio session, because your app never went into the background — but the secondaryAudioShouldBeSilencedHint may now have become true.

To hear about this, register for AVAudioSession.silenceSecondaryAudioHint-Notification. To respond to this notification, examine the AVAudioSessionSilence-SecondaryAudioHintTypeKey entry in the notification's userInfo dictionary; this will be a UInt encoding an AVAudioSession.SilenceSecondaryAudioHintType, either .begin or .end:

```
NotificationCenter.default.addObserver(forName:
    AVAudioSession.silenceSecondaryAudioHintNotification,
    object: nil, queue: nil) { n in
        let why = n.userInfo![AVAudioSessionSilenceSecondaryAudioHintTypeKey]
            as! UInt
        let type = AVAudioSession.SilenceSecondaryAudioHintType(rawValue:why)!
        switch type {
        case .begin:
            // pause secondary audio
        case .end:
            // resume secondary audio
        @unknown default: fatalError()
        }
}
```

Routing Changes

Your audio is routed through a particular output (and input). External events, such as a phone call arriving, can cause a change in audio routing, and the user can also make changes in audio routing — for instance, by plugging headphones into the device, which causes sound to stop coming out of the speaker and to come out of the headphones instead. You can and should register for the AVAudioSession.route-ChangeNotification to hear about routing changes and respond to them.

The notification's userInfo dictionary is chock full of useful information about what just happened. Here's the console log of the dictionary that results when I detach headphones from the device:

```
AVAudioSessionRouteChangeReasonKey = 2;
AVAudioSessionRouteChangePreviousRouteKey =
    <AVAudioSessionRouteDescription: 0x174019ee0,
        inputs = (null);
        outputs = (
            <AVAudioSessionPortDescription: 0x174019f00,
                type = Headphones;
                name = Headphones;
                UID = Wired Headphones;
                selectedDataSource = (null)>
        )>;
```

Upon receipt of this notification, I can find out what the audio route is now, by calling AVAudioSession's `currentRoute` method; here's the result logged to the console:

```
<AVAudioSessionRouteDescription: 0x174019fc0,
    inputs = (null);
    outputs = (
        <AVAudioSessionPortDescription: 0x17401a000,
            type = Speaker;
            name = Speaker;
            UID = Speaker;
            selectedDataSource = (null)>
    )>
```

The classes mentioned here — AVAudioSessionRouteDescription and AVAudio-SessionPortDescription — are value classes. The `AVAudioSessionRouteChangeReason-Key` refers to an AVAudioSessionRouteChangeReason; the value in this instance, 2, is `.oldDeviceUnavailable` — we stopped using the headphones and started using the speaker, because there are no headphones any longer.

A routing change may not of itself interrupt your sound, but Apple suggests that in this particular situation you should respond by stopping your audio deliberately, because otherwise sound may now suddenly be coming out of the speaker in a public place.

Audio Player

The easiest way to play sounds is to use an *audio player* (AVAudioPlayer). AVAudio-Player is part of the AV Foundation framework; you'll need to `import AVFoundation`.

An audio player is initialized with its sound, using a local file URL or Data; optionally, the initializer can also state the expected sound file format. A wide range of sound types is acceptable, including MP3, AAC, and ALAC, as well as AIFF and WAV. Starting in iOS 11, FLAC is an acceptable format, as well as Opus (a lossy compression codec commonly used for streaming and VoIP). A single audio player can possess and play only one sound; but you can have multiple audio players, they can play separately or simultaneously, and you can synchronize them. You can set a sound's volume and stereo pan features, loop a sound, change the playing rate, and set playback to begin somewhere in the middle of a sound. You can even execute a fade in or fade out over time.

Having created and initialized an audio player, you must *retain it*, typically by assigning it to an instance property. Assigning an audio player to a *local* variable and telling it to play, and hearing nothing — because the player has gone out of existence immediately, before it even has a chance to start playing — is a common beginner mistake.

To play the sound, first make sure your audio session is configured correctly. Now tell the audio player to prepareToPlay, causing it to load buffers and initialize hardware; then tell it to play. The audio player's delegate (AVAudioPlayerDelegate) is notified when the sound has finished playing, through a call to audioPlayerDid-FinishPlaying(_:successfully:); do *not* repeatedly check the audio player's isPlaying property to learn its state.

The playAtTime(_:) method allows playing to be scheduled to start at a certain time. The time should be described in terms of the audio player's deviceCurrentTime property. Other useful methods include pause and stop; the chief difference between them is that pause doesn't release the buffers and hardware set up by prepareToPlay, but stop does, so you'd want to call prepareToPlay again before resuming play. Neither pause nor stop changes the playhead position, the point in the sound where playback will start if play is sent again; for that, use the currentTime property.

Devising a strategy for instantiating, retaining, and releasing your audio players is up to you. In one of my apps, I define a class called Player, which implements a play-File(atPath:) method expecting a string path to a sound file. This method creates a new AVAudioPlayer, stores it as a property, and tells it to play the sound file; it also sets itself as that audio player's delegate, and notifies its own delegate when the sound finishes playing (by way of a PlayerDelegate protocol that I define). In this way, by maintaining a single Player instance, I can play different sounds in succession:

```
protocol PlayerDelegate : class {
    func soundFinished(_ sender: Any)
}
class Player : NSObject, AVAudioPlayerDelegate {
    var player : AVAudioPlayer!
    weak var delegate : PlayerDelegate?
    func playFile(atPath path:String) {
        self.player?.delegate = nil
        self.player?.stop()
        let fileURL = URL(fileURLWithPath: path)
        guard let p = try? AVAudioPlayer(contentsOf:fileURL) else {return}
        self.player = p
        self.player.prepareToPlay()
        self.player.delegate = self
```

```
            self.player.play()
        }
        func audioPlayerDidFinishPlaying(_ player: AVAudioPlayer,
            successfully flag: Bool) {
                self.delegate?.soundFinished(self)
    }
```

Here are some useful AVAudioPlayer properties:

pan, volume
> Stereo positioning and loudness, respectively.

numberOfLoops
> How many times the sound should repeat after it finishes playing; 0 (the default) means it doesn't repeat. A negative value causes the sound to repeat indefinitely (until told to stop).

duration
> The length of the sound (read-only).

currentTime
> The playhead position within the sound. If the sound is paused or stopped, play will start at the currentTime. You can set this property in order to "seek" to a playback position within the sound.

enableRate, rate
> These properties allow the sound to be played at anywhere from half speed (0.5) to double speed (2.0). Set enableRate to true *before* calling prepareToPlay; you are then free to set the rate.

isMeteringEnabled
> If true (the default is false), you can call updateMeters followed by average-Power(forChannel:) or peakPower(forChannel:) periodically to track how loud the sound is. Presumably this would be so you could provide some sort of graphical representation of this value in your interface.

settings
> A read-only dictionary describing features of the sound, such as its bit rate (AVEncoderBitRateKey), its sample rate (AVSampleRateKey), and its data format (AVFormatIDKey). You can alternatively learn the sound's data format from the format property.

An audio player handles certain types of interruption seamlessly; in particular, if your sound was forced to stop playing when your app was moved to the background, then when your app comes to front, the audio player reactivates your audio session and resumes playing — and you won't get any interruption notifications. But resumption

Figure 14-1. The software remote controls in the control center

of play is not automatic for every kind of interruption, so you may still need to register for interruption notifications, as I described earlier.

Remote Control of Your Sound

Various sorts of signal constitute *remote control*. There is hardware remote control, such as the buttons on certain models of earbuds. There is also software remote control — the playback controls that you see in the control center (Figure 14-1) and in the lock screen.

Your app can arrange to be targeted by *remote control events* reporting that the user has tapped a remote control, and can then respond to the remote play/pause button (probably by playing or pausing its sound). For this to work, your app's audio session category must be Solo Ambient or Playback, and your app must actually produce some sound; this causes your app's sound to become the device's *now playing* sound. The rule is that the running app that is capable of receiving remote control events and actually produced sound most recently is the target of remote control events. The Music app is the default remote control event target if no other app takes precedence by this rule.

To configure your app to receive remote control events, use the Media Player framework (`import MediaPlayer`). You talk to the *remote command center*, through the shared command center that you get from the MPRemoteCommandCenter `shared` class method, and configure its commands to send you messages, to which you then respond as appropriate. There are two ways to perform such configuration: you can give a command a target–action pair, or you can hand it a function directly.

Let's say that our app plays audio, and we want to respond to remote commands to pause or resume this audio. We will need to configure the play command and the pause command, because they are triggered by the software play/pause button, as well as the play/pause command, because it is triggered by an earbud button. I'll demonstrate the target–action style of configuration. This code could appear in our view controller's `viewDidLoad`:

```
let scc = MPRemoteCommandCenter.shared()
scc.playCommand.addTarget(self, action:#selector(doPlay))
scc.pauseCommand.addTarget(self, action:#selector(doPause))
scc.togglePlayPauseCommand.addTarget(self, action: #selector(doPlayPause))
```

Obviously, that code won't compile unless we also have doPlay, doPause, and doPlay-Pause methods. Each of these methods will be sent the appropriate remote command event (MPRemoteCommandEvent). Assuming that `self.player` is an AVAudio-Player, our implementations might look like this:

```
@objc func doPlayPause(_ event:MPRemoteCommandEvent)
    -> MPRemoteCommandHandlerStatus {
        let p = self.player
        if p.isPlaying { p.pause() } else { p.play() }
        return .success
}
@objc func doPlay(_ event:MPRemoteCommandEvent)
    -> MPRemoteCommandHandlerStatus {
        let p = self.player
        p.play()
        return .success
}
@objc func doPause(_ event:MPRemoteCommandEvent)
    -> MPRemoteCommandHandlerStatus {
        let p = self.player
        p.pause()
        return .success
}
```

This works! Once our app is playing a sound, that sound can be paused and resumed using the control center or an earbud switch. (It can also be paused and resumed using the lock screen, but only if our app is capable of playing sound in the background; I'll explain in the next section how to arrange that.)

However, we are not quite finished. Having registered a target with the remote command center, we must remember to unregister when that target is about to go out of existence; otherwise, there is a danger that the remote command center will attempt to send a remote command event to a nonexistent target, resulting in a crash. If we registered in our view controller's `viewDidLoad`, we can conveniently unregister in its `deinit`:

```
deinit {
    let scc = MPRemoteCommandCenter.shared()
    scc.togglePlayPauseCommand.removeTarget(self)
    scc.playCommand.removeTarget(self)
    scc.pauseCommand.removeTarget(self)
}
```

Having formed the connection between our app and the software remote control interface, we can proceed to refine that interface. One refinement is to specify what information is displayed about what's being played. For that, we use the MPNow-PlayingInfoCenter. Call the class method `default` and set the resulting instance's `now-PlayingInfo` property to a dictionary. The relevant keys are listed in the class documentation; many of these are actually MPMediaItem properties, and will make more sense after you've read Chapter 16. Here we make the command center show the title and artist of the sound file our app is playing:

```
let mpic = MPNowPlayingInfoCenter.default()
mpic.nowPlayingInfo = [
    MPMediaItemPropertyArtist: "Matt Neuburg",
    MPMediaItemPropertyTitle: "About Tiagol",
]
```

To make the progress view appear in the software remote control interface, display-ing our sound's duration and the current play position within it, we need to tell the MPNowPlayingInfoCenter what that duration is. If we also tell it that we are actively playing, it will automatically increment its display of the current play position as the time goes by. So, when we start playing, we would say something like this:

```
let mpic = MPNowPlayingInfoCenter.default()
mpic.nowPlayingInfo = [
    MPMediaItemPropertyArtist: "Matt Neuburg",
    MPMediaItemPropertyTitle: "About Tiagol",
    MPMediaItemPropertyPlaybackDuration: self.player.duration,
    MPNowPlayingInfoPropertyElapsedPlaybackTime: 0,
    MPNowPlayingInfoPropertyPlaybackRate: 1
]
```

The MPNowPlayingInfoCenter is not actually watching our sound play; it just blindly advances the current play position display. Therefore, if our sound pauses or resumes, we need to keep the MPNowPlayingInfoCenter updated. When the sound pauses, we need to tell it not only that we have paused, but also what the current play position is; otherwise, it will assume that the play position is zero:

```
let p = self.player
let mpic = MPNowPlayingInfoCenter.default()
if var d = mpic.nowPlayingInfo {
    d[MPNowPlayingInfoPropertyPlaybackRate] = 0
    d[MPNowPlayingInfoPropertyElapsedPlaybackTime] = p.currentTime
    mpic.nowPlayingInfo = d
}
```

Figure 14-2. Using Capabilities to enable background audio

If we don't want the user to be able to slide the slider that would tell our app to change the current play position, we must use the MPRemoteCommandCenter to disable it:

```
let scc = MPRemoteCommandCenter.shared()
scc.changePlaybackPositionCommand.isEnabled = false
```

The MPRemoteCommandCenter offers many other commands you can configure. When you do so, the appropriate software remote control interface springs to life. For instance, if you assign a target–action pair to the likeCommand, a menu button appears in the control center; the user taps this button to see an action sheet that includes your like command button.

Playing Sound in the Background

When the user switches away from your app to another app, by default, your app is suspended and stops producing sound. But if the business of your app is to play sound, you might like your app to continue playing sound in the background. To play sound in the background, your app must do these things:

- In your *Info.plist*, you must include the "Required background modes" key (UIBackgroundModes) with an array value that includes "App plays audio or streams audio/video using AirPlay" (audio). The simplest way to arrange that is to add the Background Modes capability in the Signing & Capabilities tab of the target editor, and then check "Audio, AirPlay, and Picture in Picture" (Figure 14-2).
- Your audio session's policy must be active and must be Playback.

If those things are true, then the sound that your app is playing in the foreground will go right on playing when the user clicks the Home button and dismisses your app, or when the user switches to another app, or when the screen is locked. Your app is now running in the background for the purpose of playing sound.

Your app, playing in the background, may be interrupted by the foreground app's audio session policy. However, having registered for the AVAudio-Session.interruptionNotification, your app may receive this notification in the background, and, if the AVAudioSession.InterruptionType is .ended, may be able to resume playing — still in the background.

Remote control events continue to work when your app is in the background. In fact, even if your app was *not* actively playing at the time it was put into the background, it may nevertheless be the remote control target (because it *was* playing sound earlier, as explained in the preceding section). In that case, if the user causes a remote control event to be sent, your app, if suspended in the background, will be woken up (still in the background) in order to receive the remote control event, and can then begin playing sound. Your app may also be able to start playing in the background if it is mixable (.mixWithOthers, see earlier in this chapter), even if it was not playing previously.

While your app is playing sound in the background, there's an interesting byproduct: a Timer can fire. This is remarkable, because many other sorts of activity are forbidden when your app is running in the background. The timer must have been created and scheduled in the foreground, but after that, it will fire even while your app is in the background, unless your app is currently not playing any sound.

Another curious byproduct of your app playing sound in the background has to do with app delegate events (see Appendix A). Typically, your app delegate will probably never receive the applicationWillTerminate(_:) message, because by the time the app terminates, it will already have been suspended and incapable of receiving any events. However, an app that is playing sound in the background is obviously *not* suspended, even though it is in the background. If it is terminated while playing sound in the background, it *will* receive applicationWillTerminate(_:).

AVAudioRecorder

AVAudioRecorder is the simplest way to record sound through the device's microphone. To use it, your audio session category will need to be .record (or .playAndRecord). You will also need the user's *permission* to use the microphone. You'll need to have a meaningful entry in your *Info.plist* under the "Privacy — Microphone Usage Description" key (NSMicrophoneUsageDescription) explaining to the user why you want to use the microphone. You don't have to request authorization explicitly; the system will put up an authorization request dialog on your behalf as soon as you try to use microphone. If you do want to request authorization explicitly, check your AVAudioSession's recordPermission to learn whether we have authorization, and call its requestRecordPermission, if it is .undetermined, to request authorization. A user who denies your app microphone authorization may grant it later in Settings. (See "Checking for Authorization" on page 861 for detailed discussion of user authorization requests.)

Here's a minimal example of recording through an AVAudioRecorder. The recorder is created with a file URL where the recording is to be saved, along with information about the format of the sound file to be created. It is then assigned to an instance property, just like an AVAudioPlayer, and told to `record`:

```
var recorder : AVAudioRecorder?
let recurl : URL = {
    let temp = FileManager.default.temporaryDirectory
    return temp.appendingPathComponent("rec.m4a")
}()
func startRecording() {
    try? AVAudioSession.sharedInstance().setCategory(.record, mode:.default)
    try? AVAudioSession.sharedInstance().setActive(true)
    let format = AVAudioFormat(settings: [
        AVFormatIDKey : Int(kAudioFormatMPEG4AAC),
        AVSampleRateKey : 44100.0,
        AVEncoderBitRateKey : 192000,
        AVNumberOfChannelsKey : 2
    ])
    do {
        let rec = try AVAudioRecorder(url:self.recurl, format:format!)
        self.recorder = rec
        rec.record(forDuration: 10)
    } catch {
        print("oops")
    }
}
```

Our little sound recording app would presumably also have a way to tell the recorder to `stop`, but just in case, I've limited the recording time to ten seconds.

AVAudioEngine

AVAudioEngine is modeled after a mixer board. You can construct and manipulate a graph of sound-producing objects in real time, varying their relative volumes and other attributes, mixing them down to a single sound. This is a deep topic; I'll provide an introductory overview.

The key classes are:

AVAudioEngine

The overall engine object, representing the world in which everything else happens. You'll probably make and retain just one at a time; it is perfectly reasonable to replace your engine with a new one, as a way of starting over with a clean slate. Its chief jobs are:

- To connect and disconnect *nodes* (AVAudioNode), like configuring the patch cords on a mixer board. The engine itself has three built-in nodes — its `inputNode`, its `mixerNode`, and its `outputNode` — and you can add others.

- To start and stop the production of sound. The engine must be running if any sound is to be produced; on the other hand, configuration changes generally need to be made with the engine stopped.

AVAudioNode

An abstract class embracing the various types of object for producing, processing, mixing, and receiving sound. An audio node is useful only when it has been attached to the audio engine. An audio node has inputs and outputs, and the audio engine can connect the output of one node to the input of another. It is also possible to put a *tap* on a node, copying the node's sound data off into a buffer as it passes through the node; this might be for analysis, monitoring, or saving into a file. Some subclasses are:

AVAudioMixerNode

A node with an output volume; it mixes its inputs down to a single output. The AVAudioEngine's built-in `mixerNode` is an AVAudioMixerNode.

AVAudioIONode

A node that patches through to the system's (device's) own input (AVAudioInputNode) or output (AVAudioOutputNode). The AVAudioEngine's built-in `inputNode` and `outputNode` are AVAudioIONodes.

AVAudioPlayerNode

A node that produces sound, analogous to an AVAudioPlayer. It can play from a file or from a buffer.

AVAudioSourceNode
AVAudioSinkNode

New in iOS 13. Nodes that let you produce or process a buffer's contents directly.

AVAudioEnvironmentNode

Gives three-dimensional spatial control over sound sources (suitable for games). With it, a bunch of additional AVAudioNode properties spring to life.

AVAudioUnit

A node that processes its input with special effects before passing it to the output. Built-in subclasses include:

AVAudioUnitTimePitch

Independently changes the pitch and rate of the input.

AVAudioUnitVarispeed

Changes the pitch and rate of the input together.

AVAudioUnitDelay
>   Adds to the input a delayed version of itself.

AVAudioUnitDistortion
>   Adds distortion to the input.

AVAudioUnitEQ
>   Constructs an equalizer, for processing frequency bands separately.

AVAudioUnitReverb
>   Adds a reverb effect to the input.

To give an idea of what working with AVAudioEngine looks like, I'll start by simply playing a file. Our AVAudioEngine has already been instantiated and assigned to an instance property, `self.engine`, so that it will persist for the duration of the exercise. We will need an AVAudioPlayerNode and an AVAudioFile. We attach the AVAudioPlayerNode to the engine and patch it to the engine's built-in mixer node. (In this simple case, we could have patched the player node to the engine's output node; but the engine's mixer node is already patched to the output node, so it makes no difference.) We associate the file with the player node, supplying a completion function that stops the engine so as not to waste resources after the file finishes playing. Finally, we start the engine running and tell the player node to play:

```
let player = AVAudioPlayerNode()
let url = Bundle.main.url(forResource:"aboutTiagol", withExtension:"m4a")!
let f = try! AVAudioFile(forReading: url)
let mixer = self.engine.mainMixerNode
self.engine.attach(player)
self.engine.connect(player, to: mixer, format: f.processingFormat)
player.scheduleFile(f, at: nil) { [unowned self] in
    delay(0.1) {
        if self.engine.isRunning {
            self.engine.stop()
        }
    }
}
self.engine.prepare()
try! self.engine.start()
player.play()
```

(Instead of stopping the engine in our player node's completion function, we can configure the engine to stop automatically by setting its `isAutoShutdownEnabled` property to `true`.)

So far, we've done nothing that we couldn't have done with an AVAudioPlayer. But now let's start patching some more nodes into the graph. I'll play two sounds simultaneously, the first one directly from a file, the second one through a buffer — which will allow me to loop the second sound. I'll also pass the first sound through a time-pitch effect node and then through a reverb effect node. And I'll set the volumes and pan positions of the two sounds:

```
// first sound
let player = AVAudioPlayerNode()
let url = Bundle.main.url(forResource:"aboutTiagol", withExtension:"m4a")!
let f = try! AVAudioFile(forReading: url)
self.engine.attach(player)
// add some effect nodes to the chain
let effect = AVAudioUnitTimePitch()
effect.rate = 0.9
effect.pitch = -300
self.engine.attach(effect)
self.engine.connect(player, to: effect, format: f.processingFormat)
let effect2 = AVAudioUnitReverb()
effect2.loadFactoryPreset(.cathedral)
effect2.wetDryMix = 40
self.engine.attach(effect2)
self.engine.connect(effect, to: effect2, format: f.processingFormat)
// patch last node into engine mixer and start playing first sound
let mixer = self.engine.mainMixerNode
self.engine.connect(effect2, to: mixer, format: f.processingFormat)
player.scheduleFile(f, at: nil) {
    delay(0.1) {
        if self.engine.isRunning {
            self.engine.stop()
        }
    }
}
self.engine.prepare()
try! self.engine.start()
player.play()
// second sound; loop it
let url2 = Bundle.main.url(forResource:"Hooded", withExtension: "mp3")!
let f2 = try! AVAudioFile(forReading: url2)
let buffer = AVAudioPCMBuffer(
    pcmFormat: f2.processingFormat, frameCapacity: UInt32(f2.length))
try! f2.read(into:buffer!)
let player2 = AVAudioPlayerNode()
self.engine.attach(player2)
self.engine.connect(player2, to: mixer, format: f2.processingFormat)
player2.scheduleBuffer(buffer!, at: nil, options: .loops)
// mix down a little, start playing second sound
player.pan = -0.5
player2.volume = 0.5
player2.pan = 0.5
player2.play()
```

You can split a node's output between multiple nodes. Instead of calling connect(_:to:format:), you call connect(_:to:fromBus:format:), where the second argument is an array of AVAudioConnectionPoint objects, each of which is simply a node and a bus. In this example, I'll split my player's output three ways: I'll connect it simultaneously to a delay effect and a reverb effect, both of which are connected to the output mixer, and I'll connect the player itself directly to the output mixer as well:

```
let effect = AVAudioUnitDelay()
effect.delayTime = 0.4
effect.feedback = 0
self.engine.attach(effect)
let effect2 = AVAudioUnitReverb()
effect2.loadFactoryPreset(.cathedral)
effect2.wetDryMix = 40
self.engine.attach(effect2)
let mixer = self.engine.mainMixerNode
// patch player node to _both_ effect nodes _and_ the mixer
let cons = [
    AVAudioConnectionPoint(node: effect, bus: 0),
    AVAudioConnectionPoint(node: effect2, bus: 0),
    AVAudioConnectionPoint(node: mixer, bus: 1),
]
self.engine.connect(player, to: cons,
    fromBus: 0, format: f.processingFormat)
// patch both effect nodes into the mixer
self.engine.connect(effect, to: mixer, format: f.processingFormat)
self.engine.connect(effect2, to: mixer, format: f.processingFormat)
```

Finally, I'll demonstrate how to process sound into a file. When AVAudioEngine appeared in iOS 8, I was hoping that the processing might be done rapidly in the background, but that turned out to be impossible; you had to play the sound in real time, install a tap on a node to collect its sound into a buffer, and write the buffer into a file. Starting in iOS 11, rapid offline rendering through AVAudioEngine is possible.

To demonstrate, I'll pass a sound file through a reverb effect and save the output into a new file. Initial configuration is much as you would expect:

```
let url = Bundle.main.url(forResource:"Hooded", withExtension: "mp3")!
let f = try! AVAudioFile(forReading: url)
let player = AVAudioPlayerNode()
self.engine.attach(player)
// patch the player into the effect
let effect = AVAudioUnitReverb()
effect.loadFactoryPreset(.cathedral)
effect.wetDryMix = 40
self.engine.attach(effect)
self.engine.connect(player, to: effect, format: f.processingFormat)
let mixer = self.engine.mainMixerNode
self.engine.connect(effect, to: mixer, format: f.processingFormat)
```

We create an output file with an appropriate format:

```
let fm = FileManager.default
let doc = try! fm.url(for:.documentDirectory, in: .userDomainMask,
    appropriateFor: nil, create: true)
let outurl = doc.appendingPathComponent("myfile.aac", isDirectory:false)
let outfile = try! AVAudioFile(forWriting: outurl, settings: [
    AVFormatIDKey : kAudioFormatMPEG4AAC,
    AVNumberOfChannelsKey : 1,
    AVSampleRateKey : 22050,
])
```

Now comes the interesting part. Before we start playing through the audio engine, we configure it for offline rendering:

```
var done = false
player.scheduleFile(f, at: nil)
let sz : UInt32 = 4096
try! self.engine.enableManualRenderingMode(.offline,
    format: f.processingFormat, maximumFrameCount: sz)
self.engine.prepare()
try! self.engine.start()
player.play()
```

We have told the engine to start and the player to play, but nothing happens. That's because it's up to us to *pull* the sound data through the engine into a buffer one chunk at a time, and write the buffer into a file. I create the buffer, and then loop repeatedly until all the sound data has been read:

```
let outbuf = AVAudioPCMBuffer(
    pcmFormat: f.processingFormat, frameCapacity: sz)!
var rest : Int64 { return f.length - self.engine.manualRenderingSampleTime }
while rest > 0 {
    let ct = min(outbuf.frameCapacity, UInt32(rest))
    let stat = try! self.engine.renderOffline(ct, to: outbuf)
    if stat == .success {
        try! outfile.write(from: outbuf)
    }
}
```

The result is that the input file is processed very quickly into the output file. I have one quibble with the result: our reverb effect is not given a chance to fade away at the end of the output, because we stop writing to the output file as soon as the input file is exhausted. One solution might be to add a couple of seconds arbitrarily onto the size of rest; another might be to examine the contents of outbuf and keep looping after reading the input file until the amplitude of the sound data falls below some threshold.

MIDI Playback

Playing a MIDI file is as simple as playing an audio file. In this example, I'm already armed with a MIDI file, which provides the music, and a SoundFont file, which provides the instrument that will play it; self.player will be an AVMIDIPlayer:

```
let midurl = Bundle.main.url(forResource: "presto", withExtension: "mid")!
let sndurl = Bundle.main.url(forResource: "Piano", withExtension: "sf2")!
self.player = try! AVMIDIPlayer(contentsOf: midurl, soundBankURL: sndurl)
self.player.prepareToPlay()
self.player.play()
```

A MIDI player can also act as a source in an AVAudioEngine. In this case, you'll want an AVAudioUnitSampler as your starting AVAudioUnit. The MIDI file will be parsed by an AVAudioSequencer; this is not part of the audio engine node structure, but rather it *has* the audio engine as a property, so you'll need to retain it in a property (self.seq in this example):

```
let midurl = Bundle.main.url(forResource: "presto", withExtension: "mid")!
let sndurl = Bundle.main.url(forResource: "Piano", withExtension: "sf2")!
let unit = AVAudioUnitSampler()
self.engine.attach(unit)
let mixer = self.engine.outputNode
self.engine.connect(unit, to: mixer, format: mixer.outputFormat(forBus:0))
try! unit.loadInstrument(at:sndurl)
self.seq = AVAudioSequencer(audioEngine: self.engine)
try! self.seq.load(from:midurl)
self.engine.prepare()
try! engine.start()
try! self.seq.start()
```

That code is rather mysterious: where's the connection between the AVAudio-Sequencer and the AVAudioUnitSampler? The answer is that the sequencer just finds the first AVAudioUnitSampler in the audio engine graph and proceeds to drive it. If that isn't what you want, get the AVAudioSequencer's tracks property, which is an array of AVMusicTrack; now you can set each track's destinationAudioUnit explicitly.

Text to Speech

Text can be transformed into synthesized speech using the AVSpeechUtterance and AVSpeechSynthesizer classes. As with an AVAudioPlayer, you'll need to retain the AVSpeechSynthesizer (self.talker in my example); here, I also use the AVSpeech-SynthesisVoice class to make sure the device speaks the text in English, regardless of the user's language settings:

```
let utter = AVSpeechUtterance(string:"Polly, want a cracker?")
if let v = AVSpeechSynthesisVoice(language: "en-US") {
    utter.voice = v
    self.talker.delegate = self
    self.talker.speak(utter)
}
```

You can set the utterance's speech rate; the value ranges between 0 and 1, where 0.5 is normal. You can also set pitch (higher or lower voice) and volume (louder or softer). The delegate (AVSpeechSynthesizerDelegate) is told when the speech starts, when it comes to a new range of text (usually a word), and when it finishes.

To get the user's current language, call the AVSpeechSynthesisVoice class method `currentLanguageCode`. Instead of specifying a voice by language, you can use the system's `identifier`. To get a list of all voices, call the class method `speechVoices`.

If a word within your AVSpeechUtterance needs extra pronunciation guidance, you can write it out using the international phonetic alphabet (IPA):

1. Form an NSMutableAttributedString from your overall phrase.

2. Call `addAttribute(_:value:range:)`:

    • The first parameter is `NSAttributedString.Key(rawValue: AVSpeech-SynthesisIPANotationAttribute)`.

    • The second parameter is the IPA notation to be substituted at the range of that word.

3. Form the speech utterance from the attributed string with the initializer `init(attributedString:)`.

Speech to Text

Your app can participate in the same speech recognition engine used by Siri and the virtual keyboard's Dictate button. In this way, you can transcribe speech to text. To do so, you'll use the Speech framework (`import Speech`).

Use of the speech recognition engine requires authorization from the user. You'll need to have a meaningful entry in your *Info.plist* under the "Privacy — Speech Recognition Usage Description" key (`NSSpeechRecognitionUsageDescription`) explaining to the user why you want to do speech recognition. In your code, check the value of `SFSpeechRecognizer.authorizationStatus()`. If it is `.notDetermined`, request authorization by calling `SFSpeechRecognizer.requestAuthorization`. The system will put up an alert requesting authorization from the user for your app to do speech recognition. A user who denies your app speech recognition authorization may grant it later in Settings.

Once you have authorization, the basic procedure is simple. You form a speech recognition request and hand it off to an SFSpeechRecognizer. Recognition can be performed in various languages, which are expressed as locales; to learn what these are, call the `supportedLocales` class method. The device's current locale is used by default, or you can specify a locale when you initialize the SFSpeechRecognizer.

There are two modes of speech recognition:

Over the air

In this mode (present also in iOS 12 and earlier), recognition is performed by Apple's servers. This is a resource-heavy operation. It requires an internet connection, with the work being done by Apple's servers; such a connection can fail. Apple also warns that recognized snippets must be short, and that excessive use of the server may result in access being throttled.

On the device

In this mode (new in iOS 13), recognition is performed on the device. This may be less accurate than over-the-air recognition, and only ten languages are recognized; but no internet connection is required, and there is no limit on the number and frequency of recognitions you can perform. To specify this mode, ask the SFSpeechRecognizer for its `supportsOnDeviceRecognition` and, if `true`, set the speech recognition request's `requiresOnDeviceRecognition` to `true`.

There are also two *kinds* of speech recognition: transcription of an existing file, and transcription of live speech. For transcription of a file, your speech recognition request will be an SFSpeechURLRecognitionRequest initialized with the file URL. In this example, I have a recording of myself saying "This is a test." I speak American English, so just to be on the safe side, I initialize my SFSpeechRecognizer with the "en-US" locale. Interestingly, none of the objects needs to be retained in an instance property:

```
let f = Bundle.main.url(forResource: "test", withExtension: "aif")!
let req = SFSpeechURLRecognitionRequest(url: f)
let loc = Locale(identifier: "en-US")
guard let rec = SFSpeechRecognizer(locale:loc)
    else {return} // no recognizer
rec.recognitionTask(with: req) { result, err in
    if let result = result {
        let trans = result.bestTranscription
        let s = trans.formattedString
        print(s)
        if result.isFinal {
            print("finished!")
        }
    } else {
        print(err!)
    }
}
```

In that code, we're calling `recognitionTask(with:resultHandler:)` with an anonymous function. The function is called several times, passing us an SFSpeechRecognitionResult containing possible `transcriptions` (an array of SFTranscription). We ignore these, asking instead for the `bestTranscription` and extracting its `formattedString`. We know when we've been called for the last time because the recognition result's `isFinal` is `true`. In real life, it might be sufficient to extract the transcription only on the final pass, but for the purposes of this demonstration, I've logged every call to the function; the resulting console log looks like this:

```
This
This is
This is
This is
This is a test
This is a test
finished!
```

For transcription of live speech, your app is going to be using the device's microphone, so you'll need microphone usage permission, as I described earlier in this chapter. Once you have authorization for both speech recognition and microphone usage, the procedure is almost exactly the same as before — except that the speech recognition request will be an SFSpeechAudioBufferRecognitionRequest, and we need a way to pass the microphone input to it. A buffer recognition request has an `append` method whose parameter is an AVAudioPCMBuffer. To obtain an AVAudioPCMBuffer, we can use AVAudioEngine and put a tap on a node. Here, that node will be the audio engine's `inputNode`, representing the device's microphone:

```swift
let engine = AVAudioEngine()
let req = SFSpeechAudioBufferRecognitionRequest()
func doLive() {
    let loc = Locale(identifier: "en-US")
    guard let rec = SFSpeechRecognizer(locale:loc)
        else {return} // no recognizer
    let input = self.engine.inputNode
    input.installTap(onBus: 0, bufferSize: 4096,
        format: input.outputFormat(forBus: 0)) { buffer, time in
            self.req.append(buffer)
    }
    self.engine.prepare()
    try! self.engine.start()
    // provide the user with "recording" feedback
    rec.recognitionTask(with: self.req) { result, err in
        // ... and the rest is as before ...
    }
}
```

You must provide the user with a clear indication in the interface that the microphone is now live and the speech recognition engine is listening. You must also provide a way for the user to *stop* recognition, signaling that the speech is over (like the

Done button in the dictation interface). That's why our buffer recognition request is an instance property (`self.req`): the buffer recognition request has an `endAudio` instance method, which we need to able to call when the user taps our Done button. I also stop the audio engine and remove the tap from its input node, so as to be ready if the user wants to do more speech recognition later:

```
@IBAction func endLive(_ sender: Any) {
    self.engine.stop()
    self.engine.inputNode.removeTap(onBus: 0)
    self.req.endAudio()
    // take down "recording" feedback
}
```

Instead of calling `recognitionTask(with:resultHandler:)`, you can call `recognitionTask(with:delegate:)`, providing an adopter of the SFSpeechRecognitionTaskDelegate protocol. Here you can implement any of half a dozen optional methods, called at various stages of the recognition process, to allow your response to be more fine-grained. You can also assist the recognition request with hints, retrieve confidence levels and alternatives from the segments of a transcription, and move the task messages onto a background queue.

Further Topics in Sound

iOS is a powerful milieu for production and processing of sound; its sound-related technologies are extensive. This is a big topic, and an entire book could be written about it (in fact, such books do exist). I'll talk in Chapter 16 about accessing sound files in the user's music library. Here are some further topics that there is no room to discuss here (and see Apple's *Core Audio Overview* in the documentation archive):

Other audio session policies

If your app accepts sound input or does audio processing, you'll want to look into audio session policies such as Record, Play and Record, and Audio Processing. In addition, if you're using Record or Play and Record, there are modes — voice chat, video recording, and measurement (of the sound being input) — that optimize how sound is routed and how it is modified.

Audio queues

Audio queues — Audio Queue Services, part of the Audio Toolbox framework — implement sound playing and recording through a C API with more granularity than the Objective-C AVAudioPlayer and AVAudioRecorder (though it is still regarded as a high-level API), giving you access to the buffers used to move chunks of sound data between a storage format (a sound file) and sound hardware.

Extended Audio File Services

A C API for reading and writing sound files in chunks. It is useful in connection with technologies such as audio queues.

Audio Converter Services

Originally, a C API for converting sound files between formats. Starting in iOS 9, the AVAudioConverter class (along with AVAudioCompressedBuffer) gives this API an object-oriented structure.

Streaming audio

Audio streamed in real time over the network, such as an internet radio station, can be played with Audio File Stream Services, in connection with audio queues.

Audio units

Plug-ins that generate sound or modify sound as it passes through them. Starting in iOS 9, the API was migrated from C into Objective-C and given a modern object-oriented structure; audio units can vend interface (AUViewController); and an audio unit from one app can be hosted inside another (audio unit extensions).

Core MIDI

The CoreMIDI framework manages direct communication with MIDI devices.

Core Haptics

New in iOS 13, the Core Haptics framework lets you construct precise vibration patterns to be played on certain iPhone models (iPhone 8 and higher); these are typically used to supplement and reinforce sounds.

CHAPTER 15

Video

Video playback is performed using classes provided by the AV Foundation framework (`import AVFoundation`), such as AVPlayer. An AVPlayer is not a view; rather, an AVPlayer's content is made visible through a CALayer subclass, AVPlayerLayer, which can be added to your app's interface. An AV Foundation video playback interface can be wrapped in a simple view controller, AVPlayerViewController: you provide an AVPlayer, and the AVPlayerViewController *automatically* hosts an associated AVPlayerLayer in its own main view, providing standard playback transport controls so that the user can start and stop play, seek to a different frame, and so forth. AVPlayerViewController is provided by the AVKit framework; you'll need to `import AVKit`.

A simple interface for letting the user trim video (UIVideoEditorController) is also supplied. Sophisticated video editing can be performed in code through the AV Foundation framework, as I'll demonstrate later in this chapter.

If an AVPlayer produces sound, you may need to concern yourself with your application's audio session; see Chapter 14. You almost certainly want the category to be `.playback`. AVPlayer deals gracefully with the app being sent into the background: it will pause when your app is backgrounded and resume when your app returns to the foreground.

A movie file can be in a standard movie format, such as *.mov* or *.mp4*, but it can also be a sound file. An AVPlayerViewController is an easy way to play a sound file, including a sound file obtained in real time over the internet, along with standard controls for pausing the sound and moving the playhead — unlike AVAudioPlayer, which, as I pointed out in Chapter 14, lacks a transport interface.

A web view (Chapter 11) supports the HTML5 `<video>` tag. This can be a simple lightweight way to present video and to allow the user to control playback. Both web view video and AVPlayer support AirPlay.

AVPlayerViewController

An AVPlayerViewController is a view controller whose view contains an AVPlayer-Layer and transport controls. It must be assigned a `player`, which is an AVPlayer. An AVPlayer can be initialized directly from the URL of the video it is to play, with `init(url:)`. You'll instantiate AVPlayerViewController, create and set its AVPlayer, and get the AVPlayerViewController into the view controller hierarchy. You can instantiate an AVPlayerViewController in code or from a storyboard; look for the AVKit Player View Controller object in the Library.

The simplest approach is to use an AVPlayerViewController as a presented view controller. In this example, I present a video from the app bundle:

```
let av = AVPlayerViewController()
let url = Bundle.main.url(forResource:"ElMirage", withExtension: "mp4")!
let player = AVPlayer(url: url)
av.player = player
self.present(av, animated: true)
```

The AVPlayerViewController is presented fullscreen. (This is a good example of the new iOS 13 `.automatic` modal presentation style in action: normally, this would resolve to `.pageSheet`, but for an AVPlayerViewController it is `.fullScreen`.) It knows that it's being shown as a fullscreen presented view controller, so it provides fullscreen video controls, including a Done button which automatically dismisses the presented view controller. There is literally no further work for you to do.

Figure 15-1 shows a fullscreen presented AVPlayerViewController. Exactly what controls you'll see depends on the circumstances; in my case, at the top there's the Done button (which appears as an X), the zoom button, and a volume slider, and at the bottom are transport controls including the current playhead position slider, along with the AirPlay button. The user can hide or show the controls by tapping the video.

If the AVPlayer's file is in fact a sound file, the central region is blacked out, and the controls can't be hidden.

Instead of a *presented* AVPlayerViewController, you might *push* the AVPlayerView-Controller onto a navigation controller's stack. Again, the AVPlayerViewController behaves intelligently. The controls include a fullscreen button, which results in almost exactly the same interface shown in Figure 15-1. There is now no Done button, because the user can tap the back button when finished with this screen. Ensuring that the back button is visible is up to you! You might set the navigation

Figure 15-1. A presented AVPlayerViewController

controller's `hidesBarsWhenVerticallyCompact` to `false` and the AVPlayerViewController's `edgesForExtendedLayout` to `[]`.

If you want the convenience and the control interface that come from using an AVPlayerViewController, while displaying its view as a subview of your own view controller's view, make your view controller a *parent* view controller with the AVPlayerViewController as its *child*, adding the AVPlayerViewController's view in good order (see "Container View Controllers" on page 375):

```
let url = Bundle.main.url(forResource:"ElMirage", withExtension:"mp4")!
let player = AVPlayer(url:url)
let av = AVPlayerViewController()
av.player = player
av.view.frame = CGRect(10,10,300,200)
self.addChild(av)
self.view.addSubview(av.view)
av.didMove(toParent:self)
```

Once again, the AVPlayerViewController behaves intelligently, reducing its controls to a minimum to adapt to the reduced size of its view. On my device, at the given view size, there is room for a fullscreen button, a volume button, a play button, a playhead position slider, and the AirPlay button (Figure 15-2). From here, the user can enter fullscreen mode, either by tapping the fullscreen button or by pinching outward on the video view, and now the full complement of controls is present (exactly as in Figure 15-1).

New in iOS 13, the AVPlayerViewController's `delegate` (AVPlayerViewControllerDelegate) can be notified when the user enters and exits fullscreen mode. There are

Figure 15-2. An embedded AVPlayerViewController's view

two relevant delegate methods; when you build against iOS 13, they are backward compatible to iOS 12:

- `playerViewController(_:willBeginFullScreenPresentationWithAnimation-Coordinator:)`

- `playerViewController(_:willEndFullScreenPresentationWithAnimation-Coordinator:)`

The user can start to enter fullscreen mode with an outward pinch without completing the gesture; to find out whether the user *really* entered fullscreen mode, check the transition coordinator to see whether the transition was cancelled:

```
func playerViewController(_ av: AVPlayerViewController,
    willBeginFullScreenPresentationWithAnimationCoordinator
    coordinator: UIViewControllerTransitionCoordinator) {
        coordinator.animate(alongsideTransition: { con in
            // ...
        }) { con in
            if con.isCancelled {
                // ...
            } else {
                // really went fullscreen!
            }
        }
}
```

Other AVPlayerViewController Properties

An AVPlayerViewController has very few properties:

player
> The view controller's AVPlayer, whose AVPlayerLayer will be hosted in the view controller's view. You can set the player while the view is visible, to change what video it displays (though you are more likely to keep the player and tell *it* to change the video). It is legal to assign an AVQueuePlayer, an AVPlayer subclass; an AVQueuePlayer has multiple items, and the AVPlayerViewController will

treat these as chapters of the video. An AVPlayerLooper object can be used in conjunction with an AVQueuePlayer to repeat play automatically. (I'll give an AVQueuePlayer example in Chapter 16, and an AVPlayerLooper example in Chapter 17.)

`showsPlaybackControls`

If `false`, the controls are hidden. This could be useful if you want to display a video for decorative purposes, or if you are substituting your own controls.

`contentOverlayView`

A UIView to which you are free to add subviews. These subviews will appear overlaid in front of the video but behind the playback controls. Starting in iOS 11, the content overlay is sized to fit its contents, or you can give it constraints to size it as you prefer.

`videoGravity`

How the video should be positioned within the view. Possible values are (AVLayerVideoGravity):

- `.resizeAspect` (the default)
- `.resizeAspectFill`
- `.resize` (fills the view, possibly distorting the video)

`videoBounds`
`isReadyForDisplay`

Read-only. The video position within the view, and the ability of the video to display its first frame and start playing, respectively. If the video is not ready for display, we probably don't yet know its bounds either. In any case, `isReadyForDisplay` will initially be `false` and the `videoBounds` will initially be reported as `.zero`. This is because, with video, things take time to prepare. I'll explain in detail later in this chapter.

`updatesNowPlayingInfoCenter`

If `true` (the default), the AVPlayerViewController keeps the MPNowPlayingInfoCenter (Chapter 14) apprised of the movie's duration and current playhead position. If `false`, it doesn't do that, leaving your code in charge of managing the MPNowPlayingInfoCenter. New in iOS 13, you can leave this property at `true` and still govern what information appears in the remote control interface, by setting the player item's `externalMetadata`; here's an example (without further comment):

Figure 15-3. The picture-in-picture button appears

```
let metadata = AVMutableMetadataItem()
metadata.keySpace = .common
metadata.key = AVMetadataKey.commonKeyTitle as NSString
metadata.value = "El Mirage" as NSString
av.player?.currentItem?.externalMetadata = [metadata]
```

`entersFullScreenWhenPlaybackBegins`

`exitsFullScreenWhenPlaybackEnds`

If `true`, a child AVPlayerViewController's view switches to and from fullscreen mode automatically when play begins and ends.

Everything else there is to know about an AVPlayerViewController comes from its `player`, an AVPlayer. I'll discuss AVPlayer in more detail in a moment.

Picture-in-Picture

An iPad capable of running iOS 13 supports picture-in-picture video playback (unless the user turns it off in the Settings app). This means that the user can move your video into a small system window that floats in front of everything else on the screen. This floating window persists if your app is put into the background.

Your iPad app will support picture-in-picture if it supports background audio, as I described in Chapter 14: you check the checkbox in the Signing & Capabilities tab of the target editor (Figure 14-2), and your audio session's policy must be active and must be Playback. If you want to do those things *without* your app being forced to support picture-in-picture, set the AVPlayerViewController's `allowsPictureIn-PicturePlayback` to `false`.

If picture-in-picture is supported, an extra button appears among the upper set of playback controls (Figure 15-3). When the user taps this button, the video is moved into the system window (and the AVPlayerViewController's view displays a place-holder). The user is now free to leave your app while continuing to see and hear the video. Moreover, if the video is being played fullscreen when the user leaves your app, the video is moved into the picture-in-picture system window *automatically*.

The user can move the system window to any corner. Buttons in the system window, which can be shown or hidden by tapping, allow the user to play and pause the video or to dismiss the system window. There's also a button to dismiss the system window plus return to your app; if the user taps it while the video is playing, the video goes right on playing as it moves back into place within your app.

If your AVPlayerViewController is being presented fullscreen when the video is taken into picture-in-picture mode, then the presented view controller, by default, *is dismissed*. If the user tries to return to your app from the system picture-in-picture window, the video has no place to return to. To handle this situation, give the AVPlayerViewController a `delegate` (AVPlayerViewControllerDelegate) and deal with it in a delegate method. You have two choices:

Don't dismiss the presented view controller
Implement this method:

- `playerViewControllerShouldAutomaticallyDismissAtPictureInPicture-Start(_:)`

Return `false`. Now the presented view controller remains, and the video has a place in your app to which it can be restored.

Recreate the presented view controller
Implement this method:

- `playerViewController(_:restoreUserInterfaceForPictureInPicture-StopWithCompletionHandler:)`

Do what the name tells you: restore the user interface! The first parameter is your original AVPlayerViewController; all you have to do is get it back into the view controller hierarchy. At the end of the process, *call the completion function.*

I'll demonstrate the second approach:

```
func playerViewController(_ pvc: AVPlayerViewController,
    restoreUserInterfaceForPictureInPictureStopWithCompletionHandler
    ch: @escaping (Bool) -> ()) {
        self.present(pvc, animated:true) {
            ch(true)
        }
}
```

Other delegate methods inform you of various stages as picture-in-picture mode begins and ends. One good reason for being conscious that you've entered picture-in-picture mode is that at that point you are effectively a background app, and you should reduce resources and activity so that playing the video is *all* you're doing until picture-in-picture mode ends.

Introducing AV Foundation

The video display performed by AVPlayerViewController is supplied by classes from the AV Foundation framework. This is a big framework with a lot of classes, but there's a good reason for that: video has a lot of structure and can be manipulated in many ways, and AV Foundation very carefully and correctly draws all the distinctions needed for good object-oriented encapsulation. I'll just point out some of the principal classes, features, and techniques associated with video. Further AV Foundation examples will appear in Chapters 16 and 17.

Some AV Foundation Classes

The heart of AV Foundation video playback is AVPlayer. AVPlayer is not a UIView, but rather is the locus of video transport; the actual video, if shown, appears in an AVPlayerLayer associated with the AVPlayer. AVPlayerViewController provides a play button, but what if you wanted to start video playback in code? You'd talk to the AVPlayerViewController's `player` — an AVPlayer. You'd tell it to `play` or set its `rate` to 1.

An AVPlayer's video is its `currentItem`, an AVPlayerItem. In the examples earlier in this chapter we initialized an AVPlayer directly from a URL, with no reference to any AVPlayerItem; but that was just a shortcut. AVPlayer's *real* initializer is `init(playerItem:)`, which takes an AVPlayerItem; when we called `init(url:)`, the AVPlayerItem was created for us.

An AVPlayerItem, too, can be initialized from a URL with `init(url:)`, but again, this is just a shortcut. AVPlayerItem's *real* initializer is `init(asset:)`, which takes an AVAsset. An AVAsset is an actual video resource, and comes in one of two subclasses:

AVURLAsset
: An asset specified through a URL.

AVComposition
: An asset constructed by editing video in code. I'll give an example later in this chapter.

To configure an AVPlayer using the complete "stack" of objects that constitute it, you could say something like this:

```
let url = Bundle.main.url(forResource:"ElMirage", withExtension:"mp4")!
let asset = AVURLAsset(url:url)
let item = AVPlayerItem(asset:asset)
let player = AVPlayer(playerItem:item)
```

Once an AVPlayer exists and has an AVPlayerItem, that player item's tracks, as seen from the player's perspective, are AVPlayerItemTrack objects, which can be individually enabled or disabled. That's different from an AVAssetTrack, which is a fact about an AVAsset. This distinction is a good example of how AV Foundation encapsulates its objects correctly: an AVAssetTrack is a hard and fast reality, but an AVPlayerItemTrack lets a track be manipulated for purposes of playback on a particular occasion.

Things Take Time

Working with video is time-consuming. Just because you give an AVPlayer a command or set a property doesn't mean that it obeys immediately. All sorts of operations, from reading a video file and learning its metadata to transcoding and saving a video file, take a significant amount of time. The user interface must not freeze while a video task is in progress, so AV Foundation relies heavily on threading (Chapter 24). In this way, AV Foundation covers the complex and time-consuming nature of its operations; but your code must cooperate. You'll frequently use key–value observing and callbacks to run your code at the right moment.

Here's an example; it's slightly artificial, but it illustrates the principles and techniques you need to know about. There's an elementary interface flaw when we create an embedded AVPlayerViewController:

```
let url = Bundle.main.url(forResource:"ElMirage", withExtension:"mp4")!
let asset = AVURLAsset(url:url)
let item = AVPlayerItem(asset:asset)
let player = AVPlayer(playerItem:item)
let av = AVPlayerViewController()
av.view.frame = CGRect(10,10,300,200)
av.player = player
self.addChild(av)
self.view.addSubview(av.view)
av.didMove(toParent: self)
```

There are two issues here:

- The AVPlayerViewController's view is initially appearing empty in the interface, because the video is not yet ready for display. Then there's a visible flash when the video appears, because now it *is* ready for display.

- The proposed frame of the AVPlayerViewController's view doesn't fit the actual aspect ratio of the video, which results in the video being letterboxed within that frame (visible in Figure 15-2).

Fixing those issues requires us to grapple with the fact that it takes time to learn when the video is ready for display and what its aspect ratio is.

Key–value observing a property

To prevent the flash, we can start out with the AVPlayerViewController's view hidden, and not show it until `isReadyForDisplay` is `true`. But how will we know when that is? *Not* by repeatedly polling the isReadyForDisplay property! That sort of behavior is absolutely wrong. Rather, we should use KVO to register as an observer of this property. Sooner or later, isReadyForDisplay will become true, and we'll be notified. Now we can unregister from KVO and show the AVPlayerViewController's view:

```
av.view.isHidden = true
var ob : NSKeyValueObservation!
ob = av.observe(\.isReadyForDisplay, options: [.initial, .new]) { vc, ch in
    guard let ok = ch.newValue, ok else {return}
    self.obs.remove(ob)
    DispatchQueue.main.async {
        vc.view.isHidden = false
    }
}
self.obs.insert(ob) // obs is a Set<NSKeyValueObservation>
```

Note that, in that code, I make no assumptions about what thread KVO calls me back on: I intend to operate on the interface, so I step out to the main thread.

Asynchronous property loading

Next, let's talk about setting the AVPlayerViewController's view.frame in accordance with the video's aspect ratio. An AVAsset has tracks (AVAssetTrack); in particular, an AVAsset representing a video has a video track. A video track has a naturalSize, which will give me the aspect ratio I need. But we cannot access these properties immediately. For the sake of efficiency, these and many other AV Foundation object properties don't even *have* a value unless we specifically request that they be evaluated — and when we do, it takes time to fulfill our request.

AV Foundation objects that behave this way conform to the AVAsynchronousKeyValueLoading protocol. You call loadValuesAsynchronously(forKeys:completionHandler:) ahead of time, for any properties you're going to be interested in. When your completion function is called, you check the status of a key and, if its status is .loaded, you are now free to access the property.

To obtain the video's aspect ratio, I'm going to need to do that twice — first for the AVAsset's tracks property, in order to get the video track, and then for the video track's naturalSize property, in order to get the aspect ratio. Let's go all the way back to the beginning. I'll start by creating the AVAsset *and then stop*, waiting to hear in the completion function that the AVAsset's tracks property is ready:

```
let url = Bundle.main.url(forResource:"ElMirage", withExtension:"mp4")!
let asset = AVURLAsset(url:url)
let track = #keyPath(AVURLAsset.tracks)
asset.loadValuesAsynchronously(forKeys:[track]) {
    let status = asset.statusOfValue(forKey:track, error: nil)
    if status == .loaded {
```

```
        DispatchQueue.main.async {
            self.getVideoTrack(asset)
        }
    }
}
```

When the `tracks` property is ready, my completion function is called, and I call my `getVideoTrack` method. Here, I obtain the video track *and then stop* once again, waiting to hear in the completion function that the video track's `naturalSize` property is ready:

```
func getVideoTrack(_ asset:AVAsset) {
    let visual = AVMediaCharacteristic.visual
    let vtrack = asset.tracks(withMediaCharacteristic: visual)[0]
    let size = #keyPath(AVAssetTrack.naturalSize)
    vtrack.loadValuesAsynchronously(forKeys: [size]) {
        let status = vtrack.statusOfValue(forKey: size, error: nil)
        if status == .loaded {
            DispatchQueue.main.async {
                self.getNaturalSize(vtrack, asset)
            }
        }
    }
}
```

When the video track's `naturalSize` property is ready, my completion function is called, and I call my `getNaturalSize` method. Here, at long last, I get the natural size and use it to finish constructing the AVPlayer and to set AVPlayerController's frame:

```
func getNaturalSize(_ vtrack:AVAssetTrack, _ asset:AVAsset) {
    let sz = vtrack.naturalSize
    let item = AVPlayerItem(asset:asset)
    let player = AVPlayer(playerItem:item)
    let av = AVPlayerViewController()
    av.view.frame = AVMakeRect(
        aspectRatio: sz, insideRect: CGRect(10,10,300,200))
    av.player = player
    // ... and the rest is as before ...
}
```

AVPlayerItem provides another way of loading an asset's properties: initialize it with `init(asset:automaticallyLoadedAssetKeys:)` and then observe its `status` using KVO. When that `status` is `.readyToPlay`, you are guaranteed that the player item's `asset` has attempted to load those keys, and you can query them just as you would in `loadValuesAsynchronously`.

Actually, Apple recommends that, as a matter of best practice, you should use KVO to observe the player item's `status` in any case. The reason is that if that status changes to `.failed`, you're going to want to know about it. Fetch the player item's `error` property to find out more. For possible errors, consult the AVError documentation. If the error is `.mediaServicesWereReset`, the media services daemon is hosed (similar to `AVAudioSession.mediaServicesWereResetNotification` in Chapter 14), and you should recreate your AVFoundation objects from scratch.

Remote assets

An AVURLAsset's URL doesn't have to be a local file URL; it can point to a resource located across the internet. Now things *really* take time: the asset has to arrive by way of the network, which may be slow, interrupted, or missing in action. There's a buffer, and if it isn't sufficiently full of your AVAsset's data, playback will stutter or stop.

Before iOS 10, you had to use your AVPlayer's AVPlayerItem as the locus of information about the arrival and playback of your AVAsset from across the network, keeping track of properties such as `playbackLikelyToKeepUp` and the `accessLog`, along with notifications such as `AVPlayerItemPlaybackStalled`, to keep abreast of any issues, pausing and resuming to optimize the user experience.

Starting in iOS 10, Apple made this entire procedure much easier: just tell the AVPlayer to play and stand back! Play won't start until the buffer has filled to the point where the whole video can play without stalling, and if it *does* stall, it will resume automatically. To learn what's happening, check the AVPlayer's `timeControlStatus`; if it is `.waitingToPlayAtSpecifiedRate` and you want to know why, check the AVPlayer's `reasonForWaitingToPlay`. To learn the actual current play rate, call `CMTimebaseGetRate` with the AVPlayerItem's `timebase`.

Time Is Measured Oddly

Another peculiarity of AV Foundation is that time is measured in an unfamiliar way. This is necessary because calculations using an ordinary built-in numeric class such as CGFloat will always have slight rounding errors that quickly begin to matter when you're trying to specify a time within a large piece of media. Therefore, the Core Media framework provides the CMTime class, which under the hood is a pair of integers; they are called the `value` and the `timescale`, but they are simply the numerator and denominator of a rational number.

When you call the CMTime initializer `init(value:timescale:)` (equivalent to C `CMTimeMake`), that's what you're providing. The denominator represents the degree of granularity; a typical value is 600, sufficient to specify individual frames in common video formats.

In the convenience initializer `init(seconds:preferredTimescale:)` (equivalent to C `CMTimeMakeWithSeconds`), the two arguments are *not* the numerator and denominator; they are the time's equivalent in seconds and the denominator. For instance, `CMTime(seconds:2.5, preferredTimescale:600)` yields the CMTime (1500,600).

Constructing Media

AV Foundation allows you to construct your own media asset in code as an AVComposition, an AVAsset subclass, using *its* subclass, AVMutableComposition. An AVComposition is an AVAsset, so given an AVMutableComposition, we could make an AVPlayerItem from it (by calling `init(asset:)`) and hand it over to an AVPlayerViewController's player; we will be creating and displaying our own movie!

Cutting and pasting

In this example, I start with an AVAsset (`asset1`, a video file) and assemble its first 5 seconds of video and its last 5 seconds of video into an AVMutableComposition (`comp`):

```
let type = AVMediaType.video
let arr = asset1.tracks(withMediaType: type)
let track = arr.last!
let duration : CMTime = track.timeRange.duration
let comp = AVMutableComposition()
let comptrack = comp.addMutableTrack(withMediaType: type,
    preferredTrackID: Int32(kCMPersistentTrackID_Invalid))!
try! comptrack.insertTimeRange(CMTimeRange(
    start: CMTime(seconds:0, preferredTimescale:600),
    duration: CMTime(seconds:5, preferredTimescale:600)),
    of:track, at:CMTime(seconds:0, preferredTimescale:600))
try! comptrack.insertTimeRange(CMTimeRange(
    start: duration - CMTime(seconds:5, preferredTimescale:600),
    duration: CMTime(seconds:5, preferredTimescale:600)),
    of:track, at:CMTime(seconds:5, preferredTimescale:600))
```

This works perfectly. But we are not very good video editors, as we have forgotten the corresponding soundtrack from `asset1`. Let's go back and get it and add it to our AVMutableComposition (`comp`):

```
let type2 = AVMediaType.audio
let arr2 = asset1.tracks(withMediaType: type2)
let track2 = arr2.last!
let comptrack2 = comp.addMutableTrack(withMediaType: type2,
    preferredTrackID:Int32(kCMPersistentTrackID_Invalid))!
try! comptrack2.insertTimeRange(CMTimeRange(
    start: CMTime(seconds:0, preferredTimescale:600),
    duration: CMTime(seconds:5, preferredTimescale:600)),
    of:track2, at:CMTime(seconds:0, preferredTimescale:600))
try! comptrack2.insertTimeRange(CMTimeRange(
    start: duration - CMTime(seconds:5, preferredTimescale:600),
    duration: CMTime(seconds:5, preferredTimescale:600)),
    of:track2, at:CMTime(seconds:5, preferredTimescale:600))
```

To display our edited movie in an AVPlayerViewController, we would talk to its player, replacing its player item with a new player item made from our AVMutable-Composition:

```
let item = AVPlayerItem(asset:comp)
let p = vc.player! // vc is an AVPlayerViewController
p.replaceCurrentItem(with: item)
```

Adding tracks

We can use the same technique to overlay *another* audio track from *another* asset; this might be, let's say, some additional narration taken from a sound file (comp is the AVMutableComposition from the previous example):

```
let type3 = AVMediaType.audio
let s = Bundle.main.url(forResource:"aboutTiagol", withExtension:"m4a")!
let asset2 = AVURLAsset(url:s)
let arr3 = asset2.tracks(withMediaType: type3)
let track3 = arr3.last!
let comptrack3 = comp.addMutableTrack(withMediaType: type3,
    preferredTrackID:Int32(kCMPersistentTrackID_Invalid))!
try! comptrack3.insertTimeRange(CMTimeRange(
    start: CMTime(seconds:0, preferredTimescale:600),
    duration: CMTime(seconds:10, preferredTimescale:600)),
    of:track3, at:CMTime(seconds:0, preferredTimescale:600))
```

Transitions

You can apply audio volume changes, and video opacity and transform changes, to the playback of individual tracks. I'll continue from the previous example, applying a fadeout to the second half of the narration track (comptrack3) by creating an AVAudioMix:

```
let params = AVMutableAudioMixInputParameters(track:comptrack3)
params.setVolume(1, at:CMTime(seconds:0, preferredTimescale:600))
params.setVolumeRamp(fromStartVolume: 1, toEndVolume:0,
    timeRange:CMTimeRange(
        start: CMTime(seconds:5, preferredTimescale:600),
        duration: CMTime(seconds:5, preferredTimescale:600)))
let mix = AVMutableAudioMix()
mix.inputParameters = [params]
```

The audio mix must be applied to a playback milieu, such as an AVPlayerItem. So when we make an AVPlayerItem out of our AVComposition, we can set its audioMix property to our AVAudioMix:

```
let item = AVPlayerItem(asset:comp)
item.audioMix = mix
```

Filters

You can add a CIFilter (Chapter 2) to be applied to your video. In this example, I'll apply a sepia filter to my entire edited video (comp from the previous examples):

```
let vidcomp = AVVideoComposition(asset: comp) { req in
    // req is an AVAsynchronousCIImageFilteringRequest
    let f = "CISepiaTone"
    let im = req.sourceImage.applyingFilter(
        f, parameters: ["inputIntensity":0.95])
    req.finish(with: im, context: nil)
}
```

Like an AVAudioMix, an AVVideoComposition must be applied to a playback milieu:

```
let item = AVPlayerItem(asset:comp)
item.videoComposition = vidcomp
```

You can also use an AVVideoComposition to dictate how video tracks are to be composited.

Synchronizing animation with video

An intriguing feature of AV Foundation is AVSynchronizedLayer, a CALayer subclass that effectively crosses the bridge between video time (the CMTime within the progress of a movie) and Core Animation time (the time within the progress of an animation). This means that you can coordinate animation in your interface (Chapter 4) with the playback of a movie! You attach an animation to a layer in more or less the usual way, but the animation takes place in movie playback time: if the movie is stopped, the animation is stopped; if the movie is run at double rate, the animation runs at double rate; and the current "frame" of the animation always corresponds to the current frame of the video within its overall duration.

The synchronization is performed with respect to an AVPlayer's AVPlayerItem. To demonstrate, I'll draw a long thin gray rectangle containing a little black square; the horizontal position of the black square within the gray rectangle will be synchronized to the movie playhead position:

```
let vc = self.children[0] as! AVPlayerViewController
let p = vc.player!
// create synch layer, put it in the interface
let item = p.currentItem!
let syncLayer = AVSynchronizedLayer(playerItem:item)
syncLayer.frame = CGRect(10,220,300,10)
syncLayer.backgroundColor = UIColor.lightGray.cgColor
self.view.layer.addSublayer(syncLayer)
// give synch layer a sublayer
let subLayer = CALayer()
subLayer.backgroundColor = UIColor.black.cgColor
subLayer.frame = CGRect(0,0,10,10)
```

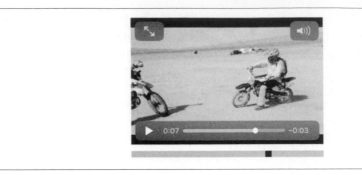

Figure 15-4. The black square's position is synchronized to the movie

```
syncLayer.addSublayer(subLayer)
// animate the sublayer
let anim = CABasicAnimation(keyPath:#keyPath(CALayer.position))
anim.fromValue = subLayer.position
anim.toValue = CGPoint(295,5)
anim.isRemovedOnCompletion = false
anim.beginTime = AVCoreAnimationBeginTimeAtZero // important trick
anim.duration = item.asset.duration.seconds
subLayer.add(anim, forKey:nil)
```

The result is shown in Figure 15-4. The long gray rectangle is the AVSynchronized-Layer, tied to our movie. The little black square inside it is its sublayer; when we animate the black square, that animation will be synchronized to the movie, changing its position from the left end of the gray rectangle to the right end, starting at the beginning of the movie and with the same duration as the movie. Although we attach this animation to the black square layer in the usual way, that animation is frozen: the black square *doesn't move* until we start the movie playing. Moreover, if we pause the movie, the black square stops. The black square is *automatically* representing the current play position within the movie. This may seem a silly example, but if you were to suppress the video controls it could prove downright useful.

Adding layers to video

Instead of adding a CALayer to the interface, you can *render* a CALayer into the video itself. In effect, you treat the video itself as a layer, combine it with other layers however you like, and then package everything into a new video.

Suppose, for instance, that we want to add a caption, title, or other text to our video. If the video itself is a layer, the text is obviously a CATextLayer in front of it. I'll describe the procedure backward, starting with some boilerplate.

To render layers into a video, you have to *export* the video to a file on disk. That requires an AVExportSession. To demonstrate, I'll export comp, the AVMutable-

Composition from the earlier examples, and load the exported video into our AVPlayerViewController:

```
let pre = AVAssetExportPresetHighestQuality
guard let exporter = AVAssetExportSession(asset:comp, presetName:pre) else {
    print("oops")
    return
}
// create a URL to export to
let fm = FileManager.default
var url = fm.temporaryDirectory
let uuid = UUID().uuidString
url.appendPathComponent(uuid + ".mov")
exporter.outputURL = url
exporter.outputFileType = AVFileType.mov
// warning: this can take a long time!
exporter.exportAsynchronously() {
    DispatchQueue.main.async {
        let item = AVPlayerItem(url: url)
        let p = vc.player! // vc is an AVPlayerViewController
        p.replaceCurrentItem(with:item)
    }
}
```

(In real life, you'd probably want to put up some kind of interface to cover the fact that exporting can take a significant amount of time.) The result of that code isn't very interesting, because we didn't make any *change* to our video. To make a change — in particular, to render the video as a layer along with other layers — we need to attach an AVVideoComposition to the exporter:

```
exporter.videoComposition = vidcomp
```

Very well, but what's vidcomp? I'll continue with some more boilerplate. First, we construct our layer architecture. At a minimum, you need two layers — a parent layer with the video layer as its sublayer:

```
let vidtrack = comp.tracks(withMediaType: .video)[0]
let sz = vidtrack.naturalSize
let parent = CALayer()
parent.frame = CGRect(origin: .zero, size: sz)
let child = CALayer()
child.frame = parent.bounds
parent.addSublayer(child)
```

Next, we package up that layer architecture into an *animation tool*, and attach it to an AVVideoComposition. There's a lot of boilerplate here, but if you don't perform this complete dance, you can crash at runtime or end up with a black video:

```
let tool = AVVideoCompositionCoreAnimationTool(
    postProcessingAsVideoLayer: child, in: parent)
let vidcomp = AVMutableVideoComposition()
vidcomp.animationTool = tool
```

```
vidcomp.renderSize = sz
vidcomp.frameDuration = CMTime(value: 1, timescale: 30)
let inst = AVMutableVideoCompositionInstruction()
let dur = comp.duration
inst.timeRange = CMTimeRange(start: .zero, duration: dur)
let layinst = AVMutableVideoCompositionLayerInstruction(assetTrack: vidtrack)
inst.layerInstructions = [layinst]
vidcomp.instructions = [inst]
```

If we now attach `vidcomp` to `exporter` as we export `comp`, we still end up with a video that looks like `comp` itself. But that's not bad; it's good! Our boilerplate is working, and now at long last we are ready to introduce more layers into the architecture. Let's go back and add our text layer:

```
let lay = CATextLayer()
lay.string = "This is cool!"
lay.alignmentMode = .center
lay.foregroundColor = UIColor.black.cgColor
lay.frame = child.bounds
child.addSublayer(lay)
// ... and the rest is as before ...
```

The exported version of `comp` now displays the words "This is cool!" superimposed in front of it.

We've accomplished our original goal, but let's go further. These are CALayers. That means we can animate them! To demonstrate, I'll cause our text to fade in slowly, starting one second after the start of the video. To do so, I simply add an opacity animation to the text layer (`lay`). As with a synchronized layer, it is crucial to coordinate our timing by starting at `AVCoreAnimationBeginTimeAtZero`:

```
let ba = CABasicAnimation(keyPath: #keyPath(CALayer.opacity))
ba.duration = 1
ba.fromValue = 0
ba.toValue = 1
ba.beginTime = AVCoreAnimationBeginTimeAtZero + 1 // crucial
ba.fillMode = .backwards
lay.add(ba, forKey: nil)
```

AVPlayerLayer

An AVPlayer is not an interface object. The corresponding interface object — an AVPlayer made visible, as it were — is an AVPlayerLayer (a CALayer subclass). It has no controls for letting the user play and pause a movie and visualize its progress; it just shows the movie, acting as a bridge between the AV Foundation world of media and the CALayer world of things the user can see.

An AVPlayerViewController's view hosts an AVPlayerLayer for you automatically; otherwise you would not see any video in the AVPlayerViewController's view. But there may be situations where you find AVPlayerViewController too heavyweight, where you don't need the standard transport controls, where you don't want the video to be expandable or to have a fullscreen mode — you just want the simple direct power that can be obtained only by putting an AVPlayerLayer into the interface yourself.

Here, I'll display the same movie as before, but without an AVPlayerViewController:

```
let m = Bundle.main.url(forResource:"ElMirage", withExtension:"mp4")!
let asset = AVURLAsset(url:m)
let item = AVPlayerItem(asset:asset)
let p = AVPlayer(playerItem:item)
self.player = p // might need a reference later
let lay = AVPlayerLayer(player:p)
lay.frame = CGRect(10,10,300,200)
self.playerLayer = lay // might need a reference later
self.view.layer.addSublayer(lay)
```

As before, if we want to prevent a flash when the video becomes ready for display, we can postpone adding the AVPlayerLayer to our interface until its isReadyForDisplay property becomes true — which we can learn through KVO.

In a WWDC 2016 video, Apple suggests an interesting twist on the preceding code: create the AVPlayer *without* an AVPlayerItem, create the AVPlayerLayer, and *then* assign the AVPlayerItem to AVPlayer, like this:

```
let m = Bundle.main.url(forResource:"ElMirage", withExtension:"mp4")!
let asset = AVURLAsset(url:m)
let item = AVPlayerItem(asset:asset)
let p = AVPlayer() // *
self.player = p
let lay = AVPlayerLayer(player:p)
lay.frame = CGRect(10,10,300,200)
self.playerLayer = lay
p.replaceCurrentItem(with: item) // *
self.view.layer.addSublayer(lay)
```

Apparently, there is some increase in efficiency if you do things in that order. The reason, it turns out, is that when an AVPlayerItem is assigned to an AVPlayer that doesn't have an associated AVPlayerLayer, the AVPlayer assumes that only the audio track of the AVAsset is important — and then, when an AVPlayerLayer *is* assigned to it, the AVPlayer must scramble to pick up the video track as well.

The movie is now visible in the interface, but it isn't doing anything. We haven't told our AVPlayer to play, and there are no transport controls, so the user can't tell the video to play either. That's why I kept a reference to the AVPlayer in a property! We can start play either by calling play or by setting the AVPlayer's rate. Here, I imagine that we've provided a simple play/pause button that toggles the playing status of the movie by changing its rate:

```
@IBAction func doButton (_ sender: Any) {
    let rate = self.player.rate
    self.player.rate = rate < 0.01 ? 1 : 0
}
```

Without trying to replicate the full transport controls, we might also like to give the user a way to jump the playhead back to the start of the movie. The playhead position is a feature of an AVPlayerItem:

```
@IBAction func restart (_ sender: Any) {
    let item = self.player.currentItem!
    let time: CMTime = CMTime(seconds:0, preferredTimescale:600)
    item.seek(to:time, completionHandler:nil)
}
```

If we want our AVPlayerLayer to support picture-in-picture, then (in addition to making the app itself support picture-in-picture, as I've already described) we need to call upon AVKit to supply us with an AVPictureInPictureController. This is *not* a view controller; it merely endows our AVPlayerLayer with picture-in-picture behavior. You create the AVPictureInPictureController (checking first to see whether the environment supports picture-in-picture in the first place), initialize it with the AVPlayerLayer, *and retain it*:

```
if AVPictureInPictureController.isPictureInPictureSupported() {
    let pic = AVPictureInPictureController(playerLayer: self.playerLayer)
    self.pic = pic
}
```

There are no transport controls, so there is no picture-in-picture button. Supplying one is up to you. Don't forget to hide the button if picture-in-picture isn't supported! When the button is tapped, tell the AVPictureInPictureController to startPicture-InPicture:

```
@IBAction func doPicInPic(_ sender: Any) {
    if self.pic.isPictureInPicturePossible {
        self.pic.startPictureInPicture()
    }
}
```

You might also want to set yourself as the AVPictureInPictureController's delegate (AVPictureInPictureControllerDelegate). As with the AVPlayerViewController delegate, you are informed of stages in the life of the picture-in-picture window so that you can adjust your interface accordingly. When the user taps the button that dismisses the system window and returns to your app, then if the AVPlayerLayer is still sitting in your interface, there may be no work to do. If you removed the AVPlayerLayer from your interface, and you now want to restore it, implement this delegate method:

- pictureInPictureController(_:restoreUserInterfaceForPictureInPicture-StopWithCompletionHandler:)

In your implementation, configure your interface so that the AVPlayerLayer is present. Make sure that the AVPlayerLayer that you now put into your interface is *the same one* that was removed earlier; in other words, your player layer must continue to be the same as the AVPictureInPictureController's `playerLayer`.

Further Exploration of AV Foundation

Here are some other things you can do with AV Foundation:

- Extract single images (sometimes referred to as *thumbnails* or *poster images*) from a movie (AVAssetImageGenerator). Displaying a poster image of a video's initial frame can help cover up for the delay before the video is ready to start playing.

- Export a movie in a different format (AVAssetExportSession), or read/write raw uncompressed data through a buffer to or from a track (AVAssetReader, AVAssetReaderOutput, AVAssetWriter, AVAssetWriterInput, and so on).

- Capture audio, video, and stills through the device's hardware (AVCaptureSession and so on). I'll say more about that in Chapter 17.

- Tap into video and audio being captured or played, including capturing video frames as still images (AVPlayerItemVideoOutput, AVCaptureVideoDataOutput, and so on; and see Apple's *Technical Q&A QA1702*).

The media capabilities of AV Foundation are nicely summarized in a classic WWDC video, *https://developer.apple.com/videos/play/wwdc2011/415/*.

UIVideoEditorController

UIVideoEditorController is a view controller that presents an interface where the user can trim video. Its view and internal behavior are outside your control, and you're not supposed to subclass it. You are expected to treat the view controller as a presented view controller on the iPhone or as a popover on the iPad, and respond by way of its delegate.

 UIVideoEditorController is one of the creakiest pieces of interface in iOS. It dates back to iOS 3.1, and hasn't been revised since its inception — and it looks like it. It has *never* worked properly on the iPad, and still doesn't. I'm not going to dwell on its bugginess or we'd be here all day.

Before summoning a UIVideoEditorController, be sure to call its class method `can-EditVideo(atPath:)`. (This call can take some noticeable time to return.) If it returns `false`, don't instantiate UIVideoEditorController to edit the given file. Not every video format is editable, and not every device supports video editing. You must also set the UIVideoEditorController instance's `delegate` and `videoPath` before presenting it; the delegate should adopt both UINavigationControllerDelegate and

UIVideoEditorControllerDelegate. You must manually set the video editor controller's modalPresentationStyle to .popover on the iPad (a good instance of the creakiness I was just referring to):

```
let path = Bundle.main.path(forResource:"ElMirage", ofType: "mp4")!
let can = UIVideoEditorController.canEditVideo(atPath:path)
if !can {
    print("can't edit this video")
    return
}
let vc = UIVideoEditorController()
vc.delegate = self
vc.videoPath = path
if UIDevice.current.userInterfaceIdiom == .pad {
    vc.modalPresentationStyle = .popover
}
self.present(vc, animated: true)
if let pop = vc.popoverPresentationController {
    let v = sender as! UIView
    pop.sourceView = v
    pop.sourceRect = v.bounds
    pop.delegate = self
}
```

The view's interface (on the iPhone) contains Cancel and Save buttons, a trimming box displaying thumbnails from the movie, a play/pause button, and the movie itself. The user slides the ends of the trimming box to set the beginning and end of the saved movie. The Cancel and Save buttons do *not* dismiss the presented view; you must do that in your implementation of the delegate methods. There are three of them, and you should implement all three and dismiss the presented view in all of them:

- videoEditorController(_:didSaveEditedVideoToPath:)
- videoEditorControllerDidCancel(_:)
- videoEditorController(_:didFailWithError:)

Implementing the second two delegate methods is straightforward:

```
func videoEditorControllerDidCancel(_ editor: UIVideoEditorController) {
    self.dismiss(animated:true)
}
func videoEditorController(_ editor: UIVideoEditorController,
    didFailWithError error: Error) {
        self.dismiss(animated:true)
}
```

Saving the trimmed video is more involved. Like everything else about a movie, it takes time. When the user taps Save, there's a progress view while the video is trimmed and compressed. The trimmed video has *already* been saved to a file in your app's temporary directory by the time the delegate method `videoEditor-Controller(_:didSaveEditedVideoToPath:)` is called.

 `videoEditorController(_:didSaveEditedVideoToPath:)` is actually called *twice* in quick succession. That's more of its creaky bugginess.

Doing something useful with the saved file at this point is up to you; if you merely leave it in the temporary directory, you can't rely on it to persist. In this example, I copy the edited movie into the Camera Roll album of the user's photo library, by calling `UISaveVideoAtPathToSavedPhotosAlbum`. For this to work, our app's *Info.plist* must have a meaningful "Privacy — Photo Library Additions Usage Description" entry (`NSPhotoLibraryAddUsageDescription`) so that the runtime can ask for the user's permission on our behalf:

```
func videoEditorController(_ editor: UIVideoEditorController,
    didSaveEditedVideoToPath path: String) {
        self.dismiss(animated:true)
        if UIVideoAtPathIsCompatibleWithSavedPhotosAlbum(path) {
            UISaveVideoAtPathToSavedPhotosAlbum(path, self,
                #selector(savedVideo), nil)
        } else {
            // can't save to photo album, try something else
        }
}
```

The function reference `#selector(savedVideo)` in that code refers to a callback method that must take three parameters: a String (the `path`), an Optional wrapping an Error, and an UnsafeMutableRawPointer. It's important to check for errors, because things can still go wrong. In particular, the user could deny us access to the photo library (see Chapter 17 for more about that). If that's the case, we'll get an Error whose `domain` is `ALAssetsLibraryErrorDomain`:

```
@objc func savedVideo(at path:String, withError error:Error?,
    ci:UnsafeMutableRawPointer) {
        if let error = error {
            print("error: \(error)")
        }
}
```

CHAPTER 16

Music Library

An iOS device can be used for the same purpose as the original iPod — to hold and play music, podcasts, and audiobooks. These items constitute the device's *music library*. iOS provides the programmer with various forms of access to the music library; you can:

- Explore the music library.
- Play an item from the music library.
- Control the Music app's music player.
- Present a standard interface where the user can select a music library item.

These features are all provided by the Media Player framework; you'll need to import MediaPlayer.

This chapter assumes that the user's music library consists of sound files that are actually present on the device. However, the user might be using the iCloud Music Library (iTunes Match); and, starting in iOS 11, MusicKit allows your app to interface on the user's behalf with the cloud-based Apple Music service. That's beyond the scope of this book; see the *Apple Music API Reference* for information about it.

Music Library Authorization

Access to the music library requires authorization from the user. You'll need to include in your *Info.plist* a meaningful entry under the "Privacy — Media Library Usage Description" key (NSAppleMusicUsageDescription) justifying to the user your desire for access, to be displayed in the authorization alert that will be presented to the user on your behalf (Figure 16-1).

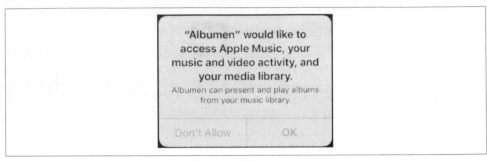

Figure 16-1. The system prompts for music library access

The system, by default, will automatically present the authorization alert the first time your app attempts to access the music library. But instead of letting that happen, you will probably want to take control by checking for authorization yourself and requesting it if necessary. To learn whether you already have authorization, call the MPMediaLibrary `authorizationStatus` class method. The result is an MPMedia-LibraryAuthorizationStatus:

`.notDetermined`
> Authorization has never been requested. You should request authorization, causing the system's authorization alert to appear.

`.authorized`
> You're already authorized. Go ahead and access the music library.

`.denied`
> You have been refused authorization. If your app depends upon music library access, you might put up an alert begging for authorization. The alert can even take the user directly to the spot in the Settings app where the user can provide authorization:
>
> ```
> let url = URL(string:UIApplication.openSettingsURLString)!
> UIApplication.shared.open(url)
> ```

`.restricted`
> You have been refused authorization and the user may not have the power to authorize you. There's no point harassing the user about this, so it is best to do nothing.

If the authorization status is `.notDetermined` and you want to request authorization, call the MPMediaLibrary class method `requestAuthorization`. This method executes asynchronously. To hear about the user's response to the alert, you pass a completion function as parameter; it will be called, possibly on a background thread, when the user dismisses the alert, with an MPMediaLibraryAuthorizationStatus parameter. If the status is now `.authorized`, you can go ahead and access the music library. (The sidebar "Checking for Authorization" encapsulates this entire procedure into a general utility function.)

Exploring the Music Library

Everything in the user's music library, as seen by your code, is an MPMediaEntity. This is an abstract class. It has two concrete subclasses:

MPMediaItem
    An MPMediaItem is a single item (a "song").

MPMediaCollection

> An MPMediaCollection is an ordered list of MPMediaItems, rather like an array; it has a `count`, and its `items` property *is* an array.

MPMediaEntity endows its subclasses with the ability to describe themselves through key–value pairs called *properties*. The property keys have names like `MPMediaItemPropertyTitle`. To fetch a property's value, call `value(forProperty:)` with its key. You can fetch multiple properties with `enumerateValues(forProperties:using:)`. As a convenience, MPMediaEntity and its subclasses also have instance properties whose names correspond to the property key names. With an MPMediaItem, for instance, you can say either `myItem.value(forProperty:MPMediaItemPropertyTitle)` or `myItem.title`, and in most cases you will surely prefer the latter. But you'll still need the full property key name if you're going to form an MPMediaPropertyPredicate, as I'll demonstrate later.

An MPMediaItem has a type (`mediaType`, or `MPMediaItemPropertyMediaType`); it might be music, a podcast, or an audiobook. Different types of item have slightly different properties; these will be intuitively familiar from your use of iTunes. A song (music) has a title, an album title, a track number, an artist, a composer, and so on; a podcast, in addition to its normal title, has a podcast title.

A playlist is an MPMediaPlaylist, a subclass of MPMediaCollection. Its properties include its name, along with its attributes (`playlistAttributes`), an option set that tells you (for instance) whether this is a "smart" playlist.

An item's artwork image is available through an instance of the MPMediaItemArtwork class. From this, you are supposed to be able to get the image itself scaled to a specified size by calling `image(at:)`. My experience is that in reality you'll receive an image of any old size the system cares to give you, so you may have to scale it further yourself (see "UIImage Drawing" on page 100).

Querying the Music Library

Obtaining actual information from the music library involves a *query*, an MPMediaQuery. Querying the music library can be time-consuming; it is perfectly reasonable to do this work on a background thread (see Chapter 24).

Forming a query

First, you *form* the query. There are three main ways to do this:

Without limits

> Create a simple MPMediaQuery by calling `init` (that is, `MPMediaQuery()`). The result is an unlimited query; it asks for everything in the music library.

With a convenience constructor

MPMediaQuery provides several class methods that form a query asking the music library for a limited subset of its contents — all of its songs, or all of its podcasts, and so on:

- `songs`
- `podcasts`
- `audiobooks`
- `playlists`
- `albums`
- `artists`
- `composers`
- `genres`
- `compilations`

With filter predicates

You can limit a query more precisely by attaching to it one or more MPMedia-PropertyPredicate instances. These predicates filter the music library according to criteria you specify; to be included in the result, a media item must success-fully pass through all the filters (in other words, the predicates are combined using logical-and). A predicate is a simple comparison. It has three aspects:

A property

The key name of the property you want to compare against. Not every prop-erty can be used in a filter predicate; the documentation makes the distinc-tion clear, and you can get additional help from an MPMediaEntity class method, `canFilter(byProperty:)`.

A value

The value that the property must have in order to pass through the filter.

A comparison type (optional)

An MPMediaPredicateComparison. In order to pass through the filter, a media item's property value can either *match* the value you provide (`.equal-To`, the default) or *contain* the value you provide (`.contains`).

The two ways of forming a limited query are actually the same; a convenience con-structor is just a quick way of obtaining a query already endowed with a filter predicate.

A query also *groups* its results, according to its `groupingType` (MPMediaGrouping). Your choices are:

- `.title`
- `.album`
- `.artist`
- `.albumArtist`
- `.composer`
- `.genre`
- `.playlist`
- `.podcastTitle`

The query convenience constructors all involve a `groupingType`. Indeed, the grouping is often the salient aspect of the query. An `albums` query, for instance, is merely a `songs` query grouped by album.

Performing a query

After you form the query, you *perform* the query. You do this by asking for the query's properties:

- You can ask for its `items`, an array of MPMediaItems, if you don't care about the groups returned from the query.
- Alternatively, you can ask for its `collections`, an array of MPMediaItemCollections each of which represents one group.

An MPMediaItemCollection has a `representativeItem` property that can come in handy when it is obtained from a grouped query. It gives you just one item from the collection, and the reason you need it is that properties of a group collection are often embodied in its items rather than in the collection itself. For example, an album has no title; rather, its items have album titles that are all the same. So to learn the title of an album, you ask for the album title of a representative item.

To illustrate, I'll discover the titles of all the albums:

```
let query = MPMediaQuery.albums() // form the query
guard let result = query.collections else {return} // perform the query
// prove we've performed the query, by logging the album titles
for album in result {
    print(album.representativeItem!.albumTitle!)
}
/*
Bach, CPE, Symphonies
Beethoven Canons
Beethoven Dances
Scarlatti Continuo
*/
```

Now let's make our query more elaborate; we'll get the titles of all the albums whose name contains "Beethoven." We simply add a filter predicate to the previous query:

```
let query = MPMediaQuery.albums()
let hasBeethoven = MPMediaPropertyPredicate(value:"Beethoven",
    forProperty:MPMediaItemPropertyAlbumTitle,
    comparisonType:.contains)
query.addFilterPredicate(hasBeethoven)
guard let result = query.collections else {return}
for album in result {
    print(album.representativeItem!.albumTitle!)
}
/*
Beethoven Canons
Beethoven Dances
*/
```

Similarly, we can get the titles of all the albums containing any songs whose name contains "Sonata." This is like the previous example, but here we are concerned with the song's own title rather than its album title:

```
let query = MPMediaQuery.albums()
let hasSonata = MPMediaPropertyPredicate(value:"Sonata",
    forProperty:MPMediaItemPropertyTitle,
    comparisonType:.contains)
query.addFilterPredicate(hasSonata)
guard let result = query.collections else {return}
for album in result {
    print(album.representativeItem!.albumTitle!)
}
/*
Scarlatti Continuo
*/
```

An album is a collection of songs (MPMediaItems). Let's modify the output from our previous query to print the titles of all the matching songs in the first album returned. We don't have to change our query, so I'll start at the point where we perform it; result is the array of collections returned from our query, so result[0] is an MPMediaItemCollection holding the filtered songs of one album:

```
// ... same as before ...
let album = result[0]
for song in album.items {
    print(song.title!)
}
/*
Sonata in E minor Kk 81 - I Grave
Sonata in E minor Kk 81 - II Allegro
Sonata in E minor Kk 81 - III Grave
Sonata in E minor Kk 81 - IV Allegro
... and so on ...
*/
```

Persistence and Change in the Music Library

One of the properties of an MPMediaEntity is its `persistentID`, which uniquely identifies it. All sorts of things have persistent IDs — entities in general, songs (media items), albums, artists, composers, and more. Two songs or two playlists can have the same title, but a persistent ID is unique. It is also persistent: using the persistent ID, you can retrieve again at a later time the same song or playlist you retrieved earlier, even across launches of your app.

While you are maintaining the results of a search, the contents of the music library may themselves change. The user might connect the device to a computer and add or delete music with iTunes. This can put your results out of date. For this reason, the library's own modified date is available through the MPMediaLibrary class. Call the class method `default` to get the actual library instance; now you can ask for its `lastModifiedDate`.

You can also register to receive a notification, `.MPMediaLibraryDidChange`, when the music library is modified. This notification is not emitted unless you first call the MPMediaLibrary instance method `beginGeneratingLibraryChangeNotifications`; you should eventually balance this with a call to `endGeneratingLibraryChangeNotifications`.

Music Player

The music player (MPMusicPlayerController) is the Media Player framework class for playing an MPMediaItem. Actually the music player plays from a *queue* of items. This behavior is familiar from iTunes and the Music app. In the Music app, when you tap the first song of a playlist to start playing it, when the end of that song is reached, we proceed by default to the next song in the playlist. That's because tapping the first song of a playlist causes the queue to be the totality of songs in the playlist. The music player behaves the same way: when it reaches the end of a song, it proceeds to the next song in its queue.

Your methods for controlling playback reflect the music player's queue-based orientation. In addition to the expected `play`, `pause`, and `stop` commands, there's a `skipToNextItem` and `skipToPreviousItem` command. Anyone who has ever used iTunes or the Music app (or, for that matter, an old-fashioned iPod) will have an intuitive grasp of this and everything else a music player does. You can even set a music player's `repeatMode` and `shuffleMode`, just as in iTunes.

The music player has a `prepareToPlay` method that takes a completion function where you can receive an error parameter; but I find that this is not useful, because you can get an error here and nevertheless be able to play. In fact, in my experience the player starts playing more reliably if you omit `prepareToPlay` altogether.

The music player comes in two flavors, depending on which class property you use to get an instance:

`systemMusicPlayer`

> The very same player used by the Music app. This might already be playing an item, or it might be paused with a current item, at any time while your app runs; you can learn or change what item this is. The system music player continues playing independently of the state of your app. It has a complete built-in user interface, namely the Music app itself, where the user can at any time alter what it is doing. It communicates automatically with the remote playback controls (Figure 14-1).

`applicationQueuePlayer`

> A separate player, independent of the Music app; the song it is playing can be different from the Music app's current song. Nevertheless, this player isn't entirely inside your app. It has its own audio session. Telling it to play interrupts your app's audio session; if your app's capabilities include the Audio background mode (Chapter 14), then the player will keep playing when your app is backgrounded, even if your app's audio session category is not Playback. Like the `systemMusicPlayer`, it communicates automatically with the remote playback controls, allowing the user to control it by pausing, seeking, and skipping forward or backward in the queue.

Setting the Queue

To provide a music player with its queue, you call `setQueue(with:)`. The parameter can be:

A query

> You hand the music player an MPMediaQuery. The query's `items` are the items of the queue.

A collection

> You hand the music player an MPMediaItemCollection. This might be derived from a query you performed, but you can also assemble your own collection of MPMediaItems in any way you like, putting them into an array and calling MPMediaItemCollection's `init(items:)`.

A descriptor

You hand the music player an MPMusicPlayerQueueDescriptor. This class was introduced in iOS 10.1 to allow the queue to contain Apple Music songs. It is abstract; its concrete subclasses are:

- MPMusicPlayerMediaItemQueueDescriptor
- MPMusicPlayerPlayParametersQueueDescriptor
- MPMusicPlayerStoreQueueDescriptor

MPMusicPlayerMediaItemQueueDescriptor has two initializers, `init(query:)` and `init(itemCollection:)`. You don't need this class merely to set a music player's queue, but you can use it if you like; it will come in handy particularly when you want to *modify* a music player's queue, as I'll explain a little later. (The other two descriptor classes have to do with Apple Music, and I'm not going to discuss them further.)

My experience is that the player can behave in unexpected ways if you don't ask it to play immediately after setting the queue; apparently the queue does not actually take effect until you do that. In addition, setting the queue seems to be most reliable if you tell the player to `stop` beforehand. It may also be useful to insert a brief delay between setting the queue and starting to play; otherwise, the player might silently fail to play, or you can even crash. Finally, both players behave much better, in my experience, if you keep a persistent reference to your player as an instance property.

In this example, we collect all songs actually present in the library that are shorter than 30 seconds, and set them playing in random order using the application queue player (`self.player`):

```
DispatchQueue.global(qos:.userInitiated).async {
    let query = MPMediaQuery.songs()
    let isPresent = MPMediaPropertyPredicate(value:false,
        forProperty:MPMediaItemPropertyIsCloudItem,
        comparisonType:.equalTo)
    query.addFilterPredicate(isPresent)
    guard let items = query.items else {return}
    let shorties = items.filter {
        let dur = $0.playbackDuration
        return dur < 30
    }
    guard shorties.count > 0 else {
        print("no songs that short!")
        return
    }
    let queue = MPMediaItemCollection(items:shorties)
    DispatchQueue.main.async {
        if self.player.playbackState == .playing {
            self.player.stop()
        }
```

```
        self.player.shuffleMode = .songs
        self.player.setQueue(with:queue)
        delay(0.2) {
            self.player.play()
        }
    }
}
```

Modifying the Queue

You can modify a player's existing queue. There are two distinct approaches:

Play next and play later

Call prepend(_:) or append(_:). Apple characterizes these as equivalent to Play Next and Play Later functionality; prepend(_:) inserts into the queue just after the currently playing item, while append(_:) inserts at the end of the queue. The parameter is an MPMusicPlayerQueueDescriptor.

Insert and remove

This feature is available only for the application queue player:

1. Call perform(queueTransaction:completionHandler:). Be careful with this call; if calls overlap, you can crash ("Only one queue transaction may be performed at a time").

2. Inside the queueTransaction: function, the parameter is an MPMusicPlayer-ControllerMutableQueue. This is a mutable subclass of MPMusicPlayerCon-trollerQueue; you can use its items property to examine the queue.

3. Call insert(_:after:) or remove(_:) on the mutable queue. The first parameter of insert(_:after:) is an MPMusicPlayerQueueDescriptor.

4. In the completionHandler: function, the first parameter is an MPMusic-PlayerControllerQueue, so you can examine the effect of your insertion or removal on the queue. The second parameter tells you whether there was an error. You can have an empty completionHandler: function body, but you can't omit the function altogether.

Player State

You can ask a music player for its nowPlayingItem, and since this is an MPMedia-Item, you can learn all about it through its properties. You can ask a music player which song within the queue is currently playing (indexOfNowPlayingItem). Unfortunately, you can't ask the system music player for its actual queue! You can obtain the application queue player's current queue by misusing perform(queue-Transaction:completionHandler:). You can learn that the application queue

player's queue has changed by registering for the `.MPMusicPlayerControllerQueue-`
`DidChange` notification.

A music player has a `playbackState` that you can query to learn what it's doing
(whether it is playing, paused, stopped, or seeking). Do not use the music player's
`currentPlaybackRate` to learn whether the player is playing; it is not as reliable as the
`playbackState`. The music player also emits notifications informing you of changes
in its state:

- `.MPMusicPlayerControllerPlaybackStateDidChange`

- `.MPMusicPlayerControllerNowPlayingItemDidChange`

- `.MPMusicPlayerControllerVolumeDidChange`

These notifications are not emitted until you tell the music player to `begin-`
`GeneratingPlaybackNotifications`. (You should eventually balance this call with a
call to `endGeneratingPlaybackNotifications`.) This is an instance method, so you
can arrange to receive notifications from either of the two music players. If you are
receiving notifications from both, you can distinguish them by examining the Notification's `object` and comparing it to each player.

To illustrate, I'll extend the previous example to set the text of a UILabel in our interface (`self.label`) every time a different song starts playing. Before we start the
player playing, we insert these lines to generate the notifications:

```
self.player.beginGeneratingPlaybackNotifications()
NotificationCenter.default.addObserver(self,
    selector: #selector(self.changed),
    name: .MPMusicPlayerControllerNowPlayingItemDidChange,
    object: self.player)
```

And here's how we respond to those notifications:

```
@objc func changed(_ n:Notification) {
    self.label.text = ""
    let player = self.player
    guard let obj = n.object, obj as AnyObject === player else {return}
    guard let title = player.nowPlayingItem?.title else {return}
    if player.playbackState != .playing {return}
    let ix = player.indexOfNowPlayingItem
    guard ix != NSNotFound else {return}
    player.perform(queueTransaction: { _ in }) { q,_ in
        self.label.text = "\(ix+1) of \(q.items.count): \(title)"
    }
}
```

There's no periodic notification as a song plays and the current playhead position
advances. To get that information, you'll have to resort to polling. This is not objectionable as long as your polling interval is reasonably sparse; your display may occasionally fall a little behind reality, but that won't usually matter. To illustrate, let's add

to our existing example a UIProgressView (`self.prog`) showing the current percentage of the current song being played by the music player. I'll use a Timer to poll the state of the player every second:

```
self.timer = Timer.scheduledTimer(timeInterval:1,
    target: self, selector: #selector(self.timerFired),
    userInfo: nil, repeats: true)
self.timer.tolerance = 0.1
```

When the timer fires, the progress view displays the state of the currently playing item:

```
@objc func timerFired(_: Any) {
    let player = self.player
    guard let item = player.nowPlayingItem,
        player.playbackState != .stopped else {
            self.prog.isHidden = true
            return
    }
    self.prog.isHidden = false
    let current = player.currentPlaybackTime
    let total = item.playbackDuration
    self.prog.progress = Float(current / total)
}
```

MPVolumeView

The Media Player framework offers a slider for letting the user set the system output volume, along with an AirPlay route button if appropriate; this is an MPVolumeView. It is customizable similarly to a UISlider (Chapter 12); you can set the images for the two halves of the track and the thumb for both the normal and the highlighted state (while the user is touching the thumb).

For further customization, you can subclass MPVolumeView and override `volumeSliderRect(forBounds:)`. (An additional overridable method is documented, `volumeThumbRect(forBounds:volumeSliderRect:value:)`, but in my testing it is never called; I regard this as a bug.)

Playing Songs with AV Foundation

MPMusicPlayerController is convenient and easy, but it's also restrictive. The music player doesn't really belong to you. It has a fixed set of music playing behaviors, similar to iTunes or the Music app. Its audio session isn't your audio session. It takes control of the remote command center. What if that isn't what you want? How else might you play an MPMediaItem?

An MPMediaItem representing a file in the user's music library has an `assetURL` property whose value is a file URL. Therefore, everything from Chapters 14 and 15 comes into play. Having obtained an MPMediaItem's asset URL, you can use that URL to initialize an AVAudioPlayer, an AVAsset, or an AVPlayer (which might be wrapped in an AVPlayerViewController).

In this example, I'll use an AVQueuePlayer (an AVPlayer subclass) to play a sequence of MPMediaItems, just as an MPMusicPlayerController does. The queue player is retained in an instance property, `self.qp`. We might be tempted to treat it as a playlist, handing it the entire array of songs to be played:

```
let arr = // array of MPMediaItem
let items = arr.map {
    let url = $0.assetURL!
    let asset = AVAsset(url:url)
    return AVPlayerItem(asset: asset)
}
self.qp = AVQueuePlayer(items:items)
self.qp.play()
```

Instead of adding a whole batch of AVPlayerItems to an AVQueuePlayer all at once, we should probably add just a few AVPlayerItems to start with, and then append each additional AVPlayerItem when an item finishes playing. So I'll start out by storing the array in a property (`self.items`) and adding just three AVPlayerItems to the queue player. Then I'll use key–value observing to watch for changes in the AVQueuePlayer's currentItem:

```
let arr = // array of MPMediaItem
self.items = arr.map {
    let url = $0.assetURL!
    let asset = AVAsset(url:url)
    return AVPlayerItem(asset: asset)
}
let seed = min(3,self.items.count)
self.qp = AVQueuePlayer(items:Array(self.items.prefix(upTo:seed)))
self.items = Array(self.items.suffix(from:seed))
// use .initial option so that we get an observation for the first item
let ob = qp.observe(\.currentItem, options: .initial) { _,_ in
    self.changed()
}
self.obs.insert(ob) // self.obs is a Set<NSKeyValueObservation>
self.qp.play()
```

In our changed method, we pull an AVPlayerItem off the front of our items array and add it to the end of the AVQueuePlayer's queue. The AVQueuePlayer itself deletes an item from the start of its queue after playing it, so in this way the queue never exceeds four items in length:

```
guard let item = self.qp.currentItem else {return}
guard self.items.count > 0 else {return}
let newItem = self.items.removeFirst()
self.qp.insert(newItem, after:nil) // means "at end"
```

Now let's go further. Since we're already being notified each time a new song starts playing, we can insert some code to update a label's text with the title of each successive song. This will demonstrate how to extract metadata from an AVAsset by way of an AVMetadataItem. Here, we fetch the `AVMetadata.commonKeyTitle` and get its `value` property — the inverse of what I did in Chapter 15, when I set a player item's external metadata:

```
var arr = item.asset.commonMetadata
arr = AVMetadataItem.metadataItems(from:arr,
    withKey:AVMetadataKey.commonKeyTitle,
    keySpace:.common)
let met = arr[0]
let value = #keyPath(AVMetadataItem.value)
met.loadValuesAsynchronously(forKeys:[value]) {
    if met.statusOfValue(forKey:value, error:nil) == .loaded {
        guard let title = met.value as? String else {return}
        DispatchQueue.main.async {
            self.label.text = "\(title)"
        }
    }
}
```

Going even further, we can also update a progress view to reflect the current item's current time and duration. Unlike an MPMusicPlayerController, we don't need to poll with a Timer; an AVPlayer can have a *time observer*. We need to retain the time observer in a property:

```
self.timeObserver = self.qp.addPeriodicTimeObserver(
    forInterval: CMTime(seconds:0.5, preferredTimescale:600),
    queue: nil) { [unowned self] t in
        self.timerFired(time:t)
}
```

To get our AVPlayerItems to load their `duration` property, we'll need to go back and modify the code we used to initialize them:

```
let url = $0.assetURL!
let asset = AVAsset(url:url)
return AVPlayerItem(asset: asset,
    automaticallyLoadedAssetKeys: [#keyPath(AVAsset.duration)])
```

Our time observer now causes our `timerFired` method to be called periodically, reporting the current time of the current player item; we obtain the current item's `duration` and update our progress view (`self.prog`):

```
func timerFired(time:CMTime) {
    if let item = self.qp.currentItem {
        let asset = item.asset
        let dur = #keyPath(AVAsset.duration)
        if asset.statusOfValue(forKey:dur, error: nil) == .loaded {
            let dur = asset.duration
```

```
            self.prog.setProgress(Float(time.seconds/dur.seconds),
                animated: false)
        }
    }
}
```

Media Picker

The media picker (MPMediaPickerController), supplied by the Media Player framework, is a view controller whose view is a self-contained navigation interface in which
the user can select a media item from the music library, similar to the Music app. You
are expected to treat the picker as a presented view controller. As with any access to
the music library, the media picker requires user authorization ("Checking for
Authorization" on page 861); if you don't have authorization, don't present the
picker.

You can use the initializer, init(mediaTypes:), to limit the type of media items displayed. You can make a prompt appear at the top of the navigation bar (prompt). You
can govern whether the user can choose multiple media items or just one, with the
allowsPickingMultipleItems property. You can filter out items stored in the cloud
by setting showsCloudItems to false.

 Starting in iOS 9, the mediaTypes: values .podcast and .audioBook don't work.
I believe that this is because podcasts are considered to be the purview of the
Podcasts app, and audiobooks are considered to be the purview of the Books app
— not the Music app. You can see podcasts and audiobooks as MPMediaEntity
objects in the user's music library, but *not* by way of an MPMediaPicker-
Controller.

While the media picker controller's view is showing, you learn what the user is doing
through two delegate methods (MPMediaPickerControllerDelegate); the presented
view controller is not automatically dismissed, so it is up to you dismiss it in these
delegate methods:

- mediaPicker(_:didPickMediaItems:)

- mediaPickerDidCancel(_:)

The behavior of the delegate methods depends on the value of the controller's allows-
PickingMultipleItems:

The controller's allowsPickingMultipleItems *is* false *(the default)*
    There's a Cancel button. When the user taps a media item, your media-
    Picker(_:didPickMediaItems:) is called, handing you an MPMediaItem-
    Collection consisting of that item; you are likely to dismiss the presented view
    controller at this point. When the user taps Cancel, your mediaPickerDid-
    Cancel(_:) is called.

The controller's `allowsPickingMultipleItems` *is* `true`

There's a Done button. Every time the user taps a media item, it is checked to indicate that it has been selected. When the user taps Done, your `media-Picker(_:didPickMediaItems:)` is called, handing you an MPMediaItem-Collection consisting of all items the user selected — unless the user selected no items, in which case your `mediaPickerDidCancel(_:)` is called.

In this example, we put up the media picker; we then play the user's chosen media item(s) with the application queue player. The example works equally well whether `allowsPickingMultipleItems` is `true` or `false`:

```
func presentPicker (_ sender: Any) {
    checkForMusicLibraryAccess {
        let picker = MPMediaPickerController(mediaTypes:.music)
        picker.delegate = self
        self.present(picker, animated: true)
    }
}
func mediaPicker(_ mediaPicker: MPMediaPickerController,
    didPickMediaItems mediaItemCollection: MPMediaItemCollection) {
        let player = MPMusicPlayerController.applicationQueuePlayer
        player.stop()
        player.setQueue(with:mediaItemCollection)
        delay(0.2) {
            player.play()
        }
        self.dismiss(animated:true)
}
func mediaPickerDidCancel(_ mediaPicker: MPMediaPickerController) {
    self.dismiss(animated:true)
}
```

On the iPad, the media picker can be displayed as a fullscreen presented view, but it also works reasonably well in a popover, especially if we increase its `preferred-ContentSize`. This code presents as fullscreen on an iPhone and as a reasonably sized popover on an iPad:

```
let picker = MPMediaPickerController(mediaTypes:.music)
picker.delegate = self
picker.modalPresentationStyle = .popover
picker.preferredContentSize = CGSize(500,600)
self.present(picker, animated: true)
if let pop = picker.popoverPresentationController {
    if let b = sender as? UIBarButtonItem {
        pop.barButtonItem = b
    }
}
```

CHAPTER 17

Photo Library and Camera

The stored photos and videos accessed by the user through the Photos app constitute the device's photo library:

- The UIImagePickerController class can be used to give the user an interface for exploring the photo library and choosing a photo.

- The Photos framework, also known as PhotoKit, lets you access the photo library and its contents programmatically — including the ability to modify a photo's image. You'll need to `import Photos`.

The user's device may include one or more cameras, and your app might want to let the user take (*capture*) a photo or video:

- The UIImagePickerController class can be used to give the user an interface similar to the Camera app, letting the user capture photos and videos.

- At a deeper level, the AV Foundation framework (Chapter 15) provides direct control over the camera hardware. You'll need to `import AVFoundation`.

The two subjects are related, especially because having allowed the user to capture an image, you will typically store it in the photo library, just as the Camera app does. So this chapter treats them together.

Constants such as `kUTTypeImage`, referred to in this chapter, are provided by the Mobile Core Services framework; you'll need to `import MobileCoreServices`.

Browsing with UIImagePickerController

UIImagePickerController is a view controller providing an interface in which the user can choose an item from the photo library, similar to the Photos app. You are expected to treat the UIImagePickerController as a presented view controller.

The documentation says that on the iPad you should make this a popover, but personally I find a fullscreen presentation more usable.

Image Picker Controller Presentation

To let the user choose an item from the photo library, first call the UIImagePicker-Controller class method isSourceTypeAvailable(_:) with a parameter of .photo-Library; if it returns false, stop. Now instantiate UIImagePickerController and assign .photoLibrary to its sourceType.

 There's another source type, .savedPhotosAlbum; I don't recommend its use. In theory, it should mean the user is confined to the contents of the Camera Roll album, which would be great. Instead, ever since iOS 8, the user sees the Moments interface and all items in the library are shown. To add insult to injury, in iOS 13 the Photos app no longer has the Moments interface, so the interface displayed in the UIImagePickerController may be unfamiliar and confusing.

You'll probably want to specify an array of mediaTypes you're interested in. This array will usually contain kUTTypeImage, kUTTypeMovie, or both; or you can specify all available types by calling the class method availableMediaTypes(for:).

A UIImagePickerController can also return a live photo as a live photo if the following two conditions are met:

- The picker's mediaTypes includes both kUTTypeLivePhoto and kUTTypeImage. The results from availableMediaTypes(for:) do *not* include kUTTypeLive-Photo; you have to add it to the mediaTypes explicitly.

- The picker's allowsEditing property is false (the default).

I'll talk later about how to display a live photo as a live photo. If you fail to include kUTTypeLivePhoto in the mediaTypes array, then if the user chooses a live photo, you'll receive it as an ordinary still image.

The videoExportPreset property lets you set the transcoding format to be used if the user chooses a video. For the preset names, consult the AVAssetExportSession documentation.

Optionally, you can set the picker's allowsEditing property to true. In the case of an image, the interface then allows the user to scale the image up and to move it so as to be cropped by a preset rectangle; in the case of a movie, the user can trim the movie as with a UIVideoEditorController (Chapter 15).

After configuring the picker as desired, and having supplied a delegate (adopting UIImagePickerControllerDelegate and UINavigationControllerDelegate), present the picker:

```
let src = UIImagePickerController.SourceType.photoLibrary
guard UIImagePickerController.isSourceTypeAvailable(src)
    else {return}
guard let arr UIImagePickerController.availableMediaTypes(for:src)
    else {return}
let picker = UIImagePickerController()
picker.sourceType = src
picker.mediaTypes = arr
picker.delegate = self
picker.videoExportPreset = AVAssetExportPreset640x480 // or whatever
self.present(picker, animated: true)
```

Image Picker Controller Delegate

When the user has finished working with the image picker controller, the delegate
will receive one of these messages:

`imagePickerController(_:didFinishPickingMediaWithInfo:)`
> The user selected an item from the photo library. The `info:` parameter describes
> it; I'll give details in a moment.

`imagePickerControllerDidCancel(_:)`
> The user tapped Cancel.

If a UIImagePickerControllerDelegate method is not implemented, the view controller is dismissed automatically at the point where that method would be called; but
rather than relying on this, you should probably implement both delegate methods
and dismiss the view controller yourself in each.

The `info` parameter in the first delegate method is a dictionary of information about
the chosen item. The keys in this dictionary (UIImagePickerController.InfoKey)
depend on the media type:

An image
> The `.mediaType` key's value will be `kUTTypeImage`. The other keys are:
>
> `.phAsset`
>> A PHAsset representing the image in the photo library; I'll discuss how to
>> access PHAsset information later in this chapter.
>
> `.originalImage`
>> A UIImage.
>
> `.imageURL`
>> A file URL to a copy of the image data saved into a temporary directory.
>
> If the picker's `allowsEditing` was `true`, these further keys may be present:

`.cropRect`
> An NSValue wrapping a CGRect.

`.editedImage`
> A UIImage. This becomes the image you are expected to use.

A live photo
> The `.mediaType` key's value will be `kUTTypeLivePhoto`. In addition to the image keys, there's a further key:

`.livePhoto`
> A PHLivePhoto (a type supplied by the Photos framework). But in iOS 13 this is always `nil`; I'll explain later what to do about that.

A movie
> The `.mediaType` key's value will be `kUTTypeMovie`. The other keys are:

`.phAsset`
> A PHAsset representing the video in the photo library; I'll discuss how to access PHAsset information later in this chapter.

`.mediaURL`
> A file URL to a copy of the movie data saved into a temporary directory.

 Many of these keys will yield `nil` values unless you have previously obtained user authorization! Merely *presenting* an image picker controller does *not* require user authorization to access the photo library, presumably because an image is just an image. But getting the full repertoire of information in the delegate method *does* require user authorization; without it, you'll get the image (for a still image) and a file URL, but that's all. Obtaining user authorization to access the photo library is discussed later in this chapter.

Here's an implementation of the first delegate method that picks up all the needed keys; the idea is that we then dismiss the picker and proceed to deal with the chosen item in the completion function:

```
func imagePickerController(_ picker: UIImagePickerController,
    didFinishPickingMediaWithInfo
    info: [UIImagePickerController.InfoKey : Any]) {
        let asset = info[.phAsset] as? PHAsset
        let url = info[.mediaURL] as? URL
        var im = info[.originalImage] as? UIImage
        if let ed = info[.editedImage] as? UIImage {
            im = ed
        }
        let live = info[.livePhoto] as? PHLivePhoto
        let imurl = info[.imageURL] as? URL
```

```
        self.dismiss(animated:true) {
            // do something with the chosen item here
        }
    }
```

Dealing with Image Picker Controller Results

The preceding code gathered all the information from the UIImagePickerController about the user's chosen photo library item; but it didn't *do* anything with it. That's the job of the dismiss completion function — where I left a blank. Let's fill it in.

A common reason for presenting a UIImagePickerController is to display the user's chosen item in your interface. In that case, you'll want to deal differently with each possible type that the user can choose.

You might suppose that the info dictionary's .mediaType would sufficiently distinguish the possible types — kUTTypeImage, kUTTypeLivePhoto, or kUTTypeMovie. Indeed, that was true up through iOS 10. But iOS 11 introduced two new possible image types that might be present in the photo library, so the .mediaType turns out to be insufficiently fine-grained. Instead, use the PHAsset returned by the .phAsset key, and examine its playbackStyle. (Recall that without user authorization, the .phAsset value will be nil.)

There are five possible playbackStyle values (PHAsset.PlaybackStyle):

.image
> You have received (im) a UIImage, suitable for display in a UIImageView. The image may be very large; to save memory, you should downsize it to the largest size and resolution needed for actual display in the interface (see "UIImage Drawing" on page 100, along with the discussion of the Image I/O framework in Chapter 22).

.imageAnimated
> You have received an animated GIF. Unfortunately, iOS doesn't include any native ability to display an animated GIF as animated in your interface. You can display the UIImage you have already received (im) as a still image, or you can use the image URL (imurl) to load the GIF data and convert it yourself into a sequence of images for animated display.

.livePhoto
> You have received a PHLivePhoto. To display it in your interface, use a PHLive-PhotoView (supplied by the Photos UI framework; import PhotosUI). This view has many powerful properties and delegate methods, but you don't need any of them just to display the live photo; the live photo is treated as a live photo automatically, meaning that the user can use press it to show the accompanying movie. The only properties of the PHLivePhotoView that you really need to set,

besides its `livePhoto`, are its `frame` and possibly its `contentMode` (similar to a UIImageView).

 The PHLivePhoto should arrive by way of the `.livePhoto` key, but it appears that this is always `nil` in iOS 13. I regard this as a bug. The workaround is to use the PHAsset to fetch the live photo manually from photo library by way of a PHImageManager, as I'll explain later in this chapter.

`.video`

> You have received (`url`) the file URL of the exported video in the temporary directory, suitable for display with AVPlayer and other AVFoundation and AVKit classes discussed in Chapter 15.

`.videoLooping`

> You have received a live photo to which the Loop or Bounce effect has been applied. It comes to you as a video file URL (`url`), but implementing the looping is up to you. You can do this easily using an AVPlayerLooper object (mentioned in Chapter 15). Start with an AVQueuePlayer rather than an AVPlayer, configure the AVPlayerLooper and retain it in an instance property, and use the AVQueuePlayer to show the video:

```
let av = AVPlayerViewController()
let player = AVQueuePlayer(url:url)
av.player = player
self.looper = AVPlayerLooper(
    player: player, templateItem: player.currentItem!)
// ... and so on ...
```

Still image metadata can be obtained from the image data stored at the `.imageURL`, using the Image I/O framework to extract the metadata as a dictionary (`import ImageIO`, and see Chapter 22):

```
let src = CGImageSourceCreateWithURL(imurl! as CFURL, nil)!
let d = CGImageSourceCopyPropertiesAtIndex(src,0,nil) as! [AnyHashable:Any]
```

Photos Framework

The Photos framework (`import Photos`), also known as PhotoKit, does for the photo library roughly what the Media Player framework does for the music library (Chapter 16), letting your code explore the library's contents — and then some. You can manipulate albums, add photos, and even perform edits on the user's photos.

The photo library itself is represented by the PHPhotoLibrary class, and by its shared instance, which you can obtain through the `shared` method; you do not need to retain the shared photo library instance. Then there are the classes representing the kinds of things that inhabit the library (the *photo entities*):

PHAsset
> A single photo or video file.

PHCollection
> An abstract class representing collections of all kinds. Its concrete subclasses are:

PHAssetCollection
>> A collection of photos. Albums and smart albums are PHAssetCollections.

PHCollectionList
>> A collection of asset collections. A folder of albums, or a smart folder, is a collection list.

Finer typological distinctions are drawn, not through subclasses, but through a system of types and subtypes, which are properties:

- A PHAsset has `mediaType` and `mediaSubtypes` properties.
- A PHAssetCollection has `assetCollectionType` and `assetCollectionSubtype` properties.
- A PHCollectionList has `collectionListType` and `collectionListSubtype` properties.

A PHAsset might have a type of `.image` and a subtype of `.photoPanorama`; a PHAsset-Collection might have a type of `.album` and a subtype of `.albumRegular`; and so on. Smart albums on the user's device help draw further distinctions: a PHAsset-Collection with a type of `.smartAlbum` and a subtype of `.smartAlbumPanoramas` contains all the user's panorama photos. A PHAsset's `playbackStyle` (discussed earlier in this chapter) draws the distinction between a still image and an animated GIF, and between a video and a looped or bounced live photo.

The photo entity classes are actually all subclasses of PHObject, an abstract class that endows them with a `localIdentifier` property that functions as a persistent unique identifier.

Access to the photo library requires user authorization. You'll use the PHPhoto-Library class for this. To learn what the current authorization status is, call the class method `authorizationStatus`. To ask the system to put up the authorization request alert if the status is `.notDetermined`, call the class method `request-Authorization(_:)`. The *Info.plist* must contain some meaningful text that the system authorization request alert can use to explain why your app wants access. For the photo library, the relevant key is "Privacy — Photo Library Usage Description" (`NSPhotoLibraryUsageDescription`). See "Checking for Authorization" on page 861 for a discussion of authorization strategy.

Querying the Photo Library

When you want to know what's in the photo library, start with the photo entity class that represents the type of entity you want to know about. It will supply class methods whose names begin with `fetch`; you'll pick the class method that expresses the kind of criteria you're starting with. So to fetch one or more PHAssets, you'll call a PHAsset `fetch` method; you can fetch by local identifier, by media type, or by containing asset collection. Similarly, to fetch one or more PHAssetCollections, you'll call a PHAssetCollection `fetch` method; you can fetch by identifier, by type and subtype, or by whether they contain a given PHAsset.

In addition to the various `fetch` method parameters, you can supply a PHFetch-Options object letting you refine the results even further. You can set its `predicate` to limit your request results, and its `sortDescriptors` to determine the results order. Its `fetchLimit` can limit the number of results returned, and its `includeAssetSource-Types` can specify where the results should come from, such as eliminating cloud items.

What you get back from a `fetch` method query is not images or videos but *information*. A `fetch` method returns a list of PHObjects of the type to which you sent the `fetch` method originally; these *refer* to entities in the photo library, rather than handing you an entire file (which would be huge and might take considerable time). The list itself is expressed as a PHFetchResult, which behaves very like an array: you can ask for its `count`, obtain the object at a given index, look for an object within the collection, extract objects into an array, and enumerate the objects with an `enumerate` method.

 You cannot directly enumerate a PHFetchResult with `for...in` in Swift, even though you can do so in Objective-C. I regard this as a bug (caused by the fact that PHFetchResult is a generic).

Let's list all albums created by the user. An album is a PHAssetCollection, so the relevant class is PHAssetCollection:

```
let result = PHAssetCollection.fetchAssetCollections(
    with: .album, subtype: .albumRegular, options: nil)
let albums = result.objects(at: IndexSet(0..<result.count))
for album in albums {
    let count = album.estimatedAssetCount
    print("\(album.localizedTitle!):",
        "approximately \(count) photos")
}
```

In that code, we can learn how many assets are in each album only as its `estimated-AssetCount`. This is probably the right answer, but to obtain the real count, we'd have to dive one level deeper and fetch the album's actual assets. Let's do that: given an album, let's list its contents. An album's contents are its assets (photos and videos), so the relevant class is PHAsset:

```
let result = PHAsset.fetchAssets(in:album, options: nil)
let assets = result.objects(at: IndexSet(0..<result.count))
for asset in assets {
    print(asset.localIdentifier)
}
```

If the `fetch` method you need seems not to exist, don't forget about PHFetchOptions. There is no PHAsset `fetch` method for fetching from a certain collection all assets of a certain type; you cannot specify, for instance, that you want all photos (but no videos) from the user's Camera Roll. But you can perform such a fetch by setting a PHFetchOptions object's `predicate` property. To illustrate, I'll fetch ten ordinary photos (no videos, and no HDR photos) from the user's Recent smart album:

```
let recentAlbums = PHAssetCollection.fetchAssetCollections(
    with: .smartAlbum, subtype: .smartAlbumRecentlyAdded, options: nil)
guard let rec = recentAlbums.firstObject else {return}
let options = PHFetchOptions()
let pred = NSPredicate(
    format: "mediaType == %d && !((mediaSubtype & %d) == %d)",
    PHAssetMediaType.image.rawValue,
    PHAssetMediaSubtype.photoHDR.rawValue,
    PHAssetMediaSubtype.photoHDR.rawValue)
options.predicate = pred // photos only, please, no HDRs
options.fetchLimit = 10 // let's not take all day about it
let photos = PHAsset.fetchAssets(in:rec, options: options)
```

Modifying the Library

Structural modifications to the photo library are performed through a *change request class* corresponding to the class of photo entity we wish to modify. The name of the change request class is the name of a photo entity class followed by "ChangeRequest." For PHAsset, there's the PHAssetChangeRequest class — and so on.

To use a change request, you'll call a `performChanges` method on the shared photo library. Typically, that method will be `performChanges(_:completionHandler:)`, which takes two functions. The first function, the *changes function*, is where you describe the changes you want performed; the second function, the *completion function*, is called back after the changes have been performed.

Each change request class comes with methods that ask for a change of some particular type. Here are some examples:

PHAssetChangeRequest
> Class methods include `deleteAssets(_:)`, `creationRequestForAssetFrom-Image(atFileURL:)`, and so on.

If you're creating an asset and what you're starting with is raw data, use the PHAssetCreationRequest class; it's a subclass of PHAssetChangeRequest that provides instance methods such as `addResource(with:data:options:)`.

PHAssetCollectionChangeRequest

Class methods include `deleteAssetCollections(_:)` and `creationRequestFor-AssetCollection(withTitle:)`.

In addition, there are initializers like `init(for:)`, which takes an asset collection, along with instance methods `addAssets(_:)`, `removeAssets(_:)`, and so on.

A `creationRequest` class method also returns an instance of the change request class. You can throw this away if you don't need it for anything. Its purpose is to let you perform further changes as part of the same batch. For example, once you have a PHAssetChangeRequest instance, you can use its properties to initialize the asset's features, such as its creation date or its associated geographical location; those would be read-only if accessed through the PHAsset.

To illustrate, let's create an album called "Test Album." An album is a PHAsset-Collection, so we start with the PHAssetCollectionChangeRequest class and call its `creationRequestForAssetCollection(withTitle:)` class method in the `perform-Changes` function. This method returns a PHAssetCollectionChangeRequest instance, but we don't need that instance for anything, so we simply throw it away:

```
PHPhotoLibrary.shared().performChanges({
    let t = "TestAlbum"
    typealias Req = PHAssetCollectionChangeRequest
    Req.creationRequestForAssetCollection(withTitle:t)
})
```

(The class name PHAssetCollectionChangeRequest is very long, so purely as a matter of style I've shortened it with a type alias.)

It may appear, in that code, that we didn't actually *do* anything — we asked for a creation request, but we didn't tell it to do any creating. Nevertheless, that code is sufficient; generating the creation request for a new asset collection in the `perform-Changes` function constitutes an instruction to create an asset collection.

All the same, that code is rather silly. The album was created asynchronously, so to use it, we need a completion function (see Appendix C). Moreover, we're left with no reference to the album we created. For that, we need a PHObjectPlaceholder. This minimal PHObject subclass has just one property — `localIdentifier`, which it inherits from PHObject. That's sufficient to permit a reference to the created object to survive into the completion function, where we can do something useful with it, such as saving it off to an instance property:

```
var ph : PHObjectPlaceholder?
PHPhotoLibrary.shared().performChanges({
    let t = "TestAlbum"
    typealias Req = PHAssetCollectionChangeRequest
    let cr = Req.creationRequestForAssetCollection(withTitle:t)
    ph = cr.placeholderForCreatedAssetCollection
}) { ok, err in
    if ok, let ph = ph {
        self.newAlbumId = ph.localIdentifier
    }
}
```

Now suppose we subsequently want to populate our newly created album. Let's say we want to make the first asset in the user's Recently Added smart album a member of our new album as well. No problem! First, we need a reference to the Recently Added album; then we need a reference to its first asset; and finally, we need a reference to our newly created album (whose identifier we've already captured as self.newAlbumId). Those are all basic fetch requests, which we can perform in succession, and we then use their results to form the change request:

```
// find Recently Added smart album
let result = PHAssetCollection.fetchAssetCollections(
    with: .smartAlbum, subtype: .smartAlbumRecentlyAdded, options: nil)
guard let rec = result.firstObject else { return }
// find its first asset
let result2 = PHAsset.fetchAssets(in:rec, options: nil)
guard let asset1 = result2.firstObject else { return }
// find our newly created album by its local id
let result3 = PHAssetCollection.fetchAssetCollections(
    withLocalIdentifiers: [self.newAlbumId], options: nil)
guard let alb2 = result3.firstObject else { return }
// ready to perform the change request
PHPhotoLibrary.shared().performChanges({
    typealias Req = PHAssetCollectionChangeRequest
    let cr = Req(for: alb2)
    cr?.addAssets([asset1] as NSArray)
})
```

A PHObjectPlaceholder has a further use. What if we created, say, an asset collection and wanted to add *it* to something (presumably to a PHCollectionList), all in one batch request? Requesting the creation of an asset collection gives us a PHAssetCollectionChangeRequest instance; you can't add *that* to a collection. And the requested PHAssetCollection itself hasn't been created yet! The solution is to obtain a PHObjectPlaceholder. Because it is a PHObject, it can be used as the argument of change request methods such as addChildCollections(_:).

Being Notified of Changes

When the library is modified, whether by your code or by some other means while your app is running, any information you've collected about the library — information which you may even be displaying in your interface at that very moment — may become out of date. To cope with this possibility, you should, perhaps very early in the life of your app, register a change observer (adopting the PHPhotoLibraryChange-Observer protocol) with the photo library:

```
PHPhotoLibrary.shared().register(self)
```

The outcome is that, whenever the library changes, the observer's `photoLibraryDid-Change(_:)` method is called, with a PHChange object encapsulating a description of the change. The observer can then probe the PHChange object by calling `change-Details(for:)`. The idea is that if you're hanging on to information in an instance property, you can use what the PHChange object tells you to modify that information (and possibly your interface). The parameter can be one of two types:

A PHObject
> The parameter is a single PHAsset, PHAssetCollection, or PHCollectionList you're interested in. The result is a PHObjectChangeDetails object, with properties like `objectBeforeChanges`, `objectAfterChanges`, and `objectWasDeleted`.

A PHFetchResult
> The result is a PHFetchResultChangeDetails object, with properties like `fetch-ResultBeforeChanges`, `fetchResultAfterChanges`, `removedObjects`, `inserted-Objects`, and so on.

Suppose my interface is displaying a list of album names, which I obtained originally through a PHAssetCollection fetch request. And suppose that, at the time that I performed the fetch request, I also retained as an instance property (`self.albums`) the PHFetchResult that it returned. Then if my `photoLibraryDidChange(_:)` method is called, I can update the fetch result and change my interface accordingly:

```
func photoLibraryDidChange(_ changeInfo: PHChange) {
    if self.albums !== nil {
        let details = changeInfo.changeDetails(for:self.albums)
        if details !== nil {
            self.albums = details!.fetchResultAfterChanges
            // ... and adjust interface if needed ...
        }
    }
}
```

Fetching Images

Sooner or later, you'll probably want to go beyond information about the structure of the photo library and fetch an actual photo or video for display in your app. The process of obtaining an image can be time-consuming: not only may the image data be large, but also it may be stored in the cloud. Therefore you will typically supply a completion function that can be called back *asynchronously* with the data (see Appendix C).

To obtain an image, you'll need an *image manager*, which you'll get by calling the PHImageManager `default` class method. You then call a method whose name starts with `request`, supplying a completion function. For an image, you can ask for a UIImage or the original data; for a video, you can ask for an AVPlayerItem or an AVAsset configured for display of the video, or an AVAssetExportSession suitable for exporting the video to a new file (see Chapter 15). The result comes back to you as a parameter passed into your completion function.

Asking for a UIImage

If you're asking for a UIImage, information about the image may increase in accuracy and detail in the course of time — with the curious consequence that your completion function may be called multiple times. The idea is to give you *some* image to display as fast as possible, with better versions of the image arriving later. If you would rather receive just *one* version of the image, you can specify that through a PHImageRequestOptions object (as I'll explain in a moment).

The various `request` methods take parameters letting you refine the details of the data-retrieval process. When asking for a UIImage, you supply these parameters:

`targetSize:`
> The size of the desired image. It is a waste of memory to ask for an image larger than you need for actual display, and a larger image may take longer to supply (and a photo, remember, is a *very* large image). The image retrieval process performs the desired downsizing so that you don't have to. For the largest possible size, pass `PHImageManagerMaximumSize`.

`contentMode:`
> A PHImageContentMode, either `.aspectFit` or `.aspectFill`, with respect to your `targetSize`. With `.aspectFill`, the image retrieval process does any needed cropping so that you don't have to.

`options:`
> A PHImageRequestOptions object. This is a value class representing a grab-bag of additional tweaks, such as:

.version

> Do you want the original image (.original) or the edited image (.current)?

.resizeMode

> Do you want the image sized exactly to your targetSize (.exact), or will you accept a larger version (.fast)?

.normalizedCropRect

> Do you want custom cropping?

.isNetworkAccessAllowed, .progressHandler

> Do you want the image fetched over the network if necessary, and if so, do you want to install a progress callback function?

.deliveryMode

> Do you want one call to your completion function, or many (.opportunistic)? If one, do you want a degraded thumbnail which will arrive quickly (.fastFormat), or the best possible quality which may take some considerable time (.highQualityFormat)?

.isSynchronous

> Do you want the image fetched synchronously? If you do, you will get only *one* call to your completion function — but then you *must* make your call *on a background thread*, and the image will arrive on that same background thread (see Chapter 24).

In this simple example, I have a view controller called DataViewController, good for displaying one photo in an image view (self.iv). It has a PHAsset property, self.asset, which is assumed to have been set when this view controller instance was created. In viewDidLoad, I call my setUpInterface utility method to populate the interface:

```
func setUpInterface() {
    guard let asset = self.asset else { return }
    let opts = PHImageRequestOptions()
    opts.resizeMode = .exact
    PHImageManager.default().requestImage(for: asset,
        targetSize: CGSize(300,300), contentMode: .aspectFit,
        options: opts) { im, info in
            if let im = im {
                self.iv.image = im
            }
    }
}
```

This may result in the image view's image being set multiple times, as the requested image is supplied repeatedly, with its quality improving each time; but there is nothing wrong with that. Using this technique with a UIPageViewController, you can easily write an app that allows the user to browse photos one at a time.

The second parameter in an image request's completion function is a dictionary whose elements may be useful in certain circumstances. Among the keys are:

PHImageResultRequestIDKey

Uniquely identifies a single image request for which this result function is being called multiple times. This value is also *returned* by the original request method call (I didn't bother to capture it in the previous example). You can also use this identifier to call cancelImageRequest(_:) if it turns out that you don't need this image after all.

PHImageCancelledKey

Reports that an attempt to cancel an image request with cancelImage-Request(_:) succeeded.

PHImageResultIsInCloudKey

Warns that the image is in the cloud and that your request must be resubmitted with the PHImageRequestOptions isNetworkAccessAllowed property set to true.

Canceling and caching

If your interface is a table view or collection view, the asynchronous, time-consuming nature of image fetching is clearly significant. As the user scrolls, a cell comes into view and you request the corresponding image. But as the user keeps scrolling, that cell goes out of view, and now the requested image, if it hasn't arrived, is no longer needed, so you cancel the request. (I'll tackle the same sort of problem with regard to internet-based images in a table view in Chapter 23.)

There is also a PHImageManager subclass, PHCachingImageManager, that can help do the opposite: you can prefetch some images *before* the user scrolls to view them, improving response time. For an example that displays photos in a UICollection-View, look at Apple's SamplePhotosApp sample code (also called "Example app using Photos framework"). It uses the PHImageManager class to fetch individual photos; but for the UICollectionViewCell thumbnails, it uses PHCachingImage-Manager.

 Even the default shared PHImageManager does some caching when it performs a request. This can cause the image manager to get out of sync with the photo library, and I have not found a way to tell it to clear its cache. The workaround is to call PHImageManager() instead of PHImageManager.default().

Live photos, videos, and data

If a PHAsset represents a live photo, you can call the PHImageManager `requestLive-Photo` method, parallel to `requestImage`; what you get in the completion function is a PHLivePhoto. I mentioned earlier that in iOS 13 a UIImagePickerControllerDelegate doesn't receive a PHLivePhoto through the `.livePhoto` key, so you have to use the PHAsset to fetch the live photo from the photo library instead. Here, I'll fetch the live photo and display it in the interface:

```
func fetchLivePhoto(from asset:PHAsset?) {
    if let asset = asset {
        PHImageManager.default().requestLivePhoto(
            for: asset, targetSize: self.redView.bounds.size,
            contentMode: .aspectFit, options: nil) { photo, info in
                if let photo = photo {
                    self.showLivePhoto(photo)
                }
        }
    }
}
func showLivePhoto(_ ph:PHLivePhoto) {
    let v = PHLivePhotoView(frame:self.redView.bounds)
    v.contentMode = .scaleAspectFit
    v.livePhoto = ph
    self.redView.addSubview(v)
}
```

Fetching a video resource is far simpler, and there's little to say about it. In this example, I fetch a reference to the first video in the user's photo library and display it in the interface (using an AVPlayerViewController); unlike an image, I am not guaranteed that the result will arrive on the main thread, so I must step out to the main thread before interacting with the app's user interface:

```
func fetchMovie() {
    let opts = PHFetchOptions()
    opts.fetchLimit = 1
    let result = PHAsset.fetchAssets(with: .video, options: opts)
    guard let asset = result.firstObject else {return}
    PHImageManager.default().requestPlayerItem(
        forVideo: asset, options: nil) { item, info in
            if let item = item {
                DispatchQueue.main.async {
                    self.display(item:item)
                }
            }
        }
}
func display(item:AVPlayerItem) {
    let player = AVPlayer(playerItem: item)
    let vc = AVPlayerViewController()
    vc.player = player
```

```
        vc.view.frame = self.v.bounds
        self.addChild(vc)
        self.v.addSubview(vc.view)
        vc.didMove(toParent: self)
    }
```

You can also access an asset's various kinds of data directly through the PHAsset-ResourceManager class. The `request` method takes a PHAssetResource object based on a PHAsset or PHLivePhoto. You can retrieve an image's RAW and JPEG data separately. For a list of the data types we're talking about here, see the documentation on the PHAssetResourceType enum.

Editing Images

Astonishingly, PhotoKit allows you to *change* an image in the user's photo library. Why is this even legal? There are two reasons:

- The user will have to give permission every time your app proposes to modify a photo in the library, and will be shown the proposed modification beforehand.

- Changes to library photos are undoable, because the original image remains in the database along with the changed image that the user sees, and the user can revert to that original at any time.

How to change a photo image

To change a photo image is a three-step process:

1. You send a PHAsset this message:

   - `requestContentEditingInput(with:completionHandler:)`

   Your completion function is called, and is handed a PHContentEditingInput object. This object wraps some image data which you can display to the user (`displaySizeImage`), along with a pointer to the real image data as a file (`full-SizeImageURL`).

2. You create a PHContentEditingOutput object by calling its initializer:

   - `init(contentEditingInput:)`

   The argument is the PHContentEditingInput object. The PHContentEditing-Output object has a `renderedContentURL` property, representing a file URL. Your mission is to *write the edited photo image data to that URL*. What you'll typically do is:

   a. Fetch the image data from the PHContentEditingInput object's `fullSize-ImageURL`.

   b. Process the image.

    c. Write the resulting image data to the PHContentEditingOutput object's `renderedContentURL`.

3. You notify the photo library that it should pick up the edited version of the photo. To do so, you call `performChanges(_:completionHandler:)` and, inside the changes function, create a PHAssetChangeRequest and set its `content-EditingOutput` property to the PHContentEditingOutput object. The user will now be shown the alert requesting permission to modify this photo; your completion function is then called, with a first parameter of `false` if the user refuses (or if anything else goes wrong).

Handling the adjustment data

So far, so good. However, if you do *only* what I have just described, your attempt to modify the photo will fail. The reason is that I have omitted something: before the third step, you *must* set the PHContentEditingOutput object's `adjustmentData` property to a newly instantiated PHAdjustmentData object. The initializer is:

- `init(formatIdentifier:formatVersion:data:)`

What goes into the initializer parameters is completely up to you, but the goal is to store with the photo a message to your future self in case you are called upon to edit the *same* photo again on some *later* occasion. In that message, you describe to yourself how you edited the photo on *this* occasion.

Your handling of the adjustment data works in three steps, interwoven with the three steps I already outlined. As you start to edit the photo, first you say whether you *can* read its existing PHAdjustmentData, and then you *do* read its existing PHAdjustmentData and use it as part of your editing; when you have finished editing the photo, you make a *new* PHAdjustmentData, ready for the *next* time you edit this same photo:

1. When you call `requestContentEditingInput`, the first argument (`with:`) should be a PHContentEditingInputRequestOptions object. You have created this object and set its `canHandleAdjustmentData` property to a function that takes a PHAdjustmentData and returns a Bool. This Bool will be based mostly on whether you recognize this photo's PHAdjustmentData as yours — typically because you recognize its `formatIdentifier`. That determines what image you'll get when you receive your PHContentEditingInput object:

    Your `canHandleAdjustmentData` *function returns* `false`
        The image you'll be editing is the edited image displayed in the Photos app.

Your `canHandleAdjustmentData` *function returns* `true`

The image you'll be editing is the *original* image, stripped of your edits. This is because, by returning `true`, you are asserting that you can reconstruct your edits based on what's in the PHAdjustmentData's `data`.

2. When your completion function is called and you receive your PHContent-EditingInput object, it has (you guessed it) an `adjustmentData` property, which is an Optional wrapping a PHAdjustmentData object. If this isn't `nil`, and if you edited this image previously, its `data` is the `data` you put in the last time you edited this image, and you are expected to extract it and use it to recreate the edited state of the image.

3. After editing the image, when you prepare the PHContentEditingOutput object, you give it a *new* PHAdjustmentData object whose `data` summarizes the *new* edited state of the photo from your point of view — and so the whole cycle can start again if the same photo is to be edited again later.

Example: Before editing

An actual implementation is quite straightforward and almost pure boilerplate. The details will vary only in regard to the actual editing of the photo and the particular form of the `data` by which you'll summarize that editing — so, in constructing an example, I'll keep that part very simple. Recall my example of a custom "vignette" CIFilter called MyVignetteFilter ("CIFilter and CIImage" on page 106). I'll provide an interface whereby the user can apply that filter to a photo. My interface will include:

- A slider that allows the user to set the *degree* of vignetting that should be applied (MyVignetteFilter's `inputPercentage`).

- A button that lets the user remove *all* vignetting from the photo, even if that vignetting was applied in a previous editing session.

First, I'll plan the structure of the PHAdjustmentData:

`formatIdentifier`

This can be any unique string; I'll use `"com.neuburg.matt.PhotoKit-Images.vignette"`, a constant that I'll store in a property (`self.myidentifier`).

`formatVersion`

This is likewise arbitrary; I'll use `"1.0"`.

`data`

This will express the only thing about my editing that is adjustable — the `input-Percentage`. The `data` will wrap an NSNumber which itself wraps a Double whose value is the `inputPercentage`.

As editing begins, I construct the PHContentEditingInputRequestOptions object that determines whether a photo's most recent editing belongs to me. Then, starting with the photo that is to be edited (a PHAsset), I ask for the PHContentEditingInput object:

```
let options = PHContentEditingInputRequestOptions()
options.canHandleAdjustmentData = { adjustmentData in
    return adjustmentData.formatIdentifier == self.myidentifier
}
var id : PHContentEditingInputRequestID = 0
id = self.asset.requestContentEditingInput(with: options) { input, info in
    // ...
}
```

In the completion function, I receive my PHContentEditingInput object as a parameter (input). I'm going to need this object later when editing ends, so I immediately store it in a property. I then unwrap its adjustmentData, extract the data, and construct the editing interface; in this case, that happens to be a presented view controller, but the details are irrelevant and are omitted here:

```
guard let input = input else {
    self.asset.cancelContentEditingInputRequest(id)
    return
}
self.input = input
let im = input.displaySizeImage! // show this to user during editing
if let adj = input.adjustmentData,
adj.formatIdentifier == self.myidentifier {
    if let vigNumber = try? NSKeyedUnarchiver.unarchivedObject(
        ofClass: NSNumber.self, from: adj.data),
    let vigAmount = vigNumber as? Double {
        // ... store vigAmount ...
    }
}
// ... present editing interface, passing it the vigAmount ...
```

The important thing about that code is how we deal with the adjustmentData and its data. The question is whether we *have* data, and whether we recognize this as *our* data from some previous edit on this image. This will affect how our editing interface needs to behave. There are two possibilities:

It's our data

> If we were able to extract a vigAmount from the adjustmentData, then the displaySizeImage is the original, unvignetted image. Therefore, our editing interface initially applies the vigAmount of vignetting to this image — *reconstructing* the vignetted state of the photo as shown in the Photos app, while allowing the user to *change* the amount of vignetting, or even to remove all vignetting entirely.

It's not our data

On the other hand, if we *weren't* able to extract a `vigAmount` from the `adjustmentData`, then there is nothing to reconstruct; the `displaySizeImage` is the actual photo image from the Photos app, and our editing interface will apply vignetting to it directly.

Example: After editing

Let's skip ahead now to the point where the user's interaction with our editing interface comes to an end. If the user cancelled, that's all; the user doesn't want to modify the photo after all. Otherwise, the user either asked to apply a certain amount of vignetting (`vignette`) or asked to remove all vignetting; in the latter case, I use an arbitrary `vignette` value of `-1` as a signal.

Up to now, our editing interface has been using the `displaySizeImage` to show the user a *preview* of what the edited photo would look like. Now the time has come to perform the vignetting that the user is asking us to perform — that is, we must apply this amount of vignetting to the *real* photo image, which has been sitting waiting for us all this time, untouched, at the PHContentEditingInput's `fullSizeImageURL`. This is a big image, which will take significant time to load, to alter, and to save (which is why we haven't been working with it in the editing interface).

So, depending on the value of `vignette` requested by the user, I either pass the input image from the `fullSizeImageURL` through my vignette filter or I don't:

```
let inurl = self.input.fullSizeImageURL!
let output = PHContentEditingOutput(contentEditingInput:self.input)
let outurl = output.renderedContentURL
var ci = CIImage(contentsOf: inurl, options: [.applyOrientationProperty:true])!
let space = ci.colorSpace!
if vignette >= 0.0 {
    let vig = MyVignetteFilter()
    vig.setValue(ci, forKey: "inputImage")
    vig.setValue(vignette, forKey: "inputPercentage")
    ci = vig.outputImage!
}
```

Don't forget about setting the PHContentEditingOutput's `adjustmentData`! My goal here is to send a message to myself, in case I am asked later to edit this same image again, stating what amount of vignetting is already applied to the image. That amount is represented by `vignette` — so that's the value I store in the `adjustment-Data`:

```
let data = try! NSKeyedArchiver.archivedData(
    withRootObject: vignette, requiringSecureCoding: true)
output.adjustmentData = PHAdjustmentData(
    formatIdentifier: self.myidentifier, formatVersion: "1.0", data: data)
```

Finally, I must write a JPEG to the PHContentEditingOutput's `renderedContentURL`:

```
try! CIContext().writeJPEGRepresentation(of:ci, to:outurl, colorSpace:space)
```

Some of that code is time-consuming, particularly where I read and write the data with these methods:

- CIImage `init(contentsOf:options:)`
- CIContext `writeJPEGRepresentation(of:to:colorSpace:)`

So in real life I call it on a background thread (Chapter 24), and I also show a UIActivityIndicatorView to let the user know that work is being done.

We conclude by telling the photo library to retrieve the edited image. This will cause the alert to appear, asking the user whether to allow us to modify this photo. If the user taps Modify, the modification is made, and if we are displaying the image, we should get onto the main thread and redisplay it:

```
PHPhotoLibrary.shared().performChanges({
    typealias Req = PHAssetChangeRequest
    let req = Req(for: self.asset)
    req.contentEditingOutput = output // triggers alert
}) { ok, err in
    if ok {
        // if we are displaying image, redisplay it — on main thread
    } else {
        // user refused to allow modification, do nothing
    }
}
```

You can also edit a live photo, using a PHLivePhotoEditingContext: you are handed each frame of the video as a CIImage, making it easy to apply a CIFilter. For a demonstration, see Apple's Photo Edit sample app (also known as Sample Photo Editing Extension).

Photo Editing Extension

A photo editing extension is photo-modifying code supplied by your app that is effectively injected into the Photos app. When the user edits a photo *from within the Photos app*, your extension appears as an option and can modify the photo being edited.

To make a photo editing extension, create a new target in your app, specifying iOS → Application Extension → Photo Editing Extension. The template supplies a storyboard containing one scene, along with the code file for a corresponding UIViewController subclass. This file imports not only the Photos framework but also the Photos UI framework, which supplies the PHContentEditingController protocol, to which the view controller conforms. This protocol specifies the methods through which the runtime will communicate with your extension's code.

A photo editing extension works almost exactly the same way as modifying photo library assets in general, as I described in the preceding section. The chief differences are:

- You don't put a Done or a Cancel button into your editing interface. The Photos app will wrap your editing interface in its own interface, providing those buttons when it presents your view.
- You must situate the pieces of your code so as to respond to the calls that will come through the PHContentEditingController methods.

The PHContentEditingController methods are:

canHandle(_:)
　　You will not be instantiating PHContentEditingInput; the runtime will do it for you. Therefore, instead of configuring a PHContentEditingInputRequestOptions object and setting its canHandleAdjustmentData, you implement this method; you'll receive the PHAdjustmentData and return a Bool.

startContentEditing(with:placeholderImage:)
　　The runtime has obtained the PHContentEditingInput object for you. Now it supplies that object to you, along with a very temporary initial version of the image to be displayed in your interface; you are expected to replace this with the PHContentEditingInput object's displaySizeImage. Just as in the previous section's code, you should retain the PHContentEditingInput object in a property, as you will need it again later.

cancelContentEditing
　　The user tapped Cancel. You may well have nothing to do here.

finishContentEditing(completionHandler:)
　　The user tapped Done. In your implementation, you get onto a background thread (the template configures this for you) and do *exactly* the same thing you would do if this were not a photo editing extension — get the PHContentEditing-Output object and set its adjustmentData; get the photo from the PHContent-EditingInput object's fullSizeImageURL, modify it, and save the modified image as a full-quality JPEG at the PHContentEditingOutput object's renderedContent-URL. When you're done, *don't* notify the PHPhotoLibrary; instead, call the completionHandler that arrived as a parameter, handing it the PHContent-EditingOutput object.

　　During the time-consuming part of this method, the Photos app puts up a UIActivityIndicatorView, just as I suggested you might want to do in your own app. When you call the completionHandler, there is no alert asking the user to confirm the modification of the photo; the user is already *in* the Photos app and has explicitly asked to edit the photo, so no confirmation is needed.

Using the Camera

Use of the camera requires user authorization. You'll use the AVCaptureDevice class for this (part of the AV Foundation framework; `import AVFoundation`). To learn what the current authorization status is, call the class method `authorization-Status(forMediaType:)`. To ask the system to put up the authorization request alert if the status is `.notDetermined`, call the class method `requestAccess(forMedia-Type:completionHandler:)`. The media type (AVMediaType) will be `.video`; this embraces capturing both still photos and movies. Your app's *Info.plist* must contain some meaningful text that the system authorization request alert can use to explain why your app wants camera use; the relevant key is "Privacy — Camera Usage Description" (`NSCameraUsageDescription`).

If your app will let the user capture movies (as opposed to still photos), you will also need to obtain permission from the user to access the microphone. The same methods apply, but with argument `.audio`. Your app's *Info.plist* must contain some explanatory text under the "Privacy — Microphone Usage Description" key (`NSMicrophoneUsageDescription`). See "Checking for Authorization" on page 861 for discussion of authorization strategy.

 Use of the camera is greatly curtailed, and is interruptible, under iPad multitasking. Watch WWDC 2015 video 211 for details.

Capture with UIImagePickerController

The simplest way to prompt the user to take a photo or video is with the same UIImagePickerController class discussed earlier in this chapter. It provides an interface that is effectively a limited subset of the Camera app.

The procedure is similar to what you do when you use UIImagePickerController to browse the photo library. First, check `isSourceTypeAvailable(_:)` for `.camera`; it will be `false` if the user's device has no camera or the camera is unavailable. If it is `true`, call `availableMediaTypes(for:.camera)` to learn whether the user can take a still photo (`kUTTypeImage`), a video (`kUTTypeMovie`), or both. Now instantiate UIImagePickerController, set its source type to `.camera`, and set its `mediaTypes` in accordance with which types you just learned are available; if your setting is an array of both `kUTTypeImage` and `kUTTypeMovie`, the user will see a Camera-like interface allowing a choice of either one. Finally, set a delegate (adopting UINavigation-ControllerDelegate and UIImagePickerControllerDelegate), and present the picker:

```
let src = UIImagePickerController.SourceType.camera
guard UIImagePickerController.isSourceTypeAvailable(src)
    else {return}
guard = UIImagePickerController.availableMediaTypes(for:src) != nil
```

```
    else {return}
let picker = UIImagePickerController()
picker.sourceType = src
picker.mediaTypes = arr
picker.delegate = self
self.present(picker, animated: true)
```

For video, you can also specify the `videoQuality` and `videoMaximumDuration`. More-over, these additional properties and class methods allow you to discover the camera capabilities:

`isCameraDeviceAvailable:`
> Checks to see whether the front or rear camera is available, using one of these values as argument (UIImagePickerController.CameraDevice):
>
> - `.front`
> - `.rear`

`cameraDevice`
> Lets you learn and set which camera is being used.

`availableCaptureModes(for:)`
> Checks whether the given camera can capture still photos, video, or both. You specify the front or rear camera; returns an array of integers. Possible modes are (UIImagePickerController.CameraCaptureMode):
>
> - `.photo`
> - `.video`

`cameraCaptureMode`
> Lets you learn and set the capture mode (still photo or video).

`isFlashAvailable(for:)`
> Checks whether flash is available.

`cameraFlashMode`
> Lets you learn and set the flash mode (or, for a movie, toggles the LED "torch"). Your choices are (UIImagePickerController.CameraFlashMode):
>
> - `.off`
> - `.auto`
> - `.on`

When the view controller's view appears, the user will see the interface for taking a picture, familiar from the Camera app, possibly including flash options, camera selection button, photo/video option (if your `mediaTypes` setting allows both), and Cancel and shutter buttons. If the user takes a picture, the presented view offers an opportunity to use the picture or to retake it.

Allowing the user to edit the captured image or movie (`allowsEditing`), and handling the outcome with the delegate messages, is the same as I described earlier for dealing with an image or movie selected from the photo library, with these additional points regarding the `info` dictionary delivered to the delegate:

- There won't be any `.phAsset` key, because the image isn't in the photo library.

- There won't be any `.imageURL` key; if the user takes a still image, no copy is saved as a file.

- There won't be any `.livePhoto` key; the user can't capture a live photo with the UIImagePickerController camera interface.

- A still image might be accompanied by a `.mediaMetadata` key containing the metadata for the photo.

The photo library was not involved in the process of media capture, so no user permission to access the photo library is needed. But if you *now* propose to save the media into the photo library, you *will* need permission. Suppose that the user takes a still image, and you now want to save it into the user's Camera Roll album. Creating the PHAsset is sufficient:

```
func imagePickerController(_ picker: UIImagePickerController,
    didFinishPickingMediaWithInfo
    info: [UIImagePickerController.InfoKey : Any]) {
        var im = info[.originalImage] as? UIImage
        if let ed = info[.editedImage] as? UIImage {
            im = ed
        }
        let m = info[.mediaMetadata] as? NSDictionary
        self.dismiss(animated:true) {
            let mediatype = info[.mediaType]
            guard let type = mediatype as? NSString else {return}
            switch type as CFString {
            case kUTTypeImage:
                if im != nil {
                    checkForPhotoLibraryAccess {
                        let lib = PHPhotoLibrary.shared()
                        lib.performChanges({
                            typealias Req = PHAssetChangeRequest
                            Req.creationRequestForAsset(from: im!)
                        })
                    }
                }
            default:break
            }
        }
}
```

In that code, the metadata associated with the photo is received (m), but nothing is done with it, and it is not folded into the PHAsset created from the image (im). To attach the metadata to the photo, use the Image I/O framework (import ImageIO) to make a copy of the image data along with the metadata. Now you can use a PHAsset-CreationRequest to make the PHAsset from the data:

```
let jpeg = im!.jpegData(compressionQuality:1)
let src = CGImageSourceCreateWithData(jpeg as CFData, nil)!
let data = NSMutableData()
let uti = CGImageSourceGetType(src)!
let dest = CGImageDestinationCreateWithData(
    data as CFMutableData, uti, 1, nil)!
CGImageDestinationAddImageFromSource(dest, src, 0, m)
CGImageDestinationFinalize(dest)
let lib = PHPhotoLibrary.shared()
lib.performChanges({
    let req = PHAssetCreationRequest.forAsset()
    req.addResource(with: .photo, data: data as Data, options: nil)
})
```

You can customize the UIImagePickerController image capture interface. If you need to do that, you should probably consider dispensing entirely with UIImagePicker-Controller and instead designing your own image capture interface from scratch, based around AV Foundation and AVCaptureSession, which I'll introduce in the next section. Still, it may be that a modified UIImagePickerController is all you need.

In the image capture interface, you can hide the standard controls by setting shows-CameraControls to false, replacing them with your own overlay view, which you supply as the value of the cameraOverlayView. That removes the shutter button, so you're probably going to want to provide some new means of allowing the user to take a picture! You can do that through these methods:

- takePicture
- startVideoCapture
- stopVideoCapture

The UIImagePickerController is a UINavigationController, so if you need additional interface — possibly to let the user vet the captured picture before dismissing the picker — you can push it onto the navigation interface.

Capture with AV Foundation

Instead of using UIImagePickerController, you can control the camera directly using the AV Foundation framework (Chapter 15). You get no help with interface, but you get vastly more power than UIImagePickerController can give you. For stills, you can control focus and exposure directly and independently, and for video, you can determine the quality, size, and frame rate of the resulting movie.

To understand how AV Foundation classes are used for image capture, imagine how the Camera app works. When you are running the Camera app, you have, at all times, a "window on the world" — the screen is showing you what the camera sees. At some point, you might tap the button to take a still image or start taking a video; now what the camera sees goes into a file.

Think of all that as being controlled by an engine. This engine, the heart of all AV Foundation capture operations, is an AVCaptureSession object. It has inputs (such as a camera) and outputs (such as a file). It also has an associated layer in your interface. When you start the engine running, by calling `startRunning`, data flows from the input through the engine; that is how you get your "window on the world," displaying on the screen what the camera sees.

As a rock-bottom example, let's start by implementing just the "window on the world" part of the engine. Our AVCaptureSession is retained in an instance property (`self.sess`). We also need a special CALayer that will display what the camera is seeing — namely, an AVCaptureVideoPreviewLayer. This layer is not really an AVCaptureSession output; rather, the layer receives its imagery by association with the AVCaptureSession. Our capture session's input is the default camera. We have no intention, as yet, of capturing anything to a file, so no output is needed:

```
self.sess = AVCaptureSession()
guard let cam = AVCaptureDevice.default(for: .video),
    let input = try? AVCaptureDeviceInput(device:cam)
    else {return}
self.sess.addInput(input)
let lay = AVCaptureVideoPreviewLayer(session:self.sess)
lay.frame = // ... some reasonable frame ...
self.view.layer.addSublayer(lay)
self.sess.startRunning()
```

Presto! Our interface now displays a "window on the world," showing what the camera sees.

Suppose now that our intention is that, while the engine is running and the "window on the world" is showing, the user is to be allowed to tap a button that will capture a still photo. Now we *do* need an output for our AVCaptureSession. This will be an AVCapturePhotoOutput instance. We should also configure the session with a preset (AVCaptureSession.Preset) to match our intended use of it; in this case, the preset will be `.photo`.

So let's modify the preceding code to give the session an output and a preset. We can do this directly before we start the session running. We can also do it while the session is already running (and in general, if you want to reconfigure a running session, doing so while it is running is far more efficient than stopping the session and starting it again), but then we must wrap our configuration changes in `beginConfiguration` and `commitConfiguration`:

```
self.sess.beginConfiguration()
guard self.sess.canSetSessionPreset(self.sess.sessionPreset)
    else {return}
self.sess.sessionPreset = .photo
let output = AVCapturePhotoOutput()
guard self.sess.canAddOutput(output)
    else {return}
self.sess.addOutput(output)
self.sess.commitConfiguration()
```

The session is now running and is ready to capture a photo. The user taps the button that asks to capture a photo, and we respond by telling the session's photo output to `capturePhoto(with:delegate:)`. The first parameter is an AVCapturePhotoSettings object. It happens that for a standard JPEG photo a default instance will do, but to make things more interesting I'll specify explicitly that I want the camera to use automatic flash and automatic image stabilization:

```
let settings = AVCapturePhotoSettings()
settings.flashMode = .auto
settings.isAutoStillImageStabilizationEnabled = true
```

As part of our configuration of the AVCapturePhotoSettings object, if we intend to display the user's captured photo in our interface, we should request a preview image explicitly. It's a lot more efficient for AV Foundation to create an uncompressed preview image of the correct size than for us to try to display or downsize a huge photo image. Here's how we might ask for the preview image:

```
let pbpf = settings.availablePreviewPhotoPixelFormatTypes[0]
let len = // desired maximum dimension
settings.previewPhotoFormat = [
    kCVPixelBufferPixelFormatTypeKey as String : pbpf,
    kCVPixelBufferWidthKey as String : len,
    kCVPixelBufferHeightKey as String : len
]
```

Another good idea, when configuring the AVCapturePhotoSettings object, is to ask for a thumbnail image. This is different from the preview image: the preview image is for you to display in your interface, but the thumbnail image is stored with the photo and is suitable for rapid display by other applications. Here's how to request a thumbnail image at a standard size (160×120):

```
settings.embeddedThumbnailPhotoFormat = [
    AVVideoCodecKey : AVVideoCodecType.jpeg
]
```

When the AVCapturePhotoSettings object is fully configured, we're ready to call `capturePhoto(with:delegate:)`, like this:

```
guard let output = self.sess.outputs[0] as? AVCapturePhotoOutput
    else {return}
output.capturePhoto(with: settings, delegate: self)
```

In that code, I specified `self` as the `delegate` (an AVCapturePhotoCaptureDelegate adopter). Functioning as the delegate, we will now receive a sequence of events. The exact sequence depends on what sort of capture we're doing; in this case, it will be:

1. `photoOutput(_:willBeginCaptureFor:)`

2. `photoOutput(_:willCapturePhotoFor:)`

3. `photoOutput(_:didCapturePhotoFor:)`

4. `photoOutput(_:didFinishProcessingPhoto:error:)`

5. `photoOutput(_:didFinishCaptureFor:)`

The `for:` parameter throughout is an AVCaptureResolvedSettings object, embodying the settings actually used during the capture; for instance, we could use it to find out whether flash was actually used.

The delegate event of most interest to our example is the fourth one. This is where we receive the photo! It will arrive in the second parameter as an AVCapturePhoto object. This object contains a lot of information. It provides the resolved settings in its `resolvedSettings` property. Its `previewPixelBuffer` property contains the data for the preview image, if we requested one in our AVCapturePhotoSettings. We can extract the image data from the AVCapturePhoto by calling its `fileData-Representation` method. (There is also a longer form of the same method, `fileData-Representation(with:)`, allowing you to do such things as modify the metadata and the thumbnail.)

In this example, we implement the fourth delegate method to store the preview image as a property, for subsequent display in our interface, and then save the actual image as a PHAsset in the user's photo library:

```
func photoOutput(_ output: AVCapturePhotoOutput,
    didFinishProcessingPhoto photo:
    AVCapturePhoto, error: Error?) {
        if let cgim =
            photo.previewCGImageRepresentation()?.takeUnretainedValue() {
                let orient = // work out desired UIImage.Orientation
                self.previewImage = UIImage(
                    cgImage: cgim, scale: 1, orientation: orient)
        }
        if let data = photo.fileDataRepresentation() {
            let lib = PHPhotoLibrary.shared()
            lib.performChanges({
                let req = PHAssetCreationRequest.forAsset()
                req.addResource(with: .photo, data: data, options: nil)
            })
        }
    }
```

Image capture with AV Foundation is a huge subject, and our example of a simple photo capture has barely scratched the surface. AVCaptureVideoPreviewLayer provides methods for converting between layer coordinates and capture device coordinates; without such methods, this can be a very difficult problem to solve. You can scan bar codes, shoot video at 60 frames per second (on some devices), and more. You can turn on the LED "torch" by setting the back camera's `torchMode` to `AVCaptureTorchModeOn`, even if no AVCaptureSession is running. You get direct hardware-level control over the camera focus, manual exposure, and white balance. You can capture bracketed images; starting in iOS 10, you can capture live images on some devices, and you can capture RAW images on some devices; and since iOS 11 even more new features have been introduced, such as depth-based image capture and multicamera capture. There are very good WWDC videos about all this, stretching back over the past several years, and the AVCam-iOS and AVCamManual sample code examples are absolutely superb, demonstrating how to deal with tricky issues such as orientation that would otherwise be very difficult to figure out.

CHAPTER 18

Contacts

The user's contacts constitute a database. The user can interact with this database through the Contacts app. Your code can access the user's contacts database programmatically through the Contacts framework. You'll need to import Contacts. An interface similar to the Contacts app for letting the user interact with the contacts database from within your app is provided by the Contacts UI framework. You'll need to import ContactsUI.

Access to the contacts database requires user authorization. You'll use the CNContact-Store class for this. To learn what the current authorization status is, call the class method authorizationStatus(for:) with a CNEntityType of .contacts. (This is a curious requirement, as .contacts is the *only* CNEntityType!) To ask the system to put up the authorization request alert if the status is .notDetermined, call the instance method requestAccess(for:completionHandler:). The *Info.plist* must contain some meaningful text that the system authorization request alert can use to explain why your app wants access. The relevant key is "Privacy — Contacts Usage Description" (NSContactsUsageDescription). See "Checking for Authorization" on page 861 for a discussion of authorization strategy.

Contact Classes

Here are the chief object types you'll be concerned with when you work with the user's contacts:

CNContactStore

> The contacts database is accessed through an instance of the CNContactStore class. You do not need to keep a reference to an instance of this class. When you want to fetch a contact from the database, or when you want to save a created or modified contact into the database, instantiate CNContactStore, do your fetching

or saving, and let the CNContactStore instance vanish. CNContactStore instance methods for fetching and saving information can take time. Therefore, they should be called on a background thread (see Chapter 24).

CNContact

An individual contact is an instance of the CNContact class. Its properties correspond to the fields displayed in the Contacts app. In addition, it has an `identifier` which is unique and persistent. A CNContact that comes from the CNContactStore has no connection with the database; it is safe to preserve it and to pass it around between objects and between threads. It is also immutable by default (its properties are read-only). To create your own CNContact, start with its mutable subclass, CNMutableContact; to modify an existing contact, call `mutableCopy` to make it a CNMutableContact.

The properties of a CNContact are matched by constant key names designating those properties. For instance, a CNContact has a `familyName` property, and there is also a `CNContactFamilyNameKey`. This should remind you of MPMediaItem (Chapter 16), and indeed the purpose is similar: the key names allow you, when you fetch a CNContact from the CNContactStore, to state which properties of the CNContact you want populated. By limiting the properties to be fetched, you fetch more efficiently and quickly.

Most properties of a CNContact have familiar types such as String or an enum. However, the Contacts framework defines a number of specialized types as well; a phone number is a CNPhoneNumber, and a postal address is a CNPostalAddress. Such types tend to be wrapped up in a generic CNLabeledValue, whose purpose I'll explain later. Dates, such as a birthday, are not Date objects but rather DateComponents; this is because they do not necessarily require full date information (I know when someone's birthday is without knowing the year they were born).

CNContactFormatter, CNPostalAddressFormatter

A formatter is an engine for displaying aspects of a CNContact as a string. A CNContactFormatter whose `style` is `.fullName`, for instance, assembles the name-related properties of a CNContact into a name string. A formatter will tell you which properties it needs in order to form its string, so that you can easily include them among the contact properties that you fetch initially from the store.

The contacts database can change while your app is running. To detect this, register for the `.CNContactStoreDidChange` notification. The arrival of this notification means that any contacts-related objects that you are retaining, such as CNContact instances, may be outdated.

Fetching Contact Information

You now know enough to get started! Let's fetch some contacts. When we perform a fetch, there are two parameters to provide in order to limit the information to be returned to us:

A predicate

An NSPredicate. CNContact provides class methods that will generate the predicates you're allowed to use. You are most likely to call `predicateForContacts(matchingName:)` or `predicateForContacts(withIdentifiers:)`; there are also predicates for fetching by email address and fetching by phone number.

Keys for properties to be fetched

An array of objects adopting the CNKeyDescriptor protocol; such an object will be either a string key name, such as `CNContactFamilyNameKey`, or a descriptor provided by a formatter such as CNContactFormatter.

Fetching a Contact

I'll start by finding the contact that represents me in my contacts database. To do so, I'll fetch all contacts whose name is Matt Neuburg and assume that the first one is me. I'll call the CNContactStore instance method `unifiedContacts(matching:keysToFetch:)` with the `matchingName` predicate. Lots of combinations will work as the name: `"Matt Neuburg"`, `"Neuburg Matt"`, `"Neuburg, Matt"`, and so on.

To prove that I've found myself, I don't need more than the first name and the last name of those contacts, so those are the keys I'll ask for. There are some parts of the process that I'm not bothering to show: we are using a CNContactStore fetch method, so everything should be done on a background thread, and the fetch should be wrapped in a `do...catch` construct because it can throw:

```
let pred = CNContact.predicateForContacts(matchingName: "Matt Neuburg")
let matts = try CNContactStore().unifiedContacts(matching: pred,
    keysToFetch: [
        CNContactFamilyNameKey as CNKeyDescriptor,
        CNContactGivenNameKey as CNKeyDescriptor
])
guard let moi = matts.first else {
    print("couldn't find myself")
    return
}
print(moi)
// CNContact: 0x10331dce0; givenName=Matt, familyName=Neuburg, ...
```

Alternatively, I could call `enumerateContacts(with:usingBlock:)`, which hands me contacts one at a time. The parameter is a CNContactFetchRequest, a simple value class; in addition to `keysToFetch` and `predicate`, it has some powerful properties allowing me to retrieve CNMutableContacts instead of CNContacts, to dictate the sort order, and to suppress the unification of linked contacts (I'll talk later about what that means). One should perhaps regard `enumerateContacts(with:usingBlock:)` as the *primary* way to fetch contacts. I don't need those extra features here, but I'll demonstrate anyway. Again, assume we're in a background thread and inside a `do...catch` construct:

```
let pred = CNContact.predicateForContacts(matchingName:"Matt Neuburg")
let req = CNContactFetchRequest(keysToFetch: [
    CNContactFamilyNameKey as CNKeyDescriptor,
    CNContactGivenNameKey as CNKeyDescriptor
])
req.predicate = pred
var matt : CNContact? = nil
try CNContactStore().enumerateContacts(with:req) { con, stop in
    matt = con
    stop.pointee = true
}
guard let moi = matt else {
    print("couldn't find myself")
    return
}
```

A commonly asked question is: where's the predicate for fetching information about *all* contacts? There isn't one. Simply call `enumerateContacts(with:usingBlock:)` without a predicate.

Repopulating a Contact

The contact that I fetched in the preceding examples is only partially populated. That means I can't use it to obtain any further contact property information. To illustrate, let's say that I now want to access my own email addresses. If I were to carry on directly from the preceding code by reading the `emailAddresses` property of `moi`, I'd crash because that property isn't populated:

```
let emails = moi.emailAddresses // crash
```

If I'm unsure what properties of a particular contact are populated, I can test for safety beforehand with the `isKeyAvailable(_:)` method:

```
if moi.isKeyAvailable(CNContactEmailAddressesKey) {
    let emails = moi.emailAddresses
}
```

But even though I'm not crashing any more, I still want those email addresses. One solution, obviously, would have been to plan ahead and include `CNContactEmailAddressesKey` in the list of properties to be fetched. Unfortunately, I failed to do that.

Luckily, there's another way; I can go back to the store and *repopulate* this contact, based on its identifier:

```
let moi2 = try CNContactStore().unifiedContact(withIdentifier: moi.identifier,
    keysToFetch: [
        CNContactFamilyNameKey as CNKeyDescriptor,
        CNContactGivenNameKey as CNKeyDescriptor,
        CNContactEmailAddressesKey as CNKeyDescriptor
])
let emails = moi2.emailAddresses
```

Labeled Values

Now let's talk about the structure of the thing I've just obtained — the value of the emailAddresses property. It's an array of CNLabeledValue objects.

A CNLabeledValue has a label and a value (and an identifier). This class handles the fact that some contact attributes can have more than one value, each intended for a specific purpose described by the label; for instance, I might have both a home email address and a work email address. This is not a dictionary; the values are not keyed by their labels. That's because the same label can be used with more than one value — I can have *two* work email addresses. The label is just a piece of information paired with the value. You can make up your own labels, or you can use the built-in labels; the latter are very strange-looking strings like "_$!<Work>!$_", but there are also some constants that you can use instead, such as CNLabelWork.

Carrying on from the previous example, I'll look for all my work email addresses:

```
let workemails = emails.filter{ $0.label == CNLabelWork }.map{ $0.value }
```

A phone number is a CNLabeledValue whose value is a CNPhoneNumber object. A postal address is a CNLabeledValue whose value is a CNPostalAddress, which is mostly a value class providing properties such as street, city, state, and country.

Contact Formatters

When presenting the user with contact information as a string, you should look to see whether there's a formatter for that information. For a name string, there's CNContactFormatter; for a CNPostalAddress string, there's CNPostalAddress-Formatter.

To illustrate, let's say that I want to present the full name and work email of the moi contact to the user, as a string. I should not assume that the full name is to be constructed as givenName followed by familyName, nor that those are the only two pieces that constitute it. Rather, I should rely on the intelligence of a CNContactFormatter:

```
let full = CNContactFormatterStyle.fullName
let keys = CNContactFormatter.descriptorForRequiredKeys(for:full)
let moi3 = try CNContactStore().unifiedContact(withIdentifier: moi.identifier,
    keysToFetch: [
        keys,
        CNContactEmailAddressesKey as CNKeyDescriptor
])
if let name = CNContactFormatter.string(from: moi3, style: full) {
    print("\(name): \(workemails[0])") // Matt Neuburg: matt@tidbits.com
}
```

CNPostalAddressFormatter turns a CNPostalAddress into a string, nicely lineated and dealing with the numerous international variations. An intriguing feature of CNPostalAddressFormatter is that it can also provide an *attributed* string, marked with a custom attribute called CNPostalAddressPropertyAttribute (see "Custom Attributes" on page 641). This attribute is applied to each piece of the address, with the attribute's value indicating *which* piece of the address this is. We could use this to present a formatted address to the user, modifying the style of particular semantic stretches. In this example, I'll obtain a contact's postal address, derive the attributed string, learn what range of that string contains the contact's country name, and underline it:

```
let pred = CNContact.predicateForContacts(matchingName:"Charlotte Wilson")
let c = try CNContactStore().unifiedContacts(matching: pred,
    keysToFetch: [CNContactPostalAddressesKey as CNKeyDescriptor])[0]
let addr = c.postalAddresses[0]
let form = CNPostalAddressFormatter()
let attr = form.attributedString(from:addr.value, withDefaultAttributes:[:])
let s = attr.string as NSString
let range = NSRange(location: 0, length: s.length)
let key = NSAttributedString.Key(rawValue:CNPostalAddressPropertyAttribute)
attr.enumerateAttributes(in: range, options: []) { result, r, stop in
    if let val = result[key] as? String {
        if val == "country" {
            // r is the range of the country name; I'll prove it...
            print("country is:", s.substring(with: r)) // New Zealand
            // underline it
            if let mas = attr.mutableCopy() as? NSMutableAttributedString {
                mas.addAttributes([
                    .underlineStyle: NSUnderlineStyle.single.rawValue
                ], range: r)
                // ... do something with the attributed string ...
            }
            stop.pointee = true
        }
    }
}
```

Figure 18-1. A contact created programmatically

Saving Contact Information

All saving of information into the user's contacts database involves a CNSaveRequest object. You describe to this object your proposed changes by calling instance methods such as add(_:toContainerWithIdentifier:), update(_:), and delete(_:). The CNSaveRequest object batches those proposed changes. Then you hand the CNSaveRequest object over to the CNContactStore with execute(_:), and the changes are performed in a single transaction.

In this example, I'll create a contact for Snidely Whiplash with a Home email snidely@villains.com and add him to the contacts database:

```
let snidely = CNMutableContact()
snidely.givenName = "Snidely"
snidely.familyName = "Whiplash"
let email = CNLabeledValue(label: CNLabelHome,
    value: "snidely@villains.com" as NSString)
snidely.emailAddresses.append(email)
snidely.imageData = UIImage(named:"snidely")!.pngData()
let save = CNSaveRequest()
save.add(snidely, toContainerWithIdentifier: nil)
try CNContactStore().execute(save)
```

Sure enough, if we then check the state of the database through the Contacts app, our Snidely contact exists (Figure 18-1).

Contact Sorting, Groups, and Containers

Contacts are naturally sorted either by family name or by given name, and the user can choose between them (in the Settings app) in arranging the list of contacts to be displayed by the Contacts app and other apps that display the same list. The

CNContact class provides a comparator, through the `comparator(forNameSort-Order:)` class method, suitable for use with NSArray methods such as `sorted-Array(comparator:)`. To make sure your CNContact is populated with the properties needed for sorting, call the class method `descriptorForAllComparator-Keys`. Your sort order choices (CNContactSortOrder) are:

- `.givenName`
- `.familyName`
- `.userDefault`

Contacts can belong to groups, and the Contacts application in macOS provides an interface for manipulating contact groups — though the Contacts app on an iOS device does not. A group in the Contacts framework is a CNGroup; its mutable subclass, CNMutableGroup, allows you to create a group and set its name. All manipulation of contacts and groups — creating, renaming, or deleting a group, adding a contact to a group or removing a contact from a group — is performed through CNSaveRequest instance methods.

Contacts come from sources. A contact or group might be on the device or might come from an Exchange server or a CardDAV server. The source really does, in a sense, own the group or contact; a contact can't belong to two sources. A complicating factor, however, is that the same real person might be listed in two different sources as two different contacts; to deal with this, it is possible for multiple contacts to be *linked*, indicating that they are the same person. That's why the methods that fetch contacts from the database describe the resulting contacts as "unified" — the linkage between linked contacts from different sources has already been used to consolidate the information into a single CNContact object. In the rare event that you *don't* want unification of linked contacts across sources as you fetch contacts, call `enumerateContacts(with:usingBlock:)` with a CNContactFetchRequest whose `unifyResults` property is `false`.

In the Contacts framework, a source is a CNContainer. When I called the CNSaveRequest instance method `add(_:toContainerWithIdentifier:)` earlier, I supplied a container identifier of `nil`, signifying the user's default container.

Contacts Interface

The Contacts UI framework endows your app with an interface similar to the Contacts app, where the user can perform common tasks involving the listing, display, and editing of contacts in the database. The framework provides two UIViewController subclasses:

CNContactPickerViewController
> Presents a navigation interface, effectively the same as the Contacts app but without an Edit button: it lists the contacts in the database and allows the user to pick one and view the details.

CNContactViewController
> Presents an interface showing the properties of an individual contact. It comes in three variants:

> *Existing contact*
>> Displays the details, possibly editable, of an existing contact fetched from the database.

> *New contact*
>> Displays editable properties of a new contact, allowing the user to save the edited contact into the database.

> *Unknown contact*
>> Displays a proposed contact with a partial set of properties, for editing and saving or merging into an existing contact in the database.

Some of the Contacts UI framework view controllers allow the user to select (tap) a property of a contact in the interface. Therefore, they need a way to package up the information about that property so as to communicate to your code *what* property this is, such as "Matt Neuburg's work email whose value is `matt@tidbits.com`." For this purpose, the Contacts framework provides the CNContactProperty class. This a value class, consisting of a `key` (effectively the name of the property), a `value`, a `label` (in case the property comes from a CNLabeledValue), a `contact`, and an `identifier`. The contact arrives fully populated, so we can access all its properties from here without returning to the CNContactStore.

 You do *not* need user authorization to use these view controllers, and in the case of an editable CNContactViewController you *cannot* prevent the user from saving the edited contact into the database.

CNContactPickerViewController

A CNContactPickerViewController is a UINavigationController. With it, the user can see a list of all contacts in the database, and can filter that list by group and by searching.

To use CNContactPickerViewController, instantiate it, assign it a delegate (CNContactPickerDelegate), and present it as a presented view controller:

```
let picker = CNContactPickerViewController()
picker.delegate = self
self.present(picker, animated:true)
```

That code works — the picker appears, and there's a Cancel button so the user can dismiss it. When the user taps a contact, that contact's details are pushed onto the navigation controller. When the user taps a piece of information among the details, some default action is performed: for a postal address, it is displayed in the Maps app; for an email address, it becomes the addressee of a new message in the Mail app; for a phone number, the number is dialed; and so on.

However, we have so far provided no way for any information to travel from the picker *to our app*. For that, we need to implement the delegate method `contact-Picker(_:didSelect:)`. This method comes in two basic forms:

The second parameter is a CNContact
When the user taps a contact name, the contact's details are *not* pushed onto the navigation controller. Instead, the delegate method is called, the tapped contact is passed to us, and the picker is dismissed.

The second parameter is a CNContactProperty
When the user taps a contact name, the contact's details *are* pushed onto the navigation controller. If the user now taps a piece of information among the details, the delegate method is called, the tapped property is passed to us, and the picker is dismissed.

(If we implement both forms of this method, it is as if we had implemented only the first form. However, it's possible to change that, using the `predicateForSelectionOf-Contact` property, as I'm about to explain.)

You can perform additional configuration of what information appears in the picker and what happens when it is tapped, by setting properties of the picker before you present it. These properties are all NSPredicates:

`predicateForEnablingContact`
The predicate describes the contact. A contact will be enabled in the picker only if the predicate evaluates to `true`. A disabled contact cannot be tapped, so it can't be selected and its details can't be displayed.

`predicateForSelectionOfContact`
The predicate describes the contact. If the predicate evaluates to `true`, tapping the contact calls the *first* delegate method (the parameter is the contact). Otherwise, tapping the contact displays the contact details.

`predicateForSelectionOfProperty`
The predicate describes the property (in the detail view). If the predicate evaluates to `true`, tapping the property calls the *second* delegate method (the parameter is a CNContactProperty). Otherwise, tapping the property performs the default action.

You can also determine *what* properties appear in the detail view, by setting the `displayedPropertyKeys` property.

Let's say we want the user to pass us an email address, and that's the only reason we're displaying the picker. Then a reasonable configuration would be:

```
picker.displayedPropertyKeys =
    [CNContactEmailAddressesKey]
picker.predicateForEnablingContact =
    NSPredicate(format: "emailAddresses.@count > 0")
```

We would then implement only the second form of the delegate method (the parameter is a CNContactProperty). Our code then effectively says: "Only enable contacts that have email addresses. When the user taps an enabled contact, show the details. In the details view, show only email addresses. When the user taps an email address, report it to the delegate method and dismiss the picker."

It is also possible to enable multiple selection. To do so, we implement a different pair of delegate methods:

`contactPicker(_:didSelect:)`
    The second parameter is an array of CNContact.

`contactPicker(_:didSelectContactProperties:)`
    The second parameter is an array of CNContactProperty.

This causes a Done button to appear in the interface, and our delegate method is called when the user taps it.

 The interface for letting the user select multiple properties, if incorrectly configured, can be clumsy and confusing, and can even send your app into limbo. Experiment carefully before deciding to use it.

CNContactViewController

A CNContactViewController is a UIViewController. It comes, as I've already said, in three flavors, depending on how you instantiate it:

- Existing contact: `init(for:)`
- New contact: `init(forNewContact:)`
- Unknown contact: `init(forUnknownContact:)`

The first and third flavors display a contact initially, with an option to show a secondary editing interface. The second flavor consists *solely* of the editing interface

Unfortunately, as of this writing, there are problems with the CNContactView-Controller interface. In all three flavors, the view controller behaves incorrectly with respect to the navigation bar: the navigation bar becomes transparent, and the view controller's main view underlaps it. In the second flavor, if the user taps the Cancel button while the keyboard is showing, the view controller is not dismissed. These are cosmetic issues, but test thoroughly before electing to use this view controller.

You can configure the initial display of the contact in the first and third flavors, by means of these properties:

`allowsActions`
Refers to extra buttons that can appear in the interface if it is `true` — things like Share Contact, Add to Favorites, and Share My Location. Exactly what buttons appear depends on what categories of information are displayed.

`displayedPropertyKeys`
Limits the properties shown for this contact.

`message`
A string displayed beneath the contact's name.

There are two delegate methods (CNContactViewControllerDelegate):

`contactViewController(_:shouldPerformDefaultActionFor:)`
Used by the first and third flavors, in the initial display of the contact. This is like a live version of the picker `predicateForSelectionOfProperty`, except that the meaning is reversed: returning `true` means that the tapped property should proceed to trigger the Mail app or the Maps app or whatever is appropriate. This includes the message and mail buttons at the top of the interface. You are handed the CNContactProperty, so you know what was tapped and can take action yourself if you return `false`.

`contactViewController(_:didCompleteWith:)`
Used by all three flavors. Called when the user dismisses the editing interface. If the user taps Done in the editing interface, you receive the edited contact, *which has already been saved into the database.* (If the user cancels out of the editing interface, then if this delegate method is called, the received contact will be `nil`.)

Existing contact

To display an existing contact in a CNContactViewController, call `init(for:)` with a CNContact that has *already* been populated with all the information needed to display it in this view controller. For this purpose, CNContactViewController supplies a class method `descriptorForRequiredKeys`, and you will want to call it to set the keys

when you fetch your contact from the store, prior to using it with a CNContactView-
Controller. Here's an example:

```
let pred = CNContact.predicateForContacts(matchingName: "Snidely Whiplash")
let keys = CNContactViewController.descriptorForRequiredKeys()
let snides = try CNContactStore().unifiedContacts(matching: pred,
    keysToFetch: [keys])
guard let snide = snides.first else {
    print("no snidely")
    return
}
```

We now have a sufficiently populated contact, snide, and can use it in a subsequent
call to CNContactViewController's init(for:).

 Handing an insufficiently populated contact to CNContactViewController's
init(for:) will crash your app.

Having instantiated CNContactViewController, you set its delegate (CNContact-
ViewControllerDelegate) and *push* the view controller onto an existing
UINavigationController's stack.

An Edit button appears at the top right, and the user can tap it to edit this contact in a
presented view controller — unless you have set the view controller's allowsEditing
property to false, in which case the Edit button is suppressed.

Here's a minimal working example; I'll display the Snidely Whiplash contact that I
obtained earlier. Note that, if we were in a background thread earlier when we
fetched snide from the database, we need to be on the main thread now:

```
let vc = CNContactViewController(for:snide)
vc.delegate = self
vc.message = "Nyah ah ahhh"
self.navigationController?.pushViewController(vc, animated: true)
```

New contact

To use a CNContactViewController to allow the user to create a new contact, instantiate it with init(forNewContact:). The parameter can be nil, or it can be a
CNMutableContact that you've created and partially populated; but your properties
will be only suggestions, because the user is going to be shown the contact editing
interface and can change anything you've put.

Having set the view controller's delegate, you then do a little dance: you instantiate a
UINavigationController with the CNContactViewController as its root view controller, and *present the navigation controller* as a presented view controller. Here is a
minimal implementation:

```
let con = CNMutableContact()
con.givenName = "Dudley"
con.familyName = "Doright"
let npvc = CNContactViewController(forNewContact: con)
npvc.delegate = self
self.present(UINavigationController(rootViewController: npvc),
    animated:true)
```

You must dismiss the presented navigation controller yourself in your implementation of `contactViewController(_:didCompleteWith:)`.

Unknown contact

To use a CNContactViewController to allow the user to edit an unknown contact, instantiate it with `init(forUnknownContact:)`. You must provide a CNContact parameter, which you may have made up from scratch using a CNMutableContact. You must set the view controller's `contactStore` to a CNContactStore instance; if you don't, it's not an error, but the view controller is then useless. You then set a delegate and *push* the view controller onto an existing navigation controller:

```
let con = CNMutableContact()
con.givenName = "Johnny"
con.familyName = "Appleseed"
con.phoneNumbers.append(CNLabeledValue(label: "woods",
    value: CNPhoneNumber(stringValue: "555-123-4567")))
let unkvc = CNContactViewController(forUnknownContact: con)
unkvc.message = "He knows his trees"
unkvc.contactStore = CNContactStore()
unkvc.delegate = self
unkvc.allowsActions = false
self.navigationController?.pushViewController(unkvc, animated: true)
```

The interface contains these two buttons (among others):

Create New Contact
The editing interface is presented, with a Cancel button and a Done button.

Add to Existing Contact
The contact picker is presented. The user can tap Cancel or tap an existing contact. If the user taps an existing contact, that contact is presented for editing, with fields from the partial contact merged in, along with a Cancel button and an Update button.

If the framework thinks that this partial contact is the same as an existing contact, there will be a third button offering explicitly to update that particular contact. The result is as if the user had tapped Add to Existing Contact and picked this existing contact. In the editing interface, if the user taps Cancel, you'll never hear about it; `contactViewController(_:didCompleteWith:)` won't even be called.

CHAPTER 19

Calendar

The user's calendar information constitutes a database of calendar events. This database also includes reminders. The user can interact with the calendar events through the Calendar app, and with the reminders through the Reminders app. Your code can access the database through the EventKit framework. You'll need to import `EventKit`. An interface for allowing the user to interact with the calendar from within your app is also provided, through the EventKit UI framework. You'll need to import `EventKitUI`.

The database is accessed as an instance of the EKEventStore class. This instance is expensive to obtain but lightweight to maintain, so your usual strategy will be to instantiate and retain one EKEventStore instance. There is no harm in initializing a property or global as an EKEventStore instance and keeping that reference for the rest of the app's lifetime:

```
let database = EKEventStore()
```

In the examples in this chapter, my EKEventStore instance is called `self.database` throughout.

Access to the database requires user authorization. You'll use the EKEventStore class for this. Although there is one database, access to calendar events and access to reminders are considered two separate forms of access and require separate authorizations. To learn what the current authorization status is, call the class method `authorizationStatus(for:)` with an EKEntityType, either `.event` (for access to calendar events) or `.reminder` (for access to reminders). To ask the system to put up the authorization request alert if the status is `.notDetermined`, call the instance method `requestAccess(to:completion:)`. The *Info.plist* must contain some meaningful text that the system authorization request alert can use to explain why your app wants access. The relevant key is either "Privacy — Calendars Usage Description"

(`NSCalendarsUsageDescription`) or "Privacy — Reminders Usage Description" (`NSRemindersUsageDescription`). See "Checking for Authorization" on page 861 for a discussion of authorization strategy.

Calendar Database Contents

Starting with an EKEventStore instance, you can obtain two kinds of object — a calendar or a calendar item.

Calendars

A calendar represents a named (`title`) collection of calendar items, meaning events or reminders. It is an instance of EKCalendar. But an EKCalendar instance doesn't contain or link to its calendar items; to obtain and create calendar items, you work directly with the EKEventStore itself. A calendar's `allowedEntityTypes`, despite the plural, will probably return just one entity type; you can't create a calendar that allows both.

Calendars themselves come in various types (`type`, an EKCalendarType), reflecting the nature of their origin: a calendar can be created and maintained by the user locally (`.local`), but it might also live remotely on the network (`.calDAV`, `.exchange`); the Birthday calendar (`.birthday`) is generated automatically from information in the contacts database; and so on.

The `type` is supplemented and embraced by the calendar's `source`, an EKSource whose `sourceType` (EKSourceType) can be `.local`, `.exchange`, `.calDAV` (which includes iCloud), and so forth; a source can also have a `title`, and it has a unique identifier (`sourceIdentifier`). You can get an array of all `sources` known to the EKEventStore, or specify a source by its identifier. You'll probably use the `source` exclusively and ignore the calendar's `type` property.

There are three ways of requesting a calendar:

All calendars
> Fetch all calendars permitting a particular calendar item type (`.event` or `.reminder`), by calling `calendars(for:)`. You can send this message either to the EKEventStore or to an EKSource.

Particular calendar
> Fetch an individual calendar from the EKEventStore by means of a previously obtained `calendarIdentifier`, by calling `calendar(withIdentifier:)`.

Default calendar
> Fetch the default calendar for a particular calendar item type, by asking for the `defaultCalendarForNewEvents` or `defaultCalendarForNewReminders` of the

EKEventStore; this is appropriate particularly if your intention is to create a new calendar item.

You can also create a calendar, by means of the initializer `init(for:eventStore:)`. At that point, you can specify the source to which the calendar belongs. I'll give an example later.

Depending on the source, a calendar will be modifiable in various ways. The calendar's `isSubscribed` might be `true`. If the calendar's `isImmutable` is `true`, you can't delete the calendar or change its attributes; but its `allowsContentModifications` might still be `true`, in which case you can add, remove, and alter its events.

Calendar Items

A calendar item (EKCalendarItem) is either a calendar event (EKEvent) or a reminder (EKReminder). Think of it as a memorandum describing when something happens. As I mentioned a moment ago, you don't get calendar items from a calendar; rather, a calendar item *has* a `calendar`, but you get it from the EKEventStore as a whole. There are two chief ways of getting a calendar item:

By predicate
   Fetch all events or reminders according to a predicate (NSPredicate):

   - `events(matching:)`

   - `enumerateEvents(matching:using:)`

   - `fetchReminders(matching:completion:)`

   EKEventStore methods starting with `predicateFor` supply the needed predicate. I'll give an example later.

By identifier
   Fetch an individual calendar item by means of a previously obtained `calendarItemIdentifier`, by calling `calendarItem(withIdentifier:)`.

Calendar Database Changes

Changes to the database can be atomic. There are two prongs to the implementation of this feature:

- The EKEventStore methods for saving and removing calendar items and calendars have a `commit:` parameter. If you pass `false` as the argument, the changes that you're ordering are batched without performing them; later, you can call `commit` (or `reset` if you change your mind). If you pass `false` and fail to call `commit` later, your changes will never happen.

- An abstract class, EKObject, functions as the superclass for all the other persistent object types, such as EKCalendar, EKCalendarItem, EKSource, and so on. It endows those classes with methods refresh, rollback, and reset, along with read-only properties isNew and hasChanges.

The database can change while your app is running (the user might sync, or the user might edit with the Calendar app), which can put your information out of date. You can register for a single EKEventStore notification, .EKEventStoreChanged; if you receive it, you should assume that any calendar-related instances you're holding are invalid. This situation is made relatively painless by the fact that every calendar-related instance can be refreshed with refresh. Keep in mind that refresh returns a Boolean; if it returns false, this object is *really* invalid and you should stop working with it entirely (it may have been deleted from the database).

Creating Calendars, Events, and Reminders

You now know enough for an example! Let's start by creating an events calendar. We need to assign a source type (EKSourceType); we'll choose .local, meaning that the calendar will be created on the device itself. We can't ask the database for the local source directly, so we have to cycle through all sources looking for it. When we find it, we make a new calendar called "CoolCal" (saving into the database can fail, so assume we're running inside a do...catch construct):

```
let locals = self.database.sources.filter {$0.sourceType == .local}
guard let src = locals.first else {
    print("failed to find local source")
    return
}
let cal = EKCalendar(for:.event, eventStore:self.database)
cal.source = src
cal.title = "CoolCal"
try self.database.saveCalendar(cal, commit:true)
```

 On a device where the calendar is subscribed to a remote source, .local calendars are inaccessible. The examples in this chapter use a local calendar, because I don't want to risk damaging your online calendars; to test the examples, you'll need to turn off iCloud for your Calendar app temporarily.

Events

Now let's create an event. EKEvent is a subclass of EKCalendarItem, from which it inherits some of its properties. If you've ever used the Calendar app in iOS or macOS, you already have a sense for how an EKEvent can be configured. It has a title and optional notes. It is associated with a calendar, as I've already said. It can have one or more alarms and one or more recurrence rules; I'll talk about those in a moment. All of that is inherited from EKCalendarItem.

EKEvent itself adds the `startDate` and `endDate` properties; these are Dates and involve both date and time. If the event's `isAllDay` property is `true`, the time aspect of its dates is ignored; the event is associated with a day or a stretch of days as a whole. If the event's `isAllDay` property is `false`, the time aspect of its dates matters; an event will then typically be bounded by two times on the same day.

Making an event is simple, if tedious. You *must* provide a `startDate` and an `endDate`! The simplest way to construct dates, and to do the date math that you'll often need in order to derive one date from another, is with DateComponents. I'll create an event and add it to our new calendar. First, I need a way to locate the new calendar. I'll locate it by its title. I really should be using the `calendarIdentifier`; the title isn't reliable, since the user might change it, and since multiple calendars can have the same title. However, it's only an example:

```
func calendar(name:String ) -> EKCalendar? {
    let cals = self.database.calendars(for:.event)
    return cals.filter {$0.title == name}.first
}
```

Now I'll create an event, configure it, and add it to our CoolCal calendar:

```
guard let cal = self.calendar(name:"CoolCal") else {
    print("failed to find calendar")
    return
}
// form the start and end dates
let greg = Calendar(identifier:.gregorian)
var comp = DateComponents(year:2019, month:8, day:10, hour:15)
let d1 = greg.date(from:comp)!
comp.hour = comp.hour! + 1
let d2 = greg.date(from:comp)!
// form the event
let ev = EKEvent(eventStore:self.database)
ev.title = "Take a nap"
ev.notes = "You deserve it!"
ev.calendar = cal
(ev.startDate, ev.endDate) = (d1,d2)
// save it
try self.database.save(ev, span:.thisEvent, commit:true)
```

Alarms

An alarm is an EKAlarm, a very simple class; it can be set to fire either at an absolute date or at a relative offset from the event time. On an iOS device, a calendar alarm fires through a local notification (Chapter 13); if the user turns off local notifications for the Calendar app, there will be no indication that the alarm has fired. We could easily have added an alarm to our event as we were configuring it:

```
let alarm = EKAlarm(relativeOffset:-3600) // one hour before
ev.addAlarm(alarm)
```

Recurrence

Recurrence is embodied in a recurrence rule (EKRecurrenceRule); a calendar item can have multiple recurrence rules, which you manipulate through its `recurrence-Rules` property and `addRecurrenceRule(_:)` and `removeRecurrenceRule(_:)` methods. A simple EKRecurrenceRule is described by three properties:

Frequency
> By day, by week, by month, or by year.

Interval
> Fine-tunes the notion "by" in the frequency. A value of 1 means "every." A value of 2 means "every other." And so on.

End
> Optional, because the event might recur forever. It is an EKRecurrenceEnd instance, describing the limit of the event's recurrence either as an end date or as a maximum number of occurrences.

The options for describing a more complex EKRecurrenceRule are best summarized by its initializer:

```
init(recurrenceWith type: EKRecurrenceFrequency,
              interval: Int,
         daysOfTheWeek: [EKRecurrenceDayOfWeek]?,
        daysOfTheMonth: [NSNumber]?,
       monthsOfTheYear: [NSNumber]?,
        weeksOfTheYear: [NSNumber]?,
         daysOfTheYear: [NSNumber]?,
          setPositions: [NSNumber]?,
                   end: EKRecurrenceEnd?)
```

The meanings of all those parameters are mostly obvious from their names and types. The EKRecurrenceDayOfWeek class allows specification of a week number as well as a day number so that you can say things like "the fourth Thursday of the month." Many of the numeric values can be negative to indicate counting backward from the last one. Numbers are all 1-based, not 0-based. The `setPositions:` parameter is an array of numbers filtering the occurrences defined by the rest of the specification against the interval; for instance, if `daysOfTheWeek` is Sunday, `-1` means the final Sunday.

An EKRecurrenceRule is intended to embody the RRULE event component in the iCalendar standard specification (*http://datatracker.ietf.org/doc/rfc5545*); in fact, the documentation tells you how each EKRecurrenceRule property corresponds to an RRULE attribute, and if you log an EKRecurrenceRule, what you're shown *is* the underlying RRULE. RRULE can describe some amazingly sophisticated recurrence rules, such as this one:

```
RRULE:FREQ=YEARLY;INTERVAL=2;BYMONTH=1;BYDAY=SU
```

That means: "Every Sunday in January, every other year." Let's form this rule. Observe that we should attach it to an event whose `startDate` and `endDate` actually obey the rule — that is, the event should fall on a Sunday in January. Fortunately, DateComponents makes that easy:

```
let everySunday = EKRecurrenceDayOfWeek(.sunday)
let january = 1 as NSNumber
let recur = EKRecurrenceRule(
    recurrenceWith:.yearly, // every year
    interval:2, // no, every *two* years
    daysOfTheWeek:[everySunday],
    daysOfTheMonth:nil,
    monthsOfTheYear:[january],
    weeksOfTheYear:nil,
    daysOfTheYear:nil,
    setPositions: nil,
    end:nil)
let ev = EKEvent(eventStore:self.database)
ev.title = "Mysterious biennial Sunday-in-January morning ritual"
ev.addRecurrenceRule(recur)
ev.calendar = cal // assume we have our calendar
// need a start date and end date
let greg = Calendar(identifier:.gregorian)
var comp = DateComponents(year:2019, month:1, hour:10)
comp.weekday = 1 // Sunday
comp.weekdayOrdinal = 1 // *first* Sunday
ev.startDate = greg.date(from:comp)!
comp.hour = 11
ev.endDate = greg.date(from:comp)!
try self.database.save(ev, span:.futureEvents, commit:true)
```

In that code, the event we save into the database is a recurring event. When we save or delete a recurring event, we must specify a `span:` argument (EKSpan). This is either `.thisEvent` or `.futureEvents`, and corresponds to the two buttons the user sees in the Calendar interface when saving or deleting a recurring event (Figure 19-1). The buttons and the span types reflect their meaning exactly: the change affects either this event alone, or this event plus all *future* (not past) recurrences. This choice determines not only how this and future recurrences of the event are affected now, but also how they relate to one another from now on.

Reminders

A reminder (EKReminder) is very similar to an event (EKEvent); the chief difference is that EKReminder was invented some years after EKEvent and so its API is a little more modern. They both inherit from EKCalendarItem, so a reminder has a calendar (which the Reminders app refers to as a "list"), a title, notes, alarms, and recurrence rules.

Figure 19-1. The user specifies a span

A remainder has an `isCompleted` property and a `completionDate`. Setting the `isCompleted` property to `true` sets the `completionDate`, and *vice versa*.

Instead of a start date and an end date, a reminder has a start date (`startDate-Components`) and a due date (`dueDateComponents`). As the names suggest, these are expressed directly as DateComponents, so you can supply any desired degree of detail.

You are free to create a reminder with no date information, and that's a common thing to do:

```
let cal = self.database.defaultCalendarForNewReminders()
let rem = EKReminder(eventStore:self.database)
rem.title = "Get bread"
rem.calendar = cal
try self.database.save(rem, commit:true)
```

Here's how to change that to a reminder for tomorrow:

```
// ... create rem as before ...
let greg = Calendar(identifier:.gregorian)
let tomorrow = greg.date(byAdding: DateComponents(day:1), to: Date())
let comps : Set<Calendar.Component> = [.year, .month, .day]
rem.dueDateComponents = greg.dateComponents(comps, from:tomorrow!)
try self.database.save(rem, commit:true)
```

But although we have set the reminder's due date, this reminder will not actively remind the user of anything! If we want to alert the user when the due date arrives, we must also add an EKAlarm to the reminder.

The reminder's `startDateComponents` are needed only if you attach a recurrence rule to the reminder. You'll typically want the reminding to start immediately. Unlike a recurring calendar event, a recurring reminder doesn't generate multiple reminders stretching out into the future; instead, it generates one reminder that automatically generates the next reminder upon completion.

Proximity Alarms

A proximity alarm is triggered by the user's approaching or leaving a certain location (also known as *geofencing*). This is appropriate particularly for reminders: one might wish to be reminded of some task when approaching the place where that task can be accomplished. To form the location, you'll need to use the CLLocation class (see Chapter 21). Here, I'll attach a proximity alarm to a reminder (rem); the alarm will fire when I'm near my local Trader Joe's:

```
let alarm = EKAlarm()
let loc = EKStructuredLocation(title:"Trader Joe's")
loc.geoLocation = CLLocation(latitude:34.271848, longitude:-119.247714)
loc.radius = 10*1000 // meters
alarm.structuredLocation = loc
alarm.proximity = .enter // "geofence": we alarm when *arriving*
rem.addAlarm(alarm)
```

Use of a proximity alarm requires Location Services authorization, but that's of no concern here, because the app that needs this authorization is not our app but the Reminders app! Now that we've placed a reminder with a proximity alarm into the database, the Reminders app will request authorization, if needed, the next time the user brings it frontmost. If you add a proximity alarm to the event database and the Reminders app can't perform background geofencing, the alarm will not fire (unless the Reminders app is frontmost).

 You can also construct a local notification based on geofencing without involving reminders or the Reminders app. See Chapter 21.

Fetching Events and Reminders

Now let's talk about how to extract an event from the database. One way, as I mentioned earlier, is by its identifier (calendarItemIdentifier). Not only is this identifier a fast and unique way to obtain an event, but also it's just a string, which means that it persists even if the EKEventStore subsequently goes out of existence, whereas an actual EKEvent drawn from the database loses its meaning and its usability if the EKEventStore instance is destroyed.

You can also extract events from the database by matching a predicate (NSPredicate). To form this predicate, you specify a start and end date and an array of eligible calendars, and call this EKEventStore method:

- predicateForEvents(withStart:end:calendars:)

That's the only kind of predicate you can use, so any further filtering of events is then up to you. In this example, I'll look through the events of our CoolCal calendar to find the nap event I created earlier; because I have to specify a date range, I ask for events occurring over a two-year span. Because calling enumerate-Events(matching:using:) can be time-consuming, it's a good idea to run it on a background thread (Chapter 24):

```
let greg = Calendar(identifier:.gregorian)
let d = Date() // today
let d1 = greg.date(byAdding:DateComponents(year:-1), to:d)!
let d2 = greg.date(byAdding:DateComponents(year:2), to:d)!
let pred = self.database.predicateForEvents(withStart:
    d1, end:d2, calendars:[cal]) // assume we have our calendar
DispatchQueue.global(qos:.default).async {
    self.database.enumerateEvents(matching:pred) { ev, stop in
        if ev.title.range(of:"nap") != nil {
            self.napid = ev.calendarItemIdentifier
            stop.pointee = true
        }
    }
}
```

When you fetch events from the database, they are provided in no particular order; the convenience method compareStartDate(with:) is provided as a sort selector to put them in order by start date:

```
events.sort { $0.compareStartDate(with:$1) == .orderedAscending }
```

When you extract events from the database, event recurrences are treated as separate events. Recurrences of the same event will have different start and end dates but the same calendarItemIdentifier. When you fetch an event by identifier, you get the *earliest* event with that identifier. This makes sense, because if you're going to make a change affecting this and future recurrences of the event, you'll want to start with the earliest possible recurrence (so that "future" means "all").

Fetching reminders is similar to fetching events, but simpler. When you call fetch-Reminders(matching:completion:), the possible predicates let you fetch all reminders in given calendars, incomplete reminders, or completed reminders. You don't have to call it on a background thread, because it calls your completion function asynchronously.

Calendar Interface

The EventKit UI framework provides three view controller classes that manage views for letting the user work with events and calendars:

EKEventViewController
    Shows the description of a single event, possibly editable.

EKEventEditViewController
    Allows the user to create or edit an event.

EKCalendarChooser
   Allows the user to pick a calendar.

These view controllers automatically listen for changes in the database and, if needed, will automatically call `refresh` on the information being edited, updating their display to match. If a view controller is displaying an event in the database and the event is deleted while the user is viewing it, the delegate will get the same notification as if the user had deleted it.

EKEventViewController

EKEventViewController displays an event in the manner familiar from the Calendar app, listing the event's title, date and time, calendar, alert, and notes. To use EKEventViewController, instantiate it, give it an event from the database, assign it a delegate (EKEventViewDelegate), and *push* it onto an existing navigation controller:

```
let ev = self.database.calendarItem(withIdentifier:self.napid) as! EKEvent
let evc = EKEventViewController()
evc.event = ev
evc.delegate = self
self.navigationController?.pushViewController(evc, animated: true)
```

 Do *not* use EKEventViewController for an event that isn't in the database, or at a time when the database isn't open! It won't function correctly if you do.

If `allowsEditing` is `true`, an Edit button appears in the navigation bar, and by tapping this, the user can edit the various aspects of an event in an interface just like the Calendar app, including the Delete button at the bottom. If the user ultimately deletes the event, or edits it and taps Done, the change is saved into the database.

If the user deletes the event, you will be notified in the delegate method, `eventViewController(_:didCompleteWith:)`. The second parameter is an EKEventViewAction, which will be `.deleted`; it is then up to you to pop the navigation controller:

```
func eventViewController(_ controller: EKEventViewController,
    didCompleteWith action: EKEventViewAction) {
        if action == .deleted {
            self.navigationController?.popViewController(animated:true)
        }
}
```

 Even if `allowsEditing` is `false` (the default), the user can change what calendar this event belongs to, can change the event's alert firing time, and can delete the event. I regard this as a bug.

EKEventEditViewController

EKEventEditViewController (a UINavigationController) presents the interface for editing an event. To use it, set its `eventStore` and `editViewDelegate` (EKEventEdit-ViewDelegate, *not* `delegate`), and optionally its `event`, and *present* it as a presented view controller (which looks best on the iPad as a popover). The event can be `nil` for a completely empty new event; it can be an event you've just created (and possibly partially configured) and not stored in the database; or it can be an existing event from the database.

The delegate method `eventEditViewControllerDefaultCalendar(forNewEvents:)` may be implemented to specify what calendar a completely new event should be assigned to. If you're partially constructing a new event, you can assign it a calendar then, and of course an event from the database already has a calendar.

You must implement the delegate method `eventEditViewController(_:did-CompleteWith:)` so that you can dismiss the presented view controller. The second parameter is an EKEventEditViewAction telling you what the user did; possible actions are that the user cancelled (`.canceled`), saved the edited event into the database (`.saved`), or deleted an already existing event from the database (`.deleted`). You can get a reference to the edited event as the view controller's `event`.

EKCalendarChooser

EKCalendarChooser displays a list of calendars, choosable by tapping; a chosen calendar displays a checkmark. To use it, instantiate it with its initializer:

- `init(selectionStyle:displayStyle:entityType:eventStore:)`

The `selectionStyle` dictates whether the user can pick one or multiple calendars; the `displayStyle` states whether all calendars or only writable calendars will be displayed. Now set a `delegate` (adopting the EKCalendarChooserDelegate protocol) and do a little dance: make the EKCalendarChooser the root view controller of a UINavigationController and *present the navigation controller* as a presented view controller (which looks best as a popover on the iPad). Two properties, `showsCancel-Button` and `showsDoneButton`, determine whether these buttons will appear in the navigation bar. You can perform additional customizations through the view controller's `navigationItem`.

There are three delegate methods, the first two being required:

- `calendarChooserDidFinish(_:)` (the user tapped Done)
- `calendarChooserDidCancel(_:)`
- `calendarChooserSelectionDidChange(_:)`

In the `finish` and `cancel` methods, you should dismiss the presented view controller.

In this example, we offer to delete the selected calendar. Because this is potentially destructive, we pass through an action sheet for confirmation:

```
@IBAction func deleteCalendar (_ sender: Any) {
    let choo = EKCalendarChooser(
        selectionStyle:.single, displayStyle:.allCalendars,
        entityType:.event, eventStore:self.database)
    choo.showsDoneButton = true
    choo.showsCancelButton = true
    choo.delegate = self
    choo.navigationItem.prompt = "Pick a calendar to delete:"
    let nav = UINavigationController(rootViewController: choo)
    self.present(nav, animated: true)
}
func calendarChooserDidCancel(_ choo: EKCalendarChooser) {
    self.dismiss(animated:true)
}
func calendarChooserDidFinish(_ choo: EKCalendarChooser) {
    let cals = choo.selectedCalendars
    guard cals.count > 0 else { self.dismiss(animated:true); return }
    let calsToDelete = cals.map {$0.calendarIdentifier}
    let alert = UIAlertController(title:"Delete selected calendar?",
        message:nil, preferredStyle:.actionSheet)
    alert.addAction(UIAlertAction(title:"Cancel", style:.cancel))
    alert.addAction(UIAlertAction(title:"Delete", style:.destructive) {_ in
        for id in calsToDelete {
            if let cal = self.database.calendar(withIdentifier:id) {
                try? self.database.removeCalendar(cal, commit: true)
            }
        }
        self.dismiss(animated:true) // dismiss *everything*
    })
    choo.present(alert, animated: true)
}
```

CHAPTER 20

Maps

Your app can imitate the Maps app, displaying a map interface and placing annotations and overlays on the map. The relevant classes are provided by the Map Kit framework. You'll need to `import MapKit`. The types that describe locations in terms of latitude and longitude, whose names start with "CL," come from the Core Location framework, but you won't need to import it explicitly if you're already importing the Map Kit framework.

Map Views

A map is displayed through a UIView subclass, an MKMapView. You can instantiate an MKMapView in code like any other view. Alternatively, in the nib editor, the Objects library contains an MKMapView object that you can drag into your interface as you design it; you might need to link to the MapKit framework manually (in the app target's Link Binary With Libraries build phase) to prevent the app from crashing as the nib loads.

A map has a `type`, which is usually one of the following (MKMapType):

- `.standard`
- `.satellite`
- `.hybrid`

(A further MKMapType, `.mutedStandard`, dims the map elements so that your additions to the map view stand out.)

Figure 20-1. A map view

Displaying a Region

The area displayed on the map is its `region`, an MKCoordinateRegion. This is a struct comprising two things:

`center`
> A CLLocationCoordinate2D. The latitude and longitude of the point at the center of the region.

`span`
> An MKCoordinateSpan. The quantity of latitude and longitude embraced by the region (and hence the scale of the map).

In this example, I'll initialize the display of an MKMapView (`self.map`) to show a place where I like to go dirt biking (Figure 20-1):

```
let loc = CLLocationCoordinate2DMake(34.927752,-120.217608)
let span = MKCoordinateSpan(latitudeDelta: 0.015, longitudeDelta: 0.015)
let reg = MKCoordinateRegion(center:loc, span:span)
self.map.region = reg
```

An MKCoordinateSpan is described in degrees of latitude and longitude. It may be, however, that what you know is the region's proposed dimensions in meters. To convert, call this MKCoordinateRegion initializer:

- `init(center:latitudinalMeters:longitudinalMeters:)`

The ability to perform this conversion is important, because an MKMapView shows the world through a Mercator projection, where longitude lines are parallel and equidistant, and scale increases at higher latitudes. I happen to know that the area I want to display is about 1200 meters on a side, so this is another way of displaying roughly the same region:

```
let loc = CLLocationCoordinate2DMake(34.927752,-120.217608)
let reg = MKCoordinateRegion(
    center:loc, latitudinalMeters:1200, longitudinalMeters:1200)
self.map.region = reg
```

Another way of describing a map region is with an MKMapRect, a struct built up
from MKMapPoint and MKMapSize. The earth has already been projected onto the
map for us, and now we are describing a rectangle of that map, in terms of the units
in which the map is drawn. The exact relationship between an MKMapPoint and the
corresponding location coordinate is arbitrary and of no interest; what matters is that
you can ask for the conversion, along with the ratio of points to meters (which will
vary with latitude):

- MKMapPoint(_:) (coerces from CLLocationCoordinate2D)

- coordinate (coerces to CLLocationCoordinate2D)

- distance(to:) (meters between map points)

- MKMetersPerMapPointAtLatitude(_:)

- MKMapPointsPerMeterAtLatitude(_:)

To determine what the map view is showing in MKMapRect terms, use its visible-
MapRect property. So this is yet another way of displaying approximately the same
region:

```
let loc = CLLocationCoordinate2DMake(34.927752,-120.217608)
let pt = MKMapPoint(loc)
let w = MKMapPointsPerMeterAtLatitude(loc.latitude) * 1200
self.map.visibleMapRect =
    MKMapRect(x:pt.x - w/2.0, y:pt.y - w/2.0, width:w, height:w)
```

In none of those examples did I bother with the question of the actual dimensions of
the map view itself. I simply threw a proposed region at the map view, and it decided
how best to portray the corresponding area. Values you assign to the map view's
region and visibleMapRect are unlikely to be the exact values it adopts, because the
map view will optimize for display without distorting the map's scale. You can perform this same optimization in code by calling these methods:

- regionThatFits(_:)

- mapRectThatFits(_:)

- mapRectThatFits(_:edgePadding:)

Scrolling and Zooming

By default, the user can zoom and scroll the map with the usual gestures; you can
turn this off by setting the map view's isZoomEnabled and isScrollEnabled to

false. Usually you will set them both to `true` or both to `false`. New in iOS 13, you can limit how far the user can zoom and scroll, using these properties:

cameraZoomRange

> An MKMapView.CameraZoomRange. How far the "camera" (the eye through which the map view is looking at the earth) is permitted to be from the center of the region displayed. The initializer takes a maximum distance, a minimum distance, or both (in meters).

cameraBoundary

> An MKMapView.CameraBoundary. The maximum region of the earth that the map view can display; the map view cannot be scrolled so as to reveal anything outside this region. Can be expressed as an MKCoordinateRegion or as an MKMapRect, just like the visible region of the map view.

Here, I'll modify my map view to restrict how far the user can zoom and scroll from the initial display:

```
self.map.cameraBoundary = MKMapView.CameraBoundary(
    coordinateRegion: MKCoordinateRegion(
        center: loc, span: MKCoordinateSpan(
            latitudeDelta: 0.6, longitudeDelta: 0.6)))
self.map.cameraZoomRange = MKMapView.CameraZoomRange(
    maxCenterCoordinateDistance: 130_000)
```

You can change programmatically the region displayed, optionally with animation, by calling these methods:

- `setRegion(_:animated:)`
- `setCenter(_:animated:)`
- `setVisibleMapRect(_:animated:)`
- `setVisibleMapRect(_:edgePadding:animated:)`

Even programmatically, you cannot violate the limits set by the map view's `camera-ZoomRange` and `cameraBoundary`.

The map view's delegate (MKMapViewDelegate) is notified as the map loads and as the region changes (including changes triggered programmatically):

- `mapViewWillStartLoadingMap(_:)`
- `mapViewDidFinishLoadingMap(_:)`
- `mapViewDidFailLoadingMap(_:withError:)`
- `mapViewDidChangeVisibleRegion(_:)`
- `mapView(_:regionWillChangeAnimated:)`
- `mapView(_:regionDidChangeAnimated:)`

Other Map View Customizations

An MKMapView has Bool properties such as `showsCompass`, `showsScale`, and `shows-Traffic`; set these to dictate whether those elements of the map should be displayed. Starting in iOS 11, the compass and the scale legend can be displayed as independent views, an MKCompassButton and an MKScaleView; if you use these, you'll probably want to set the corresponding Bool property to `false` so as not to get two compasses or scales. Both views are initialized with the map view as parameter, so that their display will reflect the rotation and zoom of the map. The MKCompassButton, like the internal compass, is a button; if the user taps it, the map is reoriented with north at the top. The visibility of these views is governed by properties (`compassVisibility` and `scaleVisibility`) whose value is one of these (MKFeatureVisibility):

- `.hidden`
- `.visible`
- `.adaptive`

The `.adaptive` behavior (the default) is that the compass is visible only if the map is rotated, and the scale legend is visible only if the map is zoomed.

New in iOS 13, you can dictate what sorts of POI (point of interest) are displayed on the map. In iOS 12 and before, your only choices were to show or suppress points of interest as a whole (`showsPointsOfInterest`). In iOS 13, the MKPointOfInterest-Category class consists of static properties (representing strings) that draw fine-grained distinctions, such as `.bakery` and `.brewery`. Use these to initialize an MKPointOfInterestFilter with `init(excluding:)` or `init(including:)`, and assign the filter to the map view's `pointOfInterestFilter`.

You can also enable 3D viewing of the map (`pitchEnabled`), and there's a large and powerful API putting control of 3D viewing in your hands. Discussion of 3D map viewing is beyond the scope of this chapter; an excellent WWDC 2013 video surveys the topic. Starting in iOS 9, there are 3D flyover map types `.satelliteFlyover` and `.hybridFlyover`; a WWDC 2015 video explains about these.

Map Images

To capture a map display as an image, use an MKMapSnapshotter. This is useful when you want to display a mere picture of a map (that is, a noninteractive map). The result is an MKMapSnapshotter.Snapshot whose `image` is the screenshot. The screenshot captures a runtime-generated map, not *your* map view; therefore, your map view's annotations and overlays are not included. Use the snapshotter's options (MKMapSnapshotter.Options) to configure the region displayed:

```
let opts = MKMapSnapshotter.Options()
opts.region = self.map.region
let snap = MKMapSnapshotter(options: opts)
snap.start { shot, err in
    if let shot = shot {
        let im = shot.image
        // ...
    }
}
```

New in iOS 13, you can configure the types of POI shown in the snapshot by setting the options object's `pointOfInterestFilter`.

In iOS 13, a map view will switch to dark mode automatically. An MKMapSnapshotter will portray a light mode map or a dark mode map, according to the `trait-Collection` you assign to its `options`; but the resulting image does not magically change just because the user changes modes, so arranging to change images when the mode changes is up to you.

Annotations

An *annotation* is a marker associated with a location on a map. To make an annotation appear on a map, two objects are needed:

The object attached to the MKMapView
> The annotation itself is attached to the MKMapView. It is an instance of any class that adopts the MKAnnotation protocol, which specifies a `coordinate`, a `title`, and a `subtitle` for the annotation. You might have reason to define your own class to handle this task, or you can use the simple built-in MKPoint-Annotation class. The annotation's coordinate is crucial; it says where on earth the annotation should be drawn. The title and subtitle are optional.

The object that draws the annotation
> An annotation is drawn by an MKAnnotationView, a UIView subclass. This can be extremely simple. In fact, even a `nil` MKAnnotationView might be perfectly satisfactory, because the runtime will then automatically supply a view for you. In iOS 10 and before, this automatic view was a realistic rendering of a physical pin, red by default but configurable to any color, supplied by the built-in MKPin-AnnotationView class. Starting in iOS 11, it is an MKMarkerAnnotationView, by default portraying a pin schematically in a circular red "balloon."

Not only does an annotation require two distinct objects, but in fact those two objects do not initially exist together. An annotation object has no pointer to the annotation view object that will draw it. Rather, it is up to you to supply the annotation view object in real time, on demand. This architecture may sound confusing, but in fact it's a clever way of reducing the amount of resources needed at any given moment.

Figure 20-2. A simple annotation

An annotation itself is merely a lightweight object that a map can always possess; the corresponding annotation view is a heavyweight object that is needed only so long as that annotation's coordinates are within the visible portion of the map.

Let's add the simplest possible annotation to our map. The point where the annotation is to go has been stored in an instance property (`self.annloc`):

```
let annloc = CLLocationCoordinate2DMake(34.923964,-120.219558)
```

We create the annotation, configure it, and add it to the MKMapView:

```
let ann = MKPointAnnotation()
ann.coordinate = self.annloc
ann.title = "Park here"
ann.subtitle = "Fun awaits down the road!"
self.map.addAnnotation(ann)
```

That code is sufficient to produce Figure 20-2. I didn't take any steps to supply an MKAnnotationView, so the MKAnnotationView is `nil`. But a `nil` MKAnnotationView, as I've already said, means an MKMarkerAnnotationView that produces a drawing of a pin in a red balloon.

By default, an MKMarkerAnnotationView displays its `title` below the annotation. This differs markedly from an MKPinAnnotationView, whose `title` and `subtitle` are displayed in a separate *callout* view that appears above the annotation view only when the annotation is *selected* (because the user taps it, or because you set the MKAnnotationView's `isSelected` to `true`). A selected MKMarkerAnnotationView is drawn larger and displays the `subtitle` in addition to the `title`.

Customizing an MKMarkerAnnotationView

MKMarkerAnnotationView has many customizable properties affecting its display:

`markerTintColor`
    The balloon color.

glyphTintColor
> The color used to tint the glyph portrayed inside the balloon. Has no effect on the default pin image.

glyphText
> One or two characters, portrayed as the image in the middle of the balloon.

glyphImage
> Replaces the glyphText; a 40×40 image, which will be sized down automatically to 20×20 when the view is not selected. Alternatively, supply both a larger and a smaller image, the selectedGlyphImage and glyphImage respectively. An iOS 13 symbol image works fine here as well. The image is treated as a template image; setting the rendering mode to .alwaysOriginal has no effect.

titleVisibility
subtitleVisibility
> The visibility of the title and subtitle. These are MKFeatureVisibility enums, where .adaptive is the default behavior that I've already described. The subtitleVisibility has no effect unless you also set the titleVisibility.

Doubtless you are now thinking: that's all very well, but *what* MKMarkerAnnotation-View are we talking about? No such view appears in our code, so there is no object whose properties we can set!

One way to access the annotation view is to give the map view a delegate and implement the MKMapViewDelegate method mapView(_:viewFor:). The second parameter is the MKAnnotation for which we are to supply a view. In our implementation of this method, we can *dequeue* an annotation view from the map view, passing in a string reuse identifier:

dequeueReusableAnnotationView(withIdentifier:for:)
> In the minimal case, pass as the identifier: the constant MKMapViewDefault-AnnotationViewReuseIdentifier. The second argument should be the annotation that arrived as the second parameter of the delegate method.

If we have taken no steps to the contrary, this will give us the default view, which in this case is an MKMarkerAnnotationView. Having obtained an annotation view, our mapView(_:viewFor:) can configure it; ultimately, it will return the annotation view.

The notion of view reuse here is similar to the reuse of table view cells (Chapter 8). The map may have a huge number of annotations, but it needs to display annotation views only for the annotations within its current region. So annotation views that have been scrolled out of view can be reused, and are held for us by the map view in a cache for exactly this purpose.

Figure 20-3. Customizing a marker annotation view

In this example, I check to see that my MKAnnotationView is indeed an MKMarker-AnnotationView, as expected. I also attempt to distinguish this particular annotation by looking at its title; that's not a very good way to distinguish annotation types, but I'll postpone further discussion of the matter until later:

```
func mapView(_ mapView: MKMapView,
    viewFor annotation: MKAnnotation) -> MKAnnotationView? {
        let id = MKMapViewDefaultAnnotationViewReuseIdentifier
        if let v = mapView.dequeueReusableAnnotationView(
            withIdentifier: id, for: annotation) as? MKMarkerAnnotationView {
                if let t = annotation.title, t == "Park here" {
                    v.titleVisibility = .visible
                    v.subtitleVisibility = .visible
                    v.markerTintColor = .green
                    v.glyphText = "!"
                    v.glyphTintColor = .black
                    return v
                }
        }
        return nil
}
```

The result is shown in Figure 20-3.

Changing the Annotation View Class

Instead of accepting the default MKMarkerAnnotationView as the class of our annotation view, we can substitute a different MKAnnotationView subclass. This might be our own MKMarkerAnnotationView subclass, or some other MKAnnotationView subclass, or MKAnnotationView itself. The way to do that is to *register* our class with the map view, associating it with the reuse identifier, by calling this method beforehand:

- `register(_:forAnnotationViewWithReuseIdentifier:)`

To illustrate, I'll use MKAnnotationView itself as our annotation view class. We won't get the default drawing of a balloon and a pin, because we're not using MKMarkerAnnotationView any longer; instead, I'll set the MKAnnotationView's

Figure 20-4. A custom annotation image

image property directly. We also won't get the title and subtitle drawn beneath the image; instead, I'll set the annotation view's canShowCallout to true, and the title and subtitle will appear in the callout when the annotation view is selected.

So, assume that I have an identifier declared as an instance property:

```
let bikeid = "bike"
```

And assume that I've registered MKAnnotationView as the class that goes with that identifier:

```
self.map.register(MKAnnotationView.self,
    forAnnotationViewWithReuseIdentifier: self.bikeid)
```

Then my implementation of mapView(_:viewFor:) might look like this:

```
func mapView(_ mapView: MKMapView,
    viewFor annotation: MKAnnotation) -> MKAnnotationView? {
        let v = mapView.dequeueReusableAnnotationView(
            withIdentifier: self.bikeid, for: annotation)
        if let t = annotation.title, t == "Park here" {
            v.image = UIImage(named:"clipartdirtbike.gif")
            v.bounds.size.height /= 3.0
            v.bounds.size.width /= 3.0
            v.centerOffset = CGPoint(0,-20)
            v.canShowCallout = true
            return v
        }
        return nil
}
```

The dirt bike image is too large, so I shrink the view's bounds before returning it; I also move the view up a bit, so that the bottom of the image is at the coordinates on the map. The result is shown in Figure 20-4.

Custom Annotation View Class

A better way to write the preceding example might be for us to create our own MKAnnotationView subclass and endow it with the ability to draw itself. This will allow us to move the code that configures the image and the callout out of the delegate method and into the subclass itself, where it more properly belongs.

A minimal implementation of an MKAnnotationView subclass should override the `annotation` property with a setter observer, so that every time the view is reused and a new `annotation` value is assigned, the view is reconfigured. It might also override the designated initializer, `init(annotation:reuseIdentifier:)`, and possibly declare some additional instance variables; but for purposes of this example, I'll simply move what I was previously doing in the delegate method directly into my `annotation` setter observer:

```
class MyBikeAnnotationView : MKAnnotationView {
    override var annotation: MKAnnotation? {
        willSet {
            self.image = UIImage(named:"clipartdirtbike.gif")
            let scale = UIScreen.main.scale
            self.bounds.size.height /= 3.0 / scale
            self.bounds.size.width /= 3.0 / scale
            self.centerOffset = CGPoint(0,-20)
            self.canShowCallout = true
        }
    }
}
```

We register our custom annotation view class to associate it with our identifier:

```
self.map.register(MyBikeAnnotationView.self,
    forAnnotationViewWithReuseIdentifier: self.bikeid)
```

Our implementation of `mapView(_:viewFor:)` now has much less work to do:

```
func mapView(_ mapView: MKMapView,
    viewFor annotation: MKAnnotation) -> MKAnnotationView? {
        let v = mapView.dequeueReusableAnnotationView(
            withIdentifier: self.bikeid, for: annotation)
        if let t = annotation.title, t == "Park here" {
            // nothing else to do!
            return v
        }
        return nil
}
```

If, in fact, MyBikeAnnotationView is the *only* annotation view type we will ever use, we can go even further: we can register MyBikeAnnotationView *as the default*:

```
self.map.register(MyBikeAnnotationView.self,
    forAnnotationViewWithReuseIdentifier:
        MKMapViewDefaultAnnotationViewReuseIdentifier)
```

At that point, we can delete our implementation of `mapView(_:viewFor:)` entirely! It has no work to do, because it has no choices to make; our MKBikeAnnotationView, which configures itself, will be the annotation view class *automatically*.

Custom Annotation Class

Let's suppose precisely the opposite of what I just said — namely, that our implementation of `mapView(_:viewFor:)` *does* have choices to make. Depending on the nature of the annotation, it must configure our annotation view class differently, or even pick a different annotation view class. Some annotations might show a dirt bike, but other annotations might show a different image.

This difference will need to be expressed somehow as part of *the annotation itself.* Different annotation types must therefore be somehow distinguishable from one another. So far, I've been avoiding that issue entirely by having my `mapView(_:viewFor:)` implementation examine the incoming annotation's `title`; but that is obviously a fragile and inappropriate solution. The proper way is to use one or more *custom annotation classes* that allow the desired distinction to be drawn.

A minimal custom annotation class will look like this:

```
class MyBikeAnnotation : NSObject, MKAnnotation {
    dynamic var coordinate : CLLocationCoordinate2D
    var title: String?
    var subtitle: String?
    init(location coord:CLLocationCoordinate2D) {
        self.coordinate = coord
        super.init()
    }
}
```

When we create our annotation and add it to the map, our code looks like this:

```
let ann = MyBikeAnnotation(location:self.annloc)
ann.title = "Park here"
ann.subtitle = "Fun awaits down the road!"
self.map.addAnnotation(ann)
```

In `mapView(_:viewFor:)`, we can decide what to do just by looking at the class of the incoming annotation:

```
if annotation is MyBikeAnnotation {
    let v = mapView.dequeueReusableAnnotationView(
        withIdentifier: self.bikeid, for: annotation)
    // ...
    return v
}
return nil
```

You can readily see how this architecture gives our implementation room to grow. At the moment, every MyBikeAnnotation is drawn the same way, but we could now add another property to MyBikeAnnotation that tells us what drawing to use. We could also give MyBikeAnnotation further properties saying such things as which way the bike should face, what angle it should be drawn at, and so on. Each MyBikeAnnotationView instance will end up with a reference to a MyBikeAnnotation instance (as its `annotation` property), so it will be able to read those properties and configure the drawing of its own image appropriately.

Annotation View Hiding and Clustering

Annotation views don't change size as the map is zoomed in and out, so if there are several annotations and they are brought close together by the user zooming out, the display can become crowded. Moreover, if too many annotation views are being drawn simultaneously in a map view, scroll and zoom performance can degrade.

Before iOS 11, the only way to prevent this was to respond to changes in the map's visible region — typically in the delegate method `mapView(_:regionDidChange-Animated:)` — by removing and adding annotations dynamically. MKMapView has extensive support for adding and removing annotations, and its `annotations(in:)` method efficiently lists the annotations within a given MKMapRect. Also, given a bunch of annotations, you can ask your MKMapView to zoom in such a way that all of them are showing (`showAnnotations(_:animated:)`). Nevertheless, deciding which annotations to eliminate or restore, and when, was left up to you, and was decidedly a tricky problem.

Starting in iOS 11, annotation views can *automatically* show and hide themselves as the display becomes crowded. And the built-in solution goes even further: if annotations are hidden, they can be replaced by a special *cluster annotation* so that the user *knows* there are hidden annotations. MKAnnotationView has properties that allow you to customize what happens:

displayPriority
:   An MKFeatureDisplayPriority struct, which works rather like a layout constraint priority: a value of `.required`, corresponding to `1000`, means that the view shouldn't be hidden, and values `defaultHigh` and `defaultLow`, corresponding to `750` and `250`, give some alternative priorities, but you can set any value you like through the struct's `init(rawValue:)` initializer. If all your annotation views have a `displayPriority` of `.required` (the default), your map view will not participate at all in automatic annotation view hiding.

clusteringIdentifier
:   A string. The idea is that birds of a feather should flock together: if two annotation views have the same clustering identifier, then the same cluster annotation

can be used to represent them when they are hidden. This will in fact happen only if the runtime judges that they are sufficiently close to one another when they are hidden. If you don't set an annotation view's `clusteringIdentifier`, it won't participate in clustering. Giving all annotation views the same `clusteringIdentifier` gives the runtime permission to cluster them however it sees fit.

collisionMode

An MKAnnotationView.CollisionMode. Two annotation views with the same `clusteringIdentifier` will be replaced by a cluster annotation if the map is zoomed out so far that they collide. But what constitutes a collision between two annotation views? To know that, we need a collision edge. It might be:

.rectangle

The edge is the view's frame.

.circle

The edge is the largest circle inscribable in and centered within the view's frame.

If you need to offset or resize the boundary of the rectangle or circle that describes the collision edge, use the annotation view's `alignmentRectInsets`.

To make your annotation views opt in to both hiding and clustering, a minimal approach would be to set the `displayPriority` of all your annotation views to `.defaultHigh` and the `clusteringIdentifier` of all your annotation views to some single string.

A cluster annotation is a real annotation — an MKClusterAnnotation. Its `member-Annotations` are the annotations whose views have been hidden and subsumed into this cluster. It has a `title` and `subtitle`; by default, these are based on the `memberAnnotations`, but you can customize them.

A cluster annotation's view is a real annotation view. It has, itself, a `displayPriority` and a `collisionMode`. (The `displayPriority` is, by default, the highest `displayPriority` among the annotation views it replaces.) If an annotation view has been hidden and replaced by a cluster annotation view, its `cluster` property points to the cluster annotation view. The default cluster annotation view corresponds to a reuse identifier `MKMapViewDefaultClusterAnnotationViewReuseIdentifier`.

You can customize a cluster annotation view as you would any other annotation view. You can substitute your own MKAnnotationView subclass by registering or dequeuing it, exactly as in the earlier examples. Your `mapView(_:viewFor:)` will know that this annotation is a cluster annotation because it will be an MKCluster-Annotation. Or you can register your custom cluster annotation view as the class for

`MKMapViewDefaultClusterAnnotationViewReuseIdentifier`, in which case you might not need an implementation of `mapView(_:viewFor:)` at all.

Other Annotation Features

When an MKPinAnnotationView initially appears on the map, if its `animatesDrop` property is `true`, it drops into place from above. When an MKMarkerAnnotationView initially appears on the map, if its `animatesWhenAdded` property is `true`, it grows slightly into place.

In like fashion, we can add our own animation to an annotation view as it initially appears on the map. To do so, we implement the map view delegate method `mapView(_:didAdd:)`, which hands us an array of MKAnnotationViews. When this method is called, the annotation views have been added but the redraw moment has not yet arrived (Chapter 4); so if we animate a view, that animation will be performed as the view appears onscreen. Here, I'll animate the opacity of our annotation view so that it fades in, while growing the view from a point to its full size; I identify the view type through its `reuseIdentifier`:

```
func mapView(_ mapView: MKMapView, didAdd views: [MKAnnotationView]) {
    for aView in views {
        if aView.reuseIdentifier == self.bikeid {
            aView.transform = CGAffineTransform(scaleX: 0, y: 0)
            aView.alpha = 0
            UIView.animate(withDuration:0.8) {
                aView.alpha = 1
                aView.transform = .identity
            }
        }
    }
}
```

Certain annotation properties and annotation view properties are automatically animatable through view animation, provided you've implemented them in a KVO compliant way. In MyBikeAnnotation, the `coordinate` property *is* KVO compliant (because we declared it `dynamic`); therefore, we are able to animate shifting the annotation's position:

```
self.map.addAnnotation(ann)
// ...
UIView.animate(withDuration:0.25) {
    var loc = ann.coordinate
    loc.latitude = loc.latitude + 0.0005
    loc.longitude = loc.longitude + 0.001
    ann.coordinate = loc
}
```

MKMapView has methods allowing annotations to be selected or deselected programmatically, doing in code the same thing that happens when the user taps. The delegate has methods notifying you when the user selects or deselects an annotation, and you are free to override your custom MKAnnotationView's set-Selected(_:animated:) if you want to change what happens when the user taps an annotation. You could show and hide a custom view instead of, or in addition to, the built-in callout.

A callout can contain left and right accessory views; these are the MKAnnotation-View's leftCalloutAccessoryView and rightCalloutAccessoryView. They are UIViews, and should be small (less than 32 pixels in height). There is also a detail-CalloutAccessoryView which replaces the subtitle; you could supply a multiline label with smaller text. You can respond to taps on these views as you would any view or control. The map view's tintColor (see Chapter 12) affects such accessory view elements as template images and button titles.

An MKAnnotationView can optionally be draggable by the user; set its draggable property to true. If you're using a custom annotation class, its coordinate property must also be settable. In our custom annotation class, MyBikeAnnotation, the coordinate property *is* settable; it is explicitly declared as a read-write property (var), as opposed to the coordinate property in the MKAnnotation protocol which is read-only. You can also customize changes to the appearance of the view as it is dragged, by implementing your annotation view class's setDragState(_:animated:) method.

Overlays

An *overlay* differs from an annotation in being drawn entirely with respect to points on the surface of the earth. Whereas an annotation's size is always the same, an overlay's size is tied to the zoom of the map view.

Overlays are implemented much like annotations. You provide an object that adopts the MKOverlay protocol (which itself conforms to the MKAnnotation protocol) and add it to the map view. When the map view delegate method mapView(_:renderer-For:) is called, you provide an MKOverlayRenderer and hand it the overlay object; the overlay renderer then draws the overlay on demand. As with annotations, this architecture means that the overlay itself is a lightweight object, and the overlay is drawn only if the part of the earth that the overlay covers is actually being displayed in the map view. An MKOverlayRenderer has no reuse identifier; it isn't a view, but rather a drawing engine that draws into a graphics context supplied by the map view.

Some built-in MKShape subclasses adopt the MKOverlay protocol: MKCircle, MKPolygon, and MKPolyline (and its subclass MKGeodesicPolyline). In parallel to those, MKOverlayRenderer has built-in subclasses MKCircleRenderer, MKPolygon-Renderer, and MKPolylineRenderer, ready to draw the corresponding shapes. New in iOS 13, multiple polygons or polylines can be combined into an MKMultiPolygon or

Figure 20-5. An overlay

MKMultiPolyline and drawn by an MKMultiPolygonRenderer or MKMultiPolyline-Renderer; this can be useful because renderers, even though they are not views, do involve overhead, so one would like as few separate overlays as possible on the screen simultaneously.

As with annotations, you can base your overlay entirely on the power of existing classes. In this example, I'll use MKPolygonRenderer to draw an overlay triangle pointing up the road from the parking place annotated in our earlier examples (Figure 20-5). We add the MKPolygon as an overlay to our map view, and supply its corresponding MKPolygonRenderer in our implementation of `mapView(_:renderer-For:)`. First, the MKPolygon overlay:

```
let lat = self.annloc.latitude
let metersPerPoint = MKMetersPerMapPointAtLatitude(lat)
var c = MKMapPoint(self.annloc)
c.x += 150/metersPerPoint
c.y -= 50/metersPerPoint
var p1 = MKMapPoint(x:c.x, y:c.y)
p1.y -= 100/metersPerPoint
var p2 = MKMapPoint(x:c.x, y:c.y)
p2.x += 100/metersPerPoint
var p3 = MKMapPoint(x:c.x, y:c.y)
p3.x += 300/metersPerPoint
p3.y -= 400/metersPerPoint
var points = [p1, p2, p3]
let tri = MKPolygon(points:&points, count:3)
self.map.addOverlay(tri)
```

Second, the delegate method, where we provide the MKPolygonRenderer:

```
func mapView(_ mapView: MKMapView,
    rendererFor overlay: MKOverlay) -> MKOverlayRenderer {
        if let overlay = overlay as? MKPolygon {
            let r = MKPolygonRenderer(polygon:overlay)
            r.fillColor = UIColor.red.withAlphaComponent(0.1)
            r.strokeColor = UIColor.red.withAlphaComponent(0.8)
```

```
                r.lineWidth = 2
                return r
        }
        return MKOverlayRenderer()
    }
```

Custom Overlay Class

The triangle in Figure 20-5 is rather crude; I could draw a better arrow shape using a CGPath (Chapter 2). The built-in MKOverlayRenderer subclass that lets me do that is MKOverlayPathRenderer. To structure things similarly to the preceding example, I'd like to supply the CGPath when I add the overlay instance to the map view. No built-in class lets me do that, so I'll use a custom class, MyPathOverlay, that adopts the MKOverlay protocol.

A minimal overlay class looks like this:

```
class MyPathOverlay : NSObject, MKOverlay {
    var coordinate : CLLocationCoordinate2D {
        get {
            let pt = MKMapPoint(
                x:self.boundingMapRect.midX,
                y:self.boundingMapRect.midY)
            return pt.coordinate
        }
    }
    var boundingMapRect : MKMapRect
    init(rect:MKMapRect) {
        self.boundingMapRect = rect
        super.init()
    }
}
```

Our actual MyPathOverlay class will also have a path property; this will be a UIBezierPath that holds our CGPath and supplies it to the MKOverlayPathRenderer.

Just as the coordinate property of an annotation tells the map view where on earth the annotation is to be drawn, the boundingMapRect property of an overlay tells the map view where on earth the overlay is to be drawn. Whenever any part of the boundingMapRect is displayed within the map view's bounds, the map view will have to concern itself with drawing the overlay. With MKPolygon, we supplied the points of the polygon in earth coordinates and the boundingMapRect was calculated for us. With our custom overlay class, we must supply or calculate it ourselves.

At first it may appear that there is a typological impedance mismatch: the bounding-MapRect is an MKMapRect, whereas a CGPath is defined by CGPoints. However, it turns out that these units are interchangeable: the CGPoints of our CGPath will be translated for us directly into MKMapPoints on the same scale — that is, the *distance* between any two CGPoints will be the distance between the two corresponding

MKMapPoints. However, the *origins* are different: the CGPath must be described relative to the top-left corner of the boundingMapRect. To put it another way, the boundingMapRect is described in earth coordinates, but the top-left corner of the boundingMapRect is .zero as far as the CGPath is concerned. (You might think of this difference as analogous to the difference between a UIView's frame and its bounds.)

To make life simple, I'll think in meters; actually, I'll think in chunks of 75 meters, because this turns out to be a good unit for positioning and laying out this particular arrow. A line one unit long would in fact be 75 meters long if I were to arrive at this actual spot on the earth and discover the overlay literally drawn on the ground. Having derived this chunk (unit), I use it to lay out the boundingMapRect, four units on a side and positioned slightly east and north of the annotation point (because that's where the road is). Then I simply construct the arrow shape within the 4×4-unit square, rotating it so that it points in roughly the same direction as the road:

```
// start with our position and derive a nice unit for drawing
let lat = self.annloc.latitude
let metersPerPoint = MKMetersPerMapPointAtLatitude(lat)
let c = MKMapPoint(self.annloc)
let unit = CGFloat(75.0/metersPerPoint)
// size and position the overlay bounds on the earth
let sz = CGSize(4*unit, 4*unit)
let mr = MKMapRect(
    x:c.x + 2*Double(unit), y:c.y - 4.5*Double(unit),
    width:Double(sz.width), height:Double(sz.height))
// describe the arrow as a CGPath
let p = CGMutablePath()
let start = CGPoint(0, unit*1.5)
let p1 = CGPoint(start.x+2*unit, start.y)
let p2 = CGPoint(p1.x, p1.y-unit)
let p3 = CGPoint(p2.x+unit*2, p2.y+unit*1.5)
let p4 = CGPoint(p2.x, p2.y+unit*3)
let p5 = CGPoint(p4.x, p4.y-unit)
let p6 = CGPoint(p5.x-2*unit, p5.y)
let points = [start, p1, p2, p3, p4, p5, p6]
// rotate the arrow around its center
let t1 = CGAffineTransform(translationX: unit*2, y: unit*2)
let t2 = t1.rotated(by:-.pi/3.5)
let t3 = t2.translatedBy(x: -unit*2, y: -unit*2)
p.addLines(between: points, transform: t3)
p.closeSubpath()
// create the overlay and give it the path
let over = MyPathOverlay(rect:mr)
over.path = UIBezierPath(cgPath:p)
// add the overlay to the map
self.map.addOverlay(over)
```

The delegate method, where we provide the MKOverlayPathRenderer, is simple. We pull the CGPath out of the MyPathOverlay instance; we hand the CGPath to the

Figure 20-6. A nicer overlay

MKOverlayPathRenderer; and we tell the MKOverlayPathRenderer how to stroke and fill that path:

```
func mapView(_ mapView: MKMapView,
    rendererFor overlay: MKOverlay) -> MKOverlayRenderer {
        if let overlay = overlay as? MyPathOverlay {
            let r = MKOverlayPathRenderer(overlay:overlay)
            r.path = overlay.path.cgPath
            r.fillColor = UIColor.red.withAlphaComponent(0.2)
            r.strokeColor = .black
            con.setLineWidth(2)
            return r
        }
        return MKOverlayRenderer()
    }
```

The result is a much nicer arrow (Figure 20-6), and of course this technique can be generalized to draw an overlay from any CGPath we like.

Custom Overlay Renderer

For full generality, you could define your own MKOverlayRenderer subclass; your subclass must override and implement draw(_:zoomScale:in:). The first parameter is an MKMapRect describing a tile of the visible map (not the size and position of the overlay); the third parameter is the CGContext into which you are to draw. Your implementation may be called several times simultaneously on different background threads, one for each tile, so be sure to draw in a thread-safe way. The overlay itself is available through the inherited overlay property, and MKOverlayRenderer instance methods such as rect(for:) are provided for converting between the map's MKMapRect coordinates and the overlay renderer's graphics context coordinates. The graphics context arrives already configured such that our drawing will be clipped to the current tile. (All this should remind you of CATiledLayer, Chapter 7.)

In our example, we can move the entire functionality for drawing the arrow into an MKOverlayRenderer subclass, which I'll call MyPathOverlayRenderer. Its initializer takes an angle: parameter, with which I'll set its angle property; now our arrow can point in any direction. Another nice benefit of this architectural change is that we can use the `zoomScale:` parameter to determine the stroke width. For simplicity, my implementation of `draw(_:zoomScale:in:)` ignores the incoming MKMapRect value and just draws the entire arrow every time it is called:

```
var angle : CGFloat = 0
init(overlay:MKOverlay, angle:CGFloat) {
    self.angle = angle
    super.init(overlay:overlay)
}
override func draw(_ mapRect: MKMapRect,
    zoomScale: MKZoomScale, in con: CGContext) {
        con.setStrokeColor(UIColor.black.cgColor)
        con.setFillColor(UIColor.red.withAlphaComponent(0.2).cgColor)
        let scale = UIScreen.main.scale
        con.setLineWidth(2/(zoomScale/scale))
        let unit =
            CGFloat(self.overlay.boundingMapRect.width/4.0)
        let p = CGMutablePath()
        let start = CGPoint(0, unit*1.5)
        let p1 = CGPoint(start.x+2*unit, start.y)
        let p2 = CGPoint(p1.x, p1.y-unit)
        let p3 = CGPoint(p2.x+unit*2, p2.y+unit*1.5)
        let p4 = CGPoint(p2.x, p2.y+unit*3)
        let p5 = CGPoint(p4.x, p4.y-unit)
        let p6 = CGPoint(p5.x-2*unit, p5.y)
        let points = [start, p1, p2, p3, p4, p5, p6]
        let t1 = CGAffineTransform(translationX: unit*2, y: unit*2)
        let t2 = t1.rotated(by:self.angle)
        let t3 = t2.translatedBy(x: -unit*2, y: -unit*2)
        p.addLines(between: points, transform: t3)
        p.closeSubpath()
        con.addPath(p)
        con.drawPath(using: .fillStroke)
}
```

To add the overlay to our map, we still must determine its MKMapRect:

```
let lat = self.annloc.latitude
let metersPerPoint = MKMetersPerMapPointAtLatitude(lat)
let c = MKMapPoint(self.annloc)
let unit = 75.0/metersPerPoint
// size and position the overlay bounds on the earth
let sz = CGSize(4*CGFloat(unit), 4*CGFloat(unit))
let mr = MKMapRect(
    x:c.x + 2*unit, y:c.y - 4.5*unit,
    width:Double(sz.width), height:Double(sz.height))
let over = MyPathOverlay(rect:mr)
self.map.addOverlay(over, level:.aboveRoads)
```

The delegate method, providing the overlay renderer, now has very little work to do; in our implementation, it merely supplies an angle for the arrow:

```
func mapView(_ mapView: MKMapView,
    rendererFor overlay: MKOverlay) -> MKOverlayRenderer {
        if overlay is MyPathOverlay {
            let r = MyPathOverlayRenderer(overlay:overlay, angle: -.pi/3.5)
            return r
        }
        return MKOverlayRenderer()
}
```

Other Overlay Features

Our MyPathOverlay class, adopting the MKOverlay protocol, implements the
coordinate property by means of a getter method to return the center of the
boundingMapRect. This is crude, but it's a good minimal implementation. The purpose of this property is to specify the position where you would add an annotation
describing the overlay:

```
// ... create overlay and assign it a path as before ...
self.map.addOverlay(over, level:.aboveRoads)
let annot = MKPointAnnotation()
annot.coordinate = over.coordinate
annot.title = "This way!"
self.map.addAnnotation(annot)
```

The MKOverlay protocol also lets you provide an implementation of
intersects(_:) to refine your overlay's definition of what constitutes an intersection
with itself; the default is to use the boundingMapRect, but if your overlay is drawn in
some nonrectangular shape, you might want to use its actual shape as the basis for
determining intersection.

Overlays are maintained by the map view as an array and are drawn from back to
front starting at the beginning of the array. MKMapView has extensive support for
adding and removing overlays, and for managing their layering order. When you add
the overlay to the map, you can say where you want it drawn among the map view's
sublayers. This is also why methods for adding and inserting overlays have a level:
parameter. The levels are (MKOverlayLevel):

- .aboveRoads (and below labels)

- .aboveLabels

Perhaps you have your own topo map or your own transit map, and you want to use
this as the *content* of the map view. The MKTileOverlay class, adopting the MKOverlay protocol, lets you supplement or replace Apple's map content with your own custom map drawing. You provide a set of tiles at multiple sizes to match multiple zoom
levels, and the map view fetches and draws the tiles needed for the current region
and degree of zoom. It takes a lot of tiles to draw an area of any size, so the

MKTileOverlay class is initialized with a URL, which can be a remote URL for tiles to be fetched across the internet.

Map Kit and Current Location

A device may have sensors that can report its current location. Map Kit provides integration with these facilities. Keep in mind that the user can turn off these sensors or can refuse your app access to them (in the Settings app, under Privacy → Location Services), so trying to use these features may fail. Also, determining the device's location can take time.

The real work here is being done by a CLLocationManager instance, which needs to be created and retained; the usual thing is to initialize a view controller instance property by assigning a new CLLocationManager instance to it:

```
let locman = CLLocationManager()
```

Moreover, you must obtain user authorization, and your *Info.plist* must state the reason why you want it (as I'll explain in more detail in Chapter 21):

```
self.locman.requestWhenInUseAuthorization()
```

You can then ask an MKMapView in your app to display the device's location just by setting its showsUserLocation property to true; the map will automatically put an annotation at that location. This will be an MKUserLocation, adopting the MKAnnotation protocol. The map view's userLocation property will also point to this annotation. If your map view delegate's implementation of mapView(_:viewFor:) returns nil for this annotation, or if there is no such implementation, you'll get the default user location annotation view; you are free to substitute your own annotation view.

An MKUserLocation has a location property, a CLLocation, whose coordinate is a CLLocationCoordinate2D; if the map view's showsUserLocation is true and the map view has actually worked out the user's location, the coordinate describes that location. It also has title and subtitle properties, which appear in a callout if the annotation view is selected; plus you can check whether it currently isUpdating.

MKMapViewDelegate methods keep you informed of the map's attempts to locate the user:

- mapViewWillStartLocatingUser(_:)
- mapViewDidStopLocatingUser(_:)
- mapView(_:didUpdate:) (provides the new MKUserLocation)
- mapView(_:didFailToLocateUserWithError:)

In this cheeky example, I use `mapView(_:viewFor:)` to substitute my own title —
though if that's all I want to do, it might be simpler to implement `mapView(_:did-`
`Update:)` instead:

```
func mapView(_ mapView: MKMapView,
    viewFor annotation: MKAnnotation) -> MKAnnotationView? {
        if let annotation = annotation as? MKUserLocation {
            annotation.title = "You are here, stupid!"
            return nil // or could substitute my own MKAnnotationView
        }
        return nil
}
```

You can ask the map view whether the user's location, if known, is in the visible
region of the map (`isUserLocationVisible`). But what if it isn't? Assigning an
appropriate value to the map's `region` — that is, actually *showing* the part of the
world where the user is located — is a separate task. The simplest way is to take
advantage of the MKMapView's `userTrackingMode` property, which determines how
the user's real-world location should be tracked *automatically* by the map display;
your options are (MKUserTrackingMode):

.none
> If `showsUserLocation` is `true`, the map gets an annotation at the user's location,
> but that's all; the map's `region` is unchanged. You could set it manually in
> `mapView(_:didUpdate:)`.

.follow
> Setting this mode sets `showsUserLocation` to `true`. The map automatically cen-
> ters the user's location, and scales itself appropriately. When the map is in this
> mode, you should *not* set the map's `region`, as you'll be struggling against the
> tracking mode's attempts to do the same thing.

.followWithHeading
> Like .`follow`, but the map is also rotated so that the direction the user is facing is
> up. In this case, the `userLocation` annotation also has a `heading` property, a
> CLHeading; I'll talk more about headings in Chapter 21.

This code, then, turns out to be sufficient to start displaying the user's location:

```
self.map.userTrackingMode = .follow
```

When the `userTrackingMode` is one of the .`follow` modes, if the user is left free to
zoom and scroll the map, the `userTrackingMode` may be automatically changed back
to .`none` (and the user location annotation may be removed). You'll probably want to
provide a way to let the user turn tracking back on again, or to toggle among the
three tracking modes.

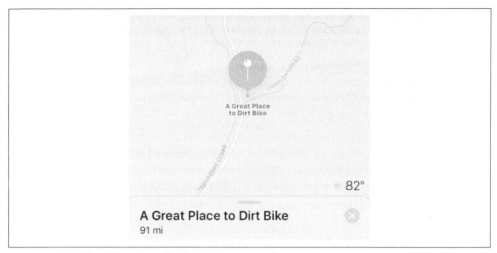

Figure 20-7. The Maps app displays our point of interest

One way to do that is with an MKUserTrackingBarButtonItem, a UIBarButtonItem subclass. You initialize MKUserTrackingBarButtonItem with a map view, and its behavior is automatic from then on: when the user taps it, it switches the map view to the next tracking mode, and its icon reflects the current tracking mode. A map view delegate method tells you when the MKUserTrackingMode changes:

- `mapView(_:didChange:animated:)`

Alternatively, you can use an MKUserTrackingButton; like an MKScaleView or MKCompassButton, it has the advantage that it can be used anywhere (not just in a toolbar or navigation bar).

Communicating with the Maps App

Your app can communicate with the Maps app. Instead of displaying a point of interest in a map view in our own app, we can ask the Maps app to display it. The user could then bookmark or share the location. The channel of communication between your app and the Maps app is the MKMapItem class.

Here, I'll ask the Maps app to display the same point marked by the annotation in our earlier examples, on a standard map portraying the same region of the earth that our map view is currently displaying (Figure 20-7):

```
let p = MKPlacemark(coordinate:self.annloc, addressDictionary:nil)
let mi = MKMapItem(placemark: p)
mi.name = "A Great Place to Dirt Bike" // label to appear in Maps app
let coord = self.map.region.center
let span = self.map.region.span
mi.openInMaps(launchOptions:[
```

```
    MKLaunchOptionsMapTypeKey: MKMapType.standard.rawValue,
    MKLaunchOptionsMapCenterKey: coord as NSValue,
    MKLaunchOptionsMapSpanKey: span as NSValue
])
```

 The need to convert the CLLocationCoordinate2D and MKCoordinateSpan manually to an NSValue is new in iOS 13. I regard this as a bug.

If you start with an MKMapItem returned by the `forCurrentLocation` class method, you're asking the Maps app to display the device's current location. This call doesn't attempt to determine the device's location, nor does it contain any location information; it merely generates an MKMapItem which, when sent to the Maps app, will cause *it* to attempt to determine (and display) the device's location:

```
let mi = MKMapItem.forCurrentLocation()
mi.openInMaps(launchOptions:[
    MKLaunchOptionsMapTypeKey: MKMapType.standard.rawValue
])
```

Geocoding, Searching, and Directions

Map Kit provides your app with three services that involve performing queries over the network:

Geocoding
> Translation of a street address to a coordinate and *vice versa*. What address am I at right now? Or conversely, what are the coordinates of my home address?

Searching
> Lookup of possible matches for a natural language search. What are some Thai restaurants near me?

Directions
> Lookup of turn-by-turn instructions and route mapping from a source location to a destination location. How do I get to that Thai restaurant from here?

These services take time and might not succeed at all, as they depend upon network and server availability; moreover, results may be more or less uncertain. Therefore, they involve a completion function that is called back *asynchronously* on the main thread (see Appendix C). The completion function is called with a single response object plus an Error, each wrapped in an Optional. If the response object is `nil`, the Error tells you what the problem was.

Geocoding

Geocoding functionality is encapsulated in the CLGeocoder class. You call one of these methods:

- geocodeAddressString(_:completionHandler:)
- geocodePostalAddress(_:completionHandler:)

The second method takes a CNPostalAddress, from the Contacts framework, so you'll need to import Contacts (see Chapter 18).

The response, if things went well, is an array of CLPlacemark objects, a series of guesses from best to worst; if things went *really* well, the array will contain exactly one CLPlacemark. A CLPlacemark can be used to initialize an MKPlacemark, a CLPlacemark subclass that adopts the MKAnnotation protocol, and is therefore suitable to be handed directly over to an MKMapView for display.

Here is a simplified example that allows the user to enter an address in a UISearchBar (Chapter 12) to be displayed in an MKMapView:

```
guard let s = searchBar.text else { return }
let geo = CLGeocoder()
geo.geocodeAddressString(s) { placemarks, error in
    guard let placemarks = placemarks else { return }
    let p = placemarks[0]
    let mp = MKPlacemark(placemark:p)
    self.map.addAnnotation(mp)
    self.map.setRegion(
        MKCoordinateRegion(center:mp.coordinate,
            latitudinalMeters:1000, longitudinalMeters:1000),
        animated: true)
}
```

By default, the resulting annotation's title contains a nicely formatted string describing the address.

The converse operation is *reverse geocoding*: you start with a coordinate — actually a CLLocation, which you'll obtain from elsewhere, or construct from a coordinate using init(latitude:longitude:) — and then, in order to obtain the corresponding address, you call this method:

- reverseGeocodeLocation(_:completionHandler:)

The address is expressed through the CLPlacemark postalAddress property; this is a CNPostalAddress, so you'll need to import Contacts. Recall that you can ask the CNPostalAddress for its street, city, state, and other properties, and that you can use a CNPostalAddressFormatter to format the address nicely. Alternatively, you can consult directly such CLPlacemark properties as subthoroughfare (a house number), thoroughfare (a street name), locality (a town), and administrativeArea (a state).

In this example of reverse geocoding, we have an MKMapView that is already tracking the user, and so we have the user's location as the map's `userLocation`; we ask for the corresponding address:

```
guard let loc = self.map.userLocation.location else { return }
let geo = CLGeocoder()
geo.reverseGeocodeLocation(loc) { placemarks, error in
    guard let ps = placemarks, ps.count > 0 else {return}
    let p = ps[0]
    if let addy = p.postalAddress {
        let f = CNPostalAddressFormatter()
        print(f.string(from: addy))
    }
}
```

Searching

The MKLocalSearch class, along with MKLocalSearch.Request and MKLocal-Search.Response, lets you ask the server to perform a natural language search for you. This is less formal than forward geocoding, described in the previous section; instead of searching for an address, you can search for a point of interest by name or description. It can be useful, for some types of search, to constrain the area of interest by setting the request's `region`. New in iOS 13, you can characterize a request's result types as `.address` or `.pointOfInterest` (or both), and you can assign an MKPointOf-InterestFilter to the request's `pointOfInterestFilter` to limit the applicable categories of POI result.

In this example, I'll do a natural language search for a Thai restaurant near the user location currently displayed in the map (illustrating the new iOS 13 POI filtering), and I'll display the first (and probably closest) result as an annotation in our map view:

```
guard let loc = self.map.userLocation.location else { return }
let req = MKLocalSearch.Request()
req.naturalLanguageQuery = "Thai"
req.region = MKCoordinateRegion(center: loc.coordinate,
    span: MKCoordinateSpan(latitudeDelta:1, longitudeDelta:1))
req.resultTypes = .pointOfInterest
let filter = MKPointOfInterestFilter(including: [.restaurant])
req.pointOfInterestFilter = filter
let search = MKLocalSearch(request:req)
search.start { response, error in
    guard let response = response else { print(error); return }
    self.map.showsUserLocation = false
    let mi = response.mapItems[0] // I'm feeling lucky
    let place = mi.placemark
    let loc = place.location!.coordinate
    let reg = MKCoordinateRegion(center:loc,
        latitudinalMeters:1200, longitudinalMeters:1200)
```

```
        self.map.setRegion(reg, animated:true)
        let ann = MKPointAnnotation()
        ann.title = mi.name
        ann.subtitle = mi.phoneNumber
        ann.coordinate = loc
        self.map.addAnnotation(ann)
    }
```

MKLocalSearchCompleter lets you use the MKLocalSearch remote database to suggest completions as the user types a search query. In effect, you are performing the search after every character that the user types; most likely you'll use a UISearchController (Chapter 8). Initialize and configure the MKLocalSearchCompleter object and give it a `delegate` (MKLocalSearchCompleterDelegate); new in iOS 13, an MKPointOfInterestFilter can be applied to the completer. Each time the search bar text changes, set the completer's `queryFragment` with the current contents of the search field. When the delegate method `completerDidUpdateResults(_:)` is called, grab the completer's `results`, which is an array of MKLocalSearchCompletion objects. These have string properties `title` and `subtitle` suitable for display in a table view; you'll probably set your table view data source model object to the completer's `results` and tell the table to reload.

Directions

The MKDirections class, along with MKDirections.Request, looks up walking or driving directions between two locations expressed as MKMapItem objects. The resulting MKDirections.Response includes an array of MKRoute objects; each MKRoute includes an MKPolyline suitable for display as an overlay in your map, as well as an array of MKRoute.Step objects, each of which provides its own MKPolyline plus instructions and distances. The response also has its own `source` and `destination` MKMapItems, which may be different from what we started with.

To illustrate, I'll continue from the Thai food example in the previous section, starting at the point where we obtained the Thai restaurant's MKMapItem:

```
// ... same as before up to this point ...
let mi = response.mapItems[0] // I'm still feeling lucky
let req = MKDirectionsRequest()
req.source = MKMapItem.forCurrentLocation()
req.destination = mi
let dir = MKDirections(request:req)
dir.calculate { response, error in
    guard let response = response else { print(error); return }
    let route = response.routes[0] // I'm feeling insanely lucky
    let poly = route.polyline
    self.map.addOverlay(poly)
```

```
    for step in route.steps {
        print("After \(step.distance) meters: \(step.instructions)")
    }
}
```

The step-by-step instructions appear in the console; in real life, of course, we would presumably display these in our app's interface. The route is drawn in our map view, provided we have an appropriate implementation of `mapView(_:rendererFor:)`, such as this:

```
func mapView(_ mapView: MKMapView,
    rendererFor overlay: MKOverlay) -> MKOverlayRenderer {
        if let overlay = overlay as? MKPolyline {
            let r = MKPolylineRenderer(polyline:overlay)
            r.strokeColor = UIColor.blue.withAlphaComponent(0.8)
            r.lineWidth = 2
            return r
        }
        return MKOverlayRenderer()
}
```

You can also ask MKDirections to estimate the time of arrival, by calling `calculate-ETA(completionHandler:)`, and there is arrival time estimation for some public transit systems (and you can tell the Maps app to display a transit directions map).

CHAPTER 21

Sensors

A device may contain hardware for sensing the world around itself — where it is located, how it is oriented, how it is moving.

Information about the device's current location and how that location is changing over time using its WiFi, cellular networking, and GPS capabilities, along with information about the device's orientation relative to north using its magnetometer, is provided through the Core Location framework.

Information about the device's change in speed and attitude using its accelerometer is provided through the UIEvent class (for device shake) and the Core Motion framework, which provides increased accuracy by incorporating the device's gyroscope, if it has one, as well as the magnetometer. In addition, the device may have an extra chip that analyzes and records the user's activity, such as walking or running, and even a barometer that reports changes in altitude; the Core Motion framework provides access to this information as well.

A challenge associated with writing code that takes advantage of the sensors is that different devices have different hardware. If you don't want to impose stringent restrictions on what devices your app will run on in the first place (`UIRequired-DeviceCapabilities` in the *Info.plist*), your code must be prepared to fail gracefully, perhaps providing a subset of your app's full capabilities, when it turns out that the current device lacks certain features.

Even on a device that has the necessary hardware, certain sensors may be switched off or may experience momentary inadequacy; for instance, Core Location might not be able to get a fix on the device's position because it can't see cell towers, GPS satellites, or both. And some sensors take time to "warm up," so that the values you'll get from them initially will be invalid. You'll want to respond nimbly to such changes in the external circumstances, in order to give the user a decent experience of your application regardless.

One final consideration: all sensor usage means battery usage, to a lesser or greater degree — sometimes to a *considerably* greater degree. There's a compromise to be made here: you want to please the user with your app's convenience and usefulness, without disagreeably surprising and annoying the user through rapid depletion of the device's battery charge.

Core Location

The Core Location framework (`import CoreLocation`) provides facilities for the device to determine and report its location (*location services*). It takes advantage of three sensors:

WiFi
> The device, if WiFi is turned on, may scan for nearby WiFi networks and compare these against an online database.

Cell
> The device, if it has cell capabilities and they are not turned off, may detect nearby telephone cell towers and compare them against an online database.

GPS
> The device's GPS, if it has one, may be able to obtain a position fix from GPS satellites. The GPS is obviously the most accurate location sensor, but it takes the longest to get a fix, and in some situations it will fail, such as when the user is indoors or among tall buildings where the device can't "see" enough of the sky.

Core Location will automatically use whatever facilities the device has available; all *you* have to do is ask for the device's location. Core Location allows you to specify how accurate a position fix you want; trying to get a more accurate fix may require more time.

To help you test code that depends on where the device is, Xcode lets you pretend that the device is at a particular location on earth. The Simulator's Debug → Location menu lets you enter a location; the Scheme editor lets you set a default location (under Options); and the Debug → Simulate Location menu lets you switch among locations. You can set a built-in location or supply a standard GPX file containing a waypoint. You can also set the location to None; it's important to test for what happens when no location information is available.

Location Manager and Delegate

Use of Core Location requires a *location manager* object, an instance of CLLocationManager. This object needs to be created on the main thread and retained thereafter.

A standard strategy is to pick an instance that persists throughout the life of your app — your app delegate, or your root view controller, is a good place — and initialize an instance property with a location manager:

```
let locman = CLLocationManager()
```

Your location manager will generally be useless without a *delegate* (CLLocation-ManagerDelegate). You don't want to change a location manager's delegate, so you'll want to set it once, early in the life of the location manager. This delegate will need to be an instance that persists together with the location manager. If `locman` is, say, a constant property of our root view controller, then we can set the root view controller as its delegate. It's a good idea to do this as early as possible; the root view controller's initializer is a good place:

```
required init?(coder: NSCoder) {
    super.init(coder:coder)
    self.locman.delegate = self
}
```

Location Services Authorization

You must explicitly request authorization from the user when you first start tracking the device's location. There are two types of authorization:

When In Use authorization
> When In Use authorization allows your app to use Core Location when the app is running. "Running" here means in the foreground or running (not suspended) in the background. New in iOS 13, an app with When In Use authorization can use *any* Core Location features.

Always authorization
> Always authorization permits your app to configure the system to perform certain Core Location activities on your behalf even when your app is not running. I'll describe later what those activities are.

The user can turn off location services as a whole. The CLLocationManager class method `locationServicesEnabled` reports whether location services are switched off. If location services are off, don't bother with authorization.

However, even if location services are off, you might like to try to use Core Location anyway. The reason is that this may cause the runtime to put up an alert on your behalf offering to switch to the Settings app so that the user can turn location services on (Figure 21-1). The attempt to learn the device's location will fail, but this failure may also cause the user to see the system alert:

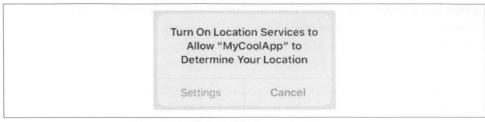

Figure 21-1. Location services are turned off

```
if !CLLocationManager.locationServicesEnabled() {
    self.locman.startUpdatingLocation()
    return
}
```

The user may see the alert, may tap Settings, and may turn on Core Location. The user just might even find your app's listing in Settings and grant it authorization then and there. But don't count on the user doing that, and don't count on the alert actually appearing.

Once location services are enabled, you'll call the CLLocationManager class method `authorizationStatus` to learn your app's actual authorization status. There are two types of authorization, so there are two status cases reporting that you have authorization: `.authorizedWhenInUse` and `.authorizedAlways`. If the status is `.notDetermined`, you can request that the system put up the authorization request alert on your behalf by calling one of two instance methods, either `requestWhenInUseAuthorization` or `requestAlwaysAuthorization`. You must also have a corresponding meaningful entry in your app's *Info.plist* providing the body of the authorization request alert; these are "Privacy — Location When In Use Description" (`NSLocationWhenInUseUsageDescription`) and "Privacy — Location Always and When In Use Usage Description" (`NSLocationAlwaysAndWhenInUseUsageDescription`) — and if you're planning to call `requestAlwaysAuthorization`, you will need both of them.

Because location tracking is both battery-intensive and a potential invasion of privacy, Apple wants the user to feel confident that secret or inadvertent location tracking is not taking place. At the same time, Apple wants to give your app a chance to demonstrate to the user its use of Core Location, in order to encourage the user to give your app the authorization it needs. Therefore iOS 13 provides a revised user interface for authorizing your app, intended to maximize your chances of obtaining authorization from a confused or mistrustful user. I'll talk about When In Use authorization now, postponing the rarer Always authorization until later.

New in iOS 13, the alert that the user sees when you request When In Use authorization includes an Allow Once option (Figure 21-2). This gives the user an opportunity to let your app use location services on a limited basis. If the user taps Allow Once, your app will get When In Use authorization, just as if the user had tapped Allow

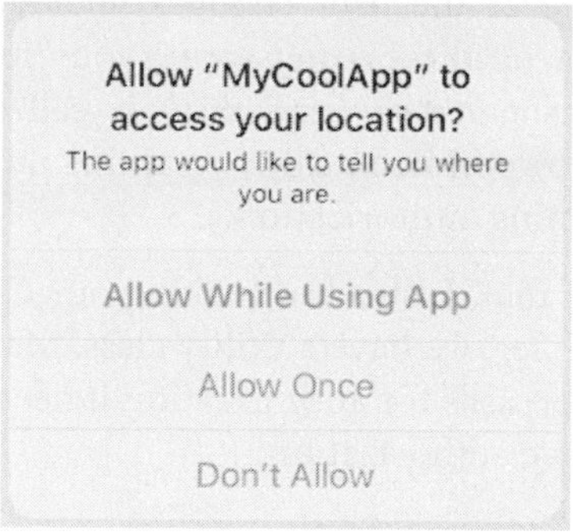

Figure 21-2. Authorization alert for When In Use authorization

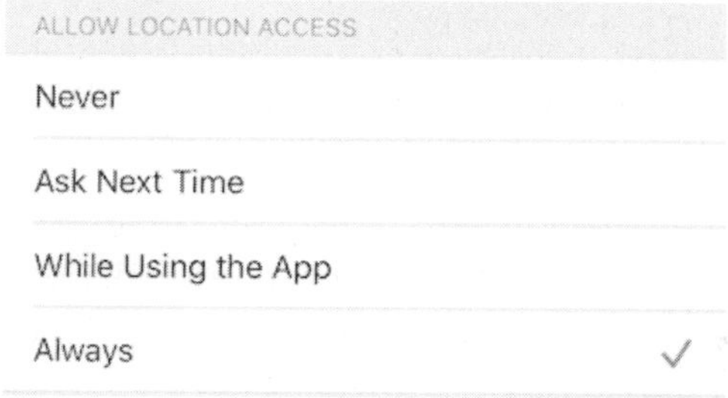

Figure 21-3. Authorization choices in Settings

While Using App — but the next time your app goes into the background and is suspended, your authorization will be revoked. Then the next time your app runs, you'll discover that your authorization status is `.notDetermined`, and you can ask for authorization again (and the alert will appear again).

The user can also change your app's authorization at any time. The Settings app lets the user turn on and off location access for your app (Figure 21-3). There are four possibilities: Never, Ask Next Time, While Using the App, and Always (which will appear only if your app has actually requested Always authorization). The second option, Ask Next Time, is new in iOS 13: it returns your authorization status to `.notDetermined`, so you can ask for authorization again (and the alert will appear again).

Oddly, the `request` methods do not take a completion function. Your code just continues blithely on. If you call `requestWhenInUseAuthorization` and then attempt to track the device's location by calling `startUpdatingLocation`, you might succeed if the user grants authorization, but you might fail because the user denies it. The Core Location API provides no simple way for you to proceed only after you know the outcome of the authorization request.

On the other hand, whenever the user changes your authorization status, in the authorization request alert or the Settings app, your location manager delegate's `locationManager(_:didChangeAuthorization:)` is called. So if you were to *store* whatever action you want to perform *before* obtaining authorization, you could *perform* that action *after* obtaining authorization.

Here's a strategy for doing that. Instead of making our CLLocationManager a property of the root view controller, we have a utility class, ManagerHolder; it creates and retains the location manager, asks for authorization if needed, and stores the function we want to call when we have authorization:

```
class ManagerHolder {
    let locman = CLLocationManager()
    var doThisWhenAuthorized : (() -> ())?
    func checkForLocationAccess(always:Bool = false,
        andThen f: (()->())? = nil) {
            // no services? try to get alert
            guard CLLocationManager.locationServicesEnabled() else {
                self.locman.startUpdatingLocation()
                return
            }
            let status = CLLocationManager.authorizationStatus()
            switch status {
            case .authorizedWhenInUse:
                if always { // try to step up
                    self.doThisWhenAuthorized = f
                    self.locman.requestAlwaysAuthorization()
                } else {
                    f?()
                }
            case .authorizedAlways:
                f?()
            case .notDetermined:
                self.doThisWhenAuthorized = f
                always ?
                    self.locman.requestAlwaysAuthorization() :
                    self.locman.requestWhenInUseAuthorization()
            case .restricted: break // do nothing
            case .denied: break // do nothing, or beg for authorization
            @unknown default: fatalError()
            }
    }
}
```

With the ManagerHolder utility class, ownership and authorization of the location manager is encapsulated. I'll attach a ManagerHolder instance to the root view controller. The root view controller initializer creates and stores a ManagerHolder instance as an instance property, bringing the location manager to life as early as possible. For convenience, I'll give the root view controller a `locman` property, but this will be a computed property that bounces to the ManagerHolder's location manager instance:

```
class ViewController: UIViewController, CLLocationManagerDelegate {
    let managerHolder = ManagerHolder()
    var locman : CLLocationManager {
        return self.managerHolder.locman
    }
    required init?(coder: NSCoder) {
        super.init(coder:coder)
        self.locman.delegate = self
    }
    // ...
}
```

Acting as the location manager delegate, the root view controller can implement locationManager(_:didChangeAuthorizationStatus:) to call the function stored in the ManagerHolder:

```
func locationManager(_ manager: CLLocationManager,
    didChangeAuthorization status: CLAuthorizationStatus) {
        switch status {
        case .authorizedAlways, .authorizedWhenInUse:
            self.managerHolder.doThisWhenAuthorized?()
            self.managerHolder.doThisWhenAuthorized = nil
        default: break
        }
}
```

If we now call our ManagerHolder's checkForLocationAccess before tracking location, everything will work correctly. If we pass a completion function in our call to checkForLocationAccess, then if we already have authorization, that function will be called immediately; if our status is .notDetermined and the authorization request alert is presented, that function will be called as soon as the user authorizes us.

Location Tracking

The primary use of a location manager is to track the user's location. Make sure the location manager has a delegate, configure the location manager further as needed (I'll go into more detail in a moment), and then tell the location manager to start-UpdatingLocation.

The location manager will then begin calling the delegate's locationManager(_:did-UpdateLocations:) method repeatedly. The delegate will deal with each such call as it arrives. In this way, you will be kept more or less continuously informed of where the device is. This will go on until you call stopUpdatingLocation; don't forget to call it when you no longer need location tracking! Your delegate should also implement locationManager(_:didFailWithError:) to receive error messages.

That pattern is common to virtually *all* uses of the location manager. The location manager can do various kinds of tracking, but they all work the same way: you'll tell it to start, a corresponding delegate method will be called repeatedly (or you'll receive an error), and ultimately you'll tell the location manager to stop.

Here are some location manager configuration properties that are useful to set *before* you start location tracking:

desiredAccuracy
>   Your choices are:
>
>   - kCLLocationAccuracyBestForNavigation
>   - kCLLocationAccuracyBest
>   - kCLLocationAccuracyNearestTenMeters
>   - kCLLocationAccuracyHundredMeters
>   - kCLLocationAccuracyKilometer
>   - kCLLocationAccuracyThreeKilometers
>
>   It might be sufficient for your purposes to know quickly but roughly the device's location; in that case, use kCLLocationAccuracyKilometer or kCLLocation-AccuracyThreeKilometers. At the other end of the scale, highest accuracy may cause the highest battery drain; indeed, kCLLocationAccuracyBestFor-Navigation is supposed to be used only when the device is connected to external power. The accuracy setting is not a filter: the location manager will send you whatever location information it has, even if it isn't as accurate as you asked for, and checking a location's horizontalAccuracy to see if it's good enough is up to you.

distanceFilter
>   Perhaps you don't need a location report unless the device has moved a certain distance since the previous report. This property can help keep you from being bombarded with events you don't need. The distance is measured in meters. To turn off the distance filter entirely, set this property to kCLDistanceFilterNone (the default).

pausesLocationUpdatesAutomatically
>   A Bool. The default, true, means that your setting for the location manager's activityType is significant. Your activityType choices are (CLActivityType):
>
>   - .fitness
>   - .automotiveNavigation
>   - .otherNavigation

- `.other` (the default)

Think of these as an autopause setting, based on the movement of the device; if we don't seem to be moving sufficiently to warrant updates based on the activity type, updates can pause and we'll conserve power.

The idea here is that the user may have stopped working out, driving, or whatever, but has forgotten to turn off your app's location tracking. A paused location manager does *not* automatically resume updates; it's up to you to implement the delegate method `locationManagerDidPauseLocationUpdates(_:)` and configure updates to resume when appropriate. Apple suggests that, as an alternative, you might save power by setting `pausesLocationUpdatesAutomatically` to `false` but accepting the broadest `desiredAccuracy` (namely `kCLLocation-AccuracyThreeKilometers`), which will probably mean that the GPS isn't used.

Here's a basic example, taking advantage of the authorization strategy described in the previous section. Presume that we want to get a very accurate location as soon as possible and keep tracking the user's location until we say to stop:

```
self.managerHolder.checkForLocationAccess {
    self.locman.desiredAccuracy = kCLLocationAccuracyBest
    self.locman.distanceFilter = kCLDistanceFilterNone
    self.locman.activityType = .other
    self.locman.pausesLocationUpdatesAutomatically = false
    self.locman.startUpdatingLocation()
}
```

In that code, we have requested authorization if needed, and if we have or can get authorization, we have configured the location manager and started tracking location. Now we must sit back and wait for our implementation of `location-Manager(_:didUpdateLocations:)` to be called. The second parameter is an array of CLLocation, a value class that encapsulates the notion of a location. Its properties include:

coordinate
    A CLLocationCoordinate2D, a struct consisting of two Doubles representing latitude and longitude.

altitude
    A CLLocationDistance, which is a Double representing a number of meters.

speed
    A CLLocationSpeed, which is a Double representing meters per second.

course
    A CLLocationDirection, which is a Double representing degrees (*not* radians) clockwise from north.

`horizontalAccuracy`
> A CLLocationAccuracy, which is a Double representing meters.

`timestamp`
> A Date.

In this situation, the array that we receive is likely to contain just one CLLocation — and even if it contains more than one, the *last* CLLocation in the array is guaranteed to be the newest. So it suffices for our `locationManager(_:didUpdateLocations:)` implementation to extract the last element of the array:

```
let REQ_ACC : CLLocationAccuracy = 10
func locationManager(_ manager: CLLocationManager,
    didUpdateLocations locations: [CLLocation]) {
        let loc = locations.last!
        let acc = loc.horizontalAccuracy
        print(acc)
        if acc < 0 || acc > REQ_ACC {
            return // wait for the next one
        }
        let coord = loc.coordinate
        print("You are at \(coord.latitude) \(coord.longitude)")
}
```

It's instructive to see, from the console logs, how the accuracy improves as the sensors warm up and the GPS obtains a fix:

```
1285.19869645162
1285.19869645172
1285.19869645173
65.0
65.0
30.0
30.0
30.0
10.0
You are at ...
```

Where Am I?

Rather than tracking location continuously, you might like to get *one* location *once*. A common beginner mistake is to call `startUpdatingLocation` and implement `locationManager(_:didUpdateLocations:)` to stop updating as soon as it is called:

```
func locationManager(_ manager: CLLocationManager,
    didUpdateLocations locations: [CLLocation]) {
        let loc = locations.last!
        let coord = loc.coordinate
        print("You are at \(coord.latitude) \(coord.longitude)")
        manager.stopUpdatingLocation() // this won't work!
}
```

As I demonstrated in the preceding section, however, the sensors take time to warm up, and many calls to `locationManager(_:didUpdateLocations:)` may be needed before a reasonably accurate CLLocation arrives. The correct strategy would be to do just what I did in the preceding section, and then call `stopUpdatingLocation` at the very end, when a sufficiently accurate location has in fact been received. But that's a lot of work to get just one reading, and there's a simpler way. Instead of calling `start-UpdatingLocation`, call `requestLocation`:

```
self.locman.desiredAccuracy = kCLLocationAccuracyBest
self.locman.requestLocation()
```

Your `locationManager(_:didUpdateLocations:)` will be called *once* with a good location, based on the `desiredAccuracy` you've already set:

```
func locationManager(manager: CLLocationManager,
    didUpdateLocations locations: [CLLocation]) {
        let loc = locations.last!
        let coord = loc.coordinate
        print("You are at \(coord.latitude) \(coord.longitude)")
}
```

Calling `requestLocation` will *not* magically cause an accurate location to arrive any faster! It's a great convenience that `locationManager(_:didUpdateLocations:)` will be called just once, but some considerable time may elapse before that call arrives. You do not have to call `stopUpdatingLocation`, though you can do so if you change your mind and decide before the location arrives that it is no longer needed.

 If you call `requestLocation` soon after calling it previously, you may get a cached value rather than a new position fix.

Continuous Background Location

Continuous background location is an extension of basic location tracking. You tell the location manager to `startUpdatingLocation`, and when the app goes into the background it keeps running and keeps receiving updates. Use of Core Location to perform continuous background updates is parallel to production of sound in the background (Chapter 14):

- In your app's *Info.plist*, the "Required background modes" key (`UIBackground-Modes`) should include `location`; you can set this up easily by adding the Background Modes capability in the Signing & Capabilities tab when editing the target, and checking "Location updates."

- You must also set your location manager's `allowsBackgroundLocationUpdates` to `true`. You should do this only at moments when you actually need to start getting background location updates — ideally, just as you go into the background (see Appendix A). You should set it back to `false` as soon as you no longer need background updates.

The result is that if you have a location manager to which you have sent `start-UpdatingLocation` and the user sends your app into the background, your app is not suspended: the use of location services continues, and your delegate keeps receiving location updates.

 You cannot *start* tracking locations when your app is *already* in the background (well, you can try, but in all probability your app will be suspended and location tracking will cease).

How the device lets the user know that you're tracking location in the background depends on what sort of authorization you have:

Your app has only When In Use authorization
> The device will make the user aware that your app is doing background location tracking by displaying a blue status bar. The user can tap this to summon your app to the front. (If you see the blue bar *momentarily* as your app goes into the background, that's because you didn't do what I said a moment ago: set `allows-BackgroundLocationUpdates` to `true` only when you really are going to track location in the background.)

Your app has Always authorization
> The blue status bar doesn't appear, because the user has already agreed to let you use location services always. But Apple recommends that you set the location manager's `showsBackgroundLocationIndicator` to `true` so the blue status bar *does* appear.

Background use of location services can cause a power drain, but if you want your app to function as a positional data logger, it may be the only way. You can help conserve power by making judicious choices, such as:

- By setting a coarse `distanceFilter` value.
- By not requiring overly high accuracy.
- By being correct about the `activityType` and allowing updates to pause.

Location Monitoring

Location monitoring is not something your app does; it's something the system does on your behalf. It *doesn't* require your app to run continuously in the background; in fact, your app doesn't need to be running at all! You do *not* have to set the `UIBackgroundModes` of your *Info.plist*.

Your app still requires a location manager with a delegate, and it needs appropriate user authorization. In general, this will be Always authorization. New in iOS 13, even if your app has only When In Use authorization, it can receive delegate messages from location monitoring any time it is running (including running in the background to receive location updates).

Always authorization

The only reason you would ever need Always authorization is that you want the system to do location monitoring for you even when your app is suspended or not running. How will you get it?

New in iOS 13, when you ask for Always authorization, the user is *not* informed of that fact. Instead, there are two possibilities:

The authorization status is `.notDetermined`
    If you ask for Always authorization when the authorization status is `.notDetermined`, the alert that appears to the user is the same as Figure 21-2. The user's choices are Allow While Using App and Allow Once.

The authorization status is `.authorizedWhenInUse`
    No alert appears.

Okay, so when *does* the user get to provide Always authorization explicitly? Here's what happens (this is all new in iOS 13):

1. If the user has granted you authorization at all, then when you ask for Always authorization you receive it *immediately.*

2. When your app next goes into the background, you must actually *use* your mighty Always powers to begin location monitoring.

3. If you do that, then at some future moment, such as when your app comes back to the foreground or the user returns to the device from the lock screen, the user will be informed that your app has been using location services when it isn't running, and is offered a chance to permit that to continue (Figure 21-4). The user is determining, in effect, whether your authorization status after this moment will be `.authorizedAlways` or `.authorizedWhenInUse`.

Forms of location monitoring

There are four distinct forms of location monitoring:

Significant location change monitoring
    Check this class method:

    - `significantLocationChangeMonitoringAvailable`

    If it returns true, you can call this method:

    - `startMonitoringSignificantLocationChanges`

Figure 21-4. The Always authorization alert

Implement this delegate method:

`locationManager(_:didUpdateLocations:)`
> Called whenever the device's location has changed significantly.

Visit monitoring
> By tracking significant changes in your location along with the *pauses* between those changes, the system decides that the user is visiting a spot. Visit monitoring is basically a form of significant location change monitoring, but requires even less power and notifies you less often, because locations that don't involve pauses are filtered out.

Check this class method:

- `significantLocationChangeMonitoringAvailable`

If it returns `true`, you can call this method:

- `startMonitoringVisits`

Implement this delegate method:

`locationManager(_:didVisit:)`
> Called whenever the user's location pauses in a way that suggests a visit is beginning, and again whenever a visit ends. The second parameter is a CLVisit, a simple value class wrapping visit data; in addition to `coordinate` and `horizontalAccuracy`, you get an `arrivalDate` and `departureDate`. If this is an arrival, the `departureDate` will be `Date.distantFuture`. If this is a departure and we were not monitoring visits when the user arrived, the `arrivalDate` will be `Date.distantPast`.

Region monitoring

Region monitoring depends upon your defining one or more *regions*. A region is a CLRegion, which basically expresses a *geofence*, an area that triggers an event when the user enters or leaves it (or both). This class is divided into two subclasses, CLBeaconRegion and CLCircularRegion. CLBeaconRegion is used in connection with iBeacon monitoring; I'm not going to discuss iBeacon in this book, so that leaves us with only CLCircularRegion. Its initializer is init(center:radius:identifier:); the center: parameter is a CLLocation-Coordinate2D, and the identifier: serves as a unique key. The region's notify-OnEntry and notifyOnExit properties are both true by default; set one to false if you're interested only in the other type of event.

Check this class method:

- isMonitoringAvailable(for:CLCircularRegion.self)

If it returns true, then you can call this method:

- startMonitoring(for:)

Call that method for each region in which you are interested. Regions being monitored are maintained as a set, which is the location manager's monitored-Regions. A region's identifier serves as a unique key, so that if you start monitoring for a region whose identifier matches that of a region already in the monitoredRegions set, the latter will be ejected from the set. Implement these delegate methods:

- locationManager(_:didEnterRegion:)
- locationManager(_:didExitRegion:)
- locationManager(_:monitoringDidFailFor:withError:)

Geofenced local notifications

This is a special case of region monitoring where everything is handled through the local notification mechanism (Chapter 13); therefore, you only need When In Use authorization, you don't start monitoring or stop monitoring, and you don't implement any delegate methods.

You configure a local notification request (UNNotificationRequest) whose trigger is a UNLocationNotificationTrigger. Create the trigger by calling its initializer, init(region:repeats:), supplying a CLRegion. If repeats: is true, the notification won't be unscheduled after it fires; rather, it will fire again whenever the user crosses the region boundary in the specified direction again (depending on the CLRegion's notifyOnEntry and notifyOnExit settings).

Delegate method calls when your app isn't running

If your app isn't in the foreground at the time the system wants to send your location manager delegate a location monitoring event, there are two possible states in which your app might find itself:

Your app is suspended in the background
> Your app is woken up (remaining in the background) long enough to receive the delegate event and do something with it.

Your app is not running at all
> Your app is relaunched (remaining in the background), and your app delegate will be sent `application(_:didFinishLaunchingWithOptions:)` with the `options:` dictionary containing the `.location` key, allowing you to discern the special nature of the situation. As soon as possible, you need to make sure you have a location manager with a delegate so that you can receive the appropriate delegate events. (This is another reason why you should create a location manager and assign it a delegate *early* in the lifetime of the app.)

Location monitoring best practices

Location monitoring is less battery-intensive than full-fledged location tracking. That's because it relies on cell tower positions to estimate the device's location. Since the cell is probably operating anyway — if the device is a phone, the cell is usually on and concerned with what cell towers are available — little or no additional power is required. Apple says that the system will also take advantage of other clues requiring no extra battery drain to decide that there may have been a change in location: for instance, the device may observe a change in the available WiFi networks, strongly suggesting that the device has moved.

Nevertheless, location monitoring does use the battery, and over the course of time the user will notice this. Therefore, you should use it only during periods when you need it. Every `startMonitoring` method has a corresponding `stopMonitoring` method. Don't forget to call that method when location monitoring is no longer needed! The system is performing this work on your behalf, and it will continue to do so until you tell it not to.

 It is *crucial* that you remember to stop location monitoring. A failure to do this will eventually drain the battery significantly. The user can figure out, by looking at the Battery screen in Settings, that your app is responsible, and if you have provided no other way to turn location monitoring off, the user will have no choice but to delete your app.

Heading

For appropriately equipped devices, Core Location supports use of the magnetometer to determine which way the device is facing (its *heading*). Although this information is accessed through a location manager, you do *not* need location services merely to use the magnetometer to report the device's orientation with respect to *magnetic* north; you *do* need location services to report *true* north, as this depends on the device's location.

As with location, you'll first check that the desired feature is available (`heading-Available`); then you'll configure the location manager, and call `startUpdating-Heading`. The delegate will be sent `locationManager(_:didUpdateHeading:)` repeatedly until you call `stopUpdatingHeading` (or else `locationManager(_:didFail-WithError:)` will be called).

A heading object is a CLHeading instance; its `magneticHeading` and `trueHeading` properties are CLLocationDirection values, which report degrees (*not* radians) measured clockwise from the reference direction (magnetic or true north, respectively). If the `trueHeading` is not available, it will be reported as `-1`. The `trueHeading` will *not* be available unless both of the following are true in the Settings app:

- Location services are turned on (Privacy → Location Services).
- Compass calibration is turned on (Privacy → Location Services → System Services).

Beyond that, explicit user authorization is *not* needed in order to get the device's heading with respect to true north.

If you want the system's compass calibration alert to be permitted to appear if needed, implement this delegate method to return `true`:

- `locationManagerShouldDisplayHeadingCalibration(_:)`

In this example, I'll use the device as a compass. The `headingFilter` setting is to prevent us from being bombarded constantly with readings. For best results, the device should probably be held level (like a tabletop, or a compass); we are setting the `headingOrientation` so that the reported heading will be the direction in which the top of the device (the end away from the Home button) is pointing:

```
guard CLLocationManager.headingAvailable() else {return} // no hardware
self.locman.headingFilter = 5
self.locman.headingOrientation = .portrait
self.locman.startUpdatingHeading()
```

In the delegate, I'll display our heading as a rough cardinal direction in a label in the interface (`self.lab`). If we have a `trueHeading`, I'll use it; otherwise I'll use the `magneticHeading`:

```swift
func locationManager(_ manager: CLLocationManager,
    didUpdateHeading newHeading: CLHeading) {
        var h = newHeading.magneticHeading
        let h2 = newHeading.trueHeading // -1 if no location info
        if h2 >= 0 {
            h = h2
        }
        let cards = ["N", "NE", "E", "SE", "S", "SW", "W", "NW"]
        func degToName(_ d:Double) -> String {
            let divCount = cards.count
            let angularRange = 360.0 / Double(divCount)
            let bucket = Int((d + angularRange/2.0)/angularRange)
            return cards[bucket % divCount]
        }
        let dir = degToName(h)
        if self.lab.text != dir {
            self.lab.text = dir
        }
        if self.lab.text != dir {
            self.lab.text = dir
        }
}
```

Heading is not the same as course. A boat may be *facing* north (its heading) but *moving* northeast (its course). There are times, however, when what you are interested in really is course. In a moving automobile, how the user is holding the device is usually unimportant to you: what you want to know is which way the car is moving. If the runtime concludes, from the nature of the device's motion, that when you ask for heading you probably mean course, it will provide the course as the heading.

If that's not what you want, then instead of using Core Location to determine heading, you can use Core Motion (discussed in the next section) to obtain the device's orientation in space as a CMDeviceMotion object's `heading` property.

Acceleration, Attitude, and Activity

Acceleration results from the application of a force to the device, and is detected through the device's accelerometer, supplemented by the gyroscope if the device has one. Gravity is a force, so the accelerometer always has something to measure, even if the user isn't applying a force to the device, and the device can use acceleration detection to report its attitude relative to the vertical.

Acceleration information can arrive in two ways:

As a prepackaged UIEvent
You can receive a UIEvent notifying you of a predefined gesture performed by accelerating the device. At present, the only such gesture is the user shaking the device.

With the Core Motion framework
> You instantiate CMMotionManager and then obtain information of a desired type. You can ask for accelerometer, gyroscope, or device motion information; device motion combines the gyroscope data with data from other sensors to give you the best possible description of the device's attitude in space, along with magnetometer and heading information.

Shake Events

A shake event is a UIEvent (Chapter 5). Receiving shake events involves the notion of the first responder. To receive shake events, your app must contain a UIResponder which:

- Returns `true` from `canBecomeFirstResponder`.
- Is in fact first responder.

This responder, or a UIResponder further up the responder chain, should implement some or all of these methods:

`motionBegan(_:with:)`
> Something has started to happen that might or might not turn out to be a shake.

`motionEnded(_:with:)`
> The motion reported in `motionBegan` is over and has turned out to be a shake.

`motionCancelled(_:with:)`
> The motion reported in `motionBegan` wasn't a shake after all.

It might be sufficient to implement `motionEnded(_:with:)`, because this arrives if and only if the user performs a shake gesture. The first parameter will be the event subtype, but this is guaranteed to be `.motionShake`, so testing it is pointless.

The view controller in charge of the current view is a good candidate to receive shake events. A minimal implementation might look like this:

```
override var canBecomeFirstResponder : Bool {
    return true
}
override func viewDidAppear(_ animated: Bool) {
    super.viewDidAppear(animated)
    self.becomeFirstResponder()
}
override func motionEnded(_ motion: UIEvent.EventSubtype, with e: UIEvent?) {
    print("hey, you shook me!")
}
```

Suppose some other object is first responder and is of a type that supports undo, such as a UITextField. Then (assuming you have not set the shared UIApplication's applicationSupportsShakeToEdit property to `false`) a shake event that percolates all the way to the top of the responder chain will be handled by the runtime: it will display an Undo or Redo alert, and will perform undo or redo on that object. Your view controller might not want to rob any responders in its view of this capability. A simple way to avoid doing so is to test whether the view controller is itself the first responder; if it isn't, we call `super` to pass the event on up the responder chain:

```
override func motionEnded(_ motion: UIEvent.EventSubtype, with e: UIEvent?) {
    if self.isFirstResponder {
        print("hey, you shook me!")
    } else {
        super.motionEnded(motion, with: e)
    }
}
```

 New in iOS 13, double tap or left swipe with three fingers signifies Undo, and shake gestures will probably diminish in importance.

Using Core Motion

The standard pattern for using the Core Motion framework (`import CoreMotion`) is reminiscent of how you use Core Location:

1. You start by instantiating CMMotionManager; retain the instance somewhere, typically as an instance property. There is no reason not to initialize the property directly:

    ```
    let motman = CMMotionManager()
    ```

2. Confirm that the desired hardware is available by checking the appropriate instance property, such as `isAccelerometerAvailable`.

3. Set the interval at which you wish the motion manager to update itself with new sensor readings by setting the appropriate property, such as `accelerometer-UpdateInterval`.

4. Call the appropriate `start` method, such as `startAccelerometerUpdates`.

5. You probably expect me to say now that the motion manager will call into a delegate. Surprise! A motion manager has no delegate. You have two choices:

    Pull
    > Poll the motion manager whenever you want data, asking for the appropriate `data` property. The polling interval doesn't have to be the same as the motion manager's update interval; when you poll, you'll obtain the motion manager's *current* data — that is, the data generated by its most recent update, whenever that was.

Push

If your purpose is to collect *all* the data, then instead of calling a simple `start` method, you can call a related method that takes a function that will be called back, preferably on a background thread managed by an OperationQueue (Chapter 24). The name of this method will have the form `start...Updates(to:withHandler:)`. For example, for accelerometer updates, instead of `startAccelerometerUpdates`, you would call `startAccelerometerUpdates(to:withHandler:)`.

6. Don't forget to call the corresponding `stop` method, such as `stopAccelerometerUpdates`, when you no longer need data.

So there are two ways to get motion manager data — pull and push. Which approach should you use? It depends on what you're trying to accomplish. Polling (pull) is a good way to learn the device's instantaneous state at some significant moment. A stream of callbacks (push) is a good way to detect a gesture, typically by recording the most recent data into a circular buffer for subsequent analysis. It's perfectly possible to use *both* methods; having configured push, you can perform an occasional pull.

Raw Acceleration

If the device has an accelerometer but no gyroscope, you can learn about the forces being applied to it, but some compromises will be necessary. The chief problem is that, even if the device is completely motionless, its acceleration values will constitute a normalized vector pointing toward the center of the earth, popularly known as *gravity*. The accelerometer is constantly reporting a combination of gravity and user-induced acceleration. This is good and bad. It's good because it means that, with certain restrictions, you can use the accelerometer to detect the device's attitude in space. It's bad because gravity values and user-induced acceleration values are mixed together. Fortunately, there are ways to separate them mathematically:

With a low-pass filter
A low-pass filter will damp out user acceleration so as to report gravity only.

With a high-pass filter
A high-pass filter will damp out the effect of gravity so as to detect user acceleration only, reporting a motionless device as having zero acceleration.

In some situations, it is desirable to apply both a low-pass filter and a high-pass filter, so as to learn both the gravity values and the user acceleration values. A common additional technique is to run the output of the high-pass filter itself through a low-pass filter to reduce noise and small twitches. Apple provides some nice sample code for implementing a low-pass or a high-pass filter; see especially the AccelerometerGraph example, which is also helpful for exploring how the accelerometer behaves.

The technique of applying filters to the accelerometer output has some serious downsides, which are inevitable in a device that lacks a gyroscope:

- It's up to you to apply the filters; you have to implement boilerplate code and hope that you don't make a mistake.

- Filters mean *latency*. Your response to the accelerometer values will lag behind what the device is actually doing; this lag may be noticeable.

Gravity and attitude

In this example, I will simply report whether the device is lying flat on its back. I start by configuring my motion manager; then I launch a repeating timer to trigger polling:

```
guard self.motman.isAccelerometerAvailable else { return }
self.motman.accelerometerUpdateInterval = 1.0 / 30.0
self.motman.startAccelerometerUpdates()
self.timer = Timer.scheduledTimer(
    timeInterval:self.motman.accelerometerUpdateInterval,
    target: self, selector: #selector(pollAccel),
    userInfo: nil, repeats: true)
```

My `pollAccel` method is now being called repeatedly. In it, I ask the motion manager for its accelerometer data. This arrives as a CMAccelerometerData object, which is a timestamp plus a CMAcceleration; a CMAcceleration is simply a struct of three values, one for each axis of the device, measured in Gs:

- The positive x-axis points to the right of the device.

- The positive y-axis points toward the top of the device.

- The positive z-axis points out the front of the screen.

The two axes orthogonal to gravity, which are the x- and y-axes when the device is lying more or less on its back, are much more accurate and sensitive to small variation than the axis pointing toward or away from gravity. So our approach is to ask first whether the x and y values are close to zero; only then do we use the z value to learn whether the device is on its back or on its face. To keep from updating our interface constantly, we implement a crude state machine; the state property (`self.state`) starts out at `.unknown`, and then switches between `.lyingDown` (device on its back) and `.notLyingDown` (device not on its back), and we update the interface only when there is a state change:

```
guard let data = self.motman.accelerometerData else {return}
let acc = data.acceleration
let x = acc.x
let y = acc.y
let z = acc.z
let accu = 0.08
if abs(x) < accu && abs(y) < accu && z < -0.5 {
```

```
        if self.state == .unknown || self.state == .notLyingDown {
            self.state = .lyingDown
            self.label.text = "I'm lying on my back... ahhh..."
        }
    } else {
        if self.state == .unknown || self.state == .lyingDown {
            self.state = .notLyingDown
            self.label.text = "Hey, put me back down on the table!"
        }
    }
```

This works, but it's sensitive to small motions of the device on the table. To damp this sensitivity, we can run our input through a low-pass filter. The low-pass filter code comes straight from Apple's own examples, and involves maintaining the previously filtered reading as a set of properties:

```
func add(acceleration accel:CMAcceleration) {
    let alpha = 0.1
    self.oldX = accel.x * alpha + self.oldX * (1.0 - alpha)
    self.oldY = accel.y * alpha + self.oldY * (1.0 - alpha)
    self.oldZ = accel.z * alpha + self.oldZ * (1.0 - alpha)
}
```

Our polling code now starts out by passing the data through the filter:

```
guard let data = self.motman.accelerometerData else {return}
self.add(acceleration: data.acceleration)
let x = self.oldX
let y = self.oldY
let z = self.oldZ
// ... and the rest is as before ...
```

As I mentioned earlier, instead of polling (pull), you can receive callbacks to a function (push). This approach is useful particularly if your goal is to collect updates or to receive updates on a background thread (or both). To illustrate, I'll rewrite the previous example to use this technique; to keep things simple, I'll ask for my callbacks on the main thread (the documentation advises against this, but Apple's own sample code does it). We now start our accelerometer updates like this:

```
self.motman.startAccelerometerUpdates(to: .main) { data, err in
    guard let data = data else {
        print(err)
        self.stopAccelerometer()
        return
    }
    self.receive(acceleration:data)
}
```

receive(acceleration:) is just like our earlier pollAccel, except that we already have the accelerometer data:

```
func receive(acceleration data:CMAccelerometerData) {
    self.add(acceleration: data.acceleration)
    let x = self.oldX
    let y = self.oldY
    let z = self.oldZ
    // ... and the rest is as before ...
}
```

Force applied by the user

In this next example, the user is allowed to slap the side of the device into an open
hand — perhaps as a way of telling it to go to the next or previous image or whatever
it is we're displaying. We pass the acceleration input through a high-pass filter to
eliminate gravity (again, the filter code comes straight from Apple's examples):

```
func add(acceleration accel:CMAcceleration) {
    let alpha = 0.1
    self.oldX = accel.x - ((accel.x * alpha) + (self.oldX * (1.0 - alpha)))
    self.oldY = accel.y - ((accel.y * alpha) + (self.oldY * (1.0 - alpha)))
    self.oldZ = accel.z - ((accel.z * alpha) + (self.oldZ * (1.0 - alpha)))
}
```

What we're looking for, in our polling routine, is a high positive or negative x value.
A single slap is likely to consist of several consecutive readings above our threshold,
but we want to report each slap only once, so we take advantage of the timestamp
attached to a CMAccelerometerData, maintaining the timestamp of our previous
high reading as a property and ignoring readings that are too close to one another in
time. Another problem is that a sudden jerk involves both an acceleration (as the user
starts the device moving) and a deceleration (as the device stops moving); a left slap
might be preceded by a high value in the opposite direction, which we might interpret wrongly as a right slap. We can compensate crudely, at the expense of some
latency, with delayed performance:

```
@objc func pollAccel(_: Any) {
    guard let data = self.motman.accelerometerData else {return}
    self.add(acceleration: data.acceleration)
    let x = self.oldX
    let thresh = 1.0
    if x < -thresh {
        if data.timestamp - self.oldTime > 0.5 || self.lastSlap == .right {
            self.oldTime = data.timestamp
            self.lastSlap = .left
            self.canceltimer?.invalidate()
            self.canceltimer = .scheduledTimer(
                withTimeInterval:0.5, repeats: false) { _ in
                    print("left")
            }
        }
    } else if x > thresh {
        if data.timestamp - self.oldTime > 0.5 || self.lastSlap == .left {
```

```
                    self.oldTime = data.timestamp
                    self.lastSlap = .right
                    self.canceltimer?.invalidate()
                    self.canceltimer = .scheduledTimer(
                        withTimeInterval:0.5, repeats: false) { _ in
                            print("right")
                    }
                }
            }
        }
```

The gesture we're detecting is a little tricky to make: the user must slap the device into an open hand *and hold it there*; if the device jumps out of the open hand, that movement may be detected as the last in the series, resulting in the wrong report (left instead of right, or *vice versa*). And the latency of our gesture detection is very high.

Of course we might try tweaking some of the magic numbers in this code to improve accuracy and performance, but a more sophisticated analysis would probably involve storing a stream of all the most recent CMAccelerometerData objects in a circular buffer and studying the buffer contents to work out the overall trend.

Gyroscope

The inclusion of an electronic gyroscope in the panoply of onboard hardware in some devices makes a huge difference in the accuracy and speed of gravity and attitude reporting. A gyroscope has the property that its attitude in space remains constant, so it can detect any change in the attitude of the containing device. This has two important consequences for accelerometer measurements:

- The accelerometer can be supplemented by the gyroscope to detect quickly the difference between gravity and user-induced acceleration.

- The gyroscope can observe pure rotation, where little or no acceleration is involved and so the accelerometer would not have been helpful. The extreme case is constant attitudinal rotation around the gravity axis, which the accelerometer alone would be unable to detect (because there is no user-induced force, and gravity remains constant).

It is possible to track the raw gyroscope data: make sure the device has a gyroscope (isGyroAvailable), and then call startGyroUpdates. What we get from the motion manager is a CMGyroData object, which combines a timestamp with a CMRotationRate that reports the *rate of rotation* around each axis, measured in radians per second, where a positive value is *counterclockwise* as seen by someone whose eye is pointed to by the positive axis. (This is the opposite of the direction graphed in Figure 1-11.)

But there's a problem: the gyroscope values are *scaled* and *biased*. This means that the values are based on an arbitrary scale and are gradually increasing (or decreasing) over time at a roughly constant rate. So in real life you are unlikely to want raw gyroscope data. Instead, you'll use device motion.

Device motion

The most reliable way to obtain the device's attitude is through a combination of at least the gyroscope and the accelerometer. The mathematics required to combine the data from these sensors can be daunting. Fortunately, there's no need to know anything about that. Core Motion will happily package up the calculated combination of data as a device motion instance (CMDeviceMotion), with the effects of the sensors' internal bias and scaling already factored out.

CMDeviceMotion consists of the following properties, all of which provide a triple of values corresponding to the device's natural 3D frame (x increasing to the right, y increasing to the top, z increasing out the front):

gravity
> A CMAcceleration expressing a vector with value 1 pointing to the center of the earth, measured in Gs.

userAcceleration
> A CMAcceleration describing user-induced acceleration, with no gravity component, measured in Gs.

rotationRate
> A CMRotationRate describing how the device is rotating around its own center. This is essentially the CMGyroData rotationRate with scale and bias already accounted for.

magneticField
> A CMCalibratedMagneticField describing (in its field, a CMMagneticField) the magnetic forces acting on the device, measured in microteslas. The sensor's internal bias has already been factored out. The accuracy is one of the following (CMMagneticFieldCalibrationAccuracy):
>
> * .uncalibrated
> * .low
> * .medium
> * .high

attitude
> A CMAttitude, descriptive of the device's instantaneous attitude in space. The attitude is measured against a reference frame (CMAttitudeReferenceFrame) which you specify when you ask the motion manager to start generating updates,

having first called the class method `availableAttitudeReferenceFrames` to ascertain that the desired reference frame is available on this device. In every case, the negative z-axis points at the center of the earth; what varies between reference frames is where the x-axis is (and the y-axis is then orthogonal to the other two):

`.xArbitraryZVertical`
>   The x-axis could be pointing anywhere.

`.xArbitraryCorrectedZVertical`
>   The same as the previous option, but the magnetometer is used to maintain accuracy (preventing drift of the reference frame over time).

`.xMagneticNorthZVertical`
>   The x-axis points toward magnetic north.

`.xTrueNorthZVertical`
>   The x-axis points toward true north. This value will be inaccurate unless you are also using Core Location to obtain the device's location.

The `attitude` value's numbers can be accessed through various CMAttitude properties corresponding to three different systems, each being convenient for a different purpose:

`pitch, roll, yaw`
>   The device's angle of offset from the reference frame, in radians, around the device's natural x-axis, y-axis, and z-axis respectively (also known as Euler angles).

`rotationMatrix`
>   A CMRotationMatrix struct embodying a 3×3 matrix expressing a rotation in the reference frame.

`quaternion`
>   A CMQuaternion describing an attitude. (Quaternions are commonly used in 3D contexts such as SceneKit and Metal.)

`heading`
>   A Double giving the device's orientation as a number of degrees (*not* radians) clockwise from north, in accordance with the reference frame which must be `.xMagneticNorthZVertical` or `.xTrueNorthZVertical` (otherwise, you'll get a value of `-1`). Unlike a Core Location CLHeading, it is a pure orientation reading, without the course folded into it. Not only the magnetometer but also the accelerometer and gyroscope are used, helping to eliminate errors caused by local magnetic anomalies.

Absolute attitude

In this example, we turn the device into a simple compass/clinometer, merely by asking for its `attitude` with reference to magnetic north and taking its `pitch`, `roll`, and `yaw`. We begin by making the usual preparations; notice the use of the `showsDevice-MovementDisplay` property, intended to allow the runtime to prompt the user if the magnetometer needs calibration:

```
guard self.motman.isDeviceMotionAvailable else { return }
let r = CMAttitudeReferenceFrame.xMagneticNorthZVertical
guard CMMotionManager.availableAttitudeReferenceFrames().contains(r) else {
    return
}
self.motman.showsDeviceMovementDisplay = true
self.motman.deviceMotionUpdateInterval = 1.0 / 30.0
self.motman.startDeviceMotionUpdates(using: r)
let t = self.motman.deviceMotionUpdateInterval * 10
self.timer = Timer.scheduledTimer(timeInterval:t,
    target:self, selector:#selector(pollAttitude),
    userInfo:nil, repeats:true)
```

In `pollAttitude`, we wait until the magnetometer is ready, and then we start taking attitude readings (converted to degrees):

```
guard let mot = self.motman.deviceMotion else {return}
let acc = mot.magneticField.accuracy.rawValue
if acc <= CMMagneticFieldCalibrationAccuracy.low.rawValue {
    return // not ready yet
}
let att = mot.attitude
let to_deg = 180.0 / .pi
print("\(att.pitch * to_deg), \(att.roll * to_deg), \(att.yaw * to_deg)")
```

The values are all close to zero when the device is level (flat on its back) with its x-axis (right edge) pointing to magnetic north, and each value increases as the device is rotated *counterclockwise* with respect to an eye that has the corresponding positive axis pointing at it. A device held upright (top pointing at the sky) has a `pitch` approaching 90; a device lying on its right edge has a `roll` approaching 90; and a device lying on its back with its top pointing north has a `yaw` approaching -90.

There are some quirks in the way Euler angles operate mathematically:

- `roll` and `yaw` increase with counterclockwise rotation from 0 to π (180 degrees) and then jump to -π (-180 degrees) and continue to increase to 0 as the rotation completes a circle; but `pitch` increases to π/2 (90 degrees) and then decreases to 0, then decreases to -π/2 (-90 degrees) and increases to 0. This means that `attitude` alone, if we are exploring it through `pitch`, `roll`, and `yaw`, is insufficient to describe the device's attitude, since a `pitch` value of, say, π/4 (45 degrees) could mean two different things. To distinguish those two things, we can supplement `attitude` with the z-component of `gravity`:

```
let g = mot.gravity
let whichway = g.z > 0 ? "forward" : "back"
print("pitch is tilted \(whichway)")
```

- Values become inaccurate in certain orientations. In particular, when `pitch` approaches ±90 degrees (the device is upright or inverted), `roll` and `yaw` become erratic. (You may see this effect referred to as "the singularity" or "gimbal lock.") I believe that, depending on what you are trying to accomplish, you can solve this by using a different expression of the attitude, such as the `rotationMatrix`, which does not suffer from this limitation.

Relative attitude

This next example illustrates a use of CMAttitude's `rotationMatrix` property. Our goal is to make a CALayer rotate in response to the current attitude of the device. We start as before, except that our reference frame is `.xArbitraryZVertical`; we are interested in how the device moves from its initial attitude, without reference to any particular fixed external direction such as magnetic north. In `pollAttitude`, our first step is to store the device's current attitude in a CMAttitude property, `self.ref`:

```
guard let mot = self.motman.deviceMotion else {return}
let att = mot.attitude
if self.ref == nil {
    self.ref = att
    return
}
```

That code works correctly because on the first few polls, as the attitude-detection hardware warms up, `att` is `nil`, so we don't get past the `return` call until we have a valid initial attitude. Our next step is highly characteristic of how CMAttitude is used: we call the CMAttitude instance method `multiply(byInverseOf:)`, which transforms our attitude so that it is relative *to the stored initial attitude*:

```
att.multiply(byInverseOf: self.ref)
```

Finally, we apply the attitude's rotation matrix directly to a layer in our interface as a transform. Well, not quite directly: a rotation matrix is a 3×3 matrix, whereas a CATransform3D, which is what we need in order to set a layer's `transform`, is a 4×4 matrix. However, it happens that the top left nine entries in a CATransform3D matrix constitute its rotation component, so we start with an identity matrix and set those entries directly:

```
let r = att.rotationMatrix
var t = CATransform3DIdentity
t.m11 = CGFloat(r.m11)
t.m12 = CGFloat(r.m12)
```

```
t.m13 = CGFloat(r.m13)
t.m21 = CGFloat(r.m21)
t.m22 = CGFloat(r.m22)
t.m23 = CGFloat(r.m23)
t.m31 = CGFloat(r.m31)
t.m32 = CGFloat(r.m32)
t.m33 = CGFloat(r.m33)
let lay = // whatever
CATransaction.setAnimationDuration(1.0/10.0)
lay.transform = t
```

The result is that the layer apparently tries to hold itself still as the device rotates. The example is rather crude because we aren't drawing a three-dimensional object, but it illustrates the principle well enough.

There is a quirk to be aware of in this case as well: over time, the transform has a tendency to drift. Even if we leave the device stationary, the layer will gradually rotate. That is the sort of effect that `.xArbitraryCorrectedZVertical` is designed to help mitigate, at the expense of some CPU and battery usage, by bringing the magnetometer into play.

Core Motion best practices

Here are some additional considerations to be aware of when using Core Motion:

- Your app should create only one CMMotionManager instance.

- Core Motion requires that various sensors be turned on, such as the magnetometer and the gyroscope. This can result in some increased battery drain, so try not to use any sensors you don't have to, and remember to stop generating updates as soon as you no longer need them.

- Use of Core Motion is legal while your app is running in the background. To take advantage of this, your app would need to be running in the background for some *other* reason; there is no Core Motion `UIBackgroundModes` setting in an *Info.plist*. You might run in the background because you're using Core Location, and take advantage of this to employ Core Motion as well.

- If your app will *not* be running in the background, then you should tell the motion manager explicitly to stop generating updates when your app goes into the background.

Other Core Motion Data

In addition to CMDeviceMotion, the Core Motion framework lets you obtain four other types of data:

CMMotionActivityManager

Some devices have a motion coprocessor chip with the ability to detect, analyze, and keep a record of device motion even while the device is asleep and with very little drain on power. This is *not* a form of location determination; it is an analysis of the device's physical motion and attitude in order to draw conclusions about what the user has been doing while carrying or wearing the device. You can learn that the user is walking, or walked for an hour, but not *where* the user was walking.

Start by maintaining a CMMotionActivityManager instance, typically as an instance property. To find out whether the device has a motion coprocessor, call the CMMotionActivityManager class method `isActivityAvailable`. There are two ways to query the motion activity manager:

Real-time updates

This is similar to getting motion manager updates with a callback function. You call this method:

- `startActivityUpdates(to:withHandler:)`

Your callback function is called periodically. When you no longer need updates, call `stopActivityUpdates`.

Historical data

The motion coprocessor stores about a week's-worth of the most recent data. You ask for a chunk of that recorded data by calling this method:

- `queryActivityStarting(from:to:to:withHandler:)`

It's fine to query the historical data while the motion activity manager is already delivering updates.

CMPedometer

The pedometer is a step counter, deducing steps from the back and forth motion of the device; it can also be used to receive events alerting you that the user has started or stopped activity. The pedometer may work reliably under circumstances where Core Location doesn't.

Start by maintaining a CMPedometer instance, typically as an instance property. Before using the pedometer, check the `isStepCountingAvailable` class method. Different devices add further capabilities. Some devices can deduce the size of the user's stride and compute distance (`isDistanceAvailable`); some devices can use barometric data to estimate whether the user mounted a flight of stairs (`isFloorCountingAvailable`). You can also ask for instantaneous cadence (`isCadenceAvailable`) and pace (`isPaceAvailable`).

Pedometer data is queried just like motion activity data:

Real-time updates

You can ask for constant updates with this method:

- `startUpdates(from:withHandler:)`

Historical data

You can ask for the stored history with this method:

- `queryPedometerData(from:to:withHandler:)`

Each bit of data arrives as a CMPedometerData object.

To be notified of changes in the user's motion, call `startEvent-Updates(handler:)`; the `handler:` function receives a CMPedometerEvent whose `type` (CMPedometerEventType) is `.pause` or `.resume`.

CMAltimeter

Some devices have an altimeter — in essence, a barometer. The idea here is not so much to tell you the user's absolute altitude, since atmospheric pressure can vary considerably at a fixed altitude, but to alert you to changes in the user's relative altitude during activity.

Start by maintaining a CMAltimeter instance, typically as an instance property. Before using the altimeter, check the `isRelativeAltitudeAvailable` class method. Then call `startRelativeAltitudeUpdates(to:withHandler:)` to start delivery of CMAltitudeData objects; the key metric is the `relativeAltitude` property, an NSNumber wrapping a Double representing meters. It starts life at 0, and subsequent CMAltitudeData objects provide a measurement relative to that initial base.

CMSensorRecorder

Some devices can record the output of the accelerometer over time in the background. Before using the recorder, check the `isAccelerometerRecording-Available`. Then instantiate CMSensorRecorder (you do *not* need to retain the instance) and call `recordAccelerometer(forDuration:)`. Recording is done by the system, 50 times per second, on your behalf, regardless of whether your app is in the foreground or even whether it is running, and stops automatically when the `duration` is over.

To retrieve the data, instantiate CMSensorRecorder again, and call `accelerometerData(from:to:)`. You are given a CMSensorDataList, which unfortunately is rather tricky to deal with. First, you'll need to make CMSensor-DataList conform to Sequence by means of an extension:

```
extension CMSensorDataList: Sequence {
    public typealias Iterator = NSFastEnumerationIterator
    public func makeIterator() -> NSFastEnumerationIterator {
        return NSFastEnumerationIterator(self)
    }
}
```

Now you can iterate over CMSensorDataList to get CMRecordedAccelerometer-Data instances, each consisting of a `timestamp` and an `acceleration` (a CMAcceleration, discussed earlier in this chapter):

```
let rec = CMSensorRecorder() // and d1 and d2 are Dates
if let list = rec.accelerometerData(from: d1, to: d2) {
    for datum in list {
        if let accdatum = datum as? CMRecordedAccelerometerData {
            let accel = accdatum.acceleration
            let t = accdatum.timestamp
            // do something with data here
        }
    }
}
```

All four types of data have in common that you need user authorization to obtain them (and even if you obtain such authorization, the user can later use the Settings app to withdraw it). Your *Info.plist* must contain an entry under the "Privacy — Motion Usage Description" key (`NSMotionUsageDescription`) explaining your purpose. Oddly, there is no `requestAuthorization` method. In the past, there wasn't even any easy way to learn in advance whether we had authorization; the technique was to "tickle" the appropriate class by trying to query it for data and see if you got an error. In this example, I have a Bool property, `self.authorized`, which I set based on the outcome of trying to query the motion activity manager:

```
guard CMMotionActivityManager.isActivityAvailable() else { return }
let now = Date()
self.actman.queryActivityStarting(from:now, to:now, to:.main) { arr, err in
    let notauth = Int(CMErrorMotionActivityNotAuthorized.rawValue)
    if err != nil && (err! as NSError).code == notauth {
        self.isAuthorized = false
    } else {
        self.isAuthorized = true
    }
}
```

On the first run of that code, the system puts up the authorization request alert if necessary. The completion function is not called until the user deals with the alert, so the outcome tells you what the user decided. On subsequent runs, that same code reports the current authorization status.

Starting in iOS 11, there's an easier way: you can ask the class in question for its authorizationStatus. This returns a status enum with the usual four cases. You *still* need to "tickle" the class to summon the authorization alert if the status is .notDetermined. This allows us to use a strategy similar to the one devised earlier ("Checking for Authorization" on page 861). I assume here that self.actman is a CMMotionActivityManager instance:

```
func checkAuthorization(andThen f:(()->())? = nil) {
    let status = CMMotionActivityManager.authorizationStatus()
    switch status {
    case .notDetermined: // bring up alert
        let now = Date()
        self.actman.queryActivityStarting(from: now, to:now, to:.main) {
            _,err in
            print("asked for authorization")
            if err == nil {
                f?()
            }
        }
    case .authorized: f?()
    case .restricted: break // do nothing
    case .denied: break // could beg for authorization here
    @unknown default: fatalError()
    }
}
```

I'll illustrate querying for historical motion activity manager data by fetching the data for the past 24 hours. I have prepared an OperationQueue property, self.queue:

```
let now = Date()
let yester = now - (60*60*24)
self.actman.queryActivityStarting(
    from: yester, to: now, to: self.queue) { arr, err in
        guard var acts = arr else {return}
        // ...
}
```

We now have an array of CMMotionActivity objects representing every *change* in the device's activity status. This is a value class. It has a startDate, a confidence (a CMMotionActivityConfidence, .low, .medium, or .high) ranking the activity manager's faith in its own categorization of what the user was doing, and a bunch of Bool properties actually categorizing the activity:

- stationary
- walking
- running
- automotive

- cycling

- unknown

A common first response to the flood of data is to pare it down (sometimes referred to as *smoothing* or *decimating*). To help with this, I've extended CMMotionActivity with a utility method that summarizes its Bool properties as a string:

```
extension CMMotionActivity {
    private func tf(_ b:Bool) -> String {
        return b ? "t" : "f"
    }
    func overallAct() -> String {
        let s = tf(self.stationary)
        let w = tf(self.walking)
        let r = tf(self.running)
        let a = tf(self.automotive)
        let c = tf(self.cycling)
        let u = tf(self.unknown)
        return "\(s) \(w) \(r) \(a) \(c) \(u)"
    }
}
```

As a straightforward way of paring down the data, I remove every CMMotionActivity with no definite activity, or with a low degree of confidence, or with an activity that is the same as its predecessor. Then I set an instance property with my data, ready for use:

```
let blank = "f f f f f f"
acts = acts.filter {act in act.overallAct() != blank}
acts = acts.filter {act in act.confidence == .high}
for i in (1..<acts.count).reversed() {
    if acts[i].overallAct() == acts[i-1].overallAct() {
        acts.remove(at:i)
    }
}
DispatchQueue.main.async {
    self.data = acts
}
```

PART IV

Final Topics

This part of the book is a miscellany of topics:

- Chapter 22 is about files and how your app can store data persistently. It also discusses sharing files with the user and with other apps, plus the document architecture and iCloud, and surveys some common file formats.

- Chapter 23 introduces networking, with an emphasis on downloading of data, along with some specialized forms of networking such as on-demand resources and in-app purchases.

- Chapter 24 is about making your code multithreaded.

- Chapter 25 describes how to support undo in your app.

- Appendix A discusses the lifetime event messages sent to your app.

- Appendix B is a catalog of some useful Swift utility functions that I've written.

- Appendix C is an excursus on asynchronous code execution.

CHAPTER 22

Persistent Storage

Your app can save data into files that persist on the device when your app isn't running or the device is powered down. This chapter is about how and where files are saved and retrieved. It also talks about some of the additional ways in which files can be manipulated, such as how apps can share documents with one another and with the cloud. The chapter also explains how user preferences are maintained in User-Defaults, and describes some specialized file formats and ways of working with their data, such as XML, JSON, SQLite, Core Data, PDF, and images.

The Sandbox

The device's file contents as a whole are not open to your app's view. Instead, a limited region of the device's persistent storage is dedicated to each app: this is the app's *sandbox*. The idea is that every app, seeing only its own sandbox, is hindered from impinging on the files belonging to other apps, and in turn is protected from having its own files impinged on by other apps. Your sandbox, and hence your data, will be deleted if the user deletes your app; otherwise, it should reliably persist.

Standard Directories

The preferred way to refer to a file or directory is with a *file URL*, a URL instance. The other possible way is with a file path, or *pathname,* which is a string; if necessary, you can convert from a file URL to a file path by asking for the URL's `path`, or from a pathname to a file URL with the URL initializer `init(fileURLWithPath:)`. But on the whole, you should try to stick with URL objects.

The sandbox contains some standard directories, and there are built-in methods for referring to them You can obtain a URL for a standard directory by starting with a

FileManager instance, which will usually be `FileManager.default`, and calling `url(for:in:appropriateFor:create:)`, like this:

```
do {
    let fm = FileManager.default
    let docsurl = try fm.url(for:.documentDirectory,
        in: .userDomainMask, appropriateFor: nil, create: false)
    // use docsurl here
} catch {
    // deal with error here
}
```

A question that will immediately occur to you is: where should I put files and folders that I want to save now and read later? The Documents directory can be a good place. But if your app supports file sharing (discussed later in this chapter), the user can see and modify your app's Documents directory, so you might not want to put things there that the user isn't supposed to see and change. A good alternative is the Application Support directory. In iOS, each app gets a private Application Support directory in its own sandbox, so you can safely put files directly into it. This directory may not exist initially, but you can obtain it and create it at the same time:

```
do {
    let fm = FileManager.default
    let suppurl = try fm.url(for:.applicationSupportDirectory,
        in: .userDomainMask, appropriateFor: nil, create: true)
    // use suppurl here
} catch {
    // deal with error here
}
```

Temporary files whose loss you are willing to accept (because their contents can be recreated) can be written into the Caches directory (`.cachesDirectory`) or the Temporary directory (the FileManager's `temporaryDirectory`). You can write temporary files into the Application Support folder, but by default this means they can be backed up by the user through iTunes or iCloud; to prevent that, exclude such a file from backup by way of its attributes:

```
var rv = URLResourceValues()
rv.isExcludedFromBackup = true
try myFileURL.setResourceValues(rv)
```

Inspecting the Sandbox

While developing your app, you might like to peek inside its sandbox for debugging purposes, to make sure your files are being saved as you expect. The Simulator's sandbox for your app is a folder on your Mac that you can, with some cunning, inspect visually. In your app's code, print to the Xcode console the `path` of your app's Documents directory. Copy that value from the console, switch to the Finder, choose Go → Go to Folder, paste the path into the dialog that appears, and click Go. Now

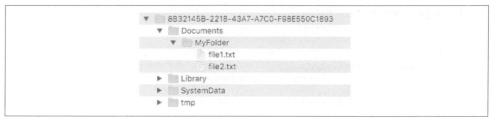

Figure 22-1. An app's sandbox in the Simulator

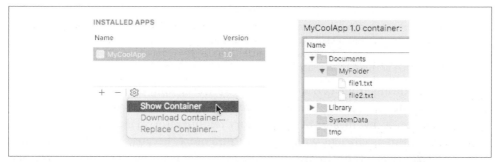

Figure 22-2. Summoning and displaying an app's sandbox on a device

you're looking at your app's Documents directory in the Finder; to see more of the sandbox, press Command-Up arrow.

Figure 22-1 displays my app's sandbox. The Documents folder contains a folder and a couple of files that I've created programmatically (the code that created them will appear later in this chapter).

You can also view the file structure of your app's sandbox on a device. When the device is connected, choose Window → Devices and Simulators, and switch to the Devices tab. Select your device on the left; on the right, under Installed Apps, select your app. Click the Gear icon and choose Show Container; after an extremely long delay, your app's sandbox hierarchy is displayed in a modal sheet (Figure 22-2). Alternatively, choose Download Container to copy your app's sandbox to your computer; the sandbox arrives on your computer as an *.xcappdata* package, and you can open it in the Finder with Show Package Contents.

Basic File Operations

Let's say we intend to create a folder *MyFolder* inside the Documents directory. We already know how to use a FileManager instance to get a URL pointing at the Documents directory; from this, we can generate a reference to the *MyFolder* folder. Using that reference, we can ask the FileManager to create the folder if it doesn't exist already:

```
let foldername = "MyFolder"
let fm = FileManager.default
let docsurl = try fm.url(for:.documentDirectory,
    in: .userDomainMask, appropriateFor: nil, create: false)
let myfolder = docsurl.appendingPathComponent(foldername)
try fm.createDirectory(at:myfolder, withIntermediateDirectories: true)
```

To learn what files and folders exist within a directory, you can ask for an array of the directory's contents:

```
let fm = FileManager.default
let docsurl = try fm.url(for:.documentDirectory,
    in: .userDomainMask, appropriateFor: nil, create: false)
let arr = try fm.contentsOfDirectory(at:docsurl,
    includingPropertiesForKeys: nil)
arr.forEach{ print($0.lastPathComponent) } // MyFolder
```

The array resulting from `contentsOfDirectory` lists full URLs of the directory's immediate contents; it is *shallow*. For a *deep* traversal of a directory's contents, you can enumerate it by means of a directory enumerator (FileManager.Directory-Enumerator); this is efficient with regards to memory, because you are handed just one file reference at a time. In this example, *MyFolder* is in the Documents directory, and I am looking for two *.txt* files that I have saved into *MyFolder* (as explained in the next section); I find them by doing a deep traversal of the Documents directory:

```
let fm = FileManager.default
let docsurl = try fm.url(for:.documentDirectory,
    in: .userDomainMask, appropriateFor: nil, create: false)
let dir = fm.enumerator(at:docsurl, includingPropertiesForKeys: nil)!
for case let f as URL in dir where f.pathExtension == "txt" {
    print(f.lastPathComponent) // file1.txt, file2.txt
}
```

A directory enumerator also permits you to decline to dive into a particular subdirectory (`skipDescendants`), so you can make your traversal even more efficient.

Consult the FileManager class documentation for more about what you can do with files, and see also Apple's *File System Programming Guide* in the documentation archive.

Saving and Reading Files

Four Cocoa classes provide a `write` instance method that saves an instance to a file, and an initializer that creates an instance by reading from a file. The file is represented by its file URL:

NSString and NSData
> NSString and NSData objects map directly between their own contents and the contents of a file. Here, I'll generate a text file in *MyFolder* directly from a string:

```
try "howdy".write(to: myfolder.appendingPathComponent("file1.txt"),
    atomically: true, encoding:.utf8)
```

NSArray and NSDictionary

NSArray and NSDictionary objects are written to a file as a *property list*. This means that all the contents of the array or dictionary must be *property list types*, which are:

- NSString
- NSData
- NSDate
- NSNumber
- NSArray
- NSDictionary

If you have an array or dictionary containing only those types (or Swift types that are bridged to them), you can write it out directly to a file with `write(to:)`. Here, I create an array of strings and write it out as a property list file:

```
let arr = ["Manny", "Moe", "Jack"]
let temp = FileManager.default.temporaryDirectory
let f = temp.appendingPathComponent("pep.plist")
try (arr as NSArray).write(to: f)
```

But how do you save an object of some *other* type to a file? The strategy is to *serialize* it to an NSData object (Swift Data). This, as we already know, can be saved directly to a file, or can be part of an array or dictionary to be saved to a file — and so the problem is solved.

Serializing means that we describe the object in terms of the values of its properties. There are two approaches to serializing an object as Data — the older Cocoa way (NSCoding) and the newer Swift way (Codable).

NSCoding

The NSCoding protocol is defined in Cocoa's Foundation framework. If an object's class adopts NSCoding, that object can be converted to NSData and back again, by way of the NSCoder subclasses NSKeyedArchiver and NSKeyedUnarchiver. This means that the class implements encode(with:) to archive the object and init(coder:) to unarchive the object.

Many built-in Cocoa classes adopt NSCoding — and you can make your own class adopt NSCoding as well. This can become somewhat involved, because an object can refer (through a property) to another object, which may also adopt NSCoding, and you can end up saving an entire graph of interconnected objects. I'll confine myself to illustrating a simple case (and for more, see Apple's *Archives and Serializations Programming Guide*, in the documentation archive).

Let's say that we have a simple Person class with a firstName property and a lastName property. We'll declare that it adopts the NSCoding protocol. For this to work, the properties must themselves adopt NSCoding. We can declare them as Swift Strings because String is toll-free bridged to NSString, which adopts NSCoding. Starting in iOS 12, Apple encourages us to step up our game to NSSecureCoding, a protocol that adopts NSCoding; to do so, we implement the static supportsSecureCoding property to return true:

```
class Person: NSObject, NSSecureCoding {
    static var supportsSecureCoding: Bool { return true }
    var firstName : String
    var lastName : String
    override var description : String {
        return self.firstName + " " + self.lastName
    }
    init(firstName:String, lastName:String) {
        self.firstName = firstName
        self.lastName = lastName
```

```
        super.init()
    }
    // ...
}
```

So far so good, but our code does not yet compile, because we do not yet conform to NSCoding (or to NSSecureCoding). We need to implement `encode(with:)` and `init(coder:)`.

In `encode(with:)`, we must first call `super` if the superclass adopts NSCoding — in this case, it doesn't — and then call the `encode` method for each property we want preserved:

```
func encode(with coder: NSCoder) {
    // do not call super in this case
    coder.encode(self.lastName, forKey: "last")
    coder.encode(self.firstName, forKey: "first")
}
```

In `init(coder:)`, we call a secure `decode` method for each property stored earlier, restoring the state of our object. We must also call `super`, using either `init(coder:)` if the superclass adopts NSCoding or the designated initializer if not:

```
required init(coder: NSCoder) {
    self.lastName = coder.decodeObject(
        of: NSString.self, forKey:"last")! as String
    self.firstName = coder.decodeObject(
        of: NSString.self, forKey:"first")! as String
    // do not call super init(coder:) in this case
    super.init()
}
```

We can test our code by creating, configuring, and saving a Person instance as a file:

```
let fm = FileManager.default
let docsurl = try fm.url(for:.documentDirectory,
    in: .userDomainMask, appropriateFor: nil, create: false)
let moi = Person(firstName: "Matt", lastName: "Neuburg")
let moidata = try NSKeyedArchiver.archivedData(
    withRootObject: moi, requiringSecureCoding: true)
let moifile = docsurl.appendingPathComponent("moi.txt")
try moidata.write(to: moifile, options: .atomic)
```

We can retrieve the saved Person at a later time:

```
let fm = FileManager.default
let docsurl = try fm.url(for:.documentDirectory,
    in: .userDomainMask, appropriateFor: nil, create: false)
let moifile = docsurl.appendingPathComponent("moi.txt")
let persondata = try Data(contentsOf: moifile)
let person = try NSKeyedUnarchiver.unarchivedObject(
    ofClass: Person.self, from: persondata)!
print(person) // "Matt Neuburg"
```

Even though Person now adopts NSCoding, an NSArray containing a Person object still cannot be written to a file using NSArray's write(to:), because Person is still not a property list type. But the array can be archived with NSKeyedArchiver and the resulting Data object *can* be written to a file. That's because NSArray conforms to NSCoding and, if its elements are Person objects, all its elements conform to NSCoding as well.

Codable

The Codable protocol was introduced in Swift 4; it is a combination of two other protocols, Encodable and Decodable. An object can be serialized (archived) as long as it conforms to Encodable, and can be restored from serial form (unarchived) as long as it conforms to Decodable. When the goal is to save to disk, an object will usually conform to both, and this will be expressed by having it adopt Codable. There are three modes of serialization:

- Property list
    - Use PropertyListEncoder encode(_:) to encode.
    - Use PropertyListDecoder decode(_:from:) to decode.
- JSON
    - Use JSONEncoder encode(_:) to encode.
    - Use JSONDecoder decode(_:from:) to decode.
- NSCoder
    - Use NSKeyedArchiver encodeEncodable(_:forKey:) to encode.
    - Use NSKeyedUnarchiver decodeDecodable(_:forKey:) to decode.

You'll probably prefer to use Swift Codable rather than Cocoa NSCoding wherever possible. A class instance, a struct instance, or even a RawRepresentable enum instance can be encoded, and most built-in Swift types are Codable right out of the box. Moreover, in most cases, *your* object type will be Codable right out of the box! There are encode(to:) and init(from:) methods, similar to NSCoding encode(with:) and init(coder:), but you usually won't need to implement them because the default methods, inherited through a protocol extension, will suffice.

To illustrate, I'll rewrite my Person class to adopt Codable instead of NSCoding:

```
class Person: NSObject, Codable {
    var firstName : String
    var lastName : String
    override var description : String {
        return self.firstName + " " + self.lastName
    }
    init(firstName:String, lastName:String) {
        self.firstName = firstName
```

```
            self.lastName = lastName
            super.init()
        }
    }
```

That's all! Person conforms to Codable with no further effort on our part. The primary reason is that our properties are Strings, and String is itself Codable. To save a Person to a file, we just have to pick an encoding format. I recommend using a property list unless there is some reason not to; it is simplest, and is closest to what NSKeyedArchiver does under the hood:

```
let fm = FileManager.default
let docsurl = try fm.url(for:.documentDirectory,
    in: .userDomainMask, appropriateFor: nil, create: false)
let moi = Person(firstName: "Matt", lastName: "Neuburg")
let moidata = try PropertyListEncoder().encode(moi)
let moifile = docsurl.appendingPathComponent("moi.txt")
try moidata.write(to: moifile, options: .atomic)
```

And here's how to retrieve our saved Person later:

```
let fm = FileManager.default
let docsurl = try fm.url(for:.documentDirectory,
    in: .userDomainMask, appropriateFor: nil, create: false)
let moifile = docsurl.appendingPathComponent("moi.txt")
let persondata = try Data(contentsOf: moifile)
let person = try PropertyListDecoder().decode(Person.self, from: persondata)
print(person) // "Matt Neuburg"
```

To save an array of Codable Person objects, do exactly the same thing. Array conforms to Codable, so use PropertyListEncoder to encode the array into a Data object and call `write(to:options:)`, precisely as we did for a single Person object. To retrieve the array, read the data from the file as a Data object and use a PropertyList-Decoder to call `decode([Person].self, from:data)`.

When your goal is to serialize your own object type to a file, there usually won't be any more to it than that. Your Codable implementation may be more elaborate when the format of the encoded data is out of your hands, such as when you are communicating through a JSON API dictated by a server. I'll illustrate later in this chapter.

The existence of Codable does not mean that you'll never need to use NSCoding. Cocoa is written in Objective-C; its encodable object types adopt NSCoding, not Codable. And the vast majority of your objects will be Cocoa objects. If you want to turn a UIColor into a Data object, you'll use an NSKeyedArchiver, not a PropertyList-Encoder; UIColor adopts NSCoding, not Codable. You can combine Swift Codable with Cocoa NSCoding, thanks to the NSCoder subclass methods `encode-Encodable(_:forKey:)` and `decodeDecodable(_:forKey:)`.

File Coordinators

In spite of sandboxing, a file can be exposed to more than one app. For example, you might permit the Files app to see into your Documents directory, as I'll explain later in this chapter. This raises the danger of simultaneous access. The low-level way to deal with that danger is to read and write through an NSFileCoordinator. Instantiate NSFileCoordinator along with an NSFileAccessIntent appropriate for reading or writing, to which you have handed the URL of your target file. Then call a coordinate method.

I'll demonstrate the use of `coordinate(with:queue:byAccessor:)`. The `accessor:` is a function where you do your actual reading or writing in the normal way, except that the URL for reading or writing now comes from the NSFileAccessIntent object. Here, I write a Person out to a file under the auspices of an NSFileCoordinator:

```
let fc = NSFileCoordinator()
let intent = NSFileAccessIntent.writingIntent(with:moifile)
fc.coordinate(with:[intent], queue: .main) { err in
    do {
        try moidata.write(to: intent.url, options: .atomic)
    } catch {
        print(error)
    }
}
```

And later I'll read that Person back from the same file:

```
let fc = NSFileCoordinator()
let intent = NSFileAccessIntent.readingIntent(with: moifile)
fc.coordinate(with: [intent], queue: .main) { err in
    do {
        let persondata = try Data(contentsOf: intent.url)
        // do something with data
    } catch {
        print(error)
    }
}
```

File Wrappers

A file needn't be a simple block of data. It can be a *file wrapper,* essentially a folder disguised as a file. On the desktop, a TextEdit *.rtfd* file, used when a styled TextEdit file contains images, is a file wrapper.

A file wrapper will usually contain multiple files along with some sort of file *manifest* reporting what the files are. The format of the manifest is up to you; it's a note to yourself that you configure when you save into the file wrapper, so that you can retrieve files from the file wrapper later.

In this simple example, I'll save the data for three UIImages into a file wrapper (at the file URL fwurl). The manifest will be a simple property list representation of an array of the names of the image files:

```
let d = FileWrapper(directoryWithFileWrappers: [:])
let imnames = ["manny.jpg", "moe.jpg", "jack.jpg"]
for imname in imnames {
    d.addRegularFile(
        withContents:
            UIImage(named:imname)!.jpegData(compressionQuality: 1)!,
        preferredFilename: imname)
}
let list = try PropertyListEncoder().encode(imnames)
d.addRegularFile(withContents: list, preferredFilename: "list")
try d.write(to: fwurl, originalContentsURL: nil)
```

The resulting file wrapper now contains four file wrappers, which can be accessed by name through its fileWrappers property. So here's how to extract the images later:

```
let d = try FileWrapper(url: fwurl)
if let list = d.fileWrappers?["list"]?.regularFileContents {
    let imnames = try PropertyListDecoder().decode([String].self, from:list)
    for imname in imnames {
        if let imdata = d.fileWrappers?[imname]?.regularFileContents {
            // do something with the image data
        }
    }
}
```

User Defaults

The UserDefaults class acts a gateway to persistent storage of the user's preferences. User defaults are little more, really, than a special case of an NSDictionary property list file. You talk to the UserDefaults standard object much as if it were a dictionary; it has keys and values, and you set and fetch values by their keys. The dictionary is saved for you automatically as a property list file; you don't know where or when, and you don't care.

 Actual saving of the dictionary to disk might not take place until several seconds after you make a change. When testing, be sure to allow sufficient time to elapse between runs of your app.

Because user defaults is actually a property list file, the only legal values that can be stored in it are property list values. Therefore, everything I said in the preceding section about saving objects applies. If an object type is not a property list type, you'll have to archive it to a Data object if you want to store it in user defaults. If the object type is a class that belongs to Cocoa and adopts NSCoding, you'll archive it through an NSKeyedArchiver. If the object type belongs to you, you might prefer to make it adopt Codable and archive it through a PropertyListEncoder.

To provide the value for a key before the user has had a chance to do so — the default default, as it were — call `register(defaults:)`. What you're supplying here is a transient dictionary whose key–value pairs will be held in memory but not saved; a pair will be used only if there is no pair with the same key already stored in the user defaults dictionary. Here's an example from one of my apps:

```
UserDefaults.standard.register(defaults: [
    Default.hazyStripy : HazyStripy.hazy.rawValue,
    Default.cardMatrixRows : 4,
    Default.cardMatrixColumns : 3,
    Default.color1 : try! NSKeyedArchiver.archivedData(
        withRootObject: UIColor.blue, requiringSecureCoding:true),
    Default.color2 : try! NSKeyedArchiver.archivedData(
        withRootObject: UIColor.red, requiringSecureCoding:true),
    Default.color3 : try! NSKeyedArchiver.archivedData(
        withRootObject: UIColor.green, requiringSecureCoding:true),
])
```

The idea is that we call `register(defaults:)` extremely early as the app launches. Either the app has run at some time previously and the user has set these preferences, in which case this call has no effect and does no harm, or not, in which case we now have initial values for these preferences with which to get started. In the game app from which that code comes, we start out with a hazy fill, a 4×3 game layout, and the three card colors blue, red, and green; but the user can change this at any time.

You will probably want to offer your user a way to interact explicitly with the defaults. One possibility is that your app provides some kind of interface. The game app from which the previous code comes has a tab bar interface; in the second tab, the user explicitly sets the preferences whose default values are configured in that code (Figure 22-3).

Alternatively, you can provide a *settings bundle*, consisting mostly of one or more property list files describing an interface and the corresponding user defaults keys and their initial values; the Settings app is then responsible for translating your instructions into an actual interface, and for presenting it to the user. Writing a settings bundle is described in Apple's *Preferences and Settings Programming Guide* in the documentation archive.

Using a settings bundle means that the user has to leave your app to access preferences, and you don't get the kind of control over the interface that you have within your own app. Also, the user can set your preferences while your app is backgrounded or not running; you'll need to register for `UserDefaults.didChangeNotification` in order to hear about this.

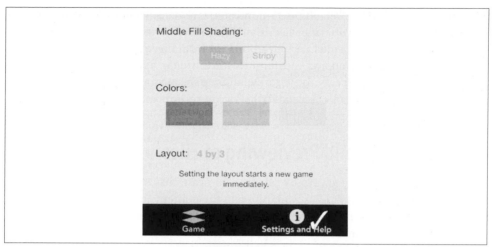

Figure 22-3. An app's preferences interface

Still, a settings bundle has some clear advantages. Keeping the preferences interface out of your app can make your app's own interface cleaner and simpler. You don't have to write any of the "glue" code that coordinates the preferences interface with the user defaults values. And it may be appropriate for the user to be able to set at least some preferences for your app when your app isn't running.

Moreover, you can transport your user directly from your app to your app's preferences in the Settings app (and a Back button then appears in the status bar, making it easy for the user to return from Settings to your app):

```
let url = URL(string:UIApplication.openSettingsURLString)!
UIApplication.shared.open(url)
```

Every method in your app can access the UserDefaults `standard` object, so it often serves as a global "drop" where one instance can deposit a piece of information for another instance to pick up later, when those two instances might not have ready communication with one another or might not even exist simultaneously. (New in iOS 13, the scene session's `userInfo` might be a more appropriate choice.)

UserDefaults is also often used for general data storage. My Zotz! app (Figure 22-3), in addition to using the user defaults to store the user's explicit preferences, also records the state of the game board and the card deck into user defaults every time these change, so that if the app is terminated and then launched again later, we can restore the game as it was when the user left off. One might argue that the contents of the card deck are not a user preference, so I am misusing the user defaults to store state data. However, while purists may grumble, it's a very small amount of data and I don't think the distinction is terribly significant in this case.

Yet another use of UserDefaults is to communicate data between your app and an extension provided by your app. Let's say you've written a today extension (Chapter 13) whose interface details depend upon some data belonging to your app. After configuring your extension and your app to constitute an app group, both the extension and the app can access the UserDefaults associated with the app group (call `init(suiteName:)` instead of `standard`). For more information, see the "Handling Common Scenarios" chapter of Apple's *App Extension Programming Guide*.

Simple Sharing and Previewing of Files

iOS provides basic passageways by which a file can pass safely in and out of your sandbox. File sharing lets the user manipulate the contents of your app's Documents directory. UIDocumentInteractionController allows the user to tell another app to hand a copy of a document to your app, or to tell your app to hand a copy of a document to another app; it also permits previewing a document, provided it is compatible with Quick Look.

File Sharing

File sharing means that an app's Documents directory becomes accessible to the user. The user connects the device to a computer and opens iTunes (or, in macOS Catalina, a Finder window) to see a list of apps on the device that support file sharing. The user can copy files and folders between the app's Documents directory and the computer, and can delete items from the app's Documents directory.

It could be appropriate for your app to support file sharing if it works with common types of file that the user might obtain elsewhere, such as PDFs or JPEGs. To support file sharing, set the *Info.plist* key "Application supports iTunes file sharing" (`UIFile-SharingEnabled`) to YES.

Once your entire Documents directory is exposed to the user this way, you are unlikely to use the Documents directory to store private files. As I mentioned earlier, I like to use the Application Support directory instead.

Your app doesn't get any automatic notification when the user has altered the contents of the Documents directory. Noticing that the situation has changed and responding appropriately is entirely up to you; Apple's DocInteraction sample code demonstrates an approach using the kernel-level `kqueue` mechanism.

Document Types and Receiving a Document

Your app can declare itself willing to open documents of a certain type. In this way, if another app obtains a document of this type, it can propose to hand a copy of the document over to your app. The user might download the document with Mobile

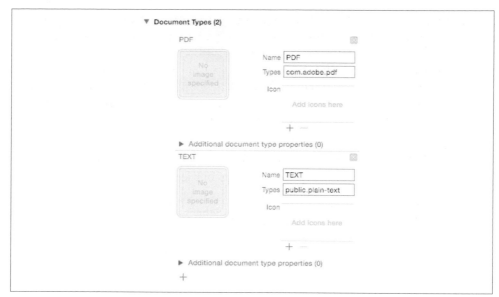

Figure 22-4. Creating a document type

Safari, or receive it in a mail message with the Mail app; now we need a way to get it from Safari or Mail to you.

To let the system know that your app is a candidate for receiving a certain kind of document, you will configure the "Document types" (CFBundleDocumentTypes) key in your *Info.plist*. This is an array, where each entry will be a dictionary specifying a document type by using keys such as "Document Content Type UTIs" (LSItem-ContentTypes), "Document Type Name" (CFBundleTypeName), CFBundleTypeIcon-Files, and LSHandlerRank.

The simplest way to configure the *Info.plist* is through the interface available in the Info tab when you edit the target. Suppose I want to declare that my app opens PDFs and text files. In my target's Info tab in Xcode, I would edit the Document Types section to look like Figure 22-4.

(The values in the Types fields in Figure 22-4 are *UTIs* — uniform type identifiers. PDFs and text files are common types, so they have standard UTIs. To find out the standard UTI for a common file type, look in Apple's *Uniform Type Identifiers Reference* in the documentation archive.)

Now suppose the user receives a PDF in an email message. The Mail app can display this PDF, but the user can also tap Share to bring up an activity view offering, among other things, to copy the file to some other app. The interface will resemble Figure 22-5; various apps that can deal with a PDF are listed here, and my app (MyCoolApp) is among them.

Figure 22-5. The Mail app offers to hand off a PDF

So far, so good. But what if the user actually *taps* our icon to send the PDF over to my app? Then my app delegate's `application(_:open:options:)` is called. New in iOS 13, with window scene support, this would be the scene delegate's `scene(_:open-URLContexts:)` instead (see Chapter 13). When that happens, our job is to open the document whose URL has arrived in the second parameter. The system has already copied the document into an *Inbox* folder which it has created in my Documents directory for exactly this purpose.

 If your app implements file sharing, the user can see the *Inbox* folder; you may wish to delete the *Inbox* folder when you're done retrieving files from it.

In this simple example, my app has just one view controller, which has an outlet to a web view where we will display any PDFs that arrive in this fashion. So my scene delegate contains this code:

```
func scene(_ scene: UIScene,
    openURLContexts URLContexts: Set<UIOpenURLContext>) {
        if let vc = self.window?.rootViewController as? ViewController,
            let url = URLContexts.first?.url {
                vc.displayDoc(url: url)
        }
}
```

And my view controller contains this code (`self.wv` is the web view):

```
func displayDoc (url:URL) {
    let req = URLRequest(url: url)
    self.wv.loadRequest(req)
}
```

In real life, things might be more complicated. We might check to see whether this really *is* a PDF. Also, our app might be in the middle of something else, possibly displaying a completely different view controller's view; we may have to be prepared to drop whatever we were doing and display the incoming document instead.

What happens if our app is launched from scratch by the arrival of this URL? In iOS 12 and before, the app delegate's `application(_:open:options:)` is still called. But

Figure 22-6. The document Open In activity view

in iOS 13 with window scenes, that won't happen, and `scene(_:openURLContexts:)` won't be called either. Instead, you need to implement `scene(_:willConnect-To:options:)` to check the `options:` parameter for its `urlContexts` property. If this isn't empty, you've got an incoming URL to deal with. This may call for some duplication of code:

```
func scene(_ scene: UIScene,
    willConnectTo session: UISceneSession,
    options connectionOptions: UIScene.ConnectionOptions) {
        let cons = connectionOptions.urlContexts
        if let vc = self.window?.rootViewController as? ViewController,
            let url = cons.first?.url {
                vc.loadViewIfNeeded()
                vc.displayDoc(url: url)
        }
}
```

The example I've been discussing assumes that the UTI for the document type is standard and well-known. It is also possible that your app will operate on a new document type, that is, a type of document that the app itself defines. In that case, you'll also want to add this UTI to your app's list of exported UTIs in the *Info.plist*. I'll give an example later in this chapter.

Handing Over a Document

The converse of the situation in the previous section is that your app has somehow acquired a document and wants to let the user hand over a copy of it to some other app. This is done through the UIDocumentInteractionController class.

Assuming we have a file URL `url` pointing to a stored document file, presenting the interface for handing the document over to some other application could be as simple as this (`sender` is a button that the user has just tapped):

```
let dic = UIDocumentInteractionController(url: url)
let v = sender as! UIView
dic.presentOpenInMenu(from:v.bounds, in: v, animated: true)
```

The interface is an activity view (Figure 22-6; see Chapter 13). There are actually two activity views available, each of which is summoned by either of two methods (the first method of each pair expects a CGRect and a UIView, while the second expects a UIBarButtonItem):

```
presentOpenInMenu(from:in:animated:)
presentOpenInMenu(from:animated:)
```
Presents an activity view listing apps to which the document can be copied.

```
presentOptionsMenu(from:in:animated:)
presentOptionsMenu(from:animated:)
```
Presents an activity view listing apps to which the document can be copied, along with other possible actions, such as Message, Mail, Copy, and Print.

Previewing a Document

A UIDocumentInteractionController can be used for an entirely different purpose: it can present a preview of the document, if the document is of a type for which preview is enabled, by calling `presentPreview(animated:)`. You must give the UIDocument-InteractionController a delegate (UIDocumentInteractionControllerDelegate), and the delegate must implement `documentInteractionControllerViewControllerFor-Preview(_:)`, returning an existing view controller that will contain the preview's view controller. So, here we ask for the preview:

```
let dic = UIDocumentInteractionController(url: url)
dic.delegate = self
dic.presentPreview(animated:true)
```

In the delegate, we supply the view controller; it happens that, in my code, this delegate *is* a view controller, so it simply returns `self`:

```
func documentInteractionControllerViewControllerForPreview(
    _ controller: UIDocumentInteractionController) -> UIViewController {
        return self
}
```

If the view controller returned were a UINavigationController, the preview's view controller would be pushed onto it; in this case it isn't, so the preview's view controller is a presented view controller with a Done button. The preview interface also contains a Share button that lets the user summon the Options activity view.

There is another way for the user to reach this interface. If you call `presentOptions-Menu` on your UIDocumentInteractionController, and if its delegate implements `documentInteractionControllerViewControllerForPreview(_:)`, then the activity view will contain a Quick Look icon that the user can tap to summon the preview interface.

Additional delegate methods allow you to track what's happening in the interface presented by the UIDocumentInteractionController. Probably most important are those that inform you that key stages of the interaction are ending:

- documentInteractionControllerDidDismissOptionsMenu(_:)
- documentInteractionControllerDidDismissOpenInMenu(_:)
- documentInteractionControllerDidEndPreview(_:)
- documentInteractionController(_:didEndSendingToApplication:)

Quick Look Previews

Previews are actually provided through the Quick Look framework. You can skip the UIDocumentInteractionController and present the preview yourself through a QLPreviewController; you'll need to import QuickLook. It's a view controller, so to display the preview you show it as a presented view controller or push it onto a navigation controller's stack, just as UIDocumentInteractionController would have done.

A nice feature of QLPreviewController is that you can give it more than one document to preview; the user can move between these, within the preview, by paging sideways or using a table of contents summoned by a button at the bottom of the interface. Apart from this, the interface looks like the interface presented by the UIDocumentInteractionController.

In this example, I may have somewhere in my Documents directory one or more PDF or text documents. I acquire a list of their URLs and present a preview for them (self.exts has been initialized to a set consisting of ["pdf", "txt"]):

```
self.docs = [URL]()
do {
    let fm = FileManager.default
    let docsurl = try fm.url(for: .documentDirectory,
        in: .userDomainMask, appropriateFor: nil, create: false)
    let dir = fm.enumerator(at: docsurl, includingPropertiesForKeys: nil)!
    for case let f as URL in dir {
        if self.exts.contains(f.pathExtension) {
            if QLPreviewController.canPreview(f as QLPreviewItem) {
                self.docs.append(f)
            }
        }
    }
    guard self.docs.count > 0 else { return }
    let preview = QLPreviewController()
    preview.dataSource = self
    preview.currentPreviewItemIndex = 0
    self.present(preview, animated: true)
} catch {
    print(error)
}
```

You'll notice that I haven't told the QLPreviewController what documents to preview. That is the job of QLPreviewController's data source. In my code, I (self) am also the data source. I simply fetch the requested information from the list of URLs, which I previously saved into self.docs:

```
func numberOfPreviewItems(in controller: QLPreviewController) -> Int {
    return self.docs.count
}
func previewController(_ controller: QLPreviewController,
    previewItemAt index: Int) -> QLPreviewItem {
        return self.docs[index] as QLPreviewItem
}
```

The second data source method requires us to return an object that adopts the QLPreviewItem protocol. By a wildly improbable coincidence, URL *does* adopt this protocol, so the example works.

By giving your QLPreviewController a `delegate` (QLPreviewControllerDelegate), you can cause a presented QLPreviewController to appear by zooming from a view in your interface. You'll implement these delegate methods:

- `previewController(_:frameFor:inSourceView:)`
- `previewController(_:transitionImageFor:contentRect:)`
- `previewController(_:transitionViewFor:)`

New in iOS 13, a QLPreviewController can permit the user to apply Markup to images and PDFs, and to trim and rotate videos. Implement these delegate methods:

- `previewController(_:editingModeFor:)` (return `.disabled`, `.updateContents`, or `.createCopy`)
- `previewController(_:didUpdateContentsOf:)`
- `previewController(_:didSaveEditedCopyOf:at:)`

For document types that you own, you can supply your own Quick Look preview. I'll discuss that later in this chapter.

Document Architecture

A *document* is a file of a specific type. If your app's basic operation depends on opening, saving, maintaining, and possibly creating documents of a certain type, you may want to take advantage of the *document architecture*. At its simplest, this architecture revolves around the UIDocument class. Think of a UIDocument instance as managing the relationship between your app's internal model data and a document file that stores that data.

Interacting with a stored document file involves a number of pesky issues. The good news is that UIDocument handles all of them seamlessly:

- Reading or writing your data might take some time, so UIDocument does those things on a background thread.

- Your document data needs to be synchronized to the document file. UIDocument provides autosaving behavior, so that your data is written out automatically whenever it changes.

- A document owned by your app may be exposed to reading and writing by other apps, so your app must read and write to that document coherently without interference from other apps. The solution is to use an NSFileCoordinator. UIDocument does that for you.

- Information about a document can become stale while the document is open. To prevent this, the NSFilePresenter protocol notifies editors that a document has changed. UIDocument participates in this system.

- Your app might be able to open a document stored in another app's sandbox. To do so, you need special permission, which you obtain by treating the document's URL as a security scoped URL. UIDocument does that automatically.

- With iCloud, your app's documents on one of the user's devices can automatically be mirrored onto another of the user's devices. UIDocument can act as a gateway for allowing your documents to participate in iCloud.

Getting started with UIDocument is not difficult. You'll declare a UIDocument subclass, and you'll override two methods:

load(fromContents:ofType:)
> Called when it's time to open a document from its file. You are expected to convert the `contents` value into a model object that your app can use, and to store that model object, probably in an instance property.

contents(forType:)
> Called when it's time to save a document to its file. You are expected to convert the app's model object into a Data instance (or, if your document is a package, a FileWrapper) and return it.

To instantiate a UIDocument, call its designated initializer, init(fileURL:). This sets the UIDocument's fileURL property, and associates the UIDocument with the file at this URL; typically, this association will remain constant for the rest of the UIDocument's lifetime. You will then probably store the UIDocument instance in an instance property, and use it to create (if necessary), open, save, and close the document file:

Make a new document

Having initialized the UIDocument with a file URL pointing to a nonexistent file, send it `save(to:for:completionHandler:)`; the first argument will be the document's own `fileURL`, and the second argument (a UIDocument.SaveOperation) will be `.forCreating`. This, in turn, causes `contents(forType:)` to be called, and the contents of an empty document will be saved out to a file. Your UIDocument subclass will need to supply some default value representing the model data when there is no data.

Open an existing document

Send the UIDocument instance `open(completionHandler:)`. This, in turn, causes `load(fromContents:ofType:)` to be called.

Save an existing document

There are two approaches to saving an existing document:

Autosave

Usually, you'll simply mark the document as "dirty" by calling `updateChange-Count(_:)`. From time to time, the UIDocument will notice this situation and will save the document to its file for you, calling `contents(forType:)` as it does so.

Manual save

On certain occasions, waiting for autosave won't be appropriate. We've already seen one such occasion — when the document file needs to be created on the spot. Another case is that the app is going into the background; we will want to preserve our document there and then, in case the app is terminated. To force the document to be saved right now, call `save(to:for:completionHandler:)`; the second argument will be `.forOverwriting`. Alternatively, if you know you're finished with the document (perhaps the interface displaying the document is about to be torn down), you can call `close(completionHandler:)`.

The `open`, `save`, and `close` methods take a `completionHandler:` function. This is UIDocument's solution to the fact that reading and saving may take time. The file operations take place on a background thread; your completion function is then called on the main thread.

A Basic Document Example

We now know enough for an example! I'll reuse my Person class from earlier in this chapter. Imagine a document effectively consisting of multiple Person instances; I'll call each such document a *people group*. Our app, People Groups, will list all people group documents in the user's Documents folder; the user can then select any people

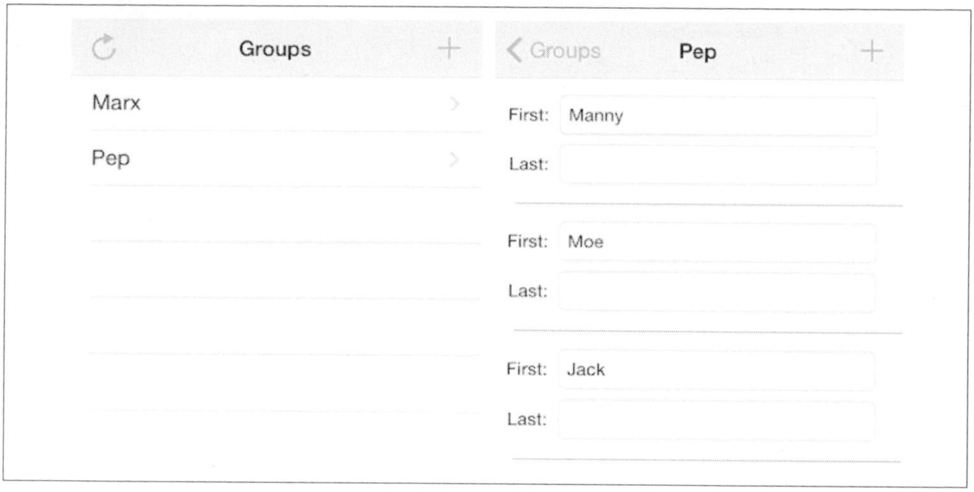

Figure 22-7. The People Groups interface

group document and our app will open that document and display its contents, allowing the user to create a new Person and to edit any existing Person's `firstName` or `lastName` (Figure 22-7).

My first step is to edit the app target and use the Info tab (Figure 22-8) to configure the *Info.plist.* I define (export) a custom UTI, associating a file type `com.neuburg.pplgrp` with a file extension `"pplgrp"`. I also define a corresponding document type, declaring that my app is the origin of this UTI (`Owner`) and that it is able to open and save documents (`Editor`).

In Figure 22-8, when I export my UTI, the entries under "Conforms To" are of particular importance:

Inheritance

I give this UTI a place in the UTI hierarchy. It inherits from no existing type, so it conforms to `public.content`, the base type.

File type

I declare that this UTI represents a simple flat file (`public.data`) as opposed to a package.

Now let's write our UIDocument subclass, which I'll call PeopleDocument. A document consists of multiple Persons, so a natural model implementation is a Person array. PeopleDocument has a public `people` property, initialized to an empty Person array; this will not only hold the model data when we have it, but will also give us something to save into a new empty document. Since Person implements Codable, a Person array can be archived directly into a Data object, and our implementation of the loading and saving methods is straightforward:

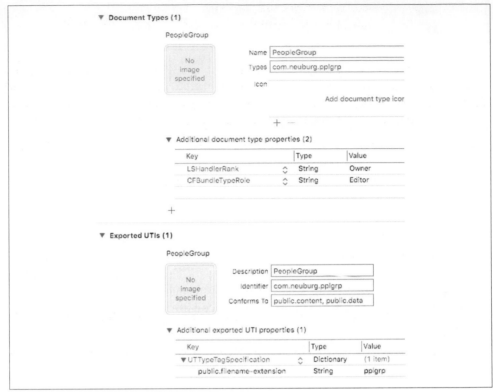

Figure 22-8. Defining a custom UTI

```swift
class PeopleDocument: UIDocument {
    var people = [Person]()
    override func load(fromContents contents: Any,
        ofType typeName: String?) throws {
            if let contents = contents as? Data {
                if let arr = try? PropertyListDecoder().decode(
                    [Person].self, from: contents) {
                        self.people = arr
                        return
                }
            }
            // if we get here, there was some kind of problem
            throw NSError(domain: "NoDataDomain", code: -1, userInfo: nil)
    }
    override func contents(forType typeName: String) throws -> Any {
        if let data = try? PropertyListEncoder().encode(self.people) {
            return data
        }
    }
```

```
        // if we get here, there was some kind of problem
        throw NSError(domain: "NoDataDomain", code: -2, userInfo: nil)
    }
}
```

The first view controller, GroupLister, is a master table view (its view appears on the left in Figure 22-7). It merely looks in the Documents directory for people group documents and lists them by name; it also provides an interface for letting the user create a new people group. None of that is challenging, so I won't discuss it further.

The second view controller, PeopleLister, is the detail view; it too is a table view (its view appears on the right in Figure 22-7). It displays the first and last names of the people in the currently open people group document. This is the only place where we actually work with PeopleDocument, so let's focus our attention on that.

PeopleLister's designated initializer demands a fileURL: parameter pointing to a people group document, and uses it to set its own fileURL property. From this, it instantiates a PeopleDocument, keeping a reference to it in its doc property. People-Lister also has a people property, acting as the data model for its table view; this is nothing but a pointer to the PeopleDocument's people property.

As PeopleLister comes into existence, the document file pointed to by self.fileURL might not yet exist. If it doesn't, we create it; if it does, we open it. In both cases, our people data are now ready for display, so the completion function reloads the table view:

```
let fileURL : URL
var doc : PeopleDocument!
var people : [Person] { // point to the document's model object
    get { return self.doc.people }
    set { self.doc.people = newValue }
}
init(fileURL:URL) {
    self.fileURL = fileURL
    super.init(nibName: "PeopleLister", bundle: nil)
}
required init(coder: NSCoder) {
    fatalError("NSCoding not supported")
}
override func viewDidLoad() {
    super.viewDidLoad()
    self.title =
        (self.fileURL.lastPathComponent as NSString).deletingPathExtension
    // ... interface configuration goes here ...
    let fm = FileManager.default
    self.doc = PeopleDocument(fileURL:self.fileURL)
    func listPeople(_ success:Bool) {
        if success {
            self.tableView.reloadData()
        }
```

```
        }
        if let _ = try? self.fileURL.checkResourceIsReachable() {
            self.doc.open(completionHandler: listPeople)
        } else {
            self.doc.save(to:self.doc.fileURL,
                for: .forCreating, completionHandler: listPeople)
        }
    }
```

Displaying people, creating a new person, and allowing the user to edit a person's first and last names, are all trivial uses of a table view (Chapter 8). Let's proceed to the only other aspect of PeopleLister that involves working with PeopleDocument, namely saving.

When the user performs a significant editing maneuver, such as creating a person or editing a person's first or last name, PeopleLister updates the model (self.people) and the table view, and then tells its PeopleDocument that the document is dirty, allowing autosaving to take it from there:

```
self.doc.updateChangeCount(.done)
```

When the app is about to go into the background, or when PeopleLister's own view is disappearing, PeopleLister forces PeopleDocument to save immediately:

```
func forceSave(_: Any?) {
    self.tableView.endEditing(true)
    self.doc.save(to:self.doc.fileURL, for:.forOverwriting)
}
```

That's all it takes! Adding UIDocument support to your app is easy, because UIDocument is merely acting as a supplier and preserver of your app's data model object. The UIDocument class documentation may give the impression that this is a large and complex class, but that's chiefly because it is so heavily customizable both at high and low levels; for the most part, you won't need any customization. You might work with your UIDocument's undo manager to give it a more sophisticated understanding of what constitutes a significant change in your data; I'll talk about undo managers in Chapter 25. For further details, see Apple's *Document-based App Programming Guide for iOS* in the document archive.

If your app's *Info.plist* key "Application supports iTunes file sharing" (UIFile-SharingEnabled) is set to YES (because your app supports file sharing), and if the *Info.plist* key "Supports opening documents in place" (LSSupportsOpeningDocuments-InPlace) is also set to YES, then files in your app's Documents directory will be visible in the Files app, and the user can tap a people group file to call your app delegate's application(_:open:options:) or your scene delegate's scene(_:open-URLContexts:), as described earlier in this chapter. That's safe only if your app accesses files by way of NSFilePresenter and NSFileCoordinator — and because you're using UIDocument, it does.

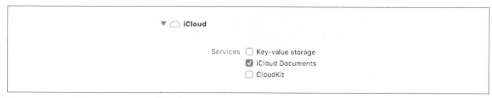

Figure 22-9. Turning on iCloud support

iCloud

Once your app is operating through UIDocument, basic iCloud compatibility effectively falls right into your lap. You have just two steps to perform:

Obtain iCloud entitlements

Edit the target and, in the Signing & Capabilities tab, add the iCloud capability and check iCloud Documents (Figure 22-9). New in Xcode 11, you may also need to create a ubiquity container; click the Plus button to make a container and give it a name. Names should be of the form `"iCloud.com.yourDomain.yourApp-ID"`. Check the checkbox to make your container the default container.

Obtain an iCloud-compatible directory

Early in your app's lifetime, call FileManager's `url(forUbiquityContainer-Identifier:)` (typically passing `nil` as the argument), on a background thread, to obtain the URL of the cloud-shared directory. Any documents your app puts here by way of your UIDocument subclass will be automatically shared into the cloud.

So, with my entitlements file in hand, I can make my People Groups app iCloud-compatible with just two code changes. In the app delegate, as my app launches, I step out to a background thread (Chapter 24), obtain the cloud-shared directory's URL, and then step back to the main thread and retain the URL through a property, `self.ubiq`:

```
DispatchQueue.global(qos:.default).async {
    let fm = FileManager.default
    let ubiq = fm.url(forUbiquityContainerIdentifier:nil)
    DispatchQueue.main.async {
        self.ubiq = ubiq
    }
}
```

When I determine where to seek and save people groups, I specify `ubiq` — unless it is `nil`, implying that iCloud is not enabled, in which case I specify the user's Documents folder:

```
var docsurl : URL {
    let del = UIApplication.shared.delegate
    if let ubiq = (del as! AppDelegate).ubiq {
        return ubiq
    } else {
        do {
            let fm = FileManager.default
            return try fm.url(for:.documentDirectory, in: .userDomainMask,
                appropriateFor: nil, create: false)
        } catch {
            print(error)
        }
    }
    return NSURL() as URL // shouldn't happen
}
```

To test, iCloud Drive must be turned on under iCloud in my device's Settings. I run the app and create a people group with some people in it. I then switch to a different device and run the app there, and tap the Refresh button. This is a very crude implementation, purely for testing purposes; we look through the docsurl directory for pplgrp files and download any cloud-based files:

```
do {
    let fm = FileManager.default
    self.files = try fm.contentsOfDirectory(at: self.docsurl,
        includingPropertiesForKeys: nil).filter {
            if fm.isUbiquitousItem(at:$0) {
                try fm.startDownloadingUbiquitousItem(at:$0)
            }
            return $0.pathExtension == "pplgrp"
    }
    self.tableView.reloadData()
} catch {
    print(error)
}
```

Presto, the app on this device now displays my people group documents created on a different device! It's quite thrilling.

My Refresh button approach, although it works (possibly after a couple of tries), is decidedly crude. My UIDocument works with iCloud, but my app is not a good iCloud citizen. The truth is that I should not be using FileManager like this; instead, I should be running an NSMetadataQuery. The usual strategy is:

1. Instantiate NSMetadataQuery and retain the instance.

2. Configure the search. This means giving the metadata query a search scope of NSMetadataQueryUbiquitousDocumentsScope and supplying a serial queue for it to run on (OperationQueue, see Chapter 24).

3. Register for notifications such as `.NSMetadataQueryDidFinishGathering` and `.NSMetadataQueryDidUpdate`.

4. Start the search by calling `start`. The NSMetadataQuery instance then remains in place, with the search continuing to run more or less constantly, for the entire lifetime of the app.

5. When a notification arrives, check the NSMetadataQuery's `results`. These will be NSMetadataItem objects, whose `value(forAttribute:NSMetadataItem-URLKey)` is the document file URL.

Similarly, in my earlier code I called `checkResourceIsReachable`, but for a cloud item I should be calling `checkPromisedItemIsReachable` instead.

Another problem with our app is that, by turning on iCloud support in this way, we have turned *off* the ability of the Files app to see our files (because they are now cloud-based and not in the Documents directory). I'll give a solution in the next section.

Further iCloud details are outside the scope of this discussion; see Apple's *iCloud Design Guide* in the documentation archive. Getting started is easy; making your app a good iCloud citizen, capable of dealing with the complexities that iCloud may entail, is not. What if the currently open document changes because someone edited it on another device? What if that change is in conflict with changes I've made on *this* device? What if the availability of iCloud changes while the app is open — for example, if the user switches iCloud itself on or off? Apple's own sample code habitually skirts these knotty issues.

Document Browser

The document browser (UIDocumentBrowserViewController), introduced in iOS 11, can improve a document-based app in two ways:

- An iOS device has no universal file browser parallel to the Mac desktop's Finder. So if your app maintains document files, it must also implement for itself the nitty-gritty details of user file management, listing your documents and letting the user delete them, rename them, move them, and so forth. That sounds daunting! The document browser solves the problem; it injects into your app a standard file management interface similar to the Files app.

- If your UIDocument-based app saves documents into iCloud, and if your app uses the document browser, the Files app (and document browsers in other apps) will be able to see your app's files in the cloud. Moreover, we can ignore everything I said in the preceding section about how to make our app participate in iCloud; with UIDocumentBrowserViewController, our app participates in iCloud *automatically,* with no need for any entitlements or added cloud management code.

Let's convert our People Groups app to use the document browser. The easiest way to get started is from the template provided by Apple; choose File → New → Project and iOS → Application → Document Based App. The template provides three features:

Info.plist configuration
> The template gives us a start on the configuration of our *Info.plist*. In particular, it includes the "Supports Document Browser" key (`UISupportsDocument-Browser`) with its value set to YES.

Classes and storyboard
> The template provides a basic set of classes:
>
> - A UIDocumentBrowserViewController subclass (DocumentBrowserView-Controller)
> - A UIDocument subclass (Document)
> - A view controller (DocumentViewController) intended for display of documents of that class
>
> The template puts instances of the two view controllers into the storyboard.

Structure
> The template makes the UIDocumentBrowserViewController instance our app's root view controller. The remainder of our app's interface, where the user views the contents of a document, must be displayed through a fullscreen presented view controller.

In adapting People Groups to this architecture, we can eliminate the GroupLister view controller class that has been acting as a master view controller to list our documents (left side in Figure 22-7), because the document browser will now fill that role; Document and DocumentViewController, meanwhile, are parallel to, and can be replaced by, our PeopleDocument and PeopleLister classes.

We begin by customizing DocumentBrowserViewController. The template gets us started, setting this class as its own delegate (UIDocumentBrowserViewController-Delegate) and configuring the document browser's capabilities:

```
override func viewDidLoad() {
    super.viewDidLoad()
    self.delegate = self
    self.allowsDocumentCreation = true
    self.allowsPickingMultipleItems = false
}
```

The template also implements delegate methods for when the user selects an existing document or copies a document from elsewhere; both call a custom method, `present-Document(at:)`, for which the template provides a stub implementation:

```
func documentBrowser(_ controller: UIDocumentBrowserViewController,
    didPickDocumentURLs documentURLs: [URL]) {
        guard let sourceURL = documentURLs.first else { return }
        self.presentDocument(at: sourceURL)
}
func documentBrowser(_ controller: UIDocumentBrowserViewController,
    didImportDocumentAt sourceURL: URL,
    toDestinationURL destinationURL: URL) {
        self.presentDocument(at: destinationURL)
}
```

Providing a real implementation of `presentDocument(at:)` is up to us. We are no longer in a navigation interface, but PeopleLister expects one; so when I instantiate PeopleLister, I wrap it in a navigation controller before presenting it:

```
func presentDocument(at documentURL: URL) {
    let lister = PeopleLister(fileURL: documentURL)
    let nav = UINavigationController(rootViewController: lister)
    nav.modalPresentationStyle = .fullScreen
    self.present(nav, animated: true)
}
```

Finally, we come to the really interesting case: the user asks the document browser to create a People Groups document. This causes the delegate's `document-Browser(_:didRequestDocumentCreationWithHandler:)` to be called. Our job is to provide the URL of *an existing empty document file* and call the `handler:` function with that URL. But where are we going to get a document file? Well, we already know how to create an empty document; we proved that in our earlier example. So I'll create that document in the Temporary directory and feed its URL to the `handler:` function. That is exactly the strategy advised by the documentation on this delegate method, and my code is adapted directly from the example code there.

I'm a little uncertain, though, about what we're intended to do about the *name* of the new file. In the past, Apple's advice was not to worry about this — any unique name would do — but that was before the user could *see* file names in a standard interface. My solution is to present a UIAlertController where the user can enter the new document's name, creating the new document in the OK button's action function. Observe that I call the `importHandler` function under every circumstance:

```
func documentBrowser(_ controller: UIDocumentBrowserViewController,
    didRequestDocumentCreationWithHandler importHandler:
    @escaping (URL?, UIDocumentBrowserViewController.ImportMode) -> Void) {
        var docname = "People"
        let alert = UIAlertController(
            title: "Name for new people group:",
            message: nil, preferredStyle: .alert)
        alert.addTextField { tf in
            tf.autocapitalizationType = .words
        }
        alert.addAction(UIAlertAction(title: "Cancel", style: .cancel) { _ in
```

```
            importHandler(nil, .none)
        })
        alert.addAction(UIAlertAction(title: "OK", style: .default) {_ in
            if let proposal = alert.textFields?[0].text {
                if !proposal.trimmingCharacters(in: .whitespaces).isEmpty {
                    docname = proposal
                }
            }
            let fm = FileManager.default
            let temp = fm.temporaryDirectory
            let fileURL = temp.appendingPathComponent(docname + ".pplgrp2")
            let newdoc = PeopleDocument(fileURL: fileURL)
            newdoc.save(to: fileURL, for: .forOverwriting) { ok in
                guard ok else { importHandler(nil, .none); return }
                newdoc.close() { ok in
                    guard ok else { importHandler(nil, .none); return }
                    importHandler(fileURL, .move)
                }
            }
        })
        self.present(alert, animated: true)
    }
```

If the user cancels or if something else goes wrong, I call `importHandler` with a `nil` URL. Just one path of execution calls `importHandler` with an actual file URL. If that happens, our delegate method `documentBrowser(_:didImportDocumentAt:to-DestinationURL:)` is called — and so our PeopleLister view controller is presented, displaying the new empty document.

Custom Thumbnails

Now that the user can see our document files represented in the file browser, we will probably want to give some attention to their icons. A document icon is called its *thumbnail*. A straightforward approach is to have our UIDocument subclass write a thumbnail into the file when saving:

```
override func fileAttributesToWrite(to url: URL,
    for saveOperation: UIDocument.SaveOperation)
    throws -> [AnyHashable : Any] {
        let icon = UIImage(named:"smiley")!
        let sz = CGSize(1024,1024)
        let im = UIGraphicsImageRenderer(
            size:sz, format:icon.imageRendererFormat).image {_ in
                icon.draw(in: CGRect(origin:.zero, size:CGSize(1024,1024)))
        }
        var d = try super.fileAttributesToWrite(to: url, for: saveOperation)
        let key1 = URLResourceKey.thumbnailDictionaryKey
        let key2 = URLThumbnailDictionaryItem.NSThumbnail1024x1024SizeKey
        d[key1] = [key2:im]
        return d
    }
```

▼ NSExtension	○	Dictionary	(3 items)
▼ NSExtensionAttributes		Dictionary	(2 items)
▼ QLSupportedContentTypes		Array	(1 item)
Item 0		String	com.neuburg.pplgrp
QLSupportsSearchableItems		Boolean	NO
NSExtensionMainStoryboard		String	MainInterface
NSExtensionPointIdentifier		String	com.apple.quicklook.preview

Figure 22-10. Defining a preview extension's document type

An alternative approach, introduced in iOS 11, is to provide a *thumbnail extension* that is consulted *in real time* whenever a document browser wants to portray one of our documents. But I have not been able to get this to work in iOS 13, so I'm not going to discuss it.

Custom Previews

There are lots of places in the interface where the user can be shown a Quick Look preview of a file. I talked about UIDocumentInteractionController and QLPreview-Controller earlier in this chapter. In places such as the Files app or a mail message with an attachment, the user can long press a file and ask for a Quick Look preview. All of that works for a standard document type such as a PDF or text file, but not for our custom People Group document type. Let's fix that.

To do so, we can add a *Quick Look preview extension* to our People Groups app. Quick Look preview extensions, introduced in iOS 11, allow your app to supply a Quick Look preview for a custom document type that it exports.

Let's try it! Add a target; choose iOS → Application Extension → Quick Look Preview Extension. The template provides a view controller class, PreviewViewController, and a storyboard containing a PreviewViewController instance and its main view. When the user tries to preview a document of our custom type, this view controller will be instantiated and its main view will be displayed in the Quick Look preview interface.

For this to work, our extension's *Info.plist* must declare, in the `QLSupportedContent-Types` array, the UTI of the document type for which it provides a preview (Figure 22-10). I've also turned off the `QLSupportsSearchableItems` setting (it's for Spotlight searches, with which we're not concerned here).

We must now implement `preparePreviewOfFile(at:completionHandler:)` in our PreviewViewController. We are handed a file URL pointing to a document file. Our job is to examine that file, configure our view controller and its view, and call the `completionHandler:` function with a parameter of `nil` (or with an Error object if there was an error)

I'll configure PreviewViewController as a reduced version of PeopleLister. Similar to the right side of Figure 22-7, it will be a UITableViewController whose table shows the first and last names of the people in this group. However, the text fields will be disabled — we don't want the user trying to edit a preview! — and there is no need to implement document saving, or even to maintain a reference to a PeopleDocument. Instead, our PeopleDocument will serve only as a temporary conduit to construct the `people` array from the document file; it stores the array in an instance property so that our table view data source methods can access it:

```
func preparePreviewOfFile(at url: URL,
    completionHandler handler: @escaping (Error?) -> Void) {
        let doc = PeopleDocument(fileURL:url)
        doc.open { ok in
            if ok {
                self.people = doc.people
                self.tableView.register(
                    UINib(nibName: "PersonCell", bundle: nil),
                    forCellReuseIdentifier: "Person")
                self.tableView.reloadData()
                handler(nil)
            } else {
                handler(NSError(domain: "NoDataDomain",
                    code: -1, userInfo: nil))
            }
        }
}
```

Document Picker

The document picker (UIDocumentPickerViewController) is a simple way to let the user view a list of document files and choose one (or several). You can open the file directly (probably in conjunction with UIDocument) or copy it into your app's sandbox temporarily. The document picker can also be configured to let the user pick a place to copy a document to.

The document picker can see into the same places as the document browser and the Files app, and its interface looks a lot like theirs, but it's a lightweight momentary dialog. You can use it without declaring any document types, without making your app participate in iCloud in any other way, and without changing your app's architecture. You just present the picker; the user chooses a file or cancels, and the picker is dismissed automatically.

In this example, I'll assume that the user has somehow saved an *.mp3* file into iCloud Drive. We'll permit the user to locate and play this file. In response to a button tap, we instantiate and configure the UIDocumentPickerViewController, providing the UTIs of the types of file to be chosen and a mode in which the picker is to operate; `.import` means that we want the file copied into our app's sandbox (in the

Temporary directory). We make ourselves the document picker's `delegate` (UIDo-cumentPickerDelegate) and present the picker. If the user chooses an *.mp3* file, the delegate method is called, and we present an AVPlayerViewController to let the user play it:

```
@IBAction func doButton(_ sender: Any) {
    let picker = UIDocumentPickerViewController(
        documentTypes: [kUTTypeMP3 as String], in: .import)
    picker.delegate = self
    self.present(picker, animated: true)
}
func documentPicker(_ controller: UIDocumentPickerViewController,
    didPickDocumentsAt urls: [URL]) {
        guard urls.count == 1 else {return}
        guard let vals =
            try? urls[0].resourceValues(forKeys: [.typeIdentifierKey]),
            vals.typeIdentifier == kUTTypeMP3 as String
            else {return}
        let vc = AVPlayerViewController()
        vc.player = AVPlayer(url: urls[0])
        self.present(vc, animated: true)
}
```

A document picker has a few properties for customizing it. Starting in iOS 11, `allows-MultipleSelection` permits the user to choose more than one file. New in iOS 13, `directoryURL` sets the folder whose contents the picker will initially display. Also new, the document type can be kUTTypeFolder, allowing the user to choose an entire folder of files; to deal with the files inside it, call `startAccessingSecurityScoped-Resource` and use an NSFileCoordinator.

XML

XML is a flexible and widely used general-purpose text file format for storage and retrieval of structured data. You might use it yourself to store data that you'll need to retrieve later, or you could encounter it when obtaining information from elsewhere, such as the internet.

On macOS, Cocoa provides a set of classes (XMLDocument and so forth) for reading, parsing, maintaining, searching, and modifying XML data in a completely general way; but iOS does *not* include these. I think the reason must be that their tree-based approach is too memory-intensive. Instead, iOS provides XMLParser.

XMLParser is a relatively simple class that walks through an XML document, sending delegate messages as it encounters elements. With it, you can parse an XML document once, but what you do with the pieces as you encounter them is up to you. The general assumption here is that you know in advance the structure of the particular XML data you intend to read, and that you have provided classes for representation of the same data in object form, with some way of transforming the XML pieces into that representation.

To illustrate, let's return once more to our Person class with a `firstName` and a `lastName` property. Imagine that, as our app starts up, we would like to populate it with Person objects, and that we've stored the data describing these objects as an XML file in our app bundle, like this:

```
<?xml version="1.0" encoding="utf-8"?>
<people>
    <person>
        <firstName>Matt</firstName>
        <lastName>Neuburg</lastName>
    </person>
    <person>
        <firstName>Snidely</firstName>
        <lastName>Whiplash</lastName>
    </person>
    <person>
        <firstName>Dudley</firstName>
        <lastName>Doright</lastName>
    </person>
</people>
```

This data could be mapped to an array of Person objects, each with its `firstName` and `lastName` properties appropriately set. Let's consider how we might do that. (This is a deliberately easy example, of course; not all XML is so readily expressed as objects.)

Using XMLParser is not difficult in theory. You create the XMLParser, handing it the URL of a local XML file (or a Data object, perhaps downloaded from the internet), set its delegate, and tell it to `parse`. The delegate starts receiving delegate messages. For simple XML like ours, there are only three delegate messages of interest:

`parser(_:didStartElement:namespaceURI:qualifiedName:attributes:)`
> The parser has encountered an opening element tag. In our document this would be `<people>`, `<person>`, `<firstName>`, or `<lastName>`.

`parser(_:didEndElement:namespaceURI:qualifiedName:)`
> The parser has encountered the corresponding closing element tag. In our document this would be `</people>`, `</person>`, `</firstName>`, or `</lastName>`.

`parser(_:foundCharacters:)`
> The parser has encountered some text between the starting and closing tags for the current element. In our document this would be `"Matt"` or `"Neuburg"` and so on.

In practice, responding to these delegate messages poses challenges of maintaining state. If there is just one delegate, it will have to bear in mind at every moment what element it is currently encountering; this could make for a lot of properties and a lot of if-statements in the implementation of the delegate methods. To aggravate the issue, `parser(_:foundCharacters:)` can arrive multiple times for a single stretch of text; that is, the text may arrive in pieces, which we must accumulate into a property.

An elegant way to meet these challenges is by resetting the XMLParser's delegate to *different delegate objects* at different stages of the parsing process. We make each delegate responsible for parsing one type of element; when a child of that element is encountered, the delegate object makes a new child element delegate object and repoints the XMLParser's `delegate` property at it. The child element delegate is then responsible for making the parent the delegate once again when it finishes parsing its own element. This is slightly counterintuitive because it means `parser(_:didStart-Element:...)` and `parser(_:didEndElement:...)` for the same element are arriving at *two different objects*.

To see what I mean, think about how we could implement this in our example. We are going to need a PeopleParser that handles the `<people>` element, and a PersonParser that handles the `<person>` elements. Now imagine how PeopleParser will operate when it is the XMLParser's delegate:

1. When `parser(_:didStartElement:...)` arrives, the PeopleParser looks to see if this is a `<person>`. If so, it creates a PersonParser, handing to it (the PersonParser) a parent reference to itself (the PeopleParser) — and makes the PersonParser the XMLParser's delegate.

2. Delegate messages now arrive at this newly created PersonParser. We can assume that `<firstName>` and `<lastName>` are simple enough that the PersonParser can maintain state as it encounters them; when text is encountered, `parser(_:found-Characters:)` will be called, and the text must be accumulated into a corresponding property.

3. Eventually, `parser(_:didEndElement:...)` arrives. The PersonParser now uses its parent reference to make the PeopleParser the XMLParser's delegate once again. The PeopleParser, having received from the PersonParser any data it may have collected, is now ready in case another `<person>` element is encountered (and the old PersonParser might now go quietly out of existence).

This approach may seem like a lot of work to configure, but in fact it is neatly object-oriented, with parser delegate classes corresponding to the elements of the XML. Moreover, those delegate classes have a great deal in common, which can readily be factored out and encapsulated into a delegate superclass from which they all inherit.

JSON

JSON (*http://www.json.org*) is often used as a universal lightweight structured data format for server communication. Typically, you'll send an HTTP request to a server using a URL constructed according to prescribed rules, and the reply will come back as JSON that you'll have to parse:

```
let sess : URLSession = {
    let config = URLSessionConfiguration.ephemeral
    let s = URLSession(configuration: config)
    return s
}()
@IBAction func doGo(_ sender: Any) {
    var comp = URLComponents()
    comp.scheme = "https"
    comp.host = "quotesondesign.com"
    comp.path = "/wp-json/wp/v2/posts"
    var qi = [URLQueryItem]()
    qi.append(URLQueryItem(name: "orderby", value: "rand"))
    qi.append(URLQueryItem(name: "per_page", value: "1"))
    comp.queryItems = qi
    if let url = comp.url {
        let d = self.sess.dataTask(with: url) { data,_,_ in
            if let data = data {
                DispatchQueue.main.async {
                    self.parse(data) // now what?
                }
            }
        }
        d.resume()
    }
}
```

That's a request to a server that dispenses quotations; the actual network communication will be explained in Chapter 23. The request returns a Data object representing a JSON string that looks something like this (I've edited and truncated the string for clarity):

```
[{
    "id": 2237,
    "date": "2014-03-28T09:01:07",
    "title": {
        "rendered": "Wim Hovens"
    },
    "content": {
        "rendered":
            "<p>Good design is in all the things you notice.
            Great design is in all the things you don&#8217;t.</\/p>\n",
        "protected": false
    },
    // ...
}]
```

We are calling our `parse` method with that Data object, and we want to parse it. How? Well, we know in advance the expected format of the JSON response, so we have prepared by declaring a nest of structs matching that format and adopting the

Decodable protocol (discussed earlier in this chapter). Now we can instantiate JSON-Decoder and call decode(_:from:). In this example, our goal is to extract just the "title" and "content" entries, so those are the only properties our struct needs:

```
struct Item : Decodable {
    let rendered : String
}
struct Quote : Decodable {
    let title : Item
    let content : Item
}
```

Our Quote struct matches the JSON's inner dictionary, but the JSON itself is an array containing that dictionary as an element. Therefore, our call to decode the JSON looks like this:

```
func parse(_ data:Data) {
    if let arr = try? JSONDecoder().decode([Quote].self, from: data) {
        let quote = arr.first!
        // ...
    }
}
```

The JSON is now parsed into a Quote instance, and we can refer to the author and the quotation as quote.title.rendered and quote.content.rendered. Now we can do whatever we like with those values, such as displaying them in our app's interface.

The JSONDecoder class also comes with properties that allow you to specify the handling of certain specially formatted values, such as dates and floating-point numbers (though we didn't need to use any of those properties in our example).

Coding Keys

When we are receiving JSON structured data, the structure is defined by the server, right down to the names of the keys. The JSON dictionary that we are receiving has keys "title" and "content", so we are forced to name our Quote struct's properties title and content. This seems unfair. But there's a workaround: declare a nested enum called CodingKeys with a String raw value and conforming to the CodingKey protocol. Now you can give your struct properties any names you like, using the enum cases and their string raw values to map the JSON dictionary key names to the struct property names:

```
struct Item : Decodable {
    let value : String
    enum CodingKeys : String, CodingKey {
        case value = "rendered"
    }
}
struct Quote : Decodable {
    let author : Item
```

```
        let quotation : Item
        enum CodingKeys : String, CodingKey {
            case author = "title"
            case quotation = "content"
        }
    }
```

The outcome is that we can extract the author and quotation as `quote.author.value` and `quote.quotation.value`, which reads more clearly than `quote.title.rendered` and `quote.content.rendered`.

Custom Decoding

We have changed the names of our struct properties, but the overall structure of the JSON is *still* defined by the server. For instance, in the JSON we're receiving, a dictionary's `title` value is itself a dictionary with a `rendered` key. I'm using two structs with an extra level of nesting because the JSON has an extra level of nesting. My Quote struct's `author` and `quotation` properties are Item objects, and to fetch the value I really want, I have to drop down an extra level: I've been saying `quote.author.value` and `quote.quotation.value` even though the only thing I'm *ever* going to be interested in is the `value`. I don't want to have to talk like this. I want my `author` and `quotation` properties to be strings, not Items. I don't want them to *lead* to the Item's `"rendered"` value; I want them to *be* the Item's `"rendered"` value.

The solution is to supply an implementation of `init(from:)`. This initializer is required by the Decodable protocol. But so far, instead of writing it, we have been allowing it to be synthesized for us. Instead, we can write it ourselves — and then we are free to parse the JSON into our object's properties in any way we like.

When you write an implementation of `init(from:)`, the parameter is a Decoder object. Start by extracting an appropriate container. For a JSON dictionary, this will be a KeyedDecodingContainer, obtained by calling `container(keyedBy:)`; we still need a CodingKey adopter to serve as the source of key names. You can then call `decode(_:forKey:)` to get the value for a key. Now you are free to manipulate values and assign the results to your properties in any way you like. The only requirement is that, as with any initializer, you must initialize all your properties.

So here's my rewrite of Quote, with `author` and `quotation` declared as String, and an explicit `init(from:)` implementation. I have kept the Item struct purely as a way of extracting the `"rendered"` value, but I've made it a private nested type that the caller is unaware of:

```
struct Quote : Decodable {
    let author : String
    let quotation : String
    enum CodingKeys : String, CodingKey {
        case author = "title"
```

```
            case quotation = "content"
        }
        private struct Item : Decodable {
            let value : String
            enum CodingKeys : String, CodingKey {
                case value = "rendered"
            }
        }
        init(from decoder: Decoder) throws {
            let con = try decoder.container(keyedBy: CodingKeys.self)
            let author = try con.decode(Item.self, forKey: .author)
            self.author = author.value
            let quotation = try con.decode(Item.self, forKey: .quotation)
            self.quotation = quotation.value
        }
    }
```

Now my `quote.author` and `quote.quotation` are strings, and I can display them in the interface directly.

Another common reason for writing a custom `init(from:)` implementation is that there is something indeterminate about the structure of the JSON you're receiving from the server. A typical situation is that there are dictionary keys whose names you don't know in advance. To deal with this, you need a special "mop-up" CodingKey adopter:

```
struct AnyCodingKey : CodingKey {
  var stringValue: String
  var intValue: Int?
  init(_ codingKey: CodingKey) {
    self.stringValue = codingKey.stringValue
    self.intValue = codingKey.intValue
  }
  init(stringValue: String) {
    self.stringValue = stringValue
    self.intValue = nil
  }
  init(intValue: Int) {
    self.stringValue = String(intValue)
    self.intValue = intValue
  }
}
```

(I owe that formulation to Hamish Knight.) When you call `container(keyedBy: Any-CodingKey.self)`, the resulting container can be sent the `allKeys` message to obtain a list of all keys in this dictionary, and you can use any of those keys to fetch the corresponding value.

Yet another common problem is that a value's type may vary. A typical situation is that the same key yields sometimes a String, sometimes an Int. The way to cope with that is to declare a *union* — that is, a Decodable enum with two cases, one with an associated String value, the other with an associated Int value. Your custom `init(from:)` just tries each of them in turn. A widely used formulation runs something like this:

```
enum IntOrString: Decodable {
    case int(Int)
    case string(String)
    init(from decoder: Decoder) throws {
        let container = try decoder.singleValueContainer()
        if let int = try? container.decode(Int.self) {
            self = .int(int)
        } else if let string = try? container.decode(String.self) {
            self = .string(string)
        } else {
            throw DecodingError.typeMismatch(
                IntOrString.self,
                DecodingError.Context(
                    codingPath: decoder.codingPath,
                    debugDescription: "Neither String nor Int"))
        }
    }
}
```

SQLite

SQLite (*http://www.sqlite.org/docs.html*) is a lightweight, full-featured relational database that you can talk to using SQL, the universal language of databases. This can be an appropriate storage format when your data comes in rows and columns (records and fields) and needs to be rapidly searchable. Also, the database as a whole is never loaded into memory; the data is accessed only as needed. This is valuable in an environment like an iOS device, where memory is at a premium.

To use SQLite, say `import SQLite3`. Talking to SQLite involves an elaborate C interface which may prove annoying; fortunately, there are a number of lightweight front ends. In my example, I'll use `fmdb` (*https://github.com/ccgus/fmdb*); it's Swift-friendly, but it's written in Objective-C, so we'll need a bridging header in which we `#import "FMDB.h"`.

To illustrate, I'll create a database and add a `people` table consisting of `lastname` and `firstname` columns:

```
let db = FMDatabase(path:self.dbpath)
db.open()
do {
    db.beginTransaction()
    try db.executeUpdate(
        "create table people (lastname text, firstname text)",
        values:nil)
    try db.executeUpdate(
```

```
        "insert into people (firstname, lastname) values (?,?)",
        values:["Matt", "Neuburg"])
    try db.executeUpdate(
        "insert into people (firstname, lastname) values (?,?)",
        values:["Snidely", "Whiplash"])
    try db.executeUpdate(
        "insert into people (firstname, lastname) values (?,?)",
        values:["Dudley", "Doright"])
    db.commit()
} catch {
    db.rollback()
}
```

At some later time, I come along and read the data from that database:

```
let db = FMDatabase(path:self.dbpath)
db.open()
if let rs = try? db.executeQuery("select * from people", values:nil) {
    while rs.next() {
        if let firstname = rs["firstname"], let lastname = rs["lastname"] {
            print(firstname, lastname)
        }
    }
}
db.close()
/*
Matt Neuburg
Snidely Whiplash
Dudley Doright
*/
```

You can include a previously constructed SQLite file in your app bundle, but you can't write to it there; the solution is to copy it from your app bundle into another location, such as the Documents directory, before you start working with it.

Core Data

The Core Data framework (`import CoreData`) provides a generalized way of expressing objects and properties that form a relational graph; moreover, it has built-in facilities for maintaining those objects in persistent storage — typically using SQLite as a file format — and reading them from storage only when they are needed, making efficient use of memory. A person might have not only multiple addresses but also multiple friends who are also persons; expressing persons and addresses as explicit object types, working out how to link them and how to translate between objects in memory and data in storage, and tracking the effects of changes, such as when a person is deleted, can be tedious. Core Data can help.

Core Data is *not* a beginner-level technology. It is difficult to use and extremely difficult to debug. It expresses itself in a verbose, rigid, arcane way. It has its own peculiar way of doing things — everything you already know about how to create, access, alter, or delete an object within an object collection becomes completely irrelevant! — and trying to bend it to your particular needs can be tricky and can have unintended side effects. Nor should Core Data be seen as a substitute for a true relational database.

A full explanation of Core Data would require an entire book; indeed, such books exist, and if Core Data interests you, you should read some of them. See also Apple's *Core Data Programming Guide* in the documentation archive, and the other resources referred to there. Here, I'll just illustrate what it's like to work with Core Data.

I will rewrite the People Groups example from earlier in this chapter as a Core Data app. This will still be a master–detail interface consisting of two table view controllers, GroupLister and PeopleLister, just as in Figure 22-7. But we will no longer have multiple documents, each representing a single group of people; instead, we will now have a single document, maintained for us by Core Data, containing all of our groups and all of their people.

To construct a Core Data project from scratch, it is simplest to specify the Master–Detail App template (or the Single View App template) and check Use Core Data in the second screen. Among other things, this gives you template code in the app delegate class for constructing the Core Data *persistence stack*, a set of objects that work together to fetch and save your data; in most cases there will no reason to alter this template code significantly.

The persistence stack consists of three objects:

- A *managed object model* (NSManagedObjectModel) describing the structure of the data
- A *managed object context* (NSManagedObjectContext) for communicating with the data
- A *persistent store coordinator* (NSPersistentStoreCoordinator) for dealing with actual storage of the data as a file

Starting in iOS 10, the entire stack is created for us by an NSPersistentContainer object. The template code provides a lazy initializer for this object, along these lines:

```
lazy var persistentContainer: NSPersistentContainer = {
    let con = NSPersistentContainer(name: "PeopleGroupsCoreData")
    con.loadPersistentStores { desc, err in
        if let err = err {
            fatalError("Unresolved error \(err)")
        }
    }
    return con
}()
```

The managed object context is the persistent container's `viewContext`. This will be our point of contact with Core Data. The managed object context is the world in which your data objects live and move and have their being: to obtain an object, you fetch it from the managed object context; to create an object, you insert it into the managed object context; to save your data, you save the managed object context. The template provides a method for saving:

```
func saveContext() {
    let context = self.persistentContainer.viewContext
    if context.hasChanges {
        try? context.save()
    }
}
```

To provide the rest of the app with easy access to the managed object context, our root view controller has a `managedObjectContext` property, and the app delegate's `application(_:didFinishLaunchingWithOptions:)` — or, if we're using window scenes, the scene delegate's `scene(_:willConnectTo:Options:)` — configures it to point back at the persistent container's `viewContext`:

```
let nav = self.window!.rootViewController as! UINavigationController
let tvc = nav.topViewController as! GroupLister
let del = UIApplication.shared.delegate as! AppDelegate
tvc.managedObjectContext = del.persistentContainer.viewContext
```

To describe the structure and relationships of the objects constituting your data model (the managed object model), you design an object graph in a data model document. Our object graph is very simple: a Group can have multiple Persons (Figure 22-11). The attributes, analogous to object properties, are all strings, except for the timestamps which are dates, and the Group UUID which is a UUID. (The timestamps will be used for determining the sort order in which groups and people will be displayed in the interface.)

Group and Person are not classes; they are *entity* names. And their attributes, such as `name` and `firstName`, are not properties. All Core Data model objects are instances of NSManagedObject, and make themselves dynamically KVC-compliant for attribute names. Core Data knows, thanks to our object graph, that a Person entity is to have a `firstName` attribute, so if an NSManagedObject represents a Person entity, you can set its `firstName` attribute by calling `setValue(_:forKey:)` with a key `"firstName"`, and you can retrieve its `firstName` attribute by calling `value(forKey:)` with a key `"firstName"`.

If that sounds maddening, that's because it *is* maddening. Fortunately, there's a simple solution: you configure your entities, in the Data Model inspector, to perform *code generation* of class definitions (Figure 22-12). Code generation allows us to treat entity types as classes, and managed objects as instances of those classes. When we compile our project, class files will be created for our entities (here, Group and

Figure 22-11. The Core Data model for the People Groups app

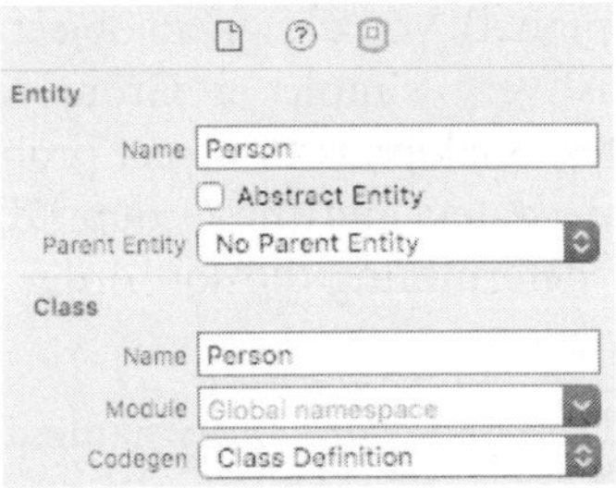

Figure 22-12. Configuring code generation

Person) as NSManagedObject subclasses endowed with properties corresponding to the entity attributes. So now Person *is* a class, and it *does* have a `firstName` property.

Now let's talk about the first view controller, GroupLister. Its job is to list groups and to allow the user to create a new group (Figure 22-7, on the left). How will Group-Lister get a list of groups? The way you ask Core Data for a model object is with a fetch request; and when Core Data model objects are the model data for a table view, fetch requests are conveniently managed through an NSFetchedResultsController.

Once again, the template gives us an excellent head start. It provides a fetched results controller stored in a property, ready to perform the fetch request and to supply our table view's data source with the actual data. My code essentially copies the template code; the first two lines demonstrate not only that Group is now a class with a fetch-Request method, but also that both NSFetchedResultsController and NSFetch-Request are generics:

```
lazy var frc: NSFetchedResultsController<Group> = {
    let req: NSFetchRequest<Group> = Group.fetchRequest()
    req.fetchBatchSize = 20
    let sortDescriptor = NSSortDescriptor(key:"timestamp", ascending:true)
    req.sortDescriptors = [sortDescriptor]
    let frc = NSFetchedResultsController(
        fetchRequest:req,
        managedObjectContext:self.managedObjectContext,
        sectionNameKeyPath:nil, cacheName:nil)
    frc.delegate = self
    do {
        try frc.performFetch()
    } catch {
        fatalError("Aborting with unresolved error")
    }
    return frc
}()
```

Now we need to hook our table view's data source to the NSFetchedResultsController somehow. New in iOS 13, this is particularly easy, because the fetched results controller vends an NSDiffableDataSourceSnapshotReference wrapping a snapshot with generic types String and NSManagedObjectID. So we'll declare a diffable data source with those types:

```
lazy var ds : UITableViewDiffableDataSource<String,NSManagedObjectID> = {
    UITableViewDiffableDataSource(tableView: self.tableView) { tv,ip,id in
        let cell = tv.dequeueReusableCell(
            withIdentifier: self.cellID, for: ip)
        cell.accessoryType = .disclosureIndicator
        let group = self.frc.object(at: ip)
        cell.textLabel!.text = group.name
        return cell
    }
}()
```

But we still have not configured a way of populating the diffable data source. The first step is to "tickle" our lazy instance properties by referring to self.frc in our view-DidLoad implementation:

```
override func viewDidLoad() {
    super.viewDidLoad()
    _ = self.frc // "tickle" the lazy vars
    // ...
}
```

Next, acting as the fetched results controller's delegate (NSFetchedResultsController-Delegate), we implement `controller(_:didChangeContentWith:)`. This method, new in iOS 13, provides our snapshot wrapped up in a snapshot reference (which is just a sort of type eraser). We cast this down to its actual generic snapshot and apply it to our diffable data source:

```
func controller(_ con: NSFetchedResultsController<NSFetchRequestResult>,
    didChangeContentWith snapshot: NSDiffableDataSourceSnapshotReference) {
    let snapshot =
        snapshot as NSDiffableDataSourceSnapshot<String,NSManagedObjectID>
    self.ds.apply(snapshot, animatingDifferences: false)
}
```

GroupLister's table now automatically reflects the contents of the fetch results controller. However, it is initially empty because our app starts life with no data. When the user asks to create a group, I put up an alert asking for the name of the new group. In the `handler:` function for its OK button, I create a new Group object in the managed object context and navigate to the detail view, PeopleLister:

```
let context = self.frc.managedObjectContext
let group = Group(context: context)
group.name = av.textFields![0].text!
group.uuid = UUID()
group.timestamp = Date()
let pl = PeopleLister(group: group)
self.navigationController!.pushViewController(pl, animated: true)
```

The detail view controller class is PeopleLister (Figure 22-7, on the right). It lists all the people in a particular Group, so I don't want PeopleLister to be instantiated without a Group; therefore, its designated initializer is `init(group:)`. As the preceding code shows, when I want to navigate from the GroupLister view to the People-Lister view, I instantiate PeopleLister and push it onto the navigation controller's stack. I do the same sort of thing when the user taps an existing Group name in the GroupLister table view:

```
override func tableView(_ tableView: UITableView,
    didSelectRowAt indexPath: IndexPath) {
        let pl = PeopleLister(group: self.frc.object(at:indexPath))
        self.navigationController!.pushViewController(pl, animated: true)
}
```

PeopleLister, too, has an `frc` property that's an NSFetchedResultsController. However, a PeopleLister instance should list only the People belonging to *one particular group*, which has been stored as its `group` property. So PeopleLister's implementation of the `frc` initializer contains these lines (`req` is the fetch request we're configuring):

```
let pred = NSPredicate(format:"group = %@", self.group)
req.predicate = pred
```

The PeopleLister interface consists of a table of text fields. Populating the table is just like what GroupLister did; I can use a Person's `firstName` and `lastName` to set the text of the text fields.

When the user *edits* a text field to change the first or last name of a Person, I hear about it as the text field's delegate and update the data model (the first part of this code should be familiar from Chapter 8):

```
func textFieldDidEndEditing(_ textField: UITextField) {
    var v : UIView = textField
    repeat { v = v.superview! } while !(v is UITableViewCell)
    let cell = v as! UITableViewCell
    let ip = self.tableView.indexPath(for:cell)!
    let object = self.frc.object(at:ip)
    object.setValue(textField.text!, forKey: (
        (textField.tag == 1) ? "firstName" : "lastName"))
}
```

When the user asks to make a *new* Person, I create a new Person object in the managed object context and configure its attributes with an empty first name and last name:

```
@objc func doAdd(_:AnyObject) {
    self.tableView.endEditing(true)
    let context = self.frc.managedObjectContext
    let person = Person(context:context)
    person.group = self.group
    person.lastName = ""
    person.firstName = ""
    person.timestamp = Date()
}
```

The result is that the delegate method `controller(_:didChangeContentWith:)` is called, I obtain the snapshot and apply it to the diffable data source, and the new empty person is displayed in the table view, waiting for the user to type into its text fields.

It remains only to save the managed object context at key moments in the life of the app, such as when a view controller disappears or the app goes into the background:

```
(UIApplication.shared.delegate as! AppDelegate).saveContext()
```

Core Data files are not suitable for use as iCloud documents. If you want to reflect structured data into the cloud, a better alternative is the CloudKit framework. In effect, this allows you to maintain a database online, and to synchronize changed data up to and down from that database. You might use Core Data as a form of *local* storage, but you'd still use CloudKit as an intermediary, to communicate the data between different devices. New in iOS 13, NSPersistentCloudKitContainer provides automatic linkage between Core Data and CloudKit. See the Core Data framework documentation for more information.

PDFs

Up to this point, I have displayed the contents of a PDF file by means of a web view or in a Quick Look preview. Starting in iOS 11, PDF Kit (`import PDFKit`), brought over from macOS, provides a native UIView subclass, PDFView, whose job is to display a PDF nicely.

Basic use of a PDFView is simple. Initialize a PDFDocument, either from data or from a file URL, and assign it as the PDFView's document:

```
let v = PDFView(frame:self.view.bounds)
self.view.addSubview(v)
let url = Bundle.main.url(forResource: "notes", withExtension: "pdf")!
let doc = PDFDocument(url: url)
v.document = doc
```

There are many other configurable aspects of a PDFView. A particularly nice touch is that a PDFView can embed a UIPageViewController for layout and navigation of the PDF's individual pages:

```
v.usePageViewController(true)
```

A PDFDocument consists of pages, represented by PDFPage objects. You can manipulate those pages, adding and removing pages from the document. You can even draw a PDFPage's contents yourself, meaning that you can create a PDF document from scratch.

As a demonstration, I'll create a PDF document consisting of one page with the words "Hello, world!" in the center. I start with a PDFPage subclass, MyPage, where I override the `draw(with:to:)` method. The parameters are a PDFDisplayBox that tells me the page size, along with a CGContext to draw into. There's just one thing to watch out for: a PDF graphics context is flipped with respect to the normal iOS coordinate system. So I apply a transform to the context before I draw into it:

```
override func draw(with box: PDFDisplayBox, to context: CGContext) {
    UIGraphicsPushContext(context)
    context.saveGState()
    let r = self.bounds(for: box)
    let s = NSAttributedString(string: "Hello, world!", attributes: [
        .font : UIFont(name: "Georgia", size: 80)!
    ])
    let sz = s.boundingRect(with: CGSize(10000,10000),
        options: .usesLineFragmentOrigin, context: nil)
    context.translateBy(x: 0, y: r.height)
    context.scaleBy(x: 1, y: -1)
    s.draw(at: CGPoint(
        (r.maxX - r.minX) / 2 - sz.width / 2,
        (r.maxY - r.minY) / 2 - sz.height / 2
```

```
    ))
    context.restoreGState()
    UIGraphicsPopContext()
}
```

To create and display my PDFPage in a PDFView (v) is simple:

```
let doc = PDFDocument()
v.document = doc
doc.insert(MyPage(), at: 0)
```

If my document consisted of more than one MyPage, they would now all draw the same thing. If that's not what I want, my `draw(with:to:)` code can ask what page of the document this is:

```
let pagenum = self.document?.index(for: self)
```

In addition, a host of ancillary PDF Kit classes allow you to manipulate page thumbnails, selection, annotations, and more.

Image Files

The Image I/O framework provides a way to open image files, to save image files, to convert between image file formats, and to read metadata from standard image file formats, including EXIF and GPS information from a digital camera. You'll need to `import ImageIO`. The Image I/O API is written in C, not Objective-C, and it uses CFTypeRefs, not objects. Unlike Core Graphics, there is no Swift "renamification" overlay that represents the API as object-oriented; you have to call the framework's global C functions directly, casting between the CFTypeRefs and their Foundation counterparts. But that's not hard to do.

Use of the Image I/O framework starts with the notion of an *image source* (CGImageSource). This can be created from the URL of a file (actually CFURL, to which URL is toll-free bridged) or from a Data object (actually CFData, to which Data is toll-free bridged).

Here we obtain the metadata from a photo file in our app bundle:

```
let url = Bundle.main.url(forResource:"colson", withExtension: "jpg")!
let opts : [AnyHashable:Any] = [kCGImageSourceShouldCache : false]
let src = CGImageSourceCreateWithURL(url as CFURL, opts as CFDictionary)!
let d = CGImageSourceCopyPropertiesAtIndex(src, 0, opts as CFDictionary)
    as! [AnyHashable:Any]
```

Without having opened the image file as an image, we now have a dictionary full of information about it, including its pixel dimensions (keys `kCGImagePropertyPixel-Width` and `kCGImagePropertyPixelHeight`), its resolution, color model, color depth, and orientation — plus, because this picture comes originally from a digital camera, the EXIF data such as the aperture and exposure at which it was taken, and the make and model of the camera.

To obtain the image as a CGImage, we can call `CGImageSourceCreateImageAtIndex`. Alternatively, we can request a *thumbnail* of the image. This is a very useful thing to do, and the name "thumbnail" doesn't really do justice to its importance. If your purpose is to display this image in your interface, you don't care about the original image data; a thumbnail is *precisely* what you want, especially because you can specify any size for this "thumbnail" all the way up to the original size of the image! This is splendid, because to assign a large image to a small image view wastes all the memory reflected by the size difference.

To generate a thumbnail at a given size, you start with a dictionary specifying the size along with other instructions, and pass that, together with the image source, to `CGImageSourceCreateThumbnailAtIndex`. The only pitfall is that, because we are working with a CGImage and specifying actual pixels, we must remember to take account of the scale of our device's screen. Let's say we want to scale our image so that its largest dimension is no larger than the width of the UIImageView (`self.iv`) into which we intend to place it:

```
let url = Bundle.main.url(forResource:"colson", withExtension: "jpg")!
var opts : [AnyHashable:Any] = [kCGImageSourceShouldCache : false]
let src = CGImageSourceCreateWithURL(url as CFURL, opts as CFDictionary)!
let scale = UIScreen.main.scale
let w = self.iv.bounds.width * scale
opts = [
    kCGImageSourceShouldAllowFloat : true,
    kCGImageSourceCreateThumbnailWithTransform : true,
    kCGImageSourceCreateThumbnailFromImageAlways : true,
    kCGImageSourceShouldCacheImmediately : true,
    kCGImageSourceThumbnailMaxPixelSize : w
]
let imref =
    CGImageSourceCreateThumbnailAtIndex(src, 0, opts as CFDictionary)!
let im = UIImage(cgImage: imref, scale: scale, orientation: .up)
self.iv.image = im
```

To save an image using a specified file format, we need an *image destination*. I'll show how to save our image as a TIFF. We never open the image as an image! We save directly from the image source to the image destination:

```
let url = Bundle.main.url(forResource:"colson", withExtension: "jpg")!
let opts : [AnyHashable:Any] = [kCGImageSourceShouldCache : false]
let src = CGImageSourceCreateWithURL(url as CFURL, opts as CFDictionary)!
let fm = FileManager.default
let suppurl = try! fm.url(for:.applicationSupportDirectory,
    in: .userDomainMask, appropriateFor: nil, create: true)
let tiff = suppurl.appendingPathComponent("mytiff.tiff")
```

```
let dest =
    CGImageDestinationCreateWithURL(tiff as CFURL, kUTTypeTIFF, 1, nil)!
CGImageDestinationAddImageFromSource(dest, src, 0, nil)
let ok = CGImageDestinationFinalize(dest)
```

CHAPTER 23

Basic Networking

Networking is difficult and complicated, not least because it's ultimately out of your control. You can ask for a resource from across the network, but at that point anything can happen. The resource might not be found; it might take a while to arrive; it might *never* arrive. The server or the network might be unavailable, or even worse, might vanish after the resource has partially arrived. There are numerous technicalities to deal with, not to mention the need for extensive background threading so that nothing interferes with the operation of your app's interface. Fortunately, iOS handles all of that behind the scenes, and makes basic networking easy.

Earlier chapters have described interface and frameworks that network for you automatically. Put a web view in your interface (Chapter 11) and poof, you're networking; the web view does all the grunt work, and it does it a lot better than you'd be likely to do it from scratch. The same is true of AVPlayer (Chapter 15), MKMapView (Chapter 20), and so on. Think of that as implicit networking. This chapter discusses explicit networking.

 A device used for development has a Network Link Conditioner switch in Settings (under Developer). Use it to simulate different networking situations to stress-test your networking code.

HTTP Requests

An HTTP request is made through a URLSession object. A URLSession is a kind of grand overarching environment in which network-related tasks are to take place.

Obtaining a Session

There are three chief ways to obtain a URLSession:

The shared session

The URLSession class vends a singleton shared session object through its `shared` class property. This object is supplied and configured by the runtime; it is good for very simple, occasional use, where you don't need configuration, authentication, dedicated cookie storage, and so forth. You can't interact with the session while it's performing a networking task for you, because you have no delegate. All you can do is order some task to be performed and then stand back and wait for it to finish.

Session configured without a delegate

You create the URLSession by calling `init(configuration:)`. This means that the session is yours, not shared. You'll hand the session a URLSessionConfiguration object describing the desired environment. This means that you can configure the URLSession. But you still can't interact with the session while it's performing a networking task for you, because you still have no delegate.

Session configured with a delegate

You create the URLSession by calling `init(configuration:delegate:delegate-Queue:)`. Like the preceding initializer, you'll hand the session a URLSessionConfiguration object. Now the session is yours and you can configure it — and you also have a delegate that can receive various callbacks during the course of a networking task (and you even get to say whether those callbacks should occur on the main thread or in the background). Clearly this is the most powerful approach; it is also more complicated than the others, but that complexity can be worthwhile.

The shared session is owned by the runtime, so there's no need to retain it; you simply access it and tell it what you want it to do. But if you create a URLSession with a configuration, you'll probably want it to persist. Your app will typically need to create only one URLSession object; it is reasonable to store it in a global variable, or in an instance property of some object that will persist throughout your app's lifetime, such as the app delegate or the root view controller.

Session Configuration

To initialize a URLSession, you'll start by creating a URLSessionConfiguration and setting its properties. The configuration object dictates various options to be applied to the session. (A legitimate reason for creating multiple URLSession objects might be that you need them to have different configurations.)

There are three URLSessionConfiguration class members that you can use to obtain a URLSessionConfiguration instance:

`default`

A basic vanilla URLSessionConfiguration. This is what you'll use most of the time.

`ephemeral`

Configures a URLSession whose cookies and caches are maintained in memory only; they are never saved. You can actually configure a `default` URLSession-Configuration to give the same behavior, so this is purely a convenience.

`background(withIdentifier:)`

Configures a URLSession that will proceed with its networking tasks independently of your app at some future time. I'll discuss background sessions later.

Here are some of the basic URLSessionConfiguration properties:

`allowsExpensiveNetworkAccess`

New in iOS 13. Effectively supersedes `allowsCellularAccess`. The notion "expensive" currently embraces both cellular and device hotspots. If you set this property to `false` and the network is "expensive," attempting to network will get you a URLError whose `networkUnavailableReason` is `.expensive`.

`allowsConstrainedNetworkAccess`

New in iOS 13. The notion of "constrained" network access corresponds to Low Data Mode in Settings (under Cellular and WiFi). The idea is that the user can mark a route as low-bandwidth; the system will respond by turning off background app refresh and so forth, and your app should respond by reducing its network activity and not fetching large resources if a smaller resource (or no resource) will do. If you set this property to `false` and the network is "constrained," attempting to network will get you a URLError whose `network-UnavailableReason` is `.constrained`.

waitsForConnectivity

If true, the session will try again later if the network is unavailable initially. Apple says that it is better to use this property, and let the URLSession do the work, than to try to determine reachability for yourself (by using SCNetwork-Reachability or similar).

httpMaximumConnectionsPerHost

The maximum number of simultaneous connections to the remote server.

Timeout values

There are two of them:

timeoutIntervalForRequest

The maximum time you're willing to wait *between* pieces of data. The timer starts when the connection succeeds, and then starts over each time a piece of data is received. A timeout means that things have stalled in the middle. If this is not a background session, the timeout will trigger failure of the download. The default is one minute.

timeoutIntervalForResource

The maximum time for the *entire* download to arrive. The timer starts when the networking task is told to start, and just keeps ticking until completion. This is appropriate for limiting the request's overall time-to-live. Failure to complete in the required time will always trigger failure of the download. The default is seven days.

There are also numerous cookie, caching, credential, proxy, and protocol properties.

Session Tasks

To use a URLSession to perform a networking task, you need a URLSessionTask object, representing a single communication exchange. You do not instantiate a task yourself; rather, you ask the URLSession for a task of the desired type, which will be an appropriate subclass:

URLSessionDataTask

A URLSessionTask subclass. You ask for a resource and the data is provided incrementally to your app as it arrives across the network. You should not use a data task for a large hunk of data, because the data is accumulating in memory throughout the download.

URLSessionDownloadTask

A URLSessionTask subclass. You ask for a resource, but the data never passes through your app's memory; instead, it is accumulated into a file, and the saved file URL is handed to you at the end of the process. The file is outside your sandbox and will be destroyed, so preserving it (or its contents) is up to you.

URLSessionUploadTask

A URLSessionDataTask subclass. You can provide a file to be uploaded and stand back, though you can also hear about the upload progress if you wish.

URLSessionStreamTask

A URLSessionTask subclass. This type of task makes it possible to deal conveniently with streams.

URLSessionWebSocketTask

New in iOS 13. A web socket is a persistent two-way connection between client and server (a "bidirectional stream").

URLSessionTask itself is an abstract superclass, embodying various properties common to all types of task, such as:

- A `taskDescription` and `taskIdentifier`; the former is up to you, while the latter is a unique identifier within the URLSession.

- The `originalRequest` and `currentRequest` (the request can change because there might be a redirect).

- The `priority`; a Float between 0 and 1, used as a hint to help rank the relative importance of your tasks. For convenience, URLSessionTask vends three constants:

  - `URLSessionTask.lowPriority` (0.25)

  - `URLSessionTask.defaultPriority` (0.5)

  - `URLSessionTask.highPriority` (0.75)

- An initial `response` from the server.

- Various `countOfBytes...` properties allowing you to track progress.

- A `progress` property that vends a Progress object; this is probably a better way to track progress than the `countOfBytes...` properties.

- A `state`, which might be:

  - `.running`

  - `.suspended`

  - `.canceling`

  - `.completed`

- An `error` if the task failed.

You can tell a task to `resume`, `suspend`, or `cancel`. A task is *born suspended*, it does *not* start until it is told to resume for the first time. Typically you'll obtain the task, configure it, and then tell it to `resume` to start it. The Progress object vended by a task's `progress` property is a second gateway to these methods; telling the Progress object to `resume`, `pause`, or `cancel` is the same as telling the task to `resume`, `suspend`, or `cancel` respectively.

Once you've obtained a new session task from the URLSession, the session retains it; you can keep a reference to the task if you wish, but you don't have to. The session will provide you with a list of its tasks in progress; call `getAllTasks(completion-Handler:)` to receive the existing tasks in the completion function. The session releases a task after the task is cancelled or completed; a URLSession with no running or suspended tasks has no tasks at all.

There are two ways to ask your URLSession for a new session task. Which one you use depends on how you obtained the URLSession; in turn, they entail two different ways of working with the task:

With a completion function
> Take this approach if you are using the `shared` session or a session configured without a delegate. You'll call a convenience method that takes a `completion-Handler:` parameter, such as `downloadTask(with:completionHandler:)`. You supply a completion function, typically an anonymous function, to be called when the task ends.

Without a completion function
> Take this approach if you gave the URLSession a delegate when you created it. You'll call a method *without* a `completionHandler:` parameter, such as `download-Task(with:)`. The delegate is called back at various stages of the task's progress.

For a data task or a download task, the `with:` parameter can be either a URL or a URLRequest. A URL is simpler, but a URLRequest allows you more power to perform additional configurations.

 Apple says that it is reasonable to call `resume` on a background queue. By specifying the queue's quality of service (`qos`), you can rank the priority of this task. See Chapter 24.

Session Delegate

If you create a session by calling `init(configuration:delegate:delegateQueue:)`, you'll specify a delegate, along with the queue (roughly, the thread — see Chapter 24) on which the delegate methods are to be called. For each type of session task, there's a delegate protocol, which may inherit from other protocols:

Data delegate
> For a data task, we would want a data delegate — an object conforming to the URLSessionDataDelegate protocol, which itself conforms to the URLSessionTask-

Delegate protocol, which in turn conforms to the URLSessionDelegate protocol, resulting in about a dozen delegate methods we could implement, though only a few are crucial:

URLSession(_:dataTask:didReceive:)
> Some data has arrived, as a Data object (the third parameter). The data will arrive piecemeal, so this method may be called many times during the download process, supplying new data each time. Our job is to accumulate all those chunks of data; this involves maintaining state between calls.

URLSession(_:task:didCompleteWithError:)
> If there is an error, we'll find out about it here. If there's no error, this is our signal that the download is over; we can now do something with the accumulated data.

Download delegate

For a download task, we would want a download delegate, conforming to the URLSessionDownloadDelegate protocol, which conforms to the URLSession-TaskDelegate protocol, which conforms to the URLSessionDelegate protocol. Here are some useful download delegate methods:

URLSession(_:downloadTask:didResumeAtOffset:expectedTotalBytes:)
> This method is of interest only in the case of a resumable download that has been paused and resumed.

URLSession(_:downloadTask:didWriteData:totalBytesWritten:totalBytes-ExpectedToWrite:)
> Called periodically, to keep us apprised of the download's progress. It might be more convenient to keep a reference to the task's Progress object.

URLSession(_:downloadTask:didFinishDownloadingTo:)
> Called at the end of the process. The last parameter is a file URL; we must grab the downloaded file immediately from there, as it will be destroyed.

URLSession(_:task:didCompleteWithError:)
> Unlike with a data task, this delegate method is not crucial for a download task. Still, if there was a communication problem, this is where you'd hear about it.

Some delegate methods provide a completionHandler: parameter. These are delegate methods that require a response from you. In the case of a data task, URLSession(_:dataTask:didReceive:completionHandler:) arrives when we first connect to the server. The third parameter is the response (URLResponse), and we could now check its status code. We must also return a response of our own, saying whether or not to proceed (or whether to convert the data task to a download task, which could certainly come in handy). But because of the multithreaded, asynchronous nature of networking (see Appendix C), we do this, not by returning a value directly, but by *calling the completion function* and passing our response into it.

The various delegate protocols also inherit this method from the URLSessionTask-Delegate protocol:

`urlSession(_:taskIsWaitingForConnectivity:)`
> Called only if the session configuration has its `waitsForConnectivity` set to `true`. The task has tried to start and has failed; instead of giving up with an error (as it would have done if `waitsForConnectivity` were `false`), it will wait and try again later. You might respond by updating your interface somehow.

HTTP Request with Task Completion Function

At long last, we are ready for some examples! I'll start by illustrating the utmost in simplicity. This is the absolute minimum approach to downloading a file:

- We use the shared URLSession, which takes no configuration.
- We obtain a download task, handing it a remote URL and a completion function. When the download is complete, the completion function will be called with a file URL; we retrieve the data from that URL and do something with it.

Having obtained the session and the task, don't forget to call `resume` to start the download! Our overall code looks like this:

```
let s = "https://www.someserver.com/somefolder/someimage.jpg"
let url = URL(string:s)!
let session = URLSession.shared
let task = session.downloadTask(with:url) { loc, resp, err in
    // ... completion function body goes here ...
}
task.resume()
```

All that remains is to write the body of the completion function. The downloaded data (here, an image file) is stored temporarily; if we want to do something with it, we must retrieve it right now. We must make no assumptions about what thread the completion function will be called on; indeed, unless we take steps to the contrary, it will be a background thread. In this particular example, the URL points to an image that I intend to display in my interface; therefore, I step out to the main thread (Chapter 24) in order to talk to the interface:

```
let task = session.downloadTask(with:url) { fileURL, resp, err in
    if let url = fileURL, let d = try? Data(contentsOf:url) {
        let im = UIImage(data:d)
        DispatchQueue.main.async {
```

```
            self.iv.image = im
        }
    }
}
```

That's all there is to it! If there's an error or a negative response from the server (such as "File not found"), url will be nil and we'll do nothing. Optionally, you might like to have the completion function report those conditions:

```
guard err == nil else { print(err); return }
let status = (resp as! HTTPURLResponse).statusCode
guard status == 200 else { print(status); return }
```

A data task is similar, except that the data itself arrives as the first parameter of the completion function:

```
let task = session.dataTask(with:url) { data, resp, err in
    if let d = data {
        let im = UIImage(data:d) // ... and so on
```

A session task vends a Progress object (starting in iOS 11). This means that we can track the progress of our task even without a session delegate. If we have a UIProgressView (self.prog) in our interface, displaying the task's progress to the user could be as simple as this:

```
self.prog.observedProgress = task.progress
```

Recall, too, that one Progress object can act as the parent of other Progress objects (Chapter 12). If we are going to perform multiple tasks simultaneously, our UIProgressView's observedProgress can be configured to show the *overall* progress of those tasks.

New in iOS 13, the Combine framework endows a URLSession with a data task *publisher*. To obtain it, call dataTaskPublisher(for:) with a URL or URLRequest. This provides a publish-and-subscribe alternative to a completion function, and you can encapsulate analysis and processing of the response within the pipeline:

```
let _ = session.dataTaskPublisher(for: url)
    .tryMap { data, response -> UIImage? in
        if (response as? HTTPURLResponse)?.statusCode != 200 {
            throw NSError(domain: "wrong status", code: 0)
        }
        return UIImage(data:data)
    }.receive(on: DispatchQueue.main)
    .sink(receiveCompletion: { comp in
        if case let .failure(err) = comp {
            print(err)
        }
    }) { im in
        self.iv.image = im
    }
```

HTTP Request with Session Delegate

Now let's go to the other extreme and be very formal and complete:

- We'll start by creating and configuring a URLSessionConfiguration object.

- We'll create and retain our own URLSession.

- We'll give the session a delegate, implementing delegate methods to deal with the session task as it proceeds.

- When we request our session task, instead of a mere URL, we'll start with a URL-Request.

We are now creating our own URLSession, rather than borrowing the system's `shared` session. Since one URLSession can perform multiple tasks, there will typically be just one URLSession; so I'll make a lazy initializer that creates and configures it, supplying a URLSessionConfiguration and setting the delegate:

```
lazy var session : URLSession = {
    let config = URLSessionConfiguration.ephemeral
    config.allowsExpensiveNetworkAccess = false
    let session = URLSession(configuration: config, delegate: self,
        delegateQueue: .main)
    return session
}()
```

I've specified, for purposes of the example, that no caching is to take place and that data downloading via cell is forbidden; you could configure things much more heavily and meaningfully, of course. I have specified `self` as the delegate, and I have requested delegate callbacks on the main thread.

When I ask for the session task, I'll supply a URLRequest instead of a URL:

```
let url = URL(string:s)!
let req = URLRequest(url:url)
// ask for the task
```

In my examples in this chapter, there is very little merit in using a URLRequest instead of a URL to form our task. Still, a URLRequest can come in handy, and an upload task requires one; this is where you configure such things as the HTTP request method, body, and header fields.

 Do *not* use the URLRequest to configure properties of the request that are configurable through the URLSessionConfiguration. There is no point setting the URLRequest's `timeoutInterval`, for instance, as it is the URLSessionConfiguration's timeout properties that are significant.

Download task

I'll recast the image file download task from the previous example. I blank out the image view, to make the progress of the task more obvious for test purposes, and I create and start the download task:

```
self.iv.image = nil
let s = "https://www.someserver.com/somefolder/someimage.jpg"
let url = URL(string:s)!
let req = URLRequest(url:url)
let task = self.session.downloadTask(with:req)
task.resume()
```

Here are some delegate methods for responding to the download:

```
func urlSession(_ session: URLSession,
    downloadTask: URLSessionDownloadTask,
    didWriteData bytesWritten: Int64,
    totalBytesWritten writ: Int64,
    totalBytesExpectedToWrite exp: Int64) {
        print("downloaded \(100*writ/exp)%")
}
func urlSession(_ session: URLSession,
    task: URLSessionTask,
    didCompleteWithError error: Error?) {
        print("completed: error: \(error)")
}
func urlSession(_ session: URLSession,
    downloadTask: URLSessionDownloadTask,
    didFinishDownloadingTo fileURL: URL) {
        if let d = try? Data(contentsOf:fileURL) {
            let im = UIImage(data:d)
            DispatchQueue.main.async {
                self.iv.image = im
            }
        }
}
/*
downloaded 23%
downloaded 47%
downloaded 71%
downloaded 100%
completed: error: nil
*/
```

Instead of implementing URLSession(_:downloadTask:didWriteData:totalBytes-Written:totalBytesExpectedToWrite:) to track the progress of the download, we could use the task's progress object. We would configure that when we obtain the download task:

```
self.ob = task.progress.observe(\.fractionCompleted) { prog, change in
    print("downloaded \(Int(100*prog.fractionCompleted))%")
}
```

Data task

A data task leaves it up to you to accumulate the data as it arrives in chunks. You'll want to keep a mutable Data object on hand; I'll use an instance property:

```
var data = Data()
```

To get started, I prepare `self.data` by giving it a zero count, and then I create and start the data task:

```
self.iv.image = nil
self.data.count = 0 // *
let s = "https://www.someserver.com/somefolder/someimage.jpg"
let url = URL(string:s)!
let req = URLRequest(url:url)
let task = self.session.dataTask(with:req) // *
task.resume()
```

As the chunks of data arrive, I keep appending them to `self.data`. When all the data has arrived, it is ready for use:

```
func urlSession(_ session: URLSession,
    dataTask: URLSessionDataTask,
    didReceive data: Data) {
        self.data.append(data)
}
func urlSession(_ session: URLSession,
    task: URLSessionTask,
    didCompleteWithError error: Error?) {
        if error == nil {
            DispatchQueue.main.async {
                self.iv.image = UIImage(data:self.data)
            }
        }
}
```

One Session, One Delegate

The URLSession delegate architecture dictates that the delegate belongs to the *session as a whole*, not to each task individually. Because of this architecture, the preceding data task code is broken. To see why, ask yourself: What happens if our session is asked to perform another data task while this data task is still in progress? Our one session delegate is accumulating the chunks of data into a single Data property, `self.data`, without regard to what data task this chunk of data comes from. Clearly this is a potential train wreck: we're going to interleave the data from two different tasks, ending up with nonsense.

Let's revise the data task code to fix the problem. We need a way to *separate* the data streams belonging to the different tasks. Fortunately, a session task has a unique identifier — its `taskIdentifier`, which is an Int. So instead of a single Data property, we can maintain a dictionary keyed by each data task's `taskIdentifier`, where the corresponding value is a Data object:

```
var data = [Int:Data]()
```

Our code for obtaining and starting a new data task now adds an entry to the `data` dictionary, like this:

```
let task = self.session.dataTask(with:req)
self.data[task.taskIdentifier] = Data() // *
task.resume()
```

As a chunk of data arrives, we append it to the correct entry in the dictionary:

```
func urlSession(_ session: URLSession,
    dataTask: URLSessionDataTask,
    didReceive data: Data) {
        self.data[dataTask.taskIdentifier]!.append(data)
}
```

When a task's data has fully arrived, we pluck it out of the dictionary and remove that dictionary entry (so that data from stale tasks doesn't accumulate), and proceed to use the data:

```
func urlSession(_ session: URLSession,
    task: URLSessionTask,
    didCompleteWithError error: Error?) {
        let d = self.data[task.taskIdentifier]!
        self.data[task.taskIdentifier] = nil
        if error == nil {
            DispatchQueue.main.async {
                self.iv.image = UIImage(data:d)
            }
        }
}
```

Delegate Memory Management

A URLSession does an unusual thing: it *retains its delegate*. This is understandable, as it would be disastrous if the delegate could simply vanish in the middle of an asynchronous time-consuming process; but it means that all the preceding delegate examples are broken in yet another way. We have a retain cycle! Our view controllers are leaking. That's because the view controller has a URLSession instance property `self.session`, but the URLSession is retaining the view controller (`self`) as its delegate.

The way to break the cycle is to *invalidate* the URLSession at some appropriate moment. There are two ways to do this:

finishTasksAndInvalidate

Allows any existing tasks to run to completion. Afterward, the URLSession *releases* the delegate and cannot be used for anything further.

invalidateAndCancel

Interrupts any existing tasks immediately. The URLSession *releases* the delegate and cannot be used for anything further.

If the delegate caught in this retain cycle is a view controller, then `viewWill-Disappear(_:)` could be a good place to invalidate the URLSession; we cannot use `deinit`, because `deinit` won't be called unless we have *already* invalidated the URL-Session (that's what it means to have a retain cycle):

```
override func viewWillDisappear(_ animated: Bool) {
    super.viewWillDisappear(animated)
    self.session.finishTasksAndInvalidate()
}
```

Session and Delegate Encapsulation

The solution in the preceding section works, but it is not very satisfying. We are still creating a retain cycle between the session and its delegate, the view controller; to break it, we must remember to invalidate the session. It is not easy to find a place to do that; `viewWillDisappear` can be called many times in the life of a view controller, and invalidating the session there might not be appropriate. It would be much better if we could invalidate the session automatically when the view controller goes out of existence. And it would be even better if there were never any retain cycle to start with!

We can achieve that goal by encapsulating the session and its delegate:

- Start with an instance of some *separate* class whose job is to hold the URLSession in a property.
- Make the URLSession's delegate an instance of yet *another* class — an instance that is not retained by any object other than the URLSession.

Now our memory management problems are over. The URLSession retains its delegate, so there is no need for any *other* object to retain it. The delegate does not retain the session or the instance that holds the session, so there is no retain cycle. And there is no entanglement with the memory management of a view controller. Our URLSession-holding instance can live anywhere — and if it is being retained by a view controller, then it will go out of existence in good order when the view controller goes out of existence.

To illustrate, I'll design a Downloader class that holds a URLSession and creates its delegate. I imagine that our view controller will create and maintain an instance of Downloader early in its lifetime, as an instance property:

```
let downloader : Downloader = {
    // ...
    return Downloader( /* ... */ )
}()
```

In that code, I omitted the initialization of Downloader. How should this work? The
Downloader object will create its own URLSession, but I think the client should be
allowed to configure the session. So let's posit that Downloader's initializer takes a
URLSessionConfiguration parameter:

```
let downloader : Downloader = {
    let config = URLSessionConfiguration.ephemeral
    config.allowsExpensiveNetworkAccess = false
    return Downloader(configuration:config)
}()
```

Now let's design Downloader itself. It creates and retains the URLSession, and makes
its delegate an instance of a private class, DownloaderDelegate — an instance that
only the URLSession itself will retain. Since there is no retain cycle, Downloader can
cancel its own session *automatically* when it goes out of existence:

```
class Downloader: NSObject {
    let config : URLSessionConfiguration
    lazy var session : URLSession = {
        return URLSession(configuration:self.config,
            delegate:DownloaderDelegate(), delegateQueue:.main)
    }()
    init(configuration config:URLSessionConfiguration) {
        self.config = config
        super.init()
    }
    // ...
    deinit {
        self.session.invalidateAndCancel()
    }
}
```

Suppose the client is a view controller with a downloader property, as I suggested earlier. There is no retain cycle, so the view controller can go out of existence in good
order when the view controller hierarchy is through with it. And when that happens,
its downloader will go out of existence too, taking the URLSession and its delegate
with it.

Next, let's decide how a client will communicate with a Downloader object. The client will hand a URL to the Downloader instance; the Downloader will obtain the
URLSessionDownloadTask and start it. The DownloaderDelegate will be told when
the download is over. At that point, the DownloaderDelegate has a file URL for the
downloaded object, which it needs to hand back to the client immediately.

One way to arrange this is that the client, when it hands the Downloader a URL to initiate a download, should also supply a *completion function* (see Appendix C) to be called when the download is over. In that way, we deal with the asynchronous nature of networking, as well as keeping Downloader independent and agnostic about who the caller is. To return the file URL at the end of a download, the DownloaderDelegate *calls* the completion function, passing it the file URL as a parameter. I can even define a type alias naming my completion function type:

```
typealias DownloaderCH = (URL?) -> ()
```

From the client's point of view, then, the process will look something like this:

```
let s = "https://www.someserver.com/somefolder/someimage.jpg"
let url = URL(string:s)!
self.downloader.download(url:url) { url in
    if let url = url, let d = try? Data(contentsOf: url) {
        let im = UIImage(data:d)
        self.iv.image = im // assume we're called back on main thread
    }
}
```

Now let's implement this architecture within Downloader. We have posited a method download(url:completionHandler:). When that method is called, Downloader stores the completion function; it then asks for a new download task and sets it going:

```
@discardableResult
func download(url:URL,
    completionHandler ch : @escaping DownloaderCH) -> URLSessionTask {
        let task = self.session.downloadTask(with:url)
        // ... store the completion function somehow ...
        task.resume()
        return task
}
```

(We're returning a reference to the task, so that the client can subsequently cancel the task if need be.)

When the download finishes, the DownloaderDelegate calls the completion function:

```
func urlSession(_ session: URLSession,
    downloadTask: URLSessionDownloadTask,
    didFinishDownloadingTo url: URL) {
        let ch = // ... retrieve the completion function somehow ...
        ch(url)
}
```

In my carefree speculative coding design, I have left a blank — the storage and retrieval of the completion function corresponding to each download task. Let's use the same technique I used earlier for accumulating the data of multiple data tasks, namely a dictionary keyed by the task's taskIdentifier. This will be a private property of DownloaderDelegate, along with a public method:

```
private var handlers = [Int:DownloaderCH]()
func appendHandler(_ ch:@escaping DownloaderCH, task:URLSessionTask {
    self.handlers[task.taskIdentifier] = ch
}
```

We are now ready to fill in the blank in Downloader's download(url:completion-Handler:) method. By the time this method is called by the client, the delegate has already been created and handed to the session, and only the session has a reference to it; so we obtain the delegate from the session and call the append-Handler(_:task:) method that we gave it for this purpose:

```
func download(url:URL,
    completionHandler ch : @escaping DownloaderCH) -> URLSessionTask {
        let task = self.session.downloadTask(with:url)
        let del = self.session.delegate as! DownloaderDelegate
        del.appendHandler(ch, task: task)
        task.resume()
        return task
}
```

All that remains is to write the delegate methods for DownloaderDelegate. There are two of them that we need to implement. When the download arrives, we find the completion function corresponding to this download task and call it, handing it the file URL where the downloaded data has been stored:

```
func urlSession(_ session: URLSession,
    downloadTask: URLSessionDownloadTask,
    didFinishDownloadingTo url: URL) {
        let ch = self.handlers[downloadTask.taskIdentifier]
        ch?(url)
}
```

When the task completes, we purge the completion function from the dictionary — and, if there was an error, we pass nil to the completion function, guaranteeing that the completion function will be called under all circumstances:

```
func urlSession(_ session: URLSession,
    task: URLSessionTask,
    didCompleteWithError error: Error?) {
        let ch = self.handlers[task.taskIdentifier]
        self.handlers[task.taskIdentifier] = nil
        if let error = error {
            ch?(nil)
        }
}
```

As written, DownloaderDelegate's delegate methods are being called on the main thread. That's not necessarily a bad thing, but it may be preferable to run that code on a background thread. I'll describe in Chapter 24 how to do that.

Downloading Table View Data

To exercise Downloader, I'll tackle a pesky problem that arises quite often in real life: we have a UITableView where each cell displays text and an image, and the image needs to be downloaded from the internet.

What will our implementation of `tableView(_:cellForRowAt:)` do? It must *not* try to network synchronously — that is, it mustn't wait around for the image to arrive before returning the cell. We must not gum up the works; this method needs to return a cell *immediately*. The correct strategy, if we don't have the image yet, is to put a placeholder (or no image at all) in the cell, return the cell, and *then* see about downloading the image. When we have the image, *then* we can insert it into the cell.

The model object for a table row will be an instance of a dedicated Model class, which is nothing but a bundle of properties:

```
class Model {
    init(text: String, picurl: URL) {
        self.text = text
        self.picurl = picurl
    }
    var text : String // text for the cell's text label
    var picurl : URL // url for downloading the image
    var im : UIImage? // image for the cell's image view; initially nil
    var task : URLSessionTask? // current download task, if any
}
```

Presume, for simplicity, that we have only one section, and our table view model is an array of Model. When the table turns to the data source for a cell in `table-View(_:cellForRowAt:)`, the data source will turn to the model and consult the Model object corresponding to the requested row, asking for its `im` property, which is supposed to be its image. Initially, this will be `nil`. In that case, the data source will display no image in this cell, and will immediately return a cell without an image.

We also want to request that the image be downloaded from this Model object's `picurl`. Later, when the image arrives and this Model object's `im` is no longer `nil`, we can *reload* the row, and this time `tableView(_:cellForRowAt:)` will find that image and display it in the cell.

This is an opportunity to exercise a feature of UITableView (and UICollectionView) that I didn't mention in Chapter 8 — *prefetching*. We assign to our table view's `prefetchDataSource` property some object adopting the UITableViewDataSource-Prefetching protocol. The runtime will then call that object's delegate method `table-View(_:prefetchRowsAt:)` before calling `tableView(_:cellForRowAt:)` — not only when the user *is* scrolling a cell onto the screen, but also when the user *might* scroll a cell onto the screen.

This architecture allows us to separate provision of the data from provision of the cell. Let's say that initially the first 12 rows of the table are displayed. Then the runtime will call `tableView(_:prefetchRowsAt:)` for the *next* 12 rows — because if the user scrolls at all, those are the rows that will come into view.

Presume, then, that we (`self`, the view controller) adopt UITableViewDataSource-Prefetching, and that we have configured the table view accordingly in our `viewDidLoad`:

```
override func viewDidLoad() {
    super.viewDidLoad()
    self.tableView.prefetchDataSource = self // turn on prefetching
}
```

Our implementation of `tableView(_:cellForRowAt:)` is trivial, just as it should be; everything we need to know is right there in the Model object for this row. The image displayed in the image view will be a downloaded UIImage or `nil`, depending on whether the Model has acquired the image for this row:

```
override func tableView(_ tableView: UITableView,
    cellForRowAt indexPath: IndexPath) -> UITableViewCell {
        let cell = tableView.dequeueReusableCell(
            withIdentifier: self.cellID, for: indexPath)
        let m = self.model[indexPath.row]
        cell.textLabel?.text = m.text
        cell.imageView?.image = m.im // image or nil
        return cell
}
```

Meanwhile, the runtime is busy calling `tableView(_:prefetchRowsAt:)` for us. Here we deal directly with the model data. We examine the Model for the given row; if it already has an image, obviously the image was already downloaded, so there's nothing more to do. We also examine the Model's `task`; if it is not `nil`, that's a marker that this image is currently being downloaded, so there's nothing more to do. Otherwise, we start the download, storing a reference to the download task in the Model's `task` as a sign that the download for this row has been requested:

```
func tableView(_ tableView: UITableView,
    prefetchRowsAt indexPaths: [IndexPath]) {
        for ip in indexPaths {
            let m = self.model[ip.row]
            guard m.im == nil else { continue } // we have an image already
            guard m.task == nil else { continue } // already downloading
            m.task = self.downloader.download(url:m.picurl) { url in
                // ... this is the completion function! ...
            }
        }
}
```

When the download finishes, our completion function is called. In my usual speculative coding style, I left it empty; now I'll fill it in. We reset the Model's `task` to `nil`, because we are no longer downloading. If the image data has been successfully downloaded, we store it in the Model. Now we call `reloadRows` for this row. There's no telling when this will happen; remember, the completion function is being called asynchronously. But that doesn't matter. If the row is visible on the screen, `tableView(_:cellForRowAt:)` will be called for this row, and the image will be displayed now; if the row is no longer visible on the screen, there are no ill effects, and the image is still stored, ready for the next time the row becomes visible:

```
m.task = self.downloader.download(url:url) { url in
    m.task = nil
    if let url = url, let data = try? Data(contentsOf: url) {
        m.im = UIImage(data:data)
        tableView.reloadRows(at:[ip], with: .none)
    }
}
```

That completes our implementation of `tableView(_:prefetchRowsAt:)`.

But there's still a problem: when the table view initially appears, the images are all missing from the visible rows. That's because the runtime calls `tableView(_:prefetchRowsAt:)` for *future* table rows, but not for the rows that are initially visible! (I regard that as a bug in the table view architecture.) However, it's easy to deal with that; at the end of `tableView(_:cellForRowAt:)`, I can call `tableView(_:prefetchRowsAt:)` myself:

```
// ... same as before ...
cell.imageView!.image = m.im // image or nil
if m.task == nil && m.im == nil {
    self.tableView(tableView, prefetchRowsAt:[indexPath])
}
return cell
```

Our table view is now working perfectly!

Further details are merely a matter of progressive refinement. If these are large images, we could end up retaining many large images in the model array, which might cause us to run out of memory. There are lots of ways to deal with that. We might start by reducing each image, as it arrives, to the size needed for display (preferably on a serial background thread). If that's still too much memory, we can implement `tableView(_:didEndDisplaying:forRowAt:)` to expunge each image from its Model (by setting the Model object's `im` to `nil`) when the cell scrolls out of sight; if the cell comes back into view, we would then automatically download the image again. Or, as we expunge the image from the Model, we might save it to disk and substitute the file URL as its `picurl` (with appropriate adjustments in the rest of the code).

Background Session

If your app goes into the background while in the middle of a big networking task, the task might not be completed. You can ask for extra time to complete an operation in case the app goes into the background (and I'll talk in Chapter 24 about how to do that); but if it isn't crucial to perform this task right now, it might be nice to defer it so that it can be performed at a better time. The way to do that is to make the URL-Session a *background session* by assigning it a URLSessionConfiguration created with the class method `background(withIdentifier:)`. The task should be an upload or download task.

A background session hands the work of uploading or downloading over to the system. Your app can be suspended or terminated and the download will still be taken care of. As with location monitoring (Chapter 21), your app does not formally run in the background just because you have a background session with tasks, so you do not have to set the `UIBackgroundModes` of your *Info.plist*. But the session still serves as a gateway for putting your app in touch with the networking task as it proceeds; in particular, you need to provide the URLSession with a delegate so that you can receive messages informing you of how things are going.

The argument that you pass to `background(withIdentifier:)` is an arbitrary string identifier intended to distinguish your background session. It should be unique within your app, and a good approach is to use your app's bundle ID as its basis.

For large data, you may want to set the URLSessionConfiguration's `isDiscretionary` to `true`. This will permit the system to postpone network communications to some moment that will conserve bandwidth and battery — when WiFi is available and the device is plugged into a power socket. Of course, that might be days from now! But this is part of the beauty of background downloads.

There is no need to set a background session's `waitsForConnectivity`; it is `true` automatically, and cannot be changed. Similarly, a task does not fail if a background session's `timeoutIntervalForRequest` arrives; the background session will simply try again. However, a task is abandoned if the `timeoutIntervalForResource` arrives.

You can also set your URLSessionTask's `earliestBeginDate`. This is a date in the future; the start of the networking task is delayed until after that date. In addition, you might implement this delegate method:

`urlSession(_:task:willBeginDelayedRequest:completionHandler:)`
> Called only if your URLSessionTask's `earliestBeginDate` was set. The begin date has arrived, and the system is thinking of starting the networking task. Your app can now change its mind about this task, possibly canceling it or even substituting a different request. The completion function takes two parameters; your

job is to call it, passing as its first argument a URLSession.DelayedRequest-Disposition stating your decision:

- `.cancel`
- `.continueLoading`
- `.useNewRequest`

The second completion function argument will be `nil`, unless the first argument is `.useNewRequest`, which case it will be the new URLRequest.

Once the background session is configured and the task is told to `resume`, the system will need to get back in touch with your code when it has a delegate message to send you. How it does this depends on what state your app is in at that moment:

Your app is frontmost and still running
> Your app may have gone into the background one or more times, but it was never terminated, and it is frontmost now. In that case, your background URL-Session still exists and is still hooked to its delegate, and the delegate messages are simply sent as usual.

Your app is not frontmost or was terminated
> Your app is in the background or not running, or it is frontmost but it was terminated since the time you told your task to `resume`. Now the system needs to perform a handshake with your URLSession in order to get in touch with it. To make that handshake possible, you must implement these two methods:

`application(_:handleEventsForBackgroundURLSession:completion-Handler:)`
> This message is sent *to the app delegate*. The `session:` parameter is the string identifier you handed earlier to the configuration object; you might use this to identify the session, or to create and configure the session if you haven't done so already. You do *not* call the completion function now! Instead, you must *store* it, because it will be needed later.

`urlSessionDidFinishEvents(forBackgroundURLSession:)`
> This message is sent *to the session delegate*. This is the moment when you must *call* the previously stored completion function.

When the system wants to send you a delegate message, if your app is not frontmost, it is awakened in the background. If it is not running, it is launched in the background. In the latter case, you should *immediately* create a URLSession, giving it a URLSessionConfiguration initialized by calling `background(withIdentifier:)` with the *same identifier* as before, *and assign a session delegate*, which will then be able to receive delegate messages.

This is all much easier if the app delegate and the session delegate are one and the same object. In this example, the app delegate holds the URLSession property, which is created lazily; it also provides storage for the completion function:

```
lazy var session : URLSession = {
    let id = "com.neuburg.matt.backgroundDownload"
    let config = URLSessionConfiguration.background(withIdentifier: id)
    config.allowsExpensiveNetworkAccess = false
    // could set config.isDiscretionary here
    let sess = URLSession(
        configuration: config, delegate: self, delegateQueue: .main)
    return sess
}()
var ch : (() -> ())!
```

The URLSessionDownloadDelegate methods are as before, plus we have the two required handshake methods in case the system needs to get back in touch with us:

```
func application(_ application: UIApplication,
    handleEventsForBackgroundURLSession identifier: String,
    completionHandler: @escaping () -> ()) {
        self.ch = completionHandler
        _ = self.session // *
}
func urlSessionDidFinishEvents(forBackgroundURLSession session: URLSession) {
    self.ch?()
}
```

The starred line will "tickle" the session lazy initializer and bring the background session to life if needed.

 If the user kills your app in the background by way of the app switcher interface, pending background downloads will *not* be completed. The system assumes that the user doesn't want your app coming magically back to life in the background.

On-Demand Resources

Your app can store resources, such as images and sound files, on Apple's server instead of including them in the app bundle that the user initially installs on the device. Your app can then download those resources as needed when the app runs. Such resources are *on-demand resources*.

To mark something as an on-demand resource in Xcode, you assign it one or more *tags* (arbitrary strings); you can do this in many places in the Xcode interface. A tag may be assigned to an individual resource or to a folder. Any resources to which you have assigned tags are *not* copied into the app when you build it; they will have to be downloaded to the user's device as on-demand resources.

Figure 23-1. An on-demand resource

Your on-demand resource configuration is summarized and managed in the Resource Tags tab of the target editor. Figure 23-1 shows the Resource Tags tab displaying the `"pix"` tag, which has been attached to a folder called *images* in my app bundle.

How do you obtain an on-demand resource? In your code, you instantiate an NSBundleResourceRequest, handing it the tags of the resources you want to use. Let's call this the *request object*. You will likely want to retain the request object, typically in an instance property (I'll talk more about that in a moment). You then toggle access to the resources associated with those tags by sending the request object these messages:

beginAccessingResources(completionHandler:)
> Your completion function is called when the resources are available (which could be immediately if they have already been downloaded). *Do not assume that the completion function runs on the main thread.* The parameter is an Optional Error. If it is `nil`, you can now use the resources.

endAccessingResources
> Lets the runtime know that you are no longer actively using these resources. After this call, you can no longer access the resources; that doesn't mean they will be deleted, but they might be. You should now abandon use of this NSBundleResourceRequest instance! Its life cycle is finished. If you need to access the same resources again, start over by creating a new NSBundleResourceRequest and calling `beginAccessingResources` again.

If your app is terminated before you call `endAccessingResources`, then on relaunch you obviously have no NSBundleResourceRequest instance. But that doesn't matter, because you just keep following the same rules about how to access the resources. When you need access to them, you create an NSBundleResourceRequest and call `beginAccessingResources`; your resources might still be present, in which case you will get access immediately.

If your call to `beginAccessingResources` causes the resources to start downloading, you can track the download progress using the NSBundleResourceRequest's `progress` property, which is a Progress object. This might be desirable if the download causes a perceptible delay in your app's action and you need to let the user know what's happening. Optimally, you might use a more proactive strategy to prefetch the resources so that they are present by the time the user needs them. The `progress.fractionCompleted` of an NSBundleResourceRequest that is not actively downloading may be either `0` or `1`. It can be `0` after completion because you said `beginAccessing` at a time when the resource was already present.

I mentioned earlier that you'll want your request object to persist, most likely as an instance property of a view controller. That's because if a resource request object goes out of existence, the runtime will assume that you no longer need those resources. Because an individual NSBundleResourceRequest instance is tied to a specific set of tags, and hence to a specific bunch of resources, you might need to keep multiple request objects stored simultaneously. One reasonable strategy might be to declare each instance property as an Optional of type `NSBundleResourceRequest?`. That way, you can set the property to `nil` when you're done with that request instance, so that you won't accidentally use it again. A more sophisticated approach might be to maintain a single mutable dictionary of type `[Set<String>:NSBundleResourceRequest]`, keyed by the request object's `tags`.

Your code that actually accesses on-demand resources does so in the normal way. If the resource is an image, you can access it using UIImage's `init(named:)`. If it's a data set in the asset catalog, you can access it using NSDataAsset's `init(name:)`. If it is a resource at the top level of the main bundle, you can get its URL by calling `url(forResource:withExtension:)` on the bundle. And so forth. An attempt to access an on-demand resource in this way *will fail in good order* — you'll get `nil` — until you have successfully called `beginAccessingResources`. After a call to `begin-AccessingResources` and a signal of success in its completion function, the resources spring to life and you can access them. After calling `endAccessingResources`, any attempt to access the resources will yield `nil` again (even if they have not actually been deleted).

How on earth does this architecture work? Is it a violation of the rule that your app bundle can't be modified? No; it's all an ingenious illusion. Your on-demand resources are stored *outside* the app bundle, in your app's *OnDemandResources* directory, but the methods that access resources are rejiggered so as to point to them, or to return `nil`, as appropriate.

There are two special categories of on-demand resource tags (visible in Figure 23-1) — *initial install* tags and *prefetch* tags.

Initial install tags

> Resources with initial install tags are downloaded *at the same time* the app is installed; in effect, they appear to be part of the app.

Prefetch tags

> Resources with prefetch tags are downloaded automatically by the system *after* the app is installed.

Neither of these special categories relieves you of the responsibility to call `begin-Accessing` before you actually use a tagged resource, nor does it prevent the resources from being deleted if you are not accessing them. The difference is that the desired resources will probably be already present when you call `beginAccessing` early in the lifetime of the app.

 Amazingly, you can test on-demand resources directly by running your app from Xcode. Also, you can check the status of your on-demand resources in the Disk gauge of the Debug navigator.

In-App Purchases

An in-app purchase is a specialized form of network communication: your app communicates with the App Store to permit the user to buy something there, or to confirm that something has already been bought there. This is a way to make your app itself inexpensive or free to download, while providing an optional increased price in exchange for increased functionality later. In-app purchases are made possible through the Store Kit framework; you'll need to `import StoreKit`.

There are various kinds of in-app purchase — consumables, nonconsumables, and subscriptions. You'll want to examine Apple's *In-App Purchase Programming Guide* in the documentation archive and the "Offer In-App Purchases" section of the *App Store Connect Help*.

To configure an in-app purchase, you need first to use App Store Connect to create, in connection with your app, something that the user can purchase; this is easiest to do if your app is already available through the App Store. For a simple nonconsumable purchase, you are associating your app's bundle ID with a name and arbitrary product ID representing your in-app purchase, along with a price.

Here's an example from an actual game app of mine, which offers a single nonconsumable purchase: it unlocks functionality allowing users to involve their own photos in the game. When the user taps the Choose button, if the in-app purchase has *not* been made, a pair of dialogs will appear, offering and describing the purchase (Figure 23-2); if the in-app purchase *has* been made, a UIImagePickerController is presented instead (Chapter 17).

Figure 23-2. Interface for an in-app purchase

For a nonconsumable in-app purchase, the app must provide the following interface (all of which is visible in Figure 23-2):

- The description of the in-app purchase. You do not hard-code this description into your app; rather, it is downloaded in real time from the App Store, using the Display Name and Description (and price) that you entered at App Store Connect.

- A button that launches the purchase process.

- A button that *restores* an existing purchase. The idea here is that the user has performed the purchase, but is now on a different device or has deleted and reinstalled your app, so that the persistent flag signaling that the purchase has been performed is missing. The user needs to be able to contact the App Store to get your app to recognize that the purchase has been performed and turn on the purchased functionality.

In my app, the purchase process proceeds in two stages. In my first view controller, if the user taps the Learn More button (on the left in Figure 23-2), I first confirm that the user has not been restricted from making purchases; then I create an SKProducts-Request, which will attempt to download an SKProductsResponse object embodying the details about the in-app purchase corresponding to my single product ID:

```
if !SKPaymentQueue.canMakePayments() {
    // ... put up alert saying we can't do it ...
    return
}
let req = SKProductsRequest(productIdentifiers: ["DiabelliChoose"])
req.delegate = self
req.start()
```

This kicks off some network activity, and eventually the delegate of this SKProducts-Request, namely `self` (conforming to SKProductsRequestDelegate), is called back with one of two delegate messages. If we get `request(_:didFailWithError:)`, I put up an apologetic alert (unless the error code is `.paymentCancelled`), and that's the end. But if we get `productsRequest(_:didReceive:)`, the request has succeeded, and we can proceed to the second stage.

In `productsRequest(_:didReceive:)`, the response from the App Store arrives as the second parameter. It is an SKProductsResponse object containing an SKProduct representing the proposed purchase. I get on to the main thread (Chapter 24), create my second view controller, give it a reference to the SKProduct, and present it (on the right in Figure 23-2):

```
func productsRequest(_ request: SKProductsRequest,
    didReceive response: SKProductsResponse) {
        let p = response.products[0]
        DispatchQueue.main.async {
            let s = StoreViewController2(product:p)
            if let presenter = self.presentingViewController {
                self.dismiss(animated: true} {
                    presenter.present(s, animated: true)
                }
            }
        }
    }
```

My second view controller has a `product` property that was set in its initializer. In its `viewDidLoad`, it populates its interface based on the information that the `product` contains (for my `lend` utility, see Appendix B):

```
self.titleLabel.text = self.product.localizedTitle
self.descriptionLabel.text = self.product.localizedDescription
self.priceLabel.text = lend { (nf : NumberFormatter) in
    nf.formatterBehavior = .behavior10_4
    nf.numberStyle = .currency
    nf.locale = self.product.priceLocale
}.string(from: self.product.price)
```

If the user taps the Purchase button, I dismiss the presented view controller, load the SKProduct into the default SKPaymentQueue, and stand back:

```
self.dismiss(animated: true) {
    let p = SKPayment(product:self.product)
    let q = SKPaymentQueue.default()
    q.add(p)
}
```

The system is now in charge of presenting a sequence of dialogs, confirming the purchase, asking for the user's App Store credentials, and so forth. My app knows nothing about that. If the user *performs* the purchase, the runtime will call `paymentQueue(_:updatedTransactions:)` on my *transaction observer*. This is an object adopting the SKPaymentTransactionObserver protocol, whose job it will be to receive messages from the payment queue. But how does the runtime know what object that is? When my app launches, it must *register* the transaction observer:

```
func application(application: UIApplication,
    didFinishLaunchingWithOptions launchOptions:
    [UIApplication.LaunchOptionsKey : Any]?) -> Bool {
        SKPaymentQueue.default().add(
            self.window!.rootViewController
                as! SKPaymentTransactionObserver)
        return true
}
```

As you can see, I've made my root view controller the transaction observer. It adopts the SKPaymentTransactionObserver protocol. There is only one required method — paymentQueue(_:updatedTransactions:). It is called with a reference to the payment queue and an array of SKPaymentTransaction objects. My job is to cycle through these transactions and, for each one, do whatever it requires, and then, if there was an actual transaction (or an error), send finishTransaction(_:) to the payment queue, to clear the queue.

My implementation is extremely simple, because I have only one purchasable product, and because I'm not maintaining any separate record of receipts. For each transaction, I check its transactionState (SKPaymentTransactionState). If its state is .purchased, I pull out its payment, confirm that the payment's productIdentifier is my product identifier (it had darned well better be, since I have only the one product), and, if so, I get onto the main thread and set the UserDefaults flag that indicates to my app that the user has performed the purchase:

```
func paymentQueue(_ queue: SKPaymentQueue,
    updatedTransactions transactions: [SKPaymentTransaction]) {
        for t in transactions {
            switch t.transactionState {
            case .purchasing, .deferred: break // do nothing
            case .purchased, .restored:
                let p = t.payment
                if p.productIdentifier == "DiabelliChoose" {
                    DispatchQueue.main.async {
                        UserDefaults.standard.set(true, forKey: self.CHOOSE)
                        // ... put up an alert thanking the user ...
                    }
                }
                queue.finishTransaction(t)
            case .failed:
                queue.finishTransaction(t)
            }
        }
    }
}
```

Finally, let's talk about what to do when the user taps the Restore button (on the left in Figure 23-2). It's very simple; I just tell the default SKPaymentQueue to restore any existing purchases:

```
self.dismiss(animated: true) {
    SKPaymentQueue.default().restoreCompletedTransactions()
}
```

Again, what happens now in the interface is out of my hands; the system will present the necessary dialogs. If the purchase is restored, my transaction observer will be sent `paymentQueue(_:updatedTransactions:)` with a `transactionState` of `.restored`. We pass through exactly the same case in my switch as if the user had freshly purchased the app; as before, I set the UserDefaults flag indicating that the user has performed the purchase.

There remains one piece of the puzzle: what if the user taps the Restore button and the purchase is *not* restored? This might happen because the user is lying or mistaken about having previously made this purchase. In that case, `paymentQueue(_:updatedTransactions:)` is *not* called. (I regard this as a bug in the store architecture; in my opinion, we should be called with a `.failed` transaction state.)

As a workaround, we can implement the SKPaymentTransactionObserver method `paymentQueueRestoreCompletedTransactionsFinished(_:)`. It is called after any restoration attempt where communication with the store was successful. This method still gives us no way to learn definitively what happened; but if `paymentQueue(_:updatedTransactions:)` is called, it is called first, so if we find in `paymentQueueRestoreCompletedTransactionsFinished(_:)` that the UserDefaults flag has not been set, we can guess that restoration failed because the user has never made the purchase in the first place.

Before releasing your app to the general public, you'll want to test your app's in-app purchase interface and functionality. One way to do that is to create a special Apple ID, called a *sandbox* ID, for testing purposes. Sandbox IDs are created and managed in the Users and Roles section of App Store Connect. When you build your app onto your device and run it, if you make an in-app purchase, your sandbox ID is used and you are not charged for the purchase. A downside of this approach is that you have to remember your sandbox account password. A simpler approach is to upload your app to App Store Connect and make it available through TestFlight. When a TestFlight tester uses your app's in-app purchase feature, the tester's normal account and password are used, but no actual charge is made. Unfortunately, in neither scenario are the alerts that the system displays identical to those that a real user would see while making the in-app purchase. As a result, testing in-app purchase functionality is always something of a gamble.

CHAPTER 24

Threads

A *thread* is a subprocess of your app that can execute even while other subprocesses are also executing. Such simultaneous execution is called *concurrency*. The iOS frameworks use threads all the time; if they didn't, your app would be less responsive to the user — perhaps completely unresponsive. For the most part, the iOS frameworks use threads behind the scenes on your behalf; you don't have to worry about threads because the frameworks are worrying about them for you.

Suppose your app is downloading something from the network (Chapter 23). This download doesn't happen all by itself; somewhere, someone is running code that interacts with the network and obtains data. Yet none of that interferes with your code, or prevents the user from tapping and swiping things in your interface. The networking code runs "in the background." That's concurrency in action.

This chapter discusses concurrency that involves *your* code in the use of background threads. It would have been nice to dispense with this topic altogether. Background threads can be tricky and are always potentially dangerous, and should be avoided if possible. But sometimes you *can't* avoid them. So this chapter introduces threads. But beware: background threads entail complications and subtle pitfalls, and can make your code hard to debug. There is much more to threads, and especially to making your threaded code safe, than this chapter can possibly touch on. For detailed information about the topics introduced in this chapter, read Apple's *Concurrency Programming Guide* and *Threading Programming Guide* in the documentation archive.

Main Thread

Distinguish between the *main* thread and all other threads. There is only one main thread; other threads are background threads.

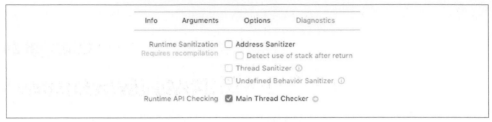

Figure 24-1. The Main Thread Checker is watching you

All your code must run on some thread, but you are not usually conscious of this fact, because that thread is usually the main thread. Why? Well, the only reason your code *ever* runs is that Cocoa calls it — and Cocoa usually calls your code from the main thread.

The main thread is the interface thread. This means that the main thread is the meeting-place between you and your user. When the user interacts with the interface, those interactions are reported as events *on the main thread*. When your code interacts with the interface, it must do so *on the main thread*. Of course that will usually happen automatically, because your code normally runs on the main thread. But when you are involved with background threads, you must be careful.

So pretend now that I'm banging the table and shouting: If your code touches the interface, it *must* do so *on the main thread*. Don't *fetch* any interface-related values on a background thread. Don't *set* any interface-related values on a background thread. Whenever you use background threads, there is a chance you might touch the interface on a background thread. *Don't!*

Touching the interface on a background thread is a very common beginner mistake. A typical sign of trouble is an unaccountable delay of several seconds. In some cases, the console may help with a warning. Also, Xcode's Main Thread Checker will automatically report runtime violations; it's a diagnostic in your scheme's Run and Test actions (Figure 24-1), and is turned on by default.

Since you and the user are both using the main thread, the main thread is a very busy place. Imagine how things proceed in your app:

1. An event arrives — on the main thread. If the user has tapped a button, this is reported to your app as a UIEvent, which passes to the button through the touch delivery mechanism (Chapter 5) — on the main thread.

2. The button emits a control event (Chapter 12) that causes your code (the button's action method) to be called — on the main thread. Your code now runs — on the main thread. *While your code runs, nothing else can happen on the main thread.* Your code might perform some changes in the interface; this is safe, because your code is running — where? — on the main thread.

3. Your code finishes. The main thread's run loop is now free to report more events, and the user is free to interact with the interface once again.

The bottleneck here is the running of your code. Your code runs on the main thread. That means the main thread can't do anything else while your code is running. No events can arrive while your code is running. The user can't interact with the interface while your code is running. Two things can't happen on the main thread at the same time, so main thread code *blocks* the main thread and therefore *blocks* the interface. But this is usually no problem, because:

Your code is fast
Your code executes really fast. It's true that the user can't interact with the interface while your code runs, but this is such a tiny interval of time that the user will probably never notice.

Blocking briefly is good
Your code, as it runs, blocks the user from interacting with the interface. As long as your code finishes quickly, that's actually a good thing! Your code, in response to what the user does, might update the interface; it would be insane if the user could do something else in the interface while you're in the middle of updating it.

Background Threads

The iOS frameworks frequently operate on background threads. This usually doesn't affect you, because the frameworks usually talk to *your* code on the *main* thread:

- During an animation (Chapter 4), the interface remains responsive to the user, and it is possible for your code to run. The Core Animation framework is running the animation and updating the presentation layer on a background thread. But your delegate methods and completion functions are called on the main thread.

- A web view's fetching and loading of its content is asynchronous (Chapter 11); that means the work is done in a background thread. But your delegate methods are called on the main thread.

- Sounds are played asynchronously (Chapters 14 and 16). Loading, preparation, and playing of movies happens asynchronously (Chapter 15). But your delegate methods are called on the main thread.

- Saving a movie file takes time (Chapters 15 and 17). So the saving takes place on a background thread. UIDocument saves and reads on a background thread (Chapter 22). But your delegate methods and completion functions are called on the main thread.

You can (and should) usually ignore the existence of background threads and just keep plugging away on the main thread. Nevertheless, there are two kinds of situation in which your code will need to be explicitly aware of background threads:

Your code is called back, but not on the main thread

Some frameworks explicitly inform you in their documentation that callbacks are not guaranteed to take place on the main thread. The documentation on CATiledLayer (Chapter 7) warns that `draw(_:in:)` is called on a background thread. By implication, our `draw(_:)` code, triggered by CATiledLayer to update tiles, is running on a background thread. (Fortunately, drawing into the current graphics context is thread-safe.)

Similarly, the documentation on AV Foundation (Chapters 15 and 17) warns that its completion functions and notifications can arrive on a background thread. So if you intend to update the user interface, or use a value that might also be used by your main thread code, you'll need to switch explicitly to the main thread.

Your code takes significant time

If your code takes significant time to run, you might need to run that code on a background thread, rather than letting it block the main thread and prevent anything else from happening there:

During launch and other app state transitions

In Chapter 22, we called `URL(forUbiquityContainerIdentifier:)` during app launch. The documentation told us to call this method on a background thread, because it can take some time to return; we don't want to block the main thread waiting for it, because the app is trying to launch on the main thread, and the user won't see our interface until the launch process is over.

Similarly, when the app is in the process of being suspended into the background, or resumed from the background, our code should not occupy the main thread; it must act quickly and get out of the way.

When the user can see or interact with the app

In Chapter 19, we called `enumerateEvents(matching:using:)` on a background thread, because it can take some time to run. If we were to call this method on the main thread, then when the user taps the button that triggers this call, the button might stay highlighted for a significant amount of time, during which the interface would be completely frozen. We would be perceptibly blocking the main thread.

Similarly, in a table view data source (Chapter 8), `tableView(_:cellForRowAt:)` needs to be fast. Otherwise, the user won't be able to scroll the table view; we'll be freezing the interface because we are blocking the main thread.

Moving time-consuming code off the main thread, so that the main thread is not blocked, isn't just a matter of aesthetics or politeness: the system "watchdog" will summarily *kill the app* if it discovers that the main thread is blocked for too long.

Why Threading Is Hard

The one certain thing about computer code is that it just clunks along the path of execution, one statement at a time. Successive lines of code are performed in the order in which they appear, and nothing else happens between them. With threading, that certainty goes right out the window.

If you have code that can be performed on a background thread, then *you don't know* when your code will be performed. Your code is now *concurrent.* This means that any line of your background-thread code could be *interleaved* between any two lines of your main-thread code. Indeed, under certain circumstances, your background-thread code can be called multiple times on multiple background threads, meaning that any line of your background-thread code could be interleaved between any two lines of *itself.*

The reason this can be problematic is because of *shared data.* There are variables in your app, such as instance properties, that persist and can be accessed from multiple places. Background threads mean that such variables can be accessed at unexpected moments. That is a really scary thought. Suppose, while one thread is in the middle of using a variable, another thread changes it. Who knows what horrors might result?

You can't work around this issue by mere logic. Suppose you try to make access to a variable safe with a condition, as in this pseudocode:

```
if no other thread is touching this variable {
    ... do something to the variable ...
}
```

Such logic is specious. Suppose the condition succeeds: no other thread is touching this variable. But between the time when that condition is evaluated and the time when the next line executes and you start to do something to the variable, another thread can still come along and start touching the variable!

It is possible to request assistance at a deeper level to ensure that a section of code is not run by two threads simultaneously. For example, you can implement a *lock* around a section of code. But locks generate an entirely new level of potential pitfalls. In general, a lock is an invitation to forget to use the lock, or to forget to remove the lock after you've set it. And threads can end up contending for a lock in a way that permits neither thread to proceed.

Another problem has to do with thread *lifetimes.* The lifetime of a thread is independent of the lifetimes of other objects in your app. When an object is about to go out of existence and its `deinit` has been called and executed, you are supposed to be guaranteed that none of your code in that object will ever run again. But a thread might still be running, and might try to talk to your object, even after your object has supposedly gone out of existence. This can result in a crash, if you're lucky; if you're not lucky, your object might become a kind of zombie.

Not only is threaded code hard to get right; it's also hard to test and hard to debug. It introduces indeterminacy, so you can easily make a mistake that never appears in your testing, but that does appear for some user. The real danger is that the user's experience will consist only of distant consequences of your mistake, long after the point where you made it, making the true cause of the problem extraordinarily difficult to track down.

Perhaps you think I'm trying to scare you away from using threads. You're right! For an excellent (and suitably frightening) account of some of the dangers and considerations that threading involves, see Apple's technical note "Simple and Reliable Threading with NSOperation" in the documentation archive. If terms like *race condition* and *deadlock* don't strike fear into your veins, look them up on Wikipedia.

Naturally, Xcode provides lots of aids to assist you in studying your app's use of threads:

- The Debug navigator distinguishes threads; you can even see pending calls and learn when a call was enqueued.
- When you call `NSLog` or `os_log`, the output in the console displays a number identifying the thread on which it was called.
- In Instruments, the Time Profiler records activity on different threads.
- The Thread Sanitizer (visible in Figure 24-1) can help catch possible race conditions and other issues (look up "Thread Sanitizer" in the documentation).

Blocking the Main Thread

To illustrate making your code multithreaded, I need some code that is worth making multithreaded. I'll use as my example a simple app that draws the Mandelbrot set in black and white. (This code is adapted from a small open source project found on the internet.) That's a sufficiently elaborate calculation to introduce a significant delay, depending on the speed of the device and the number of iterations. The idea is to see how we can safely get that delay off the main thread.

The app contains a UIView subclass, MyMandelbrotView, which has one property, a CGContext called `bitmapContext`. Here's MyMandelbrotView:

```
let MANDELBROT_STEPS = 100 // determines how long the calculation takes
var bitmapContext: CGContext!
// jumping-off point: draw the Mandelbrot set
func drawThatPuppy () {
    self.makeBitmapContext(size: self.bounds.size)
    let center = self.bounds.center
    self.draw(center: center, bounds: self.bounds, zoom: 1)
    self.setNeedsDisplay()
}
// create bitmap context
func makeBitmapContext(size:CGSize) {
    var bitmapBytesPerRow = Int(size.width * 4)
    bitmapBytesPerRow += (16 - (bitmapBytesPerRow % 16)) % 16
    let colorSpace = CGColorSpaceCreateDeviceRGB()
    let prem = CGImageAlphaInfo.premultipliedLast.rawValue
    let context = CGContext(data: nil,
        width: Int(size.width), height: Int(size.height),
        bitsPerComponent: 8, bytesPerRow: bitmapBytesPerRow,
        space: colorSpace, bitmapInfo: prem)
    self.bitmapContext = context
}
// draw pixels of bitmap context
func draw(center:CGPoint, bounds:CGRect, zoom:CGFloat) {
    func isInMandelbrotSet(_ re:Float, _ im:Float) -> Bool {
        var fl = true
        var (x, y, nx, ny) : (Float, Float, Float, Float) = (0,0,0,0)
        for _ in 0 ..< MANDELBROT_STEPS {
            nx = x*x - y*y + re
            ny = 2*x*y + im
            if nx*nx + ny*ny > 4 {
                fl = false
                break
            }
            x = nx
            y = ny
        }
        return fl
    }
    self.bitmapContext.setAllowsAntialiasing(false)
    self.bitmapContext.setFillColor(red: 0, green: 0, blue: 0, alpha: 1)
    var re : CGFloat
    var im : CGFloat
    let maxi = Int(bounds.size.width)
    let maxj = Int(bounds.size.height)
    for i in 0 ..< maxi {
        for j in 0 ..< maxj {
            re = (CGFloat(i) - 1.33 * center.x) / 160
            im = (CGFloat(j) - 1.0 * center.y) / 160
            re /= zoom
            im /= zoom
            if (isInMandelbrotSet(Float(re), Float(im))) {
                self.bitmapContext.fill(
```

```
                    CGRect(CGFloat(i), CGFloat(j), 1.0, 1.0))
                }
            }
        }
    }
    // turn pixels of bitmap context into CGImage, draw into ourselves
    override func draw(_ rect: CGRect) {
        if self.bitmapContext != nil {
            let context = UIGraphicsGetCurrentContext()!
            let im = self.bitmapContext.makeImage()
            context.draw(im!, in: self.bounds)
        }
    }
}
```

The `draw(center:bounds:zoom:)` method, which calculates the pixels of `self.bitmapContext`, is time-consuming, and we can see this by running the app on a device. If the entire process is kicked off by tapping a button whose action method calls `drawThatPuppy`, there is a significant delay before the Mandelbrot graphic appears in the interface, during which time the button remains highlighted and the interface is frozen. This is a sure sign that we are blocking the main thread.

We need to move the calculation-intensive part of this code onto a background thread, so that the main thread is not blocked by the calculation. In doing so, we have two chief concerns:

Synchronization of threads

> The button is tapped, and `drawThatPuppy` is called, on the main thread. And `setNeedsDisplay`, and therefore `draw(_:)`, are also called on the main thread — rightly, since they affect the interface. In between, the calculation-intensive `draw(center:bounds:zoom:)` is to be called on a background thread. Yet these methods must still run *in order*: `drawThatPuppy` on the main thread, then `draw(center:bounds:zoom:)` on a background thread, then `setNeedsDisplay` and `draw(_:)` on the main thread. But background threads are concurrent, so how will we ensure this?

Shared data

> The property `self.bitmapContext` is referred to in three different methods — in `makeBitmapContext(size:)`, and in `draw(center:bounds:zoom:)`, and in `draw(_:)`. But we have just said that those three methods involve two different threads; they must not be permitted to touch the same property in a way that might conflict or clash. Indeed, because `draw(center:bounds:zoom:)` runs on a background thread, it might run on multiple background threads simultaneously; the access to `self.bitmapContext` by `draw(center:bounds:zoom:)` must not be permitted to conflict or clash *with itself*. How will we ensure this?

Manual Threading

A naïve way of dealing with our time-consuming code would involve spawning off a background thread as we reach the calculation-intensive part of the procedure, by calling `performSelector(inBackground:with:)`. This is a very bad idea, and you should *not* imitate the code in this section. I'm showing it to you only to demonstrate how horrible it is.

Adapting your code to use `performSelector(inBackground:with:)` is not at all simple. There is additional work to do:

Pack the arguments
> The method designated by the selector in `performSelector(inBackground:with:)` can take only one parameter, whose value you supply as the second argument. So if you want to pass more than one piece of information into the thread, you'll need to pack it into a single object. Typically, this will be a dictionary.

Set up an autorelease pool
> Background threads don't participate in the global autorelease pool. So the first thing you must do in your threaded code is to wrap everything in an autorelease pool. Otherwise, you'll probably leak memory as autoreleased objects are created behind the scenes and are never released.

We'll rewrite MyMandelbrotView to use manual threading. Because our `draw(center:bounds:zoom:)` method takes three parameters, the argument that we pass into the thread will have to pack that information into a dictionary. Once inside the thread, we'll set up our autorelease pool and unpack the dictionary. This will all be much easier if we interpose a trampoline method between `drawThatPuppy` and `draw(center:bounds:zoom:)`. So our implementation now starts like this:

```
func drawThatPuppy () {
    self.makeBitmapContext(size:self.bounds.size)
    let center = self.bounds.center
    let d : [AnyHashable:Any] =
        ["center":center, "bounds":self.bounds, "zoom":CGFloat(1)]
    self.performSelector(inBackground: #selector(reallyDraw), with: d)
}
// trampoline, background thread entry point
@objc func reallyDraw(_ d: [AnyHashable:Any]) {
    autoreleasepool {
        self.draw(center: d["center"] as! CGPoint,
            bounds: d["bounds"] as! CGRect,
            zoom: d["zoom"] as! CGFloat)
        // ...
    }
}
```

In the trampoline method `reallyDraw(_:)`, the comment with the ellipsis indicates a missing piece of functionality: we have yet to call `setNeedsDisplay`, which will cause the actual drawing to take place. This call used to be in `drawThatPuppy`, but that is now too soon; the call to `performSelector(inBackground:with:)` launches the thread and returns immediately, so our `bitmapContext` property isn't ready yet. Clearly, we need to call `setNeedsDisplay` *after* `draw(center:bounds:zoom:)` has finished generating the pixels of the graphics context.

But `reallyDraw(_:)` runs in a background thread. Because `setNeedsDisplay` is a form of communication with the interface, we should call it on the main thread, with `performSelector(onMainThread:with:waitUntilDone:)`. It will probably be best to implement a second trampoline method:

```
// trampoline, background thread entry point
func reallyDraw(_ d: [AnyHashable:Any]) {
    autoreleasepool {
        self.draw(center: d["center"] as! CGPoint,
            bounds: d["bounds"] as! CGRect,
            zoom: d["zoom"] as! CGFloat)
        self.performSelector(onMainThread: #selector(allDone), with: nil,
            waitUntilDone: false)
    }
}
// called on main thread! background thread exit point
@objc func allDone() {
    self.setNeedsDisplay()
}
```

This works, in the sense that when we tap the button, it is highlighted momentarily and then immediately unhighlighted; the time-consuming calculation is taking place on a background thread. But the seeds of nightmare are already sown:

- We now have a single object, MyMandelbrotView, some of whose methods are to be called on the main thread and some on a background thread; this invites us to become confused at some later time.

- The main thread and the background thread are constantly sharing a piece of data, the instance property `self.bitmapContext`; this is messy and fragile. And what's to stop some other code from coming along and triggering `draw(_:)` while `draw(center:bounds:zoom:)` is in the middle of manipulating the bitmap context that `draw(_:)` draws?

To solve these problems, we might need to use locks, and we would probably have to manage the thread more explicitly. Such code can become quite elaborate and difficult to understand; guaranteeing its integrity is even more difficult. There are much better ways, and I will now demonstrate two of them.

Operation

An excellent strategy is to turn to the Operation and OperationQueue classes. The essence of Operation is that it encapsulates a *task*, not a thread. You don't concern yourself with threads directly; the threading is determined for you by an Operation-Queue. You describe the task as an Operation, and you add that Operation to an OperationQueue to set it going. You can arrange to be notified when the task ends, typically by the Operation posting a notification. (You can also safely query both the queue and its operations from outside with regard to their state.)

We'll rewrite MyMandelbrotView to use Operation and OperationQueue. We need an OperationQueue object. I'll make this an instance property (`self.queue`), and I'll create the queue and configure it in the property's initializer:

```
let queue : OperationQueue = {
    let q = OperationQueue()
    // ... further configurations can go here ...
    return q
}()
```

We also have a new class, MyMandelbrotOperation, an Operation subclass. (It is possible to take advantage of a built-in Operation subclass such as BlockOperation, but I'm deliberately illustrating the more general case by subclassing Operation itself.) Our implementation of `drawThatPuppy` creates an instance of MyMandelbrot-Operation, configures it, registers for its notification, and adds it to the queue:

```
func drawThatPuppy () {
    let center = self.bounds.center
    let op = MyMandelbrotOperation(
        center: center, bounds: self.bounds, zoom: 1)
    NotificationCenter.default.addObserver(self,
        selector: #selector(operationFinished),
        name: MyMandelbrotOperation.mandelOpFinished, object: op)
    self.queue.addOperation(op)
}
```

Our time-consuming calculations will be performed by MyMandelbrotOperation. An Operation subclass, such as MyMandelbrotOperation, will typically have at least two methods:

A designated initializer
> The Operation may need some configuration data. Once the Operation is added to a queue, it's too late to talk to it, so you'll usually hand it this configuration data as you create it, in its designated initializer.

A main *method*
> This method will be called automatically by the OperationQueue when it's time for the Operation to start.

MyMandelbrotOperation has three private properties `center`, `bounds`, and `zoom`, to be set in its initializer; it must be told MyMandelbrotView's geometry explicitly because it is completely separate from MyMandelbrotView. MyMandelbrot-Operation also has its own CGContext property, `bitmapContext`; it must be publicly gettable so that MyMandelbrotView can retrieve the finished graphics context. Note that this is different from MyMandelbrotView's `bitmapContext`, helping to solve the problem of sharing data promiscuously between threads:

```
static let mandelOpFinished = Notification.Name("mandelOpFinished")
private let center : CGPoint
private let bounds : CGRect
private let zoom : CGFloat
private(set) var bitmapContext : CGContext! = nil
init(center c:CGPoint, bounds b:CGRect, zoom z:CGFloat) {
    self.center = c
    self.bounds = b
    self.zoom = z
    super.init()
}
```

`makeBitmapContext(size:)` and `draw(center:bounds:zoom:)`, the methods that perform the time-consuming calculation, can be transferred from MyMandelbrot-View to MyMandelbrotOperation unchanged; the only difference is that when these methods refer to `self.bitmapContext`, that now means MyMandelbrotOperation's `bitmapContext` property:

```
let MANDELBROT_STEPS = 100
func makeBitmapContext(size:CGSize) {
    // ... same as before
}
func draw(center:CGPoint, bounds:CGRect, zoom:CGFloat) {
    // ... same as before
}
```

Finally we come to MyMandelbrotOperation's `main` method. First we check the Operation `isCancelled` property to make sure we haven't been cancelled while sitting in the queue; this is good practice. Then we do exactly what `drawThatPuppy` used to do, initializing our graphics context and drawing into its pixels. At that point, the calculation is over and it's time for MyMandelbrotView to come and fetch our data. There are two ways in which MyMandelbrotView can learn this; either `main` can post a notification through the NotificationCenter, or MyMandelbrotView can use key-value observing to be notified when our `isFinished` property changes. We've chosen the former approach; observe that we check one more time to make sure we haven't been cancelled:

```
override func main() {
    guard !self.isCancelled else {return}
    self.makeBitmapContext(size: self.bounds.size)
    self.draw(center: self.center, bounds: self.bounds, zoom: self.zoom)
```

```
        if !self.isCancelled {
            NotificationCenter.default.post(
                name: MyMandelbrotOperation.mandelOpFinished, object: self)
        }
    }
```

Now we are back in MyMandelbrotView, hearing through the notification that MyMandelbrotOperation has finished. We must immediately pick up any required data, because the OperationQueue is about to release this Operation. However, we must be careful: the notification may have been posted on a background thread, in which case our method for responding to it will also be called on a background thread. We are about to set our own graphics context and tell ourselves to redraw; those are things we want to do on the main thread. So we immediately step out to the main thread (using Grand Central Dispatch, described more fully in the next section). We remove ourselves as notification observer for this operation instance, copy the operation's `bitmapContext` into our own `bitmapContext`, and we're ready to redraw:

```
// warning! called on background thread
@objc func operationFinished(_ n:Notification) {
    if let op = n.object as? MyMandelbrotOperation {
        DispatchQueue.main.async {
            NotificationCenter.default.removeObserver(self,
                name: MyMandelbrotOperation.mandelOpFinished, object: op)
            self.bitmapContext = op.bitmapContext
            self.setNeedsDisplay()
        }
    }
}
```

Adapting our code to use Operation has involved some work, but the result has many advantages that help to ensure that our use of multiple threads is coherent and safe:

The background task is encapsulated

> Because MyMandelbrotOperation is an object, we've been able to move all the code having to do with drawing the pixels of the Mandelbrot set into it. The *only* MyMandelbrotView method that can be called in the background is operation-Finished(_:), and that's a method we'd never call explicitly ourselves, so we won't misuse it accidentally — and it immediately steps out to the main thread in any case.

The data sharing is rationalized

> Because MyMandelbrotOperation is an object, it has its own `bitmapContext` property. The only moment of data sharing comes in operationFinished(_:), when we must set MyMandelbrotView's `bitmapContext` to MyMandelbrot-Operation's `bitmapContext` — and that happens on the main thread, so there's no danger. Even if multiple MyMandelbrotOperation objects are added to the

```
```

queue, they are separate objects with separate `bitmapContext` properties, which MyMandelbrotView retrieves only on the main thread, so there is no conflict.

The threads are synchronized

The calculation-intensive MyMandelbrotOperation doesn't start until MyMandelbrotView calls `self.queue.addOperation(op)` to enqueue it. After that, MyMandelbrotView takes its hands off the steering wheel and makes *no* attempt to draw itself. If `draw(_:)` is unexpectedly called by the runtime, `self.bitmapContext` will be `nil` or will contain the results of an earlier calculation operation, and no harm done. Nothing else happens until the operation ends and the notification arrives (`operationFinished(_:)`); then and only then does MyMandelbrotView update the interface — on the main thread.

If we are concerned with the possibility that more than one instance of MyMandelbrotOperation might be added to the queue and executed concurrently, we have a further line of defense — we can set the OperationQueue's maximum concurrency level to 1:

```
let q = OperationQueue()
q.maxConcurrentOperationCount = 1
```

This turns the OperationQueue into a *serial* queue: every operation on the queue must be completely executed before the next can begin. This might cause an operation added to the queue to take longer to execute, if it must wait for another operation to finish before it can even get started; however, this delay might not be important. What *is* important is that by executing the operations on this queue separately from one another, we guarantee that only one operation at a time can do any data sharing. A serial queue is therefore implicitly a safe and reliable form of data locking.

Because MyMandelbrotView can be destroyed (if its view controller is destroyed), there is a risk that it will create an operation that will outlive it. So a MyMandelbrotOperation might try to access a MyMandelbrotView that no longer exists. We can reduce that risk by canceling all operations in our queue as MyMandelbrotView goes out of existence:

```
deinit {
    self.queue.cancelAllOperations()
}
```

There is more to know about Operation; it's a powerful tool. One Operation can have another Operation as a *dependency*, meaning that the former cannot start until the latter has finished, even if they are in different OperationQueues. Moreover, the behavior of an Operation can be customized; for instance, an Operation subclass can redefine what `isReady` means and so can control when it is capable of execution. Using these features, operations can be combined to express your app's logic, guaranteeing the order in which things happen (cogently argued in a brilliant WWDC 2015 video).

Grand Central Dispatch

Grand Central Dispatch, or *GCD*, is a sort of low-level analogue to Operation and OperationQueue; in fact, OperationQueue uses GCD under the hood. When I say GCD is low-level, I'm not kidding; it is effectively baked into the operating system kernel. It can be used by any code whatsoever and is tremendously efficient.

GCD is like OperationQueue in that it uses queues: you express a task and add it to a queue, and the task is executed on a thread as needed. A GCD queue is represented by a *dispatch queue* (DispatchQueue), a lightweight opaque pseudo-object consisting essentially of a list of functions to be executed. You can use a built-in system queue or you can make your own; if you make your own, your queue by default is a *serial* queue, with each task on that queue finishing before the next is started — which, as I've already said, is a form of data locking.

We'll rewrite MyMandelbrotView to use GCD. We start by creating a queue; I'll store it in an instance property:

```
let MANDELBROT_STEPS = 100
var bitmapContext: CGContext!
let draw_queue = DispatchQueue(label: "com.neuburg.mandeldraw")
```

Our goal is to eliminate data sharing, so our `makeBitmapContext(size:)` method now returns a graphics context rather than setting a property directly:

```
func makeBitmapContext(size:CGSize) -> CGContext {
    // ... as before ...
    let context = CGContext(data: nil,
        width: Int(size.width), height: Int(size.height),
        bitsPerComponent: 8, bytesPerRow: bitmapBytesPerRow,
        space: colorSpace, bitmapInfo: prem)
    return context!
}
```

For the same reason, our `draw(center:bounds:zoom:)` method now takes an additional `context:` parameter — the graphics context to draw into — and operates on that `context` without ever referring to `self.bitmapContext`:

```
func draw(center:CGPoint, bounds:CGRect, zoom:CGFloat, context:CGContext) {
    // ... as before, but we refer to local context, not self.bitmapContext
}
```

Now for the implementation of `drawThatPuppy`. This is where all the action is:

```
func drawThatPuppy () {
    let center = self.bounds.center
    let bounds = self.bounds ❶
    self.draw_queue.async { ❷
        let bitmap = self.makeBitmapContext(size: bounds.size) ❸
        self.draw(center: center, bounds: bounds, zoom: 1, context: bitmap)
        DispatchQueue.main.async { ❹
            self.bitmapContext = bitmap ❺
            self.setNeedsDisplay()
        }
    }
}
```

That's all there is to it: *all* our app's multithreading is concentrated in those few lines! There are no notifications; there is no sharing of data between threads; and the synchronization of our threads is expressed directly through the sequential order of the code.

Our code makes two calls to the DispatchQueue `async` method, which takes as its parameter a function — usually, an anonymous function — expressing what we want done asynchronously on this queue. This is the GCD method you'll use most, because asynchronous execution will be your primary reason for using GCD in the first place.

Our two calls to `async` are *nested* — the first call takes an anonymous function, which contains the second call, which takes another anonymous function. This nesting is crucial, because trailing anonymous functions are closures that can see the higher surrounding scope. As a result, we don't need to pass any parameters from an outer scope to an inner scope. The local variables `center` and `bounds` simply "fall" into the anonymous function of the first call to `async`, and the local variable `bitmap` simply "falls" into the anonymous function of the second call to `async`. There is no data sharing, because values *cascade sequentially* from one scope into the next.

Here's how `drawThatPuppy` works:

❶ We begin by calculating our `center` and `bounds` (on the main thread). These local variables will be visible within the subsequent anonymous functions, because a function body's code can see its surrounding context and capture it.

❷ Now comes the task to be performed in a separate background thread on our queue, `self.draw_queue`. We specify this task with the `async` method. We describe what we want to do on the background thread in an anonymous function.

❸ In the anonymous function, we begin by declaring `bitmap` as a *local* variable. This is our graphics context. We call `makeBitmapContext(size:)` to create it, and then call `draw(center:bounds:zoom:context:)` to set its pixels. Those calls

---

1104 | Chapter 24: Threads

are made on a *background* thread, because `self.draw_queue` is a background queue.

❹ Now we need to step back out to the *main* thread. How do we do that? With the `async` method again! This time, we specify the main queue (which is effectively the main thread), whose name is `DispatchQueue.main`. We describe what we want to do on the main queue in *another* anonymous function.

❺ Here we are in the second anonymous function. Because the first function is part of the second function's surrounding context, the second function can see the first function's local `bitmap` variable. Using it, we set our `bitmapContext` property and call `setNeedsDisplay` — on the main thread! — and we're done.

The benefits of GCD as a form of concurrency management are stunning:

No data sharing
  The only time we ever refer to a property of `self` is at the start (`self.bounds`) and at the end (`self.bitmapContext`), when we are *on the main thread*. The bitmap context where all the drawing action takes place is a *local* variable, `bitmap`, confined to each individual call to `drawThatPuppy`. Moreover, that drawing action is performed on a serial queue, so no two drawing actions can ever overlap.

Transparent synchronization of threads
  The threads are correctly synchronized, and this is *obvious*, because the nested anonymous functions are executed *in succession*, so any instance of `bitmap` must be completely filled with pixels before being used to set the `bitmapContext` property.

Maintainability and readability
  Our code is easy to maintain, because the entire task on all threads is expressed within the single `drawThatPuppy` method; indeed, the code is modified only very slightly from the original nonthreaded version. The code is also easy to read and understand, because the path of execution passes sequentially from the first line of `drawThatPuppy` to the last line — the very thing we were worried might *not* happen when we adopted background threading in the first place.

You might object that we still have the methods `makeBitmapContext(size:)` and `draw(center:bounds:zoom:context:)` hanging around MyMandelbrotView, and that we must therefore still be careful not to call them on the main thread, or indeed from anywhere except from within `drawThatPuppy`. If that were true, we could at this point destroy both methods and move their functionality completely into `drawThat-Puppy`. But we don't have to, because these methods are now *thread-safe*: they are self-contained utilities that touch no properties or persistent objects, so it doesn't matter what thread they are called on. Still, I'll demonstrate later how we can intercept an accidental attempt to call a method on the wrong thread.

Commonly Used GCD Methods

The most important DispatchQueue methods are:

`async(execute:)`
> Pushes a function onto the end of a queue for later execution; the queue will determine when the function will execute, and meanwhile we *proceed immediately* with the next line of our own code without waiting for that to happen (see Appendix C). Commonly, there is *no* next line of our own code; an `async` call is usually the last statement in its scope. Use this method to execute code in a background thread, or from *within* a background thread to step back onto the main thread.

`asyncAfter(deadline:execute:)`
> Similar to `async`, but the enqueued function runs only after a certain amount of time has been permitted to elapse following the call (*delayed performance*). Many examples in this book have made use of this method (through my `delay` utility function; see Appendix B).

`sync(execute:)`
> Pushes a function onto the end of a queue for later execution, and *waits* until the function has executed before proceeding with our own code. You should use this method only in special circumstances, typically where you need the queue as a lock (mediating access to a shared resource) but you also need to *use a result* that the function is to provide.

Synchronous Execution

The use of `sync(execute:)` is sufficiently unusual that it deserves an example. Let's say we'd like to revise the Downloader class from Chapter 23 so that the delegate methods are run on a background thread, taking some strain off the main thread (and hence the user interface) while these messages are flying around behind the scenes. This is reasonable and safe, because the URLSession and its delegate are packaged inside the Downloader object, isolated from our view controller.

To begin with, we'll need our own background OperationQueue, which we can maintain as an instance property of Downloader:

```
let queue = OperationQueue()
```

Our session is now configured and created using this background queue:

```
lazy var session : URLSession = {
    return URLSession(configuration:self.config,
        delegate:DownloaderDelegate(), delegateQueue:self.queue)
}()
```

This means that `urlSession(_:downloadTask:didFinishDownloadingTo:)` will be called on our background queue. So what will happen when we call back into the client through the completion function that the client handed us at the outset? To avoid involving the client in threading issues, we'll step out to the main thread as we call the completion function. But we cannot do this by calling `async`:

```
let ch = self.handlers[downloadTask.taskIdentifier]
DispatchQueue.main.async { // bad idea!
    ch?(url)
}
```

The reason is that the downloaded file is slated to be *destroyed* as soon as we return from `urlSession(_:downloadTask:didFinishDownloadingTo:)` — and if we call `async`, we will return *immediately*, the downloaded file *will* be destroyed, and `url` will end up pointing at nothing by the time the client receives it! The solution is to use `sync` instead:

```
let ch = self.handlers[downloadTask.taskIdentifier]
DispatchQueue.main.sync {
    ch?(url)
}
```

That code steps out to the main thread and also postpones returning from `url-Session(_:downloadTask:didFinishDownloadingTo:)` until the client has had an opportunity to do something with the file pointed to by `url`. In this way we lock down the shared data (the downloaded file). We are blocking our background OperationQueue, but this is legal, and in any case we're blocking very briefly and in a coherent manner.

 Do not call `DispatchQueue.main.sync` if you are already *on* the main queue! That's an instant deadlock and your code will grind to a complete halt.

Dispatch Groups

A dispatch group effectively combines independent tasks into a single task; we proceed only when *all* of them have completed. Its usage is structured as in Example 24-1.

Example 24-1. Dispatch group usage

```
let group = DispatchGroup()
// here we go...
group.enter()
queue1.async {
    // ... do task here ...
    group.leave()
}
group.enter()
queue2.async {
    // ... do task here ...
    group.leave()
}
group.enter()
queue3.async {
    // ... do task here ...
    group.leave()
}
// ... more as needed ...
group.notify(queue: DispatchQueue.main) {
    // finished!
}
```

In Example 24-1, each task to be performed asynchronously is preceded by a call to our dispatch group's enter and is followed by a call to our dispatch group's leave. The queues on which the tasks are performed do not have to be different queues; the point is that it doesn't matter if they are. Only when every enter has been balanced by a leave will the completion function in our dispatch group's notify be called. This is effectively a way of *waiting* until *all* the tasks have completed independently, before proceeding with whatever the notify completion function says to do.

One-Time Execution

Sometimes you need a thread-safe way of ensuring that code is run only once; this is often used to help vend a singleton. In Objective-C, you'd use dispatch_once, which is part of GCD; in Swift, however, dispatch_once is unavailable (because it can't be implemented in a thread-safe way). The Swift workaround is *not* to use GCD, but rather to take advantage of the built-in lazy initialization feature of global and static variables.

In this example, my view controller has a constant property oncer whose value is an instance of a struct Oncer that has a doThisOnce method; the actual functionality of that method is embedded in the initializer of a private static property once. The result is that, no matter how many times we call self.oncer.doThisOnce() in the course of this view controller's lifetime, that functionality will be performed only once:

```
class ViewController: UIViewController {
    struct Oncer {
        private static var once : Void = {
            print("I did it!")
        }()
        func doThisOnce() {
            _ = Oncer.once
        }
    }
    let oncer = Oncer()
    override func viewDidLoad() {
        super.viewDidLoad()
        self.oncer.doThisOnce() // I did it!
        self.oncer.doThisOnce() // nothing
    }
}
```

To change the temporal scope of the "onceness," change the semantic scope of oncer. If oncer is defined at the top level of a file, its once functionality can be performed only once in the entire lifetime of the app.

Concurrent Queues

Besides serial dispatch queues, there are also *concurrent* dispatch queues. A concurrent queue's functions are started in the order in which they were submitted to the queue, but a function is allowed to start while another function is still executing. Obviously, you wouldn't want to submit to a concurrent queue a task that touches a shared resource! The advantage of concurrent queues is a possible speed boost when you don't care about the order in which multiple tasks are finished, as when you want to do something with regard to every element of an array.

The built-in global queues, available by calling DispatchQueue.global(qos:), are concurrent. You specify which built-in global queue you want by means of the qos: argument, which can be (DispatchQoS.QoSClass):

- .userInteractive
- .userInitiated
- .default
- .utility
- .background

("QoS" is an acronym for "quality of service.")

You can also create a concurrent queue yourself by calling the DispatchQueue initializer init(label:attributes:) with a .concurrent attribute.

Checking the Queue

A question that sometimes arises is how to make certain that a method is called only on the correct queue. Recall that in our Mandelbrot drawing example, we may be concerned that a method such as `makeBitmapContext(size:)` might be called on some other queue than the background queue that we created for this purpose. This sort of problem can be solved quite elegantly by calling the `dispatch-Precondition(condition:)` global function. It takes a DispatchPredicate enum, whose cases are:

- `.onQueue`
- `.onQueueAsBarrier`
- `.notOnQueue`

These cases each take an associated value which is a DispatchQueue. (I told you it was elegant!) To assert that we are on our `draw_queue` queue, we would say:

```
dispatchPrecondition(condition: .onQueue(self.draw_queue))
```

The outcome is similar to Swift's native `precondition` function: if our assertion is `false`, we'll crash.

App Backgrounding

A problem arises if your app is backgrounded and suspended (Appendix A) while your code is running. The system doesn't want to stop your code while it's executing; on the other hand, some other app may need to be given the bulk of the device's resources now. So as your app goes into the background, the system waits a very short time (less than 5 seconds) for your app to finish doing whatever it may be doing, and it then suspends your app.

This shouldn't be a problem from your main thread's point of view, because your app shouldn't have any time-consuming code on the main thread in the first place; you now know that you can avoid this by using a background thread. On the other hand, it could be a problem for lengthy background tasks, including asynchronous tasks performed by the frameworks.

What we'd like to do in this situation is *protect* a lengthy background task against interruption, requesting extra time for completion just in case the app is backgrounded. There's a way to do that:

1. You call UIApplication's `beginBackgroundTask(expirationHandler:)` to announce that a lengthy task is beginning; it returns an identification number. This tells the system that if your app is backgrounded, you'd like to be granted some extra time to complete this task. (My experience is that the time granted is usually about 30 seconds.)

2. At the end of your lengthy task, you call UIApplication's `endBackground-Task(_:)`, passing in the *same identification number* that you got from your call to `beginBackgroundTask(expirationHandler:)`. This tells the system that your lengthy task is over and that there is no need to grant you any more background time.

The function that you pass as the argument to `beginBackgroundTask(expiration-Handler:)` is the *expiration function*. It does *not* express the lengthy task! It expresses what you will do *if your extra time expires* before you finish your lengthy task. This is a chance for you to clean up. At the very least, your expiration function *must* call `end-BackgroundTask(_:)`! Otherwise, the runtime won't know that you've run your expiration function, and your app may be killed as a punishment for trying to use too much background time. If your expiration function *is* called, you should make no assumptions about what thread it is running on.

There are two routes by which `endBackgroundTask(_:)` might be called: either our lengthy operation was cancelled because we ran out of time, or it ran to completion. So we end up with a pattern like this:

```
var bti : UIBackgroundTaskIdentifier = .invalid
bti = UIApplication.shared.beginBackgroundTask {
    // ... we didn't finish! do any cleanup ...
    UIApplication.shared.endBackgroundTask(bti) // cancellation
}
// ... do lengthy operation ...
UIApplication.shared.endBackgroundTask(bti) // completion
```

That pattern is so common in my code that it makes sense to encapsulate it. To do so, I've created an Operation subclass, which I call BackgroundTaskOperation:

```
class BackgroundTaskOperation: Operation {
    var whatToDo : (() -> ())?
    var cleanup : (() -> ())?
    override func main() {
        guard !self.isCancelled else { return }
        var bti : UIBackgroundTaskIdentifier = .invalid
        bti = UIApplication.shared.beginBackgroundTask {
            self.cleanup?()
            self.cancel()
            UIApplication.shared.endBackgroundTask(bti) // cancellation
        }
        guard bti != .invalid else { return }
        whatToDo?()
        guard !self.isCancelled else { return }
        UIApplication.shared.endBackgroundTask(bti) // completion
    }
}
```

Let's use MyMandelbrotView as an example. Let's say that if `drawThatPuppy` is started, we'd like it to be allowed to finish, even if the app is suspended in the middle of it, so that our `bitmapContext` property is updated as requested. We have created a global serial background operation queue:

```
let backgroundTaskQueue : OperationQueue = {
    let q = OperationQueue()
    q.maxConcurrentOperationCount = 1
    return q
}()
```

When we call our lengthy `self.draw(center:bounds:zoom:context:)`, we embed it in a BackgroundTaskOperation:

```
let center = self.bounds.center
let bounds = self.bounds
let bitmap = self.makeBitmapContext(size: bounds.size)
let task = BackgroundTaskOperation()
task.whatToDo = {
    self.draw(center: center, bounds: bounds, zoom: 1, context: bitmap)
    DispatchQueue.main.async {
        self.bitmapContext = bitmap
        self.setNeedsDisplay()
    }
}
backgroundTaskQueue.addOperation(task)
```

There are three possibilities here:

The app doesn't go into the background
If the app doesn't go into the background while the lengthy background task is running, then our use of `beginBackgroundTask` and `endBackgroundTask` makes no difference. These calls are asking for extra time *if* we go into the background. We didn't. `self.draw(center:bounds:zoom:context:)` is performed on a background queue because `backgroundTaskQueue` is a background queue, and all is as it was before.

We finish in the background
If the app goes into the background and we finish the lengthy background task before time runs out, the whole operation is performed in good order. If the user subsequently brings the app back to the foreground (and assuming that the app has not been terminated in the background), there's MyMandelbrotView displaying the result.

We run out of time
If the app goes into the background and we *don't* finish the lengthy background task before time runs out, we call `endBackgroundTask` and the app is suspended in good order. If the user subsequently brings the app back to the foreground (and assuming that the app has not been terminated in the background), our code *resumes* and finishes the drawing.

If the app *is* terminated in the background, our code has been interrupted in the middle and will never complete. This is a tricky situation. Since we don't know, when we run out of time, whether we will ever be able to continue, it is best to assume that the operation might *never* finish and clean up immediately. In the whatToDo function, I usually get a weak reference to task and use it to check task.isCancelled often so that I can stop quickly at a good spot if we run out of time.

Background Processing

New in iOS 13, instead of continuing a current task a bit longer in case the app goes into the background, you can request that a task be performed *only* while the app is in the background. The idea is that this would be some lengthy calculation or operation that isn't crucial to perform while the user is looking at the app, but would be nice to do at some future time when the device is more or less idle. This is called *background processing:*

- Background processing is a background mode, so you'll need to add the Background Modes capability in the Signing & Capabilities tab of the target editor and check "Background processing."

- Background processing uses the Background Tasks framework, so in your code, you'll need to import BackgroundTasks.

- In the *Info.plist,* you *must* add entries under the "Permitted background task schedule identifiers" key (BTTaskSchedulerPermittedIdentifiers); these are arbitrary strings (typically using reverse domain notation) identifying your tasks.

There are two classes involved:

BGProcessingTaskRequest
 A value class describing your background task. You initialize it with an identifier, which must match one of your *Info.plist* background task schedule identifiers; you can also set three properties:

requiresExternalPower
 The task should be performed when the device is being charged. The default is false.

requiresNetworkConnectivity
 The task should be performed when networking is available. The default is false.

earliestBeginDate
 A date in the future. Apple recommends a time somewhere between fifteen minutes from now and a week from now. The default is nil.

BGTaskScheduler

Your gateway for communicating with the runtime about background processing tasks. You'll talk to the `shared` instance. In your app delegate's `application(_:didFinishLaunchingWithOptions:)`, you *must* call this method:

`register(forTaskWithIdentifier:using:launchHandler:)`

The `identifier:` parameter must match one of your *Info.plist* background task schedule identifiers. The `using:` parameter is a dispatch queue. The last parameter is a function that will be called on that queue. This function is the task! It takes one parameter, a BGTask object. In the function, you have two responsibilities with regard to this object:

- You *must* immediately set the BGTask's `expirationHandler` to a function that will be called if your background time expires.

- You *must* call `setTaskCompleted` with a Bool parameter indicating whether your task finished. At a minimum, in your `expirationHandler` function you'll call `setTaskCompleted(false)`, and at the end of your task function you'll call `setTaskCompleted(true)`. This should remind you of how we implemented `beginBackgroundTask` and `endBackground-Task` in the previous section.

When you go into the background and you want to ask for your task to be performed, you'll talk to the `shared` BGTaskScheduler again: you'll call `submit(_:)` with a BGProcessingTaskRequest.

Here's an artificial example, using MyMandelbrotView to provide us with a lengthy task:

```
let taskid = "com.neuburg.matt.lengthy"
func application(_ application: UIApplication,
    didFinishLaunchingWithOptions launchOptions:
    [UIApplication.LaunchOptionsKey : Any]?) -> Bool {
        let v = MyMandelbrotView(frame:CGRect(0,0,500,500))
        let ok = BGTaskScheduler.shared.register(
            forTaskWithIdentifier: taskid,
            using: DispatchQueue.global(qos: .background)) { task in
                task.expirationHandler = {
                    task.setTaskCompleted(success: false)
                }
                let context = v.makeBitmapContext(size: CGSize(500,500))
                v.draw(center: CGPoint(250,250),
                    bounds: CGRect(0,0,500,500),
                    zoom: 1, context: context)
                task.setTaskCompleted(success: true)
        }
        // might check `ok` here
        return true
}
```

```
func applicationDidEnterBackground(_ application: UIApplication) {
    // might check to see whether it's time to submit this request
    let req = BGProcessingTaskRequest(identifier: self.taskid)
    try? BGTaskScheduler.shared.submit(req)
}
```

To help you test, there's a secret dance that lets you trigger your background task artificially. Here's how I would do the dance for my test app:

1. Pepper the registered task function with `print` statements or breakpoints.

2. Run the app on a device from Xcode.

3. On the device, send the app into the background; then bring it back to the foreground.

4. In Xcode, pause the running app.

5. In the console, give the following mysterious command (all on one line, using your actual task identifier):

    ```
    (lldb) e -l objc -- (void)[[BGTaskScheduler sharedScheduler]
        _simulateLaunchForTaskWithIdentifier:@"com.neuburg.matt.lengthy"]
    ```

    The console replies: "Simulating launch for task with identifier…"

6. Still in the console, say `continue`. The task function runs, printing its `print` statements and pausing at its breakpoints.

7. When we get to `task.setTaskCompleted(success: true)`, the console reports "Marking simulated task complete," and the experiment is over.

You can also test whether your expiration function is called in good order. To do that, perform the first six steps and pause again inside the task function at a point after the expiration handler has been set. Now say this in the console:

```
(lldb) e -l objc -- (void)[[BGTaskScheduler sharedScheduler]
    _simulateExpirationForTaskWithIdentifier:@"com.neuburg.matt.lengthy"]
```

Then say `continue`, and if all goes well, the console will reply "Expiring simulated task" and then "Marking simulated task complete."

 A second type of background task request, BGAppRefreshTaskRequest, supersedes the use of methods like `application(_:performFetchWithCompletion-Handler:)` to implement background app refresh. I don't discuss background app refresh in this book, but if you've been using it, you should switch to the Background Tasks framework.

Undo

The idea of undo is that the user can reverse a recently performed action. Behind the scenes, the app maintains an internal stack of undoable actions; undoing reverses the action at the top of the stack, and also makes that action available for redo through a secondary stack.

A pervasive undo capability is characteristic primarily of desktop macOS applications, but some iOS apps may also benefit from a limited undo facility, and certain built-in views — in particular, those that involve text entry (Chapter 10) — implement it already. UIDocument (see Chapter 22) integrates with your undo facility to update the document's "dirty" state automatically.

Undo operates through an *undo manager* — an instance of UndoManager. Every time the user performs an action that is to be undoable, you *register* that action with the undo manager. When the user asks to undo, you send undo to the undo manager; when the user asks to redo, you send redo to the undo manager. In both cases, the undo manager performs the registered action and adjusts its internal undo and redo stacks appropriately.

I'll introduce the UndoManager class with a simple example; for more information, read Apple's *Undo Architecture* in the documentation archive, along with the class documentation.

Target–Action Undo

I'll illustrate an UndoManager for a simple app that has just one kind of undoable action. In my example, the user can drag a small square around the screen. Our goal is to make the drag undoable.

We'll start with an instance of a UIView subclass, MyView, to which has been attached a UIPanGestureRecognizer to make it draggable; the gesture recognizer's action target is the MyView instance itself, which implements the typical drag action function described in Chapter 5:

```
@objc func dragging (_ p : UIPanGestureRecognizer) {
    switch p.state {
    case .began, .changed:
        let delta = p.translation(in:self.superview!)
        var c = self.center
        c.x += delta.x; c.y += delta.y
        self.center = c
        p.setTranslation(.zero, in: self.superview!)
    default:break
    }
}
```

We will need an UndoManager instance. Let's store it in a property of MyView itself, `self.undoer`:

```
let undoer = UndoManager()
```

To test my app's undo capability, the interface also contains two buttons: an Undo button that sends undo to the view's undo manager, and a Redo button that sends redo to the view's undo manager.

We need to tell the undo manager to *register* the drag action as undoable. There are two main ways of doing that. One way is to call this UndoManager method:

- `registerUndo(withTarget:selector:object:)`

This method uses a target–action architecture: you provide a target, a selector for an action method that takes one parameter, and a value that will *be* that parameter. Later, if the UndoManager is sent the undo or redo message, it calls the action method on that target with the object as argument. The job of the action method is to undo whatever it is that needs undoing.

Let's use `registerUndo(withTarget:selector:object:)` to configure undo in our app. How? Well, what we want to undo here is the setting of our center property:

```
var c = self.center
c.x += delta.x; c.y += delta.y
self.center = c // *
```

We need to express this as a method taking one parameter, so that the undo manager can call it as the selector: action method. So, in our dragging(_:) method, instead of setting self.center to c directly, we now call a secondary method:

```
var c = self.center
c.x += delta.x; c.y += delta.y
self.setCenterUndoably(c) // *
```

We have posited a method setCenterUndoably(_:) that doesn't exist. Let's write it. What should it do? At a minimum, it should do the job that setting self.center used to do! At the same time, we want the undo manager to be able to call this method. The undo manager doesn't know the *type* of the parameter that it will be passing to us, so its object: parameter is typed as Any. Therefore, the parameter of this method also needs to be typed as Any:

```
func setCenterUndoably (_ newCenter:Any) {
    self.center = newCenter as! CGPoint
}
```

This works, in the sense that the view is draggable exactly as before; but we have not yet made this action undoable — because we have not called registerUndo(with-Target:selector:object:). To do so, we must ask ourselves what message the UndoManager would need to send in order to undo the action we are about to perform. Clearly, we would want the UndoManager to set self.center back to the value it has *now*. And what method would the UndoManager call in order to do that? It would call setCenterUndoably(_:), the very method we are implementing! So now we have this:

```
@objc func setCenterUndoably (_ newCenter:Any) {
    self.undoer.registerUndo(withTarget: self,
        selector: #selector(setCenterUndoably),
        object: self.center)
    self.center = newCenter as! CGPoint
}
```

That code works; it makes our action undoable!

Not only is our action now undoable; it is also redoable as well. *How can this be?* Well, it turns out that UndoManager has an internal state, and responds differently to registerUndo(withTarget:selector:object:) depending on that state. If the UndoManager is sent registerUndo(withTarget:selector:object:) *while it is undoing*, it puts the target–action information on the redo stack instead of the undo stack (because redo *is* the undo of an undo, if you see what I mean).

Confused? Here's how our code works to undo and then redo an action:

1. We set self.center by way of setCenterUndoably(_:), which calls register-Undo(withTarget:selector:object:) with the *old* value of self.center. The UndoManager adds this to its *undo* stack.

2. Now suppose we want to undo that action. We send undo to the UndoManager.

3. The UndoManager calls setCenterUndoably(_:) with the *old* value that we passed it in step 1. So we are going to set the center back to that old value. But before we do that, we send registerUndo(withTarget:selector:object:) to the UndoManager with the *current* value of self.center. The UndoManager

knows that it is currently undoing, so it understands this registration as something to be added to its *redo* stack.

4. Now suppose we want to redo that undo. We send `redo` to the UndoManager, and sure enough, the UndoManager calls `setCenterUndoably(_:)` with the value that we previously undid! And, once again, we call `registerUndo(with-Target:selector:object:)` with an action that goes onto the UndoManager's *undo* stack — and we're back to step 1.

Undo Grouping

So far, so good. But our implementation of undo is very annoying, because we are adding a new object to the undo stack every time `dragging(_:)` is called — and it is called many times during the course of a single drag! This means that undoing once merely undoes the tiny increment corresponding to one individual `dragging(_:)` call. What we'd like is for undoing to undo an *entire* dragging gesture. We can implement this through *undo grouping*. As the gesture begins, we start a group; when the gesture ends, we end the group:

```
func dragging (_ p : UIPanGestureRecognizer) {
    switch p.state {
    case .began:
        self.undoer.beginUndoGrouping() // *
        fallthrough
    case .changed:
        let delta = p.translation(in:self.superview!)
        var c = self.center
        c.x += delta.x; c.y += delta.y
        self.setCenterUndoably(c)
        p.setTranslation(.zero, in: self.superview!)
    case .ended, .cancelled:
        self.undoer.endUndoGrouping() // *
    default:break
    }
}
```

This works: each complete drag gesture, from the time the user's finger first touches the view and drags it to the time the user's finger is lifted, is now undoable (and redoable) as a single unit.

A further refinement would be to animate the "drag" that the UndoManager performs when it undoes or redoes a user drag gesture. To do so, we take advantage of the fact that we can examine the UndoManager's state by way of its `isUndoing` and `isRedoing` properties; we animate the `center` change when the UndoManager is "dragging," but not when the user is dragging:

```
@objc func setCenterUndoably (_ newCenter:Any) {
    self.undoer.registerUndo(withTarget: self,
        selector: #selector(setCenterUndoably),
        object: self.center)
    if self.undoer.isUndoing || self.undoer.isRedoing {
        UIView.animate(withDuration:0.4, delay: 0.1, animations: {
            self.center = newCenter as! CGPoint
        })
    } else { // just do it
        self.center = newCenter as! CGPoint
    }
}
```

Functional Undo

I said earlier that there are two main ways of registering an action as undoable with the undo manager. The second way is to call this UndoManager method:

- `registerUndo(withTarget:handler:)`

The `handler:` is a function that will be called when we call `undo` or `redo`. It must take one parameter, which will be whatever you pass here as the `target:` argument. This is a more modern idiom than the target–action architecture for expressing the registration of an action. If we adopt this approach, then our `setCenterUndoably(_:)` no longer needs to take an Any as its parameter; it can take a CGPoint:

```
func setCenterUndoably (_ newCenter:CGPoint) {
    self.undoer.registerUndo(withTarget: self) {
        [oldCenter = self.center] myself in
        myself.setCenterUndoably(oldCenter)
    }
    if self.undoer.isUndoing || self.undoer.isRedoing {
        UIView.animate(withDuration:0.4, delay: 0.1, animations: {
            self.center = newCenter
        })
    } else { // just do it
        self.center = newCenter
    }
}
```

Let's look more closely at my call to `registerUndo(withTarget:handler:)` and the anonymous `handler:` function that accompanies it:

```
self.undoer.registerUndo(withTarget: self) {
    [oldCenter = self.center] myself in
    myself.setCenterUndoably(oldCenter)
}
```

The example shows what the `target:` parameter is for — it's to avoid retain cycles. By passing `self` as the `target:` argument, I can retrieve it as the parameter in the handler: function (I've called the parameter myself). In the body of the handler: function, I never have to refer to self and there is no retain cycle.

I've also taken advantage of a little-known feature of Swift anonymous function capture lists, allowing me to get the value of self.center as it is *now* and capture it in a local reference (oldCenter) inside the anonymous function. The reason is that if the anonymous function were to call setCenterUndoably(myself.center), we'd be using the value that myself.center will have *at undo time*, and would be pointlessly setting the center to itself.

Our code works perfectly, but we can go further. We are failing to take full advantage of the fact that we now have the ability to register with the undo manager a full-fledged function body rather than a mere function call. That fact means that the handler: function can contain *everything* that should happen when undoing, including the animation:

```
self.undoer.registerUndo(withTarget: self) {
    [oldCenter = self.center] myself in
    UIView.animate(withDuration:0.4, delay: 0.1, animations: {
        myself.center = oldCenter
    })
    myself.setCenterUndoably(oldCenter)
}
```

But we can go further still. Let's ask ourselves: Why are we setting self.center here at all? We can do it back in the gesture recognizer's dragging(_:) action method, just as we were doing before we added undo to this app. And in that case, we no longer need a separate setCenterUndoably method! True, we still need some function that calls registerUndo with a call to itself, because that's how we get redo registration during undo; but this can be a local function inside the dragging(_:) method. Our dragging(_:) method can provide a complete undo implementation internally, resulting in a far more legible and encapsulated architecture:

```
@objc func dragging (_ p : UIPanGestureRecognizer) {
    switch p.state {
    case .began:
        self.undoer.beginUndoGrouping()
        fallthrough
    case .began, .changed:
        let delta = p.translation(in:self.superview!)
        var c = self.center
        c.x += delta.x; c.y += delta.y
        func registerForUndo() {
            self.undoer.registerUndo(withTarget: self) {
                [oldCenter = self.center] myself in
                UIView.animate(withDuration:0.4, delay: 0.1, animations: {
                    myself.center = oldCenter
                })
                registerForUndo()
```

```
            }
        }
        registerForUndo() // *
        self.center = c // *
        p.setTranslation(.zero, in: self.superview!)
    case .ended, .cancelled:
        self.undoer.endUndoGrouping()
    default: break
    }
}
```

Undo Interface

We must also decide how to let the user request undo and redo. While I was developing the code from the preceding section, I used an Undo button and a Redo button. This can be a perfectly reasonable interface, but let's talk about some others.

Shake-To-Edit

By default, your app supports *shake-to-edit*. This means that the user can shake the device to bring up an undo/redo interface. We discussed this briefly in Chapter 21. If you don't turn off this feature by setting the shared UIApplication's application-SupportsShakeToEdit property to false, and if the user doesn't turn it off in Settings, then when the user shakes the device, the runtime walks up the responder chain, starting with the first responder, looking for a responder whose inherited undo-Manager property returns an actual UndoManager instance. If it finds one, it puts up an alert with an Undo button, a Redo button, or both; if the user taps a button, the runtime communicates directly with that UndoManager, calling its undo or redo method for us.

You will recall what it takes for a UIResponder to be first responder in this sense: it must return true from canBecomeFirstResponder, and it must actually be made first responder through a call to becomeFirstResponder. Let's have MyView satisfy those requirements. We might call becomeFirstResponder at the end of dragging(_:), like this:

```
override var canBecomeFirstResponder : Bool {
    return true
}
@objc func dragging (_ p : UIPanGestureRecognizer) {
    switch p.state {
    // ... the rest as before ...
    case .ended, .cancelled:
        self.undoer.endUndoGrouping()
        self.becomeFirstResponder()
    default: break
    }
}
```

Figure 25-1. The shake-to-edit undo/redo alert

Then, to implement undo through shake-to-edit, we have only to provide a getter for the undoManager property that returns our undo manager, self.undoer:

```
let undoer = UndoManager()
override var undoManager : UndoManager? {
    return self.undoer
}
```

This works: shaking the device now brings up the undo/redo alert, and its buttons work correctly. However, I don't like the way the buttons are labeled; they just say Undo and Redo. To make this interface more expressive, we should provide the undo manager with a string describing each undoable action. We do that by calling set-ActionName(_:); we can call it at the same time that we register our undo action:

```
self.undoer.setActionName("Move")
```

Now the undo/redo alert has more informative labels, as shown in Figure 25-1.

Built-In Gestures

New in iOS 13, three gestures are interpreted as asking for undo and redo:

- Double tap with three fingers means undo.
- Swipe left with three fingers means undo.
- Swift right with three fingers means redo.

The idea is probably to make shake-to-edit obsolete, as it is rather violent and somewhat unreliable.

The response when the user makes one of these gestures is comparable to shake-to-edit: the runtime walks up the responder chain looking for a responder with an UndoManager in its undoManager property. Unlike shake-to-edit, when it finds this responder it doesn't put up an alert; it simply sends the undo manager undo or redo directly. It also puts up a little caption at the top of the screen explaining what's happening (Figure 25-2).

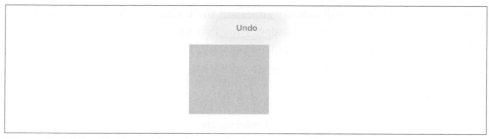

Figure 25-2. The Undo caption

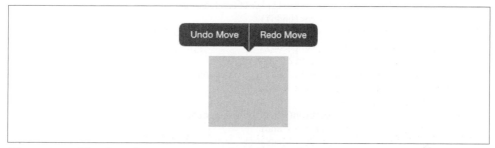

Figure 25-3. The shared menu as an undo/redo interface

The caption is not a button, nor is the user offered a choice; the gesture is obeyed, and when the caption appears, the undo or redo has already been performed. The caption text does not consult the undo manager's action name; it merely reads Undo or Redo. I regard this as unfortunate.

Undo Menu

Another possible undo/redo interface is through a menu (Figure 25-3). This is the same menu used by a UITextField or UITextView for displaying menu items such as Select, Select All, Copy, and Paste ("Text Field Menu" on page 658). The requirements for summoning this menu are effectively the same as those for shake-to-edit: we need a responder chain with a first responder at the bottom of it. So the code we've just supplied for making MyView first responder remains applicable.

Let's cause the menu to appear in response to a long press on our MyView instance. We'll attach another gesture recognizer to MyView. This will be a UILongPress-GestureRecognizer, whose action method is called longPress(_:).

To configure the menu, we get the singleton global UIMenuController object and specify an array of custom UIMenuItems as its menuItems property. To make the menu appear, we send the UIMenuController the showMenu(from:rect:) message. (This method is new in iOS 13, superseding setMenuVisible(_:animated:), which is deprecated.)

A particular menu item will actually appear in the menu only if we also return `true` from canPerformAction(_:withSender:) for that menu item's action. Delightfully, the UndoManager's canUndo and canRedo properties tell us what value canPerform-Action(_:withSender:) should return. We can also get the titles for our custom menu items from the UndoManager itself, through its undoMenuItemTitle and redo-MenuItemTitle properties:

```swift
@objc func longPress (_ g : UIGestureRecognizer) {
    if g.state == .began {
        let m = UIMenuController.shared
        let mi1 = UIMenuItem(title: self.undoer.undoMenuItemTitle,
            action: #selector(undo))
        let mi2 = UIMenuItem(title: self.undoer.redoMenuItemTitle,
            action: #selector(redo))
        m.menuItems = [mi1, mi2]
        m.showMenu(from: self, rect: self.bounds)
    }
}
override func canPerformAction(_ action: Selector,
    withSender sender: Any?) -> Bool {
        if action == #selector(undo) {
            return self.undoer.canUndo
        }
        if action == #selector(redo) {
            return self.undoer.canRedo
        }
        return super.canPerformAction(action, withSender: sender)
}
@objc func undo(_: Any?) {
    self.undoer.undo()
}
@objc func redo(_: Any?) {
    self.undoer.redo()
}
```

Lifetime Events

The fundamental events that notify you of stages in the lifetime of your app as a whole, giving your code an opportunity to run in response, are extraordinarily important. This appendix is devoted to a survey of them, along with some typical scenarios in which they will arrive.

Application States

In the very early days of iOS — before iOS 4 — the lifetime of an app was extremely simple: either it was running or it wasn't. The user tapped your app's icon in the home screen, and your app was launched and began to run. The user used your app for a while. Eventually, the user clicked the Home button and your app was terminated — it was no longer running. The user had *quit* your app. Launch, run, quit: that was the entire life cycle of an app. If the user decided to use your app again, the whole cycle started over.

The reason for this simplicity was that an iOS device, with its slow processor and its almost brutal paucity of memory and other resources, compensated for its own shortcomings by a simple rule: it could run *only one app at a time*. While your app was running, it occupied not only the entire screen but the vast majority of the device's resources, leaving room only for the system and some hidden built-in processes; it had, in effect, sole and complete control of the device.

Starting in iOS 4, that changed. Apple devised an ingenious architecture whereby, despite the device's limited resources, more than one app could run simultaneously — sort of. The Home button changed its meaning and its effect upon your app. In iOS 4 and later, when the user clicks the Home button to leave your app, your app does not die; technically, the Home button does not terminate your app. Instead, when your app occupies the screen, it is *in the foreground* (or *frontmost*); then, when some other app occupies the screen, your app is *backgrounded and suspended*.

Suspension means that your app is essentially freeze-dried; its process still exists, but it isn't actively running, and it isn't getting any events — though notifications can be stored by the system for later delivery in case your app comes to the front once again. And because it isn't running, it isn't using so much of the device's precious resources. In particular, it's not using the CPU, and some memory may be freed up by clearing the backing store of layers. Later, when the user returns to your app after having left it to use some other app for a while, your app is found in the *very same state* as when the user left it. The app was not terminated; it simply stopped and froze, and waited in suspended animation. Returning to your app no longer means that your app is *launched*, but merely that it is *resumed*.

All of this is not to say, however, that your app can't be terminated. It can be — though not by the user clicking the Home button. The user might switch off the device; that will certainly terminate your app. And a savvy user might force-terminate your app from the app switcher. The most common scenario, however, is that the system quietly *kills* your app while it is suspended. This undermines the app's ability to resume; when the user returns to your app, it will have to launch from scratch, just as in the pre–iOS 4 days. The death of your app under these circumstances is rather like that of the scientists killed by HAL 9000 in *2001: A Space Odyssey* — they went to sleep expecting to wake up later, but instead their life-support systems were turned off while they slept. The iOS system's reasons for killing your app are not quite as paranoid as HAL's, but they do have a certain Darwinian ruthlessness: your app, while suspended, continues to occupy a chunk of the device's memory, and the system needs to reclaim that memory so some other app can use it.

Over time, successive iOS systems have complicated the picture:

- Some apps can be backgrounded *without* being suspended. This is a special privilege, accorded in order that your app may perform a limited range of highly focused activities. An app that is playing music or tracking the device's location when it goes into the background may be permitted to continue doing so in the background. (See Chapters 14 and 21.)

- An app that has been suspended can be woken briefly, *remaining in the background*, in order to receive and respond to a message — in order to be told, for instance, that the user has crossed a geofence, or that a background download has completed. (See Chapters 21 and 23.)

- There is also an intermediate state in which your app can find itself, where it is neither frontmost nor backgrounded. This happens, for instance, when the user summons the control center or notification center in front of your app. In such situations, your app may be *inactive* without actually being backgrounded.

- A modern iPad that does iPad multitasking (Chapter 9) is capable of running two apps at once: they are *both* active (in the foreground) at the same time.

So your app's code can be running even though the app is not frontmost. If your code needs to know the app's state in this regard, it can ask the shared UIApplication object for its `applicationState` (UIApplication.State), which will be one of these:

- `.active`
- `.inactive`
- `.background`

In iOS 13 with scene support, things are more complicated if your app supports multiple windows on the iPad. One window can go into the background while another window remains active in the foreground. To describe these possibilities, UIScene has an `activationState` (UIScene.ActivationState), which will be one of these:

- `.unattached`
- `.foregroundActive`
- `.foregroundInactive`
- `.background`

The app's own state is then considered to be the *highest* state of any of its scenes. If any of its scenes is in the `.foregroundActive` state, the app is in the `.active` state. If all of its scenes are in the `.background` state, the app is in the `.background` state. Just as an app can be killed in the background to save memory, a window scene can be disconnected and disposed of in the background to save memory, leaving only its session as a placeholder (see Chapter 9).

Delegate Events

When your app launches, the `UIApplicationMain` function creates its one and only UIApplication instance as the `shared` application object, along with the app delegate, which adopts the UIApplicationDelegate protocol. In iOS 13, with the addition of scene support, `UIApplicationMain` also creates a scene and a scene delegate, which adopts the UIWindowSceneDelegate protocol. (See "How an App Launches" on page 4.) The runtime then proceeds to report lifetime events to these delegates through calls to the methods declared in those protocols. Other objects can also register to receive some of these events as notifications.

If your app has scene support, some of the app delegate lifetime events, such as `applicationDidBecomeActive(_:)` and `applicationDidEnterBackground(_:)`, are suppressed. Corresponding messages are sent to the scene delegate instead. In this discussion, I'll assume that you've compiled your app against iOS 13 and that it *does* have scene support. If you want to know what the app delegate messages are when there is *no* scene support, consult an earlier edition of this book.

 App delegate methods start with the word `application`; scene delegate methods start with the word `scene`.

The suite of basic lifetime events that may be sent to your app delegate and scene delegate is surprisingly limited and considerably less informative than one might have hoped:

`application(_:didFinishLaunchingWithOptions:)`
> The app has started up from scratch. You'll typically perform initializations here. But in iOS 13 in an app with scene support, these initializations should not involve views or view controllers; that's the job of the scene delegate.

`scene(_:willConnectTo:options:)`
> The scene is being created or reconnected. Perhaps the app has started up from scratch; perhaps a new window has been created in a multiple window app; perhaps this scene was disconnected from its session and is being connected again. Regardless, this is the place to prepare your window's root view controller if needed. If an app doesn't have a main storyboard, or is ignoring the main storyboard at launch time, this is the place to ensure that the scene has a window, to set the window's root view controller, and to show the window ("App Without a Storyboard" on page 6). If the app is launching because of an incoming quick action or URL, this is your chance to respond to it (Chapters 13 and 22).

`sceneWillEnterForeground(_:)`
> The scene is coming to the front. This message is sent both when the scene was previously in the background and when the app is launched from scratch. That's interesting, because in an app without scene support, `applicationWillEnter-Foreground(_:)` is *not* sent on launch to the app delegate. Always followed by `sceneDidBecomeActive(_:)`.

`sceneDidBecomeActive(_:)`
> The scene is now well and truly frontmost. Received after `sceneWillEnter-Foreground(_:)`. Also received after the end of any situation that caused the scene delegate to receive `sceneWillResignActive(_:)`.

`sceneWillResignActive(_:)`
> The scene is entering a situation where it is neither frontmost nor backgrounded; it will be *inactive*. Perhaps something has blocked the interface — the user has summoned the notification center, or a local notification alert has appeared, or there's an incoming phone call. Whatever the cause, the scene delegate will receive `sceneDidBecomeActive(_:)` when this situation ends.

Alternatively, the scene may be about to go into the background (and will then probably be suspended); in that case, this event was purely transient, and `scene-DidEnterBackground(_:)` will follow almost immediately.

`sceneDidEnterBackground(_:)`

The scene has been backgrounded. Always preceded by `sceneWillResign-Active(_:)`. Your app itself may now be backgrounded, in which case it will probably be suspended; before that happens, you have a little time to finish up last-minute tasks, such as relinquishing unneeded memory (see Chapter 6), and if you need more time for a lengthy task, you can ask for it (see Chapter 24).

`applicationWillTerminate(_:)`

The application is about to be killed dead. Surprisingly, even though every running app will eventually be terminated, it is quite unlikely that your app will *ever* receive this event! The reason is that, by the time your app is terminated by the system, it is usually already suspended and incapable of receiving events. (I mentioned an exceptional case in Chapter 14, and I'll mention some more in the next section.)

Lifetime Scenarios

A glance at some typical scenarios will demonstrate the chief ways in which your delegates will receive lifetime events. I find it helpful to group these scenarios according to the general behavior of the events.

Major State Changes

During very significant state changes, such as launching, being backgrounded, or coming back to the front, the app and scene delegates receive a sequence of events:

The app launches from scratch

Your delegates receive these messages:

- `application(_:didFinishLaunchingWithOptions:)`
- `scene(_:willConnectTo:options:)`
- `sceneWillEnterForeground(_:)`
- `sceneDidBecomeActive(_:)`

The user clicks the Home button

If your scene was frontmost, the scene delegate receives these messages:

- `sceneWillResignActive(_:)`
- `sceneDidEnterBackground(_:)`

The user summons your backgrounded scene to the front
    The scene delegate receives these messages:

- sceneWillEnterForeground(_:)
- sceneDidBecomeActive(_:)

The screen is locked
    If your scene is frontmost, the scene delegate receives these messages:

- sceneWillResignActive(_:)
- sceneDidEnterBackground(_:)

The screen is unlocked
    If your scene was frontmost, the scene delegate receives these messages:

- sceneWillEnterForeground(_:)
- sceneDidBecomeActive(_:)

Paused Inactivity

Certain user actions effectively pause the foreground-to-background sequence in the middle, leaving the scene inactive and capable of being either backgrounded or foregrounded, depending on what the user does next. When the scene becomes active again, it might or might not be coming from a backgrounded state:

The user enters the app switcher
    If your scene is frontmost, the scene delegate receives this message:

- sceneWillResignActive(_:)

The user, in the app switcher, chooses another app
    If your scene was frontmost, the scene delegate receives this message:

- sceneDidEnterBackground(_:)

The user, in the app switcher, chooses your scene
    If this scene was frontmost, then it was never backgrounded, so the scene delegate receives just this message:

- sceneDidBecomeActive(_:)

The user summons the control center or notification center
    If your scene is frontmost, the scene delegate receives this message:

- sceneWillResignActive(_:)

Actually, we get `willResignActive` as the user *starts* to pull down the notification center, and then if the user pulls it all the way down, we get `didBecome-Active` and `willResignActive` in quick succession. I regard this as unfortunate.

The user dismisses the control center or notification center
If your scene was frontmost, the scene delegate receives this message:

- `sceneDidBecomeActive(_:)`

But if the user has summoned the notification center, there's another possibility: the user might tap a notification alert to switch to that app. In that case, the scene will continue on to the background, and the scene delegate will receive this message:

- `sceneDidEnterBackground(_:)`

The user holds down the screen-lock button
The device offers to shut itself off. If your scene is frontmost, the scene delegate receives this message:

- `sceneWillResignActive(_:)`

The user, as the device offers to shut itself off, cancels
If your scene was frontmost, the scene delegate receives this message:

- `sceneDidBecomeActive(_:)`

The user, as the device offers to shut itself off, accepts
If your scene was frontmost, the app delegate receives this message:

- `applicationWillTerminate(_:)`

Transient Inactivity on the iPad

There are certain circumstances where your scene may become inactive and then active again in quick succession. These have mostly to do with multitasking on the iPad. If this happens, the scene delegate may receive these messages:

- `sceneWillResignActive(_:)`
- `sceneDidBecomeActive(_:)`

The chief case in point is when the user toggles between split sizes. When the scene is resized, it undergoes transient inactivity. If your view controller is notified of a change of size and possibly trait collection, this will happen *during* the period of transient inactivity, while the scene's activation state is `.foregroundInactive` (and the app's application state will probably be `.inactive` as well).

Multiple Windows

Here are some special cases that arise in a multiple window app on iPad, when your app manipulates the windows directly:

Your app creates a window

    If your app creates a window by calling `requestSceneSessionActivation`, your scene delegate receives these messages:

- `scene(_:willConnectTo:options:)`
- `sceneWillEnterForeground(_:)`
- `sceneDidBecomeActive(_:)`

Your app closes a window

    If your app closes a window by calling `requestSceneSessionDestruction`, then assuming this is not the last window, your delegates receive these messages:

- `sceneDidEnterBackground(_:)`
- `sceneDidDisconnect(_:)`
- `application(_:didDiscardSceneSessions:)`

Scene Death in the App Switcher

The case where the user enters the app switcher and swipes your scene up to remove it is extraordinarily confusing. What happens seems to depend on the device type and the app architecture:

On an iPhone

    If the scene was frontmost, you get these delegate messages:

- `sceneDidEnterBackground`
- `applicationWillTerminate(_:)`

On an iPad, if the app does not support multiple windows

    If the scene was frontmost, you get these delegate messages:

- `sceneDidDisconnect(_:)`
- `application(_:didDiscardSceneSessions:)`
- `applicationWillTerminate(_:)`

    (The lack of a `sceneDidEnterBackground` call here is surprising.)

On an iPad, if the app does support multiple windows

    If the scene was frontmost, you get these delegate messages:

- sceneDidEnterBackground

- applicationWillTerminate(_:)

But if there's another window still in existence, then the app might not terminate and you won't get applicationWillTerminate(_:). In that case, you might get sceneDidDisconnect(_:) and possibly application(_:didDiscardScene-Sessions:) later.

If the scene that the user swipes up was *not* frontmost, you'll get nothing; this scene already received sceneDidEnterBackground, and you won't get applicationWill-Terminate(_:) now because the app isn't running.

Lifetime Event Timing

The delegate lifetime messages may be interwoven with the lifetime events received by other objects. View controllers ("View Controller Lifetime Events" on page 401) are the primary case in point. There are circumstances where the root view controller may receive its initial lifetime events, such as viewDidLoad and viewWillAppear(_:), before application(_:didFinishLaunchingWithOptions:) (or, with scene support, scene(_:willConnectTo:options:)) has even finished running. That may come as a surprise.

Different systems can also introduce changes in timing. When I started programming iOS, back in the days of iOS 3.2, I noted the opening sequence of events involving the app delegate and the root view controller; they arrived in this order:

1. application(_:didFinishLaunchingWithOptions:)

2. viewDidLoad

3. viewWillAppear(_:)

4. applicationDidBecomeActive(_:)

5. viewDidAppear(_:)

Relying on that order, I typically used the root view controller's viewDidAppear(_:) to register for UIApplication.didBecomeActiveNotification in order to be notified of *subsequent* activations of the app.

That worked fine for some years. But iOS 8 brought with it a momentous change: the app delegate now received applicationDidBecomeActive(_:) *after* the root view controller received viewDidAppear(_:), like this:

1. application(_:didFinishLaunchingWithOptions:)

2. viewDidLoad

3. viewWillAppear(_:)

4. `viewDidAppear(_:)`

5. `applicationDidBecomeActive(_:)`

This was a disaster for many of my apps, because the notification I had just registered for in `viewDidAppear(_:)` arrived *immediately*.

Then, in iOS 9, the order returned to what it was in iOS 7 and before — knocking my apps into confusion once again. Then, in iOS 11, the order reverted back to what it was in iOS 8!

In iOS 13 with window scene support, the sequence is like this:

1. `application(_:didFinishLaunchingWithOptions:)`

2. `scene(_:willConnectTo:options:)`

3. `sceneWillEnterForeground(_:)`

4. `viewDidLoad`

5. `viewWillAppear(_:)`

6. `sceneDidBecomeActive(_:)`

7. `viewDidAppear(_:)`

Such changes from one system version to the next are likely to pose challenges for the longevity and backward compatibility of your app. The moral is that you should not, as I did, rely upon the timing relationship between lifetime events of different objects.

Some Useful Utility Functions

As you work with iOS and Swift, you'll develop a personal library of frequently used convenience functions. Here are some of mine. Each of them has come in handy in my own life; I keep them available in Xcode's Snippets library, so that I can use them in any project. Many of them have been mentioned earlier in this book.

Core Graphics Initializers

The Core Graphics `CGRectMake` function needs no argument labels when you call it. But Swift cuts off access to this function! Instead, you're forced to use various CGRect initializers that *do* need argument labels. Calls with labels take far longer to enter into your code, and the labels are superfluous because we know what each argument signifies. My solution is a CGRect initializer *without* labels (Chapter 1):

```
extension CGRect {
    init(_ x:CGFloat, _ y:CGFloat, _ w:CGFloat, _ h:CGFloat) {
        self.init(x:x, y:y, width:w, height:h)
    }
}
```

As long as we're doing that, we may as well supply label-free initializers for the other common Core Graphics structs:

```
extension CGSize {
    init(_ width:CGFloat, _ height:CGFloat) {
        self.init(width:width, height:height)
    }
}
extension CGPoint {
    init(_ x:CGFloat, _ y:CGFloat) {
        self.init(x:x, y:y)
    }
}
```

```
extension CGVector {
    init (_ dx:CGFloat, _ dy:CGFloat) {
        self.init(dx:dx, dy:dy)
    }
}
```

The examples throughout this book, including the rest of this appendix, rely on those extensions.

Center of a CGRect

One frequently wants the center point of a CGRect; even the shorthand `CGPoint(rect.midX, rect.midY)` becomes tedious. You can extend CGRect to do the work for you:

```
extension CGRect {
    var center : CGPoint {
        return CGPoint(self.midX, self.midY)
    }
}
```

A related value that I often need is a CGRect centered at the center point of my CGRect:

```
extension CGRect {
    func centeredRectOfSize(_ sz:CGSize) -> CGRect {
        let c = self.center
        let x = c.x - sz.width/2.0
        let y = c.y - sz.height/2.0
        return CGRect(x, y, sz.width, sz.height)
    }
}
```

Adjust a CGSize

There's a CGRect method `insetBy(dx:dy:)`, but there's no comparable method for changing an existing CGSize by a width delta and a height delta. Let's make one:

```
extension CGSize {
    func withDelta(dw:CGFloat, dh:CGFloat) -> CGSize {
        return CGSize(self.width + dw, self.height + dh)
    }
}
```

Delayed Performance

Delayed performance is of paramount importance in iOS programming, where we often need to finish the current run loop and commit the current CATransaction, allowing the interface to settle down, before we proceed to the next command. It isn't difficult to call `asyncAfter` (Chapter 24), but we can simplify even more with a utility function:

```
func delay(_ delay:Double, closure: @escaping ()->()) {
    let when = DispatchTime.now() + delay
    DispatchQueue.main.asyncAfter(deadline: when, execute: closure)
}
```

Call it like this:

```
delay(0.4) {
    // do something here
}
```

Dictionary of Views

When you generate constraints from a visual format string by calling NSLayout-Constraint's `constraints(withVisualFormat:options:metrics:views:)`, you need a dictionary of string names and view references as the last argument (Chapter 1). Forming this dictionary is tedious. Let's make it easier.

There are no Swift macros (because there's no Swift preprocessor), so you can't write the equivalent of Objective-C's `NSDictionaryOfVariableBindings`, which forms the dictionary from a literal list of view names. You can, however, generate a dictionary with *fixed* string names, like this:

```
extension Array where Element:UIView {
    func dictionaryOfNames() -> [String:UIView] {
        var d = [String:UIView]()
        for (ix,v) in self.enumerated() {
            d["v\(ix+1)"] = v
        }
        return d
    }
}
```

That method starts with a list of views and simply makes up string names for them, of the form `"v1"`, `"v2"`, and so on, in order. Knowing the rule by which the string names are generated, you then use those string names in your visual format strings. If you generate the dictionary by calling `[mainview, myLabel].dictionaryOfNames()`, then in any visual format string that uses this dictionary as its `views:` dictionary, you will refer to `mainview` by the name v1 and to `myLabel` by the name v2.

Constraint Issues

These are UIView methods aimed at helping to detect and analyze constraint issues (referred to in Chapter 1):

```
extension UIView {
    func reportAmbiguity(filtering:Bool = false) {
        let has = self.hasAmbiguousLayout
        if has || !filtering {
            print(self, has)
        }
        for sub in self.subviews {
            sub.reportAmbiguity(filtering:filtering)
        }
    }
    func listConstraints(recursing:Bool = true,
        up:Bool = false, filtering:Bool = false) {
        let arr1 = self.constraintsAffectingLayout(for:.horizontal)
        let arr2 = self.constraintsAffectingLayout(for:.vertical)
        var arr = arr1 + arr2
        if filtering {
            arr = arr.filter {
                $0.firstItem as? UIView == self ||
                    $0.secondItem as? UIView == self }
        }
        if !arr.isEmpty {
            print(self); arr.forEach { print($0) }; print()
        }
        guard recursing else { return }
        if !up { // down
            for sub in self.subviews {
                sub.listConstraints(up:up)
            }
        } else { // up
            self.superview?.listConstraints(up:up)
        }
    }
}
```

You can call those methods in your code, though you should remove those calls before shipping the app. Another possibility is to call them while paused in the debugger, like this:

```
(lldb) e self.view.reportAmbiguity(filtering:true)
```

Named Views

Giving a view a string identifier helps with debugging and can even come in handy in code. I feel so strongly about this that I inject a name property into all views. That's easy to do because every view has a layer, and CALayer has a name property that generally isn't used for anything. While we're up, we may as well make this property settable from the nib editor:

```
extension UIView {
    @IBInspectable var name : String? {
        get { return self.layer.name }
        set { self.layer.name = newValue }
    }
}
```

Subviews of Given Class

One often needs to find all subviews that belong to a certain class. For example, I might need to find all the UIButtons within my view. Here's a utility function that gives that information:

```
extension UIView {
    func subviews<T:UIView>(ofType WhatType:T.Type,
        recursing:Bool = true) -> [T] {
            var result = self.subviews.compactMap {$0 as? T}
            guard recursing else { return result }
            for sub in self.subviews {
                result.append(contentsOf: sub.subviews(ofType:WhatType))
            }
            return result
    }
}
```

Configure a Value Class at the Point of Use

A recurring pattern in Cocoa is that a value class instance is created and configured beforehand for one-time use:

```
let para = NSMutableParagraphStyle()
para.headIndent = 10
para.firstLineHeadIndent = 10
para.tailIndent = -10
para.lineBreakMode = .byWordWrapping
para.alignment = .center
para.paragraphSpacing = 15
content.addAttribute(
    .paragraphStyle,
    value: para,
    range: NSMakeRange(0,1))
```

First we create the NSMutableParagraphStyle; then we set its properties; then we use it once; then we throw it away. That feels clunky, procedural, and wasteful.

It would be clearer and more functional, as well as reflecting the natural order of thought, if the creation and configuration of para could happen at the actual moment when we *need* this object, namely when we supply the value: argument. Here's a generic function that permits us to do that:

```
func lend<T> (_ closure: (T)->()) -> T where T:NSObject {
    let orig = T()
    closure(orig)
    return orig
}
```

Now we can express ourselves like this:

```
content.addAttribute(
    .paragraphStyle,
    value: lend { (para:NSMutableParagraphStyle) in
        para.headIndent = 10
        para.firstLineHeadIndent = 10
        para.tailIndent = -10
        para.lineBreakMode = .byWordWrapping
        para.alignment = .center
        para.paragraphSpacing = 15
    },
    range: NSMakeRange(0,1))
```

Downsize a UIImage

A frequent need in iOS programming is to downscale a UIImage so as not to waste memory by handing a UIImageView an image larger than actually needed for display (Chapter 2). Here's a general utility that does that:

```
extension UIImage {
    func scaledDown(into size:CGSize) -> UIImage {
        var (targetWidth, targetHeight) = (self.size.width, self.size.height)
        var (scaleW, scaleH) = (1 as CGFloat, 1 as CGFloat)
        if targetWidth > size.width {
            scaleW = size.width/targetWidth
        }
        if targetHeight > size.height {
            scaleH = size.height/targetHeight
        }
        let scale = min(scaleW,scaleH)
        targetWidth *= scale; targetHeight *= scale
        let sz = CGSize(targetWidth, targetHeight)
        return UIGraphicsImageRenderer(size:sz).image { _ in
            self.draw(in:CGRect(origin:.zero, size:sz))
        }
    }
}
```

How Asynchronous Works

Beginners sometimes don't quite understand what it means for their code to run *asynchronously*. Asynchronous code runs at an indefinite time. More important, it runs *after* the surrounding code. This means that the order in which the code appears is not the order in which it will run.

Consider the following (and see Chapter 23):

```
func doSomeNetworking() {
    // ... prepare url ...
    let session = URLSession.shared ❶
    let task = session.downloadTask(with:url) { loc, resp, err in ❷
        // ... completion function body goes here ... ❹
    }
    task.resume() ❸
}
```

The method `downloadTask(with:completionHandler:)` calls its completion function asynchronously. It calls it when the networking finishes — and networking takes time. The order in which the chunks of code run is the numerical order of the numbered lines:

❶   The code before the call.

❷   The call itself.

❸   The code after the call, including the return from the surrounding function `doSomeNetworking`. Your code has now come to a complete stop!

❹   The code inside the completion function. This is the asynchronous code. It runs *later* — possibly much later, and certainly after the surrounding function `doSomeNetworking` has returned.

So asynchronous means that your code runs out of order. And that, in turn, means that the surrounding function *cannot* return a value from the asynchronous code.

Beginners sometimes try to write this sort thing:

```
func doSomeNetworking() -> UIImage? { // vain attempt to return an image
    // ... prepare url ...
    var image : UIImage? = nil
    let session = URLSession.shared
    let task = session.downloadTask(with:url) { loc, resp, err in
        if let loc = loc, let d = try? Data(contentsOf:loc) {
            let im = UIImage(data:d)
            image = im // too late!
        }
    }
    task.resume()
    return image // can only be nil!
}
```

The author of that code hopes that the image will be downloaded and returned from the surrounding function doSomeNetworking. But that can never work, because the last line, `return image`, will execute well before the line `image = im` even has a chance to execute! Therefore, the returned UIImage will always be `nil`.

Beginners might then think: So maybe I can wait until my asynchronous code has finished. That is *wrong!* Asynchronous means you *don't* wait. (If you wait, you block your thread, turning asynchronous into synchronous and defeating the whole purpose of being asynchronous.) When you obtain a value in some asynchronous code and you want to do something with that value, do it in the asynchronous code.

Suppose our goal is to update the interface with the downloaded image. Then we update the interface in the asynchronous code, after the image has been downloaded:

```
func doSomeNetworking() {
    // ... prepare url ...
    let session = URLSession.shared
    let task = session.downloadTask(with:url) { loc, resp, err in
        if let loc = loc, let d = try? Data(contentsOf:loc) {
            let im = UIImage(data:d)
            DispatchQueue.main.async {
                self.iv.image = im // update the interface _here_
            }
        }
    }
    task.resume()
}
```

That's an excellent solution. But let's go further. Let's say you really do want to hand back a value from the asynchronous code somehow to whoever called the surrounding function in the first place, leaving it up to the caller what to do with it.

We've already established that you can't return the value. But you can call back to whoever called the surrounding function in order to hand them the value. A typical architecture is that you allow the caller to hand you a *completion function* as one of the parameters of your method (usually the last parameter). Inside your asynchronous code, you then call the caller's completion function, like this:

```
func doSomeNetworking(callBackWithImage: @escaping (UIImage?) -> ()) {
    let s = "https://www.apeth.net/matt/images/phoenixnewest.jpg"
    let url = URL(string:s)!
    let session = URLSession.shared
    let task = session.downloadTask(with:url) { loc, resp, err in
        if let loc = loc, let d = try? Data(contentsOf:loc) {
            let im = UIImage(data:d)
            callBackWithImage(im) // call the caller's completion function
        }
    }
    task.resume()
}
```

Let's look at that example from the caller's point of view. The caller of doSome-Networking(callBackWithImage:) passes in a completion function that does whatever the caller ultimately wants done. Here, once again, our goal is to update the interface with the downloaded image:

```
doSomeNetworking { im in
    // this is the completion function!
    DispatchQueue.main.async {
        self.iv.image = im
    }
}
```

That works perfectly. But there is one further thing to be aware of. That completion function, too, is asynchronous! The caller here doesn't know when or whether this completion function will be called back, and perhaps not even what thread it will be called on. The caller knows only this: when and if the completion function is called back, the image will arrive as its parameter — and now the caller can dispose of it as desired.

Use of a completion handler, then, *propagates asynchronousness*. That is the pattern used throughout Cocoa. You should understand this pattern, become comfortable with it, and implement it in your own code.

Index

today extension, 788

About the Author

Matt Neuburg started programming computers in 1968, when he was 14 years old, as a member of a literally underground high school club, which met once a week to do timesharing on a bank of PDP-10s by way of primitive teletype machines. He also occasionally used Princeton University's IBM-360/67, but gave it up in frustration when one day he dropped his punch cards. He majored in Greek at Swarthmore College, and received his PhD from Cornell University in 1981, writing his doctoral dissertation (about Aeschylus) on a mainframe. He proceeded to teach Classical languages, literature, and culture at many well-known institutions of higher learning, most of which now disavow knowledge of his existence, and to publish numerous scholarly articles unlikely to interest anyone. Meanwhile he obtained an Apple IIc and became hopelessly hooked on computers again, migrating to a Macintosh in 1990. He wrote some educational and utility freeware, became an early regular contributor to the online journal *TidBITS*, and in 1995 left academe to edit *MacTech* magazine. In August 1996 he became a freelancer, which means he has been looking for work ever since. He is the author of *Frontier: The Definitive Guide*, *REALbasic: The Definitive Guide*, and *AppleScript: The Definitive Guide*.

Colophon

The animal on the cover of *Programming iOS 13* is a kingbird, one of the 13 species of North American songbirds making up the genus *Tyrannus*. A group of kingbirds is called a "coronation," a "court," or a "tyranny."

Kingbirds eat insects, which they often catch in flight, swooping from a perch to grab the insect midair. They may also supplement their diets with berries and fruits. They have long, pointed wings, and males perform elaborate aerial courtship displays.

Both the genus name (meaning "tyrant" or "despot") and the common name ("kingbird") refer to these birds' aggressive defense of their territories, breeding areas, and mates. They have been documented attacking red-tailed hawks (which are more than twenty times their size), knocking bluejays out of trees, and driving away crows and ravens. (For its habit of standing up to much larger birds, the gray kingbird has been adopted as a Puerto Rican nationalist symbol.)

"Kingbird" most often refers to the Eastern kingbird (*T. tyrannus*), an average-size kingbird (7.5–9 inches long, wingspan 13–15 inches) found all across North America. This common and widespread bird has a dark head and back, with a white throat, chest, and belly. Its red crown patch is rarely seen. Its high-pitched, buzzing, stuttering sounds have been described as resembling "sparks jumping between wires" or an electric fence.

Many of the animals on O'Reilly covers are endangered; all of them are important to the world.

The cover illustration is by Karen Montgomery, based on a black and white engraving from *Cassell's Natural History*. The cover fonts are Gilroy Semibold and Guardian Sans. The text font is Adobe Minion Pro; the heading font is Adobe Myriad Condensed; and the code font is Dalton Maag's Ubuntu Mono.

O'REILLY®

There's much more where this came from.

Experience books, videos, live online training courses, and more from O'Reilly and our 200+ partners—all in one place.

Learn more at oreilly.com/online-learning